Fundamentals of
Management Science
Custom Edition

by
Efraim Turban
California State University-Long Beach
Jack R. Merideth
University of Cincinnati

The McGraw-Hill Companies, Inc.
Primis Custom Publishing

*New York St. Louis San Francisco Auckland Bogota
Caracas Lisbon London Madrid Mexico Milan Montreal
New Delhi Paris San Juan Singapore Sydney Tokyo Toronto*

The McGraw·Hill Companies

To the memory of my parents, Devora and Itzak
>   E.T.

To Jeremy
>   J.R.M.

In honor of C. West Churchman on his 80th birthday
>   E.T.
>   J.R.M.

Fundamentals of Management Science, Sixth Edition, by Efraim Turban and Jack R. Merideth.
©Irwin/McGraw-Hill, A Division of The McGraw-Hill Companies, 1994.

FUNDAMENTALS OF MANAGEMENT SCIENCE, CUSTOM EDITION

ISBN 0-07-229333-0

Printed in the United States of America.

 2 3 4 5 6 7 8 9 0 XRC 0 9 8

Printer/Binder: Xerographic Reproduction Center, Inc.

Preface

Today, the techniques of management science are known to business leaders, urban planners, farmers, military strategists, space scientists, and public administrators in a host of fields. Words such as *systems, models, optimization, simulation,* and *cost-benefit* are now common in the public vocabulary. The need is thus great for an introductory text that explains, with a minimum of mathematics, how to *formulate* decision problems, how to *solve* them using management science concepts, and how to *apply* the solutions obtained.

The Sixth Edition

This sixth edition provides a "re-engineered" text for the teaching of management science. We all are aware of recent developments in information technology that are having a major impact on how management science is being practiced. Some interesting papers have been published during the last few years discussing these developments and suggesting changes in the manner in which management science is being taught. In the previous editions of our book we started to incorporate some of these suggestions. In this edition we are incorporating much more. Yet, we are preserving the basic philosophy that a management science book must cover all the tools of the trade (similarly, a statistics text must cover all the tools of statistics). What we have changed is the *approach* and the *emphasis*.

The following are some of the unique features of this edition.

1. We believe that management science is strongly related to managerial decision making. Therefore, a detailed understanding of the decision making process is provided (Chapter 2).

2. Similarly, we believe that the *process* of *modeling* needs to be emphasized (e.g., see Marks and McClure [6]). This is done in Chapter 2 and throughout the text.

3. Our text emphasizes *problem formulation, applications,* and *understanding of*

what practitioners do, as suggested by a special task force of The Institute of Management Sciences (see Borsting et al. [2]).

4. We recognize that management science, decision support systems and artificial intelligence/expert systems are all interrelated (Adams and Song [1], Geoffrion [2], Fordyce et al. [3]). This philosophy is presented in Section 1.2 and in the special sections of Chapter 17 on decision support systems, expert systems, genetic algorithms and neural computing.

5. We recognize the end-user computing movement and the possibility that managers are starting to build their own MS/OR models. This could change the notion that an introductory course should be aimed at management science consumers (Borsting et al. [2]) to the philosophy that the course should also be aimed at management science *producers*, or "self-starters," as suggested by Lee et al. [5].

6. Software support is essential for any management science course. Unique support is provided by this text (see instructional support).

7. A "problem first" approach, as suggested by Samson [7], is incorporated in two ways. We present several problems at the end of Chapter 2 for the purpose of illustrating many aspects of modeling. In addition, we start each "tool" chapter with an illustrative problem.

8. Relevance to the real world (as suggested by Borsting et al. [2]) is illustrated by examples of many real world applications (throughout the text).

9. The use of heuristics is becoming important both as a computational tool for complex numerical problems and as a search mechanism in expert systems. This neglected topic (per Tingley [8]) is presented in Chapter 17.

10. There is an increased recognition of the importance of multi-criteria decision making. Chapter 8 dealing with this topic is supported by Expert Choice software, which is based on the analytic hierarchy process.

11. We recognize the importance of globalization and internationalization and thus added more cases and problems with international aspects in this edition.

12. Many new problems were added to the chapters.

13. The text has been reorganized in its chapter sequence, the material within each chapter has been tightened up and footnotes largely eliminated, several chapters and sections were combined, and the overall size of the book was reduced significantly.

14. A set of illustrative, comprehensive, integrated cases concludes the text. These cases allow the use of multiple management science techniques to arrive at a solution, rather than being restricted to one particular set of techniques described in a chapter.

In the first two chapters, the foundations of the field are outlined. The reader is introduced to the topic of management science in Chapter 1. Its characteristics and processes are then outlined in Chapter 2, which focuses on the relation of management science to decision making.

Chapters 3–16 are concerned with formulating managerial problems from many different fields and finding solutions to them using management science models. The chapters are intentionally written to be independent of each other so the instructor may cover only the topics desired for the course. Chapters in this part of the book are frequently divided into two segments: "Basics" and "Extensions." The book was written with the express aim of allowing coverage in a course ranging from one quarter (if only the "Basics" are covered) to two quarters (if the entire text is covered). The essence of each topic is presented in the former at a minimal level of mathematical sophistication—typically, only algebra or elementary statistics is needed. The segments in the "Extensions" elaborate on some of the basic models at a somewhat higher level of sophistication. These segments are typically also independent of each other and may thus be selected at will by the instructor for further class study. The mathematical and statistical background needed for the book, as well as a few additional topics (such as "present value"), are included in Appendix A, Mathematics, and Appendix B, Statistics. Appendix C includes requisite tables for the text and, lastly, the *answers* (not solutions) to most of the even-numbered problems are given in Appendix D.

Each chapter typically begins with a brief episode showing the student how a particular decision problem arises. When possible, this example is carried throughout the chapter to illustrate the concepts being developed. We have attempted to present a variety of decision situations from a number of fields to emphasize the flexibility of the management science approach. Chapter 4 in particular presents a wide array of applications of linear programming. In lieu of presenting the mathematical theorems and proofs that form the basis of many of the models in each chapter, we appeal to intuitive reasoning and logic. The chapters thus include one or more cases to help the student apply the tools and techniques learned in the chapter to a realistic situation. The chapters then conclude with a glossary of chapter terms.

Chapter 17 includes an examination of the new tools of decision support systems, expert systems, genetic algorithms, and neural computing. Realistic integrated case studies conclude our emphasis on application in Chapter 18. These cases typically require the use of a variety of MS techniques to find a solution.

Instructional Support

This edition is supported by:

1. *Instructor's Manual*. This manual includes solutions to all the problems and cases. In addition, you will find extensive suggestions for organizing the course and many transparency masters.

2. *Test Bank*. The test bank is divided into two parts: conceptual questions and problems. Multiple choice format is used in both cases and problems. The test bank is available both in a printed version and on a disk (with Computest).

3. *Software support*. This edition is supported by the following software.

   a. Lotus spreadsheet templates (by Scott Shafer) for many of the models in this book. These templates are free to adopters.

   b. Preprogrammed management science software (DSS MS/OR, second edition by Vahid Lotfi and Carl Pegels) for most of the models in this book. This software is available packaged with the text.

4. *Student Solutions Manual* by Elizabeth Rivers.

5. *Operations Management Primer* by Scott Shafer is available packaged with the text for combination courses.

Acknowledgments

The number of persons to whom we owe thanks for their contributions to the development of this book defies enumeration. Of particular help in this edition were the suggestions and advice offered to us by James A. Bartos, Ohio State University; Sharad Chitgopekar, Illinois State University; Damodar Golhar, Western Michigan University; Han Kim, South Dakota State University; Ching-Chung Kuo, Pennsylvania State University; Constance McLaren, Indiana State University; David Pentico, Duquesne University; Carl Schultz, University of New Mexico; Rex Toh, Seattle University.

We would also like to thank the reviewers of previous editions: James A. Bartos, Ohio State University; F. Douglas Holcombe, Marshall University; Michael Middleton, University of San Francisco; Thomas Tucker, University of Houston at Clear Lake; Ross E. Lanser, San Jose State University; John Anderson, University of Minnesota; A. J. Waltz, University of South Florida; Peter M. Ellis, Utah State University; Richard Ehrhardt, University of North Carolina, Greensboro; Fatollah Salimian, Salisbury State College, Pennsylvania; Samuel Wagner, Franklin and Marshall College; Timothy Riggle, Baldwin-Wallace College; Peter Zanetich, Franciscan University of Steubenville; Richard McClure, Miami University; Thomas Schuppe, Air Force Institute of Technology; and Clive Sanford, University of Maine. Also, we acknowledge the work of Elizabeth Rivers who prepared the student guide.

We gratefully acknowledge the ideas and constructive suggestions of Carol Meredith in this and previous editions. Special thanks go to Sharon Turban who helped in proofing the entire manuscript. Finally, we greatly acknowledge the extensive contribution of Judy Lang who helped us with the test bank.

Software support is an extremely important feature in this text. Several people deserve acknowledgment. First, we thank Scott Shafer who prepared the Lotus Templates and Vahid Lotfi and Carl Pegels who authored the Decision Support Systems software. Second, we appreciate the support given by Ernest Forman from George Washington University who contributed the material on Expert Choice.

Efraim Turban
Jack Meredith

References

1. Adams, C.R., and J. H. Song. "Integrating Decision Technologies: Implications for Management Curriculum." *MIS Quarterly,* June 1989.
2. Borsting, J. R., et al. "A Model for a First MBA Course in Management Science/Operations Research." *Interfaces,* Sept.–Oct. 1988.
3. Fordyce, K., et al. "Artificial Intelligence and Management Science Practitioner: Links Between Operations Research and Expert Systems." *Interfaces,* July–August 1987.
4. Geoffrion, A. M. "Can MS/OR Evaluate Fast Enough?" *Interfaces,* Feb. 1983.
5. Lee, S. M. et al. "The Decentralization of Management Science and the Birth of Self-Starters," *Journal of the Operations Research Society,* Vol. 40, #3, 1984.
6. Marks, N. B. and R. H. McClure, "A First Step Toward Teaching Modeling Rather Than Models," *OR/MS Today,* Dec. 1989.
7. Samson, D. "Comment on the Paper by Borsting et al., A Model for a First MBA Course in MS/OR," *Interfaces*, Nov.–Dec. 1988.
8. Tingley, G. A., "Can MS/OR Sell Itself Well Enough?" *Interfaces,* July–Aug. 1987.

Contents in Brief

Contents

Introduction

This book is about the application of the scientific approach to managerial decision making. Management science can be a tremendous aid to the manager faced with decisions. It can sort out the complex array of data, show what is relevant and what is not, focus on the lack of certain crucial information, provide an objective and consistent basis of choosing the best (or a good enough) solution, and even help quantify the manager's feelings and preferences for solution outcomes. In short, it can be used to make better decisions and improve the management of organizations.

This chapter begins with a definition of management science, and then presents its major characteristics and a description of its historical development. The chapter ends with a discussion of the benefits and limitations of management science.

1.1   What's It All About?

Before we delve into management science—what it is, what it can be used for, and what it cannot be used for—let us briefly look at the term *management*. **Management** is a *process* used to achieve certain *goals* through the utilization of *resources* (people, money, energy, materials, space, time). The resources are considered the inputs, and the attainment of the goals the output of the process. The degree of success of the manager's job is often measured by the ratio of the value of the outputs to the value of the inputs. This ratio is an indication of the organization's **productivity**.

Productivity—a measure of success

Productivity is a major concern for any organization since it determines the well-being of the organization and its participants. Productivity is also one of the most important issues at the national level. National productivity is the sum of the productivities of all organizations and individuals, and it determines the standard of living, the employment rate, and the economic well-being of the country.

The level of productivity, or the success of management, depends primarily on the execution of certain *managerial functions* such as planning, organizing, directing, and controlling. To carry out these functions, managers engage in a continuous process of making decisions. Therefore, *management* is considered by many as synonymous with *decision making*.

Decision making— art or science?

For years, managers have considered decision making to be a pure art—a talent acquired over a long period of time through experience (learning by trial and error). It has been considered an art because a variety of individual styles can be used in approaching and successfully solving the same type of managerial problems in actual business practice. These styles are often based on creativity, judgment, intuition, and experience rather than on a systematic analytical approach.

However, the environment in which management must operate is changing. Technological advancement is altering the manner in which organizations are structured and operate. Such advances in technology cannot possibly be made or sustained without concurrent advances in the management of organizations. Such unusual strides have been possible only because the art of management has increasingly been supplemented by science.

The importance of a single decision

If one examines the reasons for bankruptcies of small and even large corporations, one frequently finds that the bankruptcy is the result of a single wrong decision. For example, many corporations borrowed unwisely in the 1980s and then collapsed in the recession of the early 1990s. The list included banks, airlines, and savings and loans.

FIGURE 1.1

Factors affecting decision making

Factor	Trend	Results
Technology	Increasing	More alternatives
Information/computers	Increasing	to choose from
Organizational size	Increasing	Larger cost of
Structural complexity	Increasing	making errors
Competition	Increasing	
International impacts	Increasing	More uncertainty
Consumerism	Increasing	regarding the
Government intervention	Increasing	future

Management Science in Practice

Ability to Make Decisions Rated First in Survey

NEW YORK (AP)—In almost any survey of what constitutes good management, you are likely to find prominently mentioned the ability to make clear-cut decisions when needed.

It is not surprising, therefore, to hear that the ability to make crisp decisions was rated first in importance in a study of 6,500 managers in more than 100 companies, many of them large, blue-chip corporations.

As managers entered a training course at Harbridge House, a Boston-based firm, they were asked how important it was that managers employ certain management practices. They also were asked how well, in their estimation, managers performed these practices.

It was from a statistical distillation of these answers that Harbridge ranked "making clear-cut decisions when needed" as the most important of ten management practices.

And it was from these evaluations they concluded that only 20 percent of the managers performed "very well" on any given managerial practice.

Ranked second in managerial importance was "getting to the heart of problems rather than dealing with less important issues," a finding that seems to show up in all such studies. Most of the remaining eight management practices were related directly or indirectly to decision making.

Source: *Stars and Stripes*, May 10, 1987.

Greater complexity and cost of errors

Business and its environment are more complex today than ever before, and the trend toward increasing complexity is continuing. Figure 1.1 shows the changes in the major factors (on the left) that have an impact on managerial decision making. The results (on the right) indicate that making decisions today is much more complicated than in the past for three reasons. First, the number of alternatives is usually much larger. Second, the cost of making errors has become larger and larger, mainly due to the size of operations, competition, and a resulting chain-reaction situation in which the impact of an error may be felt in many places due to complex interrelationships. Finally, the consequences of the decisions are more difficult to predict due to increased international and governmental uncertainty.

Philip Morris

To illustrate how critical the impact of a single decision can be, consider the following example. On April 2, 1993, Philip Morris Companies announced their decision to aggressively discount Marlboro cigarettes, their premier product line, in order to compete with lower-priced rivals and generic cigarettes. Investors abandoned the once-popular stock in droves, sending its stock price down 23 percent and wiping out $13.2 billion in the value of the firm's stock. The news also triggered a broad sell-off in other popular consumer products companies, including Quaker Oats and Procter & Gamble, and resulted in a significant decline in the stock market that day.

As a result of these trends and changes, it is very difficult to rely on a trial-and-error approach to management, especially in decisions involving the factors shown in Figure 1.1. Managers must become more sophisticated—they must learn to utilize new tools and techniques that are being developed in their field. No one can imagine a successful physician using the medicines and equipment of the turn of the century. Yet, in management, one can find executives using management tools of that time.

1.2 Managerial Decision Making

Managerial decision making can be approached from two different perspectives: behavioral and decision support. Our major concern is with the latter.

A Framework for Decision Support

Decision support

In order to better understand the content of this book and its relationship to decision making, a framework for decision support is presented. This framework was proposed by Gorry and Scott-Morton [8], integrating the work of Simon [12] and Anthony [3].

In the first half of the framework, the decision-making process spans a continuum that ranges from highly structured (sometimes referred to as *programmed*) to highly unstructured (*nonprogrammed*). *Structured* processes are used for routine and repetitive

Fuzzy problems

problems for which standard solutions exist. *Unstructured* processes are for "fuzzy," complex problems for which there are no standard solution methods.

Focusing on decision making also requires an understanding of the decision-making process. This process is divided into three phases: *intelligence*—searching for conditions that call for decisions; *design*—inventing, developing, and analyzing possible courses of action; and *choice*—selecting a course of action from those available.

A *fully structured* problem is one in which *all* these phases are structured. A structured phase is a phase whose procedures are standardized, whose objectives are clear, and whose input and output are clearly specified.

An *unstructured* problem is one in which none of the three phases is structured. Decisions where some, but not all, of the phases are structured are referred to as *semistructured*.

In a structured problem, the procedures for obtaining the best (or at least a good enough) solution are known, as shown by the various models described in Part II of this book. Whether the problem involves finding an appropriate inventory level or deciding on an optimal investment strategy, the objectives are clearly defined.

Using intuition

In an unstructured problem, human intuition is still the basis for decision making. Typical unstructured problems include planning of new services to be offered and hiring an executive. The semistructured problems fall between the structured and the unstructured, involving a combination of both standard solution procedures and individuals' judgment. The following are examples of semistructured problems: trading bonds, setting marketing budgets for consumer products, and performing capital acquisition analyses.

The second half of this framework defines three broad categories that encompass all managerial activities:

1. *Strategic planning*—the long-range goals and policies for resource allocation.
2. *Management control*—the acquisition and efficient utilization of resources in the accomplishment of the organizational goals.
3. *Operational control*—the efficient and effective execution of specific tasks.

Nine-cell framework   These taxonomies can be combined in a nine-cell table (see Figure 1.2) to create a decision support framework. The right-hand column indicates the tools needed to support the various decisions.

Decision Making and Support

Several techniques were developed to support managerial decision making. These techniques, which can be used individually or can be *integrated*, form the discipline of **decision sciences**. The nature of support provided by the various tools corresponds to the framework proposed in Figure 1.2.

Support of Structured Decisions

These decisions are supported by quantitative analysis, especially at the operational and managerial control levels. There are many tools that can be used in supporting structured decisions, such as the *management science* models that are described in this book, as well as statistical, financial, accounting, and other quantitative models.

Support of Semistructured and Unstructured Decisions

Gorry and Scott-Morton [8] suggest that conventional management science and other quantitative models are insufficient *by themselves* to deal with these situations. There-

FIGURE 1.2

Decision support framework

Type of Decision \ Type of Control	Operational Control	Managerial Control	Strategic Planning	Support Needed
Structured	Accounts receivable, Order entry [1]	Budget analysis, Short-term forecasting, Personnel reports, Make or buy analysis [2]	Financial management (investment), Warehouse location, Distribution systems [3]	Management science and other quantitative models
Semistructured	Production scheduling, Inventory control [4]	Credit evaluation, Budget preparation Plant layout, Project scheduling, Reward systems design [5]	Build new plant, Mergers, Acquisitions, New product planning, Compensation planning, Quality assurance plans [6]	DSS ES
Unstructured	Selecting a cover for a magazine, Buying software, Approving loans [7]	Negotiation, Recruiting an executive, Buying hardware, Lobbying [8]	R & D planning New technology development, Social and responsibility planning [9]	DSS ES

Same models used

fore, they propose the use of a *supportive information system,* which they call a **decision support system**—DSS (see Turban [13]). A DSS utilizes models. Some of the models are the same as those used for structured decisions, while others are specifically constructed for the DSS. For this reason, some people view DSS as a tool of management science, while others feel that management science is a part of DSS. The technique of simulation, which is most suitable for difficult problems, is often used with DSS. The least structured problems, especially those involving managerial control and strategic planning, require *expertise.* A form of computerized expertise can be provided by an expert system—ES.

This book deals mainly with structured decisions. We describe simulation, DSS, and ES only in general terms. These topics are broad and are usually covered by special courses.

The Management Science Approach

The management science approach adopts the view that a substantial portion of decision making consists of analyzing phenomena that can be measured, determining relationships that can be represented quantitatively, and determining cause-and-effect relationships whose internal consistency can be tested experimentally. Thus, the objective of this approach is to bring as many management phenomena as possible into the domain of standardized or "programmed" decisions.

1.3   Definitions of Management Science (MS)

Management science has had several definitions. Two classical definitions are:

1. Operations research [management science] is the application of scientific methods, techniques, and tools to problems involving the operations of systems so as to provide those in control of the operations with optimum solutions to the problems [4, p. 9].
2. The application of the scientific method to the study of the operations of large, complex organizations or activities. [The Committee on Operations Research of the National Research Council in Great Britain.]

In this text, **management science** is defined as:

The application of the scientific method to the analysis and solution of managerial decision-making problems.

Other names

Other names often used to connote more or less the same general area are operations research, operational research, operations analysis, quantitative analysis, quantitative methods, systems analysis, and decision analysis. The reason for so many names (most of which have their own professional societies) is that the entire field is relatively new and there is no general agreement yet on what body of knowledge it includes.

Note that the term *management science* has become more closely associated with decision making that employs quantitative techniques in the analysis of managerial problems. **Operations research** is typically used to denote the study and development of the *mathematics* that underlie the techniques. Frequently, however, these two terms are used interchangeably.

In addition to the formal definition of MS, and sometimes instead of such a definition, it is customary to list the special characteristics of the field.

1.4   The Characteristics of Management Science

The major characteristics of management science are:

1. A primary focus on managerial decision making.
2. The application of the scientific approach to decision making.
3. The examination of the decision situation from a broad perspective; that is, the application of a *systems approach*.
4. The use of methods and knowledge from several disciplines.
5. A reliance on mathematical and other quantitative models.
6. The extensive use of electronic *computers*.

These characteristics will be discussed in detail in Chapter 2.

1.5   The Tools of Management Science

The role of the management scientist can be viewed as that of a staff assistant or a consultant who is called on to diagnose an opportunity or a problem, propose an approach, and, sometimes, implement the approach. In such a capacity, the management scientist works with tools that enable him or her to analyze a situation (diagnosis), to predict the future development of the situation (prognosis), and to suggest the best approach (solution).

Standard tools for recurring decision situations

Managerial decision situations are analogous to diseases. Some of these situations are fairly standard (structured); for example, an improper level of inventories. These *standard situations* can be treated with *standard tools*. For certain types of allocation situations, a tool named linear programming was developed. For more complex allocation situations, the tools of integer programming and dynamic programming were developed.

Borrowed tools

In addition to such tools, management scientists also use tools borrowed from other disciplines. For example, statistical tools are used in determining significant differences between proposed solutions, and forecasting models are used in predicting the consequences of proposed treatments. Similarly, econometric, financial, marketing, and even organizational behavior models are frequently incorporated into the analysis. Finally, for complex situations, the management scientist may build special tools for which the technology of DSS can be employed. A manager must be aware of such tools, know how to use and interpret some of them, and know when to consult with a specialist. The application of one of these tools, simulation, is illustrated in the accompanying Management Science in Practice (MSIP) sidebar.

Special tools for unique problems

Management Science in Practice

Searching for the Sunken *SS Central America* and Its Treasure

On September 3, 1857, the wooden-hulled, sidewheeled steamship *Central America* left Panama with about 600 passengers and 6,000 pounds of gold bound for New York. On the 9th, about 60 miles off the coast of Florida, a storm began to rise that developed into a hurricane by the next day. By the 11th, a leak had developed that eventually smothered the ship's boilers. The passengers and crew bailed all night in the fury of the hurricane, but by the next day it was clear the *Central America* would sink. The captain signaled a nearby brig, the *Marine,* and 100 people were transferred before darkness prevented further rescues. Another ship, the schooner *El Dorado,* also approached the area, standing by to pick up survivors as the doomed steamship's captain relayed his last estimated position. Just after 8 P.M., the *Central America* sank in 8,000 feet of water. Fifty people were rescued during the night by another nearby ship, the bark *Ellen,* with the last survivors picked up by 9 A.M. the next morning.

Some 427 people, including the captain, lost their lives in this tragedy, the most famous shipwreck of the 19th century and one comparable to the loss of the *Titanic* in the 20th century. Additionally, the loss of the gold cargo contributed to a panic in the U.S. financial markets that wiped out several banks and cost hundreds of thousands of people their jobs. (The value of the gold alone was estimated to exceed $20,000,000.)

Over the years, several expeditions attempted to locate the wreck to recover the treasure. They all failed. The information provided in 1857 was confused and inaccurate, the ocean is large, bottom sands covered what was left of the steamship, and perhaps most important, probability theory was not used.

In 1985, the Columbus-America Discovery Group was formed to achieve a number of objectives, one of which was to locate, explore, and recover the remains of the *SS Central America.* One of the critical tasks facing the group was the synthesis of all the relevant and known information about the shipwreck into a search pattern using an advanced-technology wide-scanning ship-towed sonar with a range of 1.5 miles. This task consisted of two steps: (1) developing a probability map showing the likelihood of the *Central America* being in any particular point in the ocean and (2) developing an efficient search routine for the ship towing the sonar over the relevant grids.

Analyzing all the historical information in logs, records, and newspaper reports resulted in three possible scenarios that would indicate where the *Central America* went down. The first scenario was based on the location relayed from the captain of the *Central America* to the *El Dorado.* Reports of the disaster indicated that the captain had taken a sextant-based celestial fix of the ship's location during a slight lull in the hurricane at 7 A.M. on the fatal day, 13 hours before the steamship sank. Thus, the drift of the ship during the 13 hours before sinking had to be taken into consideration.

The second scenario was based on the celestial fix taken by the captain of the *Ellen* at 8 A.M., after the storm, when survivors were being picked up. The third scenario was based on the location of the *Marine* when they sighted the *Central America* at about noon. However, the captain's last celestial fix was made 30 hours earlier, so wind and ocean current drift corrections were also required for the *Marine.*

All of the locations, coordinates, drifts, and directions had uncertainties associated with them that had to be factored into the probability calculations. When this was done, a computer simulation program was employed to make 4,000 runs, using those probabilities. The result was an overall probability distribution for the location of the *Central America* for each scenario in terms of grids four miles on a side. Next, the three scenarios were combined by weighting each one with a confidence number based on the reliability of the reports that were used to create the scenario and the intuitive beliefs of the team members. The values were 23 percent for the first scenario, 72 percent for the second, and 5 percent for the third. Again, these scenarios were subjected to a simulation program and an overall probability distribution was derived, shown in Figure 1.3. A search pattern based on these probabilities was then developed.

In the summer of 1986, the search commenced. Early in the search, in one of the very high probability grids (see Figure 1.3), a contact was made that indicated a mound resembling a pile of coal, which is used

FIGURE 1.3

Ship locations and contours of constant-probability grids

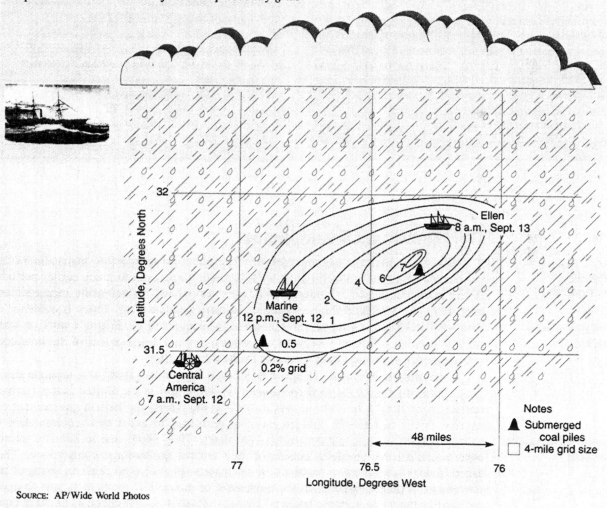

SOURCE: AP/Wide World Photos

to power a steamship. In the summer of 1987, the team returned to this contact with a remote-controlled underwater vehicle called *Nemo* and identified the wreck of a wooden-hulled ship, from which they extracted artifacts consisting of coal, pieces of iron, ceramic dishes dating from the early 1850s, and articles belonging to women and children. However, nothing else was found there, not even the identity of the wreck.

During the ensuing year, other sonar contacts were examined more closely, and one found near the end of the search in a lower-probability grid (see Figure 1.3) looked quite promising. Thus, in the summer of 1988 this site was scanned by *Nemo,* and two large iron-side wheels were spotted. Later, the bell of the *Central America* was brought up, providing proof that this was indeed the site of the tragedy. Toward the end of the summer a gold bar and several smaller pieces of gold were recovered. Over the following summers, more than a ton of gold and gold coins was brought up from the wreck. The total treasure is now estimated to be worth a billion dollars.

The Columbus-America Discovery Group was actually the second team to search for the *Central America* with this sonar system. Another group, using the same sonar system, failed to find the wreck in the early 1980s. The reason why the Columbus-America team was successful is that a management science approach based on probability theory and simulation was used to help identify the most probable location of the wreck.

Source: L.D. Stone, "Search for the *SS Central America:* Mathematical Treasure Hunting," *Interfaces,* January–February 1992, pp. 32–54.

Questions:

1. Where did the *Central America* actually sink on the probability map?
2. Simulation consists of picking a series of random numbers, which are used for each of the probability distributions (error north, drift west, and so on), and then calculating where the ship sank, given those values. This process is then repeated a number of times (here, 4,000). How then is the probability of sinking in a particular four-mile-wide grid determined?

1.6   Historical Development

F. W. Taylor's scientific management

It is difficult to mark the beginning of MS. The scientific approach to management can be traced back to the era of the Industrial Revolution and even to much earlier periods. In the late 19th century, Frederick W. Taylor formalized his **scientific management** approach, which marked the beginning of industrial engineering. There is evidence of

The use of math models

the use of mathematical models at the turn of the century (e.g., Erlang's work on waiting line problems, Edison's work on war games, and the development of the inventory management Economic Order Quantity formula by Harris).

It was not until World War II that MS began to establish itself as a separate discipline, both in England (termed *operational research*) and in the United States (termed *operations research*). In order to maximize their war effort, the British government organized teams of scientific and engineering personnel to assist field commanders in

Cross-fertilization in science

solving perplexing strategic and tactical problems. They found that technically trained experts could solve problems outside of their normal professional competency. They asked biologists to examine problems in electronics, physicists to think in terms of the movement of people rather than the movement of molecules, mathematicians to apply probability theory to improve soldiers' chances of survival, and chemists to study equilibria in systems other than chemical ones. Teams of specialists studied problems ranging from the evaluation of cost and effectiveness of complete military systems (such as the defense system of a country) to the best allocation of depth charges in antisubmarine warfare.

The success of the British operational research teams led the United States to institute a similar effort in 1942 (small-scale projects dated back to 1937). The initial project involved the deployment of merchant marine convoys to minimize losses from enemy submarines.

From wartime use to industry

Following the war, operations research extended into industry—first into the process-type industries such as oil refineries and steel and paper mills. These industries are characterized by large volumes of relatively few products. The savings were high because even a penny a unit on a large volume could total up to millions of dollars. In addition, a high capital-to-worker ratio in these automated industries meant relatively fewer employees, whose duties were mainly in supervision, control, and maintenance. Therefore, the employees showed little resistance to changes introduced by MS.

The period after World War II saw a dramatic development and refinement of MS techniques, with a corresponding expansion to almost all industries and services. Furthermore, the complexity of managerial problems attacked by MS increased significantly, especially with the introduction of the technique of simulation and large, efficient computing systems.

Trend toward public sector decision making

In the 1970s, the use of MS expanded into large social and urban systems such as criminal justice, health care, and education. Then the 1980s introduced a new dimension into MS—its integration with management information systems. This integration is taking place in a rapidly developing area termed decision support systems (DSS). Finally, recent developments in the areas of artificial intelligence, neural computing, and genetic algorithms are providing the management scientist with some sophisticated tools to address more complex situations.

All of these developments are evident in the MS departments that emerged at many universities, several of which grant a doctoral degree in the field. In the United States alone there are about 10,000 members in The Institute of Management Sciences (TIMS) and in related professional societies. About 15 English-language periodicals deal with theories and applications of MS. There are also many interesting careers in MS (see the special issue of *OR/MS Today,* April 1992).

1.7   Extent of Use and Limitations

Although relatively few studies have been published on the extent and success of using MS, the research that has been published reveals impressive results. An early survey reported by the American Management Association [2] gives some indication of both the possible savings and the difficulties of measuring them. For example, of the 324 responding companies using MS, 130 reported "considerable improvement" and "appreciable net savings." Actual figures of $100,000 or more were reported by 17 companies, anticipated savings of $300,000 or more by 18 companies. Many indicated that directly measurable dollar savings were only a *small part* of the benefit obtained.

Dollar and other benefits surveyed

Only two of the 324 companies indicated an intent to decrease MS activities, and not one indicated plans to discontinue using them.

Other surveys, although failing to give savings figures, indicated that virtually all practitioners were satisfied with MS and planned to continue its use. Evidence of its benefits may also be seen in the constantly increasing rate of application of MS in industrial firms; some of the more common areas of application are shown in Table 1.1. One of these surveys [14] revealed that 44 percent of the largest U.S. industrial and service corporations have an MS unit at their corporate headquarters. Another [6] found that statistical analysis, simulation, PERT/CPM, and linear programming are used most frequently. A similar ranking is reported in [11]. For the frequency of use of these tools over a 15-year period, see [9].

Management science, like any other management tool, is no substitute for good management practice. The manager must still decide what to investigate, what to do about the factors that cannot be quantified, and how to interpret the results of scientific analysis. MS requires capable, well-qualified, and experienced personnel. It also frequently consumes a great deal of time and may become very costly. Attempting shortcuts by superficially examining the problems, or using inappropriate models or inaccurate data, may produce results that, if applied, will be far more costly than simply using the dictates of subjective judgment.

Only a costly tool?

TABLE 1.1   Number of Firms Applying MS Techniques in Specific Areas

	Survey			
Area of application	*1959* *[2]* *631 firms*	*1965* *[10]* *65 firms*	*1975* *[7]* *275 firms*	*1983* *[6]* *62 firms*
Production	24	68	49	57
Long-range planning	23	55		
Advertising, sales, and marketing	25	20	16	47
Inventory	21	68	31	52
Transportation	15	41	8	
Top management	15			
Research	14			
Finance	13			
Accounting	11	13		
Purchasing	8			
Personnel	8			33
Quality control		38	20	42
Maintenance		24	19	38
Plant location		24	11	
Equipment replacement		20	12	
Capital budgeting		29	20	
% of companies using MS		61.5	48.4	

Management science—benefits and limitations

The results of MS cannot be guaranteed; the potential benefits, however, may be enormous and well worth the time, effort, and expense required. The main benefits and limitations of MS are:

Benefits

1. Provides a systematic and logical approach to decision making.
2. Helps communication within the organization through consultation with experts in various areas.
3. Permits a thorough analysis of a large number of alternative options.
4. Enables evaluation of situations involving uncertainty.
5. Allows decision makers to judge how much information to gather in a given problem.
6. Increases the effectiveness of the decision.
7. Enables quick identification of the best available solution.
8. Allows quick and inexpensive examination of a large (sometimes infinite) number of alternatives.
9. Enables experimentation with different alternatives using models, thus eliminating the cost of making errors while experimenting with reality.

Limitations

1. Time-consuming.
2. Lack of acceptance by decision makers.
3. Assessments of uncertainties are difficult to obtain.
4. Evaluates the decision in terms of a sometimes oversimplified model of reality, possibly leading to erroneous recommendations.
5. Can be expensive to undertake, relative to the size of the problem.
6. Studies may be abandoned for various reasons, resulting in an unproductive expense.

One question that managers frequently ask is, "Where have these techniques been applied?" The list of applications is growing continuously. Examples of typical managerial problems where MS techniques have been applied are:

Areas of application

- Inventory control.
- Facility design.
- Product-mix determination.
- Portfolio analysis (of securities).

- Scheduling and sequencing.
- Merger-growth analysis.
- Transportation planning.
- Design of information systems.
- Allocation of scarce resources.
- Investment decisions (new plants and the like).
- Project management—planning and control.
- New product decisions.
- Sales force decisions.
- Market research decisions.
- Research and development decisions.
- Oil and gas exploration decisions.
- Pricing decisions.
- Competitive bidding decisions.
- Quality control decisions.
- Machine setup problems in production.
- Distribution decisions.
- Manpower planning and control decisions.
- Credit policy analysis.
- Research and development effectiveness.

Illustrations of such applications will be shown throughout this book.

1.8   Review Questions

1. Give an example that will illustrate the equivalence of management and decision making.

2. Explain why the management style of "trial and error" is becoming less and less attractive.

3. Explain why decision making today is more complex than 40 years ago.

4. Examine the definitions of MS. Can you give a personal example of an MS situation that will fit these definitions?

5. Explain how the standard tools of MS were developed.

6. Discuss the major advantages of MS.

7. Discuss the major limitations of MS.

8. List some managerial problems that would seem amenable to MS techniques. List some that would *not*.

9. Define structured, semistructured, and unstructured decisions.

10. Categorize managerial activities (according to Anthony).

11. Give additional examples for each of the cells in the DSS framework.

12. Observe an organization with which you are familiar. List five decisions it makes in each of the following categories: *strategic planning, management control (and tactical planning)*, and *operational control*.

13. Explain: "MS models are used in structured situations. However, they can also be used as part of a DSS in semistructured or unstructured problems."

Glossary

Decision science   The collection of disciplines and techniques whose main interest is the study of decision making.

Decision support systems (DSS)   A model-based information system to support managers as they make decisions.

Management   Mobilization of resources in order to attain the organization's goals.

Management science   The application of the scientific approach to the analysis and solution of managerial decision-making problems.

Operations research   Similar to management science with emphasis on mathematical support.

Productivity   Ratio of outputs (results) to inputs (resources).

Scientific management   A school of management thought headed by F. W. Taylor that focused on economic efficiency as the productive core of the organization.

References and Bibliography

1. Alpar, P., and S. Reeves. "Predictors of MS/OR Application in Small Businesses," *Interfaces* 20, no. 2, (March–April 1990), pp. 2–11.

2. AMA Management Report No. 10. *Operations Research Considered.* New York: AMA, 1958.

3. Anthony, R. N. *Planning and Control Systems: A Framework for Analysis.* Boston: Harvard Business School, 1965.

4. Churchman, C. W.; R. L. Ackoff; and E. L. Arnoff. *Introduction to Operations Research.* New York: John Wiley & Sons, 1957.

5. Ford, F. N.; D. A. Bradbard; W. N. Ledbetter; and J. F. Cox "Use of Operations Research In Production Management," *Production and Inventory Management,* 28, no. 3 (1987), pp. 59–63.

6. Forgionne, G. A. "Corporate Management Science Activities." *Interfaces* 13 (June 1983), pp. 20–28.

7. Gaither, N. "The Adoption of Operations Research Techniques by Manufacturing Organizations." *Decision Sciences* 6 (1975), pp. 797–813.

8. Gorry, G. M., and M. S. Scott-Morton. "A Framework for Management Information Systems." *Sloan Management Review,* Fall 1971.

9. Harpell, J. L., M. S. Lane, and A. H. Mansour. "Operations Research in Practice: A Longitudinal Study." *Interfaces* 19 (May–June 1989) pp. 65–78.

10. Schumacher, C. D., and B. E. Smith. "A Sample Survey of Industrial Operations-Research Activities II." *Operations Research* 13 (1965), pp. 1023–27.

11. Shannon, R. E., et al. "Operations Research Methodologies in Industrial Engineering: A Survey." *AIEE Transactions* 12 (1980).

12. Simon, H. *The New Science of Management Decisions.* Rev. ed. Englewood Cliffs, N.J.: Prentice-Hall, 1977.

13. Turban, E. *Decision Support and Expert Systems,* 3rd ed., New York: Macmillan, 1993.

14. Turban, E. "A Sample Survey of Operations Research Activities at the Corporate Level." *Operations Research* 20 (1972), pp. 708–21.

Management Science and Decision Making

Decision making, which is of prime interest to management science, can be viewed as a systematic process. Such a perspective enables the development of quantitative tools with which managers can make better decisions.

Chapter 2 discusses the characteristics that are common to the quantitative tools and then describes the various steps of the management science process, emphasizing the task of modeling. Through the exposition of these topics, the foundation for the entire book is laid.

2.1 Introduction

In this chapter, the use of management science (MS) for managerial decision making is examined from three perspectives: its *characteristics,* its *process,* and its *tools*. The characteristics of MS consist primarily of the following:

1. A primary interest in managerial decision making.
2. The employment of a scientific approach.
3. An interdisciplinary framework is attempted.
4. Mathematical models are used.
5. Computers are very frequently employed.
6. Problems and decisions are viewed from a systems perspective.

These characteristics, which are exhibited to a greater or lesser degree in all MS projects, are discussed first. This is then followed by a description of the MS process, a very systematic approach to decision making. Finally, the tools or techniques of MS are described. These standard tools were created as a response to certain forms of problems that kept reappearing in managerial situations. These problems, the appropriate tools, and the relationships between the problems and the tools are also discussed.

Decision Making: A Primary Focus

A *decision* is the conclusion of a *process* by which one chooses between two or more available alternative courses of action for the purpose of attaining a goal(s). The process is called *decision making*. According to Herbert A. Simon [9], managerial decision making is synonymous with the whole process of management. To illustrate the idea, let us examine the important managerial function of *planning*. Planning involves a *series of decisions* such as: What should be done? When? How? Where? By whom? Hence, planning implies decision making. Other functions of management such as organizing and controlling can also be viewed as composed of making decisions.

Planning: A series of decisions

In the real world, decisions are made either by individuals or by **groups;** most major decisions are made collectively. Whereas management science tools can be used to provide analysis to either groups and/or individuals, it is also possible to support the *decision process* of a group (see [6]), either manually or by a computerized technology called group support systems. A major premise of MS is that decision making, regardless of the situation involved, can be considered as a generic process, consisting of the following major steps:

Decision making: A generic process

1. Defining the problem.
2. Searching for alternative courses of action.
3. Evaluating the alternatives.
4. Selecting one alternative.

Much confusion exists between the terms *decision making* and *problem solving*. One way to distinguish between the two is to consider the entire process (steps 1–4 above) as *problem solving;* the specific step of "selecting an alternative" (step 4 above) is the *decision* or the proposed *solution* to the problem. Another viewpoint is that steps 1–4 constitute decision making that ends with a recommendation, whereas problem solving further includes the *implementation* of the recommendation.

However, in the interest of consistency with many other texts, the terms *decision making* and *problem solving* will be considered as equivalent in this text and will be used interchangeably. Regardless of its name, the process is similar to the general process of scientific analysis. This similarity provides the basis for the management science approach to decision making, as will be shown in the following section.

A Scientific Approach

The scientific approach (or method) is a formalized reasoning process to which many of the scientific discoveries since Descartes can be credited.* It consists of the following steps:

The steps of the scientific method

Step 1. The problem for analysis is defined, and the conditions for observation are determined.

Step 2. Observations are made under different conditions to determine the behavior of the system containing the problem.

Step 3. Based on the observations, a hypothesis is conceived that describes how the factors involved are thought to interact, or what is the best solution to the problem.

Step 4. To test the hypothesis, an experiment is designed.

Step 5. The experiment is executed, and measurements are obtained and recorded.

Step 6. The results of the experiment are analyzed, and the hypothesis is either accepted or rejected.

The six steps of the scientific method can be applied to decision making. For example, the *evaluation* of alternatives is done scientifically through *experimentation*. The overall relationship of the scientific approach to the decision-making process is shown in Figure 2.1.

An Interdisciplinary Approach

The team approach

Many managerial problems have physical, psychological, biological, mathematical, sociological, engineering, and economic aspects. By bringing together a team with a variety of backgrounds, new and advanced approaches to old problems are often obtained.

---

*Descartes was a French philosopher and mathematician of the 17th century, considered the father of modern philosophy. He emphasized the use of reason as the chief tool of inquiry.

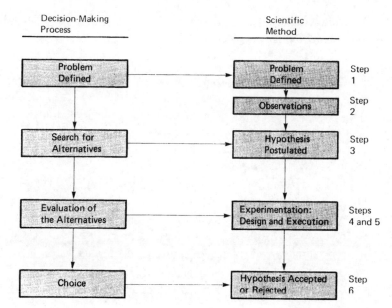

FIGURE 2.1

Relationship of the scientific approach to the decision-making process

The scientific mind from each discipline attempts to extract the essence of the problem and relate it structurally to other similar problems encountered in one's own particular field. Having drawn some analogies, the researcher can then determine if the problem under study is amenable to solution methods traditionally successful in his or her field. When scientists from several disciplines do this collectively, the pool of possible approaches is large enough to reinforce individual disciplines (e.g., see [1]).

Therefore, many complex management science problems are attacked by teams (the average size is three persons). A team approach, however, has some potential dangers. Working as a committee, the team approach may suffer from the potential deficiencies and weaknesses of committees, such as inefficiency, compromised decisions, lack of leadership, and poor communication.

Frequently, however, there is no economic justification for a team, in which case the "one-person show" is appropriate. Many problems are simple enough to be handled by a single qualified researcher, especially one with an interdisciplinary training. Also, thanks to the advance of computers, it is easy for a scientist in one field to retrieve information about other disciplines.

The problems of committees

Models

A **model** defined

Simplification and representation of reality

The use of models, especially mathematical models, is the backbone of management science. A **model** is a *simplified representation* or abstraction of reality. It is usually simplified because reality is too complex to copy exactly and because much of the complexity is actually irrelevant to the specific problem. But these characteristics of *simplification* and *representation* are difficult to simultaneously achieve in practice. For example, a model can be simple but not represent the true situation.

The following are the major reasons why MS employs models in general and mathematical models in particular.

Benefits of models

a. Models enable the compression of time. Years of operations can be simulated in minutes or even seconds of computer time.
b. Manipulating the model is much easier than manipulating the real system. Therefore, experimentation is easier.
c. The cost of making mistakes during a trial-and-error experiment is much smaller when done on the model.
d. Today's environment involves considerable uncertainty. The use of modeling allows a manager to compute *calculated risks* in the decision-making process.
e. The cost of the modeling analysis is much lower than if a similar experiment were conducted with the real system.
f. Models enhance and reinforce learning.
g. The use of mathematical models enables quick identification and analysis of a very large, sometimes almost infinite number of possible solutions.

Use of Computers

Many managerial problems are complex, involving numerous interrelated variables. The search for and evaluation of alternative solutions may become a gigantic computational project. In many cases, a manual or a hand calculator approach to the analysis is impractical or even impossible, because it may take more than a lifetime to solve the problem. Thus, many problems are solvable only with the aid of high-speed computational devices.

The need for high-speed computers

In addition to the use of the computer for the execution of the necessary calculations in solving the models, computers are also used in data collection, storage, retrieval, and analysis (e.g., identifying frequency distributions) and in the validation of the models. Computers are also used to assist in implementation, using "what if" capabilities and graphic presentation that make it easier for managers to understand and use the model results.

Faster, cheaper, more accurate

The use of computers has become closely associated with quantitative analysis and MS. Computers have the important advantage of being a relatively inexpensive means of rapid calculation and possess the accuracy and flexibility invaluable in experimenting with and solving managerial decision models.

Obsolete analyses in the past

The computer has provided a means for solving those problems that have long been quantifiable but computationally too complex or time consuming for human calculation. By the time decisions were made, the information on which they were based was often obsolete, so that poor consequences resulted. As time passed, the availability of computers increased and the cost of processing data and computing results decreased. Thus, more and more use was made of computers in MS.

2.2 The Systems Point of View

A system defined

A **system** is a collection of people, resources, concepts, and procedures that is intended to perform some identifiable function, or to serve a goal. A clear definition of the function or purpose of a system is most important. The *purpose* of an air defense system, for instance, is to protect the targets on the ground, not just to destroy attacking aircraft or missiles.

A hierarchy of systems

The notion of *levels* (or a *hierarchy*) of systems reflects the fact that all systems are subsystems, because all are contained within some larger system. For example, a bank would include within itself *subsystems* such as: (1) the commercial loan department, (2) the trust department, (3) the savings department, and (4) the operations department. Also, the bank itself may be a subsidiary of a holding company; for example, the Bank of America, which is a subsystem of the California banking system, which is a part of the national banking system, which is a part of the national economy, and so on. The connections and interactions between the subsystems are termed *interfaces*.

A systems viewpoint

Management science recognizes that a decision made in one segment of the organization may have a significant effect, not only on the operation of that particular segment, but on the operation of other segments as well. Therefore, when possible, the overall organizational point of view is adopted. Such an approach is termed a *systems point of view* or a *systems approach*.

The Structure of a System

Systems as inputs, processes, and outputs

Systems are divided into three distinct parts: *inputs, processes,* and *outputs*. They are surrounded by an environment (Figure 2.2) and are frequently connected by a feedback mechanism.

Inputs
Inputs include those elements that enter the system. Examples of inputs are raw materials to a chemical plant, or students to a university.

Processes
All the elements necessary to *convert* the inputs into outputs are included in the processes. For example, in a chemical plant, a process may include energy, operating procedures, materials handling, and the use of employees and machines. In a university, a process may include teaching, learning, examinations, and the use of faculty, laboratories, and libraries.

Outputs
Outputs describe the finished products or the consequences of being in the system. For example, fertilizers are one output of a chemical plant and graduates are the output of universities.

FIGURE 2.2

The system and its environment

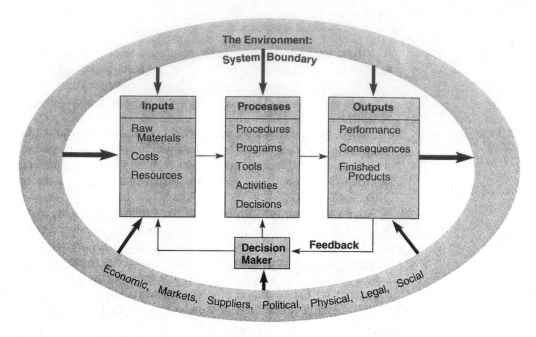

Feedback, the essence of control

Feedback

The flow of information to the decision maker concerning the system's output is called feedback. Based on this information, the decision maker can modify the inputs, or the processes, or both, as shown in Figure 2.2.

What is the environment?

The Environment

There are several elements that lie outside the system in the sense that they are not inputs, outputs, or processes. However, they have an impact on the system's performance and consequently on the attainment of its goals. These are termed the **environment.** One way to identify the elements of the environment is by answering two questions as suggested by Churchman [2]:

1. Is it possible to manipulate this element?
2. Does the element matter relative to the system's goals?

If and only if the answer to the first question is "no," and the answer to the second is "yes," should the element be considered part of the environment. Environmental elements can be social, political, legal, physical, economic, and the like. For example, in a chemical plant, the suppliers, competitors, and customers are elements of the environment. In a university, the neighboring universities, the community, and the regional accrediting agency represent some elements of the environment.

The Boundary

A boundary to separate

A system is separated from its environment by a boundary. The system is inside the boundary and the environment lies outside. The boundaries may be physical (e.g., the system is a department in building C), or the boundary may be some nonphysical factor. For example, a system can be bounded by time, such as when we analyze an organization for a period of only one year.

When systems are being studied, it is often necessary to define the boundaries in order to simplify the analysis. Such boundaries are related to the concept of closed and open systems.

Closed and Open Systems

Because every system can be considered a subsystem of another, the application of systems analysis may never end. Therefore, it is necessary, as a matter of practicality, to confine the analysis to defined boundaries. Such confinement is termed *closing* the system.

A *closed system* represents an extreme along a continuum; an *open system* is at the other extreme. The continuum reflects the degree of independence of the system. Closed systems are totally independent, while open systems are interdependent with their environments. A closed system is considered to be isolated from environmental influences. The system accepts inputs from the environment and may deliver outputs into the environment, but there are no interactions during the transformation process.

A black box

A special type of closed system is called a "black box." In a black box, the inputs and outputs are well defined but the process itself is not specified. Managers frequently treat MS models and computer systems as black boxes. That is, they do not care *how* the models or the computer work; they care only about the inputs and the results. They consider the models as they would a telephone or an airplane; they use them but do not care how they function to achieve the effect they do.

Open systems exchange information, material, or energy with the environment. Living systems are the best examples of open systems. And most organizations are also open systems that continually adapt to changes in their environment.

Many of the MS models are confined to a closed system. Decision support systems, on the other hand, attempt to deal with systems that are relatively open. Such systems are less structured and analyzing them involves checking the impacts on the environment. In a closed system, however, it is not necessary to conduct such checks because it is assumed that the system is isolated from the environment.

System Effectiveness and Efficiency

Effectiveness is defined as the *extent to which goals are achieved*. It is thus concerned with the *results* or the *outputs* of a system. As such, effectiveness is synonymous with performance.

Effectiveness versus efficiency

Effectiveness is frequently confused with **efficiency.** Effectiveness measures the degree of a goal's attainment; efficiency measures how well resources are being utilized. Effectiveness does not necessarily imply efficiency. A system may be effective but very *inefficient* if it attains its goals but at tremendous expense.

Management science is interested in improving managerial decisions. At the extreme, an attempt is made to arrive at decisions that will result in the highest level of productivity.

In many managerial systems, and especially those involving the delivery of human services (such as education, health, or recreation), the measurement of the system's effectiveness and efficiency constitutes a major problem. The reason for the difficulty is due to the existence of several, often nonquantifiable, goals, as well as the indirect costs and benefits that are involved. In recent years, several methodologies have been developed under the names of *cost-effectiveness, cost-benefit analysis, benefit-cost ratios,* and *systems analysis* that attempt to measure the effectiveness and efficiency of such systems. For further discussion and references, see [10].

Cost-benefit analysis

2.3   The Management Science Process

The MS process is illustrated in Figure 2.3. The six-step process starts with the definition of the problem and ends with the implementation of a solution. The details of this process and the methodological problems that are involved in its execution are discussed next.

FIGURE 2.3

The process of management science and the roles of the manager and the management scientist

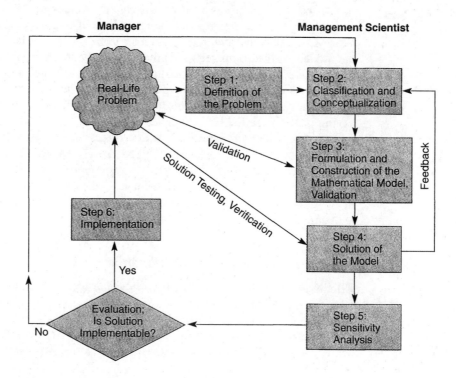

Step 1: Definition of the Problem

By the "definition of the problem" we mean recognizing that a problem (or an opportunity) exists, determining its magnitude, defining it precisely, and noting what its *symptoms* are. Often, what is described as a problem (e.g., excessive costs) may only be a *symptom* of a problem (e.g., improper inventory levels). Because so-called real-world problems are usually complicated by many interrelated factors, it is sometimes difficult to distinguish between symptoms and problems. The existence of a problem in an organization can best be appraised by monitoring the productivity level. In order to do so, it is necessary to study the organization's inputs, processes, and outputs. The measurement of productivity, as well as the construction of models, is based on data.

Symptoms versus the problem elements

Data Collection

The collection of historical data and the estimation of past and future data is one of the most difficult tasks for the management scientist. The following are some of the issues that could arise during data estimation or collection.

Time. Outcome variables may occur over an extended period of time, with revenues (or profits) and expenses being recorded at different points of time. To overcome this difficulty, a *present-value* approach should be used for all calculations involving future monies. The issue of what interest rate to select for the discounting is a special concern and is usually addressed by the financial/accounting staff.

Subjective Approach. It is often necessary to use a subjective approach to data estimation. One such method is where optimistic, pessimistic, and most likely estimates are used.

Future Conditions. It is assumed that the data used for the assessment and modeling are representative of future conditions. If not, it is necessary to predict the *nature of the change* and include it in the analysis.

Step 2: Classification of the Problem

This step involves the *conceptualization* of a problem in an attempt to classify it into a definable *category*. As mentioned earlier, problems can be classified into two major categories: *standard* (also called structured or **programmed**) and unstructured (called nonprogrammed). In addition to classifying the problem into a major category, it is necessary to classify it into a precise *prototype* (see Section 2.4). Only then is it possible to proceed with formulating the problem.

Decision situations are also frequently classified on the basis of what the decision maker knows (or believes) about the situation. It is customary to divide the degree of

FIGURE 2.4

*The categories of
decision making*

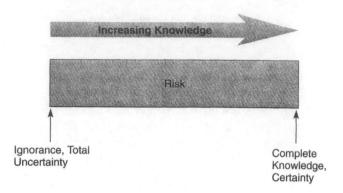

Decision categories

knowledge into three categories (see Figure 2.4), ranging from complete knowledge, on the right, to ignorance, on the left. Specifically, these categories are:

1. Certainty.
2. Risk.
3. Uncertainty.

Decision Making Under Certainty

In decision making under **certainty,** it is assumed that complete information is available so that the decision maker knows exactly what the outcome of each course of action will be. The decision maker thus becomes a perfect predictor of the future. For example, the alternative to invest in U.S. Savings Bonds is one in which it is reasonable to assume complete availability of information about the future return on the invest-

Deterministic
decisions

ment. Such situations are also termed **deterministic.** They occur most often with short time horizons. For example, with decisions whose impact will be felt after three months it is more reasonable to assume certainty than in a decision whose impact will be felt after two years.

Decision Making Under Risk

Probabilistic
decisions

A decision under **risk** (also known as a *probabilistic* or **stochastic** decision situation) is one in which there could be two or more possible results for each alternative. For example, investing in stocks may result in an annual rate of return on investment of either 15 percent, 3 percent, or negative 2 percent, depending on the state of the economy. The reason there could be more than one result is that the possible states of nature are uncontrollable by the decision maker. If we assume that the *chance* of occurrence of each of the states of nature is known, then we say that the decision situation is *under risk;* otherwise, we call it **uncertainty.** *Note:* The definitions of the terms *risk* and *uncertainty,* as presented here, were suggested by Professor F. H. Knight of the University of Chicago in 1933. Several other definitions can be found in the literature.

Less information is available than in decision making under certainty, because it is not definitely known which outcome will occur. The actual outcome depends on which *state of nature* occurs. For example, the number of umbrellas a store sells in a month depends on how much rain falls during the month.

In risk situations, it is assumed that the long-run probabilities of occurrence of the given states of nature (and their conditional outcomes) are known or can be estimated. A classic example of such a situation is roulette. The roulette board is divided into 37 equal parts: 18 are black, 18 are red, and 1 is marked with zero. The player knows the probabilities of each state of nature represented by parts of the roulette field (e.g., 18/37 for red, 1/37 for zero). In making a decision, the player knows the long-run probability of winning the bet and therefore can assess the degree of risk assumed (termed a **calculated risk**).

Calculated risk

Decision Making Under Uncertainty

In decision making under uncertainty, the decision maker considers situations in which several outcomes are possible for each course of action. However, in contrast to the risk situation, the decision maker *does not know,* or cannot estimate, the probability of occurrence of the possible states of nature. This is not necessarily the case of ignorance, however, because he or she at least knows the possible states of nature. For example, it may be impossible to assess the probability of the success of a brand new product. Thus, uncertainty situations contain even less information than risky situations.

Uncertainty or risk?

Step 3: Model Types and Formulation

Types of Models

The representation of systems or problems through models can be done at various degrees of abstraction. Models are classified, according to their degree of abstraction, into three groups:

Iconic (scale).   An **iconic model,** the least abstract, is a physical replica of a system, usually based on a different scale than the original. These may appear in three dimensions such as airplane, car, or bridge models made to scale, or a production line. Photographs and computer icons are other types of iconic scale models but in only two dimensions.

Analog.   An **analog model** does not look like the real system but behaves like it. These are usually *two-dimensional* charts or diagrams; that is, they are physical models, but their shape *differs* from that of the system. Some examples are:

- Organization charts that depict structure, authority, and responsibility relationships.
- A map where different colors represent water or mountains.
- Stock market charts.

- Blueprints of a machine or a house.
- An oil dipstick.

Analog models are more abstract than iconic models.

Mathematical.   The complexity of relationships in some systems cannot be represented physically, or the physical representation may be cumbersome and take time to construct or manipulate. Therefore, a more abstract model is used with the aid of mathematics. Most MS analysis is executed with the aid of **mathematical models.** They can describe diverse situations and be easily manipulated for purposes of experimentation and prediction. Lately, however, iconic and analog models are becoming more common, especially with simulation and decision support systems.

Management science uses mathematical models

Static and Dynamic Models

Static models take a single snapshot of a situation. During this snapshot, everything occurs in a single interval that can be short or long in duration. Most of the situations in this book are static. For example, a monthly schedule of employees' workhours assumes that only one schedule is made, at the beginning of the month, and that all data remain unchanged during the month.

Dynamic models are used to evaluate scenarios that change over time; for example, an investment decision where the return is computed for five years, at yearly intervals. Each year, the results are examined and may trigger additional decisions. Dynamic models are therefore *time dependent*. Dynamic models show trends and patterns over time.

Formulation

Modeling or *formulating* the problem involves the conceptualization of the problem and its abstraction to a mathematical form. All of the relevant variables are identified and the equations describing their relationships are established. Simplifications are made, whenever necessary, through a set of *assumptions*. For example, a relationship between two variables may be assumed to be linear. It is necessary to find a proper balance between the level of simplification of the model and the degree of representation of reality. The simpler the model, the easier the manipulations and the solutions, but the less representative it will be of the real problem, as noted earlier.

The role of assumptions

The need to simplify the problems in the model

The task of modeling involves a multitude of interrelated activities and methodological issues. The most important of these are:

a. The components of the model.
b. Analytical and numerical models.
c. The mathematical relationships.
d. The validity of the model.

a. The Components of Mathematical Models

All mathematical models are comprised of three basic components: *result variables, decision variables,* and *uncontrollable factors.* These components are connected by mathematical (logical) relationships, as shown in Figure 2.5. Examples of these components are given in Table 2.1.

The Result Variables

The result variables reflect the *level of effectiveness* of the system. That is, they tell how well the system performs or attains its goals. The result variables are **dependent** variables, which means that for the event described by this variable to occur, another event must occur first. In this case, the result variables depend on the occurrence of the deci-

FIGURE 2.5

The general structure of a model

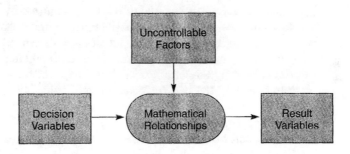

TABLE 2.1   Examples of the Components of Models

Area	Decision variables	Result variables	Uncontrollable variables
Financial investment	Investment amounts Period of investment Timing of investment	Total profit Rate of return Earnings per share Liquidity	Inflation rate Prime rate Competition
Marketing	Advertising budget Number of models Zonal sales reps	Market share Customer satisfaction	Disposable income Competitor's actions
Manufacturing	Production amounts Inventory levels Incentive plan	Total cost Quality level Spoilage	Machine capacity Technology Materials prices
Accounting	Audit schedule Use of computers Depreciation schedule	Data processing cost Error rate	Legal requirements Tax rates Computer technology
Transportation	Shipments	Total transport cost	Delivery distance Regulations
Services	Number of servers	Customer satisfaction	Demand for service

sion variables and the uncontrollable factors. The result variables also have other names:

- Outputs of the system.
- Measures of performance.
- Measures of effectiveness.
- Payoffs.
- Outcomes.
- Objectives.

The Decision Variables

Decision variables describe elements in the problem for which a choice must be made. These variables are *manipulable* and *controllable* by the decision maker. Examples are the quantities of products to produce, the number of units to be ordered, and the number of tellers to use in a bank (others are shown in Table 2.1). Decision variables are also called "unknowns" and are classified mathematically as being independent. They are denoted by the letters x_1, x_2, and so on, or by x, y, z. The aim of management science is to find the best (or good enough) values of the decision variables.

The Uncontrollable Factors

In any decision situation, there are factors (variables, constants, parameters) that affect the result variables but that are not under the control of the decision maker. Examples are the prime interest rate, building codes, tax regulations, and prices of supplies (others are shown in Table 2.1). Most of these factors are uncontrollable because they emanate from the environment surrounding the decision maker.

b. Analytical and Numerical Models

Analytical models for direct result

Analytical Models

Analytical models use mathematical formulas to directly (in one step) either *derive* an optimal solution or *predict* a certain result. As such, analytical models are *deductive* in character, in contrast to numerical procedures, which are essentially *inductive* in character.

Heuristic models for "good-enough" result

Heuristic Models

Heuristics are step-by-step procedures or rules that, in a finite number of steps, arrive at a good-enough solution. These rules are based on either experimentation or else sound, logical concepts. They are fast and easy to apply but have some limitations. Heuristics may be, in some cases, the only practical or economic way to solve complex management problems. Heuristics also play an important role in the problem-solving procedures of expert systems.

Numerical Models

Numerical techniques consist of a trial-and-error comparison of several proposed solutions, either optimal or nonoptimal. The numerical models that yield optimal solutions consist of those that are based on *complete enumeration* and those that are based on *algorithms*.

Complete, Exhaustive Enumeration

When one checks *every possible* solution, one performs a complete **enumeration.** This technique is useful only when the number of alternatives is relatively small; otherwise, it is a lengthy, tedious, or even impossible approach.

Algorithms

An **algorithm** is a step-by-step process of searching for an optimal solution by *gradually improving each solution.* Thus, in contrast to complete enumeration, an algorithm checks only a *portion* of all solutions.

Simulation

This is a numerical technique for conducting experiments with a system by checking the performance of different configurations or scenarios of the system. The approach usually is based on a computerized mathematical model of a management system operating for an extended period of time.

An Illustration

To illustrate the use of numerical techniques, one might consider a control box. The box has knobs on it representing different independent controllable variables, and dials (gauges) representing the dependent variables that measure the system's effectiveness. The uncontrollable variables are built into the operation of the box through internal wiring. When the decision maker wants to explore the consequence of a given alternative course of action, he or she merely turns the knobs (each combination setting of the knobs represents an alternative course of action) and watches the dials.

The illustration in Figure 2.6 represents a control box for an inventory model. The box has only one dial, representing the cost of inventory, the chosen measure of the system's effectiveness. The knobs represent two controllable variables: x_1 is the number of orders placed each year and x_2 is the quantity of safety stock the company keeps. The decision maker, sitting in front of this box, would manipulate the knobs. For example, the decision maker may set $x_1 = 2$ orders per year and $x_2 = 400$ units of safety stock. Then the dial that shows the resulting cost, $7,000, can be observed.

To find a solution in the case of *complete enumeration,* one would have to experiment with *all* combinations of the knobs. For example, $x_1 = 2$ and $x_2 = 400$ is one combination shown in Figure 2.6. Each time a combination is attempted, the inventory cost is recorded. When *all* possible combinations have been tried, the *optimal* solution can be identified.

FIGURE 2.6

*A control box for an
inventory problem*

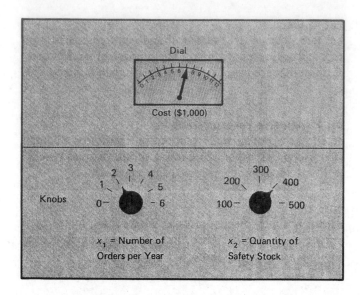

In the case of using an *algorithm,* there is no need to check *all* alternatives; using a theory, one attempts to generate new combinations of knobs such that the resultant inventory cost *continuously decreases* until the least cost combination is found. The time and cost of using an algorithm is significantly less than that of complete enumeration, because fewer combinations of knobs are checked.

Finally, management can decide not to check all combinations of the knobs, but only some of them. Two options are available. First, management may use some rules of thumb or *heuristics* that are equivalent to a few or even one setting of the knobs. Second, a *simulation* approach may be used, where *experimentation* will continue until a certain level of success is achieved. In either case, the solution is not guaranteed to be optimal.

The management science tools discussed in this text are classified in Figure 2.7, according to the solution techniques discussed above.

c.   *The Mathematical Relationships in the Model*

Mathematical
expressions to tie
the components
together

Two types of
relationships

The components of a mathematical model are tied together by sets of mathematical expressions such as equations or inequalities. Figure 2.8 is an example of a model of a manufacturing system. In MS, however, the arrows in the picture are replaced by mathematical expressions. The mathematical relations in an MS model may include two major parts: the *objective function* and the *constraints*.

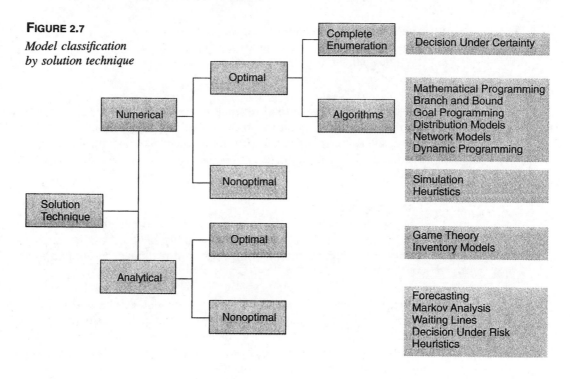

FIGURE 2.7

Model classification by solution technique

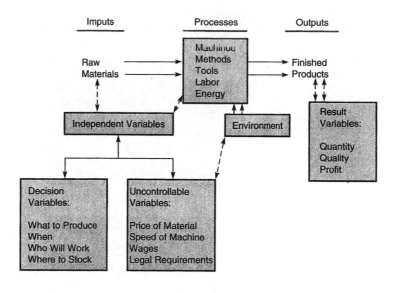

FIGURE 2.8

A manufacturing systems model

The Objective Function

The objective function expresses the dependent variables in the model as they relate to the independent variables. For example, an objective function may look like:

$$R = 5x_1 + 2x_2$$

where R symbolizes the total revenue to a manufacturer (dependent variable); x_1 and x_2 are the quantities of the two products that are produced and sold (decision variables); and 5 and 2 are the prices set by the marketplace (uncontrollable factors). The objective, or goal, is to maximize the revenue. Such an objective is usually limited by *constraints*.

The Constraints

The **constraints** express the limitations and requirements imposed on managerial systems due to regulations, competition, scarcity of resources, technology, or other such factors. For example, a marketing constraint might be represented by:

$$x_1 + x_2 \leq 50$$

That is, the total quantity of the two products that can be sold is 50 or less.

Figure 2.9 illustrates this manufacturer's model. The model can be interpreted as: Find the value of the decision variables x_1 and x_2 such that the total revenue R (result variable) is maximized, subject to the marketing limitation and market prices, which are uncontrollable by the manufacturer.

d. Validating the Model

After a model has been constructed, it is necessary to know how well the model represents reality. Often, the accuracy of a model cannot be assessed until model solutions are generated. Validation requires answering such questions as: Are the predictions

FIGURE 2.9
A simplified model of a manufacturing situation

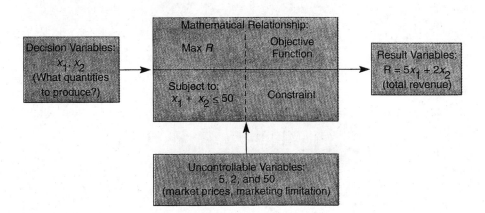

made by the model empirically accurate? and, Is the model representative of the system's behavior under real-world circumstances?

Validation may be viewed as a two-step process. The first step is to determine whether the model represents the system (or phenomena) it is supposed to represent. The second step is to determine whether the model is *internally* correct in a logical and programming sense.

Model validation is necessary

One way to validate a model is to try different possible sets of data and see if the solutions resemble the historical behavior of the system. For example, if a model describes sales behavior as a function of interest rates, then it can be tested by "plugging in" several values of interest rates, say, 4, 5, . . . , 19 percent, examining what level of sales is predicted in each case, and comparing this to historical data. Obviously, if the model was unable to successfully describe historical occurrences, it should not be considered valid for making future predictions; therefore, changes are necessary in the model. Another way to validate a model is to solve small problems and see if the results make sense to the user.

Step 4: Solving the Model

Definition: A *solution* to a model means finding a specific set of values of the decision variables that result in a desirable output level.

As previously stated, solution procedures to standard problems are well developed and computer codes exist for all of them. The user, therefore, is relieved of the task of developing these procedures. However, it is important that the user understand some of the concepts and the methodological issues that are involved in this step.

Criteria for Choice

The choice of a solution approach

The solution procedure depends on what we are trying to achieve. Are we trying to get the best? Or will any acceptable result be sufficient? That is, how are we going to *evaluate* the proposed alternative? This issue involves selecting a **principle of choice,** a decision regarding the acceptability of a solution approach. It reflects the attitudes, policies, and objectives of the decision makers. Is the best possible alternative sought, or will a "good enough" solution do? Are we willing to assume risk or do we prefer a conservative approach? Of the various principles of choice, the following are of prime interest:

The *best* way

Normative models

Optimization. An optimal alternative is one that is demonstrably the *best* of *all* possible alternatives. To find it, one should examine *all* alternatives and prove that the one selected is indeed the best. Optimization *prescribes* the course of action that the decision maker *should take*. Therefore, models designed to optimize are referred to as **normative** models. Such a model must possess a decision criterion for selecting the *best* alternative and proving that the selected alternative is indeed optimal.

Normative decision theory is based on the following *assumptions*:

1. Man is an economic being whose objective is to maximize personal goals; that is, the decision maker is *rational*.

The "economic man" assumptions

2. In a given decision situation, all alternative courses of action and their possible consequences are known.

3. The decision maker has a criterion of preference that enables him or her to rank the desirability of all consequences of the analysis.

In operational terms, **optimization** can be achieved in one of two basic ways:

1. Get the *highest level* (maximum) of goal attainment from a *given* set of resources (or at a given cost).

2. Find the alternative with the *lowest cost* (minimization of resources) that will fulfill a required level of goal(s).

Suboptimization.   By definition, the use of optimization requires that the decision maker consider the impact of each alternative course of action on the entire organization. The reason for this is that a decision made in one area may have significant effects in other areas. Take as an example a production department that plans its own schedule. For that department, it would be beneficial to produce only a few products, but in large quantities to reduce manufacturing costs. However, such a plan may result in high and costly inventories as well as marketing difficulties due to lack of a variety of products.

Using a systems point of view affords consideration of the impact on the entire organization. Thus, the production department should make its plans in conjunction with other departments. Such an approach, however, may require a complicated, expensive, and time-consuming effort. Therefore, as a matter of practice, the management scientist may "close" the system within narrow boundaries, considering only *part* of the organization or problem under study. Such an approach is called *suboptimization*.

Optimal or suboptimal?

If a decision is made in one part of the organization *without paying attention* to the rest of it, then a solution that is *optimal* from the point of view of that single part may be **suboptimal** from the point of view of the whole, producing inferior or even damaging results. In addition, the model builder may face great difficulties in the selection of the decision criteria because lower-level objectives may be inconsistent with higher-level criteria.

The praticality of suboptimization

Suboptimization, however, may still be a very practical approach and therefore many problems are first approached from this perspective. The primary reason for this is that analyzing only a portion of a system allows some tentative conclusions to be made without getting bogged down in a deluge of details. Also, the modeling is faster, yielding more accurate results. Once a solution is proposed, its potential effects on the remaining departments of the organization can be checked. If no significant negative effects can be traced, the solution may then be considered optimal from a systems point of view.

Good Enough or "Satisficing."   According to Simon [9], most human decision making, whether organizational or individual, involves a willingness to settle for a satisfactory solution, "something less than the best." This is because optimization is usually unattainable due to the time and cost required. In a **satisficing** mode, the decision maker sets up an *aspiration* (desired) level of goals and then searches the alternatives until one is found that meets the goals.

Satisficing to an aspiration level

An example of selecting a satisfactory alternative is when an individual wants to sell some land. According to the optimization approach, the seller should examine *all* offers and select the *highest* offer, assuming that the objective is to maximize the proceeds from the sale. In reality, this process is not followed. What the seller normally does is assess the market and set up a desired price (the aspiration level), say, $55,000. The first buyer to offer $55,000 (or more) will get the property. If the seller is unsuccessful in getting a bid of $55,000 within a certain period, he or she will change the asking price, say, to $53,000, which in essence means reducing the seller's level of aspiration. If the seller then sells the property for at least $53,000, the seller is satisficing a new goal.

Descriptive models

Satisficing as a principle of choice is used in those MS tools that are labeled **descriptive.** Descriptive models describe things *as they are*. Their major use in MS is to investigate the outcomes or consequences of various alternative courses of action, as reflected by the system's performance. However, because the descriptive analysis checks the effectiveness of the system for given conditions (or given alternatives) rather than for *all* conditions, there is no *guarantee* that an alternative selected with the aid of descriptive analysis is optimal. Descriptive models are usually applied in decision situations where normative models are not applicable. They are also used when the objective is to define the problem or to assess its seriousness rather than to select the best alternative. Descriptive models are especially useful in *predicting the behavior* of a system under various assumptions.

Predicting behavior with descriptive models

Using the Model to Select an Alternative

Once the principle of choice is determined, the search for the "best" or a "good enough" solution may begin. In general, this activity involves five steps:

1. Generate alternatives.
2. Predict the outcome of each alternative.
3. Relate outcomes to goals.
4. Compare the alternatives.
5. Select an alternative.

1. Generate Alternatives
The decision-making process presented in Section 2.1 involves a search for alternative courses of action that are candidate solutions to the problem. In management science,

such alternative courses of action may be either given or else generated by the model. In the first case, the model is used to *evaluate* the given alternatives; in the second case, it is used to generate and then evaluate alternatives.

There are several methods of searching for alternatives (see [4]). At the very least, the search process requires resources such as money, labor, and time. Because these are usually limited, the search must be terminated sooner or later.

2. Predict the Outcome of Each Alternative
In order to evaluate an alternative, it is necessary to predict its outcome in the future. The topic of forecasting is fully covered in a separate chapter.

3. Relate Outcomes to Goals
The value of an outcome is judged in terms of the goal's attainment. Sometimes, an outcome is expressed directly in terms of a goal. For example, *profit* is an outcome, whereas *profit maximization* is the goal, and both are expressed in dollar terms. In other cases, an outcome may be expressed in terms other than those of the goal. For example, the outcome may be in terms of machine downtime, but the goal can be expressed in terms of dollars. In such cases, it is necessary to transform the outcome so it is expressed in terms of the goal.

4. Compare the Alternatives
Once the previous activities have been completed, the decision maker can compare the alternatives and select one. Some of the difficult issues considered in this stage are the following.

Multiple goals.   The models described in this book are frequently based on the analysis of one goal, such as "maximization of profit." In reality, several goals may exist simultaneously.

Sensitivity to change.   The result variables may be particularly sensitive to changes or errors in some of the independent variables. The model builder should check this sensitivity to avoid highly sensitive alternatives.

What constitutes a significant difference between alternatives?   In comparing alternatives, one may find that alternative A will bring $323,200, while alternative B will bring $323,150. Is alternative A superior to B? In theory, the answer is yes. Practically speaking, the two alternatives are basically the same. The accuracy of data is such that $50 out of $323,000 is not a significant factor.

In general, it is important to determine when an alternative is indeed superior. Because we deal with models, we simplify reality. Alternative A may bring $50 extra, but it might also make some employees unhappy. In this text, a choice is usually made based on quantitative results, but other factors should also be considered, especially when the quantitative difference seems to be small.

5. Select an Alternative

The process ends with a choice, namely the selection and recommendation of a solution (or an alternative course of action).

Classification of Solutions

Solutions can be classified as being *feasible* or *infeasible, optimal* or *nonoptimal,* and *unique* or *multiple*.

Feasible and Infeasible Solutions

Feasible

A *feasible* solution is one that satisfies *all* the requirements and constraints imposed on the problem and, therefore, could be implemented. Violating one or more of these requirements results in an unacceptable, **infeasible** solution.

Infeasible solutions

For example, there are many ways of getting dressed. As a matter of fact, there are $n!$ (n factorial) different ways of getting dressed with n pieces of clothing. With $n = 10$ there are 3,628,800 different ways of getting dressed. Suppose that you want to determine the fastest way of getting dressed; do you have to check all 3,628,800 alternatives? Of course not! You can start with your socks, then shoes, then shirt, and so on. But you cannot put your socks on after your shoes are on—this is obviously an *infeasible* solution. By identifying and eliminating the infeasible solutions early, it is possible to narrow down the number of alternatives requiring evaluation.

Optimal and Nonoptimal Solutions

Optimal

An *optimal* solution is the *best* of all feasible solutions. For a solution to be declared optimal there must be proof that *all* feasible solutions were checked and that the proposed solution is better than any other solution. A feasible solution that cannot be classified as optimal is considered *nonoptimal*.

Unique and multiple solutions

Unique and Multiple Solutions

If there exists only one optimal solution, it is called *unique*. If two or more equivalent optimal solutions can be identified, then there exist *multiple* solutions. The latter case is usually preferred by managers because it gives them greater flexibility in implementing a solution.

Step 5: Sensitivity Analysis

Sensitivity analysis for insight and confidence in the results

Sensitivity analysis is an attempt to help managers when they are uncertain about the accuracy of their information. In sensitivity analysis, the information in question is altered to find what effects, if any, changes will have on the proposed solution. In other words, the purpose of sensitivity analysis is to determine the effect of *changes* in the independent variables on the values of the dependent variables. For example, an optimal solution that was based on an assumed prime interest rate of 7 percent may have prescribed an investment in real estate rather than in stocks or bonds. Suppose that the interest rate is 6 percent or 9 percent—is real estate still the best investment?

Of special interest are questions such as:

Questions a
sensitivity analysis
can answer

1. What change can occur in a certain independent variable before a change occurs in the recommended solution?
2. What is the magnitude of a change in the proposed solution resulting from a change in an independent variable(s)?
3. Which independent variables are most sensitive? That is, which variables will, when changed only slightly, cause the value of the dependent variables to change significantly? Which independent variables are insensitive?
4. Is a proposed solution highly sensitive? That is, does the solution include sensitive variables that, when changed slightly, will alter the solution so that it will no longer be optimal? Conversely, insensitive solutions will hold with a wide range of variations in the independent variables.

Insensitive solutions are usually easier to implement, because their predicted results are more certain to occur and because management can modify the proposed solution with a small loss in the effectiveness of the system.

Step 6: Evaluation and Implementation

The results generated by a model represent a solution to a simplified scenario of reality. Also, in many cases the solution appears in an abstract format (e.g., mathematical symbols) or in technical terminology. Therefore, before the solution is submitted to management, it needs to be *evaluated*. Evaluation also involves such issues as determining the *meaning* of the proposed solution in terms of solving the problem (similar to an "impact analysis").

The management scientist's role does not end with the submission of a recommended solution. To complete the process, a solution must be implemented. Implementing an MS solution is a difficult process; on many occasions, it is harder to implement a solution than to build and solve a model.

2.4 Managerial Problems and the Tools of Management Science

Models for generic
managerial
problems

Throughout the history of management, certain types of problems have been encountered repeatedly. The structure of these has been abstracted and analyzed so as to yield "generic" problems. To handle these generic problems, a set of standard solution procedures (also called *tools* or *techniques*) has been developed. Thus, whenever a management problem is recognized as a generic problem, it can be molded into a standard format and the appropriate tool can be applied for its solution.

The Generic Managerial Problems

Some common **generic managerial problems** discussed in this text are:

Allocation Problems

These problems arise when (1) there are a number of activities to be performed, (2) there exist two or more different ways to perform these activities, and (3) resources or facilities are scarce. The problem then is to find the best utilization of resources; namely, which activities to pursue and in what magnitude, so that effectiveness will be maximized.

Distribution Problems

Moving a commodity (e.g., oil or corn) from several sources to several destinations at minimum cost constitutes a *transportation problem*. Several types of problems (e.g., production scheduling) can be viewed and solved as transportation problems. A related topic is the *assignment problem,* in which certain items such as a person or an activity are to be assigned, on a one-to-one basis, to other items such as facilities or services. The objective is to minimize the cost or to maximize the effectiveness of the assignment.

Network and Project Management Problems

Network problems describe flows of commodities, activities, information, or other resources between locations. For example, in the construction of a bridge, many activities, information, and resources flow as time passes. The problem is to find the best activity plan for such systems.

Competitive Situations

When the results of a decision are determined not only by one's own course of action but also by that of a competitor, a competitive situation exists. This situation may be viewed as a game that each party attempts to win.

Inventory Control

The proper level of inventories of materials, money, finished products, or persons is a major problem in many organizations. The costs of carrying inventories are high, but inventories can result in large savings by preventing shortages, providing discounts on large quantities purchased or produced, eliminating changes in the level of production, and reducing ordering and setup costs. The problem is to find the proper level of inventory, which is determined by the decisions "when" and "how much" to order, such that the total cost will be minimized.

Waiting Line Problems

Whenever persons or objects that require service arrive at a service facility, a waiting line is likely to occur, especially in rush periods. Typically, in such situations there is a waiting line during certain periods, but the facility may be idle during other "slack" periods. In general, the larger the facility, the costlier its operation, but the smaller the waiting time for service. The problem is to find the appropriate size of the facility as well as to determine its operating procedures (e.g., give priority to certain customers) in such a way as to minimize the sum of the relevant costs.

Predicting the Behavior of a System

Management is frequently interested in predicting the behavior of a system under different conditions or scenarios. Although this is not classified as a prototype problem by itself, it can be used in constructing prototype procedures and/or evaluating solutions.

Other Problems

Several other managerial problems are of interest to management scientists. The most important are:

- Sequencing (which task to do next) and routing (what path minimizes travel time between points).
- Maintenance (how often to repair) and replacement (which items, how often).
- Scheduling of work, people, or vehicles.
- Search (which items to consider first, or locating an item such as a sunken ship).
- Bidding (what strategy, how high or low).
- Unstructured, "fuzzy," and qualitative situations.
- Diagnosis of problems from symptoms.

The Tools of Management Science

To solve the above managerial problems, a body of standard MS tools have been developed.

Mathematical Programming

Mathematical programming attempts to maximize the attainment level of one goal subject to a set of requirements and limitations. In this text, the following models will be covered: *linear programming; transportation* and *assignment models;* and *integer* and *goal programming*.

Branch and Bound

Branch and bound is a step-by-step procedure used when a *very large* (or even infinite) number of alternatives exist for certain managerial problems. It is also used to solve integer programming problems.

Decision Tables

Allocation and investment problems involving a relatively small number of possible solutions can be presented in a tabular form known as a decision table.

Decision Trees
The extension of decision tables for situations involving several decision periods takes the shape of a "tree."

Forecasting
To predict the outcome of managerial decisions, various forecasting approaches are employed. Many of these are based on statistics.

Network Models
This is a family of tools designed for the purpose of planning and controlling complex projects. The best known models are *PERT* (Program Evaluation Review Technique) and *CPM* (Critical Path Method).

Inventory Models
For certain types of inventory control problems, special models that attempt to minimize the cost associated with ordering and carrying inventories have been developed.

Markov Chains
Markov chains are used for predicting the outcome of processes where systems or units change their condition over time.

Waiting Line (Queuing) Models
For certain types of problems involving waiting lines, special models have been developed to predict the performance of service systems.

Simulation Models
For the analysis of complex systems where all other models fail, management science uses descriptive-type simulation models.

Heuristic Programming
The use of either quantitative and/or qualitative decision rules (heuristics) can facilitate the solution of complex problems.

Dynamic Programming
Dynamic programming is an approach to decisions that are basically sequential in nature or can be reformulated so as to be considered sequential.

Game Theory
Game theory provides a systematic approach to decision making in competitive environments and a framework for the study of conflicts.

The Relationships Between Managerial Problems and the Tools

The one-to-one matching of a problem to a technique does not always hold. In some instances, a particular tool can be used for several prototype problems; and in other situations, one problem can be addressed with several tools. Although selection of a specific tool may depend on the specific problem, there are certain relationships that *usually* hold true. These are presented in Table 2.2.

Decision making is a complicated process consisting of certain steps and elements common to all decision situations. Such generalization makes it a potential subject for scientific analysis. The importance and complexity of the decision-making process has attracted investigators from several disciplines, resulting in various approaches to the study. One of these approaches is management science.

TABLE 2.2   The Major Relationships Between Problems and Tools

Problem type / Tools	Mathematical programming	Goal programming	Transportation, assignment	Branch and bound	Decision tables	Decision trees	Forecasting	PERT/CPM	Inventory	Markov chains	Waiting lines	Simulation	Heuristic programming	Game theory	Dynamic programming
Allocation	X	X		X	X	X							X		X
Distribution	X	X	X	X											
Network								X							X
Competitive decision making												X		X	
Inventory	X								X			X			X
Waiting lines											X	X			
Predicting a system's behavior					X	X	X			X	X	X			
Complex, semistructured, unstructured, fuzzy		X										X			
Combinatorial, or qualitative													X		

2.5 Review Questions

1. What is the difference between making decisions and solving problems? Give an example.

2. Apply a scientific approach process to the following problems:
   a. Can vitamin C cure colds?
   b. Will a new product be accepted in the market?
   c. Should an airline add an additional flight between Chicago and New York?

3. Analyze a managerial system of your choice and identify the following:
   a. The components.
   b. The environment.
   c. The inputs.
   d. The system's goals.
   e. The decision variables.

4. What are some of the "measures of effectiveness" in a manufacturing plant; in a restaurant; in an educational institution; in the U.S. Congress?

5. Give an example of a managerial problem where an interdisciplinary team is desirable. Explain why.

6. Give an example of a mathematical model used by management.

7. What are some of the controllable and uncontrollable variables in the following systems: automotive manufacturer, hospital, courthouse, airline, restaurant, hotel, bank, oil refinery, atomic power plant?

8. What is meant by an objective function?

9. Why are computers an integral part of MS? Under what conditions should computers *not* be used by a management scientist?

10. Give examples of three programmed decisions in an organization with which you are familiar.

11. Give examples of two nonprogrammed decisions in an organization.

12. Apply the MS process to the problem of deciding whether to open a new fast-food outlet. What should the principle of choice be?

13. The city of Toulouse in France is debating whether or not to build a public transportation system. What should the principle of choice be?

14. Compare and contrast normative versus descriptive approaches to decision making.

15. Give an example that illustrates the difference between optimization and suboptimization.

16. Distinguish between numerical and analytical solution techniques. Between an algorithm and a simulation.

17. Give an example to illustrate the simultaneous existence of several goals in organizations.

18. How can a model that predicts the movement of the Tokyo stock market be validated?

19. Describe a situation that will demonstrate the meaning of sensitivity analysis.

20. Give an example of an infeasible solution.

21. Define a "unique" solution.

22. Describe the role of decision support systems in managerial decision making.

23. Distinguish between risk and uncertainty.

2.6 Problems

The problems in this section, especially 4–6, describe typical management problems in order to introduce you to some of the actual complexities of management as they relate to this book. Our purpose is to show you why management science techniques can be of help in solving such problems. Obviously at this time you are not equipped with the appropriate tools to solve these six problems; just do the best you can. (Answers to the even-numbered problems are given in Appendix D.)

As you will see later on, it is not necessarily easy to identify the right tool (or tools) to deal with each situation. In later chapters, the problems at the end of each chapter can be solved with the tools presented in that chapter. We hope that you enjoy your journey through this set of managerial problems. We start here with some short problems and move to more comprehensive ones.

1. A European manufacturer of solar energy devices has two models available: Alpha, which costs $800 per unit and sells for $1,000, and Beta, which costs $1,150 per unit and sells for $1,500.
   a. The company's objective is profit maximization; write the profit function.
   b. The company's objective is to maximize sales (number of units); write the objective function in this case.

2. Express, mathematically, the following requirements and constraints for the preceding problem.
   a. The market for the Alpha devices is limited to no more than 400 units a month.
   b. The total number of devices produced will be at least 540 per month.
   c. Production capability is limited to no more than 720 units per month.
   d. The capital available for production is $50,000 per month.

3. The fixed annual cost of a company's model T product is $55,000. It sells for $1,000, while its variable cost is $740. The company's goal is profit maximization. Write the profit function if the company produces X units each year. Write a model for finding the break-even (zero profit) point.

4. Amuse Corporation is planning to build a theme park in the city of Mid America. They have also discussed a plan for the parking lot, which is to be an independent business unit. Presently, they are discussing the size of the parking lot and the pricing policy. It is estimated that 20 to 25 percent of the users of the parking lot will not go to the amusement park.

Among the options discussed are:
a. Very high parking fees with reimbursement to the amusement park guests.
b. Free parking for everybody.
c. Low fees and no reimbursement.

All these options are being used in shopping centers, theaters, and other theme parks in town.

Amuse Corporation is a private corporation whose objective is to maximize net revenues from the park as a whole. Use the concepts of optimization and suboptimization to discuss the three options.

5. For generations, a two-pan scale used to be the only instrument available for weighing small products. It is still in use in many open-air markets all over the world. This instrument shows whether two amounts are the same or not and which amount is heavier (see figure). Normally, the user places a standard weight (e.g., 1 pound or 1 kilogram) on one of the pans and then tries to put enough of the product on the second pan to achieve a balance.

   A trader's problem is as follows. He just received 12 gold coins. He knows that one of them is irregular (either lighter or heavier) but they all look the same, and he does not have any standard weight to compare them against. Using a two-pan scale, help him devise a procedure to identify the irregular coin. *Note:* While this is not a typical managerial problem today, it is a challenging exercise.
   a. Describe the process you would suggest the trader use to identify the irregular coin.
   b. How many tests (weighings) are needed in order to arrive at a solution?

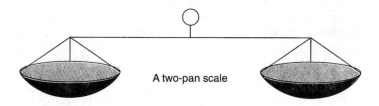

A two-pan scale

c. Now, try to do it in three weighings. (*Hint:* Stop after 15 minutes if you are unsuccessful. If you know the answer, do not tell the other students).

6. Before the days of telemarketing, home shopping, traffic jams, and complex shopping centers, salespersons used to travel a lot. Assume that you work for the MBI Corporation as a salesperson. You have 10 cities that you need to visit each time you go on the road. Obviously, you want to return home at the end of your trip. Also, corporate policy allows you to visit each city once and only once. *Note:* This is known as the "traveling salesperson problem."

   a. Build an analog model of this problem—that is, show it on a map for 10 cities.

   b. Identify some important data concerning the problem (such as distances). Use your imagination. Enter the data into the model.

   c. Define the problem.

   d. Show one possible solution.

   e. List any assumptions that were necessary for your solution.

   f. How many feasible alternative solutions would you guess exist for such a problem?

   g. You are doing a great job in sales, so your boss just added five more cities to your territory. Answer question f now.

   h. List five factors that may be encountered in real life that would make this problem more complicated than what you have shown in questions *a–h*. Explain the impacts of each of these complexities.

   i. What type of model is this? Static or dynamic? Deterministic or stochastic? Is the situation one of certainty, risk, or uncertainty?

Glossary

Algorithm   A set of logical steps to follow to reach a solution.

Analog model   A physical model in a different form from the actual system being modeled.

Analytical   Considering the individual subparts of a system to deduce a result.

Calculated risk   The ability to compute the chance of winning or losing over the long run.

Certainty   The decision environment when there is only one possible payoff for a decision. This situation occurs when only one state of nature exists.

Constraints   Limitations on actions.

Dependent variables   System measures of effectiveness.

Descriptive   Nonoptimizing; describes how a system operates.

Deterministic   Perfect knowledge of the outcome; certainty.

Dynamic models   Models that deal with multiperiod scenarios.

Effectiveness   The degree of goal attainment.

Efficiency   Ratio of output to input.

Enumeration   Listing of possible items to consider.

Environment   Uncontrollable elements outside the system that affect it.

Expert system   A form of artificial intelligence that incorporates the decision rules of an expert within the computer.

Generic managerial problems   Common organizational decision situations such as a "resource allocation" problem.

Group decision making   A decision that is made collectively.

Heuristic   A logical rule to efficiently search for "good enough" solutions.

Iconic model   A physical, scaled replica.

Infeasible   Not acceptable; can't be done.

Inputs   The forms of resources introduced into a system for transformation into outputs.

Mathematical model   A system of mathematical symbols and expressions to represent a real situation.

Model   An abstraction of reality.

Normative   Prescribes how a system *should* operate.

Numerical   Trial-and-error inductive comparisons.

Optimization   The best solution possible.

Outputs   The result of a transformation process in a system.

Principle of choice   The criterion for basing a choice among alternatives.

Programmed problems   Repetitive, routine problems for which standard models have been developed.

Risk   A decision situation where several states of nature exist and their likelihood (probability) of occurrence is known.

Satisfice   A solution that is acceptable.

Sensitivity analysis   Measuring the effect of a change in one variable on a proposed solution.

Simulation   An imitation of reality.

Static models   Models that are confined to one period, taking a single snapshot of a situation.

Stochastic   A situation that involves risk; where the outcome is uncertain.

Suboptimal   Best for a subsystem of the total system.

System   A set of elements that are considered to act as a single, goal-oriented entity.

Uncertainty   The decision environment in which several states of nature exist but their chances of occurring are not known.

References and Bibliography

1. Batson, R. G. "The Modern Role of MS/OR Professionals in the Interdisciplinary Teams." *Interfaces,* May–June 1987.
2. Churchman, C. West. *The Systems Approach.* Rev. ed. New York: Delacort Press, 1975.
3. Clemer, R. T. *Making Hard Decisions: An Introduction to Decision Analysis.* Boston: PWS-Kent, 1991.
4. Etzioni, A. "Humble Decision Making." *Harvard Business Review,* July–Aug., 1989.
5. Harrison, E. F. *The Managerial Decision-Making Process.* 2nd ed. Boston: Houghton Mifflin, 1981.
6. Jessup, L. M., and J. S. Valacich. *Group Support Systems.* New York: Macmillan, 1993.
7. Saaty, T. L., and J. H. Alexander. *Thinking with Models.* Elmsford, N.Y.: Pergamon Press, 1981.
8. Scheer, A. W. *Enterprise-Wide Data Modeling.* New York: Springer-Verlag, 1988.
9. Simon, H. A. *The New Science of Management Decisions.* Rev. ed. Englewood Cliffs, N.J.: Prentice-Hall, 1977.
10. Van Gigch, J. P. *Applied General Systems Theory.* 2nd ed. New York: Harper & Row, 1978.

A Preview
Chapters 3–7

Mathematical Programming

Mathematical programming is the name for a family of tools designed to help solve managerial problems in which the decision maker must allocate scarce (or limited) resources among various activities to optimize a measurable goal. For example, distribution of machine time (the resource) among various products (the activities) is a typical allocation problem. Allocation problems usually display the following characteristics and necessitate making certain assumptions.

Characteristics

1. A limited quantity of economic resources (such as labor, capital, machines, or water) is available for allocation.
2. The resources are used in the production of products or services.
3. There are two or more ways in which the resources can be used. Each is called a solution or a program. (Usually the number of ways is very large, or even infinite.)
4. Each activity (product or service) in which the resources are used yields a return (or reward) in terms of the stated goal.
5. The allocation is usually restricted by several limitations and requirements called constraints.

Assumptions

1. Returns from different allocations can be compared; that is, they can be measured by a common unit (such as dollars or utility).
2. All data are known with certainty.
3. The resources are to be used in the most economical manner.

In the case of linear programming, two additional assumptions are:

4. The return from any allocation is independent of other allocations.
5. The total return is the sum of the returns yielded by the different activities.

The allocation problem can generally be stated as: Find the way of allocating a set of limited resources to various activities so the total reward is maximized. Allocation problems usually have many possible alternative solutions. Depending on the underlying assumptions, the number of solutions can be either infinite or finite. Also, different solutions yield different rewards. Of the available solutions, one (sometimes more) is the *best*, in the sense that the degree of goal attainment associated with it is the highest (i.e., total reward is maximized). This is called the *optimal* solution.

Many problems in organizations are related to the allocation of resources (money, people, time, power, space, equipment). The reasons are limited resources, various ways of allocation, the difficulty of measuring the contribution of the allocation to the goals, and disagreement concerning the importance of the results. Mathematical programming provides a relatively unbiased approach to this allocation problem.

The mathematical programming topics covered in this text include:

Linear Programming—Foundations (Chapter 3)   Linear programming deals with allocation problems in which the goal (or objective) and all the requirements imposed on the problem are expressed by linear functions (see Appendix A).

Linear Programming—Applications (Chapter 4)   This chapter presents a variety of example applications for which linear programming is most appropriate.

Integer Linear Programming (Chapter 6)   When the requirement that some or all of the decision variables must be integers (whole numbers) is added to a linear programming problem, it becomes one of integer (linear) programming. Integer programming is used as an auxiliary tool for solving a host of difficult managerial problems.

Nonlinear Programming (Chapter 6)   Mathematical programming problems, where the goal and/or one or more of the requirements imposed on the problem are expressed by nonlinear functions (see Appendix A), are nonlinear programming problems.

Distribution Problems (Chapter 7)   The transportation of a commodity from sources of supply to destinations, at minimum cost (or maximum profit), and the assignment of workers (or equipment) to jobs are *distribution problems*. These are also a special case of linear programming.

Goal Programming (Chapter 8)   This variant of linear programming is used when multiple goals exist.

The uses of mathematical programming, especially linear programming, are so common that software programs are now found in just about any organization with a computer. A glance at professional or trade journals reveals many applications of mathematical programming. For instance, the petroleum industry makes extensive use of linear programming techniques, and integer programming is increasingly applied to the complex problems of scheduling operations. Process industries such as chemicals, food, steel, and rubber are known as especially heavy users of mathematical programming.

3 Linear Programming— Foundations

Part A: Basics

Part B: Extensions

Linear programming (LP) is one of the best known tools of management science. The most general statement of its objective is that it is used to determine an optimal allocation of an organization's limited resources among competing demands. Many managerial problems can be considered allocation problems. These range from product-mix and blending problems to bus scheduling and dietary planning. Linear programming deals with a special class of allocation problems; namely, those in which all the mathematical functions in the model are linear. Part A presents the general formulation of the LP problem and the graphical technique for its solution. In Part B, the simplex method of solution, a most efficient algorithm of linear programming, is presented.

PART A: BASICS

The Sekido Corporation—Part I

Suji Okita and his wife Keiko were heartily enjoying their dinner of fresh shrimp, their first unhurried meal in days. Final tests had just been successfully completed on the new "slit matrix" television projection system Suji had developed, and the outlook was encouraging. "They'll be installing the system on two models for initial sales next week," he was saying to Keiko. "I wish we had a larger work force, more machine time, and better marketing capabilities; I'm sure we could make considerably more profit. But even as it is, we don't know how many of each model to produce."

Keiko was thinking about her problem at the Toshida Paint Company. A new, expensive, special-purpose paint, Sungold, was becoming very popular, and the production manager had asked Keiko to see if she could find a combination of two new ingredients, code-named Alpha and Beta, that would result in an equivalent brilliance and hue but at less cost than the original ingredients. She felt confident she could.

Keiko did not realize that her problem, a typical *blending* problem, was in many ways equivalent to Suji's, a typical *product-mix* problem.

3.1 The Nature of Linear Programming (LP) Problems

Two prototype LP problems

Allocation problems appear in several forms. Two of the most common are the **product-mix problem** faced by Suji and the **blending problem** faced by Keiko.

The Product-Mix Problem

In a product-mix problem, there are two or more *products* (also called *candidates* or *activities*), such as TV models, competing for limited resources, such as limited production capacity. The problem is to find out *which products* to include in the production plan *and in what quantities* these should be produced (product mix) in order to maximize profit, market share, or some other goal.

Maximize profit with fixed resources

Allocating scarce resources

Although a solution to a product-mix problem does specify the quantities to be produced, what it tells more generally, in effect, is *how to allocate* scarce resources. This is because the technology of production is given and once a decision has been made on the products and quantities to produce, a determination has actually been made of what resources to use and in what quantities.

The Blending Problem

Blending problems involve the determination of the *best blend* of available ingredients to form a certain quantity of a product under strict specifications. The best blend means the least-cost blend of the required inputs. Blending problems are especially important in the process industries such as petroleum, chemicals, and food.

The blending problem is similar to the product-mix problem. However, the objectives usually differ. In the product-mix problem, the profit derived from selling the

Minimize resource
use to obtain a fixed
output

products made from the given amount of resources is to be maximized. In blending, the cost of certain ingredients is to be minimized, while adhering to given specifications. Therefore, a blending problem is also considered a problem of allocating resources in the best manner.

3.2 Formulation

The Linear Programming Model

Management science models are composed of three components: the *decision* (controllable) variables, the *environment* (uncontrollable) parameters, and the *result* (dependent) variables. The LP model is composed of the same components, but they assume different names, as shown in Figure 3.1.

a. The Decision Variables
The decision variables in LP depend on the type of LP problem being considered. The variables can be the quantities of the resources to be allocated, or the number of units to be produced. The decision maker is searching for the value of these unknown variables (usually denoted by $x_1, x_2, \ldots$ or $x, y,$ and z) that will provide an **optimal solution** to the problem.

b. The Objective Function
An LP model attempts to optimize a single goal, written as a **linear function;** for example, total profit $= 5x_1 + 7x_2 + 1x_3$. That is, it attempts to find either the maximum level of a desired goal, such as total share of the market or total profit, or the minimum level of some undesirable outcome, such as total cost.

c. The Constraints
The decision maker is searching for the values of the decision variables that will maximize (or minimize) the value of the objective function. Such a process is usually subject to several uncontrollable restrictions, requirements, or regulations that are called **constraints.** These constraints are expressed as linear inequalities and/or equations.

FIGURE 3.1

*The linear
programming model*

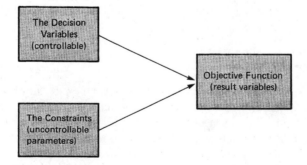

Two Examples

Let us return to the product-mix and blending problems and present both with the relevant data. Then we will formulate both problems in the general structure of the linear programming model.

Example: The Product-Mix (maximization) Problem

The two models of color TV sets produced by the Sekido Corporation will be designated as A and B. The company is in the market to maximize profit. The profit realized is $300 from set A and $250 from set B. Obviously, the more sets produced and sold, the better. The trouble is that there are certain limitations that prevent Sekido Corporation from producing and selling thousands of sets daily. These limitations are:

1. Availability of only 40 hours of labor each day in the production department (a labor constraint).
2. A daily availability of only 45 hours of machine time (a machining constraint).
3. Inability to sell more than 12 sets of model A each day (a marketing constraint).

Sekido's problem is to determine *how many sets of each model to produce each day so that the total profit will be as large as possible.*

The LP approach is divided into two steps: first, the problem is set up or *formulated* as a model. Then the model is solved.

Formulation of the Product-Mix Problem

The Decision Variables

Decision variables

The decision variables in this case are:

$$x_1 = \text{Number of sets of model A to be produced daily}$$

$$x_2 = \text{Number of sets of model B to be produced daily}$$

Objective function

The Objective Function

The daily profit realized from selling sets of model A is $300x_1$ (i.e., the profit per unit times the number of units). Similarly for model B, a profit of $250x_2$ will be realized. The total profit, z, is, therefore, $300x_1 + 250x_2$. This total profit is called the **objective function.** Sekido wishes to maximize the objective function z.

The Constraints on the System

Constraints

1. Labor Constraint. There are 40 hours of labor available each day. Each unit of model A requires two hours of labor, whereas each set of model B requires only one hour. This situation can be expressed as:

Demand for labor		Supply
Total labor for model A	Total labor for model B	Total labor available
$2x_1$ +	$1x_2$ ≤	40

Note that the less-than-or-equal-to sign ($\leq$) is used to represent this linear inequality. That is, 40 hours is the *available* capacity, which does not necessarily have to be used in full.

2. Machine Time Constraint.   There are up to 45 machine-hours available per day. Machine processing time for one unit of model A is one hour and for one unit of model B, three hours. This limitation can be expressed as:

$$1x_1 + 3x_2 \leq 45$$

3. Marketing Constraint.   It is only possible to sell *up to* 12 units of model A each day. This can be expressed as:

$$1x_1 + 0x_2 \leq 12$$

Note that all variable coefficients are included (e.g., 0 and 1), to follow standard LP form.

4. Nonnegativity Constraint.   Finally, it is impossible to produce a negative number of sets; that is, both x_1 and x_2 must be **nonnegative** (zero or positive). This constraint is expressed as:

$$1x_1 \geq 0, \quad 1x_2 \geq 0$$

Note: In later sections of this book, we often do *not* write these latter constraints in the formulation of problems. However, they are always implied, and the reader should remember their existence. Also, in most LP computer programs, it is not necessary to input these constraints; they are automatically assumed.

In summary, the problem is to find the best daily production plan so that the total profit will be maximized. The problem, then, can now be written in standard form as follows. Find x_1 and x_2 that maximize z, the objective function, subject to constraints (shown in standard form).

$$\text{maximize } z = 300x_1 + 250x_2$$
subject to:

$2x_1 + 1x_2 \leq 40$	(labor constraint)
$1x_1 + 3x_2 \leq 45$	(machine time constraint)
$1x_1 + 0x_2 \leq 12$	(marketing constraint)
$1x_1 + 0x_2 \geq 0$	(nonnegativity constraints)
$0x_1 + 1x_2 \geq 0$	

Note: Because production continues day after day, it is not necessary to complete all sets at the end of the day; that is, a fractional number of sets is permissible (e.g., 5.73 sets). However, had it been necessary to complete all sets at the end of the day, additional constraints limiting x_1 and x_2 to whole numbers would have been added. Such an addition changes the problem to one of *integer programming*.

We shall return to the solution of this problem later.

Example: The Blending Problem (minimization)

In preparing Sungold paint, it is required that the paint have a brilliance rating of at least 300 degrees and a hue level of at least 250 degrees. Brilliance and hue levels are determined by two ingredients: Alpha and Beta. Both Alpha and Beta contribute equally to the brilliance rating, one ounce (dry weight) of either producing one degree of brilliance in one drum of paint. However, the hue is controlled entirely by the amount of Alpha, one ounce of it producing three degrees of hue in one drum of paint. The cost of Alpha is 45 cents per ounce, and the cost of Beta is 12 cents per ounce. Assuming that the objective is to minimize the cost of the ingredients, then the problem is to find the quantity of Alpha and Beta to be included in the preparation of each drum of paint. The problem is shown graphically in Figure 3.2.

FIGURE 3.2

The blending problem

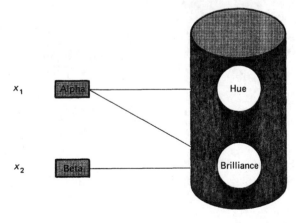

Formulation of the Blending Problem

The problem is formulated for only one drum of paint. The reason is that an optimal answer for one drum of paint will remain optimal for any number of drums as long as the relationships are linear. The total quantity of paint to be produced is, of course, larger than one drum, and it is determined mainly by the demand and the manufacturing technology.

Decision variables

The *decision variables* are:

x_1 = Quantity of Alpha to be included, in ounces, in each drum of paint

x_2 = Quantity of Beta to be included, in ounces, in each drum of paint

The cost of Alpha is 45 cents per ounce, and because x_1 ounces are going to be used in each drum, then the cost per drum is $45x_1$. Similarly, for Beta the cost is $12x_2$. The total cost is, therefore, $45x_1 + 12x_2$, and as our objective function, it is to be *minimized* subject to the following constraints:

Objective function

Constraints

1. To provide a brilliance rating of at least 300 degrees in each drum. Because each ounce of Alpha or Beta increases the brightness by one degree, the following relationship exists:

Supplied by Alpha		Supplied by Beta		Demand
$1x_1$	$+$	$1x_2$	$\geq$	300

2. To provide a hue level of at least 250 degrees. The effect of Alpha (alone) on hue can similarly be written as:

Supplied by Alpha		Supplied by Beta		Demand
$3x_1$	$+$	$0x_2$	$\geq$	250

A math model of the blending problem

In summary, the blending problem is formulated as follows. Find x_1 and x_2 such that:

$$\text{minimize } z = 45x_1 + 12x_2$$
subject to:
$$1x_1 + 1x_2 \geq 300 \quad \text{(brightness specification)}$$
$$3x_1 + 0x_2 \geq 250 \quad \text{(hue specification)}$$

As mentioned before, the nonnegativity requirement will not be stated.

The blending problem is going to be solved later in the chapter. At this time, the reader may note that the blending problem is very similar in structure to the product-mix problem. One difference, however, is that here we wish to minimize the value of the objective function, whereas in the product-mix problem we were maximizing the objective function.

Note: In our example, all the maximization constraints are of the less than or equal to ($\leq$) type, and all the minimization constraints are of the greater than or equal to ($\geq$) type. In reality, when we deal with larger problems, we find all types of constraints, $\leq$, $\geq$, and $=$ in both types of problems, as will be demonstrated later.

3.3 Mathematical Formulation and Terminology

In the previous section, two classical managerial problems were formulated. Let us now generalize the formulation.

Components of a Linear Programming Problem

LP components

Every LP problem is composed of:

Decision Variables
The variables whose values are unknown and are searched for. Usually they are designated by x_1, x_2, and so on.

Objective Function
This is a mathematical expression, given as a linear function, that shows the relationship between the decision variables and a *single goal* (or objective) under consideration. The objective function is a measure of goal attainment. Examples of such goals are total profit, total cost, share of the market, and the like.

Multiple goals

If the managerial problem involves several goals, one can use the following two-step approach.

1. Select a primary goal whose level is to be maximized or minimized.
2. Transform the other goals into constraints, which must only be satisfied.

For example, one may attempt to maximize profit (the primary goal) subject to a growth rate of at least 12 percent per year (a secondary goal). An alternative approach is to combine several goals into one, for example through trade-offs.

Optimization.   Linear programming attempts to either maximize or minimize the values of the objective function.

Profit or Cost Coefficients.   The coefficients of the variables in the objective function (e.g., 300 and 250 in the product-mix example or 45 and 12 in the blending problem) express the *rate* at which the value of the objective function increases or decreases by including in the solution one unit of each of the decision variables.

Constraints

The maximization (or minimization) is performed subject to a set of constraints. There-fore, LP can be defined as a *constrained optimization problem*. These constraints are ex-pressed in the form of linear inequalities (or, sometimes, equalities). They reflect the fact that resources are limited or that other limiting factors must be considered.

Input-Output (Technology) Coefficients.   The coefficients of the constraints' vari-ables are called the *input-output* coefficients. They indicate the rate at which a given re-source is depleted or utilized. They appear on the left-hand side of the constraints.

Capacities.   The capacities (or availability) of the various resources, usually expressed as some upper or lower limit, are given on the *right-hand side* of the constraints. The right-hand side also expresses minimum requirements.

The Mathematical LP Model

The general LP problem can be presented in the following mathematical terms. Let:

a_{ij} = Input-output coefficients c_j = Cost (profit) coefficients

b_i = Capacities (right-hand side) x_j = Decision variables

Find a vector $(x_1, \cdots, x_n)$ that minimizes (or maximizes) a linear objective function $F(x)$ where:

$$F(x) = c_1 x_1 + c_2 x_2 + \cdots + c_j x_j + \cdots + c_n x_n \tag{3.1}$$

subject to the linear constraints:

$$
\left.
\begin{aligned}
a_{11} x_1 + a_{12} x_2 + \cdots + a_{1n} x_n &\leq b_1 \\
a_{21} x_1 + a_{22} x_2 + \cdots + a_{2n} x_n &\leq b_2 \\
\cdots \quad\quad \cdots \quad\quad \cdots \quad\quad \cdots \quad\quad \cdots \\
a_{i1} x_1 + a_{i2} x_2 + \cdots + a_{in} x_n &\leq b_i \\
\cdots \quad\quad \cdots \quad\quad \cdots \quad\quad \cdots \quad\quad \cdots \\
a_{m1} x_1 + a_{m2} x_2 + \cdots + a_{mn} x_n &\leq b_m
\end{aligned}
\right\} \tag{3.2}
$$

and the nonnegativity constraints:

$$x_1 \geq 0, \, x_2 \geq 0, \, \ldots \, x_n \geq 0 \tag{3.3}$$

Example

The LP model for the blending problem is shown next.

Decision variables	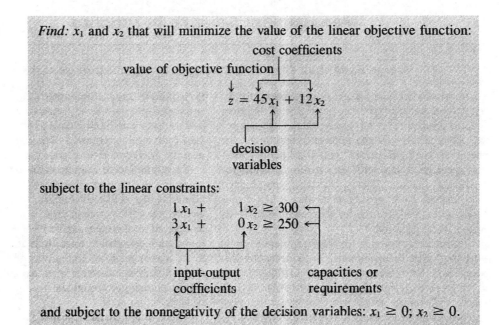
Objective function	
Constraints	
Nonnegativity	

Find: x_1 and x_2 that will minimize the value of the linear objective function:

cost coefficients

value of objective function

$$z = 45 x_1 + 12 x_2$$

decision variables

subject to the linear constraints:

$$1 x_1 + 1 x_2 \geq 300$$
$$3 x_1 + 0 x_2 \geq 250$$

input-output coefficients

capacities or requirements

and subject to the nonnegativity of the decision variables: $x_1 \geq 0$; $x_2 \geq 0$.

3.4 Advantages, Limitations, and Solution Methods

The advantages and limitations of LP are described below. The general solution methodology is also overviewed, in order to introduce the more detailed descriptions in the remainder of the chapter.

Advantages of Linear Programming

LP can be used to solve allocation-type problems that are very common and extremely important in organizations. Their solution is difficult due to the fact that an infinite number of feasible solutions may exist. LP not only provides the optimal solution, but does so in a very efficient manner. Further, it provides additional information concerning the value of the resources that are allocated.

Specifically, the advantages of LP are as follows:

1. Finds an optimal solution(s).
2. Fast determination of the solution, especially if a computer is used.
3. Finds solutions to a wide variety of problems that can be formulated with LP (e.g., see Chapter 4).
4. Finds solutions to problems with a very large or infinite number of possible solutions.
5. Provides a natural sensitivity analysis.

Management Science in Practice

Surge Staffing at Canada Systems Investment Fund Services

In the spring of 1984, the volume of transactions for investment fund services (IFS) in the Financial Services Division of Canada Systems Group, Inc., virtually exploded. Both unforeseen and unplanned-for transaction volumes grew over 100 percent in a short period, forcing management to cope with the situation in an ad hoc and inefficient manner. Delays, overtime, rework, and turnover soared. Additional costs of almost half a million dollars, as well as a major deterioration in IFS's reputation, were incurred.

The transaction explosion involved registered retirement savings plans contributions, a tax-deductible investment used for retirement, similar to IRAs in the United States, that must be paid before the end of February. IFS was the only firm in the transaction processing business large enough to handle these accounts. The investment period, though over a year's duration, was inevitably little used until the last few weeks, approximately the beginning of February to mid-March.

IFS, determined not to see a repeat of the 1984 problem, planned ahead of time for the seasonal crush. A new operations manager and two staff members with business school training were hired to plan for the 1985 season. The situation was complicated by a number of constraints (e.g., number of terminals, space) as well as the variety of possible alternatives. After deciding to model the problem and then to analyze the nature of the situation, a linear programming model was chosen for implementation.

First, historical records and subjective estimates were used to determine a 1985 forecast of transaction volumes over each week of the seven-week season. Two major tasks had to be completed for each transaction—data preparation (sorting, coding, error checking, and grouping) and data entry (keying in the data).

Sources of personnel for the task were chosen from nonregular employees for economic and psychological reasons (e.g., burnout). Two alternative sources were available: temporary hires for just a three-month period (includes training) and on-call clerks with task-specific training from Manpower Temporary Services. Either set of personnel could be assigned to either weekdays or weekends, on the first, second, or third shift. Also, they could be assigned to either data preparation or data entry, because they would generally be trained for each. The decision variable was thus to hire from source j, for shift i, on days t, for task k. The objective was to minimize the total cost of this labor hiring and leasing.

Constraints were numerous and included the maximum size of the source pools, the limiting number of terminals, the skill availabilities, the space limitations, and so on. Other constraints included the expected number of transactions arriving in a week, the data preparation completion rates, backlog estimates, and so forth. Based on historical productivity figures, break and rest periods, learning rates, and fatigue effects, the available capacity could be computed and thereby matched to the need.

The resulting model consisted of 225 variables and 202 constraints. The solution was immediately implementable and, because the forecast turned out to be quite close to reality, the model never had to be rerun. Only about 15 percent of the hiring variables were noninteger and needed rounding, which was not a problem because the values were so large anyway. The optimal solution involved building up a major backlog of transactions in the queue toward the end of February and then working them off in the early weeks of March.

The incremental cost of operations during the 1985 season was $170,000, almost $330,000 less than 1984, in spite of higher wage rates and a 25 percent increase in volume. This represented a 64 percent productivity gain over 1984. IFS's reputation was also restored.

Source: C. H. von Lanzenauer et al., "RRSP Flood: LP to the Rescue," *Interfaces*, July–August 1987, pp. 27–33.

Questions:

1. Why is rounding the number of new hires not a problem if the value is large?

2. A major backlog developed in 1984 and was extremely expensive. Why then was another backlog the optimal solution for 1985?

3. Where did the 64% productivity gain come from? The $330,000 cost savings?

Limitations of Linear Programming Due to Assumptions

Eight limiting assumptions

The applicability of LP is limited by several assumptions. As in all mathematical models, assumptions are made for reducing the complex real-world problem into a simplified form. The major assumptions are:

Certainty
It is assumed that all the data in the LP are known with certainty. In problems under risk, the expected value of the input data can be considered as a constant, thus enabling the treatment of risky situations by LP.

Linear Objective Function
It is assumed that the objective function is linear. This means that per unit cost, price, and profit are assumed to be unaffected by changes in production methods or quantities produced or sold.

Linear Constraints
It is also assumed that the constraints are linear. The linearity assumptions in LP are reflected in additivity, independence, and proportionality.

Additivity
It is assumed that the total utilization of each resource is determined by adding together that portion of the resource required for the production of each of the various products or activities. The **assumption of additivity** also means that the effectiveness of the joint performance of activities, under any circumstances, equals the sum of the effectiveness resulting from the individual performance of these activities.

Independence
Complete independence of coefficients is assumed, both among activities and among resources. For example, the price of one product has no effect on the price of another.

Proportionality
The requirement that the objective function and constraints must be linear is a proportionality requirement. This means that the amount of resources used, and the resulting value of the objective function, will be proportional to the value of the decision variables.

Nonnegativity
Negative activity levels (or negative production) are not permissible. It is required, therefore, that all decision variables take nonnegative values.

Divisibility
Variables can, in general, be classified as continuous or discrete. Continuous variables are subject to *measurement* (e.g., weight, temperature), whereas discrete variables are those that can be *counted*: 1, 2, 3, . . . In LP, it is assumed that the unknown variables

$x_1, x_2, \ldots,$ are continuous, that is, they can take any fractional value (**divisibility assumption**). If the variables are restricted to whole numbers and thus are indivisible, a problem in **integer programming** exists.

Solving Linear Programs

A set of decision variables, each having a value, is called a *solution.* For example, $x_1 = 5$ and $x_2 = 0$ is a solution for the Sekido Corporation problem. Proposed solutions to an LP problem that *satisfy all the constraints* are called *feasible.* The collection of **feasible solutions** is called the **feasible solution space** or **area.** Any proposed solution that violates one or more of the constraints is termed **infeasible.**

Feasible or infeasible?

Once a problem has been formulated, one of several available methods of solution can be applied. Normally, this is done with the aid of a computer. With the exception of Karmarkar's Algorithm, described below, only two of all the solution methods have a significant value. They are (1) the *graphical method,* whose main purpose is to illustrate the concepts involved in the solution process; and (2) the general, computationally powerful **simplex method** and its variants.

The simplex method

The Ellipsoid Algorithm

This method was developed by a Russian mathematician, L. G. Khachian [6]. The approach involves shrinking an ellipsoid that surrounds the feasible solution space until it converges on the optimum solution. Its advantage was purported to be that it solved problems in a period of time that related linearly to the complexity of the problem, rather than exponentially, as is characterized by the simplex method. However, in practice, it was found that the linear increase was so great that it provided no major improvement over the simplex method for most practical-sized problems.

The Karmarkar Algorithm

In this method, the algorithm moves to a point *within* the solution space instead of on the boundary, and creates sequences of spheres that converge on a desired vertex (basic solution) until the optimum vertex is reached. It, too, solves LP problems in a linear amount of time, but it is much more efficient for large problems than either the ellipsoid algorithm or the simplex [7, 9, 10]. This method is most efficient with problems having many thousands of variables and/or constraints. A software program called KORBX utilizes the Karmarkar algorithm; it is marketed by AT&T.

3.5   The Graphical Method of Solution

A graphical solution

The graphical method is used mainly to illustrate certain characteristics of LP problems and to help in explaining the simplex method. The only case where it has a practical value is in the solution of small problems with two decision variables and only a few constraints, or problems with two constraints and only a few variables.

Example 1: A Maximization Problem

In order to illustrate the graphical method, let us reproduce the product-mix problem discussed previously:

Model of the
product-mix problem

$$\text{maximize } z = 300x_1 + 250x_2$$
subject to:
$$2x_1 + 1x_2 \leq 40 \quad \text{(labor constraint)}$$
$$1x_1 + 3x_2 \leq 45 \quad \text{(machining constraint)}$$
$$1x_1 + 0x_2 \leq 12 \quad \text{(marketing constraint)}$$

Graphical Analysis

Originated by
Descartes

The plotting of algebraic equations and **inequalities** in terms of geometric lines and curves was initiated by the French philosopher Descartes in the 17th century. Two straight lines intersecting at right angles are used as a reference and points are located by giving two coordinates (distances from each of the lines). The plane formed by the two lines is divided into four regions called quadrants. An example of such a system is shown in Figure 3.3. We use x_1 and x_2 to designate the lines. Sometimes x and y are used instead.

Because the nonnegativity constraints appear in all LP problems, we are limited to the 1st quadrant only ($x_1 \geq 0$, $x_2 \geq 0$). The graphical solution procedure consists of two phases: (*a*) graphing the feasible area, and (*b*) identifying the optimal solution.

FIGURE 3.3

Feasible and infeasible quadrants on the two-dimensional grid

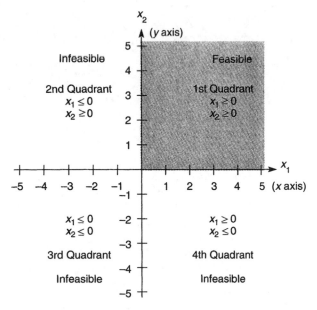

Phase 1: Graphing the Feasible Area

Graphing the
constraints

The feasible area is established through graphing all of the inequalities and equations that describe the constraints.

Graphing the First (Labor) Constraint (Figure 3.4)

This constraint is expressed as $2x_1 + 1x_2 \leq 40$. The steps in drawing the constraint are:

Step 1. An inequality of the type *less than or equal to* has two parts. We will first consider only the equality part of the constraint: $2x_1 + 1x_2 = 40$. Because an equation can be shown graphically as a straight line, it is sufficient to find the coordinates of two points to graph the entire equation as a line. To do so, first set x_1 to zero and then solve the equation for x_2. We get: $2(0) + x_2 = 40$. Thus, $x_2 = 40$. This yields a point (0, 40) which is shown as point **A**. This solution means that if only model B sets are produced, it will be at a rate of 40 per day. To find a second point, we set x_2 to zero:

$$2x_1 + 0 = 40$$

Solving this we get $x_1 = 20$. This is shown as point B (20, 0) in Figure 3.4.

Step 2. Joining points A and B by a straight line is a representation of the equation $2x_1 + x_2 = 40$. However, it is not just the equation that is of interest, but also the in-

Inequality represents
an area

equality $2x_1 + x_2 < 40$. This inequality is represented by an *area* below and to the bottom left of the equality (Figure 3.4). Because the original constraint was of the $\leq$ type, the area of interest includes both the line and the shaded area below it.

FIGURE 3.4

The labor constraint

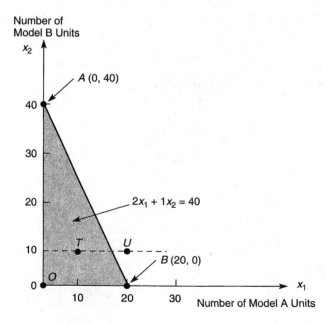

This area represents all the combinations that use 40 or less units of labor and therefore we call it a *feasible* area.

> *Note: How to find the side of the constraint on which the feasible area is located.* Sometimes it is not obvious which side of the line represents the feasible area. Of the several methods that can be used, the following is the simplest. Take an arbitrary point and check if it is feasible. If the point is feasible, then the entire area is feasible. For example, point T in Figure 3.4, which is inside the area, has coordinates of (10, 10). If we substitute these coordinates into the constraint $2x_1 + 1x_2 \leq 40$, we get $2(10) + 1(10) = 30$. Because 30 is smaller than 40, the point is in the feasible area. Point $U = (20, 10)$, on the other hand, is not feasible, since $2(20) + 1(20) = 50$.

The inequality area in Figure 3.4 would normally include negative values of x_1 and x_2, except for the fact that in LP, negative values are excluded by the nonnegativity constraints $x_1 \geq 0$ and $x_2 \geq 0$. The end result is a feasible area inside (and including the boundary of) the triangle O-A-B in Figure 3.4 (shaded).

Graphing the Second (Machine Time) Constraint
Similarly, the shaded area O-C-D in Figure 3.5a represents the area of feasible solutions for the machining constraint $1x_1 + 3x_2 \leq 45$.

FIGURE 3.5

The second and third constraints

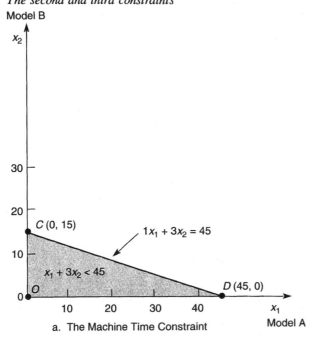

a. The Machine Time Constraint

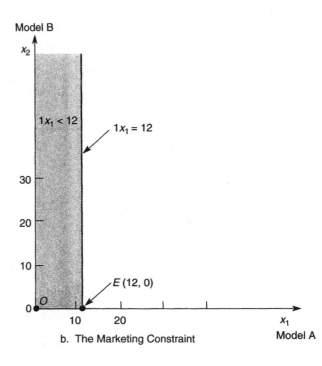

b. The Marketing Constraint

Graphing the Third (Marketing) Constraint

Next, the equality part $x_1 = 12$ of the marketing constraint $x_1 \le 12$ is plotted as a straight line, vertically from point E and parallel to the x_2 axis (Figure 3.5b). Again, the feasible area is left of, and including, the line.

Feasible—the area within *all* constraints

Combining the Constraints

Once all the constraints have been drawn, they can be put on one graph. As a matter of practicality, they can be built on one graph from the beginning. We used the graphs of Figures 3.4 and 3.5 for instructional purposes only. The combination of all constraints is shown in Figure 3.6. The shaded area $O\text{-}C\text{-}G\text{-}E$ is the area that is to the lower left of all equations simultaneously. Therefore, any solution in this area (Figure 3.7) is *feasible* with respect to *all* the constraints.

Phase 2: *Identifying an Optimal Solution*

Infinite number of possible solutions

Any point in the shaded area of Figure 3.7 and its boundary is a feasible solution. Because there are an infinite number of points in this area, there are an *infinite number of feasible solutions* for this problem. To find an optimal one, it is necessary to identify a solution (point) in the feasible area that maximizes the profit (objective) function.

How can this task be accomplished? Let us examine a feasible solution inside the feasible area; say, point H. This point is a solution plan that calls for five sets of model A ($x_1 = 5$) and three sets of model B ($x_2 = 3$). This solution is not optimal, because production of x_1 can be increased from point H to point K (12 units of x_1 and 3 of x_2),

FIGURE 3.6

All three constraints simultaneously

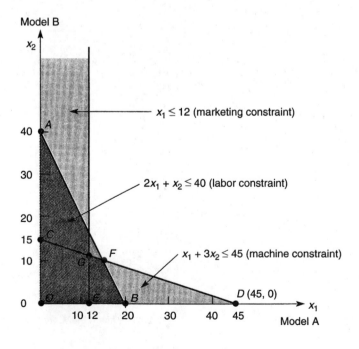

FIGURE 3.7

The feasible area

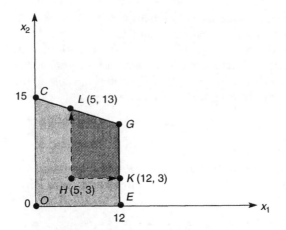

resulting in a higher profit. Notice that such an increase may continue only until we are limited by a constraint. Similarly, point L, where more x_2 is produced than at H, will result in a higher profit than point H.

The reason that both points K and L are better than point H is because both yield a higher profit, because the coefficients of the objective function are positive (more units, more profit). It can, however, be shown that no matter what sign the coefficients of the objective function have, there will always be at least one point somewhere *on a boundary* of the feasible area that is *superior* to any point inside the area. Therefore, an optimal solution to a linear programming problem can *never* be inside the feasible area but must be on a boundary. Furthermore, it can be shown that an optimal solution must be at a corner (called a vertex or *extreme* point) where two constraints intersect. *Note:* If only one optimal solution exists, it must be on a vertex. If more than one optimal solution exists, then *at least* two optimal solutions *must* be on two adjoining vertices, and the others will be on the boundary connecting them.

On the boundary

To a corner

Therefore, an efficient search for an optimal solution need only consider corner points (O, C, G, and E in our case). Two methods can be used for such a search.

Enumeration

Method 1. Enumeration of All Corner Points
In this method, the solution values at all the corner points are compared. This is done by determining the coordinates of all corner points and then computing and comparing the values of the objective function at these points. Let us demonstrate: For points O, C, and E, the exact coordinates can be read directly from Figure 3.7, as given below:

Point	x_1	x_2
O	0	0
C	0	15
E	12	0
G	?	?

For point G, the approximate coordinates can be read from the graph, or exact co-ordinates can be computed as follows: Point G is at the intersection of two straight lines. Therefore, the value at point G (as given by x_1 and x_2) must be the same for the two intersecting lines. Such a value can be found by simultaneously solving the two intersecting linear equations, one of which describes the marketing constraint and the other the machine time constraint. In this case:

$$\text{Equation 1:} \quad 1x_1 = 12 \qquad \text{(marketing constraint)}$$

$$\text{Equation 2:} \quad 1x_1 + 3x_2 = 45 \quad \text{(machine constraint)}$$

The solution is simple in this situation, because the value of one decision variable, x_1, is already known to be 12. This value is introduced into Equation 2, which can then be solved. We get:

$$1x_1 + 3x_2 = 12 + 3x_2 = 45, \qquad \text{or} \qquad 3x_2 = 33, \qquad \text{or} \qquad x_2 = 11$$

Therefore, the coordinates of point G are (12, 11).

Now the profits at each corner point can be calculated, using the objective function $300x_1 + 250x_2$. The results are shown in Table 3.1.

Identify the best corner

The point that yields the greatest profit is point G. The optimal solution, therefore, is to produce 12 units of TV model A and 11 units of TV model B. The total profit is $6,350.

The process of comparing profits at all corner points may be very lengthy, because in larger linear programming problems many corners exist. A graphical method can also be used to evaluate the corners. This method is presented next.

Method 2. The Use of Isoprofit (Constant Profit) Lines

Slope of the objective function

According to this procedure, the optimal solution can be found by using the *slope* of the objective function as a guide. Let us illustrate.

In examining solution H (5, 3) in Figure 3.7, it was indicated that better solutions are available such as K (12, 3). The question is: In what direction should one move to find better solutions? The answer to this question is found from the objective function. If the objective function (a profit function in our example) is graphed and the direction of increasing profit is identified, then when one starts moving the profit function in that direction, the profit will increase and increase. The limit to the increase is reached when the function touches the farthest point(s) on the boundary of the feasible area (if

---

TABLE 3.1   Profit Values at Corner Points

Point (corner)	Solution coordinates	Total profit $300x_1 + 250x_2 = z$	
O	(0, 0)	$300\,(0) + 250\,(0) = 0$	
C	(0, 15)	$300\,(0) + 250(15) = \$3,750$	
E	(12, 0)	$300(12) + 250\,(0) = \$3,600$	
G	(12, 11)	$300(12) + 250(11) = \$6,350$	← *Maximum*

the feasible area is bounded). (The unbounded situation will be discussed in a later section.) This point is then an optimal solution. The graphical method accomplishes this task in a systematic fashion.

Graphing an Objective Function. Profit functions (such as $z = 300x_1 + 250x_2$) describe an infinite number of equations that depend on the value of z and, therefore, cannot be presented as a single line. To overcome this difficulty, a *family* of linear equations, called **isoprofit lines** (or isocost lines, in the minimization case) is constructed. An isoprofit line is a line (a collection of points), each of whose points designates a solution with the *same* profit. By assigning various values to z, we get different profit lines. Graphically, such a family can be plotted as many lines *parallel* to each other (see Figure 3.8).

Isoprofit lines

To start, we pick a value for z. Any arbitrary profit figure will work. However, it is simple to pick a profit number that gives an integer as an answer to x_1 when we set $x_2 = 0$, and vice versa. A good choice is to use a number that is divided easily by the coefficients of both variables. For example, $1,500 \div 300 = 5$, and $1,500 \div 250 = 6$. Thus, let us assume that $z = 1,500$. Then, the profit equation $300x_1 + 250x_2 = 1,500$ can be drawn as a straight line exactly in the same manner as the equality constraints were drawn. This line intersects the x_1 axis at point N in Figure 3.8 (where $x_2 = 0$ and

FIGURE 3.8

Family of isoprofit equations $z = 300x_1 + 250x_2$

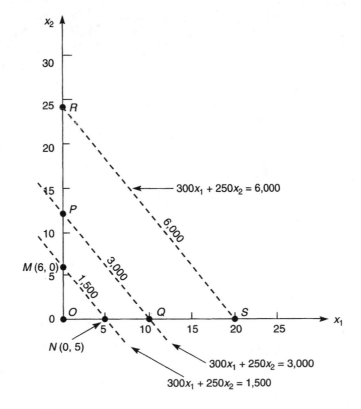

$x_1 = 5$) and the x_2 axis at point M (where $x_1 = 0$ and $x_2 = 6$). Point N tells us how many units of product x_1 *alone* are required to produce a profit of \$1,500. Because the profit contribution per unit of product x_1 is \$300, the answer is $1,500 \div 300 = 5$ units of x_1. Similarly, because the per unit profit contribution of x_2 is \$250, it takes 6 units of x_2, if only x_2 is produced (as indicated by point M), to produce a profit of \$1,500. All points on the isoprofit line MN are within the shaded area, representing feasible solutions, giving a total profit of \$1,500.

In a similar fashion, other isoprofit lines could be drawn, yielding different levels of profits. For example, line PQ in Figure 3.8 represents a \$3,000 isoprofit level, and the line RS represents a \$6,000 isoprofit level. An examination of lines MN, PQ, and RS shows that they are *parallel* to each other. Note also that profit levels increase as the isoprofit lines get *farther away* from the origin (point O).

Moving parallel

A little reflection will show that an even higher profit can be achieved if additional isoprofit lines can be drawn farther away from the origin. The question is: Where is the farthest *isoprofit* line? Let us see how this question can be answered.

Farthest away from the origin

Finding the Optimal Solution(s). The feasible area is reproduced from Figure 3.7 as Figure 3.9. Superimposed on the figure is the isoprofit line MN.

Now, if one starts building parallel isoprofit lines in the northeast direction (see the heavy arrow), these lines will represent higher and higher profits. We shall now show how to build such parallel lines and how to find the farthest possible isoprofit line.

To build parallel lines to MN, take a ruler and a 90-degree triangle. Hold the ruler perpendicular to line MN and keep one side of the triangle on the line MN. To find the farthest isoprofit line, move the triangle slowly to the northeast until the point where it is about to leave the feasible area $OCGE$.

FIGURE 3.9

Moving to an optimal solution

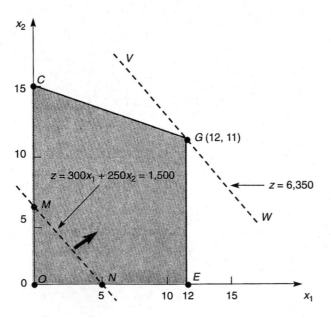

The optimal solution

> In our example, the farthest isoprofit line (*VW*) hits point *G*, which is declared the *optimal solution*. The coordinates of this point were previously computed as 12 and 11. The value of the objective function at that point is $300(12) + 250(11) = 6,350$. Therefore, line *VW* designates an isoprofit line $z = 6,350$.

When employing the above method, one of two cases may be expected. First, the farthest isoprofit line may intersect one corner point, providing a single optimal solution. Second, the farthest isoprofit line may coincide with one of the boundary lines of the feasible area. (This second case is discussed in more detail later.) This procedure

A vertex or a boundary?

reaffirms the previous comment that an optimal solution must be on the boundary and not inside the feasible area and that the optimal solution (if only one exists) must always occur at a vertex.

Note that if the optimal values of x_1 and x_2 are introduced into the inequality constraints, the solution will fully utilize only the second and the third resources in this

Binding constraint

case. That is, the labor constraint is not fully utilized (*binding*). This can be clearly seen in Figure 3.6 where the labor constraint does not intersect the optimal point.

Example 2: A Minimization Problem

Minimization

The graphical method can be used for minimization problems in a manner similar to the maximization case. To illustrate, let us examine the *blending problem* discussed earlier.

The problem is reproduced below:

A model of the blending problem

> minimize $z = 45x_1 + 12x_2$
> subject to:
> $1x_1 + 1x_2 \geq 300$
> $3x_1 + 0x_2 \geq 250$

To begin with, the inequality constraints are considered equations. They are drawn in Figure 3.10. Because the inequalities are of the *greater-than-or-equal-to* type, the feasible area is formed by considering the area to the *upperright* side of each equation (away from the origin, the shaded area in Figure 3.10). Next, a family of lines that represents various levels of the objective function is drawn (broken lines in Figure 3.10).

Isocost lines

These lines, in the minimization case, are called **isocost** lines.

In the diagram, a value of $z = 2,700$ is arbitrarily selected. The isocost equation is:

$$45x_1 + 12x_2 = 2,700$$

This isocost line is shown as line *MN* in Figure 3.10; note that the line *does not* intersect the feasible solution space. Therefore, this isocost line must be moved *toward* the feasible area until it first intersects a point (or points) in this region (point *K*). The co-

FIGURE 3.10

The blending problem

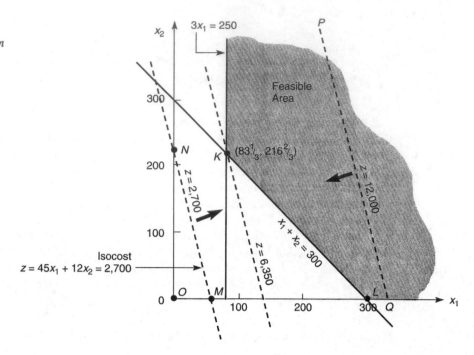

ordinates of point K can be read from the graph, or they can be computed as the intersection of the two linear equations. The solution for point K is:

$$x_1 = 83\tfrac{1}{3}$$

$$x_2 = 216\tfrac{2}{3}$$

The solution

This means that for every drum of the finished paint, the following raw materials should be used: $83\tfrac{1}{3}$ ounces of Alpha at a cost of 45 cents $\times$ $83\tfrac{1}{3}$ = 3,750 cents; and $216\tfrac{2}{3}$ ounces of Beta at a cost of 12 cents $\times$ $216\tfrac{2}{3}$ = 2,600 cents. The total cost is, therefore, 3,750 cents + 2,600 cents = 6,350 cents. If the isocost line is constructed inside the feasible area, like line PQ in Figure 3.10, then the search moves in the direction of the arrow, toward the origin. Because the objective is cost minimization, we search for the *lowest* level isocost that is still feasible.

Graphing an Equality

Equality means *on* the line.

Thus far, we have graphed only inequalities. If a constraint appears as an equality, then the feasible region of solutions is not an area anymore but a *line segment*, directly on the line describing the equality constraint. Generally speaking, the use of equations should be minimized in LP because it introduces inflexibility.

Solved Problem by the Graphical Solution

Given 5 constraints:

1) $2x_1 + 2x_2 \leq 8$
2) $x_1 + 2x_2 \leq 6$
3) $x_1 + 5x_2 \geq 4$

4) $4x_1 + x_2 \geq 6$
5) $x_2 \leq 2$

a) Show the feasible area. This is graphed in Figure 3.11.

FIGURE 3.11

The feasible area

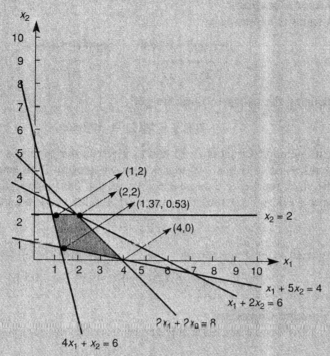

b) Find the solution with four different objective functions:

The objective functions	The solutions
1) Max $z = 5x_1 + 4x_2$	$z = 20$; $(x_1 = 4, x_2 = 0)$
2) Max $z = x_1 + 3x_2$	$z = 8$; $(x_1 = 2, x_2 = 2)$
3) Min $z = x_1 + x_2$	$z = 1.895$; $(x_1 = 1.37, x_2 = 0.53)$
4) Min $z = 6x_1 + x_2$	$z = 8$; $(x_1 = 1, x_2 = 2)$

c) Suppose that constraint #4 is changed to: $4x_1 + x_2 = 6$. What will be the optimal solution for the following objective functions?

Objective functions	The solutions
1) Max $z = 5x_1 + 4x_2$	$z = 13$; $(x_1 = 1, x_2 = 2)$
2) Min $z = 8x_1 + 2x_2$	$z = 12$, infinite number of solutions, including points $(1, 2)$ and $(1.37, 0.53)$

Note: In the last two cases the feasible area is the line segment $(1, 2)$ to $(1.37, 0.53)$.

3.6 Utilization of the Resources—Slack and Surplus Variables

Slack Variables

The optimal solution for the product-mix problem calls for $x_1 = 12$ and $x_2 = 11$. Let us examine now what will happen to the constraints if the optimal solution is used.

1. The Labor Constraint
This constraint is expressed as:

$$\underbrace{2x_1 + 1x_2}_{\text{Demand for labor}} \quad \leq \quad \overbrace{40}^{\text{Supply of labor}}$$

Introducing the optimal values, we get:

$$2(12) + 1(11) = 35 \text{ hours}$$

That is, the demand for labor is 35 hours, whereas the supply is 40. Therefore, there would be $40 - 35 = 5$ hours of *unused* labor potential. This unused supply is called *slack*. The slack must take only nonnegative values. Designating this **slack variable** by s_1 (where the 1 designates the first constraint), the labor constraint can be rewritten as:

Slack variables

$$2x_1 + 2x_2 + s_1 = 40$$

transforming the constraint into an equality. The solution for s_1 is:

$$s_1 = 40 - (2x_1 + 1x_2) = 40 - 2(12) - 1(11) = 5$$

2. The Machine Constraint
Similarly, the machine slack variable can be inserted into the constraint as:

$$x_1 + 3x_2 + s_2 = 45$$

Substituting the values of the optimal solution and solving for s_2:

$$s_2 = 45 - (1x_1 + 3x_2) = 45 - 12 - 33 = 0$$

Full utilization: No slack

In this case, the machine time is *fully utilized* (no slack exists). A fully utilized constraint is also called a *binding* constraint and it constitutes a *bottleneck* in the organization's operations.

3. The Marketing Constraint
Similarly:

$$1x_1 + s_3 = 12$$

Solving:

$$s_3 = 12 - 1x_1 = 12 - 12 = 0$$

The implication again is that there is no slack; the constraint is being exactly met.

Note: A glance at Figures 3.6 and 3.9 will show that a constraint with zero slack intersects the optimal solution point. A constraint with positive slack does not intersect the point of the optimal solution.

Surplus Variables

Any larger-than-or-equal-to constraint has a surplus variable.

Example 1

Assume that a fourth constraint is added:

$$2x_1 + 3x_2 \geq 50$$

Let the optimal solution be:

$$x_1 = 12; x_2 = 11$$

Introducing these values into the left side of the inequality, we get:

$$2(12) + 3(11) = 57$$

The value of the left side of the inequality is larger than the value of the right side. The difference, 7 in this case, is called a **surplus variable.** It indicates how much the requirements of the right-hand side are exceeded.

The fourth constraint is now written with a surplus variable that can either be positive or zero. It is written as:

$$2x_1 + 3x_2 - s_4 = 50$$

Introducing the values of the decision variables and solving for s_4:

$$s_4 = (2x_1 + 3x_2) - 50 = 2(12) + 3(11) - 50 = 7$$

Example 2

Taking the first constraint of the blending problem:

$$1x_1 + 1x_2 - s_1 = 300$$
$$s_1 = 1x_1 + 1x_2 - 300 = 83\tfrac{1}{3} + 216\tfrac{2}{3} - 300 = 0$$

The value of the surplus is zero, which indicates that the minimum specification is just being met.

Note 1: An LP inequality can be multiplied or divided by a constant without changing the optimal solution. For example, the inequality $3x_1 + 6x_2 \geq 15$ can be rewritten $x_1 + 2x_2 \geq 5$. However, if this is done, the magnitude of the surplus (or slack) variable will be changed. Therefore, one *should not* change the original constraints unless it is absolutely necessary (e.g., for a computer solution). The slack and surplus variables also play an important role in the simplex method.

Note 2: The addition of slack and surplus variables helps standardize the LP problem, as required by the simplex method.

Summary

Each smaller-than-or-equal-to constraint has a slack variable whose value is either positive or zero. Each larger-than-or-equal-to constraint has a surplus variable whose value is either positive or zero. Each equality constraint has neither slack nor surplus. Any constraints that intersect at the point of the optimal solution have zero slack or surplus.

Management Science in Practice

Farming with Linear Programming Software

Farmers and other businesspeople have always faced problems of finding the best feed mix for their chickens, the best blend for their products, or the best route for their trucks. Now, user-friendly software can help even small businesses formulate their problems in an LP format on their PCs and solve them quickly. Sometimes the user is asked to put the problem in the format of a spreadsheet, with which many people are familiar.

A number of firms are offering this software in various options and at a variety of prices, ranging from $100 to $1,000. Some packages are specifically oriented to farming, trucking, and other specific industries, and are thus even more user friendly.

A Chicago director of nursing, for example, is saving her hospital over $100,000 a year in overtime costs by better scheduling of her nurses. And a Texas rancher is saving money during drought periods by feeding his cattle more inexpensive cottonseed rather than alfalfa hay. A New York coal wholesaler is able to meet customers'

demands for particular ash, sulfur, and heating values in their coal with a cheaper mix.

But the use of these programs isn't limited to small users. The president of Newfoundland Energy, for example, now solves his firm's regular purchasing decisions regarding what crudes to buy on a personal computer rather than the company mainframe, thereby saving thousands of dollars of expensive computer time.

Source: "The Right Mix: New Software Makes the Choice Much Easier," *The Wall Street Journal*, March 27, 1987.

Questions:

1. What would the rows and columns of the spreadsheet represent for the farmer? the director of nursing?
2. How does LP use the spreadsheet data?

3.7 Concluding Remarks

LP is a powerful tool of MS, designed to solve allocation problems. Such problems appear in dozens of forms and complications. The major difficulty is that there are an infinite number of feasible solutions; therefore, finding the optimal or the *best of all possible* solutions is not usually possible by complete enumeration.

LP models the allocation problem with two parts: a linear objective function that is to be maximized or minimized, and a set of linear constraints that describes the limitations and requirements subject to which the maximization or minimization is attempted.

The model is solved by an efficient search algorithm called the simplex method. This method is presented in Part B of this chapter. The graphical method that was presented in Part A is very restricted in use. Part B of this chapter deals with various topics and extensions that relax some of the limiting assumptions, enabling LP to be applied to a wide range of situations.

3.8 Problems for Part A*

1. Nitron Corp. of Canada produces two products. Unit profit for product A is $60; for product B, $50. Each must pass through two machines, P and Q. Product A requires 10 minutes on machine P and 8 minutes on machine Q. Product B requires 20 minutes on machine P and 5 minutes on machine Q. Machine P is available 200 minutes a day, whereas machine Q is available 80 minutes a day. The company must produce at least two units of product A and five of product B each day. Units that are not completed in a given day are finished the next day; that is, a portion of a product can be produced in the daily plan. What is the most profitable daily production plan?
   a. Formulate.
   b. Solve graphically (specifically show all constraints and the objective function as well as the optimal solution).
   c. How should the resources be allocated?

2. Given:

   maximize $z = 5x_1 + 5x_2$

   subject to:
   1) $1x_1 + 2x_2 \leq 30$
   2) $1x_1 + 1x_2 \leq 19$
   3) $8x_1 + 3x_2 \leq 120$

   a. Solve the problem graphically.
   b. If the problem has more than one optimal solution, explain why this is so and list all the optimal solutions.
   c. Find the slacks, or surpluses, or both, on all constraints.

3. Given a set of constraints:

   1) $10x_1 + 8x_2 \leq 120$
   2) $5x_1 + 5x_2 \geq 30$
   3) $1x_1 \qquad \geq 2$
   4) $\qquad 1x_2 \leq 10$
   5) $\qquad 1x_2 \geq x_1$

   a. Graphically display the feasible area.
   b. Compute the coordinates of all feasible corner (intersection) points.

---

*A large number of LP problems for formulation and computer solution are available in Part B of this chapter, as well as in the following three chapters.

c. If the objective function is:

$$\text{maximize } z = 5.5x_1 + 3x_2$$

find the value of the objective function at all corner points. Which corner point is the best one?

d. Graphically draw the slope of the objective function. Confirm the findings of part (c).

e. Find the slacks/surpluses on all constraints.

f. Given: minimize $z = 5.5x_1 + 3x_2$
What will the optimal solution be now?

4. Given:

$$\text{maximize } z = 8x_1 + 6x_2$$
subject to:
1) $5x_1 + 2x_2 \leq 60$
2) $2x_1 + 4x_2 \leq 48$
3) $3x_1 \qquad \geq 15$
4) $5x_1 - 4x_2 \leq 40$

a. Graphically show the feasible solution area.

b. Compute the coordinates of all intersecting feasible corners.

c. Find the optimal solution.

d. Find the value of the objective function.

e. Find the slacks/surpluses on all constraints.

f. Compute the utilization of resources (as a percent).

g. Suppose that the last constraint is changed to a strict equality. What will the optimal solution be now?

5. A store sells men's and ladies' tennis shoes. It makes a profit of $1 a pair on the men's shoes and $1.20 a pair on the ladies'. It takes two minutes of a salesperson's time and two minutes of a cashier's time to sell a pair of men's shoes. It takes three minutes of a salesperson's time and one minute of a cashier's time per pair of women's shoes. The store is open eight hours per day, during which time there are two salespersons and one cashier on duty. How much of the salespersons' and the cashier's time should be allocated to the men's and ladies' shoes and how many shoes should the store sell to maximize profit?

a. List all the assumptions that are necessary to formulate this as an LP problem. What is the objective of the store?

b. Formulate as an LP problem.

c. Solve graphically. Calculate the profit.

6. A knitting machine can produce 1,000 pairs of pants or 3,000 shirts (or a combination of the two) each day. The finishing department can handle either 1,500 pairs of pants or 2,000 shirts (or a combination of the two) each day. The marketing department requires that at least 400 pants be produced each day. The company's stated objective is profit maximization.

a. If the profit from a pair of pants is $4 and that derived from a shirt is $1.50, how many of each type should be produced? Solve graphically.

b. Assume that the profit from a shirt increases to $2. What should be the *minimum* profit derived from selling a pair of pants that will justify production of pants only (i.e., $X_{shirts} = 0$)?

c. Examine the solutions to (a) and (b) and interpret the difference between them. Can this interpretation be generalized to all LP graphical solutions?

7. The owner of Black Angus Ranch of Australia is trying to determine the correct mix of two types of beef feed, A and B, which cost 50 cents and 75 cents per pound, respectively. Five essential ingredients are contained in the feed, as shown in the table below, which also indicates the minimum daily requirements of each ingredient:

Ingredient	Percent per pound of feed		Minimum daily requirements (pounds)
	Feed A	Feed B	
1	20	25	30
2	30	10	50
3	0	30	20
4	24	15	60
5	10	20	40

Find the least-cost daily blend for the ranch; that is, how many pounds of feed A and feed B will be included in the mix? (Solve graphically.)

8. Korean Valves, Inc., produces drainage valves. Two alternative production lines are available. The company just received an order for producing 1,000 Mark I valves. Line 1 can produce the valves at a rate of 15 minutes for each valve. The production capacity on line 2 is 5 valves per hour. Line 1 is available, for this order, for not more than 200

hours at 80,000 Korean won an hour. Line 2 is available, for this order, for not more than 170 hours at 50,000 won an hour.
Find the best production plan.

  a. Formulate in two different ways. (*Hint:* In one of the ways, the decision variables are in terms of hours.)
  b. Solve graphically.
  c. Discuss the best allocation of resources.

9. a. Given a constraint $3x_1 + 5x_2 - 1x_3 \le 80$; the optimal solution is: $x_1 = 5$, $x_2 = 6$, $x_3 = 1$; find the slack on this constraint.
   b. Given a constraint $5x_1 + 2x_2 + 8x_3 \ge 120$; the optimal solution is: $x_1 = 20$, $x_2 = 10$, $x_3 = 0$; find the surplus on this constraint.

10. Given two LP graphical solutions; the optimal solution is marked by x. In each case, find:
   a. Which constraints are redundant.
   b. Which constraints will have a slack.
   c. Which constraints will have a surplus.

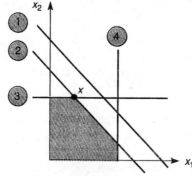

a. Maximization

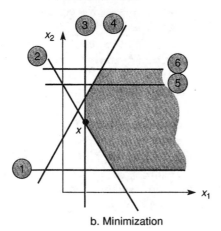

b. Minimization

11. Solve the following LP problem graphically:

   maximize $z = 5x_1 - 3x_2$
   subject to:
   $$\begin{aligned} x_1 + x_2 &\le 5 \\ x_1 \quad\;\; &\le 2 \\ 3x_1 + x_2 &\le 9 \end{aligned}$$

12. Graph the following constraints:
   a. $2x_1 \qquad\;\; \le x_2$
   b. $2x_1 + \;\; x_2 \le 0$
   c. $15x_1 + 10x_2 \ge 800$

13. Formulate the constraint:
   A machine can produce 50 units of product A, or 100 units of product B, or any linear combination of the two products.

14. Given an LP problem:

   minimize $z = 6x_1 + 14x_2$
   subject to:
   $$\begin{aligned} 4x_1 + \;\; 7x_2 &= 56 \\ 4.5x_1 + 2.5x_2 &\le 45 \\ x_2 &\ge 3 \\ x_1 \qquad\; &\le 12 \end{aligned}$$

   a. Draw the feasible area.
   b. Compute the value of all intersecting feasible points.
   c. Solve graphically.

15. For each of the following constraints and proposed solutions find:
   a. Is the solution feasible?
   b. The value of the slack or surplus.

   1) $2x_1 + 2.5x_2 - 0.5x_3 \ge 40$; solution $(2, 4, 2)$
   2) $5x_1 + \;\; 3x_2 + \;\; x_3 \le 60$; solution $(10, 2, 4)$
   3) $2x_1 + \;\; x_2 \qquad\;\; \ge 3$; solution $(4, 3)$

16. Solve the following LP problem graphically:

   maximize $z = 3x_1 + 2x_2$
   subject to
   $$\begin{aligned} x_1 \qquad\; &\le 8 \\ x_2 &\le 10 \\ x_1 + x_2 &\le 22 \\ 1.5x_1 + x_2 &\le 15 \end{aligned}$$

PART B: EXTENSIONS

3.9   The Simplex Method

The simplex method is an **iterative** algorithm for efficiently solving LP problems. The iterative simplex procedure obtains an optimal solution by sequentially improving the previous solution. The improvement procedure follows the same steps each time; that is, it "iterates" through the same process in each pass.

LP developed in 1947

LP was first developed in 1947 by G. B. Dantzig and his associates in the U.S. Department of the Air Force. Some revisions in the method have since been made in order to increase computation efficiency, but the basic approach remains the same. The simplex method and its variations have now been programmed and coded for practically all makes and types of computers. Before launching into the simplex process, however, it will be worthwhile to spend some time visualizing, in graphic terms, what the simplex process does algebraically.

Graphical Explanation of the Simplex Process

The simplex method

It was pointed out during the graphical solution procedure that the search for an optimal solution can be limited to only the corner points of the feasible solution space. This was easy enough to do by hand for a problem with only two variables and three constraints, but for larger problems a more efficient procedure for identifying and evaluating corner points is necessary. This is one of the main objectives of the simplex method.

Moving to adjacent corners

In the simplex method, the search usually starts at the origin and moves to that *adjacent corner* that increases (for maximization problems) the value of the objective function the most. An adjacent corner is a "neighboring" corner. For example, in Figure 3.12 corner E is adjacent to corners O and G. In two dimensions, each corner has two adjacent corners, but in higher dimensions there are more; for example, there are three adjacent corners for each corner on a cube. On reaching such a corner, the search moves, if possible, to an even better corner adjacent to the new one. The process continues until no further improvement is possible. To illustrate this process in two dimensions, we reproduced Figure 3.6 as Figure 3.12. The search starts at the origin O and moves to corner E and then to the optimal point, corner G. *Note:* The simplex method will move to corner E first because the *rate of increase* in the objective function for x_1 is greater than for x_2.

Optimality by iteration

The simplex process must always reach the optimum solution (if a solution exists) because in each iteration, the objective function improves, and there are only a finite number of corner points in a feasible solution space. Also, the optimum will be reached regardless of the initial direction of the process. In Figure 3.12, for example, going first to point C would not have affected the ultimate solution, nor the number of iterations, though in other situations different routes will result in a different number of iterations.

FIGURE 3.12

The product-mix problem (corner solution points)

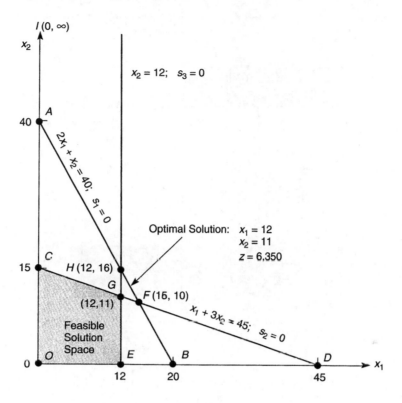

The Simplex Process

The computational process of the simplex involves six steps, as depicted in Figure 3.13. These steps are:

The steps

Step 1. Standardize the problem into a linear programming tableau.

Step 2. Generate an initial solution, called a **basis.**

Step 3. Test the solution for optimality. If the solution is not optimal, improve it (go to step 4); otherwise go to step 6.

The improvement of a nonoptimal solution is done in two steps:

Step 4. Generate an improved solution by identifying one variable that will leave the basis and one variable that will enter the basis.

Step 5. The improved solution is checked (see step 3) for optimality. If it is not optimal, then steps 4 and 5 are repeated. If it is optimal, step 6 is undertaken.

Step 6. Find if more than one optimal solution exists.

FIGURE 3.13

Schematic presentation of the simplex method

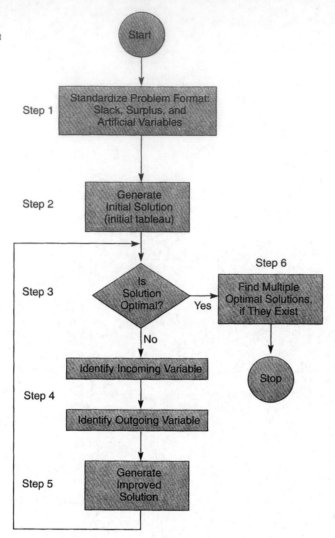

This process guarantees that an optimal solution, if it exists, will be found in a finite number of iterations. The process will be illustrated through a product-mix example.

Example

Let us reproduce the product-mix problem that was previously solved graphically.

maximize $z = 300x_1 + 250x_2$
subject to:
$$2x_1 + 1x_2 \leq 40$$
$$1x_1 + 3x_2 \leq 45$$
$$1x_1 + 0x_2 \leq 12$$

The graphical solution of the problem is shown in Figure 3.12.

Step 1: Standardize the Problem

A standard form

Because only corner points of the feasible solution space are to be checked, and because these points are defined by the intersection of equations, it is necessary to convert the inequalities in the problem statement into equations in order to find the coordinates of the intersecting points. Such a conversion depends on the type of constraints involved.

Constraints with Inequalities of the Smaller-Than-or-Equal-To Type

Slack variable

A slack variable is added to each of these type constraints. For example, the labor constraint in the product-mix problem is:

$$2x_1 + 1x_2 \leq 40$$

Adding a slack variable:

$$2x_1 + 1x_2 + 1s_1 = 40$$

where s_1 = slack of labor and $s_1 \geq 0$.

Note that if *no* sets, either A or B, were produced ($x_1 = x_2 = 0$ is a common starting point in the simplex procedure), then the slack s_1 would be 40:

$$2 \times 0 + 1 \times 0 + 1s_1 = 40$$

Constraints with Inequalities of the Larger-Than-or-Equal-To Type

Surplus variable

Let us examine the blending constraint $x_1 + x_2 \geq 300$. Once a solution is found and the values of the variables are introduced into the constraint, then the left side can be either equal to *or* larger than 300. In the latter case, there will be a *surplus*. Let us call it s_2. It is possible, therefore, to write the inequality $x_1 + x_2 \geq 300$ as:

$$1x_1 + 1x_2 - 1s_2 = 300$$

where $s_2 \geq 0$.

Artificial Variables

Artificial variable

Note that if no Alpha or Beta is included ($x_1 = x_2 = 0$, a starting point in the simplex), then the equation $1x_1 + 1x_2 - 1s_2 = 300$ will result in the solution $s_2 = -300$, which is not allowable. Neither a slack nor a surplus can be negative. To overcome this difficulty, an auxiliary variable, called an **artificial variable,** is introduced into the equation. This allows us to form the initial basis. The constraint is then written as:

$$1x_1 + 1x_2 - 1s_2 + 1a_2 = 300$$

where a_2 is the artificial variable for the constraint ($a_2 \geq 0$). When x_1, x_2, and s_2 are set to zero, then $a_2 = 300$.

A large penalty (*M*)

Because the sole objective of the artificial variable is to form an initial basis, it does not have any physical meaning and must be kept out of any final solution. To do so, a penalty (usually denoted by the symbol M) is assigned as a coefficient to the corresponding variable in the objective function. The magnitude of M should be large enough to *ensure* that the artificial variable will be so undesirable that it will not enter an optimal solution.

Constraints with an Equality. Consider a constraint given as an equality, say:

$$3x_1 + 1x_2 = 10$$

If, as an initial simplex solution, the two variables x_1 and x_2 are set to zero, a value of $0 = 10$ is obtained, which is unacceptable. This difficulty is again solved by adding an artificial variable:

$$3x_1 + 1x_2 + a_3 = 10$$

Then, when x_1 and x_2 are set to zero, $a_3 = 10$.

Standard Form

Once the constraints have been modified, the problem can be written in a *standard form.*

Example a: The Product-Mix Problem Because all the constraints in this example are of the type $\leq$, then it is necessary to add three slacks, one for each constraint. *The slack variables will have a coefficient of zero in the objective function* because "producing" slack (i.e., not using a resource) does not generate any profit, nor does it have any costs. The problem then, can be written in a *standard form* as shown in Table 3.2.

Example b: The Blending Problem The blending problem was formulated as:

minimize $z = 45x_1 + 12x_2$
subject to:
 $1x_1 + 1x_2 \geq 300$
 $3x_1 + 0x_2 \geq 250$

Because the constraints are of the larger-than-or-equal-to type, it is necessary to add an artificial variable and subtract a surplus variable to make each constraint an equation. The resulting standard form is shown in Table 3.3. The surpluses have a coefficient of zero in the objective function because they incur no cost. To ensure that the artificial variables are kept out of the final solution, they are given a large cost penalty of $+M$ in the objective function (use $-M$ in a maximization problem).

Before proceeding to step 2, let us explain again in graphical terms what the simplex method does once the problem is written in standard form.

TABLE 3.2 Standard Form for the Product-Mix Problem

Objective function:		maximize $z = 300x_1 + 250x_2 + 0s_1 + 0s_2 + 0s_3$
subject to:	(1)	$2x_1 + 1x_2 + 1s_1 + 0s_2 + 0s_3 = 40$
	(2)	$1x_1 + 3x_2 + 0s_1 + 1s_2 + 0s_3 = 45$
	(3)	$1x_1 + 0x_2 + 0s_1 + 0s_2 + 1s_3 = 12$

TABLE 3.3 **Standard Form for the Blending Problem**

Objective function:	minimize $z = 45x_1 + 12x_2 + 0s_1 + 0s_2 + Ma_1 + Ma_2$						
subject to:	(1)	$1x_1 +$	$1x_2 -$	$1s_1$		$+ 1a_1$		$= 300$
	(2)	$3x_1 +$	$0x_2$		$- 1s_2$		$+ 1a_2$	$= 250$

Basic Variables and a Basis

The product-mix maximization problem, as presented in Table 3.2, consists of a system of three linear equations describing the constraints and a family of isoprofit functions. To determine corner points, the intersection coordinates of the constraints must be calculated. In order to do so, it is necessary to solve the three linear equations simultaneously. In general, two cases are distinguished.

Basic solutions

The *basis*

1. Solutions with exactly m nonzero variables, where m is the number of constraints, are called *basic solutions*. The m variables in these solutions are called **basic variables** and they constitute the *basis* of the solution. The remaining variables have values of zero.
2. Solutions that include more than m nonzero variables are called *nonbasic* solutions.

Note that in our example there exist five unknown variables: x_1, x_2, s_1, s_2, and s_3; but there are only three constraint equations. A solution to a system of linear equations requires that the number of equations equal the number of variables; otherwise, there will be an infinite number of solutions. To overcome this problem, two of the five variables are set to zero, thus giving only basic solutions.

Feasible—Infeasible

The *basic* solutions can be further divided into two groups: *feasible* and *infeasible*. The *feasible solutions* are those that satisfy *all* the constraints; that is, they are in the *feasible area* and the value of *all* their variables must be nonnegative.

Basic feasible

The simplex algorithm searches for *basic feasible solutions* only (the corner points of the feasible area). In large LP problems, such solutions are a small part of all basic solutions. Thus, the amount of search is much less than that required by complete enumeration of all corner points.

Graphical Illustration: The Product-Mix Problem (from Figure 3.12)

With three equations and five unknowns, there are 10 possible ways of setting two of the variables to zero and solving the remaining three variables. Thus, there are 10 bases listed in Table 3.4.

Each of these bases is a *basic solution,* as shown in Figure 3.12. But only the corner points O, C, G, and E have nonnegative values for *all five* variables in Table 3.4. (Slack variables cannot take negative values; therefore, points such as A and H correspond to infeasible solutions.) Therefore, only *these* corner points (listed in Table 3.5) constitute the *feasible* basic solutions of Table 3.4. The search for an optimal solution is now narrowed from 10 points to 4.

TABLE 3.4   The 10 Possible Bases for the Product-Mix Problem (Basic Solutions)

Basis No.	Variables in the Solution					Corner points in Figure 3.12	Feasible?
	x_1	x_2	s_1	s_2	s_3		
1	0	0	40	45	12	O	Yes
2	0	40	0	−75	12	A	No
3	0	15	25	0	12	C	Yes
4	0	∞	−∞	−∞	0	I	No
5	20	0	0	25	−8	B	No
6	45	0	−50	0	−33	D	No
7	12	0	16	33	0	E	Yes
8	15	10	0	0	−3	F	No
9	12	16	0	−15	0	H	No
10	12	11	5	0	0	G	Yes

TABLE 3.5   The Feasible Corner Points (Basic Feasible Solutions)

Corner	x_1	x_2	s_1	s_2	s_3
O	0	0	40	45	12
C	0	15	25	0	12
G	12	11	5	0	0
E	12	0	16	33	0

Notice in Table 3.5 that each succeeding corner includes all but one of the same basic variables, though their *values* may differ. That is, C has two of the same basic variables, (s_1 and s_3) that O has, with x_2 replacing s_2. Similarly, G has the same basis as C except for x_1 replacing s_3. And in E, s_2 replaces x_2 of G. Returning to the origin O, s_3 replaces x_1 of E. Therefore, each pair of succeeding bases represents *adjacent corners* of the feasible solution space in Figure 3.12.

This then, will be the solution procedure of the simplex method. The search starts with a solution at the origin, O. Then it moves to an adjacent corner where the objective function achieves the largest initial improvement. It continues on from corner to corner, improving, if possible, the value of the objective function each time. At some point, no further improvement will be possible, signaling the attainment of the optimal solution. *Note:* In some cases, the origin is not a feasible starting solution. This situation is handled in a special way, as will be shown later.

Step 2: Generate an Initial Solution

The expression of the LP problem in the standard form of step 1 suggests an easy initial solution that is both basic and feasible. For example, the product-mix problem expressed in Table 3.2 has three constraint equations and five variables. Thus, there must be $5 - 3 = 2$ nonbasic variables with zero values and 3 basic variables to solve for. Reproducing these equations:

$$2x_1 + 1x_2 + 1s_1 = 40$$
$$1x_1 + 3x_2 + 1s_2 = 45$$
$$1x_1 + 0x_2 + 1s_3 = 12$$

A natural solution to this set of equations would be to set x_1 and x_2 as the nonbasic variables with s_1, s_2, and s_3 as the basic variables. This is because x_1 and x_2 appear in more than one equation, whereas s_1, s_2, and s_3 each appear only once and in different equations and can thus be solved easily. Setting $x_1 = x_2 = 0$ and solving for s_1, s_2, and s_3 yields:

$$s_1 = 40, \qquad s_2 = 45, \qquad s_3 = 12$$

The resulting profit is found from the objective function as:

$$z = 300x_1 + 250x_2 + 0s_1 + 0s_2 + 0s_3$$
$$= 300(0) + 250(0) + 0(40) + 0(45) + 0(12) = 0$$

Obtaining such a simple initial solution is, of course the purpose of starting the simplex solution process with a standard format. The simplex process then *continues to maintain* this simplified solution format through the *Gauss-Jordan method* of solving simultaneous equations (see Section A5 of Appendix A). That is, each iteration of the simplex involves again expressing the set of equations such that each basic variable appears in only one, a different one, of the equations. This is not as difficult as it may sound, because the simplex begins from such a point (as in Table 3.2) and then switches only *one* of the basic variables for one of the nonbasic variables at a time, as we saw in Table 3.5. Thus, reexpressing the equations in this special form only requires eliminating one basic variable from all but one equation.

The Gauss-Jordan method

To facilitate the required manipulations of the equations, the simplex process makes use of a specialized adaptation of the standard LP form shown in Table 3.2. This adaptation is called a "tableau" (*tabulated coefficients*).

The Structure of a Tableau

Figure 3.14 illustrates the initial tableau of the product-mix problem. Explanations of its major parts are included.

FIGURE 3.14

A tableau explanation

Basic Rows	Basis	Unit profits	Quantity	x_1	x_2	s_1	s_2	s_3
	s_1	0	40	2	1	[1]	0	0
	s_2	0	45	1	3	0	[1]	0
	s_3	0	12	1	0	0	0	[1]

Column headers (top): List of basic variables → Basis; Coefficients of objective function → Unit profits; Quantity in solution → Quantity; **Main body**: Decision variables (x_1, x_2); Slack (surplus) variables (s_1, s_2, s_3).

c_j row (coefficients of objective function)

300	250	0	0	0

z_j row (new coefficient: per unit "losses")

0	0	0	0	0

$c_j - z_j$ row (the simplex criterion or evaluator)

300	250	0	0	0

Value of objective function = 0

Discussion and Economic Interpretation

The tableau includes three rows, one for each constraint. This correspondence will be maintained throughout the entire simplex manipulations.

The main body of the tableau corresponds to the standard format of the problem, as shown in Table 3.2. Notice, however, that the variables are not repeated in each row but are summarized on the top. The column "Basis" identifies the proposed initial solution variables.

The z_j Row. The row denoted z_j is labeled "per unit 'losses.'" It shows the amount of profit the objective function will be *reduced* by when one unit of the variable in each column is brought into the basis. Initially, all z_j's have values of zero. The reason for this is that only slack variables are in the first tableau and their coefficients in the objective function are initially zero. If there had been $\geq$ or $=$ constraints in this problem, then some of the z_j's would have had nonzero values.

Each value in this row is found as follows:

> ***Rule:*** For each variable, multiply, on a row-by-row basis, the value in the "Unit profits" column by the corresponding value in that variable's column in the main body of the tableau and add the resulting products. For example, the z_j for column x_2 is: $0(1) + 0(3) + 0(0) = 0$.

***The Simplex Criterion (Evaluator) Row:* $c_j - z_j$.** The bottom row, $c_j - z_j$, shows the *net* impact on the value of the objective function of bringing one unit of each of the column variables into the basis. The c_j's tell us how much will be gained while the z_j's tell us how much will simultaneously be lost. If the difference between the two is *positive,* then the value of the objective function can be *increased* by introducing one unit of the variable into the solution. In maximization problems, this is an indication of a possible *improvement;* that is, if one (or more) of the $c_j - z_j$ values is positive, then the solution is not *optimal.* This is the basis of the analysis to be conducted in step 3.

Find if improvement is possible

Economic Interpretation. The value $c_j - z_j$ represents the *opportunity cost* of not having one unit of the corresponding value in the solution. That is, it shows the marginal impact on the value of the objective function, or the net marginal contribution to profit. (The value $c_j - z_j$ of the slack variables is related to the concept of the *dual variables* to be presented later.) *Note:* The value $z_j - c_j$ designates the value by which the objective function will be reduced if variable j is introduced into the optimal solution. This value is referred to as the reduced cost.

The Value of the Objective Function z. Finally, the value of the objective function can be computed by multiplying each "Unit profit" by its corresponding quantity, and then totaling the results. For example, the value of the objective function (total profit) in Figure 3.14 is:

$$0(40) + 0(45) + 0(12) = 0$$

Step 3: Test for Optimality

This test is made by examining the $c_j - z_j$ row and using the following rule.

> **Rule for Optimality**
>
> If, in a maximization problem, all the coefficients of the $c_j - z_j$ row are nonpositive (either zero or negative), then the solution given by the tableau is optimal.

That is, if bringing any other variable into the basis can only either decrease the profit or leave it unchanged, then the current solution must be optimal.

Because both coefficients of x_1 and x_2 are positive in the $c_j - z_j$ row of our first tableau in Table 3.6, then introducing either x_1 or x_2 into the basis will *increase* the profit. Therefore, the current solution is *not* optimal. The solution can be improved by exchanging one variable. The improvement is done by:

- Identifying an incoming variable.
- Identifying an outgoing variable.
- Building an improved tableau.

TABLE 3.6   The Initial Product-Mix—Tableau I

	Basis	Unit profits	Incoming x_1	x_2	s_1	s_2	s_3	Quantity	b_i/a_{ij} Ratio
	s_1	0	2	1	☐1	0	0	40	40/2 = 20
	s_2	0	1	3	0	☐1	0	45	45
Outgoing	s_3	0	①	0	0	0	☐1	12	12
	c_j (unit profits)		300	250	0	0	0		
	z_j (unit losses)		0	0	0	0	0		
	$c_j - z_j$		300	250	0	0	0		

Step 4: Identify the Incoming and Outgoing Variables

The Incoming Variable

First, *an incoming variable* (currently nonbasic, to be changed to a basic variable) is chosen by inspecting the $c_j - z_j$ row of the current solution for that variable with the *largest positive* coefficient. In this example, x_1, with a coefficient of 300, is chosen. This is also known as the *pivot column* (shaded in Table 3.6). *Note:* It is not mandatory to select the column with the largest positive coefficient. Any column with a positive $c_j - z_j$ is a good candidate. However, it is customary to use the column with the *largest* value.

> **Rule for Determining the Incoming Variable (in maximization)**
>
> Select the nonbasic variable (in the column) with the largest positive coefficient in the $c_j - z_j$ row.

The Outgoing Variable

Once the incoming variable has been identified, it is necessary to identify an outgoing variable. The procedure for determining the *outgoing basic variable* (either s_1, s_2, or s_3 in the example) is somewhat more involved. In essence, the outgoing variable is that basic variable that is first reduced to zero as x_1 (the incoming variable) increases from zero. This is done as follows. For each basis row in the tableau, form the ratio of the "Quantity" to the coefficient of the incoming variable (or b_i/a_{ij}). In this case, the incoming variable is x_1, so the three ratios are 40/2 = 20, 45/1 = 45, and 12/1 = 12, which are listed in the rightmost column of the tableau. Select the row with the smallest nonnegative ratio. (Negative ratios indicate no limit for the incoming variable.) This row's basic variable will be the *outgoing* variable. In Table 3.6, the smallest positive ratio is 12, so the outgoing variable is s_3.

The coefficient of the incoming variable in the outgoing (*pivot*) row is called the *pivot element*, 1 in Table 3.6, and is circled for later reference.

(margin notes:) Incoming   Outgoing   Pivot element

The above procedure is summarized in the following rule.

Rule for Determining the Outgoing Variable

Look down the column of the incoming (nonbasic) variable and consider only non-negative elements (coefficients). Then, divide the quantity of each constraint by the corresponding coefficient in the column of the incoming variable. The current basic variable with the smallest ratio (it may be zero) is selected as the outgoing variable.

Step 5: Generate an Improved Solution

The solution is improved by introducing the incoming variable into the basis and removing the outgoing variable. This is done row by row on the old tableau, forming, in the process, a new one. The procedure starts with transforming the row of the outgoing variable, then the other basic rows, and finally transforming the c_j, z_j, and $c_j - z_j$ rows.

Transformation of the Outgoing Row

Rule: Divide the main body elements and the "Quantity" of the outgoing row by the pivot element.

Because the pivot element is 1 in this case, the row is unchanged. Note that in the new row, x_1 replaces s_3 in the "Basis" column, and is thus boxed; as a result, the unit profit has been changed from 0 to 300. This information is now entered into the improved tableau (Table 3.7).

TABLE 3.7   First Improved Solution—Tableau II

Basis	Unit profits	x_1	x_2	s_1	s_2	s_3	Quantity	Ratio
s_1	0	0	1	☐1	0	−2	16	16
s_2	0	0	③	0	☐1	−1	33	11
x_1	300	☐1	0	0	0	1	12	limit = ∞
c_j		300	250	0	0	0		
z_j		300	0	0	0	300		
$c_j - z_j$		0	250	0	0	−300		

Transformation of the Other Rows   The transformation, again, deals only with the columns of the main body and the "Quantity." The process involves three activities:

1. Identify the coefficient at the intersection of the row to be transformed and the income column. For example, the coefficient for the first row in Table 3.6 is 2; for the second one it is 1.
2. Multiply, in turn, every element of the transformed pivot row (the new third row here) by the number identified in activity #1.
3. Subtract the result of the second activity from the old row (to be transformed) to derive the new transformed row.

Example: Transforming the First Row

The coefficient for this row in the incoming column is 2.

	x_1	x_2	s_1	s_2	s_3	*Quantity*
The new third row (Table 3.7)	1	0	0	0	1	12
The row to be transformed (first row, Table 3.6)	2	1	1	0	0	40
Minus: 2 × New third row	−2	0	0	0	−2	−24
Result: New first row (Table 3.7)	0	1	1	0	−2	16

This is the first row in the improved tableau (Table 3.7). Notice that the "Basis" and the "Unit profits" are transformed unchanged. The reason for this is that s_1 remains a basic variable.

Example: Transforming the Second Row

Here, the coefficient is 1 and the mathematical manipulations are:

	x_1	x_2	s_1	s_2	s_3	*Quantity*
Second row	1	3	0	1	0	45
Minus: 1 × New third row	−1	0	0	0	−1	−12
Result: New second row (Table 3.7)	0	3	0	1	−1	33

Transformation of the c_j Row
This row is transformed unchanged (always).

Computing the New z_j Row

Multiply the "Unit profits" in each row by the main body column coefficients and sum the results.

For the value in Table 3.7 under columns x_1 to s_3:

$$
\begin{array}{llll}
x_1 & 0(0) & + 0(0) & + 300(1) = 300 \\
x_2 & 0(1) & + 0(3) & + 300(0) = 0 \\
s_1 & 0(1) & + 0(0) & + 300(0) = 0 \\
s_2 & 0(0) & + 0(1) & + 300(0) = 0 \\
s_3 & 0(-2) & + 0(-1) & + 300(1) = 300
\end{array}
$$

Computing the New $c_j - z_j$ Row

Simply subtract z_j from c_j.

Computing the New Value of the Objective Function

The improved solution calls for $s_1 = 16$, $s_2 = 33$, and $x_1 = 12$ ($x_2 = 0$ and $s_3 = 0$ being nonbasic variables). The value of the objective function is thus:

$$
z = 12(300) + 16(0) + 33(0) = \$3,600
$$

Step 3 (repeat): Test for Optimality

The new solution must now be tested for optimality. It can be seen that the variable x_2 in the new $c_j - z_j$ row has a *positive coefficient;* therefore, the current solution is not optimal.

Step 4 (repeat): Identify Incoming and Outgoing Variables

The Incoming Variable

In Tableau II (Table 3.7), x_2 has the largest positive coefficient in the $c_j - z_j$ row, (250) and therefore it is the *incoming variable*.

The Outgoing Variable

Because the incoming variable is x_2, the ratios are:

$$
\text{For constraint 1:} \quad \frac{16}{1} = 16
$$

$$
\text{For constraint 2:} \quad \frac{33}{3} = 11 \leftarrow \textit{Smallest}
$$

$$
\text{For constraint 3:} \quad \frac{12}{0} = \text{limit at } \infty
$$

The second row has the smallest nonnegative ratio. This row contains the variable s_2 as a basic variable (boxed in Table 3.7). Hence, the variable s_2 is the outgoing variable. The exchange of x_2 for s_2 is equivalent to a move from corner E to corner G in Figure 3.12.

Note: The existence of a zero in the body of the tableau indicates that this variable provides no limit to the value of the incoming variable—it could increase without limit toward infinity.

Step 5 (repeat): Generate an Improved Solution

The rows of the tableau of the *old solution* (Tableau II, Table 3.7) are transformed one at a time to a *new solution* (Tableau III, Table 3.8).

Step 3 (repeat): Test of Optimality

It is optimal!

Inspection of the new $c_j - z_j$ row in Table 3.8 reveals that there are no positive coefficients; hence, the second improved solution is optimal.

Interpretation of the Results
The results of Table 3.8 can be read as follows:

The Constraint Rows.   The solution values of the variables are:

Optimal solution

Row (3) $x_1 = 12$:   Produce 12 model A sets
Row (2) $x_2 = 11$:   Produce 11 model B sets
Row (1) $s_1 = 5$:   Constraint one has a slack of 5; that is, only 35 hours of labor out of 40 hours will be utilized

Interpretation of Coefficients.   Note that all basic variables have a coefficient of 1. The other coefficients in the main body—for example, $-\frac{1}{3}$, where constraint (1) intersects with s_2—are called the *marginal rates* (or ratios) *of substitution* between the row and column variables. They designate the trade-offs that occur when a nonbasic variable becomes a basic variable.

Marginal rates of substitution

TABLE 3.8   Second Improved Solution—Tableau III

Basis	Unit profits	x_1	x_2	s_1	s_2	s_3	Quantity
s_1	0	0	0	$\boxed{1}$	$-\frac{1}{3}$	$-\frac{5}{3}$	5
x_2	250	0	$\boxed{1}$	0	$\frac{1}{3}$	$-\frac{1}{3}$	11
x_1	300	$\boxed{1}$	0	0	0	1	12
c_j		300	250	0	0	0	
z_j		300	250	0	250/3	650/3	
$c_j - z_j$		0	0	0	$-250/3$	$-650/3$	

The Value of the Objective Function (Profit). The final profit can be calculated as:

$$0(5) + 250(11) + 300(12) = \$6,350$$

Step 6: Check for Other Optimal Solutions

It is important to know if only one optimal solution exists (unique solution) or if there is more than one. **Multiple optimal solutions** allow management greater flexibility in implementing a solution.

The check for other optimal solutions is simple. If the coefficient of one of the *nonbasic* variables in the final $c_j - z_j$ row is zero, then multiple optimal solutions exist. A coefficient of zero means that this variable can enter the basis, creating another feasible solution, but with the *same* value of the objective function. If two solutions exist, then there must be an infinite number of optimal solutions that are linear combinations of these two solutions (on the line joining them). In Table 3.8, there are no zero coefficients of nonbasic variables; hence, there is only one optimal solution to this problem.

Only one optimal solution

3.10 Computerization

Real-life LP problems are almost always too large and complex for graphical or manual simplex solutions. Therefore, they are solved with computers, usually by the *revised simplex method* (see [8]) or other derivatives of the simplex method. Dozens of LP packages exist and are commercially available for both microcomputers and mainframes.

As an example of an LP computer routine, we will use the Lotfi and Pegels software package [12] to solve the Sekido product-mix example presented and solved earlier in this chapter. (See Figures 3.15 for the input data and 3.16 for the results.)

First, the computer asks the user questions regarding the input data. An example of such a dialogue is given in Figure 3.15 with the user's responses shown. Note that the nonnegativity constraints are omitted, because this information is preprogrammed in the computer. Also, it is not necessary to enter the data in a standard form here (and in many other programs).

Once the data have been entered, the computer repeats, if desired, the information entered (so that any corrections can be made) and then computes and prints the results. The printout in Figure 3.16 provides the complete solution, as discussed in this chapter, plus the *shadow prices* (dual variables), to be discussed later. Most LP packages can generate the intermediate and final simplex tableaus on request. In addition, the value of the *reduced cost* is provided. This tells us how much the value of the objective function will be penalized when we enter into the optimal solution one unit of a decision variable not currently in the optimal solution.

Reduced cost is computed

FIGURE 3.15

LP computer program: Entering data

```
Problem title: PRODUCT MIX
Minimize or Maximize objective (MIN/MAX): MAX
Enter number of constraints: 3
Enter number of variables: 2


              ████████████████████████████████

              : Continue with coefficients (Y/N) Y:

              ████████████████████████████████


 p Input    Edit    Print    File    Solve    Quit    Setup

 :
 :         A              B           C     D      E
 :1                       x1          x2           RHS Val.
 :2   Objective       300.000     250.000
 :3   Row1              2.000       1.000   < =    40.000
 :4   Row2              1.000       3.000   < =    45.000
 :5   Row3              1.000       0.000   < =    12.000
 :6   Lower Bnd         0.000       0.000
 :7   Upper Bnd    999999.000  999999.000
```

FIGURE 3.16

LP computer program: Solution

```
F1-Help                    LINEAR PROGRAMMING               File:
                        ***** Optimal Solution *****

Problem Title : PRODUCT MIX
Number of iterations = 2              Objective =      6350.000

        Decision Variables Section:

        Variable        Status        Value        Reduced Cost
        --------        --------      ---------     ------------
        x1              Basic         12.000            0.000
        x2              Basic         11.000            0.000

        Slack Variables Section:

        Row       Variable   Status      Value     Shadow Price
        --------  --------   -------     -----     ------------
        Row1      Slack1     Basic       5.000         0.000
        Row2      Slack2     Lower Bnd   0.000        83.333
        Row3      Slack3     Lower Bnd   0.000       216.667

Do sensitivity analysis (Y/N)?  N
```

3.11 Special Situations in the Simplex Method

There are several special LP situations that require adjustments in the simplex procedure. Nine cases are described below.

Case 1: The Simplex Method: Minimization

The simplex method solves minimization problems in essentially the same manner as it solves maximization problems. There are two alternative approaches for minimization problems.

Two ways to solve

Direct Approach

The first approach is to solve the problem as a minimization problem directly, but this requires a slight change in the simplex procedure. The method of solving a minimization problem is basically the same as with a maximization problem, except that all the coefficients in the $c_j - z_j$ row should be nonnegative for the optimality test and the incoming variable is that variable in the $c_j - z_j$ row with the most *negative* coefficient (provides the greatest cost reduction, per unit, for minimization). This method will not be pursued here.

Conversion

The second approach is to convert the problem into a maximization problem, solve it as a maximization problem, and then translate the results in the light of the minimization objective.

Because minimizing a function is equivalent to maximizing the *negative* of that function, the only change required in order to convert an LP problem from minimization to maximization (or vice versa) is to multiply the objective function by -1. The constraints remain untouched.

Example 1. Given:

$$\text{minimize } z = 2x_1 - 5x_2$$

The problem is converted to:

Multiply by -1

$$\text{maximize } w = -2x_1 + 5x_2$$

When the solution is obtained (say, $x_1 = 12$, $x_2 = 3$) the results should be substituted back into the *original* minimization objective function to obtain the minimized value of z; $z = 2(12) - 5(3) = 9$.

Example 2. Given:

$$\text{minimize } z = 5x_1 + 1x_2 - 2x_3$$

The problem is converted to:

$$\text{maximize } w = -5x_1 - 1x_2 + 2x_3$$

Example: Solving the Blending Problem

To illustrate this approach, as well as to demonstrate the procedure for handling artificial variables, the blending problem of Part A will be solved, starting from the standard form in Table 3.3. First, however, the objective function must be converted to maximization:

$$\text{maximize } w = -45x_1 - 12x_2 - 0s_1 - 0s_2 - Ma_1 - Ma_2$$

where M is a very large number (e.g., 1,000).

The equivalent tableau is given in Table 3.9. Note the inferiority of the initial "profit" solution (value of the objective function).

$$Z = -M(300) - M(250) = -550M$$

The tableaus in Tables 3.10 and 3.11 illustrate the solution process. Tableau III represents an optimal solution, because all the coefficients in the $c_j - z_j$ row are negative or zero ($12 - M$ in Table 3.11 is a large negative number). The answer is thus:

$$x_1 = 83.33 \text{ ounces of Alpha}$$
$$x_2 = 216.67 \text{ ounces of Beta}$$
$$\text{"Profit"} = -12(216.67) - 45(83.33) = -6350 \text{ cents or}$$
$$\text{Cost} = -\text{"Profit"} = 6,350 \text{ cents per drum}$$

Note that once an artificial variable leaves the basis, it will never enter again because of the large penalty of M associated with it (1,000 could have been used here instead of M).

Case 2: Two Incoming Variables

If two or more variables have the same largest coefficient in the $c_j - z_j$ row (see Table 3.12), then either may be arbitrarily chosen as the incoming variable. This will not affect the final solution.

TABLE 3.9   Tableau for the Blending Problem

Basis	Unit profits	x_1	x_2	s_1	s_2	a_1	a_2	Quantity	Ratio
a_1	$-M$	1	1	-1	0	$\boxed{1}$	0	300	300
a_2	$-M$	③	0	0	-1	0	$\boxed{1}$	250	250/3
c_j		-45	-12	0	0	$-M$	$-M$		
z_j		$-4M$	$-M$	M	M	$-M$	$-M$		
$c_j - z_j$		$-45 + 4M$	$-12 + M$	$-M$	$-M$	0	0		

TABLE 3.10   Second (Improved) Tableau (II)

Basis	Unit profits	x_1	x_2	s_1	s_2	a_1	a_2	Quantity	Ratio
a_1	$-M$	0	①	-1	$\frac{1}{3}$	☐1	$-\frac{1}{3}$	216.67	216.67
x_1	-45	☐1	0	0	$-\frac{1}{3}$	0	$\frac{1}{3}$	83.33	limit $= \infty$
c_j		-45	-12	0	0	$-M$	$-M$		
z_j		-45	$-M$	M	$(15 - M/3)$	$-M$	$(-15 + M/3)$		
$c_j - z_j$		0	$-12 + M$	$-M$	$(M/3 - 15)$	0	$(15 - 4M/3)$		

TABLE 3.11   Third (Optimal) Tableau (III)

Basis	Unit profits	x_1	x_2	s_1	s_2	a_1	a_2	Quantity	Ratio
x_2	-12	0	☐1	-1	$\frac{1}{3}$	1	$\frac{1}{3}$	216.67	
x_1	-45	☐1	0	0	$-\frac{1}{3}$	0	$\frac{1}{3}$	83.33	
c_j		-45	-12	0	0	$-M$	$-M$		
z_j		-45	-12	12	11	-12	-11		
$c_j - z_j$		0	0	-12	-11	$(12 - M)$	$(11 - M)$		

TABLE 3.12   Tie for Incoming Variable

	x_1	x_2	x_3	$x_4 \ldots$
	↓		↓	
$c_j - z_j$	7	4	7	-15

? (tie between x_1 and x_3)

Case 3: Two Outgoing Basic Variables (degeneracy)

The situations presented thus far had the property that the number of variables in the solution was the same as the number of constraints (not counting the nonnegativity constraints). If the number of positive variables in the solution is *less* than the number of constraints, the solution is "degenerate." An example of **degeneracy** occurs when three or more constraints intersect in the solution of a problem with two variables. This is shown in Figure 3.17.

Three intersect

In the simplex procedure, degeneracy occurs when two b_i/a_{ij} ratios tie for the smallest value (see Table 3.13). The problem is: Which of the two should go? Again, the choice for outgoing basic variable may be made arbitrarily without affecting the final solution.

FIGURE 3.17

Degeneracy in a two-variable problem

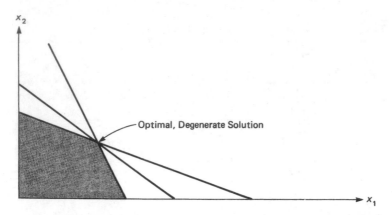

Optimal, Degenerate Solution

TABLE 3.13   Example of Degeneracy in a Tableau

Tie for outgoing variable:

Basis	Unit profits	x_1	x_2	x_3	s_1	s_2	Quantity	Ratio
s_1	—	0	0	①←	1	2	50	$50/1 = 50$ ←
x_1	—	1	0	④←	0	1	200	$200/4 = 50$ ← Minimum
x_2	—	0	1	2	0	5	250	$250/2 = 125$
$c_j - z_j$		0	0	3	0	1		

Improved tableau with s_1 arbitrarily selected as outgoing variable:

Basis	Unit profits	x_1	x_2	x_3	s_1	s_2	Quantity	Ratio
x_3	—	0	0	1	1	2	50	
x_1	—	1	0	0	−4	−7	0	
x_2	—	0	1	0	−2	0	150	
$c_j - z_j$		0	0	0	−3	−5		

Final solution: $x_3 = 50$, $x_1 = 0$ (just like nonbasic variables), $x_2 = 150$.

Case 4: Unbounded Solutions

An infinitive value

Graphically, in this case, the feasible solution space extends indefinitely—creating an **unbounded problem** (see Figure 3.18 for a maximization case). The result in the simplex is that there is no outgoing basic variable; the ratios are either infinite or negative (see Table 3.14). Therefore, the optimal solution is infinite. Such a result could mean that an error was made, the problem was misstated, or an incorrect assumption was made.

FIGURE 3.18

*An unbounded
maximization problem*

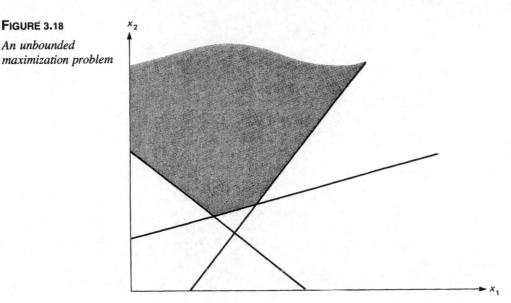

TABLE 3.14   No Outgoing Variable

Basis	Unit profits	x_1	x_2	s_1	s_2	Quantity	Ratio
s_1	—	1	−1	$\boxed{1}$	0	180	180/−1 (ignore)
s_2	—	5	0	0	$\boxed{1}$	55	55/0 limit = ∞
$c_j - z_j$		−2	3	0	0		

Case 5: Unconstrained Decision Variables

Negative solutions

Occasionally, a problem arises when some of the decision variables are *not* constrained to be nonnegative. In this case, the problem statement is modified slightly before employing the simplex. The modification is to replace the unconstrained variable, say, x_i, throughout the problem statement with the difference of two variables $(y_i - w_i)$, where both $y_i \geq 0$ and $w_i \geq 0$. The optimal simplex solution will then either have $y_i = 0$, in which case $x_i = -w_i$, or else $w_i = 0$ and $x_i = y_i$.

For example, suppose the following problem statement is given and x_2 is a temperature (°F) that may be either positive or negative.

maximize $z = 40x_1 + 65x_2 - 8x_3$
subject to:
$$1x_1 + 1x_2 + 1x_3 \geq 1,000$$
$$2x_1 + 0x_2 - 1x_3 \leq 783$$
$$1x_1 + 0x_2 + 0x_3 \geq 0$$
$$0x_1 + 0x_2 + 1x_3 \geq 0$$

103

Then the problem would be recast as:

maximize $z = 40x_1 + 65y_2 - 65w_2 - 8x_3$
subject to:

$$1x_1 + 1y_2 - 1w_2 + 1x_3 \geq 1,000$$
$$2x_1 + 0y_2 + 0w_2 - 1x_3 \leq 783$$

and $\quad x_1, \quad y_2, \quad w_2, \quad x_3 \geq 0$

Case 6: Negative Right-Hand Quantity (b_i)

If one of the b_i quantities is negative, then multiply the entire constraint by -1, and the constraint will be in proper form. Note that if the constraint was an inequality, multiplying by -1 will *reverse* the direction of the inequality ($\geq$ instead of $\leq$, and vice versa), which may thereby necessitate adding an artificial variable to obtain an initial basis.

For example, if one of the constraints in a problem is:

$$1x_1 - 2x_2 + 1x_3 \leq -10$$

then multiplying by -1 yields:

$$-1x_1 + 2x_2 - 1x_3 \geq 10$$

Adding *surplus* and artificial variables further results in:

$$-1x_1 + 2x_2 - 1x_3 - 1s_1 + 1a_1 = 10$$

Case 7: No Feasible Solution

No feasible solutions

In some cases, there will not be a feasible solution to the problem. Graphically, no solution space that simultaneously satisfies all constraints exists—See Figure 3.19. The clue to this situation, when using the simplex process, is that the "optimal" solution will

FIGURE 3.19

No feasible solution space (shaded regions are infeasible)

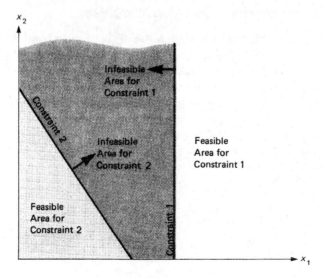

TABLE 3.15 **No Feasible Solution**

Basis	Unit profits	x_1	x_2	s_1	s_2	a_1	a_2	Quantity	Ratio
x_2	—	2	$\boxed{1}$	6	-1	0	0	370	
a_2	—	1	0	2	0	-3	$\boxed{1}$	120	
$c_j - z_j$		$(-M - 6)$	0	-17	$-2M$	-8	0		

still continue an *artificial* variable and the value of the $c_j - z_j$ row will still be on the order of $-M$ (see Table 3.15).

Case 8: Multiple Optimal Solutions

This solution is shown, for a maximization case, in Figure 3.20. The objective function, when moved as far as possible from the origin to the right, does not touch a corner point but rather a line segment between two points (P and Q). This happens when the isoprofit line is parallel to an "active" (binding) constraint (2). In such a case, there are optimal solutions at corner P, at corner Q, and at an infinite number of points on the line segment PQ.

This situation can be recognized in the simplex procedure by the fact that one of the nonbasic variables in the $c_j - z_j$ row will have a value of zero (see Table 3.16). Hence, a nonbasic variable may be brought into the solution basis, thereby creating a new solution with the same value of the objective function.

FIGURE 3.20
Multiple solutions case

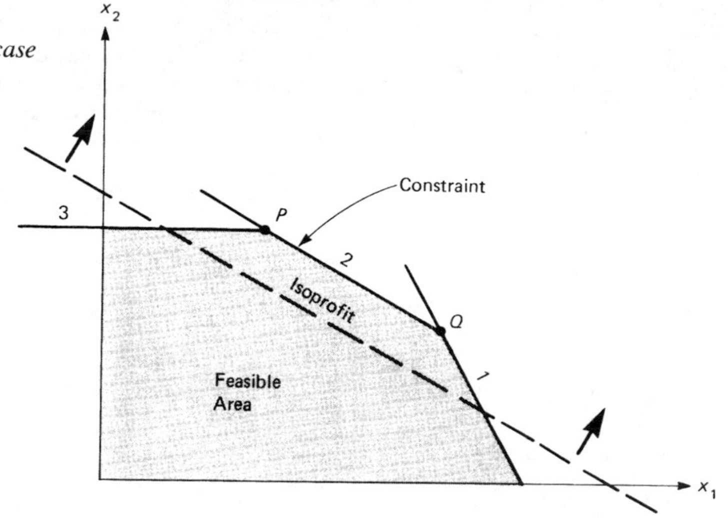

TABLE 3.16   The Multiple Solutions Situation

Basis	Unit profits	x_1	x_2	s_1	s_2	Quantity	Ratio
x_2	—	2	$\boxed{1}$	2	0	6	$6/2 = 3$
s_2	—	6	0	3	$\boxed{1}$	18	$18/3 = 6$
$c_j - z_j$		−3	0	0	0		

Case 9: Redundant Constraint

A constraint that does not intersect the feasible area of solutions is called **redundant**. It can be removed from the problem without affecting the optimal solution. The constraint $2x_1 + 1x_2 \leq 40$ in Figure 3.12 illustrates such a constraint. Note that a redundant constraint will *not* affect the simplex process.

3.12 Problems for Part B

17. In 1717, Edward Teach, better known as "Blackbeard," sailed his ship into the harbor of Arecibo in the West Indies and attacked and looted the town. His plunder consisted of 29,000 pounds of gold (worth 350 shillings per troy ounce), 21,000 pounds of silver (worth 25 shillings/oz.), and 9,000 pounds of gems and jewelry (worth 200 shillings/oz). Blackbeard's ship includes three holds: the forward hold has a capacity of 11,000 pounds or 900 cubic feet, the center hold has a capacity of 15,000 pounds or 1,400 cubic feet, and the aft hold has a capacity of 8,000 pounds or 500 cubic feet. How much of each type of plunder should Blackbeard put in each hold to maximize his haul? *Note:* There are 12 troy ounces in each pound and gold occupies a quarter of a cubic foot per pound when stored for shipping, silver takes a third of a cubic foot per pound, and the gems/jewelry two-thirds of a cubic foot per pound.

18. COM Food Corporation specializes in menu preparation for British restaurants, institutions, and individual families. The major idea of the service is to provide an adequate (and tasteful) diet at a minimal cost. Given below is a *simplified* diet problem.

    The minimum daily nutrient requirements for a certain group of adults are:

Calories	2,860
Protein	80 grams
Iron	15 milligrams
Niacin	20 milligrams
Vitamin A	20,000 units

A menu, when recommended by COM Food, must supply *at least* these minimum daily requirements. In this simplified problem, we shall assume that COM Food prepares one menu only. (In actual cases, a different menu would be prepared for every day of the week, or even every day of the month.)

The following table lists foods and prices (pounds sterling per pound, £) offered to the customers.

Food	Price per pound (£)
Beef	1.00
Butter	.79
Bread	.26
Carrots	.15
Halibut	.80
Eggs	.34
Cheese	1.10

The quantities of calories, protein, iron, niacin and vitamin A included in each 100 grams of the above foods are given below:

	Food	Calories	Protein (grams)	Iron (mg)	Niacin (mg)	Vitamin A (units)
A	Beef	309	26.0	3.1	4.1	0
B	Butter	716	.6	0	1	3,330
C	Bread	276	8.5	.6	.9	0
D	Carrots	42	1.2	.6	.4	12,000
E	Halibut	182	26.2	.8	10.5	0
F	Eggs	162	12.8	2.7	.3	1,140
G	Cheese	368	21.5	.5	.4	1,240

Find the least-cost food mix of the daily menu that satisfies minimum daily requirements.
a. Set up the problem as a linear program.
b. How many foods will be included in the optimal solution? Why? (Answer this *before* attempting to solve the problem.)
c. Review your answer to (b). Under what circumstance(s) will the answer to (b) be different?
d. Solve the problem: Give the quantities of the foods to be included and the total daily cost. (A computer is recommended.)
e. In what nutritional elements will you have a surplus? In what quantities?
f. The customers are unhappy with the proposed menu solution because it does not include beef and it includes too much bread and eggs, so the following requirements are imposed:
  (1) The menu must include at least 100 grams of beef.
  (2) The menu should not include more than 500 grams of bread and 200 grams of eggs.
  Resolve the problem and find the optimal menu now. What is the additional cost and in what nutritional elements will there be a surplus? (How much?)

19. A commodities wholesaler maintains a 400-ton capacity warehouse to buy, sell, and store cocoa beans. Cocoa purchased in one month cannot be sold until the first day of the following month. The wholesaler's current stock is 200 tons of beans and the cost of storage is $30/ton/month. The wholesaler believes that the buy and sell prices for cocoa beans for the next four months will be about: July 900 (buy) and 1,100 (sell), August 800/1,200, September 1,000/900, October 1,100/1,200. Formulate a buying and selling plan for the wholesaler to maximize her profits.

20. Given:

minimize $z = 5x_1 + 4x_2$
subject to:
$$4x_1 + 2.5x_2 \geq 60$$
$$2x_1 + 5x_2 \geq 60$$
$$5x_1 + 4x_2 \geq 82$$

a. Solve the problem graphically.
b. Explain the uniqueness of the problem.
c. Solve the problem by the simplex method.
d. How is the uniqueness of this problem reflected in the simplex procedure?
e. Assume that the second constraint is changed to $2x_1 + 6x_2 \geq 60$. What will the impact of this change be? How will it be reflected in the simplex solution now?

21. A pharmaceutical firm produces two grades of mouthwash for the retail market. The firm must supply 600 gallons of green mouthwash and 200 gallons of blue mouthwash a day. It uses two vats whose capacities are 25 (Vat A) and 50 (Vat B) gallons to produce the mouthwashes. It takes an hour to produce a batch in Vat A, costing $30/hour, and 1.5 hours per batch in Vat B, which costs $35/hour. The company works a two-shift day (16 hours). Green mouthwash sells for $5/gallon and must include at least 45 percent of liquid "p" (which costs $2/gallon) and not more than 25 percent of specially-distilled water (cost of $0.50/gallon). Blue mouthwash sells for $4/gallon and must include at least 25 percent of liquid p and not more than 50 percent water. The remaining ingredients consist of special fillers that cost $1/gallon. What is the best daily schedule to maximize profits, considering the batching requirements?

22. Given a problem:

maximize $z = 5x_1 + 3x_2$
subject to:
$$4x_1 + 2x_2 \leq 10$$
$$2x_1 + 2x_2 \leq 8$$

Solve the problem by the simplex method and/or graphically.

23. Solve Problem 22, adding a third constraint: $1x_1 \geq 2$.

24. Solve Problem 22 if the $\leq$ sign in the first constraint is changed to an equality ($=$).

25. Solve Problem 22 if the constraint $4x_1 + 2x_2 \leq 10$ is replaced by $1x_1 - 1x_2 \leq -1$.

26. Solve Problem 22 if both constraints are replaced by:

$$
\begin{aligned}
1x_1 - 1x_2 &\leq -1 \\
1x_1 \quad\quad &\leq \quad 1
\end{aligned}
$$

27. Solve Problem 22 if the additional constraint $1x_1 \geq 3$ is added.

28. Western Swiss Machine shop makes deluxe and regular skis on a weekly schedule for the area skiing enthusiasts. They have a contract with Apple Hill to supply 18 regular pairs of skis per week. They also sell both regular and deluxe skis to local sporting goods stores. A deluxe pair of skis requires 40 minutes for roughing and 20 minutes for finishing, whereas a regular pair of skis requires 20 minutes for roughing and $26\frac{2}{3}$ minutes for finishing. With only 1,000 minutes for roughing and 800 minutes of finishing time available per week and a profit realization of 4 SFr (Swiss francs) and 3 SFr for the deluxe and regular, respectively, what weekly mix of the two types of skis should be produced to meet the contract's requirement and maximize profits?

   a. Formulate as a LP in two *different ways*.

   b. Solve graphically (the formulation with the three constraints).

   c. Solve by the simplex method.

29. Solve by the simplex method:

   a. maximize $z = 8x_1 + 6x_2$

   subject to:

$$
\begin{aligned}
4x_1 + 2x_2 &\leq 60 \\
2x_1 + 4x_2 &\leq 48 \\
1x_1 \quad\quad &\geq 5 \\
3x_2 &\geq 5
\end{aligned}
$$

   b. minimize $z = 2x_1 + 4x_2 + x_3$

   subject to:

$$
\begin{aligned}
1x_1 + 2x_2 - 1x_3 &\geq 5 \\
2x_1 - \quad x_2 + 2x_3 &= 2 \\
-1x_1 + 2x_2 + 2x_3 &\geq 1 \\
1x_3 &\leq 2
\end{aligned}
$$

30. The Indian Valve Company is developing an alloy to be used in the manufacture of valves. The research department has determined that the alloy can be formed by mixing the alloying metals of iron, nickel, and chrome, provided that the proportions of the materials fall within certain limits. The chemists have set the following proportional limits on the quantities of iron, nickel, and chrome that may be used.

Limit	Iron	Nickel	Chrome
Upper	5	1	—
Lower	3	1	—
Upper	3	—	1
Lower	2	—	1
Upper	—	1	3
Lower	—	1	3

The upper limit means that, for example, *no more* than 5 parts of iron should be used for each part of nickel; the lower limit means that at least 3 parts of iron should be used for each part of nickel, and so on.

If the unit costs of iron, nickel, and chrome are 1, 2, and 3 rupees, respectively, what is the lowest-cost mixture per unit of alloy that will satisfy the quality requirements?

a. Formulate as a LP problem.

b. Solve (use a computer).

Note: More LP problems are available in the next chapter.

3.13 CASE
THE DAPHNE JEWELRY COMPANY*

The Daphne Jewelry Company markets the bulk of its products through seven salespersons operating in seven separate sales territories (on a one-to-one basis). This is due to the fact that other area salespersons use Daphne's products only as a supplement to some other distributor's line. The seven salespersons follow just the opposite practice, using the products of other manufacturers to augment the Daphne line. For this reason the firm sets periodic sales quotas only for the seven salespersons.

The firm sells nine product lines. These are listed in Table 1, where each column shows how $1 in sales in each of the seven territories is distributed among the various product lines. For example, the .07 coefficient for the first product, belts, indicates that on the average, 7 cents of every dollar's worth of merchandise sold in territory 1 is generated by belts. These distributions were found to be quite stable over time, regardless of the size of the account.

The market potential of each sales territory for the next planning period is presented in Table 2. This is Daphne's estimate of "potential" demand for its products next year for each of the seven territories at the present level of advertising. These demand forecasts

were based on past sales records, information gathered from trade associations and governmental agencies, as well as independent forecasts made by consulting firms that specialize in economic analysis of trade areas.

The cost of a dollar's worth of merchandise required in the production of each product line, together with the

TABLE 2   Daphne's Market Potential in each of Seven Selling Areas

Sales territory	Market potential (maximum)
No. 1	$ 225,000
No. 2	135,000
No. 3	150,000
No. 4	100,000
No. 5	210,000
No. 6	80,000
No. 7	250,000
Total	$1,150,000

TABLE 1   Dollar Distribution Value of Sales for Nine Products in Seven Territories

Product lines	Sales territory						
	No. 1	*No. 2*	*No. 3*	*No. 4*	*No. 5*	*No. 6*	*No. 7*
1. Belts	.07	.02	.01	.15	.18	.15	.00
2. Buckles	.05	.00	.00	.10	.10	.07	.00
3. Package goods	.20	.35	.30	.25	.25	.25	.50
4. Necklaces	.07	.07	.07	.10	.15	.10	.03
5. Earrings	.15	.15	.15	.15	.15	.15	.15
6. Bracelets	.10	.20	.10	.10	.10	.10	.05
7. Gold stone	.18	.10	.17	.10	.05	.05	.12
8. Hematite	.15	.08	.17	.02	.02	.10	.12
9. Job turquoise	.03	.03	.03	.03	.00	.03	.03
Total	1.00	1.00	1.00	1.00	1.00	1.00	1.00

TABLE 3   Material Costs and Sales Commission for the Nine Product Lines

Product lines	Cost of $1 in merchandise	Sales commission on $1 in merchandise
1–6 inclusive	$.50	$.15
7–9 inclusive	.67	.10

corresponding sales commission paid on each dollar of sales, is depicted in Table 3. The production capacity of the nine product lines is given in Table 4.

During recent years, the company's sales and profits have been growing very slowly. Last year, the company netted about $200,000 on sales of about $650,000. Mr. Brown, the president of Daphne Jewelry, was not pleased with the results. He felt there was a large quantity of unutilized production capacity as well as market potential. Mrs. Grant, the vice president of marketing,

TABLE 4   Product Line Capacity

Product line	Product line capacity
1	$ 70,000
2	20,000
3	210,000
4	70,000
5	150,000
6	100,000
7	150,000
8	150,000
9	30,000

disagreed with Brown's assessment. She felt that the company was at or near optimal operating conditions, and that very little could be done within the framework of the existing conditions.

Last Monday, the president called the executive management team together and requested proposals for improving the situation. The vice president for marketing suggested an increase in marketing efforts, especially in territories 2, 4, and 6, where current market potential is the lowest. The vice president for production suggested increasing production of those product lines that yield the highest return. The controller suggested dropping the least profitable products or territories, or both. The president was reluctant to accept any of these suggestions, because both the market potential and the production capacity were underutilized. Furthermore, the specific marketing plan proposed violated the production capabilities, and the proposed increase in certain product lines violated the marketing capabilities.

The president finally decided to call in a management scientist who was asked to prepare a report to include the following items:

a. Evaluate the existing situation; determine if the company is indeed close to optimal operating conditions.

b. Analyze the marketing and production proposals brought forth by the vice presidents and the controller.

c. Submit other proposals; determine their feasibility and profitability.

d. Analyze the pricing and commission policies; submit recommendations.

*Case developed by Dr. Malcolm Golden, University of Miami, and Dr. Alan Parker, Florida International University. Reproduced with permission.

Glossary

Additivity assumption   An assumption in LP that the returns are independent of each other and can be added together proportionally.

Adjacent corner   A neighboring vertex in the feasible solution space.

Allocation problem   A problem involving the best allocation of scarce resources, commonly solved by LP.

Artificial variable   A fictitious constraint parameter used in the simplex to obtain an initial solution.

Basic variable   One of the variables currently in the basis.

Basis   A solution in m variables of a system of m equations with n unknowns, where $n \geq m$. The other $n - m$ variables have the value zero.

Blending problem   One of the two major types of LP problems: minimizing the cost of a fixed amount of output.

Constraints   Restrictions on the problem solution arising from limited resources, policy requirements, and so on.

Degeneracy   A situation in the simplex where a basic variable takes on the value zero, just like a nonbasic variable.

Divisibility assumption   An assumption in LP that the resources are infinitely divisible.

Feasible area   The solution space or region that satisfies all the constraints simultaneously.

Feasible solution   A solution inside or on the boundary of the feasible area.

Inequality constraint   A restriction on some combinations of the variables such that they must be greater than, less than, or equal to a particular value.

Infeasible solution   A solution that violates at least one constraint.

Integer programming   A linear program where one or more of the decision variables is indivisible.

Isocost (isoprofit) lines   Lines of constant objective function cost (profit) on a graph, each line parallel to the others.

Iteration   One pass through an algorithmic process, such as the simplex.

Linear function   A mathematical expression in which the variables appear in separate terms and are raised to the first power.

Multiple optimal solutions   When alternative optima exist.

Nonnegativity constraint   The restriction in LP that all decision variables must be positive or zero.

Objective function   The statement of the goal of the program (the result variable) in mathematical form.

Optimal solution   The best of all feasible solutions.

Product-mix problem   One of the two basic LP forms: maximizing the output with given resources.

Redundant constraint   A constraint that does not affect the feasible region of solutions.

Simplex method   An algorithm for LP that only investigates feasible corner points of the solution space.

Slack variable   A variable representing the difference between the use of a resource and its availability.

Surplus variable   A variable representing the difference between the use of a resource and a minimum requirement.

Unbounded problem   A case where the feasible solution extends indefinitely.

Vertex   A corner point of the solution space corresponding to the intersection of two or more constraints.

References and Bibliography

1. Bazaraa, M. S., and J. J. Jarvis. *Linear Programming and Network Flows.* New York: John Wiley & Sons, 2nd ed., 1990.
2. Best, M. J., and K. Ritter. *Linear Programming: Action Set Analysis and Computer Programs.* Englewood Cliffs, N.J.: Prentice-Hall, 1985.
3. Clavert, J. E., and W. L. Voxman. *Linear Programming.* New York: Harcourt, Brace, Jovanovich, 1989.
4. Dantzig, G. B. *Linear Programming and Extensions.* Princeton, N.J.: Princeton University Press, 1963.
5. Darst, R. B. (ed.) *Introduction to Linear Programming: Applications and Extensions.* New York: Dekker, 1990.
6. Friendly, J. "Shazam! A Shortcut for Computers." *New York Times,* November 11, 1979, p. E7.
7. Hooker, J. N. "Karmarkar's Linear Programming Algorithm." *Interfaces,* July–August 1986, pp. 75–90, and January–February 1987, p. 128.
8. Jeter, M. W. *Mathematical Programming—An Introduction to Optimization.* New York: Dekker, 1986.

9. Karmarkar, N. "A New Polynomial-time Algorithm for Linear Programming." *Combinatorica* 4, no. 4 (1984), pp. 373–95.

10. Kolata, G. "A Fast Way to Solve Hard Problems." *Science,* September 21, 1984, pp. 1379–80.

11. Lev, B., and H. J. Weiss. *Introduction to Mathematical Programming*. New York: Elsevier North-Holland, 1982.

12. Lotfi, V. and C. C. Pegels. *Decision Support Systems for MS/OR Software,* 2nd ed., Homewood, IL: Irwin, 1992.

13. Nazareth, J. L. *Computer Solution of Linear Programming*. New York: Oxford University Press, 1987.

14. Stryer, J. K. *Linear Programming and Its Applications*. New York: Springer-Verlag, 1989.

Linear Programming— Applications

The power and richness of linear programming are demonstrated in this chapter through nine diverse examples. Although the examples are simplified—the original problems had hundreds of variables and constraints—they do provide illustrations of typical problems solved by LP. In addition, the formation of complex and difficult situations is illustrated in many of the examples. The problems at the end of the chapter are intended to enhance formulation skills.

4.1 Crude Oil Refining

CAM Oil Company produces four products in its refinery: gasoline, heating oil, jet fuel, and lubricating oil. These products are made from four available crude oils. The process is schematically shown in Figure 4.1.

The first three crudes are processed in unit I; the fourth crude is processed in either unit I or unit II. Only unit II is capable of producing lube oil in addition to the other three products.

Resource (Input) Availability (in barrels per week)

Crude 1 and 3: up to 200,000 each

Crude 2: up to 150,000

Crude 4: up to 250,000

Input-Output Coefficients

Table 4.1 shows the input-output relationship between crudes (inputs) and products (outputs). These are the yields. For example, a barrel of crude 1 yields .5 barrels of gasoline, .3 barrels of heating oil, and .1 barrels of jet fuel.

Marketability

Each week, CAM can sell up to 250,000 barrels of gasoline; 120,000 barrels of heating oil; 30,000 barrels of lube oil; and 100,000 barrels of jet fuel.

FIGURE 4.1

CAM Oil Company production process

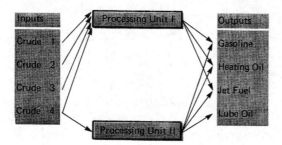

TABLE 4.1   **Input-output Coefficients**

	Gasoline	Heating oil	Lube oil	Jet fuel	Loss
Unit I					
Crude 1	.5	.3	0	.1	.1
2	.4	.2	0	.2	.2
3	.6	.2	0	.1	.1
4	.5	.1	0	.2	.2
Unit II					
Crude 4	.4	.1	.3	.1	.1

Profit

For each barrel of crude 1 refined, CAM realizes $1.50 profit, crude 2 brings $2.00 per barrel, crude 3 brings $1.10 per barrel, and crude 4 brings $2.00 per barrel if processed in unit I and $3.00 per barrel if processed in unit II. The objective of CAM is to maximize profits. The problem is: How much crude oil of each available type should CAM refine each week to meet the profit maximization objective?

Formulation

1. Define the Decision Variables

x_1 = Amount of crude 1 to be processed
x_2 = Amount of crude 2 to be processed
x_3 = Amount of crude 3 to be processed
x_4 = Amount of crude 4 to be processed in unit I
x_5 = Amount of crude 4 to be processed in unit II
$(x_4 + x_5)$ = Amount of crude 4 processed

2. The Objective Function to be Maximized is the Total Profit:

$$\text{maximize } z = 1.5x_1 + 2.0x_2 + 1.1x_3 + 2.0x_4 + 3.0x_5$$

3. The Constraints

$$1x_1 \leq 200,000$$
$$1x_2 \leq 150,000$$
$$1x_3 \leq 200,000$$
$$1x_4 + 1x_5 \leq 250,000$$

Technology and marketability:

$$.5x_1 + .4x_2 + .6x_3 + .5x_4 + .4x_5 \leq 250,000 \quad \text{(for gasoline)}$$
$$.3x_1 + .2x_2 + .2x_3 + .1x_4 + .1x_5 \leq 120,000 \quad \text{(heating fuel)}$$
$$.3x_5 \leq 30,000 \quad \text{(lube oil)}$$
$$.1x_1 + .2x_2 + .1x_3 + .2x_4 + .1x_5 \leq 100,000 \quad \text{(jet fuel)}$$

The Optimal (computerized) Solution

x_1 = 150,000 barrels $x_3 = 0$ x_5 = 100,000 barrels

x_2 = 150,000 barrels x_4 = 150,000 barrels   Total profit = $1,125,000 (each week)

4.2 Paper Trimming

The Northwestern Paper Company produces rolls of paper, 12 inches wide × 1,000 feet long. These standard rolls are purchased by many of its clients. However, some clients prefer to receive special sizes; namely, 2-inch, $3\frac{1}{2}$-inch, or 5-inch rolls, all 1,000 feet long. The minimum amount of rolls demanded is 500 of 2-inch, 2,000 of $3\frac{1}{2}$-inch, and 1,500 of 5-inch rolls. The special rolls can be cut out of the 12-inch standard rolls.

The company is considering six cutting alternatives, each of which results in 1 inch of waste or less. These are shown in Table 4.2, which lists the number of rolls in each cutting alternative. Find the best cutting program to minimize the waste.

Formulation

1. The Decision Variables
Let x_1 = number of 12-inch rolls to be cut according to alternative 1, x_2 = number of rolls to be cut according to alternative 2, and so on.

2. The Objective Function to be Minimized is the "Total Waste":

$$\text{minimize} = z = 0x_1 + 0x_2 + 1x_3 + 0x_4 + 1x_5 + \tfrac{1}{2}x_6$$

3. The Constraints (Minimum Demand)

$$
\begin{aligned}
6x_1 + 1x_2 + 2x_3 + 0x_4 + 3x_5 + 4x_6 &\geq 500 \quad \text{(for 2-inch rolls)} \\
2x_3 + 2x_4 + 1x_6 &\geq 2{,}000 \quad \text{(for } 3\tfrac{1}{2}\text{-inch rolls)} \\
2x_2 + 1x_4 + 1x_5 &\geq 1{,}500 \quad \text{(for 5-inch rolls)}
\end{aligned}
$$

Solution (by computer)

$$x_1 = 41.67, \; x_2 = 250, \; x_3 = 0, \; x_4 = 1{,}000, \; x_5 = 0, \; x_6 = 0$$

Total waste (objective function) is zero. This solution will result in exactly 500 rolls of 2 inches, 2,000 rolls of $3\frac{1}{2}$ inches, and 1,500 rolls of 5 inches. *Note:* If cutting 41.67 of alternative 1 cannot be achieved by averaging over multiple trim runs, then the problem should be formulated as an integer program.

TABLE 4.2 **Paper Trimming Alternatives**

	Size of rolls			
Alternatives	*2-inch*	*$3\frac{1}{2}$-inch*	*5-inch*	*Waste*
1	6	0	0	0
2	1	0	2	0
3	2	2	0	1
4	0	2	1	0
5	3	0	1	1
6	4	1	0	$\frac{1}{2}$

4.3   Agriculture

Sam Green just acquired a five-acre orange grove in South Florida. The U.S. Department of Agriculture recommends that orange groves be fertilized twice a year. The quantities of chemicals recommended by the Agriculture Department, per acre, per application of fertilizer, are:

> Nitrogen—at least 20 lbs.
>
> Phosphoric acid—at least 25 lbs.
>
> Potash—at least 30 lbs.
>
> Chlorine—no more than 36 lbs.

Fertilizers are sold on the market under various brands, in standard bags of either 25 lbs. or 50 lbs. Each brand is designated by a system of three numbers. For example, 8–10–6 means that each bag contains 8 percent (by weight) nitrogen, 10 percent phosphoric acid, and 6 percent potash.

Sam is shopping for fertilizers, determined to pay as little as possible; at the same time, he wants to follow the recommendations of the Agriculture Department.

The fertilizers currently available on the market are:

Brand	Designation	Cost per bag	Chlorine content (percent)	Weight
A	4–6–8	$5.50	8	50 lbs.
B	8–8–8	6.00	6	50 lbs.
C	6–6–20	5.00	5	25 lbs.

Find:

    a. How many bags of each type Sam should buy each year.

    b. Sam's yearly budget for fertilizers.

    c. The excess amount of chemicals that the grove will receive each year.

    d. The actual amount of chlorine provided to the grove yearly, as compared to the recommended amount.

Formulation

This blending-type problem can be formulated in two different ways, depending on the definition of the decision variables. The problem is first solved for one application of the fertilizers per acre.

Formulation A

1. The Decision Variables

x_1 = No. of pounds of brand A, per application per acre

x_2 = No. of pounds of brand B, per application per acre

x_3 = No. of pounds of brand C, per application per acre

2. The Objective Function

Each pound of brand A costs: $\$5.50/50 = \$0.11$

Each pound of brand B costs: $\$6.00/50 = \$0.12$

Each pound of brand C costs: $\$5.00/25 = \$0.20$

Therefore, the objective function for total cost, z, is:

$$\text{minimize } z = .11x_1 + .12x_2 + .20x_3$$

3. The Constraints

a. Provide at least 20 pounds of nitrogen. Nitrogen is provided by the three fertilizers according to the percentage designated; that is:

$$\underbrace{.04x_1}_{\substack{\text{provided by} \\ \text{brand A}}} + \underbrace{.08x_2}_{\substack{\text{provided by} \\ \text{brand B}}} + \underbrace{.06x_3}_{\substack{\text{provided by} \\ \text{brand C}}} \geq 20$$

b. Provide at least 25 pounds of phosphoric acid. Similarly:

$$.06x_1 + .08x_2 + .06x_3 \geq 25$$

c. Provide at least 30 pounds of potash. Similarly:

$$.08x_1 + .08x_2 + .20x_3 \geq 30$$

d. Provide no more than 36 pounds of chlorine. Similarly:

$$.08x_1 + .06x_2 + .05x_3 \leq 36$$

Solution (by computer)

$$x_1 = 0 \qquad\qquad x_3 = 35.71$$
$$x_2 = 285.71 \qquad z = \$41.43$$

Note that this solution, even for five acres, results in a noninteger number of bags. Thus, the problem can either be solved by "integer programming" or the unused fertilizer can be saved for the following year. Another formulation of this problem, intended to get around the integer difficulty, is given below.

Formulation B

1. The Decision Variables

They are the number of bags of each brand:

y_1 = No. of bags of brand A, per acre, per application
y_2 = No. of bags of brand B, per acre, per application
y_3 = No. of bags of brand C, per acre, per application

2. The Objective Function

$$\text{minimize } z = 5.5y_1 + 6.0y_2 + 5.0y_3$$

3. The Constraints

The nitrogen constraint:

$$.04(50)y_1 + .08(50)y_2 + .06(25)y_3 \geq 20$$

The student is encouraged to complete the formulation and solution of this problem. Can you see why this formulation is no better than the one in A in solving the integer difficulty?

4.4   Finance (Banking)

Palmetto National Savings & Loan makes five kinds of loans. These loans, with the yearly interest rate charged to customers, are shown in the table below:

Type of loan	Interest charged (percent)
Commercial loans	15
Home mortgage (first mortgage)	10
Home improvements	13.6
Home mortgage (second mortgage)	14
Short-term revolving loan	18

The bank has $53 million in available funds. Its objective is to maximize yield on investment.

The Demand for Funds

The demand for short-term revolving loans never exceeds $5 million. All other demands are unlimited.

Policies and Regulations

a. Home improvement loans cannot be higher than 20 percent of first mortgage loans.

b. Commercial loans must be smaller than or equal to the second mortgage loans.

c. The bank must invest at least 60 percent of the loans outstanding (total loans) in mortgages.

d. For safety reasons, there must be at least $2 invested in first mortgage loans for every dollar invested in second mortgage loans.

e. Short-term loans cannot exceed $5 million.

Find the best bank fund investment plan.

Formulation

1. The Decision Variables

x_1 = Dollars invested in commercial loans
x_2 = Dollars invested in first mortgages
x_3 = Dollars invested in home improvements
x_4 = Dollars invested in second mortgages
x_5 = Dollars invested in short-term loans

2. The Objective Function

$$\text{maximize } z = .15x_1 + .10x_2 + .136x_3 + .14x_4 + .18x_5$$

3. The Constraints

Monthly availability: $1x_1 + 1x_2 + 1x_3 + 1x_4 + 1x_5 \leq 53{,}000{,}000$
Policy a: $1x_3 \leq .2x_2$
b: $1x_1 \leq 1x_4$
c: $1x_2 + 1x_4 \geq .6(1x_1 + 1x_2 + 1x_3 + 1x_4 + 1x_5)$
d: $1x_2 \geq 2x_4$
e: $1x_5 \leq 5{,}000{,}000$

Note: c is rewritten *as* $.6x_1 - .4x_2 + .6x_3 - .4x_4 + .6x_5 \leq 0$

Solution (by computer)

$x_1 = 10{,}900{,}000$ $x_3 = 4{,}360{,}000$ $x_5 = 5{,}000{,}000$

$x_2 = 21{,}800{,}000$ $x_4 = 10{,}900{,}000$ $z = \$6{,}838{,}808$

4.5 Paper Manufacturing

A paper mill produces two types of paper: paper for books and paper for magazines. Each ton of paper for books requires 2 tons of spruce and 3 tons of fir; each ton of paper for magazines requires 2 tons of spruce and 2 tons of fir. The company must supply at least 25,000 tons of paper for books and 100,000 tons of paper for magazines a year. The yearly availability of materials is 278,000 tons of spruce and 426,000 tons of fir. The marketing department requires that the amount of paper manufactured for magazines be at least 1.5 times that which is manufactured for books. Each ton of paper for books is sold for $750, whereas that for magazines is sold for $685 per ton. The cost of spruce is $100 per ton, whereas a ton of fir costs $112.

Find:

  a. The most profitable production plan.
  b. The best use of the resources.
  c. The annual profit.

Formulation

1. The Decision Variables

$$x_1 = \text{Paper produced for books (in tons)}$$

$$x_2 = \text{Paper produced for magazines (in tons)}$$

2. The Objective Function

Cost of materials for books: $2(100) + 3(112) = 536$

Revenue $= 750$. Thus, gross profit $= 750 - 536 = \$214$ per ton

Cost of materials for magazines: $2(100) + 2(112) = \$424$

Revenue $= 685$. Thus, gross profit $= 685 - 424 = \$261$ per ton

The objective function is:

$$\text{maximize } z = 214x_1 + 261x_2$$

3. The Constraints

$2x_1 + 2x_2 \leq 278{,}000$	(spruce availability)
$3x_1 + 2x_2 \leq 426{,}000$	(fir availability)
$1x_1 \quad\ \geq 25{,}000$	(supply requirement)
$\quad\ 1x_2 \geq 100{,}000$	(supply requirement)
$\quad\ 1x_2 \geq 1.5x_1; \text{ or: } 1.5x_1 - x_2 \leq 0$	(marketing requirement)

Solution

    a. The optimal solution is: $x_1 = 25,000$, $x_2 = 114,000$.

    b. The spruce is used in full (slack = 0).
        The fir is only partially utilized.
        (There is a slack of 123,000 tons.)

    c. The annual gross profit is $z = \$35,104,000$ (before processing expenses).

4.6   Marketing

The Everglade Shoe Company plans to allocate some or all of its monthly advertising budget of $82,000 in the Miami Metropolitan area. It can purchase local radio spots at $120 per spot, local TV spots at $600 per spot, and local newspaper advertising at $220 per insertion.

    The company's policy requirements specify that the company must spend at least $40,000 on TV and allow monthly newspaper expenditures up to either $60,000 or 50 percent of the TV expenditures, whichever is most profitable, overall, for the company.

    The payoff from each advertising medium is a function of the size of its audience. The general experience of the firm is that the values of insertions and spots in terms of "audience points" (an arbitrary unit), are as given below:

Radio	40 audience points per spot
TV	180 audience points per spot
Newspapers	320 audience points per insertion

Find the optimal allocation of advertising expenditures among the three media.

Formulation

1. The Decision Variables

$$x_1 = \text{No. of spots allocated to radio}$$

$$x_2 = \text{No. of spots allocated to TV}$$

$$x_3 = \text{No. of insertions allocated to newspapers}$$

2. The Objective Function

$$\text{maximize } z = 40x_1 + 180x_2 + 320x_3$$

3. The Constraints

$$\begin{array}{rl} (1) & 120x_1 + 600x_2 + 220x_3 \le 82{,}000 \\ (2) & 600x_2 \ge 40{,}000 \end{array}$$

and either: $(3a)$ $\qquad 220x_3 \le 60{,}000$

or: $(3b)$ $\qquad 220x_3 \le 300x_2$

and x_1, x_2, x_3 are integers.

Solution

The problem must be solved twice, once for each set of "either/or" constraints, and the better solution selected. The solution is:

When $(3a)$ is used: $x_2 = 66\frac{2}{3}$, $x_3 = 190.9$, $z = 73{,}090.9$

When $(3b)$ is used: $x_2 = 91.1$, $x_3 = 124.24$, $z = 56{,}157.6$

The first solution is better. Rounding to integers but keeping within the constraints:

$$x_2 = 67,\ x_3 = 190,\ z = 72{,}860 \text{ audience points}$$

Note: An alternative approach is to use $0-1$ auxiliary variables; see Chapter 6.

4.7 Auditing

Arthur and Son, P.A., is an auditing firm that conducts both financial and operational audits. Arthur can conduct 90 financial audits (FAs) per year if he spends full time on just FAs, *or* 180 operational audits (OAs) per year full time, or any *linear combination* of both. (*Note:* A linear combination means that because the capacity required for 1 FA is the same as that for 2 OAs (90 to 180 ratio), Arthur can conduct such combinations as 89 FAs plus 2 OAs, or 88 FAs plus 4 OAs, and so on.) Son processes the reports made by Arthur. Son can prepare 180 financial audit reports or 150 operational audit reports per year, or any linear combination thereof. The office staff finalizes the reports submitted by Son. They can handle no more than 160 reports of any kind, per year. Arthur and Son have calculated that to keep their association solvent, they must produce at least 30 FAs and 50 OAs each year.

The profit from each FA has averaged $720 in the past and for each OA has been about $650. How many FAs and OAs should Arthur and Son attempt to conduct each year to maximize their firm's profits?

Formulation

1. The Decision Variables

$$y = \text{Number of FAs},\ x = \text{Number of OAs}$$

2. The Objective Function z, to be Maximized

$$\text{maximize } z = 720y + 650x$$

3. The Constraints

The formulation of the constraints is more complicated. To show how they are derived, let us graph the situation for Arthur (Figure 4.2).

Arthur can conduct 90 FAs at maximum capacity. This information is shown as point A, that is, zero OAs and 90 FAs. Similarly, point B (180, 0) designates that Arthur can conduct 180 OAs and zero FAs at maximum capacity. The straight line connecting points A and B indicates all other possible combinations for Arthur. For example, point C designates 90 OAs and 45 FAs. The problem is to find the equation of the straight line that designates the constraint. From geometry, it is known that if the coordinates of two points are (x_1, y_1) and (x_2, y_2), then the equation of the straight line connecting these two points is:

$$y = \frac{y_2 x_1 - y_1 x_2}{x_1 - x_2} + \left(\frac{y_1 - y_2}{x_1 - x_2}\right)x$$

Thus, the equation of the straight line between (0, 90) and (180, 0) is:

$$y = 90 - \left(\frac{90}{180}\right)x = 90 - .5x$$

or:
$$y + .5x = 90$$

and the inequality constraint is: $y + .5x \leq 90$

FIGURE 4.2

Capacity of Arthur

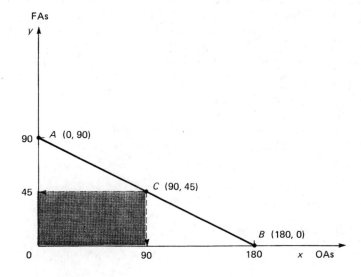

Similarly, for Son:

$$y + 1.2x \leq 180$$

The office staff and solvency constraints are expressed as:

$$y + x \leq 160, y \geq 30, x \geq 50$$

Summary of Formulation

maximize $z = 720y + 650x$
subject to:
$$1y + .5x \leq 90$$
$$1y + 1.2x \leq 180$$
$$1y + 1x \leq 160$$
$$1y \geq 30$$
$$1x \geq 50$$

The solution of this problem is $y = 30$, $x = 120$, and the maximum profit = \$99,600.

4.8 Hospital Scheduling

Palm General Hospital is concerned with the staffing of its emergency department. A recent analysis indicated that a typical day may be divided into six periods. In each period, a different demand level, measured by "cases," is experienced.

Time period	Average number of cases
7 A.M.–11 A.M.	80
11 A.M.– 3 P.M.	60
3 P.M.– 7 P.M.	120
7 P.M.–11 P.M.	60
11 P.M.– 3 A.M.	40
3 A.M.– 7 A.M.	20

Past experience indicates that one emergency room (ER) nurse can handle 2.5 cases each hour. Thus, for example, between 7 A.M. and 8 A.M. there is a need for eight nurses to handle the 20 cases (80 cases per 4 hours).

ER nurses work in shifts of eight hours. The normal shifts are: 7 A.M.–3 P.M.; 3 P.M.–11 P.M.; and 11 P.M.–7 A.M. However, three nurses said that they are willing to start an eight-hour shift at 11 A.M., if necessary, and two said that they will start a shift at 7 P.M., if asked.

Find the least-cost schedule that will assure complete coverage of the emergency room.

Formulation

The problem is to find the minimum number of nurses, assuming that they all receive the same wages. Thus, the least-cost schedule means the minimum number of nurses.

1. The Decision variables

x_1 = Number of nurses starting at 7 A.M.
x_2 = Number of nurses starting at 11 A.M.
x_3 = Number of nurses starting at 3 P.M.
x_4 = Number of nurses starting at 7 P.M.
x_5 = Number of nurses starting at 11 P.M.
x_6 = Number of nurses starting at 3 A.M.

2. The Objective Function

$$\text{minimize } z = x_1 + x_2 + x_3 + x_4 + x_5 + x_6$$

3. The Constraints

To structure the constraints, it is necessary to assume first that the demand in each time period is constant regardless of the hour observed. This enables the computation of the minimum number of required nurses:

Time period	7–11	11–3	3–7	7–11	11–3	3–7
Required nurses	8	6	12	6	4	2

The demand constraints are thus:

$1x_1 + 1x_6 \geq 8$ (for the 7 A.M.–11 A.M. time period)
$1x_1 + 1x_2 \geq 6$ (for 11–3)
$1x_2 + 1x_3 \geq 12$ (for 3–7)
$1x_3 + 1x_4 \geq 6$ (for 7–11)
$1x_4 + 1x_5 \geq 4$ (for 11–3)
$1x_5 + 1x_6 \geq 2$ (for 3–7)

The supply constraints are: $x_2 \leq 3$ and $x_4 \leq 2$.

The Optimal Solution (by computer)

$$x_1 = 8, \; x_2 = 3, \; x_3 = 9, \; x_4 = 2, \; x_5 = 2, \; x_6 = 0$$

for a total of 24 nurses. *Note:* There are multiple optimal solutions to this problem.

4.9   Multiperiod Production Scheduling

Linear programming can be used to determine a production schedule over several production periods in cases of fluctuating demand for a product. The following example illustrates such a situation.

Calpal is a small manufacturer of a special engineering workstation. The company operates one plant with a monthly capacity of 3,000 units. In addition, 750 units can be produced on an overtime basis, which is 30 percent more expensive, on the average. The labor cost when producing on regular time is $1,000; it is $1,300 on overtime (per workstation produced). The company may use inventories to reduce fluctuations in production, but carrying inventories costs money. The cost of carrying one finished unit in inventory is $80 per unit per month.

Management is preparing a six-month production plan with the following stipulations:

a. All demand must be met according to the following schedule.

Month	1	2	3	4	5	6
Units	2,500	3,200	3,800	3,500	5,000	3,000

b. There should be no inventory left at the end of the sixth month.

c. There is no inventory at the present time.

The problem is to find the production schedule for the next six months that minimizes total cost.

Formulation

The Decision Variables

x_i = quantity produced in month i, on a regular time basis, for $i = 1,2,3,4,5,6$

y_i = quantity produced on overtime in month i

v_i = quantity in inventory at the end of month i; note that $v_6 = 0$

The Objective Function

$$\text{minimize } z = 1,000(x_1 + x_2 + x_3 + x_4 + x_5 + x_6)$$
$$+1,300(y_1 + y_2 + y_3 + y_4 + y_5 + y_6)$$
$$+80(v_1 + v_2 + v_3 + v_4 + v_5)$$

The Constraints

a. Production is limited to 3,000 units per month on a regular basis. Six constraints express this limitation.

$$x_1 \leq 3,000,\ x_2 \leq 3,000,\ x_3 \leq 3,000,\ x_4 \leq 3,000,\ x_5 \leq 3,000,\ x_6 \leq 3,000$$

b. Similarly, we find the following overtime limitations:

$$y_1 \leq 750,\ y_2 \leq 750,\ y_3 \leq 750,\ y_4 \leq 750,\ y_5 \leq 750,\ y_6 \leq 750$$

c. Six constraints (one for each month) can be written to show how the demand is to be met. For month 1:

$$x_1 + y_1 - v_1 = 2,500$$

That is, the total produced in regular and overtime, minus what is carried on for the future, must equal the demand.

Similarly, for months 2–6 we get:

$$
\begin{aligned}
x_2 + y_2 - v_2 + v_1 &= 3,200 \\
x_3 + y_3 - v_3 + v_2 &= 3,800 \\
x_4 + y_4 - v_4 + v_3 &= 3,500 \\
x_5 + y_5 - v_5 + v_4 &= 5,000 \\
x_6 + y_6 - 0 + v_5 &= 3,000
\end{aligned}
$$

Solution

The model involves 17 decision variables and 18 constraints. Its solution is left as a homework exercise for the student.

Note: This problem can be expanded in the real world to include variable monthly production capability, back orders (unfilled orders) and their penalties, variable costs, and so on. When more complexity is added, LP may not be a sufficient tool, and we may need to employ a more powerful tool, such as dynamic programming or simulation.

4.10   Concluding Remarks

The examples presented in this chapter illustrate some of the wide range of applications of LP. Many other applications can be found throughout business, engineering, government, economics, science, and almost every field. The problems that follow provide additional examples of this diversity.

However, LP is even more powerful than has been demonstrated so far. The solution to LP problems can also provide important supplementary information. This will be demonstrated in the next chapter, where the topics of duality and sensitivity analysis are addressed.

4.11 Problems

1. Carlo's International manufactures blue jeans. Three brands are considered: A, B, and C. The manufacture of brand A requires 2 minutes machine time, 30 minutes labor, and costs $7. Brand B requires 2.5 minutes machine time, 40 minutes labor, and costs $10 to produce. Finally, brand C, the top of the line, requires 3 minutes machine time, 1 hour labor, and costs $13 to produce. Brand A sells for $12, brand B for $14, and brand C for $20.

   The company works on a weekly schedule of five days, with two shifts of 7.5 hours (net time) each. It has four machines available for production and 50 employees on each shift. Its weekly manufacturing budget is $10,000. Its declared objective is profit maximization.
   a. Formulate the problem as a linear program.
   b. Solve the problem (use the computer).

2. The Swiss Construction Company is building roads on the side of the Alps. It is necessary to use explosives to blow up the underground boulders to make the surface level. There are three ingredients (A, B, C) in the explosive used. It is known that at least 10 grams of the explosive must be used to get results. If more than 20 grams are used, the explosion will be too damaging. Also, for an explosion, at least $\frac{1}{4}$ gram of ingredient C must be used for every gram of ingredient A, and at least 1 gram of ingredient B must be used for every gram of ingredient C. The costs of ingredients A, B, and C are 6 Swiss francs (SFr), 18 SFr, and 20 SFr per gram, respectively. Find the least-cost explosive mix necessary to produce a safe explosion.

3. Westcan Corporation is considering producing five different types of special computers that yield the following unit profits:

Type	A	B	C	D	E
Net profit ($000)	16	8	11	6	10

   The company has $1 million capital to invest in production and a capability of 10,000 working days.

   The capital and labor requirements for each type of computer are given below.

Type	Required capital per unit ($000)	Required per unit working days
A	20	200
B	15	120
C	16	150
D	10	80
E	14	100

   Find the best production plan:
   a. If the company's objective is *profit maximization*.
   b. If the company's objective is to produce the *maximum number of total units* (of all types combined).

4. Sun Electric can produce three chips:

   A, which costs $6 per unit and sells for $9 per unit.
   B, which costs $5 per unit and sells for $6 per unit.
   C, which costs $8 per unit and sells for $9 per unit.

   The company's declared objective is profit maximization. The company is planning a monthly production schedule. The marketing department requires the production of at least 100 units of chip C and no more than 1,000 units of chip A. The production department cannot produce more than 4,000 units of all chips. Products are made on the "chipping" machine, which can produce 20, 30, or 40 units of chips A, B, or C, respectively, per hour. The machine is available for up to 100 hours each month. The marketing department also requires that there be at least twice as many units of B as of C in the monthly schedule. The finance department has set an upper budget of $15,000 for the schedule.

   How many units of A, B, and C should the company produce?

5. Atlantic Chemical produces three products, A, B, and C, which can be extracted and blended from three ores: b_1, which costs $2 a ton and up to 1,000 tons are available a month; b_2, which costs $1.50 a ton and up to 800 tons a month are available; and b_3,

which costs $3 a ton and is available in unlimited quantities. The company wishes to determine how much of each product to make from the available ores so as to maximize the profit from the overall operation. The ore requirements, per ton of product, are:

Product A requires: 5 tons b_1, 10 tons b_2, 10 tons b_3.
Product B requires: 7 tons b_1, 8 tons b_2, 5 tons b_3.
Product C requires: 10 tons b_1, 5 tons b_2, no tons b_3.

Sales price per ton: A = $130, B = $140, C = $100.

a. What important assumption, which is not usually implied in an LP problem, is necessary to formulate this problem in LP terms?
b. Formulate as an LP problem.

6. A French market research firm wishes to conduct home visit interviews according to the quotas specified in the first column of the following table:

Type of household	Desired number of responding calls (quota)	Probability of response to calls		
		Morning	Afternoon	Evening
Single person	50	.1	.1	.5
Married, no children	100	.5	.4	.7
Married, with children	150	.75	.6	.9

Because not all persons are at home at the time of the visit and not all persons cooperate, there is only a certain "probability of response" to the home visits (calls). This probability is shown in the table. Thus, the following requirements exist:

a. The total number (responding and nonresponding) of planned morning calls must not exceed the total number of afternoon calls.
b. The total number of responding evening calls must be at least 20 percent and no more than 30 percent of the total number of all responding calls.
c. An evening call costs twice as much as a morning or an afternoon call.

Decide how the calls should be distributed among the three types of households (by the three times during the day) such that the desired quotas are fulfilled at minimum cost. Formulate only.

7. Glades Discount Store is opening a new department with a storage area of 10,000 square feet. Management considers four products for display.

Product A: Costs $55, sells for $80, and requires 24 square feet per unit for storage.
Product B: Costs $100, sells for $130, and requires 20 square feet per unit for storage.
Product C: Costs $200, sells for $295, and requires 36 square feet per unit for storage.
Product D: Costs $300, sells for $399, and requires 50 square feet per unit for storage.

It is required that at least 10 units of each product be on display. The company's objective is profit maximization.

Find out how many units of each product should be on display if the company has $600,000 available for purchasing the product. Formulate as a linear programming problem (assuming divisibility of the products; that is, ignore the fact that the answer should be in integer form).

8. The Canadian Safety Council has allocated $500,000 for projects designed to prevent automobile accidents. Four proposals were submitted: (a) TV advertisements, (b) teenage safety education, (c) improved airbags, and (d) enforcement of driving laws. The projects are expected to result in the reduction of both fatalities and property damage, as shown in the table below.

Project	Expected reduction in fatalities per $1,000	Average property damage averted per $1,000
a	.25	300
b	.32	500
c	.15	0
d	.28	250

The council has decided that no single project will be awarded more than $250,000. They also wish to award at least $50,000 for teenage education. Finally, they want to award at least $1 for improved airbags for each dollar awarded for TV advertisements. The federal government, for internal analysis purposes, has assessed the average value of a human life as being $400,000.

a. Assume that the council's only objective is fatality prevention. Formulate as a linear programming problem to find the best fund allocation.

b. Reformulate the problem for the case that *both* fatalities and damage aversion are the objectives of the funds' allocation.

9. Korea National Bank is preparing to invest up to 5 billion won of its cash reserves. The bank is considering the following alternatives:

Alternative	Expected rate of return (percent)	Risk factor
Treasury securities	7.6	0
Corporate bonds	8.9	1
Loans to corporations	10.3	2
Stocks	14.0	5

The expected return is measured in percent over one year. The risk factor is a projection for next year, based on experience.

The bank's investment policy requires that:

a. The amount loaned to corporations will not exceed the amount invested in Treasury securities.

b. The *weighted* risk factor will not exceed 1.9.

c. For every won invested in stocks, there will be at least 0.5 won invested in Treasury securities.

d. The amount invested in stocks will not exceed 25 percent of the total amount invested.

Find the investment portfolio that will maximize the bank's return on investment. (*Hint:* To find the weighted risk factor, multiply the amounts invested in the corresponding risk factor and divide by the total investment.)

10. Paint Fair Company advertises its weekly sales in newspapers, television, and radio. Each dollar spent in advertising in newspapers is estimated to reach an exposure of 12 buying customers, each dollar in TV reaches an exposure of 15 buying customers, and each dollar in radio reaches an exposure of 10 buying customers. The company has an agreement with all three media services that it will spend not less than 20 percent of its total money in each medium. Further, it is agreed that the combined newspaper and television budget will not be larger than three times the radio budget.

The company has just decided to spend no more than $17,000 on advertising. The problem is: How much should the company budget for each medium if it is interested in reaching as many buying customers as possible?

11. The ABC Corporation produces two types of paint, I and II, which it sells at $2.20 and $1.80 per gallon, respectively. Three different raw materials can be used to make the paint. Raw material 1 costs $1 per gallon and contains 70 percent of ingredient A, 20 percent of ingredient B, and 10 percent of ingredient C. Raw material 2 costs $1.50 per gallon and contains 30 percent, 40 percent, and 30 percent of ingredients A, B, and C, respectively. Raw material 3 costs $0.80 per gallon and contains 50 percent ingredient A and 50 percent ingredient C. The product specification of paint type I calls for at least 40 percent each of ingredients A and C. Paint type II requires at least 30 percent of ingredient B, no more than 50 percent of ingredient C and exactly 10 percent of A.

a. Management would like to know the relative amount of raw materials (in percent) to be used in regular production so as to maximize total profit. Formulate, but do not solve.

b. Separate the problem into two independent problems and explain why this is possible in this case.

c. Formulate the same problem with the assumption that the company cannot use raw material 3 more than twice the rate of raw material 2.

d. How would the problem change if there is a waste of 5 percent of ingredient A in the production process?

12. Sunoil sells two types of Gasohol: regular and premium. Gasohol is prepared by mixing gasoline and alcohol. Sunoil can buy up to 100,000 barrels per week of gasoline at $40 per barrel, and up to 12,000 barrels per week of alcohol at $47 per barrel. Regular Gasohol is made by blending 9 portions of gasoline with one portion of alcohol, whereas premium Gasohol is made of 87 percent gas and 13 percent alcohol.

Each barrel is equivalent to 42 gallons. A gallon of regular Gasohol sells for $1.35 and a gallon of premium Gasohol sells for $1.43. The company must provide at least 600,000 gallons of premium and 1 million gallons of regular each week. In addition, the amount of regular Gasohol produced must be at least twice the amount of premium produced.

Find the most profitable production plan. *Note:* This problem can be formulated either with two or with four decision variables.

Find:

a. The quantities of gasoline and alcohol used.
b. The quantities of regular and premium produced.
c. The total cost.
d. The total profit.

13. The ABC Company makes four types of radios. Each radio can be made by two different methods, each of which has three processes. Data on the operation are given below:

	Radio type			
	1	*2*	*3*	*4*
Price to distributor	80	60	50	45
Cost method X	45	40	60	60
Cost method Y	60	50	40	25
Quantity that can be sold	3,000	5,000	8,000	15,000

		Radio type				
		1	*2*	*3*	*4*	*Hours available*
		Manufacturing time, hours				
Method X, Process	A	—	3.0	1.8	2.5	8,000
	B	9.4	8.6	6.2	4.2	30,000
	C	2.2	—	1.0	—	8,000
Method Y, Process	D	—	6.0	1.2	1.8	12,000
	E	14.0	15.0	3.0	1.2	12,000
	F	10.0	—	6.0	3.0	6,000

Formulate to find the best production plan.

14. Robin, Inc., produces two different concrete products with the following price and input data.

	Input requirements			
	Selling price ($)	Material (lb.)	Power consumed (kWh)	Labor (hr)
Construction blocks	0.75	4	0.1	0.04
Decorative blocks	1.75	3	0.2	0.10

Labor cost is $5 per hour, materials cost $0.05 per pound, and power costs $1.00 per kWh. The company is limited to 100,000 lbs. of material, 9,000 kWh of power, and 1,200 hrs. of labor. The demand for decorative blocks is at most 3,500.

a. Formulate to maximize profits.
b. Solve graphically.
c. Solve with a computer. Find the slack on material and power.

15. Great Scott! Steel Corp. has two iron reduction refineries, designated by the index **r.** Each refinery processes iron ore into two different ingot stocks, designated by the index **s.** The ingot stocks are then shipped to any of three different fabricating plants, index **f,** each of which makes two products, index **p.** Over the coming production planning horizon, the firm wants to minimize the total tonnage of iron ore processed in its reduction refineries, subject to certain production and demand requirements. Let:

x = total tonnage of iron ore processed by both refineries.

y_{sfr} = total tonnage of iron ore processed into ingot stock s for shipment to fabricating plant f by refinery r.

z_{spf} = total tonnage of ingot stock s manufactured into product p at fabricating plant f.

a_{sr} = tonnage yield of ingot stock s from one ton of iron ore processed at refinery r.

b_{spf} = total yield of product from one ton of ingot stock s manufactured into product p at fabricating plant f.

c_r = maximum tonnage of iron ore that can be processed by reduction refinery r.

k_f = maximum tonnage of all stocks that can be manufactured into products at fabricating plant f.

d_p = tonnage demand for product p.

The production demand requirements are:

1. The total tonnage of iron ore processed by both reduction refineries must equal the total tonnage processed into ingot stocks for shipment to the fabricating plants by the reduction refineries.
2. The total tonnage of iron ore processed by each reduction refinery cannot exceed the refinery's available capacity.
3. The total tonnage of ingot stock manufactured into products at each fabricating plant must equal the total tonnage of ingot stock shipped to it by the reduction refineries.
4. The total tonnage of ingot stock manufactured into products at each fabricating plant cannot exceed the plant's available capacity.
5. The total tonnage of each product manufactured must equal its demand requirement.

   a) Formulate this problem as an LP.
   b) Reformulate the problem with an objective function that might be more appropriate.

16. The minimum daily requirement of vitamin D for patients following surgery is 180 units, whereas the minimum amount of B_{12} that they may receive is 150 units. The hospital dietitian is considering liver and steak for the daily diet. Each pound of liver costs $1.50, whereas a pound of steak costs $4.00. On the average, two ounces of liver and five ounces of steak provide the minimum daily need for vitamin D. An ounce of liver yields 30 units of vitamin D and 20 units of vitamin B_{12}. A pound of steak yields 480 units of B_{12} and an undetermined amount of vitamin D. (*Hint:* You can find it yourself.)

Find the least-cost diet, per patient, per day. *Note:* There are 454 grams in a pound and 16 ounces in a pound.

17. As Blackbeard left the harbor of Arecibo (see Problem 17 in Chapter 3) after plundering the town, the ship became unstable and nearly capsized. To maintain trim, the weight in each hold (in pounds) must be proportional to the capacity of the hold (in pounds). How should Blackbeard rearrange his booty among the holds to keep the ship in trim? Formulate only.

18. Sherwood Acres, a central Kentucky farm, grows tobacco and soybeans on its 350 acres of land. An acre of soybeans brings a $150 profit and an acre of tobacco brings a $500 profit. Because of state agricultural regulations, no more than 150 acres can be planted in tobacco. Each acre of tobacco requires 100 worker-hours of labor over the growing season and each acre of soybeans requires 20 worker-hours. There are 16,000 worker-hours of labor available during the growing season. How many acres should be planted in tobacco and how many in soybeans to maximize profit?
    a. Formulate.
    b. Solve graphically.
    c. Solve with a computer. Find the slacks on all constraints.

19. Complete formulation B in Section 4.3, compare to A, and discuss the results.

References and Bibliography

1. Calvert, J. E., et al. *Linear Programming*. New York: Harcourt Brace Jovanovich, 1989.
2. Hayhurst, G. *Mathematical Programming Applications*. New York: Macmillan, 1987.
3. Schrage, L. *Linear, Integer, and Quadratic Programming with LINDO*. 3rd ed. Palo Alto, Calif.: Scientific Press, 1986.
4. Sposito, V. A. *Linear Programming with Statistical Applications*. Ames, Iowa: Iowa State University Press, 1989.
5. Strayer, J. K. *Linear Programming and Its Applications*. New York: Springer-Verlag, 1989.

5 Duality, Postoptimality Analysis, and Computerization

Linear programming modeling provides the user not only with the optimal solution but also with the possibility of conducting a postoptimality analysis. Furthermore, the use of the simplex method enables an interesting economic interpretation of the problem and its solution. In this chapter we present these topics as well as some computerized packages and their interpretation.

The Sekido Corporation—Part II

The optimal daily production plan suggested by Suji Okita (12 units of type A TV sets and 11 of type B) was submitted to Sekido's executive committee for approval. During their weekly Monday morning meeting, the members of the committee raised the following questions:

1. Should additional resources (labor, machine time) be committed to the production of these TV sets? If so, how much?
2. If the available supply of Sekido's resources should happen to change, what effect will it have on the company's profit?
3. Would it be worthwhile to increase Sekido's marketing effort to increase potential sales from 12 to 13, 14, or even more? How much should the company be willing to invest in such a promotion?
4. What is the best production plan if some of the input variables (per unit profit contribution, production technology) change?
5. How does the restriction of producing a whole number of units each day affect the results?

On returning home, Suji found that Keiko was faced with similar questions at her office. For example: What effect will certain changes in the paint specifications have on the total production cost? And what will happen to the optimal blending plan if other objectives are also considered?

Two very useful extensions of LP can be used to answer these and similar questions:

- Duality.
- Sensitivity analysis.

5.1 Duality

The primal and the dual

With every LP maximization problem, there is an associated minimization problem, and vice versa. Therefore, LP problems exist in pairs. The original problem is called the **primal,** and the complementary problem is termed the **dual.**

Duality plays an important role for these reasons:

An important economic interpretation

1. The dual problem has an *important economic interpretation*.
2. Several theories that are used to develop methods for efficient computational shortcuts to the simplex method are based on the concept of duality.
3. In some cases, the use of the dual helps *overcome some computer capacity limitations*.
4. Some special procedures developed for *testing optimal solutions* are based on duality.
5. The dual is used in developing the MODI algorithm for the transportation model (Chapter 7).

Theoretically, the dual problem is the same problem as the primal, but mathematically transformed. Therefore, the solution of the primal (by the simplex method) gives the solution to the dual, and vice versa.

Major Properties

The following are some properties of duality:

1. If the primal is a maximization problem, the dual is a minimization problem, and vice versa.
2. An optimal solution to the dual exists only when the primal has an optimal solution (and vice versa).
3. The value of the objective function of the optimal solution in both problems is the same.
4. The dual of the dual is the primal.
5. The solution of the dual problem can be obtained from the solution of the primal problem, and vice versa (if solved by a procedure such as the simplex method).
6. The dual variables may assume negative values.
7. The dual variables have important economic interpretations.

Negative values
are OK

Formulation of the Dual to a Maximization Problem—an Example

The product-mix problem discussed in Chapter 3 is reproduced below as the *primal:*

maximize $z = 300x_1 + 250x_2$
subject to:

$2x_1 + 1x_2 \leq 40$	(labor constraint)
$1x_1 + 3x_2 \leq 45$	(machine time constraint)
$1x_1 + 0x_2 \leq 12$	(marketing constraint)

Writing the Dual

The Objective.   Because the original problem calls for *maximization,* the dual will be a *minimization* problem.

The Decision Variables.   For each constraint in the primal, there is one corresponding decision variable in the dual. Thus, there will be, in this example, three dual variables, to be denoted u_1, u_2, and u_3.

One-to-one
correspondence

The Objective Function.   Remember that each dual variable corresponds to a constraint in the primal. The coefficient of each variable in the objective function of the dual is equal to the right-hand side (capacity, b_i) of the corresponding constraint in the primal. For example, the capacity of the labor (first) constraint in the primal is 40; thus, the coefficient of u_1 in the dual's objective function is 40. The objective function for the dual is:

$$\text{minimize } w = 40u_1 + 45u_2 + 12u_3$$

The Constraints. For each decision variable in the primal, there is a corresponding constraint in the dual. Because there are two primal variables, there will be two constraints in the dual. Before structuring the dual constraints, all primal constraints should be transformed to $\leq$ in maximization; $\geq$ in minimization. The right-hand side of the dual's constraints is the same as the corresponding coefficients of the objective function in the primal. For example, the coefficient of the *first* variable in the primal objective is 300, and so will be the right-hand side of the dual's *first* constraint.

The coefficients of the constraints in the dual are formed from the coefficients of the primal's constraints by writing each column of these coefficients as a row. The coefficients of the primal's constraints are:

$$\begin{matrix} 2 & 1 \\ 1 & 3 \\ 1 & 0 \end{matrix}$$

With each column written as a row, the result is:

Previous first column: 2 1 1
Previous second column: 1 3 0

Thus, the dual's constraints are:

$$2u_1 + 1u_2 + 1u_3 \geq 300$$
$$1u_1 + 3u_2 + 0u_3 \geq 250$$

Standardization of the Primal

The primal problem presented earlier contained only $\leq$ type constraints, and it was to be maximized. If a primal problem deviates from such a structure, it must first be transformed into the required standard format.

Example 1

Given a primal:

minimize $y = 3x_1 + 4x_2 - 2x_3$
subject to:
  (1) $1x_1 + 2x_2 - 3x_3 \geq 40$
  (2) $3x_1 + 5x_2 + 1x_3 \leq 80$
  (3) $0x_1 + 3x_2 + 2x_3 = 30$

Step 1. If the objective function is to be minimized, convert it into maximization by multiplying it by -1. We get:

$$\text{maximize } z = -3x_1 - 4x_2 + 2x_3$$

Step 2. Multiply each $\geq$ constraint by -1 in order to convert it to a $\leq$ type. Constraint (1) thus becomes:

$$-1x_1 - 2x_2 + 3x_3 \leq -40$$

Step 3. Split each equality constraint into two inequalities; one $\leq$ and the other $\geq$. (Mathematically, an equation is equivalent to two inequalities, one $\leq$ and one $\geq$.)
Thus, constraint (3) is expressed as:

$$(3a) \quad 0x_1 + 3x_2 + 2x_3 \leq 30$$

$$\text{and } (3b) \quad 0x_1 + 3x_2 + 2x_3 \geq 30$$

However, because constraint (3b) is of the $\geq$ type, it has to be multiplied by -1 in order to convert it to a $\leq$ type. That is:

$$(3b) \qquad - 3x_2 - 2x_3 \leq -30$$

Conclusion
The original problem can now be rewritten as on the left, with its dual on the right.

Standardized primal	Dual
maximize $z = -3x_1 - 4x_2 + 2x_3$ subject to: $(1) \ -1x_1 - 2x_2 + 3x_3 \leq -40$ $(2) \ \ \ \ 3x_1 + 5x_2 + 1x_3 \leq 80$ $(3a) \ \ 0x_1 + 3x_2 + 2x_3 \leq 30$ $(3b) \ \ 0x_1 - 3x_2 - 2x_3 \leq -30$	minimize $w = -40u_1 + 80u_2 + 30u_3 - 30u_4$ subject to: $-1u_1 + 3u_2 + 0u_3 + 0u_4 \geq -3$ $-2u_1 + 5u_2 + 3u_3 - 3u_4 \geq -4$ $\ \ 3u_1 + 1u_2 + 2u_3 - 2u_4 \geq 2$

Example 2

The standardized or canonical form

In the previous example, a primal minimization problem was converted to a standard maximization problem and then its dual was derived. Alternatively, the primal problem can be standardized as a minimization problem where all the constraints are of the $\geq$ type. Let us examine another example.
Given a primal:

minimize $z = 2x_1 + 3x_2 - 1x_3$
subject to:
$(1) \quad 5x_1 + 1x_2 + 1x_3 \geq 20$
$(2) \quad 2x_1 + 1x_2 + 3x_3 = 24$
$(3) \quad 1x_1 + 2x_2 - 1x_3 \leq 18$

Standardization

Constraints (2) and (3) are not in the required form.

Step 1. Split constraint (2) into two constraints:

$$(2a) \quad 2x_1 + 1x_2 + 3x_3 \leq 24$$

$$(2b) \quad 2x_1 + 1x_2 + 3x_3 \geq 24$$

Multiply ($2a$) by -1 to reverse the direction of the inequality:

$$(2a) \quad -2x_1 - 1x_2 - 3x_3 \geq -24$$

Step 2. Reverse the inequality of constraint (3) by multiplying it by -1:

$$(3) \quad -1x_1 - 2x_2 + 1x_3 \geq -18$$

Conclusion

Now the standardized primal and its dual can be written:

Standardized primal	Dual
minimize $z = 2x_1 + 3x_2 - 1x_3$	maximize $w = 20u_1 - 24u_2 + 24u_3 - 18u_4$
subject to:	subject to:
(1) $\quad 5x_1 + 1x_2 + 1x_3 \geq 20$	$5u_1 - 2u_2 + 2u_3 - 1u_4 \leq 2$
($2a$) $-2x_1 - 1x_2 - 3x_3 \geq -24$	$1u_1 - 1u_2 + 1u_3 - 2u_4 \leq 3$
($2b$) $\quad 2x_1 + 1x_2 + 3x_3 \geq 24$	$1u_1 - 3u_2 + 3u_3 + 1u_4 \leq -1$
(3) $-1x_1 - 2x_2 + 1x_3 \geq -18$	

The general form of the primal-dual relationship is:

Primal	Dual
maximize $z = \sum\limits_{j=1}^{n} c_j x_j$	minimize $w = \sum\limits_{i=1}^{m} b_i u_i$
subject to:	subject to:
$\sum\limits_{j=1}^{n} a_{ij} x_j \leq b_i$	$\sum\limits_{i=1}^{m} a_{ij} u_i \geq c_j$

for $i = 1, 2, \ldots, m$; and $j = 1, 2, \ldots, n$

Summary

The primal-dual relationship is shown pictorially in Figure 5.1. The dual, once formulated, can be solved as any regular LP problem. In addition, the use of the simplex method automatically gives the solution to the dual when the primal is being solved.

FIGURE 5.1

*The primal-dual
relationship*

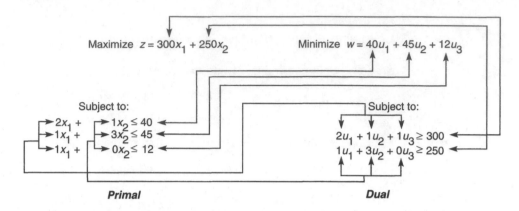

5.2 Solution to the Dual

The dual problem, once formulated, can be solved like any other LP problem. However, given a simplex solution to the primal, it is not necessary to solve the dual, because the final tableau of the primal's solution provides *both* the optimal values of the primal and the dual problems. The dual's solution is $u_j = -(c_j - z_j)$.

Let us reproduce the final tableau of the product-mix problem (Table 3.8) in Table 5.1. The optimal solution to the dual problem can be read directly in the $c_j - z_j$ row of the tableau, because $u_j = -(c_j - z_j)$. The column s_1, which is related to the first constraint, has a $c_j - z_j$ value of zero; that is, $u_1 = 0$. Similarly, $u_2 = 250/3$ (take the negative of the value shown) and $u_3 = 650/3$. Because the dual problem has two constraints, it has two surplus dual variables, t_1, and t_2, whose values can also be found in the primal's optimal tableau. Examining the $c_j - z_j$ row in the tableau, we see that t_1's value is zero under the x_1 column; that is, the surplus t_1 of the first dual's constraint (which is associated with the primal x_1 variable) is zero. Similarly, the surplus t_2 of the second dual's constraint is zero.

TABLE 5.1   Reproduction of Table 3.8

Basis	Unit Profit	x_1	x_2	s_1	s_2	s_3	Quantity
s_1	0	0	0	1	$-1/3$	$-5/3$	5
x_2	250	0	1	0	$1/3$	$-1/3$	11
x_1	300	1	0	0	0	1	12
c_j		300	250	0	0	0	
z_j		300	250	0	$250/3$	$650/3$	
$c_j - z_j$		0	0	0	$-250/3$	$-650/3$	
Dual's solution		$-t_1$	$-t_2$	$-u_1$	$-u_2$	$-u_3$	

Note: In solving dual problems, irregularities may be encountered, such as negative right-hand "Quantity" values in the constraints. Special extensions of the simplex method, such as the dual-simplex algorithm, can then be used. For details, see the bibliography.

5.3 Economic Interpretation Using the Dual Variables

The dual variables have an interesting economic interpretation. They are called the **shadow prices,** the **marginal values** of the constraints, or the *opportunity costs* per unit of each primal's resource (constraint). These imaginary variables can be used for making various managerial decisions, such as examining the profitability of purchasing additional resources and evaluating the trade-offs among them.

Shadow prices (margin)

Example

The dual variables express the change in the value of the objective function of the primal when one additional unit of a specific resource is added. If, for example, in our product-mix problem, machine capacity is increased from 45 hours (the current machine time available) to 46 hours, the total profit will increase by $u_2 = \frac{250}{3} = \$83\frac{1}{3}$. The reverse is also true; if capacity decreases from 45 to 44, the profit will decline by $\$83\frac{1}{3}$. Similarly, if the marketability of model A is increased from 12 sets to 13 sets, the total profit will increase by $u_3 = \frac{650}{3} = \$216\frac{2}{3}$. This assumes that the structure of the optimal solution remains unchanged; that is, that the same variables participate in the optimal solution. See Section 5.7 for further discussion.

The Value of the Resources

The value $u_2 = \$83\frac{1}{3}$ can be viewed as the *value* of the one unit of machine time (marginal value of the resource). Therefore, the total current value of the resource "machine time" is $83\frac{1}{3} \times 45 = \$3,750$. Similarly, the value of one unit of "marketability" is $u_3 = 216\frac{2}{3}$; the total value of marketability is therefore $12 \times 216\frac{2}{3} = \$2,600$. However, if labor availability is increased from 40 to 41 units, there will be *no gain* ($u_1 = 0$). The reason is that *labor is not utilized in full* at present; this is clearly shown by the fact that $s_1 = 5$ (i.e., slack in labor exists). A resource that is not fully utilized is considered a *free good* and obviously an increase in its supply will not increase profits. When the dual's unit value of the resources is multiplied by the available quantities (right-hand side of the constraints), a total value function is constructed as follows:

Marginal values (margin)

Free good (margin)

$$\text{Total value of labor} \quad = u_1 \left(\frac{\text{Dollars}}{\text{Hour}} \right) \times 40 \text{ hours} = \$40u_1$$

$$\text{Total value of machine} \quad = u_2 \left(\frac{\text{Dollars}}{\text{Hour}} \right) \times 45 \text{ hours} = \$45u_2$$

$$\text{Total value of marketing} = u_3 \left(\frac{\text{Dollars}}{\text{Unit}} \right) \times 12 \text{ units} = \$12u_3$$

The total value of all resources is $40u_1 + 45u_2 + 12u_3 = \$3,750 + \$2,600 + 0 = \$6,350$, which is exactly the value of the objective function in the primal and in the dual.

Interpretation of the Value of the Dual's Objective Function

The objective of the manufacturer is to *minimize* the value of the resources used. Therefore, the dual's objective function is: minimize $z = 40u_1 + 45u_2 + 12u_3$. This minimization is subject to two constraints.

The Interpretation of the Constraints

It is given that one unit of TV model A requires two hours of labor, one hour of machine time, and one unit of marketing effort. Because the *profit* (or *contribution margin*) made from each TV model A is $300, it can be said that the value of the invested resources *must* be *at least* $300, or $2u_1 + 1u_2 + 1u_3 \geq 300$. This is the first constraint of the dual.

Similarly, the constraint for model B is:

$$1u_1 + 3u_2 \geq 250$$

Marginal contribution

Remember that these values are accounting or shadow price values that do not measure *cost* but measure potential, *marginal contribution* to profit.

The Relationship Between the Dual's Variables and the Objective Function

The dual variables, by definition, measure the change in the value of the objective function of the primal when the right-hand side of the primal's constraints are changed by one unit. The following relationship thus exists between the two:

Right-hand Side	If Dual Variable is	Then Objective Function Value will
add one unit	positive	increase by the amount of the dual
add one unit	negative	decrease by the amount of the dual
add one unit	zero	remain unchanged
delete one unit	positive	decrease by the amount of the dual
delete one unit	negative	increase by the amount of the dual
delete one unit	zero	remain unchanged

Notes:

- There is one dual variable for every constraint in the primal.
- If the change in the right-hand side is less than one unit, then the change in the objective function will be proportional. For example, if the right-hand side is increased by .5, then the value of the objective function will increase by one half of the value of the dual variable.

- If the change in the right-hand side is more than one unit, then the change in the objective function will be proportionally greater. Such a change can be made only up to a certain limit, as will be discussed in the sections on sensitivity analysis.

The Relationship Between the Dual Variables and the Slack (Surplus) Variables
One dual variable exists for each constraint. It was shown earlier that each inequality constraint will also have either a slack or a surplus variable. The question is: What kind of relationship exists between the two types of variables? As stated earlier, a dual whose value is zero signifies a free good for the constraint (or resource) it represents. Such a case occurs when the resource is *not* fully utilized; that is, when it has a slack. In general, the following relationships, known as the *Kuhn-Tucker conditions,* exist for each constraint (whenever there is a unique optimal solution and the problem is nondegenerate).

Kuhn-Tucker
conditions

	Dual	**Primal's Slack or Surplus**
Condition 1	If: 0	Then: Nonnegative
Condition 2	If: Nonzero	Then: 0

Note that when the dual is *nonzero,* the resource is fully utilized (no slack or surplus). The reason for this is that if a constraint is fully utilized and one increases the supply of this constraint (right-hand side), it should increase the profit, because more units can be produced (in the case of maximization). Increasing the supply of a non-fully utilized resource (one with a slack) will not do any good; that is, the value of the objective function will not be changed.

5.4 Managerial Applications

Management can use the dual for making decisions regarding addition, deletion, and trade-offs of resources. We illustrate with the Sekido example.

Consider the cost of
the change

Example 1: Adding machine capacity

Suppose that management is considering increasing the available machine time. The estimated daily cost is $50 per hour increase. Should management increase the machine time? In order to answer this question, one of two approaches may be used.

1. Re-solve the problem, changing the machine constraint to $x_1 + 3x_2 \le 46$; keep all other data unchanged. The new solution calls for $x_1 = 12$, $x_2 = 11\frac{1}{3}$, and $z = 6,433\frac{1}{3}$. Because the addition to profit, $6,433\frac{1}{3} - 6,350 = \$83\frac{1}{3}$, is larger than the $50 required investment, it is recommended.

2. Use the dual. Because the "worth" of machine time, $u_2 = \$83\frac{1}{3}$, is larger than the investment, the investment should be recommended. If a change of one unit is recommended, then it makes sense to add even more. The limit for the change is given by a sensitivity analysis.

Example 2: Cut back in resources

Suppose the advertising budget is cut so that only 11, rather than 12, units of model A can be sold each day. What is the impact on profit? The marketing people claim that is $300 per day, because the profit contribution of model A is $300 per unit. The fact is that only $u_3 = \$216\frac{2}{3}$ will be lost. The reason for this is that reducing x_1 to 11 releases one unit of machine time, which enables the production of one third of model B (from 11 to $11\frac{1}{3}$). Such a change is worth $\$83\frac{1}{3}$, as seen before. Therefore, the net impact is $\$300 - \$83\frac{1}{3} = \$216\frac{2}{3}$.

Example 3: Should capacity be changed?

Given the solution $x_1 = 5$, $x_2 = 1$, $z = \$50$ to a new LP maximization problem. The problem includes a space constraint of $3x_1 + 5x_2 \le 20$ (square feet) with a corresponding dual variable value of $1.80. Management is considering changing the space availability. An increase in availability costs $2 per square foot; a decrease in availability reduces expenses by $1.60. What should management do and why?

If management increases the available space, the cost increase will be $2 per square foot, while the contribution to profit will only be $1.80. Therefore, this is not advisable. If management decreases the available space, the contribution to profit will decrease by $1.80, but the expenses will be reduced by only $1.60. Therefore, this is not advisable either. Thus, management should not change the space availability.

Discussion

What is the maximum justifiable investment?

The shadow price gives the *maximum value that should be paid to obtain one additional unit of the resource* (over the relevant range). However, one should be careful when determining this maximum. It should include only those costs of making the changes that have not been included in the calculation of the per unit contribution of the basic decision variables (the coefficients of the objective function). The reason for this is that by expanding the resources, we create more products; some of the cost of creating the resources (the variable cost) is included in the cost of the unit, as expressed in the objective function. (The coefficients of the objective function are computed on a per unit basis: Contribution = Revenue − Cost.) Therefore, the decision of whether or not to increase the resource should consider only the nonvariable cost of increasing that resource (which is not reflected in the objective function). Similar considerations are made when the issue of *decreasing* capacities is being investigated (as in Example #3).

Negative Shadow Price

As stated earlier, the dual variables may assume a negative value. This means that if the value of a constraint is increased by one unit, the value of the objective function will decrease. This can be a desirable situation in the case of minimization.

Example

Given a minimization problem with a labor constraint of $x_1 + 3x_2 \leq 42$ and a corresponding dual of -1.2. The interpretation here is that if we increase the availability of labor from 42 to 43, the value of the objective function (cost in the case of minimization) will be decreased by $1.20.

Based on the above discussion and examples, we can summarize the problem that the dual represents (for the case of maximization).

The Dual's Problem

The problem is to determine the value of each unit of the primal's resources (or constraints) such that the value of the total resources, whose availability is given, is minimized. This minimization is subject to the requirement that the resource value per unit of input will be greater than (or equal to) the value of each unit produced (in the primal problem). The dual's values tell management the contributions of each resource to the profit.

5.5 Postoptimality Analysis

The optimal solution to an LP problem is based on a set of assumptions and on forecasting of future data such as prices. In a **deterministic model,** there is no provision for risk or uncertainty. Therefore, it is important for management to know *what* will happen to the optimal solution *if* changes occur in the input data on which the LP model is based. Because such analysis is done *after* the optimal solution is found, the approach is called postoptimality analysis. Several analyses can be made in a postoptimality analysis; the most common one is sensitivity analysis. The name *sensitivity analysis* derives from the fact that an analysis is made to find out how sensitive the optimal solution (after it was obtained) is to changes in the input data.

What-if

Why a Sensitivity Analysis?

Impacts of changes

One of the major purposes of sensitivity analysis is to provide the decision maker with additional information to adapt to changing conditions. For example, the availability of resources in an actual situation may change from day to day. Sensitivity analysis permits one to change the solution to maintain optimality in light of these changes without constantly having to resolve the problem. Sensitivity analysis also provides the decision maker with information as to which parameter estimates are most critical in the formulation.

There are two approaches for conducting sensitivity studies.

1. A Trial-and-Error Approach

According to this approach, one may change the input data (e.g., by using the *edit* capability in most computer programs), hence forming a new problem. Then the problem is solved from the beginning and the results are compared with that of the old problem. This process is repeated for all desired changes. The deficiency of this approach is that it may become very lengthy, because there are large numbers of possible changes in the data. Another possible deficiency is that resolving a problem may be expensive or time-consuming for large-scale problems.

2. Use of an Analytical Approach

When an analytical approach is used, there is no need to completely resolve the LP problems each time a change is made. Furthermore, information such as the "permissible range of change," which is directly provided by the analytical approach, can be provided by the trial-and-error approach only after an extremely lengthy experimentation period. The analytical approach presented here finds the effects on the optimal solution of each of the following changes, one at a time, in the input data:

- Changes in the coefficients in the objective function.
- Changes in the right-hand "quantity" side of the constraints.
- Changes in the input-output coefficients in the constraints.
- Adding or deleting a constraint.

It should be noted that the optimal solution may be changed in various ways: the value of the objective function (but not the basis) may be changed, its composition (the basic variables) may be changed, or the solution may become infeasible.

5.6 Sensitivity Analysis: Objective Function

Changes in the coefficients of the objective function are basically *product pricing* decisions. Assuming that the unit cost of producing a given product remains the same, two important managerial questions can be answered by the analysis:

- When does a price (or profit) *decrease* of a product, currently in the optimal solution, justify discontinuing or reducing its production?
- How much of a price (or profit) *increase* in a product, currently *not* in the optimal solution, justifies its production (inclusion in the optimal plan)?

Similar questions regarding price ratios and limits can also be answered.

Graphical Explanation of the Changes in the Coefficients

Example 1

Let us reproduce the product-mix problem:

maximize $z = 300x_1 + 250x_2$
subject to:
$$2x_1 + 1x_2 \leq 40$$
$$1x_1 + 3x_2 \leq 45$$
$$1x_1 + 0x_2 \leq 12$$

The decision as to whether or not the optimal solution should include a particular product, and how much, depends on its relative contribution to profit, as expressed in the objective function. In graphical terms, such a decision depends on the *slope* of the objective function. Let us examine the optimal graphical solution to the product-mix problem (Figure 5.2). The existing objective function (line *KL*) yields a solution at point *G* (12 units of x_1 and 11 of x_2). However, if we change the slope of the objective function so it is parallel to line *MN*, then the optimal solution will be at point *C* (produce 15 of x_2). The slope of the objective function can change if the coefficient of x_1 changes, the coefficient of x_2 changes, or the ratio between the coefficients of x_1 and x_2 is changed.

FIGURE 5.2

Solution to the product-mix problem

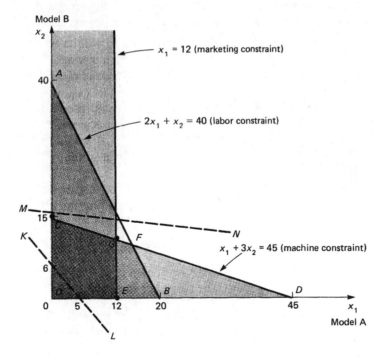

A change in solution from point G to point C will be achieved when the coefficient of x_2 is more than three times that of x_1. The reason for this is that with a ratio of exactly one to three, the objective function will be parallel to the machine constraint CD, with both points C and G being optimal. A smaller x_2/x_1 ratio means that G is the solution; a larger ratio means that C is the solution.

Limits on the Coefficients

Consider Figure 5.2. The current solution involves both product A (i.e., x_1) and B (x_2). Assume that the profit contribution of x_1 remains 300, whereas the profit contribution of x_2 increases. This increase will change the slope of the line KL toward that of MN. When the profit contribution reaches 900 (exactly 3 times 300), the line will be parallel to CD and both points C and G will be in the optimal solution. Thus, 900 is the upper limit of the coefficient of x_2. If the profit contribution of B is *more* than 900, the solution will then be at point C. On the other hand, the solution may move from point G to point E (produce A only). For this to happen, assuming that the profit contribution of x_1 remains 300, the profit contribution of x_2 would have to decrease to *below* zero. If the profit contribution of x_2 is *exactly* zero, then both points G and E will be optimal. Thus, the upper limit on the coefficient of x_2 is 900, and the lower limit is zero.

Let us now consider the variable x_1. If the coefficient of x_2 remains 250, then the *lower* limit of the coefficient of x_1 is $83\frac{1}{3}$ (i.e., $\frac{1}{3}$ of 250). If the profit contribution of x_1 becomes *less* than $83\frac{1}{3}$, then x_1 will not appear in the optimal solution (which will move to point C).

The upper limit on x_1 is the amount required to move the solution from G to E. This can happen only if the coefficient of x_2 is negative. Because the coefficient of x_2 is 300, no matter what the coefficient of x_1, point G will be superior to E. Thus, the upper limit of x_1 is ∞. The limits on x_1 and x_2 are summarized in the computer printout of Section 5.9. These limits are computed by the use of the simplex method as will be illustrated next.

Note: The example so far has dealt only with products that are in the solution. However, assume that the optimal solution was at point C to begin with (product x_2 only). Again, by figuring the appropriate slope, it would have been possible to figure the necessary increase in the coefficient of x_1 that would result in the inclusion of x_1 in the optimal solution.

The graphical analysis is limited, of course, to two decision variables. A similar analysis for any number of variables is possible using the simplex method.

Use of the Simplex Method to Determine the Range of c_j

The aim of the sensitivity analysis presented here is to find the *range* of no change in the composition of the basis. The range is composed of two limits: lower and upper. As long as a variable's coefficient is within this range, the current optimal solution will remain unchanged, though the objective function will change in value. Should the coefficient go above or below these limits, there will be a change in the basis and optimal solution. The limits of the range that were explained graphically above will now be computed with the help of the simplex tableau.

Example 1

Given a product-mix problem:

maximize $z = 5x_1 + 4.5x_2 + 1x_3$
subject to:
$$15x_1 + 15.8x_2 + 0 x_3 \leq 150$$
$$5x_1 + 6.4x_2 + 15 x_3 \leq 77$$
$$0x_1 + 2.8x_2 + 11.8x_3 \leq 36$$

The optimal tableau of this problem is shown below.

Basis	Unit Profits	x_1	x_2	x_3	s_1	s_2	s_3	Quantity
x_1	5	1	1.053	0	.067	0	0	10
x_3	1	0	.076	1	−.022	.067	0	1.8
s_3	0	0	1.924	0	.258	−.773	1	15.12
c_j		5	4.5	1	0	0	0	
z_j		5	5.342	1	.311	.067	0	
$c_j - z_j$		0	−.842	0	−.311	−.067	0	

The simplex approach distinguishes between an analysis of the coefficients of basic variables and nonbasic variables.

Analysis of Basic Variables

The analysis will be conducted on products x_1 and x_3, which are in the basis.

Analysis for x_1

Step 1   Copy the $c_j - z_j$ row of the optimal solution.

Step 2   Copy the x_1 row; enter it just below the $c_j - z_j$ row.

Step 3   Divide each $c_j - z_j$ row entry, *for variables not in the solution* (x_2, s_1, and s_2), by the associated variable a_{ij} from the x_1 row.

	x_1	x_2	x_3	s_1	s_2	s_3
$c_j - z_j$ row	0	−.842	0	−.311	−.067	0
x_1 row	1	1.053	0	.067	0	0
$\dfrac{c_j - z_j \text{ row}}{x_1 \text{ row}}$	—	$\dfrac{-.842}{1.053} = -.8$	—	$\dfrac{-.311}{.067} = -4.64$	$\dfrac{-.067}{0} = -\infty$	—

Interpretation   The *smallest positive number* in the last row of the new table tells by how much the profit of x_1 can be increased before the solution is changed. Because there are *no positive values*, there is no limit; that is, the profit can be increased to infinity and the solution will not change.

The *largest negative number (smallest absolute value)*, $-.8$ in this case, indicates by how much the coefficient of x_1 can be decreased without changing the solution.

The range is those two numbers within which the price of x_1 can be changed from the current level of 5. The lower limit is $5 - 0.8 = 4.2$, and the upper limit is $5 + \infty = \infty$.

Analysis for x_3   A similar analysis is conducted for x_3 and is shown below.

	x_2	s_1	s_2
$c_j - z_j$ row	$-.842$	$-.311$	$-.067$
x_3 row	$.076$	$-.022$	$.067$
$\dfrac{c_j - z_j \text{ row}}{x_3 \text{ row}}$	$\dfrac{-.842}{.076} = -11.09$	$\dfrac{-.311}{-.022} = 14.13$	$\dfrac{-.067}{.067} = -1$

The largest negative number is -1.
The smallest positive number is 14.13.

The range is:

$$\text{Lower limit} = 1 - 1 = 0$$

$$\text{Upper limit} = 1 + 14.13 = 15.13$$

Conclusion

a. If the profit contribution of x_3 exceeds 15.13, then s_1 will enter into the solution; if this happens, then x_1 will not be produced and the optimal solution will involve producing only x_3.

b. For product x_3 to be removed from the solution (s_2 would enter), its profit contribution will have to be less than zero (i.e., negative). A similar interpretation would be made for variable x_1.

Summary

The preceding analysis is generalized in Equations 5.1 and 5.2.

$$\text{Upper limit} = \text{minimize} \left[c_i + \frac{c_j - z_j}{a_{ij}} \right] \text{ for all } a_{ij} < 0 \qquad (5.1)$$

$$\text{Lower limit} = \text{maximize} \left[c_i + \frac{c_j - z_j}{a_{ij}} \right] \text{ for all } a_{ij} > 0 \qquad (5.2)$$

where:

c_i = profit contribution of basic variable i

j = index of nonbasic variable j

a_{ij} = substitution ratio, in the optimal tableau, between basic variable i and nonbasic variable j

Range for Nonbasic Variables

If there is a variable, j, not participating in the optimal basis, then, in order for this variable to be included in the optimal solution, its coefficient in the objective function will have to change from the existing c_j to a new level, c_j (new). This level is given by Inequality 5.3.

$$c_j \text{ (new)} \geq z_j \tag{5.3}$$

Computations

The only nonbasic decision variable is x_2 (with a coefficient c_2). By using Inequality 5.3:

$$c_2 \text{ (new)} \geq z_2 = 5.342$$

That is, if the profit contribution of x_2 increases from 4.5 to more than 5.342, then x_2 will be included in the solution.

This is the *upper limit* on the range of c_2. There is no *lower limit* on the range of c_2 because this is a maximization problem. Therefore, a coefficient of x_2 lower than the existing 4.5 will make it *even less desirable*. (Essentially, the lower range for nonbasic variables in maximization is $-\infty$.)

Range of Optimality

Another way to view the above is to view it as a *range* of optimality. Specifically, we are looking for the range within which each coefficient of the objective function can change without changing the decision variable value in the optimal solution.

5.7 Sensitivity Analysis: Right-Hand Side

The right-hand side (RHS) of the constraints expresses the capacities, limitations of the resources, or it makes explicit certain requirements. Management may be interested in finding out the effect of changes in these values (b_i's) on the optimal solution. Such changes may not affect the optimal solution, may change the composition of the basis, or may affect only the value of the objective function (same basis variables with different values). Of special interest is the impact on the dual's variables. Graphically, a change in any b_i is shown as a movement of the constraint, *parallel to itself*.

Example

Given:

maximize $z = 3x_1 + 4x_2$
subject to:
   (1) $3x_1 + 5x_2 \leq 15$
   (2) $2x_1 + 1x_2 \leq 8$
   (3) $0x_1 + 1x_2 \leq 2$

The graphical solution of this problem is shown in Figure 5.3, where point C is the optimal solution. Moving a binding constraint (such as 1 or 2) will change the location of the optimal solution. For example, if the capacity of constraint (2) is increased from 8 to 9 (x_2, line ST), then the optimal solution will move to point G. On the other hand, slightly moving constraint (3) will not affect the optimal solution at all (because the constraint is not binding). However, moving it much farther may change the location of the optimal solution. Management may be interested in finding the range of such changes. For example, moving constraint (2) more to the right will result in a situation where the solution is at point F (5 units of x_1, 0 of x_2). This will happen when the capacity of constraint (2) is 10; that is, 10 is the upper limit on constraint (2).

FIGURE 5.3

Changes in capacity

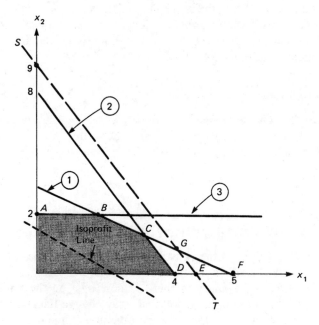

Use of the Simplex Method to Determine the Range of b_i

Range of feasibility

The dual variable, as shown earlier, can tell management the impact on the objective function of a marginal (one unit) change in the right-hand-side values (b_i's). If a change in one unit is desirable, then management may want to find if a change of two, three, or more units is feasible with respect to the dual variable. Specifically, management would like to know the range of b_i over which the dual variable will remain valid. The answer is automatically provided.

The simplex method is going to be used in the following manner:

Step 1   List the "Quantity" column of the optimal table.
Step 2   List the substitution ratios of the constraint whose range of b_i is analyzed.
Step 3   Divide the Quantity by the substitution ratio.
Step 4   Identify the smallest positive number and the smallest number with a negative sign.

Example

Let us analyze the product-mix problem that was solved graphically (Figure 5.3). The optimal simplex solution is given in Table 5.2.

Analysis for the First Constraint

Quantity, Q	s_1	Q/s_1	
3.57	−.143	−24.96	
1.143	−.286	−3.99	← smallest negative
.857	.286	3.00	← smallest positive

The smallest positive Q/s_1 (3.00 in our case) tells us how much the existing $b_1 = 15$ can be *decreased* (to $15 - 3 = 12$).

TABLE 5.2   Optimal Simplex Solution of the Product-Mix Problem

Basis	Unit Profit	x_1	x_2	s_1	s_2	s_3	Quantity
x_1	3	1	0	−.143	.714	0	3.57
s_3	0	0	0	−.286	.428	1	1.143
x_2	4	0	1	.286	−.428	0	0.857
$c_j - z_j$		0	0	−.714	−.428	0	

Next, the smallest number with a negative sign (3.99 in our case) tells us by how much the existing $b_1 = 15$ can be *increased*. Thus, the *range* over which b_1 can be changed is:

$$\text{Lower limit} = 15 - 3.00 = 12.00$$
$$\text{Upper limit} = 15 + 3.99 = 18.99$$

Analysis for the Second Constraint

Quantity	s_2	Q/s_2	
3.57	.714	5	
1.143	.428	2.67	← smallest positive
.857	−.428	−2	← smallest negative

$$\text{Lower limit} = 8 - 2.67 = 5.33$$
$$\text{Upper limit} = 8 + 2 = \quad 10.00$$

Analysis for the Third Constraint.   This is not a binding constraint, therefore the upper limit on b_3 is ∞. Because there is slack on this constraint, adding more capacity will not do us any good.

Quantity	s_3	Q/s_3	
3.57	0	∞	
1.143	1	1.143	← smallest positive
.857	0	∞	

$$\text{Upper limit} = \infty$$
$$\text{Lower limit} = 2 - 1.143 = 0.857$$

The Logic of the Analysis

Introducing a positive slack into a constraint is equivalent to reducing the value of the right-hand side by the value of the slack. For example, in the constraint:

$$5x_1 + 2x_2 + s_1 = 20$$
$$\text{if } s_1 = 2, \text{ then } 5x_1 + 2x_2 = 18$$

The same is true for a negative slack.

Thus, introducing a slack is equivalent to decreasing (increasing) the right-hand side. Therefore, in order to determine the *range* of the RHS, one should determine the maximum amount of slack (positive and negative) that can be introduced. This is done by analyzing the slack (surplus) of each constraint in the final simplex tableau. The maximum amount that can be introduced is found by:

> The smallest positive Q/slack ratio, which tells us how much the value of the right-hand side can be *decreased*.
>
> The largest negative Q/slack ratio, which tells us how much the value of the right-hand side can be *increased*.

Summary

The sensitivity analysis for the constraint RHS values involves finding the range of RHS values that will not change the basis. The smallest positive b_i/a_{ij} from the optimal tableau says how much the existing b_i can be decreased. The largest negative b_i/a_{ij} says how much the existing b_i can be increased. The upper limit for b_i is:

$$b_i \quad \max[b_i/a_{ij}] \qquad \text{for all } i, \text{ where } a_{ij} < 0$$

and the lower limit is:

$$b_i - \min[b_i/a_{ij}] \qquad \text{for all } i, \text{ where } a_{ij} > 0$$

These limits are very important, because they tell management how much a capacity limit can be changed before the existing optimal basis changes. Note that if there are no positive or negative values, then the associated limits are infinity. The a_{ij} values are the final cell values in the column of the optimal A matrix that was in the initial basis for the ith constraint whose right-hand-side range is being determined.

Range of Feasibility

The above analysis tells management the ranges over which each RHS value may change while the variables in the optimal solution remain feasible. During this range, the values of the dual variables remain unchanged. This is very important, because it tells management the limits within which resources can be changed based on the dual's analysis.

5.8 Other Changes

In the case of two decision variables, a change in the input-output coefficients (left-hand side) of the constraints is equivalent to either changing the slope of the constraint or moving the constraint parallel to itself (if the ratio of the coefficients remains the same). As a result of such a change, the area of feasible solutions will be changed. The impact on the optimal solution depends on the magnitude of the change. An analytical treatment of this topic is beyond the scope of this text.

Adding or Deleting Constraints

The addition of a new constraint can lead to one of the following results. First, the constraint may be redundant in the sense that it does not further restrict the feasible solution set. In that case, the optimal solution remains the same. Second, the constraint may decrease the feasible area, but the optimal solution will remain the same. Third, the additional constraint may reduce the feasible area so as to make the current optimal solution *infeasible*, thereby creating the need for finding a new optimal solution.

To find the impact of an added constraint on the optimal solution, all one has to do is to insert the value of the variables of the optimal solution into the new constraint. If the constraint is *not* violated, it belongs to the first or the second result above, and there is no change in the optimal solution. If the constraint is violated, then the problem must be resolved.

When deleting a constraint, one should check if the constraint is fully utilized (zero slack or surplus). If the answer is yes, the problem must be resolved; otherwise, there will be no change in the optimal solution.

5.9 Computerization

Most real-life problems are too large or complex for a graphical or manual simplex solution. Therefore, they are solved with the aid of computer programs. Dozens of computer programs are available from software companies, computer manufacturers, textbook publishers, and universities. As with other software, LP packages were developed both for mainframe and for mini- and microcomputers.

The inputs to the computer are typically simple: the objective function and the constraints. The most common outputs include:

a. The value of the decision variables.
b. The value of the objective function.
c. The value of the slack and surplus variables.
d. The value of the dual's variables.
e. Limited sensitivity analysis.

Example 1

So far, we have examined the following product-mix problem using both a graphical solution and the simplex approach.

$$\text{maximize } z = 3x_1 + 4x_2$$

subject to:
$$3x_1 + 5x_2 \leq 15$$
$$2x_1 + 1x_2 \leq 8$$
$$0x_1 + 1x_2 \leq 2$$

Data Input

The data input to the LP problem are sufficient for the sensitivity analysis. All the user has to do is to request "sensitivity analysis" from the menu.

Solution

A typical computer printout (Lotfi and Pegel's software) includes four parts. These are shown in Table 5.3 and are arranged in a way that shows the *relationship* among the parts. The meaning of the solution is explained next.

Interpretation of the Results

The solution is divided into four parts.

I. Decision Variable Analysis

This solution includes:

1. The value of the objective function.

$$z = 14.143$$

2. The name of the variables.
3. The status (either basic, or at lower bound or at their upper bound).
4. The value of the decision variables.

$$x_1 = 3.571, \qquad x_2 = 0.857$$

5. Reduced cost (coefficient of sensitivity). This coefficient measures how much the cost per unit must be decreased (or profit per unit increased) to bring another variable not currently in the solution into the solution.

II. Slack Variable Analysis

Here, all the constraints are listed with their slack (surplus) and shadow (dual) prices. Notice that if the slack is zero, the shadow price is nonzero; if the slack is nonzero, then the shadow price is zero.

TABLE 5.3 Sensitivity Analysis

```
                    ***** Optimal Solution *****
              Problem Title : Example 1
              Number of Iterations = 2
```

I Decision Variables Section :

Objective = 14.143

Variable	Status	Value	Reduced Cost
x1	Basic	3.571	0.000
x2	Basic	0.857	0.000

II Slack Variables Section :

Row	Variable	Status	Value	Shadow Price
Row1	Slack1	Lower Bnd	0.000	0.714
Row2	Slack2	Lower Bnd	0.000	0.429
Row3	Slack3	Basic	1.143	0.000

III Sensitivity Analysis–Objective Function Coefficients Ranges

Variable	Lower Limit	Original Coefficient	Maximum Increase	Maximum Decrease	Upper Limit
x1	2.400	3.000	5.000	0.600	8.000
x2	1.500	4.000	1.000	2.500	5.000

IV Sensitivity Analysis–Right-Hand Side Ranges

Row	Lower Limit	Original RHS	Maximum Increase	Maximum Decrease	Upper Limit
Row1	12	15.000	4.000	3.000	19.000
Row2	5.333	8.000	2.000	2.667	10.000
Row3	.857	2.000	Infinity	1.143	No Limit

III. Objective Function Ranging: Sensitivity Analysis
We consider each column in turn.

1. Variable name:

   This is the name assigned to the decision variable (e.g., x_1).

2. Lower limit:

   The limit to which the coefficients in the objective function can be reduced (one at a time) without changing the current optimal solution. For example, if the profit contribution of variable 1 (currently 3) goes below 0.6, at least one of the variables in the currently optimal solution will change.

3. Original value:

   The current value of the coefficient for the variable in the objective function.

4. Maximum increase:

   The value that creates the upper limit.

5. Maximum decrease:

   The value that creates the lower limit.

6. Upper limit:

   The maximum level of a coefficient, expressed as an upper limit, that is possible without changing the current optimal solution. For example, the upper limit for variable x_1 is 8.

7. Incoming variable, lower:

   The current nonbasic variable that will enter the optimal solution if the maximum decrease is violated.

8. Incoming variable, upper:

   The current nonbasic variable that will enter the optimal solution if the maximum increase is violated.

   (7 and 8 are not shown in this example.)

IV. RHS: Sensitivity Analysis
We consider each column in turn.

1. Constraint number:

   This refers to the number of the constraint, in the same sequence that it was entered in the problem.

2. Lower limit:

   The minimum level, a lower limit, in the current right-hand-side (RHS) value of a constraint that is possible before the value of the corresponding shadow price is changed. In other words, the downward range over which the shadow price associated with the constraint remains valid.

3. Original value:

   This is the value of the RHS of the original problem or the most current version of the problem, for each constraint.

4. Maximum increase: The value that creates the upper limit.
5. Maximum decrease: The value that creates the lower limit.
6. Upper limit: The maximum level of the current RHS value of a constraint that is possible before the value of the shadow price is changed. The upper value is 19 for constraint (1).
7. Outgoing variable, lower: The current basic variable that will be forced out of the solution if the lower limit is violated. In other words, if more than an allowable amount of decrease is removed from the RHS of the constraint, this variable will leave the solution.
8. Outgoing variable, upper: The current basic variable that will be forced out of the solution if the upper limit is violated.

(7 and 8 are not shown in this example.)

Note: In Table 5.3, changes *within* the limits of part III will impact part I but not part II. Changes *within* the limits of part IV will impact II but not I.

Example 2

Let us examine the product-mix problem discussed in Section 5.2. Given:

maximize $z = 5x_1 + 4.5x_2 + 1x_3$
subject to:
$$15x_1 + 15.8x_2 + 0x_3 \leq 150$$
$$5x_1 + 6.4x_2 + 15x_3 \leq 77$$
$$0x_1 + 2.8x_2 + 11.8x_3 \leq 36$$

The computer solution printout is given in Table 5.4.

Interpreting the Output

The first part of the table lists the variables, their values in the optimal solution, and their coefficients in the objective function. Notice that the second variable is not in the solution and, therefore, has a nonzero value in the Reduced Cost column.

The objective function coefficients explanation is given earlier in the text for this example. Notice, however, that there are differences in the values of the limits. The reason is that the computer program used is accurate only to two decimal places, whereas the manual solution is more accurate (in this case). Rounding errors tend to accumulate in a computer and this can be a major problem in computer applications.

The interpretation of the right-hand-side analysis is the same as in the previous example.

TABLE 5.4 **Computer Solution for Example 2**

```
                         Solution Summary
                      Problem Title: Example 2
                     ***** Optimal Solution *****
       No. of Iterations =  2          Objective =       51.800
```

Decision Variables Section

Variable	Status	Value	Reduced Cost
x1	Basic	10.000	0.000
x2	Lower Bnd	0.000	0.842
x3	Basic	1.800	0.000

Slack Variables Section

Row	Variable	Status	Value	Shadow Price
Row1	Slack1	Lower Bnd	0.000	0.311
Row2	Slack2	Lower Bnd	0.000	0.067
Row3	Slack3	Basic	14.760	0.000

Sensitivity Analysis–Right-Hand Side Ranges

Row	Original RHS	Maximum Increase	Upper Limit	Maximum Decrease	Lower Limit
Row1	150.000	81.000	231.000	56.288	93.712
Row2	77.000	18.763	95.763	27.000	50.000
Row3	36.000	No Limit	No Limit	14.760	21.240

Sensitivity Analysis–Objective Function Coefficients Ranges

Variable	Original Coefficient	Maximum Increase	Upper Limit	Maximum Decrease	Lower Limit
x1	5.000	No Limit	No Limit	0.800	4.200
x2	4.500	0.842	5.342	No Limit	No Limit
x3	1.000	14.000	15.000	1.000	0.000

5.10 Concluding Remarks

Linear programming provides an optimal solution to complex allocation problems. In addition, the tool can be used to conduct a quick postoptimality analysis that provides interesting managerial information concerning the problem. Two major topics were discussed in the chapter. First, duality with its resource analysis and utilization information was presented and then several options for conducting a sensitivity analysis were performed. The most important sensitivity analyses concern changes in the coefficients of the objective function and capacity changes. In both cases, ranges of optimality and/or feasibility are identified.

Note that the sensitivity analysis described in this chapter is based on the assumption that we change only one value at a time (with all other values remaining fixed). Although there are methods that permit simultaneous changes in several variables, they are very limited. An alternative approach is to re-solve the problem with the new data and use a trial-and-error approach to answer managerial questions.

5.11 Problems

1. Write the dual to the blending problem given in Section 3.2. Solve graphically.

2. Write the dual to Problem 3.29a. Solve by the simplex method. Compare to the simplex solution of the primal.

3. Given a linear programming problem:

   minimize $z = 6x_1 + 5x_2$
   subject to:
   - (1) $4x_1 + 8x_2 \geq 80$
   - (2) $6x_1 + 4x_2 \geq 100$
   - (3) $5x_1 + 5x_2 \geq 95$
   - (4) $6x_1 + 3x_2 \geq 110$

   a. Write the dual to the problem.
   b. Solve the dual manually by the simplex method (or by computer).
   c. What is the solution of the primal? (Answer *without* solving the primal.)
   d. What is the total value of each constraint?

4. Write the dual to the following problems:

   a. maximize $5x_1 + 3x_2 + x_3$
      subject to:
      $$5x_1 + 3x_2 \qquad \leq 50$$
      $$2x_2 + x_3 \geq 20$$
      $$2x_1 + 3x_2 - x_3 = 26$$

   b. minimize $6x_1 - 2x_2$
      subject to:
      $$3x_1 + 4x_2 \geq 50$$
      $$x_1 + 2x_2 = 20$$
      $$2x_1 + 3x_2 \leq 45$$

5. The solution to an LP minimization problem is $x_1 = 8$, $x_2 = 3$, $x_3 = 5$, $z = \$84$. There is a raw material constraint that is expressed as:

   $$7x_1 + 3x_2 - x_3 \leq 60$$

   The dual variable of this constraint is $\$-2.6$. Management is considering changing the availability of the raw material. Increasing the availability costs $2.50 per unit, whereas decreasing raw material by one unit reduces expenses by $2.70. What would you advise management to do and why?

6. Given an LP problem:

   minimize $z = 300x_1 + 800x_2$
   subject to:
   - (1) $2x_1 + 2x_2 \leq 1$
   - (2) $4x_1 + 2x_2 \geq 1$
   - (3) $10x_1 + 20x_2 \geq 6$
   - (4) $x_1 + x_2 = .5$

   a. Solve the problem graphically and by the simplex method.
   b. Which of the constraints are fully utilized?
   c. Use the shadow prices to find the impact on the objective function of the following changes:
      (1) Increase the right-hand side of constraint (1) by .5.
      (2) Decrease the right-hand side of constraint (1) by .1.
      (3) Increase the right-hand side of constraint (2) by .1.
      (4) Decrease the right-hand side of constraint (2) by .5.

(5) Decrease the right-hand side of constraint (3) by .5.

(6) Increase the right-hand side of constraint (4) by .1.

d. Verify the answer to (b) through observation of the graphical solution.

7. Write the dual to Problem 6. Solve by computer. Compare to the results of Problem 6.

8. Given the LP problem:

maximize $z = 5,000x_1 + 4,000x_2$
subject to:
$$x_1 + x_2 \geq 5$$
$$x_1 \quad 3x_2 \leq 0$$
$$10x_1 + 15x_2 \leq 150$$
$$20x_1 + 10x_2 \leq 160$$
$$30x_1 + 10x_2 \geq 135$$

Find:

a. The lower and upper limits of the coefficients of the basic variables.
b. The limit on the coefficients of the nonbasic variables.
c. The upper and lower limits of all five right-hand-side constraints.

9. Given:

maximize $z = 2.5x_1 + 2.25x_2 + .5x_3$
subject to:
$$7.5x_1 + 7.9x_2 \qquad \leq 75$$
$$2.5x_1 + 3.2x_2 + 7.5x_3 \leq 38.5$$
$$1.4x_2 + 5.8x_3 \leq 18$$

Find:
a. How much should the profit coefficient of x_2 be increased in order for it to be included in the optimal solution?
b. How much can the profit of x_1 be decreased without it dropping out of the optimal solution?
c. Change the right-hand side of the first constraint to 45; what impact will such a change have on the solution? Change it to 46 and check again. What can you conclude from the results?

10. Given a linear programming problem:

maximize $z = 70x_1 + 30x_2$
subject to:
$$2x_1 + x_2 \leq 1$$
$$x_1 + 8x_2 \leq 4$$

a. Solve graphically.
b. What profit coefficient should the product, currently not in the optimal solution, have in order to be included in the optimal solution?
c. How much can the right-hand side of constraint (2) change before the optimal solution is changed? What will the impact of the change be?
d. How much can the coefficient of x_1 in constraint (1) change before the optimal solution is changed?
e. What will be the impact of the following additional constraint on the solution?

$$2x_1 + 5x_2 = 4$$

11. Refer to the blending problem in Chapter 3.
a. What price will x_1 have to assume in order for it to be eliminated from the optimal solution?
b. What change in the brightness requirement needs to occur in order to change the optimal solution?
c. What change in the coefficients of the hue constraint (a_y) must occur in order to change the optimal solution?

12. Given an LP problem and its computerized solution:

MAXIMIZATION PROBLEM
$3.75X1 + 7.63X2 + 8.07X3$
SUBJECT TO:
$$1.5X1 + 2X2 + 1X3 \leq 9,600$$
$$4X1 + 5X2 + 10X3 \leq 38,400$$
$$1X1 + 1.5X2 + 1X3 \leq 6,000$$
$$0X1 + 1X2 + 0X3 \geq 1,000$$
$$0X1 + 0X2 + 1X3 \geq 3,000$$

Optimal Solution

Problem Title: LP 12
Objective = 37028.399

Decision Variables Section:

Variable	Status	Value	Reduced Cost
x1	Lower Bnd	0.000	2.354
x2	Basic	1680.000	0.000
x3	Basic	3000.000	0.000

Slack Variables Section:

Row	Variable	Status	Value	Shadow Price
Row1	Slack1	Basic	3240.000	0.000
Row2	Slack2	Lower Bnd	0.000	1.526
Row3	Slack3	Basic	480.000	0.000
Row4	Slack4	Basic	680.000	0.000
Row5	Slack5	Lower Bnd	0.000	−7.190

Right-Hand Side Ranges

Row	Original RHS	Maximum Increase	Upper Limit	Maximum Decrease	Lower Limit
Row1	9600.000	Infinity	No Limit	3240.000	6360.000
Row2	38400.000	1600.000	40000.000	3400.000	35000.000
Row3	6000.000	Infinity	No Limit	480.000	5520.000
Row4	1000.000	680.000	1680.000	Infinity	No Limit
Row5	3000.000	340.000	3340.000	240.000	2760.000

Objective Function Coefficients Ranges

Variable	Original Coefficient	Maximum Increase	Upper Limit	Maximum Decrease	Lower Limit
x1	3.750	2.354	6.104	Infinity	No Limit
x2	7.630	Infinity	No Limit	2.942	4.688
x3	8.070	7.190	15.260	Infinity	No Limit

This is a product-mix problem with:

$$X1 = \text{Units of budget}$$

$$X2 = \text{Units of regular}$$

$$X3 = \text{Units of deluxe}$$

Constraint:

(1) cutting (minutes)
(2) sewing (minutes)
(3) packing (minutes)
(4) marketing (units)
(5) marketing (units)

Objective function value is in dollars. Answer the following questions:

a. Should management increase the capacity of sewing by 10 hours if the cost of such a change is $120? Why or why not?

b. The cost of making one unit of a "budget" is $10. What should this product sell for in order to be included in the solution?

c. What is the utilization (in percent) of the cutting department?

d. Which constraints are not fully utilized?

e. Can you have a production plan of product X2 (regular) only? Why or why not?

f. Can you have a production plan of product X3 only? Why or why not?

g. What will be the total profit if we make 2,990 units of deluxe (instead of 3,000) in the optimal manner?

h. Why is there "no limit" on the RHS analysis of constraint (4)?

13. Refer to Problem 7 in Chapter 3. The current solution is: $x_A = 181.8, = x_B = 109.1$.

a. Assume that the cost coefficient of x_A is 50. What must the cost coefficient of x_B be for:

(1) The solution to be at the intersection of constraints 3 and 5?

(2) The solution to be at the intersection of constraint 2 with the x_B axis?

b. Describe, with examples, two ways to reduce the total cost.

c. Which constraints will have a non-zero dual variable?

14. Given a linear programming problem:

minimize $z = 50x_1 + 80x_2 + 15x_3 + 180x_4$
subject to:
(1) $300x_1 + 1,000x_2 + 10x_3 + 1,500x_4$
   $\geq 2,500$; (color)
(2) $20x_1 + 110x_2 + 10x_3 + 0x_4$
   ≥ 200; (strength)
(3) $15x_1 + 10x_2 + 8x_3 + 48x_4$
   ≥ 100; (weight)
(4) $x_1 \leq 2$
(5) $x_2 \leq 1.5$

and the following computerized solution, find the quantities of the four ingredients x_1, x_2, x_3, and x_4 that will provide sufficient color, strength, and weight to a blend but still minimize the overall cost. Answer the following questions.

a. What will the total cost of the blend be?

b. How much will the blend weigh?

c. Which ingredients are not included in the solution?

d. What should the cost of the absent ingredient(s) be to be included in the solution?

e. How strong is the blend going to be?

f. What is the utilization level of constraint (4)?

g. Suppose that we introduce into the blend one additional pound of x_1; what will the total cost be?

h. Why is the dual of constraint (4) equal to zero?

i. Refer to the RHS ranging; why is there no limit on constraint (2)? On constraint (4)?

j. Why is there an upper and lower limit on constraint (5), but not on (4)?

k. How much can we save by *decreasing* the color requirement by 10 percent?

l. What will happen if the cost of ingredient 4 is increased 10 percent? What if it is increased 20 percent?

```
                        Optimal Solution

Problem Title : LP 14
Number of Iterations = 2               Objective =        335.234

        Decision Variables Section :

        Variable        Status        Value        Reduced Cost

           x1        Lower Bnd        0.000           4.297
           x2        Basic            1.500           0.000
           x3        Basic            6.901           0.000
           x4        Basic            0.621           0.000

        Slack Variables Section :

        Row      Variable    Status        Value      Shadow Price

        Row1     Slack1    Lower Bnd       0.000        -0.063
        Row2     Slack2    Basic          34.010        0.000
        Row3     Slack3    Lower Bnd       0.000        -1.797
        Row4     Slack4    Basic           2.000        0.000
        Row5     Slack5    Lower Bnd       0.000        0.469
```

Sensitivity Analysis–Right-Hand Side Ranges

Row	Original RHS	Maximum Increase	Upper Limit	Maximum Decrease	Lower Limit
Row1	2500.000	816.250	No Limit	893.750	45.703
Row2	200.000	34.010	80.469	Infinity	No Limit
Row3	100.000	715.000	15.164	26.120	1.200
Row4	2.000	Infinity	202.000	2.000	179.316
Row5	1.500	0.905		0.245	

Sensitivity Analysis–Objective Function Coefficients Ranges

Variable	Original Coefficient	Maximum Increase	Maximum Decrease
x1	50.000	Infinity	4.297
x2	80.000	0.469	Infinity
x3	15.000	0.164	13.800
x4	180.000	22.000	0.684

15. Which of the five constraints in Problem 14 should be considered for investigation? Why?

16. Assume that the RHS of constraint #3 in Problem 14 changes to 110. a. What will happen to the value of the objective function? b. Is such a change feasible? Why or why not?

17. A glance at the sensitivity analysis coefficients of the *objective function* portion can tell us if there is a multiple optimal solution. Explain how.

5.12 CASE
HENSLEY VALVE CORP. (A)

It was Monday morning and the weekly meeting of the Executive Committee was in full swing. There were two primary items on the agenda and both directly affected Hensley's profit margin.

> Agenda Item A: The Proposed Tax Increase on Diesel Fuel
> Agenda Item B: Record Interest Rates

"Gus, as regional manager in our largest selling region, what will be the result of our raising prices to offset this possible increase in our trucking costs?"

"Well J. B., it certainly won't help our sales effort. Valve JBH-1 is only marginally profitable now, but takes twice the time to sell as our more profitable JBH-2s. I'm afraid a price increase might wipe out the viability of our JBH-1 valves altogether."

"That's what I was afraid of, too. Pat, how about the effect of that cancellation of the second NC machine we were hoping would help our productivity? I know you were counting on that to increase our output rate, but with the latest two big jumps in the prime rate we simply can't afford it at this time."

"Yes, I realize that, J. B. I certainly hadn't expected the prime rate to go quite this high. Basically, our output rates will remain limited, especially on old line 3, which produces the JBH-1 and -2 valves. Given the limited floor space and equipment and working three shifts on this line, we can still produce at most 600 JBH-1s or 100 JBH-2s a week, or any combination in between. I wondered if it would be worthwhile to have Tim Moran in our controller's office look at the interacting effect of all these changes? It seems that because so many things are happening at once, it may be best to totally change our product mix as well as our prices."

"I agree, Pat. It seems appropriate to undertake a complete contingency analysis of what we should do given any specific change in the market or combination of changes. I'll work up a memo to Tim this afternoon."

MEMO

TO: Tim Moran, Controller's Assistant
FROM: J. B. Hensley, President
SUBJECT: Reanalysis of Product Line

Please undertake a review of our JBH-1 and -2 valves for the next meeting of the Executive Committee on Monday morning. For this purpose you may assume their profitability to be $10 and $40 each, respectively. We have figured that a JBH-1 takes, on average, 4 hours to sell and a -2 takes 2 hours to sell. Sales has at most 1,000 hours a week available. Check with Pat Johnson for production figures on line 3. Items we would specifically like to know include:

- Given our limited capacities, how many of each valve should we currently be producing and selling to maximize our profits?
- What is an extra hour of sales time worth?
- At what hour sales effort is it not worth producing JBH-1s any longer?
- What is an increase in the capacity of line 3 worth?
- At what JBH-1 profitability will only JBH-1s be worth producing?
- What will be the effect on the solution of improving the JBH-1 marketing effort so it only takes 2.5 hours to sell a unit? What per unit investment is this worth?

Please add any other information you find to be relevant. Thank you.

Help Tim Moran to accomplish his assignment.

Glossary

Deterministic model   A model where all parameters are assumed to be known with certainty, such as LP.

Dual problem   An LP complementary problem that is associated with an original LP (primal) problem.

Dual variable   The decision variable of the dual problem.

Marginal value   The additional return from having one more unit available.

Objective function range of optimality   The range within which the optimal solution remains unchanged in terms of the composition and quantity of the decision variables in the basis.

Postoptimality analysis   A sensitivity analysis conducted after an optimal solution is derived.

Primal problem   An original LP problem.

Right-hand side range of feasibility   The range of RHS values for which the shadow prices and the basic solution composition remain unchanged.

Sensitivity analysis   An analysis of the impact of changes in the input data to an LP problem on its optimal solution.

Shadow price   The value that is added to the objective function when one unit is added to an LP constraint (right-hand side). This value equals the *dual variable* of the resource.

References and Bibliography

1. Gal, T. *Postoptimal Analysis, Parametric Programming, and Related Topics*. New York: McGraw-Hill, 1979.
2. Ignizio, J. P. *Linear Programming in Single and Multiple Objective Systems*. Englewood Cliffs, N.J.: Prentice-Hall, 1982.
3. Jeter, M. W. *Mathematical Programming—An Introduction to Optimization*. New York: Dekker, 1986.
4. Lev, B., and H. J. Weiss. *Introduction to Mathematical Programming*. New York: Elsevier North-Holland Publishing, 1982.
5. Minoux, M. *Mathematical Programming*. New York: John Wiley & Sons, 1986.

CHAPTER 6

Integer Programming and Extensions

Chapters 2–5 introduced the reader to the topic of linear programming, its variants, and some solution methodologies. This chapter is dedicated primarily to the concept of integer programming. With integer programming, the decision variables in the solution must be an integral number of units: 14 people, three planes. Special types of integer programming models are described and methods of solution are illustrated. Of special interest is the zero-one formulation, where variables can assume only one of two values (e.g., yes or no) that are designated as zero and one. The technique of branch and bound, which is useful for solving integer programming problems, is then presented, followed by a brief discussion of nonlinear programming.

Jack Smith, the administrator of Southern General Hospital, just returned from a meeting with the hospital board. He was in a gloomy mood, because the board only approved funds for a minor expansion, $210,000, to be used for not more than 10 hospital beds. He wanted to make the most of this authorization; that is, to get as much additional income as possible to improve the hospital's cash flow situation. So he called his assistant, Ruth Green, and asked her advice. There were two places where the additional beds could be added— in ward A and/or ward B. Each additional bed in ward A would generate $20 profit a day, versus $25 in ward B. For a moment, he thought of placing all the additional beds in ward B; however, he remembered that the board insisted on at least two beds for ward A. Also, the expansion would cost $24,600 per bed in ward B and only $20,000 per bed in ward A. Thus, he could add more beds in ward A. The problem, therefore, was how many beds to add to each ward (say, x_1 to ward A and x_2 to ward B).

6.1 Integer Programming—an Overview

Jack Smith's problem differs from the problems introduced in the previous chapters in one major way. The decision variables (i.e., the number of beds in wards A and B) *must* assume integer values such as five or six. As will be shown soon, the problem is a typical allocation problem and as such can be formulated as a linear program. However, the integer requirement must be added. Many practical problems involve integers. For example, it is impossible to have 2.7 elevators in a building, to admit 12.6 patients to a hospital, or to have 30.3 seats in a classroom.

Integer programming is important not only because it allows us to solve practical problems with indivisibility requirements, but also because it can be used as a computational tool in the solution of several complicated problems that cannot otherwise be solved (or cannot otherwise be solved effectively). For example, many nonlinear as well as combinatorial problems can be reduced to integer programming form. (A combinatorial problem consists of finding, from among a finite set of feasible solutions—usually very large—a solution that optimizes the value of the objective function.)

Integer programming is different from LP in several ways:

a. Cost of indivisibility—Adding the indivisibility requirement results in additional constraints. This means that the optimal integer solution will be either inferior (the usual case) or, at best, as good as the optimal noninteger solution. In other words, there is a cost attached to imposing the indivisibility requirement.

b. Solution method—In contrast to LP, which can be solved by the simplex method, there is no simple solution to the integer programming problem. For that reason one may use near-optimal rather than optimizing techniques. Algorithmic solution models can be very slow, even if executed by fast computers.

c. Number of solutions—Although integer programming has only a finite number of possible solutions (as compared to an infinite number in LP), this finite number may still be astronomical.

d. Special cases—The transportation and assignment models (Chapter 7) are special cases of integer programming.

e. LP codes—General-purpose mixed-integer LP codes can be used to solve some special cases of integer programming problems. However, the sensitivity analyses generated by these codes do not usually have any meaning.

f. Optimal solutions—With LP, there is either one optimal solution or an infinite number of them. With integer programming, there is either one or several optimal solutions.

6.2 Solving the Southern General Hospital Problem

Jack gave Ruth all the information he had, and instructed her to go to work on the problem. Ruth, having just completed a course in management science, immediately realized that she was dealing with an allocation problem. As she formulated it, she was very pleased to find out that it was a linear programming problem, as follows:

maximize $z = 20x_1 + 25x_2$
subject to:
$$1x_1 + 1x_2 \leq 10 \quad \text{(total bed limitation)}$$
$$\$20,000x_1 + \$24,600x_2 \leq \$210,000 \quad \text{(budget constraint)}$$
$$1x_1 + 0x_2 \geq 2 \quad \text{(at least two beds in ward A)}$$

With only two variables and three constraints, it seemed natural to try the graphical method (Figure 6.1). Ruth did so, and found an optimal solution of 2 beds in ward A and 6.9 beds in ward B, with a total daily profit of \$212.50 (point P in Figure 6.1). Examining the solution, Ruth immediately realized that she was dealing with integer requirements, because 6.9 beds is obviously not feasible. Before she had a chance to re-examine the solution, she was surprised by Jack.

"I don't know what they teach you there at school, but you have been working on the problem for more than half an hour; let me try it." At that stage, Ruth had no choice but to look at Jack's attempt. Jack rationalized that in this case there are only a few alternatives; they are listed in Table 6.1. Obviously, alternatives a_0 and a_1 should not be considered, because there must be at least two beds in ward A. He also realized that alternatives a_2, a_3, a_4, a_5, a_6, and a_7 exceeded the available budget. Left with only alternatives a_8, a_9, and a_{10}, he computed their profits and declared: "It is best to build eight beds in ward A and two in ward B; it will cost us \$209,200, and it will generate a daily profit of \$210. As you see, we do not need your LP."

Ruth returned, disheartened, to her desk. After all, why spend so much time on LP? Nevertheless, she decided to return to the graphical solution. As she examined the

FIGURE 6.1

*Graphical approach to
bed allocation*

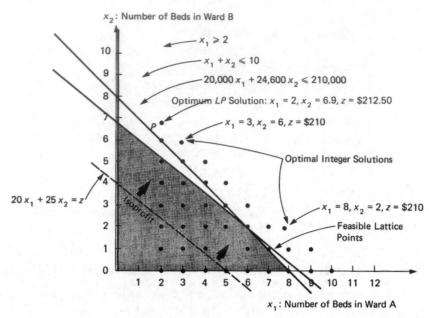

x_2: Number of Beds in Ward B

$x_1 \geq 2$

$x_1 + x_2 \leq 10$

$20{,}000\,x_1 + 24{,}600\,x_2 \leq 210{,}000$

Optimum *LP* Solution: $x_1 = 2$, $x_2 = 6.9$, $z = \$212.50$

$x_1 = 3$, $x_2 = 6$, $z = \$210$

Optimal Integer Solutions

$20\,x_1 + 25\,x_2 = z'$

isoprofit

$x_1 = 8$, $x_2 = 2$, $z = \$210$

Feasible Lattice
Points

x_1: Number of Beds in Ward A

TABLE 6.1   Bed Alternatives

Alternatives	Beds in Ward A	Beds in Ward B	Required Expenses	Daily Profit
a_0	0	10	$246,000	(infeasible)
a_1	1	9	241,000	(infeasible)
a_2	2	8	236,800	(infeasible)
a_3	3	7	232,200	(infeasible)
a_4	4	6	227,600	(infeasible)
a_5	5	5	223,000	(infeasible)
a_6	6	4	218,400	(infeasible)
a_7	7	3	213,800	(infeasible)
a_8	8	2	209,200	$210
a_9	9	1	204,600	$205
a_{10}	10	0	200,000	$200

points marked with a (•) in Figure 6.1 (feasible integer solution points), it took her only
a moment to notice that there was another solution. She called Jack and declared: "To
get a daily profit of $210, it is sufficient to build only six beds in ward B and three in A
at a total cost of $207,600, a savings of $1,600 in the required investment." Jack was
surprised; he checked and rechecked and finally admitted that the investment in "that
LP course" was perhaps not so worthless. The Southern General Hospital case demonstrates one type of integer programming (IP) problem and one approach to its solution.
In the following sections, we will attempt to generalize the technique.

6.3 Types of Integer Programming Models

Integer programming problems can be divided into two general classes: integer linear programming and integer nonlinear programming. The discussion in this chapter is limited to the former. However, the following subclassifications are valid for both.

a. All-integer model This model adds a requirement that all decision variables (x_1, x_2, etc.) must be integers. Other than that, the problem is basically an LP (or non-LP) problem.

b. Mixed integer model In this model, there is a requirement that some, but not all, of the decisions variables must be integers. Other than that, the problem is again either LP or non-LP.

c. Zero-one integer model In this model there are sets of decision variables and/or auxiliary (support) variables whose value is limited to either zero or one. Such problems are important because a set of $0-1$ values can represent situations such as "yes" and "no": to undertake a project, invest in a certain stock, etc.

The solution procedures outlined in this chapter may be limited to only one type of model, or may be good for several types of models.

Some Applications of Integer Programming

1. Exxon's Baton Rouge Refinery
As described in the MSIP at the end of Section 6.4, this project involved an economic assessment of energy improvement projects over an extended period. The objective was to maximize energy savings, less expenses, subject to technology and other constraints. A mixed IP formulation was used and resulted in a savings of $100 million over 15 years.

2. Kelly-Springfield Tire Company
This project involved complex production planning and distribution decisions associated with setting up a specific line of tire production. The decision was modeled as a $0-1$ integer programming problem. The solution saves about $8 million each year. (Source: *Interfaces*, Dec. 1980.)

3. Intercollegiate Women's Gymnastics
The problem was to assign members of a team to four events conducted at an NCAA meeting so as to maximize the team's overall expected score, subject to certain constraints (Source: *Interfaces*, May–June 1984.)

4. Flying Tiger Lines
Using mixed integer programming, this cargo transportation company solved two problems simultaneously. The first was to design a service network involving 33 cities and 8 hubs. The second was to select and deploy their aircraft fleet.

5. AT&T

Mixed integer programming was used to help their clients determine the best site locations for their telemarketing centers. Savings were estimated to be one million dollars a year. (Source: *Interfaces*, Jan.–Feb. 1990.)

6.4 Methods of Solution

Complete Enumeration

Complete enumeration

What Jack attempted to do in the hospital expansion case was to list all possible solutions, eliminate those that violate the constraints, and select the best solution by comparing the profits. Such a process is called an *enumeration;* and if *all* feasible solutions are checked, it is termed a **complete enumeration.** What Jack did was to assume that he should enumerate only the alternatives involving 10 beds (a partial enumeration), neglecting alternatives of 9 or fewer beds.

Because most integer programming problems have a finite number of feasible solutions, these can be solved by complete enumeration. To do so, it is necessary to assign all possible integer values to all variables and to check all possible feasible solution combinations to determine that combination that yields the best value of the objective function. In cases with a small number of variables and possible combinations, this method is efficient. However, in many practical problems, there is a very large number of possible solution combinations and the enumeration method is therefore impractical.

The zero-one algorithm

There is one special case in which complete enumeration might be used to advantage: in the 0–1 formulation. For such cases, an implicit enumeration search, named the *zero-one algorithm,* has been developed. This method has, for example, been used in the problem of allocating funds to research and development projects and found to be very efficient with as many as 50 projects.

Rounding the Noninteger Solution

A practical approach to an integer programming problem in some cases is to solve it as a regular LP problem and then round off the optimal results. The major advantage of such an approach is the saving of time and cost that would have been required for formulating and solving an integer programming model. The major disadvantage of the rounding approach is that the resultant solution may differ significantly from the optimal integer solution and, furthermore, may even be infeasible.

Although the infeasibility problem can be avoided when rounding (by making sure that the constraints are not violated), it is impossible to tell offhand how close the rounded solution is to the optimal integer one. However, it is possible to tell how close the rounded integer solution is to the otherwise optimal noninteger solution. If the difference between the two is not large, there is very little sense in investing time and money in an attempt to identify the optimal integer solution. The logic for this approach is that the optimal integer solution must be in between the noninteger solution and the rounded solution. If the difference between these two is small, then the difference between the rounded and the true optimal integer solution is minimal.

Trial and error

A variant of the rounding method is the *trial-and-error* approach, in which one enumerates *selected* feasible integer solutions in the neighborhood of the optimal LP solution. For example, using this approach, Ruth would have investigated the solutions: (3,6) [i.e., $x_1 = 3$, $x_2 = 6$]; (2,6); (3,5); (4,5); and (5,4).

The Graphical Method

Integer programming problems with either two unknown variables (or two constraints) can be solved by the graphical method. Its major advantages are its simplicity and its applicability for solving both the all-integer and mixed-integer problems. Ruth used this method in the hospital expansion case.

The feasible solution space

The graphical approach for integer programming problems is similar to the graphical approach for solving regular LP problems; the difference lies in the nature of the *feasible solution spaces* for the two problems (see Figure 6.1). Whereas in the LP case, the set of feasible solutions is a *space* bounded by the linear constraints, in integer programming, the feasible area is a collection of *all-integer points*. Once such points are marked, the isoprofit line is moved away from the origin until it covers the last lattice points in the feasible area—points (3,6) and (8,2) in Figure 6.1. (A lattice point here refers to a point with all-integer coordinates.)

Branch and Bound

This is a special type of enumeration procedure and is discussed in Section 6.6.

More Complicated Methods

A host of more complicated methods are available for larger and more complex problems. All require computers. Of special interest are the methods based on Gomory's "cutting plane" algorithm (following). Dynamic programming can also be used to solve certain types of integer programming problems. Finally, heuristic methods have also been developed for special integer programming problems.

The Gomory Cutting Plane Method*

Cutting planes

Gomory's major idea was to construct a convex area covering all lattice points. He accomplished this by constructing "cutting planes," with the aid of additional constraints imposed on the problem. These "cutting planes," which are introduced *one at a time,*

---

*Based on Loomba and Turban [2, pp. 261–262]

reduce the original feasible area to the desired integer configuration. Gomory's constraints have the following properties.

1. They usually cut a convex area out of the previous feasible area.
2. The cutting plane goes through *at least* one lattice point (not necessarily a feasible one).
3. Each cut approaches the *smallest area* that is required to cover all feasible lattice points.

The method ensures us an optimal solution in a finite number of iterations. The Gomory method is described below.

First we solve the problem without paying any attention to the integer constraints. Then we examine the optimal solution. If each variable is an integer, the problem is solved. Otherwise, we construct a Gomorian constraint and impose it on the original problem. This constraint is our "cutting plane." The addition of the Gomorian constraint turns the optimal and feasible (noninteger) solution into an optimal but infeasible (noninteger) solution. Hence, the next step is to employ the dual-simplex method to arrive at a new optimal and feasible solution. If this is an all-integer solution, the problem is solved. Otherwise, we keep on adding Gomorian constraints, one at a time, until an optimal integer solution is obtained. These steps are summarized in Figure 6.2.

FIGURE 6.2

Gomory method steps

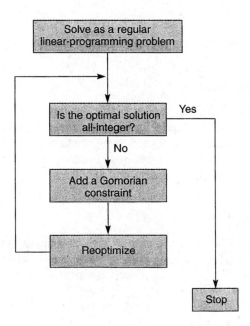

Management Science in Practice

Minimizing Family Relocations at Boston's Orient Heights Housing Project

In the late 1980s, the Boston Housing Authority (BHA) was planning for the modernization of the Orient Heights housing project in East Boston. One of their primary concerns was with finding a procedure for relocating the current tenants with a minimum of disruption.

The housing project consisted of seven row houses with three two-bedroom and three three-bedroom units each, and 13 apartment buildings, each containing 24 or fewer units of varying size. The BHA was also contemplating the addition of 15 new townhouses to the project. At the time, there were over 250 households residing in the project, rendering the buildings partially occupied. However, the redevelopment project could not proceed sequentially on one building at a time for construction reasons. Rather, the fewer the number of construction phases, the better.

There were a number of conflicting objectives in the relocation and redevelopment project. First, it was desired to minimize the duration of the entire redevelopment process. But it was also desired to minimize the amount of relocation the existing tenants must endure. Additionally, neither the tenants nor the BHA wanted to temporarily relocate tenants to off-site locations while the redevelopment was proceeding; it was preferable to move them to currently vacant units within the existing project, if enough units were available. Of course, once a building was redeveloped, its newly available units could be used to house tenants from other buildings while they were being redeveloped. There was also the complication that the units available might be smaller than the units the tenants were vacating so the BHA preferred minimizing the extent of temporary "underhousing" that might occur, too. And finally, the BHA wanted to delay, as much as possible, the need to build the 15 new townhouses, because they were not sure that they would even be able to obtain the funding for their construction.

What the BHA needed from the analysis was a sequence for redevelopment of the buildings and relocation of the tenants while work proceeded. To evaluate all the sequences of 20 buildings leads to 20 factorial (20!) different construction sequences, with 400 binary decision variables. This magnitude of problem was out of the question for BHA. Therefore, buildings were instead grouped into superunits of about three buildings

each and analyzed in this fashion, giving just 7! sequences (5,040). The groupings were based on geographical proximity and construction similarity and effort.

The problem was formulated as an integer linear program, including some ancillary scheduling heuristics. Five scenarios, representing different assumptions about BHA's preferences, were considered in the formulation.

- a: All relocation is on-site and no underhousing is allowed.
- b: All relocation is on-site with underhousing limited to one room at most.
- c: Relocate 12 households in 1 superunit off-site, the remainder as with scenario A.
- d: Same as C but with one room underhousing at most.
- e: Same as C but continue relocating households off-site as needed to delay the need for the townhouses to the end of the project.

Solving the models indicated that some of the scenarios were infeasible and others were not very realistic. In essence, either the townhouses had to be made available or substantial off-site relocation had to occur. Even with the townhouses, on-site relocation still required some degree of underhousing. The BHA found the study extremely helpful in clarifying the feasibility of their alternatives and structuring the nature of the problem so they could make a more informed decision regarding the relocation problem at Orient Heights.

Source: E. H. Kaplan and O. Berman, "OR Hits the Heights: Relocation Planning at the Orient Heights Housing Project," *Interfaces*, November–December 1988, pp. 14–22.

Questions:

1. What is the objective function of the IP model?
2. What are the decision variables?
3. How much realism was lost by forming "superunits"? Do you think some better alternatives might have surfaced?
4. Because no money was saved what was the value in this study?

Logical variables

6.5 The Zero-One Model

A special and important application of integer programming is the case where the value of the decision variables is limited to two "logical" variables. For example, a variable may be either yes or no, or match or not. These are symbolized by the values 0 and 1 and known as **zero-one variables.** Several computer packages can address these problems (See Section 6.8).

Examples

a. Research and Development (R&D) or Capital Budgeting

Companies frequently face the situation of selecting one or more R&D projects or investment opportunities from among several competing projects. For example, consider the list below. If $25 million is available, which projects should be selected?

Competing Projects	Cost ($ million)	Expected Utility
Crime prevention (x_1)	5	20
Housing improvement (x_2)	20	18
Health-care center (x_3)	12	13
Geriatric research (x_4)	7	30
Gifted child education (x_5)	4	15

Formulation.   Each decision variable can assume one of two values, either 0 (not selected) or 1 (selected). Thus, $x_1 = 0$ means to not select the crime prevention project. The objective function is:

maximize $z = 20x_1 + 18x_2 + 13x_3 + 30x_4 + 15x_5$
subject to:
$\quad 5x_1 + 20x_2 + 12x_3 + 7x_4 + 4x_5 \le 25$
and
$\quad x_i = 0, 1$ for all i

Solution.   The optimal solution, using the Lotfi and Pegels [3] software package, is:

$$x_1 = 1, x_4 = 1, x_5 = 1, z = 70.$$

b. The Knapsack Problem

Four items are considered for loading on an airplane. The weights and values of the items are shown below. Which items should be loaded on the plane, which has a capacity of 11 tons, to maximize the value of the cargo transported (in units of importance)?

Item	Weight (tons)	Value
A	2	18
B	4	25
C	5	30
D	3	20

Formulation. The decision variables are 0 (do not load) or 1 (load). The objective function is:

maximize $z = 18x_A + 25x_B + 30x_C + 20x_D$

subject to:

$$2x_A + 4x_B + 5x_C + 3x_D \leq 11$$

and

$$x_i = 0,1 \text{ for all } i$$

Note: A variation of this problem is solved by dynamic programming in Chapter 16.

c. The Fixed-Charge Problem

Many real-life problems involve a combination of fixed and variable costs. The fixed costs are incurred only if certain projects are undertaken or a certain capacity level is exceeded. A common example is machine scheduling.

Eastland Corporation is planning to produce at least 900 pollution control valves. Three production lines are available with the setup costs, unit processing (variable) costs, and capacities given below. Find which lines to use in order to minimize the total cost.

Line	Setup Cost	Unit Processing Cost	Maximum Capacity
A	$850	$20	500
B	150	58	700
C	520	36	620

Formulation. Let x_A, x_B, and x_C represent the quantities to be produced on lines A, B, and C; d_A, d_B, and d_C indicate whether a line is to be used (1) or not (0). The objective function is

$$\text{minimize } z = \underbrace{(850d_A + 150d_B + 520d_C)}_{\text{Fixed cost}} + \underbrace{(20x_A + 58x_B + 36x_C)}_{\text{Variable cost}}$$

subject to:

$$\begin{aligned} x_A + x_B + x_C &\geq 900 \\ x_A &\leq 500d_A \\ x_B &\leq 700d_B \\ x_C &\leq 620d_C \end{aligned}$$

and

$$d_i = 0,1 \quad \text{for all } i$$

(*Note:* This problem is actually a mixed-integer programming problem, because only *some* of the variables are restricted to 0 or 1 values.)

d. Capacity Planning

A company is considering whether to expand a warehouse or not. If so, the amount of the expansion, x, should be at least 2,000 units but not more than 10,000. Disregarding other information, this condition can be written as two constraints:

$$(1) \quad x - 10,000d \leq 0$$

$$(2) \quad x - 2,000d \geq 0$$

where:

$$d = 0,1$$

Now, if $d = 1$ in the solution, the x can assume any value between 2,000 and 10,000. But if $d = 0$ in the solution, then $x = 0$.

e. Mutually Exclusive Constraints

In many real-life situations, an optimization is to be made subject to one constraint (or a set of constraints) or another, but not both. In this case, the problem can be separated into two or more problems, each solved separately, and then the one with the highest payoff is selected. Or, an elegant integer-programming approach can be used. For example:

> maximize $5x_1 + 7x_2$
> subject to one (only) of the following:
> $2x_1 + x_2 \leq 5,000$
>
> or:
> $3x_1 + 7x_2 \leq 14,000$
>
> or:
> $5x_1 + 6x_2 \leq 12,500$

The equivalent integer programming presentation is:

$$\text{maximize } 5x_1 + 7x_2 + 0d_1 + 0d_2 + 0d_3$$

subject to:

$$
\begin{aligned}
2x_1 + x_2 &\leq 5{,}000 + Md_1 \\
3x_1 + 7x_2 &\leq 14{,}000 + Md_2 \\
5x_1 + 6x_2 &\leq 12{,}500 + Md_3 \\
d_1 + d_2 + d_3 &= 1
\end{aligned}
$$

where M is a very large number compared to the RHS values (say, 100,000) and d_1, d_2, and d_3 are either 0 or 1. This is another mixed-integer programming problem, because only the ds are required to have integer values.

f. Assignment

The assignment problem in Chapter 7 uses 0–1 variables when it is converted into a linear program.

Solved Problem 6.1: Zero-One Algorithm

The production of model A involves \$2,000 in fixed cost and \$50 in variable cost. The production of model B involves \$4,000 in fixed cost and \$30 per unit variable cost. Finally, model C requires \$10,000 of fixed cost and \$25 variable cost per unit.

The production time required for the three models is: four hours for A, six for B and seven for C. The total available production time is 44,000 hours per quarter. The company must produce 200 units of model C. The company sells the products for: Model A: \$75, model B: \$50, and model C: \$33. Formulate as a zero-one model.

Formulation. Let X_A = units of model A, X_B = units of model B, X_C = units of C.

$$d_A = 0; \text{ do not produce product A}$$

$$d_A = 1; \text{ produce product A}$$

Also,

$$d_B = 0,1, \text{ and } d_C = 0,1$$

The Objective Function is:
Max. $z = (75 - 50)X_A + (50 - 30)X_B + (33 - 25)X_C - 2000d_A - 4000d_B - 10{,}000d_C$
Subject to:

$$
\begin{aligned}
4X_A + 6X_B + 7X_C &\leq 44{,}000 \\
X_C &\geq 200
\end{aligned}
$$

This is a mixed integer, zero-one problem because X_A and X_B can take noninteger values and the ds are restricted to the values of 0 or 1.

Solution. $X_A = 10{,}650$; $X_B = 0$; $X_C = 200$; $z = 267{,}850$

Management Science in Practice

Exxon Optimizes Energy Use with Integer Programming

Exxon Corporation is a 100 year old enterprise with branches in over 100 countries. It is focused on exploring, producing, refining, and marketing petroleum products. But as a large, fully-integrated energy company, it is also a major *user* of energy. In fact, the refining industry alone accounts for about 4 percent of total domestic energy consumption.

In the 1970s, energy demand began to outstrip the previously plentiful supply and prices increased markedly. Thus, the refining industry began massive energy conservation projects during the 1970s to reduce these costs, achieving an 18 percent reduction between just 1972 and 1978 alone. Exxon achieved a 25 percent reduction between 1972 and 1978. Yet the energy portion of refining costs still remained high, running several million dollars a day for Exxon's five refineries and two plants. Moreover, the changes taking place in the industry, such as the switch from leaded to unleaded gasoline, were requiring even more energy.

However, by 1980 most of the obvious efficiency gains had already been accomplished. Hence, a new approach was called for. At Exxon, this was termed a "Site Energy Project" and involved improving the movement of heat by a medium such as steam between units that have excess heat and units that need heat. However, most of the improvements consisted of installing more expensive capital equipment.

Exxon studied several operation strategies, each having hundreds of discrete energy improvement projects for which there would be three to five alternative methods of executing the project. The timing and sequencing of the projects was also interdependent, creating an extremely complex problem for evaluation and selection of the best strategies, projects, and alternatives. Thus, the projects and their interactions were modeled as a multi-time period mixed integer program. Input data included energy consumption or production, capital investment required, operating costs, and expense and downtime costs for each project. The objective function was to maximize the net present value of the total energy savings less the capital investment and expenses. The constraints were utility balances (steam pressures, condensates, hot oil, hot water), as well as any project limitations.

Over 600 separate projects were identified for the program at a test site in Baton Rouge, Louisiana. The actual optimized solution then identified the approximately 200 economically "best" projects, which involved 74 different processing units. The model also identified minor utility imbalances resulting from the requirement of integer numbers of project selections (cannot have 0.84 units of a project selected; either it is or is not selected). These projects are now in the stage of being implemented. It is estimated that this will save Exxon on the order of $100 million dollars over 15 years. The model is now being used at many of Exxon's other sites to produce additional savings.

The use of the integer programming model is believed to have resulted in three major benefits to Exxon: (1) approximately 10 percent more was saved than would have been otherwise; (2) about one year was saved in conducting the analysis, resulting in energy and cost savings one year sooner; and (3) more than five engineering man-years were saved due to the discipline this model brought to the problem. It played a key role in the organization of the data, the systemization of the procedures, and the pre-specification of the assumptions. The model was also believed to contribute to the firm's increased analysis capabilities, improved reaction to change, and ability to transfer modeling support to other sites.

Source: W. L. McMahan and P. A. Roach. "Site Energy Optimization, A Math Programming Approach", *Interfaces,* December 1982, pp. 66–82.

Questions:

1. How do you think Exxon's "Site Energy Project" differed from previous energy conservation projects?

2. If the Baton Rouge investment is expected to save $100 million over the next 15 years (payback period), what would you estimate the capital investment to be?

3. What was the imputed value of the integer programming solution? Do you think the costs of obtaining the data or running the program should be subtracted from these savings?

4. Using the figures given, about how much was one year's earlier implementation worth to Exxon?

6.6 The Branch and Bound Method

The branch and bound method is an intelligent search procedure for either an optimal or, with less computational effort, a close-to-optimal solution to certain managerial problems, including all-integer and mixed-integer problems.

The Process in General

Dividing into subproblems

The process consists of dividing a problem into two or more *subproblems* (**branching**) and setting two *bounds* on the value of the objective function. The manner of determining bounds depends on the type of problem. A distinction is then made between *feasible bounding solutions* and *infeasible bounding solutions*. The subproblems are then solved. All subproblems whose objective functions are worse than the established feasible bounds are eliminated from further consideration. The remaining subproblems are used to modify the bounds and then subdivided and investigated. The process is repeated until no further subdivision is possible, at which point the optimal (or near optimal) solution has been reached.

Example

Let us illustrate by solving a problem of finding the best assignment of three employees to three machines on a one-to-one basis. Table 6.2 shows the profits (determined from prior experience) derived from assigning each employee to each machine. For example, if Jim is assigned to a drilling machine, a profit of 2 is realized.

Solution

First, the maximum possible profit is computed. To do so, the highest possible profit in the first row, which is 3, is selected; accordingly, Jim is assigned to the lathe (a to y, or ay). Next is the second row; 4 is the highest profit. Therefore, an assignment of b to y is made. Similarly, c is assigned to z. The profit for this assignment (ay, by, cz) is: $3 + 4 + 3 = 10$. This solution is *infeasible* because two employees were assigned to

Upper bound

machine y, violating the one-to-one requirement. (If this solution had been feasible, it would also have been optimal and the problem would have been solved.) This solution,

---

TABLE 6.2 An Assignment Problem

Machine Employee	Mill (x)	Lathe (y)	Drill (z)
Jim (a)	0	3	2
Bill (b)	2	4	1
Joe (c)	2	1	3

with the highest possible profit, is now used as the *upper bound* (UB), an infeasible bound in this case.

First Branching.   By changing *one assignment* in the *infeasible solution,* and leaving the others the same, three new problems are formed. Suppose a change in the assignment to the milling machine (x) is chosen: then, three subproblems will involve assigning a, b, and c consecutively to x. First, a is assigned to x. The original assignments of b and c (by, cz) are kept. This solution is *feasible* with a value of 7 (see Figure 6.3).

Lower bound

Being a feasible solution, it is declared the *first lower bound* (LB). Because the LB is less than the UB, we continue. Second, b is assigned to x. In this case the (feasible) solution is: ay, bx, and cz, with a value of 8. Because this is a better feasible solution than the previous one, the previous solution is dropped. Finally, c is assigned to x for the solution: cx, ay, and by (which is infeasible), with a value of 9.

The original problem has now been partitioned into three new problems, with a best (but infeasible) solution of 9 instead of 10. Therefore, 9 becomes the *new upper bound*. New bounds are generated at each branching because the partitioning of the problem totally replaces the previous problem. It is still an infeasible solution, but it has a value closer to the feasible area than the previous upper bound had. The optimal solution must now be between the *lower bound* of 8 and the *upper bound* of 9. Now the ax solution can be dropped from further consideration because it is *below* the lower bound.

New bounds at each branching

Second Branching.   The next branching is from cx, because this is the current best but infeasible solution. This time two branches are possible, ay and by (see Figure 6.4).

Again, solutions whose value is less than the current lower bound are dropped; thus, ay with a profit of 6 is dropped. Because no further branching is possible (only feasible solutions remain and feasible solutions are not partitioned), the optimal solution has been reached. At that point, the old UB is replaced with the new one (8) at the

FIGURE 6.3

First branching

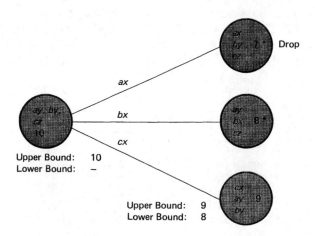

Upper Bound: 10
Lower Bound: –

Upper Bound: 9
Lower Bound: 8

* Feasible.

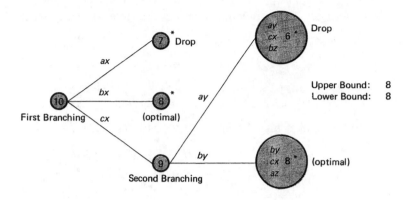

FIGURE 6.4

Second branching

* Feasible.

optimal solution UB = LB. Here, two optimal solutions with a profit of 8 have been identified:

1. *b* to *x*, *a* to *y*, *c* to *z*.
2. *c* to *x*, *b* to *y*, *a* to *z*.

Flexibility of branch and bound

The procedure for bounding is very flexible—in the example above, for instance, the initial upper bound could have been found by selecting the largest value in each *column* rather than in each row.

Use in Solving Integer Programming Problems

The branch and bound technique can be used to solve integer programming problems. The first step is to solve the problem by linear programming without paying attention to the integer requirements. Then, if the solution is noninteger, a branching procedure is employed. This procedure splits the problem into two subproblems based on two integer values that are immediately above and below the noninteger value.

Example

The Worthy Company is a large manufacturer of household appliances. Recently, its board of directors approved $25 million for constructing additional plants and/or warehouses. The construction of each warehouse will cost $2 million, and management does not want more than eight warehouses. The construction of each plant will cost $4 million, and management does not plan to construct more than five. It is estimated that each warehouse will contribute $31,000 per month to the company's profit, while each plant will contribute $60,000 per month. The problem is to determine the optimal number of plants and warehouses. Because fractions of plants or warehouses cannot be built, the problem is an integer programming one.

Formulation. The problem can be stated as follows (data are in thousands of dollars):

$$\text{maximize } z = 31x_1 + 60x_2$$

subject to:

$$2x_1 + 4x_2 \leq 25$$
$$x_1 \qquad \leq 8$$
$$x_2 \leq 5$$

and both x_1 and x_2 must be nonnegative integers, where:

$$x_1 = \text{Number of warehouses}$$

$$x_2 = \text{Number of plants}$$

Solution

A graphic presentation of the problem is shown in Figure 6.5.

Step 1. The optimal, noninteger solution is:

$$x_1 = 8 \text{ warehouses}$$

$$x_2 = 2.25 \text{ plants}$$

$$z = 383 \text{ (thousand dollars) profit}$$

FIGURE 6.5

The Worthy Company's solution

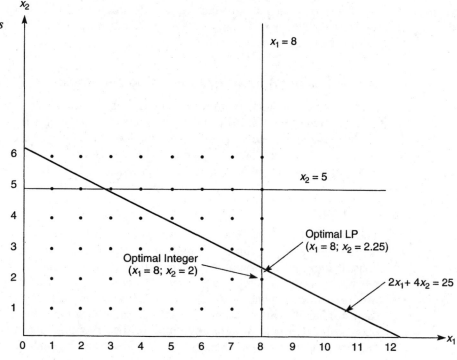

The solution is not acceptable, because x_2 is not an integer. The value of $z = 383$ is set as the initial *upper bound*.

Step 2. The next step is to set a lower bound. The lower bound, in the case of maximization, must be *feasible*. (Remember that the upper bound is usually *not* feasible.) One way to find a feasible solution is to *round* the optimal one, making sure that the constraints are not violated. The rounded solution is: $x_1 = 8$; $x_2 = 2$, $z = 368$. The value $z = 368$ is set as the LB.

Step 3. Compare the UB and LB. If they are equal, stop. This is the optimal solution. Otherwise, go to step four.

Step 4. Branch from the node with the current UB. That is, branch from the noninteger (infeasible) solution. In this case, there is only one noninteger variable (x_2), and therefore we branch from this variable. In general, however, branching is done from the variable farthest from being integral. The branching results in two subproblems. In our case, because $x_2 = 2.25$, the branching results in subproblems with $x_2 \leq 2$ and $x_2 \geq 3$.

The two subproblems created are:

Subproblem A	Subproblem B
maximize $z = 31x_1 + 60x_2$	maximize $z = 31x_1 + 60x_2$
subject to:	subject to:
$2x_1 + 4x_2 \leq 25$	$2x_1 + 4x_2 \leq 25$
$x_1 \leq 8$	$x_1 \leq 8$
$x_2 \leq 5$	$x_2 \leq 5$
$x_2 \leq 5$	$x_2 \leq 5$
$x_2 \geq 3$	$x_2 \leq 2$

Optimal solution for subproblems A and B:

For subproblem A: $x_1 = 6.5$, $x_2 = 3$, and $z = 381.5$

For subproblem B: $x_1 = 8$, $x_2 = 2$, and $z = 368$

This information is shown in Figure 6.6 in tree form. The search of subproblem B is stopped, because it has the all-integer feasible solution $z = 368$, which equals the lower bound established earlier. Subproblem A is searched further, because it has a *noninteger solution* and the value of its objective function is greater than the current lower bound of 368. Thus, it is possible that the optimal integer solution to A will yield a value of z larger than 368. The second *upper bound* is set to 381.5, replacing the initial upper bound of 383.

Next, the solution of subproblem A is branched into two other subproblems: subproblem C, where an additional constraint of $x_1 \leq 6$ is added, and subproblem D, where an additional constraint of $x_1 \geq 7$ is added. The reason for adding these con-

Figure 6.6

*Branch and bound
solution*

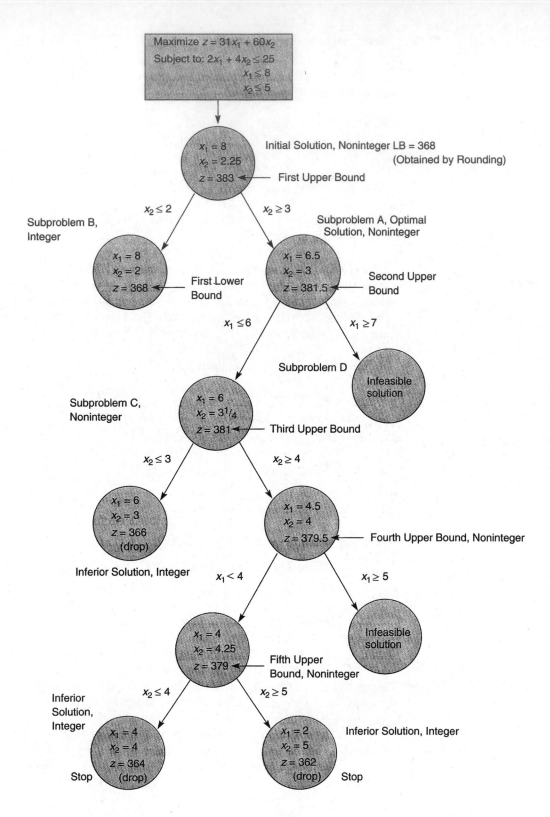

straints is that because $x_1 = 6.5$ is noninteger, then the feasible integer solution *must* be with either $x_1 \le 6$ *or* $x_1 \ge 7$.

Subproblem C	Subproblem D
maximize $z = 31x_1 + 60x_2$	maximize $z = 31x_1 + 60x_2$
subject to:	subject to:
$2x_1 + 4x_2 \le 25$	$2x_1 + 4x_2 \le 25$
$x_1 \le 8$	$x_1 \le 8$
$x_2 \le 5$	$x_2 \le 5$
$x_2 \ge 3$	$x_2 \ge 3$
$x_1 \le 6$	$x_1 \ge 7$

Subproblem D has no feasible solution, because any value for x_1 (only ≥ 7 and ≤ 8 are considered) will violate the constraints $x_2 \ge 3$ or $2x_1 + 4x_2 \le 25$ and, therefore, its solution is not considered. Subproblem C has a noninteger solution with a new third *upper bound* of $z = 381$ (see Figure 6.6). The process is continued until no further branching is possible, or until the new upper bound becomes equal to or smaller than the *lower bound*. In this case, the process stops with integer feasible solutions that are inferior to the lower bound $z = 368$; and, therefore, the optimal solution is:

$$x_1 = 8, \ x_2 = 2, \quad \text{and} \quad z = 368.$$

Notes: (1) In our example, the lower bound was not changed. Usually, the lower bound will change, increasing in value toward the upper limit. (2) If two noninteger solutions (J and K) result from a branching, use the one with the largest z value for the next branching (say, J). If the branching of J results in a noninteger problem with a z value lower than that of K, then it is necessary to branch from problem K as well. (3) Branch and bound can also be used to solve 0–1 integer programming problems. See Problem 13.

Branch and bound can be efficiently coded into a computer routine (e.g., IFPS/Optimum in Chapter 18); it works well in problems containing a few integer-valued variables. However, in problems with large numbers of integer-valued variables and in cases where the noninteger solution is far from optimal, then the number of required iterations may be too large for efficient application. For such cases, a more complicated procedure (e.g., heuristics) is required.

6.7 Nonlinear Programming

A nonlinear programming problem is a mathematical programming problem in which the objective function and/or one or more of the constraints are nonlinear.

Nonlinear Functions

Functional relationships that contain such terms as $2x^3$, $\log 1/x$, and $2e^x$, as well as discontinuous functions, are termed *nonlinear functions*. In general, any functional relation that does not meet linearity conditions (see Appendix A) is considered nonlinear.

Examples of Nonlinear Programming Problems

1. minimize $z = 3x^2 - 2y$ (Nonlinear objective function and linear
   subject to: constraints)
   $$3x + 4y \geq 12$$
   $$x - y \geq 3$$

2. minimize $z = 2xy - \dfrac{2}{x}$ (Nonlinear objective function and nonlinear
   subject to: constraints)
   $$3x^2 + 2y \leq 100$$
   $$x + y^3 \leq 80$$

3. maximize $z = 5x + 7y$ (Linear objective function and nonlinear
   subject to: constraints)
   $$x^2 + 2y^3 \leq 65$$
   $$2x^2 + y \leq 50$$

Note: Nonlinear programs can be even more complex if integer requirements are imposed.

Solution Methods

As opposed to the simplex method, which is a general method for solving LP problems, there is no general method for solving *all* nonlinear programming problems. Instead, various computational techniques, some of which are mathematically complicated, have been developed to solve different categories of nonlinear programs. These special computational methods are limiting factors in the use of nonlinear programming.

In this text, we will not solve any nonlinear programming problems. For methods of solution, see Jeter [1].

Quadratic Programming

Some of the less complicated types of nonlinear problems are those involving **quadratic programming.** These deal with the problem of minimizing a quadratic (second degree) objective function, subject to linear constraints. Examples of quadratic functions are:

$$x_1^2 = 20; \qquad (x_1 - 2)^2 = 0;$$

and

$$x_1^2 + x_2^2 - 2x_1 + x_2 = 42$$

Many practical problems can be formulated as quadratic programs. Fairly efficient solution techniques have been developed for quadratic programming problems but are beyond the scope of this text. See Minoux [4].

6.8 Computer Programs

There are many computer programs for mathematical programming. A representative list is given in Table 6.3. The list includes integer and certain nonlinear programming models. In the area of integer programming, there are programs for mixed-integer, all-integer and zero-one.

Example 1   (Derived with the LINDO [6] software)

The problem (all-integer requirement):
maximize $z = 6x_1 - 2x_2 + 10x_3 + x_4$
subject to:

$$
\begin{aligned}
x_2 + 2x_3 &\leq 5 \\
3x_1 - x_2 + x_3 + x_4 &\leq 10 \\
x_1 + x_3 + x_4 &\leq 8
\end{aligned}
$$

The solution, using the GIN command, is:

```
OPTIMAL SOLUTION = 36.000
VARIABLE          VALUE           REDUCED COST
      X1          3.000                .000
      X2          1.000                .000
      X3          2.000              -8.000
      X4           .000               1.000


    ROW     SLACK OR SURPLUS      DUAL PRICES
     2)             .000               .000
     3)             .000              2.000
     4)            3.000               .000

NO.  ITERATIONS=       7
```

TABLE 6.3   **Representative Programs for Integer and Linear Programming**

IFPS/Optimum:	Comshare, Inc. (LP, integer) Ann Arbor, Mich.
MPI-MP8:	Miscellaneous mathematical programming models. SCI Computing, Wilmette, Ill.
LINDO, LINDO/PC, GINO, VINO:	LINDO Systems, Inc., Chicago, Ill. Student version—The Scientific Press.
MPS III:	Ketron, Inc., Arlington, Va.
OSL, MPSX:	IBM, Armonk, N.Y.
GAMS/MINOS:	Stanford University, Stanford, Calif. Student version—The Scientific Press.
LP 83, MIP83,XA:	Sunset Software, San Marino, Calif.
XPRESS MP:	Data Assoc. Ltd./Math PRO, Washington, D.C
CPLEX:	CPLEX Optimization, Inc., Houston, Tex.
SAS/OR:	SAS Institute, Cary, N.C.

Example 2   (Derived with LINDO [6]; for 0−1 variables):

Min. $x_1 + 3x_2 + 2x_3$
subject to:
$$2.5x_1 \qquad\qquad + 3.1x_3 \geq 2$$
$$.2x_1 + .7x_2 + .4x_3 \geq .5$$

Solution

Using an INTEGER command for all three variables activates a branch and bound algorithm. The optimal solution (found in eight iterations) is:

```
        OBJECTIVE FUNCTION VALUE 3.000
   VARIABLE   VALUE    REDUCED COST

      X1      1.000       1.000
      X2      0.000       3.000
      X3      1.000       2.000


   ROW    SLACK/SURPLUS   DUAL PRICES

   2)        3.6000         0.000
   3)        0.1000         0.000
```

The program provides other information such as: Bound on optimum = 2.257 (value of noninteger solution) and Branches = 3

6.9 Concluding Remarks

Many real-world problems impose integer requirements on the decision variables. For such cases, integer programming must be used. This procedure is less efficient than the regular simplex method and requires innovative approaches for solutions. A special methodology, the branch and bound technique, can be used to solve integer programming problems. Finally, many other complex problems are nonlinear in nature, but their complex solution procedures are beyond the scope of this text.

6.10 Problems

1. Solve by branch and bound:

   maximize $z = 130x_1 + 140x_2 + 80x_3 + 100x_4$
   subject to:
   $$9x_1 + 3x_2 + 6x_3 \qquad\quad \leq 15$$
   $$5x_1 + 6x_2 + 3x_3 + 4x_4 \leq 15$$

   and x_1, x_2, x_3, and x_4 are either 0 or 1.

2. Graphics, Inc., is considering several potential sites for its manufacturing plants. The proposed locations are shown in the table, together with the estimated costs (per unit shipped) to their five existing distribution centers. The supply at each proposed plant is currently considered unlimited, with identical variable manufacturing costs. However, the monthly fixed cost at each plant varies. Find where the plant should be constructed and the monthly shipment to minimize the total cost. Formulate. *Hint:* Use auxiliary variables.

Proposed	Distribution Centers					Monthly Fixed
Locations	A	B	C	D	E	Costs
Chicago	6	8	3	8	5	8,000
Denver	10	4	5	12	8	11,000
Los Angeles	4	8	6	15	9	12,000
Miami	12	8	9	4	7	7,500
New York	11	5	6	8	7	8,900
Monthly demand	100	120	150	80	60	

3. Given:

maximize $z = x_1 + x_2$
subject to:
$$2x_1 + x_2 \leq 5$$
$$x_1 + 2x_2 \leq 5$$
$$x_1, x_2 \text{ integer}$$

a. Solve by complete enumeration.
b. Solve graphically.
c. Solve by rounding the noninteger LP solution.
d. Find the cost of indivisibility.

4. The navy is considering three types of attack aircraft to equip its carriers: a supersonic type, a subsonic type, and a boost glide type. The effectiveness of any air vehicle to the fleet is determined by the expected military value of targets the aircraft can "kill" during military engagements of a certain length. These have been estimated for the three types mentioned as follows:

Type	Expected Value of Target "Killed"
Supersonic	30
Subsonic	24
Boost glide	25

The following numbers of aircraft could be accommodated if the entire deck is allocated to one specific type. In other words, the deck can contain (if full) 60 supersonic, or 120 subsonic, or 160 boost glide, or any linear combination of these types.

Type of Aircraft	Number of Full Deck
Supersonic	60
Subsonic	120
Boost glide	160

Personnel requirements and monthly maintenance costs are as follows:

Type	Personnel Per Aircraft	Maintenance Cost Per Aircraft
Supersonic	15	$5,000
Subsonic	13	3,000
Boost glide	17	6,000

A carrier has facilities for 1,500 personnel, and the navy's monthly maintenance budget for aircraft is $650,000 per carrier.

The problem is to find how many of each of the three types of aircraft should be purchased per carrier in order to maximize the value of the attack capability of a carrier. Formulate as an integer programming problem: Define the decision variables, establish the objective function, and determine the constraint relationships.

5. Canadian Aviation Company organizes summer charter flights from Toronto to London. The company uses three types of aircraft whose operating cost and capacities are shown below.

Type of Aircraft	Passenger Capacity	Cost Per Flight	Maximum Possible Flights	Required Crew
M-1	100	$ 6,000	15	4
M-2	180	8,000	12	12
M-3	270	10,000	6	17

The company can spare a crew of only 140 for the entire mission. Thirty-two hundred students signed up for the summer, each paying $110.

All students *must* be flown. Find how many flights of each type should be used in order to maximize profit. Formulate as a mathematical program.

6. Venezuela-Grand Hospital has recently modernized one of its operating rooms so that it now contains the very latest in a variety of equipment. Only two types of operations are considered. The hospital desires to schedule as many operations as possible in this room, which can handle up to 12 operations of type A, or 30 operations of type B (or any linear combination) per day. Each A-type operation requires 4 pints of blood, and each B-type operation requires 5.5 pints of blood. The hospital has a blood inventory of 100 pints. At least 7 type A operations and no more than 20 type B operations should be performed. Find the best possible schedule.

   a. Set up the problem as an integer linear program.
   b. Solve the problem graphically and show the feasible area.
   c. Comment on the resource utilization in the optimal solution.
   d. Suppose that the value of each operation of type A is three times as important as that of type B. Reformulate, solve the problem, and comment on the result.

7. The Singapore Mower Blade Company wishes to market a deluxe and a regular model lawn mower blade. The deluxe requires 5 units of carbon steel and 8 units of alloy steel per 150 blades, whereas the regular blade requires 10 units of carbon steel and no alloy steel per 150 blades. Due to market conditions (a recent boom), the company is left with only 300 units of carbon steel and 200 units of alloy steel. The deluxe blade also requires 2 hours of grinding time and 1.25 hours of finishing time per 150 blades, whereas the regular needs 1 hour of grinding and .5 hours of finishing. The grinding department states that it has at most 50 hours available in the time period concerned, and the finishing department can contribute 30 hours toward the production of the blades.

   a. How can the firm maximize profit if $2 profit from a deluxe blade and $1.50 from a regular blade is realized? (Solve graphically.)

   b. What is the best production plan if an *integer number of batches* must be produced? (Solve graphically.) *Hint:* Formulate the problem in batches of 150 blades.

8. Flamingo Computing Corporation manufactures two types of small computers, A and B. The company can produce up to seven computers a week. Of its 10 available production teams, 2 are required for the production of each type A computer every week and 3 are required for the production of each type B computer.

   The company profit (in thousands of dollars) for each unit of type A sold is $8 - 2x_1$ (where x_1 is the amount sold of type A) and $5 - x_2$ for each unit of type B. All computers must be completed by the end of each week.

   The problem is to find the most profitable weekly production plan for the company. (Formulate only; do not solve.)

9. Solve Problem 3 by branch and bound.

10. Given an assignment problem: The cost of assigning jobs A, B, and C to machines M, N, O, and P is shown below.

   Find the best assignment. Solve by branch and bound.

Job \ Machine	M	N	O	P
A	6	7	5	9
B	8	5	6	7
C	10	8	5	6

11. In branch and bound:
   a. Discuss the role of the lower bound in minimization problems.
   b. Discuss the role of the upper bound in minimization problems.
   c. At what point can branches be dropped from consideration?
   d. Discuss three ways of bounding the assignment example in Section 6.6. Which is best?

12. Explain why the value of the objective function in a product-mix integer programming problem can never

exceed that of a similar LP problem where there is no integer requirement.

13. Give an example that will illustrate a case where there exists an LP problem that has a *noninteger* optimal solution value of z, and an integer requirement is imposed on the problem. The optimal integer solution also has a value of z, exactly the same as the noninteger solution. That is, the cost of indivisibility is zero. Use a graphical presentation.

14. Hong Kong Importers, Ltd., is looking for potential sites for their warehouses. The expected construction time is two years and the available funds are $50 million the first year and $36 million the second year. The projected costs and returns (all in present values) are shown in the table below for four potential locations. The company wishes to maximize the projected return value. Formulate as an integer program using 0–1 variables.

Site	Projected Cost ($M)		Projected Return (Points Value)
	Year 1	*Year 2*	
A	12	15	100
B	20	31	160
C	17	30	150
D	32	15	155

15. Consider a zero-one model for the R&D or capital budgeting problem. Assume that you have five projects like the ones in Example *a* of Section 6.5. Now assume that there are the *additional constraints* expressed below. Write the equalities (or inequalities) for these constraints:

a. Any two of the first four projects *must* be undertaken.

b. Projects x_1 and x_3 must be taken simultaneously or not taken at all.

c. Project x_1 will be undertaken *only* if x_3 is undertaken but x_3 is *not* conditional on x_1 (i.e., you can have x_3 without x_1, but you cannot have x_1 unless x_3 is undertaken).

16. A U.S. student organization is chartering flights to Europe each summer. For 1995, 2,000 students registered for the flights. The WW Company, which provides the airplanes, has three available types: type I can carry up to 90 students, with a crew of five and

a cost of $8,000 (15 such flights available); type II can carry up to 150 students, with a crew of 9 and cost of $11,000 (10 such flights available); and type III can carry up to 360 students, with a crew of 18 and a cost of $25,000 (only one such flight available). The company can spare 120 crewmen for the entire mission. Find the best schedule for the WW company.

17. Products A, B, and C, are to be made on three machines. Net profit per unit of A, B, and C, respectively, is $21, $26, and $22. Each product is processed by three different machines. Processing time per unit of production and data on machine availability are shown in the table below:

Machine	Product			Machine Availability (Minutes Per Two-Week Scheduling Period)
	A	*B*	*C*	
1	273	221	374	9282
2	273	442	187	9282
3	91	182	159	4732

Assuming no set-up requirements, find the best product mix (that is, what products should be produced and in what quantities) if the production schedule must meet all-integer constraints; that is, no fractions of products can be produced.

a. Formulate.

b. Solve using a computer.

c. Find the opportunity cost of indivisibility with the aid of the dual's optimal variables.

18. Given:

$$\max. z = 2.5x_1 + 2.25x_2 + 0.5x_3$$

subject to:

$$7.5x_1 + 7.9x_2 \leq 75$$

and either

$$2.5x_1 + 3.2x_2 + 7.5x_3 \leq 38.5$$

or

$$1.4x_1 + 5.8x_3 \leq 18$$

a. Formulate the problem as a mixed-integer programming problem. *Hint:* Use IP for the either-or constraint or else solve the LP twice.

b. Solve the problem, using a computer.

19. Given:

$$\max. \; z = 3x_1 + 2x_2$$

subject to:

$$\frac{20}{3}x_1 + 10x_2 \le 100$$
$$10x_1 + 5x_2 \le 100$$

a. Find an all-integer solution graphically.
b. Find an all-integer solution, using a computer.
c. Assuming that either the first or the second constraint holds, set up the problem as an all-integer programming problem. Solve graphically.

20. The Elster Machine Corporation has a department specializing in job-shop orders. One day the foreman received an order for three jobs, the processing times of which (on several available machines with equivalent capabilities) are:

Job	Time (Hours)
A	4
B	6
C	7

Each job is processed through one machine only. Once a job is started on a machine it must be completed. The department can spare only one employee for the order. The employee can handle no more than two machines simultaneously. The foreman's objective is to minimize the total elapsed time required for one production run. Find the best scheduling.
a. Solve by enumeration.
b. Set up as a mixed-integer program, but do not solve.

Assume:
1. No setups are involved.
2. Processing times are constant.
3. The machines work without interruptions.
4. Only one job can be processed on a machine at a time.

21. The research department of ABC is selecting projects for the next two years. Seven proposed projects are to be evaluated. The yearly cost of each product in man-hours required and the data on available man-hours are given in the table below. Also, the expected profits (discounted to time zero) are given. The research department wants to maximize its profits. Find the projects they should select.
a. Set up as a mixed-integer programming problem.
b. Solve (use common sense if you have difficulties in getting results with Gomorian constraints).

Project	Man-Hours Required		Discounted Expected Profits in Thousands of Dollars
	1st Year	2nd Year	
A	1000	4000	120
B	1200	2000	100
C	1800	1600	80
D	2000	2400	140
E	1200	1800	100
F	2600	2000	160
G	2200	2200	140
Available Man-Hours/ Year	10,000	12,000	

22. Four different processes are available for producing a certain paint. The processing cost of each gallon in any of the four available processes, the maximum capacity of each process, and the set-up costs are given in the table below. Assume that a daily demand of 35,000 gallons must be supplied. Find the best processing schedule (minimize total costs). Base your solution on an elasped time of one day.

Process	Set-up Cost, Dollars	Processing Cost, Cents Per Gallon	Maximum Capacity, Gallons
A	500	6	20000
B	600	5	15000
C	1000	4	40000
D	600	3	25000

  a. Formulate the problem as an integer-programming problem.

  b. Which processes should be used, and to what extent, in order to minimize total cost? Solve this part with the aid of a computer.

  c. Find the best and the second-best production schedule by a common-sense approach.

23. The ABC Company is producing three types of canned beef. Type I is packed in half-pound cans, type II is packed in one-pound cans, and type III is packed in three-pounds cans. Net profit from selling each pound of canned beef is 14 cents for type I, 20 cents for type II, and 10 cents for type III. Production is subject to the following constraints:

$$6x_1 + 10x_2 + 3x_3 \le 100 \text{ pounds}$$

$$8x_1 + 10x_2 + 6x_3 \le 120 \text{ pounds}$$

$$4x_1 + 8x_2 + 9x_3 \le 150 \text{ pounds}$$

where x_i is the number of pounds of product i. The objective of the company is profit maximization.

  a. Find the best product mix if the number of cans produced must be integer. (*Hint:* A transformation is advisable.) *Note:* If you do not have a computer program for integer programming, stop after three iterations. Try to enumerate for optimal solution.

  b. Determine the best production plan if the number of cans produced must be integer, and if at least 10 cans and no more than 40 cans of beef type I should be in the program. *Note:* If you do not have a computer program, try to enumerate.

24. Given:

$$\min z = 3x_1 - x_2 + 2x_3$$
subject to:

(1)	$x_1 + x_2 + x_3 \ge 16$	
(2)	$2x_1 + x_2 - x_3 \ge 18$	
(3)	$x_1 + 3x_2 + 5x_3 \ge 24$	
(4)	$x_1 - x_2 + x_3 \ge 10$	

Use integer programming to express the following:

  a. At least three of the constraints must hold.

  b. No more than any two constraints must hold.

  c. No more than any single constraint must hold.

CASE 6.11
HENSLEY VALVE CORP. B

It was Monday morning and the weekly meeting of the Executive Committee was in full swing. There were two primary items on the agenda and both directly affected Hensley's profit margin.

Agenda Item A: The Proposed Tax Increase on Diesel Fuel.

Agenda Item B: Record Interest Rates.

"Gus, as regional manager in our largest selling region, what will be the result of our raising prices to offset this possible increase in our trucking costs?"

"Well J. B., it certainly won't help our sales effort. Valve JBH-1 is only marginally profitable now, but takes twice the time to sell as our more profitable JBH-2s. I'm afraid a price increase might wipe out the viability of our JBH-1 valves altogether."

"That's what I was afraid of, too. Pat, how about the effect of that cancellation of the second NC machine we were hoping would help our productivity? I know you were counting on that to increase our output rate, but with the latest two big jumps in the prime rate we simply can't afford it at this time."

"Yes, I realize that, J. B. I certainly hadn't expected the prime rate to go quite this high. Basically, our output rates will remain limited, especially on old line 3, which produces the JBH-1 and -2 valves. Given the limited floor space and equipment and working three shifts on this line, we can still produce at most 600 JBH-1s or 100 JBH-2s a week, or any combination in between. I wondered if it would be worthwhile to have Tim Moran in our controller's office look at the interacting effect of all these changes? It seems that since so many things are happening at once, it may be best to totally change our product mix as well as our prices."

"I agree, Pat. It seems appropriate to undertake a complete contingency analysis of what we should do given any specific change in the market or combination of changes. I'll work up a memo to Tim this afternoon."

MEMO

TO: Tim Moran, Controller's Assistant
FROM: J. B. Hensley, President
SUBJECT: Reanalysis of Product Line

Please undertake a review of our JBH-1 and -2 valves for the next meeting of the Executive Committee on Monday morning. For this purpose you may assume their profitability to be $10 and $40 each, respectively. We have figured that a JBH-1 takes, on average, 4 hours to sell and a -2 takes 2 hours to sell. Sales has at most 1,000 hours a week available. Check with Pat Johnson for production figures on line 3. Items we would specifically like to know include:

- Given our limited capacities, how many of each valve should we currently be producing and selling to maximize our profits?
- What is an extra hour of sales time worth?
- At what hour sales effort is it not worth producing JBH-1s any longer?
- What is an increase in the capacity of line 3 worth?
- At what JBH-1 profitability will only JBH-1s be worth producing?
- What will be the effect on the solution of improving the JBH-1 marketing effort so it only takes 2.5 hours to sell a unit? What per unit investment is this worth?

Please add any other information you find to be relevant. Thank you.

(Refer to Section 5.12, Hensley Valve Corp. (A.))

Show Tim how to use the branch and bound technique in order to find the all-integer solution.

Glossary

All-integer   An integer programming problem where *all* the decision variables must be whole numbers.

Branch and bound   An intelligent search procedure for optimal or near-optimal solutions.

Branching   Dividing a managerial problem into subproblems.

Complete enumeration   A comparison of *all* possible solution values.

Indivisibility   A requirement that the values of a variable be restricted to whole numbers.

Integer programming   A mathematical programming problem requiring that some or all of the decision variables be whole numbers.

Mixed integer   An integer programming problem where some, but not all, of the decision variables must be whole numbers.

Nonlinear programming   A problem where the objective function and/or one or more constraints are nonlinear.

Quadratic programming   A mathematic programming problem with a quadratic (second degree) objective function and linear constraints.

Zero-one variables   Decision variables that must take a value of either 0 or 1.

References and Bibliography

1. Jeter, M. W. *Mathematical Programming—An Introduction to Optimization*. New York: Dekker, 1986.
2. Loomba, P. and E. Turban. *Applied Programming for Management*. New York: Holt, Rinehart & Winston, 1974.
3. Lotfi, V. and C. C. Pegels. *Decision Support Systems for MS/OR Software*, 2nd ed. Homewood, IL: Irwin, 1992.
4. Minoux, M. *Mathematical Programming*. New York: John Wiley & Sons, 1986.
5. Nemhauser, G. L., and L. A. Wolsey, *Integer and Combinatorial Optimization*. New York: John Wiley & Sons, 1988.
6. Schrage, L. *LINDO User's Manual (release 5.0)*, San Francisco, Scientific Press, 1991.
7. von Randow, R. (ed.) *Integer Programming and Related Areas*. Berlin: Springer-Verlag, 1990.
8. Walukiewicz, S. *Integer Programming*. New York: Kluwer Academic, 1991.

Part A: Basics

Part B: Extensions

Distribution problems are a special type of linear programming problem. Due to their special structure, these problems can be solved by special computational procedures in an efficient manner. There are two main types of distribution problems: the transportation problem and the assignment problem. The transportation problem deals with shipments from a number of sources to a number of destinations. Typically, each source is supply limited, each destination has a known demand, and the shipping costs between sources and destinations are given. The object is to find the cheapest shipping schedule that satisfies demand without violating supply constraints.

The assignment problem deals with finding the best one-to-one match for each of a given number of "candidates" to a number of "positions." Typical situations include assigning workers to machines, teachers to classes, and so on. Different benefits or costs are involved in each match, and the goal is to maximize the total reward or minimize the total cost.

Due to their special structure, these problems can be solved by special computational procedures in an efficient manner.

PART A: BASICS

Bill Grout, Tuff's operations manager, knew he would have to face this problem sooner or later. Finally, here it was on his desk. Tuff Cement Company had opened a new warehouse in New York to serve the fast-growing demand for cement in that region. Management now wondered which plants should supply it and to what extent. As manager of operations, Bill was responsible for making those decisions. Although the problem did not look complicated, he was having trouble matching demand to supply. The situation was as follows:

Tuff Cement Company has two processing plants, one in Allentown, Pennsylvania (A), with a supply capacity of 100 tons per day, and one in Baltimore, Maryland (B), with a supply capacity of 110 tons a day. Tuff now has three warehouses: R in Easton, Pennsylvania, S in Philadelphia, and the newly added T on Long Island in New York. The warehouses need, if possible, 80, 120, and 60 tons of cement each day, respectively, to meet their distribution demands.

The shipping costs from each plant to each warehouse are given below:

From	To	Cost Per Ton
A (Allentown)	R (Easton)	1
A (Allentown)	S (Philadelphia)	2
A (Allentown)	T (New York)	3
B (Baltimore)	R (Easton)	4
B (Baltimore)	S (Philadelphia)	1
B (Baltimore)	T (New York)	5

Tuff's distribution scheme is shown in Figure 7.1.

Bill's problem is to plan the shipments at the least possible cost. The managerial tool that will assure him of a least-cost solution is called the *transportation* model.

7.1 The Transportation Problem—Characteristics and Assumptions

Transportation—a special type of distribution problem

Tuff's transportation situation is typical of a class of distribution problems that exhibit the following characteristics:

1. *The supply.* A *limited quantity* of items, such as cement or oil, is available at certain **sources** (or origins), such as factories or refineries.
2. *The demand.* There is a demand for the items at several **destinations** such as warehouses, distribution centers, or stores.
3. *The quantities.* The quantities of *supply* at each source and the demand or *requirements* at each destination are known.

FIGURE 7.1

Tuff's distribution problem

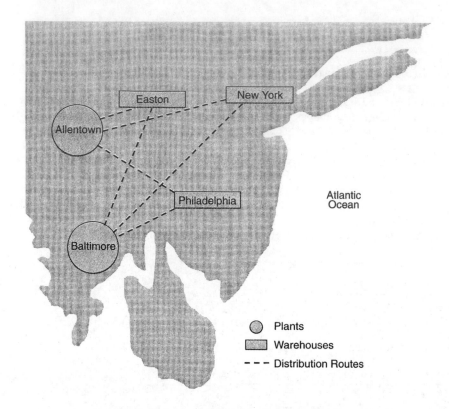

Find the best shipment plan

4. *The shipping cost.* The per unit costs of transporting the commodity from each source to each destination are assumed to be known. Usually, they are based on the distance between the two points or they are negotiated. Moving companies and the post office are examples of users of a similar cost system in their deliveries.

5. *It is assumed* that no shipments are allowed between sources or between destinations. Allowing such transshipments would require special adjustments in the model. (See Section 7.9).

6. *All supply and demand* quantities are given in whole numbers (integers).

7. *The problem* is to determine how many units should be shipped from each source to each destination (i.e., what routes to use and in what capacity) so that all demands are satisfied (if possible) at the minimum total shipping cost.

Presentation in a Tabular Form

Transportation problems are presented in tabular form because it is a convenient form for applying special solution procedures. Table 7.1 shows Tuff's distribution problem.

TABLE 7.1   Tabular Presentation of Tuff's Problem

From plant \ To warehouse	Easton R	Philadelphia S	New York T	Supply
Allentown (A)	[1] x_{AR}	$c_{AS} = 2$ x_{AS}	[3] x_{AT}	$b_A = 100$
Baltimore (B)	[4] x_{BR}	[1] x_{BS}	[5] X_{BT}	$b_B = 110$
Demand	$d_R = 80$	$d_S = 120$	$d_T = 60$	210 ← *Total supply*
			260	

Total demand

Explanation of the Table

Using a tabular form

Left side.   The sources of supply (plants) are listed on the left. Each source is represented by a row.

Top.   The destination points (warehouses) are listed at the top. Each destination is represented by a column.

Right side.   The column designates the capacity (supply) at the sources.

Bottom.   The requirements (demand) of each destination are listed here.

Center.   The center of the table is composed of cells. In this case, there are six. Each is designated by the letter of its row and column; for example, cell AS is in row A and column S. The corresponding shipping costs (per ton) are in the upper right-hand corner of each cell. For example, the shipping cost from plant A to warehouse S is 2. In each cell, there is also a decision variable. For example, in cell AR the variable is x_{AR}. This variable designates the quantity to be shipped from plant A to warehouse R.

Presentation as a Linear Program

Formulation as an LP

Any transportation problem can be presented in the form of a linear programming problem. As such, it includes an objective function and constraints.

The Objective Function
The objective function calls for minimization of the total shipping cost, which is computed by multiplying the quantity shipped from each source i to each destination j (labeled x_{ij}), by its per unit shipping cost, c_{ij}, and totaling the results.

For example, using the data of Table 7.1, the objective function can be written as:

$$\text{minimize } z = 1x_{AR} + 2x_{AS} + 3x_{AT} + 4x_{BR} + 1x_{BS} + 5x_{BT}$$

In general, the objective function can be written as:

$$\text{minimize } z = c_{11}x_{11} + c_{12}x_{12} + \cdots + c_{21}x_{21} + c_{22}x_{22} + \cdots + c_{mn}x_{mn} \qquad (7.1)$$

where:

$$m = \text{Number of sources}$$

$$n = \text{Number of destinations}$$

The Supply and Demand Constraints

We consider three possible problem situations involving the supply and demand constraints: Either the total supply is less than, the same as, or more than the total demand.

a. *Total supply < total demand:* In this case (Table 7.1), all the supply (b_i) will be shipped from all points i, but not all demand (d_j) will be satisfied for all destinations j. Such a situation can be expressed as:

$$x_{i1} + x_{i2} + \cdots + x_{in} = b_i \qquad \text{for each supply point } i \qquad (7.2)$$

$$x_{1j} + x_{2j} + \cdots + x_{mj} \le d_j \qquad \text{for each demand point } j \qquad (7.3)$$

In our example, this results in:

$$\left. \begin{array}{l} x_{AR} + x_{AS} + x_{AT} = 100 \\ x_{BR} + x_{BS} + x_{BT} = 110 \end{array} \right\} \text{ supply constraints}$$

$$\left. \begin{array}{l} x_{AR} + x_{BR} \qquad \le \ \ 80 \\ x_{AS} + x_{BS} \qquad \le 120 \\ x_{AT} + x_{BT} \qquad \le \ \ 60 \end{array} \right\} \text{ demand constraints}$$

b. *Total supply = Total demand:* In this situation, all the constraints are equalities (=).

c. *Total supply > Total demand:* In this case, the demand constraints are equalities and the supply constraints are of the $\le$ form (i.e., there will be an excess supply in the optimal solution).

Notes:

1. Although all transportation problems can be represented as LP problems, it is not efficient in most cases to do so. Special solution methods can do the job much better. Almost any medium or large transportation problem becomes a huge LP model with many variables and constraints.

Inefficient solution
with LP

2. Most transportation problems are really integer problems, but they can be solved by LP because the theory guarantees optimal integer solutions if supply and demand are all integer-valued.

Solving the Transportation Model

Many, many solutions

A transportation problem has a very large, sometimes infinite, number of feasible solutions. For example, consider the simple problem given in Table 7.2. Five feasible solutions are shown in Table 7.3. There are many others.

Several solution approaches

Solution Method: Complete Enumeration

One approach is to generate solutions, as was done in Table 7.3, and then find and compare the total cost of each solution. But even if only nonfractional solutions are considered, there may still exist a large number of them. Therefore, this method could be cumbersome and time-consuming.

TABLE 7.2   An Example Problem

Source \ Destination	1	2	Supply
A	6	8	60
B	10	7	70
Demand	80	50	130 / 130

TABLE 7.3   Feasible Solutions to Table 7.2

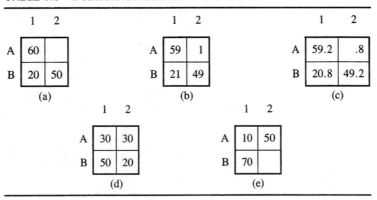

	1	2
A	60	
B	20	50

(a)

	1	2
A	59	1
B	21	49

(b)

	1	2
A	59.2	.8
B	20.8	49.2

(c)

	1	2
A	30	30
B	50	20

(d)

	1	2
A	10	50
B	70	

(e)

Solution Method: Linear Programming

Because the transportation problem is indeed an LP problem, it can be solved as such. However, presentation of a large transportation problem in an LP format results in considerable computational effort, significantly more than the special transportation method. For example, if we have 50 sources and 30 destinations, we will have $50 \times 30 = 1,500$ decision variables and $50 + 30 = 80$ constraints.

Solution Method: Transportation Method

The transportation method provides a computationally efficient procedure for solving large transportation problems. Section 7.2 presents this method.

7.2 The Transportation Method

A five-step procedure

The transportation method is a search and evaluation algorithm, similar to that of the simplex method in LP. The process involves the following five steps, as shown in Figure 7.2

Step 1. Arrange the Data in Tabular Form

The transportation problem must first be arranged in tabular form. An example of such an arrangement for Tuff's problem was given in Table 7.1 with an explanation.

Step 2. Balance the Table

Balance—a must

The use of the transportation solution technique requires that the problem be **balanced;** that is, the *total supply* must equal the *total demand*. If the table is not balanced, this must first be done. Two causes of imbalance are excess supply and excess demand.

    1. Excess supply. Table 7.4 shows an example of an unbalanced table, where the total supply of 300 exceeds the total demand of 260. In this case, there will be 40 unshipped units. Such a table is balanced by adding an artificial destination column to "absorb" the excess supply (sometimes labeled a "dummy" destination). The amount in this **dummy column** equals the excess supply, as shown in Table 7.5. x_{AD} is the excess supply at source A and x_{BD} is the excess supply at source B. The cost of "shipments" to the dummy is usually set at zero, as an unreal shipment implies no real cost. However, in some cases, no shipment may still incur a cost, such as with idled production. In this case, a penalty cost should be entered.

Adding a dummy destination

    2. Excess demand. When the total demand exceeds the total supply, as in Tuff's problem (see Table 7.6), a **dummy** source **row** is added to "meet" the extra demand (50, in this case). Again, the per unit shipping costs for the dummy row are set to zero. The results are shown in Table 7.7.

Adding a dummy source

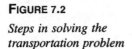

FIGURE 7.2

Steps in solving the transportation problem

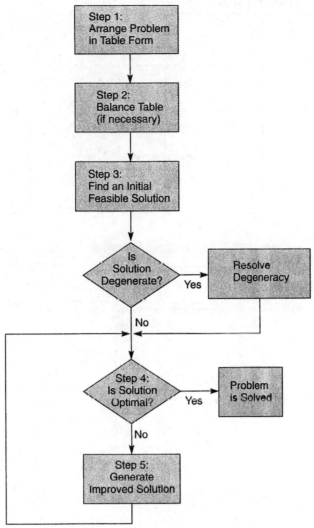

TABLE 7.4   Unbalanced Table (Excess Supply)

Source \ Destination	R	S	T	Supply
A	1	2	3	200
B	4	1	5	100
Demand	80	120	60	300 / 260

TABLE 7.5   Table 7.4 Balanced

Source \ Destination	R	S	T	D (Dummy)	Supply
A	1	2	3	0 x_{AD}	200
B	4	1	5	0 x_{BD}	100
Demand	80	120	60	40 (excess supply)	300 / 300

TABLE 7.6   Unbalanced Table (Excess Demand)

Source \ Destination	R	S	T	Supply
A	1	2	3	100
B	4	1	5	110
Demand	80	120	60	210 / 260

TABLE 7.7   Table 7.6 Balanced

Source \ Destination	R	S	T	Supply
A	1	2	3	100
B	4	1	5	110
D (dummy)	0	0	0	50 (excess demand)
Demand	80	120	60	260 / 260

Step 3. The Initial Feasible Solution

An initial feasible solution is needed to initiate the solution procedure. It can be found by any of several available procedures. Two of these are demonstrated in this text. A third method that gives an efficient initial solution is the Vogel approximation method (VAM). For details, see the references and bibliography.

Northwest Corner Rule

1. Initial Assignment by the Northwest Corner Rule

> *a.* Starting with the northwest corner (left, uppermost in the table), allocate the *smaller amount* of either the row supply or the column demand.
>
> *b.* Subtract from the row supply *and* from the column demand the amount allocated.
>
> *c.* If the column demand is now zero, move to the cell next on the right; if the row supply is zero, move down to the cell in the next row. If both are zero, move first to the next cell on the right, then down one cell.
>
> *d.* Once a cell is identified as per step (*c*), it becomes a northwest cell. Allocate to it an amount as per step (*a*).
>
> *e.* Repeat the above steps (*a*)–(*d*) until all the remaining supply and demand is gone.

Purely mechanical

The advantage of this rule is that it is a simple mechanical process. The problem presented in Table 7.1 is balanced in Table 7.8 and serves as an example to illustrate an assignment by the Northwest Corner Rule.

TABLE 7.8 Initial Solution by the Northwest Corner Rule

Source \ Destination	R	S	T	Supply	Remaining Supply
A	[1] 80	[2] 20	[3]	100	~~20~~ 0
B	[4]	[1] 100	[5] 10	110	~~10~~ 0
D (dummy)	[0]	[0]	[0] 50	50	0
Demand	80	120	60	260 / 260	
Remaining demand	0	~~100~~ 0	~~50~~ 0		

Initially, an amount of 80 tons is allocated to cell AR, out of the 100 available in source A, meeting all the demand of destination R. The remaining supply of 20 tons at source A is then allocated to cell AS. The capacity of row A has now been exhausted, but the demand of S has not yet been fully satisfied. Therefore, 100 tons of the 110-ton supply of source B is allocated to cell BS, in order to meet the entire demand of destination S. Then, moving to the right in row B, the remaining supply of B (10 tons) is allocated to cell BT. This exhausts the supply in row B, but the destination T still needs 50 units. Moving down column T, the remainder (50 tons) is allocated to cell DT. In this fashion, the entire supply has been used and the entire demand has been satisfied. Cells that receive allocations are called *occupied* cells, to distinguish them from the remaining empty or unoccupied ones.

Compute total cost

The initial solution shown in Table 7.8 calls for shipments of:

80 tons from A to R at a cost of 80 × 1 =	$ 80
20 tons from A to S at a cost of 20 × 2 =	40
200 tons from B to S at a cost of 100 × 1 =	100
10 tons from B to T at a cost of 10 × 5 =	50
50 tons from D to T at no cost =	0
Total cost...	$270

The total cost is easily computed ($270). Note that warehouse T supposedly obtains 50 tons from D (dummy); that is, there is a shortage (unsatisfied demand) of 50 tons at warehouse T.

Good initial solutions by least-cost

2. The Least-Cost (Largest Profit) Method

The least-cost method yields not only an initial feasible solution but also one that is close to optimal in small problems. The method is "heuristic" in nature. To illustrate the method, another example using cost data, is shown in Table 7.9.

Solution

The least-cost method prescribes that the first allocation be made to the cell with the lowest cost (the highest profit in a maximization case). (*Note:* If a dummy is added, start with one of the dummy cells with a cost of zero.) In this example, there is an additional consideration, because cells AD and CE both have the lowest cost of $1. Cell AD is selected first because more units can be allocated to it (70) than to cell CE (50). Thus, an allocation of 70 is made to cell AD. As a result, the supply of A is reduced to 30 and the demand at D is completely satisfied.

Assign to low-cost cells first.

Next, an allocation of 50 (maximum possible) is made to cell CE, reducing the supply of C to 70. The process continues in this fashion, seeking the unoccupied cell with the lowest cost. The next search yields BF and CF, which each have a cost of $2. (BE is not considered because E is satisfied already.) Cell CF is filled in first, since a larger quantity (120 − 50 = 70) can be placed there. Then, the remaining requirement of 30 for column F is allocated to cell BF and source B's supply is reduced to 30.

TABLE 7.9 Initial Solution by the Least-Cost Method

Source \ Destination	D	E	F	G	Supply
A	[1] 70	[5]	[3]	[4] 30	100
B	[4]	[2]	[2] 30	[5] 30	60
C	[3]	[1] 50	[2] 70	[4]	120
Demand	70	50	100	60	280 / 280

Next, an allocation is made to cells with a cost of $4, because assignment to the cells with a cost of $3 is not possible under the supply and demand constraints. The only cell with a cost of $4 to which an assignment can be made is AG. The maximum possible quantity of 30 is assigned there. Finally, the remaining demand (30 in column G) is assigned to BG to complete the initial feasible solution.

Once an initial feasible solution is achieved (by any method), a test for optimality is conducted.

Step 4. Testing for Optimality

The purpose of the optimality test is to see if the proposed solution just generated can be improved or not.

"Basic" variables in the occupied cells

The procedure for testing optimality is analogous to that of the simplex method. A distinction is made between *basic* variables, those associated with the occupied cells, and *nonbasic* variables, those associated with the empty cells. For each empty cell, the effect of changing it to an occupied cell is examined. If any of these changes are favorable, the solution is not optimal and a new solution must be designed. (A favorable change means an increase in the value of the objective function in maximization problems or a decrease in minimization problems.)

Two procedures for calculating the effect of such a change are:

1. Stepping-stone (discussed next).
2. Modified distribution (MODI—discussed in Part B).

Degeneracy

Note: In both procedures, the solution to be checked for optimality must be nondegenerate; that is:

> the number of occupied cells must be $m + n - 1$

where m = number of sources and n = number of destinations. The reason for this and a method to handle degeneracy are given in Section 7.8.

The Stepping-Stone Procedure

Example (Tuff's Problem)

Table 7.10 presents the initial (Northwest Corner) solution to Tuff's problem.

The **stepping-stone procedure** executes the final *two steps* of the transportation method.

Step 4: Testing for Optimality.   This is done by calculating the **cell evaluators** for all the empty cells.

Step 5: Improving a Nonoptimal Solution.

1. Identifying the incoming cell.
2. Designing an improved solution.

TABLE 7.10   Table 7.8 Reproduced

Source \ Destination	R	S	T	Supply
A	1 80	2 20	3	100
B	4	1 100	5 10	110
D (dummy)	0	0	0 50	50
Demand	80	120	60	260 / 260

Finding the cell
evaluator from a
closed loop

Details of Step 4: Start with Building a Path that Forms a Closed Loop. A cell evaluator for an empty cell is a number designating the cost change that results from occupying that cell (that is, shipping one unit through it) rather than one of the currently occupied cells. In order to occupy an empty cell, a transfer has to be made from a currently occupied cell. Such a transfer, subject to the supply and demand constraints, will affect an even number of four or more cells. The evaluator is calculated by determining the overall effect on the total cost of shifting *one unit* to that empty cell. The signs of the cell evaluators enable us to test for optimality.

In Table 7.11, a demonstration is given of how to calculate the cell evaluator for the empty cell AT. One unit is moved from the occupied cell AS to AT (follow the top double arrow). Cell AT is called the *gaining cell* and a "+" sign is placed there; cell AS is labeled the *losing cell* and a "−" sign is placed there. However, because one unit is moved to cell AT, column T will now have $1 + 10 + 50 = 61$, which is more than the 60 required. Therefore, in order to maintain the demand requirement, one unit is moved from the occupied cell, BT, to occupied cell BS (follow bottom double arrow). The new number of units in each cell is now circled.

As a result of this transaction, the row supply requirements are maintained:

$$\text{For row A: } 80 + 19 + 1 = 100$$

$$\text{For row B: } 101 + ⑨ \quad = 110$$

and so are the column demands:

$$\text{For column S: } ⑲ + ⑩⑴ \quad = 120$$

$$\text{For column T: } ① + \quad ⑨ + 50 = 60$$

TABLE 7.11   Evaluation of Cell AT

Source \ Destination	R	S	T	Supply
A	80 [1]	⑲ [2] 2̶0̶ −	① [3] ⇒ + Start	100
B	[4]	⑩⑴ [1] 1̶0̶0̶ +	⑨ [5] ↓ 1̶0̶ −	110
D (dummy)	[0]	[0]	[0] 50	50
Demand	80	120	60	260 / 260

The entire movement process is indicated by a **closed loop** of arrows. Such a closed loop will involve an even number of at least four, and sometimes more, cells. *Note:* The direction of all arrows can be reversed by moving the first unit from BT to AT.

Stepping over cells

> **Rule for Drawing Each Closed Loop**
>
> When tracing a closed loop, start with the empty cell to be evaluated and, going clockwise, draw an arrow from it to an *occupied cell* in the same row (or column). Next, move vertically or horizontally (but never diagonally) to another *occupied* cell, "stepping over" unoccupied or occupied cells (if necessary) without changing them. Follow the same procedure to other occupied cells until returning to the original empty cell.
>
> At each turn of the loop (the loop may cross over itself at times), plus and minus signs are alternately placed in the cells, starting with a + sign in the empty cell. One further important restriction is that there must be exactly one cell with a + sign and exactly one cell with a − sign in any row or column in which the loop turns. This restriction is imposed to ensure that the requirements of supply and demand will not be violated when the units are shifted. Note that an even number of at least four cells must participate in a loop and the occupied cells can be visited once and only once. Also, in a nondegenerate problem, there is only one possible way of drawing the loop for each empty cell. Finally, remember that all cells that receive a + or −, except the first one, must be occupied.

Cell evaluator

Evaluation of Cell AT.   Let us calculate the cost effect of the changes arising from the decision to ship one unit to the empty cell AT. In cells AT and BS, one unit is added, so the additional cost is $3 + 1 = 4$. In cells BT and AS, one unit is deleted, and the cost is reduced by $5 + 2 = 7$. Thus, by executing this exchange, we simultaneously *increase* the total cost by 4 and *reduce* the total cost by 7; that is, we alter the total cost by $4 - 7 = -3$.

This value of -3 is then the *cell evaluator* of cell AT. The minus sign indicates a *possible cost reduction;* that is, the solution tested is improvable and therefore not optimal. At this stage we can either improve the solution or else continue to evaluate unoccupied cells. The latter is done in large problems because it results in the most gain for each improvement iteration, and thus, possibly fewer iterations.

Finding the Value of the Cell Evaluators for the Unoccupied Cells

Evaluation of Cell DR (Involving Six Cells).   In Table 7.12, the test is applied to cell DR. This time, six cells participate in the evaluation.

TABLE 7.12 Evaluation of Cell DR

Source \ *Destination*	R	S	T	Supply
A	[1] ~~80~~ (79) −	[2] + ~~20~~ (21)	[3]	100
B	[4]	[1] (99) − ~~100~~	[5] (11) + ~~10~~	110
D (dummy)	[0] (1) + Start	[0]	[0] − ~~50~~ (49)	50
Demand	80	120	60	260 / 260

A move of one unit to DR will result in the addition of one unit to AS and BT and the deletion of one unit each from AR, BS, and DT. The total cost impact of this closed loop is:

Gaining (+) Cells	*Added Cost*	*Losing (−) Cells*	*Saved Cost*
DR	0	AR	1
AS	2	BS	1
BT	5	DT	0
Total	7	Total	2

Thus, such a move will add to the value of the objective function a cost of 7 (from the gaining cells) and subtract a cost of 2 (from the losing cells). The value of the cell evaluator DR is hence $7 - 2 = +5$. The plus sign indicates that a transfer to this cell increases cost and is *not* favorable because it will *increase* the value of the objective function by 5.

Another way to interpret this situation is: A gaining cell (cell with a + sign) means an *increase* in the value of the objective function and a losing cell (− sign) means a *decrease*. Because the total increase (7) is larger than the total decrease (2), the value of the objective function will *increase* by $7 - 2 = 5$, an undesirable case in *minimization*.

Cost Analysis.   By drawing these closed loops, *all* the empty cells of Table 7.12 can be evaluated. The results (details not shown) are:

Empty Cell	Cell Evaluator
AT	−3
BR	+4
DR	+5
DS	+4

Test of Optimality

Once the cell evaluators for *all* the empty cells have beem computed, their signs are examined.

Quality Test

If one or more of the cell evaluators is negative (positive) in a minimization (maximization) problem, the existing solution is not optimal. *Note:* A cell evaluator of 0 indicates the existence of another solution just as good as the current solution. Thus, in the final solution, if cell evaluators of 0 exist, this indicates the existence of multiple optimal solutions.

A minus evaluator means a possible cost reduction

The logic for this test is that an empty cell with a negative cell evaluator will reduce the total cost if it becomes occupied. In the example just presented, cell AT has a negative evaluator. Thus, the initial solution of Table 7.8 is *not optimal*.

Step. 5 Improving a Nonoptimal Solution

The operations in this step are:

1. *Identify the "incoming" cell (the empty cell to be occupied).* In a minimization case, the incoming cell is located by identifying the *most negative* cell evaluator. (If two or more cells have the same value, then either may be selected.) In the example, the incoming cell is AT (because only this cell has a negative evaluator).

Shifting units from cell to cell

2. *Design an improved solution.* Once the incoming cell has been identified, an improvement is made by shifting *as many units as possible* (along the closed loop) into that empty cell. The quantity limit to this shifting process is reached when one of the "losing" cells becomes empty. If two or more of the "losing" cells contain the same number of units, both will become empty simultaneously and a "degenerate" solution will result (see discussion in Part B

of this chapter). In our case, of the two "losing" cells in Table 7.11, AS and BT, cell BT becomes empty first, when 10 units are shifted around the closed loop (10 from BT to BS, 10 from AS to AT).

Shift as many units as possible

Rule for Shifting Units

In general, compare the number of units among all losing cells (−) in the loop of the most improvable empty cell (AT in our case). Select the *smallest* number (10 in this case). Add this number to all cells with a + sign and subtract it from all cells with a − sign. The result here is given in Table 7.13.

Once an improved solution is generated, the optimality test (step 4) is repeated.

Optimality Test

The evaluators of all the empty cells are again computed for the improved solution of Table 7.13. The results (details not shown) are:

Empty Cell	Cell Evaluator
BR	+4
BT	+3
DR	+2
DS	+1

TABLE 7.13 Improved Solution

Source \ Destination	R	S	T	Supply
A	80 `[1]`	− `[2]` 20 − 10 = 10	+ `[3]` 0 + 10 = 10	100
B	`[4]`	+ `[1]` 100 + 10 = 110	− `[5]` 10 − 10 = 0	110
D (dummy)	`[0]`	`[0]`	`[0]` 50	50
Demand	80	120	60	260 / 260

Because *all* the empty cells have nonnegative cell evaluators, an optimal solution has been obtained. This optimal solution calls for a shipment of:

80 units from A to R at a cost of $1 per ton, total	$ 80
10 units from A to S at a cost of $2 per ton, total	20
10 units from A to T at a cost of $3 per ton, total	30
110 units from B to S at a cost of $3 per ton, total	110
50 units from dummy to T at no cost	0
Total cost	$240

The total cost

This, compared with the original solution, represents a reduction in cost of $30. Notice that the demand requirements of destination T have, in reality, not been completely satisfied, because 50 units are shipped to T out of the dummy source D.

The stepping-stone method is efficient for small-sized transportation problems. For larger problems, however, the MODI method is recommended (see Part B).

MODI for large problems

Summary of the Stepping-Stone Method

1. Compute the cell evaluators for all empty cells. This is done by subtracting the total cost of the losing cells from that of the gaining cells in the closed loop.

2. If *all* cell evaluators are nonnegative (in a minimization case), then the solution is optimal. Otherwise, an improvement (or alternate solution in the case of 0 evaluators) is possible.

3. Generating an improved solution involves identifying the incoming cell and transferring *as much as possible* to it. Once this has been done, a new solution is generated by adjusting the quantities in all losing and gaining cells along the loop.

4. The improved solution is then tested. If it is not optimal, another improvement is made. Eventually, an optimal solution (if one exists) will be reached.

The Maximization Case

If a transportation problem involves maximization, the same method can be used. The only difference is the test of optimality. A *positive* cell evaluator points to an improvement. An optimal solution will show no positive cell evaluators.

Positive cell evaluator

Some Notes on Transportation Problems

Prohibited or Impossible Transportation Routes

There are cases where shipments from a certain source to a certain destination are not possible, due to a physical or legal obstacle. In this case, the appropriate cell may either be completely crossed out or a *very large* per-unit transportation cost assigned to it (M). (In maximization problems, assign $-M$).

Multiple Optimal Solutions

A solution to a transportation problem can be either *unique* or multiple. These situations are indicated when the value of one of the cell evaluators is zero. An example of a multiple optimal solution (minimization) is given below.

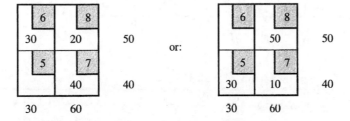

"Capacited" Transportation Problems

In some cases, there are upper capacity limits on the amounts that can be shipped by a certain route. In other cases, a minimum amount must be shipped from some source to some destination. In these situations, the problem should be transformed into a regular LP problem and the additional requirements added as constraints.

7.3 Applications

The commonality of transportation-type problems

Several production planning problems, routing problems, and scheduling problems can be formulated as transportation problems, thus increasing the applicability of the model.

Example 1: Production Scheduling

Three garment plants are available for monthly production of four styles of men's shirts. The capacities of the three plants are 45,000, 93,000, and 60,000 shirts. The number of shirts required in styles *a* through *d* are 28,000, 65,000, 35,000, and 70,000, respectively. The profits, in dollars per shirt, at each plant for each style, are shown in Table 7.14. Find how many shirts of each type to produce in each plant so that profit is maximized.

Formulation as a Transportation Problem

Let the plants be considered as "sources" and the styles as "destinations." The capacities of the plants are the supply, and the required number of shirts of each style are the demand. The transportation table that describes the production scheduling problem is shown in Table 7.15. Note that this is a *maximization* problem.

TABLE 7.14   The Garment Plants' Profits

Plant \ Style	a	b	c	d
1	8	12	−2	6
2	13	4	3	10
3	0	7	11	8

TABLE 7.15   Formulation of Table 7.14

Plant \ Style	a	b	c	d	Supply
1	8	12	−2	6	45,000
2	13	4	3	10	93,000
3	0	7	11	8	60,000
Requirements	28,000	65,000	35,000	70,000	198,000 / 198,000

Solution

Solving by the stepping-stone method, the results are:

Plant 1	manufactures 45,000 of style *b*
Plant 2	manufactures 28,000 of style *a* and 65,000 of style *d*
Plant 3	manufactures 20,000 of style *b*, 35,000 of style *c*, and 5,000 of style *a*
Total profit	$2,119,000

Example 2: International Trade

Three countries—the United States, Russia, and Korea—all both consume and grow rice, soybeans, and corn. It is known how much labor is needed to produce 1 ton of each crop per acre in each country. The problem is to find the best domestic planting and import program for each country that satisfies all demands.

TABLE 7.16   International Trade

Country / Crop	U.S.	Russia	Korea	Demand (millions of Acres)
Rice	8	13	9	92
Soybeans	7	11	9	28
Corn	6	12	8	30
Acres available (millions)	90	12	48	150 / 150

The data are shown in Table 7.16, where numbers in the upper right-hand boxes are the labor cost per acre. Each x_{ij} in the final solution will give the amount of crop i to be raised by country j so as to gain the greatest "comparative advantage" with respect to labor (tariffs and transportation costs are not considered). This is a minimization problem, of course.

Solution
The United States should grow 44 million acres of rice, 16 of soybeans, and 30 of corn. Russia should grow 12 million acres of soybeans, and Korea should grow 48 million acres of rice. The total labor cost of all three countries is $1,208 (million).

Example 3: Multiperiod Production Scheduling

The transportation method can be applied to certain multiperiod problems. As an example, consider a production situation (Table 7.17) where we are dealing with a single plant and a single commodity, but different methods of producing the commodity and different periods of demand. The objective is to minimize the costs of monthly production plus storage, subject to the constraints of meeting monthly sales demands, capacity limitations, and desired initial and ending inventory levels.

The "sources" are the different production methods in the various periods and include regular time production, overtime production, and subcontracting. Constraints on production capacity may also be included but the problem then may require a regular LP formulation. The "destinations" are the different monthly demands, where September represents the required ending August inventory. A dummy column ("Unused")

TABLE 7.17   **Multiperiod Scheduling**

		June	July	August	(September)	Unused	Available
Beginning Inventory		0	2	4	6	0	200
June	Regular time	50	52	54	56	0	500
	Overtime	60	62	64	66	0	100
	Subcontract	65	67	69	71	0	300
July	Regular time	55	50	52	54	0	500
	Overtime	65	60	62	64	0	100
	Subcontract	70	65	67	69	0	300
August	Regular time*	60	55	50	52	0	250
	Overtime*	70	65	60	62	0	50
	Subcontract	75	70	65	67	0	300
Demand		1,000	700	500	150	250	2600 / 2600

*Two-week vacation in August.

picks up any slack in the "Available" production capacity of the sources (far right column).

The cost of using each supply source for each of the month's sales is shown in the appropriate cell. Note that backordering is possible (e.g., July production for June), but at a cost of $5 extra per unit per month. Holding inventory is also possible for future months, but with a carrying charge of $2 per unit per month. The solution to the example is assigned as a problem.

Solved Problem 7.1

Florida Electric and Light operates three power plants in Florida. These plants, A, B, and C, are shown on the map. Electricity cost, per kilowatt-hour, is $.03 at plant A, $.05 at plant B, and $.04 at plant C. Electricity is transmitted to five transforming stations (one each in the company's five regions) at an average cost of $.01 per kilowatt-hour. The demand at each transforming station (1–5) is marked on the map. The arrows on the maps show existing electrical cables. Finally, plant A is capable of generating 500 kilowatts, plant B is capable of generating 650 kilowatts, and plant C is capable of generating 360 kilowatts.

Find the transmission plan (from plants to transforming stations) that will minimize the cost of electricity.

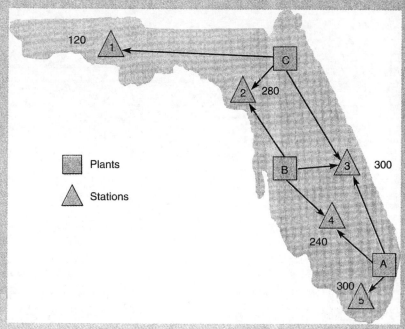

Formulation

The information can be arranged as a transportation table. The data in the cells involves the sum of the production plus transportation costs.

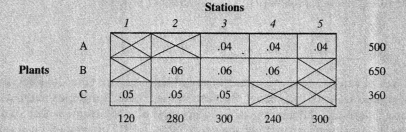

		Stations					
		1	*2*	*3*	*4*	*5*	
	A			.04	.04	.04	500
Plants	B		.06	.06	.06		650
	C	.05	.05	.05			360
		120	280	300	240	300	

The crossed-out cells mean there are no power lines from these sources to these destinations.

Solution

In order to solve this problem, we must put relatively high costs on the cells that are unusable (e.g., $1 per kilowatt-hour). Plus, it's necessary to add a dummy to balance demand and supply. The calculations are done for one hour of operation.

Optimal Solution

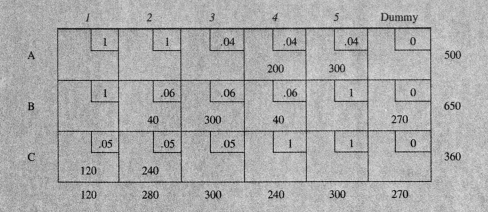

	1	2	3	4	5	Dummy	
A	1	1	.04	.04	.04	0	500
				200	300		
B	1	.06	.06	.06	1	0	650
		40	300	40		270	
C	.05	.05	.05	1	1	0	360
	120	240					
	120	280	300	240	300	270	

The total cost is: $60.80 (per hour). Cell A3 has an evaluator of zero, indicating multiple optimal solutions (within the loop A3, A4, B3 and B4).

7.4 The Assignment Problem

A second type of distribution problem is the "assignment" problem.

Example

The management of a utility company wants to assign three service teams to three geographical zones, one team to each zone. Because of each team's differing familiarity with each zone, there are differences in the efficiency of each team, a fact that is reflected in the different service costs, as shown in Table 7.18. For example, assigning team S_2 to zone Z_3 will result in a cost of $33,000. The problem is to find that assignment that minimizes the total cost.

Management Science in Practice

Developing a Logistics System for Marshalls' Retail Stores

Marshalls, Inc., a subsidiary of Melville Corporation, is an off-price retail chain experiencing 30 percent annual growth from the addition of retail outlets. The constant change in volume and spatial demands for goods stretched Marshalls' existing logistics planning system to its capacity. Moreover, heavy competition in this market has increased the importance of logistical systems that can respond quickly to customer demands while reducing the costs of distribution, primarily by supplying precisely (and only) the goods desired in the marketplace.

Thus, in the mid-1980s, Marshalls formed a team of consultants and in-house planners to design a new logistics planning system (LPS). The final system that was developed comprised three primary modules based on transportation/network algorithms for determining inbound sourcing, outbound reshipment points, and the location of a set of market service centers that supply the retail stores. Although some of the networks have over 20,000 links, the entire system runs on the transportation division's microcomputer, which gives the transportation division very fast overall turnaround time.

The LPS consists of four basic components: a demand data management system, a network data management system, the network optimization process using the transportation algorithms, and postanalysis processing. The demand data management system manipulates the vendor supply and retail store demand among data files for review and editing by the user. Reports can also be printed to summarize supply and demand data if desired.

The network data management system is written for dBASE III to provide the information needed by the network optimization routine. It organizes and maintains facility data (vendors, processing plants, inbound consolidators, outbound pools, and retail stores), product-related data (costs and capacities from each facility), and transportation costs (by traffic mode and weight category).

The network optimization process incorporates four basic components. First, a network of nodes and links is generated from the demand and data files. Then an editor allows the user to change the network nodes and links as desired, including costs, demands, and constraints. At this point, the optimization algorithm operates to optimize the flows across the updated network. Finally, a postprocessor downloads the results into dBASE III files for further analysis.

The postanalysis processor prepares both routine and demand reports. The routine reports present operating and cost information in a range of formats appropriate to the managers and needs involved. The demand reports are generated through a dBASE III file to allow individual manipulation for the characteristics of interest.

The optimization algorithm actually consists of three separate optimization models. The first, the "regional network inbound model," optimizes flows from 350 vendors through 20 intermediate warehouses to 5 processing facilities. The second, the "outbound model," optimizes the flows from the 5 processing facilities through the 20 warehouses to the 300 retail stores. The third, the "fixed-charge outbound model," identifies the best set among the 20 market service center warehouses to handle the flows at lowest cost while meeting constraints on the capacities of the facilities.

Marshalls first used LPS to select the site of their next distribution center planned for the 1990s in southern California. This site will eliminate a $1.4 million annual cost Marshalls now pays for transportation. Marshalls has also used the system to help them develop five-year strategic plans, set monthly tactical budgets, evaluate new distribution opportunities, test the location of consolidation centers, and generally reduce their logistical costs (estimated savings of $250,000 annually).

Source: D. P. Carlisle, et al., "A Turnkey, Microcomputer-Based Logistics Planning System," *Interfaces,* July–August 1987, pp. 16–26.

Questions

1. Identify the sources, destinations, costs, supplies, and demands in the LPS.
2. Why are three optimization models needed?
3. How is Marshalls saving $1.4 million? Is that the net savings? What costs will increase?

TABLE 7.18   Service Costs of Different Team Assignments (In $ Thousands)

Service Team \ Zone	Z_1	Z_2	Z_3
S_1	20	15	31
S_2	17	16	33
S_3	18	19	27

Characteristics of the Assignment Problem

The problem just presented is typical of a class of managerial problems with the following characteristics:

1. The objects under consideration, such as service teams, jobs, employees, or projects, are finite in number.

One-to-one basis

2. The objects have to be assigned on a *one-to-one* basis to other objects.
3. The result of each assignment can be expressed in terms of payoffs such as costs or profits.
4. The aim is to assign all objects (if possible) in such a way that the total cost is minimized (or the total profit is maximized).

Assignment—a common problem

Several practical allocation problems can appear as assignment-type problems. For example, a supervisor assigns subordinates to various jobs every morning, an employment agency matches employees and employers, a real estate agency matches houses to potential buyers, and teachers are assigned to classes.

Presentation of the Assignment Problem

1. *Table form.* The assignment problem is usually arranged in a tabular form. For example, Table 7.19 presents the utility company problem of Table 7.18. The assignment table is very similar to the transportation table. Indeed, the assignment problem is

Assignment problem is a transportation problem

considered as a special transportation problem in which the supply at each source and the demand at each destination are always one unit. (Because the supply and demand are always equal to one unit in each row and column, there is no need to write them in the assignment table.) As in the transportation problem, assignment problems can be balanced or not. In a balanced case, the number of objects to be assigned equals the number of objects to which they are assigned. Unbalanced problems can be balanced by adding a dummy (or dummies) with zero cost coefficients.

2. *Presentation as a linear program.* The assignment problem can also be presented as an LP problem with the following formulation.

TABLE 7.19 The Assignment Table

Service Team \ Zone	Z_1	Z_2	Z_3	Supply
S_1	20	15	31	1
S_2	17	16	33	1
S_3	18	19	27	1
Demand	1	1	1	

The Decision Variables

Let x_{ij} be an assignment of the ith source (e.g., service team) to the jth destination (e.g., zone). Each of these decision variables can take only one of two values: 0 or 1. We assign the value of $x_{ij} = 1$ if there is a match between i and j. The value $x_{ij} = 0$ means no match. No other value can be assigned.

Zero-one variables

The Objective Function

The objective function expresses the total cost (or profit) of the assignment.

The Constraints

There are two types of constraints: supply and demand.

Example

The utility company's problem is presented as a linear program.

$$\text{minimize } z = 20x_{11} + 15x_{12} + 31x_{13} + 17x_{21} + 16x_{22}$$
$$+ 33x_{23} + 18x_{31} + 19x_{32} + 27x_{33}$$

subject to:

All constraints equal one

$$\left.\begin{array}{l} x_{11} + x_{12} + x_{13} = 1 \\ x_{21} + x_{22} + x_{23} = 1 \\ x_{31} + x_{32} + x_{33} = 1 \end{array}\right\} \text{ (supply constraints)}$$

and to:

$$\left.\begin{array}{l} x_{11} + x_{21} + x_{31} = 1 \\ x_{12} + x_{22} + x_{32} = 1 \\ x_{13} + x_{23} + x_{33} = 1 \end{array}\right\} \text{ (demand constraints)}$$

and: x_{ij} either 0 or 1 for all i, j.

Because all x_{ij} can be either 0 or 1, there will be only one assignment in each supply constraint and one assignment in each demand constraint. The general formulation is as follows.

Let c_{ij} be the *cost* associated with an assignment of i to j. The assignment problem can then be stated as follows:

$$\text{minimize } z = \sum_{i=1}^{m} \sum_{j=1}^{n} c_{ij} x_{ij}$$

subject to the linear constraints (in a balanced case):

$$\sum_{j=1}^{n} x_{ij} = 1 \quad i = 1, 2, \ldots, m; \qquad \sum_{i=1}^{m} x_{ij} = 1 \quad j = 1, 2, \ldots, n \qquad (7.4)$$

and x_{ij} can take either the value of one or the value of zero.

Unbalanced Problems

Balancing an assignment problem

Notice that the constraints in the LP formulation are given as equations. The reason this can be done is that the problem is balanced. In an unbalanced problem, the number of items to be assigned differs from the number of objects to be assigned to and *must be* balanced before proceeding. The balancing is done by adding dummy supply or demand items. For example, if there are three jobs to be done on five machines, two dummy jobs must be added. A machine with a dummy job will, of course, in actually be matched with nothing. Therefore, the cost (or profit) or such a match is considered to be zero.

Balancing of the problem is only required for the **Hungarian method** (to be presented next). If a conversion to LP is used, the following rules apply.

If there are more rows (items) to be assigned than columns, then all the supply constraints will be of the $\leq$ type and all the demand constraints will be of the $=$ type (i.e., not all items will be assigned). If there are more columns, then all the demand constraints will be of the $\leq$ type and all the supply constraints will be of the $=$ type.

Note: If the assignment problem is solved as a transportation problem, it is necessary to add only one dummy whose value shows the difference between the number of columns and rows.

Methods for Solving Assignment Problems

Complete Enumeration

n! solutions

The assignment problem is usually a balanced problem with n items to be assigned to n objects. As such, there are $n!$ (n factorial) different solutions to the problem. One way to find the optimal solution is to list and compare *all* $n!$ solutions. This is called a complete enumeration approach. However, it is often impractical because the number of solutions for even a relatively small problem is unmanageably large. For example, for $n = 10$, $n! = 3,628,800$. These can be enumerated in seconds by a high-speed computer. However, for a larger n, say 20, even a computer is overwhelmed. For the problem presented in Table 7.19, there are only 3! or six solutions. These are listed in Table 7.20. Comparing all the possibilities indicates that alternative 3, which yields 59 (i.e., $59,000), is the optimal solution.

TABLE 7.20   **Assignment Alternative Solutions**
(By Enumeration)

Alternative	Combination	Total Cost
1	S_1Z_1 S_2Z_2 S_3Z_3	$20 + 16 + 27 = 63$
2	S_1Z_1 S_3Z_2 S_2Z_3	$20 + 19 + 33 = 72$
3	S_2Z_1 S_1Z_2 S_3Z_3	$17 + 15 + 27 = 59 \leftarrow$ *Minimum*
4	S_2Z_1 S_3Z_2 S_1Z_3	$17 + 19 + 31 = 67$
5	S_3Z_1 S_2Z_2 S_1Z_3	$18 + 16 + 31 = 65$
6	S_3Z_1 S_1Z_2 S_2Z_3	$18 + 15 + 33 = 66$

The Simplex Method

The simplex method can be used, but it is rather inefficient for solving the assignment problem. For example, an assignment problem of 10×10 will be transformed to a linear program with 100 variables, 20 constraints, and 20 artificial variables, resulting in a large matrix. The simplex method is much slower than the Hungarian method.

The Transportation Model

Any assignment problem can be solved by the transportation method, because the assignment problem is a special case of the transportation problem. However, there are more efficient methods.

"Near-optimal" Methods

Various computational methods are available for arriving at a near-optimal solution in a rapid way. These are mainly heuristic in nature.

Branch and Bound

The branch and bound method can also be used to solve the assignment problem.

The Hungarian Method

The Hungarian method is the most efficient way of solving large assignment problems. It is named after the Hungarian mathematician Konig, who first proved (1916) a theorem necessary to the development of the method.

The Hungarian Method

First, balance the matrix

The Hungarian method is a fast, efficient solution procedure for solving large, *balanced* assignment problems. The procedure is supported by the following theorem:

> If one subtracts (or adds) a constant number from all entries in any row or column of the assignment matrix, then the total cost of each of the $n!$ possible assignments is reduced (or increased) by the constant number subtracted (or added).

FIGURE 7.3

Solution steps for the assignment problem

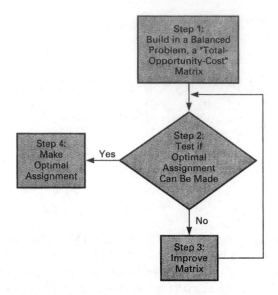

Therefore, one can make these additions or subtractions to rows or columns without changing the ultimate optimal assignment. The total costs are changed, but not the *relative* ones. The Hungarian method is next illustrated for the case of *cost minimization.*

The Procedure

After assuring that the problem is balanced, the solution procedure involves four major steps, as shown in Figure 7.3.

Example

The method will be illustrated with the example in Table 7.19.

Step 1: Build a Balanced "Total-Opportunity-Cost" Matrix.   This step involves the transformation of the cost matrix to what is termed a *total-opportunity-cost* matrix. It involves two operations.

A total opportunity cost matrix

First, the element with the lowest value (including zero and negative numbers, where negative numbers represent profit, in a cost table, or cost, in a profit table) in each row is subtracted from all the other elements in that row. All negative numbers *disappear* in this step. In our example, the lowest element is 15, so it is subtracted from all the numbers as shown in Table 7.21.

Second, the smallest element (including zero) in each column of the new matrix is subtracted from all the elements of that column. The result is the total-opportunity-cost matrix as shown in Table 7.22.

TABLE 7.21 New Matrix

20	15	31
17	16	33
18	19	27

Original Matrix

→

$20 - 15 = 5$	$15 - 15 = 0$	$31 - 15 = 16$
$17 - 16 = 1$	$16 - 16 = 0$	$33 - 16 = 17$
$18 - 18 = 0$	$19 - 18 = 1$	$27 - 18 = 9$

→

5	0	16
1	0	17
0	1	9

New Matrix

TABLE 7.22 Total-Opportunity-Cost Matrix

$5 - 0 = 5$	$0 - 0 = 0$	$16 - 9 = 7$
$1 - 0 = 1$	$0 - 0 = 0$	$17 - 9 = 8$
$0 - 0 = 0$	$1 - 0 = 1$	$9 - 9 = 0$

→

5	0	7
1	0	8
0	1	0

Notice that this matrix now contains *at least* one zero in each row and column.

Step 2: The Optimality Test. Because all entries in the total-opportunity-cost matrix are nonnegative, the minimum value of the objective function (i.e., total cost) *cannot* be negative, no matter what assignments are made. Hence, the *minimum possible* cost is zero in the relative terms of the new table. (The *real* cost with the *real* solution will, of course, be greater. The absolute values are calculated later.) Therefore, *if* a feasible assignment with a total opportunity cost of zero is found, this assignment must have the *lowest possible cost;* that is, it is optimal.

The "lowest possible cost" can be achieved if all assignments are made to cells with a value of zero. Thus, in testing for optimality, one needs to know whether there are enough zeros in the table to permit a "zero" assignment for each row and each column on a one-to-one basis.

Rather than using the trial-and-error approach, we use a simple procedure that tests whether this can be done.

Draw the minimum number of lines

1. Draw the *minimum* necessary number of straight lines, horizontally and vertically, so that all zeros in the matrix are covered. Draw the lines by trial and error but always try to cover two or more zeros with one line.

2. Count the number of these lines. If it equals *n* (the number of rows or columns), an optimal assignment can be made. If it is smaller than *n*, an improvement is possible.

Note: In some cases, there are several alternative ways of drawing the minimum number of lines. Any of these may be chosen.

Let us find the minimum number of lines necessary to cover all the zeros in our case. The total-opportunity-cost matrix of Table 7.22 is reproduced in Table 7.23.

TABLE 7.23   The Optimality Test

Service Team \ Zone	Z_1	Z_2	Z_3
S_1	5	0	7
S_2	1	0	8
S_3	0	1	0

Note that the table has four "zero" cells. It is possible to cover all the zeros with two lines (shown as dashed lines in Table 7.23); one through row S_3 and the other through column Z_2. According to the optimality test, because only two lines are needed to cover all the zeros, an optimal assignment cannot be made at this stage and an improved solution is possible.

Step 3: Improve the Total-Opportunity-Cost Matrix.   An improved total-opportunity-cost matrix is derived by the following three operations:

An improved solution

1. Find the *smallest* entry in the *uncovered* cells (cells with no lines through them) and subtract it from *all* entries in the uncovered cells, as shown in Table 7.24. In our case, the lowest entry is 1 (cell $S_2 Z_1$).
2. Add the same *smallest* entry to those cells in which the lines intersect (cells with two lines through them). In our case, there is only one such cell, $S_3 Z_2$.
3. Cells with one line through them, such as $S_1 Z_2$, are transferred *unchanged* to the improved table.

The result is the *first improved total-opportunity-cost matrix,* Table 7.25. The *optimality test* is now applied to this matrix. Using the line-drawing procedure of step 2, a minimum of *three* lines is needed to cover all the zeros in Table 7.25. This means that an optimal assignment can now be made.

In those problems where the first improvement *does not yield* an optimal solution,

TABLE 7.24   First Operation for the Improved Matrix

Service Team \ Zone	Z_1	Z_2	Z_3
S_1	$5 - 1 = 4$	0	$7 - 1 = 6$
S_2	$1 - 1 = 0$	0	$8 - 1 = 7$
S_3	0	$1 + 1 = 2$	0

TABLE 7.25 First Improved Total Opportunity Cost Matrix

Team	Zone Z_1	Z_2	Z_3
S_1	4	☐0	6
S_2	☐0	0	7
S_3	0	2	☐0

we *keep on* improving the solution (by repeating step 3) until an optimal solution is achieved.

Step 4: Make an Optimal Assignment. An optimal assignment can now be made to cells with a zero entry, maintaining the one-to-one requirement. If only one solution exists, a fast procedure for finding it is to locate a row or column with only one zero in it and make that assignment. Then drop the row and column of that cell from the matrix and repeat the procedure. If the solution is *not* unique, there will be two or more zeros in a column or row to choose from. The choice, then, is done by trial and error.

Multiple optimal solutions are possible

The optimal assignment for our example is shown in Table 7.25 (squares around the zeros): S_1 to Z_2, S_2 to Z_1, and S_3 to Z_3. The total cost in this case is $15 + 17 + 27 = 59$ (thousand dollars). If more than one optimal solution exists, a trial-and-error approach can be used to find all possible combination assignments in the zero cells.

The Maximization Case

Convert to minimization

The example just demonstrated was a minimization one. In maximization cases, a convenient solution procedure involves transforming the problem into a minimization problem (an opportunity loss table) by the following procedure (see example in Table 7.26).

1. Find the *largest profit* coefficient in the entire table (11 here).
2. Subtract each entry in the original table from the largest profit coefficient (see Table 7.26b).

TABLE 7.26 a. Maximize (Before Transformation)

	R	S	T
A	8	6	10
B	11	9	6
C	4	7	5

b. Minimize (After Transformation)

	R	S	T
A	$11 - 8 = 3$	$11 - 6 = 5$	$11 - 10 = 1$
B	$11 - 11 = 0$	$11 - 9 = 2$	$11 - 6 = 5$
C	$11 - 4 = 7$	$11 - 7 = 4$	$11 - 5 = 6$

FIGURE 7.4

Flowchart of the Hungarian method

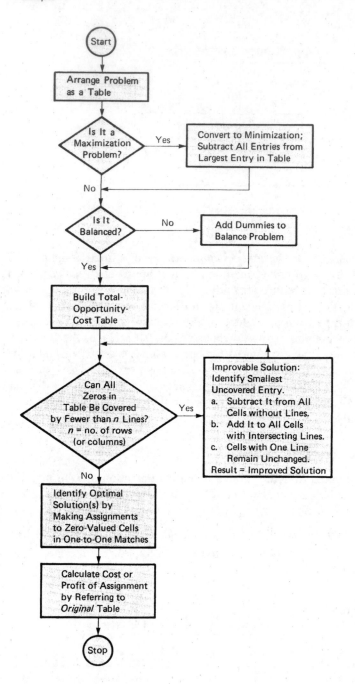

Once the transformed table is constructed, the Hungarian method can then be employed to solve the problem. Once a solution is obtained, the total profit can be computed using the original profit coefficients in the original table.

The process of the Hungarian method is summarized in Figure 7.4.

Notes:

Impossible Assignment

If a certain match is not feasible, assign a large cost (M) to this cell. In maximization, a large loss ($-M$) is assigned.

Multiple Solutions

These are very common in assignment problems and occur when there are alternative feasible ways to assign the zeros.

Line Drawing

The following is an alternative procedure that guarantees that the minimum number of lines are drawn and simultaneously identifies unique allocations: If there is a row

---

Solved Problem 7.2

Three salesmen, A, B and C, are to be assigned to serve the following zones: (1) Northern New Jersey and Newark, (2) Southern New Jersey, (3) Western Pennsylvania and Pittsburgh, and (4) Eastern Pennsylvania and Philadelphia. The anticipated profit from executing one sale during one week in each zone is given below:

Zone	Profit
1	$18,000
2	8,000
3	12,000
4	18,000

The probability of executing one sale in any given zone during the week is a function of a salesman's familiarity with the zone as well as his personal ability. These probabilities are given in the matrix below:

		Zone			
		1	2	3	4
	A	0.5	0.8	0.2	0.6
Salesman	B	0.6	0.6	0.4	0.5
	C	0.4	0.7	0.5	0.4

Solved Problem 7.2 continued

Find:

a) The optimal assignment plan if the objective is profit maximization.

b) The total profit in this case.

c) Reformulate with the objective of maximizing the overall probability of sales and then solve.

d) Comment on the differences between the two goals and the results.

Solution:

a. First we build an expected profit table (in thousands of dollars). Each cell shows the expected values. For example, A to 1 is ($18,000 × the probability of .5) = $9,000; C to 2 is $8,000 × .7 = $5,600. The assignment table is shown below, and because it is unbalanced, we have balanced it with the aid of a dummy salesman.

		Zone			
		1	2	3	4
	A	9	6.4	2.4	10.8
Salesman	B	10.8	4.8	4.8	9.0
	C	7.2	5.6	6.0	7.2
	Dummy	0	0	0	0

Now we have an assignment problem with *profit* coefficients. We can employ any desired method to solve this assignment problem. One approach may be to build the "relative cost matrix" by subtracting all profits from the highest profit in the table and then employing the Hungarian Method.

The Optimal Solution is:

Salesman A to zone #4
Salesman B to zone #1
Salesman C to zone #3

b. The total expected profit is: $27,600 per month.

c. If the company's objective is to maximize the overall probability of sales, we must use the original probability matrix as the assignment matrix with "profit" coefficients. To simplify computations we multiply all data by 10. Again, we can employ any desired method; for example, we can build the "relative cost matrix" as shown below:

		Zone			
		1	2	3	4
Salesman	A	3	0	6	2
	B	2	2	4	3
	C	4	1	3	4
	Dummy	0	0	0	0

The Hungarian Method calls for an optimal solution of:

Salesman	to	Zone	Sales Probability
A		2	.8
B		1	.6
C		3	.5
		Overall	1.9

at a total profit of $23,200. An alternative optimal solution exists in this case; it calls for

A	to	4
B	to	1
C	to	2

at a total profit of $27,200 and overall "probability" again of 1.9. Because both solutions give us the same overall value (1.9) and the second solution promises higher profit, we should adopt the second solution.

d. Sales maximization does not necessarily lead to profit maximization, especially in the short run. For example, a sales promotion may initially be very expensive, but should result in long term profits and other benefits.

Management Science in Practice

Assigning American League Umpires to Games

The American Baseball League consists of 14 professional baseball teams organized into two divisions: Western and Eastern. Generally, the baseball season lasts about 26 weeks and each team plays approximately 52 series during that time, each consisting of either two, three or four games. Each week, one series is usually scheduled for Monday through Thursday and another for Friday through Sunday. Constructing the game schedule is a very difficult task. Typically, the schedule is made up the winter before the season begins and includes such complicating factors as balancing the number of home and away trips for each team, avoiding conflicts in cities that also have National League teams, and so on.

A related problem is the assignment of umpire crews to each series. The two main objectives here are to minimize the total travel costs and to balance the crew assignments among the teams over the season. This balance includes considering the number of home/away series for each crew, distributing the assignments of each crew to each team somewhat evenly over the season, and limiting the number of times a crew is exposed to each team in total.

Two of the constraints are that a crew must have a day off between any assignment to a west coast series followed by an assignment to a midwest or east coast series (or vice versa) and no crew should be assigned to the same team for more than two consecutive series.

The basic crew scheduling problem can be solved with an assignment model where the seven crews are assigned to each of the seven simultaneous series on a series-by-series basis, moving progressively forward in time. The costs of each assignment are represented by the travel costs; if an assignment violates a restriction, then the travel cost is set infinitely high to avoid that assignment. Travel penalties are also used to allow the scheduler to accommodate the balance objectives while still observing the constraints.

This approach was implemented in a microcomputer-based decision support system (DSS) for the umpire crew scheduler for the American League. Additional flexibility was incorporated in the software to allow the scheduler to follow several heuristic rules that have been found to work well in practice. For example, a crew should remain in a city whenever a two-game series is preceded or followed by a three-game series, a crew should remain on the same coast for two to three series, and the general flow of crews should follow a smooth east-to-west pattern (or vice-versa).

Using the system, the time for the scheduler to generate a crew schedule has been significantly decreased. The quality of the schedule has also increased in terms of, for example, crew exposure balance. And finally, travel costs were reduced by about four percent, representing a savings of approximately $30,000 per year.

Source: J. R. Evans "Scheduling American League Umpires: A Microcomputer-Based DSS", *DSI Proceedings*, Honolulu, 1986, pp. 914-916.

Questions

1. Does the assignment model address the entire problem of 52 series of games? What aspects does it address? What aspects must the scheduler still solve?

2. If the DSS doesn't solve the entire problem, in what ways is it still helpful to the scheduler?

3. What was the approximate original cost of creating an umpire crew schedule? What is the cost now? Does this cost seem reasonable?

4. Would a league scheduler be an interesting job to you?

5. The assignment model is the core of the system. Why is the system called a DSS?

(column) with only a single zero in it, draw a line through that zero's column (row). Continue this procedure, progressively reducing the matrix of uncovered zeros until no more such zeros remain, leaving either the unique optimal solution or alternative solutions (pairs).

7.5 Concluding Remarks

The transportation and assignment models are special cases of LP. However, formulation and solution of such problems in the format of LP is too cumbersome. Due to their special structure, these problems are formulated as special algorithms that are extremely efficient when compared to the LP format. The larger the problem, the greater is the advantage of the special algorithms.

In addition to actual transportation problems, there are several production and scheduling problems that can be formulated as transportation-type problems, thus increasing the applicability of the model.

7.6 Problems for Part A

1. Solve the transportation problem (with cost coefficients).

From \ To	1	2	3	Supply
A	67	42	51	250
B	61	24	39	400
C	29	47	60	300
D	43	31	42	200
Demand	400	150	600	1150

a. Find an initial solution using the least-cost method.
b. Find the optimal solution (use the stepping-stone method).

2. Given a transportation problem (with cost coefficients):

Sources \ Destinations	1	2	3	4	Supply
A	1	5	3	4	100
B	4	2	2	4	60
C	3	1	2	4	120
Demand	70	50	100	60	280

a. Find an initial solution by the Northwest Corner Rule.
b. Find an initial solution by the least-cost method.
c. Find an optimal solution by the stepping-stone method: Start with the results of part (*a*).
d. Are there any other optimal solutions?
e. Based on findings of part (*d*), comment on the number of occupied cells in an optimal solution.

3. The Aztec Silver Mine has two operating mines in Chile and three distributing warehouses located in different parts of South America. The company ships the ore by trucks. The capacity of mine I is 500 tons a week and that of mine II is 1,300 tons per week. The weekly sales potential of the three warehouses is 1,200 tons, 500 tons, and 700 tons. The shipping cost per ton from each mine to each warehouse is given below:

From Mine Number	To Warehouse Number	Shipping Cost (pesos per ton)
I	I	8
I	II	13
I	III	9
II	I	11
II	II	14
II	III	5

Find the best shipment schedule if the company's objective is to minimize the transportation cost.
a. Formulate as a transportation model.
b. Solve the problem (start with the northwest corner).

4. Given below is a transportation problem with *profit* coefficients:
   a. Find the best solution (start with the northwest corner).
   b. Present as an LP problem (do not solve).

From \ To	1	2	Supply
A	6	4	50
B	3	5	80
C	8	7	60
D	5	9	40
Demand	80	100	

5. Continental Electric Company buys fuel once a month for its five operational zones. Demand (in hundreds of thousands of barrels) in each of the zones is given below:

Zone	Demand
A	28
B	60
C	36
D	45
E	16
Total	185

There are three bidders who wish to supply the demand: one in Texas, one in California, and one in Canada. The prices per barrel (FOB) and the maximum quantities available (in hundreds of thousands of barrels) are given below:

	Price	Maximum Supply
California	$10.00	80
Texas	11.50	60
Canada	9.50	120

Transportation costs between each bidder and each zone are given below (in $ per barrel):

From \ To Zone	A	B	C	D	E
California	1.8	1.6	1.3	.6	.3
Texas	1.6	1.2	.9	.2	.6
Canada	.8	1.0	1.1	1.2	1.6

Bids can be accepted for the entire quantity or for portions of it. Continental Electric's objective is to supply all demand in all zones at minimal total cost. Find the contract award policy that Continental Electric should follow.

6. The Pollution Control Board of Pardo Province has 100 employees: 20 live in city A, 35 in city B, and 45 in city C. The employees have interchangeable skills and are to be assigned to various laboratories. The Water Laboratory requires 40 employees, the Air Lab requires 30 employees, the Solid Waste Lab requires 20 employees, and the Central Lab requires 10 employees. The distance between the cities and the labs is shown on the following map (in miles along the available streets).
   Workers travel by the shortest available route along the streets shown. What worker-to-lab

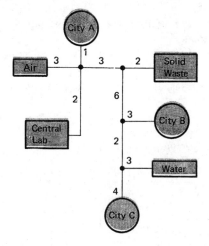

arrangement minimizes the total distances traveled by all the employees?

a. Formulate as a transportation problem.

b. Solve.

c. What assumptions are necessary in this case?

7. A firm owns facilities at five geographically remote locations. It has manufacturing plants at points *A* and *B* with daily production capacities of 60 and 40 units, respectively. At points *C*, *D*, and *E* it has warehouses with daily demands of 20, 30, and 50 units, respectively. Shipping costs between these points are exactly proportional to the distances between them, which are indicated in miles below:

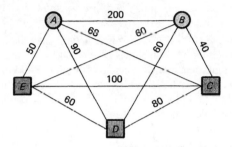

a. Given that the firm wishes to minimize its total transportation costs, formulate as a transportation problem.

b. Find the optimal solution; use the least-cost method to generate an initial solution.

   Note: Shipments between plants, and also between warehouses, are prohibited.

8. The energy czar is planning shipments of gasoline from two sources to three destinations. Per ton transportation costs are given in the following table:

From \ To	C	D	E
A	6	7	9
B	9	4	6

There are 1,000 tons available at A and 1,300 available at B. Because the destinations want as much as possible, the czar has decided to ship out *all* available quantities. His objective is to minimize total shipment cost.

a. Formulate as a transportation problem.

b. Solve.

c. Formulate as an LP.

9. Taiwan Electronics produces three models of CB radios: A, B, and C. The estimated monthly demand for the three models is 10,000, 12,000, and 7,000 units, respectively. The radios can be produced on one of four available production lines; Q, R, S, and T, the production capacities of which are: 6,000, 15,000, 20,000, and 5,000 units, respectively. The manufacturing costs vary among the production lines and are shown in the table below (in $ per unit):

	Production Line			
Model	Q	R	S	T
A	60	53	61	50
B	80	75	81	70
C	75	70	75	65

The company's objective is to meet all estimated demand at the lowest possible manufacturing cost. Use the transportation model to find the best monthly production schedule.

10. The cost of assigning jobs A, B, and C on machines M, N, O, and P is shown below:

Job \ Machine	M	N	O	P
A	6	7	5	9
B	8	5	6	7
C	10	8	6	6

a. Use the Hungarian method to find the least-cost assignment.

b. Formulate as an LP.

c. Formulate as a transportation problem.

11. In a small job shop department there are three tasks to be assigned to three workers. The table below indicates the weekly profit achieved by assigning each worker to each job. (For example, assigning worker B

242 Chapter 7

to job III brings $3 profit.) Find the assignment that will maximize profit.

Worker \ Job	I	II	III
A	5	4	7
B	6	7	3
C	8	11	2

a. Solve by complete enumeration.
b. Solve by the Hungarian method.
c. Formulate as an LP.

12. Fraser City has a group of five social workers. The director of the group wishes to assign each of the workers to a residential area in the "best possible" manner. It was suggested that workers be rotated in the various areas for a few weeks and their efficiency measured by the number of complaints received. The table below gives the number of complaints in each area against each worker in one month of service.

Worker \ Zone	I	II	III	IV	V
A	3	5	4	8	2
B	9	4	3	6	7
C	11	6	8	10	9
D	6	10	4	12	5
E	3	5	6	4	9

a. Suggest the best assignment of workers to zones. Solve by the Hungarian method. (*Hint:* Attempt to minimize the total number of complaints.)
b. Specify the necessary assumptions.

13. Given below is a table that shows the cost of the row personnel doing the column job. The cost figures in the matrix reflect the effectiveness of the person for the particular job weighted by the person's rate of pay.

Personnel \ Job	Bed Making	Patient Care	Patient Examination
Physicians	—	20	11
Nurses	14	6	30
Nurses aids	5	11	—

Find the optimal assignment of personnel to jobs. Use the Hungarian method.

Note: Some assignments are not feasible (e.g., physicians do not make beds.) In such a case, simply ignore the cell.

14. Indian Electronics Ltd., manufactures computers in two plants. The capacities of the plants are: plant A, 150 units per month; plant B, 120 units a month. The company has three buyers who distribute the product to a chain of stores. Demand is deterministic at the following constant rate:

Buyer I	60 units
Buyer II	120 units
Buyer III	80 units

Transportation costs are given in the table below (in rupees per unit).

From Plant	To Buyer I	II	III
A	27	40	60
B	35	28	42

Find the quantities to be shipped from A and B to I, II, and III so as to minimize the total transportation costs.
a. Solve by the transportation method.
b. Formulate as an LP. Solve (use a computer).

15. A caterer must supply napkins for dinners in seven consecutive days, according to the following demand:

Day	Demand
1	50
2	100
3	40
4	20
5	80
6	50
7	100

Napkins can be cleaned for 5 cents each with regular service (four days) or for 8 cents each with two-day express service. An immediate supply of napkins can be purchased for 15 cents each.

Assuming we have a single week to plan, what is the optimal scheduling program of the caterer? How many napkins should he buy, have cleaned using regular service, and have cleaned using express service each day, if he is to meet all demand at a minimum cost?

16. The Tilt Lumber Company has four lumberyards, A, B, C, and D, with the following capacities:

A	3,000 tons
B	2,000 tons
C	1,800 tons
D	6,000 tons

The company has received a contract to supply lumber for three construction projects: Project I, with a maximum demand of 5,200 tons and a selling price of $70 per ton; Project II, with a maximum demand of 10,000 tons and a selling price of $50 per ton; and Project III, with maximum demand of 10,000 tons and a selling price of $45 per ton.

Transportation costs in dollars per ton are given in the following table.

Lumber-Yard	To		
	Project 1	Project 2	Project 3
A	10	15	30
B	18	12	20
C	25	10	25
D	35	20	12

Find the best schedule for the Tilt Lumber Company. Start with the least-cost method, proceed with the stepping-stone method.

17. An airline operates between New York and Chicago seven days a week. The timetable is given below (in EST):

Flight Number		Depart	Arrive
1		6:30 A.M.	8:00 A.M.
2		7:30 A.M.	9:15 A.M.
3	*Westbound*	10:00 A.M.	12:00 P.M.
4		12:15 P.M.	2:00 P.M.
5		2:00 P.M.	4:00 P.M.
6		6:30 P.M.	8:15 P.M.
7		10:30 P.M.	12:15 A.M.

Flight Number		Depart	Arrive
11		5:30 A.M.	7:30 A.M.
12		8:00 A.M.	9:45 A.M.
13	*Eastbound*	10:30 A.M.	12:30 P.M.
14		1:00 P.M.	3:00 P.M.
15		3:30 P.M.	5:45 P.M.
16		7:30 P.M.	9:30 P.M.
17		11:30 P.M.	1:30 A.M.

Crews must return always to their base, which can be either in New York or in Chicago. Crews must have a minimum layover of six hours between flights. Because overtime is paid for layover outside the base, the company likes to minimize the time spent on the ground away from home.
a. Match each of the New York–Chicago flights with each of the Chicago–New York flights.
b. Where should each of the seven crews be based?

18. Without balancing the profit situation below, formulate as an LP. Solve by computer.

	I	II
A	6	9
B	12	5
C	4	13
D	11	8

Ambulance Team	Region			
	A	B	C	D
1	12	8	10	6
2	6	6	4	8
3	10	10	8	12
4	12	10	12	10

19. AMA's maintenance shop has three groups of employees who have varying proficiencies in their skills: Group G-1, three skilled employees; group G-2, four semiskilled; and group G-3, two specialists. Six jobs to be performed are relatively easy and three are complex (nine jobs total). Assigning one worker per job, find the best assignment schedule if the objective is to minimize total cost.

The table below gives the cost of the repairs:

If Done by Worker of Group	Easy Repair	Complex Repair
G-1	10	24
G-2	9	28
G-3	12	20

a. Formulate as a transportation problem.
b. Solve.
c. Formulate (do not solve) as an assignment problem. (*Hint:* Nine variables are required.)

20. The town of Beersheba must determine how to deploy its four ambulances among its four regions in the most effective manner. The teams differ in their abilities and the special equipment at their disposal. An accurate measure of the health cost in each region would be the average weekly monetary loss owing to illness and death. Based on historical records and judgment, the table below shows the expected monetary loss that could be prevented if each of the four ambulances were to be assigned to each of the four regions (in 1,000 Israeli shekels per week). Determine the optimal assignments.

21. Use the transportation model to solve the following production scheduling problem. The demand for ABC's product fluctuates seasonally according to the following pattern:

1st quarter—100 units

2nd quarter—300 units

3rd quarter—450 units

4th quarter—270 units

The demand (in the short run) is considered as constant. The maximum manufacturing capacity of the plant is 260 units per quarter, except during the third quarter, when the capacity is only 240 units because of the yearly shutdown. Management policy is to supply all demand. If capacity is insufficient, a subcontractor is used (without any limit) at a cost of $50 more per unit than the production in the plant. Top management encourages production in slack quarters to supply demand in peak quarters; however, there is a storage cost of $25 per unit per quarter ($100 per unit per year). Assume that we have a one-year planning horizon. Find ABC's production and purchasing schedule that will minimize its total relevant costs. In all cases assume that beginning and closing inventories are zero.

22. The French army is testing four antitank missiles against five targets. At its proving ground in Toulouse, the "effective damage" ratings shown below were ascertained. If each missile is devoted to only one type of target, what would be the best assignments?

Antitank Missile	Target				
	A	B	C	D	E
Python	26	36	40	30	28
Rattler	18	50	34	40	22
Asp	28	40	30	42	20
Coral	20	30	36	32	18

23. Solve the problem formulated in Table 7.17 and comment on the result.

24. A firm that markets one product has four salespersons, A, B, C, and D, and three customers, I, II, and III. The firm's profit for selling one unit of its product to customer I is $100, to customer II is $120, and to customer III is $150. Sales of the firm's product to each customer depend on the salesperson-customer rapport. The probability matrix for the sale

of a unit of the product to each customer by each salesperson is as follows:

Salesperson \ Customer	I	II	III
A	.7	.6	.6
B	.5	.7	.7
C	.4	.8	.5
D	.8	.6	.4

(For example, the probability that salesperson B can sell a unit of product to customer III is 0.7.) If only one salesperson can be assigned to each customer, what is the optimal assignment?

PART B: EXTENSIONS

7.7 The Modified Distribution Procedure (MODI)

MODI uses the LP dual

An efficient procedure for solving large transportation problems is the **MODI (modified distribution) procedure,** which is based on the *dual* to the transportation problem. The reader will recall that every LP problem has a dual. The transportation problem, being a special case of LP, has its own dual.

When the *dual* is solved, its solution yields two types of variables:

Implicit costs

$u_i =$ Implicit cost (or shadow price) of source i
(value of one more unit at source i)

$v_j =$ Implicit cost of destination j (value of one more unit at j)

The MODI procedure uses the values of u_i and v_j to find the cell evaluators. *Note:* u_i and v_j can be found by transforming the problem to an LP and solving it by the simplex method. However, the MODI procedure *does not require,* as will be shown, the transformation to an LP in order to find u_i and v_j.

The Theoretical Basis of MODI

In an *optimal solution* for a minimization transportation problem, Equations 7.5 and 7.6 must hold by definition:

$$c_{ij} - u_i - v_j \geq 0 \tag{7.5}$$

where c_{ij} is the per unit shipping cost between i and j, and:

$$x_{ij}(c_{ij} - u_i - v_j) = 0 \tag{7.6}$$

where x_{ij} is the quantity to be shipped between i and j.

Two cases may occur

These two conditions imply that when optimality is reached, one of two things may occur:

Case a

If $x_{ij} \neq 0$ (occupied cell), then $c_{ij} - u_i - v_j = 0$, or $c_{ij} = u_i + v_j$, which means that an allocation i to j will be made if, and only if, the actual cost of transportation c_{ij} is equal to the sum of the implicit cost of source i plus the implicit cost of destination j. In such a case, x_{ij} is called a basic variable; that is, cell ij is occupied. (Alternatively, x_{ij} may be a nonbasic variable that has the potential of being in the basis as an alternative optimal solution; that is, when the cell evaluator equals zero.)

Case b

If $x_{ij} = 0$, then one of two things may happen:

1. $c_{ij} > u_i + v_j$. In this case, an allocation i to j is *not* made, because the actual cost is larger than the sum of the implied costs of the source i and the destination j.
2. $c_{ij} = u_i + v_j$. In this case, the nonbasic variable has the potential of being in the basis as an alternative optimal solution.

Note: c_{ij} *cannot* be smaller than $u_i + v_j$ without violating Equation 7.5.

The conditions just presented are the foundation for MODI, which follows the same solution steps as the stepping-stone:

The MODI steps

Step 1. Find an initial feasible solution.
Step 2. Calculate the cell evaluators and test for optimality. If the solution is not optimal, improve it (next step).
Step 3. Identify the "incoming" cell and design an improved solution.
Step 4. Recycle until an optimal solution is obtained.

The major difference between MODI and the stepping-stone procedure is in using different calculations for the optimality test.

The Concept of Cell Evaluators

Let K_{ij} denote the cell evaluator, defined as:

$$K_{ij} = c_{ij} - (u_i + v_j) = c_{ij} - u_i - v_j \qquad (7.7)$$

The cell evaluator from the implicit costs

The cell evaluator, thus, is the difference between the actual cost of shipping one unit from i to j, c_{ij}, and the sum of the implicit costs of source i and destination j.

Let us investigate the concept of the cell evaluators by examining in Table 7.27 the initial solution of a previous example. In the initial feasible solution, there are five occupied cells.

Now, if one assigns a complete set of row auxiliary numbers, u_i (to be placed at the extreme right-hand side of the table), and a complete set of column auxiliary numbers, v_j (to be placed at the bottom of the table), in such a way that the shipping cost per unit of *each* of the *occupied* cells equals the sum of its *row and column auxiliary numbers,* that is:

$$u_i + v_j = c_{ij} \qquad (7.8)$$

Cell evaluators for occupied cells are zero

then the condition that the cell evaluator of each occupied cell be zero will be satisfied. Further, for the *empty* cells, the sum of the row and column auxiliary numbers will normally be different from the actual cost of the cell, c_{ij}. This difference is the value of the cell evaluator.

TABLE 7.27   Table 7.8 Reproduced

Source \ Destination	R	S	T	Supply
A	[1] 80	[2] 20	[3]	100
B	[4]	[1] 100	[5] 10	110
D (dummy)	[0]	[0]	[0] 50	50
Demand	80	120	60	260 / 260

Assigning Auxiliary Row and Column Numbers

From each *occupied* cell, u_i and v_j are selected so that c_{ij} equals the sum of u_i and v_j. For the occupied cell AR, for example, u_1 and v_1 are chosen so $c_{11} = u_1 + v_1$. Similarly, for the occupied cell AS, u_1 and v_2 are selected so $c_{12} = u_1 + v_2$. This process must be carried out for *all* the occupied cells.

One arbitrary value

To determine all the row and column auxiliary numbers, one *arbitrary* number, serving as either a row or a column number, must first be chosen. (This is necessary because there is one less occupied cell $(m + n - 1)$ than the number of auxiliary variables $(m + n)$. The rest will be determined from the occupied cells by using the relationship $c_{ij} = u_i + v_j$. Insofar as *any* arbitrary number can be chosen to represent one of the u_i's or v_j's, we shall follow the practice of *making u_1 take the value zero.* (It is even more efficient to let the u_i or v_j of the row or column with the *most occupied cells* take the value zero.)

An Example of MODI

To illustrate the steps of MODI, the problem presented in Table 7.27 is used.

Step 1: Find an Initial Solution
The initial solution shown in Table 7.27 will be used.

Step 2: Calculate the Cell Evaluators for all the Empty Cells and Test for Optimality
Arbitrarily, a value of zero for u_1 is chosen. The next question is: What value must be given to v_1 so that for the first occupied cell AR, $c_{11} = u_1 + v_1$, or $1 = 0 + v_1$? Obviously, v_1 must take a value of 1. Again, what value must be given to v_2 so that $c_{12} = u_1 + v_2$, or $2 = 0 + v_2$? The value of v_2 must be 2. We can skip cell AT because it is unoccupied. Now, what value must be given to u_2 so that $c_{22} = u_2 + v_2$, or $1 = u_2 + 2$? Obviously, $u_2 = -1$. In a similar manner, v_3 is found to be 6 and u_3 to be -6.

All the row and column numbers are entered in Table 7.28 in the new row v_j and the new column u_i.

Computing the Cell Evaluators.   Let us now calculate the cell evaluator for the empty cell BR. For cell BR, the cell evaluator, according to Equation 7.7, is $K_{21} = c_{21} - u_2 - v_1 = 4 + 1 - 1 = 4$. Similarly, the cell evaluators of the other empty cells are calculated and summarized below:

Empty Cell	Cell Evaluator K_{ij}	
BR	$c_{21} - u_2 - v_1 = 4 + 1 - 1 =$	4
AT	$c_{13} - u_1 - v_3 = 3 - 0 - 6 =$	-3
DR	$c_{31} - u_3 - v_1 = 0 + 6 - 1 =$	5
DS	$c_{32} - u_3 - v_2 = 0 + 6 - 2 =$	4

TABLE 7.28 Finding the Implicit Costs

Source \ Destination	R	S	T	Supply	u_i
A	1 80	2 20	3	100	$u_i = 0$
B	4	1 100	5 10	110	$u_2 = -1$
D (dummy)	0	0	0 50	50	$u_3 = -6$
Demand	80	120	60	260 / 260	
v_j	$v_1 = 1$	$v_2 = 2$	$v_3 = 6$		

Test of Optimality. The optimality test is identical to that of the stepping-stone method. Namely, an optimal solution requires that all cell evaluators be nonnegative (in minimization). Because the cell evaluator of AT is negative, the solution of Table 7.27 is *not optimal.* An improved solution is thus called for.

Step 3: Identify the "Incoming" Cell and Design an Improved Solution

Shifting units along a closed loop

The incoming cell for a minimization case is located by identifying, as in the stepping-stone method, the most negative cell evaluator. (The largest positive evaluator in the case of maximization.) In this case, the incoming cell is AT. The improved solution is obtained by shifting as many units as possible around a closed path into AT without violating the demand and supply requirements. The improved solution is shown in Table 7.29.

Step 4: Recycle (Until Optimality is Achieved)

The next step is to test the solution of Table 7.29 for optimality. All cell evaluators for the empty cells are computed by first recalculating the u_i's and v_j's. This is accomplished by again using the equation $c_{ij} = u_i + v_j$ for the *occupied* cells.

The new u_i's and v_j's are entered in Table 7.29. The cell evaluators for the empty cells of Table 7.29 are calculated as:

Empty Cell	Cell Evaluator
BR	+4
BT	+3
DR	+2
DS	+1

Because *all* cell evaluators are positive, the solution in Table 7.29 is optimal.

TABLE 7.29   **First Improved Solution**

Source \ Destination	R	S	T	Supply	u_i
A	[1] 80	[2] 10	[3] 10	100	0
B	[4]	[1] 110	[5]	110	−1
D (dummy)	[0]	[0]	[0] 50	50	−3
Demand	80	120	60	260 / 260	
v_j	1	2	3		

Economic Interpretation of u_i and v_j

Implicit costs

The variables u_i and v_j used in the MODI procedure have an interesting economic interpretation. They are, in effect, the dual variables and, as such, represent implicit costs associated with the i sources and j destinations:

u_i is the value of one unit of the product at source i. In other words, u_i represents the *implicit cost of source i.*

v_j is the value of one unit of the product delivered at destination j. In other words, v_j is the *implicit cost of the destination j.*

u_i and v_j are *relative* costs

Because, in this procedure, one value of u_i (or v_j) is assigned arbitrarily, the values u_i and v_j are *relative* rather than absolute. Hence, u_i measures the *comparative locational disadvantage* of the various sources. Similarly, v_j measures the comparative disadvantage of the various destination locations.

For example, in the optimal solution:

$$v_1 = 1 \text{ (for warehouse R)}$$

$$v_3 = 3 \text{ (for warehouse T)}$$

This means that if the demand of warehouse T is increased by 1 ton and, at the same time, the requirement of warehouse R is decreased by 1 ton, then the total shipment cost will be *increased* by 2 ($v_3 - v_1 = 3 - 1 = 2$). In other words, warehouse T is less efficient. The policy implication is that if it is impossible to meet all the demand, warehouse T should be supplied only after all the demand at R is met.

Similarly, comparing v_2 and v_3, it can be seen that warehouse S is more efficient than warehouse T. This explains why, in the optimal solution (Table 7.29), the demand for warehouse T is not fully satisfied. It receives only 10 of the required demand of 60 tons.

Summary of MODI

Preparation: MODI requires a balanced transportation table.

Step 1. Derive an initial solution.

Step 2. Use equation $c_{ij} = u_i + v_j$ to compute all implicit costs of the occupied cells. Then, compute the cell evaluators of all empty cells, using equation $K_{ij} = c_{ij} - u_i - v_j$. Test for optimality as in the stepping-stone method.

Step 3. Identify an incoming cell and design an improved solution, as in the stepping-stone method.

Step 4. Recycle the process until an optimal solution is found.

7.8 Degeneracy

$m + n - 1$ occupied cells

$m + n - 1$ active constraints

A transportation problem has m supply constraints and n demand constraints, or a total of $m + n$ constraints. Because transportation problems are either balanced to begin with or, if not, can be converted to a balanced problem, the total demand is assumed to equal the total supply. As a result of such equality, it is possible to express one of the constraints in terms of the others: thus, one constraint is always redundant. Therefore, there are only $m + n - 1$ active constraints. This suggests that the transportation problem should have $m + n - 1$ active variable (occupied cells) in every *basic feasible solution* as well as in the *optimal solution*. For example, in a 3×3 problem, only five of the nine cells are normally occupied.

Whenever the number of occupied cells is *less than* $(m + n - 1)$ the solution is called *degenerate*. To handle **degeneracy,** the previous solution techniques must be slightly modified.

Two types of degeneracy

Degeneracy can develop in one of two ways. First, it can appear in the initial solution if the supply equals the demand for any cell in which an assignment is to be made. (More generally, the *remaining supply* (after some assignment) equals the remaining demand). Table 7.30 represents such a case (see cell AR). Note that the number of occupied cells in Table 7.30 is three instead of four; that is, $m + n - 1 = 2 + 3 - 1 = 4$.

Degeneracy can also develop during the improvement of solutions. If the quantities of two or more "losing" cells of a nondegenerate solution are the same, they will become empty simultaneously when an incoming variable is introduced. The resultant solution will then be degenerate.

Degeneracy impedes the optimality test

A degenerate solution cannot be tested for optimality by the methods previously outlined. Therefore, a special treatment is called for.

TABLE 7.30   Degenerate Solution

Source \ Destination	R	S	T	Supply
A	[1] 100	[3]	[6]	100
B	[5]	[3] 30	[2] 40	70
Demand	100	30	40	170 / 170

How to Resolve Degeneracy

Case 1: Degeneracy in the Very First Assignment

E is nil

In this case, an extremely small amount, designated by E, (almost zero) of the commodity to be shipped is allocated to one (or more) of the empty cells of the first solution to bring the number of occupied cells to $m + n - 1$. In a minimization problem, E is allocated to the empty cell with the lowest cost and that still allows the optimality check (in maximization problems, to the cell with the highest profit coefficient). The problem is then solved as if it were nondegenerate. The assignment of E should be made so the solution permits a check on optimality. If the configuration of occupied cells is such that after assigning E to the lowest cost cell, and now having $m + n - 1$ occupied cells, a check on optimality is not possible, then E should be assigned to the second lowest cost cell instead, and so on. Sometimes when E is assigned to one of the unoccupied cells, a check on optimality is not possible. This situation can be avoided during the construction of the initial basic feasible solution by assigning E to the row or column where the degeneracy actually occurs (when the supply and demand constraints are met simultaneously).

Example

Table 7.31A is a minimization example of a transportation problem in which degeneracy will develop when the initial solution is generated by the Northwest Corner Rule (Table 7.31B). The solution of Table 7.31B cannot be checked for optimality because the test requires $m + n - 1$ occupied cells (i.e., $2 + 2 - 1 = 3$). The requirement can be met by adding the quantity E to the low-cost cell AS. It is then possible to test for optimality, whereupon it will be found that the solution is not optimal. One improvement gives the solution shown in Table 7.31C, which is both optimal and nondegenerate.

TABLE 7.31A   A Degenerate Problem

From \ To	R	S	Supply
A	3	3	50
B	4	6	30
Demand	50	30	80 / 80

TABLE 7.31B   Initial Solution (Degenerate)

From \ To	R	S	Supply
A	3 / 50	3 / E	50
B	4	6 / 30	30
Demand	50	30	80 / 80

TABLE 7.31C   A Degenerate Problem

From \ To	R	S	Supply
A	3 / 20	3 / 30	50
B	4 / 30	6	30
Demand	50	30	80 / 80

TABLE 7.32A   Initial Solution

From \ To	R	S	T	Supply
A	5 50	4 20	2	70
B	6	3 30	2 20	50
C	1	5	1 10	10
Demand	50	50	30	130 / 130

TABLE 7.32B   First Improved Solution (Degenerate)

From \ To	R	S	T	Supply
A	5 50	4	2 20	70
B	6	3 50	2 E	50
C	1	5	1 10	10
Demand	50	50	30	130 / 130

TABLE 7.32C   Second Improved and Optimal Solution (Degenerate)

From \ To	R	S	T	Supply
A	5 40	4	2 30	70
B	6	3 50	2 E	50
C	1 10	5	1	10
Demand	50	50	30	130 / 130

254

Case 2: Degeneracy in Intermediate Solution Stages

In this case, E is assigned to one (or more) of the *newly vacated* cells. As mentioned earlier, the assignment must be made so that $m + n - 1$ cells will be "occupied" and an optimality check is possible.

Example

Where to place E

Table 7.32A contains an initial solution for a minimization problem. It is not optimal, and AT is in the incoming cell. Table 7.32B shows the first improved solution. The solution is degenerate. In order to test optimality, E is added to cell BT (the newly vacated cell with the lowest cost coefficient). The solution of Table 7.32b is not optimal; and hence a second improved solution, Table 7.32C, is derived. The second improved solution is still degenerate, but on checking, turns out to be optimal. To interpret the final solution, the value E is ignored. The total cost is $420.

7.9 The Transshipment Problem

The regular transportation model does not permit shipments among sources or destinations. However, it might be economically wise in certain instances to practice **transshipment** among origins and/or destinations. This would permit any origin, destination, or other distribution point to serve as an intermediate source.

In a transshipment model, there must always be a material balance at every point; that is,

$$Gross\ supply = Amount\ in + amount\ produced$$
$$= Amount\ shipped\ out + Amount\ consumed$$

The transshipment problem can be solved as an LP problem. But for larger problems, a transformation to a transportation model is more efficient.

Transshipment Example

Nippon Machinery Corporation makes popcorn machines. These are stored in three warehouses (I, II, and III) and are shipped once a month to four selling centers (A, B, C, and D). The warehouses can deliver 30, 40, and 30 units each month, respectively, and the zones (A, B, C, and D) require 50, 20, 10, and 20 units a month, respectively. Given in Table 7.33 are the shipping costs per unit (in hundreds of dollars) from warehouses to the zones. It is also possible to ship from zones to warehouses (at the same cost of shipping as from the warehouses to zones) and between warehouses (charges are shown in Table 7.34). Finally, it is possible to ship machines between zones (Table 7.35).

Shipments OK between sources or destinations

The problem is to find the shipment schedule that will minimize total transportation cost.

TABLE 7.33   Costs (In $ Hundreds)

		To Zone			
		A	B	C	D
From	I	$6	$10	$5	$7
Warehouse	II	5	9	4	8
	III	4	8	3	9

TABLE 7.34   Costs (In $ Hundreds)

		To Warehouse		
		I	II	III
From	I	$0	$1	$2
Warehouse	II	1	0	1
	III	2	1	0

TABLE 7.35   Costs (In $ Hundreds)

		To Zone			
		A	B	C	D
From	A	$0	$4	$1	$1
Zone	B	4	0	5	3
	C	1	5	0	2
	D	1	3	2	0

Solution

Step 1: Write the Combined Cost Matrix.   The cost information given in Tables 7.33, 7.34, and 7.35 is combined as shown in Table 7.36. Note that the cost from the source to the same destination (itself) is zero.

Step 2: Build the Transportation Equivalent of the Transshipment Problem.   The transportation equivalent of the transshipment problem is built as follows:

1. Determine a quantity S such that:

$$S = \sum_{i=1}^{m} b_i = \sum_{j=1}^{n} d_j$$

TABLE 7.36 Combined Cost Matrix

		Warehouses			Zones				Supply
		I,II,III			A	B	C	D	
	I	0 1 2			6	10	5	7	30
Warehouses	II	1 0 1			5	9	4	8	40
	III	2 1 0			4	8	3	9	30
	A	6 5 4			0	4	1	1	0
Zones	B	10 9 8			4	0	5	3	0
	C	5 4 3			1	5	0	2	0
	D	7 8 9			1	3	2	0	0
Demand		0 0 0			50	20	10	20	100 / 100

where S = total demand (or total supply). If total demand does not equal total supply, a dummy row or column must be added to balance supply and demand. In our case, $S = 30 + 40 + 30 = 100$.

2. Add this quantity to all the supply and demand numbers of the combined cost matrix of step 1. The result is the equivalent transportation problem, as summarized in Table 7.37.

Step 3: Solve the Equivalent Transportation Problem. We now have a standard transportation problem. The optimal solution is given in Table 7.38.

TABLE 7.37 The Equivalent Transportation Problem

	I	II	III	A	B	C	D	Modified Supply
I	0	1	2	6	10	5	7	130
II	1	0	1	5	9	4	8	140
III	2	1	0	4	8	3	9	130
A	6	5	4	0	4	1	1	100
B	10	9	8	4	0	5	3	100
C	5	4	3	1	5	0	2	100
D	7	8	9	1	3	2	0	100
Modified Demand	100	100	100	150	120	110	120	800 / 800

TABLE 7.38 Optimal Solution (Total Cost = $590)

	I	II	III	A	B	C	D	Modified Supply
I	100	30						130
II		70	70					140
III			30			100		130
A				60			40	100
B					100			100
C				90		10		100
D					20		80	100
Modified Demand	100	100	100	150	120	110	120	800 / 800

Interpretation of the Results

The "self-port" shipments (warehouse I to warehouse I, II to II, etc.) along the north-west to southeast diagonal (colored boxes) are in the optimal solution because of the zero costs of these cells. These self-port shipments are disregarded. The remaining shipments constitute the optimal solution. This solution consists of shipping 30 units from warehouse I to II and 70 units from II to III. Also, 100 units are shipped from III to C, with C keeping 10 units and forwarding 90 units on to A, which in turn sends 40 to D. Finally, 20 units are sent from D to B.

7.10 Use of Computers

The transportation problem can easily be solved by the computer.

Example

The Tuff Cement Company problem, presented in the beginning of this chapter, was solved by computer. The computer printout from the Lotfi and Pegels software is given below.

```
        Problem title: TUFF'S DISTRIBUTION

  Optimal solution: Total shipping cost :      240.00

     Ship        80.00   units from source  Allento   to dest. Easto
     Ship        10.00   units from source  Allento   to dest. Phild
     Ship       110.00   units from source  Baltim.   to dest. Phild
     Ship        10.00   units from source  Allento   to dest. NY
     Ship        50.00   units from source  Dummy     to dest. NY
```

The results are: ship 80 units from Allentown to Easton, ship 10 from Allentown to Philadephia, ship 10 from Allentown to New York, and ship 110 from Baltimore to Philadephia. The dummy source "ships" 50 to New York. The rest of the shipments are zero. The total cost is $240.

Assignment Packages

Assignment packages are less common than transportation packages. However, any assignment problem can easily be solved using a transportation package by simply balancing the problem and setting all supply and demand constraints to unity (1). A computer printout (from Lotfi and Pegels) of the assignment problem of Section 7.4 is given below.

```
               Problem title: ASSIGNMENT
           Optimal Solution: Objective value = 59

     S1          assigned to      Z2
     S2          assigned to      Z1
     S3          assigned to      Z3
```

7.11 Problems for Part B

25. In the transportation problem below, the data in the cells are profits per unit shipped. The objective of the company is profit maximization. Find the best shipment schedule.

    Note: Start with the Northwest Corner Rule: use the stepping-stone method. Watch for degeneracy.

To / From	I	II	Capacity
A	6	4	60
B	3	5	100
C	7	2	80
Requirement	60	150	

26. Solve Problem 2 by MODI. Start with the Northwest Corner Rule.

27. The Zip-Zip Fruit Company has drying facilities for fruits in several California cities. In the east, Baltimore, Atlantic City, New York City, and Philadelphia have ordered 20, 50, 100, and 60 tons, respectively. The company plans to fill these orders by shipping 70, 60, and 100 tons from Sacramento, Modesto, and Sunnyvale, respectively. Shipments can be sent through intermediate locations at a cost equal to the sum of the costs for each of the legs of the journey. Air freight charges per ton between locations are given in the following table:

Location	Plants SAC.	MOD.	SUN.	Destinations BALT.	ATL.	NYC	PHILA.
Sacramento	–	10	not poss.	50	80	55	50
Modesto	10	–	9	60	90	65	60
Sunnyvale	5	9	–	45	75	50	45
Baltimore	50	60	45	–	30	25	20
Atlantic City	80	90	75	30	–	10	10
New York	55	65	50	25	10	–	8
Philadelphia	50	60	45	20	10	8	–

a. Formulate this problem as a transshipment problem by constructing the appropriate cost and requirements table to be solved by a transportation-problem solution procedure.

b. Determine the shipping plan that minimizes the total freight cost.

28. Given the transportation cost table:

Warehouse \ Store	A	B	C	D	E	Capacity
1	4	7	3	9	6	200
2	3	2	4	6	5	400
3	5	6	2	5	3	600
4	8	4	5	7	3	700
Requirement	600	400	500	100	300	

a. Find the initial solution by the Northwest Corner Rule.

b. Find the transportation schedule that will minimize total shipping cost. Use MODI.

Hints: Watch for degeneracy and for more than one optimal solution.

29. Swedish Bakeries make three types of bread: small, standard, and large. These are baked in each of their four shops. The daily demand for the three types of bread and the selling prices are given below:

Type	Daily Demand	Selling price (Krona)
Small	500	24
Standard	1,200	29
Large	800	37

Each bakery shop is capable of baking up to 1,000 loaves of each type daily. The cost per loaf, including transportation, is given below. The difference in costs is due to baking technology and travel distances.

Shop \ Bread	Small	Standard	Large
A	12	15	20
B	13	17	19
C	11	17	22
D	14	16	18

Find how many loaves of each type of bread to bake in each shop to maximize profit.

a. Formulate as a transportation problem.

b. Solve by MODI. Start with the least-cost method.

Note: Watch for degeneracy.

30. Eastern Railroad Company serves five cities, A–E. The distances between the cities are shown below:

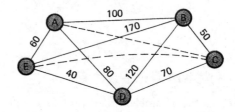

At the present time, there is no connection between cities A and C, and E and C, due to maintenance work on the rails.

On Sunday afternoon, the company has 200 identical cars at the following cities: A—40, B—60, C—70, D—30. By Monday, empty cars are needed in the following cities: B—40, D—50, and E—40.

The company wants to minimize the mileage traveled. All demands of Monday must be met. Find the best routing plan. Use MODI; start with the least-cost method.

31. Westcan Machine Shop produces three products (A, B, and C) using its four automatic machines (1, 2, 3, and 4). Each is capable (unless otherwise specified) of making the product in one operation.

The table below shows the output, in units per hour, of each machine, for each product (*X* implies impossible combinations).

Product \ Machine	1	2	3	4
A	16	10	X	6
B	8	20	10	9
C	12	X	14	1

The monthly demand for the three products is 2,000, 2,500, and 2,200, respectively. The products sell for $6, $4, and $8.20, respectively. The machines are available at a cost of $24, $30, $28, and $18 per hour. Each machine is capable of making up to 2,500 units per month. Find the optimal monthly production plan.

a. Formulate as a transportation problem.

b. Solve by MODI, start with the least-cost method.
   Hint: Watch for degeneracy.

32. Formulate and solve Problem 10 as a transportation problem.

33. Kojo Corporation is a large Korean manufacturer of heavy numerically controlled (computerized) machines. The company has two plants, one in Seoul and the other in Pusan. Machines are shipped once a month to two distribution centers, one in Chicago and one in London. From there, the machines are shipped to four sales centers, A, B, C, and D. A machine stays in a distribution center for about half a month on the average. Shipping costs per machine are listed below.

From Seoul to Pusan or back	$ 150
From Seoul to Chicago	1,100
From Seoul to London	1,250
From Pusan to Chicago	1,180
From Pusan to London	1,450
From Chicago to London	880
From Chicago to A	350
From Chicago to B	620
From A to B or B to A	538
From London to C or D	465
From C to London	590
From C to D	810

The company does not ship in routes that are not listed above (e.g., from Chicago to Seoul). The company can ship 550 units from Seoul and 670 from Pusan each month. The Chicago center can hold 800 units, whereas the one in London can hold 560. The monthly demand at the sales centers is: A = 240, B = 480, C = 190, D = 375. Storage costs in Chicago are $60 per unit per month and in London, $38 per unit per month.

Prepare the most economic monthly shipping schedule.

7.12 CASES
I. NORTHEASTERN BLOOD BANK

Northeastern General is the only hospital in a small mountain community in Wales. Dr. Alton, the chief surgeon, just completed the list of patients to be operated on the next morning, specifying the blood that will be required during the operations.

Eight patients are on the list below with their blood type and quantity required.

Patient	Blood Type	Quantity (Pints)
Able	AB	3
Brook	B	2
Cock	A	6
Dean	O	3
Elm	B	4
Flint	AB	2
Gloss	A	2
Hope	O	2

The hospital's blood bank currently has the following blood inventory. (Blood comes in 1-pint containers.)

Blood Type	Inventory (Pints)
A	4
B	10
O	11
AB	7

A patient with blood type AB is considered a universal recipient; that is, he or she can receive any type of blood. A blood type O is considered acceptable for transfusion to any type of patient.

Ann White, the director of the hospital's blood bank, has just received the list and computed the demand for blood as:

Type	Pints in Demand	Versus	Pints in Stock
A	8		4
B	6		10
O	5		11
AB	5		7

Ann realizes that she is short by four pints of type A. However, this shortage can be covered by four pints of type O.

As she was ready to deliver the blood, she remembered the meeting she had with the hospital administrator last Friday. The meeting went as follows:

John Par (the administrator): Ann, the doctors are happy with your work. The patients always receive the required amount of the proper type of blood. There is only one problem.
Ann: What do you mean?
John: Well, the cost of acquiring blood is ever increasing, and the expenses of your department are increasing much faster than those of the other departments.
Ann: What can I do about the situation? I can't buy cheaper blood; we belong to a regional blood bank and can't negotiate prices.
John: That's true, but I understand that the cost of the different types of blood isn't the same, especially when the cost of transportation and special orders is added.
Ann: I just completed a study on this. Here are the figures: Type A = $30 per pint; type B = $36 per pint; type O = $35 per pint; and type AB = $40 per pint.
John: This is interesting. It looks as though you might be able to save some money by substituting blood types.

Ann: That's possibly true, but what will the physicians say if we increase the rate of blood substitutions?

John: I don't know. Let's check and find out.

a. Find the *least* total cost blood allocation plan. Use a transportation type model.

b. How much can Ann save by following the optimal solutions, as compared to her present policy of "matching blood to needs as close as possible"?

c. Even though substitutions may be safe from a clinical point of view, the physicians may not be too happy with the optimal solution. Why?

II. Greenhill's Federal Grant

The Greenhill public hearing meeting turned stormy. Citizens from four suburbs were gathered at city hall to try to get the city's federal funds for their own suburbs.

The government recently awarded $750,000 to the city for road improvements. The city requested bids and five contractors submitted bids for work in the four suburbs. The bids are listed below (in thousands of dollars):

| Contractor | Suburb | | | |
	1	2	3	4
A	210	242	202	243
B	222	232	205	250
C	205	225	244	210
D	265	206	200	270
E	215	211	253	212

Because under the terms of the federal grant, the work must be completed fairly soon, none of the contractors are large enough to perform more than one job. That is, it will be necessary to use a different contractor for each suburb's job.

From the bids, it was clear to Greenhill's city council that the federal funds would not cover road improvements in all four suburbs. As they began to analyze the situation, they realized they needed some hard facts. Therefore, they called the finance director of Greenhill and requested the following information:

a. What is the *minimum* amount of money that the city must add to the government grant such that work may be done in all four suburbs?

b. What is the best contractor-to-suburb match?

c. Which of the contractors should not receive a job contract?

d. If the city cannot come up with any supplementary funds, only three suburbs will be repaired. Based on dollars and cents, which three suburbs should be selected such that the surplus from the government grant is maximized?

The director of finance asked you, a newly appointed assistant, to use some management science tools to answer these questions. What will your answers be?

Glossary

Balancing   Equating total supply to total demand by adding dummy sources of supply or dummy destinations for demand.

Cell evaluator   The opportunity cost involved in shipping one unit through a route that is not currently used.

Closed loop   A path showing the transfer of units in a revised transportation table.

Degeneracy (degenerate solution)   A solution to a transportation problem in which there are fewer than $m + n - 1$ occupied cells in the transportation table.

Destination   A place a shipment is directed to.

Dummy row(s), column(s)   Row(s) or column(s) that are added to the transportation and assignment tables to equalize total supply and total demand (in the case of transportation) or to equalize the number of rows and columns (in the case of assignment).

Hungarian method   An algorithm used to efficiently solve an assignment problem.

MODI (modified distribution procedure).   An algorithm used to efficiently solve a transportation problem.

Northwest Corner Rule   A procedure used to find an initial feasible solution to a transportation problem.

Source   A place a shipment originates from.

Stepping-stone procedure   An algorithm used to test a transportation solution for optimality.

Transportation method   An algorithm to efficiently solve transportation problems.

Transshipment   A problem where shipments among sources and/or destinations are permissible.

References and Bibliography

1. Bazaraa, M., J. J. Jarvis, and H. Sherali. *Linear Programming and Network Flows,* 2nd ed. New York: Wiley, 1990.
2. Harvey, C. *Operations Research, An Introduction to Linear Optimization and Decision Analysis.* New York: Elsevier North-Holland Publishing, 1979.
3. Loomba, N. P. *Linear Programming,* 2nd ed. New York: Macmillan, 1976.
4. Murty, K. *Linear Programming,* New York: Wiley, 1983.
5. Taha, H. A., *Operations Research: An Introduction.* 5th ed., New York: Macmillan, 1992.
6. Wagner, H. M. *Principles of Operations Research with Applications to Managerial Decisions.* 2nd ed. Englewood Cliffs, N.J.: Prentice-Hall, 1975.

Multiple Criteria Decision Making

Although linear programming applications can be found throughout organizations worldwide, when several competing objectives must be considered simultaneously, a more sophisticated tool is needed. The multiple criteria decision making approaches discussed in this chapter describe some of these tools. One very sophisticated approach is goal programming, the subject of Part A of this chapter. Utility theory and the analytic hierarchy process are other approaches to address situations involving multiple objectives. These two techniques are described in Part B.

PART A: GOAL PROGRAMMING

The Birch Paper Company

The Birch Paper Company (BIP) is composed of three divisions. Division A makes paperboard that is sold to divisions B and C and the outside market. Division B produces boxes that are sold to division C and to the outside market. Division C makes two specialty paper products that are sold to Sears Roebuck & Co. The company's production plan was determined in the past by an LP model. This approach permitted profit maximization. However, the approach created temporary working capital and cash reserve difficulties. As a result, the credit rating of the company was lowered and the company stock lost 15 percent of its value in one month. Cash reserves and working capital requirements were then imposed, but as a result, profits declined. The angry shareholders forced the CEO to resign. The three division heads, Bill, Gil, and Will, decided to discard the LP model in an attempt to improve the situation, but they were unable to agree on an alternative plan.

The matter was aggravated when Patricia Gray, the corporate chief financial officer (CFO), pushed for even stricter financial requirements. The division managers blamed Patricia for adding to their troubles. Patricia replied that this was nonsense: "You make the production decisions, and if you cannot improve profitability, you should go."

It was the first day of work for Judy Beer, the newly appointed CEO, when she was thrown into the midst of a heated debate between Bill and Will, who were blaming each other for a production problem. Judy paused for a moment to consider the following:

- Why was the LP model discarded?
- Can a substitute model be used?
- What will happen if the cash reserves and working capital requirements are increased or reduced?

Judy realized that the job of the CEO may not be as easy or as pleasant as many people think.

Source: This case is based on the Harvard Business School case Birch Paper Company. The GP application was suggested by R. P. Manes, "Birch Paper Company Revisited: An Exercise in Transfer Pricing," *Accounting Review* 45 (July 1970), pp. 565–72; and S. Kinory, "Goal Programming and Managerial Decision Making," *Management International Review* 18, no. 2 (1978), pp. 101–9.

8.1 Multiple Criteria Decision Making

The analysis of management decisions aims at evaluating, to the greatest possible extent, how far each alternative advances management toward its goals. Unfortunately, managerial problems are seldom evaluated in terms of a single goal such as profit maximization. Today's management systems are becoming more and more complex, and striving for just one goal is rare. Instead, managers want to attain simultaneous goals, some of which conflict with each other. Therefore, it is often necessary to analyze each alternative in light of its potential impact on several goals (or criteria).

No single goal

For example, the strict financial requirements in the Birch Paper situation interfered with production scheduling. For a generic example, consider a profit-making firm. In addition to making money, the company wants to grow, to develop its products and its employees, to provide job security to its workers, and to serve the community.

Complementary and conflicting goals

Needless to say, some of these goals complement each other and others are in direct conflict. Add to this social, legal, and ethical considerations and the system of goals begins to look quite complex.

The quantitative approach to decision theory discussed so far is based on comparing a single measure of effectiveness. In this chapter, we expand the discussion to multiple criteria. Before presenting methodologies for dealing with **multiple criteria decision making (MCDM),** it will be worthwhile to discuss some of the difficulties involved.

Some difficulties

1. It is usually difficult to obtain an explicit statement of the organization's goals.
2. Participants assess the importance (priorities) of the various goals differently.
3. The decision maker(s) may change the importance assigned to specific goals with the passage of time or in different decision situations.
4. Goals and subgoals are viewed differently at various levels of the organization and in various departments.
5. The goals themselves are dynamic in response to continuous changes in the organization and its environment.
6. It is difficult to express some of the goals in quantitative terms.
7. The relationship between alternatives and their impact on goals may be difficult to measure.

In spite of these difficulties, it is instructive to examine some methods that can be used to resolve the multiple criteria situation. Six such techniques are outlined below.

a. Goal Programming

A special method of treating certain multiple goal situations involving problems of allocation is termed *goal programming*. According to this technique, goals are ranked in order of their importance. For example, profit may be more important than share of the market. Then allocation decisions are made such that the sum of the undesirable deviations from the goals is minimized. This topic is treated in detail in Part A of this Chapter.

b. Expression of Goals as Requirements (Constraints)

Goals as system requirements

This approach is used in linear programming. The most important (primary) goal is maximized (or minimized) and all other (secondary) goals are expressed in terms of system *requirements*.

c. Conversion to a Single Scale

A single scale

Multiple goals can sometimes be expressed by a single measure, such as dollars. In this case, all the outcomes, as well as the costs of the alternatives, should be expressed in the same measure.

Example: Change in Maintenance Policy

Assume that a company is considering a change in its maintenance policy from weekly to biweekly preventive maintenance. The maintenance policy primarily affects breakdowns but also has an impact on maintenance costs, product quality, and spare parts inventory. In this case, it may be possible to express the overall effect of the two alternatives on the various goals (or measures of effectiveness) directly, in dollar terms. For example, total weekly cost = $3,000 for maintenance + $600 for product quality losses + $280 for breakdowns = $3,880.

d. Expressing One Goal in Terms of Another (Trade-offs)

Goal trade-offs

Sometimes it is possible to express two or more goals in terms of one, by using trade-offs, thus again arriving at a single measure of effectiveness.

Example: Sales and Profit Increases

The projected outcomes of two alternatives are shown in Table 8.1. The question is: Which alternative is better if both cost the same? To answer this question, it is necessary to find a single measure of effectiveness.

Suppose management decides that each 1 percent increase in profit is worth a $10,000 increase in sales. Then $50,000 and $80,000 sales increases are equivalent to a 5 percent and 8 percent increase in profit, respectively, as shown in Table 8.2.

Once the two outcomes are expressed in one measure, we can combine and compare them (14 for a_1, 12 for a_2), then select the most effective (a_1 in this case).

The trade-offs between sales and profits were linear in this example. But in other cases, the relationship may be *non*linear and it would be necessary to construct trade-off curves to accurately show the relationship between the result variables. A refinement of this approach is the *analytic hierarchy process,* which is discussed in Part B of this chapter.

e. Using a Utility System

The value of one goal in the previous example was expressed in terms of the other. Another method is to express all alternatives in terms of utilities. This method is discussed in Part B of this chapter.

TABLE 8.1   Two Outcomes

Outcomes / Alternatives	Sales Increase	Profit Increase
a_1	$50,000	9%
a_2	$80,000	4%

TABLE 8.2   Combined Outcomes

Outcomes / Alternatives	Sales Expressed as Percent Profit	Profit	Total	
a_1	$\dfrac{\$50,000}{\$10,000} \times 1\% = 5\%$	9%	5 + 9 = 14	←*Maximum*
a_2	$\dfrac{\$80,000}{\$10,000} \times 1\% = 8\%$	4%	8 + 4 = 12	

f. Multiple Objective Linear Programming

Multiple objective linear programming (MOLP) is a technique often used in solving problems with multiple goals, especially when the priorities are non-preemptive. In MOLP the objectives are stated in terms of a linear objective function instead of a pre-specified goal. In some cases MOLP has an advantage over goal programming, in which the goals are stipulated before the problem is solved. It is often useful to graphically solve a MOLP problem in objective space in order to clearly depict the nondominated extreme points.

8.2 Introduction to Goal Programming

Multiple goals

Judy's case highlights several important issues. First, BIP's situation involves **multiple goals.** In practice, many decisions are made subject to multiple criteria where a "satisfactory" solution is sought, rather than an optimal one. Second, the requirements and constraints in the real world are not always rigid; that is, deviations from targets may be acceptable, especially when trade-offs are permitted. Finally, the BIP situation seems to have many of the characteristics of LP (for example, general structure, assumptions). However, the LP solution was ineffective. What is needed is a modified approach called **goal programming (GP).**

The Basic Idea of Goal Programming

When a company is faced with multiple conflicting goals, it may not be possible to achieve every goal to the desired extent. For example, the company may not be able to grow at 15 percent a year and make $3 profit per share. The GP model attempts to obtain a satisfactory level of goal attainment that would be the best feasible solution in view of the priorities (relative importance of the goals). Thus, higher-priority goals can be attained at the expense of lower-priority goals.

Goal programming is used to perform three types of analysis:

a. Determining the required resources to achieve a set of desired objectives.
b. Determining the degree of attainment of the goals with the available resources.
c. Providing the best satisfying solution under a varying amount of resources and priorities of the goals.

Linear vs. Goal Programming

Before presenting the technique, let us examine the differences between problems that can be solved by LP and those that require the GP approach (see Table 8.3).

Linear programming has a single objective function that is to be optimized. In the formulation discussed so far, either one objective existed or, if there were several objectives, one was expressed in the objective function while the remaining objectives were expressed as constraints. For example, maximizing profit could be the primary objective, subject to at least a 10 percent share of the market (a secondary objective). Because most organizations possess several (sometimes even conflicting) goals, it is often difficult to determine which goal to maximize and which goals to express as constraints.

Another problem with LP is its inflexibility. The limits on the secondary goals cannot be violated. Thus, a solution to the BIP problem with $1 million profit and a 9.9 percent share of the market could be considered as infeasible, but a solution with $100,000 profit and a 10 percent share of the market could be declared optimal.

TABLE 8.3   Differences Between GP and LP

Dimension	Linear Programming (LP)	Goal Programming (GP)
Goals and objectives	One primary—to be maximized or minimized	All objectives are ranked, each with a target
Targets or constraints	Inflexible, no deviations are allowed	Flexible, deviations are acceptable, constraints can be relaxed
Objective function	Maximize (minimize) the value of the primary goal	Minimize the sum of the undesirable deviations (weighted by their relative importance)
Purpose	Optimization	Satisfaction
Theory	Mature	Relatively young, developing
Computer programs	Very efficient, many packages	Inefficient, few computer packages
Applications	Many and varied	Few, but increasing

8.3 Concepts for Goal Programming

Five important concepts constitute the backbone of GP: (*a*) Goal constraints, (*b*) deviations, (*c*) priorities and weights of the goals, (*d*) dimensions of the goals, and (*e*) goal setting.

a. Goal Constraints

The constraints in GP are of two types: system constraints (same as in LP) and goal constraints. In goal constraints, we are willing to allow deviations from the constraint targets (right-hand side values).

b. Deviations

Deviations are the amounts by which goals are either overachieved or underachieved. Let us look at three goals:

1. Achieve a profit of at least $300,000 per month.
2. Do not exceed 500 hours of overtime per month.
3. Maintain an inventory level of exactly 20 units.

Overachievement

The **overachievement** deviations measure the extent to which the goals are exceeded; they are labeled by the **deviational variable** d_i^+.

Example 1

If the profit is $320,000, then $d_1^+ = 320,000 - 300,000 = 20,000$; $d_1^- = 0$

If overtime is 550 hours, then $d_2^+ = 550 - 500 = 50$; $d_2^- = 0$

Note that the first deviation is desirable while the second one is not.

Underachievement

The **underachievement** deviations measure the extent by which performance is less than the goal. They are denoted as d_i^-.

Example 2

If profit level is $290,000, then $d_3^- = 300,000 - 290,000 = 10,000$; $d_3^+ = 0$

If overtime is 460 hours, then $d_3^- = 500 - 460 = 40$; $d_3^+ = 0$

Note that both d_i^+ and d_i^- must be *nonnegative* and at least one of them *must be zero*.

Desirable and Undesirable Deviations

Undesirable deviations

Deviations can be either desirable or undesirable. For example, in the case of profit, d^+ is desirable, but d^- is not. On the other hand, in the case of overtime, d^+ is undesirable, but d^- is desirable. In many cases, we observe the following relationships:

Type of Constraint on Goal	Undesirable Deviations
$\geq$	d_i^-
$\leq$	d_i^+
$=$	d_i^+ and d_i^-

According to our definition, *underachievement* is *undesirable* in the case of $\geq$ constraints. Similarly, *overachievement* is *undesirable* in the case of $\leq$ constraints. In the case of equalities, *both* under- and overachievement are undesirable. That is, a violation of the constraints is considered undesirable.

c. Prioritizing Goals

Goals in GP are prioritized in three different ways: ordinal, cardinal, and a mixture of the two.

1. *Ordinal ranking.* In this method, goals are listed in the order of their importance. P_1 designates the priority level of the most important goal, P_2 designates the second most important goal, and so on.

Priority ranking

2. *Cardinal ranking.* In this method, a specific weight is assigned to each of the deviations. These weights show the relative importance of each deviation.
3. *A mix of the two.* This approach will be illustrated later when the objective function's structure is presented.

The priorities of the goals are expressed in the objective function's coefficients, as will be demonstrated later.

d. Dimensions of the Goals

Minimize undesirable deviations

The objective function of the GP attempts to minimize the sum of the undesirable deviations weighted by their importance. This summation may make little sense, however, if the dimensions of the deviations are different. For example, d_1 may be profit measured in dollars, but d_2 may be expressed in terms of percent of market share. (The dimension problem may be solved by using weights, as will be shown later.)

e. Goal Setting

The fact that in real life not all goals may be achieved means that there will be undesirable deviations in the less important goals. This fact may have a psychological impact on the people responsible for attaining these goals. Specifically, they would not like to be labeled "nonachievers." For this reason, and because of the fact that in many cases there will be rewards attached to achievements, people may attempt to set the goals too low.

Negotiation for goal setting

Goal setting, in many cases, is a negotiated process. Methods such as management by objectives (MBO) extensively utilize negotiated goals. During a negotiation session, the employee responsible for the attainment of the goal (e.g., a department chairperson) may try to set the goal at a low level, whereas his or her superior may try to increase it. If the goals are set too low, then the GP solution will indicate that all of them can be fully achieved. This can be an easy political escape, but it is usually a poor resource allocation solution.

Recognizing this fact, companies are using a "stretching" strategy. According to this strategy, the initial goals are set through the regular negotiation process. Then, those involved in the GP situation are briefed about GP and assured that undesirable deviations are acceptable. Then, the stretching process begins, where the goals are tightened as much as possible. Only then should the GP model be initiated.

8.4 The Structure of Goal Programming

The GP model is composed of four elements:

Four elements

a. Decision variables.
b. System constraints.
c. Goal constraints.
d. Objective function.

a. Decision Variables

The decision variables are the same as in regular LP.

b. System Constraints

Regular LP constraints

System constraints are identical to LP constraints. They represent absolute restrictions and do not allow any deviations. For example, it is impossible to work more than 21 shifts (7×3) each week. These constraints are expressed as regular LP constraints and must be satisfied before *any* of the goal constraints can be considered.

c. Goal Constraints

Aspiration levels

Goal constraints represent target values to be achieved.

Example 1

Assume that the decision variables are the products to include in a product mix. Product *A* brings a $5 profit contribution, product *B* nets a $7 profit contribution, and product C brings a \$3 profit contribution. The total profit is:

$$5A + 7B + 3C$$

In regular LP, we attempt to maximize this function. In GP we first write it as:

$$5A + 7B + 3C \geq 200,000$$

where \$200,000 is a desired profit level. However, because we allow deviations, the constraint is written instead as:

$$5A + 7B + 3C + d_1^- - d_1^+ = 200,000$$

where d_1^- is the underachievement of profit and d_1^+ is the overachievement.

Example 2

Each unit of product A (above) requires two hours of labor, each unit of B requires six hours, and each unit of C requires three hours. The labor supply during regular hours is 500 hours. The constraint is:

$$2A + 6B + 3C + d_2^- - d_2^+ = 500$$

Example 3

Overtime in Example 2 should not exceed 50 hours:

$$2A + 6B + 3C - 500 + d_3^- - d_3^+ = 50$$

or

$$2A + 6B + 3C + d_3^- - d_3^+ = 550$$

The Signs in Front of the Deviations

Deviation signs

The reader will notice that a d^+ deviation is always preceded by a minus sign, while a d^- deviation is always preceded by a plus sign. The reason for this is shown in the following example. Assume that we have a profit constraint:

$$5x_1 + 7x_2 \geq 10,000$$

In GP terms, we change it to:

$$5x_1 + 7x_2 + d^- - d^+ = 10,000$$

Three cases may occur in the solution:

1. The profit $5x_1 + 7x_2$ will be exactly 10,000. In such a case, both d^- and d^+ must equal zero.
2. The profit $5x_1 + 7x_2$ will be less than \$10,000 (underachievement), say, \$9,000. In this case, we will get:

$$9,000 + d^- - d^+ = 10,000$$

that is,

$$d^- - d^+ = 10,000 - 9,000 = 1,000$$

Because deviations cannot be negative, and one of them must be zero, we get the following solution:

$$d^- = 1,000, \quad d^+ = 0$$

3. The profit is larger than 10,000; say, 12,000. The equation will then be:

$$12,000 + d^- - d^+ = 10,000$$

Solving, we get:

$$d^+ = 2,000, \quad d^- = 0$$

GP With a Single Goal

It is possible to have a GP problem with only one goal. In this case, we use the GP formulation to analyze the deviations from this single goal. Most times, however, GP deals with multiple, conflicting goals.

d. Objective Function

The objective function in GP is formulated to minimize the weighted sum of the undesirable deviations. Therefore, the structure of such a function depends on the weighting system. The following variations exist:

1. Single Objective Problem

In such a case, the objective function is:

$$\text{minimize } z = d_1^+ \tag{8.1}$$

where d_1^+ is undesirable (or minimize d_1^- if d_1^- is undesirable).

2. Multiple Objectives, Ordinal Ranking

Single and multiple objectives

The objective function is written, for example, as

$$\text{minimize } z = P_1 d_1^- + P_2 d_2^+ + P_3 d_3^- + \cdots \tag{8.2}$$

where the P_i indicates the importance of the goal ($i = 1$ is first in importance). For example, $P_1 d_1^-$ means that d_1^- is an undesirable deviation with priority level one.

There is one variation to this situation: the case where d^+ and d^- are undesirable for the same goal (produce exactly 10 units). In such a case, we can use *two* approaches. First, we give the same or different priority to the deviations. Giving a different priority (e.g., $P_1 d_1^- + P_2 d_1^+$) means that the negative deviation is much more important than the positive one. Such a designation is somewhat confusing, because P_2 is generally used to designate another, second, goal. Another way to overcome this problem is discussed later, under item 5.

In solving this type of goals presentation, the computer employs a "preemptive" philosophy. This approach allows the pursuit of the objectives in an ordinal sequence, but one based on their importance. The most important objective (labeled P_1) is pursued first until it is either attained as fully as desired (i.e., its undesirable deviation $= 0$) or found to be unattainable. Then, the deviation of the second most important goal, P_2, is driven to zero (or as close to zero as possible) within the solution space defined by the first priority goal and the system constraints. This process continues until all goals have been considered. This process can be expressed as:

$$P_1 >>> P_2 >>> P_3 >>> P_4 >>> \cdots \qquad (8.3)$$

where $P_i >>> P_{i+1}$ means that multiplication of the deviation by any number, however large it may be, cannot make P_{i+1} more important than P_i. (P_i is much more important than P_{i+1}.)

It is usually not possible to fully satisfy all the goals. As a result, there will be undesirable deviations from some of the goal targets. These deviations are analyzed in GP through a sensitivity analysis. Priorities can be changed, for example, and the impact on the solution observed (see Section 8.7).

3. Multiple Goals That Are Equally Important
If all the goals are equally important, then the objective is simply to minimize the sum of the undesirable deviations. For example,

$$\text{minimize } z = d_1^- + d_2^+ + d_3^+ + d_4^-$$

4. Multiple Goals, Use of a Cardinal Scale
In this case, a specific weight is assigned to *each* undesirable deviation. This approach is especially important when the *dimensions* of the deviations are different. An objective function in such a case may look like this:

$$\text{minimize } z = 16d_1^- + 10d_2^+ + 1d_3^- + 4d_4^+ + 5d_5^-$$

There are two problems with this approach. First, people in general have difficulty assigning specific weights to goals. Second, in this case, the problem is even more difficult, because the weights express *both* the relative importance of the goals and the dimensional relationship of the deviations.

5. Multiple Goals, Use of Cardinal and Ordinal Scales
This is an extension of the ordinal scale for a case where there exist two undesirable deviations for one goal. Let us assume that this happened in the third goal. In such a case, weights are assigned to determine which deviation is more important within the same priority level. The objective function in such a case will look like this:

$$\text{minimize } z = P_1 d_1^+ + P_2 d_2^+ + 3P_3 d_3^- + 2P_3 d_3^+ + P_4 d_4^+$$

That is, the negative deviation of the third goal is $\frac{3}{2} = 1.5$ times as important as the positive one.

Management Science in Practice

Restructuring Peoria's City Tax System

In the early 1980s, Peoria's (Illinois) industrial base began to erode as several major plants closed. Because Peoria relied heavily on property taxes for its revenues, the services it provided to its citizens were at risk as the population and property values continued to fall. In many cities, total reliance on property taxes for revenue has been replaced with other forms of taxes, for a variety of reasons; for example, during periods of rapid inflation, property tax revenues do not keep up. And as property tax rates rise, real estate market values tend to be depressed.

Peoria commissioned a study by Bradley University in 1982 to investigate the impact of a restructuring of their tax system. The study indicated that a sales tax offered the possibility of decreasing the existing property tax and maintaining solid growth as the economy improved in the future. A particular attraction was its shift of the tax burden from city residents to include nonresidents who consume the public goods and services the city offers, yet pay no property tax.

A follow-up study was then conducted to examine the desirability of a broader restructuring of the tax system that would include three major tax sources: property, sales, and gasoline.

Discussion with the city manager indicated three major objectives in the tax restructuring: (1) reducing existing property taxes, (2) minimizing the tax burden on low-income households, and (3) minimizing the flight of businesses and shoppers to the suburbs to escape higher sales taxes. Also, he wanted to be sure that in achieving these objectives, the city's current tax revenues, as well as the city's medium- and high-income households, would not be adversely affected.

This problem was modeled with a multiobjective linear program, a version of linear programming similar to goal programming. The solutions in this program are not guaranteed to be optimal but they are efficient in the sense that no other solution will improve the value of any single objective without worsening the value of at least one other objective. Additionally, the program was run in the interactive mode, with the city manager altering the objectives and constraints as the results of each iteration were presented, in an attempt to match his intuitive sense of what was politically acceptable and desirable with the program's outputs.

The first solution resulted in an unacceptably high gasoline tax; so in the next iteration a fourth objective was added—to minimize the gasoline tax. Later iterations resulted in food and drug and durable goods sales tax rates exceeding the general sales tax rate (which tends to violate the second and third objectives); so the program was again modified to constrain these rates to not exceed the general sales tax rate. More iterations involved adding limits and constraints to the tax rates as well as the low-income tax burden.

Finally, a set of acceptable solutions was produced. The solution preferred by the city manager added about 1 percent to the general sales tax and subtracted more than 1 percent from the 2.7 percent property tax, as well as eliminating the then-existing 1 percent food and drug tax. It also added about 1 percent to the durable goods sales tax and initiated a 3.3 cents per gallon gasoline tax.

The city of Peoria did restructure its tax system. It does not directly reflect the results of the study, but it is constructed along similar lines and uses the tradeoffs illustrated in the analysis. A major value of the model as it was employed and continues to be used by the city is the insight it provides to the tax planners and city managers.

Source: J. J. Chrisman, et al. "A Multiobjective Linear Programming Methodology for Public Sector Tax Planning," *Interfaces*, September–October 1989, pp. 13–22.

Questions

1. Why was a high gasoline tax unacceptable?
2. Why was a high food, drug, and durable tax rate unacceptable?
3. What implicit objectives were there in addition to the three explicit objectives?
4. Did the city manager's solution achieve the three objectives? Did it achieve the implicit additional objectives?

8.5 Formulation: The Birch Paper Co.

As the reader may recall, the Birch Paper Company (BIP) is composed of three divisions. Figure 8.1 presents the produce relationships among the divisions.

Division A produces paperboard (quantity x_1). Division B produces boxes (x_2). Division C sells up to 150 units a week of two specialty paper products to Sears: x_3 = quantity of product I and x_4 = quantity of product II. The division can acquire the materials necessary for production from two sources: either internally (divisions A and/or B) or from an outside vendor. However, the vendor will provide the materials if and only if division B agrees to provide them with boxes at prices they stipulate. As stated earlier, both A and B can also sell their products on the open market. The relevant data are shown in Table 8.4.

Find the weekly schedule

The initial problem is to determine the optimal weekly production schedule. That is, find the values of x_1, x_2, x_3, and x_4 that maximize the profit. The LP formulation follows.

Objective function:

$$\text{maximize } z = 112x_1 + 162x_2 + 192x_3 + 89x_4$$

subject to the following constraints, which were derived based on certain technological relationships between the divisions and the products:

$$x_1 + x_2 + x_3 + .333x_4 \leq 100 \quad \text{(to be called C5)}$$

$$x_2 + x_3 + .143x_4 \leq 100 \quad \text{(to be called C6)}$$

$$x_3 + x_4 \leq 150 \quad \text{(to be called C7)}$$

The linear programming solution for this problem is:

$$x_1 = 0,\ x_2 = 50,\ x_3 = 0,\ x_4 = 150;\ \text{profit} = \$21,450 \text{ per week}$$

This production plan (above) was used before the following new financial requirements were added:

(C1) $168x_1 + 288x_2 + 288x_3 + 391x_4 \geq 67,000$ (cash on hand, proportional to total cost)

(C2) $150x_1 + 80x_2 + 86x_3 + 70x_4 \geq 16,000$ (net working capital)

FIGURE 8.1

BIP production flow process

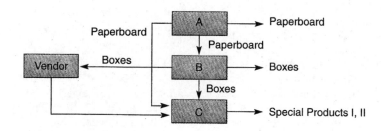

TABLE 8.4 Data for the BIP Company

Product	Quantity	Selling Price per Unit	Cost per Unit	Profit Margin
Paperboard	x_1	280	168	112
Boxes	x_2	450	288	162
Special product I	x_3	480	288	192
Special product II	x_4	480	391	89

The linear programming solution to this new problem is now:

$$x_1 = 21.44, \; x_2 = 28.55, \; x_3 = 0, \; x_4 = 150$$

for a total profit of $20,948 per week.

When the cash-on-hand requirement was later increased to $72,000, the LP computer package signaled an *infeasible* solution. Management was unable to use the LP any longer and a negotiated production plan was introduced to meet the financial requirements. However, meeting the requirements resulted in some overtime and reduced profit, a situation that caused the resignation of the former CEO. The new CEO, Ms. Beer, heard about GP and decided to try it.

The GP Approach

The System Constraints

The capacity constraints of the LP problem are technological in nature and cannot be changed. Therefore, they appear in an identical format as in the original LP problem, namely:

$$1x_1 + 1x_2 + 1x_3 + .333x_4 \leq 100 \quad \text{(constraint C5)}$$

$$0x_1 + 1x_2 + 1x_3 + .143x_4 \leq 100 \quad \text{(constraint C6)}$$

$$0x_1 + 0x_2 + 1x_3 + \quad 1x_4 \leq 150 \quad \text{(constraint C7)}$$

The Goal Constraints

In addition to the original goal of profit, there are two financial requirements: cash and net working capital. The goals are expressed in GP terms (in descending order of importance) as:

(C1) $168x_1 + 288x_2 + 288x_3 + 391x_4 + d_1^- - d_1^+ = 72,000$ (cash—most important)

(C2) $150x_1 + \quad 80x_2 + \quad 86x_3 + \quad 70x_4 + d_2^- - d_2^+ = 16,000$ (working capital)

(C3) $112x_1 + 162x_2 + 192x_3 + \quad 89x_4 + d_3^- - d_3^+ = 23,000$ (profit)

The profit target of \$23,000 is slightly higher than the old plan, but management wanted to see the degree to which this goal can be attained.

Finally, a marketing requirement was added:

$$x_1 = 20$$

which becomes:

$$(\text{C4}) \quad x_1 + d_4^- - d_4^+ = 20$$

The initial GP objective function (including only the undesirable deviations) is:

$$\text{minimize } z = P_1 d_1^- + P_2 d_2^- + P_3 d_3^- + P_4 d_4^- + P_4 d_4^+$$

Because there are two undesirable deviations within the fourth priority level (a result of the fourth constraint being $x_1 = 20$), it is advisable to set weights on the deviations; after consultation with the corporate staff, these were set as 2 on d_4^- and 9 on d_4^+. That is:

$$\text{minimize } z = P_1 d_1^- + P_2 d_2^- + P_3 d_3^- + 2 P_4 d_4^- + 9 P_4 d_4^+$$

(The computerized solution is provided in Section 8.7.)

8.6 Graphical Solution

Goal programming problems with two decision variables (or two constraints) can be solved graphically. To illustrate the technique, let us examine a simple product-mix problem:

$\text{minimize } z = P_1 d_1^- + P_2 d_2^+ + P_3 d_3^+ + P_4 d_4^-$
subject to:
(1) $\quad 20x_1 + 30x_2 + d_1^- - d_1^+ = 120 \qquad$ (profit)
(2) $\quad 10x_1 + 3x_2 + d_2^- - d_2^+ = 30 \qquad$ (capacity, machine A)
(3) $\quad 7x_1 + 8x_2 + d_3^- - d_3^+ = 56 \qquad$ (capacity, machine B)
(4) $\quad 1x_1 + 0x_2 + d_4^- - d_4^+ = 5 \qquad$ (marketing)

The problem is to find the quantities of x_1 and x_2 to be produced.

Solution

To illustrate the process, we will construct the first three constraints, one at a time.

Figure 8.2 shows the profit constraint:

$$20x_1 + 30x_2 + d_1^- - d_1^+ = 120$$

Notice that the deviational variables are ignored. Because we are attempting to minimize (or eliminate) d_1^-, it is clear that the area that fully meets the goals of no deviations must be on the right side of the line, where d_1^+ is.

FIGURE 8.2

The profit constraint

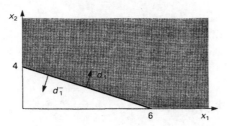

The second and third priority goals are superimposed on the profit goal, as shown in Figure 8.3. The shaded area, *ABCD*, designates an acceptable solution for the first three constraints. Any point inside this area will fully meet the requirement of no deviations in these three constraints.

No feasible solution space

Now we consider the fourth goal (produce at least five units of the first product). In order to achieve this goal, it is necessary to eliminate the area to the left of the line $x_1 = 5$. However, that cannot be done without violating constraints (2) and (3). That is, in a regular LP situation, an infeasible solution would arise. In GP, however, there is a way out! We want, then, to find a solution point that will satisfy the first three goals, yet also come as close as possible to achieving the fourth goal. Such a point can be found by observation: point *D*. Its coordinates are:

$$x_1 = 2.25; \quad x_2 = 2.5$$

FIGURE 8.3

The goal constraints

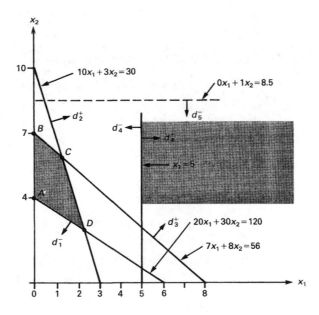

Substituting these values into the goal constraints, we find that the first two goals are fully met (intersection at the solution).

$$\text{For goal 3:}\quad 7(2.25) + 8(2.5) = 35.75$$

That is:

$$d_3^+ = 0;\ d_3^- = 56 - 35.75 = 20.25 \text{ (slack)}$$

This slack is *not* an undesirable deviation.

$$\text{For goal 4:}\quad d_4^+ = 0;\ d_4^- = 5 - 2.25 = 2.75$$

This is the only undesirable deviation.

Another goal

Now, let us assume that an additional goal is added:

$$0x_1 + 1x_2 + d_5^- - d_5^+ = 8.5$$

and the undesirable deviation is d_5^-. If we add this goal to Figure 8.3 (broken line), we see that a deviation on goal 5 is imminent. The closest feasible point to the new constraint is B and not D. However, because d_4 has higher priority, the optimal solution will stay at D. If, instead, we set weights on the deviations, then we would multiply the distances from a candidate solution point (such as B, C, or D) to the two goals by the weights, total them, and select the solution that minimizes the total deviations. (See Problem 9.)

The graphical solution to GP has the same drawbacks LP has; namely, it can only handle problems with two variables and not too many constraints. For larger problems, it is necessary to use the modified simplex method (see Ignizio [3]), which is executed by computer, as shown next.

8.7 Computer Solution to Birch Paper

The solution to BIP's problem is shown in Table 8.5. It was derived by a micro-based computer program (Lee and Shim [5]).

Interpretation of the Printout

Part a: Analysis of Deviations

Goal Constraints (Constraints C1–C4 in the Printout):

- (C1) The most important goal is fully met (cash reserve).
- (C2) The working capital is short by $875.
- (C3) Profit: A deviation of $1,985 exists; that is, the profit is only $21,015.
- (C4) The solution is $x_1 = 8.87$; that is, there is a negative deviation of 11.13.

Interpreting the results

TABLE 8.5 Solution to BIP Problem

a. Analysis of deviations

Constraint	RHS value	d+	d−
C 1	72000.00	0.00	0.00
C 2	16000.00	0.00	875.10
C 3	23000.00	0.00	1985.40
C 4	20.00	0.00	11.13
C 5	100.00	0.00	0.00
C 6	100.00	0.00	37.37
C 7	150.00	0.00	0.00

b. Analysis of decision variables

Variable	Solution value
X 2	41.18
X 1	8.87
X 4	150.00

c. Analysis of the objective function

Priority	Nonachievement
P 1	0.00
P 2	875.10
P 3	1985.40
P 4	22.26

System Constraints (C5–C7 in the Printout):

(C5) The constraint is fully satisfied.

(C6) A slack of 37.37 exists.

(C7) The constraint is fully satisfied.

Notice that in a less-than-or-equal-to type system constraint, a slack is equivalent to a d^-. (A surplus of d^+ will appear in a larger-than-or-equal-to type constraint.)

Part b: Analysis of Decision Variables

Similar to a regular LP solution, the values of x_1, x_2, and so on are computed.

Part c: Analysis of the Objective Function

This part lists the *undesirable* deviations multiplied by their importance index. This is labeled as "nonachievement." For example, for priority level 4, we get:

$$11.13 \text{ (the } d^- \text{ of C4) times 2 (the weight for } d_4^-) = 22.26$$

8.8 Sensitivity Analysis

Sensitivity analysis techniques for GP are not as well developed as those for LP. Although the questions may be similar, the techniques to find the answers are not as readily available. Most of the analysis is performed by interactively re-solving the problem with new input data. Let us examine some sensitivity analysis possibilities.

Switching Priorities

A manager may want to know the effect of changing the order of the priorities. Sometimes such a change will not alter the solution. In other cases, deviations will be switched (or be changed in magnitude).

In the BIP case, we made the following changes:

Priority changes

a. The priorities of the second and fourth goals were reversed. This resulted in no change in the solution.

b. The priorities of the first and third goals were switched. The solution changed as follows:

$$x_2 = 50; \quad x_4 = 150$$

The goals' attainments were:

1. Cash requirement goal was overachieved (by $1,064.40).
2. Working capital level was $14,504, or $1,496 short.
3. Profit increased only slightly, from $21,104 to $21,458.10 (i.e., a deviation of $1,541.90). It seems that profit is very insensitive at this level.

The requirement of making 20 units of product x_1 was completely sacrificed. That is, $d_4^- = 20$; with a weight of 2, this translates to 40 units of nonachievement.

Changing the Targets (Right-Hand Side)

If a solution indicates an attainment of the most important goals, one may want to examine the possibility of increasing the targets. Such a change may result in deviations in the most important goals, or in larger deviations in the less important goals.

Cash requirement

In the BIP case, we changed the cash requirement to $75,000. At the same time, we reduced its priority to second (working capital was changed to first priority). This resulted in the following solution: $x_1 = 21.37$, $x_2 = 28.68$, and $x_4 = 150$. The cash requirement was not fully met (70,500 instead of 75,000) and nonachievement was scored in all but the first goal.

Changing the Weights

Once a solution is observed, it may be desirable to try changing the weights assigned to the goals. Assigning a larger weight to a goal may result in a smaller (or no) deviation.

Relaxing the System Constraints

There is a sizable dual in the regular LP solution to the original BIP problem on one or more of the fully utilized constraints. In such a case, it may be advisable to relax some constraints because of the potentially large benefits associated with the large value of the dual.

Goal Seeking

If a solution to GP includes undesirable deviations in some of the goals, then one may ask, "What would be required in order to eliminate some or all of these deviations?" The answer may be more resources or changes in the priorities.

Setting up a Minimum Goal Level (or a Maximum Deviation)

Adding a constraint

Examining the solution in Table 8.5, management may find the deviation of 11.13 on x_1 to be unacceptable. Adding a system constraint $x_1 \geq 15$, for example, guarantees a solution with at least 15 units of x_1. In such a case, we obtain a solution with $x_2 = 35$ and the profit declines.

Other Changes

Other changes may include adding or deleting constraints, changing the technology coefficients (left-hand side of the constraints) and adding or deleting decision variables. By experimenting with these what-if scenarios, the analysis may reduce conflict among the managers and help in restoring the corporate image and success.

8.9 Examples of Applications

a. Advertising (Integer GP)

An advertising budget

The marketing department of E&D, Inc., uses TV and magazines for advertising. The problem is how to budget advertising if the following goals are to be pursued:

Goal 1 The funds spent on advertising should not exceed the $200,000 budget. This goal is the most important and is labeled P_1.

Goal 2 The total exposure, measured by the number of people (audience) expected to see the advertising, should be at least 20 million. This is the second highest priority goal, labeled P_2.

Goal 3 The effective exposure, that is, the audience that is assumed to be *influenced* by the advertising, should be at least 5 million, labeled P_3.

Goal 4 There should be at least eight TV inserts, each of which costs $15,000, labeled P_4.

Goal 5 There should be at least five magazine inserts, each of which costs $10,000, labeled P_5.

A TV insert reaches 2 million people, of which 800,000 are influenced. A magazine insert is read by 1 million people, of which 300,000 are influenced.

The problem is to determine how many TV inserts and how many magazine inserts to place in order to attain the above goals.

Formulation

The Decision Variables

$$x_1 = \text{Number of TV inserts to be used}$$

$$x_2 = \text{Number of magazine inserts to be used}$$

The Goal Constraints

(1)	$15{,}000x_1 + 10{,}000x_2 + d_1^- - d_1^+ = 200{,}000$		(budget constraint)
(2)	$2{,}000{,}000x_1 + 1{,}000{,}000x_2 + d_2^- - d_2^+ = 20{,}000{,}000$		(exposure constraint)
(3)	$800{,}000x_1 + 300{,}000x_2 + d_3^- - d_3^+ = 5{,}000{,}000$		(effectiveness constraint)
(4)	$x_1 + d_4^- - d_4^+ = 8$		(minimum TV inserts)
(5)	$x_2 + d_5^- - d_5^+ = 5$		(minimum magazine inserts)

The System Constraints

This is an integer programming problem, and therefore the values of x_1 and x_2 are restricted to whole numbers. No other system constraints exist.

The Objective Function

Considering only the *undesirable deviations*, we have:

$$\text{minimize } z = P_1 d_1^+ + P_2 d_2^- + P_3 d_3^- + P_4 d_4^- + P_5 d_5^-$$

b. Manufacturing

A company is planning the monthly production of three products: A, B, and C. The fabricating department can process 10 units of A in an hour or 15 units of B. Part C is fabricated in five minutes. The department has 250 hours available each month, beyond which overtime is required, at a cost of $15 per hour. Painting the products is also required, with times of: 20 minutes per unit of A, 24 minutes per unit of B, and 30 minutes per unit of C. There are three painters in the department, each working 200 hours per month.

The company cannot sell more than 3,000 units of all products, combined, in a month. It is the company's policy to produce at least 200 units of product B each month. The products' contributions to profit are $20, $28, and $40 for A, B, and C,

Production requirements

respectively. The company's priorities, in order of importance, are: (1) a desired monthly profit level of $120,000; (2) overtime of $1,000 allowed in the fabricating department; (3) painting hours should not exceed 1,200 each month; and (4) at least 200 units of B should be produced.

Formulation

The Decision Variables

$$x_1 = \text{Quantity of product A}$$
$$x_2 = \text{Quantity of product B}$$
$$x_3 = \text{Quantity of product C}$$

The System Constraints

$$x_1 + x_2 + x_3 \leq 3,000$$

The Goal Constraints

1. Profit: $20x_1 + 28x_2 + 40x_3 + d_1^- - d_1^+ = 120,000$
2. Overtime: The demand on time (in minutes) is: $6x_1 + 4x_2 + 5x_3$. The supply is 250 hours $\times$ 60 minutes = 15,000 minutes. Overtime will be paid after 15,000 minutes. That is: Overtime = $(6x_1 + 4x_2 + 5x_3) - 15,000$. The cost of overtime is $15 per hour or $0.25 per minute. The constraint is thus:

$$0.25[(6x_1 + 4x_2 + 5x_3) - 15,000] + d_2^- - d_2^+ = 1,000$$

   or: $1.5x_1 + 1x_2 + 1.25x_3 + d_2^- - d_2^+ = 4,750$
3. Painting time: $20x_1 + 24x_2 + 30x_3 + d_3^- - d_3^+ = 1,200 \times 60 = 72,000$ minutes
4. Production of product B: $x_2 + d_4^- - d_4^+ = 200$

The Objective Function

$$\text{minimize } z = P_1 d_1^- + P_2 d_2^+ + P_3 d_3^+ + P_4 d_4^-$$

Only undesirable deviations are listed.

c. Recreational Facility Funding (Integer GP)

Community services

A city parks and recreation department has been authorized a special construction budget of $3 million to expand its public recreation facilities. Four different types of facilities have long been requested by the public: basketball courts, baseball fields, tennis courts, and swimming pools. The demand by various communities within the city has been for 6 basketball courts, 4 baseball fields, 10 tennis courts, and 12 swimming pools. The information about the facilities is summarized in Table 8.6.

TABLE 8.6 Recreational Facilities Information

Facility	Cost	Required Acres per Unit	Average Usage (People per Week)
Basketball courts	$250,000	3	600
Baseball fields	100,000	10	1,200
Tennis courts	50,000	2	500
Swimming pools	200,000	2	1,000

The park management has located 45 acres of land for construction and, for public image reasons, established the following list of prioritized goals:

P_1: The department would like to spend the total budget.

P_2: The park department desires the additional facilities to be used by 10,000 people or more weekly.

P_3: The department wants to avoid using land other than the 45 acres presently available.

P_4: If the department must secure more land, they desire to limit it to 10 acres.

P_5: The department would like to meet all the demands of the public for the new facilities. However, this priority should be weighted according to the number of people estimated to use each facility.

Finally, the department *must* build at least 14 facilities altogether; this goal cannot be violated.

Formulation

Decision Variables

x_1 = Number of basketball courts
x_2 = Number of baseball fields
x_3 = Number of tennis courts
x_4 = Number of swimming pools

System Constraints

(1) $x_1 + x_2 + x_3 + x_4 \geq 14$

(2) $250,000x_1 + 100,000x_2 + 50,000x_3 + 200,000x_4 \leq 3,000,000$

Goal Constraints

P_1: $250,000x_1 + 100,000x_2 + 50,000x_3 + 200,000x_4 + d_1^- - d_1^+ = 3,000,000$
(note that d_1^+ must be zero because of system constraint number 2; d_1^- is undesirable).

P_2: $600x_1 + 1,200x_2 + 500x_3 + 1,000x_4 + d_2^- - d_2^+ = 10,000$
d_2^- is undesirable

P_3: $3x_1 + 10x_2 + 2x_3 + 2x_4 + d_3^- - d_3^+ = 45$
d_3^+ is undesirable

P_4: This priority can be expressed in two ways, either:
$(3x_1 + 10x_2 + 2x_3 + 2x_4) - 45 + d_4^- - d_4^+ = 10$ or:
$d_3^+ + d_4^- - d_4^+ = 10$
We will use the second formulation; d_4^+ is undesirable.

P_5: This goal is expressed in terms of four goal constraints. The number of users is estimated to be most for baseball fields, second for the swimming pools, and so on.

$x_1 + d_5^- - d_5^+ = 6$ (d_5^- is undesirable), basketball courts
$x_2 + d_6^- - d_6^+ = 4$ (d_6^- is undesirable), baseball fields
$x_3 + d_7^- - d_7^+ = 10$ (d_7^- is undesirable), tennis courts
$x_4 + d_8^- - d_8^+ = 12$ (d_8^- is undesirable), swimming pools

Note: The second system constraint and the first goal constraint can be combined by dropping the d_1^+ from the first goal constraint.

The Objective Function

minimize $z = P_1 d_1^- + P_2 d_2^- + P_3 d_3^+ + P_4 d_4^+ + 6P_5 d_5^- + 12P_5 d_6^- + 5P_5 d_7^- + 10P_5 d_8^-$

The deviations in goal five now receive weights, according to the number of users of each facility (in hundreds):

minimize $z = P_1 d_1^- + P_2 d_2^- + P_3 d_3^+ + P_4 d_4^+ + 6P_5 d_5^- + 12P_5 d_6^- + 5P_5 d_7^- + 10P_5 d_8^-$

Integer Constraints

Finally, x_1, x_2, x_3, and x_4 must be integer numbers. *Notes: a.* The integer requirements make the solution of this problem difficult. *b.* For goal five, we established four sets for deviations and prioritized them.

d. Investment Maximization

An investment firm's typical "bottom-level" customer earns a part-time salary of $25,000 and has $5,000 of that available to invest. The firm has a variety of opportunities available in which to invest its customers' funds, as shown below:

Decision Variable	Alternative	Expected Annual Return (Percent)
x_1	IRA (retirement)	7.4
x_2	Employer's retirement plan	18.8
x_3	Deferred income (retirement)	24
x_4	RST mutual fund	9
x_5	ABC mutual fund	32
x_6	Money market A	12
x_7	Money market B	13
x_8	Credit union savings account	11
x_9	Bank savings account	8
x_{10}	Investment club	15

The firm's per-person policies, in order of priority, are as follows:

Investment priorities

1. Invest not less than 2 percent but not more than 5 percent of the salary of $25,000 in the employer's retirement plan. But it is twice as important to keep the lower limit as the upper limit.
2. Invest at least $150 per year in the investment club.
3. Also obey the club's rule not to accept more than 15 percent of an individual's salary for investment in the club.
4. Invest 60 percent of the amount invested in the money market in mutual funds, 20 percent in the savings accounts, and 20 percent in the investment club.
5. Allot no more than 30 percent of the total moneys available for the various retirement plans.
6. Maximize the return on the sum of all investments, with a target of $7,000.
7. Invest all the moneys available.

Formulation

The decision variables are the x_i given in the problem (per investor).

System Constraints

$$x_1 + x_2 + x_3 + x_4 + x_5 + x_6 + x_7 + x_8 + x_9 + x_{10} \leq 5,000$$

Goal Constraints

$$x_2 + d_1^- = 500 \qquad \text{(2 percent of 25,000)}$$
$$x_2 - d_2^+ = 1,250 \qquad \text{(5 percent of 25,000)}$$
$$x_{10} + d_3^- = 150$$
$$x_{10} - d_4^+ = 750 \qquad \text{(15 percent of 5,000)}$$

$$x_4 + x_5 - .6x_6 - .6x_7 - d_5^+ + d_5^- = 0$$
$$- .2x_6 - .2x_7 + x_8 + x_9 - d_6^+ + d_6^- = 0$$
$$- .2x_6 - .2x_7 + x_{10} - d_7^+ + d_7^- = 0$$
$$x_1 + x_2 + x_3 - d_8^+ = 1,500$$
$$.074x_1 + .188x_2 + .24x_3 + .09x_4 + .32x_5 + .12x_6 + .13x_7 + .11x_8 + .08x_9$$
$$+ .15x_{10} - d_9^+ + d_9^- = 7,000$$
$$x_1 + x_2 + x_3 + x_4 + x_5 + x_6 + x_7 + x_8 + x_9 + x_{10} + d_{10}^- = 5,000$$

Objective Function

$$\text{minimize } z = 2P_1d_1^- + P_1d_2^+ + P_2d_3^- + P_3d_4^+ + P_4d_5^- + P_4d_5^+ + P_4d_6^+ + P_4d_6^-$$
$$+ P_4d_7^+ + P_4d_7^- + P_5d_8^+ + P_6d_9^- + P_7d_{10}^-$$

8.10 Concluding Remarks

Goal programming can expand the applicability of LP into many real-life situations that involve multiple, conflicting goals. For such situations to be treated by GP, it is necessary to rank (prioritize) the goals and, preferably, assign weights that indicate their relative importance. In addition to its ability to handle multiple goals, GP permits deviations from the desirable levels of the goals. However, an attempt is made to minimize the sum of the *undesirable* deviations.

The GP approach is currently applied efficiently only to linear situations (linear objective function and constraints). However, the what-if procedures used during the application of GP make it a very attractive tool for the practicing manager. Furthermore, this can be used to support a group of decision makers with diverse interests.

GP was not a popular tool until rather recently because it required a mainframe computer for its execution but several micro packages are now available.

8.11 Problems for Part A

1. Products A and B are considered for production. Each unit of A requires two hours of labor, three hours of machine time, and $20 capital. Each unit of B requires three hours of labor, two hours of machine time, and $25 in capital. There are available 2,000 hours of labor capacity and 2,200 hours of machine time. The profit on product A is $110; on product B it is $120.

    Management's objectives, in descending order, are:

    P_1: No idle labor.

    P_2: Produce at least 400 units of product A.

    P_3: Produce at least 400 units of product B.

    P_4: Total overtime should not exceed 250 hours.

    P_5: Make a profit of at least $120,000.

    P_6: Utilize machine time fully. However, underutilization is one half as desirable as overutilization.

    Formulate as a goal programming problem. Solve (use a computer).

2. A production order of 300 units of product A must be executed within a week by AAA Manufacturing Company. Two production lines are available, each

for 30 hours during the week. Production line I can produce five units per hour. Using production line II, it takes 15 minutes to produce each unit. Line I costs $9 per hour to operate, and line II costs $11 per hour. Overtime is available for line I at $15 per hour and for line II at $12 per hour.

Management goals, in decreasing order of importance, are:

P_1: Produce 300 units.

P_2: Maximum allowable overtime of four hours for line I.

P_3: The cost of overtime must not be greater than $800.

P_4: Underutilization of either line during the regular working hours must be avoided. Assign weights to underutilization in direct proportion to their production capability.

P_5: Producing over 300 is twice as undesirable as producing under 300.

Formulate as a goal program in order to find the best production plan.

3. Formulate a goal program to help Atlanta BanCorp invest $5 million. The company is considering investing in stocks, bonds, CDs (certificates of deposit), and gold. The anticipated annual returns are listed below.

Stocks: 5 percent dividends plus 7 percent capital gains.

Bonds: 9 percent interest plus 1 percent capital gains.

CDs: 10 percent interest.

Gold: 13 percent capital gains.

The firm's investment policies, in decreasing order of importance, are:

P_1: The amount to be invested cannot, under any circumstances, exceed $5 million.

P_2: Do not invest more than 10 percent in gold.

P_3: Make at least $500,000 total profit.

P_4: Invest no more than $1 million in stocks.

P_5: Invest at least $200,000 in CDs, for liquidity.

P_6: Derive at least $200,000 from capital gains (tax advantage).

The firm also has the following current investment guidelines:

a. Profit is twice as important as the ceiling limit on investment in stocks.

b. The limitations on stocks and CDs are considered just as important as their proportional contribution to profits.

c. The capital gains target is half as important as the CD restriction.

4. Given a computer printout of the following GP (* designates a deliberately deleted item of information):

minimize $z = P_1 d_1^- + P_2 d_2^+ + P_3 d_3^-$
$\qquad\qquad + P_4 d_4^+ + 7P_5 d_5^- + 3P_5 d_5^+$

subject to:

(1) $1x_1 + 1x_2 + d_1^- - d_1^+ = 80$
(2) $2x_1 + 3x_2 + d_2^- - d_2^+ = 120$
(3) $1x_1 + 0x_2 + d_3^- - d_3^+ = 75$
(4) $5x_1 + 2x_2 + d_4^- - d_4^+ = 100$
(5) $0x_1 + 1x_2 + d_5^- - d_5^+ = 45$
(6) $5x_1 + 2x_2 \qquad\qquad\quad \leq 200$

The solution is:

```
*****  PROGRAM OUTPUT  *****

   Analysis of decision variables

   Variable          Solution value
      X2                  66.67
      X1                  13.33

  Analysis of the objective function
   Priority          Nonachievement
      P1                   0.00
      P2                     *
      P3                  61.67
      P4                 100.00
      P5                  65.00
```

```
Analysis of deviations
Constraint    RHS Value       d+        d-
   C1           80.00       0.00      0.00
   C2          120.00     106.67      0.00
   C3           75.00       0.00        *
   C4             *        100.00      0.00
   C5           45.00         *         *
   C6          200.00       0.00        *
```

Answer the following questions:

a. What are the undesirable deviations on constraints C2 and C3?

b. What are the values of d^+ and d^- on constraint C5?

c. What is the slack (surplus) on constraint C6?

d. What is the total value of the GP objective function?

e. What is the RHS value of C4 in the optimal solution?

5. Consider a case of a single objective function in which the objective is to produce exactly 20 units. Both overachievement and underachievement are undesirable. Write the objective function for such a case.

6. A company produces two products: alpha, which sells for $30 and costs $20; and beta, which sells for $50 and costs $35. Profit is the most important goal of the company and the target for this year is $1 million.

The second most important goal for the company is the manufacturing budget of $800,000 a year (maximum).

The products are produced by a machine shop that has a capacity of 40,000 hours a year. Each unit of alpha takes 20 minutes to produce, whereas beta requires 24 minutes. The machine shop capacity can be expanded. However, the company prefers not to do it. It is a third-priority goal *not* to expand.

Fourth, for each unit of beta produced, the company would like to produce at least .7 of alpha.

Finally, marketing is an extremely important issue; however, the most the company can sell is 50,000 units of alpha in a year and 60,000 units of beta. These limits *cannot* be exceeded at all.

The company puts the following weights on their objectives: If the least important goal has a weight of one, then the next goal will be twice as important. The next goal in the ladder will then be twice as important as the second from the bottom (or four times more important than the least important), and so on.

a. Formulate as a goal program.

b. Solve, using a computer.

7. Given a GP problem:

$$\text{minimize } z = P_1 d_1^- + P_2 d_2^- + P_3 d_3^+ + P_4 d_4^- + P_5 d_5^-$$

subject to:

$$1x_1 + 1x_2 + d_1^- - d_1^+ = 40 \quad \text{(most important)}$$
$$2x_1 + 0x_2 + d_2^- - d_2^+ = 40$$
$$0.8x_1 + 1x_2 + d_3^- - d_3^+ = 50$$
$$5x_1 + 4x_2 + d_4^- - d_4^+ = 200$$
$$0x_1 + 1x_2 + d_5^- - d_5^+ = 32$$

a. Solve graphically.

b. Solve by a computer.

8. Given a GP problem:

$$P_1: \quad 1x_1 + 1x_2 + d_1^- - d_1^+ = 60 \quad \text{(profit)}$$
$$P_2: \quad 1x_1 + 1x_2 + d_2^- - d_2^+ = 75 \quad \text{(capacity)}$$
$$P_3: \quad 1x_1 + 0x_2 + d_3^- - d_3^+ = 45 \quad \text{(produce at least 45)}$$
$$P_4: \quad 0x_1 + 1x_2 + d_4^- - d_4^+ = 50 \quad (d_4^- \text{ is undesirable})$$
$$P_5: \quad 1x_1 + 0x_2 + d_5^- - d_5^+ = 10 \quad (d_5^+ \text{ is undesirable})$$

a. Write the objective function.

b. Identify the conflicting goals.

c. Solve graphically.

9. Refer to Section 8.6. Assume the importance of goals four and five are given in the objective function as $5d_4^- + 8d_5^-$. Find the optimal solution (point B, C, or D?).

10. GOAL ANALYSIS EXERCISE

a. Identify five *short-term goals* (i.e., to be completed in not more than a year) for the department or unit for which you work (or in your own career). List these goals. Tell how the information was solicited.

b. For each goal, describe how the goal's attainment can be measured and how the information is to be collected.

Example 1

Provide timely bus service to the City of Hope. Measurement: 95 percent of all buses will leave scheduled departure points no later than five minutes after the scheduled time.

Collect information through self-logging of drivers, sample survey done by supervisor, or install automated vehicle monitoring system. The goal this year is to improve the service level to 95 percent from 92 percent last year.

Example 2
Provide quality service at the information desk. Measurement: Customers' satisfaction. Ask one question: "Is the service provided to you: (5) Excellent; (4) Very good; (3) Good; (2) Fair; (1) Poor"
Survey a sample of 40 customers.
The goal is to improve average satisfaction level from 3.7 to 3.9.

c. Prioritizing the goals.
   Use any method you wish to prioritize the goals. Make sure that at least three individuals participate in this part, including your boss and one of your subordinates. Describe the process of *soliciting information* and how different opinions (if they existed) were handled.

d. What have you learned from this exercise? (one-half page)

11. Liberty Insurance Corporation is a large midwestern company with three goals: liquidity, stability and profit (given in the order of their importance). The company policies and procedures regarding these goals are:

a. Cash on hand (x_1) must equal at least 15 percent of the unpaid claims (x_2).
b. The company's investment in bonds (x_3) must be equal to or larger than the unpaid claims (x_2).
c. The ratio of assets (x_4) to premium volume (x_5) must be equal to or larger than 1.3.
d. The amount in cash (x_1), plus bonds (x_3), plus mortgages given (x_6), must be at least twice that of the loss reserves (x_7) plus the unearned premiums (x_8).
e. Returns on current investment should be at least 8.2 percent. Yields on the various investments are: cash 5.5 percent, bonds 8.3 percent, mortgages 9.8 percent.

   Find the most appropriate allocation of funds among the various investment instruments. The total money to be allocated is $200 million + 75 percent of the premium volume. Formulate as a GP.

8.12 CASE
CARTOY INTERNATIONAL

Cartoy International is a large multinational corporation with automobile manufacturing and assembly plants scattered worldwide. The company has recently developed a new model named Zentz. The Zentz will be produced in three forms: sedan, sport, and luxury. The company plans to use excess capacity available in Tokyo (3,000 cars per week), Fremont, California (1,200 cars per week), and Djakarta (2,000 cars per week).

Cartoy is primarily interested in profits, of course; however, the company would also like to minimize idle capacity, because fully utilized facilities increase the employment level in the same areas that the company sells its cars. In addition, high-capacity utilization reduces hiring and firing cost, as well as giving a better distribution of fixed costs.

Due to the international nature of the company, it is also necessary to consider distribution constraints. The cars are shipped by boat about once a month. Therefore, it is necessary to store the products near or in the manufacturing plants. A sedan requires 40 square feet, a sports car 34 square feet, and the luxury model 50 square feet. Storage capacity for one month (four weeks) is available as follows: In Tokyo, 400,000 square feet; in Fremont, 300,000 square feet; and there is no limit on the number of cars that can be stored in Djakarta.

The estimated profit contributions of the cars are: sedan—$680, sport—$1,100, luxury—$2,200. The anticipated weekly worldwide demand is 4,000 sedans, 1,300 sports cars, and 1,800 luxury.

Top management has announced the following goals and priorities (P_1 is the highest-priority goal):

P_1: To utilize plant capacity in a balanced way. This means that once the new model capacities are assigned, the leftover capacity will be the same, in number of cars, in the three countries. This goal is essential to avoid a feeling of discrimination among the different countries.

P_2: Utilize excess capacity in Djakarta twice as intensively as Tokyo or Fremont (due to the lower labor cost).

P_3: Sell as many luxury cars as possible, due to their larger contribution margin.

P_4: Do not exceed the current storage capacity.

P_5: Produce as many cars of each type as the market can absorb.

P_6: Utilize plant capacity for the new cars in proportion to the available capacity. This goal attempts to balance utilization in terms of percent idle space.

P_7: Maximize profit.

Sen Yokota, the vice president for corporate manufacturing, was displeased with these goals and priorities. Although he was delighted about the decision to produce the Zentz, he had difficulty in scheduling its production. So he called the corporate president, Su-nu, and they had the following discussion.

Sen: I do not like these goals. They impose too many restrictions and some of them clearly contradict each other.

Su-nu: Calm down, Sen. You know that we have an international responsibility.

Sen: True, but we have shareholders, too.

Su-nu: We must also consider markets, employees, international distribution, and the like.

Sen: OK, but why is profit the least priority?

Su-nu: I think that we can make a good profit even if it is the last priority. Furthermore, some of the other goals were designed to increase the profit margin.

Sen: But you are not sure how much profit we will make.

Su-nu: No, not until I see the production plan.

Required:

a. Identify the contradictions among the goals.

b. Formulate as a linear program with profit maximization as the only goal. Solve.

c. Formulate as a GP.

d. Solve (use a computer).

e. Comment on the differences between the LP and the GP solutions.

f. Change the priority of P_7 to P_2 and P_2 to P_7; solve and comment on the results.

g. Examine the LP dual prices, as derived in part (*b*); what can you learn?

PART B: UTILITY THEORY AND THE ANALYTIC HIERARCHY PROCESS

Paul sensed they were caught in a dilemma. All month, he and his girlfriend Erin had planned to go to the school's annual prom. They had even saved up the usual $70 per couple admission fee. But at the last minute, the student council raised the fee to $100 to cover the unexpected costs of hiring a well-known dance band. That seemed to doom their plans. Then one of his friends, knowing their dilemma, jokingly offered them a coin-toss gamble. If the toss showed heads, they must pay him the $70 they had saved, but if it showed tails, he would pay them $40. At the time, Paul had laughed off the gamble because it was so obviously unfair. But now, Paul wondered—perhaps it wasn't such a foolish gamble after all.

8.13 Utility and Decision Theory

Let us attempt to analyze the above situation with the expected value method, as shown in Table 8.7. The payoffs represent the money left after the gamble.

Solution

Using an expected payoff approach, Paul and Erin should reject his friend's offer, because the expected value of rejection is higher.

Analysis

Before Paul and his girlfriend reject the offer, they should do some thinking. If they consider the enjoyment they will have at the prom, they probably should accept the offer. The reason for this is that the $70 is of very little use to them, because it cannot get them to the prom; but if they win the gamble, they will have enough money ($70 + $40 = $110) to pay the admission fee and even buy a soft drink or two. What should actually be compared in this case are not the monetary values but the benefits or **utilities** that it has for Paul and Erin.

Discussion

Expected monetary value or expected utility?

EMV not valid in three cases

In the analysis of decision making under risk, the best alternative is usually selected by calculating and comparing the *expected monetary values* (EMV) of the various alternatives. However, there are at least three situations in which EMV is *not* likely to be a valid criterion. First, if the decision maker finds difficulty in expressing the values of some of the outcomes of his or her decisions in terms of monetary payoffs, the EMV cannot be used. Second, EMV assumes that the decision maker is willing to risk losing money in the short run as long as he or she is better off in the long run. In reality, however, decision makers frequently act to *avoid* risk in the short run, particularly if there is any possibility whatsoever of incurring a large initial loss. Finally, EMV assumes a linear relationship between the amount of money and its value (or utility). For example, it is assumed that the value of $20,000 is twice that of $10,000. In reality, however, it has been observed that with an increase in the amount of wealth accumulated, the value

TABLE 8.7   **The Expected Monetary Payoff**

States of Nature / Alternatives	.5 Heads	.5 Tails	Expected Payoff (EMV)	
Accept offer	0	110	55	
Reject offer	70	70	70	←Maximum

of additional money decreases. (For example, the value of a dollar added to $10 is larger than that of one added to $1,000.)

Multiple Criteria.   The concept of utility can be used not only to value different quantities of one commodity (e.g., money), but also to assess the value of different quantities of several commodities. This application is especially important in the case of MCDM where we attempt to combine several criteria that are measured on different scales.

The Basic Concept.   The application of *utility* as a measure of the *value of an outcome* was proposed by Von Neumann and Morgenstern [12]. They suggested that each individual has a measurable preference among various choices available in risk situations. This preference is called *utility* and is measured in arbitrary units called **utiles.** By suitable questioning (an example will be given later), it is possible to determine a person's utility for various amounts of money. This is called a person's *utility* (or *preference*) *function.* The graph of this function offers a profile of the individual's attitude toward risk taking. Von Neumann and Morgenstern hypothesized that in any decision involving risk, a person will choose the alternative that maximizes his or her expected utility. The mechanics of computing **expected utility** are the same as the mechanics of computing any expected value; namely, multiply the probabilities by the corresponding payoffs (this time given in units of utility called utiles) and add them up.

This idea is based on the following assumptions:

1. Utility can be measured on a cardinal scale. That is, cardinal numbers (1, 2, and so on) can describe how many utiles constitute a payoff. For example, if a certain consequence, say, a 5 percent share of the market, is twice as important as another consequence, say, a 6 percent return on investment, we describe the 5 percent share of the market as having twice as many utiles as the 6 percent return on investment.

2. Utilities of different objects can be added together (this is called the **additivity assumption**). For example, if object A is worth 10 utiles and object B is worth 5 utiles, then objects A and B together are worth 15 utiles.

Margin notes:
- Utiles
- How much is money valued?
- Utility a cardinal measure
- Utilities are additive

Certainty Equivalent

Let us return to Paul's dilemma. Paul and Erin have two alternatives: accept the offer with an EMV of $55, or reject it and save the $70. Let us assume that they are *indifferent* to the two alternatives. That is, they are willing to accept the offer at $70 but they are not willing to pay *more* than $70. It is clear that the decision of how much to pay for this gamble is *subjective.* Whereas they are willing to pay $70, someone else may not be willing to pay more than $48. We call such a subjective valuation of a risky situation (a *gamble*) the **certainty equivalent (CE)** of the decision maker for that risky situation. (That is, the $70 or $48 is the CE of the gamble.)

Margin note:
- Indifference between a gamble and certainty

The concept of certainty equivalent enables us to classify decision makers into three types:

- EMV takers whose certainty equivalent = EMV.
- Risk takers whose certainty equivalent is *larger* than the EMV of the gamble (such as Paul and Erin).
- Risk averters whose certainty equivalent is *smaller* than the EMV.

Risk Premium

We see that people's attitudes toward risk are related to the certainty equivalent (CE) and the EMV of the risk. The difference between these two is called the **risk premium (RP)**.

$$RP = EMV - CE \qquad (8.4)$$

In our example, RP = $55 − $70 = $−15. For a risk taker, the RP is negative because the CE > EMV. For a risk averter, the RP is positive. Why do people behave differently? For more insight into this issue, let us look at the solution of the school prom case.

Solution of the School Prom Case Using Utilities

Translate money to utilities

Let us examine the problem in utility terms: Because the $70 will not get Paul and his girlfriend to the prom, it is of little value to them. We may arbitrarily assume that the $70 is worth 100 utiles. Losing the $70 will leave them with no money, a situation which is worth 0 utiles. However, the additional $40 is crucial, because they will have $110 and will then be able to go to the prom. Therefore, the $110 is extremely valuable—worth, say, 500 utiles. Now the decision situation can be reevaluated (see Table 8.8) in terms of utilities.

Using the **expected utility** (EU), they should *accept* the offer, because the expected utility in the case of "accept" is: .5(0) + .5(500) = 250 utiles, which is higher than the expected utility of "reject," which is .5(100) + .5(100) = 100.

TABLE 8.8   Expected Utility (EU)

Alternatives	States of Nature	.5 Lose (Heads)	.5 Win (Tails)	EU	
Accept		0	500	250	←*Maximum*
Reject		100	100	100	

Gambling versus insurance

The above example can explain why people gamble; that is, why they are willing to spend money to assume risk. The next example of utility will show why people insure themselves; that is, why they are willing to spend money to *avoid* risk.

Example: To Insure or Not to Insure?

Insure or not?

Suppose that management is about to make a decision concerning fire insurance on a plant valued at $2 million. There is a chance of 1 in 2,000 (i.e., .0005) that a fire will destroy the plant during a one-year period. The annual premium for insurance is $1,500. Should the company insure or not? The situation is shown in the decision Table 8.9.

According to the EMV, management should not insure. In the long run, it will cost much more to insure than not to. However, because the situation is in the realm of risk, there is a chance, although very small, that fire may even occur during the very first year. The loss of $2 million would probably bankrupt the company—a situation that management could not afford. Therefore, they will buy the insurance even though it has a larger expected monetary cost. If the same situation is analyzed in utility terms, it might look like this:

The $1,500 premium is worth −1 utile to the company; zero dollars is worth zero utiles. A loss of $2 million is worth −10,000 utiles. This information is entered in Table 8.10.

TABLE 8.9   Fire Insurance, EMV Outcomes

States of Nature / Alternatives	.0005	.9995	Expected Cost (EMV)	
	Fire	*No Fire*		
Insure	$1,500	$1,500	$1,500	
Do not insure	$2,000,000	0	$1,000	←*Minimum*

TABLE 8.10   Fire Insurance, EU Outcomes

States of Nature / Alternatives	.0005	.9995	Expected Utility (EU)	
	Fire	*No Fire*		
Insure	−1	−1	−1 utile	←*Maximum*
Do not insure	−10,000	0	−5 utiles	

The results show that the expected utility of insuring is higher than that of not insuring; thus, the company will elect to insure.

Utility (Preference) Curves

The EU

From the discussion so far, it is evident that the mechanics of using utilities are similar to using money. The only difference is that the expected value is expressed in terms of expected utility (EU), instead of expected monetary value (EMV). The biggest problem, however, is the assignment of utility values as a replacement for monetary (or other) values. The relationship between money and utility can be described graphically with the help of a curve termed the **utility curve** or *utility function*.

Utility curves

If a utility curve can be constructed, then one can read off the curve the utility values that correspond to any desired monetary values. The construction of the curve, therefore, is the key to the analysis. According to the Von Neumann–Morgenstern proposal, a curve can be constructed by measuring the attitude of the decision maker toward risk. Four such curves are shown in Figure 8.4. The shape of each curve is a function of the individual's attitude toward risk. Curve *a* describes a typical risk averse person and in curve *b*, a person is described who is poor but willing to gamble to improve his standard of living. The same person, once he has accumulated wealth, will become risk averse. Once a person's utility curve is known, then it is possible to replace any monetary value by its utility equivalent for that person.

Example

A decision table with three alternatives and three states of nature is shown in Table 8.11 (with payoffs given in dollars). The objective is to maximize profit. The problem is to select the alternative that will do so.

FIGURE 8.4

Different utility curves

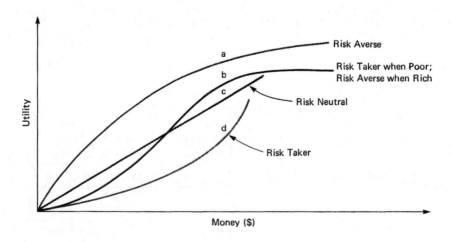

TABLE 8.11   Decision Table with Profit Figures

Alternatives \ States of Nature	.2 s_1	.5 s_2	.3 s_3	EMV	
a_1	12	6	4	6.6	←*Maximum*
a_2	15	3	−2	3.9	
a_3	6.5	6.5	6.5	6.5	

Solution by EMV

Using expected monetary value, alternative a_1, with the largest EMV at $6.6, is selected.

Solution by Expected Utility

In order to evaluate the decision table in terms of utility, it is necessary to express all nine entries in the table in utiles. The question of how to do this can be answered with the aid of the decision maker's utility curve.

How to Construct a Utility Curve

Constructing the utility curve

To illustrate how the decision maker's utility-of-money curve is obtained, let us first arbitrarily assign the value of 100 utiles to the highest outcome, $15, and 0 utiles to the worst possible outcome, $−2. (One can use any other pair of numbers instead of 100 and 0; for example, 1 and 0.) These data are graphed in Figure 8.5 (see points *A* and *B*). To build the utility curve, additional reference points are needed. The utility for $12 will be derived in order to illustrate how to obtain additional points on the curve.

A gamble

One way of doing this is to ask the decision maker, whose utility curve is to be constructed, to visualize a hypothetical gambling situation in which the decision maker has the option of investing:

a. In a lottery ticket with two possible outcomes: winning $15 (the highest outcome) or losing $2 (the worst outcome).

b. In a project that is sure to yield $12.

"Let's Make a Deal"

(The situation is similar to a former popular TV program "Let's Make a Deal.")

Gamble or take the "sure thing"?

The decision whether or not to take the lottery ticket clearly depends on the chance of making the $15; and it is a personal, subjective decision. Some people will prefer the lottery only if the odds of making $15 are very high; others will take it with lower odds. The management scientist attempts, by trial and error, to find the "*chance* of making $15," to be labeled p, that will make the decision maker *indifferent* between the two options.

FIGURE 8.5

The utility-of-money curve

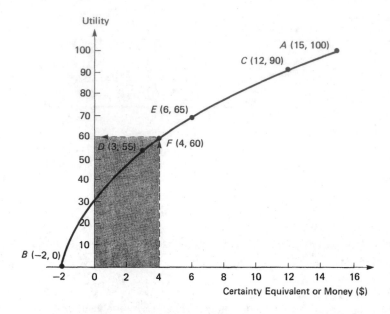

This is done in the following manner: First, the decision maker is asked if he or she *prefers* the $12 certain return over the lottery ticket with an arbitrary probability of, say, $p = .80$. If the decision maker says yes, p is *increased* slowly to say, $p = .81$, $p = .82$, and so on, until a point where the decision maker is *indifferent* between the sure return and the ticket. If the decision maker says no, the value of p is decreased slowly to the point where the decision maker expresses indifference. At the point of indifference, the $12 alternative is equivalent to the gamble. The $12 is the *certainty equivalent* of the lottery ticket.

Suppose that the analyst finds that at a probability of $p = .90$, the decision maker is indifferent between the two points. Given this information, the analyst can now find the decision maker's utility for $12, using the indifference Equation 8.5.

> Utility of a certainty equivalent = Expected utility of a lottery   (8.5)

In our case:

$$U(\$12) = pU(\$15) + (1 - p)U(\$-2)$$

The assigned values of 100 utiles to $15 and 0 utiles to $-2 are now introduced into Equation 8.5, as are the predetermined probability values:

$$U(\$12) = p(100) + (1 - p)0 = .9(100) + .1(0) = 90 \text{ utiles}$$

Thus, the utility of $12 is 90 utiles (point C in Figure 8.5).

Similarly, by the use of further hypothetical gambling situations [e.g., $6 for certain versus a lottery with a probability, p, of gaining a yield of $15 and $(1 - p)$ of

$-2]$, it is possible to obtain other values for the curve. Let us assume that the utility values for the additional points of $3 and $6 were found to be 55 and 65, respectively. These results are plotted in Figure 8.5 (points D and E). Next, a continuous curve is constructed by connecting all computed points (each marked with a dot). This curve describes the decision maker's utility for money. Note that this decision maker is some-

Risk taker or risk averse?

what risk averse.

From Figure 8.5, it is possible to read the utility values for all the monetary payoffs of Table 8.11. These utility values are shown in Table 8.12. For example, to read the utility value of $4 in Figure 8.5, go from point 4 on the horizontal axis up (follow the arrows) to point F; then turn 90 degrees to the left and go to the utility axis (reaching it at 60). The coordinates of point F are thus 4 and 60, which means that $4 is equivalent to 60 utiles.

It is now possible to compute the expected utility value (EU) of the various alternatives.

$$EU(a_1) = 90(.2) + 65(.5) + 60(.3) = 68.5$$
$$EU(a_2) = 100(.2) + 55(.5) + 0(.3) = 47.5$$
$$EU(a_3) = 70(.2) + 70(.5) + 70(.3) = 70.0 \leftarrow largest$$

The third alternative has the highest expected utility, and is therefore recommended.

A nonlinear relationship

Note that the alternative with the highest EMV (a_1), does not have the highest EU. This is not surprising, due to the nonlinear relationship that exists between monetary values and utility for this decision maker. Alternative a_1 is more speculative than a_3. The decision maker indicated, through personal preferences, that he or she is less likely to gamble.

The Concept of Risk Profile

In decision making under risk, we relate the possible results for each alternative to their respective probabilities. Such a presentation is called a **risk profile** and is slightly different from a decision table.

TABLE 8.12 Utility Values for the Profits of Table 8.10

Alternatives / *States of Nature*	.2 s_1 $	.2 s_1 Utiles	.5 s_2 $	.5 s_2 Utiles	.3 s_3 $	.3 s_3 Utiles	EMV	Expected Utility (EU)	
a_1	12	90	6	65	4	60	6.6	68.5	
a_2	15	100	3	55	-2	0	3.9	47.5	
a_3	6.5	70	6.5	70	6.5	70	6.5	70	←*Maximum*

Example

Given below are the risk profiles of two projects, A and B, for a decision maker with the utility curve of Figure 8.5. The problem is to find which project should be selected.

Project A				Project B		
Possible Result ($)	Probability	EMV		Possible Result ($)	Probability	EMV
−1,000	.1	−100		0	.1	0
6,000	.6	3,600		5,000	.5	2,500
10,000	.2	2,000		10,000	.4	4,000
15,000	.1	1,500			1.0	6,500
	1.0	7,000				

Solution

Using the utility curve, we can find the expected utility values (EU) of the two projects.

Project A				Project B			
Result	Utility	Probability	EU	Result	Utility	Probability	EU
−1,000	15	.1	1.5	0	30	.1	3.0
6,000	65	.6	39.0	5,000	63	.5	31.5
10,000	82	.2	16.4	10,000	82	.4	32.8
15,000	100	.1	10.0				67.3
			66.9				

Project B is preferred over A even though its expected monetary value is lower ($6,500 versus $7,000 for project A).

Utility Curves Expressed as Functions

Once utility curves are constructed, they can sometimes be expressed as functions, such as:

$$U(M) = 0.8M + \sqrt{9M}$$

Here, the utility is algebraically related to the amount of money by a formula. For example, if $M = \$40,000$, then its utility will be:

$$U(40,000) = .8(40,000) + \sqrt{360,000} = 32,600$$

8.14 Utility and Multiple Criteria Decision Making

Utility theory can be used to solve problems involving multiple criteria.

Example

Two alternatives are considered in light of the attainment of the four different corporate goals shown in Table 8.13. Table 8.14 gives management's utility valuation of these goals.

Relative Weights

In the example just presented, utiles were assigned and totaled, assuming that all goals carry the same weight. However, in many organizations, objectives may carry different weights and priorities. Therefore, it is appropriate to adjust the utiles before totaling them.

A weighted sum   One way to treat such situations is to compute the weighted total of utiles. For example, Table 8.15 shows the problem of Table 8.14 with weights put on each goal.

The total weighted utility is then computed, similar to the way that expected value is computed. Each utile is multiplied by its relative importance, and the results are totaled.

$$\text{For } a_1: \quad 40(2) + 60(1.2) + 20(.4) + 40(.8) = 192$$

$$\text{For } a_2: \quad 25(2) + 80(1.2) + 28(.4) + 30(.8) = 181.2$$

Thus, alternative a_1 is superior.

TABLE 8.13   **Multiple Outcomes**

Alternatives Corporate Goals	Profit	Market Share	Sales*	Cash Reserves*
a_1	5%	18%	23	.6
a_2	3%	20%	30	.3

* In millions of dollars.

TABLE 8.14   **Utility Valuation of Table 8.13**

Alternatives Corporate Goals	Profit	Market Share	Sales	Cash Reserves	Total Utility	
a_1	40	60	20	40	160	
a_2	25	80	28	30	163	←*Maximum*

TABLE 8.15   **Weighted Utilities**

Goals	Profit	Market Share	Sales	Cash	Total Weighted Utility
Weights	2.0	1.2	.4	.8	
a_1	40	60	20	40	192
a_2	25	80	28	30	181.2

←Maximum

A major problem in such an approach is assessing the relative importance, or priorities, of goals. Various methods such as ranking, pairing, allocating 100 points among the alternatives, and the like, can be used. Also, the use of experts is recommended (e.g., via the Delphi method [6]).

Delphi
The point system

A well-known variation of the use of utility is the *point system*. A point system is used by many universities in admission decisions. For example, in order to be admitted into an MBA program, the university may require a minimum of 750 points. These points are computed by multiplying the student's grade point average by 100 (e.g., a B average is 3.0, or 300 points) and adding the result achieved on the Graduate Management Admission Test (GMAT). Many firms also use a point system in their annual performance evaluation to determine various levels of merit increases.

8.15 The Analytic Hierarchy Process (AHP)*

The **Analytic Hierarchy Process (AHP)** developed by Saaty [7] helps the decision maker to arrive at the best decision and allocate resources accordingly. The AHP makes it possible to deal with both tangible and intangible factors. With it, one organizes thought and intuition in a logical fashion using a *hierarchy* and enters judgments according to understanding and experience. This approach tolerates uncertainty and allows for revision so that individuals and groups can grapple with all their concerns.

Hierarchy of facts

The answers can be tested for sensitivity to changes in judgment. Problems are broken down into smaller constituent parts so the decision maker makes only simple **pairwise comparison** judgments throughout the hierarchy to arrive at overall priorities for the alternatives of action. The decision problem may involve social, political, and technical factors; several parties; many objectives, criteria, and alternatives; and may require negotiation. The process can be used to:

• Predict likely outcomes.
• Allocate resources.

---

* Condensed from R. F. Dyer and E. H. Formen *An Analytical Approach to Marketing Decisions*, Prentice-Hall, 1991, with permission.

- Plan projected and desired futures.
- Exercise control over changes in the decision-making system.
- Evaluate employees and allocate wage increases.
- Facilitate group decision-making processes.
- Select alternatives.
- Do cost/benefit comparisons.

We illustrate the process with an example.

An AHP Problem

Bill Morgan, the national sales manager of Sundial Industries, a firm that sells decorative art objects to specialty gift shops and art stores, has the job of selecting the make and model of cars to be purchased for the firm's entire sales force of twenty-eight account representatives. Bill first narrowed the list of cars to three makes/models that his company would consider. All of these vehicles met Sundial's "must" criteria of: (1) made in the U.S.A., (2) standard extended warranty and repair clauses for fleet purchase, and (3) favorable records for repair and maintenance costs.

Bill gathered the information on the three candidate vehicles shown in Table 8.16. In addition, he took each one for a test drive. Bill felt that there were a number of key "want" criteria that should be incorporated into the fleet-purchase decision. His list of criteria included initial purchase price, miles per gallon, comfort, and style as the major factors. Table 8.16 provides quantitative data on the three vehicles on the purchase price and MPG criteria. Measures of comfort and style are not easily quantified, however. In order to assess comfort, Bill would have to consider car-interior room and design, ease of entry and exit, and so on. The style factor would have to rest on Bill's personal feelings and a very informal poll he has conducted among a few of his salespeople.

Thus Bill has a problem involving both objective and subjective factors. It would be a mistake, however, to jump to the conclusion that all quantitative factors, such as purchase price, should be treated in a completely objective fashion. For example, car A, which costs $13,000, is $4,000 more than car C, which costs $9,000. A completely

---

TABLE 8.16 **Sundial Corporation's Information About the Three Candidate Vehicles**

	Car A	*Car B*	*Car C*
Price	$13,000	$11,200	$9,000
MPG	18	23	29
Interior	Deluxe	Above avg	Standard
Body	4-door, midsize	2-door, sport	2-door, compact
Radio	AM/FM, Tape	AM/FM	AM
Engine	6-cylinder	4-cyl, Turbo	4-cylinder

objective approach would be to say that car C is 13/9 or about 1.4 times more preferable than car A with respect to purchase price. However, an individual or group in considering their utility for money (based on financial status and other needs) might judge that car C is 6 or 7 times more preferable than car A with respect to purchase price.

Such a numerical judgment—6 or 7 times—might be difficult to make and/or justify. Instead, they can, with AHP, specify that car C is, say, "strongly" more preferable than car A with respect to purchase price. Obviously, there will be a requirement for deriving *meaningful* priorities based on such verbal judgments. We will see how AHP fulfills this requirement. As noted previously, a major advantage of AHP is that it is designed to handle situations such as this, in which the subjective judgments of individuals constitute an important part of the decision process.

Developing the AHP Hierarchy

The first stage in AHP model building is to decompose the overall problem into a hierarchy. A variety of basic hierarchical structures are available to fit a wide variety of problems. These include:

- Goal, criteria, alternatives
- Goal, criteria, subcriteria, alternatives
- Goal, criteria, subcriteria, scenarios, alternatives
- Goal, actors, criteria, alternatives
- Goal, criteria, levels of intensities, many alternatives

In this book we will present only the simplest structure, consisting of the goal, criteria (and possibly subcriteria), and alternatives, as shown in Figure 8.6.

Making Judgments about the Criteria and the Decision Alternatives

An AHP evaluation is based on the decision maker's judgments about the relative importance of each criterion in terms of its contribution to the overall goal as well as his preferences for the alternatives relative to each criterion. For example, in the car-selection problem, Bill will need to specify his judgments about the relative importance of each of the four criteria. He will also need to indicate his preference for each of the three cars relative to each criterion. Judgments should be based on hard data as well as

FIGURE 8.6

Hierarchy for the decision on fleet-car purchase for the sales force

	A	B	C	D	E
A	1	1/3	1/4	1/5	1
B	3	1	1/2	1/3	2
C	4	2	1	1/2	6
D	5	3	2	1	4
E	1	1/2	1/6	1/4	1

on the decision maker's knowledge and experience, which can be expressed verbally or quantitatively.

Given the judgments about relative importance and preferences, a mathematical process is used to calculate priorities of the criteria relative to the goal and priorities for the alternatives relative to each criterion. These priorities are then synthesized to provide a ranking of the three cars in terms of overall preference. We will not illustrate how AHP utilizes pairwise comparisons to establish priority measures.

Pairwise Comparisons and AHP.   Keep in mind that Bill will need to make a series of judgments in order to complete his AHP model:

1. The relative preferences for the three cars with respect to the purchase price criterion
2. The relative preferences for the three cars with respect to the MPG criterion
3. The relative preferences for the three cars with respect to the comfort criterion
4. The relative preferences for the three cars with respect to the style criterion
5. The relative importance of the four criteria in terms of their contribution to the goal of "selecting the best car"

Pairwise comparisons are the basic measurement mode employed in the analytic hierarchy process. (Other modes include pairwise numerical, pairwise graphical, and absolute. They are available in the Expert Choice software to be discussed later.) In establishing priorities for the three cars in terms of comfort, Bill will state his relative comfort preference among the cars as the cars are considered two at a time (pairwise). In other words, Bill will compare the comfort of car A to car B, car A to car C, and car B to car C in three separate comparisons.

Another aspect of the AHP pairwise-comparison process is that a nine-point scale is utilized in order to evaluate the preferences for each pair of items. Although other methods of scaling and rating could be used with AHP, research and experience have shown that the nine-point scale offers reasonably good discrimination. The recommended scale and its underlying numerical representation are shown in Table 8.17.

TABLE 8.17   Pairwise Comparison Scale for AHP

Verbal Judgment	*Numerical Judgment*
Extremely preferred	9
Very strongly to extremely	8
Very strongly preferred	7
Strongly to very strongly	6
Strongly preferred	5
Moderately to strongly	4
Moderately preferred	3
Equally to moderately	2
Equally preferred	1

Using our fleet car decision as an example, assume that Bill has compared the comfort levels of car A with car B and is convinced that car A is more comfortable, but only slightly. AHP allows Bill to go one step further, expressing the intensity of his judgment using the nine-point scale from Table 8.17. Let's say Bill feels that car A is between equally comfortable to moderately more comfortable than car B, so he specifies equal to moderate. For notational convenience we will represent this as a 2.

Bill then indicates his preference between car A and car C (again on relative comfort). Assume that Bill's judgment is that car A is very strongly to extremely preferable to car C. Finally, Bill assesses that he strongly-to-very-strongly prefers car B to car C.

The Pairwise-Comparison Matrix. The three pairwise verbal comparisons of the cars in terms of comfort are represented in a pairwise-comparison matrix. This matrix is used to compute the unidimensional priority or utility scores for the three cars in terms of comfort. Based upon the judgments provided by Bill, the matrix is shown in Table 8.18. The remaining entries in the matrix (sometimes not shown) consist of one's on the main diagonal and the reciprocals of the ratings in the cells below the diagonal.

We next employ the same process to determine priorities with respect to each of the other criteria: purchase price, miles per gallon, and style. In addition, we will also have to determine Bill's priorities for the criteria themselves; that is, What is the relative importance of comfort, price, MPG, and style? The pairwise-comparison matrices for judgments about the alternatives relative to the three remaining criteria are shown in Table 8.19.

The same interpretation we used for the comfort factor is attached to the preference comparisons indicated in Table 8.19. For example, car B ($11,200) is considered moderately more preferable than car A ($13,000) on the purchase-price criterion.

We see that car C is preferred with respect to purchase price and MPG, while car B is preferred with respect to style. No car is the most preferred over all the criteria. In other words, before Bill can make a final decision, he must have information about the relative importance of the criteria. He will make six judgments about the relative importance of the criteria as follows (three criteria taken two at a time):

- Price versus MPG
- Price versus comfort
- Price versus style
- MPG versus comfort
- MPG versus style
- Comfort versus style

Bill's judgments (made using the verbal scale but summarized using the numerical representation) are shown in Table 8.20. We can tell that Bill places the highest importance on purchase price. However, it is interesting that he values both style and comfort over MPG. MPG, in fact, appears to be a relatively unimportant consideration in his decision process.

TABLE 8.18 Partial Pairwise Comparison Matrix

Comfort	Car A	Car B	Car C
Car A	1	2	8
Car B	1/2	1	6
Car C	1/8	1/6	1

Note: In the pairwise-comparison matrix, the value in row i and column j is the measure of preference for the car in row i over the car in column j. If the car in column j were preferred over the car in row i, the judgment would be an inverse, e.g., 1/8 instead of 8.

TABLE 8.19 Pairwise-Comparison Matrices for Price, MPG, and Style in the Example on Fleet-Car Selection

Price	Car A	Car B	Car C
Car A	1	1/3	1/4
Car B	3	1	1/2
Car C	4	2	1

MPG	Car A	Car B	Car C
Car A	1	1/4	1/6
Car B	4	1	1/3
Car C	6	3	1

Style	Car A	Car B	Car C
Car A	1	1/3	4
Car B	3	1	7
Car C	1/4	1/7	1

AHP Models and Analysis With Expert Choice Software

Expert Choice is a user-friendly software package that implements AHP on a microcomputer. We continue with the example of the fleet-car selection problem. Expert Choice allows the user to construct a graphical representation of the AHP hierarchy by using a few simple commands. To construct the hierarchy for the problem on fleet car selection, the user first starts the EC software program and specifies the file name for the model (application) and a description of the goal of the decision, such as SELECT

TABLE 8.20 Pairwise Comparison Matrix for the Four Fleet Car Purchase Criteria

Criterion	Price	MPG	Comfort	Style
Price	1	3	2	2
MPG	1/3	1	1/4	1/4
Comfort	1/2	4	1	1/2
Style	1/2	4	2	1

THE BEST FLEET CAR. Next, a rectangular box, or node, appears on the screen, with the goal description written above it. Then the user selects the **EDIT** command and next the **INSERT** option; another rectangular box appears below the goal node, and the user proceeds to type in the name of the first criterion, price, which will appear inside the box. This process continues until all four criterion nodes have been entered, as can be seen in Figure 8.7.

In Figure 8.7 we see that in addition to the names of each criterion, the criterion nodes also contain the equal values of .250. These values represent the initial weights, or priorities, of the criteria before any judgments are made.

The model-construction process continues by moving down to the first criterion node and again using the **EDIT** and **INSERT** command sequences, this time to define the decision alternative nodes. In Figure 8.8 we show the result of defining the alternatives nodes under the PRICE criterion. Note that since there are three alternatives, the initial priorities are set at .333. Using a convenient **REPLICATE** option, we place the same alternative nodes under the other three criteria.

Once you have defined the complete shell of the EC model, you can move to any part of the model with the cursor arrow keys on the keypad; a particular part of the hierarchy can be displayed with the use of the **REDRAW** command.

Using EC to Calculate Priorities: The Pairwise-Comparison Mode

Now that the hierarchy of criteria and alternatives has been defined, we are ready to make pairwise comparisons to express relative preferences for the alternatives with respect to each criterion and for the relative importance of the criteria. The hierarchy is defined "top down" but usually evaluated "bottom up" because the thinking involved in the lower-level comparisons of alternative preferences helps make better judgments about the relative importance of the criteria.

After we move to the price node, and select the option to make comparisons based upon the *preference* for the decision alternatives with respect to price, the EC software takes us to the verbal pairwise comparison screen shown in Figure 8.9.

This screen allows the user to specify the relative preferences of cars A and B with respect to the price criterion. Note that this figure illustrates the nine-point verbal com-

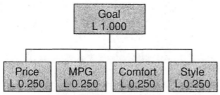

Select the Best Fleet Car

Comfort – Occupant Comfort - Seat, leg and
                 Headroom, HVAC
MPG   – Miles per gallon / Fuel efficiency
Price   – Initial purchase price of the fleet vehicles
Style   – Aesthetic appearance of vehicle

        – Local Priority: Priority Relative to Parent

FIGURE 8.8

Partial hierarchy showing price criterion with initial priorities for cars A, B, and C equal to .333

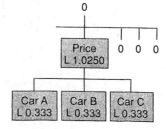

FIGURE 8.9

*Determining relative
preferences of cars
A and B with respect
to price*

FIGURE 8.10

*Pairwise comparison
matrix and priorities
of cars with respect
to price*

Judgments and Priorities with Respect to
Goal > Price

	Car A	Car B	Car C
Car A		(3.0)	(4.0)
Car B			(2.0)

Matrix entry indicates that ROW element is
1 Equally 3 Moderately 5 Strongly 7 Very Strongly 9 Extremely
more preferable than column element
unless enclosed in parenthesis.

Car A   :Car A
Car B   :Car B
Car C   :Car C

0.122
Car A

0.320
Car B

0.558
Car C

Inconsistency ratio = 0.016

Goal: Select the best fleet car
with respect to
Goal > Price

Car B
    is moderately more preferable than
Car A

    Extreme...................
    Very strong.............
    Strong......................
    Moderate................ ←
    Equal.......................

parison scale. (Judgments between each of the five words are permitted.) By moving the arrow to the word felt to be most appropriate (or between two words), the user enters his or her judgments. Figure 8.9 indicates to EC that the user feels car B is moderately more preferable than car A.

The pairwise-comparison process continues until all the possible combinations, taken two at a time, have been evaluated. After the final judgment is entered, EC automatically calculates the priorities for the cars with respect to the price criterion. Figure 8.10 displays the pairwise comparison matrix of the user's judgments, as well as the priorities in both decimal and horizontal-bar graph form.

In Figure 8.11 we can see that the decimal values in the boxes for each car now match the priorities based upon the pairwise comparisons entered by the user. The process of entering pairwise *preferences* for the cars relative to each of the other criteria is then performed in a similar manner.

Measuring the Consistency of the Decision Maker's Judgments

AHP provides a measure of the consistency of the decision maker's judgment process. Consistency is important because we would not want to base an important decision upon a set of judgments that lacked consistency. Inconsistency can result from an improper conceptualization of the hierarchy, lack of information, a mental lapse, or clerical errors.

As an example of some inconsistency in pairwise comparisons, examine the numerical representation of Bill's judgments about the relative comfort of the three cars. If his preference for A is twice B, and his preference for B is six times C, then his preference for A should be twelve times C (if he is perfectly consistent). But the numerical representation for the preference of A over C is eight, not twelve. If one mistakenly attempted to change judgments to be more consistent, which one should be changed? Are the first two correct and the third wrong, or are the second and third correct and the first judgment wrong? Most likely, none of the judgments are perfect reflections of

FIGURE 8.11

Priorities of cars with respect to price

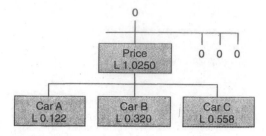

Car A – Car A
Car B – Car B
Car C – Car C
Price – Initial purchase price of the fleet vehicles
L   – Local priority: Priority relative to parent

Bill's preference, particularly since Bill used words, not numbers. They should be averaged in order to derive the priorities. This is essentially what AHP does and is also why it is not necessary for every decision maker to have the exact same interpretation of the verbal intensities.

AHP provides a method called the inconsistency ratio that calculates the degree of inconsistency of judgments. The ratio is based on a comparison with simulations of random judgments. As a rule of thumb, if the inconsistency ratio is greater than about .10 (10 percent of what would result from random judgments), one should investigate and try to ascertain the possible cause of the inconsistency. Expert Choice will calculate the inconsistency ratio almost instantaneously, as it calculates the priorities based on the set of pairwise judgments.

Synthesis of the AHP model

The overall decision is then arrived at by returning to the goal node invoking the **SYNTHESIS** command. This command is used only *after* we have entered all the data for the pairwise-comparison matrices and want to obtain an overall prioritization of the decision alternatives. Figures 8.12 and 8.13 display the results obtained. Note that the results indicate that the final priority for car B, the most preferable, is .423.

FIGURE 8.12

Synthesis details for final results of using AHP for the problem on fleet car selection

Select the Best Fleet Car
Tally for Synthesis of Leaf Nodes with Respect to Goal

Level 1	Level 2	Level 3	Level 4	Level 5
PRICE	= 0.377			
		Car C = 0.210		
		Car B = 0.120		
		Car A = 0.046		
Style	= 0.307			
		Car B = 0.202		
		Car A = 0.081		
		Car C = 0.024		
Comfort	= 0.220			
		Car A = 0.131		
		Car B = 0.075		
		Car C = 0.014		
MPG	= 0.097			
		Car C = 0.062		
		Car B = 0.026		
		Car A = 0.008		

FIGURE 8.13

End results of synthesis

Select the Best Fleet Car
Synthesis of Leaf Nodes with Respect to Goal
Overall Inconsistency Index = 0.08

Car B   0.423
Car C   0.311
Car A   0.266

1.000

Car A – CAR A
Car B – CAR B
Car C – CAR C

Performing a Sensitivity Analysis

A sensitivity analysis answers the question: How sensitive are the alternative priorities to changes we may contemplate in the weights of the criteria? After completing the model and moving back to the goal node, the user invokes the **SENSITIVITY** command. The screen displayed in Figure 8.14 appears. The dashed vertical line tells us that the priority of price (the *X* axis variable) is (.377). The height of the intersection of this dashed line with the alternative lines shows the alternatives' *overall* priorities. Thus as we saw in the synthesis, car B is the preferred alternative. If price were to become more important (i.e., by moving the dashed line to the right), the overall preferences for cars B and A decrease while that of car C increases. As can be seen from the figure, it would not take a great increase in the priority of price before we became indifferent to car B or C. Based upon this analysis, we can say that changes in the rankings of our alternatives are fairly sensitive to the priority of price.

Figure 8.15 displays the dynamic-sensitivity mode of EC. As the user adjusts the horizontal bar for any criterion (the length represents the weight attached to the criterion), the length of the alternative bars changes dynamically, representing the resulting

FIGURE 8.14

Sensitivity analysis of the price criterion

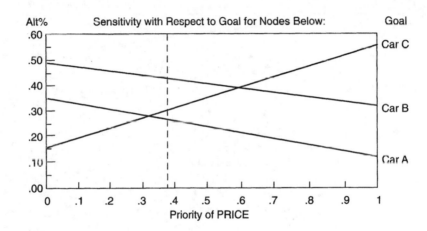

FIGURE 8.15

Expert choice's dynamic sensitivity mode

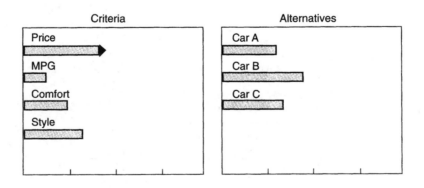

FIGURE 8.16

Increasing the weight assigned to price, using dynamic sensitivity mode

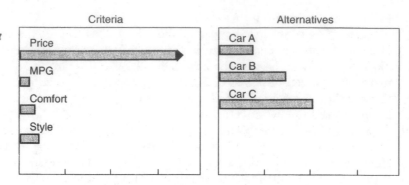

changes in alternative priorities. By moving the price bar to the right as shown in Figure 8.16, the sensitivity plot shown in Figure 8.17 results. The what-if that has been tested here examines the questions: What if more importance is placed upon price? and How much more priority would we have to assign to price for our decision to change?

FIGURE 8.17

Sensitivity plot after increasing weight of price criterion.

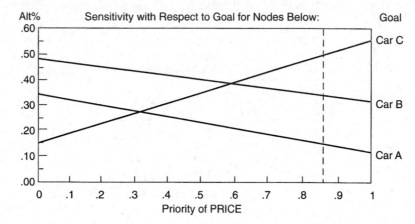

Commercial Software

Several other packages for the PC are available, each of them using a slightly different approach in setting up and computing the priorities and the weights. Representative products are:

Product	Vendor
Criterium	Sygenex, Redmond, Wash.
Decision Master	Generic Software, Inc., Bellevue, Wash.
Decision AID	Computer Software Construction, Inc., New York, N.Y.
Decision AIDE II	Kepner-Tregoe, Inc., Princeton, N.J.
Decision PAD	Apian Software, Menlo Park, Calif.
Logical Decision	Logical Decision, Inc., Point Richmond, Va.
Lightyear	Lightyear, Inc., Santa Clara, Calif.
Orion	Comshare, Inc., Ann Arbor, Mich.
SMART Edge	Haviland-Lee, Inc., Pasadena, Calif.

Management Science in Practice

Evaluating Energy Policies in Finland's Parliament

As in most countries, energy policy in Finland is a subject of wide public debate. In 1983, less than half the citizens supported nuclear power; about one-third of the representatives in Parliament were in favor of nuclear power and about one-third were against it. Studies by Finland's Department of Energy indicated that new sources of power would be needed by the mid-1990s if Finland's economy continued to grow, or not until after the year 2000 if the economy stagnated. If new nuclear power plants were to be added to the existing power grid, their planning would need to start quickly, because it takes 8 to 10 years to complete an operational nuclear power plant.

Three options were the major contenders for additional energy sources. The first two options, big nuclear plants and coal-fired plants, are the most economical. But each adds risk and/or pollution to the environment and sulfur-based acid rain from coal-fired plants was a

current major public concern. A third option employed a mix of conservation measures and decentralized small and medium-sized power plants.

To help structure the public and political debate, the Academy of Finland funded a special project proposed by the Systems Analysis Laboratory of Helsinki University of Technology. The project consisted of a computer-assisted decision aid based on the "analytic hierarchy process" (AHP). The aid would only be used by individuals, particularly members of Parliament, to help them clarify their personal views of the energy policy issue. Thus, it needed to be simple enough to be quickly comprehended by users with no prior knowledge of decision analysis and a minimal knowledge of mathematics.

The decision aid was constructed in four hierarchical levels, as shown below. At the top is society's overall benefit. This is attained through three major criteria at

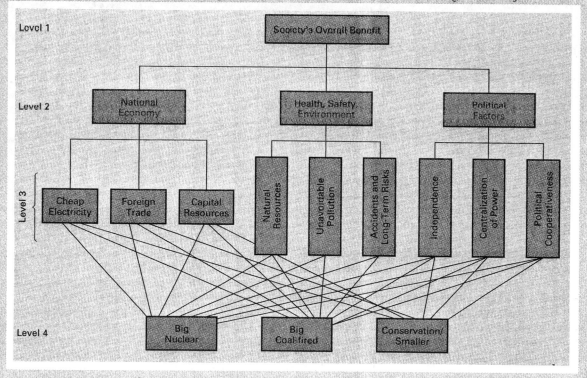

Management Science in Practice continued

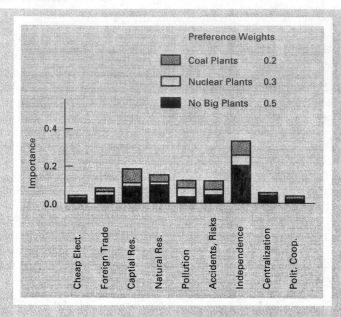

the second level: the national economy; health, safety, and the environment; and political factors. These in turn are composed of three subcriteria at the third level. The national economy consists of the subcriteria: cheap electricity, foreign trade, and capital resources. Health, safety, and environment is composed of natural resources, unavoidable pollution, and accidents and long-term risks. Last, political factors are composed of independence (from imports), centralization (of economic and political power), and political cooperativeness (between the eight political parties represented in the Parliament). The last level involved the three energy options—big nuclear, big coal-fired, and conservation/smaller—and their impacts on the nine subcriteria.

Representatives from the political parties volunteered to try out the decision aid. They made pairwise decisions regarding the quantitative priorities of the subcriteria. As their pairwise decisions were translated into preference weights for each of the criteria, they could visually see on the computer screen a graph of the overall importance weightings for each of the subcriteria, and the impact of each energy option on those weightings. One typical display is shown here.

The results of the process were that four major preference profiles emerged: two for conservation/smaller with emphases on natural resources and accidents/risks, and two for nuclear with emphases on cheap electricity and pollution. Interestingly, these are the same four as that of energy experts, which shows that the decision is not a matter of technical understanding or gathering more information but rather one of values, and *this* should be the focus of debate.

The members of Parliament believed that the aid significantly helped them clarify what they soon realized to be a very complex issue. It preserved their preliminary preferences in all cases but reversed the order of the second most-preferred alternative in three cases. The process and results were covered by the biggest daily paper in Finland in a long pro and con nuclear power article. Other newspapers and television stations further publicized the process in the evening news.

In early 1986, the power companies applied for licenses to build large nuclear power plants. Not long thereafter came the large Soviet nuclear accident in

Chernobyl and the power companies withdrew their applications. In their place, new medium-scale peat and coal plants are being built, some electricity is being imported, and investigations are being made into the possibility of building more hydroelectric plants.

Source: R. P. Hamalainen, "Computer Assisted Energy Policy Analysis in the Parliament of Finland," *Interfaces*, July–August 1988, pp. 12–23.

Questions:

1. Of the four major preference profiles, which one, if any, is shown in the bar chart?
2. How did Chernobyl affect this process?
3. Can you think of any other level subcriteria?
4. What was the value of this AHP aid? Did it save any money?

8.16 Concluding Remarks

The material presented in Part B of this chapter included two topics. First, the use of *utility* theory was introduced, permitting subjective assessments of payoffs and the additivity of different payoffs. Second, the difficulty of measuring attainment level when *multiple goals* exist was emphasized, and some techniques for solving this problem were suggested. A popular method called the analytic hierarchy process was introduced together with its support software—Expert Choice.

8.17 Problems for Part B

12. A manager expresses indifference between a certain profit of $5,000 and a venture with a 70 percent chance of making $10,000 and a 30 percent chance of making nothing. If the manager's utility scale was set at 0 utiles for $0, and 100 for $10,000, what is the utility index for $5,000? What is the risk premium?

13. The manager in Problem 12 is indifferent between two ventures: one that has a 60 percent chance of making $10,000 and a 40 percent chance of making $1,000, and a sure investment that yields $5,000. Find the value of $1,000 in utiles for this manager. Find the risk premium.

14. Below are the results of a preference test given to an executive:

    a. The executive is indifferent between an investment that will yield a certain $10,000 and a risky venture with a 50 percent chance of $30,000 profit and a 50 percent chance of a *loss* of $1,000.

    b. The executive's utility function for money has the following shape:

Money ($)	−1,000	0	5,000	20,000	30,000
Utility	−2	0	10	20	30

A new risky venture is proposed. The possible payoffs are *either* $0 or $20,000. The probabilities of the gain cannot be determined. Find what probability combination of $0 and $20,000 would make the executive indifferent to the certain $10,000.

15. A manager has an opportunity of investing $3,000 in a venture that has a .2 chance of making no profit, a .3 chance of making a $2,000 profit, a .2 chance of making a $4,000 profit, and a .3 chance of making a $6,000 profit. Her utilities for each of the outcomes are 0 for $0, .625 for $2,000, .875 for $4,000, and

1.000 for making $6,000. Draw the manager's utility curve and advise her on making the investment.

16. A Jamaican plant manager has a utility of 10 for $20,000, 6 for $11,000, 0 for $0, and -10 for a loss of $5,000.

   a. The plant manager is indifferent between receiving $11,000 for certain and a lottery with a .6 chance of winning $5,000 and a .4 chance of winning $20,000. What is the utility of $5,000 for the manager? Construct the manager's utility curve.

   b. Using this curve, find the certainty equivalent for the following gamble (i.e., the amount of cash that will make the manager *indifferent* to the gamble below):

Payoff	Probability
$-2,000	.2
0	.3
3,000	.4
10,000	.1

   c. What probability combination of $0 and $20,000 would make the manager indifferent to the certain $11,000?

   d. The manager is facing a decision about buying a new production machine that can bring a net profit of $15,000 (80 percent chance) or a loss of $1,000 (20 percent chance); alternatively, the manager can use the old machine and make a $10,000 profit. Use the utility curve to find which alternative the manager should select. Specify all necessary assumptions.

17. A survey of 10 physicians, 50 patients, and 20 nurses shows that each group allocated 100 "units of worth" among the four stated objectives of a hospital as follows:

Objectives	Physicians	Patients	Nurses
A	10	30	20
B	20	20	20
C	50	30	20
D	20	20	40
Total	100	100	100

   a. Assuming that all participants are considered to be equal, find the relative importance of the various objectives.

   b. Assume that physicians are considered twice as important as nurses and nurses are three times as important as patients. Find the relative importance of the various objectives.

18. EDX Electronic Corporation, Limited, can produce either product A, which will result in a 23 percent share of the market and a net profit of 7 percent, or product B, which will result in increasing the company's share of the market to 27 percent and a net profit of 5.5 percent. If the company considers each percent of net profit as important as a 2 percent share of the market, which product should the company produce?

19. Given below are the results of three years of operations at Computer Services Corporation:

Measure	1988	1989	1990
Sales (in million $)	6.0	6.6	7.2
Share of market (%)	15.0	13.5	16.5
Net profit ($ per share)	2.0	1.8	1.4
Equity per share ($)	4.0	4.2	4.8

The company's stated policy is that the relative importance of the objectives is as follows:

   a. Net profit is the most important objective.

   b. Equity per share is half as important as net profit.

   c. Sales are 1.2 times more important than equity per share.

   d. Share of the market is .4 times as important as net profit.

Which year was the most successful for the company's operations? Use 1988 as the base year.

20. International University uses a mathematical model for the initial screening of law school applicants. The variables considered are:

   a. The Law School Admission Test (LSAT), which has a possible score between 10 and 48.

   b. Grade point average (GPA on a 0–4 scale).

   c. An essay score on the LSAT that can vary from 0 to 80.

   d. The undergraduate school attended by the applicant, which is evaluated between 1 (poor) and 5 (excellent).

e. The applicant's involvement in extracurricular activities, which is valued from 0 (nothing) to 10 (extremely active).

The weights for the variables are: LSAT = .4, GPA = .4, essay = .1, undergraduate school = .05, extracurricular activities = .05.

John and Mary applied to the school. The necessary information on both students is given below:

	LSAT	GPA	Essay	Under-graduate School	Extra Activities
John	25	3.8	60	2	6
Mary	30	3.0	72	4	6

Use a single measure of performance to evaluate the two candidates. Which candidate is better? What assumptions are necessary to solve this problem?

21. Goodsite International is searching for a worldwide location for their new plant. Three sites are under consideration. These sites and the attributes on which they are being judged are given in the table below. Devise a methodology that will enable the company to select the most appropriate site.

	Site		
Attribute	Los Angeles	Barcelona	Tokyo
Climate	Excellent	Good	Poor
Labor availability	Plenty	Poor	Average
Regulations	Stiff	Easy	Easy
Cost of operations	High	Low	Medium
Transportation	Good	Good	Excellent
Cost of land	Very high	Low	High

22. The utility curve for a manager is given as $U(M) = 1.1M + \sqrt{20M}$.
    a. What is the attitude of this manager toward risk?
    b. Will this manager prefer investing in project P1, where there is a 30 percent chance of making $1 million and a 70 percent chance of making $2 million; or in P2, where there is a 50 percent chance of making nothing and a 50 percent chance of making $4 million?

23. A company is looking for a candidate to fill the position of a senior VP for marketing. Use the AHP to help in selecting a candidate. Specifically:
    a. Graph the hierarchy for five criteria and three candidates.
    b. List the criteria.
    c. Explain how the prioritization is to be conducted.
    d. Describe some possible difficulties in using AHP for this task.

24. Refer to the Sundial Industries fleet-selection problem in the chapter. Bring up on the computer screen the FLEETCAR model you developed for Sundial. Move to the MPG node. Experiment with each of the following modes of comparison in Expert Choice:

    Verbal pairwise comparisons
    Numerical pairwise comparisons
    The COMPARE-OTHER-WHAT IF mode using either graphic or numeric judgments

    Which method seems most appropriate here? Why? Next, highlight the STYLE node and attempt the same modes of comparison as above. Which method seems most appropriate here? Why?

25. Design an AHP model to assist you in the selection of a career or job area. Before you construct your model with Expert Choice, do the following:

    a. List some of the career/job-function areas that interest you (e.g., advertising account executive, industrial sales, product or brand manager, merchandise manager, marketing-research director).
    b. Divide a sheet of paper into two parts, mark one part PRO and the other CON; for each job you have noted list probable pros and cons.
    c. Scan the pros and cons that you have noted. You will see that you have generated some important criteria, and you are now ready to develop an Expert Choice model. In constructing your EC model, once you have entered the goal, criteria, and alternatives, begin making your pairwise comparisons from the "bottom up" (e.g., first evaluate the positions on the criteria). After you have finished evaluating all positions on all criteria, perform the pairwise comparisons to prioritize the criteria. Obtain a synthesis of your model. Finally, use the sensitivity utility to see how stable your priorities for the positions are,

given any changes in the priorities attached to criteria.

26. Bill Jennings is considering one of three graduate schools of business to pursue studies for an M.B.A. with a concentration in marketing. He has narrowed the schools down to UCLA, USC, and UC–Berkeley. Before making his final selection, Bill prepares a list of criteria. Also to get their views, he arranges appointments with a professor he has taken several courses with and the president of an advertising agency where he has worked part time in the media department.

1. Design an AHP model that includes the following elements:
   Viewpoints—professor, employer, and Bill.
   Criteria—list a few of the key factors that Bill should consider.
   Possible subcriteria linked to each parent criterion.
   Alternatives—his three potential schools.
2. What information would the synthesis of the above model provide?

Glossary

Additivity assumption   The utility of two or more items equals the sum of the utilities of the individual items.

Analytic hierarchy process (AHP)   A methodology for solving MCDM problems based on pairwise comparisons of preferences for criteria and alternatives.

Certainty equivalent (CE)   A subjective evaluation of the monetary worth of a gamble to a decision maker.

Deviational variables   The variables that measure the deviations from the goals; d^+ measures the deviation above the goal; d^- the deviation below the goal.

Deviations (from goals)   The values by which the goals are either overachieved or underachieved.

Expected utility (EU)   The long-run average utility per decision.

Goal constraints   These constraints express the desired organizational goals when deviations (d^+ and/or d^-) are tolerable.

Goal programming (GP)   A mathematical programming extension where several goals can be treated in the model if they are ranked according to their importance. The objective is to minimize the undesirable deviations from the goals.

Multiple criteria decision making (MCDM)   Same as multiple goals.

Multiple goals   A situation in which the impact of a decision is evaluated for several goals simultaneously.

Overachievement   A variable that measures by how much a goal is exceeded.

Pairwise comparisons   A method in which two of many criteria are compared to each other at a time in order to prioritize the criteria.

Preference theory   A measure of attitude toward risk using probabilities of a gamble.

Risk premium (RP)   The attitude toward risk, as measured by the difference between EMV and CE.

Risk profile   A list of the payoffs and probabilities for each alternative.

System constraints   Requirements and constraints that must be met in full. No deviations are permitted, usually due to some physical limitation (e.g., space, time). These are identical to LP constraints.

Underachievement   A variable that measures the difference between a given target and a performance lower than the standard.

Utile   A unit of measurement of utility.

Utility   The subjective value of the outcome to the decision maker.

Utility curve   The relationship between the quantity of money and its benefit to the decision maker.

Weighted goals   The relative importance of the goals as expressed by the explicit weights placed on the deviations.

References and Bibliography

1. Dyer, R. G. and E. H. Forman. *An Analytic Approach to Marketing Decisions*. Englewood Cliffs, N.J.: Prentice-Hall, 1991.

2. Hwang, C. L., and M. J. Lin. *Group Decision Making under Multiple Criteria Methods*. New York: Springer Verlag, 1987.

3. Ignizio, J. P. *Goal Programming and Extensions*. Lexington, Mass.: Lexington Books, 1976.

4. Lee, S. M., and J. P. Shim. *Micro Manager*. Dubuque, Iowa: Wm. C. Brown, 1986 (software package included).

5. Lev, B., and H. J. Weiss. *Introduction to Mathematical Programming*. New York: Elsevier North-Holland Publishing, 1982.

6. Linstone, H. A., and M. Turoff, eds. *The Delphi Method*. Reading, Mass.: Addison-Wesley Publishing, 1975.

7. Saaty, T. S. *Decision for Leaders: The Analytic Hierarchy Process*. Pittsburgh, Penn.: University of Pittsburgh, 1990.

8. Schniederjans, M. J. *Linear Goal Programming*. New York: Petrocelli Books, 1984.

9. Schniederjans, M. J. and R. L. Wilson. "Using the AHP and Goal Programming for Information Systems Project Selection," *Information and Management*, Vol. 20, 1991, pp. 333–342.

10. Steuer, R. E. *Multiple Criteria Optimization: Theory, Computation, and Applications*. New York: John Wiley & Sons, 1986.

11. Tabucanon, M. T. *Multiple Criteria Decision Making in Industry*. New York: Elsevier, 1989.

12. Von Neumann, J., and O. Morgenstern. *Theory of Games and Economic Behavior*. 3rd ed. Princeton, N.J.: Princeton University Press, 1953.

This chapter begins the presentation of the tools and techniques of management science. The major content of this chapter is the use of decision tables and trees as tools for selecting alternatives. Managerial problems are then classified and the appropriate tools and techniques are divided into three major classes: decisions under certainty (deterministic), decisions under risk (probabilistic), and decisions under uncertainty. These three classes are discussed in detail here.

PART A: BASICS

"The Dow Jones Industrial Average failed to hold above the 3,500 mark," the ticker tape calmly proclaimed. Mary Golden, vice president of Friendly Trust Company, read the message on the ticker tape over and over again. She moaned to herself: "This is the sixth time in the last four months that the famous indicator has penetrated the magic 3,500 mark but could not hold above it more than a few days." The major reason cited by most analysts for the weakness of the market was fear of an upcoming inflation and climbing interest rates. Mary was still in shock when the ticker tape brought another message: "City Bank of New York raised the prime rate by $\frac{1}{4}$ of 1 percent." This was too much for one day.

Mary was in charge of the Trust's investment department. She had just been authorized to invest a large sum of money in one (and only one) of three alternatives: corporate bonds, common stocks, or certificates of deposit (time deposits).

The Trust's objective is to maximize the yield on the investment over a one-year period. The problem is that the economic situation seemed to be uncertain and no one was able to predict the exact movements of the stock or even the bond markets. It was rather obvious to Mary that the yields (in percent of return on investment) depend on the state of the economy. Therefore, she consulted the economic research department. The researchers were not sure what the exact state of the economy would be after one year. However, they told Mary they expected the economy to be in one of three possible conditions (or states): solid growth, stagnation, or inflation. When asked for the likelihood of each condition, the researchers estimated a 50 percent chance for solid growth, a 30 percent chance of stagnation, and a 20 percent chance for inflation.

Mary examined the relationship between the yield on the possible investments and the state of the economy and concluded that past experience indicated the following trends:

1. *If* there is solid growth in the economy, bonds will yield 12 percent; stocks, 15 percent; and time deposits, 6.5 percent.
2. *If* stagnation prevails, bonds will yield 6 percent; stocks, 3 percent; and time deposits, 6.5 percent.
3. *If* inflation prevails, bonds will yield 3 percent; the value of stocks will drop 2 percent; and time deposits will yield 6.5 percent.

Mary examined all the above information and realized that the investment decision would not be simple at all.

9.1 Decision Analysis with Decision Tables

Characteristics of the Investment Problem

Mary's dilemma is a typical managerial investment problem. Mary, the *decision maker* in this case, must make a *choice* among several *courses of action*. She will attempt to evaluate the alternatives based on their yield during the next year, because the Trust's goal is to maximize its yield over that period. The difficulty is that there is *uncertainty* with respect to what is going to happen in the future. No matter which choice Mary makes, she is going to *assume some risk* that the future she has hoped for is not going to materialize. What is the degree of risk that she is assuming? How does it relate to the

Decision theory for
calculated risk

available alternatives? Can the risk be reduced? Can the risk be eliminated? *Decision theory,* a quantitative analysis procedure applied to decision making, attempts to answer such questions.

The Use of Decision Tables

The payoff table for
analyzing data

The quantitative data of many decision situations can be arranged in a standarized tabular form known as a **decision table** (or a **payoff** table). The objective of doing so is to enable a systematic analysis of the problem. Although not all decision situations are explicitly amenable to a tabular presentation, many concepts used in decision tables are common to all decision situations.

Decision tables typically contain four elements:

1. The alternative courses of action.
2. The states of nature.
3. The probabilities of the states of nature.
4. The payoffs.

Let us return to Mary's problem and arrange the information there as a decision table.

The Alternative Courses of Action

Decision making, by definition, involves two or more *options,* or **alternative courses of action,** also called strategies. One, *and only one,* of these alternatives *must* be selected. The alternative courses of action are designated as $a_1, a_2, \ldots, a_n$ (sometimes $d_1, d_2, \ldots, d_n$), where n is the number of available alternatives that may be either finite or infinite. For example, the decision to select a textbook for a particular class may involve numerous but finite alternatives. If, however, one were producing beer, the quantity of water to add to the mix may include, at least in theory, an infinite number of combinations. For example, one can add 2.1 gallons, 2.11 gallons, 2.111 gallons, and so on.

A finite number of
alternatives

In this text, the alternatives are listed on the left side of the table, one to a row (e.g., see Table 9.1). In other books or computer programs, they may be presented as columns.

In most operating circumstances, not all possible alternatives are considered, but only those within a limited range. For example, in beer making, rules of good brewing establish that the water added ought to be within the range of, say, 7 to 7.5 gallons to a 10-gallon barrel. This is the range of *feasible* solutions. It still leaves an infinite number of points between 7 and 7.5, but one might decide to structure the alternatives in only tenths of gallons, thus reducing the number to only six (7, 7.1, 7.2, 7.3, 7.4, 7.5).

Only feasible
alternatives

Decision tables are used when the number of alternatives is *finite* and usually small (e.g., less than a few hundred). In the investment problem, there are three alternatives.

The ability to generate alternatives depends on the creativity and imagination of the manager. A creative manager sees more alternatives than does a conservative one.

TABLE 9.1   Decision Table (Payoffs in Percentage Yield)

Alternatives (decision variables)	States of nature	Solid Growth s_1	Stagnation s_2	Inflation s_3	
		.5	.3	.2	← *Probabilities (uncontrollable)*
a_1 *Bonds*		12	6	3	← *Payoffs*
a_2 *Stocks*		15	3	−2	
a_3 *Time deposits (CDs)*		6.5	6.5	6.5	

For example, if Mary wants to consider investing in both stocks and bonds simultaneously, she can create more alternatives such as a_4: 50 percent stocks, 50 percent bonds; or a_5: 30 percent stocks, 70 percent bonds.

The States of Nature

Uncontrollable futures

At the top of the table, the possible **states of nature** (also called events or possible futures) are listed. They are generally labeled s_1, s_2, . . . , s_m. A state of nature can be a state of the economy (e.g, inflation), a weather condition, a political development, or other situation that the decision maker cannot control. In the investment example, there are three states of nature that are the possible states of the economy: solid growth, stagnation, and inflation. The states of nature are usually *not* determined by the action of a single individual or an organization. They are basically the result of an "act of God," or the result of many forces pushing in various directions.

The Probabilities of the States of Nature

One and only one state of nature will occur

What is the likelihood of these states of nature occurring? Whenever it is possible to answer this question in terms of explicit chances (or probabilities), the information is recorded at the top of the table. The probabilities are given either in percent or in percentage fractions; for example, 50 percent = .5. Because it is assumed that one *and only one* of the given states of nature will occur in the future, then the sum of the probabilities must always be one. This is expressed as:

$$p_1 + p_2 + \cdots + p_m = 1 \qquad \text{or:} \quad \sum_{j=1}^{m} p_j = 1 \tag{9.1}$$

where p_1 = probability of s_1 occurring, p_2 = probability of s_2 occurring, and so on. In Mary's example, p_1 = .5, p_2 = .3, and p_3 = .2. The subscript m designates the fact that m states of nature are considered.

The Payoffs

The payoff (or the *outcome*) associated with a certain alternative and a specific state is given in that cell within the body of the table located at the *intersection* of the alternative in question (given by a row) and the specific state of nature (given by a column).

The payoff is designated by o_{ij} where i indicates the row and j the column. For example, in Table 9.1, if the decision maker selects alternative a_1 and future s_2 occurs, then the outcome of the decision is predicted as a payoff (yield) of 6 percent. The payoffs can be thought of as *conditional* because a specific payoff results from a specific state of nature occurring but only after a certain alternative course of action has been taken. An important point to remember is that the payoff is measured within a *specified* period (e.g., after one year). This period is sometimes called the *decision horizon*. Alternatively, a payoff can be the *present value* of several payoffs realized at different times in the future.

Conditional payoffs

Payoffs can be measured in terms of money, market share, or other measures. The payoffs considered in most decisions are monetary. However, other consequences also will occur and should be taken into account once the quantitative answer is derived.

The General Structure of a Decision Table

The decision table as a model

Table 9.2 shows the general structure of decision tables. In terms of the elements of mathematical models, the decision table can be described as:

Decision Table	Mathematical Model
Alternative courses of action	= Independent decision variables.
States of nature	= Independent, uncontrollable parameters.
Probabilities of the states of nature	= Independent, uncontrollable parameters.
Payoffs	= Expected results (dependent variables).

TABLE 9.2 The Decision Table—General Structure

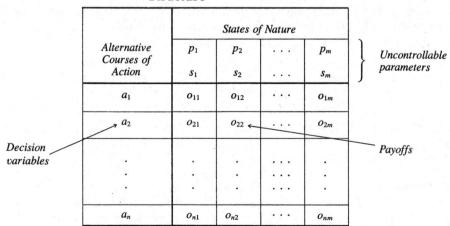

9.2 Decisions under Certainty

In decision making under **certainty,** the situation can be mapped as a table with one payoff column (one state of nature). Therefore, in making a decision, all one has to do is to compare all the entries in the payoff column and select the alternative with the highest profit or lowest cost. In executing such a comparison, one distinguishes between two cases:

Enumeration or exhaustive search

1. When the number of alternatives is relatively small. In this case, an approach known as **complete enumeration** is used.
2. When the number of alternatives is large or even infinite. In this case, a selective search for the best solution is conducted with the aid of mathematical models.

Complete Enumeration

Complete enumeration means examining every payoff, one at a time, comparing the payoffs to each other (e.g., in pairs), and discarding inferior solutions. The process continues until *all* payoffs are examined.

Example: Assignment of Employees to Machines

A maintenance crew of three machinists is to be assigned to the repair of three machines, on a one-to-one basis, in a manner that minimizes repair time. Based on historical data, the supervisor knows the exact repair time, which varies with each person-machine match. The repair times, in hours, are shown in Table 9.3. (For example, if Jack works on machine A, it takes him three hours to fix it; the repair time is the payoff in this case.)

Consider all possible matches

Solution
All alternative assignments, with their appropriate total repair times, are shown in Table 9.4. Note that the decision table has only one column of payoffs (one state of nature).

TABLE 9.3   Repair Times

Machinist \ Machine	A	B	C
Jack	3	7	4
Gene	4	6	6
Mel	3	8	5

TABLE 9.4   Assignment Payoffs

Alternatives	Total Payoff (Total Repair Time)	
a_1 Jack–A, Gene–B, Mel–C	3 + 6 + 5 =	14
a_2 Jack–A, Gene–C, Mel–B	3 + 6 + 8 =	17
a_3 Jack–B, Gene–A, Mel–C	7 + 4 + 5 =	16
a_4 Jack–B, Gene–C, Mel–A	7 + 6 + 3 =	16
a_5 Jack–C, Gene–B, Mel–A	4 + 6 + 3 =	13	←Best
a_6 Jack–C, Gene–A, Mel–B	4 + 4 + 8 =	16

By comparing the total repair times for *all* possibilities, it is found that alternative a_5 is the best, because the total repair time is the smallest. Larger assignment problems have an extremely large number of possible solutions and are therefore solved by algorithms rather than by enumeration.

Computation with Analytical Models

Although complete enumeration is an effective approach in many situations, there are two cases in which it does not work at all or works very poorly. The first is the case of an *infinite number of alternatives*. Managerial problems such as allocation of resources or blending liquid materials are examples of such situations. To cope with these problems, models such as linear programming have been developed.

Why use models?

Combinatorial problems

The second case involves problems with a *finite, but very large,* sometimes astronomical, number of alternatives. Such problems are frequently referred to as *combinatorial problems*. Several scheduling and sequencing problems are of this nature. In these cases, it is possible to enumerate all the alternatives, but it may take years to do so, even with the aid of high-speed computers. Special models such as branch and bound (Chapter 6), assignment (Chapter 7), dynamic programming (Chapter 16), and heuristic programming (Chapter 17) have been developed for effective solutions.

Summary

Decision making under certainty involves the following steps:

1. Determine the alternative courses of action.
2. Calculate (or assess) the payoffs, one for each course of action.
3. Select the one with the best payoff (e.g., largest profit or smallest cost), either by complete enumeration or by the use of an analytical model.

9.3 Decisions under Risk

Calculated risk

Decision situations in which the chance (or probability) of occurrence of each state of nature is known (or can be estimated) are defined as decisions made under **risk.** In such cases, the decision maker can assess the degree of risk that he or she is taking in terms of probability distributions. For example, a decision not to purchase fire insurance means that the decision maker takes a chance of perhaps 1 in 10,000 of losing all of his or her property in a fire.

The Concept of Probability in Decision Making

Probabilities in decision making should be viewed as a means of expressing the decision maker's judgment about an uncertain future. We all use phrases such as:

"There is a pretty good chance that interest rates will decline."

"It is likely to rain today."

"It's not likely that mortgage rates will come down."

"We are not sure how our competitor will react."

Probabilities constitute a language similar to the above but are more precise. By definition, a probability is the relative frequency of an event occurring when a situation is repeated many times under identical circumstances. But probabilities in managerial language are also used for one-time decision situations. For example, instead of saying that our new product has a pretty good chance of succeeding, we say that there is an 85 percent chance that the product will be a success.

Objective and Subjective Probabilities

There are two approaches to the assessment of the probabilities of the states of nature: objective and subjective.

Objective Probability

History or experimentation for probabilities

Objective probabilities can be derived either based on historical occurrences or based on experimentation. Alternatively, they can be derived with statistical formulas. For example, the probability of a "head" in the toss of a coin is computed statistically as one half because only two states of nature (a head or a tail) can occur; and assuming the coin is fair, there is an equal chance for each (i.e., 50 percent). Thus, the use of objective probabilities narrows the scope for judgment. Unfortunately, the use of objective probabilities requires several of the following crucial assumptions that restrict its use:

1. Objective probabilities are usually based on observation of past events, experimentation, or both. Therefore, in using objective probabilities for decision making, it must be assumed that future conditions will follow the same pattern as past conditions (or that a clear trend for future events has been established).

2. A necessary result of the assumption above is that the process observed must be stable.

3. It must be assumed that if a sample was observed for determining past behavior, it was large enough (statistically) and representative of the process under study.

Subjective Probability

Belief about the probabilities

The **subjective probability** approach measures the *degree of belief* in the likelihood of the future occurrence of a given outcome. Thus, such probabilities are a subjective appraisal of the nature of reality, in contrast to objective probabilities, which must be actual, countable, observable fact. Subjective probabilities are made by an individual(s) possessing experience with the phenomena involved. Subjective probability is used in cases in which objective probabilities cannot be used. The major problem with subjective probabilities is that different decision makers may give different estimates of the probabilities, and even change their estimates as a result of psychological, emotional, or other behavioral factors.

Note: With either objective or subjective probabilities, we incorporate *judgment* into the decision process. For example, in objective probabilities, we must judge which historical data are appropriate.

Solution Approaches to Decision Making under Risk

Several criteria

The most acceptable solution approach to decision making under risk is the use of **expected value (EV)** as a criterion of choice. Alternatively, the **expected opportunity loss (EOL)** criterion may be used. Both lead to the same result. Other criteria are the **most probable state of nature** criterion and some of those used for decision making under uncertainty (such as minimax), which is discussed in Section 9.12.

An Example of Decision Making under Risk: How to Beat Inflation

In the problem presented at the beginning of this chapter. Mary Golden was considering an investment for a trust fund in one of the following alternatives: a_1 = corporate bonds, a_2 = common stocks, or a_3 = time deposits. Suppose that the trust wants to invest in only *one alternative* with a declared objective of maximizing the yield over a one-year period. The yield (in percent of return) will depend on the state of the economy, which can be solid growth, stagnation, or inflation. The estimated yields under each alternative and state of the economy are shown in Table 9.5. The problem is to find the best investment alternative.

Solution Approach A: The Use of the Expected Payoff Criterion

Maximize expected yield

This approach prescribes that the decision maker select the alternative with the best expected (average) payoff. This alternative should be selected each time the decision maker confronts the investment situation. Over the long run, the average yearly yield will be the same as the expected payoff.

TABLE 9.5 Yields (in Percent) of Investment Alternatives

States of Nature / Alternatives	.5 Solid Growth	.3 Stagnation	.2 Inflation	←Probabilities Expected Value (Percent)	
a_1	12	6	3	8.4	←*Maximum*
a_2	15	3	−2	8.0	
a_3	6.5	6.5	6.5	6.5	

The expected payoff of an alternative is the sum of all possible payoffs of that alternative, weighted by the probabilities of those payoffs occurring.

How to compute an expected value

How to Find the Expected Payoff. The expected payoffs are computed, for each alternative, one at a time.

Step 1 Multiply each payoff by its corresponding probability. For example, for alternative a_1 of Table 9.5: $12 \times .5$, $6 \times .3$, and $3 \times .2$.

Step 2 Sum the results of the multiplications of Step 1; the total is the expected payoff.

In mathematical terms, let:
a_i = Alternative i
s_j = State of nature j
p_j = Probability that state of nature s_j will occur
o_{ij} = Payoff resulting from the selection of alternative a_i when s_j occurs

Then, the expected value $E(a_i)$ is:

$$E(a_i) = p_1 o_{i1} + p_2 o_{i2} + \cdots = \sum_{j=1}^{m} p_j o_{ij}$$

For alternative a_1 in Table 9.5, the results are:

$$E(a_1) = 12 \times .5 + 6 \times .3 + 3 \times .2 \qquad = 8.4 \text{ percent}$$
$$E(a_2) = 15 \times .5 + 3 \times .3 - 2 \times .2 \qquad = 8.0 \text{ percent}$$
$$E(a_3) = 6.5 \times .5 + 6.5 \times .3 + 6.5 \times .2 = 6.5 \text{ percent}$$

The Selection of an Alternative. Once the expected payoffs for all alternatives are determined, only the newly formed column of expected payoffs need be considered (see the right-hand column of Table 9.5). This is the dependent (or result) variable of the decision model. If the problem is one of maximization, then the *highest* expected payoff is searched for, using complete enumeration. In minimization, the alternative with the *lowest* expected payoff is sought. In the investment (maximization) example, alternative a_1 has the highest expected yield, and therefore investing in corporate bonds is recommended. The meaning of this choice is that the decision maker should invest in a_1, and only a_1, each time that he or she is confronted with the decision. Furthermore, the average yearly yield, over the long run, per decision, is 8.4 percent. *Note:* The use of this criterion, when the payoffs are expressed in dollars, is called the **expected monetary value** or the EMV criterion.

EMV = expected monetary value

Solution Approach B: The Expected Opportunity Loss (EOL) Criterion (Also Called the Regret Criterion)

Minimizing expected regret

The basic idea of this criterion is that people frequently act to minimize their anticipated average (expected) **regret. Opportunity loss** is defined as the relative loss resulting from selecting an alternative, given that a particular state of nature occurred, as compared with the *best* alternative that could have been selected. For example, if Mary Golden invests in bonds (a_1) and solid growth occurs, she will *regret* not having invested in stocks (a_2), which would have been the best alternative. Because she will make 12 percent with the bonds versus 15 percent that she could have made with stocks, her regret, or opportunity loss, is 3 percent. Table 9.6 shows the complete opportunity loss data. Within each payoff column, each payoff is subtracted from the largest payoff in the column. Once the table is constructed, the *expected* regret is computed by the same method used in computing expected payoffs, and the alternative with the *smallest expected regret* is selected. This rule is true for *any* regret table, whether derived from profit or loss data. Regret is always bad and is to be avoided or minimized.

EOL and EMV give the same result

Note also that alternative a_1 was selected under both the expected opportunity loss criterion and the expected payoff criterion. This is *not* a coincidence. Both will *always lead* to the *same choice* because the mathematical operations are basically the same.

TABLE 9.6 **Opportunity Loss Table (Percent Yield) of Table 9.5**

States of Nature / Alternatives	.5 Solid Growth	.3 Stagnation	.2 Inflation	← Probabilities Expected Regret	
a_1	15 − 12 = 3	6.5 − 6 = .5	6.5 − 3 = 3.5	3 × .5 + .5 × .3 + 3.5 × .2 =	2.35 ← *Smallest*
a_2	15 − 15 = 0	6.5 − 3 = 3.5	6.5 − (−2) = 8.5	0 × .5 + 3.5 × .3 + 8.5 × .2 =	2.75
a_3	15 − 6.5 = 8.5	6.5 − 6.5 = 0	6.5 − 6.5 = 0	8.5 × .5 + 0 × .3 + 0 × .2 =	4.25

The difference is only philosophical. These are merely two different explanations of why people make certain choices.

Solution Approach C: The "Most Probable State of Nature" Criterion

Ignoring less likely
outcomes

This criterion prescribes that as the decision maker confronts the various possible states of nature in a decision under risk, he or she ignores all but the *most probable* state. By doing so, the decision maker changes the situation to a decision under *assumed certainty*. Some nonrepetitive decisions are treated with this principle.

Example

Consider the investment decision of Table 9.5. According to the most-probable-state-of-nature criterion, the decision maker assumes that solid growth will occur because it has the largest chance of occurring. The other states of nature are ignored. Therefore, Mary Golden will select a_2 because it will give her the largest yield (15 percent) in the event that solid growth occurs. However, if the decision maker is wrong, she may end with a yield of 3 or even lose 2. If this is a repeating situation, she will only make 8 (the expected value) over the long run.

One problem with this criterion is that it ignores the magnitude of some of the payoffs. For example, according to this criterion, a decision maker would choose a_1 over a_2 in the table below no matter what the profits are under the s_2 column. In reality, a_2 would almost always be selected because of the large potential payoff.

	$p_1 = .6$ s_1	$p_2 = .4$ s_2
a_1	10	10
a_2	8	500

Solution Approach D: Criteria of Choice for Uncertainty

In Part B of this chapter, we introduce five criteria of choice for the case of uncertainty. These could be used for the case of risk as well. However, with the exception of nonrepetitive decisions, it is very unlikely that these criteria will be used when actual probabilities are available, because the criteria possess too many deficiencies and do not include the consideration of the risk level.

Note: Solution approach C ignores the relative *magnitude* of some of the outcomes, whereas solution approach D ignores the *likelihood* of each of the events occurring. The expected value criterion *combines* both the size of the consequences and their likelihood. Therefore, it is a superior criterion for most situations.

Notes on Application

Nonrepetitive Decisions

The expected value approach is based on achieving the best payoff over the long run. For example, if the decision maker of Table 9.5 selects alternative a_1, he or she will make *either* a 12, 6, or 3 percent yield each time the decision is made. Only over the *long run* will these yields average out to 8.4 percent. The question may thus be asked: Is there any justification in using an expected value approach for a one-shot, nonrepetitive decision?

There is at least one case in which the answer to this question is clearly yes. If a company is making several one-shot decisions whose payoff is more or less of the same magnitude, then the overall impact of using an expected value approach is similar to that of one repetitive decision. That is, repeating one decision 30 times, or making 30 decisions one time, results in the same mathematical expectation. In cases where an expected value cannot be justified, the criteria discussed in Section 9.11 (such as minimax) can be used, or the use of utilities, as shown in Chapter 8, may be a good approach.

Use of Mathematical Models

The evaluation of decisions under risk is made by comparing (complete enumeration) *all* expected payoffs and selecting the best one. However, this may be a long and costly procedure if many alternatives and payoffs are considered. For these types of situations, probabilistic mathematical models (such as those presented in Chapters 3–7) are available.

The Use of Utilities as Payoffs

This subject was discussed in Chapter 8.

Dominance

In certain cases, it is possible to eliminate some alternatives from evaluation because they are *inferior to* or *dominated by* other alternatives. For example, assume that alternative a_4 is added as an investment alternative to Table 9.5, where the yields are: 10 in the case of solid growth, 6 in the case of stagnation, and 2 in the case of inflation. If we compare this alternative (a_4) to a_1, we get:

	Solid Growth	Stagnation	Inflation
a_1	12	6	3
a_4	10	6	2

It can clearly be seen that the decision maker should not consider a_4 at all, because no matter what state of nature occurs, the decision maker will be as well off or better with a_1. Thus, it is said that a_1 **dominates** a_4.

A Note on the Concept of Risk

Last, in spite of the usefulness of expected value as a decision criterion for risky situations, it is always advisable to also consider the *variability* of the payoffs. For example, it may not be worthwhile to select an alternative that has an insignificantly higher expected return if it also entails the possibility of significant loss. Thus, the variability of returns should always be considered.

Also note that the concept of expected value is based on the long-run consequences. You lose one, you win one; what is important is the long-run average. Now, assume that there is a 30 percent chance that you lose. If you lose once, twice, or maybe three times in a row, you may be out of business. That is, you cannot always afford to wait for the long run. In cases like this, the concept of utility theory (Chapter 8) may be more appropriate.

Sensitivity Analysis

Assume that our company is examining a venture in which we can make $45,000 or lose $15,000. Also assume that the company uses expected value as the criterion for decision making; if the EMV of this venture is larger than zero, the company will undertake the project, but if the EMV is zero, they will be indifferent.

Denote the probability of success by p. Therefore:

$$\text{EMV} = p(45{,}000) + (1 - p)(-15{,}000)$$

If we set EMV to zero and solve for p, we will get $p = .25$. That is, if the probability of success is larger than .25, the EMV will be larger than zero. By assumption, the company should undertake the project.

Now suppose that we have estimated the probability of success to be .60; obviously the company will undertake the project. Furthermore, the probability of success could drop all the way to .25 before the company would change its decision. As the probability approaches .25, the EMV gets smaller and smaller, shrinking to exactly zero at .25 and becoming *negative* for values less than .25. This value of $p = .25$ is called the **critical probability.**

Breakeven at the
critical probability

Summary

The use of the expected payoff criterion for making decisions under risk enables the decision maker to consider the risk involved in the decision. The expected payoff is the sum of individual payoffs weighted by their probabilities of occurrence. Other criteria of choice may be used, especially in nonrepetitive situations, such as "avoid any alternative that could result in a loss greater than X."

Management Science in Practice

Evaluating the National Weather Service's Flood Forecasts

The National Weather Service (NWS) issues flood forecasts and warnings for 3,000 flood-prone areas in order to save lives and reduce property damage. The importance of this service has grown significantly in the last decade due to a number of factors such as the increasing cost of structural flood protection measures (dams, levees, diversion channels) and the growth in development of floodplains for urban, commercial, and industrial uses.

Although a late or inaccurate forecast can cause millions of dollars in preventable damage, a perfect forecast that is simply ignored by those who are in potential danger can be just as expensive. To better understand the interplay of these two factors, the NWS commissioned a study of the flood forecast-response (FFR) process that included hydrologic, organizational, behavioral, and economic factors. The study included both *normative* operation (e.g., perfect forecasts) as well as *actual* operation of the FFR. Thus, three scenarios were used in the study: (1) A *perfect* forecast combined with an *optimal* response by those in jeopardy, (2) An *actual* forecast combined with an *optimal* response to that forecast, and (3) An *actual* forecast with an *actual* response.

Data were gathered for Milton, Pennsylvania, a small community of 840 people who would be endangered by a flood of the nearby Susquehanna River. Such a flood occurs in Milton every two years, on average. Four expected losses were computed based on past data: ELN, the expected loss with no response from those in jeopardy (i.e., the expected annual damage without an FFR system); EL1, the expected loss with scenario 1 above; EL2, the expected loss with scenario 2; and EL3, the expected loss in scenario 3. The potential value of a perfect FFR system would thus be represented by the difference between ELN and EL1. Similarly, the value of an optimal response to the actual forecast would be represented by the difference between ELN and EL2. And finally, the actual value of the current FFR system is represented by the difference between ELN and EL3. The values are shown in Table 1.

TABLE 1. FFR Values and Opportunity Losses (in $1000s) for Milton, PA

	A Actual	B +2 Hours	C +120 Hours
Potential value: ELN–EL1	1827	1827	1827
Optimal value: ELN–EL2	374	474	1506
Actual value: ELN–EL3	126	210	1289
EOL(Forecast system)	1453	1353	321
EOL(Response system)	248	264	217
EOL(Total system)	1701	1617	538

The actual value of the current FFR system is $126,000, as indicated in the third line. If those in jeopardy made optimal responses to the actual forecast (instead of waiting, for example), the value would increase to $374,000. The difference of $248,000 thus represents an "expected opportunity loss" (EOL) due to the imperfect response system, as shown in the fifth line. And if, in addition, the forecasts were perfect and people responded optimally, the value would increase to $1,827,000 (first row), representing an expected opportunity loss due to the imperfect forecasts of $1,453,000, as shown in the fourth line.

Of interest to the National Weather Service is the potential advantage of being able to provide forecasts earlier than is done at present by, for example, automating some of the tasks that are currently performed manually. The effect of being able to give warnings two hours sooner than at present is illustrated in column *B* of Table 1. As we see, it enhances the optimal and actual values by about a hundred thousand dollars.

Another item of interest of NWS is the ability of those in jeopardy to respond faster to the warnings. It was found, for example, that it takes about 20 hours to avert 60 percent of the maximum preventable damage that may be averted by short-term protective action. Virtually 100 percent of the short-term preventable damage can be averted if 120 hours of warning are available. Thus, values were determined assuming 120 hours of warning were available, thereby simulating maximum response to the warning. These values are given in column *C* of Table 1. In this case we see that the optimal and actual values improve significantly, almost reaching the potential value.

The conclusions drawn by the NWS were that a combination of earlier forecasts and better response by the endangered community holds the most promise for improved flood protection.

Source: R. Krzysztofowiz and D. R. Davis, "Toward Improving Flood Forecast-Response Systems", *Interfaces*, May–June 1984, pp. 1–14.

Questions:

1. Why do you think that the value of an FFR with a perfect forecast but actual response was not included in the study?

2. In Table 1, interpret the values of the EOLs for the +2 hours column.

3. A natural question for NWS is: What is the maximum value that can be attained with as much lead time as is needed to prepare (third column of Table 1)? However, this is not the intended intrepretation of column 3. What is it? How well does it portray the intended situation?

9.4 Decision Trees

Decision making as discussed thus far has been limited to a single decision over one period of time. A decision was to be made at the beginning of the period, and the future consequences were estimated either in terms of the present value or the future worth of the results. All the information was presented in the form of a decision table. There are times, however, when a decision cannot be viewed as an isolated, single occurrence, but rather as the first of a sequence of several interrelated decisions over several future periods. Therefore, the decision maker must consider the whole series of decisions simultaneously. Such a situation is called a *sequential* or *multiperiod* decision process. Using decision tables to analyze these decisions becomes too cumbersome. The tool that

Decision trees for sequential decisions

was developed instead is called a **decision tree,** which is basically a graphical exposition of decision tables in the form of a tree.

Advantages

Decisions at a glance

Decision trees provide a graphical presentation of sequential decision processes. They show, at a glance, when decisions are expected to be made, what the possible consequences are, and what the resultant payoffs are expected to be.

Another advantage is that the results of the computations can be depicted directly on the tree, simplifying the analysis. A decision tree is composed of the following elements (see Figure 9.1): decision points, alternatives, chance points, states of nature, and payoffs.

1. Decision Points

Alternatives emerge from decision points

At a **decision point** (also called a decision *node,* act node, or decision fork), usually designated by a square, the decision maker must select *one alternative course of action*

FIGURE 9.1

*The general structure
of a decision tree*

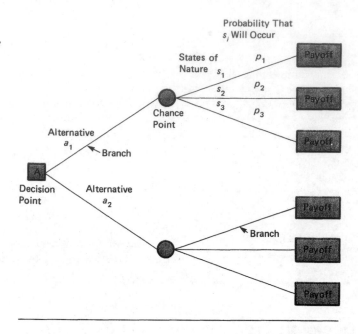

from a finite number of available ones. These are shown as **branches** or arcs emerging
out of the right side of the decision point. When there is a cost or profit associated with
the alternative, it is necessary to keep track of it along the path. The net present value
is then written at the end of each branch. Each alternative branch may result in a payoff, another decision point, or a chance point.

2. Chance Points

Events emerge from
chance points

A **chance point** (also known as an event fork or chance node), designated by a circle,
indicates that a chance event is expected at this point in the process. That is, one of a
finite number of *states of nature* is expected to occur. The states of nature are shown on
the tree as branches to the right of the chance points. Because decision trees depict decision making under risk, the assumed probabilities of the states of nature are written
above the branches. Each state of nature may be followed by a payoff, a decision point,
or by another chance point.

Constructing a Tree

A tree grows to the
right

A tree is started at the *left* of the page with a decision point. Once the decision point is
constructed, all possible alternatives are drawn branching out to the right. Then, a
chance point or other decision points are added, corresponding to events or decisions
that are expected to occur after the initial decision. Each time a chance point is added,

the appropriate states of nature, with their corresponding probabilities, branch out of it to the right. The tree continues to branch from left to right until the payoffs are reached. Figure 9.1 shows the general structure of a small tree. Larger trees involve a sequence of several decision and chance points, representing several decision periods, as shown later in both this section and in Section 9.10. The tree shown in Figure 9.1 represents a single decision and as such is equivalent to a decision table.

The process of constructing a tree may be divided conceptually into three steps:

a. Build a *logical tree,* which includes all decision points, chance points, and emerging arcs, arranged in chronological order.

b. Introduce the probabilities of the states of nature on the arcs, thus forming a *probability tree.*

c. Finally, add the conditional payoffs, thus forming the completed *decision tree.*

Example of the Equivalence of Decision Trees and Decision Tables

Table-tree equivalence

Consider the situation in Table 9.7. This table is presented as a decision tree in Figure 9.2.

Evaluating a Tree

In order to solve a tree, it is customary to divide it into segments. Two types of segments are considered: *decision points* with all their alternatives (Figure 9.3a), and *chance points* with all their emerging states of nature (Figure 9.3b).

Backward evaluation

The solution process starts with those segments ending in the final payoffs at the *right side of the tree,* and continues to the left, segment by segment, in the *reverse* order from which the tree was drawn.

Chance segments use EMV

1. *Chance point segments.* The *expected value* of all the states of nature emerging from a chance point must be computed (multiply payoffs by their probabilities and sum up the results). The expected value is then written near the chance point inside a rectangle (labeled EMV in Figure 9.2). These expected values are considered as payoffs for the next branch to the left.

Decision segments

2. *Decision point segments.* At a decision point, the payoffs given (or computed) for each alternative are compared and the best one is selected. All others are disregarded. A disregarded alternative is marked by the symbol ‖ directly on the branch (see Figure 9.2).

Thus, the decision maker *must* select one alternative at each *decision* point, and discard (prune) *all* other alternatives. The computation process continues from the right to the left. Pruning slowly reduces the size of the decision tree until only one alternative remains at the last decision point on the left side of the tree.

TABLE 9.7　Table 9.5 Reproduced

Alternatives	States of Nature	.5 Solid Growth s_1	.3 Stagnation s_2	.2 Inflation s_3	Expected Value
a_1　Bonds		12	6	3	8.4
a_2　Stocks		15	3	−2	8.0
a_3　Time deposits		6.5	6.5	6.5	6.5

FIGURE 9.2

A decision tree for Table 9.7

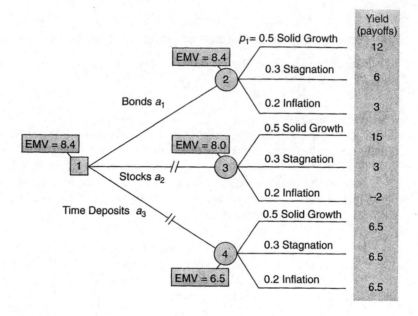

FIGURE 9.3

Segments of a tree

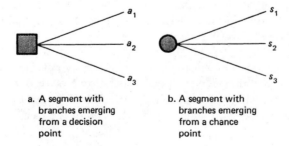

a. A segment with branches emerging from a decision point

b. A segment with branches emerging from a chance point

Evaluating the Tree of Figure 9.2

Computations at a Chance Point

The segments at the right are considered first. They are all chance points, and therefore *expected values* are computed. The expected values (designated in Figure 9.2 as EMV) are:

For point 2:

$$EMV = 12(.5) + 6(.3) + 3(.2) = 8.4$$

For point 3:

$$EMV = 15(.5) + 3(.3) - 2(.2) = 8.0$$

For point 4:

$$EMV = 6.5(.5) + 6.5(.3) + 6.5(.2) = 6.5$$

Payoffs

The EMVs are entered inside a rectangle above each chance point. They are now considered as *payoffs* for the next step.

Computations at a Decision Point

Figure 9.4 shows the situation in Figure 9.2 after EMVs for all chance points have been computed. At decision point **1**, all alternatives are compared with the EMVs considered as payoffs. Alternative a_1, the choice with the highest payoff, is recommended.

The example just presented showed a decision tree for a single-decision period (equivalent to a decision table). However, decision trees are especially useful in multiperiod situations involving sequential decisions.

The Multiperiod (Sequential Decision) Case

The multiperiod tree

Decision trees involving a sequence of decisions are nothing but a collection of smaller decision trees, each representing a single time period. All grow horizontally from left

FIGURE 9.4

Computation at a decision point

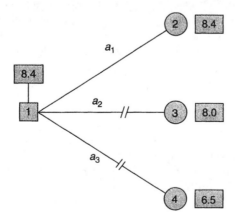

to right; the trunk is at the left and the branches at the right. The tree can be extended to the limit of forecasting ability.

Example

The Microflange Company is facing heavy demand for one of its flanges. The existing manufacturing facility is presently working at full capacity on a normal shift. The firm has two options to meet the heavy demand: either instituting overtime, an option that will cost $2,000, or installing new machinery at a cost of $20,000. There is insufficient volume to justify a second shift. The choice between the options depends mainly on what happens to sales over the next two years. During the *first year*, management estimates that there is a 70 percent chance that sales will rise and a 30 percent chance that they will fall.

The information given so far is sufficient to start building a decision tree (Figure 9.5 points **1, 2,** and **3**). After one year of operation, management will be faced with another decision, which will depend on the action taken initially, the events during the year, and the projection of second-year sales.

The Decisions after One Year

Depending on the action at time zero and the future states of nature, management could be at either point **4, 5, 6,** or **7**.

Decisions, decisions, decisions

First Decision Point (4 in Figure 9.5).   If a new machine had been installed at time zero and sales had risen, then management could either install a second machine or institute overtime. The decision at point **4** depends on the anticipated payoffs after two years. These depend on sales forecasts, which can be either high (20 percent chance), medium (70 percent), or low (10 percent). In the event that a second machine is installed, the anticipated payoffs are $80,000, $60,000, and $50,000, respectively. We assume that these figures and the rest of the payoffs and expenses in this problem are given in present values, so they can be combined and compared. This information is entered on the right side of the trees. The expected value is then computed ($63,000) and entered above chance point **8**.

However, if overtime is instituted, the profits are estimated to be $60,000 for high sales, $50,000 for medium sales, and $40,000 for low sales. This information is used to compute the expected value, which is then entered at chance point **9** in Figure 9.5 ($51,000).

Second Decision Point.   If a new machine had been installed initially and sales had fallen, then the decision maker would be at point **5** after one year. At that point, management would have no choice but to use the existing capacities to the fullest extent. Anticipated results are shown on the tree at point **10**.

FIGURE 9.5

The Microflange Company decision tree

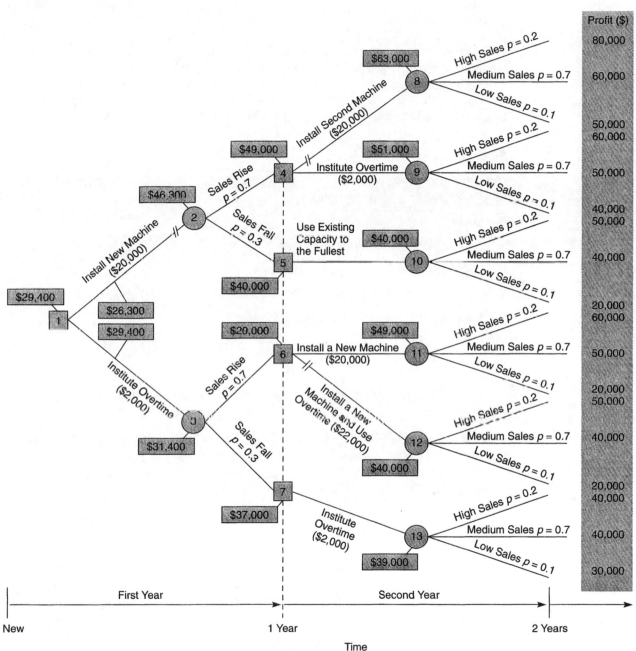

Third Decision Point. If overtime had been instituted initially and sales had risen, then management would be at decision point **6** with two alternatives open: install a new machine or install a new machine *and* use overtime. The anticipated payoffs are shown at points **11** and **12.**

Fourth Decision Point. If overtime had been instituted initially and sales had fallen, then management would be at decision point **7,** where only one alternative is assumed to be available: institute overtime. The anticipated results are shown at point **13.**

The problem is to find the best course of action the company should take *initially* and at *intermediate* stages, knowing all the information above.

Evaluation

Using the procedure previously outlined, the expected values at all chance points are computed (starting from the right).

For point 8:

$$\text{EMV} = .2 \times 80,000 + .7 \times 60,000 + .1 \times 50,000 = \$63,000$$

For point 9:

$$\text{EMV} = .2 \times 60,000 + .7 \times 50,000 + .1 \times 40,000 = \$51,000$$

Similarly, for the other points the EMVs are:

Point	⑩	⑪	⑫	⑬
EMV	$40,000	$49,000	$40,000	$39,000

Next, the computation moves leftward, thus reaching decision points **4, 5, 6,** and **7.**

Point 4. At this decision point, the alternative of a second machine ($63,000 − $20,000 = $43,000 profit) is compared with the alternative of overtime ($51,000 − $2,000 = $49,000 profit). Because the latter is more profitable, it is selected, and the EMV of $49,000 is entered above point **4.**

Point 5. There is only one alternative. The expected value of point **10** is thus recorded at point **5.**

Point 6. At this decision point, there are two alternatives: install a new machine ($49,000 − $20,000 = $29,000) or overtime plus a new machine ($40,000 − $22,000 = $18,000). The first one is better, and so an EMV of $29,000 is recorded at point **6.**

Point 7. There is only one alternative at this point. The EMV from point **13,** $39,000, is recorded (less the $2,000 expense) at point **7.**

At this stage, only the left side of the tree is considered. This information is presented in Figure 9.6.

Computation of the Left Side (Figure 9.6)

EMV of point 2 = .7 × $49,000 + .3 × $40,000 = $46,300

EMV of point 3 = .7 × $29,000 + .3 × $37,000 = $31,400

Finally, decision point **1** is considered: The expected value of installing a new machine is:

EMV = $46,300 − $20,000 = $26,200

The expected value with overtime is:

EMV = $31,400 − $2,000 = $29,400

Thus, it is better to plan now on overtime, for an expected gain of $29,400. The final decision, therefore, is to use overtime this year and, *if* sales rise, install a new machine the second year. If sales fall, however, the overtime should continue.

FIGURE 9.6

Left side of Figure 9.5

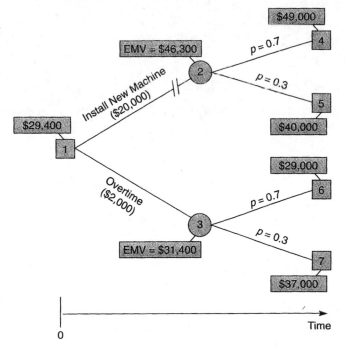

9.5 Computer Programs for Decision Tables and Trees

Computer programs for decision tables, sometimes referred to as "expected value analyses," consist of a variety of calculations and are available as a part of many standard management science or statistical packages. Typical programs include:

Inputs

The decision table.

Outputs

The expected value of all alternatives and the identification of the best (optimal) one. Normally, the expected value of perfect information is also given (see Section 9.9). A computer printout of the problem presented in Table 9.7 is given below (based on Lotfi and Pegels).

```
                    Problem Title:   INVESTMENT #1
                    Decision Making:    Under Uncertainty

        Alternative        Expected Payoff
        -----------        ---------------
        Bonds                  8.40   < === Maximum
        Stocks                 8.00
        CD's                   6.50

        Expected value of perfect information is:       2.35
```

Computerized Decision Trees

Computerized decision tree analyses are commercially available from several vendors. A typical program includes:

Inputs

a. The decision points, the alternatives emerging from each, and the point at the end of each alternative.

b. Chance points, their branches (states of nature), and the ending point for each branch.

c. Terminal points with their respective payoffs.

Outputs

a. The alternative(s) selected.

b. The expected value of the best alternative.

A printout of the decision tree described in Problem 19 is shown below (from using the Nelson [6] software package).

```
                        **INFORMATION ENTERED**

    BRANCH          BRANCH                          DECISION
    NUMBER           NAME        NODES             OR CHANCE              PAYOFF
       1              a1          1-2              Decision                  0
       2              a2          1-3              Decision                  0
       3              --          2-4                 .7                     0
       4              --          2-9                 .3       - (2000 + 500) = -2500
       5              --          3-5                 .4                     0
       6              --          3-6                 .6                     0
       7              a3          4-7              Decision    - (3000 + 500) = -3500
       8              a4          4-8              Decision    - (1000 + 500) = -1500
       9              --          5-10                .2       - (500 + 1000) = -1500
      10              --          5-11                .3       - (1000 + 1000) = -2000
      11              --          5-12                .5       - (3500 + 1000) = -4500
      12              a5          6-13             Decision    - (3000 + 1000) = -4000
      13              a6          6-14             Decision    - (4000 + 1000) = -5000
Results:    (Decision Tree Analysis)
   Selected alternatives a1 (and a4 if needed)
   Expected (conditional) payoff of the solution = -1800
```

Notes:

1. The initial expense is added to each payoff on the right-hand side (the terminal nodes).
2. A negative payoff implies a cost.

Special Packages for Decision Analysis

Several application software packages exist that can be considered as potentially useful decision aids. Representatives are as follows:

Product	*Vendor*
CRITERIUM	Sygenex, Redmond, Wash.
SUPERTREE	SDG Decision System, Menlo Park, Calif.
SUPERTREE (student version)	The Scientific Press, Redwood City, Calif.
Arborist	Texas Instruments, Dallas, Texas
Decision 1–2–Tree	Fast Decision Systems, Cambridge, Mass.

Note: Additional packages with multiple criteria decision-making capabilities were listed in Chapter 8.

Summary

The unique feature of decision trees is that they allow management to view the logical order of a sequence of decisions. They show a clear graphical presentation of the various alternative courses of action and their possible consequences. Using decision trees, management can also examine the impact of a series of decisions (multiperiod decisions) on the objectives of the organization. The graphical presentation helps in understanding the interactions among alternative courses of action, uncertain events, and future consequences.

The computations required in decision trees can usually be done manually; a computer is required only when extremely large and complicated trees are analyzed. For some practical aspects of implementation, consult [8].

9.6 Concluding Remarks

Most managerial decisions are made in one of two decision environments that are presented in this chapter, namely *certainty* or *risk*. In decisions under certainty, the payoff, or the outcome of selecting an alternative, is assumed to be known. In decisions under risk, it is assumed that it is possible to assess the chances of various outcomes occurring, but it is not possible to predict exactly which one will occur.

Decision theory has developed a methodology for analyzing managerial decisions. It uses a standard format, known as a decision (payoff) table, for arranging all the pertinent data of the situation.

In the case of certainty, the selection of the best alternative is made either by a comparison process called complete enumeration or with the aid of mathematical models. Mathematical models are used to conduct an efficient search among given alternatives, or sometimes even to generate the alternatives themselves. In either case, the choice is based on rational selection of the *best* payoff.

In the case of risky decisions, the decision maker may use one of several available criteria for making a choice. Most acceptable is the search for the alternative with the highest expected payoff.

Decision tables and trees are valuable tools to aid in decision making under risk. Decision trees also have the capability of solving sequential decisions involving different sets of decision alternatives and, in general, more complex decision situations.

Part B of this chapter discusses the third decision situation, that of uncertainty. The value of acquiring additional information about states of nature is also discussed in Part B.

Management Science in Practice

Deciding on ZIP+4 Technology

In March of 1984, the Office of Technology Assessment (OTA) conducted a review of the U.S. Postal Service's (USPS) automation strategy. In particular, OTA reviewed the USPS's use of the nine-digit ZIP code (ZIP+4) and the purchase of capital equipment to support the ZIP code strategy, an investment involving over $350 million with annual maintenance and other costs that could reach $300 million a year, yet save up to $1.5 billion a year.

The use of ZIP+4 at that time was a voluntary program but offered large-volume mailers a discount ranging from 0.5 to 0.9 cents per piece of mail. For USPS, the nine-digit ZIP code allowed automatic mail sorting to the level of city block, building, or post office box, thereby saving significant amounts of labor, even over the standard five-digit ZIP code. (Labor costs are about 85 percent of the USPS's total postal costs.) The use of optical character readers (OCRs) and bar code sorters (BCSs) allow automatic reading of the ZIP code, translation into a bar code, printing of the bar code on the envelope, and sorting of the envelope directly to a post office zone (with regular ZIP) or to an individual box or carrier (with ZIP+4).

At the time of OTA's analysis, the USPS was ready to proceed with phase 2 of their long-range postal automation strategy by purchasing another 403 OCRs and 452 BCSs. The OCRs were, however, only single-line readers and could sort to individual box or carrier only if the mailer included the ZIP+4 on the envelope, which few mailers were using. But there was now available on the market a multiline OCR capable of reading up to four lines of an address and determining and printing the correct nine-digit ZIP code, allowing the BCSs to sort to individual box or carrier.

The analysis was conducted through a complex decision tree. The tree included six alternative choices with three potential sets of uncertainties, each modeled at three levels of uncertainty: the 95th percentile (taking a probability of .185), the median (with a probability of .630), and the fifth percentile (probability of .185). Not all alternatives included all uncertainties, but the most complex alternatives did involve the analysis of 3 × 3 × 3 = 27 paths.

Option A: Single-Line OCRs

Option B: Multiline OCRs with ZIP+4. Includes the conversion of existing single-line OCRs to multiline capability.

Option C: Multiline OCRs without ZIP+4. Same as Option B but drop the ZIP+4 *discounts* for mailers and retain just the standard five-digit ZIP code.

Option D: Convert. Purchase single-line OCRs but proceed with testing and research on converting single-line to multiline OCRs and, as soon as possible, convert them over.

Option E: Hedge. Same as option D but convert only if ZIP+4 usage by mailers is still low.

Option F: Cancel. Do not purchase new equipment. Cancel the ZIP+4 discounts. Continue with the existing OCRs and BCSs and standard ZIP code.

The decision tree analysis indicated that option D was the best, with a net present value relative to option F of $1.5 billion; E was next best at $1.4 billion; and F was worse than all the other alternatives by at least $.9 billion. Internal rates of return for option D ranged from 25 to 85 percent, with incremental NPVs ranging from $.46 to $2.44 billion, depending on the outcomes of the related uncertainties.

A risk analysis of each of the options was also conducted by systematically varying the uncertainties to see which option performed best for each uncertainty combination. In all cases, option D was always better than option E.

The results of this analysis were incorporated into OTA's written and oral reports to Congress and USPS.

Source: J. W. Ulvila, "Postal Automation (ZIP+4) Technology: A Decision Analysis," *Interfaces,* March–April 1987, pp. 1–12.

Questions:

1. Why were all the options compared to F?
2. Draw the decision tree.
3. What would you guess were the three sets of uncertainties? Would all alternatives need to model all three uncertainties?

9.7 Problems for Part A

1. The demand for Swiss watches is estimated as:

Number of Units	Probability
20	.15
21	.20
22	.36
23	.19
24	.10

Days	Probability (Percent)	Days	Probability (Percent)
2	3	6	15
3	5	7	25
4	5	8	20
5	10	9	10
		10	7

Find the expected revenue if the watch sells for 399 francs.

2. An $800,000 property has a $\frac{1}{10}$ of 1 percent chance of catching fire that will cause damages of $100,000; and $\frac{1}{20}$ of 1 percent chance of catching fire that will completely destroy the property. Management decided to insure the property and it is reviewing two possible insurance policies:

   I. A policy with $50,000 deductible: that is, the insurance company covers all damages except the initial $50,000. The annual premium for such a policy is $750.

   II. A no-deduction (fully paid) policy with an annual premium of $1,000.

   a. If the company's objective is cost minimization, which policy should it purchase? Build both an opportunity loss table and a regular payoff decision table for the situation and solve both of them.

   b. Suppose the company decides *not* to insure, a practice that is called *self-insurance*. What will be the expected cost in such a case?

   c. Why is the expected cost of self-insuring *lower* than that of insuring?

   d. Why do companies insure rather than self-insure even though the expected cost of self-insuring is much lower?

3. The table below shows the length-of-stay distribution in a Toronto hospital, in days.

The hospital makes $120 net profit per day during the first four days of patients' stays, and $40 a day for the fifth day or more of stays. How much profit will the hospital make in one year (365 days) if it admits 20 patients per day, on the average?

4. Lemon Auto keeps detailed data on its car sales for the previous year. The table below summarizes these sales. For example, there were 15 days when no cars were sold at all.

	Number of Days
No cars were sold	15
One car per day was sold	30
Two cars per day were sold	87
Three cars sold	141
Four cars sold	27
Total number of days observed	300

   a. Find the frequency distribution of the sales.
   b. Find the average number of cars sold daily.
   c. Find the yearly profit of Lemon Auto if the average profit per car is $237.

5. Fire insurance for a plant valued at $1 million costs $150.

   a. Should the company take the insurance if the chance of a fire that will destroy the plant is 1 in 10,000 (base your answer on expected value)?

   b. What factor(s) may change the decision?

6. You have been offered the chance to play a dice game in which you will receive $10 each time the point

total of a toss of two dice is 4. If it costs you $1 per toss to participate, should you play or not?

7. A survey conducted over the last 20 years in Hamburg, Germany indicated that in 8 of them the winter was mild, in 7 of them it was cold, and in the remaining 5 it was very cold. A company sells 1,000 heavy coats in a mild year, 1,300 in a cold year, and 2,000 in a very cold year.

   Find the yearly expected profit of the company if a coat costs 85 deutsche marks (DM) and is sold to stores for 123 DM.

8. Find the best alternative in the following decision tables: *a* and *b* are *profits,* and *c* is *cost* data. Use both an expected value and an expected opportunity loss (EOL) approach.

a.

States of Nature	.3	.5	.2
Alternatives	s_1	s_2	s_3
a_1	5	8	3
a_2	6	5	7

b.

States of Nature	.6	.1	.2	.1
Alternatives	s_1	s_2	s_3	s_4
a_1	3	5	8	−1
a_2	6	5	2	0
a_3	0	5	6	4

c.

States of Nature	.1	.6	.3
Alternatives	s_1	s_2	s_3
a_1	5	2	1
a_2	4	3	3
a_3	2	6	1

9. A marketing agent frequently flies from Montreal to Boston. She can ride the airport bus from her hotel to the airport, which costs $3; but if she takes it, there is a .08 chance that she will miss the flight. A hotel limousine costs $7, with a .96 chance of being on time for the flight. For $15, she can take a taxi that will make 99 of 100 flights. Each time she catches the plane, she will conclude a business transaction that will produce a profit of $1,000; otherwise, she will lose the deal.

   Which mode of transportation should the marketing agent use in order to maximize her profit?

10. The yearly demand for a seasonal, profitable item follows the distribution below:

Demand (units)	Probability
1,000	.20
2,000	.30
3,000	.40
4,000	.10

The manufacturer of the item can produce it by one of three methods:

a. Use existing tools at a cost of $6 per unit.
b. Buy special equipment for $1,000. The value of the equipment at the end of the year (salvage value) is zero. The cost is $3 per unit.
c. Buy special equipment for $10,000 that can be depreciated over four years (one fourth of the value each year). The cost of using this equipment is $2 per unit.

   Which method of production should the manufacturer follow in order to maximize profit? *Hint:* Compare total annual costs. Assume production must meet all demand; each unit demanded and sold means more profit.

11. A firm needs temporary business space. It can lease the desired space for $5,000 for one year or $9,000 for two years (all rent is paid in advance). Alternatively, it can rent the space for one year for $5,000 and then if it wishes to rerent, pay $5,500 on the first day of the second year (rent for the second year). The firm estimates that there is a 25 percent

chance that they will have to depart from the city after one year. In that case, if they have rented the space for two years, they can sublet it for the second year. The chance of subletting is 60 percent, and they would receive $5,500, paid on the first day of the second year. If they are unable to sublet the space, it will remain empty for the entire second year. The interest rate that the company uses for evaluating such decisions is 10 percent.

Should the company rent the space for one year or two? Why?

12. Greenwood Groceries buys fresh fruit daily for $10 a crate. Crates sold the same day bring $15 profit contribution, each. Crates that are not sold in a day are sold later as animal food for $2.50 each. The demand for fruit fluctuates, according to the following distribution (data collected over the last 300 days):

Demand (Number of Crates)	Number of Days
10	120
11	90
12	75
13	15
Total	300

a. How many crates should the store order if Greenwood wants to maximize profit from selling fruit? Use an expected value approach.

b. What will be the average daily profit?

13. An apartment building has eight washing machines. The probability of these machines failing in any given year is:

Number of Machines Failing During the Year	Probability
3	.15
4	.30
5	.50
6	.05

Once a machine has failed, its repair will cost either $30, the minimum service charge; $70 for a moderate repair; or $120 for a major repair. The chance for a major repair is 36 percent, whereas for a moderate repair it is 44 percent for any washer. Sears offers a prepaid one-year maintenance policy that costs $45 per machine.

a. Should the owner of the apartment building buy the maintenance insurance?

b. Assume that the cost of repair is evenly distributed over the year whereas the insurance premium is prepaid. How is your analysis affected by this assumption?

14. A consultant plans to work in Bolivia, where the exchange rate is 100 pesos for $1. He plans to be there for several months, and his expenses for the period are estimated at 250,000 pesos. A skyrocketing inflation is temporarily in check while the government attempts to get a loan, the effect of which will be to lower the exchange rate by 10 percent (i.e., $1 = 90 pesos). If the loan is refused, the exchange rate will increase by 20 percent ($1 = 120 pesos). Suppose it is known that the probability of the government receiving the loan is .80. The consultant considers the following alternatives:

a_1 Immediately convert enough dollars into pesos to meet expenses for the entire period.

a_2 Wait until the loan is either granted or refused; in the meantime, hold dollars.

a_3 Hedge by converting part of the dollars to 125,000 pesos now and holding enough in dollars until the loan is either granted or refused, and then buy 125,000 additional pesos.

Assume that the decision on the loan is to be made prior to the consultant's arrival in the foreign country. Assume also that after the change in the exchange rate he will still need 250,000 pesos (regardless of the exchange rate).

If the consultant wants to minimize his dollar expense, which course of action should he take?

15. A common scene in many casinos is an old woman simultaneously playing two slot machines at a rate of 30 plays on each machine per hour. Assume that she plays the "dime" machines. The winning chances are

given below (per play, per machine):

Winning Prize	Chance
$10 (jackpot)	1 out of 400
$1	1 out of 100
50¢	1 out of 50
20¢	1 out of 10

a. Find the net gain (loss) of the woman during a four-hour period.

b. Compute the profit (loss) of the "house" from each machine in an hour.

c. The total cost of operating such a machine (including maintenance and depreciation) is $6 per day. The machine is played an average of 10 hours a day. Is the machine profitable?

d. How many plays an hour will have to be made for the casino to break even on each machine?

16. Given a decision situation with profit data:

p_i	.3	.7
	s_1	s_2
a_1	15	4
a_2	10	12
a_3	2	15

a. Find the best alternative using EMV.

b. Find the *range of probabilities* of s_1 within which the best alternative is still preferable.

17. Lime sales in Mexico are affected by both supply, which is determined by weather conditions, and demand, which is determined by the state of the economy. It is forecasted that the next year will be: cold (30 percent), mild (45 percent), warm (25 percent), and that the economy will be: stable (50 percent), in recession (30 percent), or else back in inflation.

Following are the historical annual lime sales (in kilograms):

Cold year: 200 kilos in a stable economy, 100 in a recession, 130 in inflation.

Mild year: 240 in a stable economy, 150 in a recession, 200 in inflation.

Warm year: 300 in either a stable or an inflationary economy, 200 kilos in a recession.

Find the average monthly value of sales if a kilo of limes sells for 1,700 pesos.

18. *a.* Write the following decision table in tree form:

	Futures		
Alternatives		Fire	No Fire
Insure		$ 100	$100
Do not insure		$8,000	$ 0

These figures are cost data.
There is a .01 chance of a fire.

b. What action should an individual take to minimize cost?

19. Given the decision tree below, find the best alternative and its expected value. The outcomes shown are *costs* and the investment expenses are in parentheses.

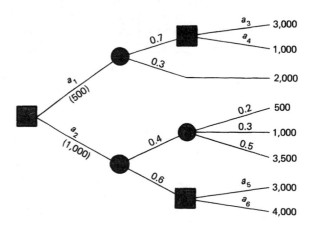

20. Given a decision tree, as shown in the figure below:
    a. Write the equivalent table form.
    b. Find the action that will minimize total cost (assume data are present values; use the tree presentation).

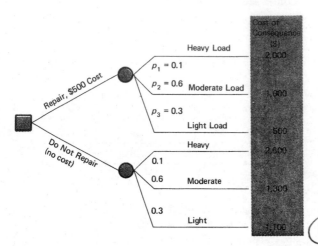

21. The future of solar energy in Africa depends on oil prices. The African Solar Company is considering the development of one of two possible home solar energy devices: Sun I and Sun II.

    The anticipated profits as they relate to oil prices are shown in the table below:

	Oil Price		
	High	*Very High*	*Extremely High*
Sun I	−50,000	73,000	500,000
Sun II	138,000	−100,000	60,000

The company economist estimates that the chances that oil prices will be high are 60 percent, very high 30 percent, and extremely high 10 percent. What device should the company develop if it is interested in maximizing profit?
a. Present as a decision tree.
b. Solve the tree; find the best alternative.

22. If you attend all class sessions, your probability of passing the course is .8; but if you only attend randomly, your probability of passing the course is .5. If you fail, you may take a makeup exam where the probabilities of passing are .6 if you attended in full and .1 if you attended at random. If passing the course is worth 5 credits, but, in terms of energy, attending full time "costs" 3 credits and attending randomly "costs" 1 credit, which attendance pattern should you adopt?

    Note: Assume that all failing students will take the makeup exam. The utility of failing is zero.

23. An oil explorer, commonly called a wildcatter, must decide whether to drill a well or sell his rights to a particular exploration site. The desirability of drilling depends on whether there is oil beneath the surface. Before drilling, the wildcatter has the option of taking seismographic readings that will give him further geological and geophysical information. This information will enable him to deduce whether subsurface structures usually associated with oil fields exist in this particular location. However, some uncertainty about the presence of oil will still exist after seismic testing because oil is sometimes found where no subsurface structure is detected, and vice versa.

    The wildcatter estimates that the cost of drilling a well would be $250,000 (in net present value terms, after making allowance for all taxes). The yield that would be expected from a typical oil well is estimated to be $1.2 million (in net present value terms, net of all taxes and operating costs, but excluding drilling costs). Seismic tests would cost $50,000 per test.

    The wildcatter could sell his rights for $230,000 before either drilling or testing. However, if he should decide to carry out seismographic readings and no subsurface structure is indicated, the site will be considered almost worthless by other wildcatters, in which case he will barely be able to sell the rights for $10,000. If substructure is indicated by the test, he can sell his rights for $300,000. If no oil is found, the value of the exploration site is considered to be zero.

The probability of getting oil from the site without any test is 41 percent. If he carries out the seismic test, he feels that the test will indicate subsurface structure with a 40 percent probability. In case of structure, he can drill with a 65 percent chance of finding oil. In the case of no structure, he can drill with a 75 percent chance of finding the well dry.

What should the wildcatter do? Draw a decision tree to solve the problem.

24. ABC's growth rate in past years has been slower than the average for the industry. The company is considering two alternatives to rectify the situation: (1) expand the number of product lines and (2) increase inventories for better service.

There is a 70 percent chance that the economy will go into a growth state, in which case there is an 80 percent chance for increased demand. If demand increases, a profit of $1 million is expected; however, if demand does not increase, only $800,000 profit is anticipated. If inventories are increased, a profit of $900,000 is anticipated in case of high demand; otherwise, $600,000 will be realized.

In the event the economy does not grow, a mild recession is anticipated. In this case, there is a 50–50 chance for either high or low demand. The profits are then estimated to be:

Expansion and high demand	$750,000
Expansion and low demand	600,000
Inventories and high demand	550,000
Inventories and low demand	400,000

Profit figures are a forecast for the end of one year of operation.

A product expansion policy requires $100,000 in cash now. Keeping inventories will cost $12,000 for the year, payable at year end. The company is using an interest rate of 10 percent for its analysis.

Should the company expand its products or work with inventories?

25. Todo Corp. operates two complex production lines on an eight-hour-per-day basis. These lines fail frequently due to the extensive workload. The daily probability of line no. 1 failing is .10 and that of line no. 2 is .15. When any line fails, the cost is 10,000 ¥ (yen) each hour; when both lines are down at the same time, the cost is 14,000 ¥ per hour.

The company is trying to decide whether to hire one or two repairpersons. The time for one person to repair a machine is five hours. If two are hired, they can work either as a team or each on one machine. If they work as a team, the repair time is three hours per machine. If a repairperson costs 8,000 ¥ per day, what would you recommend Todo do? *Note:* Repairpersons are salaried and not paid overtime, even if their workload some days requires it.

26. A machine shop received an order for 2,000 units to be made on one of its automated machines. This is a multistation operation and once it is started, it runs without interruption. The machine shop makes $2 profit on each part of acceptable quality. Each unit that is classified as "defective" needs rework at an additional cost of $3.50 before it is considered "acceptable."

Historical data indicates that if the machine is used without any special preparation, it produces 1 percent defectives (this happens 50 percent of the time), 2 percent defectives (this happens 30 percent of the time), 3 percent defectives (this happens 12 percent of the time), or 5 percent defectives in the remaining cases. With a minor adjustment that costs $42, the defective rate *above* 2 percent is reduced to 2 percent. (That is, there is *no* chance of a 3 percent or 5 percent defect rate; these occurrences will not result in a 2 percent defect rate.) With a major adjustment (cost $100), the defective rate is 1 percent.

What adjustment policy should the machine shop adopt in order to maximize profit?

PART B: EXTENSIONS

9.8 The Acquisition of Additional Information

Examining the situations of certainty, risk and uncertainty, it is clear that there is a difference between the three situations in terms of the amount of information available for making the decision. In the case of certainty, it is assumed that we have complete information. That is, each time an alternative is selected, there is only one possible outcome, which is known. In the case of risk, there are several possible outcomes associated with each alternative, and their chances of occurring are assumed to be known. Finally, the case of uncertainty, there are again several possible outcomes associated with each alternative, but the decision maker does not know the likelihood of each of these occurring. That is, there is even less information available than in risk. These situations are illustrated in Figure 9.7.

Of course, managers prefer to make decisions with as much information as possible. That is, they prefer to make decisions under certainty, if at all possible. Otherwise, they will accept risk. Only in extreme cases do they make decisions under *uncertainty*. For this reason, in many decision situations, a subdecision has to be made: whether to attempt to acquire additional information so as to convert the decision situation to one under certainty, or at least risk.

The Feasibility of Acquiring More Information

Whenever a decision about the acquisition of additional information is to be made, the following questions should be considered.

1. *What information is needed and is it available?*
2. *Is there time to acquire the information?*
3. *What is the quality of the additional information?* Information can have very different levels of quality. This issue will be explored later.
4. *What is the value of the information?*
5. *What is the cost of obtaining the information?*
6. *Should the information be acquired?*

FIGURE 9.7

The amount of information in decision situations

Situation	Amount of Information
Certainty	Most
Risk	Some
Uncertainty	Least

TABLE 9.8   Simple Decision Table

Action \ Event	.3 Rain	.7 No Rain
Take umbrella	Dry, happy	Frustrated Why did I bring it?
Do not take umbrella	Wet, mad	Thankful

Our analysis here will be based on the assumption that additional information is available and that there is sufficient time to acquire and use it.

Information Quality: Perfect versus Imperfect Information

Our discussion here will be limited only to information quality in terms of its accuracy, although there are several other dimensions of information quality that can also be important.

Perfect Information

Both perfect and imperfect information relate to decision making under risk. That is, the probability of an outcome, given a repetitive decision situation, is assumed to be known. For example, suppose you are about to make a decision on whether or not to bring an umbrella with you. A simplified decision table is shown in Table 9.8.

Assume that, on the average, there is a 30 percent chance of rain each day. Based on this information, if we can quantify the outcomes in the table, we can use an expected value approach to develop a *policy* that will tell us whether or not to take an umbrella.

However, it may make more sense to examine the weather every morning. This requires more information. If we can find a predictor that can tell us whether it will rain that day or not, and if such a predictor is *always correct* (i.e., possesses perfect information), then we must decide whether or not to acquire such **perfect information.** The concept of perfect information as compared with imperfect information is shown in Table 9.9. (*Note*: The number of predictions may be the same as the number of states of nature [2 each, here] or it may be larger [for example, "not sure" can be a prediction]).

Imperfect Information

Here, the prediction is not perfect, as in Table 9.9B. Using imperfect information, the probability of each possible state of nature occurring is *redetermined* each time a decision is made using any new information. This process changes the earlier predicted probabilities of the states of nature from their initial (*prior*) values to revised (*posterior*) values. With each additional prediction, the probabilities continue to be revised,

TABLE 9.9   The Quality of Information in Risk Situations

		Actual State of Nature				Actual State of Nature	
		Rain	No Rain			Rain	No Rain
Predicted	Rain	1	0		Rain	.8	.2
	No rain	0	1		No rain	.2	.8
		A. Perfect				B. Imperfect	

with each posterior probability considered to be the **prior probability** for the next prediction. The statistical tool used to perform such an analysis is called **Bayes' theorem.** The process of revision is discussed in Section 9.10.

9.9 The Value of Perfect Information

A crystal ball

Suppose that additional information can be obtained; what will its value be to the decision maker? This discussion will be confined to the case where the obtained information changes the situation from one of *risk* to one of *certainty*. That is, the decision maker, just prior to the time a decision is to be made, is assumed to acquire perfect information.

Example

Let us analyze the investment decision presented in Table 9.5 as reproduced in Table 9.10. The problem, solved by the expected value approach, indicated that the best alternative was a_1, yielding an average of 8.4 percent. Let us now assume that each percent of yield equals $10,000; that is, a decision maker who uses the expected value as a criterion will make, over the long run, 8.4 × $10,000 = $84,000 per decision.

TABLE 9.10   The Investment Decision (in Percent Yield)

States of Nature / Alternatives	.5 Growth	.3 Stagnation	.2 Inflation	Expected Value
a_1 Bonds	12	6	3	8.4
a_2 Stocks	(15)	3	−2	8.0
a_3 Time deposit	6.5	(6.5)	(6.5)	6.5

What Alternative Course of Action Should Be Selected, Given Perfect Information?

Assume that we deal with a repetitive situation. Suppose that in advance of making a specific decision, a market research firm is able to predict, with certainty, the state of the economy that will prevail for that decision. Thus, the decision maker can make a choice with complete certainty. The choice depends on what the research firm predicts:

- · If the research firm predicts growth, then the best choice is stocks (a_2).
- · If the research firm predicts stagnation, the choice will be time deposit (a_3).
- · If the prediction is for inflation, the choice will again be time deposit (a_3).

A varying choice

Note that, in contrast to the regular expected value situation where one alternative is continuously selected, here the choice varies among the alternatives with each decision.

The Expected Payoff with Perfect Information. Assuming that the frequency distribution of the states of the economy does not change over the long run, then 50 percent of the time the research firm will predict *growth* as the next state. The decision maker, now knowing what is going to happen for the next decision, will select a_2 and realize a 15 percent yield. Similarly, 30 percent of the time stagnation will be predicted and the decision maker will make 6.5 percent by selecting a_3, and 20 percent of the time inflation will be predicted, yielding 6.5 percent for selecting a_3. These choices are circled in Table 9.10. The decision maker's average (expected) yield will be:

> yield per decision: $.5 \times 15 + .3 \times 6.5 + .2 \times 6.5 = 10.75$ percent

Using the $10,000 per 1 percent equivalence, the average return per decision will be $107,500.

Should the Perfect Information Be Acquired? If we compare the expected yield *with* perfect information ($107,500) with the expected yield under regular conditions ($84,000), we see an improvement of $23,500. In general, decisions with perfect information yield much better results than decisions without it. The difference of $23,500 is called the **expected value of perfect information (EVPI)** and is used to answer the

EVPI

question of whether or not perfect information should be acquired.

The mathematical expression of the expected value of perfect information in the case of maximization is:

$$\text{EVPI} = \underbrace{\sum_{j=1}^{n} p_j(\max_i o_{ij})}_{\substack{\text{Expected yield with} \\ \text{perfect information}}} - \underbrace{\max_i \sum_{j=1}^{n} p_j o_{ij}}_{\substack{\text{Expected yield} \\ \text{without perfect information}}}$$

where:

p_j = Probability of state of nature j

o_{ij} = The payoff when action a_i is taken and state of nature j occurs

In the case of minimization:

$$\text{EVPI} = \begin{bmatrix} \text{Expected cost without} \\ \text{perfect information} \end{bmatrix} - \begin{bmatrix} \text{Expected cost with} \\ \text{perfect information} \end{bmatrix}$$

Note that the EVPI is the average (per decision) improvement in the objective function. If this figure is compared against the cost of acquiring the information, management can make a decision regarding the acquisition of the information. For example, if the research firm charges $15,000 per prediction, the investor stands to gain $23,500 − $15,000 = $8,500, on the average, by using the service. But if the marketing firm charges $23,500 or more for this service, then the arrangement would not be profitable.

How much to pay, at most, for the information

Thus, the EVPI tells the decision maker the *upper limit* one should be willing to pay for "perfect predicting information"; information that is 100 percent reliable. If the decision maker decides to buy the perfect information, he or she should, of course, wait for the result of each prediction and then make a choice accordingly.

Summary

To determine whether or not to purchase perfect information, one should:

1. Compute the expected payoff *without* perfect information and select the best alternative.
2. Compute the expected payoff *with* perfect information, assuming the best selection of alternatives is made.
3. Compute the EVPI by subtracting (1) above from (2). (Reverse order for cost minimization.)
4. If the difference is larger than the cost of the information, it should be purchased; otherwise, it should not.

Note: The Equivalence of EVPI and EOL

The expected value of perfect information (EVPI) in the investment example was $23,500 or 2.35 percent of yield. Examining Table 9.6, the reader will find that the expected regret or expected opportunity loss (EOL) of the *best alternative* is also 2.35 percent yield. Is this a coincidence? The answer is no! As a matter of fact, the EVPI is *always equal* to the best (smallest) EOL. The reason is that in computing EVPI we actually compute the regret, which is the difference between the best choice with perfect information and the best choice without it.

EOL = EVPI

9.10 The Value of Imperfect Information

The value of perfect information is computed with the assumption that a perfect predictor exists. In other words, each time that a prediction for a state of nature is made, this prediction comes true. In reality, however, this is a very rare case. The typical case involves predictions that may not come true all the time. Such a case is called prediction under imperfect (or sample) information, and it will be discussed next.

Bayes' Theorem

Bayes' theorem is a procedure that is used to revise the probabilities of the states of nature. This helps us decide whether to acquire the additional information needed to revise the prior probabilities.

Example

American Ecology, Inc., estimates that its new product, E-3, has a .8 chance (80 percent) of being a winner. Thus, there is a .2 chance of its being a loser. However, before the company makes a production commitment, it would like to further investigate the situation, because these initial estimates (the "prior probabilities") may not be accurate. Hence, the possibility of calling on a market researcher to conduct a special survey.

From previous experience, it is known that such a special survey can either *predict success, predict failure,* or *be inconclusive*. Statistically, it is known that of all the new products that were successful, 70 percent of the time the surveys correctly predicted success (S), 10 percent of the time they falsely predicted failure (F), and 20 percent of the time the surveys were inconclusive (I). On the other hand, an examination of all the cases that were failures (losers) indicated that in 85 percent of these cases the surveys correctly predicted failure, in 10 percent they were inconclusive, and success was incorrectly predicted in the remaining 5 percent. This information is summarized in Table 9.11.

Conditional probabilities

The probabilities in Table 9.11 are *conditional probabilities* (see Appendix B) because they tell us what the historical prediction was, *given* an actual state (winner or loser). Thus, they indicate the *reliability* of the surveys to prospective customers. These

TABLE 9.11 Reliability of the Surveys

Results of Survey	Actual State of Products	
	Winners (W)	Losers (L)
Predicted success (S)	.70	.05
Inconclusive (I)	.20	.10
Predicted failure (F)	.10	.85
Total	1.00	1.00

conditional probabilities, which describe the *track record* of the forecaster, are not easy to obtain. They may be based on personal knowledge of the past accuracy of the fore-caster, reports from other customers or users, or a simple subjective assessment. It is assumed that future prediction success will be identical to that in the past.

Using Revised Probabilities with Imperfect Information

A policy for information acquisition

The **revised probabilities** depend on the nature of the additional information, which is found only after the information is acquired. For this reason, if we analyze a situation prior to the actual acquisition of the information, we cannot prescribe the best decision alternative. Instead, we derive a *decision policy*.

A decision policy does not recommend a particular alternative as being the best. Instead, it recommends several specific alternatives, one for every possible outcome of the prediction. The use of revised probabilities in assessing the acquisition of additional information involves the following nine steps:

Step 1	The decision situation is evaluated with the prior probabilities.
Step 2	Assuming that it is impossible to obtain perfect information, the possibility of acquiring partial information is checked.
Step 3	Revised (posterior) probabilities are computed, one for each possible outcome of the prediction.
Step 4	The probabilities of each of the research outcomes ("indicators") are computed. (Step 4 can precede Step 3.)
Step 5	A decision tree is constructed.
Step 6	The tree is solved.
Step 7	The expected value of the additional information is computed.
Step 8	A decision on whether or not to acquire the information is made.
Step 9	An alternative in the original problem is selected.

Example

The marketing department of Production Unlimited, Inc., is considering whether or not to develop a new product. All the relevant information is shown in Table 9.12.

TABLE 9.12   Marketing Payoffs (Dollars)

Alternatives \ States of Nature	.2 A	.5 B	.3 C	Expected Value	
a_1 Develop	300,000	200,000	−600,000	−20,000	
a_2 Do not develop	0	0	0	0	←*Best*

Solution

Step 1. Initial Evaluation. Using the prior probabilities, the expected values can be computed. Accordingly, the product *should not* be developed (Table 9.12).

Step 2. Check Track Record. A consultant has been called in to predict, through a survey, what state of nature in the consultant's opinion will occur next. The consultant asks $50,000 for the survey. The track record of the consultant indicates that the consultant's surveys have the prediction reliabilities shown in Table 9.13. This information is called the *conditional probabilities* of the source.

For example, of all the past cases in which *B* actually occurred, 90 percent of the time the survey correctly predicted that *B* would occur, 10 percent of the time the wrong prediction of *A* was made, and 0 percent of the time the wrong prediction of *C* was made.

Step 3. Compute Revised Probabilities. Given (in Table 9.12) the prior probabilities and the reliability of the survey (Table 9.13), the revised probabilities can be calculated with the aid of Equation 9.5 (see Section 9.13).
For branch A_p:

$$P(A|A_p) = \frac{P(A)P(A_p|A)}{P(A)P(A_p|A) + P(B)P(A_p|B) + P(C)P(A_p|C)}$$

In our case:

$$P(A|A_p) = \frac{.2 \times .8}{(.2 \times .8) + (.5 \times .1) + (.3 \times .1)} = \frac{.16}{.24} = .667$$

Similarly,

$$P(B|A_p) = \frac{.5 \times .1}{(.5 \times .1) + (.2 \times .8) + (.3 \times .1)} = \frac{.05}{.24} = .208$$

and,

$$P(C|A_p) = \frac{.3 \times .1}{(.3 \times .1) + (.2 \times .8) + (.5 \times .1)} = \frac{.03}{.24} = .125$$

TABLE 9.13 **Consultant's Reliability (Conditional Probability Matrix)**

Indicators	Actual State of Nature		
	A	B	C
Survey predicted A (call this prediction A_p)	$P(A_p|A) = .80$	$P(A_p|B) = .10$	$P(A_p|C) = .10$
Survey predicted B (call this prediction B_p)	$P(B_p|A) = .10$	$P(B_p|B) = .90$	$P(B_p|C) = .20$
Survey predicted C (call this prediction C_p)	$P(C_p|A) = .10$	$P(C_p|B) = 0$	$P(C_p|C) = .70$

For branch B_p:

$$P(A|B_p) = \frac{.2 \times .1}{(.2 \times .1) + (.5 \times .9) + (.3 \times .2)} = \frac{.02}{.53} = .038$$

$$P(B|B_p) = \frac{.45}{.53} = .849$$

$$P(C|B_p) = \frac{.06}{.53} = .113$$

For branch C_p:

$$P(A|C_p) = \frac{.2 \times .1}{(.2 \times .1) + (.5 \times 0) + (.3 \times .7)} = \frac{.02}{.23} = .087$$

$$P(B|C_p) = 0$$

$$P(C|C_p) = \frac{.21}{.23} = .913$$

Step 4. Compute the Indicator (Marginal) Probabilities. In order to determine whether or not to use the consultant, it is necessary to use the probabilities that the consultant's survey will actually predict events A_p, B_p, or C_p. The probabilities (derived above as the *denominators* of the Bayes' equations) are:

Denominators of the Bayes' equation

$$P(A_p) = .24$$
$$P(B_p) = .53$$
$$P(C_p) = .23$$

Two decisions

Step 5. Construct a Decision Tree. Management must now decide whether or not to use the consultant. Then they must decide about the new product (a_1—develop, a_2—do not develop). The situation is shown in the form of a decision tree in Figure 9.8.

The upper part of the tree shows the information presented in Table 9.12. The lower part of the tree presents the situation of using the consultant. There exist three branches: branch A_p for when the survey predicts A, branch B_p for when the survey predicts B, and branch C_p for when the survey predicts C. The revised probabilities from Step 3 and the indicator probabilities from Step 4 are next entered on the tree (Figure 9.9).

Step 6. Solve the Decision Tree (Figure 9.9). The expected values at all chance points are computed. Then the best alternative at every decision point is selected. In this case, if the consultant is not used, the expected value (top branch) is zero. If the

FIGURE 9.8

A decision tree for Bayes' analysis— general structure

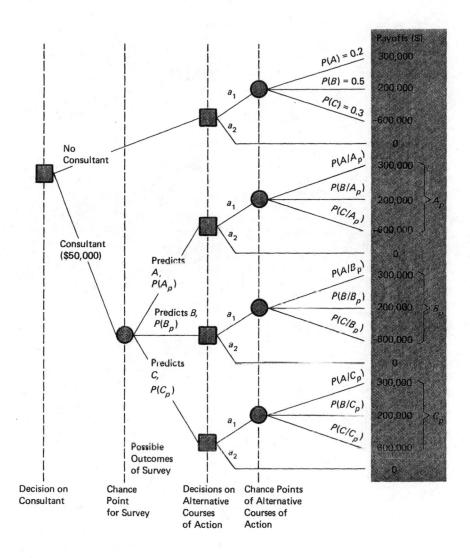

consultant is used, the expected value (rounded) using posterior probabilities is:

$$.24(\$166,700) + .53(\$113,400) + .23(\$0) = \$100,110$$

The value of imperfect information

Step 7. Compute the Expected Value of Imperfect Information. The information computed in Bayes' analysis is less than perfect, because its prediction reliability is not 100 percent. Therefore, it is interesting to determine the value of such information.

FIGURE 9.9

Decision analysis with revised probabilities

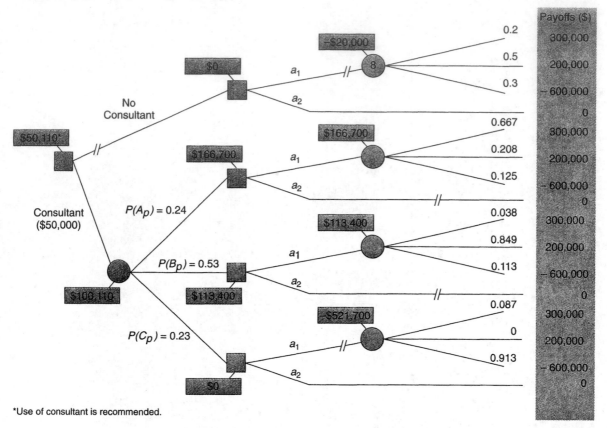

*Use of consultant is recommended.

EVSI

The **expected value,** per decision, **of the imperfect sample or survey information (EVSI)** is computed by using Equation 9.2:

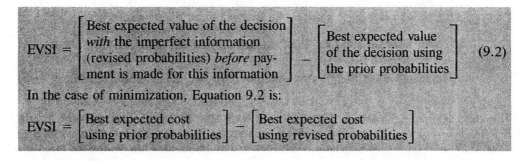

$$\text{EVSI} = \begin{bmatrix} \text{Best expected value of the decision} \\ \textit{with} \text{ the imperfect information} \\ \text{(revised probabilities) } \textit{before} \text{ pay-} \\ \text{ment is made for this information} \end{bmatrix} - \begin{bmatrix} \text{Best expected value} \\ \text{of the decision using} \\ \text{the prior probabilities} \end{bmatrix} \quad (9.2)$$

In the case of minimization, Equation 9.2 is:

$$\text{EVSI} = \begin{bmatrix} \text{Best expected cost} \\ \text{using prior probabilities} \end{bmatrix} - \begin{bmatrix} \text{Best expected cost} \\ \text{using revised probabilities} \end{bmatrix}$$

In our example:

Expected value with imperfect information = $100,110

Expected value with prior probabilities = $0

Thus, EVSI = $100,110 − 0 = $100,110. As in the case of EVPI, here too we get an indication regarding the upper limit that management should be willing to pay for the additional information. Note that the expected value of imperfect information is *smaller than* the expected value of perfect information. The reason for this is that the imperfect information is less reliable. The value of perfect information serves as an *upper limit* for the value of imperfect information. The ratio of EVSI/EVPI is called the *efficiency* of the imperfect information.

Efficiency of information

Step 8. Decide Whether or Not to Acquire the Information. The expected value of the sample information is now compared with the cost of acquiring it.

> If EVSI > Cost: Acquire the information
> If EVSI < Cost: Do not acquire the information

In our case, EVSI = $100,110 and the cost is $50,000. Therefore, the information should be acquired.

Step 9. Select an Alternative. If the consultant is not hired, select the alternative with the best expected value. If the consultant *is* hired, then wait for the additional information and make a final decision. In our case, the decision policy is:

If the survey indicates A_p, select alternative a_1
If the survey indicates B_p, select alternative a_1
If the survey indicates C_p, select alternative a_2

Note: In addition to the use of imperfect information for accepting or rejecting an opportunity to conduct research to gain additional information, one can use the methodology to select a research firm (or consultant) from among several. To do so, the track record of each contender is examined and the expected value of the sample information (EVSI) is compared against the cost (see Problem 42 at the end of this chapter).

9.11 Decisions under Uncertainty

In the condition of **uncertainty,** the decision maker recognizes different potential states of nature but cannot confidently estimate the probabilities of their occurrence. This is an undesirable but often unavoidable situation. It may occur when one faces a completely new phenomenon (e.g., the 1989 fall of Communist Europe) or when a completely new product, process, or state of nature is under consideration. In many such situations, even prominent experts cannot agree on the chances of the various states of nature occurring. In the limiting case of uncertainty, called "ignorance," some or all of the possible states of nature are not known. We will not consider this case here.

Example

The Palm Tree Hotel is considering the construction of an additional wing. Management is evaluating the possibility of adding 30, 40, or 50 rooms. The success of the addition depends on a combination of local government legislation and competition in the field; four states of nature are being considered. They are shown, together with the anticipated payoffs (in percent of yearly return on investment), in Table 9.14. Management cannot agree on the probabilities of the states of nature. The problem is: how many rooms to build in order to maximize the return on investment.

No "right" answers

Principle of choice by policy

At the present time, decision theory does not provide a single best criterion for selecting an alternative under conditions of uncertainty. Instead, there are a number of different criteria, each with its benefits and limitations. The choice among these is determined by organizational policy, the attitude of the decision maker toward risk, or both.

Criteria of Choice

Five criteria of choice are presented here:

1. The Criterion of Equal Probabilities (Laplace)

Equal chances

The user of this criterion assumes that all states of nature are *equally likely* to occur. Thus, equal probabilities are assigned to each state of nature. The expected values are then computed and the alternative with the highest expected payoff is selected.

TABLE 9.14 Payoff Table (Percent of Return on Investment)

Alternatives \ States of Nature	Positive Legislation and Low Competition s_1	Positive Legislation and Strong Competition s_2	No Legislation and Low Competition s_3	No Legislation and Strong Competition s_4
a_1 30 rooms	10	5	4	-2
a_2 40 rooms	17	10	1	-10
a_3 50 rooms	24	15	-3	-20

Example

Using the example given in Table 9.14, probabilities of $\frac{1}{4}$ are assigned to each of the *four* states of nature. The expected payoffs are:

$$E(a_1) = \frac{1}{4} \times 10 + \frac{1}{4} \times 5 + \frac{1}{4} \times 4 + \frac{1}{4} \times (-2) = \frac{17}{4}$$

$$E(a_2) = \frac{1}{4}(17 + 10 + 1 - 10) = \frac{18}{4} \text{ (largest expected yield)}$$

$$E(a_3) = \frac{1}{4}(24 + 15 - 3 - 20) = \frac{16}{4}$$

Thus, the best alternative is a_2, with an expected payoff of $\frac{18}{4}$. The major argument against this criterion is that there is absolutely no reason to assume the probabilities are all equal. Such an assumption may be as erroneous as assuming any other values.

2. Criterion of Pessimism (Maximin or Minimax)

The user of this criterion is completely pessimistic, because he or she assumes that the worst will happen, no matter which alternative is selected. To provide protection, the decision maker should select the alternative that will give as large a payoff as possible under this pessimistic assumption (best of the worsts).

Example

Let us reproduce Table 9.14 as Table 9.15 (payoffs in percent yield).

Assume that the decision maker selects a_1; then the *worst* that can happen is a loss of 2 percent when s_4 occurs. Similarly, the worst for a_2 is -10, and for a_3 is -20 (the lowest number in the row is selected in the case of maximization). This information is entered into a new column labeled Worst. From this column, the best entry is then selected (-2 in the example). The decision maker maximizes the minimum payoffs, and therefore this criterion is labeled *maximin*. (In the case of cost minimization, the decision maker will minimize the maximum possible costs; that is, the decision maker will *minimax*.) The use of this criterion will guarantee the decision maker that in the *worst possible case* the loss will be 2.

Maximin

TABLE 9.15   Pessismistic Approach in the Case of Profit

Alternatives \ *States of Nature*	s_1	s_2	s_3	s_4	*Worst (Minimum)*	*Best of Worst (Maximum of Minimums)*
a_1	10	5	4	-2	-2	-2
a_2	17	10	1	-10	-10	
a_3	24	15	-3	-20	-20	

One drawback of this criterion (which is also a drawback of all the remaining criteria) is that the decision is based on only a *small portion* of the available information. Thus, valuable information is completely disregarded, leading to poor choices. This is shown in Table 9.16, which illustrates a deliberately exaggerated case (maximization). According to the criterion of pessimism, a_2 should be selected. The decision is based on the "minimum" column, which includes only one entry from each row. The rest of the data is ignored. In reality, most decision makers will pay attention to the remaining information and consequently select a_1. The pessimistic decision maker acts in a *superconservative* manner, paying attention only to the risks and completely neglecting the opportunities.

Neglects opportunities

3. Criterion of Optimism (Maximax or Minimin)

Maximax

An optimistic decision maker assumes that the very best outcome will occur and selects the alternative with the best possible payoff. To do so, the decision maker searches for the best possible payoff for each alternative. These are placed in a new column to the right of the decision table. The alternative with the best payoff in this newly added column is then selected (best of bests). If the data were costs, then the optimistic decision maker would select as best the *lowest* cost payoff for each alternative and then select the *lowest* of these lowests. Such an approach is labeled *minimin*.

Example

Reproducing the data of Table 9.14 in Table 9.17, the "best" column is created. According to the maximax criterion, alternative a_3 would be selected.

The gambler

Notice again that no consideration is given to most of the available information; only the highest payoff is considered. Thus, an optimistic decision maker is a gambler who *disregards* the risks and looks forward only to the opportunities.

4. Coefficient of Optimism (Hurwicz Criterion)

Middle-of-the-road types

Most decision makers are neither completely optimistic nor completely pessimistic. Therefore, it was suggested, by Hurwicz, that a degree of optimism labeled alpha, α, be measured on a 0 to 1 scale (0 = completely pessimistic, 1 = completely optimistic).

TABLE 9.16 Profits under Two Alternatives

Alternatives \ States of Nature	s_1	s_2	s_3	Minimum (Worst)	
a_1	40,000	20,000	500	500	
a_2	550	520	510	510	← *Maximum (best)*

TABLE 9.17 **Maximax Choice**

Alternatives \\ States of Nature	s_1	s_2	s_3	s_4	Best	
a_1	10	5	4	−2	10	
a_2	17	10	1	−10	17	
a_3	24	15	−3	−20	24	← *Best of bests*

Hurwicz

Hurwicz suggested that the best alternative is the one with the highest (in maximization) weighted value, where the weighted value, *WV*, for each alternative (each row in the decision table) is expressed by:

$$(WV)_i = \alpha \,[\text{best } o_{ij}] + (1 - \alpha)[\text{worst } o_{ij}] \tag{9.3}$$

where o_{ij} is the payoff. Then the best $(WV)_i$ is selected.

Example

Examining Table 9.17 with α given as .7 we get:

$$WV(a_1) = .7 \times 10 + (1 - .7) \times (-2) = 6.4$$
$$WV(a_2) = .7 \times 17 + (1 - .7) \times (-10) = 8.9$$
$$WV(a_3) = .7 \times 24 + (1 - .7) \times (-20) = 10.8 \leftarrow (\text{maximum})$$

Thus, alternative a_3 is the best. *Note:* In the case of minimization (such as with costs), where the best is lowest, select the alternative with the *lowest WV*.

The major difficulty in applying this criterion is the measurement of alpha (e.g., see [4], pg. 283). Note that use is made of more information than in minimax, yet only the two extreme payoffs are considered and the remaining information is ignored.

Savage's "regret"

5. The Criterion of Regret (Savage's Criterion)

I wish I had done . . .

A pessimistic approach

The concept of regret is equivalent to the determination of *opportunity loss*, discussed in Section 9.3. Both concepts represents the important economic concept of *opportunity cost*, which indicates the magnitude of *the loss incurred by not selecting the best alternative*. Savage argued that the decision maker should attempt to *minimize the largest anticipated regret*. That is, employ a **minimax** approach to the **regret** data (in a basically pessimistic manner).

TABLE 9.18   Regret Table for Table 9.14

States of Nature / Alternatives	s_1	s_2	s_3	s_4	Largest Regret (Worst)	
a_1	$24 - 10 = 14$	$15 - 5 = 10$	$4 - 4 = 0$	$-2 - (-2) = 0$	14	
a_2	$24 - 17 = 7$	$15 - 10 = 5$	$4 - 1 = 3$	$-2 - (-10) = 8$	8	←Minimum
a_3	$24 - 24 = 0$	$15 - 15 = 0$	$4 - (-3) = 7$	$-2 - (-20) = 18$	18	

Example

Let us use the hotel example of Table 9.14.

Solution

Minimax regret

Step 1. Build a regret (opportunity loss) table. This is done according to the method exhibited in Table 9.6. The result is shown in Table 9.18.

Step 2. Minimax the regret. This is done by finding the worst (largest) regret in each row, and then selecting the lowest regret in the newly formed column.

In the example, the lowest regret is for alternative a_2. This selection guarantees that regardless of what happens, the decision maker will never have a regret larger than 8. Note again that use is made only of a small portion of the available information.

Note: The value of regret, by definition, can never be negative.

Summary

Decision making under uncertainty is more difficult than it is for risk or certainty. All five different criteria presented here have some deficiencies and will usually point to different selections of alternatives. In the real world, decision making under uncertainty is usually avoided because the results can be disastrous. Instead, enough information should be acquired so that decisions can be made under calculated risk or, at best, under certainty.

9.12 Use of Computers

Perfect Information

An example of perfect information computer computations from Table 9.10 is shown below. The computations, executed with Nelson's software [6], are self-explanatory.

```
          THE EXPECTED VALUE OF PERFECT INFORMATION  (EVPI)

                    Problem Name:  Table 9.10

                  EMV without Perfect Information:          8.40

                   EMV with Perfect Information:           10.75

                 Problem Type:  PAYOFF Maximization
     EMV with PI      -     EMV without PI    =      EVPI
        10.75                   8.40                 2.35
```

Imperfect Information

The revision of probabilities using Bayes' theorem and its application for the decision regarding the acquisition of additional information is easily programmed for a computer. The following illustration follows the computations executed manually in Section 9.10. Furthermore, Nelson's MSS package [6] is capable of conducting a comparative study in which the acquisition of information from several sources (vendors) is compared. The input to the program includes the original decision table (Table 9.12) and the source reliabilities (conditional probabilities) in Table 9.13.

To begin with, the program computes the expected value of the imperfect ("survey") information. This value is compared to the cost, and the net gain is computed. If several sources (vendors) are involved, the analysis includes a comparative study to identify the best one.

```
          THE EXPECTED VALUE OF PERFECT INFORMATION  (EVPI)
Problem name:  Table 9.12              Problem Type:  PAYOFF Maximization
EMV with PI - EMV without PI  =  EVPI
  160,000.00         0.00        160,000.00

             THE EXPECTED VALUE OF SURVEY INFORMATION  (EVSI)  AND
             THE EXPECTED NET GAIN FROM SURVEY INFORMATION  (ENGSI)

EMV with SI - EMV without SI  =  EVSI      Survey Cost      ENGSI
  100,110.00         0.00       100,110.00   50,000.00     50,110.00
```

Next, the revised (posterior) probabilities are depicted.

	STATES OF NATURE			
INDICAT.	A	B	C	P(I)
Ap	0.6667	0.2083	0.1250	0.2400
Bp	0.0377	0.8491	0.1132	0.5300
Cp	0.0870	0.0000	0.9130	0.2300
P(Si)	0.2000	0.5000	0.3000	

Finally, the decision tree computation is performed and, optionally, a node-by-node analysis is given.

```
Problem Name: Table 9.12                    Problem Type: Payoff Maximization
                    Total Nodes in Tree: 14


      Initial Tree Branch Selected: Imperfect Information Source #1
                        Expected Value:        50,110.00
      If Information Indicator Ap
            Then Select Decision Alternative a1
                        Expected Value:       116,666.67
      If Information Indicator Bp
            Then Select Decision Alternative a1
                        Expected Value:        63,207.54
      If Information Indicator Cp
            Then Select Decision Alternative a2
                        Expected Value:       -50,000.00
                  DECISION TREE NODE INFORMATION



      Node Number:           1                         Type: Chance
Node is on tree branch:  a1               Expected Value:  -20,000.00
                     Branches      P(Si)        Payoff
                     --------      -----        ------
                        A         0.2000      300,000.00
                        B         0.5000      200,000.00
                        C         0.3000     -600,000.00
```

Uncertainty

All the computation approaches described in this chapter are easily computerized, as shown below for the problem in Table 9.14, a maximization problem using the Nelson package. Similar computations are available for the other methods of treating uncertainty.

```
            **LAPLACE CRITERION VALUE  (EQUAL P(Si) VALUES)**
            Problem Name: Table 9.14


      Decision Alternative                 LaPlace Value
      --------------------                 -------------
            A 1                                4.25
            A 2                                4.50      ←MAXIMUM
            A 3                                4.00
```

```
                              **MAXIMIN PAYOFF**
            Problem Name: Table 9.14

      Decision Alternative                    Minimum Payoff

              A 1                                  -2.00    ←MAXIMUM
              A 2                                 -10.00
              A 3                                 -20.00
```

9.13 Appendix *Calculating Revised Probabilities*

We use the example of Section 9.10 to show the calculation of revised probabilities.

Formulation

Let $P(W)$ be the prior probability of the product being a winner. Given:

$$P(W) = .80$$

$$P(L) = .20; \text{ (the probability of the product being a loser)}$$

The conditional probabilities of Table 9.11 are given as:

1. In the Event the Product Is Actually a Winner:

$P(S|W)$ = Probability of the survey predicting success, given the product is actually a winner. $P(S|W) = .70$

$P(I|W)$ = The probability of the survey being inconclusive, given the product is actually a winner. $P(I|W) = .20$

$P(F|W)$ = The probability of the survey predicting failure, given the product is actually a winner. $P(F|W) = .10$

2. In the Event the Product Is Actually a Loser:

$P(S|L)$ = Probability of the survey predicting success (given . . .) = .05

$P(I|L)$ = Probability that the survey is inconclusive (given . . .) = .10

$P(F|L)$ = Probability of the survey predicting failure (given . . .) = .85

The point to remember here is that all this information is known *before* the survey is actually taken.

Revision of the Probabilities of the States of Nature

Suppose the survey is taken and it predicts *success*. The prior probability of $P(W)$ will be changed now to a posterior probability, $P(W|S)$, which is the probability of the product being a winner *given* that the survey predicts success. This probability can be computed by using the Bayes' formula for two variables, as given in Equation 9.4:

$$P(W|S) = \frac{P(W)P(S|W)}{P(S)} = \frac{P(W)P(S|W)}{P(W)P(S|W) + P(L)P(S|L)} \quad (9.4)$$

This formula is adapted from the general formula for Bayes' formula (see Equation 9.5):

$$P(N_i|B) = \frac{P(N_i)P(B|N_i)}{\sum\limits_{i=1}^{n} P(N_i)P(B|N_i)}$$

$$= \frac{P(N_i)P(B|N_i)}{P(N_1)P(B|N_1) + P(N_2)P(B|N_2) + \cdots + P(N_n)P(B|N_n)} \quad (9.5)$$

where:

B = Outcome predicted by the research (or new information), which is, in our example, either success (S), inconclusive (I), or failure (F)

N_i = A possible state of nature (either a winner $[W]$ or loser $[L]$ in our example.)

i = 1, 2, 3, . . . n, where n = the number of states (two states here, winner and loser)

Equation 9.5 states that the posterior probabilities of the states of nature (N_i: winner or loser), after observing some survey evidence (B: success, inconclusive, or failure), is proportional to the product of the prior probability of N_i and the conditional probability of B given state N_i.

Computing the Revised Probabilities

In the Event the Survey Predicts Success

Using Equation 9.4, we get:

$$P(W|S) = \frac{.8 \times .7}{(.8 \times .7) + (.2 \times .05)} = \frac{.56}{.57} = .9825$$

That is, the probability of a winner is increased from 80 to 98.25 percent due to the fact that the additional information predicted success. Similarly:

$$P(L|S) = \frac{P(L)P(S|L)}{P(L)P(S|L) + P(W)P(S|W)} = \frac{.2 \times .05}{(.2 \times .05) + (.8 \times .7)} = \frac{.01}{.57}$$

$$= .0175$$

It is possible to compute $P(L|S)$ in a shorter manner. Because the product can be either a winner or a loser, $P(W|S) + P(L|S)$ must sum to 1.0. Therefore:

$$P(L|S) = 1 - P(W|S) = 1 - .9825 = .0175$$

An important question that one may ask is: What is the probability of the survey predicting success? This probability is designated $P(S)$ and is computed from Equation 9.6.

$$P(S) = P(W)P(S|W) + P(L)P(S|L) \tag{9.6}$$

Note that this value is exactly the denominator in Equation 9.4. In our example:

$$P(S) = (.8 \times .7) + (.2 \times .05) = .57$$

In the Event the Survey Is Inconclusive

Using Equation 9.5, we get:

$$P(W|I) = \frac{P(W)P(I|W)}{P(W)P(I|W) + P(L)P(I|L)} = \frac{.8 \times .2}{(.8 \times .2) + (.2 \times .1)} = .8889$$

Similarly:

$$P(L|I) = 1 - .8889 = .1111$$

Also, the possibility of the survey predicting inconclusiveness, $P(I)$, is computed as .18 (the denominator of the $P(W|I)$ equation).

In the Event the Survey Predicts Failure

$$P(W|F) = \frac{P(W)P(F|W)}{P(W)P(F|W) + P(L)P(F|L)} = \frac{.8 \times .1}{(.8 \times .1) + (.2 \times .85)} = \frac{.08}{.25} = .32$$

(Notice the drastic revision, from 80 percent to 32 percent!) And similarly,

$$P(L|F) = 1 - .32 = .68$$

The chance of the survey predicting failure, $P(F)$, is .25 (the denominator of the $P(W|F)$ equation).

What Will the Survey Predict?

Revision without the survey

We showed that it is possible to revise the initial probabilities *without actually taking the survey*. Of course, the answers that we received are *conditional, depending on the outcome of the survey*. For example, *if* the survey predicts success, then the probability of having a winner, $P(W/S)$, is 98.25 percent, and so on. In decision making, it is important to find out, *before* the survey is taken, the chance that the survey will predict success, failure, or will be inconclusive. In deriving the solution above, it was found that:

$$P(S) = \text{Probability that the survey will indicate success} = .57$$

$$P(I) = \text{Probability that the survey will be inconclusive} = .18$$

$$P(F) = \text{Probability that the survey will indicate failure} = .25$$

Note that because these are the only possible survey outcomes, they must sum to 1.0.

Figures 9.10 and 9.11 summarize the process and the results obtained in the example above.

FIGURE 9.10

Summary of the Bayes' process

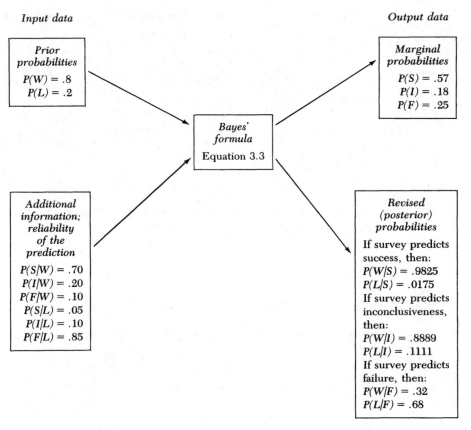

Input data

Prior probabilities
$P(W) = .8$
$P(L) = .2$

Additional information; reliability of the prediction
$P(S/W) = .70$
$P(I/W) = .20$
$P(F/W) = .10$
$P(S/L) = .05$
$P(I/L) = .10$
$P(F/L) = .85$

Bayes' formula
Equation 3.3

Output data

Marginal probabilities
$P(S) = .57$
$P(I) = .18$
$P(F) = .25$

Revised (posterior) probabilities

If survey predicts success, then:
$P(W/S) = .9825$
$P(L/S) = .0175$
If survey predicts inconclusiveness, then:
$P(W/I) = .8889$
$P(L/I) = .1111$
If survey predicts failure, then:
$P(W/F) = .32$
$P(L/F) = .68$

FIGURE 9.11

Tree representation of the Bayes' process

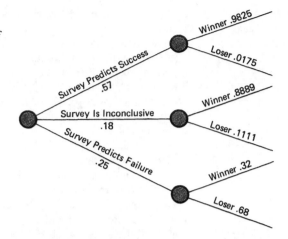

9.14 Problems for Part B

27. Find the expected value of perfect information in Problem 8 (*a*), (*b*), and (*c*). Compare the results to the EOL.

28. Review Problem 12. Assume that the store can buy information that will enable it to predict, with certainty, the daily demand. How much should the store be willing to pay for such information?

29. Review Problem 14. Find the value of perfect information and comment on it.

30. Given two decision tables below, find the best alternative in each by the following criteria:
    a. Equal probabilities (Laplace)
    b. Pessimism.
    c. Optimism.
    d. Coefficient of optimism (Hurwicz) with $\alpha = .4$
    e. Regret (Savage).

31. Consider a decision in which the possible outcomes can be classified as either acceptable (*x*) or not acceptable (*y*). Given below is a payoff table.

Futures / Alternatives	s_1	s_2	s_3
a_1	x	x	y
a_2	x	y	x

   a. If the probabilities of the futures, s_1, s_2, and s_3, are unknown (call them p_1, p_2, and p_3), which alternative would you select? Why?
   b. Describe under what conditions the two alternatives would be of equal value to the decision maker.
       Hint: Naturally, the utility of *x* is larger than that of *y*. Use the "expected value criterion." Assume a repetitive situation.

32. The manager of an advertising agency has to make a decision between three available programs (a_1, a_2, a_3). There are three possible futures that can be expected: s_1 = market rises, s_2 = market falls,

TABLE 1

	s_1	s_2	s_3	s_4
a_1	5	8	3	1
a_2	7	4	5	2
a_3	3	6	6	4

TABLE 2

	s_1	s_2	s_3
a_1	7	2	−1
a_2	3	6	2
a_3	0	3	8

s_3 = no change in the market. The manager can estimate the yields in each case (given in the table below, in percent of return) but cannot estimate the probabilities of the various futures occurring.

Programs \ Futures	s_1	s_2	s_3
a_1	3	6	−1
a_2	8	5	4
a_3	−4	7	12

Which program will the manager select if he uses the following decision approaches:

a. Equal probabilities (Laplace).
b. Pessimistic approach.
c. Optimistic approach.
d. Hurwicz criterion with $\alpha = .55$.
e. Minimax regret (Savage).

33. Italian Investor's Bank is evaluating two investment proposals involving 3 billion lire. The first is to buy Italian class A bonds with a 7.3 percent return. The second is to buy some land in Easton, Pennsylvania. The land is intended for development into an industrial park, in which case a 17 percent return is expected. However, the land is close to a planned new highway, and the government may purchase the land to build a rest area. In this case, the government will pay the bank 4.5 percent above the purchase price.

Assuming a one-year decision horizon, what would you advise the bank to do if the probability of the government action is unknown? What assumption must be made in order to solve this problem?

34. The probability of the government action in Problem 33 is unknown. However, there exists a theoretical probability that will make the two alternatives *equal*. Find that probability.

35. Review a decision made by an organization. Describe how the decision was made. Was the decision a case of certainty? Uncertainty? Risk? Could a decision table approach be applied? Why or why not?

36. It is said that managers will avoid making decisions under uncertainty. Why?

37. A patient calls her doctor complaining that she is sick. Based on the described symptoms and the knowledge of the kind of diseases currently epidemic in the city, the physician suspects that there is a 40 percent chance that the patient has disease D_1 and a 60 percent chance that she has disease D_2.

On arrival at the physician's office, the patient is subjected to a test that has either a *negative* or a *positive* result.

The physician knows that there is a .6 likelihood that the results discovered in the test are associated with D_1. That is, in all past cases of D_1, the test was positive 60 percent of the time. Also, the physician knows that there is only a .2 likelihood that the results are associated with D_2.

a. Find the revised probabilities of D_1 and D_2. Assume that the patient has either D_1 or D_2.
b. What is the probability that a test will yield negative results?

38. Given a decision matrix (profits in thousands of dollars):

	S_1	S_2
a_1	5	8
a_2	9	3
a_3	−1	10

The probability of S_1 is .35 and that of S_2 is .65. A research company's track record showed that it had three predictions (p_1, p_2, and p_3) with respect to the states of nature as shown below.

	S_1	S_2
p_1	.8	0
p_2	.1	.1
p_3	.1	.9

a. Draw a decision tree for the situation, including the decision regarding the employment of the research company.

b. Show all revised (posterior) probabilities.

c. What is the probability of predicting p_3?

d. The research company charges $2,700 per prediction; would you advise using it?

39. The following is the payoff profit matrix for two alternate plans:

Futures / Alternatives	$p = .75$ Market Receptive	$p = .25$ Market Unfavorable
Plan a	$20,000	$6,000
Plan b	$25,000	$3,000

a. Which plan do you recommend adopting, using the expected value criterion?

b. What is the expected value of perfect information?

c. It is known from past experience that of all the cases when the market was receptive, a research company predicted it in 90 percent of the cases. In the other 10 percent, they predicted an unfavorable market. Also, of all the cases when the market proved to be unfavorable, the research company predicted it correctly in 85 percent of the cases. (In the other 15 percent of the cases, they predicted it incorrectly.) Find the posterior probabilities of all states of nature.

d. Using the posterior probabilities, which plan would you recommend now?

e. How much should one be willing to pay (maximum) for the research survey?

40. Eeetee Phones of England can either make or purchase the electronic innards for its phones. The profits in thousands of pounds per year are given in the table below.

	Sales Level			
Make	I: Low	II: Mod	III: High	IV: Very High
Make	−20	40	100	300
Buy	10	60	80	240

a. The probabilities of each of the sales levels are: .1, .2, .6, and .1 for levels I through IV. Build a decision tree, compute the EVPI, and find the best alternative.

b. A research study costing £3,000 can be bought. It may result in one of two conclusions, with the conditional probabilities ("track record") given below. Should Eeetee purchase the research?

	I	II	III	IV
Conclusion A	.05	.25	.80	.90
Conclusion B	.95	.75	.20	.10

41. Management is considering replacing an energy-saving device with a new one. The new device has a probability of 60 percent of being superior to the old one. A testing service is called on to test it.

From experience, it is known that when a new device was actually superior, the testing service predicted this superiority in 80 percent of the cases. However, when the new device was really inferior, the testing service predicted it to be superior 50 percent of the time.

a. Suppose a test is undertaken and superiority for the new device is predicted. What will management's revised probabilities be of the device being superior?

b. Suppose the test indicates that the device is inferior. How would the probabilities be changed now?

c. What is the probability that the test will indicate a superior device?

42. Use the decision situation below (profits in millions of dollars) in this problem.

	s_1	s_2	s_3	s_4	s_5
a_1	10	8	3	−2	12
a_2	−4	12	8	11	5
a_3	0	3	6	10	2
Probabilities	.2	.1	.3	.3	.1

Two vendors submit bids for conducting (imperfect) predictions. Vendor A wants $350,000 per prediction and Vendor B wants $600,000 per prediction. The conditional probabilities that reflect the anticipated reliability of the vendors are given below.

			Vendor A		
Indicator	s_1	s_2	s_3	s_4	s_5
I_1	.6	0	.1	0	0
I_2	.1	.7	0	.1	0
I_3	0	.2	.7	.1	0
I_4	.1	.1	0	.8	0
I_5	.1	0	.1	0	.9
I_6	.1	0	.1	0	.1

			Vendor B		
Indicator	s_1	s_2	s_3	s_4	s_5
I_1	.8	.1	0	.05	0
I_2	0	.8	.1	0	0
I_3	.1	0	.9	.05	.1
I_4	.1	0	0	.9	0
I_5	0	.1	0	0	.9

Use a computer to answer the following questions:

a. How much should the company pay, at the most, for perfect information?

b. Which vendor should they hire (if any) and why?

c. What is the chance that Vendor A will be inconclusive (indicator I_6)?

d. What is the chance that Vendor B will predict I_3?

e. Build the decision tree for Vendor A and show all the computations at the nodes.

f. List the revised probabilities for the five states of nature if Vendor A makes prediction I_2.

43. The City of Hope is recognizing its social work department. Based on past experience, it is estimated that the number of cases to be treated annually is distributed as follows:

Cases	3,500	4,000	4,500	5,000
Probability	.12	.29	.48	.11

A social worker is paid $25,000 per year and he or she can treat 300 cases on the average. The federal government reimburses the city $80 for each case.

a. How many workers are needed if the policy is to treat all cases whenever demanded? What will be the annual cost to the city?

b. How many workers are needed if the city's objective is to minimize the budget this year? (The federal money is considered part of the budget). However, at least 3,500 cases must be treated.

c. How much should the city pay to get perfect information about the demand?

44. EToy Corp. specializes in E.T.-related products. A new product, ET3M, sells for $19.95 and is planned for the forthcoming holiday season. Projected sale figures are: 10,000 units if the economy is strong (45 percent chance), 7,000 in a moderate economy (35 percent), and 4,000 in a weak economy. Because of the seasonal nature of the product, the company will have to discount all *unsold* items by 55 percent at the end of the season in order to clear the stock.

The company can use one of two production methods. If the items are produced with the existing equipment, the cost is $8 per unit, plus $10,000 fixed cost. Alternatively, special equipment can be leased at $25,000. In this case, the cost per unit is $5. Marketing and overhead costs in either case are $4 per unit.

a. What production method would you recommend, and why?

b. What quantity should be produced?

c. What is the maximum the company should be willing to pay for a perfect prediction of the demand? What assumptions are needed in such a case?

d. A marketing research company charges $10,000 per prediction. Their track record is good, but not perfect. In the past, of the 15 times the sales were strong, the company predicted it correctly 14 times (one time they predicted moderate sales). Of the 10 times that sales were moderate, they predicted it correctly 8 times (one time they overestimated and one time they underestimated). Of the six times that sales were a bust, they predicted it correctly four times (twice they overestimated). Would you advise using the marketing research service?

e. Should the marketing research service be used, what quantity should the company produce and what production method should be utilized?

45. A manufacturer must decide whether to manufacture and market a new seasonal novelty that has just been developed to sell at $1.50 per unit. If he decides to manufacture it, he will have to purchase special machinery that will be scrapped after the season is over. If a machine costing $1,000 is bought, the variable cost of manufacturing will be $1 per unit; if a machine costing $5,000 is bought, the variable manufacturing cost will be $.50 per unit. In either case, it will be possible to manufacture in small batches as sales actually occur and there will be no danger of having unsold merchandise left over at the end of the season. The manufacturer's probability distribution for sales volume is shown in the following table:

Sales Volume	Probability
1,000	.5
5,000	.25
10,000	.25
	1.00

a. Draw up a payoff table, remembering that there are *three* possible acts.

b. Find the "best" act.

c. Set up the opportunity loss (regret) table.

d. The manufacturer has received an offer from The Great Transcendental Swami, a soothsayer. Swami claims to be able to make a perfect sales forecast. Supposing this claim is valid, determine how much the manufacturer should be willing to pay (at most) for Swami's forecast. (Use the opportunity loss [regret] table.)

9.15 CASES
I. THE CONDOMINIUM

It was a hot summer day in Los Angeles and Dave Greenhouse was trying to make a decision before 5 P.M. Dave was in the business of buying repossessed condominium apartments from lending institutions such as savings and loan associations and banks. In the summer of 1989, during the recession, there were many such repossessions. The lending institutions' objectives were to get rid of the property as soon as possible. Dave would buy the apartments and then sell them, hopefully with a nice profit.

This time, the Aztec Savings and Loan Association offered him three units (he must take all of them or nothing) at a nonnegotiable price of $720,000. It was the last day that the offer was valid and Dave knew that he must make a fast decision. He had already had the assets appraised. The estimated selling price that he could get for the units is shown below:

Unit 1. $269,000

Unit 2. Twenty-five percent chance of $250,000; 50 percent chance of $260,000; and 25 percent of $270,000.

Unit 3. Thirty percent chance of $250,000; 40 percent of $260,000; and 30 percent chance of $270,000.

There was also a selling cost of $10,000 per unit (advertising, legal, financial, and so forth).

Dave hoped to sell the units within 60 days. This was the time limit the savings and loan association gave him to pay the $720,000. Dave estimated there was a 70 percent chance that he could do it. Any unit that was not sold within 60 days would be sold, for certainty, within the next 30 days. However, in that case, there would be a financial charge for late payment of $4400 per apartment.

Present the situation in a decision table and advise Dave on what to do.

II. MAINTAINING THE WATER VALVES

Because of the 1991–93 recession, local governments across the country became very cost conscious. Sharon Brown, Evergreen's city manager, was under continuous pressure to contain costs.

The city of Evergreen owns and operates a water system. A major expense item is water valve repair. These valves are currently repaired by the city's maintenance department. In preparing next year's budget, the water system manager, Bill White, was faced with the following situation.

The average number of valves repaired in one year is 4,120. The average time needed to repair a valve is 42 minutes. It is estimated that the labor cost next year will be $14 an hour. Parts and supplies are estimated at $3 per valve. Overhead shop expenses are computed at 40 percent of the total labor and parts cost. Some of the valves being repaired also need reworking, because of poor material or mistakes made by employees. Historical data indicate that the percentage of repaired valves that need reworking varies according to the following distribution:

Reworking Needed (Percent)	Probability
3.0	.50
4.0	.40
4.6	.10

A reworked valve is 100 percent reliable because such valves go through a special quality control check. The reworking cost is estimated to be $20 per valve.

Last month, the city manager called in all her assistants and advised them about some cost containment programs that were soon to be implemented. Specifically, she requested they each check on the possibility of eliminating inefficient in-house services that could be contracted out. Accordingly, Bill White advertised the valve repair job on a contractual basis. Western Maintenance Corp. (WMC), a reputable company, came up with the lowest bid: a $38,000 flat yearly fee plus $5 a valve with all reworking done at no additional charge.

City manager Ms. Brown requested that Mr. White evaluate WMC's proposal in terms of possible dollar savings. Mr. White's response is given in the following memo:

TO: Sharon Brown, City Manager
FROM: William White, Manager, Water System
SUBJECT: WMC's Proposal on Valve Repair Jobs

After careful evaluation of the proposal, I recommend that the contract be awarded to WMC. However, due to the budget squeeze, I will not be able to reassign the employees involved in any other jobs. Therefore, I recommend that the contract be awarded to WMC if and only if they will hire all displaced employees.

Upon receipt of this memo, Sharon Brown called the president of WMC. His response was as follows:

WMC is currently fully staffed, so hiring the city employees, some of whom are not highly skilled, will increase our cost. Therefore, WMC will be able to hire them only if the terms of the contract are changed to a flat fee of $40,000 plus $5 per valve, or else a $38,000 flat fee and $5.50 per valve.

Use a decision tree approach to advise Sharon Brown what to do.

a. Construct a decision tree and include the alternative of WMC not hiring the city employees.

b. Solve the tree; discuss the results.

c. Suppose the city agrees to the $40,000 flat fee and $5 per valve proposal, provided that the $40,000 is paid in four quarterly payments. The first payment is made with the signing of the contract. If Evergreen's cost of capital is 10 percent compounded quarterly, how will this affect the decision?

III. THE AIR FORCE CONTRACT

Nova Aviation, Inc., is considering its bidding strategy for a U.S. Air Force contract. Because of the specialization of this job, there is only one other contractor currently approved to bid on it—Sun Aircraft. The air force determines bid eligibility after lengthy investigation, and is, therefore, unlikely to approve of any additional contractors in the near future.

Due to the repetitive nature of such bids, Nova usually has special meetings to consider bidding strategy. They are considering two options: bidding "high" or

bidding "low." Marketing Director Judy Scher explained the logic behind options as follows:

"Our company's policy is to bid every time, whereas Sun's policy is to bid only 60 percent of the time. And we have only two choices: a high bid or a low one. If we bid high and Sun doesn't bid, we get the job and make $1.1 million profit. But if Sun bids, then we might get the contract or we might not, depending on their bidding level. All in all, our profit, when we place a high bid and Sun bids as well, averages out to zero. If we place a low bid, our per-bid profit averages out to $500,000 *regardless* of Sun's action."

Steve Green, Nova's director of finance, thought for a few moments: "If what you say is true, it seems that we should bid 'high' whenever our competitor doesn't bid and 'low' whenever they do."

"Exactly," replied Ms. Scher. "But," said Steve, "how can we find out what Sun might do? We could try to buy this information from someone at Sun, but not only is that unethical, it is probably illegal as well."

"Wait a minute," said Ms. Scher. "Suppose it were legal; how much should we offer for such information assuming it were 100 percent reliable?"

"That's a good question," replied Mr. Hunt, the company's president. "It seems to me, however, that we're getting off the track. What do you propose to do, Judy?"

"We could use an expected value approach to solve this problem," said Ms. Scher, "but that approach would assume that our competitor will behave in the future as they have behaved in the past, and how can we

make such an assumption? How can we know what they'll do?"

"Well," said the president, "we've tried before to predict their moves. Aviation Research Co. has provided such information before, at $100,000 a shot. Their track record isn't bad: of 30 times that Sun bid, Aviation Research predicted it correctly 24 times. On the other hand, of the 20 times that Sun didn't bid, Aviation called it right 17 times."

"What you're saying, Mr. Hunt," said Steve, "is that this research company isn't 100 percent reliable."

"You may infer that, but Aviation Research is still considered the best research company available in this market. It's getting late, and we have to make a decision."

You are Steve Green. Prepare a short report advising your boss how to handle this decision. Specifically, use the concepts of the value of perfect and imperfect information and decision policy. Work out the actual numerical values.

Glossary

Alternative course of action   An alternative (solution) open to the decision maker.

Bayes' theorem   A statistical process of revising prior probabilities based on additional information.

Branches (of a decision tree)   Lines or arcs that emerge either from a decision point to designate alternatives, or from a chance point to designate states of nature.

Certainty   The decision environment when there is only one possible payoff for a decision. This situation occurs when only one state of nature exists.

Chance point   A circle on the decision tree designating that states of nature follow.

Coefficient of optimism, α   A measure of willingness to assume risk. There exist two extremes: $\alpha = 0$, completely pessimistic; and $\alpha = 1$, completely optimistic (gambler).

Complete enumeration   A listing of all possible combinations and the comparison of their results.

Criterion of optimism   A criterion of choice under uncertainty that assumes that the best is going to occur (maximax).

Criterion of pessimism   A criterion of choice under uncertainty that assumes that the worst is coming. Thus, trying to select the best of the worsts (maximin).

Critical probability   The probability of an event that results in the EMV of an alternative equal to a desired value.

Decision point   A square on the decision tree that indicates that a choice is to be made (selection of an alternative course of action).

Decision table   Organizes the data for decision making under certainty or risk in a tabular form. The table shows all the input data as well as the expected values.

Decision tree   A graphical representation of a sequence of interrelated decisions to be made under risk.

Dominance   When one alternative is preferred to another because it is at least as good as the other and, in some outcome(s), better.

Equal probabilities (Laplace's) criterion of choice Criterion for decision making under uncertainty that assumes that probabilities of all states of nature occurring are equal.

Expected monetary value (EMV) The average gain/loss for each alternative course of action. It is computed by weighting the payoffs by their probabilities of occurrence.

Expected opportunity loss (EOL) The average opportunity loss, or regret, per decision.

Expected value (EV) A weighted average (mean), found by weighting each possible payoff by its probability (relative frequency) of occurrence.

Expected value of perfect information (EVPI) The difference in expected payoff between making a decision under risk with an expected value approach and making a decision having perfect information about which state of nature is going to occur.

Expected value of sample (or survey) information (EVSI) The difference between the best expected value with posterior probabilities and the best expected value with prior probabilities. It is a measure of the maximum (or upper limit) value of the additional information.

Minimax regret A pessimistic criterion for decision making using the regret figures as payoffs; using this criterion, one minimizes the maximum regret values.

Most probable state of nature A criterion of choice for decision making under risk that assumes that the state of nature with the highest probability will occur.

Objective probability Probability estimate based on hard data obtained from history or through experimentation (contrast with subjective probability).

Opportunity loss (or cost) The amount of loss attached to each possible outcome of an alternative, due to *not* selecting the best alternative.

Payoff The result of selecting an alternative course of action, given a specific state of nature occurring (also called outcome).

Perfect information The prior knowledge of exactly which state of nature will occur.

Prior probabilities The original probabilities of the states of nature prior to adjustments made as a result of acquiring additional information.

Regret See "Opportunity loss (or cost)."

Revised probabilities The probabilities of the states of nature after being adjusted with the aid of Bayes' theorem.

Risk A decision situation where several states of nature exist and their likelihood (probability) of occurrence is known.

State of nature Future event that impacts the result of a decision and is *not* under the control of the decision maker.

Subjective probability The probability estimate of a knowledgeable person that is based on judgment and intuition.

Uncertainty The decision environment in which several states of nature exist, but their chances of occurring are not known.

References and Bibliography

1. Bell, D. E., et al. *Decision Making*. New York: Cambridge University Press, 1988.
2. Gladwin, C. H. *Ethnographic Decision Tree Modeling*. Beverly Hills, Calif.: Sage Publications, 1989.
3. Hertz, D. D. *Practical Risk Analysis*. New York: John Wiley & Sons, 1983.
4. Luce, R. D., and H. Raiffa. *Games and Decisions*. New York: John Wiley & Sons, 1957.
5. McNamera, P., and J. Celona. *Decision Analysis with Supertree*. New York: Scientific Press, 1991.
6. Nelson, T. *The Management Science System (MSS)*. Homewood, Ill.: Richard D. Irwin, 1988.
7. Raiffa, H. *Decision Analysis*. Reading, Mass.: Addison-Wesley Publishing, 1970.
8. Ulvila, J., and R. V. Brown. "Decision Analysis Comes of Age." *Harvard Business Review*, September–October 1982, pp. 130–41.
9. Von Winterfeldt, D., and W. Edwards. *Decision Analysis and Behavioral Research*. New York: Cambridge University Press, 1986.
10. Waston, S. R., and D. M. Buede. *Decision Synthesis*. New York: Cambridge University Press, 1987.

10 Forecasting

Managers, in their decision-making activities, must be able to anticipate the future under various scenarios. They need to be able to predict the demand for their products and services, the probable development of new technology for their operations, cost trends, reactions to decisions they are contemplating, and so on. These all involve forecasting, the topic of this chapter. In some situations, data are lacking and a "qualitative" forecast must be made. In other situations, data may be plentiful and a quantitative, or statistical, forecast is possible.

In this chapter, we will consider both qualitative and quantitative forecasts and describe various approaches or models in each category. In Part A, we will focus on the qualitative approaches first and then consider some of the statistical models. Part B then develops some of the more complex approaches, finishing up with a presentation of the software packages available for forecasting.

PART A: BASICS

Bill Jacobs, administrator for the Lakeland City Health Center, was feeling frustrated in his attempts to predict next quarter's demand for service at his center, expressed in terms of *patient visits*. Lakeland City Health Center is a state-funded health clinic that serves the needs of the citizens of Lakeland, Florida. The state government requires that the center prepare a budget request each quarter for the coming quarter. The request is based largely on the forecast of demand for specific services during the next quarter. The center is currently in its fourth year of operation and is presently preparing its staffing plan for the upcoming quarter.

Demand information is available for each of the four quarters of the preceding three years and for the first two quarters of the current year. Bill has, in the past, tried using the last quarter's demand to predict the next quarter's demand for the center. He has also tried using the average of all past demand. Neither of these two approaches has proved satisfactory. The use of the last quarter's demand as a predictor of the next quarter's demand produced erratic forecasts. For example, using this method, he predicted (and staffed, scheduled, and purchased for) a demand of 3,500 visits for the second quarter of 1990, when about 8,000 visits actually resulted. Then he predicted 8,000 visits for the third quarter when only 5,500 visits materialized. Clearly this method could not sort out the fluctuations in the demand data and were therefore deemed unsatisfactory.

Bill had then turned to using the average of all demand data to predict the next quarter's demand. For the fourth quarter of 1990, he had predicted a demand of 5,667, when about 10,000 actually occurred. Bill recognized that this averaging method produced forecasts that smoothed out the fluctuations but did not adequately respond to any growth or reduction in the demand trend. As a matter of fact, the averaging method performed progressively worse as the amount of data increased. At this point, Bill had decided that he needed a more sophisticated tool for prediction.

We will return to Bill's situation and some models he might consider a bit later in this chapter.

10.1 The Forecasting Situation*

The management science process is centered around decision making. As the reader may recall, such a process involves choosing an alternative course of action by evaluating the possible consequences of the choice. Although the choice is made today, the consequences are assumed to occur sometime in the future. Thus, it is necessary to forecast the consequences. Although historical data are often extensively used in forecasting, the goal is not to fit the best curve to this data but to determine the best forecast.

Forecasting demand

Our opening case dealt with a forecast of *demand*. As the reader may imagine, demand data are used in several MS models such as inventory, decision tables and trees, queuing, transportation, and LP. Bill's problem is that the historical data fluctuate in what seems to be (at least at first sight) an irregular fashion. Furthermore, Bill is not sure how to relate the future to the past.

---

*Portions of this chapter are adapted from Jack R. Meredith, *The Management of Operations,* 4th ed. (New York: John Wiley & Sons, 1992). Copyright © 1992 John Wiley & Sons, Inc. Reprinted by permission.

The Uses of Forecasts

The major use of forecasting, as it relates to MS, is to predict the value of the model's input data, and sometimes the logical relationship of the model. The future time of interest depends on "when" we want to evaluate our options. For example, in a regular investment decision, we may be interested in income a year from today, whereas in a capital investment decision, we may be interested in projected income during the next five years. Generally speaking, we distinguish between two types of forecasts: (*a*) short run (up to one year), where the forecast is used mainly in deterministic models, and (*b*) long run (beyond one year), where the forecast is used in both deterministic and probabilistic models.

Forecasting Models and Methods

Many types of forecasting models exist because forecasting is an extremely difficult task. What is going to happen in the future depends, in many cases, on a multiplicity of factors, most of which are uncontrollable. Furthermore, data availability, accuracy, cost, and the time required to make the forecast also play an important role in creating each forecast.

Forecasting methods can be grouped in several ways. One classification scheme distinguishes between formally recognized forecasting techniques and informal approaches such as intuition, spur-of-the-moment guesses, and seat-of-the-pants predictions. Our attention in this chapter will be directed to the formal methods.

Formal methods can be divided into four categories: *judgment methods, counting methods, time-series methods,* and *association* or *causal methods* (Figure 10.1). Those methods described in this chapter are shown in Figure 10.1 with the appropriate section number. Each of the categories is briefly discussed below.

Judgment Methods

Judgment methods are those based on subjective estimates and expert opinion, rather than on hard data. They are often used for long-range forecasts, especially where external factors (e.g., political developments such as the 1989 fall of Communist Eastern Europe) may play a significant role. They also are used where historical data are very *limited* or *nonexistent,* such as in new product/service introductions.

Counting Methods

Counting methods involve some kind of experimentation or surveys of a sample with an attempt to generalize about the entire market. These methods are primarily used for forecasting demand for products/services, a part of marketing research.

The next two types of forecasting methods are quantitative in nature. They are based on hard data and are thus generally considered more objective than the previous types. They typically use historical data and are commonly divided between time-series and causal methods.

FIGURE 10.1

Classification of forecasting methods

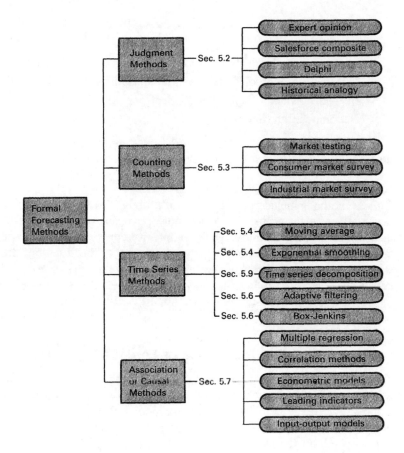

Time-Series Analysis

Time series

A **time series** is a set of values of some business or economic variable, measured at successive (usually equal) intervals of time. For example, quarterly sales over a few years make up a time series, as does the yearly growth rate of people in a city, the weekly demand for hospital beds, and so on.

If, for example, we recorded the number of automobiles sold each month of 1993 by the Schroeder Oldsmobile Co. and kept those data points *in the order in which they were recorded,* the 12 numbers would constitute a *12-period time series*. We undertake *time-series analysis* in decision making because we believe that knowledge of *past behavior* of the time series might help our understanding of (and therefore our ability to predict) the behavior of the series in the future. In some instances, such as the stock market, this assumption may be unjustified, but in managerial planning we assume that history will repeat itself and that past tendencies will continue. Time-series analysis efforts conclude with the development of a *time-series forecasting model* that can then be used to predict future events.

Time-series methods of forecasting

The analysis of a time series can be done by a host of methods ranging from fairly simple to very complicated. The following methods are described later in this chapter:

- Moving average (Section 10.4).
- Exponential and double exponential smoothing (Sections 10.4 and 10.10).
- Box-Jenkins and other methods (Sections 10.6 and 10.7).
- Decomposition (Section 10.9).

These methods analyze historical data and essentially project this data into the future; they do not attempt to find any cause-effect relationship.

Association or Causal Methods

Causal method

Causal methods include data analysis for finding statistical associations and, if possible, cause-effect relationships. They are more powerful than the time-series methods, but they are also more complex. Their complexity comes from two sources. First, they include more variables, some of which are external to the situation. Second, they employ sophisticated statistical techniques for segregating the various types of variables. Causal approaches are most appropriate for mid-term (between short- and long-term) forecasting. These methods, described in Section 10.7, usually require a computer for their execution.

Factors Influencing the Choice of Forecasting Method

Generally speaking, judgment and counting methods, which are subjective in nature, are used in those cases where quantitative methods are inappropriate or cannot be used. Time pressure, lack of data, or lack of money may prevent the use of a quantitative model. Complexity of historical data (due to interactions or fluctuations, for example) may also inhibit the use of hard data.

The method chosen to prepare a forecast depends on a number of factors, as described below.

The Historical Data Available

If historical data are available, a quantitative forecasting method can be used. Attempting to forecast without a history is almost as useful as using a crystal ball. The history need not be long, complete, or even for exactly the same item as is being forecast. But some historical database should be located if at all possible. If data are not available, an experiment can sometimes be conducted to generate the needed information.

The Money and Time Available

Cost trade-offs

The greater the limitations on time or money available for forecasting, the more likely it is that an unsophisticated method will have to be used. In general, management desires to use that forecasting method that minimizes the total cost of making the forecast and the cost of an *inaccurate* forecast. Costs of forecasting inaccuracy include the cost of making a wrong decision: for example, the costs of over- or understocking items; the costs of under- or overstaffing, and the intangible and opportunity costs associated with

FIGURE 10.2

The costs of forecasting

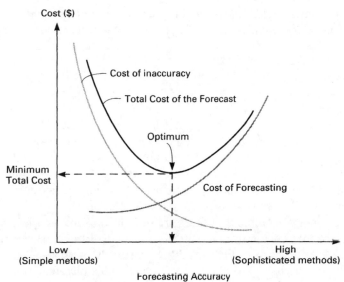

loss of customer/client goodwill because an item was not available. This trade-off situation is depicted in Figure 10.2. The best forecasting method is the one for which the combined costs are minimized, but, because some of these costs are difficult (if not impossible) to measure, a "best" method is difficult to determine.

With the advent of computers and preprogrammed forecasting routines, the cost and time of statistical forecasts based on historical data have been reduced significantly. It therefore has become more cost-effective for organizations to conduct more sophisticated forecasts, and the optimum forecasting method is thus shifting to the right in Figure 10.2.

The Accuracy Required

Short versus long range

If, for whatever reasons, the forecast must be very accurate, highly sophisticated and expensive methods are called for. Typically, very long-range (3–10 year) forecasts require the least accuracy, whereas very short-range (one week to a few months) forecasts require great accuracy, because detailed plans and actions are based on these short-range projections.

10.2 Judgmental Forecasting Methods

Some of the most significant decisions made by organizations are made on the basis of judgment. Judgment forecasts are made using information such as expert opinion, or analyses of demand information for similar products or services that have been previously introduced and for which historical data are available. An example of the latter

Forecasting by historical analogy

method, known as *historical analogy,* was the use of demand data for black-and-white television sets to predict the slope of the demand curve for color TV sets. Two judgmental forecasting methods are particularly common; these are expert opinion and Delphi.

Expert Opinion

Using expert judgment

Consider, for example, a company that has introduced, over the years, several dozen different consumer goods. It is conceivable that the experience of key managers, particularly those associated with the marketing of the products, could provide reasonable forecasts of costs, prices, or the demand for another new product. As "two heads are better than one," most expert judgment methods rely on the formation of a panel of experts who reach a consensus or compromise forecast.

The problems with committees

But panel or committee solutions to the forecasting problem are sometimes biased in favor of the opinion of one dominant member. Either that member is a better salesperson of his or her own ideas, is more "expert" than fellow committee members, or is simply more verbal than others on the panel. This bias may result in forecasts that are not as good or as well thought out as predictions based on *all* of the information available from the committee members. Several methods exist to improve the work of committees, one of which is the Delphi method.

Delphi

Using Delphi to improve expert forecasts

The **Delphi** method was developed by the RAND Corporation as a technique for group forecasting that would eliminate the undesirable effects of interaction between members of the group. The experts need not meet face-to-face, nor need they know who the other experts are. The method generally begins by having each expert provide individual written forecasts, along with any supporting arguments and assumptions. These forecasts are submitted to the Delphi coordinator, who edits, clarifies, and summarizes the data. These data are then provided as anonymous feedback to the experts along

Rounds of questions are employed

with a *second round* of questions. Questions and feedback continue in writing for several rounds, becoming increasingly more specific, until consensus among the panel members is reached or until the experts do not change their forecasts any more.

The Delphi method allows the benefits of multiple opinions and communication among group members of diverse opinions and assumptions, but avoids the negative effects of dominant behavior, "groupthink," and unwillingness to change one's mind that

Groupthink

are often associated with committee solutions. For more details, see [6].

Electronic Meeting Systems (EMS)

Although Delphi solves some of the process problems involved in face-to-face meetings, it is an expensive and lengthy process. An alternative method that has been recently developed is to conduct the meetings electronically. This is done by various EMS technologies, including Group Decision Support Systems (GDSS). These technologies enable forecasting by the group, permitting anonymity, creativity, and other positive characteristics that can improve the interactions of a group.

10.3 Counting Methods

Counting methods of forecasting employ experiments and surveys, usually based on representative samples of the entire population. The purpose is to generalize from the sample to the entire population. Of special interest are market surveys and market testing.

The Market Survey and Market Testing

Market research

New products and services are often subjected to extensive *market research* before a final decision is made regarding the introduction of this new output. Such devices as telephone surveys, mail questionnaires, consumer panels, and test markets are used to ascertain estimates of value, perceived quality, and demand. For example, both the Nielson TV ratings and the Gallup public opinion poll are based on sample surveys of public attitudes and behavior.

Test marketing can also provide data over a long period of time to track changes in shopping and/or buying trends (called *longitudinal research*). A test market is usually some specific geographical region that is selected because it represents some segment of the organization's overall market for the new output. The test market requires that the product or service actually be introduced into the limited test area. Test marketing provides management with information about actual consumer behavior.

Industrial surveys

As with consumer market surveys, it is also possible to conduct *industrial* market surveys. Here, the subjects are vendors, purchasing agents, and other individuals who are more knowledgeable than consumers.

10.4 Moving Averages and Exponential Smoothing

The two simplest time-series analysis methods are **moving averages** and **exponential smoothing.** These methods are illustrated with an example below.

Table 10.1 presents Bill Jacobs' historical data for the Lakeland City Health Center. For illustration, the data are also plotted in Figure 10.3. As you recall, Bill had decided he needed a more sophisticated forecasting methodology than just using last period's demand or the average of all the previous periods.

Moving Averages

Using only the last few periods to average

To overcome the deficiency of using a simple average, the moving average technique generates the next period's forecast by averaging the actual demand for only the last *n* (*n* is often in the range of 4 to 7) time periods, rather than for all the periods such as in

TABLE 10.1 **Patient Demand for the Lakeland City Health Center**

Year	Quarter	Period Number	Number of Patient Visits
1990	1	1	3,500
	2	2	8,000
	3	3	5,500
	4	4	10,000
1991	1	5	4,500
	2	6	6,000
	3	7	3,000
	4	8	5,500
1992	1	9	5,000
	2	10	9,500
	3	11	7,500
	4	12	15,000
1993	1	13	13,500
	2	14	17,500
	3	15	?

FIGURE 10.3

Plot of Lakeland's quarterly demand

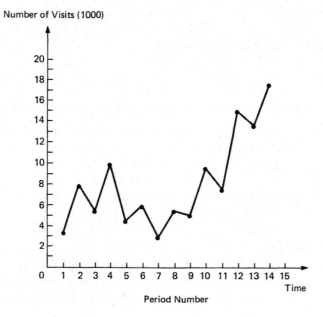

a simple average. Any data older than n are thus ignored. The choice of the value for n is usually based on the expected seasonality in the data, such as four quarters, or 12 months, in a year. Such a choice will effectively neutralize the impact of any seasonality in the data. If n must be chosen arbitrarily, then it should be based on the value that best describes the historical data when used in the model.

Mathematically, the moving average is computed as:

$$F_{t+1} = \frac{1}{n} \sum_{i=(t-n+1)}^{t} D_i \qquad (10.1)$$

where:

t = Period number for the *current* period
F_{t+1} = Forecast of demand for the *next* period
D_i = Actual demand in period i
n = Number of periods of demand to be included (known as the "order" of the moving average)

For example, to forecast demand for the next quarter of this year (i.e., quarter 3 of 1993 or period 15 in Table 10.1) using a moving average of order four (that is, $n = 4$), Bill would compute:

$$F_{14+1} = \frac{1}{4} \sum_{i=14-4+1}^{14} D_i$$

or:

$$F_{15} = \frac{1}{4} \sum_{i=11}^{14} D_i$$
$$F_{15} = (D_{11} + D_{12} + D_{13} + D_{14})/4$$
$$F_{15} = (7,500 + 15,000 + 13,500 + 17,500)/4$$
$$F_{15} = 13,375$$

The forecast for the next quarter, using a moving average forecast of order four, would therefore be 13,375 visits.

The moving average as a compromise

The moving average is a *compromise* between the last period's demand and the simple average, both of which the administrator has rejected as being unsatisfactory. The number of periods to be averaged in the moving average is dependent on the specific situation. If too few periods are included in the average, the forecast will be similar to the forecast obtained when only the last period's demand had been used as the forecast. Using too many periods in the moving average will result in a forecast similar to the forecast obtained when the simple average was used.

Weighted Moving Averages

A refinement of the moving average approach is to weight the older or, more commonly, the newer data more heavily rather than use equal weights in the moving average. For example, we might believe that the newest data point is the best indicator of where the data are headed, but to guard against a random fluctuation we also include the three prior data points, each with a decreasing level of importance. Thus, rather than using weights of 1/4, or .25, in a four-period moving average, we might use .10, .20, .30, and .40. (Note that they still sum to 1.0.) This would give the third oldest data point only half the importance, or weight, as the most recent data point. Other weights might be .20, .20, .25, .35 or .05, .10, .25, .60.

Applying the first set of weights: 10, .20, .30, .40, to the past four periods of data, we obtain the period 15 forecast of

$$F_{15} = .10D_{11} + .20D_{12} + .30D_{13} + .40D_{14}$$

$$= .10(7,500) + .20(15,000) + .30(13,500) + .40(17,500)$$

$$= 14,800$$

This compares with the equally weighted moving averages forecast of 13,375. As with regular moving averages, a longer or shorter order may be used and the weights adjusted appropriately.

Simple Exponential Smoothing

Achieving the two objectives by exponential smoothing

As noted above, we generally want to use the most current data, and at the same time, use enough earlier observations to smooth out random fluctuations. One technique perfectly adapted to meeting these two objectives is exponential smoothing.

The computation of a forecast using exponential smoothing is carried out with the following equation. If we consider demand data, for example,
New demand forecast = (α) (current demand) + $(1 - \alpha)$ (previous demand forecast)
or:

$$F_{t+1} = \alpha D_t + (1 - \alpha)F_t \tag{10.2}$$

where α is a **smoothing constant** that must be greater than or equal to zero but less than or equal to 1. The other symbols are illustrated in the diagram below.

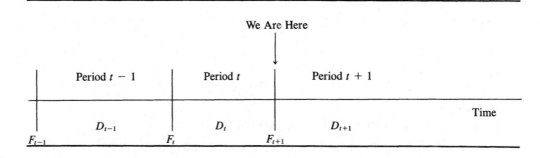

Note that Equation 10.2 is iterative in nature. That is, the previous solution (for F_t) is used to obtain the next solution (for F_{t+1}). If we substitute into Equation 10.2 the

FIGURE 10.4

Data exhibiting low and high variability

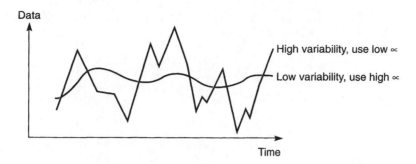

equation for F_t, and keep substituting back in the same fashion, we can obtain the equation that led to the name *exponential smoothing*. This is shown in Equation 10.3.

$$F_{t+1} = \alpha D_t + \alpha(1 - \alpha)D_{t-1} + \alpha(1 - \alpha)^2 D_{t-2} + \cdots + \alpha(1 - \alpha)^{t-1}D_1 \qquad (10.3)$$

If we consider a value of α of 0.1, Equation 10.3 becomes:

$$F_{t+1} = .1D_t + .09D_{t-1} + .081D_{t-2} + .073D_{t-3} + \cdots$$

and for a value of 0.5 it becomes:

$$F_{t+1} = .5D_t + .25D_{t-1} + .125D_{t-2} + .063D_{t-3} + \cdots$$

Thus, the exponentially decreasing contributions of earlier demands to the latest forecast can be clearly seen.

The smoothing constant as a weighting factor

The smoothing constant α can be interpreted as the *weight* assigned to the last (i.e., the current) data point. The higher the weight assigned to this current demand, the greater the influence this point has on the forecast. For example, if α is equal to 1, the demand forecast for the next period will be equal to the value of the current demand, the approach Bill used earlier.

Smoothing the data

Our objective in exponential smoothing is to choose the value of α that results in the best forecasts. With a large α, exponential smoothing will produce forecasts that react quickly to fluctuations. Generally speaking, larger values of α are used in situations in which the data can be plotted as a rather smooth curve, such as the middle curve in Figure 10.4. A low value of α should be used with widely fluctuating data, also shown in Figure 10.4. The appropriate value of α is usually determined through a trial-and-error process; values typically lie in the range of 0.01 to 0.30.

10.5 Forecasting Errors

Most forecasts tend to be somewhat, or significantly, incorrect. It is important to assess the quality of a forecast by comparing actual results to the forecast. This comparison then tells us about the magnitude of the forecast errors and the quality of the forecasting method.

MAD and bias

The two most common methods of measuring forecast error are the mean absolute deviation (**MAD**) and the **bias.**

$$MAD = \frac{1}{n}\sum_{i=1}^{n}|F_i - D_i| \qquad (10.4)$$

$$Bias = \frac{1}{n}\sum_{i=1}^{n}(F_i - D_i) \qquad (10.5)$$

where:

F_i = Forecast of demand in period i
D_i = Actual demand in period i
n = Number of periods of data analyzed
$||$ = Absolute value

Very different effects

Though very similar in appearance, these two methods measure different forecasting effects. Because the MAD only sums absolute values of errors, both positive and negative errors add to the sum and the average size of the error is determined. This gives the manager a sense of the *accuracy* of the forecasting model. A manager might use this knowledge by saying: "Our forecasts are typically only accurate within 10 percent; we should prepare for being either 10 percent *above* or *below* the forecast."

The bias, on the other hand, tells whether the forecast is typically too low or too high, and by how much. A manager knowing this might say: "We are almost always forecasting 10 percent too low; we had better add an extra 10 percent to hedge against this potential error." That is, MAD tells the average size of the error and bias tells the direction.

Example

Suppose that two methods of forecasting are tested against data for a four-month period. Method A gave forecasts for January through April of 102, 107, 106, and 113, respectively; Method B gave 104, 105, 107, 110; and the actual results were 103, 106, 106, and 111. The MAD for Method A would be $(|102 - 103| + |107 - 106| + |106 - 106| + |113 - 111|)/4 = 1$; and the bias would be $[(102 - 103) + \ldots]/4 = 0.5$. For Method B, the MAD is also 1, but the bias is 0 (check the data). Thus, Method B is the better of the two.

It may well happen that one forecasting method has a smaller MAD but a larger bias, or vice versa. In such cases, the circumstances of the situation must be considered to determine whether MAD or bias is the most important measure.

A tracking signal

The MAD is sometimes used as a **tracking signal** in certain **adaptive forecasting** models (see reference [11]). Briefly, adaptive forecasting models *self-adjust* by increas-

TABLE 10.2 **Actual and Exponentially Forecast Values of Quarterly Demand for the Lakeland Health Center (Data in Thousands)**

Year	Quarter	Actual D	Forecast ($\alpha = 0.1$) F	Forecast ($\alpha = 0.3$) F
1990	1	3.5		
	2	8.0	3.50	3.50
	3	5.5	3.95	4.85
	4	10.0	4.11	5.05
1991	1	4.5	4.69	6.53
	2	6.0	4.68	5.92
	3	3.0	4.81	5.95
	4	5.5	4.63	5.06
1992	1	5.0	4.71	5.19
	2	9.5	4.74	5.14
	3	7.5	5.22	6.44
	4	15.0	5.45	6.76
1993	1	13.5	6.40	9.23
	2	17.5	7.11	10.51
	3	?	8.15	12.61

ing or decreasing the smoothing constant α in the exponential smoothing method when the tracking signal becomes too large.

For the Lakeland City Health Center example, we will use two different smoothing factors and calculate the MAD and bias to determine the best one. Table 10.2 presents the actual historical data for patient visits and the exponentially smoothed forecasts using α values of 0.1 and 0.3. Because there were no data on which to base a forecast for period one (i.e., F_1), we used, as is common practice, the actual demand D_1; then, F_2 is computed (using $\alpha = 0.1$) as:

$$F_2 = \alpha D_1 + (1 - \alpha)F_1$$
$$F_2 = 0.1 \times 3.5 + (1 - 0.1) \times 3.5 = 3.5$$

In the same manner, we compute F_3 as:

$$F_3 = 0.1(8) + 0.9(3.5) = 3.95$$

The computations continue for F_4, F_5, and so on, using the previous forecast and the value of the current observation. The current data are weighted by α and the historical data (all of which is embodied in the previous period's forecast) by $(1 - \alpha)$. As can be seen from Table 10.2, F_{15}, the forecasts for the next quarter (using each of the two α values), are 8,150 and 12,610 visits, a considerable difference.

Comparing values of α

Table 10.3 presents the computation of the MAD and bias for the two forecasts. The results for MAD show that the error is quite high for either value of α, though 0.3

TABLE 10.3   Calculation of the Forecast Errors

Year	Quarter	Algebraic Difference (Forecast − Actual)		Absolute Difference |Forecast − Actual|	
		$\alpha = 0.1$ Bias	$\alpha = 0.3$ Bias	$\alpha = 0.1$ MAD	$\alpha = 0.3$ MAD
1990	1				
	2	− 4.50	− 4.50	4.50	4.50
	3	− 1.55	− 0.65	1.55	0.65
	4	− 5.89	− 4.95	5.89	4.95
1991	1	+ 0.19	+ 2.03	0.19	2.03
	2	− 1.32	− 0.08	1.32	0.08
	3	+ 1.81	+ 2.95	1.81	2.95
	4	− 0.87	− 0.44	0.87	0.44
1992	1	− 0.29	+ 0.19	0.29	0.19
	2	− 4.76	− 4.36	4.76	4.36
	3	− 2.28	− 1.06	2.28	1.06
	4	− 9.55	− 8.24	9.55	8.24
1993	1	− 7.10	− 4.27	7.10	4.27
	2	−10.39	− 6.99	10.39	6.99
	Sum	−46.50	−30.37	50.50	40.71
		Bias = − 3.57	Bias = − 2.33	MAD = 3.88	MAD = 3.13

seems to be the better of the two. This is because the exponential smoothing model is fairly simple and, as such, does not consider seasonal and trend impacts, which *are* considered by time-series decomposition analysis (Section 10.9). Trend and seasonal factors can also be included through more complex exponential smoothing models, called *double* or *triple exponential smoothing* (Section 10.10).

Lagging

The negative value of the bias in Table 10.3 indicates that most of the error is due to negative bias in the model, in this case consistently forecasting too low or "lagging" the demand (a typical characteristic of simple exponential forecasting models such as this one). This result is also seen in Figure 10.5, which shows the actual demand data and the forecast values using $\alpha = 0.1$ and $\alpha = 0.3$. Notice, for example, that the downturn after quarter 4 and the upturn after quarter 9 are detected more quickly by the $\alpha = 0.3$ model, as we have indicated should be the case. You may notice that both models lag behind the upward trend after quarter 9. In general, if values of alpha greater than 0.3 seem to give the best results, then exponential forecasting should probably not be used. A smoothing model like the one presented in Equation 10.2 is best used in situations where demand fluctuates around an overall level trend. If the trend is increasing or decreasing, more sophisticated models are usually more appropriate.

FIGURE 10.5

Plot of actual data and exponential forecasts

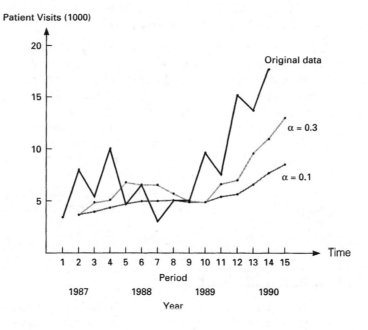

Other Measures of Error

Several other methods are used to measure forecasting errors. Some are variants of MAD and bias. Various computer programs (see Section 10.11) offer some of the following additional methods:

a. *The mean percentage deviation:* This is just the bias converted to a percentage. Each error $F_i - D_i$ is replaced by $100[(F_i - D_i)/D_i]$; using percentages allows comparisons among different series of forecasts.

b. *The mean absolute percentage deviation:* This is the MAD converted to a percentage. Each absolute value $|F_i - D_i|$ is replaced by $100\,|F_i - D_i|/D_i$. Again, using percentages allows comparisons among forecasts.

Error measure

c. *The mean squared deviation (MSE):* This measure is computed by averaging the squares of the separate deviations $(F_i - D_i)^2$. Squaring the deviations has the same effect as taking their absolute value, but it also penalizes large errors much more than small ones. This property could be important in practice, where small deviations are much easier to handle than large ones. The resulting measure is in squared units.

d. *The standard error:* This measure is based on the squared deviations as well. It computes the mean by dividing by $n - 2$ (the 2 comes from the two estimates of the regression line, the slope and the intercept) rather than by n, and then takes the square root of the average to get a measure in the same units as D_i.

10.6 Other Time-Series Methods

Adaptive filtering

In addition to simple moving averages and exponential smoothing, there exist several other methods. For example, *adaptive filtering* is a type of weighted combination of actual and estimated outcomes, systematically altered to reflect underlying data patterns. *Time-series extrapolation* involves predicting outcomes based on the extension of a least squares (regression) function fitted to a data series with time as an independent variable. A very popular method is *time-series decomposition* (Section 10.9).

Box-Jenkins

Box-Jenkins is a complex, computer-based, iterative procedure that produces an autoregressive, integrated moving average model, adjusted for trend and seasonal factors (these factors will be described in Part B of this chapter). Box-Jenkins (see reference [5]) estimates appropriate weighting parameters, tests the model, and repeats the cycle as appropriate. To some degree, the Box-Jenkins method can be considered a causal model.

10.7 Causal Methods

Considering the factors that cause demand

In the previous section, we saw that demand could be related to time; that is, the demand changed as time changed. Although a relationship existed, we could not say for sure that time *caused* the changes in demand. There are factors other than time that are often related to demand and, in fact, these factors often cause the demand changes.

Marriages as a predictor of housing demand

For example, increases in single-family housing starts during a given quarter might be highly related to the number of new marriages during the previous quarter. Although marriages do not directly *cause* new houses to be purchased, it is logical to argue that marriages are a major precondition to new housing starts. Figure 10.6 illustrates the likely relationship between new marriages (the independent variable) and single family housing starts (the dependent variable). This figure indicates a rather close relationship between the two variables. The variables are thus said to be highly *correlated*. Correlation-based forecasts predict values based on historic patterns of covaria-

FIGURE 10.6

Plot of marriages versus housing starts showing the close relationship

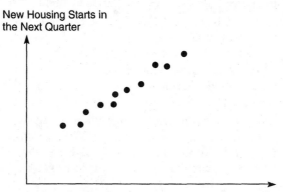

New Housing Starts in the Next Quarter

Number of Marriages in Current Quarter

tion between variables. The relationship between housing starts in one quarter and marriages in a previous quarter is an example of a *logical* association. Many causal models use such "leading indicators" to predict upcoming events.

Linear (Least Squares) Regression

Predictor variables

Least squares regression is used to estimate a trend-predicting equation such as 10.6 or 10.7 (an example is given in Section 10.9). The simple linear regression equation is:

$$Y'_x = a + bX \tag{10.6}$$

In the case of housing starts, it would be interpreted as:

Y'_x = The predicted number of new housing starts
a = The Y-axis intercept
b = The slope
X = The number of new marriages in the previous quarter

Multiple Regression

Including many causative factors through multiple regression

This linear regression methodology can be extended to situations in which more than one explanatory variable is used, called **multiple regression,** to explain the behavior of one dependent variable Y. For example, in addition to the number of marriages, the employment rate in the previous quarter might also explain some of the change in housing starts. The multiple regression equation would be of the form:

$$Y'_{x_1 x_2} = a + b_1 X_1 + b_2 X_2 \tag{10.7}$$

where:

$Y'_{x_1 x_2}$ = The predicted number of housing starts based on new marriages and the employment rate
a = The Y-axis intercept
b_1 and b_2 = The slopes (rates of change in Y') with respect to X_1 and X_2
X_1 and X_2 = The number of marriages and the employment rate, respectively, in the previous quarter

Whereas with simple linear regression we use a straight line to predict the dependent variable Y, with multiple regression with two independent (or explanatory) variables, the predicting equation represents a plane. And with three or more explanatory

Hyperplane

variables, the predicting equation is termed a *hyperplane* because it would be a plane in four- (or higher) dimensional space.

The solution of the sets of equations that determine the coefficients of the predicting equation is relatively straightforward, especially with the power of computers.

Management Science in Practice

Forecasting Demand for Aircraft Parts at American Airlines

An airline, to support its fleet of aircraft, must stock replacement parts ranging from landing gears to altimeters at the many airports it services. Because the number of replacement parts can reach into the many thousands and their unit value can be significant, deciding which items will be in demand and where they should be held is a problem involving millions of dollars in spare parts investment.

In the mid-1970s, the materials management department at American Airlines investigated the possibility of upgrading their existing spare parts forecasting and allocation computer program. American Airlines was using over 5,000 different parts averaging $5,000 each, although some (such as complex avionics computers) could cost well over $500,000 each. The existing program was difficult to use, limited in capability, and most importantly, the demand forecasts and shortage costs were of questionable accuracy. Also, to make the monthly forecasts for the approximately 5,000 different parts and verify their accuracy required several days.

The replacement computer program expanded the capability of the spare parts program significantly, allowing forecasts of future demand, ascertaining the impact of fleet changes, and adding a number of other important functions and capabilities. Moreover, the demand forecasts are now completed within one hour and there is no need for verifying their accuracy. However, to check on its operation, demand forecast samples are taken periodically to validate the system.

Originally, the demand forecasts were made using only time-series approaches that made the forecasts slow to respond to changes in aircraft utilization, not to mention major fleet expansions. The forecasts are now made in two stages: first calculating total system demand for each part and then distributing this demand across each airport.

For total system demand, linear regression is used to include the appropriate relationships between monthly demands and different functions of monthly flying hours. The system updates a rolling 18-month demand and flying hour history using the most recent month's data. After updating the history, new regression coefficients are calculated and new forecasts are made.

In the second stage, the aggregate forecast from the first stage is distributed among the airports based on weights reflecting each airport's aircraft traffic, number of maintenance checks, and past history of part demand. The forecast must also be distributed over the days of the month, because a demand for 12 items in one day is considerably different than a demand for 1 item every day for 12 days. That is, the forecast must include not only the volume of demand disaggregated by part and airport but also its distribution pattern over the month.

Many of the other segments of the parts program were upgraded at the same time. The materials management department estimates that using the new program has provided a one-time savings to American Airlines of $7 million and a recurring annual savings of nearly $1 million. In addition, the program has helped increase the productivity of the department's analysts, which in turn means faster replacements and newer data to work with, all of which improves the accuracy of the system. And the system has heightened the analyst's sensitivity to all factors affected by part allocations, allowing them to better anticipate the future effects of each day's allocation decisions.

Source: M. J. Tedone, "Repairable Part Management," *Interfaces*, July–August 1989, pp. 61–68.

Questions:

1. Why is it no longer necessary to verify the accuracy of the computerized demand forecast?
2. Identify the various forecasting tools in this application.
3. List the benefits of the computerized system.

However, the level of confidence of the forecast with additional independent variables drops off quickly. That is, one variable such as number of marriages may help a lot in predicting housing starts; but adding another variable such as employment rate may only help a little bit more. This is termed the *explained variance of Y;* the first variable explains much of the variance but the second only explains a little more. And a third may add no further explanation. For further discussion of this topic, consult the bibliography.

Simultaneous Equation Models

In many cases, the dependent and independent variables used in forecasting models are *interdependent*. That is, sales may be a function of personal income and personal income a function of sales. **Simultaneous equation models** take these interrelationships into consideration by formulating, not one regression equation, but a series of simultaneous regression equations that relate the data to all of the interdependent factors, many of which are also predicted by the model.

10.8 Problems for Part A

1. How many periods (n) should be included in a moving average for each of the following sets of data?
   a. Hourly rate of fire alarms.
   b. Daily output from a 40-hour-per-week manufacturer.
   c. Monthly sales.
   d. Quarterly earnings.
   e. Daily sales from a 24-hour convenience food store.
   f. Weekly bank deposits.

2. Plot the following data and then calculate and plot a moving average of order $n = 3$, order $n = 4$, and order $n = 5$. Interpret your results.

Period	1	2	3	4	5	6	7	8	9	10
Data	6	5	5	4	5	3	2	4	3	3

3. Use a weighted moving average with weights 0.2, 0.3, and 0.5 with the data in Problem 2. Compare the results to the unweighted moving average of order 3.

4. Use the data from periods 6 to 10 in Problem 2 to make an exponential forecast for period 11. Try three values of smoothing constants, alpha of 0.05, 0.30, and 0.90. Start with $F_1 = 6$. Compare to the moving average forecasts obtained from the answers to Problem 2.

5. Make an exponential forecast for period 5 with two values of alpha, 0.05 and 0.60, given the data below. Start with $F_1 = 32$. Compare the results.

Period	1	2	3	4
Data	32	14	41	10

6. Calculate the MAD and bias for periods 7 through 10 of the six forecasts in Problems 2 and 4 to determine the best forecast method.

7. Use the data in Problem 5 to calculate the MAD and bias for the two sets of forecasts of periods 2 through 4. How do they compare?

8. A four-period weighted moving average might weight the oldest data point only by 0.1, the next oldest by 0.2, the second most recent by 0.3, and the most recent by 0.4, thus acting much like exponential smoothing. Use these weights to calculate a forecast for the Lakeland City Health Center.

9. Recompute the exponential forecast for the Lakeland City Health Center using an alpha of 0.3, but use the

MAD as a tracking signal. Whenever the MAD exceeds 3.0, switch to an alpha of 0.8. When the MAD drops to less than 3.0, return to an alpha of 0.3. Plot the result on Figure 10.5. Is this method of "adaptive smoothing" more accurate than simple exponential smoothing for this data?

10. A conceptually simple method of adaptive smoothing is known as Chow's Method. With this approach, after the actual demand is known for the forecast period, one recalculates the last forecast two times using an alpha 0.05 larger and 0.05 smaller than what was previously used. Using the best result of the three, one then forecasts the next period, using the value that performed best in the last period. Starting with an alpha of 0.3, try this approach on the Lakeland City Health Center data of Table 10.2 and plot the results on Figure 10.5. How does this method compare with the others?

11. Following is a list of actual data for 15 periods and a computer printout of simple linear regression with forecasts for each period. Calculate the MAD, bias, mean percentage deviation, mean absolute percentage deviation, mean squared deviation, and standard error of the forecast.

12. Economists have calculated that new home sales (H) are related to the number of new family formations (F), average annual income (I), average interest rate (R), and cost of construction (C) through the following equation:

$$H = 62{,}731 + 0.74F + 5.1I - 4126R - 0.9C$$

where I and C are in dollars and R is a percentage. If it is predicted that, in 1998, F will be 100,000 new families, I will be \$50,000, R will be 26 percent, and C will be \$200,000, how many new homes will be sold? How sensitive are sales to a 1 percent increase in the interest rate; to a \$1000 increase in the cost of construction; to a \$1000 increase in average annual income? Do you think there may be any relationship between average annual income and new family formations? Or between average annual income and the cost of construction? If so, what effect might this have on your results?

Period (X)	Actual (Y)	Forecast (Y)	Error	Percent Error	Period (X)	Actual (Y)	Forecast (Y)	Error	Percent Error
1	0.50	0.90	−0.40	80.42	10	4.00	4.99	−0.99	24.81
2	1.50	1.36	0.14	9.56	11	4.75	5.45	−0.70	14.67
3	2.25	1.81	0.44	19.51	12	5.50	5.90	−0.40	7.29
4	3.00	2.27	0.73	24.48	13	6.50	6.36	0.14	2.22
5	3.25	2.72	0.53	16.31	14	7.50	6.81	0.69	9.20
6	3.50	3.17	0.33	9.30	15	8.25	7.26	0.99	11.94
7	3.50	3.63	−0.13	3.68			*Coefficient*		
8	3.50	4.08	−0.58	16.67	Intercept (a)		.447619		
9	3.75	4.54	−0.79	21.01	Slope (b)		.454464		

PART B: EXTENSIONS

10.9 Decomposition

Four components

Time-series decomposition is a procedure that separates a time series of past values into four components: (1) *trend T,* (2) *seasonal variation S,* (3) *cyclical variation C,* and (4) *random (unexplained) variation R.* Then each of the first three components is *extrapo-*

FIGURE 10.7

Three common trends

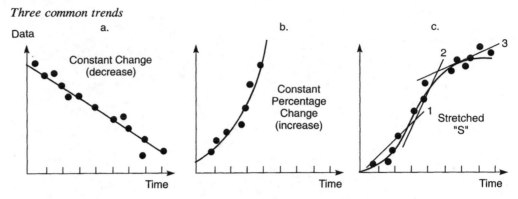

lated into the future to form the basis for a forecast through recombination of the components. A brief description of the four components follows.

The Trend (T)

The **trend** component refers to the long-term direction in which the time-series data appears to be going. Figure 10.7 illustrates three fairly common trends.

Straight-line trend

A straight-line or "linear" trend showing a constant amount of *change,* as in Figure 10.7a, could be an accurate fit to the historical data over some *limited range* of time. Figure 10.7b illustrates the situation of a constant percentage change. Here, change in

Nonlinear trends

the data depends on the current level of the data rather than being constant each period, as in Figure 10.7a. Figure 10.7c indicates a nonlinear trend line known as the

Stretched S

"stretched S" or **life cycle growth curve.** This curve could be approximated by three separate straight trend lines: 1, 2, and 3.

The Seasonal (S)

The bases for seasonal variation

Seasonal fluctuations result primarily from nature but are also brought about by human behavior. Snow tires and antifreeze enjoy brisk demand during the winter months, whereas sales of golf balls and bikinis peak in the spring and summer months. Of course, seasonal demand often *leads* or *lags* (i.e., precedes or follows) the actual season. For example, the production season to meet retailer's demand for Christmas goods is August through September. Sales of "heart-shaped" boxes of candy and Christmas trees are brought about by events that are controlled by humans. The *seasonal* variation in events need not be related to the seasons of the year, however. For example, fire alarms in New York City reach a "seasonal" peak at 7 P.M. and a seasonal low at 7 A.M. every day. And restaurants reach three "seasonal" peaks every day at 7:30 A.M., 12:30 P.M., and about 8:00 P.M. A typical seasonal is shown in Figure 10.8.

FIGURE 10.8

Seasonal variation superimposed on a trend and cycle

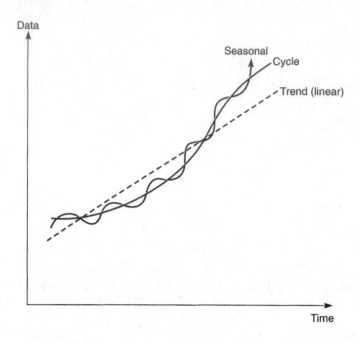

The Cycle (C)

Long-term cycles

The **cycle** component is only obvious in time series that span several years. A cycle can be defined as a *long-term oscillation* or swing of the data points around the trend line over a period of at least three complete sets of seasonals. National economic cycles of boom times and depressions and periods of war and peace are examples of such cycles. Figure 10.9 presents two complete cycles and the underlying straight-line trend of a time series where no yearly seasonal is assumed to exist. Note that the oscillations around the trend line are *not* symmetrical, as they seldom are in actual time series.

Cycles, particularly business cycles, are often difficult to explain or predict. Identification of a cyclic pattern in a time series requires the analysis of a long set of

FIGURE 10.9

Typical cycles

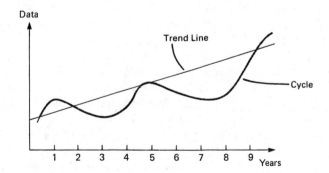

data. For example, only two cycles were completed in nine years for the time series shown in Figure 10.9. In many cases, the cycle component is not considered because it is difficult to predict the direction and magnitude of the cycle.

Random Variation (R)

Random variation is unpredictable

Random variations are, as the name implies, without specific assignable cause and without pattern. Random fluctuations can usually be explained after the fact, such as the increase in energy consumption due to abnormally harsh weather conditions, but cannot be systematically predicted.

The Decomposition Procedure

There are several approaches to decomposition and several ways that each component can be estimated. The procedure illustrated here is a fairly common one; its major steps are shown in Figure 10.10.

FIGURE 10.10

The decomposition process

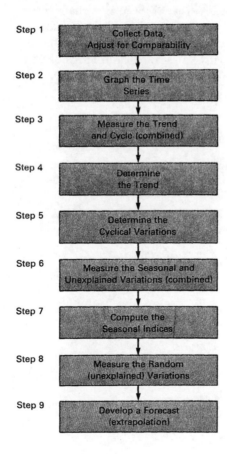

Step 1 — Collect Data, Adjust for Comparability

Step 2 — Graph the Time Series

Step 3 — Measure the Trend and Cycle (combined)

Step 4 — Determine the Trend

Step 5 — Determine the Cyclical Variations

Step 6 — Measure the Seasonal and Unexplained Variations (combined)

Step 7 — Compute the Seasonal Indices

Step 8 — Measure the Random (unexplained) Variations

Step 9 — Develop a Forecast (extrapolation)

Our approach is based on the multiplication of the components in order to get the forecast; that is, it is assumed that the time-series variable Y is a product of the variables T, C, S, and R. (Others prefer to consider Y as the sum of $T + C + S + R$.)

$$Y = T \times C \times S \times R \tag{10.8}$$

The details of the decomposition procedure are as follows:

Step 1. Collection and Adjustment of Data
The data must be reliable and in line with the purpose of the analysis. Data must be adjusted for any special situations (e.g., leap years versus regular years).

Step 2. Graphing the Time Series
It is helpful to graph the data of the time series, noting visually the presence of a long-term trend, cyclical variations, seasonal variations, and large random variations.

Example (Adapted from [10])

The Mercantile Stores Company, Inc. (MSC), is a chain of retail department stores. The sales figures of MSC for the period 1986–1993 are shown in Table 10.4. Because the sales are in terms of dollars, the data are adjusted to reflect the changes in the value of the dollar. Alternatively, sales can be shown in terms of units sold whenever possible, assuming that the units do not change much over time. The data are broken down into quarters.

TABLE 10.4   MSC Sales (in 1986 Dollars)

Year	Quarter	Sales ($ millions)	Year	Quarter	Sales ($ millions)
1986	1	48.6	1990	1	58.7
	2	54.2		2	67.1
	3	59.8		3	74.2
	4	79.8		4	102.8
1987	1	49.5	1991	1	65.3
	2	56.0		2	72.3
	3	63.5		3	78.3
	4	85.5		4	111.2
1988	1	54.7	1992	1	72.1
	2	59.9		2	82.0
	3	65.0		3	91.6
	4	89.0		4	127.5
1989	1	57.0	1993	1	82.3
	2	63.9		2	92.0
	3	68.6		3	96.7
	4	94.2		4	134.9

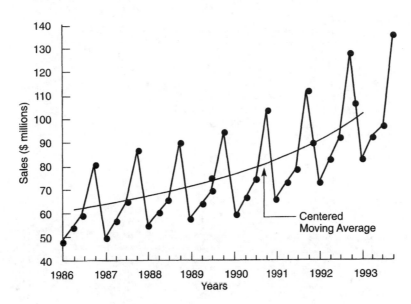

Figure 10.11

A graph of the data

Graph shows trend and seasonals

The data are graphed in Figure 10.11. From this graph it is evident that seasonal variations exist. It is also clear that there is an upward trend. The other variations (cyclical and random) are not visible from the graph.

Step 3. Measure the Trend and the Cycle ($T \times C$ Combined)

In step 3, we separate the trend and the cycle from the seasonal and random variations. One way to execute this separation is to use annual data as the basis for computation. Such a separation will eliminate seasonal differences and most of the random variations. However, in order to compare these annualized values to the original quarterly observations, they must be made comparable in both magnitude and timing. The annualized

Annualize the data

values can be made comparable in size by converting the annual total to a monthly or quarterly average (dividing the total by 12 or 4). The following procedure ensures that the annualized values and the original observations are comparable both in size and in timing.

Calculate a moving average

Calculate a 4-quarter *moving average*. This is done by averaging the first four quarters. Then the oldest quarter (1) is dropped, quarter 5 is added instead, the average of the new four quarters is computed, and so on. Each average is placed at the midpoint of the dates of the included observations (see Table 10.5). Thus, the first average refers to a point in time midway between the dates of the second and third quarterly observations, the second is a point between the third and fourth quarters, and so on.

Example

The moving average for MSC is shown in column 2 of Table 10.5. Note that this column is shown one-half line offset from the sales data. Therefore, it is necessary to

TABLE 10.5 Moving Average for MSC

Year	Quarter	(1) Sales ($ millions)	(2) Moving Average	(3) Centered Moving Average $T \times C$	(4) Ratio of Sales to Moving Average $(1) \div (3)$
1986	1	48.6			
	2	54.2			
	3	59.8 ÷ 4 =	60.60 ÷ 2 =	60.71	0.9850
	4	79.8	60.82	61.05	1.3071
1987	1	49.5	61.28	61.74	0.8017
	2	56.0	62.20	62.91	0.8902
	3	63.5	63.62	64.27	0.9880
	4	85.5	64.92	65.41	1.3071
1988	1	54.7	65.90	66.09	0.8276
	2	59.9	66.28	66.72	0.8978
	3	65.0	67.15	67.44	0.9638
	4	89.0	67.72	68.22	1.3046
1989	1	57.0	68.72	69.17	0.8241
	2	63.9	69.62	70.27	0.9093
	3	68.6	70.92	71.14	0.9643
	4	94.2	71.35	71.75	1.3129
1990	1	58.7	72.15	72.85	0.8058
	2	67.1	73.55	74.62	0.8992
	3	74.2	75.70	76.52	0.9697
	4	102.8	77.35	78.00	1.3179
1991	1	65.3	78.65	79.16	0.8249
	2	72.3	79.68	80.73	0.8956
	3	78.3	81.78	82.63	0.9476
	4	111.2	83.48	84.69	1.3130
1992	1	72.1	85.90	87.56	0.8234
	2	82.0	89.22	91.26	0.8985
	3	91.6	93.30	94.58	0.9685
	4	127.5	95.85	97.10	1.3131
1993	1	82.3	98.35	98.98	0.8315
	2	92.0	99.62	100.55	0.9150
	3	96.7	101.48		
	4	134.9			

center the moving average by averaging the two adjacent averages in column 2. This centered moving average is shown in column 3 and Figure 10.11; it represents the value $T \times C$. The first value in this column is the centered moving average for the third quarter of 1986. Thus, the first period for which a centered moving average is available is *not* the first period for which raw data are available. When quarterly data are used, two quarters are lost at the beginning and again at the end of the data.

Note: A choice of an odd number as a basis for computing the moving average would eliminate the need to center the data. However, using a four-quarter moving av-

Represent all time periods

erage has a statistical advantage over the use of three or five quarters in that all seasons are represented once and only once.

Column 4 of Table 10.5 shows the ratio of each quarterly sales value to the centered moving average. This column will be used in the computation of the seasonal and the random variations in Steps 6–8.

Step 4. Separating the Effect of the Trend (T)

Two ways to find the trend

The moving average, as computed in column 3 of Table 10.5, represents $T \times C$. Our task is to separate T from C. Several methods exist for determining the trend. Two popular methods are *freehand* and the *least square*.

a. *Freehand:* This method is straightforward; it involves the freehand fitting of a smooth line that, in the judgment of the forecaster; is a *good fit* to the moving average. This method is simple but not accurate. Therefore, projections that are made on the basis of this graphical approach can be inaccurate. A freehand fit is demonstrated in Figure 10.12. The $T \times C$ data are from column 3 of Table 10.5.

b. *Least-square (regression) analysis:* If the trend line appears to be linear, as in Figure 10.7a, or if it is possible to segment the trend line into linear portions, as in Figure 10.7c, then linear **regression analysis** can be used.

The intercept and slope of the trend line equation

In our example, the trend (Figure 10.12) appears to follow a straight line. In order to project this linear trend into the future, we must first estimate the parameters of the trend line. The parameters of a straight line are the Y-axis intercept and the slope. The *Y-axis intercept* is the value of Y where the trend line crosses the *Y-axis* (at $X = 0$).

FIGURE 10.12

Drawing a freehand trend line

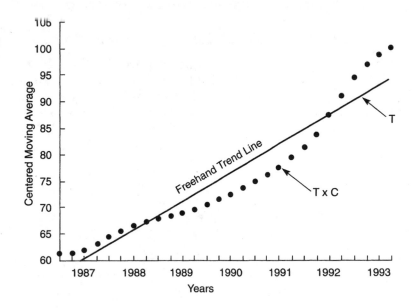

The *slope* is the amount of change in Y for a one-period change in X. There are several procedures for estimating these values, but least squares regression is the most widely used method. This method uses the following *estimated regression equation:*

$$T_x = a + bX \tag{10.9}$$

where:

> **Least squares regression is most commonly used for trend determination**

T_x = The trend *forecasted* value of sales Y for period number X
a = The estimate of the Y-axis intercept
b = The estimate of the slope of the line
X = The period number
Y = Actual sales (historical data)

The two equations used to determine a and b are:

$$b = \frac{\Sigma XY - n\bar{X}\bar{Y}}{\Sigma X^2 - n\bar{X}^2} \tag{10.10}$$

and

$$a = \bar{Y} - b\bar{X} \tag{10.11}$$

where:

ΣXY = X times Y for each period, summed over all of the periods
ΣX^2 = X squared for each period, summed over all of the periods
$\bar{X}$ = The average of the X values
$\bar{Y}$ = The average of the Y values
n = The number of periods of data used in the regression

Using Least Squares Regression for the MSC Corp.

Using the data from column 3 of Table 10.5, we can compute the slope and the intercept of the trend equation. To simplify the computations, we will arrange the data into four columns, as shown in Table 10.6. The numbers in column 3 are simply column 1 numbers squared and the numbers in column 4 are computed by multiplying the numbers in column 1 by the corresponding number from column 2. To compute the slope of the regression line (b) we need the average of column 1, which is:

$$\bar{X} = \frac{\Sigma X}{n} = \frac{406}{28} = 14.5$$

and the average of column 2, which is:

$$\bar{Y} = \frac{\Sigma Y}{n} = \frac{2126.12}{28} = 75.93$$

In addition, we need the total of columns 3 and 4. In our algebraic notation, ΣXY is the sum of column 4.

TABLE 10.6 **Least Squares Trend Data**

(1) Quarter Number X	(2) Sales ($ millions) Y	(3) X²	(4) XY
1	60.71	1	60.71
2	61.05	4	122.10
3	61.74	9	185.22
4	62.91	16	251.64
5	64.27	25	321.35
6	65.41	36	392.46
7	66.09	49	462.63
8	66.72	64	533.76
9	67.44	81	606.96
10	68.22	100	682.20
11	69.17	121	760.87
12	70.27	144	843.24
13	71.14	169	924.82
14	71.75	196	1004.50
15	72.85	225	1092.75
16	74.62	256	1193.92
17	76.52	289	1300.84
18	78.00	324	1404.00
19	79.16	361	1504.04
20	80.73	400	1614.60
21	82.63	441	1735.23
22	84.69	484	1947.87
23	87.56	529	2013.88
24	91.26	576	2190.24
25	94.58	625	2364.50
26	97.10	676	2524.60
27	98.98	729	2672.46
28	100.55	784	2815.40
$\Sigma X = 406$	$\Sigma Y = 2126.12$	$\Sigma X^2 = 7714$	$\Sigma XY = 33442$

The slope can then be computed by using Equation 10.10:

$$b = \frac{33442 - 28(14.5)75.93}{7714 - 28(14.5)^2} = 1.43$$

which means that the sales volume is, on the average, increasing by $1.43 million every quarter.

The *Y*-axis intercept is computed from Equation 10.11:

$$a = 75.93 - 1.43(14.5) = 55.20$$

which means that the initial sales volume (at time $X = 0$) would have been $55.20 million.

The estimated regression equation for the trend in sales volume is therefore (in millions of dollars):

$$T_x = 55.20 + 1.43X$$

Step 5. Computing the Cycle

Freehand or regression

In step 4, we showed how to find T, either by freehand or by finding the values of T for each quarter. If the freehand method is used, then one can read the values directly from the graph. If regression is used, one can calculate the value of T for each quarter. Table 10.7 shows the values of T, by quarter (in column 3) as calculated from the

TABLE 10.7   Computing the Trend and the Cycle

(1) Quarter X	(2) Centered Moving Average (CMA)	(3) Trend T	(4) Cycle C = CMA/T
1*	60.71	56.62	1.07
2	61.05	58.05	1.05
3	61.74	59.48	1.04
4	62.91	60.91	1.03
5	64.27	62.34	1.03
6	65.41	63.77	1.03
7	66.09	65.20	1.01
8	66.72	66.64	1.00
9	67.44	68.07	0.99
10	68.22	69.50	0.98
11	69.17	70.93	0.98
12	70.27	72.36	0.97
13	71.14	73.79	0.96
14	71.75	75.22	0.95
15	72.85	76.65	0.95
16	74.62	78.08	0.96
17	76.52	79.51	0.96
18	78.00	80.94	0.96
19	79.16	82.37	0.96
20	80.73	83.80	0.96
21	82.63	85.23	0.97
22	84.69	86.66	0.98
23	87.56	88.09	0.99
24	91.26	89.52	1.02
25	94.58	90.95	1.04
26	97.10	92.38	1.05
27	98.98	93.81	1.06
28	100.55	95.24	1.06

* Quarter 1 is the third quarter of 1986.

regression equation. For example, the value for the third quarter of 1986 ($X = 1$) is:

$$T_1 = 55.20 + 1.43(1) = 56.62$$

and for the "last" quarter (the 28th):

$$T_{28} = 55.20 + 1.43(28) = 95.24$$

Notice also that in column 2 we reproduced from Table 10.5, column 3 the values of the centered moving average (CMA). We can now calculate the values of C as:

$$C = \text{CMA}/T = \frac{T \times C}{T} \qquad (10.12)$$

where CMA represents the $T \times C$ values. For example, for the third quarter ($X = 1$) we get:

$$C = 60.71/56.62 = 1.07$$

Using this approach, the cyclical movements are expressed as a percentage of the trend. The results appear in column 4 of Table 10.7.

A mild cycle

As shown in Figure 10.13, the cyclical movements are fairly mild and the span of the cycle covers quite a few years. The trend line in Figure 10.13 is shown by the horizontal 100 percent line.

FIGURE 10.13

Graphing the cycle

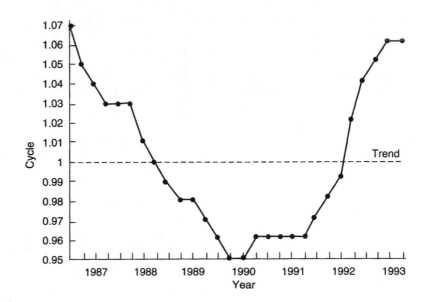

Step 6. Measuring the Combined Effects of Seasonal and Random Variations

Separating the components

The decomposition method assumes that the original data are the product of $T \times C \times S \times R$. Previously, we assumed the value of $T \times C$ to be the centered moving average. Therefore, the value of $S \times R$ can be calculated as:

$$S \times R = \frac{T \times C \times S \times R}{T \times C} = \frac{\text{Original data}}{\text{Centered Moving Average}}$$

This computation was executed in column 4 of Table 10.5. Note that the value $S \times R$ is thus expressed as a *percentage* of the corresponding moving average.

Step 7. Compute the Seasonal Variations

Repetitive patterns

The term *seasonal variation* can apply to any repetitive pattern in a time series where the interval of time to completion of the pattern is one year or less. Thus, the term could be used to describe not only a monthly or quarterly pattern within a year, but also a weekly pattern within a month, a daily pattern within a week, or even an hourly pattern within a day. By observing the graph of our original data, it seems that we do have quarterly variations.

In order to compute the value of S, we regroup the $S \times R$ values (column 4 in Table 10.5) by period. That is, all first quarters together, all second quarters, and so on. This is shown in Table 10.8.

The next task is to find the values of the quarterly indices. There are several ways to proceed in finding these values. For example, simply take the arithmetic mean of the entries in each quarter. However, it is usually considered to be more reasonable to con-

Drop extreme values

struct a modified mean. A modified mean is found by striking out the highest and lowest value for each quarter and averaging the remaining values. This is done in order to

---

TABLE 10.8   Quarterly Ratios of Sales to Centered Moving Average

Year	Quarter			
	1	*2*	*3*	*4*
1986			0.9850	1.3071
1987	0.8017	0.8902	0.9880	1.3071
1988	0.8276	0.8978	0.9638	1.3046
1989	0.8241	0.9093	0.9643	1.3129
1990	0.8058	0.8992	0.9697	1.3179
1991	0.8249	0.8956	0.9476	1.3130
1992	0.8234	0.8985	0.9685	1.3131
1993	0.8315	0.9150		

remove the influences of any unusual quarter. But when an unusually high (low) value is removed, it is necessary to remove the lowest (highest) value as well, so that the mean of the remaining values still represents a useful measure of central tendency. If the data are highly volatile, it might be desirable to strike out two or even three low values and a similar number of high values, depending on the number of years of data.

Normalize the means

The modified mean for Mercantile Stores is constructed in Table 10.9. For each column, the highest and lowest values are struck out. The remaining values are averaged. Because the averages do not total precisely to 4.00, they have to be adjusted so that their total is 4 (within the limit of rounding) by multiplying each modified mean by 4 and dividing by the actual total of modified means. These adjusted modified means are: .820, .900, .970, and 1.310, and when we multiply each by 100, we get the seasonal indices.

Seasonal Adjustment of Data

The seasonal indices will be used to compute the random variations (R). They can also be used to adjust the original data. This is done by dividing the original data by the ap-

TABLE 10.9 Computation of Seasonal Indices

	Quarter			
Year	*1*	*2*	*3*	*4*
1986			0.9850	1.3071
1987	0.8017	0.8902	0.9880	1.3071
1988	0.8276	0.8978	0.9638	1.3046
1989	0.8241	0.9093	0.9643	1.3129
1990	0.8058	0.8992	0.9697	1.3179
1991	0.8249	0.8956	0.9476	1.3130
1992	0.8234	0.8985	0.9685	1.3131
1993	0.8315	0.9150		
Modified total	4.1058	4.5004	4.8513	6.5532
Modified mean	0.82116	0.90008	0.97026	1.31064
Adjusted modified mean	0.820	0.900	0.970	1.310
Seasonal index	82.00	90.00	97.00	131.00

Calculations:

Total of modified means $= 0.82116 + 0.90008 + 0.97026 + 1.31064 = 4.00214$
Adjusted modified means:

$$\text{Quarter 1: } 0.82116 \times \frac{4.0}{4.00214} = \boxed{0.820} \qquad \text{3: } 0.97026 \times \frac{4.0}{4.00214} = \boxed{0.970}$$

$$\text{2: } 0.90008 \times \frac{4.0}{4.00214} = \boxed{0.900} \qquad \text{4: } 1.31064 \times \frac{4.0}{4.00214} = \boxed{1.310}$$

propriate index, multiplied by 100. For example, for the first quarter of 1986 (Table 10.5), we get:

$$\frac{48.6 \times 100}{82.0} = 59.2$$

This adjustment can also be done on forecasted data for any desired time period in the future, as will be shown later. There are also more sophisticated methods of seasonal adjustment (consult the bibliography).

Step 8. Measuring the Random (Unexplained) Variations
In Step 6, we identified the value $S \times R$; to compute R, all we have to do is divide this value (column 4 in Table 10.5) by the seasonal index S. For example, for quarter 1 (third quarter of 1986) we get:

$$R = \frac{S \times R}{S} = \frac{0.9850}{0.97} = 1.016$$

Risk analysis

Table 10.10 shows the random values for quarters 1 through 28. In our example, the random variations are fairly small and the forecaster may wish to ignore them. However, these variations are used in the risk analysis approach demonstrated in the next step.

Step 9. Develop a Forecast
The decomposition procedure for a time series is reversed in order to predict future values of the time series. As always, it is cautioned that any prediction is better thought of as a projection from past data. If the basic forces underlying the time series change, the future values of the time series may not reflect the behavior indicated by past values.

TABLE 10.10   The Random Variations

Quarter Number	Random R	Quarter Number	Random R
1	1.016	15	.983
2	.998	16	.991
3	.978	17	1.000
4	.989	18	1.006
5	1.019	19	1.006
6	.998	20	.995
7	1.010	21	.977
8	.998	22	1.002
9	.994	23	1.004
10	.996	24	.998
11	1.005	25	.998
12	1.010	26	1.002
13	.994	27	1.014
14	1.002	28	1.017

There are several methods of developing the forecast. One of them is briefly introduced next.

Let us assume that we would like to forecast the demand for the year 1996 and for each quarter of that year. Because we labeled the third quarter of 1986 as 1 in order to calculate the centered moving average, then the last quarter of 1993 is 30. Therefore, the four quarters of 1996 are numbered as 39, 40, 41, and 42. The computation involves four operations.

Four steps in making the forecast

a. Compute the Trend Line (Extrapolation into the Future).   The trend line was computed in step 4 as a linear equation:

$$T = 55.20 + 1.43X$$

where X designates the appropriate quarter. Using this equation for the four quarters, we get:

1st quarter 1996 (39); $y = 55.20 + 1.43(39) = 110.97$
2nd quarter 1996 (40); $y = 55.20 + 1.43(40) = 112.40$
3rd quarter 1996 (41); $y = 55.20 + 1.43(41) = 113.83$
4th quarter 1996 (42); $y = 55.20 + 1.43(42) = 115.26$

b. Seasonal Adjustment.   The trend projections for 1996 are now each multiplied by the appropriate seasonal index:

1st quarter 1996 =   (.820)110.97 =   91.10
2nd quarter 1996 =   (.900)112.40 = 101.16
3rd quarter 1996 =   (.970)113.83 = 110.42
4th quarter 1996 = (1.310)115.26 = 150.99

c. Cyclical Adjustment.   The seasonally adjusted data can now be further adjusted for the *cyclical* variation. This is a most difficult task since the cyclical movements are of an irregular nature. One approach is to use a freehand extrapolation of the business cycle. Another approach is to consult experts in the field. The cyclical adjustment can be made for each quarter or for an entire year, in terms of a decimal.

Using a freehand prediction (extending Figure 10.13), we might establish the following cyclical adjustments for the four quarters:

1st quarter 1996 = .97
2nd quarter 1996 = .96
3rd quarter 1996 = .95
4th quarter 1996 = .96

These figures are then multiplied by the seasonally adjusted data. The result, $T \times S \times C$, is:

1st quarter 1996 =   91.10 × .97 =   88.37
2nd quarter 1996 = 101.16 × .96 =   97.11
3rd quarter 1996 = 110.42 × .95 = 104.90
4th quarter 1996 = 150.99 × .96 = 144.95

d. Inclusion of the Random Variations: Risk Analysis. The R values computed in
Step 8 (Table 10.10) are used to construct a cumulative probability distribution that describes the uncertainty surrounding the forecasts based on T, S, and C. The cumulative
probability distribution for our case is shown in Figure 10.14a (and ranges from .977 to
1.019, per Table 10.10).

The forecaster can now perform a risk analysis by combining the $T \times S \times C$ information with the data in Figure 10.14a. We illustrate such a combination for the first
quarter of 1996 in Figure 10.14b. Notice that the forecast for the first quarter of 1996
was calculated as \$88.37 million. This value is aligned with the value of 1.00 in Figure
10.14b. The range of sales in this quarter is therefore predicted to be between 86.34

FIGURE 10.14

*Risk analysis based
on R values*

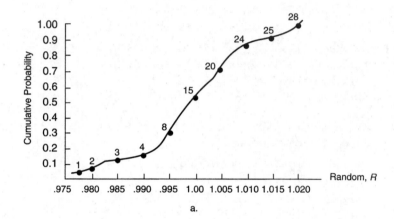

a.

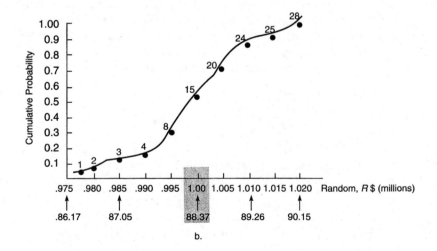

b.

Forecast variability

(i.e., 88.37 × .977) and 90.06 (88.37 × 1.019). In our case, the range is fairly narrow because the random variations are minimal. In other cases, one may see a distribution of plus or minus 20 percent or more around the mean. In such a case, the actual plans will be determined by the corporate attitude toward risk. Finally, all dollar values should, of course, be adjusted for inflation.

10.10 Double Exponential Smoothing

Trend correction can also be accomplished with exponential smoothing, as was done with the original data. In this case we add an equation to smooth the trend and then include the trend in our forecast. The original data is first averaged, smoothed, and corrected for trend with the following equation.

$$R_t = \alpha D_t + (1 - \alpha)(R_{t-1} + T_{t-1}) \tag{10.13}$$

The smoothed trend, T, is then obtained with another smoothing constant, β:

$$T_t = \beta(R_t - R_{t-1}) + (1 - \beta)T_{t-1} \tag{10.14}$$

The forecast for the next period is then:

$$F_{t+1} = R_t + T_t \tag{10.15}$$

These calculations are illustrated for the Lakeland Health Center data in Table 10.11 with $\alpha = 0.1$ and $\beta = 0.1$.

Comparing the results to Table 10.2 we see that correction for the trend improves the forecasts somewhat for the same smoothing constant (0.1). It is also possible to use exponential smoothing for the seasonals, but that is beyond the scope of this text. Consult the chapter bibliography for further information.

TABLE 10.11 **Exponential Forecasting with Trend for the Lakeland Health Center (Data in Thousands)**

Year	Quarter	A	R	T	F
1990	1	3.5	3.50	—	—
	2	8.0	3.95	.05	—
	3	5.5	4.15	.06	4.0
	4	10.0	4.79	.12	4.21
1991	1	4.5	4.87	.12	4.91
	2	6.0	5.10	.13	4.99
	3	.	.	.	5.23
	.	.	.	.	.
	.	.	.	.	.
	.	.	.	.	.

Management Science in Practice

Forecasting Hospital Nursing Requirements

The explosive growth in the costs of health care have become a major national concern. Over half the operating budget of most hospitals is for payroll, and nursing typically represents the largest single group of this portion of the budget. Thus, the more efficiently and effectively a hospital can employ its nursing pool, the better control it will have over both quality of care as well as escalating health care costs.

The major factor in planning nursing requirements is an accurate forecast of patients requiring care, disaggregated by care level required, ward location (diagnosis), and time. Given this information, nursing hour requirements can be determined through standard hospital ratios that identify the hours of nursing care required per patient. For example, surgical patients at the lowest care need level require 1.5 hours of care per patient each month whereas patients at the highest care need level require 8 hours per month.

The purpose of the study reported on here was to forecast the patient load for a 220-bed, nonprofit community hospital in an urban setting; a typical, short-term, acute-care hospital. A total of 9,687 observations constituting the patient population for a full year's duration was initially gathered to test the forecasting model. A multiple-regression model was formulated that included the major wards of the hospital, the specific times, the care levels, and a growth trend factor. The wards included intensive and coronary care (combined), psychiatric, medical, surgical, orthopedic, pediatrics, obstetrics, and nursery. The times were identified by month; day of the week; and day, evening, or night shift. The required intensity of care was divided into six different levels, numbered CL1 (easiest) through CL6 (most serious). The growth trend was captured simply by the numbered day of the year (1–365).

The resulting equations tended to correlate well with the actual data for the year and gave the hospital administrator valuable information for estimating future nursing requirements. It was found, for example, that there was a definite seasonality in the more critical care situations, with the latter months of the year having more of these serious care patients and the earlier months (January on) having fewer. This trend was present for lower care need patients also, but much less pronounced.

There was also a slight negative trend in patient growth over time. Also, less serious cases typically arrived toward the middle of the week, avoiding the weekends, whereas the more serious cases had almost no pattern. And, as might be expected, the intensive and coronary care wards generally had the more serious cases and the medical, surgical, orthopedic, obstetric, and nursery wards tended to have the less serious cases.

The model outputs have also been compared to the standard hours estimated by the nursing staff. Knowing the distribution of nursing hours by shift, day of the week, and month of the year has identified several areas for more detailed analysis by the staff. A future study will consider the skill mix among nursing types.

Source: F. T. Helmer, E. B. Oppermann, J. D. Suver, "Forecasting Nursing Staffing Requirements by Intensity-of-Care Level," *Interfaces*, June 1980, pp. 50–55.

Questions:

1. What forecasting tools were used in this application?

2. For July 17, 1993, the forecast was for 25 patients for the day shift requiring a medium level of care and 15 patients requiring a high level of care in the surgical ward. How should the administrator go about deciding how many nurses to schedule for this shift for this ward?

TABLE 10.12 Representative Micro Forecasting Packages

Name	Vendor
Autobox, BOXX	Automatic Forecasting Systems, Inc. (Hatboro, Penn.).
EXEC*U*STAT	EXEC*U*STAT Inc. (Princeton, N.J.).
ForeCalc, Forecast Pro	Business Forecast Systems, Inc. (Belmont, Md.)
Forecast GFX	Index Solutions (Needham, Mass.)
Forecast Master	Scientific Systems, Inc. (Cambridge, Mass.).
Forecast Plus	Walonick Associates (Minneapolis, Minn.).
Futurcast	Futurion Assoc., Inc. (Pittsburg, Calif.)
Smart Forecast	Smart Software, Inc. (Belmont, Mass.)
Soritec Econometrics	The Soritec Group (Springfield, Va.).
Systat	Systat Inc. (Evanston, Ill.).
Tomorrow	Isogon Corp. (New York, N.Y.)
1,2,3 Forecast	1,2,3 Forecast (Salem, Ore.).

10.11 Computerization

Forecasting methods easily lend themselves to computerization, and indeed, dozens of software packages are available on the market for any type of computer.

Table 10.12 includes 13 representative software packages for PCs. In addition, many standard statistical packages (such as SAS and SPSS) include routines for forecasting. Some of the packages allow users to include their own judgmental values.

10.12 Concluding Remarks

This chapter described the need and uses of forecasts and the factors that influence the choice of the forecasting approach. The various forecasting approaches—qualitative, counting, time-series analysis, and causal—were described and illustrated.

The most common types of qualitative forecasting approaches are market surveys, expert opinion, and Delphi. Time-series analysis includes moving averages, exponential smoothing, decomposition models, and Box-Jenkins. Causal forecasting methods consist of multiple regression, econometric models, and input-output. These complex (usually computerized) models take much skill and time for construction.

Measures of forecast accuracy include the mean absolute deviation (MAD) and bias. The MAD measures the average error, ignoring whether the error is positive or negative, of a set of forecasts compared to the actual result. The bias includes the sign (direction) of the error, positive errors meaning the forecast was too high. The forecasting method with both the smallest MAD and bias is the best.

10.13 Problems for Part B

13. Develop a linear regression equation to predict demand in the future from the data below.

Demand	23	24	31	28	29
Year	1989	1990	1991	1992	1993

14. Determine the linear regression trend equation and seasonals for the data below.

Units	5	4	3	5	6	5	4	6
Quarter	1	2	3	4	5	6	7	8

15. Determine in Problem 13 if odd-numbered years are different from even-numbered years by calculating "seasonals" for each.

16. Predict quarter 10 in Problem 14 by linear regression and seasonals and calculate the current MAD and bias.

17. Develop a demand regression equation for the data below and predict demand at a price of $4 and a price of $9.

Price, $	7	6	8	5
Demand	1,050	1,100	1,020	1,130

18. *a.* Demand for snow tires in Toronto depends on the snowfall; the history for the last 10 years follows. Use the data to develop a linear regression equation for snow tire demand. Calculate the MAD and the bias and predict 1994 demand if weather forecasters predict 22 inches of snowfall.

Year	Snowfall (inches)	Demand
1984	25.0	2050
1985	27.6	1944
1986	22.4	2250
1987	24.0	1700
1988	28.2	1842
1989	22.2	2404
1990	23.4	1756
1991	25.2	1780
1992	23.8	2144
1993	24.6	1862

b. A friend in the used auto business thinks you might get a better forecast by considering the possibility that demand *lags* snowfall by a year. That is, consider the possibility that demand is related to the snowfall in the *previous* year and develop a new regression equation, MAD, bias, and 1994 prediction. Is the result better or worse?

19. Given the following toy store data on "Rube's Triangle," a toy for children from 5 to 85 years:

Month	J	F	M	A	M	J	J	A	S	O
Demands (000s)	0.2	0.5	1.0	2	4	8	25	45	59	66

a. Forecast November demand by a three-month moving average.
b. Forecast November demand by exponential forecasting with an alpha of 0.3.
c. Forecast November demand by linear regression.
d. Plot the data and the linear trend line from (*c*). What does it look like is happening? Can you intuitively forecast November?

20. Vollo, Inc., of Sweden, is preparing a prediction of its U.S. sales for 1995. The information is as follows:

Quarter	Trend line	Cycle	Seasonal Index
Winter	80,000	1.05	.70
Spring	88,000	1.10	.90
Summer	96,000	1.00	1.10
Fall	104,000	.90	1.30

Calculate the number of units to be produced each quarter for the U.S. market.

21. The cyclical residuals of the Japanese demand for black-and-white TVs are given below.

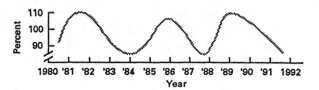

a. Estimate the cyclical values of the demand for the years 1994, 1995, and 1996.
b. The trend line for demand is forecast (in thousands of units) by the equation $y = 50 + 10x$, where x is the time ($x = 0$ in 1984) and y is the annual demand. The quarterly seasonal percent indices are: quarter 1—92; quarter 2—106; quarter 3—104; and quarter 4—98. Predict the demand for each quarter of 1995.
c. Given the cumulative distribution of the unexplained variation curve below, find the probability of demand being 140,000 units or less in 1994.

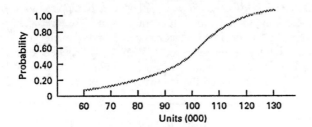

22. The sales history of Swedish Machine Parts, Ltd. is given in units below:

	Period	Value
1983	1	456.00
	2	543.00
	3	457.00
	4	486.00
1984	5	444.00
	6	534.00
	7	478.00
	8	496.00
1985	9	468.00
	10	550.00
	11	487.00
	12	490.00
1986	13	488.00
	14	560.00
	15	499.00
	16	494.00

	Period	Value
1987	17	490.00
	18	550.00
	19	502.00
	20	510.00
1988	21	570.00
	22	500.00
	23	492.00
	24	512.00
1989	25	502.00
	26	594.00
	27	513.00
	28	510.00
1990	29	498.00
	30	593.00
	31	520.00
	32	514.00
1991	33	506.00
	34	588.00
	35	510.00
	36	503.00
1992	37	550.00
	38	600.00
	39	534.00
	40	512.00
1993	41	545.00
	42	612.00
	43	542.00
	44	542.00

Use a computer package to find:
a. The forecast for period 45 by exponential smoothing ($\alpha = 0.3$).
b. Period 45 forecast by centered moving average.
c. The trend equation.
d. The seasonal indices.
e. The cycle.
f. Random variations.
g. Predict quarter 1 of 2001 and quarter 2 of 2002.
h. Predict the total for 2003.

23. Use double exponential smoothing with $\alpha = 0.3$ and $\beta = 0.1$ to predict November demand in Problem 19. Compare your answer to that found in Problem 19b.

Bardstown Box Company is a small, closely held corporation located in Bardstown, England. The stock of the company is divided among three brothers, with the principal shareholder being the founding brother, Bob Wilson. Bob formed the company 20 years ago when he resigned as a salesman for a large corrugated box manufacturer.

Bob attributes his success to the fact that he can better serve the five-district area that he considers "his territory" than can any of his large competitors. Bardstown Box supplies corrugated cartons to many regional distilleries and to several breweries. Also, standard-sized boxes are printed to order for many small manufacturing firms in the region. Bob feels that the large box manufacturers cannot economically provide this personal level of service to his accounts.

Bob recognizes the danger of becoming too dependent on any client and has enforced the policy that no single customer can account for over 20 percent of sales. Two of the distilleries account for 20 percent of sales each, and hence are limited in their purchases. Bob has convinced the purchasing agents of these two companies to add other suppliers, because this alternative supply protects them against problems Bardstown might have in shipping, paper shortages, or labor problems.

Bardstown currently has over 600 customers with orders ranging in size from a low of 100 boxes to blanket orders for 50,000 boxes per year. Boxes are produced in 16 standard sizes with special printing to customers' specifications. Bardstown's printing equipment limits their print to two colors. The standardization and limited printing allows Bardstown to be price competitive with the big producers but they also provide the service for small and "emergency" orders that large box manufacturers cannot provide.

Such personal service, however, requires tight inventory control and close production scheduling. So far, Bob Wilson has always forecast demand and prepared production schedules through experience, but because of the ever-growing number of accounts and changes in personnel in customer purchasing departments, the accuracy of his forecasting has been rapidly declining. The number of back orders is on the increase, late orders are more common, and inventory levels of finished boxes

are on the increase. A second warehouse has recently been leased due to the overcrowded conditions in the main warehouse. Plans are to move some of the slower moving boxes to the leased space.

There has always been an increase in demand for boxes prior to the Christmas holiday season, when customers begin stocking for holiday promotional demand. Such seasonality in demand has always substantially increased the difficulty of making a reliable forecast.

Bob Wilson feels that it is now important to develop an improved forecasting method. It should take both customer growth and seasonality into consideration. Bob believes that if such a method can be applied to forecasting total demand, it can also be used to forecast demand for the larger customers; the requirements of the smaller customers could then be integrated to smooth production and warehousing volume.

Bob has compiled the following demand data:

	Sales (in Thousands of Boxes)				
Month	1989	1990	1991	1992	1993
January	12	8	12	15	15
February	8	14	8	12	22
March	10	18	18	14	18
April	18	15	13	18	18
May	14	16	14	15	16
June	10	18	18	18	20
July	16	14	17	20	28
August	18	28	20	22	28
September	20	22	25	26	20
October	27	27	28	28	30
November	24	26	18	20	22
December	18	10	18	22	28
	195	216	209	230	265

Questions for Discussion

1. Develop a forecasting method for Bardstown and forecast total demand for 1994.

2. How might Bob improve the accuracy of the forecast?

3. Should Bob's experience with the market be factored into the forecast? How?

Glossary

Adaptive forecasting A method that automatically changes the smoothing constant in relation to model error.

Bias A tendency to always be high (or low); a measure of error.

Causal Identifying events that cause other events.

Cycle A long-term variation around the trend.

Delphi A special qualitative methodology for group forecasting.

Exponential smoothing Weighting a set of data with exponentially decreasing coefficients.

Least squares regression Estimation of a data series by minimizing the deviations of the estimate from the actual.

Life cycle curve, stretched S A growth curve that starts slowly, increases, and then slows again, taking the form of an S shape.

MAD Mean absolute deviation, a measure of forecasting error.

Moving average An average of only the last n data points.

Multiple regression A regression with several independent variables.

Random Unpredictable; occurring by chance.

Regression analysis A means of fitting a polynomial equation to a set of data.

Seasonal A regular periodic variation around the trend.

Smoothing constant The weight attached to the latest data point in an exponential smoothing model.

Tracking signal The measuring of forecast error to determine prediction accuracy.

Time Series A data series that changes with time.

Trend The long-term direction of a series of data.

References and Bibliography

1. Chatfield, C. "What is 'Best' Method of Forecasting?" *Journal of Applied Statistics* 15, (1988).
2. Farnum, N. R., and L. M. Stanton. *Quantitative Forecasting Methods*. PWS-Kent Publishing Co., 1989.
3. Georgoff, D. M., and R. G. Murdick. "Manager's Guide to Forecasting." *Harvard Business Review,* January-February 1986, pp. 110–20.
4. Granger, C. W. *Forecasting in Business and Economics*. 2nd ed. Academic Press, 1989.
5. Hoff, J. C. *A Practical Guide: Box-Jenkins Forecasting,* Belmont, Calif: Lifetime Learning Publications, 1983.
6. Linstone, H. A., and M. Turoff. *The Delphi Method: Techniques and Applications*. Reading, Mass.: Addison-Wesley Publishing, 1975.
7. Makridakis, S. and S. Wheelwright. *Forecasting Methods for Management*. Wiley, 1989.
8. Montgomery, D. C., et al. *Forecasting and Time Series Analysis*. 2nd ed. McGraw-Hill, 1990.
9. Newbold, P., and T. Bos. *Introductory Business Forecasting.* Cincinnati: South-Western Publishing Co., 1990.
10. Plane, D. R. *Business and Economic Statistics*. Rev. ed. Plano, Tex.: Business Publications, 1981.
11. Whybark, D. C. "A Comparison of Adaptive Forecasting Techniques." *The Logistics and Transportation Review* 8 (January 1973), pp. 13–26.
12. Willis, R. E. *A Guide to Forecasting for Planners and Managers*. Englewood Cliffs, N.J.: Prentice-Hall, 1987.

11 PERT, CPM and Other Networks

Part A: Basics

Part B: Extensions

Managerial projects involving a complex of interrelated activities can be modeled as "networks." Typical of these are large construction projects (dams, bridges) consisting of a number of subtasks; transportation networks connecting a number of cities; utility and piping systems; computer systems; the organization of a company; and similar cases in which a complex of branches connects, either literally or figuratively, a set of locations. A systematic analysis of these situations enables the manager to plan, monitor, and reorganize resources so that objectives can be attained efficiently and on schedule.

Of special interest among the network models are the Program Evaluation Review Technique (PERT) and the Critical Path Method (CPM). Other networks discussed in this chapter are the minimal spanning tree, the shortest route, and the maximum flow.

PART A: BASICS

The morning mail held exciting news for Judi Kosen, special projects manager for Restoration, Inc. As she anxiously opened the letter from the Proposal Committee, Environmental Projects Branch, Department of the Interior, her eyes spotted the words ". . . invite you to bid . . . ," ". . . activity network required . . ." Then, to be sure there was no mistake, she reread the good news. After rereading the letter, Judi settled back in her chair to contemplate the task before her.

Four months ago, Restoration, Inc., had requested that the Department of the Interior include them in the competition to revitalize Moose Lake in the northern part of the state. The company had developed a new technique to combat water pollution by increasing the basic amount of oxygen in a lake, called oxygenation.

Oxygenation of a lake is a very complex project involving several of the company's departments as well as outside suppliers. It requires specialized equipment and supplies and specially trained personnel. The contract would be for a period of more than half a year, a long enough time for significant changes to occur in the economy, in prices, and in the availability of resources. The Department of the Interior wanted the project to be completed on time. Therefore, the contract would contain a $2,000 penalty clause for each week beyond the 30-week completion time. Judi realized that there were many factors that could cause a delay in such a complex project and wondered if it were possible to use an activity network to minimize any delays.

As she examined all of the various factors, operations, and activities involved in the project, she felt that planning, monitoring, and controlling this job could be staggering. Then she remembered a course in operations management she had taken several years ago. The professor talked about the planning and control of large, complex projects using a network tool that had a long name and had to be abbreviated. It finally came back to her; yes—it was PERT.

11.1 Introduction To PERT and CPM

Characteristics of Project Management

Project versus production management

The Moose Lake situation is an example of *project management*. Project management is distinguished from production management primarily by the nonrepetitive nature of the work; a *project* is usually a one-time effort. Although similar work may have been done previously, or may be done in the future (Restoration, Inc., may receive a contract for the oxygenation of other lakes), it is not usually repeated in the identical manner such as cars or TV sets being manufactured on a production line. The management of projects is more complicated than the management of a production line due to the following characteristics, generally typical of all projects to a greater or lesser degree.

1. The duration of a project lasts weeks, months, or even years. During such a long period, many changes may occur, most of which are difficult to predict. Such changes may have a significant impact on project costs, technology, and resources. The longer the duration of the project, the more uncertain are the execution times and costs.

The complexity of projects

2. A project is complex in nature, involving many interrelated activities and participants from both within the organization and outside it (e.g., suppliers, sub-

contractors). (Our example is highly simplified for the purpose of easier demonstration.)

    3. Delays in completion time may be very costly. Penalties for delays may amount to thousands of dollars per day. Completing projects late may result in lost opportunities and ill will as well.

    4. Project activities are sequential. Some activities cannot start until others are completed.

    5. Projects are typically a unique undertaking, something that has not been encountered previously.

As a consequence of the above, the management of projects is rather complicated. Figure 11.1 summarizes the major characteristics of projects. Until the mid-1950s, there were no generally accepted formal techniques to aid in project management. Each manager had his or her own management scheme. However, the need for formal tools soon became apparent. Two of the best known tools that fill this need are **PERT (Program Evaluation Review Technique)** and **CPM (Critical Path Method)**. PERT was developed by the U.S. Navy with Booz, Allen & Hamilton Inc. and Lockheed Corporation to accelerate development of the Polaris missile system in the late 1950s. CPM was developed by Du Pont in the same time period as PERT.

PERT versus CPM *(margin note)*

Definitions Used in PERT and CPM

In order to explain the purpose, structure, and operation of PERT and CPM, it is helpful to define the following terms:

Activity: A time-consuming task *(margin note)*

Activity
An **activity** is an effort that requires resources and takes a certain amount of time for completion. Examples of activities are: studying for an examination, designing a part, connecting bridge girders, or training an employee.

FIGURE 11.1

Project management characteristics

Characteristics	Factors	Symptoms
Uniqueness	Uncertainty	Cost overruns
Extended duration	Uncontrollable	Schedule slippage
Complexity	Need for coordination	Insufficient technical performance
Significant outside participation	Need for priorities	Contract problems
Extensive interactions	Difficult planning	Communication difficulties, finger pointing
Multiple dependencies	High visibility	Uncoordination, foul-ups
High risk	Attention by top management	Big failures, public attention, anxiety
High profit potential	Attention by top management	Competition, external interest

Event

Event: A milestone

An **event** is a specific accomplishment at a recognizable point in time; a milestone, a checkpoint; for example, passing a course at a university, submission of engineering drafts, completion of a span on a bridge, or the arrival of a new machine. Events *do not* have a time duration per se. To reach an event, all the activities that precede it *must* be completed. An event can be viewed as a goal attained, whereas the activities leading to it can be viewed as the means of achieving it.

All preceding
activities must be
completed.

Project

A **project** is a collection of activities and events with a definable beginning and a definable end (the goal). For example: getting a college degree, patenting an invention, building a bridge, or installing new machinery.

Network

A **network** is a logical and chronological set of activities and events, graphically illustrating relationships among the various activities and events of the project.

Critical Activity

A **critical activity** is an activity that, if even slightly delayed, will hold up the scheduled completion date of the entire project.

A Path

A **path** is a sequence of adjacent activities that form a continuous path between two events.

Critical Path

A **critical path** is the sequence of critical activities that forms a continuous path between the start of a project and its completion.

The Major Differences and Similarities between PERT and CPM

PERT and CPM are very similar in their approach; however, two distinctions are usually made between them. The first relates to the way in which activity durations are estimated. In PERT, three estimates are used to form a weighted average of the expected completion time of each activity, based on a probability distribution of completion times. Therefore, PERT is considered a probabilistic tool. In CPM, there is only one estimate of duration; that is, CPM is a deterministic tool. The second difference is that CPM allows an explicit estimate of costs in addition to time. Thus, while PERT is basically a tool for planning and control of time, CPM can be used to control both the time and the cost of the project. Extensions of both PERT and CPM allow the user to manage other resources in addition to time and money, to trade off resources, to analyze different types of schedules, and to balance the use of resources.

PERT is probabilistic

CPM includes costs

The Purpose of PERT and CPM

Due to the complex nature of most projects, it is very difficult to completely eliminate the delays and the cost overruns that are typically associated with large projects. However, with the appropriate management systems for planning, organizing, and controlling, it is possible to reduce them to a reasonable level. The problem is that the cost of implementing and executing such systems can exceed their benefits because of the large amount of monitoring and reporting that is required.

8,000 activities in one project

For example, overhauling a Boeing 757 airplane may involve 8,000 different activities (work orders). To be completely in control, management must plan, organize, monitor, report, and act on each of these 8,000 work orders, either daily or perhaps even on a shift-by-shift basis. This will require an extreme amount of reporting. However, using the concept of "management by exception," management may elect to exercise tight control over only the most critical activities. The number of critical activities may be only 5 percent of the total activities; less control is then exercised over the remaining activities. *Note:* The same idea is used in inventory control, where a method called the A-B-C classification system is used to identify the most critical items that deserve more control.

"Management by exception"

The major purpose of PERT and CPM is to objectively identify these critical activities. Further, these techniques can tell us how close the remaining activities are to becoming critical. (This available delay is called *slack* or *float*.)

"Float"

Accordingly, any PERT or CPM program provides management with the following information at the minimum.

1. Which activities are critical.
2. Which activities are noncritical.
3. The amount of slack on each noncritical activity.

Other valuable information may also be provided by computerized programs, as will be shown later.

The Advantages of PERT and CPM

Detailed Planning
The use of PERT and CPM forces management to plan in detail and to define what must be done to accomplish the project's objectives on time.

Commitments and Communications
Management is forced to plan and make commitments regarding execution times and completion dates. The tools also provide for better communication among the various departments in an organization and between suppliers and the client.

Efficient Monitoring and Control
The number of critical activities in a network (especially in a large one) is only a small portion of the total activities. Identification of the critical activities enables the use of

an efficient monitoring system (mainly record-keeping and reports) to concentrate only on those activities.

Identifying Potential Problem Areas
The critical activities are also more likely to become problem areas. Once the activities are identified, contingency plans may be devised.

Proper Use of Resources
Employing PERT or CPM enables management to use resources more wisely by examination of the overall plan. Resources can be transferred to bottleneck or trouble areas from other activities.

Rescheduling
The tools enable management to follow up and correct deviations from schedule as soon as they are detected, thus minimizing delays.

Government Contracts
Several government agencies (such as the U.S. Department of Defense) require the submission of a PERT or CPM plan with bids.

Easily Understood
CPM and PERT can be easily understood because they provide a method for visualizing an entire project. Therefore, management can explain the tools to supervisors and employees in such a way that the chances of implementation are increased.

Adaptable to Computers
PERT and CPM are easily adaptable to computer use. Large projects can be planned by computers in seconds. The computer is even capable of diagramming the networks.

Tools for Decision Making
PERT and CPM allow management to check the effectiveness and efficiency of alternative ways of executing projects by examining possible trade-offs among resources (usually time and cost) and by answering "what-if" questions.

Assess Probability of Completion (in PERT Only)
The probabilities of successfully meeting deadlines, finishing early, or finishing late can be assessed by the use of PERT.

Cost-Time Trade-offs (in CPM Only)
CPM enables management to evaluate trade-offs between the cost of executing a job in a normal way or expediting activities (called **crashing**) at a higher cost so as to finish earlier.

FIGURE 11.2

PERT/CPM process

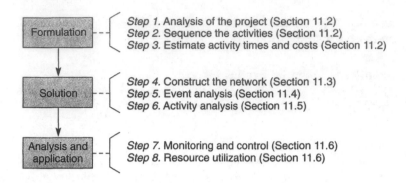

Step 1. Analysis of the project (Section 11.2)
Step 2. Sequence the activities (Section 11.2)
Step 3. Estimate activity times and costs (Section 11.2)

Step 4. Construct the network (Section 11.3)
Step 5. Event analysis (Section 11.4)
Step 6. Activity analysis (Section 11.5)

Step 7. Monitoring and control (Section 11.6)
Step 8. Resource utilization (Section 11.6)

The PERT and CPM Procedure

Three stages

The application of PERT/CPM may be divided into three phases: formulation (inputs), solution (outputs), and analysis and application. Figure 11.2 illustrates the major steps involved in each phase.

11.2 Formulation: The Basic Inputs to PERT/CPM

In order to illustrate the formulation of a PERT or a CPM network, let us return to the oxygenation problem and follow the general steps outlined in Figure 11.2.

Step 1. Analysis of the Project

After consultation with all department heads, a list of activities is agreed on (see Table 11.1). Each activity is clearly defined and responsibility is assigned to the proper department heads (not shown here).

Step 2. Sequence the Activities

Once the content of each activity is defined, the sequence of execution is determined. For example, personnel cannot be hired before proper authorization is granted (administrative setup) and equipment cannot be assembled before all parts and materials are on site. Such infomation is also shown in Table 11.1 (in the "Required immediately preceding activities" column).

Step 3. Estimate Activity Times and Costs

The next step is to determine the required **duration** (elapsed time) for each activity, designated as **expected time, t_e.** We distinguish two cases: in CPM, the activity duration is considered to be deterministic (certain). This assumption occurs when there is a wealth of experience regarding activity times (e.g., in many construction projects). In

TABLE 11.1   Moose Lake Project Activities

Activity	Description	Duration	Required Immediately Preceding Activities
a	Administrative setup	3	None
b	Hire personnel	4	a
c	Obtain materials	4	a
d	Transport materials to Moose Lake	2	c
e	Gather measuring team	4	a
f	Planning	6	c
g	Assemble equipment	3	d, b
h	Plan evaluation	1	e
i	Oxygenation	12	f, g
j	Measurement and evaluation	2	i, h

Certain or unknown

the case of PERT, however, we assume that the duration is unknown, so we use three estimates with an averaging procedure (discussed in Part B of this chapter). In both cases, we also assume that there are sufficient resources to complete the activities.

Other Input Data

In addition to time, we may also enter other information such as cost per activity (labor, parts), trade-offs between time and cost, the availability of resources, and milestone dates. The more information entered, the more output information can be provided to management.

11.3 Solving PERT and CPM

Event versus activity orientation

PERT/CPM can be solved manually (small networks) or by a computer. There are two basic network approaches: *event oriented* and *activity oriented*. Both approaches are discussed in this chapter. We will start our presentation by constructing a network and then presenting the two approaches.

Step 4. Construct the Network

The PERT (or CPM) network is a graphical representation of information such as that in Table 11.1. It shows the interrelationships among the activities, the events, and the entire project.

An activity as an arrow

To construct a PERT network, start by viewing an activity as an arrow (arc) between two events (circles). For example, the first activity of the Moose Lake Project, the "administrative setup," is shown in Figure 11.3.

The arrow points in the direction of the time flow, but its length is *not* related to the duration of the activity (it is arbitrarily set at a suitable length for drawing the dia-

An event as a node

gram). The number circled in front of the arrow, **1** in Figure 11.3, is the event that *precedes* the activity. The number circled after the arrow, **2** in Figure 11.3, is the *succeeding* event. The numbering of the events is somewhat arbitrary—several methods are used in real-life projects. The activity between events **1** and **2** is labeled *a*. It can also be labeled **1–2.**

The construction of the network starts with event **1** (the beginning of the project), which precedes the first activity, *a*. This will always be the activity (or activities) that *does not* require any preceding activity. It is placed at the left side of the diagram (similar to the start of a decision tree); the event before this activity is marked **1,** and the one after it is marked **2.** Next, the data show that activities *b*, *c*, and *e* must all be preceded by activity *a*, whose conclusion is event **2.** Therefore, all of these activities can start only after **2** has been accomplished. This is shown in Figure 11.4.

At the end of each activity, a number is assigned to designate the forthcoming event. The assignment of the numbers **3, 4,** and **5** is made as the network progresses from left to right. The representation in Figure 11.4 shows that activities *b*, *c*, and *e* can be conducted simultaneously, but none can start until activity *a* has been completed. Note that activity *c* was placed above activity *b* in the diagram; this was done merely as a matter of convenience for drawing the remaining diagram.

Project grows to the right

The construction of the entire network continues in the same manner. Out of event **3,** succeeding activities *d* and *f* are extended (Figure 11.5). Out of event **4,** the suc-

FIGURE 11.4

Precedence requirements

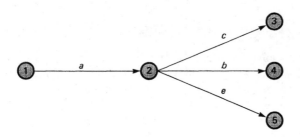

FIGURE 11.5

PERT network for Moose Lake project

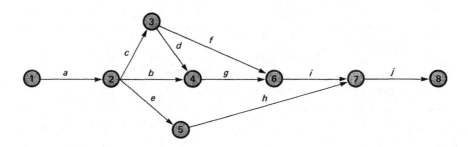

ceeding activity *g* is drawn, and out of event **5**, the succeeding activity *h* is drawn. The diagram grows to the right until all activities and events are depicted.

Some typical network relationships are illustrated in Figure 11.6. The last one includes a "dummy" activity.

Dummy Activities

Dummy activities for proper sequencing

In the construction of a network, care must be taken to assure that the activities and events are in proper sequence. One device that helps proper sequencing is **dummy activities.** Dummy activities are characterized by their use of zero time and zero resources; their only function is to designate a precedence relationship. Graphically, such activities are shown as broken lines.

Example

Given the network:

Activity	Required Preceding Activities
a	None
b	None
c	b
d	a, c
e	a
f	d, e

FIGURE 11.6

Network relationships

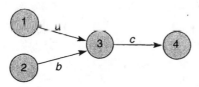

a and b can start simultaneously but c can start only after both a and b are finished.

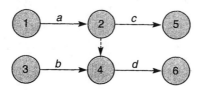

a and b can start simultaneously, c can start after a is completed but d must wait for both a and b to finish.

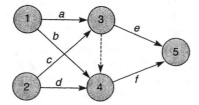

e can start after a and c are completed but f must wait until a, b, c, and d are completed.

To diagram this network, it is necessary to use a dummy activity, as shown in Figure 11.6.

FIGURE 11.7

Dummy activity

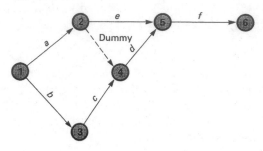

Networks Without Events (Activity-Oriented)

It is possible to draw a network composed of activities only. Figure 11.8 shows such a network (a) and its equivalent event-oriented network (b). The activity-oriented network is more cumbersome. It is used mainly in computer analysis where events are not used at all.

FIGURE 11.8

Activity- and event-oriented networks

a. Activity Oriented (no events)

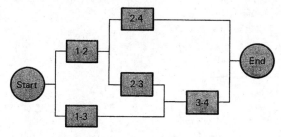

b. Event Oriented

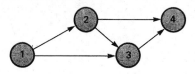

Time-Scaled Networks

A time-scaled network is one in which the activities and events are located by a time scale along the horizontal axis. The estimated duration of the activity is shown as a bar whose length is proportional to the duration. Figure 11.9 illustrates a PERT network and its equivalent bar chart. PERT can be viewed as an extension of a simple Gantt (bar) chart. The Gantt chart in Figure 11.9 shows that all activities in this project can be completed by time 6. Activity **2–4** does not start until activity **1–2** has been completed, and activity **3–4** does not start until **1–3** has been completed. Activities **1–2** and

FIGURE 11.9

Comparison of PERT and a Gantt chart

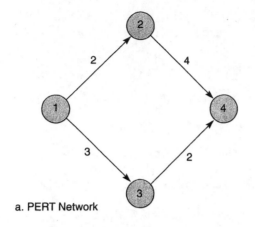

a. PERT Network

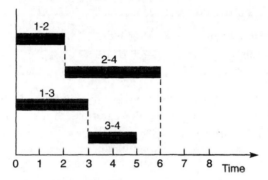

b. Equivalent Gantt Chart

2–4, however, can take place at the same time that **1–3** and **3–4** are taking place, as long as the precedence relationships are maintained.

Computer programs produce Gantt charts with dates inserted instead of elapsed time. There are several ways to depict the activities on a chart, depending on when the activities are scheduled to "start," if they are not critical.

11.4 Event Analysis (Step 5)

Event-oriented analysis is used primarily in PERT because it is especially convenient for risk analysis involving probabilities of completion.

The following procedure is used in event analysis.

a. Enter time estimates on the network.
b. Compute the earliest and latest dates for all events.

> *c*. Find the slack on the events and identify critical events.
> *d*. Find the slack on the activities and identify critical activities.
> *e*. Find the critical path.

The details of this procedure are illustrated next.

a. Enter Time Estimates on the Network

Once the network is completed, the activity durations (t_e) are entered on the diagram (in parentheses, above the arcs or arrows) as shown in Figure 11.10. (For a discussion of time estimates in PERT, see Section 11.8.)

b. Compute the Earliest and Latest Dates

This approach is based on two important concepts:

- The earliest possible event date—T_E (or ET).
- The latest allowable event date—T_L (or LT).

The Earliest Date: T_E

By definition, the **earliest date, T_E,** for an event to occur is immediately after *all* the preceding activities have been completed. For example, if a certain event is preceded by two activities, and the earliest date that activity *a* can be completed is 15 weeks, and the earliest date that activity *b* can be completed is 17 weeks, then the earliest time that the event can occur is at the conclusion of 17 weeks. Because this rule is true for every event (including the last one), then *the earliest possible date for completing the entire project is the earliest date of the last event*.

The Latest Allowable Date: T_L

The **latest allowable date** for each event, T_L, is the latest date that an event can occur *without causing a delay* in the already-determined project's completion date. The completion date for the project can be either the earliest possible completion date or any other agreed-on date. Unless otherwise stated, we will use the earliest possible completion date for our calculations. The computation is done as follows.

Earliest date of
latest activity

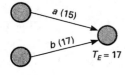

Latest date without
delay

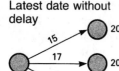

FIGURE 11.10

*Time estimates for
the project*

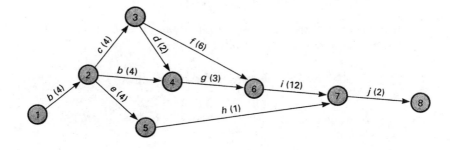

Forward pass

Path with the
longest time

Step 1. Conduct a Forward Pass: Find T_E for Each Event. In order to compute T_E for an event, the duration of each path leading to the event is computed. If several paths lead to an event, then the path with the *largest elapsed* time is selected.

Example

We will now find T_E for all events. To begin with, Figure 11.10 is reproduced as Figure 11.11.

Event **1:** This is the event at the beginning of the project. The T_E for this event is set to zero. This information is written above the event (Figure 11.11).

Event **2:** There is only one activity from event **1** to **2**; its duration is three weeks. The T_E for event **2** is thus 3.

Event **3:** Similarly, T_E for event **3** is seven weeks.

Event **4:** Note that T_E is to be determined by the longest (timewise) path leading to an event. However, it is not necessary to return to the beginning of the network to compute all paths leading to an event to figure the longest one. With the following formula, use can be made of existing information.

> Length of a path = Duration of the last activity on
> the path + T_E of the preceding event

Figure 11.12 shows the portion of the network leading to event **4.** For event **4** to be declared, both activity *d* and activity *b* must be completed. The length of the path **1–2–3–4** is determined as:

$$
\begin{array}{ll}
T_E \text{ for event } \mathbf{3} = & 7 \\
+ \text{ duration of activity } d = & \underline{2} \\
\text{Total} & 9 \\
\end{array}
$$

FIGURE 11.11

Computation of T_E and T_L

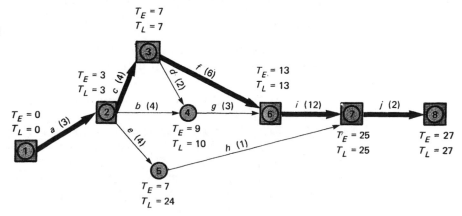

FIGURE 11.12

Event 4

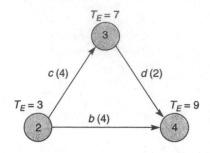

Length of a path

The length of path **1–2–4** is determined as:

$$
\begin{array}{lr}
T_E \text{ for event } \mathbf{2} = & 3 \\
+ \text{ duration of activity } b = & \underline{4} \\
\text{Total} & 7
\end{array}
$$

All paths leading to the event are now compared. Because 9 is the larger number, T_E for event **4** will be 9.

Event **5:** T_E for this event is seven weeks.

Event **6:** Two paths are considered:

path **1–2–3–6**   whose length is:

$$T_E = 7 \text{ (for event } \mathbf{3}) + 6 = 13$$

and

path **1–2–3–4–6**   whose length is:

$$9 + 3 = 12 \quad (\textit{Note:} \text{ path } \mathbf{2\text{–}3\text{–}4} \text{ is longer than } \mathbf{2\text{–}4})$$

Thus, the larger is 13 weeks.

Event **7:** Checking the two paths leading to **7**, we find T_E to be $13 + 12 = 25$.

Event **8:** This event designates the *end* of the project, because no activities emerge from it. Therefore, the earliest date for this event, 27 weeks, is the earliest date that the entire project can be completed. (This is good news for Judi, as project director, because the required complement time was 30 weeks.)

Step 2. *Conduct a Backward Pass: Find T_L for Each Event.*   (Refer to Figure 11.11)

Backward pass

To compute each T_L, start from the last event (**8**) and work backward all the way to event **1**.

For event **8:** T_L for the last event is set equal to the computed earliest completion time of the project (27 weeks).

For event **7:** Because the latest that event **8** can occur is 27 weeks, and because it takes 2 weeks to complete activity *j*, the latest allowable date that event **7** can occur is $27 - 2 = 25$ weeks.

For event **6:** Because the latest that event **7** can occur is week 25 and because activity *i* lasts 12 weeks, the latest time for event **6** is $25 - 12 = 13$.

Working backward
to find T_L

For event **5:** In a similar manner, T_L is found to be 24 (T_L for **7** is 25 minus 1 week for activity $h = 24$).

For event **4:** In a similar manner, T_L is computed as 10.

For event **3:** Here, two activities, d and f, must be considered. Because activity d lasts 2 weeks, and because it must be completed no later than the 10th week (the latest allowable time for event **4**), then activity d must start not later than $10 - 2 = 8$. Activity f takes 6 weeks; it must be completed, at the latest, by week 13 (which is T_L for event **6**). Therefore, activity f must be started *not later* than $13 - 6 = 7$.

Now, to enable both activities to start on time so that there will be no delay in the entire project, event **3** must occur, *at the latest,* by week 7, which is the *smaller* of the two T_L's. Computation is continued in the same manner, event by event, until event **1** is reached. Of special interest is event **2.** Here, three T_L's and activities must be considered. For c, $7 - 4 = 3$; for b, $10 - 4 = 6$; and for e, $24 - 4 = 20$. The *smallest one,* three weeks, is selected as T_L for event **2.** For event **1,** T_L is zero. *Note:* For the first event, T_L must be zero if $T_E = T_L$ for the last event.

Summary

Forward and
backward pass

The T_E's are computed starting from the left; this is called a **forward pass.** The T_L's are computed starting from the right side of the network, called a **backward pass.**

c. Find the Slack on the Events and Identify Critical Events

The difference between the T_L and the T_E, for each event, is defined as **slack** (S).

$$S = T_L - T_E \tag{11.1}$$

Two cases of slack

Two cases are distinguished:

1. *When $T_L = T_E$ for the last event (the end of the project).* In this case, slacks in the network can either be zero, whereupon the events are called *critical events,* or larger than zero, whereupon the events are considered to have positive slack.

In our example (Figure 11.11), we assumed $T_L = T_E$ for the final event and all critical events, which have zero slack. These are shown with a box around them to aid in quick recognition. Note that only events **4** and **5** are not critical here.

Critical events-
minimum slack

2. *When $T_L \neq T_E$ for the last event.* In this case, the *critical* events are defined as those events with the *minimum slack,* which *can* be negative (when $T_L < T_E$).

Slack as allowable
delay

What is the meaning of slack? Because T_E is the earliest that an event can be reached and T_L is the latest that the event can occur without delaying the entire project, then the difference, the slack, tells how long the event can "linger" *without* delaying the entire project. Any delay in a critical event will cause a delay in the entire project.

Let us examine event **5.** For this event, the slack is: $T_L - T_E = 24 - 7 = 17$ weeks. The meaning of this is that although event **5** can be reached in 7 weeks, management has the flexibility to reach this event at any time during the ensuing 17 weeks (up to the 24th week) without causing a delay in the entire project.

d. Find the Slack on the Activities and Identify Critical Activities

Similar to the slack on an event, there is also slack on activities. This slack tells us how long the activity can linger without delaying the entire project. Equation 11.2 can be used to find the amount of slack:

$$\text{Activity slack} = \begin{bmatrix} T_L \text{ for the event} \\ \text{at the end} \\ \text{of the activity} \end{bmatrix} - \begin{bmatrix} T_E \text{ for the event} \\ \text{at the beginning} \\ \text{of the activity} \end{bmatrix} - \begin{bmatrix} t_e \\ \text{duration} \\ \text{of the activity} \end{bmatrix} \quad (11.2)$$

Total float and free float

This slack is also called **total float (TF).** It is distinguished from a type of slack called **free float (FF),** which will be discussed later. In our example, we get the following results:

Activity	T_L	Minus	T_E	Minus	t_e	=	Slack (TF)
a	3	−	0	−	3	=	0
b	10		3		4		3
c	7		3		4		0
d	10		7		2		1
e	24		3		4		17
f	13		7		6		0
g	13		9		3		1
h	25		7		1		17
i	25		13		12		0
j	27		25		2		0

Critical activities

Again, two cases are distinguished:

1. *When $T_L = T_E$ for the last event.* In this case, an activity with zero slack is defined as a *critical activity.*
2. *When $T_L \neq T_E$ for the last event.* In this case, the activities with the *minimum slack* are the critical ones.

e. Find the Critical Path

The critical activities and events constitute the critical path

The critical path is the path(s) in the network, leading from the beginning of the project to its end, *all* of whose activities and events are critical.

This definition implies that if $T_L = T_E$ for the last event, then there is *zero slack* on the critical path. Otherwise, the critical path is that path with the minimum slack on it.

> The critical path has certain additional characteristics:
>
> 1. There can be more than one critical path in the network.
> 2. The critical path is the longest (timewise) path in the network.

In our example, the (one) critical path is:

$$1 \rightarrow 2 \rightarrow 3 \rightarrow 6 \rightarrow 7 \rightarrow 8$$

Monitoring the critical path

The importance of identifying the critical path is that it points out those activities and events that are critical and, as such, must be carefully monitored and controlled. Before getting into these topics, however, let us note some additional characteristics of the PERT/CPM network.

11.5 Activity Analysis (Step 6)

The previous method identified the critical events by computing their earliest and latest times. From this information, we derived the critical path, critical activities, and the slack. The following method can be used as an alternative for arriving at the same result. Let:

ES = **Earliest start** time for an activity. This time is equivalent to the T_E of the event from which the activity starts. We assume that all predecessor activities started at their earliest times and have been completed.

EF = **Earliest finish** time for an activity. Assuming the activity started at its ES and lasted its planned duration, t_e, then:

$$EF = ES + t_e \tag{11.3}$$

LF = **Latest finish** time for an activity. This is the latest time by which an activity can be completed without delaying the project. It is equal to the T_L of the event at the end of the activity.

LS = **Latest start** for an activity. This is the latest an activity can start without jeopardizing the project's deadline.

$$LS = LF - t_e \tag{11.4}$$

Graphical Presentation

ES, EF, LF, and LS may be presented in different ways. Three common ways are shown in Figure 11.13. Also, an event-oriented picture, (d), is included.

Example

Given: the network shown in Figure 11.14.

FIGURE 11.13

Alternative ways of presentation

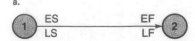

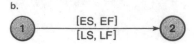

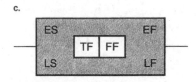

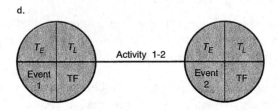

FIGURE 11.14

An example network

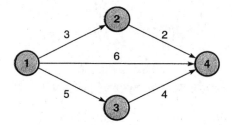

Computing ES and EF (Forward Pass)

The procedure starts from the left and moves to the right. Let the earliest start for the project be zero. (Alternatively, an actual date may be used.)

Rule for computing the ES: The earliest time for an activity is equal to the *largest value* of the earliest finish (EF) for all activities ending at the event from which the activity starts.

The computations are shown in Table 11.2.

TABLE 11.2 **Finding the ES and EF Values**

Activity	ES	EF (Eq. 11.3)
1–2	0	0 + 3 = ③
1–4	0	0 + 6 = 6
1–3	0	0 + 5 = ⑤
2–4	3	3 + 2 = 5
3–4	5	5 + 4 = 9

We start with event **1.** The ES for activities **1–2, 1–4,** and **1–3** is zero, because these are the starting activities. Next, we figure EF for these three activities using the formula EF = ES + t_e. Then, we find ES for activities **2–4** and **3–4** using the rule above. Last, we figure EF for these two activities using Equation 11.3.

Computing LF and LS (Backward Pass)

Once all ESs and EFs are computed, we start by setting the LF of all final activities to the *largest* EF (9 in our example). Alternatively, a desired finish date (larger than the largest EF) may be used (as we will discuss later) as the starting LF. Then we sequentially compute the resulting LSs, then the resulting LFs, and so on until the beginning node is reached.

> *Rule for computing the LF:* The latest finish time for an activity entering a particular event is equal to the *smallest value* of the LSs for all activities starting from that event.

The computations for Figure 11.14 are shown in Table 11.3, starting with LF=9 for event **4**.

Now, we figure the LSs for activities **2–4, 1–4,** and **3–4** using Equation 11.4 and the designated LFs. Then, we compute LF for the remaining two activities using the rule above. Finally, we compute (with Equation 11.4) the LSs for activities **1–2** and **1–3**.

TABLE 11.3 **Finding the LF and LS Values**

Activity	LF	LS (Eq. 11.4)	ES	TF (slack)
2–4	9	9 − 2 = 7	3	4
1–4	9	9 − 6 = 3	0	3
3–4	9	9 − 4 = 5	5	0
1–2	7	7 − 3 = 4	0	4
1–3	5	5 − 5 = 0	0	0

Computation of the Slack

The regular slack, also called the total float (TF), is computed as:

$$TF = LS - ES \qquad (11.5)$$

The computations are shown in Table 11.3.

Some Additional Characteristics

Regular Slack (Total Float)

Such a case is shown in Figure 11.15. Activity **1–3** has a duration of 6 weeks, whereas the path **1–2–3** has a duration of 13 weeks. Therefore, activity **1–3** can linger $13 - 6 = 7$ weeks; that is, there is a seven-week slack on the activity. Regular slack denotes the *maximum* amount of slack available, some of which may be shared.

Shared Slack (Slack on a Noncritical Path)

Whenever there are two or more noncritical activities, or noncritical events connected in a series, their slack is called **shared.** An example of **shared slack** is shown in Figure 11.16, where activities *e* and *h* are connected in series. The critical portion of the path between events **2** and **7** requires 22 weeks.

Activity *e* requires four weeks and activity *h* requires one week, a total of five weeks. Therefore, there is a slack of $22 - 5 = 17$ weeks, which can be distributed between *e* and *h* in any combination. For example, a slack of 17 on *e* and zero on *h*, 16 on *e* and 1 on *h*, and so on.

FIGURE 11.15

Regular slack

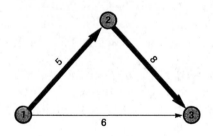

FIGURE 11.16

Shared slack, example 1

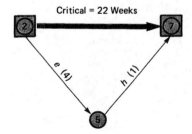

FIGURE 11.17

Shared slack, example 2

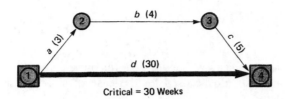

Critical = 30 Weeks

Another Example of Shared Slack. Figure 11.17 shows a situation with two noncritical events, **2** and **3,** and three noncritical activities, *a*, *b*, and *c*. Activities *a*, *b*, and *c* together require $3 + 4 + 5 = 12$ weeks. Therefore, there is a regular slack of $30 - 12 = 18$ on both events **2** and **3** (e.g., 18 on **2,** zero on **3**; 17 on **2** and 1 on **3,** and so on). That is, there is a shared slack of 18 on events **2** and **3.**

There is also a regular slack of $30 - 12 = 18$ on each of *activities a, b,* and *c,* which is shared among the three. Again, one may use the 18 weeks on activity *a* alone, or six weeks on each activity, and so on. (There are as many possibilities as there are ways of allocating 18 among three recipients.)

In a situation of shared slack, it can be viewed as being on a path, rather than on an individual activity. For example, in Figure 11.17, there is a slack of 18 on path **1–2–3–4.**

Free Float

Free float (FF) is a slack that represents the time any activity can be delayed before it delays the earliest start time of any activity immediately following. For example, in Figure 11.15, the slack of 7 on **1–3** is free, as is the slack of 17 on **5–7** in Figure 11.16. Notice that the free float on activity *e* in Figure 11.16 is zero. In general, if there are several noncritical activities in a series, only the *last one* will have a free float.

Free float is important in the case of shared slack. It means that if a slack has not been shared, it can all be used in the last sharing activity. Computer printouts typically give both the TF and the FF for each activity, as will be demonstrated later. Basically, the free float on an activity can be calculated as the early start of the successor event, minus the early finish of the activity.

The Case when $T_L \neq T_E$ for the Project

In the previous computations, we assumed that $T_L = T_E$ for the last event. However, this may not always be the case.

If T_L is larger than T_E for the last event, then the slack for the last event will be positive.

Example

In the Moose Lake project, Judi can consider T_L as 30 (the agreed-on completion time). Thus, the slack on event **8** will be $30 - 27 = 3$, and so will the slacks on all critical events. Further, the slack on all noncritical events will be three weeks larger, too. For example, for event **5**, the new $T_L = 27$; because $T_E = 7$ (unchanged), then the slack for event **5** $= 27 - 7 = 20$ weeks.

Negative slack—a delay

If T_L is smaller than T_E for the last event, a *negative slack* will result, indicating that the desired date cannot be achieved and a delay of the magnitude of the negative value is expected. Similar logic can be used for the case of starting LF calculations in an activity-oriented analysis.

A Critical Path Leading to an Event
The critical path procedure outlined previously can also be used to find the critical path leading to any desired event. For example, the critical path to event **4** is: **1–2–3–4.**

Use of Complete Enumeration
In small problems like the one in the example, the critical path may be identified by listing all possible paths leading from the beginning of the project to its end. The path with the *largest* duration is the critical path (composed of all critical activities and events). The reason for this is that in order to complete the project, all activities *must*

Compare and select the longest path

be accomplished. Because the longest path is longer than any other, its completion gives enough elapsed time to complete *all other paths*. This guarantees that every single activity in the network will be accomplished. In the Moose Lake example, the following four paths are identified:

		Total Duration (Weeks)	
Path 1	**1–2–3–4–6–7–8**	26	
Path 2	**1–2–3–6–7–8**	27	←*Maximum*
Path 3	**1–2–4–6–7–8**	24	
Path 4	**1–2–5–7–8**	10	

When *all* paths are compared (complete enumeration approach), the longest path is found to be path 2, with a duration of 27 weeks.

In large, complex networks with hundreds of activities, especially when continuous updating is required, the complete enumeration approach may take a long time. In such cases, the analytical approach is used.

Multiple Critical Paths
In our example, there is a single critical path for the project. However, in other problems, multiple paths may occur. For example, if activity *d* were three weeks, there would have been *two* critical paths. The one already identified:

Several critical paths are possible

$$1\text{–}2\text{–}3\text{–}6\text{–}7\text{–}8$$

and another one:

$$1\text{–}2\text{–}3\text{–}4\text{–}6\text{–}7\text{–}8$$

Several Starting Events

The examples given so far exhibit a single starting event. However, this is not necessary, and real projects often do have multiple starting events (e.g., see Problem 9).

11.6 Analysis and Application

Management by exception

The previous sections showed how to construct a network and find the critical activities, the noncritical activities, and the slack. Based on this information, and using the principle of *management by exception,* it is possible to construct a management system with tighter control over the critical activities and less control over the noncritical activities. Alternatively, one can use very tight control over critical activities, less control on activities with small slack, and the least control over activities with large slack. PERT/CPM can also be used to generate additional information, as will be discussed in the remainder of this section and again in Part B of this chapter.

Step 7. Monitoring and Control

Suppose that the Moose Lake project started on schedule. However, the very first activity, the administrative setup, is delayed. Although the duration of this critical activity had been estimated as three weeks, it is now clear that it will take four weeks to handle all the administrative details. Thus, when the time comes for event **2,** its T_E will be 4, rather than 3. The slack in event **2,** according to Equation 11.1, will be:

$$S = T_L - T_E = 3 - 4 = -1$$

Dealing with a delay

That is, the slack has a negative value and is labeled as *negative slack*. A negative value for a slack means that the project is behind schedule. If T_E's are now computed for all the remaining critical events, including the ending event, there will be a negative slack of 1. This implies that the *entire project* will be delayed by one week. What can management do about this?

Look, for a moment, at event **5,** which is not critical. The previous slack for this event was computed as $24 - 7 = 17$; now it will be $24 - 8 = 16$, still a positive slack.

Transferring resources to critical activities

Activities *b*, *d*, *e*, and *h* likewise possess positive slack. This means that these activities can still be delayed without delaying the entire project. Slowing down noncritical activities may release resources (such as labor, tools, and equipment) that can then be transferred to one (or more) of the critical activities. If such a transfer could reduce the completion time of any critical activity by one week, the delay could be eliminated and the project would still be completed on schedule.

A similar situation may develop if a noncritical activity such as *g* requires six, rather than three, weeks for completion. The T_E for event **6** would then be 15 weeks, and a negative slack of 2 would be formed at event **6.** Notice that the critical path will be changed to **1–2–3–4–6–7–8,** and activities *d* and *g* will become critical. In general, any deviation of the actual time from the computed duration should be reported to the project director, who in turn will recompute the critical path. Previously noncritical events and activities may become critical, and vice versa.

In addition to transferring resources to critical activities, management can correct delays by some other actions such as:

Other ways to correct delays

- Relaxing (making less strict) the technical specifications or the required quality.
- Changing the scope of the project by reducing the desired goals and consequently the amount of work.
- Changing the sequencing of activities.
- Pouring additional resources into the project.
- Expediting activities by various incentives.
- Starting activities while preceding ones are still being worked on.

Step 8. *Resource Utilization*

The regular PERT/CPM analysis is limited to planning the elapsed time. Because the planning is done prior to actual project execution, it is not always possible to know the precise resource availability, so we assume that there are sufficient resources for executing the activities as planned.

Competing for one resource

Suppose, however, that a project includes two activities that have the same early start date. In addition, they both are noncritical with three days slack and a duration of seven days. Assume that each activity requires a bulldozer throughout the duration, and it is then discovered that only one of the two bulldozers is operable. It is therefore apparent that both activities *cannot* proceed simultaneously. Because neither of them is critical, neither has a priority, and because there is not sufficient slack, then either one must be postponed, the second bulldozer must be quickly repaired, or the network must be rearranged to move one of these activities forward in time. In other words, the way that the company allocates one of its resources may affect the critical path and the completion date.

This example can be extended to cover other resources (e.g., labor, money). In general, whenever several activities need a limited resource, it is necessary to decide on how to allocate this resource. Because the regular PERT/CPM analysis essentially contains only early and late start dates for the activities, the project manager is free to decide on an actual start date between these limits. In contrast, a *resource allocation schedule* contains a scheduled start date for every activity, taking into consideration the availability of resources.

Example

The following example involves the management of labor. Assume that a project is given as shown in Figure 11.18 (times in weeks). The critical path is shown colored on the network; the earliest and latest dates for each activity are given in Table 11.4. The

FIGURE 11.18

Example of a project

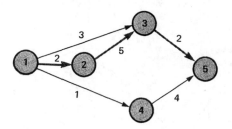

TABLE 11.4   **Earliest and Latest Dates**

Activity	Earliest Start	Latest Start	Slack (TF)	Employees
1–2	0	0	0	2
1–3	0	4	4	2
1–4	0	4	4	3
2–3	2	2	0	2
3–5	7	7	0	1
4–5	1	5	4	2

---

last column of the table lists the number of employees required each week to work on each activity. For simplicity, we assume that all the employees possess the same skill.

Solution

The project shown in Figure 11.18 is transferred to a bar chart in Figure 11.19 with each activity at its earliest starting time. In Figure 11.20, the weekly labor requirements indicate an *unbalanced demand* for labor, ranging from one to seven employees per week, that may be difficult to arrange. A more leveled schedule can be derived by delaying the noncritical activities **1–3, 1–4,** or **4–5.** Such an arrangement is shown in Figure 11.21. This arrangement reduces the peak manpower requirements to five without affecting the completion date of the project. But if only four employees are available, it would be necessary to delay the completion date of the entire project or use overtime (at an increased cost). A trial-and-error approach is used in such cases.

Finding the Best Schedule—a Trial-and-Error Approach

The reader may note that there are several different five-employee schedules with a duration of nine weeks. Similarly, more than one schedule will fit the four-employee duration. Because of this fact, the computer program that performs resource scheduling uses a trial-and-error approach with heuristics (e.g., given as priority rules) to find the *mini-*

FIGURE 11.19

Earliest start schedule

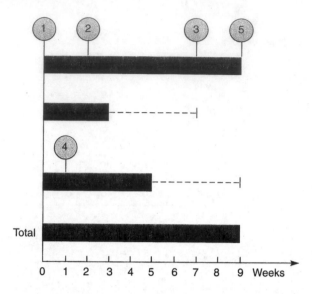

FIGURE 11.20

*Manpower require-
ment for ES schedule*

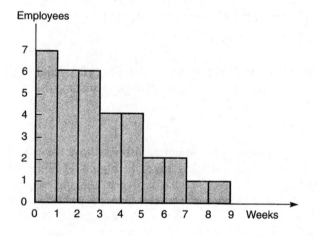

Trial-and-error
approach

mum duration. Existing programs are also able to handle multiple projects with thousands of activities that simultaneously compete for resources and to derive schedules within specified machine, facility, and manpower limitations.

Heuristic programs for resource scheduling usually take one of two forms.

1) Resource Leveling
An attempt is made to reduce peak resource requirements and to smooth the weekly (daily) requirements within a constraint on project duration.

FIGURE 11.21

Leveled schedule of labor demands

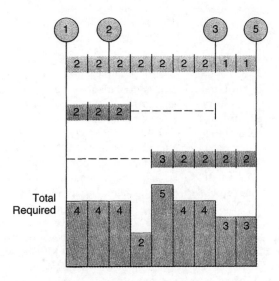

2) Resource Allocation

For a desired resource level (e.g., five employees), find the shortest possible project schedule. Examples can be found in reference [6].

Summary

The example in this section dealt with manpower as a resource. Similar analyses can be made with money (cost of activities), multiple skills, or any other resource.

Multiple Projects

Manage several projects simultaneously

In this chapter, we have presented a case of a company managing a single project. However, companies commonly execute several projects at the same time. For example, an airline may overhaul six airplanes simultaneously and a construction company may build 10 different structures at the same time. If there are dependencies among projects, such as resource constraints, the projects' management becomes very complex. Resources may be shared among projects, and employees may continuously be transferred from lower- to higher-priority activities. Fortunately, several computer programs exist to help manage multiproject activities (e.g., by Unisys, DEC, and IBM).

Actual Dates

Most commercial PERT/CPM programs are executed with actual dates (excluding weekends and holidays, if necessary) rather than with elapsed time.

Management Science in Practice

PERT Helps Move St. Vincent Hospital

When St. Vincent Hospital and Medical Center in Portland, Oregon, decided to move from its 373-bed city facility to a new 403-bed suburban facility five miles away, a sophisticated scheduling system was deemed mandatory. Because it was impractical to attempt to operate the two hospitals concurrently, the patients, equipment, staff, and supplies would all have to be moved as quickly as possible. To help keep track of the multitude of activities that were occurring concurrently, as well as identifying major milestones throughout the process, PERT was selected as the preferred planning tool.

The network was developed by starting with the major milestones that had to be reached for successful completion of the move. For each milestone, its preceding and succeeding activities were identified, as were the activities and events that must precede and follow each of these, and so on until all the myriad of details involved in the move had been identified. In this way, the project's activity dependencies were known beforehand so they did not get accidentally lost in the process and delay the overall move. The overall project critical path was also identified so that these critical activities could be closely monitored.

The complete network included hundreds of activities. These were coded to facilitate responsibility: 100–199 involved admissions and disaster planning, 500–599 involved housekeeping, and so on. All times were scaled to the date of the patient move, rather than real time, so that if the patient move date changed it would not require changing the PERT diagram. (In fact, this move date changed a number of times.) Designating the patient move date as M, the complete project ranged from M − 175 days to M + 21 days. The actual patient move was planned to take just one day (a Sunday, to minimize traffic problems) and relied on the use of military buses as well as ambulances.

Coordination and help was required not only from the military but also local merchants; the police; city traffic engineers; other local hospitals who could receive St. Vincent's emergency patients and grant temporary physician privileges; and the local media, which was publicizing the event on television. Considerable coordination was also required internally, with every employee getting training for working in the new hospital and a tour of the facility.

Move-day came as a very cold, foggy morning with 6 A.M. briefings for medical staff, department heads, nurses, ambulance crews, police officers, and volunteer staff. At 7 A.M. the patient transfer began. The patients were lined up in the lobby according to their transfer order. Five busloads and 28 ambulance loads moved the 84 infirm patients, who were then unloaded and taken directly to their rooms at the new hospital. The patients ranged from a nine-day-old premature baby to a 101-year-old nun. By 10:30 A.M., the last patient had left the old hospital.

All in all, the move went so smoothly that visitors were allowed in the new hospital by noon. The entire event, from M − 3 to M + 1, was shown on television Monday night. The moving of the rest of the hospital was completed in the next three days and by the end of the week all hospital departments were operating normally.

Throughout the move project, there were constant modifications to the plans as events and time changed many required activities. However, the basic PERT planning document remained relatively unchanged through the final seven months. It was the constant around which all other plans and activities were based and developed, reaffirming the value of detailed, advance planning with the appropriate management science tools.

Source: R. S. Hanson "Moving the Hospital to a New Location," *Industrial Engineering,* November 1972, pp. 32–38.

Questions:

1. What was unusual (the critical problem) about this move project?

2. What elements of PERT made it particularly appropriate for this use?

3. How would the probabilistic aspect of PERT be used here? Do you think it was? Why or why not?

4. What might have gone wrong in this project? How serious or costly might it have been?

11.7 Problems for Part A

(Unless stated otherwise, slack means total float, TF, in all problems.)

1. The events of the project below are designated as **1**, **2**, and so on.
   a. Draw the network.
   b. Find the critical path by complete enumeration.
   c. Find, for all events, the earliest and latest dates.
   d. Find the slacks on all the events and activities.
   e. Find the critical path, using the T_E's and T_L's.

Activity	Preceding Event	Succeeding Event	t_e (Weeks)	Preceding Activities
a	1	2	3	none
b	1	3	6	none
c	1	4	8	none
d	2	5	7	a
e	3	5	5	b
f	4	5	10	c
g	4	6	4	c
h	5	7	5	d, e, f
i	6	7	6	g

2. Given the following PERT network (times are in weeks):

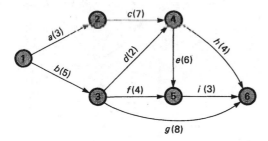

Determine:
   a. The T_E and T_L for each event.
   b. The slacks on all events and activities.
   c. The critical activities and path.
   d. The shared slacks.

3. Suppose that management has a contract to finish the project in Problem 2 in 22 weeks. *Determine:*
   a. The slack on event 3.
   b. The slack on activity g.

4. Given the following schedule for a liability work package done as part of an accounting audit in a corporation:

Activity	Duration (Days)	Preceding Activities
a. Obtain schedule of liabilities	3	None
b. Mail confirmation	15	a
c. Test pension plan	5	a
d. Vouch selected liabilities	60	a
e. Test accruals and amortization	6	d
f. Process confirmations	40	b
g. Reconcile interest expense to debt	10	c, e
h. Verify debt restriction compliance	7	f
i. Investigate debit balances	6	g
j. Review subsequent payments	12	h, i

Find:
   a. The critical path.
   b. The slack time on f (process confirmations).
   c. The slack time on c (test pension plan).
   d. The slack time on h (verify debt restriction compliance).

5. In the project network shown in the figure below, the number alongside each activity designates the activity duration (t_e) in weeks.

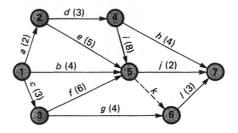

Determine:
   a. The T_E and T_L for each event.
   b. The earliest time that the project can be completed.
   c. The slack on all events and activities.

d. The critical events and activities.

e. The critical path.

f. The shared slacks.

6. Given the following information regarding a project:

Activity	t_e (Weeks)	Preceding Activities
a	3	None
b	1	None
c	3	a
d	4	a
e	4	b
f	5	b
g	2	c, e
h	3	f

a. Draw the network.

b. What is the critical path?

c. What will the scheduled (earliest completion) time for the entire project be?

d. What is the critical path to event **4** (end of activities *c* and *e*)? What is the earliest time that this event can be reached?

e. What is the effect on the project if activity *e* takes an extra week? Two extra weeks? Three extra weeks?

7. Construct a network for the project below and find its critical path. (Use a complete enumeration approach.)

Activity	t_e (Weeks)	Preceding Activities
a	3	None
b	5	a
c	3	a
d	1	c
e	3	b
f	4	b, d
g	2	c
h	3	g, f
i	1	e, h

8. Construct a network for the project:

Activity	t_e (Weeks)	Preceding Activities
a	3	None
b	5	None
c	14	a
d	5	a
e	4	b
f	7	b
g	8	d, e
h	5	g, f

a. Draw the network.

b. Find the critical path by complete enumeration.

c. Assume activity *a* took five weeks. Replan the project.

d. From where would you suggest transferring resources, and to what activities, such that the original target date may be maintained?

9. Given a PERT network:

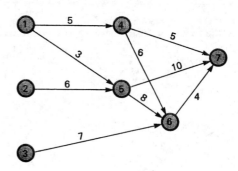

Note that three activities can start immediately. *Find:*

a. The critical path.

b. The earliest time to complete the project.

c. The slack on activities **4–6, 5–6,** and **4–7.**

10. For the project in Problem 2, find:

a. ES, EF, LS, and LF for all activities.

b. TF for all activities.

c. The critical path.

d. FF for all activities.

11. For the project in Problem 7, find ES, EF, LS, LF, TF, and FF for all activities.

12. Given the project network below:

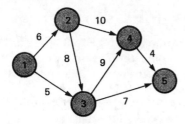

a. Draw an activity-oriented equivalent (without events).

b. Draw a bar chart; start at the *latest* possible time for all activities.

13. Assume that in Problem 2 you need two employees for each of the activities **1-2, 1-3,** and **5-6;** three employees for each of the activities **4-5** and **3-6;** and one employee for each of the remaining activities.

a. Prepare the labor demands if all activities start at their earliest times.

b. Prepare a plan that will level the labor demand, over time, as much as possible. Do not "split" jobs. Once started, they must be completed.

14. Solve the maintenance work project network below (use a computer). Find the critical path, ES, LS, EF, LF, and the regular slack.

15. Build a PERT network (do *not* use dummy activities) given the following:

Activity	Time	Immediately Preceding Activity
Drill	2	None
Cut	1	None
Punch	3	Drill
Bend	2	Drill
Inspect	6	Cut, punch
Assemble	3	Cut, punch
Test	1	Assemble
Paint	2	Bend, inspect, test

(Time column header annotated: "minutes")

Handwritten notes: CPM

Digram
Critical
Slack for each Path

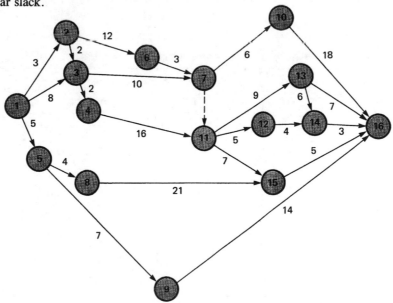

PART B: EXTENSIONS

11.8 Estimating Activity Times in PERT

Three time
estimates: optimistic,
pessimistic, and
most likely

Because the Moose Lake project was an experimental project, it was suitable for a PERT analysis. Judi asked each department to submit three estimates of duration time for each activity the department was responsible for, using the following guidelines:

Optimistic estimate (t_o): An estimate of the *shortest possible time* (duration) in which the activity can be accomplished. The probability that the activity will take less than this time is 0.01.

Most likely estimate (t_m): The duration that would occur most often if the activity were repeated under exactly the same conditions many times. Equivalently, it is the time that would be estimated most often by experts.

Pessimistic estimate (t_p): The longest time that the activity could take "when everything goes wrong." The probability that the activity will exceed this duration is 0.01.

All three estimates are entered in Table 11.5. Notice that in some cases, $t_o = t_p = t_m$; that is, the exact time duration is known.

Computing the Weighted Average

Once the three time estimates are obtained, their weighted average is computed. This average, which is called the mean time of an activity, t_e, is a *weighted average* of the

TABLE 11.5   Moose Lake Project Activities (Weeks)

Activity	Description	t_o (Opimistic)	t_m (Most Likely)	t_p (Pessimistic)	t_e (Weighted Average)
a	Administrative setup	1	3	5	3
b	Hire personnel	1	3	11	4
c	Obtain materials	3	4	5	4
d	Transport materials to Moose Lake	1	2	3	2
e	Gather measuring team	3	3	9	4
f	Planning	2	5	14	6
g	Assemble equipment	2	3	4	3
h	Plan evaluation	1	1	1	1
i	Oxygenation	12	12	12	12
j	Measurement and evaluation	1	2	3	2

three time estimates. It is computed using Equation 11.6:

$$t_e = \frac{t_o + 4t_m + t_p}{6}$$

(11.6)

where t_e is the expected duration of the activity.

A weighted average   The formula gives four times more weight to the most likely estimate than to the pessimistic or optimistic estimates. The division by 6, the sum of the weights, is to obtain a weighted average such as that shown in the "duration" column of Table 11.1. (*Note:* Equation 11.6 is based on the assumption that the Beta distribution is the probability distribution of duration times. Other weights are used in real-life problems based on experience.) For example, in Table 11.5, for activity *a*, the weighted average is:

$$t_e = \frac{1(1) + 4(3) + 1(5)}{6} = 3 \text{ weeks}$$

11.9 Finding the Probabilities of Completion in PERT (Risk Analysis)

The consideration of risk   PERT has more capabilities than just as a planning and control tool. It can also be used to give management an indication of risk in terms of project completion. This is a crucial analysis that considers the chance of completing the project on, before, or after scheduled dates.

    The three estimates of activity duration in PERT, t_o, t_m, and t_p, are assumed to follow a probability distribution called the Beta distribution, shown in Figure 11.22 for

FIGURE 11.22

Activity time distribution for activity b

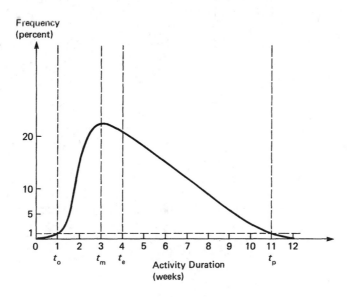

Activity Duration (weeks)

activity b as an example ($t_o = 1$, $t_m = 3$, $t_p = 11$, and their average $t_e = 4$). Even though estimates of each activity duration follow the Beta distribution, the estimate of the combined duration of several activities (such as those on the critical path) approaches the *normal* distribution. *Note:* The justification for the use of the normal distribution is based on the central limit theorem: the sum of n independent variables tends to be normally distributed as n approaches infinity (becomes "large enough").

The project estimated completion time, TS, is computed as the expected time, T_E, for the last event. (The T_E for the last event is the same as the sum of the t_e's along the critical path if the project starts at time 0). Therefore, there is a 50 percent chance that the *entire* project will be completed by its earliest projected time (27 weeks in our example from Part A). However, a "50 percent chance" is usually too low a confidence level for managerial planning. Management may want to know the chances of completing the project in other time periods, say 25 or 30 weeks. To answer such questions, an analysis involving the probability associated with the duration times is conducted.

To calculate the probabilities, it is necessary to find the *standard deviations* for the activities. The standard deviation of the Beta distribution of activity durations is given by Equation 11.7.

$$\text{Standard deviation of an activity} = \sigma = \frac{t_p - t_o}{6} \tag{11.7}$$

The variance of the activity's distribution is given by Equation 11.8.

$$\text{Variance of activity} = \sigma^2 = \left(\frac{t_p - t_o}{6}\right)^2 \tag{11.8}$$

For example, for activity b, the standard deviation is:

$$\sigma_b = \frac{11 - 1}{6} = 1.67 \text{ weeks}$$

and the variance is:

$$\sigma_b^2 = 1.67^2 = 2.79 \text{ weeks squared}$$

For activities h and i, the variance is zero, because $t_p = t_o = t_m$ for these activities. This means that no uncertainty is involved in their estimates. The larger the variance, the greater the degree of uncertainty involved.

Assuming that the durations of the activities are independent of each other, the variance of a *group* of activities (designated by V) can be computed by adding the variances of the activities in that group. The value of V is then expressed by Equation 11.9:

$$V = \sigma_1^2 + \sigma_2^2 + \cdots + \sigma_n^2 \tag{11.9}$$

where n is the number of activities in the group.

The variance along
the critical path

Of special interest are the activities that comprise the *critical path*. For example, in the Moose Lake project, the variance for the critical path is given as:

$$V = \sigma_a^2 + \sigma_c^2 + \sigma_f^2 + \sigma_i^2 + \sigma_j^2$$

$$= .44 + .11 + 4.00 + 0 + .11 = 4.66$$

A critical path to
each event

The value of V can be computed, in a similar manner, for *any event* in the network by considering the group of activities along the critical path leading to the event.

Note: The method described here is valid only if the following three assumptions hold: (1) there is a large number of activities (at least 25) on the critical path; (2) the activities' completion times are independent of each other; and (3) the noncritical paths are not relevant (i.e., we are not checking the degree of risk there). If the above assumptions are not valid, simulation must be used for the risk analysis.

Managerial Applications

The managerial questions raised at the beginning of this section—the chance of completing the project in a certain desired time and the duration necessary for obtaining any desired probability of completion—can now be answered. Let:

TS = Earliest project completion time. It is the earliest time (T_E) computed for the last event (27 weeks in the example).

D = The desired completion time (30 weeks in the example).

Z = The number of standard deviations of a normal distribution (see Appendix C, Table C1) corresponding to the probability of completing the project by the desired completion time.

$$Z = \frac{X - \mu}{\sigma} - \frac{D - TS}{\sqrt{V}} \qquad (11.10)$$

What-if analysis

Example 1: Finding the Probability of Completion within a Desired Time, D

Management wishes to know the probability of completing the Moose Lake project *on or before* the 30th week, as specified in the contract.

Thus: $D = 30$, $TS = 27$ (as computed), $V = 4.66$ (as computed). Therefore:

Using the normal
distribution

$$Z = \frac{30 - 27}{\sqrt{4.66}} = \frac{13}{2.16} = 1.39$$

The probability equivalent to $Z = 1.39$ can be found in Table Cl in Appendix C as .9177. Therefore, there is a 91.77 percent chance of completing the Moose Lake project within 30 weeks. (Remember that there is a 50 percent chance of completing the project by 27 weeks.) Figure 11.23 depicts the situation.

In a similar manner, the Z for completing the project within 25 weeks is:

$$Z = \frac{25 - 27}{2.16} = -.93$$

FIGURE 11.23

*Chance of completing
the project in 25, 27,
and 30 weeks*

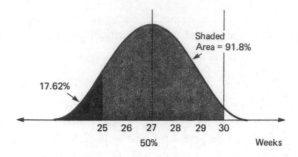

If the normal distribution tables included negative numbers, the probability could be read directly from them. Because this is usually not the case, the probability for $Z = +.93$ is read first (which is. 8238). This value is then subtracted from 1.0 (the total area under the curve); that is, $1 - .8238 = .1762$. Thus, there is only a 17.62 percent chance of completing the project in 25 weeks or less (see Figure 11.23).

Note: If Z is negative, the corresponding probability is always less than 50 percent. If Z is positive, the corresponding probability is always more than 50 percent; and if Z is 0, the corresponding probability is exactly 50 percent.

Goal-seeking
analysis

Example 2: Finding the Duration Associated with a Desired Probability

In the previous example, a chance of 91.77 percent of completing the project in 30 weeks was computed. Suppose that management would like to know for what duration they can be 80 percent sure of completion. To do so, Table C1 in Appendix C is consulted. The value of Z associated with 80 percent is searched for. The answer is $Z = .845$. Using Equation 11.10, with D as the unknown, we obtain Equation 11.11:

$$D = Z\sigma + TS \qquad (11.11)$$

$$D = .845 \times 2.16 + 27 = 28.83 \text{ weeks}$$

That is, there is an 80 percent chance of completing the project within 28.83 weeks. The computation of D enables management to make delivery commitments knowing the degree of risk assumed.

The Variance of a Noncritical Path

The danger of
noncritical paths

The probability of completing a project was found to be related to the variance of the critical path (Equation 11.10). Suppose, however, that there is a noncritical path whose variance V is *larger* than, or even similar in magnitude to, the variance of the critical path. What might its effect be on the probability of completion? If Equation 11.10 is used for the new path, then the probability of completion by the desired time might very well be *lower* than that computed using the critical path. Therefore, if more than one critical path exists, then V should be computed for *all* such paths. To be conservative, use the path with the largest V to compute probabilities of completion for dates *after* the expected completion time; use the smallest V for probabilities of completion for dates *before* the expected completion time.

11.10 The Critical Path Method (CPM): Cost-Time Relationships

Expediting projects

CPM analysis is used to evaluate various alternatives of executing projects in those cases where it is possible to *expedite* the execution of some or all of the project's activities. Expediting activities requires additional resources, which means increasing the cost of the project. However, considerable savings may be realized in projects finished ahead of schedule. An example of such a case was observed in Phoenix, Arizona, where two builders constructed two large condominium projects. With the economic slump of 1991/92, the demand for condominiums dropped considerably. One of the builders decided to expedite construction, at a considerable cost, in order to finish first. He sold 240 units in a short time, exhausting the demand. When the second builder completed his project, he could not sell the units and was forced to file for bankruptcy.

Thus, the decision of how much to expedite may be of great importance to management. The tool that enables such an analysis is CPM.

The Basic Idea

Normal or crash?

Figure 11.24 presents the relationship in CPM between cost and time. An activity can be performed in a *normal manner* (normal point in Figure 11.24) requiring T_n units of time and C_n units of money (where n designates *normal*). In an extreme case, the activity can be performed on a *crash* basis (e.g., using overtime, special services, extra tools) at a time T_c and a cost C_c (where c designates *crash*). No activity can be executed in less time than T_c or more than T_n, but one can take any value between.

The crash point and the normal point can be connected by a *straight line*. Any intermediate point X on the straight line will involve T_x time and C_x cost. The relationship between time and cost is given by the slope of the straight line (Equation 11.12).

$$\text{Slope} = \frac{C_c - C_n}{T_n - T_c}$$

(11.12)

The slope as a trade-off

The slope gives us the *cost increase* associated with a reduction of one unit of the activity duration. The assumption of a linear relationship between cost and time is not valid in all cases. In some cases, the relationships are described by a nonlinear function (the broken curve in Figure 11.24) and the solid line only approximates the broken line. In other cases, a stepwise curve is applicable. It is customary to write the normal and crash data for each activity directly on the diagram as shown in Figure 11.25 (time above the line, cost underneath). For example, for activity **1–3,** the normal time is five weeks, at a cost of $4,000; the crash time is three weeks, at a cost of $5,200.

FIGURE 11.24

CPM cost-time trade-offs for an activity

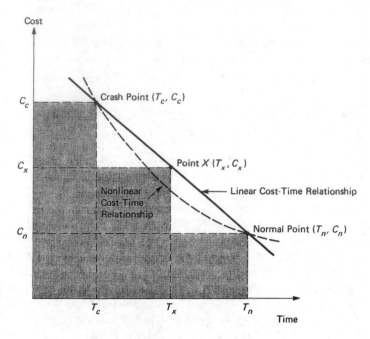

FIGURE 11.25

CPM labeling

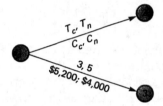

The slope of activity **1–3** is:

$$\frac{\$5,200 - \$4,000}{5 - 3} = \$600 \text{ per week}$$

This is the cost required to expedite the activity by one week. The linear relationship means that it will cost $1,200 to expedite the activity by two weeks. The true slope will actually be a negative number because the direction of the line is from northwest to southeast; however, Equation 11.12 yields a *positive* number that we use as a cost *increase*.

The CPM Analysis

The CPM analysis examines the total cost involved in executing the project at various scheduled times, starting with either the lowest cost–longest duration alternative or with the higher cost–shortest duration alternative. The additional cost of expediting the project can then be compared with the possible savings from the expedited completion (e.g., a client may pay a bonus for completion ahead of schedule).

Solve the problem twice

The CPM analysis starts by solving the problem twice. First, attention is paid only to **normal times.** Using the procedure outlined in Part A of this chapter and assuming that the normal times are the t_e's, a solution is derived, and its cost is also computed. Second, by considering only the crash times as t_e's, another solution is derived, and its cost is also computed.

Once the two solutions are computed, the cost-time trade-offs are used to find the least-cost plan for any number of weeks (days) between the *all crash* and *all normal* plans. This cost can then be compared with the anticipated benefits.

Example

A network of activities for a maintenance project is shown in Figure 11.26. The problem is to find the least-cost plan for various project durations.

The normal time (in days) and cost, as well as the crash time and cost, are shown in Table 11.6. The column "Cost slope" indicates the incremental *increase* in cost when the duration of the project is decreased by one day, computed from Equation 11.12. For example, for activity D:

$$\text{Slope} = \frac{340 - 280}{9 - 7} = \frac{60}{2} = \$30 \text{ per day}$$

Solution

The first observation that can be made from Table 11.6 is that if all activities are performed in the normal duration, the total cost will be $1,860. Second, if all activities are performed on a crash basis, the total cost will be $2,860. The *times* required to complete the project on an *all-normal* basis and on an *all-crash* basis should be determined next.

All-Normal Basis

All-normal, least-cost, longest time

Considering first *all-normal* times (disregard the normal costs, the crash time, and the crash cost), the critical path can be computed using the procedure shown in Part A of this chapter. The results are shown in Figure 11.27. The critical path is **0–1–2–4–5** for a duration of 25 days and a cost of $1,860.

FIGURE 11.26

A maintenance project

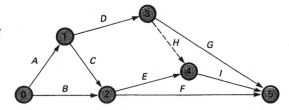

TABLE 11.6   Time and Cost Information

Activity	Normal		Crash		Cost Slope
	Time	Cost	Time	Cost	
A	5	$ 100	4	$ 140	40
B	9	200	7	300	50
C	7	250	4	340	30
D	9	280	7	340	30
E	5	250	2	460	70
F	11	400	7	720	80
G	6	300	4	420	60
I	8	80	6	140	30
Total		$1,860		$2,860	

FIGURE 11.27

All-normal solution, 25 days

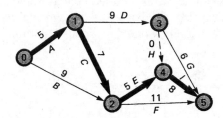

FIXED COST : 50.⁰⁰/day

FIGURE 11.28

All-crash solution, 17 days

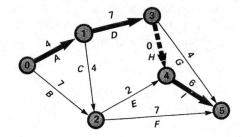

All-crash, most-expensive, shortest time

All-Crash Solution

In a similar manner, the critical path of *all-crash* duration is computed (Figure 11.28). The critical path is **0–1–3–4–5** for a duration of 17 days and a cost of $2,860. At this stage, the following analysis is performed:

  a. Determine the *minimum* cost for the crash time of 17 days.
  b. Determine the least-cost plan for any desired number of days between all-normal to all-crash.

Find the Minimum Cost for the Crash Time

So far, it was found that it is possible to perform the project in 17 days at a cost of $2,860. The question is whether it is possible to perform the project in 17 days but at a lower cost. To achieve a cost reduction, the noncritical activities could be performed at a slower pace. (This is called *expanding* the activities.) There is a simple procedure for this.

Step 1: All *noncritical* activities found in Figure 11.28 are listed with their appropriate cost slopes:

Noncritical Activities	Cost Slope
B: **0–2**	50
C: **1–2**	30
E: **2–4**	70
G: **3–5**	60
F: **2–5**	80

Step 2: The activity with the *largest* slope is selected (activity *F*) first. The largest savings can be made if this activity is expanded first. It would be desirable to expand it *as much as possible* to achieve as large a cost reduction as possible. Because activity *F* is on two noncritical paths, **0–1–2–5** and **0–2–5,** it can be expanded until one of these becomes critical.

Because path **0–2–5** now takes 14 days, it can be expanded by 3 days to make it critical (up to 17 days). However, path **0–1–2–5** now takes 15 days, and therefore only 2 days can be added to it to make it critical. Therefore, the maximum number of days that can be added to activity *F* is two (the smaller of the two).

There is another point that should be checked in expanding an activity. The crash time of activity *F* is seven days. The normal time is given as 11 days. Therefore, expansion by two days is feasible. In other cases, it *may not be feasible* to expand up to the maximum length allowed by the length of the noncritical path because of the normal time limitations that are imposed on an individual activity.

Check for feasibility

The expansion of activity *F* now yields an additional critical path, **0–1–2–5,** which will take 17 days at a cost reduction of $160.

Step 3: Activity *E*, which has the *second largest* cost reduction potential, is expanded next. Here, an expansion of only one day is possible at a $70 saving. In a similar manner, the expansion of activity *G* by two days will yield an additional $120, and finally, activity *B* can be expanded by one day, resulting in a $50 saving. Notice that because activity *F* has been expanded to nine days, the maximum that activity *B* can be expanded is to eight days ($17 - 9 = 8$). It is impossible to expand activity C, because it became *critical* as a result of the expansion of activity F.

The total cost savings are: $160 + 70 + 120 + 50 = 400$. Thus, the revised plan calls for a 17-day project, at a total cost of $2,860 - $400 = $2,460$. This new schedule is shown in Figure 11.29. Notice that all activities are now *critical;* that is, no further expansion is possible. The information is then entered into a cost-time diagram (Figure 11.30) as point A.

Determine the Least-Cost Plan for Any Desired Number of Days

The normal schedule is the *longest* (slowest) schedule for carrying out the project and costs the *least*. On the other hand, the all-crash schedule is the *fastest,* but is also the most expensive. In certain cases, management needs to know the cost of carrying out the project at some point between the fastest and the slowest. Such a situation may de-

FIGURE 11.29

Least-cost crash schedule of 17 days ($2,460)

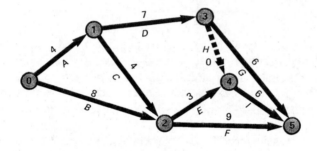

FIGURE 11.30

Cost-time trade-offs

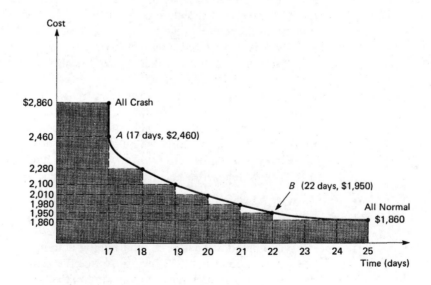

velop, for example, when a customer offers to pay a certain amount as a bonus for finishing ahead of schedule.

Example: Least-Cost Plan for 22 Days

Compress or expand?

Let us assume that management would like to find the least-cost plan for 22 days. Two approaches are available: either *compressing* the project from 25 days (all normal) to 22 days, or *expanding* the project from 17 days (all crash) up to 22. The former approach will be illustrated here.

The first step is to list all *critical activities* of the all-normal schedule (Figure 11.27). The list of these activities and their slopes follows:

Critical Activities	Slope
A: 0–1	40
C: 1–2	30
E: 2–4	70
I: 4–5	30

Multiple critical paths

The activity with the *least* slope will be compressed first, because decreasing the project time by one day will result in the smallest increase in cost. In the example, either activity C or activity I can be selected, because both have the smallest slope (lowest cost). Arbitrarily, activity C is selected.

How much can activity C be compressed? The most an activity can be compressed is up to its *crash time* (four days here). However, such a reduction may create one (or more) additional critical paths. The minute an additional critical path is created, the compression should be stopped and a cost reevaluation made. In the example, two additional critical paths are formed after activity C is reduced from seven to four days. Thus, the maximum project compression is to 22 days (see Figure 11.31) at a cost of $1,860 + 90 = $1,950 (point B in Figure 11.30).

FIGURE 11.31

A 22-day, least-cost schedule

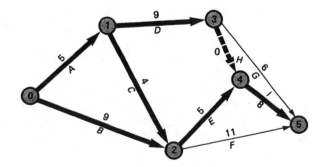

FIGURE 11.32

A 20-day, least-cost schedule

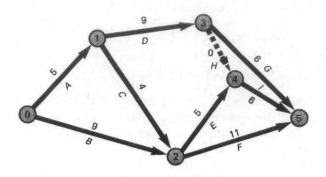

Notice that the compression to 22 days also tells us that the best plan for achieving 24 days is to cut one day from activity *C* and the best plan for 23 days is cutting two days from activity *C*.

Compression to 20 Days

In a similar manner, the best plan for 21 days can be found. Starting with 22 days, the *critical* activity *I* (Figure 11.31) is expedited, because its cost increase is now the smallest. Compressing by one day yields a 21-day schedule with a cost of $1,980. This activity could be compressed by two days to its crash time of six days. After compressing it by two days, we get a 20-day schedule at a cost of $2,010 (see Figure 11.32). This information is now entered in Figure 11.30. Note that the entire network is now critical.

Additional Compression

At this stage, a single activity can no longer be considered by itself, because there are several critical paths involved. For example, if activity *D* is reduced by one day, the critical path **0–1–3–5** will be reduced to 19 days, but other critical paths will also have to be reduced by one day. In this case, activities *E* and *F* have to be compressed by one day each and the cost effect will be felt in two places. Therefore, it is necessary to check all combinations of possible reductions to make sure that the smallest total cost is added. This is done by taking the smallest slope on a path (rather than an activity) first and adding the resultant cost impact to the other paths.

Then a computation is made for the least slope on the next path, taking into consideration the impact on the resultant cost, and so on. Finally, all alternatives are compared and the one with the least-cost increase is selected. In the example, a compression of activities *A* and *B* by one day results in a 19-day schedule at a cost of $2,010 + 40 + 50 = $2,100 (see Figure 11.33).

Further compression is done in the same manner. An 18-day schedule can be obtained with a cost of $2,280, and a 17-day schedule has a cost of $2,460. All these re-

Check all possibilities

FIGURE 11.33

A 19-day, least-cost schedule

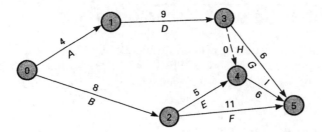

sults are entered in Figure 11.30 for the purpose of evaluation of the anticipated benefits.

Once Figure 11.30 is completed, it can be used to facilitate decisions regarding the expediting of projects. This is especially useful when one must decide whether to permit a delay or reduce it. Because the cost curves of delays and expediting run contrary to each other (see Figure 11.34), it is necessary to find the optimal strategy each time a delay develops. If, for example, the cost of delay is smaller than that of expediting, then the delay should be permitted.

FIGURE 11.34

Cost analysis

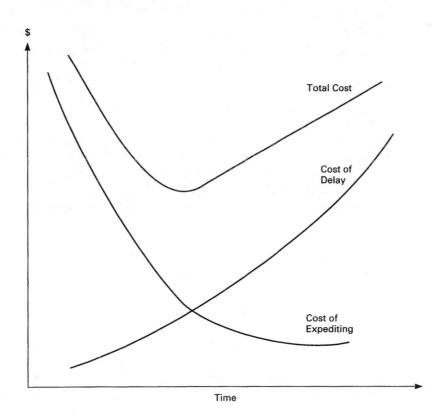

11.11 Other Network Techniques

Nonproject
networks, too

Over the years, several other network techniques have been developed. Some of these are modifications and extensions of PERT and CPM. Various techniques can be classified as either project or nonproject oriented.

Project-Oriented Techniques

PERT/Cost
The PERT technique is a time-oriented method that helps plan and control a project's duration. **PERT/Cost** is an extension that permits the planning and control of both time and cost. The basic concept of PERT/Cost is that costs are to be measured and controlled primarily on a project basis rather than, say, on a departmental basis. Thus, individual activities (or groups of activities) form cost centers for both accounting purposes and managerial control. This is in contrast to conventional cost methods, where organizational units such as departments are the cost centers.

Other Techniques
Several other planning techniques, including PERT II, PERT III, PERT IV, LESS, TOPS, COMET, and PROPT (all extensions or modifications of PERT or CPM), are available.

Graphical Evaluation and Review Technique (GERT)
The application of PERT assumes that all activities must be completed before an event can be realized, that events cannot be repeated, that all activities in the network must be completed, that estimates follow the Beta distribution, and that the critical path is the one with the longest elapsed time (sum of mean activity times), even though variances from those mean times exist. GERT is an extension of PERT, where all of the above assumptions are relaxed; that is, they are not imposed any longer. (For details, see [9].)

Nonproject-Oriented Network Techniques

Collection of nodes
and branches

The next three sections concern three special nonproject-oriented network models, all of which are recognized for their simplicity and solution efficiency. A *network* is a collection of nodes connected by branches (arcs). Figure 11.35 depicts a general network. Other examples are a decision tree and a PERT (event-oriented) diagram.

Many managerial problems can be represented by networks, even though they may not physically appear to be networks. Examples include inventory decisions and scheduling problems.

FIGURE 11.35

A general network

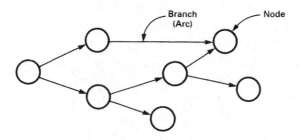

11.12 Minimal Spanning Tree

We will illustrate this topic through an example.

Example

The Northwood Telephone Company is planning a network of telephones for a small, high-class shopping center. Figure 11.36 shows the desired location of the phones (circled and numbered). The lines to every telephone must be buried to maintain the posh image of the center. The telephone company wishes, of course, to minimize the necessary digging, but due to existing electrical and utility lines, it is not possible to dig just anywhere. Figure 11.36 also shows the feasible underground lines as arcs with their distances shown. The problem is to determine which of these lines to dig such that the total distance is minimized, yet every phone is connected to the network.

Minimize the length of cables

In this case, the objective is to select a set of branches in a network, from a feasible larger set of branches, that will span (connect) *all* the nodes of the network, yet minimize the sum of the branch lengths (which equate to cost). This problem is called the **spanning tree** problem. In solving this problem, we are searching for the *minimal* spanning tree.

FIGURE 11.36

The telephone problem

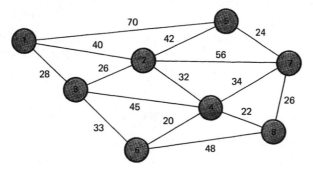

FIGURE 11.37

The optimal solution

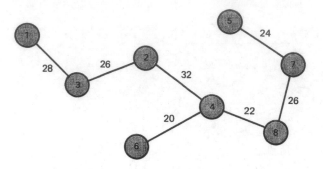

Solution Using the Greedy Algorithm

A popular solution method is commonly referred to as the **greedy algorithm,** because simply joining to the closest node at each iteration of the solution turns out to be the optimal procedure.

First, arbitrarily select any node and connect it to the nearest node. We will start with **1** and connect it to **3,** the closest node. From the connected nodes **1** and **3** (both must be considered), we search for the shortest distance to any unconnected node—**3** to **2** in our example—and connect the two. We repeat this process, always considering *all* connected nodes when searching for a new node to connect, until all nodes are connected. In our example:

> From **2** to **4**
> From **4** to **6**
> From **4** to **8**
> From **8** to **7**
> From **7** to **5**

The optimal solution is shown in Figure 11.37 with a total distance of 178.
Notes:

1. There may be more than one optimal solution.
2. The total number of connecting segments is always $n - 1$, where n is the number of nodes.
3. A more complicated problem is one in which there are *limits* on the capacities that can be transmitted along the arcs (a *capacitated* spanning tree).

11.13 Shortest Route (Path)

Shortest possible route

The **shortest route** problem can be stated as follows: Find the shortest route (in terms of distance, time, or money) from a given node in a network to any (or all) of the nodes in the network.

Example

A bank has six branches and a headquarters in the greater Los Angeles metropolitan area (see map, Figure 11.38). The distances along the streets are shown on the map. Some routes, such as from **1** directly to **5,** are not possible because of an intervening airport, railroad, or park. Note that the arcs are *not* directed; that is, they permit travel in either direction. Bank employees frequently travel from headquarters **1** to the branches. The problem is to find the shortest distance from headquarters to each branch.

Solution

The algorithm used is iterative in nature. In each iteration, the shortest distance to one node is determined. Therefore, the optimal solution will be reached in $n - 1$ iterations, where $n =$ the number of nodes.

Step 1: Determine the distance from headquarters **1** to every node that can be reached directly. Label each such destination node according to the following code:

Direct distance
↓
(1, 2) − 20
Source ↗ ↖ Destination

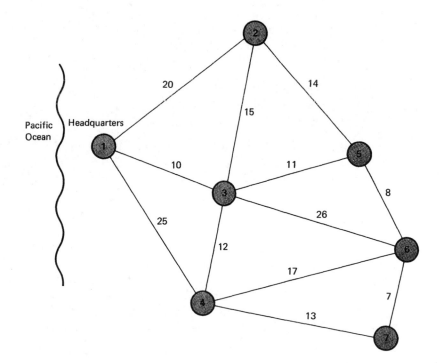

FIGURE 11.39

Initial solution

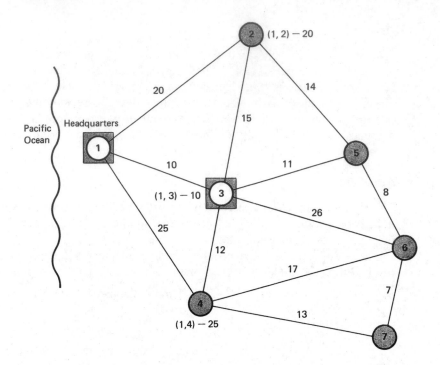

Step 2: Box the initial node, then box the closest node to the initial node (in our case, **3**). The results are shown in Figure 11.39.

Step 3: We now have three types of nodes:

a. Those that are boxed (**1** and **3**).

b. Those that are labeled (**2, 3,** and **4**).

c. Those that are not labeled (**5, 6,** and **7**).

Start from the latest boxed node, **3,** and check the distance to all unlabeled direct nodes. Because **5** and **6** are unlabeled, label them, using the distance from the initial node **1** *through* node **3**.

For **5:** The label is (**3, 5**) − 21.

For **6:** The label is (**3, 6**) − 36.

Step 4: Check the labeled nodes, **2** and **4,** for possible improvements.

For node **2:** Two alternatives exist: **1–2** for a distance of 20, or **1–3–2** for a distance of 25. Because no improvement can be achieved by going through **3,** we conclude that **1–2** is the shortest way. Therefore, **2** is boxed.

For node **4:** The previous label indicated a distance of 25. However, following route **1–3–4** results in a shorter path of 10 + 12 = 22. Therefore, the node is relabeled (**3, 4**) − 22. (Refer to Figure 11.40.)

Most flow

FIGURE 11.40

Improved solution

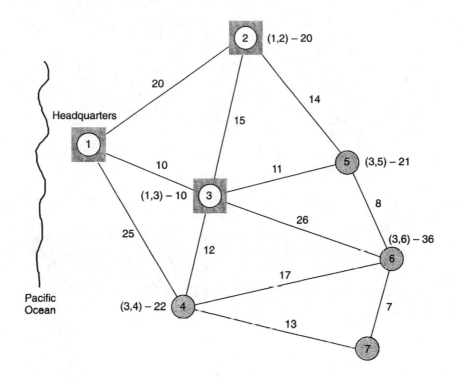

Step 5: Step 3 is repeated for node **2.** At this iteration, the label of **5** is checked and stays unchanged. Node **4** is boxed, because no improvement is possible. Also, node **7** is labeled.

Step 6: Step 4 is repeated for node **4.** The results are shown in Figure 11.41.

Step 7: Step 4 is repeated for node **5.** No improvement is possible, so the node is boxed.

Step 8: Step 4 is repeated for node **6.** Improvement is possible: $(5, 6) - 29$, so it is boxed. Finally, we check node **7.** No improvement is possible, so we box it, too. (See Figure 11.42.)

The optimal solution is then read from the labels. From **1,** the shortest paths are:

To	Path	Distance
2	1–2	20
3	1–3	10
4	1–3–4	22
5	1–3–5	21
6	1–3–5–6	29
7	1–3–4–7	35

FIGURE 11.41

Second improved solution

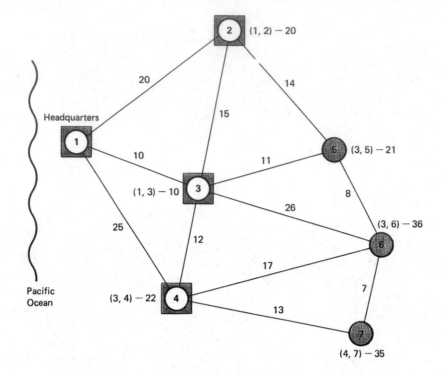

FIGURE 11.42

Optimal solution

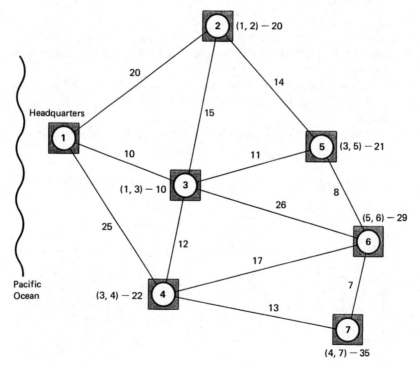

11.14 Maximum Flow

The objective in this technique is to find the **maximum** amount of **flow** of fluid, traffic, information, and so on, that can be transported through a capacitated (capacity limited) network. Such a network is composed of a **source** and a **sink** and connecting arcs and nodes. Flow in each individual arc (e.g., a water pipe) is measured by the amount that can be transported during a unit of time (e.g., six gallons per minute). Flow can only be one-way along an arc, as shown by the arrow connecting points **1** and **2** in Figure 11.43. However, it is also possible to have two direct arcs between nodes (e.g., points **2** and **3** in Figure 11.43) so that flow can be two ways.

Solution Procedure

Step 1: Trace a continuous path from the source to the sink; for example, **1–2–3–4.** (Do not consider any path where there is one or more arcs with a *zero*-flow capacity.)

Step 2: In this continuous path, determine the arc with the *minimum* flow capacity. In our example, it is arc **2–3** with a flow of **4;** thus, the most we can transport through path **1–2–3–4** is **4.**

Step 3: Reduce *all* the quantities along this path by 4 (the maximum amount transported). The result is shown in Figure 11.44.

Iteration 2

Repeat steps 1 through 3. This time, the path **1–3–4** is considered. (Note that the *order* in which paths are considered does not matter.) The minimum quantity is 6. The result is shown in Figure 11.45.

FIGURE 11.43

A capacitated network

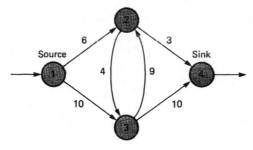

FIGURE 11.44

Network after iteration 1

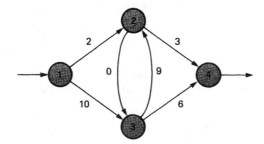

FIGURE 11.45

*Network after
iteration 2*

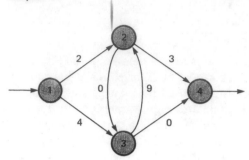

FIGURE 11.46

*Network after
iteration 3*

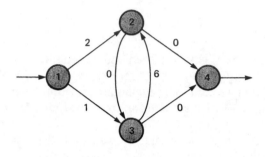

Iteration 3

Repeat steps 1 through 3. This time, path **1–3–2–4** is considered. The minimum flow is 3. The result is shown in Figure 11.46.

Step 4: Because all the paths have at least one arc with a zero capacity, we stop. The maximum flow in the entire network is $4 + 6 + 3 = 13$.

Note: In some cases, it may be desirable to *reverse* a previously assigned flow through an arc to increase the total source-to-sink flow. This is acceptable.

11.15 Computerization

PERT/CPM networks are usually very large and require frequent replanning or updating for changes. Therefore, many computer programs have been developed to perform partial or complete network analyses. A typical computer program will have, as a minimum, the input-output structure shown in Figure 11.47. An example data printout of the Moose Lake project presented in Part A is solved by activity analysis and is shown in Figure 11.48 (derived with Nelson's MSS Software [10]).

This example also includes the risk analysis for the project. The input-output information for a typical risk analysis is shown in Figure 11.49. The printout for the Moose Lake project is shown in Figure 11.50. Note that the MSS program monitors all critical paths and considers the one with the largest variance (in our example, there is only one such path).

"What-if" and "goal-seeking" analysis

Also note that the program is capable of conducting an interactive "what-if" analysis. The user enters the desired completion times (we entered four values; 30, 26, 31,

FIGURE 11.47

Computerized network models

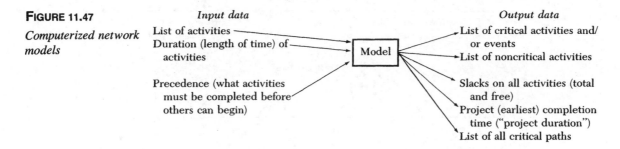

Input data

List of activities
Duration (length of time) of activities

Precedence (what activities must be completed before others can begin)

Model

Output data

List of critical activities and/or events
List of noncritical activities

Slacks on all activities (total and free)
Project (earliest) completion time ("project duration")
List of all critical paths

FIGURE 11.48

Moose Lake data printout using Nelson's software [10]

Project Name: MOOSE   Problem Type: PERT-Stochastic
Completion Time: 27   No. of Critical Paths: 1
Max. Path Variance: 4.666667   Min. Path Variance: 4.666667

Activity Name	DESCRIPT.	ES	EF	LS	LF	SLACK	T_E (Mean)	STD. DEV.	CRITICAL
A	Admin.	0.00	3.00	0.00	3.00	0.00	3.00	0.67	YES
B	Hire	3.00	7.00	6.00	10.00	3.00	4.00	1.67	NO
C	Materials	3.00	7.00	3.00	7.00	0.00	4.00	0.33	YES
D	Transport	7.00	9.00	8.00	10.00	1.00	2.00	0.33	NO
E	Team	3.00	7.00	20.00	24.00	17.00	4.00	1.00	NO
F	Planning	7.00	13.00	7.00	13.00	0.00	6.00	2.00	YES
G	Assemble	9.00	12.00	10.00	13.00	1.00	3.00	0.33	NO
H	Plan	7.00	8.00	24.00	25.00	17.00	1.00	0.00	NO
I	Oxygen	13.00	25.00	13.00	25.00	0.00	12.00	0.00	YES
J	Evaluate	25.00	27.00	25.00	27.00	0.00	2.00	0.33	YES

CRITICAL PATHS

NO.	PATH ACTIVITY NAMES	VARIANCE
1	A → C → F → I → J	4.666667

FIGURE 11.49

Risk analysis model

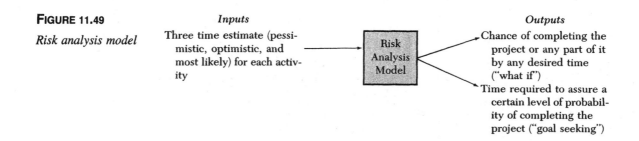

Inputs

Three time estimate (pessimistic, optimistic, and most likely) for each activity

Risk Analysis Model

Outputs

Chance of completing the project or any part of it by any desired time ("what if")
Time required to assure a certain level of probability of completing the project ("goal seeking")

FIGURE 11.50

*Moose Lake risk
analysis using Nelson's
software* [10]

Project completion time: 27	No. of critical paths: 1
Maximum path variance: 4.667	Minimum path variance: 4.667

Probability of completion by what time?	Time	Probability
	30	.917
	26	.322
	31	.968
	32	.990

and 32) and the program computes the probability of completion for each of them, as shown in Figure 11.50.

Note: Several programs can also provide an event analysis, such as Lotfi and Pegels, though theirs does not include a risk analysis.

Critical Path Method

Several management science software packages include a routine for CPM. For example, entering the input data from Table 11.6 results in the output shown in Figure 11.51. The program also allows for a least-cost what-if analysis similar to that shown in the text. The least-cost crash solution is found in four iterations. A particular comple-

FIGURE 11.51

*CPM results of
Table 11.6*

	DURATION	COST
Normal	25	$1860
First iteration	22	1950
Second iteration	20	2010
Third iteration	19	2100
Least-cost crash	17	2460
Crash	17	2860

Problem Title: CPM 1

Normal time: 25
Crash time: 8

Project completion time: 17

Indirect costs: $0.00

Direct costs:
   Normal costs $1860.00
   Crash costs $600.00

Total cost: $2460.00

| | TABLE 11.7 | **Representative PC-based Project Management Software** |

Product	Vendor
Advanced Project 6	Softcorp. Inc., Clearwater, Fla.
Artemis	Metier Management Systems, Houston, Tex.
Harvard Project Manager	Software Publishing Co., Mountain View, Calif.
InstaPlan	Instaplan Corp., Mill Valley, Calif.
MacProject	Apple Computer, Inc., Cupertino, Calif.
Microman	DOC-IT Management, Santa Monica, Calif.
Microsoft Project	Microsoft Corp., Northup Way, Bellevue, Wash.
Milestone	Digital Marketing Corp., Walnut Creek, Calif.
Planning Pro	Kepner-Tregoe, Inc., Princeton, N.J.
Project Scheduler Network	Scitor Corp., Foster City, Calif.
PC MIS	Davis and Associates, Atlanta, Ga.
Project Manager IBM	Institute of Industrial Engineering, Norcross, Ga.
Project Workbench	Applied Business Technology Corp.
Scheduling and Control	Softext Publishing Co., New York, N.Y.
Superproject Plus	Computer Associates International, San Jose, Calif.
The Project Manager	Wiley Professional Software, New York, N.Y.

tion time can also be entered, as shown. Some packages use a backward expanding approach by starting from the all-crash solution.

More Sophisticated Computer Programs

Project management software for mainframes and minis is available for all types of hardware. Typical packages are PAC II and PAC III (from AGS Management Systems), Quicknet (Project Software and Development, Inc.), and Artemis (Metier Management Systems).

Micro-based projects range in price from $50 to over $5,000. They range in their capabilities from entry level to professional applications. A representative list is provided in Table 11.7.

Capabilities of the Packages

Listed below are some of the capabilities of these computer software packages.

- Drawing network and/or Gantt charts.
- Controlling several resources: time, labor, money, and so on.
- Resource leveling.
- Conducting risk analyses.
- Providing an on-line tutorial.
- Mainframe/micro interfacing.

- Windowing.
- Providing detailed cost analyses.
- Conducting what-if and goal-seeking analyses.
- Calculating job requirements, salaries, and skill levels.
- Report writing.
- Displaying leveled manpower requirements.
- Calculating labor, cost, time, and other trade-offs.

Note: Buyer's guides for project management software are published from time to time. For an example, see *Software Review.*

Examples

Figure 11.52 presents the printout of a more sophisticated program. The analysis involves both cost and labor control. Powerful graphical capabilities are available in most new packages. For example, Nelson's [10] software generated the bar chart shown in Figure 11.53. An example of a computer-drawn network is shown in Figure 11.54.

Nonproject Network Programs

Computer programs are also available for nonproject-oriented networks such as minimal spanning tree, shortest route, and maximum flow. Figures 11.55 and 11.56 illustrate the Lotfi and Pegels computer solutions to the corresponding manually solved examples in Sections 11.12 and 11.13. Note and that the program can allow for travel in both directions (called *symmetric)* and that the network can be printed. Figure 11.57 illustrates the computer solution to the maximum flow problem in Section 11.14 (using Nelson's software).

FIGURE 11.52

Cost and labor control

```
Job $4, Develop Work Manual
───────────────────────────
              Duration = 14 days            Earliest start = 1/2/90
       Work completed = 0 days              Earliest finish = 1/20/90
      On critical path = No                   Latest start = 2/6/90
            Slack time = 25 days             Latest finish = 2/27/90
         Prerequisites = none
      Manpower skills = Skill #1, Personnel (U.S.), 40 @ 150$ per man-day
                        Skill #2, Management (U.S.), 1.0 @ 250$ pe
                        Skill #3, Spanish liaison, 2.0 @ 200$ per man-day
          Total effort = 98.0 man-days
         Manpower cost = $17500.00
           Direct cost = $5000.00
```

FIGURE 11.53

Bar charting graphical capabilities

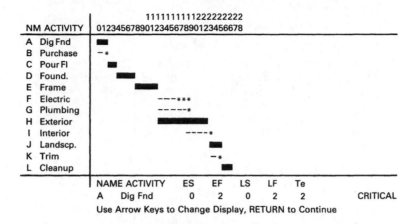

Project Name: detexp
Completion Time: 28

Project Type: PERT - Deterministic
No. of Critical Paths: 1

```
                        1111111111222222222
NM ACTIVITY            0123456789012345678901234566678
A  Dig Fnd            ██
B  Purchase          ─*
C  Pour Fl              ██
D  Found.                ██
E  Frame                  ██
F  Electric                  ───***
G  Plumbing                  ─────*
H  Exterior                  ████████
I  Interior                      ─────*
J  Landscp.                        ██
K  Trim                              ─*
L  Cleanup                            ██
```

NAME	ACTIVITY	ES	EF	LS	LF	Te	
A	Dig Fnd	0	2	0	2	2	CRITICAL

Use Arrow Keys to Change Display, RETURN to Continue

Notes: solid bar ██ designates a critical activity
dashed line ─ ─ ─ runs from early start to early finish for
non critical activities
asterisks ****** represent slack time

FIGURE 11.54

A computer-drawn network

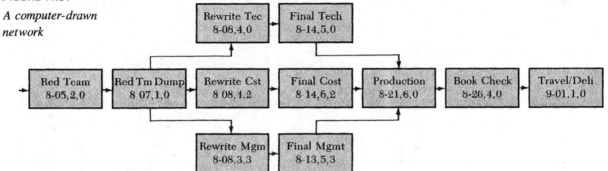

FIGURE 11.55

Minimal spanning tree solution

```
: Problem Title: EXAMPLE      Total Weight = 178   :
:     Minimum Spanning Tree                        :
:    Initial        Terminal        Distance       :
:    Node           Node            (Weight)        :
:    ───────        ────────        ──────────      :
:    Node1          Node3            28.00          :
:    Node3          Node2            26.00          :
:    Node2          Node4            32.00          :
:    Node4          Node6            20.00          :
:    Node4          Node8            22.00          :
:    Node8          Node7            26.00          :
:    Node7          Node5            24.00          :
```

493

FIGURE 11.56

Shortest route solution

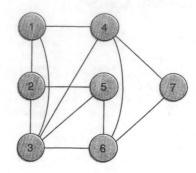

Problem Title: SHORTEST ROUTE

Total Distance =   35.00

Shortest Path Between Node 1 and Node 7

Initial Node	Terminal Node	Distance (Weight)
Node1	Node3	10.00
Node3	Node4	12.00
Node4	Node7	13.00

Problem Title: SHORTEST ROUTE

Total Distance =   29.00

Shortest Path Between Node 1 and Node 6

Initial Node	Terminal Node	Distance (Weight)
Node1	Node3	10.00
Node3	Node5	11.00
Node5	Node6	8.00

FIGURE 11.57

Maximum flow solution (using Nelson's software)

MAXIMUM FLOW

Problem Name: mf1

BRANCH	INITIAL NODE	TERMINAL NODE	CAPACITY S→E	S←E	BRANCH (ARC)	INITIAL NODE	TERMINAL NODE	CAPACITY S→E	S←E
1	1	2	2	0	2	1	3	10	0
3	2	3	0	9	4	2	4	3	0
5	3	4	6	0					

SOLUTION a) MAXIMUM FLOW OVER EACH POSSIBLE BRANCH

INITIAL NODE	TERMINAL NODE	CAPACITY	MAX FLOW
1	2	6	3
1	3	10	10
2	3	4	0
3	2	9	0
3	4	10	10
2	4	3	3

Total Flow = 13

---

b) MAXIMUM FLOW SOLUTION FROM SOURCE TO SINK

STEP	PATH SELECTED	MAX FLOW
1	1→2→4	3
2	1→3→4	10
	MAXIMUM TOTAL FLOW: 13	

11.16 Concluding Remarks

PERT and CPM are tools for planning, monitoring, and controlling large, complex projects.

Formulation

The project under consideration can be presented graphically as a network. Such a presentation is based on the following assumptions:

The assumptions:

1. The project can be subdivided into a set of predictable, independent activities, each of which has a clear beginning and end.
2. Each activity can be sequenced as to its predecessors or successors. An activity cannot start until all its predecessors are completed.
3. The network is not cyclical; that is, each activity is executed once and only once during the life of the project. Any repeating activity is considered a different activity.
4. Activity times may be estimated, either as a single-point estimate (CPM) or as a three-point estimate (PERT).
5. The durations of the activities are independent of each other.

In addition, special assumptions are made with respect to PERT and CPM.

PERT

a. Activity duration is assumed to follow the Beta distribution.
b. The variance of the length of the project is assumed to be equal to the sum of the variances of the activities on the critical path.

CPM

a. Duration of an activity has an inverse relation to its execution cost.
b. The normal time for an activity is the slowest. Executing an activity in a normal time costs the least.

As with any other models, here, too, not all the assumptions hold in all cases. However, most of these assumptions hold. Relaxing of some of these assumptions leads to more complicated network models that were discussed earlier.

Methodology and Solution Approaches

The major objective of PERT and CPM analyses is to identify the *critical activities* of a project. The search for these activities can be done through a comparison of all paths in the network (complete enumeration), looking for the longest path (which is labeled the critical path), or through a special algorithm that computes the slack times in the network. In the algorithm case, all events with no slack are situated on the critical path. PERT and CPM can also be presented as LP models.

It is also possible to use simulation to enlarge the scope of PERT/CPM analyses. For example, using simulation, it is possible to find the probabilities of any noncritical path being delayed or becoming critical for any desired discrete or continuous distribution of the activity times.

PERT versus CPM

The distinction between PERT and CPM centers around two areas. In PERT, a three-point estimate of time is used that introduces a probabilistic element into the results. In CPM, a cost-time relationship is exhibited, and the cost of shortening the project's completion time is evaluated.

Application

PERT and CPM are powerful and flexible tools for decision making. Specifically, they can be used in planning, monitoring, and controlling large projects. Due to their graphical presentation and simple conceptual basis, they are relatively easy to explain and therefore easy to implement. Further assistance in implementation is achieved through adaptability to computers. A wide range of preprogrammed computer routines is available from many software vendors.

Management by exception

Identification of critical events and activities enables management to exercise better control of the project by using a management-by-exception philosophy. In addition, control becomes even more effective because the corrective actions and replanning can take effect as soon as deviations in critical activities are reported.

In summary, PERT and CPM can be most effective amplifiers of managers' skills.

Management Science in Practice

Optimizing Truck Routes at Quality Stores

Quality Stores is a Michigan-based retail chain of about 40 stores situated within 250 miles of one centralized distribution center. Their fleet of 11 trucks delivers goods to the stores, backhauls overstocks to the distribution center for redistribution, and backhauls vendor goods from nearby suppliers. Deliveries, ranging from a half-truckload to several truckloads, are commonly made to each store twice a week. When seasonal or daily fluctuations exceed the fleet's capability, the excess is contracted to common carriers.

Even with such a small situation, the number of possible route combinations to evaluate is far beyond the capability of a human dispatcher. For example, even for just 10 stores and 10 suppliers requiring deliveries and pickups on a particular day, 3,135 alternative routes must be evaluated. Beyond this, there are various ways of grouping stores and suppliers on the routes, a fact that futher complicates the problem. Because the budget for Quality Stores' truck fleet is extremely high, even saving just a few percentage points of the total cost can significantly improve their annual profits.

The essence of the shortest route network solution is to identify the shortest routes, assign trucks to the routes, and assign drivers to the trucks. Obviously, there are legal restrictions on driving speeds, but there are also laws concerning the maximum driving time and time on the road (including loading and unloading) per truck driver. Although the trucks must start and return to the distribution center, multiple dispatches of a truck on the same day need not use the same driver. Other restrictions also complicate the problem. For example, because all the trucks are rear loaded, deliveries must generally be made before pickups. However, if the pickups are intended for the next delivery point, even this rule can be relaxed for some types of situations.

The routing optimization was done with a version of branch and bound to obtain the shortest routes. Data concerning distances, temporary road closings, delivery requirements, pickup requirements, store hours, and other such elements are also considered in the model. (The model runs on a personal computer.)

Quality Stores is currently using this system to route its trucks, saving nearly a half million dollars a year (primarily from more efficient backhauls). They are also reducing store delivery frequencies and reevaluating stocking policies, based on the results of the program. For example, they learned that overstock backhauls from their stores to the distribution center were much more expensive than they had thought, prompting them to reduce prices on overstocks to sell the goods at the stores and thus not require backhauls. Also, the loss of time spent waiting for loading and unloading at the stores made the company decide to purchase additional trailers. (The trailers could simply be dropped off and picked up later, which would avoid the expensive waiting time.) The understanding that the model has brought to the company is expected to result in a return many times the cost of the additional trailers.

Source: C. A. Yano, "Vehicle Routing for Quality Stores," *Interfaces,* March–April 1987, pp. 52–63.

Questions:

1. How does rear loading restrict the sequence of sites to visit in the routing?

2. Which policy changes were due to routing changes and which were due to better understanding of the problem? Do you think this is typical of the management science approach?

3. Is this just a routing problem? What other types of problems are included here?

11.17 Problems for Part B

(Slack in all the problems refers to "total slack/float.")

16. Given a project with the following information from a computer printout:

Activity	Standard Deviation	Critical?	Duration
a	2	yes	2
b	1		3
c	0	yes	4
d	3		2
e	1	yes	1
f	2		6
g	2	yes	4
h	0	yes	2

Find:

a. The probability of completing this project in 12 weeks (or less).

b. The probability of completing this project in 16 weeks (or less).

c. The probability of completing this project in 13 weeks (or less).

d. The number of weeks required to assure a 92.5 percent chance of completion.

17. Given the following project:

a. Find all "earliest dates," including project completion (T_E's for all events).

b. Find all "latest dates" (T_L's for all events).

c. Determine the critical path and the event slack values.

d. What is the critical path leading to event **5?**

e. What will happen if activity **4–5's** actual time slips to 9?

f. What will be the slack on activity **3–5** if activity **4–5** slips to 9 weeks and activity **5–7** takes 6 weeks?

Activity	Times (Weeks) Optimistic	Most Likely	Pessimistic
1–2	5	11	11
1–3	10	10	10
1–4	2	5	8
2–6	1	7	13
3–6	4	4	10
3–7	4	7	10
3–5	2	2	2
4–5	0	6	6
5–7	2	8	14
6–7	1	4	7

18. a. Find the probability of finishing the project in Problem 17 in 19 weeks. In 17 weeks. In 24 weeks.

b. What is the probability of completing event **5** in Problem 17 by 9 weeks?

c. If management wants to be 80 percent sure that the project will be completed by a "guaranteed" date, what date should be quoted?

19. The following event completion times have been estimated by a contracting firm:

Activity	Times Optimistic	Most Likely	Pessimistic
1–2	3	6	9
1–3	1	4	7
3–2	0	3	6
3–4	3	3	3
3–5	2	2	8
2–4	0	0	6
2–5	2	5	8
4–6	4	4	10
4–5	1	1	1
5–6	1	4	7

If the firm can complete the project within 14 days, it will be given a $20,000 bonus. If not, it must pay a one-time penalty of $3,500. Should the firm accept the contract? What other factors are probably relevant? Are there any noncritical paths whose variance might become important?

20. Given a PERT network:
Find:

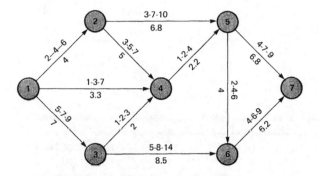

a. The estimated project completion time.
b. The critical path.
c. The slack on events **2** and **3**.
d. The slack on activities **1–4** and **2–5**.
e. The probability the project will be completed in 20 weeks or less.
f. The probability the project will be completed in 30 weeks or less.
g. The number of weeks required to complete the project with 95 percent certainty.

21. The following data were obtained from a study of the time required to overhaul a small power plant:

	Crash Schedule		Normal Schedule	
Activity	Time	Cost	Time	Cost
1–2	3	6	5	4
1–3	1	5	5	3
2–4	5	7	10	4
3–4	2	6	7	4
2–6	2	5	6	3
4–6	5	9	11	6
4–5	4	6	6	3
6–7	1	4	5	2
5–7	1	5	4	2

Note: Costs are given in thousands of dollars; time in weeks.
a. Find the all-normal schedule and cost.
b. Find the all-crash schedule and cost.
c. Find the total cost required to expedite all activities from all-normal (case *a*) to all-crash (case *b*).
d. Find the *least-cost* plan for the all-crash time schedule. Start from the all-crash problem (*b*).
e. Find the least cost for an intermediate time schedule of 17 weeks.

22. Reconsider Problem 1 under the constraint that the project *must* be completed in 16 weeks. This time, however, activities *c, f, h,* and *i* may be crashed as follows:

Activity	Crash Time (Weeks)	Additional Cost per Week
c	7	40
f	6	20
h	2	10
i	3	30

Find the best schedule and its cost.

23. The CPM network below has a normal time and a fixed cost of $90 per day. The various activities can be reduced up to their crash time with the additional costs shown:

Activity	Crash Time	Cost Increase, per Day Reduction
1–2	4	30 first day, 50 second, 70 third
2–3	6	40 first day, 45 second, 65 third
1–3	10	60 each
2–4	9	35 first, 60 second
3–4	3	—

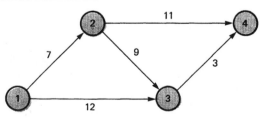

Find the least-cost schedule.

Hint: Start with normal time of 19 days
(1–2–3–4). The total cost there is $19 \times 90 =$
$1,710. Then start cutting to 18. You save $90 fixed
cost but have a cost increase of $30 when you cut
activity **1–2** by 1 day. Continue until no further
reductions are possible or the cost climbs.

24. Given the following network with normal times and
crash times (in parentheses), find the optimal
time-cost plan. Assume indirect costs are $100 per
day. The crash data are:

Activity	Time Reduction, Direct Cost Per Day
1–2	$30 first, $50 second
2–3	$80 each
3–4	$25 first, $60 second
2–4	$30 first, $70 second, $90 third

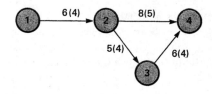

25. Given a proposed water system with the feasible
distances shown below, find the optimal layout of
pipes such that water will reach all points from the
pump to *F*.

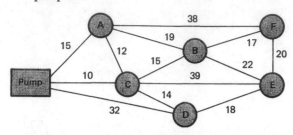

26. Your company plans to install an information system
composed of a mainframe computer and seven
terminals. The computer may be connected directly
to a terminal or a terminal may be connected to
another terminal that is connected to the computer.
The matrix of distances is given below (an *x* means
no direct connection is possible), as well as the map
of terminals and computer locations. Find the optimal
installation plan.

	Computer	Terminal Number						
		T1	*T2*	*T3*	*T4*	*T5*	*T6*	*T7*
Terminal	—	20	48	25	61	21	37	60
T1	20	—	30	32	60	50	65	85
T2	48	30	—	22	33	40	*x*	73
T3	25	32	22	—	36	18	*x*	*x*
T4	61	60	33	36	—	67	52	40
T5	21	50	40	18	67	—	*x*	*x*
T6	37	65	*x*	*x*	52	*x*	—	*x*
T7	60	85	73	*x*	40	*x*	*x*	—

27. Find the maximum flow in the following networks.

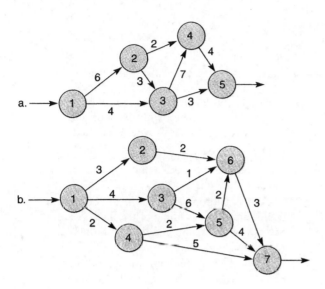

a.

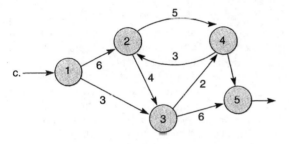

b.

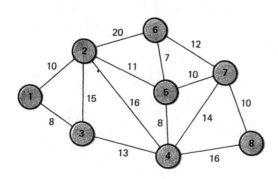

c.

28. Find the shortest route from **1** to all nodes.

29. Given the following estimates regarding the activities composing a project to be planned (the activities are numbered by initial and terminal events):

Estimated Completion Times in Months			
Activity	*Minimum, a*	*Maximum, b*	*Most likely, m*
1–2	2	3	$2\frac{3}{4}$
1–3	1	$1\frac{1}{2}$	$1\frac{1}{2}$
3–5	$\frac{1}{2}$	1	$\frac{3}{4}$
5–6	$\frac{1}{4}$	$\frac{1}{2}$	$\frac{1}{2}$
3–4	1	4	3
4–5	$\frac{1}{4}$	$\frac{3}{4}$	$\frac{1}{2}$
2–4	1	4	$2\frac{1}{4}$
2–7	1	2	$1\frac{3}{4}$
4–7	3	4	$3\frac{3}{4}$
7–5	$\frac{1}{4}$	$\frac{1}{2}$	$\frac{3}{8}$

Determine whether a 10-month completion time deadline can be met with at least 95% certainty.

30. Find the minimum spanning tree for Problem 28.

31. Given the following table of minimum and maximum times for completion of each activity, cost per unit of performance time decrease, and precedences, derive the project duration cost function for the project.

	Completion Times		*Cost per Time*	*Immediate*
Activity	*Min.*	*Max.*	*Unit Decrease*	*Predecessors*
A	4	6	8	—
B	4	8	9	—
C	3	5	3	—
D	3	3	∞	A
E	3	5	4	A
F	8	12	20	B
G	5	8	5	C,D
H	6	6	∞	E

32. Find the shortest path for the network in Figure 11.36.

11.18 CASES
CASE I. THE SHARON CONSTRUCTION CORPORATION

The Sharon Construction Corporation has been awarded a contract for the construction of a 20,000-seat stadium. The construction must start by February 15 and be completed within one year. A penalty clause of $15,000 per week of delay beyond February 15 of next year is written into the contract.

Jim Brown, the president of the company, called a planning meeting. In the meeting, he expressed great satisfaction at obtaining the contract, revealing that the company could net as much as $300,000 on the project. He was confident that the project could be completed on time, with an allowance made for the usual delays anticipated in such a large project.

Bonnie Green, the director of personnel, agreed that in a normal year, only slight delays might develop due to a shortage of labor. However, she reminded the president that for such a large project, the company would have to use unionized employees and that the construction industry labor agreements were due to expire on November 30. Past experience indicated a 50-50 chance for a strike.

Jim Brown agreed that a strike might cause a problem. Unfortunately, there was no way to change the contract. He inquired about the prospective length of a strike. Bonnie figured that such a strike would last at least 8 weeks (70 percent chance) and possibly 12 weeks (30 percent chance).

Jim was not too pleased with these prospects. However, before he had a chance to discuss contingency plans, he was interrupted by Jack White, the vice president for engineering. Jack commented that an extremely cold December had been predicted. This factor had not been taken into consideration during earlier estimates, because previous forecasts called for milder weather. Concrete pouring in a cold December would require, in one out of every three cases (depending on the temperature), special heating that costs $500 per week.

This additional information did not please Jim at all. The chances for delays were mounting. In addition to the penalty, an overhead expense of $500 per week would be incurred in case of any delay. The technical details of the project are given in the appendix to this case.

The management team was asked to consider contingency alternatives for coping with the situation. At the end of the week, five proposals were submitted.

1. Expedite the pouring of seat gallery supports. This would cost $20,000 and cut the duration of the activity to six weeks.

2. The same as proposal 1, but in addition, put a double shift on the filling of the field. A cost of $10,000 would result in a five-week time reduction.

3. The roof is very important, because it precedes several activities. The use of three shifts and some overtime could cut six weeks off the roofing, at an additional cost of only $9,000.

4. Take no special action until December 1. Then, if December is indeed cold, defer the pouring until the cold wave breaks, schedule permitting, and heat whenever necessary. If a strike occurs, wait until it is over (no other choice) and then expedite *all* remaining activities. In that case, the duration of any activity could be cut to no more than one third of its normal duration. The additional cost per activity for any week that is cut would be $3,000.

5. Do not take any special action at all; that is, hope and pray that no strike and no cold December occur (no cost).

Analyze the five proposals and make recommendations.

Appendix: Technical Details of the Stadium

The stadium is an indoor structure with a seating capacity of 20,000. The project begins with clearing the site, an activity that lasts eight weeks. Once the site is clear, the work can start simultaneously on the structure itself and on the field.

The work in the field involves subsurface drainage that lasts eight weeks, followed by filling for the playing field and track. Only with the completion of the filling (14 weeks) can the installation of the artificial playing turf take place, an activity that consumes 12 weeks.

The work on the structure itself starts with excavation, followed by the pouring of concrete footings. Each of these activities takes four weeks. Next comes the pouring of supports for seat galleries (12 weeks), followed by erecting precast galleries (13 weeks). The seats can then be poured (four weeks), and are ready for painting. However, the painting (three weeks) cannot begin until the dressing rooms are completed (four weeks). The dressing rooms can be completed only after the roof is erected (eight weeks). The roof must be erected on a steel structure that takes four weeks to install. This activity can start only after the concrete footings are poured.

Once the roof is erected, work can start simultaneously on the lights (five weeks) and on the scoreboard and other facilities (four weeks). Assume that there are 28 days in February and that February 15 falls on a Monday.

Case II. Dapshar Corporation Goes Multinational

Dapshar Corporation is an emerging company in the field of plasmascopes. Several weeks ago, the company decided to open sales and possibly manufacturing facilities in several Eastern European countries. Management is aware that such a mission would be a complex project. All executives involved were requested to prepare a list of activities for the project. These activities are described below. The numbers in parentheses following the description of each activity indicate the estimated time, in weeks, required for the completion of the activity (optimistic, most likely, and pessimistic estimates). If only one number is given, the time should be considered as constant.

A. Planning

The Training Program. In order to be able to penetrate the foreign markets, a sales force will have to be specially trained and oriented, so it is necessary to develop a training program (**7–9–11**). At the same time, management will be selecting the personnel most adaptable for this job (**2–3–4**). Next, the salespersons will be taking a five-week introductory course ("all you ever wanted to know about Eastern Europe").

The actual training program (13 weeks) will start after the introductory course. This training program will be given at the company's headquarters. On its completion, the salespersons will be taken abroad for a six-week tour of Eastern Europe. The salespersons will be given time to analyze the foreign markets, the consumer's needs, and the political climates of the countries. At the end of the tour, the participants will return to the United States, where specific assignments to foreign countries will be made based on psychological tests and interviews (**2–3–4**). Once the final selection is made, the salespersons will be dispatched to the various countries (**1**).

Preparation at the Foreign Countries. At the same time the training program is being developed in the United States, preliminary work will be started abroad. First, potential centers will be identified and appropriate office space will be rented (**9–12–15**). After that, recruiting of local staff will begin (**4–6–14**) simultaneously with legal arrangements (**5–8–11**). The local staff will receive preliminary training (**5**) and will then be sent for three weeks of training at U.S. headquarters. However, before going to the United States, the local staff will meet the U.S. salespersons in Eastern Europe before the start of the tour.

On returning from the United States, the local staff will be assigned specific jobs (**2**). However, the assignments can be executed only after all legal arrangements have been made.

Work Manual. To assure appropriate activities abroad, management will develop a work manual for the salespersons. The development of the manual can begin immediately but can be finished only after the legal arrangements in the foreign countries have been completed. The work manual will take 16 weeks, of which the last 2 will be spent on the analysis of the completed legal arrangements. The manual will be given to the U.S. salespersons *prior* to their departure for their foreign assignments but *after* they have been assigned to specific countries. Travel time and initial arrangements will take one week. At that time, the project can be regarded as completed.

Because top management is aware of the complications involved in such a project, they are interested in an appropriate planning tool. Therefore, the decision was made to utilize network planning techniques.

Questions

1. What network technique should be used?
2. Plan the project. Show graphically all pertinent information.
3. Identify the critical path(s) and the slacks on all activities.

B. Risk Analysis

The information regarding the completion of the activities given in part A is not known with certainty. Therefore, management is not 100 percent sure if the entire project can be completed on time. (What is the chance of completing the entire project on or before the earliest computed time?)

Questions

1. Management is planning a large press conference at the end of this project. However, they want to be at least 95 percent sure that the project will indeed be completed. For the purpose of hotel reservations, how many weeks from the start should rooms be reserved?
2. Management would like to know the chance of completing this project in 30 weeks or earlier.
3. Management would also like to know the chance of completing the project in 37 weeks or less.

C. Refinements

Execution with an Advanced Computer Software Package.

1. Input Data in 1994 (use actual dates)
   Starting date: 1/1/94
   Assume: Five-day workweeks
         Set actual dates for holidays
2. Skill Categories: Use at least four categories:

	Daily Cost ($)
Skill 1: U.S. personnel	100
Skill 2: Management	150
Skill 3: International staff	60
Skill 4: Instructors	80

3. Decide yourself what skill categories will be used in each activity.
4. Level the labor requirement for the project *at least one time*.
5. Make any necessary assumptions; write them down.

Glossary

Activity A specific job or task that is part of a project and requires time and resources for completion.

Backward pass Solving a network problem by starting at the end first.

CPM (critical path method) A tool that plans and monitors both time and cost where expediting of activities (crashing) is possible.

Crashing　Expediting an activity so that it will be completed in less than its normal time up to the minimum possible duration.

Critical activity　Any activity on the critical path. All of these activities have either zero slack or the same amount of minimum slack in the network.

Critical path　The longest path(s) in the network. This path has the least slack in the network. It is wholly composed of critical activities and critical events.

Dummy activity　A fictitious activity that requires no time for completion. Its main purpose is to establish the precedence relationship in a network.

Duration　Time required to complete an activity.

Earliest date (T_E)　The earliest time (counted from the beginning of the project) at which an event, or activity, may be finished.

Earliest finish (EF)　The earliest time an activity can be completed, provided it started at its ES.

Earliest start (ES)　The earliest calendar time that an activity can start.

Event　A specific accomplishment at a recognizable point in time; a milestone, a checkpoint. An event occurs when *all* preceding activities have been completed. Events use neither time nor resources.

Expected time (t_e)　Average duration time for an activity.

Forward pass　Solving a network problem by starting at the beginning and proceeding forward.

Free float (FF)　A slack that represents the time that an activity can be delayed without delaying the early start time of an immediately following activity.

Graphical evaluation and review technique (GERT)　An extension of PERT that relaxes several of PERT's assumptions, making it more realistic (and more complex).

Greedy algorithm　A solution method that incrementally solves a problem by selecting the next best element in the set.

Latest allowable date (T_L)　The latest date (counted from the beginning of the project) at which an event can occur without holding up the project's earliest completion date.

Latest finish (LF)　The latest an activity can be finished without delaying the project.

Latest start (LS)　The latest an activity can start without delaying the project.

Maximal flow　Finding the distribution of flows through a network that permits the greatest amount to flow from the source to the sink.

Most likely time estimate (t_m)　An estimate of an activity duration time that is considered to be the most likely.

Network　A graphical presentation of a project showing the sequential relationship of activities. It consists of nodes representing events and arcs representing activities.

Normal time　The lowest cost activity time in a CPM network.

Optimistic time estimate (t_o)　An estimate of an activity's duration under ideal conditions; the shortest possible time to complete the activity. Such conditions occur only 1 out of 100 times.

Path (in the network)　A sequence of activities leading from the beginning of the project to its end.

PERT (program evaluation review technique)　A planning and monitoring technique for projects based on three time estimates for each activity's duration.

PERT/Cost　An extension of PERT that allows the planning and control of both time and cost in a project.

Pessimistic time estimate (t_p)　An estimate of the activity's duration under the worst possible conditions that may occur in only 1 out of 100 cases.

Project　A collection of activities with a definable beginning and a definable end (the goal).

Shared slack　Slack shared by two or more noncritical activities.

Shortest route　Finding the shortest path from one point to another in a network.

Sink　A destination where all flows end.

Slack　The extra time that an activity (or an event) can be held up without delaying the project's completion.

Source　The point where all flows begin.

Spanning tree　A network where every node may be reached from every other node through one or more arcs.

Total float (TF)　The extra time an activity or event can be delayed without delaying the project completion, assuming that the slack is not used by another activity already.

11.20 References and Bibliography

1. Badiru, A. B. *Project Management in Manufacturing and High Technology Operations*. New York: John Wiley & Sons, 1988.

2. Dreger, J. B. *Project Management: Effective Scheduling*. New York: Van Nostrand Reinhold, 1991.

3. Kerzner, H. *Project Management: A Systems Approach to Planning, Scheduling, and Controlling*. New York: Van Nostrand Reinhold, 1989.

4. Kezsbom, D. S., D. L. Schilling, and V. A. Edward. *Dynamic Project Management*. New York: John Wiley & Sons, 1989.

5. Knudson, J. *How to Be a Successful Project Manager*. Saranac Lake, N.Y.: American Management Association, 1989.

6. Knudson, J. and I. Bitz. *Project Management: How to Plan and Manage Successful Projects*. Saranac Lake, NY: American Management Assn., 1991.

7. Levine, H. A. *Project Management Using Microcomputers*. Berkeley, Calif.: Osborne McGraw-Hill, 1986.

8. Lock, D. *Project Management*. 4th ed. Brookfield, Vt.: Gower Publishing, 1988.

9. Meredith, J. R., and S. J. Mantel, Jr. *Project Management: A Managerial Approach*. 2nd ed., New York: John Wiley & Sons, 1989.

10. Nelson, T. R. *The Management Science System*. Homewood, Ill.: Richard D. Irwin, Inc., 1988. (Software).

Inventory Models

The use of mathematical models to determine the best inventory level to maintain and the best time to reorder merchandise is one of the oldest techniques of management science. Part A of this chapter is directed toward determining a proper balance between the cost of holding an inventory and the cost of placing an order. The result is the classical "economic order quantity" (EOQ) model. Part A also covers the applicability and limitations of this model and closes with a discussion of some practical inventory systems.

The most common extension of the EOQ model is the "economic lot size" (ELS) production model, presented in Part B. Also presented are the quantity discount model, the establishment of safety stock, MRP, single-period inventories, and computerization.

PART A: BASICS

As Jed Stowe, the director of materials, walked out of the vice president's office, it was clear that he felt frustrated. Just last month, Jed recalled, the vice president had complained about the secretaries "wasting time filling out requisition (order) forms for materials." Almost in the same breath, he mentioned the possibility of an inventory shortage due to an impending strike against their major supplier. In the face of those comments, Jed thought that a simple solution for both of the vice president's concerns was to order materials in larger amounts but less frequently. Thus, the number of orders would be reduced (less work for the secretaries) and protection would exist in the event of a strike against the supplier. This strategy carried the additional advantage of allowing the company to obtain discounts given by the supplier on large orders.

Yesterday, however, the previous month's operating cost report came out and the cost of keeping the inventory had jumped to a record high. Jed was summoned to the vice president's office, where he learned that the additional inventory cost due to his larger orders caused a cash flow problem to the company. Jed concluded that there was simply no way to win.

12.1 Inventory Systems

Characteristics of the Situation

Jed Stowe's plight illustrates a typical inventory dilemma. An inventory is any stock of economic resources that is stored for future use. Jed's case called attention to the following dilemma: If a commodity is ordered frequently, then the costs of ordering (paperwork, secretarial time) are high. On the other hand, ordering more units less frequently saves on ordering costs but increases the expense of keeping a larger inventory. Thus, the proper ordering policy is a dilemma. The management problem in this case is: *How frequently should materials be ordered?*

Two conflicting costs

How frequently to order supplies?

This is a problem for management because the dilemma exists for many of the items in stock, sometimes tens of thousands of items. Further, due to continuous changes in prices, the solution should be updated periodically. What makes the situation even more complicated is that there are many (theoretically, infinite) possible solutions to the problems. An item may be ordered on a daily basis or once every 10 years. For all these reasons a trial-and-error solution is often not practical. Management science provides models that execute the search for an *optimal* solution rather quickly.

Some specific examples of inventories are:

- Items on the shelves of department and food stores.
- Unused telephone numbers the phone company is holding.

Blood, cash, spaces

- Cash on hand at the bank (reserves).
- Blood in blood banks.
- Standby pilots and flight attendants employed by airlines.
- Empty space in a warehouse for incoming shipments.

Inventories in a Production System

Several types of inventories are maintained by organizations for their production systems. Some of the major inventories are:

1. Raw materials.
2. Finished goods.
3. Semifinished products.
4. Spare parts and supplies.

The general production process is illustrated in Figure 12.1. As shown, vendors supply raw materials, supplies, spares, and even semifinished parts to the firm. These are stored as inventories and then enter the production process at the point where parts are fabricated, some of which temporarily enter the storeroom as semifinished parts, and then are sent on to assembly, where finished goods are produced for sale. The finished goods may be temporarily stocked in the storeroom or a warehouse or go directly to a customer. The former are called "made-to-stock" goods and the latter are called "made-to-order" goods. In some cases, products are fabricated "to stock" and then, as customer orders come in, assembled "to order," thereby cutting down on the lead time to customers.

The Purpose of Inventory

The following is a list of the major reasons for maintaining an inventory.

Protection Against Fluctuating Demand
Inventories are kept to meet peak demand. For example, blood is stored in hospitals in quantities sufficient to meet the needs of a major accident. Demand fluctuations are frequently related to the seasonality of the products.

Many reasons for
inventory

Protection Against Delayed Supply
A strike by the supplier's employees is one reason why deliveries may not arrive on time. Lack of material at the supplier level, strikes in the transportation network, or a snowstorm are other possible causes for shortages. Inventories are kept as a buffer that can be used until late deliveries arrive. Supply variations are sometimes also related to seasonality.

Protection Against Inflation
Inventories are often kept as a hedge against inflation. In this case, inventories are built up in anticipation of a price increase. This speculative practice is especially common in the commodity markets (such as wheat or oil).

Benefits of Large Quantities
Purchasing large quantities of an item often entitles the buyer to a price *discount* (lower per-unit price). Similarly, in the case of manufacturing large production lots, the uti-

FIGURE 12.1

*The production/
inventory process*

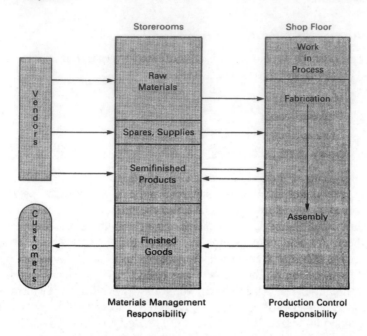

lization of more efficient automated equipment can be justified by the reduction in the per-unit manufacturing cost.

Primary Basis for Business
Retail operations involving customer examination and selection require fully stocked shelves and complete inventories.

Savings on Ordering Cost
Ordering in large quantities reduces the number of times that an order must be placed and processed. Because a fixed cost is associated with placing each order, the fewer times one places an order, the lower total cost of ordering will be.

Other Reasons
Inventories are kept for several other reasons: An inventory may improve the bargaining power of a firm with a supplier (or with its own employees) by making the company less vulnerable to delays or stoppages. Inventories also are kept so that machines can be shut down for overhauls. An inventory of labor is maintained to meet fluctuating production demands in order to reduce hiring, firing, and training costs.

The Importance of Inventory Management

Proper inventory management may be one of the most important functions of management. Tracing several bankruptcies of construction firms and agricultural machinery manufacturers has shown that overstocking was the major contributor to failure. As another example, grocery stores have a profit margin of only about 1 percent of sales;

thus, saving $20,000 in inventory costs is equivalent to a sales increase of $2 million. High-technology companies must often write off expensively produced inventories because of technological obsolescence.

Materials management

Excess inventories are costly to store but insufficient inventories may result in loss of market share or idle employees. The task of inventory control is part of a management function named *materials management*, which is concerned with acquisition, distribution, storage, and disposal of materials and parts in organizations. In this text, we will only address the topic of inventory management.

12.2 The Structure of the Inventory System

The inventory models described in the remainder of this chapter pertain only to an *individual* item in stock. This means, for example, that with an inventory system of three different items, the model must be employed three times.

Inventory ordering— a cyclical process

An inventory system involves a *cyclical process* that is assumed to run over several periods and whose major characteristics are described next.

Inventory Level

An item is stocked in a warehouse, store, or any other storage area. This stock constitutes an *inventory*. The size of the inventory is called the *inventory level* (or the inventory *on hand*).

Demand and Depletion

The inventory is *depleted* as *demand* occurs. Assume that one starts with an inventory of 100 units, as shown in Figure 12.2. As time passes, the inventory level declines due to the demand for the item in stock. The *rate of demand* determines the **depletion** rate

FIGURE 12.2

An inventory system

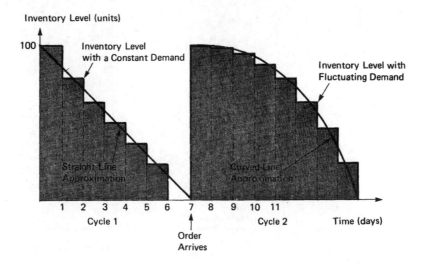

Constant or fluctuating demand

and the inventory level. The higher the rate of demand, the quicker the inventory is reduced. The rate of demand can be constant (e.g., five units per day), or may fluctuate (e.g., three units on the first day and seven on the second). A *constant demand* reduces the inventory level in equal steps. Graphically, it is shown as a stairway (see cycle 1 in Figure 12.2). The steps of the constant demand can be approximated by a straight line. A *fluctuating (variable) demand* is shown by unequal steps, as in cycle 2 of Figure 12.2, and can be approximated by a curve.

Reordering

Reorder points and lead times

To rebuild an inventory, the item is replenished periodically. When the inventory level is reduced to a certain level called the **reorder point,** a **replenishment** order is placed (see Figure 12.3). The time between reordering and receiving the shipment is called the **lead time.**

Replenishment, Shortages, and Surpluses

Shortages result from demand fluctuation or lead time variation

In some basic inventory models, it is assumed that the reordering is scheduled so that the replenishment will arrive exactly when the inventory level reaches zero. However, if the demand fluctuates and/or the lead time varies, the shipment may arrive either before or after the stock is completely depleted; that is, the depletion and replenishment do not coincide. In such a case, a surplus or a shortage will occur. If the shipment arrives *after* depletion, then the demand cannot be met and a **shortage,** (or **stockout**)

FIGURE 12.3

Reordering, replenishment, a shortage, and surplus

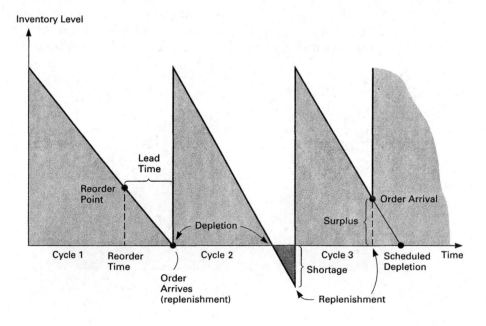

will occur. This is shown by the second cycle of Figure 12.3. When the shipment arrives *prior* to depletion, an inventory level larger than zero, or a **surplus,** exists, as demonstrated by the third cycle of Figure 12.3. (Also see Figure 12.12.)

Safety Stock

Shortages can be eliminated or reduced by establishing a *buffer* or **safety stock.** This topic is discussed in detail in Section 12.14.

The Average Inventory

For purposes of inventory decision making, as well as for other managerial uses such as insurance and taxation, the concept of an **average inventory** is used. To illustrate, let us assume that during a five-day period, the inventory levels are as follows:

Monday	Tuesday	Wednesday	Thursday	Friday
16	12	8	4	0

The average inventory is then:

$$\frac{16 + 12 + 8 + 4 + 0}{5} = 8 \text{ units}$$

This is shown in Figure 12.4.

FIGURE 12.4

Average inventory

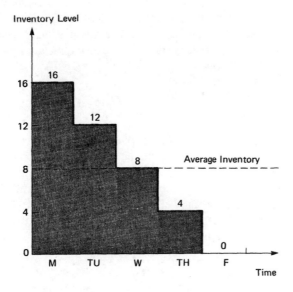

Average inventory is
one-half the
maximum

If the demand is *constant,* the average inventory can be computed by adding the inventory at the beginning of a cycle (16 in this example) to the inventory at the end of the cycle (0 in this case) and dividing it by 2. If the inventory at the end of the cycle is 0 (as in this example), the *average inventory equals exactly one-half of the initial* (or *maximum*) *inventory*. If the demand is not constant, a more complicated formulation is required.

Inventory Problems and Decisions

The major problem of inventory management is determining the *appropriate inventory level*. This problem is related to the problem of "how much" to order, because the amount ordered determines, in part, the inventory level. Also related is the problem of "when" to order. These three issues appear together in most models. A fourth issue that will affect the inventory level concerns the creation of a safety stock.

Other inventory decisions are often made by management. Some of these decisions are:

· Where to stock.
· How the inventory system should be staffed.
· Whether the inventory system should be computerized.

Such decisions are discussed in texts specializing in inventory management. See Greene [4], Silver [11], and Tersine [13].

12.3 Inventory Costs

Inventory problems are usually examined from a cost, rather than from a profit, standpoint. Generally, only relevant (or incremental) costs are considered. Therefore, in the remainder of this chapter, whenever we refer to cost, we mean an incremental one. The major costs are described below.

Ordering Cost (K)

Ordering cost includes all the expenses of placing orders. It is assumed to be a fixed cost per order; that is, each time an order is placed, the same expenses occur regardless of how many units are ordered. Included in the ordering cost may be some clerical and paperwork expenses of purchasing, receiving, bookkeeping, and data processing that are directly related to ordering, as well as the expenses of delivery, postage, and the related overhead (such as direct telephone charges). The cost of ordering can be computed by dividing the total annual cost related to ordering by the number of orders processed that year.

Example

A typical ordering cost calculation is:

Expense Category	Annual Expense for 2,000 Orders	Annual Expense for 5,000 Orders
Department head	$ 25,000	$ 25,000
Clerks (at $13,000 each)	26,000	39,000
Buyers (at $18,000 each)	18,000	36,000
Secretary	12,000	12,000
Receiving clerks (at $14,000 each)	14,000	28,000
Bookkeeping (accountant)	15,000	20,000
Supplies	1,200	2,000
Phone, postage, miscellaneous	800	1,000
Overhead	20,000	25,000
Total	$132,000	$188,000

If the company processes 2,000 orders, then the average cost per order is $132,000/2,000 = \$66$. For 5,000 orders, the cost will be $188,000/5,000 = \$37.60$. The *incremental cost,* however, is

$$(188,000 - 132,000)/(5,000 - 2,000) = \$18.67$$

If we change from 2,000 orders to 5,000 orders, the incremental cost is only \$18.67 per order, and *this* cost must be considered in the analysis. Note that some of the ordering costs are fixed or semifixed, whereas others are variable. The point here, and for the remaining costs as well, is a subtle one. Only use the costs that can indeed be *saved* by changing the ordering quantity. Usually, it is the incremental, rather than the full, cost.

Holding (Carrying) Cost (H)

The expenses of holding or carrying the inventory include such components as:

- *Cost of capital:* The interest paid on the capital invested in inventories or the opportunity cost of doing something else with the money.
- *Storage:* Cost of maintaining the storage space. This includes rental fees, light, heat, security, and janitorial services.
- *Storekeeping operations:* Expenses such as record-keeping and taking of physical inventory.
- *Insurance and taxes.*
- *Obsolescence and deterioration* of the items stored.

Holding cost can be expressed two ways

All **holding (carrying) costs** are totaled and expressed either in terms of *dollars per item per year,* or in *percentage of the value of the inventory.*

Example

A chair costs $40. To keep the chair in inventory for one year will cost $H = \$10$. Alternatively, we can say that the holding cost is 25 percent of the value of the item (25 percent of $40 is $10).

Shortage (or Stockout) Cost (G)

Shortage costs occur when an item is out of stock and demand is unsatisfied. Depending on the item under consideration, shortage costs may include the following:

In the case of raw materials: costs of idled production, spoilage of products or materials, and the cost of placing and fulfilling special expediting orders.

In the case of finished goods: cost of ill will to the seller (the loss of customers) due to inability to deliver or due to late deliveries. The cost of ill will or the loss of goodwill reflects the anticipated loss of future profits due to customers' dissatisfaction.

In the case of replacement parts: costs of idle machines, idle labor, spoilage of materials, and delays in shipment.

In other cases: the shortage of blood or ambulances may cost a life; and a shortage of fire engines may result in excessive damage caused by a fire.

Back orders versus lost sales

Shortages may be temporary (**back orders**), in which case they are eliminated when the supply arrives; or permanent, in the sense that sales are lost.

Item Cost (C)

Item (or unit) cost is the price paid for one unit of the commodity under consideration. It is not a direct inventory cost, as the items must eventually be procured anyway, but it may be influenced by inventory decisions. For example, ordering large quantities

Quantity discounts

may result in a lower per-unit price due to **quantity discounts.**

12.4 The Economic Order Quantity Model (EOQ)

The **economic order quantity (EOQ)** model, which was developed prior to World War I, is the most elementary of all inventory models. Its objective is to determine the *optimal quantity to order*. It answers the following questions:

EOQ answers five questions

1. How much should be ordered each time?
2. When should it be ordered?
3. What will the total cost be?
4. What will the average inventory level be?
5. What will the maximum inventory level be?

Assumptions

The EOQ model assumes the following:

- The demand for the item is constant over time (e.g., two units per day).
- Within the range of quantities to be ordered, the per-unit holding cost and ordering cost are independent of the quantity ordered.
- The replenishment is scheduled in such a way that shipments arrive exactly when the inventory level reaches zero. Therefore, there will never be a shortage.
- Because only one item is being considered, orders for different items are independent of each other.
- Full orders are delivered in one batch.

Simplifying assumptions

The behavior of the inventory level under the above assumptions is shown in Figure 12.5. An examination of the figure indicates that all cycles are equal, that orders arrive exactly when the inventory level reaches zero, that the order quantity Q is equal in all cycles, and that the maximum inventory level is also Q.

Example

Everglades University uses 1,200 boxes of typing paper each year. The university is trying to determine how many boxes to order at one time. The information it considers is:

$$\text{Annual demand, } D = 1,200 \text{ boxes}$$

$$\text{Ordering cost, } K = \$5 \text{ per order}$$

$$\text{Holding cost, } H = \$1.20 \text{ per box, per year}$$

FIGURE 12.5

The inventory process

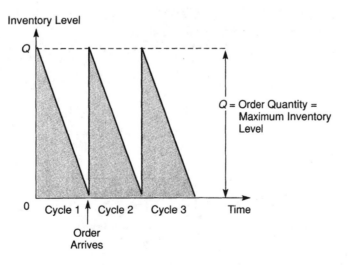

The problem is to find the quantity to be ordered, Q. (As we shall see, finding this quantity will also tell us how often to order.)

Figure 12.6 demonstrates three possible ordering policies: annually, quarterly, and monthly. Let us examine these:

1. Annual policy: Order once a year. Therefore, $Q = 1,200$ boxes.
2. Quarterly: Order once a quarter, four times a year. $Q = 1,200/4 = 300$ boxes at a time.
3. Monthly: Order once a month, 12 times a year. $Q = 1,200/12 = 100$ boxes at a time.

Which policy costs less?

Other ordering policies could also be considered; for example, once a week, semi-annually, or once every two years. The problem faced by management is: *Which ordering policy is the best?*

Solution Using a Trial-and-Error Approach

One way of solving this problem would be to compute the total annual inventory cost for each of the suggested policies. The policy with the lowest total cost is the best one. The total cost is given by Equation 12.1.

$$
\begin{matrix}
TC & = & T_O & + & T_H \\
\begin{Bmatrix} \text{Total annual} \\ \text{inventory cost} \end{Bmatrix} & = & \begin{Bmatrix} \text{Total annual} \\ \text{ordering cost} \end{Bmatrix} & + & \begin{Bmatrix} \text{Total annual} \\ \text{holding cost} \end{Bmatrix}
\end{matrix}
\tag{12.1}
$$

FIGURE 12.6
Inventory level under three different ordering policies

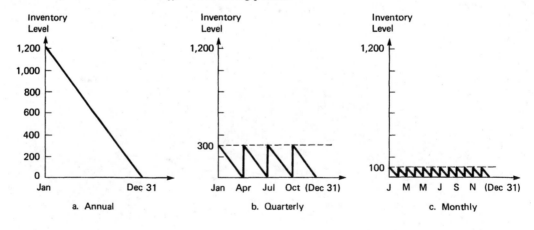

a. Annual   b. Quarterly   c. Monthly

Let us execute the calculation step by step:

Step 1. Find Total Annual Ordering Cost, T_O

The total annual ordering cost is given as the number of times an order is placed, N, multiplied by the ordering cost, K. This is expressed in Equation 12.2.

$$T_O = NK \qquad (12.2)$$

The number of times an order is placed during a year is given by the total yearly demand, D, divided by the order quantity, Q:

$$N = \frac{D}{Q} \qquad (12.3)$$

Thus, the equation for T_O is:

$$T_O = NK = \frac{D}{Q}K \qquad (12.4)$$

T_O in the three proposed policies is:

$$
\begin{aligned}
\text{Annual:} \quad & N = 1, \quad K = 5, \quad T_O = 1 \times (5) = \$\ 5 \\
\text{Quarterly:} \quad & N = 4, \quad K = 5, \quad T_O = 4 \times (5) = \$20 \\
\text{Monthly:} \quad & N = 12, \quad K = 5, \quad T_O = 12 \times (5) = \$60
\end{aligned}
$$

The above values are entered in Figure 12.7a, as points a (for the annual policy), b (for quarterly), and c (for monthly). Points a, b, and c are then connected, resulting in a *total annual ordering cost* curve. The curve indicates that as the order quantity, Q, increases, the total annual cost of ordering decreases. The reason for this is that the larger the order size, the fewer the number of orders placed per year.

Step 2. Find Total Annual Holding Cost, T_H

The total annual holding cost can be computed by multiplying the daily holding cost by the *number of units in inventory* each day of the year, and summing. However, because the inventory level is changing from day to day, the number of units in inventory fluctuates over time. Thus, it is easier to solve this problem by using the *average inventory* on hand over the year and multiplying by the yearly holding cost. When the demand is constant, the average inventory is the midway point between the highest and the lowest inventory level. Because one of the EOQ assumptions requires that the lowest inventory level be zero, the average inventory equals exactly one-half of the maxi-

FIGURE 12.7

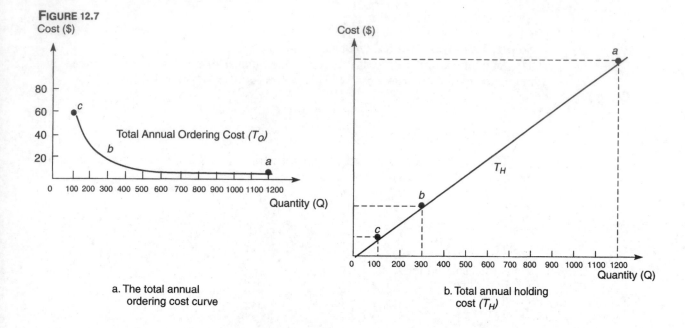

a. The total annual
   ordering cost curve

b. Total annual holding
   cost (T_H)

mum inventory. However, in the EOQ model, the maximum inventory equals the order quantity, Q. Consequently, the average inventory equals one-half of Q:

$$\text{Average inventory} = \frac{Q}{2} \tag{12.5}$$

Therefore, the total annual inventory holding cost, T_H, will be:

$$T_H = H\frac{Q}{2} \tag{12.6}$$

The total annual inventory holding for the three proposed ordering policies is:

a. Annual: $Q = 1{,}200$, $T_H = 1.20 \left(\dfrac{1{,}200}{2}\right) = \$720$

b. Quarterly: $Q = 300$, $T_H = 1.20 \left(\dfrac{300}{2}\right) = \$180$

c. Monthly: $Q = 100$, $T_H = 1.20 \left(\dfrac{100}{2}\right) = \$60$

It is evident that the value of Q will be in direct proportion to the value of T_H. This information is shown graphically in Figure 12.7b.

Step 3. Compute Total Annual Inventory Cost, *TC*

Using Equation 12.1, the total annual cost (designated *TC*, or sometimes *TC*[*Q*]) for the proposed policies is:

Policy	$T_O + T_H = TC$	
Annual	5 + 720 = 725	
Quarterly	20 + 180 = 200	
Monthly	60 + 60 = 120	←**Minimum**

Comparing the three alternatives, the best ordering policy is "Monthly," because it has the lowest total cost of $120. However, because other possible ordering policies (e.g., semiannually, weekly) were not checked, no assurance exists that monthly ordering is indeed the *optimal* policy. To check *all* possible policies may involve much computational work, especially because these calculations must be continuously updated for every item in the stock. Therefore, a more efficient method is provided through the economic order quantity (EOQ) formula.

Checking other possible policies, too

The EOQ Formula

It was shown previously that the total cost, *TC*, can be expressed as:

$$TC = T_O + T_H = \frac{DK}{Q} + \frac{HQ}{2} \tag{12.7}$$

where *D* is the annual demand, *K* is the ordering cost, *H* is the holding cost, and *Q* is the quantity to be ordered. The problem is to find that *Q* for which *TC* is the minimum.

Graphical Solution

One way to find *TC* is to combine T_O and T_H graphically and then find a minimum point on the combined curve. Figure 12.8 shows *TC* as the summation of T_O and T_H. (Summation of two curves is done as shown in Figure 12.8 for *Q* = 200 (point *A*). Take the distance *A* to *B* and add it to the distance *A* to *C*. The result is the distance *A* to *D*.) The minimum value of *TC* occurs at the intersection of T_H and T_O; that is, where T_H equals T_O. (With other forms of cost curves, the minimum point on the total cost curve may occur at a point other than the intersection.) This approach is very cumbersome.

Analytical Solution

Through calculus, the optimal value of *Q* (designated Q^*) can be found analytically. It occurs where the total annual holding cost equals the total annual ordering cost:

$$\frac{HQ^*}{2} = \frac{KD}{Q^*} \tag{12.8}$$

FIGURE 12.8

Ordering, holding, and total cost variation with order size

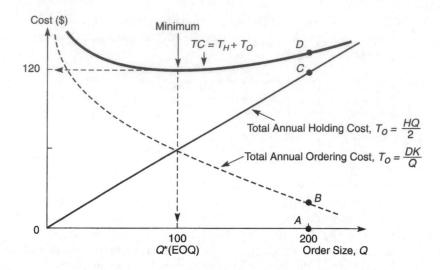

EOQ: The *optimal*

By manipulation of Equation 12.8, it is possible to compute the *optimal* value of Q; that is, the EOQ. (Multiply each side by Q; then divide each side by $H/2$.)

$$(Q^*)^2 = \frac{2KD}{H} \quad \text{or} \quad Q^* = \sqrt{\frac{2KD}{H}} \tag{12.9}$$

where K is the ordering cost (in dollars), D is the annual demand (in units), and H is the holding cost (in dollars per unit per year).

Note: The EOQ can also be obtained through calculus: $TC = HQ/2 + KD/Q$. Setting the first derivative to 0;

$$\frac{dTC}{dQ} = \frac{H}{2} - \frac{KD}{Q^2} = 0 \quad \text{or} \quad Q^* = \sqrt{\frac{2KD}{H}}$$

To verify that this is a minimum point, we check for a positive second derivative:

$$\frac{d^2TC}{dQ^2} = \frac{2KD}{Q^3} > 0$$

Because the second derivative is positive (K, D, and Q can take only positive values), the point is a minimum point indeed.

Solution to the Example

$$Q^* = \sqrt{\frac{2(5)(1,200)}{1.20}} = 100 \text{ boxes}$$

The optimal solution calls for an order size of 100 boxes at a time. For a yearly demand of 1,200, this means 12 orders per year, or once a month. Thus, the monthly order policy is indeed optimal.

Additional Information Provided by EOQ

In addition to the size of the order to be placed, the EOQ can be used to provide the following information:

Other information from the EOQ

a. *The optimal number of orders* to be placed in a year. Using Equation 12.3, we find:

$$N = \frac{D}{Q^*} = \frac{1,200}{100} = 12 \text{ times}$$

Maximum inventory = Q

b. *The maximum inventory on hand* (I_{max}) *and the average inventory level* (I_{avg}). The maximum inventory is equal to Q^* (100 in the example). The average inventory is one half of Q^* (50 in the example).

c. *The number of days' supply.* The computation of the EOQ also helps provide the number of **days' supply,** *d*. This information tells management the length of each inventory cycle. This is given in Equation 12.10.

$$d = \frac{365}{N} \tag{12.10}$$

In the example:

$$d = \frac{365}{N} = \frac{365}{12} = 30.4 \text{ days}$$

Note: If the company works less than 365 days a year, use the actual number of days worked.

d. *The dollar value of an optimal order and of the average inventory.* Sometimes it is useful to know the dollar value of the EOQ; this is obtained by multiplying Q^* by the unit cost. This information is important because the dollar value of the average inventory is useful for such purposes as cash flow determination, tax assessment, and calculation of depreciation. Assume in the example that the cost of one box of paper is $10. Thus, Q in dollars is 100(10) or $1,000. That is, the university orders $1,000 worth of supplies at a time. Similarly, the dollar value of the average inventory is:

$$\frac{100}{2}(10) = \$500$$

e. The total annual cost. Using Equation 12.7, the total annual cost (excluding the cost of the goods themselves) can now be computed.

$$TC = \frac{DK}{Q^*} + \frac{HQ^*}{2} = \frac{(1{,}200)5}{100} + \frac{1.2(100)}{2} = 60 + 60 = \$120$$

$T_H = T_O$ in the optimal solution

Notice that the two components of the total cost, the ordering cost and the holding cost, *must equal* each other whenever the optimal Q is used (\$60 each in the example).

12.5 Application of the EOQ Model

In applying the EOQ formula, the following points may be helpful:

Holding Cost Given as a Percentage of Value

It is sometimes common to express the holding cost as a percentage of the value in inventory. For example, it may be stated that the inventory holding costs are 30 percent per year. This means that if the item is worth \$20, then $H = .3 \times \$20 = \$6$ per item, per year. In general:

$$H = IC \tag{12.11}$$

where I = annual percentage and C = per-item cost.

With a 10 to 15 percent cost of capital (interest per year), it is not unusual to find that the cost of holding inventory is 30 percent or even higher.

When the Demand Is Given in Dollars

Demand in dollars

In some cases, the demand for an item is given in terms of dollars rather than in units. Two cases are then distinguished:

1. *The unit cost is given.* In this case, simply convert the demand to units by dividing the annual dollar amount by the unit cost.
2. *The unit cost is not given.* In such a case, the holding cost *must* be expressed as a percentage.

Example

A recreation department's annual budget for supplies is \$200,000. The ordering cost is \$50, and the holding cost is 20 percent of the value of the item. Find the EOQ, the optimal number of orders, and the total inventory costs.

Given:

D: Annual *dollar value* of demand = \$200,000

K: Ordering cost, in dollars = \$50

H: Holding cost = .2 (i.e., 20 percent)

Solution

Using the EOQ formula (Equation 12.9):

$$Q^* = \sqrt{\frac{2KD}{H}} = \sqrt{\frac{2(50)(200,000)}{0.2}} = \$10,000$$

Thus, the optimal policy is to order $10,000 worth of supplies at a time. Because the yearly demand is $200,000, there will be $N = 20$ orders per year (Equation 12.3).

The total annual inventory costs are:

$$TC = \frac{KD}{Q^*} + \frac{HQ^*}{2} = \frac{50(200,000)}{10,000} + \frac{(.2)10,000}{2} = \$2,000$$

Sensitivity Analysis: The Cost Impact of Deviations from the EOQ

In some situations, it is not convenient to actually order the EOQ. For example, a standard package size may differ from the EOQ, or there may be insufficient funds to purchase the EOQ amount. Using the university's supply situation in Section 12.4 as an example, the EOQ calls for 100 boxes. But suppose that they are packed 40 to a case. In such an event, it is possible to buy either 80 or 120 boxes, but not 100. Let us examine the effect of overordering (120) versus that of underordering (80).

For 80 Boxes

The total annual cost for an order of 80 will be (use Equation 12.7 with $Q = 80$):

$$TC = \frac{DK}{Q} + \frac{HQ}{2} = \frac{(1,200)5}{80} + \frac{(1.2)80}{2} = \$123$$

Compared with the cost of $120 for the EOQ of 100 (as previously computed), there is an increase of only $3 (about 2.5 percent), even though the order quantity was decreased by 20 percent.

For 120 Boxes

$$TC = \frac{(1,200)(5)}{120} + \frac{(1.2)(120)}{2} = \$122$$

Thus, overordering by 20 percent caused the total annual inventory cost to rise by less than 2 percent.

In a similar manner, it can be shown that a change of 10 percent in the order quantity increases the total inventory cost by only about 0.5 percent. In other words, *TC* in the EOQ formula is *relatively insensitive to changes in the order quantity*. This property gives management greater flexibility in implementing the EOQ because the theoretical order quantity can be changed by as much as 20 percent with only a slight impact on the total inventory cost.

Note that the sensitivity for decreasing the EOQ is *larger* than the sensitivity for increasing it (cost increase of $3 on the downside versus cost increase of $2 on the upside for a change of 20 units from EOQ). (*Note:* In other cases the reverse can be true.)

Cost insensitive to order quantity

Another example is that changing the EOQ from 100 to 50 (deviation of 50) will increase the total cost from \$120 to \$150, whereas an increase in Q of 50 (to 150) will increase cost only to \$130. A look at Figure 12.8 shows us why this is so. The curve of total cost increases faster when Q decreases, especially when Q is very small.

Rounding the Result

The computed EOQ may be noninteger; for example, 6.3 units. In such a situation, the result may be rounded to 6 or 7. The total cost for 6 should be calculated and compared to that for 7 to decide whether to round down or up. Rounding is often done to comply with required bulk quantities, such as six cartons per case.

The Sensitivity of the EOQ to Changes in Input Data

Let us examine the EOQ formula:

$$Q^* = \sqrt{\frac{2KD}{H}}$$

One can see that the quantity Q^* is proportional to the square root of the input data (K, D, and H). This means that if K or D quadruples, for example, then Q^* will be doubled, and if H quadruples, then Q^* will be halved. Table 12.1 compares the original university purchasing problem with three changes: change 1, quadruple D; change 2, quadruple K; change 3, quadruple H. In all three cases, the total cost doubled.

Nonproportional changes

The managerial implication of the sensitivity of the EOQ is that the order quantity should *not* be increased or decreased in direct proportion to the changes in the input data. Some managers make the mistake of doubling their EOQ when the demand doubles. Instead, they should increase it only by $\sqrt{2} = 1.41$, because the EOQ is directly proportional to the *square root* of the demand.

The general formula for sensitivity analysis is:

$$\frac{TC}{TC^*} = \frac{1}{2}\left(\frac{Q}{Q^*} + \frac{Q^*}{Q}\right) \tag{12.12}$$

When to Order (the Reorder Point)

The decision *when* to order does not depend on the optimal value of Q. Rather, it is a function of the demand and the lead time to resupply. For example, if the demand is 50 per week and the lead time is two weeks, then the order should be placed when the inventory level is 100 units (two weeks' supply). The reorder point (designated ROP) is a practical concept used in many inventory systems.

TABLE 12.1 Cost Effect of Data Changes

	Original Problem	*Change* ①	*Change* ②	*Change* ③
Given	$D = 1,200$ $K = 5$ $H = 1.20$	$D = 4,800$ $K = 5$ $H = 1.20$	$D = 1,200$ $K = 20$ $H = 1.20$	$D = 1,200$ $K = 5$ $H = 4.80$
Computed	$Q^* = 100$	$Q^* = 200$	$Q^* = 200$	$Q^* = 50$
Total cost	$TC = \$120$	$TC = \$240$	$TC = \$240$	$TC = \$240$

12.6 Discussion of the EOQ Assumptions

In order to derive the EOQ, a list of assumptions was outlined in Section 12.4. These assumptions enabled us to develop a rather simple inventory formula.

Assumptions Used in Developing an Inventory Formula

Constant Demand

In the EOQ model, a constant demand was assumed (e.g., five units per day). In reality, demand may fluctuate. In such a case, it is necessary to modify the EOQ formulation (e.g., by using safety stock as shown in Section 12.14 or by using special stochastic models).

Constant Unit Price

The EOQ analysis that assumes constant unit price can be extended to include variable prices due to discounts as larger quantities are ordered. This procedure is discussed in Section 12.10.

Constant Holding Cost

It is assumed that the holding cost is constant. However, as the level of inventory increases, the unit holding cost may decrease (e.g., due to storage efficiency) or increase (e.g., due to higher capital costs). Such a situation can be handled by a procedure similar to the one used for quantity discounts.

Constant Ordering Cost

This assumption is usually valid for limited ranges of order quantities. For exceptional cases, the EOQ model can be modified by computing different values for different ordering costs. Again, this situation resembles the quantity discount case discussed in Part B of this chapter.

The EOQ assumptions

No Shortages

The assumption is made that replenishment arrives exactly when the inventory level reaches zero and therefore there will never be a shortage. As long as the demand is constant and delivery time is either constant or zero, the assumption will hold. Otherwise, a safety stock should be added.

Instantaneous (or Fixed) Delivery Time

It is assumed that deliveries are received on a desired date. This can be assured by instantaneous delivery; for example, if the supplier happens to be in the same location and can deliver quickly on short notice. Alternatively, if the lead time and the demand are both constant, an order can be placed so that the delivery will arrive exactly on a desired date. But in the case of variations in the lead time or the demand, the EOQ must be modified as shown in Part B.

Independent Orders

Joint ordering

Quite often, several items are purchased from the same supplier, and the ordering cost can be reduced by ordering several items in one order. This saves paperwork, transportation costs, and may also result in discounts. Special models have been developed to deal with situations where several items are ordered together, a practice known as **joint ordering.** (See Tersine [13].)

Single Goal of Cost Minimization

This assumption is not always true. Sometimes, for example, the service level is more important (e.g., in blood inventory).

FIGURE 12.9

Summary of the EOQ model

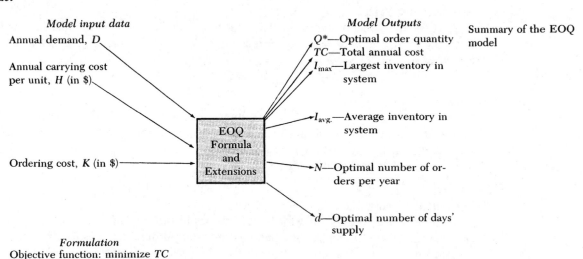

Model input data

Annual demand, D

Annual carrying cost per unit, H (in $)

Ordering cost, K (in $)

EOQ Formula and Extensions

Model Outputs

Q^*—Optimal order quantity
TC—Total annual cost
I_{max}—Largest inventory in system

$I_{avg.}$—Average inventory in system

N—Optimal number of orders per year

d—Optimal number of days' supply

Summary of the EOQ model

Formulation
Objective function: minimize TC
Constraints: satisfy demand

Summary

The EOQ model is summarized in Figure 12.9.

12.7 Inventory Systems

The A-B-C Classification System

Some organizations carry such a large number (thousands) of items in inventory that it would be impractical to try to exercise control over even a single item by using the EOQ analysis. Remember that each time any input (such as demand or ordering cost) is changed, the EOQ has to be recomputed.

A-B-C, value-volume, 80–20

One method frequently used to identify the items that deserve tight control is called the **A-B-C classification system** or the *value-volume analysis*. Other names are the *Pareto* analysis and the "80–20" method. The idea is based on an economic phenomenon observed by Pareto, an Italian economist (1848–1923), that a few items usually account for the majority of the value.

The A-B-C classification system segregates all items in stock into three groups, A, B, and C, based on the annual dollar inventory value of the items' value or criticality.

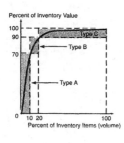

The A Group

Group A usually includes a small (e.g., 10) percent of the items that account for a large (e.g., 70) percent of the total annual inventory cost for the company. Special attention should be paid to every item in this group, and application of the EOQ formula is recommended for every one of the items.

The B Group

Items in this group constitute another small (e.g., 10) percent in inventory volume, but are worth only 20 percent or so of the total value. Accordingly, items in this group merit somewhat less control than those in group A. For example, an EOQ may still be used, but updating due to changes in input data may be done only once a month.

Adding the groups A and B together shows that perhaps 20 percent of the items account for possibly 90 percent of the dollar value of the inventory.

The C Group

The remaining 80 percent or so of the items account for perhaps only 10 percent of the inventory dollar value. These are small value items such as nuts, bolts, and nails. Control over such items should be minimal, because the potential saving rarely justifies the expense of the control exercised.

Different degrees of control

Classification into three categories is traditional but not mandatory. Classification into two, four, or even more categories can be found in some companies. What is important to remember is that some items in inventory deserve detailed and continuous planning and control, whereas others do not merit such consideration. Thus, different classes of items should be subjected to different inventory systems, as discussed next.

Management Science in Practice

Reducing Hospital Inventory Costs Through ABC

The virtual explosion of the cost of medical care in recent years has given renewed emphasis to cost containment in hospitals. Because inventories represent a major investment of a hospital's assets, many hospital administrators are seeking more systematic methods of controlling them. The objective is both to lower investment costs and to gain better control over the inventories, thus improving service at the same time. To help achieve these dual goals, the ABC method of classifying inventories for better control was applied to a group of 47 disposable stock-keeping units (SKUs) in the respiratory unit of a regional hospital. The methodology was as follows:

1. Determine the total number of units issued for each SKU.
2. Determine the average unit cost for each SKU.
3. Multiply these two values to find the total annual dollar usage.
4. Sort the SKUs in descending sequence of total annual usage.
5. Calculate the cumulative percentage of SKUs for each item in the sequence. (*Note:* This is not the same as the cumulative percentage of total items used, as indicated in the chapter.)
6. Find the cumulative total annual dollar usage for each SKU.
7. Calculate the cumulative percentage of total annual dollar usage for each SKU by dividing the cumulative amount by the grand total.
8. Decide on appropriate divisions for the ABC classes.

At Step 8, it was noticed that there was a large break in annual usage between the 10th and 11th items, with the first ten representing 21 percent of all the SKUs but 74 percent of the total annual usage value of $51,685, so the first ten items were deemed to constitute Class A. (It is interesting to note that in this setting, these ten items constituted 62 percent of all *units* used, but only 21 percent of the SKUs.)

The next class, B, was determined by both natural breaks in the annual value and informed judgment regarding the importance of individual SKUs to the goals of the hospital. The 13 items in the B class thus comprised 28 percent of the SKUs (30 percent of the units)

and 18 percent of the annual usage value. The remainder of the SKUs, 24 in total, represented 51 percent of the items (but only 8 percent of the units) and comprised only 8 percent of the annual value.

The management of these classes was then differentiated to provide better control at less cost. The class A items are monitored closely and forecasts are updated monthly. Stocks are counted and replenished weekly, or more often if the reorder point is passed. Minimum stock levels were established for these items relative to their lead times, availability of substitute SKUs, and criticality. The B items are replenished on a biweekly basis and price discounts have been negotiated through blanket order commitments with suppliers. The ordering of C items was automated for replenishment to a preestablished maximum every two to three months. A two-bin system was implemented to trigger purchases between replenishments, if necessary.

This system gave the hospital better control over their inventories with reduced inventory costs. It also offered a cost-effective inventory control policy. The ABC procedure offers a simple, yet powerful approach to managing assets such as inventories for a reasonable investment of managerial time and energy, particularly in designing control procedures.

Source: R. A. Reid "ABC Method in Hospital Inventory Management: A Practical Approach," *Production and Inventory Management Journal,* Fourth Quarter, 1987, pp. 67–70.

Questions:

1. Why is there such a difference between the percent of the SKUs and the percent of the units used? Is this different from normal manufacturing situations?

2. The listing of cumulative total annual usage showed a very slight break between items 19 and 20 and between items 28 and 29. Yet neither one of these breaks was chosen for the B-to-C break. Why?

3. Most of the C-class SKUs are used less than four times a year. Does an EOQ or two-bin system make sense for these items? (In a two-bin system, the small bin is filled with the safety stock to cover demand over the lead time and the rest of the EOQ is placed in the large bin.)

The Fixed-Quantity (Perpetual) System

The **fixed-quantity (perpetual) system** dictates that a fixed-quantity order be placed each time the inventory level reaches the reorder point. The fixed quantity could be determined by the EOQ formula. A safety stock is usually added (at a level determined by experience or by computation, as shown in Part B). This system is used mainly for type A items.

Safety stock

A special, less expensive (to administer) version of the fixed-quantity system, called the **two-bin system,** is frequently used for type B and C items. The inventory is stored in a large bin, with the exception of a safety stock kept in a smaller bin. Demand depletion of the large bin acts as a signal to reorder. While awaiting replenishment of the large bin, demand is supplied from the small bin. When the shipment arrives, the smaller bin is refilled first and the remainder then goes into the larger bin. The amount to be ordered can be based on the EOQ, but is usually based on experience. This system is practical if the stock can be conveniently separated into two bins; if not, a perpetual auditing (counting) of the amount on hand (balance) is required, increasing the cost substantially. This problem can be solved with a computerized system that automatically computes the balance.

The two-bin system

The Fixed-Time [Periodic or (s,S)] System

The **fixed-time (periodic or *s,S*) system** involves a periodic auditing (e.g., once a month) of the inventory. If at that time the stock of an item is below the predesignated level, *s*, an order is placed to return the inventory level to another predetermined, maximum level *S*. (The levels of *s* and *S* can be determined by a mathematical model or by experience.) Although amounts ordered each cycle will vary, as shown in Figure 12.10, this system allows *joint reordering* of items in the same period at a substantial savings. The major disadvantages of the (*s,S*) system are:

s,S system

Joint reordering possible

1. A large safety stock may be needed to reduce the possibility of shortages.
2. The nonuniform order sizes may be inconvenient to fill. The method is used mainly for group A items and sometimes for group B items.

A version of this method is the so-called **base-stock system,** in which orders are placed as soon as demand occurs, *regardless of the inventory level,* to bring the inventory back to its maximum level, *S*. This method is especially useful where the number of units in inventory is very small (e.g., 1–5), the units are expensive, and the ordering cost is not too high.

The base-stock system

Rule of Thumb Systems

Type C items are typically of such low value that the effort required either to determine the EOQ or audit frequently cannot be economically justified. Thus, these items are typically ordered on the basis of experience or when stock is depleted. The control imposed on such items is minimal.

FIGURE 12.10

Periodic (s, S) inventory system

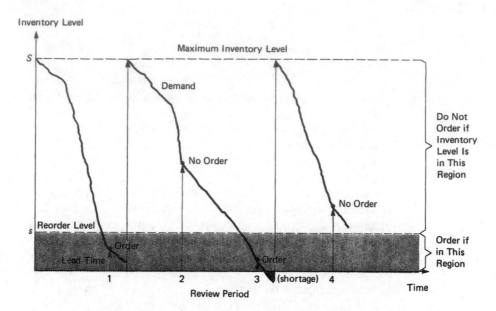

Computerized Systems (Details in Section 12.15)

Computer use is common

Inventory systems in medium- and large-sized organizations are usually computerized. The computer system follows the inventory level in a manner similar to that of a computerized banking system following a cash balance. All transactions are recorded, and the balance is computed immediately. Whenever the inventory level is at or below the reorder point, the computer signals to place a new order. The same computer may issue and print the purchase orders or send them electronically to the vendor. The reorder point and the order quantity can be computed with the aid of one of the models presented in this chapter, by the aid of more complicated models such as MRP (see Part B), with the use of simulation (see example in Chapter 15), or by using a trial-and-error approach. In addition, computers are used to prepare management reports concerning the overall inventory system.

"Zero-Inventory" Systems and the Japanese Approach

Zero inventory

Inventory holding costs may become so high that some companies adopt a "no-inventory" policy. The concept behind this system is called *total life cycle* (from acquisition to disposition), and an attempt is made to minimize or even eliminate inventories. In addition to saving holding costs, there is a savings in internal material handling as well. For example, several hospitals are using this approach by having daily deliveries from large suppliers located in the same city.

Just-in-time

Although no-inventory systems are becoming more common in the United States, their equivalent, "just-in-time" (or JIT), is very popular in Japan. The classic example of this approach is Toyota's "Kanban" system [5]. According to JIT, only the necessary products are made, at the necessary time, in the necessary quantities. All the required materials are delivered to each workstation when they are needed so there is very little work-in-process inventory.

The impetus behind JIT in Japan is usually different than in the United States, however: it is to eliminate waste, particularly in facility space, which is very expensive in Japan. Stores of unused materials are perceived as using up precious space. The goal, then, is to turn every production system into a continuously flowing system of materials, where items pass through the system one by one and are never in storage. Note that JIT is primarily used for production systems, but not for all inventories (typing paper, forms).

But the JIT system has produced many unexpected side benefits for the Japanese as well. With no stores of material sitting idle, there is little inventory cost, of course. And with each worker passing his or her completed item to the next worker, defects are caught immediately and the reason corrected. Scrap also becomes immediately apparent and, thus, efforts are made to eliminate it. And without bins of material to store, locate, and move, the scheduling and management process is much simpler. Lately, these systems are gaining popularity in the United States. For further details, see Hay [6], Schonberger [10], or Walleigh [15].

12.8 Concluding Remarks

The models presented in this chapter deal with the simplest inventory situations. Yet they are widely applied and give satisfactory results even in places where real-life conditions do not conform exactly to the models' formats and the underlying assumptions. The insensitivity of the models provides management with more flexibility, enabling deviations from optimal solutions at a small cost.

Inventory models are one of the most common applications of management science. This is partly due to their insensitivity, but mainly attributable to the possibility of realizing quick, significant, measurable savings. Further, because the application of such models only affects people minimally, human resistance to implementation is not much of a problem.

The models are basically cost models attempting to minimize the total inventory expense. This inventory expense may be extremely high in some instances, and thus, so are the potential savings.

12.9 Problems for Part A

1. The Elco Company needs 10,000 lamps annually. It costs $45 to place one order and 10 cents to store each lamp for a year. *Find:*

   a. The economic order quantity.

   b. The total inventory cost per year.

   c. How many orders will be placed each year.

2. Sunshine Corporation uses 840,000 bags of fertilizer each year for its orange groves. It costs the company $100 to place an order and 50 cents to store a bag for a year. How many months' supply should the company purchase at one time using the economic order quantity formula?

3. Columbia City buys office supplies for $500,000 each year. It costs $80 to place one order. Annual per-item holding costs are 20 percent.
   a. What is the dollar value of the EOQ?
   b. How many times should orders be placed each year?
   c. What is the total annual ordering cost?
   d. What is the total annual carrying cost?

4. Eastwood State Park uses 1,000 bags of food each month. It costs $30 to place a purchase order, and the carrying cost is $1.125 per bag per year.
   a. Find the economic order quantity.
   b. How many months' supply of food are contained in one order?

5. Assume an inventory system where a demand of 2,500 units per year must be supplied and where orders are shipped immediately.
   a. Find how often orders should be placed (how many times a year) if the ordering cost is $40 per order and the cost of the product is $1 per unit. The annual per-unit carrying cost is 20 percent of the value of the product.
   b. Find the total carrying and ordering cost.
   c. What will happen to the EOQ if demand increases to 10,000 units? What will happen to the total inventory cost?

6. American Department Store sells 4,050 vacuum cleaners a year. One cleaner occupies 6 square feet of storage space. Each cleaner costs $50, and the annual per unit holding cost is 16 percent of each cleaner. Placing an order costs $32. There is presently an area of 900 square feet for storage. Using the EOQ, would it be profitable for the store to increase the storage area if it costs 50 cents a square foot per year?

7. The Costly Company buys its raw materials 10 times a year, 100 units each time. It is known that this purchasing policy is an optimal one (most economic). The company pays $50 per unit. Annual carrying cost is 20 percent of the value stored. *Find:*
   a. The cost of placing one order (ordering cost).
   b. The total cost (ordering, carrying, and parts) for one year.
   c. Assume that the yearly demand has increased from X to $4X$; all other conditions remain the same. What will the new economic lot size be? What general conclusions may you arrive at?

8. Producers Company is using $200,000 of a certain

material per year. The inventory holding cost is 20 percent. The cost of placing an order is $50.
   a. How often should an order for the material be placed?
   b. What is the total inventory cost involved?
   c. The company wants to place four orders a year; how much more than the optimal solution found in parts (a) and (b) will it cost the company?
   d. After establishing the optimal policy, it was found that there is a price increase of 10 percent in the material. What ordering policy would you suggest now?
   e. What will the effect on the total inventory cost be if the company orders once a month? (Compare to part (b) of this problem.)

9. Find the reorder point (number of units still remaining in stock) for the following three situations:

	Annual Demand	Lead Time
Case A	5,200	2 weeks
Case B	60	1 month
Case C	600	17 days

Assume 50 working weeks and 300 working days per year.

10. The following data give expenditures for carrying light bulbs in a department store.

Annual sales (units)	10,000
Annual cost of capital	$1,200.00
Insurance (per unit)	.05
Taxes and licenses (per unit)	.03
Rent, maintenance (per unit)	.12
Annual paperwork	800.00

Find H, the annual carrying cost per unit.

11. Northwest Hospital currently buys surgical gloves in lots of 1,200 boxes once every four months. The carrying cost per box is $12.50 per unit per year, and the ordering cost is $100 per order. *Find:*
   a. The economic order quantity.
   b. The annual inventory cost. Compare it to the annual cost under the existing purchasing policy.

c. Suppose that it is possible to buy only in lots of 100 boxes. How many boxes should the hospital buy?

12. CORDON Industries produces 7,200 energy-conserving devices each year. The company sells these units at $10 apiece. CORDON's objective is to produce these units at the least possible cost. One option is to produce all the units once a year. Alternatively, the company may produce several times during the year. Each such production period is called a "run" and these runs are equal in size. Assume that the start-up cost for each product run is $300 and the holding cost is computed at 30 percent. *Find:*

a. The annual cost of one run per year.

b. The optimal size and cost of the production run.

c. The optimal number of production runs per year.

13. For what household items do you use: (*a*) a perpetual, (*b*) a periodic, or (*c*) a rule of thumb inventory system?

14. Which items in a typical household would be classified as type A items? Which as type C items (in an A-B-C classification system)?

15. What would the modification be to the EOQ formula if the carrying charge is a function of the *maximum* inventory level rather than the average?

16. Compare the concept of the A-B-C classification system with the concept of the critical path in PERT/CPM.

17. A company has sales offices in Miami, Tampa, and Jacksonville. The annual unit sales in these cities are 40,000, 8,000, and 16,000, respectively. The company is considering opening a central inventory warehouse instead of the three existing regional warehouses.

Inventory holding costs, which are $10 per unit per year, are estimated to be 20 percent lower in the central location. Ordering cost, $30 per order, is expected to stay the same. It is further expected that there will be an additional transportation cost of 10 cents per unit under the proposed centralization. Should the company use a centralized warehouse? What assumption *must* be made in order to answer this question?

PART B: EXTENSIONS

12.10 Quantity Discounts

"Cheaper by the dozen"

Sellers frequently offer buyers a price discount for purchasing large quantities ("cheaper by the dozen"). There may be several price intervals (or price breaks) such as $10 each unit for quantities up to 99, $9 each unit for 100 to 499, $8 each unit for 500 up to 999, and $7 each unit for 1,000 and over.

The practice of quantity discounts is widely spread because it offers advantages to both buyer and seller. These are listed, together with some possible disadvantages, in Table 12.2. We distinguish two cases of discounting:

Two types of discounts

a. A discount is offered at one price level.

b. A discount is offered at several levels (price breaks).

Example 1: Discount Offered at One Level

A conditional discount

The city of Northstar uses 100 replacement lamps a month for its streetlights. Each lamp costs the city $8. Ordering costs are estimated at $27 per order and the holding

TABLE 12.2 Quantity Buying Considerations

	Advantages	Disadvantages
Buyer	Lower unit price Less paperwork Cheaper transportation Fewer stockouts Uniform goods (coming from same shipment) Security (against such factors as strikes, price increases)	Larger inventories Higher holding cost Risk of deterioration and obsolescence Older stock on hand
Seller	Cheaper transportation Less paperwork Larger production runs (thus, lower production costs per unit)	Lower unit prices Less bargaining power with buyers

costs (primarily the cost of capital) are 25 percent. The city currently orders according to the EOQ. The supplier has now offered the city a 2 percent discount *if* the city will buy 600 lamps at a time. Should the city accept the offer?

Solution

Given:

$$D = 100 \text{ units per month} \times 12 \text{ months} = 1{,}200 \text{ units per year}$$

$$H = .25 \times 8.00 = \$2.00 \text{ per lamp per year}$$

$$K = \$27 \text{ per order}$$

$$\text{EOQ} = \sqrt{\frac{2 \times 27 \times 1{,}200}{2}} = 180 \text{ lamps}$$

The current total annual inventory cost is:

$$TC = \frac{27 \times 1{,}200}{180} + \frac{180 \times 2}{2} = \$360 \text{ per year}$$

To this cost should be added the item cost, which is relevant when discounts on the item cost are considered. If we let C_i be the item cost at the ith price break (only one break here), then:

$$\text{Annual cost of items} = C_i D \qquad (12.13)$$

$$= \$8 \times 1{,}200 \text{ lamps} = \$9{,}600$$

Thus, the total *system* cost is $360 + \$9,600 = \$9,960$.

Review of the Discount Offer

The analysis is conducted on an annual basis. The offer to buy 600 units at a 2 percent discount will reduce the item cost. The holding cost will be higher because the city will buy 600 units instead of 180, and the ordering cost will decrease with fewer orders. The analysis is shown in Table 12.3 and illustrated in Figure 12.11.

Conclusion

The discount offer should be rejected. The city will be at a disadvantage to accept it. A higher discount rate should be negotiated instead (e.g., a 5 percent discount is favorable).

TABLE 12.3 Cost Comparison on an Annual Basis

No Discount	*Discount*
$Q^* = 180$ $K = 27$ $D = 1,200$ $H = 2.00$	$Q = 600$ (given) $K = 27$ $D = 1,200$ $H_d = 1.96$ (2% less than previous H)
Total annual ordering cost $= \$ \quad 180$	$\dfrac{KD}{Q} = \dfrac{27 \times 1,200}{600} = \$ \quad 54$
Total annual holding cost $= \quad 180$	$\dfrac{QH}{2} = \dfrac{600 \times 1.96}{2} = \quad 588$
Total annual unit cost $= \quad 9,600$	2 percent discount $\quad 9,408$
Total cost $\quad 9,960$	10,050

Note: H has been changed in the proportion of the discount. The reason for this is that the major portion of *H* is the cost of capital. Because the unit cost decreases, the cost of capital will decrease also. The new *H* is subscripted with *d* — discount, i.e., H_d.

FIGURE 12.11

Northstar quantity discounts situation

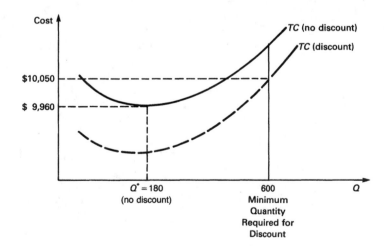

Example 2: Discounts at Several Price Breaks

General Hospital buys a certain antibiotic from a large supplier. The drug can be bought at the following prices:

Buy more—pay less
per unit

     For quantities of 1 up to 4,999—$2.75 a unit.

     For quantities from 5,000 to 9,999—$2.60 a unit.

     For quantities over 10,000 units—$2.50 a unit.

The demand (D) for the drug in the hospital is 50,000 units a year. There is an ordering cost (K) of $50 per order and a holding cost (H) of 20 percent of the cost of the item, per unit, per year. The problem is to find the optimal purchasing policy for the hospital.

Solution

Step 1

Find the EOQ (labeled Q_1^*) for the *lowest price level* ($2.50 in our case). Using the EOQ formula we get:

$$Q_1^* = \sqrt{\frac{2KD}{H}} = \sqrt{\frac{2 \times 50 \times 50{,}000}{.5}} = \sqrt{10{,}000{,}000} = 3{,}163 \text{ units}$$

(Note that $H = 20$ percent of $2.50 = .2(2.5) = \$0.5$)

Step 2

Compare Q_1^* to the quantity required for the price break (10,000 in our case). If Q_1^* is *larger* than this quantity, the problem is solved. If it is *smaller*, the solution is *not feasible* and the search for the lowest cost ordering quantity continues (in this example 3,163 is smaller than 10,000).

Step 3

Select the next higher item cost ($2.60 in this example) and calculate Q_1^*, using the EOQ formula:

$$Q_2^* = \sqrt{\frac{2 \times 50 \times 50{,}000}{.52}} = \sqrt{9{,}615{,}385} = 3{,}101 \text{ units}$$

(Notice that H has been changed to $.2(2.60) = \$0.52$.)

Step 4

Repeat step 2. Compare Q_2^* to the range that is required for the equivalent price. In this example, the price of $2.60 is for the range of 5,000–9,999. Because Q_2^* is not within this range, the solution is *not feasible* and the search continues.

upcoming run. It also includes the cost of processing the necessary paperwork. The larger the production run, the fewer times it will be repeated each year, and therefore fewer setups will be required. Another advantage is the reduction in the *unit production cost* due to the possibility of buying expensive but efficient tools and machines for producing large quantities. (A reduction in unit production cost is equivalent to a *quantity discount* and can be treated as in the previous section.)

Disadvantages

The major disadvantage of producing large lots is that the accumulated inventory has a holding cost. Thus, the production of lots that are too large may result in additional inventory costs larger than the setup costs saved.

Management is interested in finding the production quantity for a lot that minimizes the sum of the holding inventory and setup costs. Such a problem is called the **economic lot size (ELS) problem.**

Example

Energy Sol Corp. produces a certain energy-saving device. The demand for the device, D, is 1,800 units per year (or 6 units each day, assuming 300 working days in a year). The company can produce at an annual rate, P, of 7,200 units (or 24 per day). (P is the *maximum* rate when the line is running, *not* an average daily rate.) Setup cost, S, is $300. (Setup cost is the cost of preparing for a production run and is similar to the ordering cost K in the EOQ.) There is an inventory holding cost, H, of $36 per unit, per year. The problem is to find the economic lot size, which is designated by L^*.

Schematic Illustration

The process is shown in Figure 12.13. As in the regular EOQ illustration, the time axis is divided into cycles, each with the following elements:

First, produce—T_1
Then, deplete—T_2

The Production Period T_1. Let us assume that Energy Sol Corp. produces in lots of 72; that is, $L = 72$. Because the production rate is 24 per day, it will take $72/24 = 3$ days to produce one lot. This period is called T_1. In general, the length of a production period is given by Equation 12.15, where L is the given lot size.

$$T_1 = \frac{L}{P}$$

(12.15)

Note: If P is expressed in years, T_1 will be also. If P is in days, so will be T_1. And so on.

Inventory Buildup. During the first day within period T_1, Energy Sol will produce 24 units, but will also *use* 6. Thus, the inventory level at the end of the day will be (daily P) − (daily D) = 24 − 6 = 18. At the end of the second day, there will be 36 units

FIGURE 12.13

Inventory level for ELS model

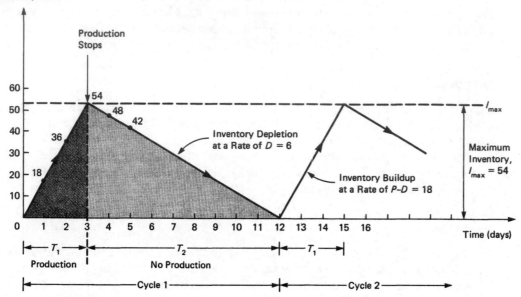

Inventory Level

in inventory and at the end of the third day, 54. (See Figure 12.13.) At that time, production will stop (at 72 units produced).

The Maximum Inventory.   The maximum inventory, I_{max}, will be reached when the production stops at the end of the third day (end of T_1). Equation 12.16 can be used to compute this level.

$$I_{max} = (P - D)T_1 = (P - D)\frac{L}{P} \tag{12.16}$$

In our case, $I_{max} = (24 - 6)3 = 54$

The Depletion Period (T_2).   Once production stops, demand is provided from the inventory during the "depletion" period, T_2. With an initial 54 units of inventory at the end of T_1, there is enough to supply $54/6 = 9$ days (days 4–12 in Figure 12.13) of demand. In general, T_2 is given by Equation 12.17.

$$T_2 = \frac{I_{max}}{D} = \frac{(P - D)L}{PD} \tag{12.17}$$

A cycle

A Cycle.   The time between two consecutive production runs is called a **cycle,** and is composed of:

$$\text{Cycle} = T_1 + T_2 \tag{12.18}$$

Other Performance Variables

Using the information given, we can find some additional performance variables as well.

The Average Inventory (I_{avg})

As in the EOQ case, the average inventory here also equals half the maximum inventory:

$$I_{avg} = (1/2)I_{max} = \frac{(P - D)L}{2P} \tag{12.19}$$

Number of Cycles Per Year

The number of cycles per year, N, is determined from the annual demand D and the lot size L.

$$N = \frac{D}{L} \tag{12.20}$$

Cost Analysis

The Annual Holding Cost

The annual holding cost is given, as in the regular EOQ, by the product of the average inventory and the annual holding cost per unit (H):

$$\text{Annual holding cost} = \frac{H(P - D)L}{2P} \tag{12.21}$$

The Annual Setup Cost

The setup cost per cycle is given as S. Therefore, the total annual setup cost is the product of S times the number of cycles. That is:

$$\text{Annual setup cost} = \frac{SD}{L} \tag{12.22}$$

The Total Annual Cost

The total annual cost is again equal to the sum of the total holding cost and the total setup cost:

$$TC = \frac{H(P - D)L}{2P} + \frac{SD}{L} \qquad (12.23)$$

Finding the ELS

The optimal lot size, L^*, is found by taking the first derivative of Equation 12.23 and setting it to zero, with the result:

$$L^* = \sqrt{\frac{2PSD}{H(P - D)}} \qquad (12.24)$$

Solution to Energy Sol's Problem

Given:

     Annual demand, $D = 1{,}800$
     Annual production capability, $P = 7{,}200$
     Setup cost, $S = \$300$
     Holding cost per unit per year, $H = \$36$

Inserting the data given into Equation 12.24:

$$L^* = \sqrt{\frac{2PSD}{H(P - D)}} = \sqrt{\frac{2(7{,}200)(300)(1{,}800)}{36(7{,}200 - 1{,}800)}} = 200 \text{ units}$$

Using Equations 12.15 through 12.23:

$$T_1 = \frac{L^*}{P} = \frac{200}{7{,}200} = .0278 \text{ years}$$

Assuming 300 working days, this will be $8\frac{1}{3}$ days.

$$I_{max} = (P - D)T_1 = 5{,}400 \times .0278 = 150 \text{ units}$$

$$I_{avg} = \frac{I_{max}}{2} = 75 \text{ units}$$

$$T_2 = \frac{I_{max}}{D} = \frac{150}{1{,}800} = .0833 \text{ years, or 25 working days}$$

A cycle $= T_1 + T_2 = .0278 + .0833 = .111$ years, or $33\frac{1}{3}$ working days

FIGURE 12.14

The Energy Sol production process

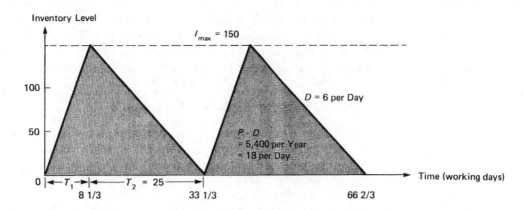

The above information is entered on Figure 12.14. Additional information that can be derived is:

$$N = \frac{D}{L^*} = \frac{1,800}{200} = 9 \text{ cycles per year}$$

$$\text{Annual holding cost} = \frac{36 \times (7,200 - 1,800)200}{2 \times 7,200} = \$2,700$$

$$\text{Annual setup cost} = \frac{300(1,800)}{200} = \$2,700$$

Note: These two costs *must* be equal in an *optimal* solution.

Total annual cost = Annual setup + Annual holding cost = \$5,400

12.12 Single-Period Inventories

The "Newsboy" problem

There exist some situations where the inventory decision is a one-period problem due to the product's high degree of perishability or obsolescence. This problem is classically known as *the Newsboy problem,* because day-old newspapers are considered worthless. Similar one-period situations are: church bake sales, Christmas tree sales, and Easter bunnies at the pet store. Seasonal products such as holiday greeting cards, spring dresses and certain holiday foods and flowers are other examples of the one-period problem. The same problem with a modified structure is the situation of those firms and people who must accept reservations or appointments for their services. This category consists of such services as motels and hotels, restaurants, airlines, doctors, and hairdressers.

Underorder or overorder?

The common element in all these situations is that the product is only ordered once, and there is a penalty associated with underordering as well as a penalty associated with overordering. The underordering penalty is the loss of potential profit (opportunity cost) plus a possible loss of customer goodwill. The overordering penalty is primarily the cost of the leftover product. There may additionally be disposal costs that add to the penalty or a salvage value that decreases the penalty.

A Discrete Demand Distribution Example

Calexico Produce buys tomatoes from Mexico once a week. A crate of tomatoes costs $6 and sells for $11 (i.e., a profit of $5 per crate sold). Any crates remaining unsold at the end of the week are sold as animal food for $2 a crate. Observations show that past sales ranged from 16 to 20 crates a week. Because demand is relatively stable, it is assumed it will continue at the same rate.

Suppose that a study, taken over the sales of the last 50 weeks, showed the following results:

Number of Crates Demanded	Number of Weeks
16	4
17	10
18	12
19	15
20	9
Total	50

The problem is to find how many crates Calexico Produce should order each week so that the profit will be maximized.

Solution Using a Decision Table

Because demand ranges between 16 and 20, there is no sense in ordering less than 16, nor more than 20. Therefore, there are only five alternatives of ordering: 16, 17, 18, 19, and 20 crates. There are five possible states of nature (demand); they are given with their respective probabilities below.

Five alternatives

16 crates with a chance of 4 out of 50 = 8 percent = .08
17 crates with a chance of 10/50 = .20
18 crates with a chance of 12/50 = .24
19 crates with a chance of 15/50 = .30
20 crates with a chance of 9/50 = .18

The information can be arranged in a decision table form (Table 12.4). To demonstrate the calculation of the numbers in the table, if 16 crates are ordered and the demand is 16 or more, a profit of $5 × 16 = $80 will be realized. It is assumed here that there is no cost for unsatisfied customers (cost of ill will). If 17 crates are ordered and there is only a demand for 16, 16 crates will be sold for $80 profit, and the 17th crate

TABLE 12.4   Calexico Produce Decision Table

			Demand			
Probabilities	.08	.20	.24	.30	.18	*Expected Value of Profit ($)*
Alternatives	16	17	18	19	20	
16	80	80	80	80	80	80.00
17	76	85	85	85	85	84.28
18	72	81	90	90	90	86.76
19	68	77	86	95	95	87.08 ←*Maximum*
20	64	73	82	91	100	84.70

will be sold at a $6 - 2 = \$4$ loss; that is, the total profit is $80 - 4 = \$76$. For every crate overordered, a loss of $4 is recorded. Thus, if 20 crates are ordered and the demand is 16, the profit will be $64: $80 - (4 \times 4) = \$64$.

Solution

Using expected value as a criterion, the best strategy is: order 19 crates each week at an expected profit of:

$$.08(\$68) + .20(\$77) + .24(\$86) + .30(\$95) + .18(\$95) = \$87.08$$

Note that, as with the EOQ, the solution is cost insensitive.

Solution by Marginal Analysis

Small inventory problems can be solved with the decision table approach rather quickly. However, the solution of problems with dozens or hundreds of possible alternatives requires excessive computations. To overcome this difficulty, marginal analysis can be used. Marginal analysis can also be used for the solution of more complicated problems involving continuous demand distributions and costs due to ill will.

The basic idea of marginal analysis is to compare two opposing costs, the cost of overordering (including holding and spoilage) and the cost of underordering (primarily shortage cost), on an "additional-unit" basis. Let us demonstrate. Let:

p = Probability of selling *at least* one more (the *marginal*) unit. This is the *cumulative* probability of "demand exceeding the current level."

$1 - p$ = Probability of *not* selling one more unit.

MP = Profit realized from selling that additional unit (marginal profit).

ML = Loss realized if the additional unit is not sold (marginal loss).

Excessive number of computations

General Formulation

The expected profit is equal to the probability of selling the unit times its marginal profit:

$$\text{Expected marginal profit} = p\,(\text{MP})$$

Similarly, the expected marginal loss is given as:

$$\text{Expected marginal loss} = (1 - p)\,\text{ML}$$

EMP should exceed EML

To find out whether or not an additional unit should be ordered (at a given level of ordering), it is necessary to compare the expected profit versus the expected loss of the next unit. As long as the expected profit is *larger* than the expected loss, a unit should be added. Units will be added, one at a time, until the point where the *expected profit* equals the *expected loss*. (Ordering more than this will produce a loss.) This condition is expressed mathematically as:

$$p\,(\text{MP}) \geq (1 - p)\,\text{ML} \tag{12.25}$$

Critical fraction or critical probability

Solving the equation portion of 12.25 for p, the critical fraction:

$$p = \frac{\text{ML}}{\text{ML} + \text{MP}} \tag{12.26}$$

In other words, in order to justify ordering (or stocking) a unit, the probability of selling that unit must be *at least* equal to p. The problem now is how to find the optimal unit.

Application to the Discrete Probability Example of Calexico Produce:

$$\text{MP} = 11 - 6 = \$5$$

$$\text{ML} = 6 - 2 = \$4, \text{ therefore: } p = \frac{4}{4 + 5} = .444$$

Cumulative probability

It is necessary now to relate p to the *cumulative probability of demand;* that is, the probability that one *or more* crates will be sold. For example, the probability of selling 19 or more crates (that is, 19 or 20) is $.18 + .30 = .48$ (see Table 12.5).

Note that the cumulative probability for 19 crates is .48, more than $p = .444$, and, hence, 19 should be stocked; but at 20 crates .18 is less than .444 and, hence, 20 cannot be justified. Therefore, the optimal order policy is 19 crates (closest to p, yet larger).

TABLE 12.5 **Cumulative Probability of Demand**

Number of Crates, N	Probability of Demand	Cumulative Probability (of Selling N or More)
16	.08	1.00
17	.20	.92
18	.24	.72
19	.30	.48←optimal
20	.18	.18

Application to Continuous Probability Situations

The same approach can be applied to situations involving continuous demand probability distributions such as normal, triangular, or uniform. In these cases, 1.0 − the cumulative probability distribution function is set equal to the critical fraction, p, to find the optimal ordering level. For example, in the last situation with Calexico Produce, if the demand had been uniformly distributed over 16–20 crates, the optimal number of crates to order, x, would be found as follows:

$$1.0 - .2(x - 16) = .444$$

and, solving for x: $x = 18.78$ crates

Note: Rounding is required, as discussed earlier.

12.13 Material Requirements Planning (MRP)

Independent versus dependent demand

Inventory control systems are designed for two distinct cases: (1) where the demand is independent, and (2) where the demand is dependent.

Independent Demand
In this case, the demand for a given item is completely independent of the demand for other items. For example, the demand for bread in the store or light bulbs in your home.

Dependent Demand
Dependent demand occurs in manufacturing and other environments where the demand for one item depends on the demand for another item(s). For example, in producing tables, the demand for legs is dependent on the demand for tables. The **demand** for a dependent item (e.g., the legs) is usually **lumpy** rather than constant. This is because many finished products are produced in batches (e.g., 2,000 in a short time). Thus, the

Lumpy dependent demand

TABLE 12.6   MRP versus EOQ System Characteristics

Characteristic	MRP Systems	EOQ Systems
Demand:	Dependent	Independent
Lead time basis:	Time point	Reorder point (in units)
Reorder basis:	Future demand	Historical demand
Safety stock:	Finished goods only, not components	All items
Item focus:	Finished goods	All parts

demand for legs can be zero for six weeks and then 1,000 per week for two weeks. Using the EOQ is not advisable in this case (EOQ assumes constant demand). It would be much better to have the legs arrive in inventory *just prior* to the time when they are needed. This is one of the major purposes of **materials requirements planning (MRP)**, a computer-based production planning and inventory control system. Table 12.6 compares the characteristics of MRP with EOQ systems.

Each product typically consists of several subcomponents—for a company with many products, the number of subcomponents and parts may reach tens of thousands. To keep track of all these parts on a *finished product* basis clearly requires a computer. Therefore, until the advent of economic computer power in the 1980s, MRP was not feasible for many situations.

MRP requires computer power

MRP as one part of MRP II

In actuality, MRP is only one element in a production planning and control system known as manufacturing resource planning (MRP II). Other required elements include order entry, engineering bills of materials, a master production schedule, forecasting, stores control, and so on. These elements tie together the various functions of business (purchasing, accounting, engineering, marketing) and maintain consistency with the manufacturing reality. According to a study published in *Datamation* (February 1, 1988), between 8,000 and 15,000 out of the 43,000 U.S. corporations with manufacturing sites of 100 employees or more are using MRP II. This number is probably even higher now.

MRP—Basic Overview

Let us assume that a company produces a walnut table in three sizes: large, medium, and small. Also, the company produces other tables (e.g., oak, teak) as well as a variety of wooden chairs. Each of the finished products includes a *bill of materials* (Figure 12.15) that details what it takes to make the product, which can be represented by a *product tree* (Figure 12.16) that shows how the materials go together to make the product.

It frequently happens that some of the materials in the products are common to a number of different tables; for example, screws and anchors. The MRP system is then executed for each product and aggregates common parts and subassemblies from the several sources according to their unique, time-phased requirements for purchase and manufacture.

FIGURE 12.15

Bill of materials for walnut table

Top		(one)	manufactured
Walnut veneer	15 ft²	(one)	purchased
Particle board	$\frac{1}{2}'' \times 15$ feet	(one)	manufactured
Veneer strip	$\frac{1}{2}'' \times 17$ feet	(one)	purchased
Apron		(one)	manufactured
Veneer strip	$3'' \times 15$ feet	(one)	purchased
Particle board	$3'' \times 5\frac{1}{2}$ feet	(two)	manufactured
Particle board	$3'' \times 2$ feet	(two)	manufactured
Wood screws	$1\frac{1}{2}''$ flathead	(eight)	purchased
Legs		(four)	manufactured
Walnut	$1\frac{1}{2}'' \times 1\frac{1}{2}'' \times 2'$	(one)	manufactured
Anchors		(one)	manufactured
$\frac{1}{16}''$ steel ribbon		(one)	purchased
6–32 screws		(two)	purchased
6–32 nuts		(two)	purchased

FIGURE 12.16

Walnut table product tree

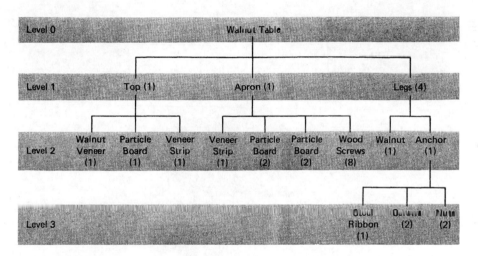

The Elements of MRP

Four sets of data requirements

The MRP system is composed of four data elements (Figure 12.17):

1. A master production schedule.
2. A bill of materials file.
3. An inventory master file.
4. Lead times.

The Master Production Schedule

The **master production schedule** (**MPS**) is a schedule listing how many of each finished product will be required and when; this is called a *time-phased* schedule. The

FIGURE 12.17

The MRP data elements

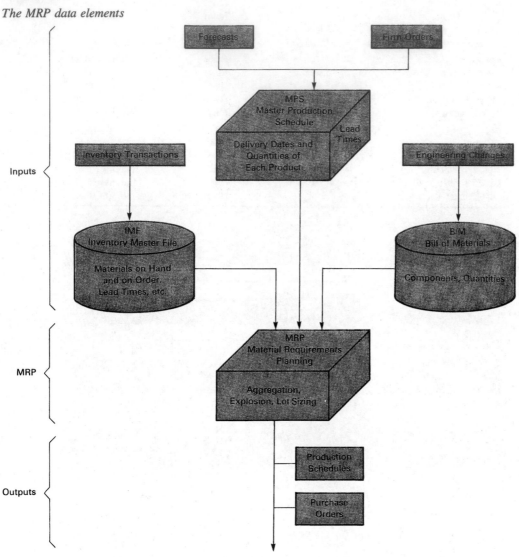

"Parent" or "Level 0"
items in the MPS

items may be finished goods, parts, or subcomponents. The demand is based on both forecasts and actual customer orders to date.

It is the MPS that drives the MRP system. To assemble the end items (called **parent** or **level 0 items**), the components must be ready on time. To have the components ready for final assembly on time, *their* subcomponents must be produced, or purchased, by the necessary dates. And so on. The time it takes to get these components and subcomponents is called their *lead time*. The MRP system takes these lead and assembly times into account in determining when to release work orders and purchase requisitions. An example of an MPS will be given soon.

The Bill of Materials

The MRP system knows what items constitute each end product and each subassembly from the **bill of materials (B/M)**. The B/M includes all of the raw materials, components, and subassemblies (and their quantities) required to produce the item.

The Inventory Master File

The **inventory master file (IMF)** contains detailed information on the lead times to make, assemble, or purchase each item and the number of items on hand in inventory, on order with suppliers, and previously committed to production items. If sufficient items are available, the system commits them to use; if not, purchase or work orders are scheduled for release at the proper time so that items will be available when needed with the least possible inventory.

Inspecting the IMF for material availability

The MRP Computation Process—An Example

Exploding the B/M to determine time-phased material requirements

As an order is entered into the MPS, the MRP system **explodes** the B/M to determine what components and subcomponents will be required in what quantities in what time periods. The "explosion" simply consists of stepping down through the B/M levels and determining the quantity and lead times of subcomponents to support the purchase, manufacture, or assembly at each level. The result is a time-phased set of production requirements to support the parent order.

An example is given in Table 12.7 for a delivery schedule of 100 tables in week 15 and 70 tables in week 18. Note that because of an on-hand inventory of 90 tables and planned receipts of 30, only $(100 + 70) - 90 - 30 = 50$ are exploded through the B/M.

The levels 1, 2, and 3 exploded schedules for a portion of the B/M are shown in Table 12.8. The gross requirements at any level are based on the planned releases at the previous level. Notice, however, that gross requirements can be accumulated for sev-

---

TABLE 12.7   Level 0 MPS for Walnut Table (Two-Week Lead Time)

	Week Number							
	12	*13*	*14*	*15*	*16*	*17*	*18*	*19*
Gross requirements				100			70	
On hand	90	90	120	120	20	20	20	0
Net requirements							50	
Planned receipts		30						
Planned releases						50		

2-week lead time

TABLE 12.8 B/M Explosion for Subcomponent Requirements

a. Level 1: Legs (One-Week Lead Time)

	Week Number							
	11	12	13	14	15	16	17	18
Gross requirements						200		
On hand	130	130	130	130	130	130	0	0
Net requirements						70		
Planned receipts								
Planned releases					(70)			

$\times 1 =$

b. Level 2: Anchors (One-Week Lead Time)

	Week Number							
	11	12	13	14	15	16	17	18
Gross requirements			10		(70)		40	
On hand	35	35	60	50	50	0	0	0
Net requirements					20		40	
Planned receipts		25						
Planned releases				(20)		(40)		

$\times 2 =$ $\times 2 =$

c. Level 3: Screws (Three-Week Lead Time)

	Week Number							
	11	12	13	14	15	16	17	18
Gross requirements		50		(40)		(80)		40
On hand	80	80	30	30	0	0	0	0
Net requirements				10		80		40
Planned receipts								
Planned releases	10		80		40			

Externally generated demands also

eral products; for example, the anchors and screws have externally generated demands on them as well. (They are also used in oak tables, but the schedule for those is not illustrated here.)

The planned release of work orders for 50 tables in week 16 (Table 12.7) generates a gross requirement of $4 \times 50 = 200$ legs in week 16. Because 130 are already in stock (Table 12.8a), only 70 need be released in week 15. This generates a gross requirement for 70 anchors in week 15 (Table 12.8b). Considering other external requirements for anchors (e.g., 10 in week 13), inventory on hand, and planned receipts, two

Work and purchase order releases

work orders are released in weeks 14 and 16 for more anchors. These work orders generate, in turn, requirements for twice as many screws, because there are two screws in an anchor, and purchase orders are thus placed for screws in weeks 11, 13, and 15 (Table 12.8c).

The Lot-Sizing Problem

Lot sizing

Note in Table 12.8b that work orders are released for anchors in weeks 14 and 16 (and purchase orders for screws in weeks 11, 13, and 15). Clearly, it may well be worthwhile to consider combining these orders and avoiding an extra setup or ordering charge. But, how many orders ahead should be included? This is known as the **lot-sizing problem.**

The best approach to the lot-sizing problem is still an unresolved question in research literature. An acceptable trial-and-error approach is shown next.

Produce to Demand

In this straightforward approach, the firm simply produces or purchases to meet demand and keeps no inventories. Holding costs are thus minimized, but the production fluctuations and possible capacity problems are a severe disadvantage. If the cost of ordering screws in Table 12.8c is $5 each time, and the holding cost is $0.01 per week, the total cost of this policy would be $15 (ordering three times).

Produce for the Entire Time Horizon

Compare several alternatives

In this approach, all the parts known to be needed over the horizon of demand are produced or ordered at the same time. Thus, in Table 12.8c, the firm would order $10 + 80 + 40 = 130$ screws. The resulting inventory cost would be:

$$\text{Carry 80 units for two weeks: } .01 \times 80 \times 2 = \$1.60$$

$$\text{Carry 40 units for four weeks: } .01 \times 40 \times 4 = \$1.60$$

for a total of $3.20, added to the one-time ordering cost of $5.00, results in a total cost for the horizon of $8.20.

Produce in Intermediate Lots

Trial-and-error approach

In this situation, different lot sizes corrresponding to different horizons can be tried to determine the most cost-effective approach. For example, the firm can order 90 in week 11 and then 40 in week 15, or 10 in week 11 and 120 in week 13, and so on. One possibility is to find the size that will make the holding and ordering costs as close to each other as possible.

Summary

MRP has emerged as the best inventory control system for job lot production with a dependent demand. It allows a *near zero* inventory level because the inventory is closely coordinated with the production schedule. In contrast to the EOQ that controls one item at a time, MRP can control several products simultaneously when they share common components or parts. Therefore, most MRP systems are large in size and require a computer for processing (see Section 12.15).

12.14 Safety Stocks and Service Levels

Stockout

So far, it has been assumed that the demand and the lead time are constant. As a result, it was possible to adopt an inventory policy whereby an item would *never be out of stock*. Running out of stock (a *stockout* or a *shortage*) implies that demand cannot be filled on time. Stockouts result from either delays in deliveries and/or from unexpected rises in demand during the lead time. These situations are depicted in Figure 12.18. Though models exist for each of these situations, this model is applicable to both, either individually or combined.

What level of safety stock?

For protection against a stockout, an order can be computed and placed so that the delivery will arrive when a certain level of inventory is still remaining, rather than at the scheduled depletion of the stock. The managerial problem is *determining the proper level* of this safety stock (SS).

Example

Assume an average demand of 10 units per day and a lead time of six days. In such a case, there is an average demand during the lead time (DDLT) of $10(6) = 60$ units. Now assume that protection against a stockout (safety stock) of up to SS = 15 units is desired. The reorder point will be: ROP = $60 + 15 = 75$ units. In general, the following relationship exists between the reorder point and the safety stock:

$$ROP = DDLT + SS \qquad (12.27)$$

The Concept of Service Level

To build up a safety stock that would prevent shortages in *all* cases could be very expensive. The cost of incurring a once-a-year shortage may be much smaller than the

FIGURE 12.18

Factors contributing to an inventory stockout

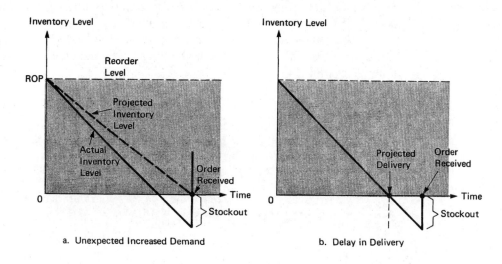

a. Unexpected Increased Demand

b. Delay in Delivery

cost of maintaining the extra safety stock. Therefore, management may wish to maintain a safety stock that will protect against a shortage not in all cases but, say, 80 percent of the time. The percentage of time that all demand is met (in this example, the 80 percent) is called the **service level.** The service level is defined as the probability of *not* running out of stock. That is:

The service level

$$\text{Service level} = 1 - \text{Probability of running out of stock} \qquad (12.28)$$

The higher the service level, the higher the required safety stock with its associated inventory cost, and the lower the chance of a shortage and its consequences. Service levels are usually determined by management policies, but may also be determined mathematically in such a way that the total cost of keeping the safety stock and incurring expenses during shortages is minimized. Let us show how.

Example

The average demand for product G3 is 10 units a day. The lead time is known to be six days. Therefore, the *average* demand during the lead time is 6 × 10, or 60. The lead time demand follows a *normal distribution* with a *standard deviation,* σ_d, of 8.59 units.

The normal distribution

With a normal distribution, there is exactly a 50 percent chance that the demand during the lead time will be more than the average of 60 units. Using the tables for the area under the normal curve (see Table C1 in Appendix C), the relationship between a desired service level (which is equivalent to the area under the normal curve) and the safety factor (number of standard deviations), Z, can be found. For example, for a 50 percent (.50) service level, $Z = 0$; for a 67 percent (.67) service level, $Z = .44$; for a 90 percent service level, $Z = 1.28$.

Suppose that management is interested in providing a 90 percent service level. To find the safety stock required for such a level, we invoke the definition of Z:

$$Z = \frac{X - \mu}{\sigma}$$

In our case:

$$Z = \frac{\text{ROP} - \text{DDLT}}{\sigma_d} = \frac{\text{SS}}{\sigma_d}$$

or:

$$\text{Safety stock} = Z \times \sigma_d \qquad (12.29)$$

where Z is the number of standard deviations equivalent to the desired service level and σ_d is the standard deviation of the demand during the reorder period (8.59 in this case).

For this example:

$$\text{Safety stock} = 1.28 \times 8.59 = 11 \text{ units}$$

This information is shown in Figure 12.19.

Note that in addition to the average demand for 60 units needed during the lead time, there is a need for a safety stock of 11 to ensure a service level of 90 percent; that is, 71 total units is the reorder point. In a similar manner, it can be found that in order to ensure a 95 percent service level, a safety stock of 14 units is required; and to ensure a 99.9 percent service level, 26.5 units of safety stock are needed.

Finding the Best Level of Safety Stock

Equation 12.29 tells management what amount of safety stock is required in order to maintain a desired service level. However, management may also be interested in knowing the cost of maintaining a desired service level. The establishment of a safety stock involves two costs:

1. The expected cost of a shortage, which declines as the safety stock increases.
2. The expected cost of keeping the safety stock, which increases as the safety stock increases.

The total cost that management is interested in is the sum of the two. Management may be interested in finding the relationship between this total cost and the service level. Management may also be interested in determining the service level for which the total cost is the lowest. The following computations illustrate such an analysis, assuming that orders are spread out enough so that only one order may be outstanding and thus short at any given point in time.

FIGURE 12.19

Service level of 90 percent

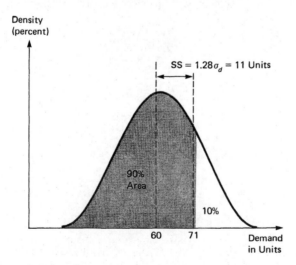

The Cost of Shortage

The expected cost of the shortage is given by:

$$\text{Annual cost of shortage} = \frac{\pi BD}{Q} \qquad (12.30)$$

where:

π = The probability of shortage (which equals 1 minus the service level)
B = Average cost of one shortage
D = Annual demand
Q = Order quantity
$\dfrac{D}{Q}$ = The number of cycles per year

The Cost of Holding Safety Stock

The expected cost of holding safety stock is given by:

$$\text{Annual holding cost} = H \times (\text{safety stock}) = HZ\sigma_d \qquad (12.31)$$

where:

H = Holding cost, per unit per year

Z = Number of standard deviations required to maintain a desired service level

σ_d = The standard deviation of demand during the lead time

The sum of the cost in Equations 12.30 and 12.31 is the total relevant cost for each service level:

$$TC = \frac{\pi BD}{Q} + HZ\sigma_d \qquad (12.32)$$

To find the best level of safety stock, the total relevant cost, *TC*, is computed for several desired service levels (e.g., 80 percent, 90 percent, 95 percent, 99 percent) and the lowest one is chosen.

Example

In the example of product G3, the following data are given:

Lead time = 6 days
Demand = 10 units per day or 2,500 per year (with 250 working days)
Standard deviation = 8.59 units during the lead time

K = Order cost = \$160 per order
H = Holding cost = \$20 per unit per year
B = Shortage cost = \$100 per shortage

Management insists that a service level of at *least* 90 percent be maintained.

·The problem is to find the cost of maintaining this 90 percent service level and whether there is one *above it* that would cost less.

Solution

First, the EOQ is computed disregarding shortages and safety stock.

$$Q^* = \sqrt{\frac{2KD}{H}} = \sqrt{\frac{2(160)2,500}{20}} = 200 \text{ units per order}$$

Computation for 90 Percent Service Level.   It was shown earlier that a safety stock of 11 units will guarantee a 90 percent service level. The total annual holding cost of a safety stock of 11 units is:

$$H \times (\text{safety stock}) = 20(11) = \$220$$

The total annual shortage cost (according to Equation 12.30) is:

$$\text{Shortage cost} = \frac{\pi BD}{Q^*} = \frac{.1(100)(2,500)}{200} = \$125$$

Therefore, the *total relevant costs* are 220 + 125 = \$345. Using a trial-and-error approach, the analyst now searches for a possible lower cost service level about 90 percent.

Try a Service Level of 95 Percent.   It was mentioned earlier that the necessary safety stock for a 95 percent service level is 14. Thus, the total annual holding cost of safety stock is (14)(20) or \$280, and the total annual shortage cost = .05 × 100 × 2,500/200 = \$62.50. Therefore, the *total relevant costs* are 280 + 62.50 = \$342.50.

Try a Service Level of 99.9 Percent.   The necessary safety stock for 99.9 percent was stated to be 26.5. Rounding to 27 units, the total annual holding cost of safety stock is 27(20) or \$540 and the total annual shortage cost is:

$$.001 \times 100 \times \frac{2,500}{200} = \$1.25$$

The *total relevant costs* are:

$$540 + 1.25 = \$541.25$$

Comparing the three service levels, 95 percent is the best. However, this process could have been continued in the same manner for any other desired service level (e.g., 96 percent) until an even lower total cost level might have been found.

Notes:

1. If the demand during the lead time follows a distribution other than the normal (e.g., Poisson, negative exponential), the appropriate statistical methodology for the standard deviation and safety factor calculations must be followed.

2. If both the demand and the lead time are stochastic (variable), a Monte Carlo simulation may be used to determine the best safety stock (see Chapter 15).

Shortage Cost on a per Unit Basis

To conduct a cost analysis with per-unit shortage costs, it is necessary to determine the average number of units short. Table 12.9 relates the average number of units short $E(K)$ to the service level. To find $E(K)$, the second column must be multiplied by σ_d. For our earlier example, $E(K)$ for a 90 percent service level = $0.0473 \times 8.59 = 0.406$ units. In general, the annual shortage cost will be:

$$\text{Shortage cost} = (D/Q^*)(G)E(K)\sigma_d \qquad (12.33)$$

where G is the cost per unit short.

Example

If $G = \$10$, then:

$$\text{Annual cost of shortage} = (2{,}500/200)(10)(.406) = \$50.75$$

TABLE 12.9 **Unit Shortage as a Function of Service Level**

Service Level	$E(K)/\sigma_d$
99	0.00441
95	0.02089
90	0.04730
85	0.07776
80	0.11156

Source: R. G. Brown. *Decision Rules for Inventory Management* (New York: Holt, Rinehart & Winston, 1967).

Management Science in Practice

Cutting the Cost of Inventories for the U.S. Navy

The U.S. Navy operates eight supply centers in the United States, each one holding about 80,000 items worth about $25 million. Order quantities are computed with a version of the EOQ model with safety stock added in to minimize the likelihood of stockouts. At the time of initiation of this study, the navy was placing about 840,000 orders per year. Each center's budget sets the average inventory investment at about 2.5 month's worth of stock with a service goal of filling 85 percent of all requisitions immediately from stock.

Although the 2.5-month stockage requirement is set by law, there is no mention regarding what percent of this requirement should be safety stock versus cycle stock. Existing policy is to maintain 1.5 months of safety stock and 1 month of cycle stock, where the cycle stock is half the EOQ (that is, 2 months' worth). These are aggregate amounts, of course, and individual items may vary considerably from these values.

The navy initiated a study to determine if these were the best policy levels, or if better service or reduced cost could be obtained with other policy levels. It was found that service is a function of two factors: the number of reorder cycles and the likelihood of a shortage on each cycle. At extreme values for either one of these factors, the service level deteriorates. That is, with large cycle stocks, there are very few replenishment cycles; yet, there is a good chance of stockouts because of the small level of safety stocks. And with many replenishment cycles and large safety stocks, there are more cycles where a stockout might occur.

The navy found that even with no safety stock (all the 2.5 months of stock going into cycle stocks with a typical workload of 112,000 orders per depot) there was still a 78 percent service level. And with a large safety stock of 2 months (only 0.5 months of cycle stocks with a workload of 289,000 orders) there was an 81 percent service level. At the current policy of 1.5 month's worth of safety stock (240,000 orders), the service level was 85 percent. However, at a 1-month safety stock (184,000 orders), the service level was still 85 percent.

Analyzing each of the supply depots separately, the minimum safety stock varied between 0.8 and 1.1 months. The policy was thus changed to specify maintaining 1 month's safety stock instead of 1.5 month's worth, with the total work orders among the eight supply depots thereby decreasing from the 840,000 currently to 670,000. This reduction was estimated to save $2 million in annual labor costs for the supply depots, obtained by reductions in the operating expense budgets of each center.

Source: E. S. Gardner, "A Top-Down Approach to Modeling U.S. Navy Inventories," *Interfaces*, July–August 1987, pp. 1–7.

Questions:

1. What is the average value of each item?
2. On average, what is the monthly order interval for each item?
3. Graph the safety stock (in months) versus service level. What does it show?
4. Comment on the supply centers' manager's incentive to conduct more studies such as this.

12.15 Use of Computers

Several computer printout examples are included in this section. The first is a regular EOQ applied to the program presented in Section 12.4 (using Nelson's software). Notice that the program computes the reorder level when the lead time is input.

```
     **  INFORMATION  ENTERED  **

     DEMAND                 :  1200
     ORDERING  COSTS        :  5
     HOLDING  COSTS         :  1.2
     LEAD  TIME  (DAYS)     :  10
     WORKING  DAYS          :  300


     RESULTS:  OPTIMAL  ECONOMIC  ORDER  QUANTITY  (EOQ):  100  UNITS  AVERAGE
               INVENTORY  LEVEL:  50


     TOTAL  ANNUAL  INVENTORY  COSTS
                   HOLDING  COST:        $  60.00
                   ORDERING  COSTS:      $  60.00
                          TOTAL:        $120.00


     OPTIMAL  REORDER  POINT:  40  UNITS
     OPTIMAL  NUMBER  OF  ORDERS  PER  YEAR:  12  TIMES
     OPTIMAL  INVENTORY  CYCLE  TIME:  25  days
```

The second example involves the ELS problem of Section 12.11, with a unit cost of $360. The Lotfi and Pegels package is used.

```
               **  INFORMATION  ENTERED  **

               DEMAND                 :  1800
               ORDERING  COSTS        :  300
               HOLDING  COSTS         :  36
               LEAD  TIME             :  0
               WORKING  DAYS          :  300
               PRODUCTION  RATE       :  7200
               PURCHASE  PRICE/UNIT   :  360


          Problem  Title  :  ELS


Results:  Production  run  size  model  with  no  shortage:

Days  between  production  runs      33.3
Length  of  run  is                   8.3
Optimal  run  size  is              200.0
Re-Production  Point  is              0.0
Max  inventory  level  is           150.0
Annual  holding  cost  is          2700.00
Annual  setup     cost  is         2700.00
Purchase  price        is        648000.00

Total  cost  is                   653400.00
```

The next example is a modification of the example given in Section 12.14. The input data include a lead time of six days with an average demand of 60 during this time and a standard deviation of 8.59. The penalty cost is $20 per unit per year. The results using Nelson's package are:

```
            ** INFORMATION ENTERED **

        DEMAND            : 2500
        ORDERING COSTS    : 160
        HOLDING COSTS     : 20
        LEAD TIME         : 6
        WORKING DAYS      : 250
        SERVICE LEVEL     : 95%
        MEAN DEMAND       : 60
        STANDARD DEV      : 8.59
        PENALTY COST      : 20


        RESULTS: ECONOMIC ORDER QUANTITY (EOQ) = 200
        SAFETY STOCK LEVEL =                      14.1735 UNITS

        EXPECTED NUMBER OF UNITS SHORT =          .1783714
        REORDER POINT (ROP) =                     74.17 UNITS
        ANNUAL HOLDING COSTS FOR SAFETY STOCK = 283.47
        ANNUAL SHORTAGE COSTS FOR SAFETY STOCK = 44.59285
        TOTAL ANNUAL SAFETY STOCK COSTS =        328.0628
        ANNUAL ORDERING COST                    2000.00
        ANNUAL HOLDING COST                     2000.00
```

Notice that the reorder level is not just usage times lead time, but also includes safety stock (of 14).

The last example depicts a marginal analysis solved with Nelson's package.

```
                         MARGINAL ANALYSIS

        NO. OF DEMAND LEVELS            5

        DEMAND LEVEL               PROBABILITY

            16                         .08
            17                         .2
            18                         .24
            19                         .3
            20                         .18


        MARGINAL PROFIT                5
        MARGINAL LOSS                  4

        RESULTS: PROBABILITY OF SELLING THE MARGINAL UNIT: .4444444
```

```
                      CUMULATIVE PROBABILITY TABLE

                                          CUMULATIVE
                           PROBABILITY    PROBABILITY
                               OF         (OF SELLING N      EXPECTED
          DEMAND             DEMAND         OR MORE)          PROFIT

            16                0.080          1.000           80
            17                0.200          0.920           84.28
            18                0.240          0.720           86.76
            19                0.300          0.480           87.08 <---BEST
            20                0.180          0.180           84.7
       OPTIMAL INVENTORY LEVEL: 19 UNITS
```

Computerized MRP

In the last few years, a large number of these packages have been written for the micro-computer. This development makes the use of MRP economically feasible for almost any size of company. Such systems can immediately reflect the effects of changes, delays, or cancellations on production schedules. It is a virtual necessity to use a computer for MRP calculations. IBM, Xerox, Micro MRP, CINCOM, UNISYS, Markem Corp., and several others have developed MRP programs. For a discussion, see reference [12].

12.16 Concluding Remarks

This chapter has presented a variety of basic inventory models, each of which is appropriate for a different set of circumstances. There exist many more inventory models based on other characteristics of demand, supply, and the costs involved. There are even dozens of variations of the basic models presented here. With the increased complexity of many of the advanced models, it is necessary to use a computer to apply them.

12.17 Problems for Part B

18. Canographic Corporation produces computer plotters for the West Coast. The monthly demand for the plotters is 20 units. The company has a production capacity of 80 units per month. There is a setup cost of $750 per production run. Each plotter kept in stock for one month costs $25 in holding cost. Management's policy is to supply *all* demand; thus, no shortage is allowed. (Assume 20 manufacturing and demand days per month.)

    a. Show the inventory cycle graphically (without any data).
    b. Find the best production plan (i.e., how many units to produce each production run). A whole number of units must be produced in each run. A production run may involve a fraction of a day.
    c. How many days of production will there be in each cycle?

d. In part (*a*), find the length of the total cycle and the maximum inventory level.

e. Assuming that the company produces 60 units in each production run, what will the effect on the total monthly cost be? (Compare to the minimum cost.)

19. Union Machine Corporation operates a punch press that produces 20 units of product M each hour. The press is in operation five hours a day. In order to set up the press for product M, it is necessary to shut down for two hours. Setup time costs the company $15 per hour.

    The demand for product M is 40 units a day, during 250 operating days in a year. The inventory carrying cost (for each unit of product M) is $1 per year. *Determine:*
    a. The optimal production lot.
    b. The production and no-production periods.
    c. The total annual inventory cost.

20. Amerland Corporation produces industrial air cleaners in the *most economical way*, in lot sizes of 600 units. Each unit costs $300. The company operates 360 days a year and is capable of producing 30 units daily. The demand rate is 300 units per month. Inventory carrying cost is 25 percent of the value stored. *Find:*
    a. The length of a production run.
    b. The maximum inventory, in units.
    c. The length of the "no-production" periods.
    d. The total yearly inventory cost.

21. Central Airlines buys special valves at $10 apiece. The company uses 24,500 valves each year. It costs $20 to place an order, and the unit carrying cost per year is considered to be 20 percent of the value stored.
    a. Find how many valves should be purchased at a time (using EOQ).
    b. Should the company accept an offer of a 2 percent discount on the valves if they are purchased quarterly?

22. Given an inventory system where:

    Yearly demand = 120 units
    Ordering cost = $45
    Price of unit = $200
    Annual carrying cost = 24 percent

Determine:
a. The economic order quantity.
b. The supplier offered a 1 percent discount on the unit price if the items are purchased in lots of 100 at a time. Should management accept the offer?
c. The minimum percentage discount that will make the offer attractive.

23. Dee's Department Store sells 25,000 type A shirts a year. The supplier offers a generous quantity discount. The price list is given below:

Quantity	Price per Shirt
0–999	$2.50
1,000–1,749	2.00
1,750–2,499	1.50
2,500 and over	1.00

Given: Order cost, $20. Inventory carrying cost, 20 percent of the value of the item.

Find the EOQ for each price level and check its feasibility. In the infeasible cases, compute cost data for the closest possible limit. Compare total cost at all quantity levels and suggest the best inventory policy for Dee's.

24. Formulate an algorithm (set of decision rules) to solve the quantity discount problem when only one price break exists.

25. A company uses a certain product that is demanded at an average rate of 10 units a working day. The company operates on a five-day-a-week schedule.

    Replenishment occurs once every six weeks. Storage cost per unit is $6 (paid only if the unit is stored for the entire six-week period). Shortage cost is $30 per unit per week. The table below gives the probability of demand during the six weeks.

Quantity Demanded	Probability
60	.05
150	.10
240	.15
300	.40
360	.15
450	.10
540	.05

Find the best safety level. Use the trial-and-error approach to check safety levels of 0, 60, 150, and 240.

26. Given an MRP system with the following information:

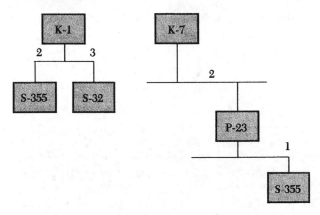

Delivery Schedule:

Item	Lead Time	On Hand	November 5	November 12	November 19	November 26	December 3
K-1	2 weeks	0		20	—	50	—
K-7	1 week	20	10	—	30	40	—
P-23	1 week	0	—	—	—	—	—
S-32	2 weeks	30	—	—	—	—	—
S-355	2 weeks	100					

Existing Orders:

K-7 (complete): 10 units to arrive on November 12. Find the planned releases for part S-355.

27. The lead time for a product is 10 days. The demand for the product is 20 units per day. It is known that the standard deviation of the demand during the lead time is 15 units. Assume a normal distribution for the demand.

Management would like to provide a service level of 85 percent or 90 percent, whichever is less expensive. The company orders 10 times a year, and the holding and shortage costs are:

H = $20 per unit per year
G = $80 per unit short per year

Should the company use the 85 percent or the 90 percent service level?

28. Tampa Electric Corp. wishes to determine the number of special batteries it should maintain. Each time the company runs out of batteries, it costs the company $700. The holding cost of a battery is $80 per year. The company now orders four times a year. The historical data on inventory levels and stockouts is:

Inventory Level	Probability of Stockout
20	.60
30	.30
40	.20
50	.10

Find:

a. The total annual inventory and stockout cost for an inventory level of 20 batteries.
b. Which of the given inventory levels will be the most desirable?

29. A company can produce 10 units of product M per day, during 250 working days per year. The cost of producing one unit is $10. The cost of setting up one production run amounts to $100. The inventory carrying cost, per year, is 30 percent of the value stored. The company sells 1,500 units of product M each year. The company's objective is profit maximization. *Find:*

a. The economic lot size.
b. The annual number of production runs.
c. The total annual cost of carrying inventory.
d. The production time (T_1).
e. The maximum inventory level.
f. The depletion period (T_2).
g. The company is considering producing a two-year supply in one production run. If they do so, they will be able to cut production cost by 10 percent. Show whether such an alternative will be profitable.

30. I produce spare parts for $5 each. If I run out of spares, I must make a special run, and those parts will cost $15 each. If my probability of demand for

spares is constant (discrete) between 1 and 10, how many spares should I produce?

31. Ambulances cost $50,000 each. Goodwill loss due to a death is X. The chance of needing two ambulances is 1 in a 100 and three is 1 in a 1,000. If the hospital buys three ambulances, what is the minimum value of X?

32. You run a restaurant with room for 100 tables that are available on a reservations-only basis. If you accept N reservations for tables, you will actually fill N-19, N-18, . . . N tables with a probability of .05 each. For each unoccupied table, you lose a potential profit of $9. Rent and other expenses are $10 per table. Each demand for a table that must be turned away because of no space (overbooking), costs you $6 in damages and $5 in bad publicity. If you accept 100 reservations, how many tables should you *rent*? If you *buy* 100 tables, how many reservations should you accept? (*Hint:* $Q^* = 100$).

33. Given the following MPS, IMF, and product tree, determine the planned releases for item 1342.

Item	Lead time	On hand	Demand in weeks (number) 11	12	13	14	15
19	1 week	100	100	0	100	200	0
1342	2 weeks	200	0	500	0	0	0
102	1 week	0	50	0	0	0	0
312	2 weeks	0	5	0	0	10	0

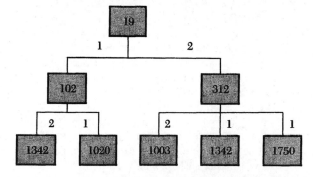

34. In part-period lot sizing, a lot size is selected that comes closest to equating the holding cost to the ordering cost. Conduct a part-period lot sizing for table legs given the following demand schedule.

Holding a leg in inventory costs $1 per week. Ordering/shipping costs $100 for any size order. Lead time is virtually instantaneous.

Week	Demand for table legs
10	85
11	40
12	25
13	40
14	105
15	75
16	80

35. Resolve the example following Equation 12.32 if the shortage cost is given as $10 *per unit* short. Consider service levels of 90, 95, and 99 percent.

36. Several airlines offer their passengers a selective food menu (e.g., fish, beef, chicken). The flight attendants admit that sometimes some passengers do not get the meal of their choice, but the vast majority of passengers do get what they ask for. Relate this situation to the concepts of "service level" and "planned shortages."

37. The lead time to make a special gear is four weeks. There are currently four gears available and two due to be finished in two weeks. The gross requirements for the gear over the next eight weeks are as follows:

Week	1	2	3	4	5	6	7	8
No. of units	3	1	2	0	1	3	2	1

If the ELS is 2 units, when should orders be released for the 8-week period?

38. Given a schedule for planned releases as derived by MRP for a plant that works on a 50-week production schedule:

Date	January 3	January 10	January 17	January 24	January 31	February 7
Quantity	50	—	120	80	40	140

The ordering cost is $100.
The item cost is $500.
The holding costs are 20 percent per unit per year.
Find the optimal lot size (ordering policy).

39. A company has used this information:

S = Setup cost = $250 per order
h = Holding cost rate = 1% per day
p = Purchase price = $5 per unit
U = Usage rate = 100 per day

to calculate the EOQ for a purchased item as 1,000 units. The following distribution of lead times has been derived from experience with suppliers' performance:

Lead Time, Days	Probability
under 3	0
3	.30
4	.30
5	.20
6	.15
7	.05
over 7	0

a. If it costs $2.50 per unit per day to be out of stock and the calculated EOQ is accepted as the proper order quantity, what should be the reorder point?
b. Explain why the calculated EOQ is incorrect and show how to calculate it.

12.10 CASES
I. VISUTECH

Visutech is a manufacturer of industrial cameras that are currently selling for $4,200 a unit. The demand for the product is stable in the quantity of 6,000 units per year.

The company has had little competition up to last year. At that time, two Japanese companies entered the market. Visutech sales started to drop. In order to boost sales, the company decided not to increase prices even though inflation pushed up the production cost by 11 percent. As a result, the company gained back its share of the market. However, earnings decreased significantly.

At present, the company produces at a rate that exactly meets the demand. In this manner, the unit cost is estimated to be $4,000. There is a $6,000 setup cost for each production start-up and the monthly production is 500 units per lot.

The company's cost containment committee met last Monday. Two proposals were submitted to the committee:

a. Change the frequency of production to produce the most economic lot sizes. The company's

maximum production capacity is estimated at 2,000 units per month.

b. Buy subassemblies in Korea and assemble them at the plant. The Koreans can ship the parts in lots of 1,000 once every two months. The cost of each subassembled unit is $3,000. The assembly work requires no setup cost; it is done continuously at a cost of $1,010 per unit. The Korean supplier will offer a 3 percent discount if Visutech is willing to receive shipments twice a year.

As a management scientist working for the cost containment committee, what would you advise them to do? (*Hint:* Consider the alternative of no change.)

General Information

The company computes its inventory carrying cost at an annual rate of 25 percent. Ordering cost for vendor's work is considered to be $60 per order. An order must be prepared for every shipment.

II. EMCO CORPORATION*

The Emco Corporation, a midwestern manufacturer of desktop publishing machines, has the public image of a well-managed corporation in a growth industry. If the company is able to maintain its present rate of growth, it will be number one in its field within a few years. Emco has sales offices in approximately 100 cities in the United States. Emco products are sold or rented to both large and small customers in a number of different in-

dustries. Exhibit 1 shows the firm's income statement for the past five years.

The company has always followed a policy of giving liberal trade-ins on Emco and non-Emco equipment to increase sales in this competitive industry. Several years ago, Mr. E. Miller, a former salesman, showed management that there was a market for these trade-ins. He was then put in charge of the used equipment department. His job was to maintain an orderly market in used equipment—maintaining high prices on the used units sold so as not to cut into the sales of new machines. The department staff, which was composed

*Adapted from a case prepared by Dean Harold Lazarus, School of Business Administration, Hofstra University, and John D. McGarr, Graduate School of Business Administration of New York University, for class discussion.

EMCO CORPORATION
Income Statement
for the Past Five Years
($ in Thousands)

	1993	*1992*	*1991*	*1990*	*1989*
Gross income	$599,000	$450,000	$330,000	$315,000	$290,000
Cost of goods sold	200,000	150,000	120,000	115,000	140,000
Gross profit	339,000	300,000	210,000	200,000	150,000
Net income	55,000	45,000	33,000	27,000	15,000

mostly of former salesmen, grew from 10 to 45. It was discovered that there was a market for machines that had been used as floor demonstrators in the sales offices. Thus, today the two major sources of used equipment are trade-ins and former demonstrators.

Some of the machines are sold, whereas others are directed into a rental program. Those sold to wholesalers or dealers are in either an as-is or reconditioned state. The as-is units are sold from any one of 10 regional headquarters when a large quantity is accumulated. All non-Emco trade-ins are sold as-is. The reconditioned units are sold from the factory, where they have been moved by company vans from the sales offices on a quarterly basis.

The machines in the rental program have all been reconditioned. Once they have been reconditioned, they are shipped to regional headquarters to await renting for periods ranging from two weeks to one year.

All Emco products have a seven-digit serial number that is used for inventory classification purposes. The inventory of used equipment is broken down into Emco trade-ins, non-Emco trade-ins, former demonstrators, and reconditioned machines in the rental program. Machines are classified as Emco trade-ins and non-Emco trade-ins at the time when a customer receives a new Emco unit. When the sales offices receive new machines for demonstration purposes, the old demonstrators are then considered former demonstrators. The demonstrators are replaced on a yearly cycle. Machines are transferred to the rental program at the discretion of the used equipment department.

Mr. S. Carlson, the controller of Emco, recently set up a profit analysis area within the finance department.

The objective of this new area is to evaluate the profitability of the firm's various operations.

The profit analysis area was called on by the controller to make an analysis of a proposal put forth by Mr. Miller. He proposed that the firm put new machines into the high profit rental program for six months and then sell them in the used market. Mr. Miller reasoned that the demand for machines in the used market was greater than the present inventory or the forecasted additions to inventory for the remainder of the year.

Mr. A. Ernst, a financial analyst, received this proposal. In order to get some background, Mr. Ernst first computed income statements for the past five years. Exhibit 2 shows these statements, whereas Exhibit 3 gives a breakdown of Exhibit 2 into the sales and rental programs of used equipment.

The statements puzzled Mr. Ernst because everyone was under the impression that the used equipment department was a profitable operation.

The factory inventory classification report for June 1994 is shown in Exhibit 4.

The used equipment department had made a forecast of trade-ins and former demonstrators that they expected to be added to the inventory for the rest of the year. They also forecasted their sales for the remainder of the year. This data is shown in Exhibit 5.

At first, Mr. Ernst thought it obvious that there were enough machines in inventory and incoming flows to cover the forecasted demand. Mr. Ernst then checked the factory on the physical inventory. He called the factory and, after speaking with several managers in the inventory area who didn't know where this information was or even if the factory had it, he finally received the

EXHIBIT 2

Income Statements
Used Equipment
($ in Thousands)

	1993	1992	1991	1990	1989
Gross income	$25,600	$19,020	$14,150	$9,100	$5,000
Net earnings before taxes	(2,504)	500	(1,700)	(1,800)	(1,000)

EXHIBIT 3

Income Statements
Used Equipment by Source
($ in Thousands)

	1993	1992	1991	1990	1989
Sales					
Gross income	$19,000	$14,000	$11,000	$7,000	n.a.
Net earnings before taxes	(4,514)	(1,630)	(2,900)	(2,900)	n.a.
Rental					
Gross income	6,600	5,020	3,050	2,100	n.a.
Net earnings before taxes	2,010	2,130	1,200	1,100	n.a.

EXHIBIT 4   Inventory Classification Report—June 1994

	Units
Emco trade-ins	17,586
Non-Emco trade-ins	9,987
Former demonstrators	29,543
Total	57,116
Used rental program	20,437*

*4,543 machines in district office warehouses awaiting rental.

EXHIBIT 5   Used Equipment Department Forecast—June 1994

	Units
July–December 1994 additions to inventory	
Emco trade-ins	19,642
Non-Emco trade-ins	7,679
Former demonstrators	23,113
Total	50,434
Sales forecast	70,445
Forecast addition to used rental program	2,000

EXHIBIT 6 **Used Equipment Physical Inventory Report—June 1994**

	Units		
	At Sales Office	At Plant	Total
Emco trade-ins	5,843	2,894	8,737
Non-Emco trade-ins	3,435	1,015	4,450
Former demonstrators	7,364	6,775	14,139
Total			27,326

June 1994 report on physical inventory. The report is shown in Exhibit 6.

When Mr. Ernst called Mr. Miller to ask about the discrepancies in the inventory figures, he found that Mr. Miller was on a trip to Los Angeles. Mr. Ernst spoke, instead, to a former salesman who had recently joined the used equipment department. The former salesman, when asked about the inventory figures, told Mr. Ernst, in a laughing manner, that some salesmen would "misplace" demonstrators and others would forget that customers had machines to trade in when the new machines were installed. The former salesman related that he had just received a letter from the New York sales office manager asking what he should do about 150 demonstrators, still in factory packaging, that had been accumulating in the office warehouse. The average age of these demonstrators was three years.

After this conversation, Mr. Ernst collected his figures (Exhibits 2–6), went to the used equipment department to pick up a copy of the letter from the manager of the New York sales office, and went to Mr. Carlson's office. After hearing Mr. Ernst's presentation, Mr. Carlson agreed to permit Mr. Ernst to make to full study of this department. The two men then began to formulate a strategy for the investigation of this operation.

Analyze this case and ascertain the nature of Emco's problem. Where are the missing machines?

Glossary

The A-B-C classification system   Inventory items are classified into three groups: A (high value, small quantity), B (medium value, larger quantity), C (small value, many items—the nuts and bolts). Classification is made for control purposes.

Average inventory   The average amount of inventory, usually on a one-year period. It is equal to one half of the maximum inventory of the EOQ model.

Back order   A temporary shortage. Items that will be delivered (or produced) later.

Base-stock system   An inventory system in which an order is placed as soon as a unit is taken from stock.

Bill of materials (B/M)   The list of raw materials, components, and subassemblies (and their quantities) needed to produce an item.

Carrying cost   Same as holding cost.

Cycle time   The length of time between placing (or receiving) two consecutive orders.

Days' supply   The length of time (days) that an inventory will last without renewal (replenishment or stockout).

Dependent demand   Demand for items that are parts of items whose production is already planned.

Depletion   Reduction of the inventory to a zero point of no inventory.

Economic lot size (ELS)   A manufacturing lot or batch size that will minimize the total annual costs of setup and holding inventory.

Economic order quantity (EOQ)   A quantity of an item that, if purchased at one time, will minimize the total annual inventory ordering and holding costs.

Explode   Stepping down through the bill of materials levels to determine what parts will be required, in what quantities, and when.

Fixed quantity (perpetual) system   An inventory system where orders for fixed amounts are placed whenever an agreed-on reorder point is reached (e.g., order whenever stock is down to 10 units).

Fixed time (periodic or *s,S*) system   An inventory system where varying-sized orders are placed periodically (e.g., once a month).

Holding cost   Costs associated with storing inventory, such as expenses of capital, insurance, renting storage space, and taxes.

Inventory master file (IMF)   The computer file that contains a listing of on-hand, on-order, and committed inventory.

Joint ordering   Placing orders for different items (usually with one supplier) as one combined order.

Lead time   The time between placing an order and its delivery.

Level   The stage of subcomponent assemblies in the bill of materials, the finished product being designated as level 0.

Lot sizing   Determining the best amount of items to produce or purchase at a given time.

Lumpy demand   Demand that comes in groups, with little or no demand occurring between the groups.

Master production schedule (MPS)   The time-phased list of products (and their quantities) that are to be produced.

Material requirements planning (MRP)   An inventory control system for independent demand items.

MRP II   Manufacturing resource planning to tie all company information systems into the manufacturing systems.

Ordering cost   The costs of placing one order for an item, including paperwork, inspection of the incoming order, and telephone calls.

Parent item   The finished product (level 0).

Planned shortage   Allowing shortages to occur from time to time rather than keeping a large inventory.

Quantity discount   A discount on the unit cost, offered by the supplier to a buyer willing to buy in large lots.

Reorder point   The inventory level at which an order for an item is placed.

Replenishment   Describes the arrival of a shipment or renewal of the inventory.

Safety stock   Inventory maintained specifically to reduce shortages when demand is high or when the lead time is too long.

Service level   The percent of time that all demand is met on request. The probability of *not* running out of stock.

Setup costs   Expenses incurred to start up a production run (paperwork, tool preparation, and clean up).

Shortage   Inability to provide the item from stock. Available inventory is insufficient to meet demand.

Stockout   Same as shortage.

Two-bin system   An inventory where items are stored in two bins: large and small. Demand is satisfied from the large bin first. Depletion of the large bin signifies the need to reorder.

References and Bibliography

1. Chikan, A., ed. *Inventory Models*. New York: Kluwer Academic, 1991.
2. Dear, A. *Inventory Management Demystified*. New York: Van Nostrand Reinhold, 1990.
3. Fuller, T. H. *Microcomputers in Production and Inventory Management*. Homewood, Ill.: Dow Jones-Irwin, 1987.
4. Greene, J. H., ed. *Production and Inventory Control Handbook*. 2nd ed. New York: McGraw-Hill, 1987.
5. Hall, R. W. *Zero Inventories*. Homewood, Ill.: Dow Jones-Irwin, 1983.
6. Hay, H. J. *The Just-in-Time Breakthrough: Implementing the New Manufacturing Basics*. New York: John Wiley & Sons, 1989.
7. Janson, R. L., *Handbook of Inventory Management*. Englewood Cliffs, N.J.: Prentice-Hall, 1989.
8. Nelson, T. *The Management Science System*. Homewood, Ill.: Richard D. Irwin, 1988.
9. Plossl, G. W. *Production and Inventory Control: Principles and Techniques*. New York: Prentice-Hall, 1985.

10. Schonberger, R. J. *Japanese Manufacturing Techniques: Nine Hidden Lessons in Simplicity*. New York: Free Press, 1982.

11. Silver, E. A., and R. Peterson, *Decision Systems for Inventory Management and Production Planning*. 2nd ed. New York: John Wiley & Sons, 1985.

12. Smith, S. B. *Computer Based Production and Inventory Control*. Englewood Cliffs, N.J.: Prentice-Hall, 1989.

13. Tersine, J. R. *Principles of Inventory and Materials Management*. 3rd ed. New York: Elsevier North-Holland, 1987.

14. Vollmann, T. E., W. L. Berry, and D. C. Whybark, *Manufacturing Planning and Control Systems*. 2nd ed. Homewood, Ill.: Richard D. Irwin, 1988.

15. Walleigh, R. C. "Getting Things Done: What's Your Excuse for Not Using JIT?" *Harvard Business Review*, March–April 1986.

A Markov analysis is a procedure that can be used to describe the behavior of a system in a dynamic situation. Specifically, it describes and predicts the movement of a system among different system states as time passes. This movement is done in a probabilistic (stochastic) environment. Movements of people, inventories, monetary accounts, taxicabs, and even people's attitudes are a few examples of situations that can be described by Markov processes. To be able to predict the future movements and condition of such a system would clearly be of value to management.

Markov analysis makes predictions such as:

1. The probability of finding a system in any particular state at any given time.
2. The long-run probabilities of being in each state.

John Byer, director of product planning for P&C Chemical Corporation, felt somewhat satisfied as he scanned the latest marketing research results of last year's big gamble. The argument, as he recalled the meeting of the executive committee, had centered around the question of competing with one's own product. P&C's original entry in the already well-established household laundry detergents markets, known inside the company by the code Brand A, had been well accepted by the market until two years ago, when a competitor moved in with a flashy promotional campaign and began luring P&C's customers away. John's suggestion to the executive committee was to bring out an improved detergent (Brand B) with a countering advertising campaign stressing the quality of the new brand based on P&C's experience with Brand A.

But the executive vice president, Bill Harmon, was deeply worried that Brand B might compete more with P&C's own Brand A than with the competitor's brand. Other members of the committee pointed out that these buyers would probably be customers P&C would have lost to the competition anyway, but this did not seem to appease Bill. Finally, John pointed out how common it was in the detergent market for companies to offer multiple brands, in stark contrast to their chemicals market. He argued that detergents, being in the consumer market, were totally unlike industrial chemicals.

The executive committee finally decided to go along with John's idea, but they were not completely convinced. Thus, the first year's report took on special importance for John. At the time of the introduction of Brand B a year ago, P&C held 40 percent of the market and the competitor had 60 percent. The 12-month report summary now indicated that Brand A's share had dropped to 27.5 percent, but that the competitor's share had almost been halved, now standing at 35 percent, the losses in each case going to the new Brand B, currently holding 37.5 percent of the market.

The detailed report showed month-to-month "brand loyalty" figures from the date of introduction of Brand B until this last month. Initially, the rate of shifting between brands changed every month, but it had now settled down to the general situation illustrated in Figure 13.1. Customers were still being drawn from Brand A to the competitor (Brand C) to the extent of 60 percent each month (the remainder divided evenly at 20 percent each between switching to B and staying with A). However, half of the competitor's market (Brand C) would return to A in any particular month, with another 20 percent switching from C to B, resulting in the competition maintaining only 30 percent of its customers. Of particular interest was the response to Brand B, with half of B's purchasers remaining loyal to B and only 40 percent switching to C, the rest going to A.

FIGURE 13.1

Month-to-month switching

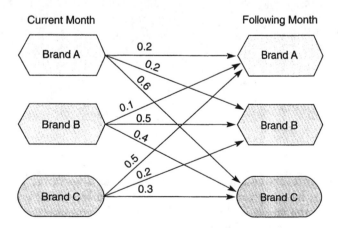

John felt that these figures substantiated his words from a year earlier and saved P&C from failing in this new market venture. Although John realized that the competition might upset this delicate balance at any moment with a new product introduction or a new marketing campaign, he wondered how the market shares would shift in the coming months, given the brand switching results above, and especially what the ultimate market shares would be.

13.1 Markov Systems

The situation presented in the preceding incident is concerned with the prediction of market shares in a dynamic market. Such predictions are based on what is termed a *Markov analysis* and can be used as a basis for determining market strategies and product planning. Notice that John Byer is not asking about how to determine the *best* marketing strategy, but rather he wishes to determine or predict the *behavior* of the "system" (the household detergent purchasers in this case). Thus, we are dealing with a **descriptive** rather than with a **normative** situation. Other features of the incident are:

Markov analysis is descriptive—not normative

Risk analysis

Transition probabilities

1. The situation occurs in a chance environment consisting of two or more possible outcomes (three here) that occur at the end of a well-defined, usually fixed period. Such a process is referred to as a **stochastic** (or probabilistic) process. Thus, we are now dealing with analysis and prediction under risk.
2. The situation involves a multiperiod (in our example, monthly) case. The customer's brand-switching propensities are followed for many months. The probabilities of switching (shown in Figure 13.1) are termed the **transition probabilities** of the stochastic process.
3. The situation is dynamic in nature because the customers make a sequence of decisions.
4. The process is observed after each transition and is governed by a matrix of transition probabilities.

Markov Processes

Stochastic process, Markov process, Markov chain

As stated before, the customer's brand switching is a *stochastic process*. If a customer's brand choice in any given month depends *only* on his or her choice the month before (i.e., not on the choice two, three, or more months previously), the stochastic process is called a **Markov process.** In addition, if the transition probabilities of a customer's switching from one brand (*state*) to another remain constant over time, then the Markov process is called a homogeneous **Markov chain** (the type of process discussed in this chapter).

The Characteristics of a Markov Analysis

Two interpretations

A Markov analysis is conducted on a system that can usually be interpreted in two different ways: either as *the fraction of a group* (e.g., percentage of Brand A sold) or *the probability of an individual* (e.g., the chance of a customer purchasing Brand A). To familiarize the reader with both of these (equivalent) interpretations, we will use both quite frequently in this chapter.

Advantage of simple manipulations

As a *descriptive tool,* the major objective of Markov chain analysis is the prediction of the future behavior of managerial systems. A *system* in this chapter can be a person, an organization, the demand for a product, a machine, or other such entity. The advantage of Markov chain analysis is that the computational work is relatively uncomplicated and can be carried out very rapidly. Small problems can be solved manually; for larger problems, a standard computer package can be used (see Section 13.7).

Necessary Assumptions

In the Markov chains discussed in Sections 13.2–13.4, the following assumptions are made:

1. The system has a finite number of discrete states, none of which is "absorbing" (a state that, once entered, cannot be left).
2. The system's condition (state) in any given period depends only on its condition in the preceding period and on the transition probabilities.
3. The transition probabilities are constant over time.
4. Changes in the system may occur once and only once each period (once a month in the example).
5. The transition periods occur with regularity.

The Assumptions as Reflected in the Detergent Incident

Finite Number of States, None of Which is Absorbing
In this example, the *condition* of the system was limited to three **states** (brands). If there was a brand from which a customer *never* switched, then this would be termed an **absorbing state.** It is assumed here that none of the states is absorbing.

Present Brand Choice is Dependent on the Previous Month's Choice
It was assumed that the brand choice in any given month was influenced *only* by the choice in the previous month. This may or may not be a realistic assumption, depending on the circumstances.

FIGURE 13.2

Information flow

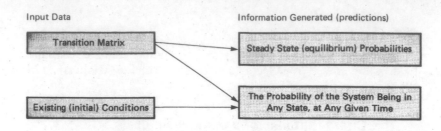

Constant Transition Probabilities

It may well be that the transition probabilities will change over time. If so, a more complicated analysis is required (consult reference [8]).

One Change (Transition) per Period

This requirement is usually satisfied by choosing a natural time period for the system. For example, consumers commonly shop once a month for detergent.

Regular Transition Periods

This assumption is satisfied because the brand purchases are monitored on a monthly basis. If purchases change faster, the time period can be shortened (e.g., a week rather than a month). Note that the periods need not be of the same time lengths; for example, classes are frequently offered on a Tuesday–Thursday basis with a cycle of one day off and then four days off.

Information Flow in the Markov Analysis

Two sets of inputs   The Markov model is based on two sets of input data, the transition matrix and the existing (initial) conditions, as shown in Figure 13.2. From these inputs, the model makes two predictions, usually expressed as vectors:

 a. The probabilities of the system being in any state at any given future time (Section 13.3).

Two predictions   *b.* The long-run (steady state) probabilities (Section 13.4). Note that the transition matrix is necessary for *both* predictions, but the initial conditions are only needed for the former.

13.2 Input Data: Transition Probabilities and Initial Conditions

The Transition Probabilities

The Markov process describes the movement of a system from a certain condition (or state) in the current stage (time period) to one of n possible states in the next stage. The system moves in an uncertain environment. All that is known is the probability associated with any possible transition. This probability, termed the *transition probability*, p_{ij}, is the likelihood that the system, currently in state i, will move to state j in the next period. The transition probability concept is the key to Markov analysis.

Transition probabilities—the key

Transition Diagram
Let us return to the detergent example. Figure 13.3 illustrates the three possible brand choices of the customers. The arrows show the probabilities of a customer (or the fraction of detergent purchasers) moving from state to state (brand to brand), as computed by the available historical data.

The Transition Matrix
Another way of expressing the system's movement is in tabular or matrix form, as shown in Table 13.1. Such a table is called a *transition matrix* (denoted by *P*).

FIGURE 13.3

Transition diagram of the Markov process

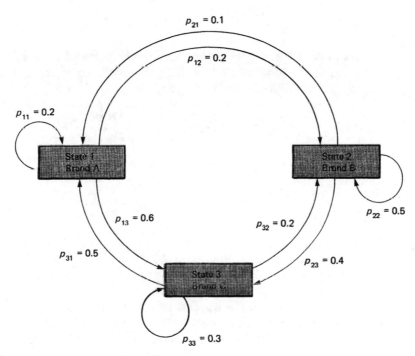

TABLE 13.1 The Transition Matrix *P*

Current Month's Brand Choice	Next Month's Brand Choice		
	P&C's Brand A	P&C's Brand B	Competitor's Brand C
P&C's Brand A	.2	.2	.6
P&C's Brand B	.1	.5	.4
Competitor's Brand C	.5	.2	.3

The general structure of a transition matrix is:

$$
\begin{array}{c}
\\
\\
\textit{From}\\
\textbf{State in the Current Period}
\end{array}
\quad
\begin{array}{cc}
 & \textit{To}\\
 & \textbf{State at the Next Period}\\
\begin{array}{c}
\\
s_1\\
\cdot\\
\cdot\\
\cdot\\
s_i\\
\cdot\\
\cdot\\
\cdot\\
s_n
\end{array}
&
\begin{array}{ccccc}
s_1 & s_2 & \cdots s_j & \cdots & s_n\\
\left[\begin{array}{ccccc}
p_{11} & p_{12} & \cdots p_{1j} & \cdots & p_{1n}\\
\cdot & \cdot & \cdot & & \cdot\\
\cdot & \cdot & \cdot & & \cdot\\
\cdot & \cdot & \cdot & & \cdot\\
p_{i1} & p_{i2} & \cdots p_{ij} & \cdots & p_{in}\\
\cdot & \cdot & \cdot & & \cdot\\
\cdot & \cdot & \cdot & & \cdot\\
\cdot & \cdot & \cdot & & \cdot\\
p_{n1} & p_{n2} & \cdots p_{nj} & \cdots & p_{nn}
\end{array}\right] & = P
\end{array}
\end{array}
$$

Note that the sum of the probabilities in every row of Table 13.1 is 1.0. That is, the customers must choose one of the three brands the next month, because these are the only brands available. Formally, for any row i:

$$p_{i1} + p_{i2} + \cdots + p_{in} = 1 \tag{13.1}$$

In abbreviated form:

$$\sum_{j=1}^{n} p_{ij} = 1$$

where p_{ij} is the probability of being in state j in the next period, given that the system is now in state i (i.e., the *conditional* probability).

The transition matrix as a set of probability vectors

The set of transition probabilities across any row (current state) is called a *probability vector* and represents all possibilities of moving from one state in the current period to one of the n states in the next period. For example, the vector [.2 .2 .6] means that there is a chance of .2 of moving *from* A *to* A, .2 from A to B, and .6 from A to C.

The transition probabilities can be obtained in a number of ways. One is through market research—asking people about their preferences and seeing how they change over time. Another is to simply monitor their actions over time. Alternatively, the flow of products can be monitored directly.

The Initial Conditions

The initial conditions describe the situation the system is currently in. For example, the market share is divided 27.5 percent to A, 37.5 percent to B, and 35 percent to C. These conditions are usually described by a row vector: [.275 .375 .350]. Initial conditions such as [0 1 0] mean that the market is totally held by brand B; or, a *given* customer has currently purchased brand B.

13.3 State Probabilities

State probability

A Markov analysis can make several predictions (see [5]). Two are discussed here: The probability q of the system being in state i in period k, called the *state probability;* and the long run (steady state) probability of finding the system in a particular state i. The state probability is denoted as $q_i(k)$ where k denotes the period; $k = 0$ is *now;* and i, the index, specifies the particular state.

Because the system must occupy one and only one of the possible states at any given period, including period 0, then the sum of all q_i values must equal 1. Formally:

$$q_1(k) + q_2(k) + \cdots + q_n(k) = 1 \quad \text{for every } k \tag{13.2}$$

Equation 13.2 can be expressed as:

$$\sum_{i-1}^{n} q_i(k) = 1$$

where:

n = Number of states

k = Number of transitions (periods ahead) = 0, 1, 2, . . .

Example

Let us consider the detergent example to illustrate the determination of these $q_i(k)$ probabilities. The states of the system—Brands A, B, and C—are designated as 1, 2, and 3, respectively. The probability $q_1(0)$ represents the probability of a customer choosing Brand A this month (time zero); $q_1(1)$ represents the probability of choosing Brand A after "one transition," that is, after one month; and so on.

State Probabilities

The probability distribution of the customer choosing any given brand (1, 2, 3) in any given month (k) can be written as a row vector:

$$Q(k) = [q_1(k), q_2(k), q_3(k)] \tag{13.3}$$

In general, for n states we can write:

$$Q(k) = [q_1(k), q_2(k), \ldots, q_n(k)] \tag{13.4}$$

Initial conditions are expressed as $Q(0)$.

Initial State Probabilities in the Detergent Example

Let us denote the month in the example as the initial state, labeled $k = 0$. The initial state probabilities were given in the case as:

$$q_1(0) = .275 \text{ current share of the market for Brand A}$$

$$q_2(0) = .375 \text{ current share of the market for Brand B}$$

$$q_3(0) = .350 \text{ current share of the market for Brand C}$$

These values can be summarized as:

$$Q(0) = [q_1(0), q_2(0), q_3(0)] = [.275, .375, .350]$$

The Transition Matrix

To compute the state probabilities, we will use the transition matrix P of Table 13.2 (Table 13.1, reproduced). The states are labeled Brand A = 1, B = 2, and C = 3.

Computing the State Probabilities for the Next Month ($k = 1$)

Three ways to choose Brand A

The value of $q_1(1)$ is first computed. This is the probability that the customer will choose Brand 1 (A) after one month. There are three ways for this to occur:

1. A customer who last purchased Brand A could continue to purchase Brand A (probability of .2).

Conditional probabilities

2. A customer could switch to Brand A from Brand B (probability of .1).
3. A customer could switch to Brand A from Brand C (probability of .5).

Note: All the above probabilities are *conditional* probabilities. That is, each depends on the customer's last purchase. Therefore, the chance of choosing Brand A in the next month, $q_1(1)$, is the sum of the following three *joint* probabilities:

1. The probability that a customer last purchased Brand A and again chooses Brand A is computed as $q_1(0)p_{11} = .275(.2)$.

Joint probabilities

2. The probability that a customer last purchased Brand B and now chooses Brand A is computed as $q_2(0)p_{21} = .375 (.1)$.
3. The probability that a customer last purchased Brand C and now chooses Brand A is computed as $q_3(0)p_{31} = .350 (.5)$.

TABLE 13.2   Transition Matrix for the Detergent Example (Table 13.1 Reproduced)

From \ To	1	2	3
1	.2	.2	.6
2	.1	.5	.4
3	.5	.2	.3

$$\rightarrow \quad P = \begin{bmatrix} .2 & .2 & .6 \\ .1 & .5 & .4 \\ .5 & .2 & .3 \end{bmatrix}$$

Formally:

$$q_1(1) = .275(.2) + .375(.1) + .350(.5) = .2675$$

This is the sum of the chance of being in each state times the chance of switching from there to Brand A. In vector notation, this can be written as:

$$q_1(1) = Q(0) \begin{bmatrix} .2 \\ .1 \\ .5 \end{bmatrix} = [.275 \ .375 \ .350] \begin{bmatrix} .2 \\ .1 \\ .5 \end{bmatrix} = .2675$$

That is: Multiply the $Q(0)$ row vector times the first column vector (Brand A) in the transition matrix P.

Similarly, the values of $q_2(1)$ and $q_3(1)$ are:

$$q_2(1) = Q(0) \begin{bmatrix} .2 \\ .5 \\ .2 \end{bmatrix} = .275(.2) + .375(.5) + .350(.2) = .3125$$

$$q_3(1) = Q(0) \begin{bmatrix} .6 \\ .4 \\ .3 \end{bmatrix} = .4200$$

Generalization

It is the probability $q_1(1)$ together with $q_2(1)$ and $q_3(1)$ that are the components of $Q(1)$. In matrix notation, $Q(1)$ is computed as the product of $Q(0)$ and P:

$$Q(1) = [q_1(1) \ q_2(1) \ q_3(1)] = Q(0)P \tag{13.5}$$

or

$$[q_1(1) \ q_2(1) \ q_3(1)] = [q_1(0) \ q_2(0) \ q_3(0)]P$$

where P is the transition probability matrix of the system. Thus:

$$Q(1) = Q(0)P \tag{13.6}$$

and by similar reasoning it can be shown that:

$$Q(2) = Q(1)P \tag{13.7}$$

Introducing the value of $Q(1)$ (Equation 13.6) into Equation 13.7 results in:

$$Q(2) = Q(1)P = Q(0)PP = Q(0)P^2 \tag{13.8}$$

Similar computations can be performed for   Q(3), Q(4), . . . In general:

$$Q(k) = Q(k - 1)P = Q(k - 2)P^2 = . . . = Q(k - k)P^k = Q(0)P^k \quad (13.9)$$

John Byer's first
question

Using Equation 13.9, John Byer could address his first question; namely, what the market shares will be the first, second, and third month from now, and so on. For example, for the first two months:

$q_3(1)$ = The probability of choosing Brand C (state 3) one month from now. This was already computed as .42 (or 42 percent).

$q_3(2)$ = The probability of choosing Brand C two months from now.

In order to find $q_3(2)$, Equation 13.9 is used with $k = 2$: $Q(2) = Q(0)P^2$. Thus, P^2 must first be calculated:

$$P^2 = \begin{bmatrix} .2 & .2 & .6 \\ .1 & .5 & .4 \\ .5 & .2 & .3 \end{bmatrix}^2 = \begin{bmatrix} .2 & .2 & .6 \\ .1 & .5 & .4 \\ .5 & .2 & .3 \end{bmatrix} \times \begin{bmatrix} .2 & .2 & .6 \\ .1 & .5 & .4 \\ .5 & .2 & .3 \end{bmatrix} = \begin{bmatrix} .36 & .26 & .38 \\ .27 & .35 & .38 \\ .27 & .26 & .47 \end{bmatrix}$$

Because $q_3(2)$ is the third entry in the row vector $Q(2) = [q_1(2), q_2(2), q_3(2)]$, it can be found by multiplying the third column of P^2 by $Q(0)$; that is:

$q_3(2) = Q(0) \times$ [the Brand C (third) column vector of P^2]

$$= [.275 \quad .375 \quad .350] \begin{bmatrix} .38 \\ .38 \\ .47 \end{bmatrix}$$

$$= .275(.38) + .375(.38) + .35(.47) = .4115, \text{ or } 41.15 \text{ percent.}$$

In a similar manner, it is possible to find $q_1(k)$, $q_2(k)$, and $q_3(k)$ for any desired k.

Tree Presentation
The relationship between the transition and state probabilities can be seen in a probability tree presentation (Figure 13.4). The tree presentation may be clearer for small problems, but its computations become very tedious for large problems.

Computation Without Matrix Algebra
From $k = 1$, we can move in a similar fashion to the month after next, $k = 2$, as shown in Figure 13.5. That is, the market share distribution is predicted to be:

A: 29.47 percent   B: 29.38 percent,   C: 41.15 percent

FIGURE 13.4

Tree presentation of transition and state probabilities

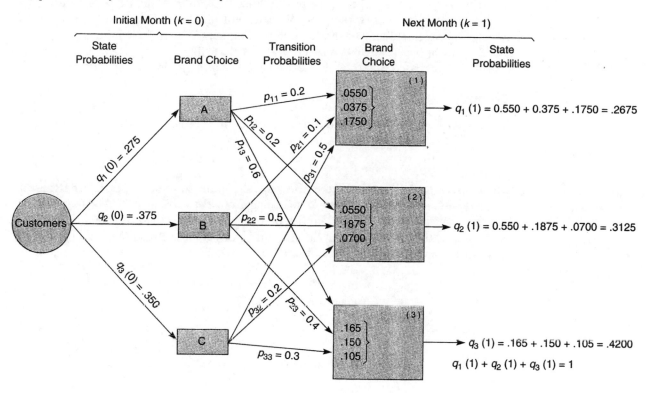

FIGURE 13.5

Tree computations for k = 2

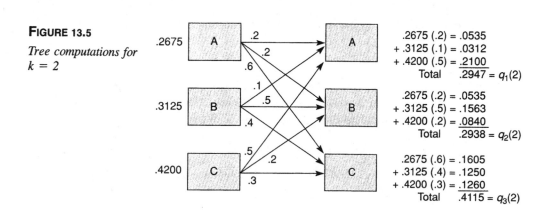

State Probabilities Given the System is in a Specific State

In the previous discussion, the state probabilities (i.e., market shares) were interpreted in terms of the fraction of the group of detergent purchasers. However, in some instances, management may be interested in finding out the state probabilities in terms of the chances of a particular purchaser buying a particular brand, *given* that he or she previously purchased Brand X. These are called *conditional state probabilities*.

Example

A customer last purchased Brand B (state 2). Find the probability that she will purchase Brand C (state 3) in two months ($k = 2$).

Solution

Let us use a tree diagram (Figure 13.6) to follow the customer's possible purchases. The tree first shows the chances of switching from Brand B to A, B, or C after one month. Then it shows the probabilities of switching among these brands in month 2. For example, the probability that the customer will purchase Brand C in month 2 is the sum of the following three probabilities:

$$
\begin{array}{rl}
.06 & \text{(switch from A to C at month 2)} \\
.20 & \text{(switch from B to C at month 2)} \\
+.12 & \text{(stay with C at month 2)} \\
\hline
\text{Total} \quad .38 &
\end{array}
$$

Similarly, the chance for the Brand B customer to purchase Brand A after two months is:

$$.02 + .05 + .20 = .27$$

and the chance of purchasing Brand B again is:

$$.02 + .25 + .08 = .35$$

Note also that the total probabilities of the purchases sum to 1.0: (.38 + .27 + .35 = 1).

Generalization

Conditional state probabilities

Conditional state probabilities can be expressed as $q_{ij}(k)$; that is, *given* initial condition i, the probability of being in state j after k transitions. Thus, $q_{23}(2)$ means: given that Brand B was initially purchased, the probability of buying Brand C after two transitions. Note that

$$\sum_{j=1}^{n} q_{ij}(k) = 1, \quad \text{for } i = 1, 2, \ldots n$$

FIGURE 13.6

Tree diagram for Brand B purchaser

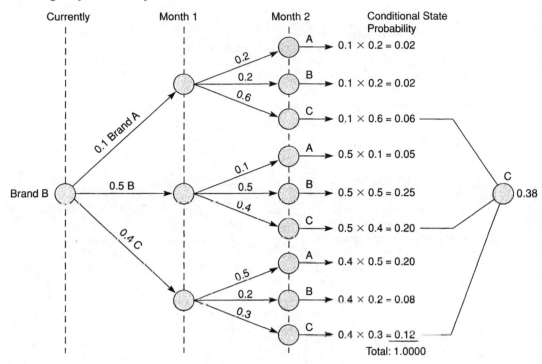

Currently | **Month 1** | **Month 2** | **Conditional State Probability**

A → $0.1 \times 0.2 = 0.02$

B → $0.1 \times 0.2 = 0.02$

C → $0.1 \times 0.6 = 0.06$

A → $0.5 \times 0.1 = 0.05$

B → $0.5 \times 0.5 = 0.25$

C → $0.5 \times 0.4 = 0.20$

A → $0.4 \times 0.5 = 0.20$

B → $0.4 \times 0.2 = 0.08$

C → $0.4 \times 0.3 = 0.12$

Total: 1.0000

C 0.38

Mathematical Presentation. The computation can be done with matrix algebra as follows:

1. Multiply the transition matrix by itself k times. For example, in the detergent case, for $k = 2$:

$$P^2 = \begin{bmatrix} .2 & .2 & .6 \\ .1 & .5 & .4 \\ .5 & .3 & .3 \end{bmatrix}^2 = \begin{bmatrix} .36 & .26 & .38 \\ .27 & .35 & .38 \\ .27 & .26 & .47 \end{bmatrix}$$

2. Each initial condition (i) is equivalent to a row, each final state (j) to a column. For example, reading from the P^2 matrix:

$$q_{23}(2) = .38$$

$$q_{31}(2) = .27$$

The computation of such state probabilities provides management with valuable descriptive information about the system's behavior. Additional valuable information is provided by analyzing the system in a "stabilized" (steady state) condition, which is discussed next.

Management Science in Practice

Adaptive Response for New York City's Fire Department

In 1968, the New York City Fire Department initiated a series of studies that continued over an extended period of years. These studies aimed at ways to improve their productivity and service while containing or reducing their cost. As a result of these studies, the fire department has instituted a series of changes that have saved over $5 million per year, reduced the workload of the fire companies, and resulted in a more equitable distribution of fire companies throughout the city.

One of the major changes that was instituted resulted from a Markovian analysis of the response policy of the fire department to an alarm. The traditional dispatch policy was to send three engine companies and two ladder companies. If the fire is serious, all of them will be needed. However, if the fire is not serious and only two engines and one ladder are needed (which is the case 97 percent of the time), these companies will not be available for other alarms, thereby stripping the area of fire protection.

The Markov decision model explicitly considers information on the current alarm and expected future events in arriving at what is now termed an *adaptive response policy*. The modeling assumptions are that alarms and their resulting extinguishment follow random processes. The state space for the Markov model includes the number of busy companies and the potential seriousness of the incoming alarms, and the decision variable is the number of companies to dispatch. The objective function is the response time to "serious" fires.

Three factors were critical in conducting the analysis: (1) the probability that this alarm is serious and requires more companies; (2) the expected alarm rate in this area, intense rates dictating fewer companies to dispatch so more will be held in reserve; and (3) the number of companies available for this area—the more available, the more dispatched. The analysis indicated that considering these factors in deciding how many companies to dispatch to an alarm, particularly the expected seriousness of the fire, significantly improved the response time to serious fires.

The results of the analysis were implemented through the following procedure: As with the previous policy, all alarms or calls are referenced to the nearest fire alarm box. A dispatch is based on the probability that an alarm from that box is serious, the type of structures in that area, and the time of day. Critical values of these variables are noted and for any particular alarm, the values identify the number of engine and ladder companies to dispatch.

Overall, the new policy sends fewer units than the traditional policy, thereby reducing the workload, yet still reduces the response time to serious fires. For example, in one simulation under the traditional policy, a second ladder company was sent to only 25 percent of the serious fires; whereas the new, adaptive response policy sends a second ladder to 42 percent of the serious fires. The difference is very significant because not sending a second ladder initially results in a long delay of four minutes before a second ladder arrives.

Sources: A. J. Swersey, "A Markovian Decision Model for Deciding How Many Fire Companies to Dispatch," *Management Science*, April 1982, pp. 352–65; E. J. Ignall, et al., "Improving the Deployment of New York City Fire Companies," *Interfaces*, February 1975, pp. 48–61.

Questions:

1. Create an example of "critical values" of structure type or time of day for an alarm box.
2. Why are the three critical variables different from the three critical analysis factors?
3. Describe the transition matrix.

13.4 Steady State (Equilibrium)

One of the major properties of Markov chains is that, in the long run, the process usually stabilizes. A stabilized system is said to approach **steady state** or **equilibrium** when the system's state probabilities have become independent of time.

The phenomenon of equilibrium probabilities is expressed as:

$$Q(k) = Q(k - 1) \tag{13.10}$$

That is, the state probabilities in period k are identical to those in the previous period. Introducing expression 13.10 into Equation 13.9, the following formulation for the steady state is obtained:

$$Q(k) = Q(k)P \quad \text{or} \quad Q = QP \tag{13.11}$$

where the deletion of the index k denotes equilibrium probabilities. Equation 13.11 can also be presented as:

$$[q_1, q_2, \cdots q_n] = [q_1, q_2, \cdots, q_n]
\begin{bmatrix}
p_{11} & p_{12} & \cdots & p_{1n} \\
p_{21} & p_{22} & \cdots & p_{2n} \\
\vdots & \vdots & & \vdots \\
p_{n1} & p_{n2} & \cdots & p_{nn}
\end{bmatrix} \tag{13.12}$$

The matrix multiplication shown in Equation 13.12 results in a system of n simultaneous linear equations, as per Equation 13.13.

$$
\begin{aligned}
q_1 &= p_{11}q_1 + p_{21}q_2 + \cdots + p_{n1}q_n \\
q_1 &= p_{12}q_1 + p_{22}q_2 + \cdots + p_{n2}q_n \\
&\quad \vdots \\
q_n &= p_{1n}q_1 + p_{2n}q_2 + \cdots + p_{nn}q_n
\end{aligned} \tag{13.13}
$$

Equation 13.13 can also be expressed as:

$$q_j = \sum_{i=1}^{n} p_{ij}q_i, \quad \text{for } j = 1, 2, \ldots, n$$

In Equation 13.13, it so happens that one equation is redundant and hence the system of equations cannot be solved for a unique solution.

Note: A redundant equation presents the same information as that given by another equation in a different form. For example, one of the following two equations is redundant: $x_1 + 2x_2 = 50$ and $2x_1 + 4x_2 = 100$. Therefore, a replacement equation must be added. Using Equation 13.2:

$$\sum_{j=1}^{n} q_j = 1$$

as the replacement, it is possible to derive a solution for the steady state vector Q. Before returning to the problem of finding Q in the detergent example, let us consider some additional examples:

The Case of Two States

The simplest case is that of a 2×2 transition matrix. In this case, Equation 13.12 is expressed as:

$$[q_1 \quad q_2] = [q_1 \quad q_2] \begin{bmatrix} p_{11} & p_{12} \\ p_{21} & p_{22} \end{bmatrix} = [q_1 p_{11} + q_2 p_{21}, \quad q_1 p_{12} + q_2 p_{22}] \quad (13.14)$$

Solving this equation and the equation $q_1 + q_2 = 1$, we obtain:

$$q_1 = \frac{p_{21}}{1 - p_{11} + p_{21}}$$

Example 1

Given a transition matrix:

$$\begin{array}{cc} & \begin{array}{cc} A & B \end{array} \\ \begin{array}{c} A \\ B \end{array} & \begin{bmatrix} .2 & .8 \\ .3 & .7 \end{bmatrix} \end{array}$$

Find the steady state probabilities, utilizing Equation 13.14:

1. $q_1 = p_{11}q_1 + p_{21}q_2 = .2q_1 + .3q_2$
2. $q_2 = p_{12}q_1 + p_{22}q_2 = .8q_1 + .7q_2$
3. Also, it is known that $q_1 + q_2 = 1$

This system can be solved by considering either the first and third equations or the second and third equations (because one of the first two equations is redundant and can be dropped).

Solution, Using Equations (1) and (3)
Equation (3) can be rewritten as $q_1 = 1 - q_2$. Introducing this value into Equation (1): $1 - q_2 = .2(1 - q_2) + .3 q_2$. Solving for q_2, the solution $q_2 = 8/11$ is obtained. In-

troducing this value into Equation (3) yields the solution for q_1; $q_1 = 3/11$. Thus, *in equilibrium,* there is a chance of 3/11 that the system will be in state A, and a chance of 8/11 that it will be in state B.

Example 2

Given a transition matrix:

$$\begin{bmatrix} .3 & 0 & .7 \\ 0 & .2 & .8 \\ .5 & .4 & .1 \end{bmatrix}$$

Find the steady state probabilities.

Equation 13.12 is utilized to find the steady state vector:

$$Q = [q_1 \quad q_2 \quad q_3] = [q_1 \quad q_2 \quad q_3] \times \begin{bmatrix} .3 & 0 & .7 \\ 0 & .2 & .8 \\ .5 & .4 & .1 \end{bmatrix}$$

Executing the multiplication, a system of three simultaneous linear equations is obtained:

$$(1) \quad q_1 = .3q_1 + 0q_2 + .5q_3$$

$$(2) \quad q_2 = 0q_1 + .2q_2 + .4q_3$$

$$(3) \quad q_3 = .7q_1 + .8q_2 + .1q_3$$

In addition, Equation 13.2 for three states contributes:

$$(4) \quad q_1 + q_2 + q_3 = 1$$

To solve this system, any two of the first three equations, plus the fourth one, may be considered. The following solution then is obtained:

$$q_1 = \frac{10}{31}, \quad q_2 = \frac{7}{31}, \quad q_3 = \frac{14}{31}$$

A simple test can be employed to assure that an equilibrium solution has been obtained. Check if Equation 13.11 holds; that is, if $Q = QP$. In the above example:

$$\begin{bmatrix} \dfrac{10}{31} & \dfrac{7}{21} & \dfrac{14}{31} \end{bmatrix} \times \begin{bmatrix} .3 & 0 & .7 \\ 0 & .2 & .8 \\ .5 & .4 & .1 \end{bmatrix} = \begin{bmatrix} \dfrac{10}{31} & \dfrac{7}{31} & \dfrac{14}{31} \end{bmatrix}$$

$$Q \qquad \times \qquad P \qquad = \qquad Q$$

Thus, it does check.

The following example will help clarify the process through which steady state is achieved:

Example 3

One half of Glade County's population lives in the city and one half in the suburbs. The initial condition of this system can therefore be described as:

$$Q(0) = [.5 \quad .5]$$

Exodus to the suburbs

There is an 80 percent chance that a suburban resident will remain in the suburbs and a 20 percent chance that he or she will move to the city within the next year. A city dweller has a 50–50 chance of staying in the city or moving to the suburbs. The transition matrix describing this process is:

$$
\begin{array}{c}
\text{Next Year:} \\
\begin{array}{cc}
Suburb & City
\end{array} \\
\text{Today:} \begin{array}{c} Suburb \\ City \end{array}
\left[\begin{array}{cc} .8 & .2 \\ .5 & .5 \end{array} \right] = P
\end{array}
$$

Using Equation 13.9, the population distribution after any desired number of years can be found. Results are shown in Table 13.3.

The probability distributions $q_1(k)$ and $q_2(k)$ of Table 13.3 show that as equilibrium is approached, the changes in the probability distribution become smaller. In the long run, about 71.43 percent of the population will reside in the suburbs and 28.57 percent in the city. Note that the same results are achieved regardless of the initial conditions. The reader is encouraged to test this statement with the extreme initial conditions $q_1(0) = 1$, $q_2(0) = 0$.

Market shares in equilibrium

Let us return now to the detergent example. With the equilibrium Equation 13.11, John Byer's second question (concerning the ultimate market shares) can be addressed.

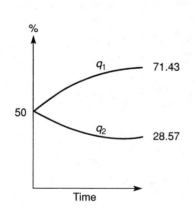

TABLE 13.3   The Approach to Steady State

(k) Year	$q_1(k)$* Percentage in Suburbs	$q_2(k)$ Percentage in City	Formula Used
0	50	50	$Q(0)$ Given
1	65	35	$Q(1) = Q(0)P$
2	69.5	30.5	$Q(2) = Q(1)P$
3	70.85	29.15	$Q(3) = Q(2)P$
4	71.255	28.745	.
.	.	.	.
.	.	.	.
n (large)	71.4286	28.5714	$Q = QP$

*q_1 and q_2, the probabilities of an individual being in the suburbs or in the city, respectively, also correspond to the percentage of the population in the suburbs and in the city. For example, after one year, 35 percent of the total population will be in the city.

The equilibrium probabilities are computed (to three decimal-place accuracy) as:

$$Q = [.297 \quad .286 \quad .417]$$

This means that once steady state has been achieved, the market shares of A, B, and C in any given month are 29.7 percent, 28.6 percent, and 41.7 percent, respectively.

Summary: How a Steady State Situation Is Recognized

As seen earlier, the state probabilities changed over time. In the detergent example, we found that:

$$\text{Initially} \qquad Q(0) = [.2750 \quad .3750 \quad .3500]$$

$$\text{After a month} \qquad Q(1) = [.2675 \quad .3125 \quad .4200]$$

That is, $Q(0) \neq Q(1)$. A steady state condition is recognized when the state probabilities remain *unchanged* from period to period. Formally, such a condition is expressed by Equation 13.10, namely: $Q(k) = Q(k - 1)$.

Characteristics of the Steady State Situation

From Equation 13.11 it can be seen that the steady state conditions can be expressed by a set of probabilities, Q, that are called the steady state (or equilibrium) probabilities. These probabilities are constant state probabilities, and they depend only on the transition matrix. In contrast, state probabilities that are *not* in (or close to) equilibrium *do* depend on the initial conditions. In a nonabsorbing situation, steady state is approached in a finite number of transitions.

Note: Not all Markov chains reach equilibrium.

Solved Problem: Promotional Policy Planning

P&C is considering two alternative policies for promoting its products.

Alternative 1. Promote Brand A only. This will cost $150,000 (invested in a lump sum) and is expected to change the transition matrix to:

From \ To	A	B	C
A	.6	.2	.2
B	.4	.4	.2
C	.6	.1	.3

Alternative 2. Promote Brand B only. This will cost $280,000 (lump sum, one shot) and is expected to change the transition matrix to:

From \ To	A	B	C
A	.1	.5	.4
B	.2	.8	0
C	.3	.5	.2

Find:

1. Which policy will bring larger increases in P&C's total share of the market in the long run?
2. Which policy will be more efficient (gain per dollar invested) in the long run?
3. Assume that each percentage of increased share in the total market is worth $10,000 to P&C; which policy (if any) should P&C take?
4. What is the break-even point for each of the two possible policies? That is, at what dollar value of worth, for each percentage gain, will the policies start to be profitable, disregarding interest rates?

Solution:

1. If only Brand A is promoted, the following market equilibrium (using the new transition matrix) is obtained:

$$A = .555, \quad B = .223, \quad C = .222 \qquad \text{(rounded)}$$

The total of Brands A and B increases from .297 + .286 = .583 to .778 (or 77.8 percent of the market). If only Brand B is promoted, the equilibrium (using the third transition matrix) is: A = .190, B = .715, C = .095, for a total of .905 to A and B. Thus, promoting B only (alternative 2) is preferable, because it will result in a larger share of the market.

2. Promoting A only is more efficient because promoting A yields a 19.5 percent increase (i.e., .778 − .297 − .286 = .195) for a $150,000 investment or .13 percent per $1,000 investment; promoting B yields a 32.2 percent increase for a $280,000 investment or .115 percent per $1,000 investment.

3. For promoting A: $10,000 × 19.5 = $195,000, less $150,000 (cost) = $45,000. For promoting B: $10,000 × 32.2 = $322,000, less $280,000 (cost) = $42,000. Thus, promoting A is better. This solution was expected because the same answer was obtained earlier in part (2), but here it is in dollar terms.

4. In promoting A only, let x be dollars per 1 percent gain. To break even, the total gain must equal the expenses; that is, 19.5 (x) = $150,000. Solving:

$$x = \$7,678 \text{ for each 1 percent gain.}$$

If only B is promoted, 32.2 (x) = $280,000. Solving:

$$x = \$8,685 \text{ for each 1 percent gain.}$$

Thus, promoting A is better, because its break-even point is lower.

13.5 Absorbing States

Cannot exit from an absorbing state

A system is said to be in an absorbing state if, once there, it cannot exit to some other state. A bankrupt business, a river or lake irreversibly destroyed by pollution and sediment, and a building destroyed by fire are examples of absorbing state situations.

Analysis of absorbing Markov chains can provide management with answers to at least four important questions:

1. What is the average number of periods that the system will be in *each* nonabsorbing state before it is absorbed?
2. How long is the system expected to stay in nonabsorbing states before it is absorbed?

Answers to four questions

3. What is the probability of moving into each absorbing state starting from each nonabsorbing state?
4. What proportion will be absorbed in each absorbing state?

Such information has an important practical value for managerial decisions in areas such as replacement of equipment, marketing, and maintenance, as will be demonstrated in the following examples and the homework problems.

A Labor Training Program

Participants in a certain labor training program can be found in one of four given states: s_1, no service (not in the training program); s_2, discharged; s_3, in training; and s_4, employed. Table 13.4 shows the proportion of the program population that has changed categories (states) in the most recent month.

The first step is to construct the *transition matrix* (assuming that the transition probabilities are constant over time). The numbers in the matrix below (derived from Table 13.4) represent the fraction of people who have transferred from one category to another during the month. States s_2 and s_4 are defined as *absorbing states* because all the entries in rows s_2 and s_4 are zero except the one corresponding to the *same* state,

TABLE 13.4 **A Training Problem**

Status on January 1, 1994	Status on February 1, 1994									
	s_1 No Service		s_2 Discharged		s_3 In Training		s_4 Employed		*Total*	
	No.	*Percent*	*No.*	*Percent*	*No.*	*Percent*	*No.*	*Percent*	*No.*	*Percent*
s_1 No Service	10	10.0	60	60.0	30	30.0	0	.0	100	100.0
s_2 Discharged	0	.0	100	100.0	0	.0	0	.0	100	100.0
s_3 In Training	60	20.0	60	20.0	150	50.0	30	10.0	300	100.0
s_4 Employed	0	.0	0	.0	0	.0	500	100.0	500	100.0

which has the value of one. *If a system is in an absorbing state, there is a zero probability of moving from that state to any other state.* For example, once employed or discharged, movement to another state is not possible.

From \ To	s_1	s_2	s_3	s_4
s_1	.1	.6	.3	0
s_2	0	1.0	0	0
s_3	.2	.2	.5	.1
s_4	0	0	0	1.0

The Fundamental Matrix

After the transition matrix is constructed, it is *rearranged* by placing the absorbing states together, either first or last. This enables us to partition the matrix and identify four submatrices, **I, O, A,** and **N,** as shown in Figure 13.7.

These four matrices are:

I = Unit (identity) matrix
O = All zero (null) matrix
A = Absorbing matrix
N = Nonabsorbing matrix

Note: A unit or identity matrix contains zeros in all elements except the diagonal from upper left to lower right, which is filled in with ones (see Appendix A).

FIGURE 13.7

A partition of the transition matrix

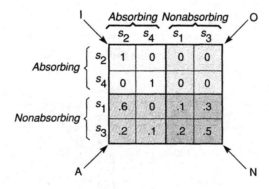

Fundamental matrix

Next, we define a new matrix, termed the *fundamental matrix (F)*, according to Equation 13.15:

$$F = (I - N)^{-1} \qquad (13.15)$$

where the -1 exponent stands for the *inverse* of the matrix (see Appendix A). In our case:

$$F = \left(\begin{bmatrix} 1 & 0 \\ 0 & 1 \end{bmatrix} - \begin{bmatrix} .1 & .3 \\ .2 & .5 \end{bmatrix} \right)^{-1} = \begin{bmatrix} .9 & -.3 \\ -.2 & .5 \end{bmatrix}^{-1} = \begin{array}{c} s_1 \\ s_3 \end{array} \begin{array}{cc} s_1 & s_3 \\ \begin{bmatrix} \dfrac{50}{39} & \dfrac{30}{39} \\ \dfrac{20}{39} & \dfrac{90}{39} \end{bmatrix} \end{array}$$

The meaning of the entries in the fundamental matrix

The entries in the fundamental matrix give the *average number of periods* (months in our case) *the system will be in each nonabsorbing state until it gets absorbed*. If an employee started in state s_1, then he or she will spend $\frac{50}{39} = 1.28$ months (on the average in state s_1 *and* $\frac{30}{39} = .77$ months in state s_3 before being absorbed; that is, either employed (state s_4) or discharged (state s_2). If the employee was in s_3, then he or she will spend $\frac{20}{39} = .51$ months in state s_1 *and* $\frac{90}{39} = 2.31$ months in state s_3 before being absorbed into either s_4 or s_2.

Time to Absorption
To find the average number of periods to absorption, add the entries in the rows of matrix F.

If an employee starts in state s_1, it will take, on the average:

$$\frac{50}{39} + \frac{30}{39} = \frac{80}{39} = 2.05 \text{ months}$$

until he or she is absorbed into either s_2 or s_4. If the employee starts in state s_3, it will take $\frac{110}{39}$ or 2.82 months until he or she is absorbed (on the average).

Conditional Probabilities
It is of interest to find the probabilities of moving from any nonabsorbing state to each absorbing state. These probabilities are given by matrix B, whose formula is:

$$B = FA \qquad (13.16)$$

In our case:

$$B = \begin{bmatrix} \dfrac{50}{39} & \dfrac{30}{39} \\ \dfrac{20}{39} & \dfrac{90}{39} \end{bmatrix} \begin{bmatrix} .6 & 0 \\ .2 & .1 \end{bmatrix} = \begin{array}{c} s_1 \\ s_3 \end{array} \begin{array}{cc} s_2 & s_4 \\ \begin{bmatrix} \dfrac{36}{39} & \dfrac{3}{39} \\ \dfrac{30}{39} & \dfrac{9}{39} \end{bmatrix} \end{array}$$

These results may be interpreted as follows: If an employee is in state s_1, there is a probability of $\frac{36}{39}$ or .92 that he or she will be absorbed by state s_2 (i.e., discharged), and a probability of $\frac{3}{39}$ or .08 that the employee will be absorbed by state s_4 (i.e., employed). Similarly, if an employee starts from s_3, there is a $\frac{30}{39} = .77$ chance that he or she will be absorbed by state s_2, and a $\frac{9}{39} = .23$ chance of being absorbed by state s_4. Note again that the sum of the probabilities in each row is 1.

Interpreting the results

The final proportion in each of the absorbing states can now be found. As the reader may recall, the initial conditions were $s_1 = 100$; $s_3 = 300$ (numbers in each nonabsorbing state). If we multiply these numbers by matrix B, we can find the total number of employees (again, the alternate Markov interpretation) in each absorbing state; namely;

$$B = \begin{array}{c} \\ s_1 \\ s_3 \end{array} \begin{array}{cc} s_2 & s_4 \\ \left[\begin{array}{cc} .92 & .08 \\ .77 & .23 \end{array} \right. & \left. \right] \end{array}$$

Total in s_2: $100(.92) + 300(.77) + 100 \text{ (already)} = 423$ discharged

Total in s_4: $100(.08) + 300(.23) + 500 \text{ (already)} = \underline{577}$ employed

Grand total 1000

The proportion in s_2 is thus 42.3 percent, and in s_4, 57.7 percent. That is, in the long run, 42.3 percent will be discharged and 57.7 percent employed.

The results obtained in the above analysis can be compared to desired standards, or to results obtained from alternative training programs. Different programs will result in different movements of employees from category to category. In other words, each program will result in a different transition matrix. Given the monthly costs of each program, the administration can determine the cost-benefit relationship of different labor training programs.

Solved Problem: Accounts Receivable

Many businesses extend credit to customers. Some of the customers pay late, others do not pay at all (a situation called a *bad debt*). The typical business will classify accounts according to their age; once an unpaid account reaches a certain age, it will often be transferred to a collection agency (which keeps a certain percentage of the successful collections) or perhaps the account is simply written off as a bad debt.

Consider a department store that classifies its accounts as:

S_1 = 0–30-day age
S_2 = 31–90-day age
S_3 = In collection agency
S_4 = Bad debt
S_5 = Paid

Solved Problem continued

Past experience indicates the following one-month transition matrix:

	S_1	S_2	S_3	S_4	S_5
S_1	0	.8	0	0	.2
S_2	0	.7	.2	0	.1
S_3	0	0	.4	.2	.4
S_4	0	0	0	1	0
S_5	0	0	0	0	1

The current situation in the department store is as follows:

$$S_1 = \$100,000; \quad S_2 = \$150,000; \quad S_3 = \$50,000$$

It would be of interest to management to know the following:

1. The long-run "fate" of a dollar currently in S_1, S_2, and S_3.
2. The average number of months it will take an account now in the hands of the collection agency to be either paid or closed.
3. The probability that an account now in category S_2 will be paid.

The solution to this problem, by computer, is given in Section 13.7.

13.6 Managerial Applications

Markov analysis is used to predict a system's behavior. The relationship between the Markov analysis and a managerial situation is shown in Figure 13.8. In this section, an extension of the detergent example is given. Other examples are given in the problems.

Sensitivity (Postoptimality) Analysis

Sensitivity analysis plays an important role in Markov analysis. The following what-if scenarios are especially important:

> Change the figures in the transition matrix to see the impact on future probabilities (e.g., market share).

FIGURE 13.8

*Managerial analysis
using Markov chains*

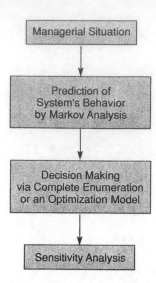

· Delete or add states (e.g., products) to find the impact on the conditional (state) probabilities and on the steady state probabilities.
· Examine the potential impact of introducing an absorbing state (see Problem 22).

Note: As stated earlier, the sensitivity analysis can be expedited by the use of the Edit function in most computer programs.

Other Predictions

Markov chain analysis can also give other information of managerial interest. (See [5] for the formulas.)

Mean First Passage Times
The average number of periods that will elapse before a system in one state first switches to another *specified* state.

Equilibrium First Passage Times
The average number of periods that will elapse before a system in one state first switches to *any* of the other states.

Expected Recurrence Times
The average number of periods that will elapse before a system in one state returns to that *same* state.

Time and Probabilities of Absorption
The average number of periods before absorption and the probabilities of being absorbed in each of the absorbing states.

The computer printouts in the next section provide the values of these predictions for our P&C brand-switching example and accounts receivable solved problem.

13.7 Use of Computers

Markov chain problems can be easily programmed for computers. Several statistical packages include Markov chain computations such as multiplication of a matrix by a vector and multiplication of a matrix by itself *n* times (raising it to the *n*th power). The input to the computer includes the transition matrix, the initial conditions (if applicable), and the number of regular and absorbing states.

Two examples of computer printouts using the Nelson software follow. The first one is the solution to the earlier P&C brand-switching example in Section 13.3. Note that the solution includes:

- *a.* The steady state (equilibrium) probabilities (market share).
- *b.* Equilibrium first passage times.
- *c.* Expected recurrence times.
- *d.* Mean first passage times.
- *e.* The transition matrix after *n* transitions (three in our case).
- *f.* The state (conditional) probabilities after *n* (3 here) periods (in period *n* + 1).

a. STEADY STATE PROBABILITIES

STATES	PROBABILITIES
Br. A	0.29670
Br. B	0.28571
Br. C	0.41758

b. EQUILIBRIUM 1ST PASSAGE TIMES

STATES	TIMES
Br. A	2.247
Br. B	3.571
Br. C	1.223

c. EXPECTED RECURRENCE TIMES

STATES	TIMES
Br. A	3.370
Br. B	3.500
Br. C	2.395

d. MEAN 1ST PASSAGE TIMES

FROM	TO Br. A	Br. B	Br. C
Br. A	0.00000	5.00000	1.84211
Br. B	4.07407	0.00000	2.36842
Br. C	2.59259	5.00000	0.00000

e. TRANSITION MATRIX AFTER 3 TRANSITIONS

FROM	TO Br. A	Br. B	Br. C
Br. A	0.28800	0.27800	0.43400
Br. B	0.27900	0.30500	0.41600
Br. C	0.31500	0.27800	0.40700

f. STATE (CONDITIONAL) PROBABILITIES IN PERIOD 4

STATES	PROBABILITIES
1	0.29408
2	0.28800
3	0.41780

The second example is the solution to the accounts receivable solved problem, including absorbing states. The absorbing states ("paid" and "bad debt") are arranged first (states 1 and 2) and the nonabsorbing states are arranged last (states 3, 4, and 5). (In some computer programs, the order may be reversed.) The solution includes:

a. The fundamental matrix F.

b. The time to absorption.

c. The state (conditional) probabilities.

d. Transition matrix.

```
    **  INFORMATION ENTERED  **

    NUMBER OF STATES          :5
    NUMBER OF ABSORPTIVE STATES:2
```

```
                    TRANSITION MATRIX

  STATES
  PAID            1       0       0       0       0
  BAD DEBT        0       1       0       0       0
  D 0-30         .2       0       0      .8       0
  D 31-90        .1       0       0      .7      .2
  COLLECTION     .4      .2       0       0      .4

              ** RESULTS **

  a. FUNDAMENTAL MATRIX

              STATES
                       TO
      FROM    D 0-30    D 31-90    Coll.

      D 0-30  1.00000   2.66667    0.88889

      D 31-90 0.00000   3.33333    1.11111

      Coll.   0.00000   0.00000    1.66667
```

b. TIME TO ABSORPTION

STATES	TIMES
3	4.55556
4	4.44444
5	1.66667

c. STATE (CONDITIONAL) PROBABILITIES

FROM	Paid	Bad.db.	ROW TOT
D 0-30	0.82222	0.17778	1.00000
D 31-90	0.77778	0.22222	1.00000
Coll.	0.66667	0.33333	1.00000

d. The transition matrix after n transitions and the state (conditional) probabilities in period n + 1 are the same as in the nonabsorbing case.

Interpretation

The *fundamental matrix* is given first. The cells of this matrix indicate the average time that an account will be in any nonabsorbing state, given that the account is in a nonabsorbing state. For example, an account now in state 0–30 days will be 2.666 months in the state 31–90 days.

Absorption Time

This is the average time (number of periods) that it will take for an entry to be absorbed by either one of the absorbing states. For example, for a 0 to 30-day account, it will take 4.555 months, on the average, to either be paid or closed (bad debt).

State (Conditional) Probabilities

This is the probability that each account in a nonabsorbing state will be absorbed in a particular absorbing state. For example, the collection agency collects .66667 (66.667 percent) of all accounts submitted to it.

With this information, one can answer the three questions posed by management.

Answer to Question 1

a. Of the $100,000 in 0–30 days, $82,222 will be paid and $17,778 will become bad debt.
b. Of the $150,000 in the 31 to 90-day category, 77.778 percent (or $116,667) will be paid, whereas 22.22 percent ($33,333) will become bad debt.
c. Of the $50,000 currently in the collection agency, 66.67 percent (or $33,334) will be paid, whereas $16,667 will become bad debt.

Thus, of the $300,000: $82,222 + $116,667 + $33,334 = $232,223 will be paid.

Answer to Question 2

On the average, it will take the collection agency 1.66667 months to collect an account or to close it.

Answer to Question 3

The probability that an account now in the 31 to 90-day category will be paid is 77.778 percent.

13.8 Concluding Remarks

Markov analysis is a descriptive tool designed to predict the behavior of a system over time. The analysis applies in a dynamic, probabilistic environment where most other management science tools are inadequate.

What Information Is Provided?

Determining system effectiveness

The analysis can provide information about the chances of a system to occupy any state at any future time. Such information can be used by management to determine the *effectiveness* of a system under various operating conditions. This enables management to compare various policies and projects by considering each relevant transition matrix.

Difficulties in Application

Using historical or subjective data

A key difficulty in the application of Markov chain analysis is that of obtaining the transition matrix. Historical data can serve this purpose in some cases. In other cases, the subjective beliefs of experts may be used.

Markov chain analysis can be applied as an auxiliary tool to a host of managerial problems that are dynamic in nature, such as replacement, maintenance, brand loyalty, investment evaluation, and management of ecology. In addition, it is used in dynamic programming [7]. Ultimately, the extent of the applications of Markov chains will depend on the ability to relax the restrictive assumptions and solve the modified models efficiently.

13.9 Problems

1. A survey of the condition of textile machines in the ABC Corporation indicated the following:

   January 1: Two hundred in excellent condition, 80 in good condition, 20 in fair condition.

   February 1: Of those found in excellent condition on January 1, 180 are still in excellent condition, 20 in good. Of those found in good condition in January, 60 are still in good condition, 16 are in excellent condition (maintenance is given routinely), and 4 are in fair condition. Of those found in fair shape in January, 2 are in good condition and 18 are in fair condition.

   Construct the transition matrix.

2. Given the following transition matrix:

$$P = \begin{array}{c} \\ s_1 \\ s_2 \end{array} \begin{array}{c} \begin{array}{cc} s_1 & s_2 \end{array} \\ \begin{bmatrix} .2 & .8 \\ .6 & .4 \end{bmatrix} \end{array}$$

   The system is now in state s_2 (i.e., $q_2(0) = 1$). Find the probability vector $Q(3)$ after three periods.

3. A survey of a two-brand market indicates that 80 percent of brand A's customers remain loyal to their brand (state 1) and 20 percent switch to brand B (state 2) each period (say, a week). It is also known that 40 percent of B's customers are loyal and that 60 percent switch to A. This information is presented as a *brand-switching* (transition) matrix:

$$\begin{array}{cc} & \text{Next week} \\ & \begin{array}{cc} A & B \end{array} \\ \begin{array}{c} \text{This} \\ \text{week} \end{array} \begin{array}{c} A \\ B \end{array} & \begin{bmatrix} .8 & .2 \\ .6 & .4 \end{bmatrix} = P \end{array}$$

   Assume that a consumer is currently buying product B. Find:
   a. The probabilities that the consumer will buy products A and B after one week.
   b. The probabilities that the consumer will buy products A and B after two weeks.
   c. The equilibrium (steady state) probabilities.

4. Continental Corporation operates a large fleet of cars for which an extensive preventive maintenance program is utilized. The cars can be classified in one of three states: good (G), fair (F), and poor (P). The transition matrix of these cars follows:

$$\begin{array}{cc} & \text{To} \\ & \begin{array}{ccc} G & F & P \end{array} \\ \text{From} \begin{array}{c} G \\ F \\ P \end{array} & \begin{bmatrix} .6 & .3 & .1 \\ .2 & .6 & .2 \\ .1 & .4 & .5 \end{bmatrix} \end{array}$$

   a. Assume that currently there are 100 cars in good shape, 60 in fair shape, and 20 in poor shape. How many cars will be found in each condition next week?
   b. How many cars will be found in each condition once the process stabilizes (steady state)?

5. Buckaday Rent-A-Car has a fleet of 1,000 cars. The company has three rental offices, A, B, and C. Cars can be picked up at and returned to any office. Customers return cars to each of the offices according to the following probabilities:

Picked up at \ Returned to	A	B	C
A	.7	.1	.2
B	.3	.5	.2
C	0	.2	.8

a. How many cars should the company keep in each office and why? What special assumption must be made in order to answer this question?
b. Near which office should the maintenance facilities be located and why?

6. A university's service department is considering leasing one of two possible computers. A computer can be found in operating condition O or nonoperating condition NO. The daily transition matrix of the two computers under identical maintenance follows:

Computer A	O	NO
O	.95	.05
NO	.90	.10

Computer B	O	NO
O	.98	.02
NO	.85	.15

a. Which computer should the university lease if the leasing charges are the same?
b. If charges are not the same, what additional information is necessary to determine which computer to lease? Under what conditions should the university lease computer A and under what conditions computer B?

7. Given below are two transition matrices.

$$
\text{Matrix 1} = \begin{array}{c} \\ A \\ B \\ C \end{array} \begin{array}{ccc} A & B & C \\ \begin{bmatrix} .8 & .1 & .1 \\ 0 & .4 & .6 \\ 0 & .6 & .4 \end{bmatrix} \end{array} \qquad
\text{Matrix 2} = \begin{array}{c} \\ A \\ B \\ C \end{array} \begin{array}{ccc} A & B & C \\ \begin{bmatrix} .2 & .1 & .7 \\ 0 & 1.0 & 0 \\ 0 & .6 & .4 \end{bmatrix} \end{array}
$$

a. Analyze these matrices and explain their uniqueness.
b. Predict the steady state probabilities. *Do not* set up any equations; use logic!

8. A company's job rotation program shows the following rotations among its employees between March and April 1991.

Dept.	Total March	Gains			Total April
		From Checking	From Loans	From Savings	
Checking	18	0	3	2	20
Loans	12	2	0	1	10
Savings	10	1	2	0	10

a. What would you expect the June results to be?
b. What assumptions were necessary in (a)?

9. A yearly follow-up of a certain metropolitan area residents' mobility showed that 6 percent of the residents in the city move to the suburbs. At the same time, 3 percent of the suburbs' residents move to the city. Assume that the moving percentages remain unchanged and the total number of people in the combined area remains constant (500,000). The average yearly tax paid by a city dweller is $1,000 per capita, and by a suburb dweller $2,000 per capita.

a. How much tax will the metro government collect (assume 100 percent collection) two years from now if 40 percent of the population currently live in the suburbs?
b. The metro government proposed to induce people to stay in the city by reducing yearly taxes for city

dwellers (only) to $500 per capita. As a *result* of this change, population movement from the city to the suburbs will be reduced from 6 percent to 5 percent, and population movement from the suburbs to the city will be changed from 3 percent to 5 percent. How much tax would be collected each year in the long run (steady state) if the proposal is rejected; that is, if the existing tax structure remains unchanged?

c. How much annual tax will be collected in the long run if the proposal is accepted?

d. If the total number of people in the metropolitan area is changing due to additions from other metropolitan areas, what pattern of change should be assumed in order to employ the Markov chain approach?

10. Three major oil companies compete in a certain marketing zone. Company A runs a promotion campaign 50 percent of the time, Company B runs one 30 percent of the time, and Company C does no advertising. All campaigns are run on a weekly basis. The average buyer shows the following purchasing habit:

a. If only one company advertises, a buyer will buy from that company.

b. If no one advertises, a buyer will buy from C.

c. If *both* A and B advertise, the buyer will review the previous week's decision. If in the previous week the buyer bought from A, he or she will do so again. If in the previous week the buyer bought from B, he or she will buy from B again. However, if in the previous week the buyer bought from C, the product will be selected at random from either A, B, or C (each with a one-third chance of being selected).

Find the long-run market distribution among the three oil companies.

11. Carefully read the following statement:

Why Worry?

There are only two things to worry about—either you are well or you are sick. If you are well, then there is nothing to worry about. But if you are sick, there are two things to worry about. Either you will get well or you will die. If you get well, there is nothing to worry about. If you die, there are only two things to worry about—either you will go to Heaven or to

Hell. If you go to Heaven, there is nothing to worry about. But if you go to Hell, you'll be so damn busy shaking hands with friends, you won't have time to worry!

a. Assume that the chances of moving among the events described are known and constant. Would it be possible to describe this process as a Markov process? Why or why not?

b. If the answer to part (a) is no, would it be possible to make certain assumptions that will turn the answer to (a) into yes? Name these assumptions.

c. Is it possible to describe the process as a decision tree (assuming that the probabilities of the events are known)? If the answer is no, explain why. If the answer is yes, draw the decision tree and comment on the relationship between Markov chains and decision trees.

12. The Chamber of Commerce of the city of Mid-America conducted a study on the size of new, high-technology businesses. Companies were classified as small (S), medium (M), or large (L). One survey was taken on January 1, 1992. It showed 400 companies, of which 200 were small, 150 were medium, and 50 were large. At the end of the year, another survey of the 400 companies was taken. This time, there were 160 small, 180 medium, and 60 large corporations. The gains and losses in terms of number of companies between the two surveys are given below:

Size	Gains from			Losses to		
	S	M	L	S	M	L
S	0	5	2	0	42	5
M	42	0	1	5	0	8
L	5	8	0	2	1	0

a. Construct the transition matrix.

b. State all the assumptions necessary to answer the following questions if a Markov chain is to be used.

c. Predict how many small, medium, and large companies will exist on January 1, 1994.

d. Predict the number of companies in each category in the long run.

13. A production line has 0.4 probability of failure during any one day. Seventy percent of the time, the failure can be fixed in exactly one day; otherwise, it requires two days. Assume that failures occur at the end of a day and that downtime costs $450 per day.
    a. Formulate this situation as a Markov chain, describe the states and assumptions, and develop the transition matrix for the situation.
    b. For $200 per day, extra tooling can be rented so that a failure is always repaired in one day. Should this be done?

14. The air in Mexico City is classified as being in one of nine levels of pollution. Observations show that the following transition probability matrix exists: (Consider one day as a period.)

From \ To	1	2	3	4	5	6	7	8	9
1	.22	.28	.20	.15	.10	.05	0	0	0
2	.10	.20	.30	.20	.10	.10	0	0	0
3	.10	.10	.20	.40	.10	.05	.05	0	0
4	.05	.10	.10	.20	.40	.10	.05	0	0
5	0	0	.10	.10	.20	.30	.20	.10	0
6	0	0	0	.07	.08	.15	.40	.20	.0
7	0	0	0	.05	.10	.15	.36	.20	.14
8	0	0	.05	.07	.08	.10	.15	.30	.25
9	0	0	.06	.06	.08	.10	.15	.25	.30

For how many days during the year (365 days) is the air polluted at each level? (Use of a computer is recommended.)

15. Hopeful Hospital is using volunteer help in three departments. On May 1, there were 20 volunteers in department A, 16 in B, and 14 in C. Volunteers are free to move between departments once a month.

    The table below shows the *gains* in volunteers, in each department, on June 1.

Depart- ment	**Gains**			Volunteers on June 1
	From A	*From B*	*From C*	
A	16	0	1	17
B	3	12	1	16
C	1	4	12	17

a. Write the formulas that will show the long-run probability distribution of volunteers among the three departments.
b. Solve the equations to find the probabilities.

16. Taxi-cab of Miami has 100 cabs; currently, 70 are located at the airport and 30 are at the beach. The probability that a car located at the beach will be called for a trip to the airport is 80 percent. The net profit of such a trip is $5. Otherwise, the cab will be called for a local trip, where a profit of $2 is realized.

    The probability that a cab located at the airport will be called to the beach is 90 percent. The net profit is $5 for such a trip. There is a 10 percent chance that the cab will be called for a trip to the airport. In this case, the cab will return to the airport parking, netting $3.

    Note: Once a trip is completed, the cabs return to the port nearest to their unloading point. *Find:*
    a. What assumption should be made so that a Markov chain approach can be used for this problem.
    b. How many cabs will be at each location after three periods.
    c. The per-period profit for the company in a steady state situation.
    d. Cab 135 (nicknamed Fair Lady) is currently parked at the airport. What is the chance of this cab being located at the beach after two trips?

17. Given the transition matrix below, find the appropriate *fundamental* matrix.

$$\begin{bmatrix} 1.0 & 0 & 0 & 0 \\ .3 & .2 & .5 & 0 \\ .1 & .6 & .1 & .2 \\ 0 & 0 & 0 & 1.0 \end{bmatrix}$$

18. Assume that a machine is currently found in either good (G), fair (F), or poor (P) condition. Suppose that management decides to stop all preventive maintenance and let the machine fail. If preventive maintenance stops, the machine will have a new state, complete failure (D). The transition matrix under these conditions is given below:

$$\text{From} \begin{array}{c} G \\ F \\ P \\ D \end{array} \overset{\begin{array}{cccc} \quad G & F & P & D \end{array}}{\begin{bmatrix} .4 & .3 & .2 & .1 \\ 0 & .5 & .3 & .2 \\ 0 & 0 & .1 & .9 \\ 0 & 0 & 0 & 1 \end{bmatrix}}$$

Assuming the machine is presently in good condition, management wants to know:

a. How many weeks the machine is expected to go before it fails.

b. How many weeks (on the average) it will operate in good, fair, and poor condition before it fails.

c. What is its probability of failing? What would this probability be, given that the machine was in fair condition to start? In poor condition?

19. Suppose a new labor training program became available. What information would you need to determine if it were better or worse than the program described in Section 13.5? If you wished to determine the cost-benefit of both programs, what information would you need and how would you conduct the analysis?

20. A department store classifies its accounts as: S_1 = paid in full, S_2 = current, S_3 = delinquent, and S_4 = bad debt. The following information is given regarding the accounts:

	Transactions during October			
Category	S_1	S_2	S_3	S_4
S_1	500,000	0	0	0
S_2	400,000	500,000	100,000	0
S_3	50,000	0	100,000	50,000
S_4	0	0	0	100,000

The amounts on October 1 were: $500,000 in S_1; $1,000,000 in S_2; $200,000 in S_3; and $100,000 in S_4.

Find:

a. How much money will be in each category on November 1 and on December 1.

b. In the long run, how much money will be classified as paid.

c. What allowance should be prepared for the possible bad debt.

d. The average number of months that it will take a current account to be closed.

21. A computer printout of a Markov chain follows. Cells marked with * were deliberately deleted. Answer the

following questions:

a. For a person now in state 4:
   (1) How long will it take to be absorbed (on the average)?
   (2) How long will he or she stay in that state (on the average)?

b. Of the 10,000 people currently in state 4, how many will be absorbed by state 1?

c. Of the 20,000 people in state 5, how many will be absorbed by state 1? By state 2?

d. There are 15,000 in state 3, 50,000 in state 1, and 100,000 in state 2. How many will be in each of the five states at the end? (Use the information from [b] and [c].)

FUNDAMENTAL MATRIX			
		TO	
FROM	3	4	5
3	3.67347	0.20408	0.81633
4	1.42857	2.85714	1.42857
5	1.02041	0.61224	*
ABSOR. TM	4.69388	*	4.08163

STATE (CONDITIONAL) PROBABILITIES			
		TO	
FROM	ABSORB 1	ABSORB 2	ROW TOT
3	0.44898	0.55102	1.00000
4	*	0.71429	1.00000
5	0.34694	*	1.00000

22. The city of Charleston, Illinois, is known for its "clean environment" efforts. Of 4,000 families (customers of energy), 25 percent use gas (average monthly cost, $73), 45 percent use heating oil (average monthly bill, $58), 25 percent use electricity ($115), and 5 percent use solar energy ($10). The total population of Charleston is fairly stable, but people move in and out and they also change energy

sources according to the following table (in percent):

From	To			
	Gas	*Oil*	*Electricity*	*Solar*
Gas	95	3	1	1
Oil	1	96	1	2
Electricity	2	3	90	5
Solar	1	1	1	97

Changes are recorded once a year. *Find:*

a. The percentage of customers that will use each type of energy during each of the next three years.

b. The total cost of energy in the city next year.

c. The long-term distribution of customers (in number of customers per energy type).

d. To reduce pollution, the city is willing to pay each customer $10 per month as a rebate. Such an action is anticipated to change the customers' usage of energy as follows:

From	To			
	Gas	*Oil*	*Electricity*	*Solar*
Gas	.94	.02	.01	.03
Oil	.01	.95	.01	.03
Electricity	.01	.02	.87	.10
Solar	.005	.005	.005	.985

(1) How will such a rebate change the usage of energy in the long run (in percent of customers)?

(2) How much money will be paid by customers for energy each year (in the long run)?

(3) How much money will the city have to pay as a rebate next year? In the long run?

e. The city would like to see *all* customers using solar energy. Assuming that this can be done, how long will it take until *all* customers will switch to solar energy?

23. The land of Oz is blessed by many things, but not by good weather. They never have two nice days in a row. If they have a sunny (nice) day they are just as likely to have snow as rain the next day. If they have snow (or rain), they have an even chance of having the same the next day. If there is a change from snow or rain, only half the time is this a change to a nice day. It is a sunny day in Oz today.

a. Show how to predict the weather in Oz for the next n days.

b. In the long run, what percentage of days will be rainy, snowy, and nice in the land of Oz?

24. The probability that a machine will be operating the next day if it is operating on a given day is $\frac{1}{2}$; if the machine is not operating on a given day, the probability that it will be operating the next day is $\frac{4}{5}$.

a. If the machine is operating this Monday, what is the probability that it will be operating Thursday? What is the probability that the machine will be operating on the Monday one year from this Monday?

b. If it costs $100 for each day the machine is not operating, what is the maximum daily amount that should be spent on preventive maintenance to change the probability (that an operating machine will also be operating the next day) from $\frac{1}{2}$ to $\frac{3}{5}$?

13.10 CASE
SPRINGFIELD GENERAL HOSPITAL

Dr. Bill Parker, medical director of Springfield General Hospital, has just been informed that an ambulance is rushing in an accident victim who may require surgery using the heart-lung machine. This hospital has only one such expensive machine, which is not in use now but is heavily scheduled for surgeries in the next few days. Dr. Parker has called the management science unit to provide him with estimates of the following:

a. The likelihood that the victim will require service on the heart-lung machine during each of the next few days.

b. The prognosis over time for such cases.

After quickly reviewing their records, the management science analysts compiled the following information:

1. In the past, 112 such victims entered the hospital. At admittance, 72 were found to be in satisfactory condition, 24 were diagnosed as fair, and 16 were considered to be in *critical condition, requiring the heart-lung machine*.

2. Of the 72 in satisfactory condition, 63 (87.5 percent) were still in satisfactory condition the following day, but the condition of 9 (12.5 percent) had deteriorated due to complications and these persons were considered to be in fair condition. None had deteriorated to the point of being in critical condition.

3. Of the 24 in fair condition, 12 (50 percent) were still in the same condition the following day, and

8 (33.3 percent) had improved to satisfactory condition; but 4 (16.7 percent) had deteriorated so much they were classified as critical.

4. Of the 16 in critical condition, 10 (62.5 percent) had improved to fair by the following day, 4 (25 percent) were still in critical condition, and 2 (12.5 percent) had improved significantly to the level of satisfactory.

With this information on hand, the management analysts can answer Dr. Parker's questions.

Questions for Discussion:

1. What is the likelihood of the patient requiring the heart-lung machine today or in the next two days?

2. What are the steady state transition probabilities?

3. Assume now that in addition to the 112 victims listed in the records, there were another 8 who were discharged. Six of these were discharged alive from "satisfactory" status and two had expired from "critical" status.

4. Starting from each nonabsorbing state, what is the average number of days a patient will be in each state and the number of days before the patient is discharged?

5. From each nonabsorbing state, what is the probability of expiring, as opposed to being discharged alive?

Glossary

Absorbing state   A state that, once entered, cannot be left.

Descriptive   Illustrating a system and how it reacts.

Equilibrium   (see Steady state).

Markov chain   A Markov process with constant transition probabilities.

Markov process   A stochastic process whose probability of being in any state depends only on its previous state and the transition matrix.

Normative   Prescriptive; that is, what *should* be done.

State   A condition that a system may be in.

Steady state   A point where the chances of finding a system in any particular condition are unchanged from period to period.

Stochastic   Probabilistic; that is, with an exhaustive set of probabilities or chances of outcomes.

Transition probability   The chance of a system moving from one state to another.

References and Bibliography

1. Anderson, W. J. *Continuous Time Markov Chains*. New York: Springer-Verlag, 1991.
2. Ethier, S. N. and T. G. Kurtz. *Markov Processes*. New York: Wiley, 1986.
3. Gillespie, D. T. *Markov Processes*. New York: Academic Press, 1991.
4. Hernandez-Lerma, O. *Adaptive Markov Control Processes*. New York: Springer-Verlag, 1989.
5. Hillier, F. S., and G. J. Lieberman. *Introduction to Operations Research*. 5th ed., San Francisco: Holden-Day, 1989.
6. Hou, D., et al. *Homogeneous Denumerable Markov Processes*. New York: Springer-Verlag, 1988.
7. Howard, R. A. *Dynamic Probabilistic Systems*. Vols. 1 and 2. New York: Wiley, 1971.
8. Kemeny, J. G., et al. *Denumerable Markov Chains*. 2nd ed. New York: Springer-Verlag, 1991.
9. Sharpe, M. *General Theory of Markov Processes*. New York: Academic Press, 1988.

CHAPTER 14 Waiting Lines

The more society becomes interdependent psychologically, economically, and technically, the more individuals encounter waiting lines, or queues, in their daily lives. People queue at doctors' offices, supermarkets, gasoline stations, and tollbooths. Waiting lines may also involve nonhumans as customers: airplanes circling airports and machines waiting for repairs. The problem of managing waiting lines is complex, because the cost of providing services of all kinds is rapidly increasing. The objective is to determine the appropriate level of service. The method of analyzing waiting line problems illustrated in this chapter is called queuing theory.

In Part A of this chapter, the queuing problem is formulated and a solution using equations for simple problems is derived. In Part B, more complex queuing systems are addressed, and tables substituting for formulas are presented to facilitate the analysis of these systems. For even more complex queuing systems, the technique of simulation, presented in Chapter 15, is necessary.

PART A: BASICS

All American Aviation Company has a specialized machine shop that serves the airlines in Plain City. At the present time, the shop employs about 400 mechanics. Willie Davis, the materials manager, just returned, troubled, from the regular Monday executive committee meeting. It was only a week ago that he placed his best employee, John, in the "toolroom," the machine shop's center for distributing specialized tools. He took this action after continuous complaints from the production manager about long waiting lines there. It appeared to Willie that the toolroom was the scapegoat for everything that went wrong with production.

This week, Willie was sure that the problem of the waiting lines had been solved, because John seemed to be handling the situation well. However, in the morning's meeting, Willie was again under the gun. He therefore started wondering if it might be necessary to add a second clerk. He reasoned that with two clerks, the waiting time at the toolroom would be reduced by one-half. However, he was not sure that such a reduction would justify the additional cost.

Willie's reasoning that doubling the capacity of the toolroom would decrease the waiting time by one-half seemed so logical and obvious that it didn't occur to him that it might be incorrect. His error will be analyzed later in this chapter.

14.1 The Queuing Situation

Characteristics of Waiting Line Situations

Fluctuating demand

The incident at the All American Aviation Company is typical of a situation that arises in the delivery of services. On the one hand, the demand for services is unstable; there are some foreseeable fluctuations during certain time periods (e.g., rush hours at the beginning and the end of shifts at the toolroom). In addition, there are unforeseeable changes in the pattern of demand. On the other hand, the length of service may vary due to particular requirements of those requesting the service. The result is difficulty in meeting demand immediately on request, especially during rush hours.

Expensive to meet peak demand

The only way that demand can be immediately supplied, all the time, is to build a large service capacity that can always meet peak demand. Such a situation can be observed in an electric utility company. In some industries, it is *very expensive* to build, operate, and maintain a service facility so that all demands will be met, all the time, on request. It may also be expensive to constantly *change* the capacity in an existing service facility to meet the demand, especially when people provide the service. Instead, service facilities are usually designed so that their capacity is less than the maximum

Formation of a queue

demand. As a result, whenever demand exceeds capacity, a *waiting line,* or a **queue,** is formed; that is, the customers do not get service immediately on request, but must wait. On other occasions, the service facility will be idle. Thus, at a high level of service capacity, the people served will have only a limited wait, but the service facility will frequently be idle (at considerable expense). At a lower, less expensive level of service capacity, there will be less idle time but people will have to wait longer.

The management of services is indeed complicated. Although management would like to satisfy the customer ("the customer is always right"), it is very expensive, sometimes even impossible, to satisfy everyone immediately, all the time. Therefore, management is interested in finding the *appropriate level of service*. The theory applied to this problem is called *queuing* (or *waiting line*) theory.

Pioneered by A. K. Erlang, a Danish engineer in the telephone industry in the early 1920s, queuing theory was extended in application, especially after World War II, to a large number of situations; for example:

- Determining access to telecommunications networks.
- Determining the capacity of an emergency room in a hospital.
- Determining the number of runways at an airport.
- Determining the number of elevators in a building.
- Determining the number of traffic lights and their frequency of operation.
- Determining the number of flights between two cities.
- Determining the number of first-class seats in an airplane.
- Determining the size of a restaurant.
- Determining the number of employees in a storeroom, in a typing pool, or in a nursing team.
- Scheduling work in large computer systems.

The Structure of a Queuing System

A queuing system (Figure 14.1) is composed of the following parts:

The Customers and Their Source (Section 14.4)
Customers are defined as those in need of service. Customers can be people, airplanes, machines, or raw materials. The customers are generated from a **population (calling population)** or a **source.** For example, a hospital's "population" would be the residents in the surrounding community and the "customers" would be those sick people in the population requiring hospitalization.

The Arrival Process (Section 14.4)
The manner in which customers show up at the service facility is called the arrival process.

FIGURE 14.1

The major components of a queuing system

The Service Facility and the Service Process (Section 14.5)

The service facility | The service is provided by a **service facility** (or facilities). This may be a person (a bank teller, a barber), a machine (elevator, gasoline pump), or a space (airport runway, parking lot, hospital bed), to mention just a few. A service facility may include one person or several people operating as a team.

The Queue (Section 14.6)

The queue | Whenever an arriving customer finds that the service facility is busy, a *queue*, or waiting line, is formed.

Examples of Queuing Systems

The following table lists some examples of queuing systems:

System	Queue	Service
Computer	Jobs	Process facilities
Bank	People	Tellers
Telephone	Callers	Switchboards
Library	Books to be shelved	Librarian's assistants
Freeway	Automobiles	Tollbooths
Airplane	People	Seats, flights
Airport	Circling planes	Runways

14.2 The Managerial Problem

The basic queuing problem: What level of service? | Looking at Willie Davis's situation, it is now possible to understand the managerial problem of waiting lines. As a responsible manager, Willie realizes that he must satisfy his customers. On the other hand, there is a cost attached to the provision of this service. In general, the basic problem of the management of waiting lines is: What is an "appropriate" level of service? In addition to this basic decision, management will have to make several related decisions regarding such factors as the priorities of service and the operating hours. These decisions will not be discussed in this text. The interested reader is referred to the end-of-chapter bibliography.

Decision variables | Decisions about an appropriate level of service are:

a. If only one service station exists, then the decision involves the *speed* of service, which can be increased by adding more personnel and/or equipment or using *faster* personnel or equipment.

b. If additional service stations can be added, then the decision is: How many more is best?

Cost Considerations

In making such decisions, the objective would be to minimize total cost. Management must consider both the cost of providing the service and the cost of customers' waiting

Opposing costs

(lost time, loss of goodwill, lost sales, and so on). Unfortunately, these costs are in direct opposition to each other, as shown in Figure 14.2. That is, the cost of providing the service increases with the service level, while the waiting time (and its cost) declines with the service level. Unfortunately, the cost of waiting, in many cases, cannot be expressed in terms of dollars. This issue is discussed later. (Note: Observe the resemblance of Figure 14.2 to the one associated with the EOQ model, although here, the minimum cost may *not* be at the intersection of the two curves.)

The Costs Involved in a Queuing Situation

The Facility Cost
The cost of providing a service includes:

1. Cost of construction (capital investment) as expressed by interest and amortization.
2. Cost of operation: labor, energy, and materials required for operations.
3. Cost of maintenance and repair.
4. Other costs: insurance, taxes, rental of space, and other fixed costs.

The Cost of Waiting Customers
In some cases, it is easy to assess the waiting cost. For example, when employees are waiting in line to use a copying machine or get tools, the cost, at minimum, is their

FIGURE 14.2

The queuing system

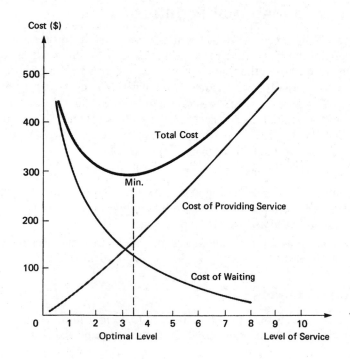

wasted wages. In addition, there is their lost contribution to profit. This is the typical situation when the customers belong to the same organization providing the service.

In other situations, such as retail sales, external customer "ill will" may be involved. Then the cost of waiting time is more difficult to assess and involves several components. For example, a waiting customer may get impatient and leave, thus resulting in a loss of revenue and possible loss of repeat business due to his or her dissatisfaction. There may also be an ill-will cost incurred; that is, when talk is spread about the poor service given at a facility, other customers may not come. A more extreme situation would be that of a patient waiting for surgery. If the patient waits too long, he or she may die. In addition to the loss of revenue to the hospital and the cost of ill will, there is an additional cost to the customer; in this case, the loss of his or her life.

The difficulties in expressing the cost of waiting are especially severe in cases where the customers are *external* to the organization providing the service and the provider of the service is a *nonprofit* organization. In such a case, one may raise such questions as: "Cost to whom (e.g., to the patient, to the doctor, or to society)?" Or, "Is the cost directly proportional to the waiting time?" The answers to such questions are not simple, because they involve personal values, social priorities, and other qualitative factors. For this reason, decisions concerning queuing systems are often made from one of the two perspectives described below.

Margin note: Ill-will costs

Margin note: Internal versus external customers

Management Objectives

Management may hold either or both of the following objectives when making decisions about an appropriate service level.

Cost Minimization
In cases where it is possible to ascribe a cost to the waiting time (usually when a company is serving its own employees or equipment), management will provide a service level such that the total cost of waiting *and* service is minimized. This approach is demonstrated in Section 14.9.

Achieving a Specified Performance Level (Service Goal)
Instead of (sometimes in addition to) minimizing costs, management will strive to achieve a certain level of service. For example:

- Telephone companies want to repair 99 percent of all inoperative telephones within 24 hours.
- Fast-food restaurants advertise that you will not have to wait more than three minutes for breakfast.
- Banks try to avoid having more than six cars in any lane of their drive-in windows at a time.
- Service facilities should be in use at least 60 percent of the time.

Margin note: Service goals

Determining the desired level of service is a matter of organizational policy and is influenced by external factors such as competition and consumer pressures.

Management Science in Practice

Evaluating Dispatch Policies for New York City's Police

The New York City Police Department (NYPD) initiated a study in 1986 into the advantages of alternative patrol car dispatching policies. NYPD is the largest police department in the United States, with a budget of $1.3 billion and a force of 28,000 personnel. In 1985, it responded to over 3.6 million emergency calls for service (CFS).

At the time, patrol cars were dispatched on a precinct basis, responding only to CFS within their precinct. To improve productivity and response to calls, this study investigated the alternative of responding to calls on a zonewide basis instead, where a zone includes two to four contiguous precincts.

Two countervailing factors complicated the analysis. Because patrol cars from any precinct in the zone could now respond to a CFS, there should be a car available more often. On the other hand, the available car would probably be further away, thus taking longer to reach the CFS. Moreover, NYPD did not want to make a change in policy that would primarily result in more cross-zone travel without a significant improvement in response time to CFS.

The problem was modeled as a queuing situation with the CFS waiting for service from the patrol cars. In addition to the concerns noted above, NYPD was also interested in the possible change in the "distribution" of service from a change in the policy. Specifically, would outlying areas now experience unacceptable delays in response time, at the benefit of more centrally located areas?

A public domain queuing/patrol car allocation computer program called the hypercube model was used to address the problem. This model requires a number of inputs to operate: the geographic distances between subareas of the precincts (called *atoms*), the distribution of CFS across the atoms, the typical "beat" of each patrol car, the dispatch rule being modeled, the busy fraction (or actual patrol time) of each patrol car, and so on. A number of dispatch rules were actually evaluated; for example, closest car within the precinct, closest available car within the zone, first free car within the precinct,

and other such policies. Also, busy fractions of 27, 41, 56, 70, and 84 percent were evaluated.

The findings of the study were that travel times would not significantly increase by switching to a zone-based dispatching policy. And in some zones, it actually decreased because of the nearness of neighboring-precinct cars. This did, however, tend to heavily increase the utilization of patrol cars whose beat was near precinct borders. Although citizens living near such borders enjoyed faster response to their CFS, citizens not living near such borders did not experience any degradation in service because the decrease in cross-beat responses left more centrally located cars available to respond.

In general, at low levels of patrol car utilization, local cars will always be available for response, so a zone-based response policy has little effect. At very high levels of utilization, cars will be spending most of their time on cross-beat responses and travel times will increase dramatically (about 60 percent at 84 percent utilization), so the zone-based policy is detrimental. But at moderate utilization levels—around 50 percent, which is a fairly realistic level of practice—the zone-based policy benefits are significant. New York City's Office of Management and Budget has used the results of this study in their ongoing assessment of city policies and practices.

Source: R. C. Larson and T. F. Rich, "Travel-Time Analysis of New York City Police Patrol Cars," *Interfaces,* March–April 1987, pp. 15–20.

Questions:

1. Would an available car in another precinct take a longer or shorter time to reach a CFS?
2. Interpret the dispatch rules mentioned.
3. Is travel time the same as response time?
4. Why did utilization of border cars increase?
5. Why is the zonal policy detrimental at high utilization? Detrimental to whom?

14.3 The Methodology of Queuing Analysis

The queuing methodology is basically a *descriptive* tool of analysis. As such, it is similar to a Markov analysis. As the reader may recall, the major objective of the Markov analysis was *prediction* of a system's behavior. Here, too, the major objective of waiting line theory is *prediction* of the behavior of a system as reflected in its *operating characteristics* or *measures of performance*. This information is needed by management to determine the most appropriate service level to the system. Although queuing theory is basically descriptive, it can also be used at times to determine the optimal number of service facilities or the optimal speed of a facility. Such normative applications are, however, limited.

The managerial application of waiting line theory involves the use of computed measures of performance for selecting an alternative solution to a queuing problem, usually among small numbers of alternatives. The entire process involves three steps, as follows.

a. Establish the Measures of Performance of the System

In this step, a model of the problem is constructed and the *measures of performance* are decided on. Examples of such measures are:

- The average waiting time per customer.
- The average number of customers in the waiting line.
- The utilization of the service facility, or else its idle time.

b. Compute the Measures of Performance

Once the problem has been formulated, one of two solution methods is employed to find the measures of performance:

1. For problems in which certain theoretical statistical distributions can describe the actual data, formulas (Section 14.8) or equivalent tables (Section 14.13) can be used.
2. For other problems, simulation (see Chapter 15) is used.

The measures of performance are computed for every course of action under consideration, compared with each other, and a decision is then made.

c. The Analysis

In queuing analysis, there are usually only a small number of alternatives to be evaluated. For example, in a decision about the number of elevators to be constructed in a new building, 10 possibilities would be a realistic consideration, but not 5,000. The number of feasible alternatives in a service system is usually small because of human, technical, financial, and legal constraints. Alternatives may differ in the size of the facility, the number of servers, the speed of service, the priorities given to customers, or in the operating procedures. For each alternative, the measures of effectiveness must be computed.

Comparing the alternatives

The alternative solutions are then compared on the basis of their overall effectiveness. One approach is the use of a total cost curve, as shown in Figure 14.2. The major problem in this step may be the cost assessment. A queuing system usually involves several measures of performance, and it is necessary to establish a common denominator (such as total cost or total utility) to quantitatively compare the alternatives. In some cases, a qualitative comparison of the alternatives is performed and no attempt is made to perform a cost analysis.

In a limited number of cases, the comparative analysis leads to an optimal solution—for example, a decision regarding the choice of the proper number of identical service facilities (see Example 2 in Section 14.13). In such cases, an explicit dollar value for the cost of waiting must be specified.

Most frequently, the analysis involves the assessment of performance levels under different system configurations. For example, if waiting time per customer is important, it is useful to know, for each alternative configuration, how long customers must wait.

But before conducting such an analysis, let us examine the structure of a queuing system. As the reader may recall, a queuing system is composed of arrivals (Section 14.4), a service facility (Section 14.5), and a waiting line (Section 14.6).

14.4 The Arrival Process

Description of Arrivals

Arriving customers are classified according to the following:

Source: Finite versus Infinite

Finite or infinite

Two cases are of primary interest: when the source (population) is basically *infinite* (or unlimited), such as the number of people visiting Niagara Falls, or when it is *finite,* as when a repair crew in a factory is responsible for maintaining a dozen machines. Unless otherwise specified, *queuing theory assumes an infinite population.* (*Note:* No population is really infinite. What is meant is that the population is *large enough* that the probability of one arrival is not significantly changed by the previous arrivals.)

Individual or group

Batch versus Individual Arrivals

Customers may arrive in *batches* (such as the arrival of a family at a restaurant) or *individually* (such as the arrival of an airplane at an airport). In this text, *individual arrivals are assumed* in all cases.

Appointment or walk-in

Scheduled versus Nonscheduled Arrivals

Customers arrive at a service facility either on a scheduled basis (by appointment) or without prior notification. If they come without prior notification, their arrival time is not exactly known, but historical data enables us to describe arrivals by some *frequency distribution.*

Quantitative Measures of Arrivals

Scheduled or unexpected arrivals?

In *scheduled* arrivals, the arrival rate is relatively predetermined, whereas in *unscheduled* arrivals, the times are **random** variables and we must therefore talk about *averages* and *frequency distributions* of the times. In both cases, the arrival process can be described by either the average **arrival rate** (the average number of arrivals per unit of time) or by the average **interarrival time** (the reciprocal of the average arrival rate).

Arrival rate and interarrival time

The Arrival Rate and the Interarrival Times (Unscheduled Arrivals)

The arrival process can be described by either the *mean arrival rate* or by the *mean interarrival time*. As an example, consider the situation at a toolroom (an area for storage and dispersal of tools) between 7 and 8 A.M. Figure 14.3 shows that seven employees arrived during the hour. Therefore, the *arrival rate* is seven per hour. The times between two consecutive arrivals vary. For example, there are eight minutes between the first arrival and the second, but there are two minutes between the second and third arrivals. These times between arrivals are called the *interarrival times*. The *average* (or *mean*) interarrival time during the first hour is $\frac{60}{7} = 8.6$ minutes $= \frac{1}{7}$ of an hour. Let us examine these times through examples.

The Average Arrival Rate (Unscheduled Arrivals), λ

Assume that the arrival times of employees to the toolroom were recorded over a period of 100 hours. Of these 100 hours, there were 5 hours within which there were 0 arrivals (5 percent of all cases), 6 hours where there was only 1 arrival, and so on. Such results can be described in the form of a frequency distribution, or *histogram,* as shown in Figure 14.4. The shape of Figure 14.4 is very similar to the theoretical **Pois-**

Poisson arrivals

FIGURE 14.3

Arrivals at the toolroom

FIGURE 14.4

The frequency distribution of arrivals

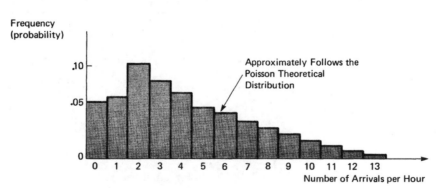

son distribution (see Appendix B). Such a distribution is very common in queuing systems.

When customers, in a given period of time, arrive *at random,* the distribution of arrivals has been shown to follow the *Poisson* distribution. Random arrival means that even if the mean number of arrivals in a time period is known, the exact moment of arrival cannot be predicted. Thus, each moment in the time span has the same chance of having an arrival. Such behavior is observed when arrivals are independent of each other; namely, when the arrival time is unaffected by preceding or future arrivals. Examples of such arrivals are customers to gasoline stations and failures of machines. The *average* arrival rate is usually designated by the Greek letter "lambda," λ.

The Average Interarrival Time (Unscheduled Arrivals), $1/\lambda$

As an alternative to the arrival rate, the interarrival time can also be used. After many observations of a certain service system, it may be possible to say that in 15 percent of the cases the time between two consecutive arrivals was 5 minutes, in 12 percent of the cases it was 7 minutes, in 10 percent of the cases it was 17 minutes, and so on. This information is recorded by the dots in Figure 14.5.

Exponential
interarrival times

If the arrival rate of Figure 14.4 follows the Poisson distribution, then the interarrival times of Figure 14.5 are distributed according to the **negative exponential** distribution (see Appendix B). The average interarrival time is designated by $1/\lambda$; for example, if $\lambda = 5$ per hour, then average interarrival time will be $\frac{1}{5}$ of an hour, or 12 minutes. (*Note:* Notice that in Figure 14.5, the distribution is described by a curve "connecting" the points. Such a distribution is a continuous distribution. The distribution of Figure 14.4, on the other hand, is composed of intervals and is called a discrete distribution.)

FIGURE 14.5
The interarrival times

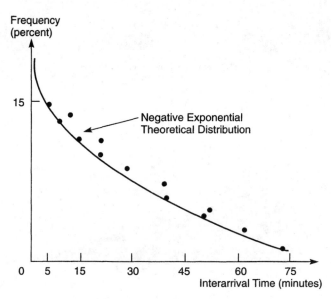

14.5 The Service Process

The Basic Arrangements of Service Facilities:

How to provide service

There are several possible ways of providing service:

1. Single facility (such as a dentist's chair).
2. Multiple, **parallel,** *identical* facilities **(multifacility),** either with a single queue (as in the post office) or with multiple queues (as in a gasoline station).
3. Multiple, parallel, but *not identical* facilities (such as express and regular checkout counters in a supermarket).
4. Service facilities that are arranged in a series (**serial** arrangement). The customer enters the first facility and gets a portion of the service, then moves on to the second facility, and so on, as though he or she is in an assembly line. An example of such an arrangement is a restaurant where you may wait first for a table, then for the food, and finally at the cashier.
5. Combinations of the above.

Figure 14.6 illustrates some of these possible service arrangements. The arrows into the boxes represent arriving and waiting customers, the boxes represent the service facilities, and the arrows out represent served customers. Some definitions follow.

A Server
The service is rendered by a server, which can be a person, group, machine, or a person-machine combination. There is a server in each facility.

A Channel
Another name used for a service facility is a channel. Thus, a system such as *b* in Figure 14.6 is called a multichannel system.

Description of the Service Time

Constant versus fluctuating service

The service given in a facility consumes time. The length of time of the service may be *constant* (e.g., exactly 10 minutes for each service), or it may *fluctuate*. A fluctuating service time may be described by a frequency distribution.

There are two ways of describing fluctuating service times. One is to describe the *average length of the service* (e.g., 15 minutes, on the average); the other is the average **service rate,** or how many customers can be served, on the average, each hour (e.g., four per hour).

The Average Length of Service (Service Time), $1/\mu$

Exponential service time

A fluctuating service time may follow one of several statistical distributions. Most common is the *negative exponential* (as in Figure 15.5). For example, the length of telephone calls is distributed in this fashion. A less common distribution is the *normal*

FIGURE 14.6

Different arrangements of service facilities

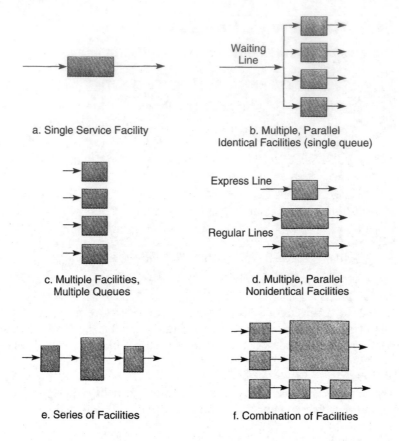

a. Single Service Facility

b. Multiple, Parallel Identical Facilities (single queue)

c. Multiple Facilities, Multiple Queues

d. Multiple, Parallel Nonidentical Facilities

e. Series of Facilities

f. Combination of Facilities

distribution (Appendix B), such as might be used in describing the time required for repairing a car. The average service time is usually designated by $1/\mu$. (*Note:* Service times may, in actuality, be affected by the length of the waiting line. If the line is long, the servers may work faster because of psychological and social pressures. In this text, the length of the line is assumed *not* to affect the service rate.)

The Average Service Rate, μ

Inverse relationship

The service rate measures the service capacity of the facility in terms of customers per unit of time. The mean service rate, μ, is the *inverse* of the mean service time. For example, if the average service time is one-half of an hour, then the mean service rate is $1 \div \frac{1}{2} = 2$ customers per hour. Note that the service rate *inherently* assumes the facility is busy. That is, it is *not* the average number of customers served over some period of time. If the service time is exponentially distributed, then the service rate can be shown to be Poisson distributed. Other service time distributions also exist, such as constant, Erlang, and "arbitrary" (which means that the mean service time and its standard deviation are known). For further discussion, see Cooper [3].

14.6 The Waiting Line

The queue discipline

A queue is formed whenever customers arrive and the facility is busy. The characteristics of the queue depend on rules and regulations that are termed the **queue discipline.**

Queue Discipline

The queue discipline describes the policies that determine the manner in which customers are selected for service. Examples of some common disciplines are:

Some priority systems

A Priority System

Priority is given to selected customers. For example, those with 10 items or less in a supermarket can go to the express lane. The handicapped and passengers with small children board airplanes first.

Emergency (Preemptive Priority) Systems

An emergency (**preemptive priority**) system is one in which an important customer not only has priority in entrance, but can even interrupt a less important customer in the middle of his or her service. For example, in an emergency case in a hospital, the doctor may leave the regular patient in the middle of the treatment. That is, the regular patient is *preempted* by the emergency one.

Last-Come, First-Served (LCFS)

In LCFS, last arrivals are served first. This system is commonly used with parts and materials in a warehouse, because it reduces handling and transportation.

First-Come, First-Served (FCFS)

In **FCFS,** customers that arrive first are served first. In this text, the FCFS queue discipline is assumed.

Queue Length

In some cases there are limits on the length of the queue; in these cases we talk about a *finite* queue length. Normally we assume no such limitations.

The Organization of the Queue

Queues may be organized in various ways. For example, customers may be screened at a main gate and then referred to one of several lines (such as in some theaters or banks), depending on the service and the queue discipline. In other cases, there is one line for several parallel service facilities. This is the organization generally assumed here.

The Behavior in a Queue

Some interesting observations of human behavior in queues are:

1. **Balking**—Customers refusing to join the queue, usually because of its length.
2. **Reneging**—Customers tiring and leaving the queue before they are served.

Human behavior

3. **Jockeying**—Customers switching between waiting lines (a common scene in a supermarket).

4. **Combining or dividing**—Combining or dividing queues at certain queue lengths (e.g., in a supermarket when a counter is closed or opened).

5. **Cycling**—Returning to the queue immediately after obtaining service. (Children taking turns at a playground or ore cars cycling at a mine.)

In this text, we assume that a customer enters the system, stays in the line (if necessary), receives the service, and leaves. If a customer behaves otherwise (according to any of the above observations), the queuing system becomes very complex, requiring simulation for its analysis.

14.7 Queuing Models and Solution Approaches

Queuing Models

Due to the large number of possible queuing systems, a notation set was developed by D. G. Kendall in 1953. This notation system is commonly used today to label queuing models. Six items of information are necessary to completely define a queuing system. The arrival process, service process, and number of servers in the system are first defined. The way in which arriving units are accepted for service (the queue discipline), the maximum size permitted for the queue, and the number of people (or units) in the population served by the queuing system are then specified. The symbols are shown below. These are also used in many computer packages.

Item	*Value*	*Notation Used*
Arrival process	Poisson	*M*
	Erlang, shape parameter-*k*	*Ek*
	Constant	*D*
	Normal	*N*
	Uniform	*U*
	Only mean and variance known	*G*
Service process	Exponential	*M*
	Erlang, shape parameter-*k*	*Ek*
	Constant	*D*
	Normal	*N*
	Uniform	*U*
	Only mean and variance known	*G*
Number of servers	One or more	*K* (actual number)
Queue discipline	First-come, first-served	*FCFS*
	Nonpreemptive priority	*PRI.*
Maximum queue length	No limit	∞
	Finite limit	*n* (actual number)
Calling population size	Infinite	∞
	Finite	*n* (actual size)

When a system is described, its symbols are summarized using a simple two-part system based on Kendall's notation. The items are shown in two sets of three items, separated by slashes. For example, a system with a Poisson arrival process; exponential service time distribution; two servers; first-come, first-served discipline; no queue size limit; and serving a large (presumed infinite) population would be labeled *M/M/* 2 *FCFS/* ∞/∞. The most common queuing systems are listed below.

Descriptive Label		*Comments*
M/M/ 1	*FCFS/* ∞/∞	Standard single server model
M/M/K	*FCFS/* ∞/∞	Standard multiserver model
M/Ek/ 1	*FCFS/* ∞/∞	Single Erlang service model
M/G/ 1	*FCFS/* ∞/∞	Service time distribution unknown
M/M/ 1	*PRI./* ∞/∞	Priority service
M/M/K	*PRI./* ∞/∞	Multiserver priority service
M/M/ 1	*FCFS/n/* ∞	Finite queue, single server
M/M/K	*FCFS/n/* ∞	Finite queue, multiserver
M/M/ 1	*FCFS/* ∞/n	Limited source, single server
M/M/K	*FCFS/* ∞/n	Limited source, multiserver

There are many variations of queuing situations; for example, truncated queues, queues with priorities, cyclic queues, and others that will not be treated here. See Cooper [3] for more discussion.

Solution Approaches

Simulation versus analytical approach

There are two basic approaches to the solution of queuing problems: analytical and simulation.

The Analytic Approach

The measures of performance are determined through the use of formulas. Unfortunately, many queuing situations are so complex that the analytic approach is completely impractical or even impossible.

Simulation

For those situations in which the analytic approach is unsuitable, the procedure of simulation can be used. The process of solving queues by simulation will be deferred to Chapter 15, where the necessary theory is first presented.

In either of the above cases, computers are now the most practical approach to solving complex queuing problems. This will be discussed further in Section 14.16.

Deterministic Queuing Systems

The simplest of all waiting line situations involves constant arrival rates at predetermined times and constant service times. Three cases can be distinguished:

1. *Arrival rate equals service rate.* Assume that people arrive every 10 minutes, to a single server, where the service takes exactly 10 minutes. Then the server

will be utilized continuously (100 percent utilization) and there will be no waiting line.

2. *Arrival rate larger than service rate.* Assume that there are six arrivals per hour (one every 10 minutes) and the service rate is only five per hour (12 minutes each). Therefore, one arrival cannot be served each hour, and a waiting line will build up (at a rate of one per hour). Such a waiting line will grow and grow as time passes and is termed an **explosive queue.**

3. *Arrival rate smaller than service rate.* Assume that there are six arrivals per hour and the service capacity is eight per hour. In this case, the facility will be utilized only $\frac{6}{8} = 75$ percent of the time. There will never be a waiting line (if the arrivals come at equally scheduled intervals).

Note that in the first case, there is no waiting line and no idle facility. In the second case, the facility is fully utilized but a waiting line is formed. In the third case, there is no waiting line but the facility is not fully utilized. *In all these cases, there cannot be a waiting line and underutilization in the same situation.* However, when nonscheduled arrivals are involved, it is common to have *both* idle facilities at times and waiting lines at other times in the same service system, as will be shown later.

14.8 The Basic Poisson-Exponential Model (*M*/*M*/1 *FCFS*/∞/∞)

The classical and probably best known of all waiting line models is the **Poisson-exponential single-server system.**

Poisson-Exponential Model Characteristics:

Arrival Rate
The arrival rate is assumed to be random and is thus described by the *Poisson* distribution. The *average* arrival rate is designated by the Greek letter "lambda," λ.

Service Time
The service time is assumed to follow the *negative exponential distribution*. The *average* service rate is designated by the Greek letter "mu," μ, and the *average* service time by $1/\mu$.

The *major assumptions* for the operation of such a single server system are:

1. Infinite source of population.
2. First-come, first-served treatment.
3. The ratio λ/μ is smaller than 1. This ratio is designated by the Greek letter "rho," ρ. The **ratio** is a measure of the **utilization** of the system. If the utilization factor is equal to or larger than 1, the waiting line will increase

Some assumptions

without bound (will be *explosive*), a situation that is unacceptable to management. Note that this is true even when $\rho = 1$ because of the *variability* of the arrivals. Remember, this is *not* the deterministic case where people arrive on schedule. Here they are *not* on time—sometimes early (but then they have to wait if someone else is being served) and sometimes late (during which the server is idle)—and λ is only the *average* arrival rate.

4. Steady state (equilibrium) exists. A system is in a "transient state" when its measures of performance are still dependent on the initial conditions. Our interest is in the "long-run" behavior of the system, commonly known as *steady state*. A steady state condition occurs when the system measures become *independent of time*.

5. Unlimited space for the waiting line exists.

Measurements of Performance (Operating Characteristics)

A queuing system is usually evaluated by one or more of the following measures of performance (given with their respective formulas). These measures depend on only two given variables, λ and μ, which must be stated in the same time dimensions.

The Average Waiting Time, *W*
The average time a customer spends in the system—waiting for the service *and* being served—is:

$$W = \frac{1}{\mu - \lambda} \tag{14.1}$$

The Average Waiting Time in the Queue, W_q
This is the average time a customer will wait, in the queue, before the service starts:

$$W_q = \frac{\lambda}{\mu(\mu - \lambda)} \tag{14.2}$$

The Average Number of Customers in the System, *L*
The average number of customers in the system; that is, counting those in the queue and those being served, is:

$$L = \frac{\lambda}{\mu - \lambda} \tag{14.3}$$

The Average Number of Customers in the Queue, L_q

The average number of customers in the queue measures the average length of the waiting line:

$$L_q = \frac{\lambda^2}{\mu(\mu - \lambda)} \tag{14.4}$$

The Probability of an Empty Facility, $P(0)$

The probability that there are no customers in the system (that the facility is idle) is:

$$P(0) = 1 - \frac{\lambda}{\mu} \tag{14.5}$$

The Probability of the System Being Busy, P_w

The probability of the system being busy, P_w, is the same as the probability of *not* finding an empty system; that is:

$$P_w = 1 - P(0) = \frac{\lambda}{\mu} \tag{14.6}$$

The Probability of Being in the System (Waiting and Being Served) Longer than Time t

The probability is:

$$P\{T > t\} = e^{-(\mu - \lambda)t} \tag{14.7}$$

where:

$$e = 2.718 \text{ (the base of the natural logarithms)}$$

$$t = \text{Specified time and}$$

$$T = \text{Time in the system}$$

Note: $P\{T \leq t\} = 1 - P\{T > t\}$

The probability of waiting (before service starts) a period of time T', which is *larger* than a designated time t', is:

$$P\{T' > t'\} = \rho e^{-(\mu - \lambda)t'} \tag{14.8}$$

The Probability of Finding Exactly N Customers in the System, $P(N)$

$$P(N) = \rho^N(1 - \rho) \tag{14.9}$$

The Probability that the Number of Customers in the System, N, Will Be Larger than a Specified Number of Customers, n.

$$P\{N > n\} = \rho^{n+1} \tag{14.10}$$

This measure is used to determine the *balking rate* (available in most computer programs). The assumption here is that if you can accommodate, say, only six people in the line and in service, then when customers arrive and see that there is no more room to wait (in systems with a limited waiting area), they will leave. Thus, the probability of finding more than six people in the system will be the balking rate (probability of not staying). When people balk, the characteristics of the system change and must be recomputed based on modified data.

Note that:

$$P\{N < n\} = 1 - P\{N > (n - 1)\} \tag{14.11}$$

For example:

$P\{N < 3\}$ means $N = 0$, 1, or 2 and $P\{N > 2\}$ means $n = 3, 4, \ldots$

Thus:

$$P\{N < 3\} = 1 - P\{N > 2\}$$

The following relationships, developed by J. D. C. Little, are extremely important because they hold for *any* queuing system and enable us to find L, L_q, W, and W_q as soon as one of these is computed.

$$
\begin{aligned}
L &= \lambda W \\
L_q &= \lambda W_q \\
W &= W_q + \frac{1}{\mu}
\end{aligned}
\tag{14.12}
$$

Managerial Use of the Measures of Performance

The measures of performance can be used in a cost analysis, as shown in the next section. Others are used to aid in determining service level policies. For example:

a. A fast-food restaurant wants to design its service facility so that a customer will not wait, on the average, more than two minutes (i.e., $W_q \leq 2$ minutes) before being served.

Example service policies

b. A telephone company desires that the probability of any customer being without telephone service more than two days be 3 percent (i.e., $P\{T > 2 \text{ days}\} = .03$).

  c. A bank's policy is that the number of customers at its drive-in facility will exceed 10 only 5 percent of the time (i.e., $P\{N > 10\} = .05$).

  d. A city information service should be busy at least 60 percent of the day (i.e., $P_w \geq .6$).

The use of the various measures of performance is further demonstrated in the examples throughout this chapter, in the problems at the end of the chapter, and in Section 14.10.

Information Flow in Waiting Line Models

As discussed earlier, it is helpful to use some measures of performance when evaluating service alternatives, particularly when a cost approach (Section 14.9) is planned. Therefore, a *solution* to a queuing problem means computing certain measures of performance. These measures are computed from three input variables:

$$\lambda, \text{ the mean arrival rate}$$

$$\mu, \text{ the mean service rate}$$

$$K, \text{ the number of servers}$$

Figure 14.7 summarizes the relationship between the input variables and the major measures of performance for most queuing models. For other models there may be additional input and/or output variables.

FIGURE 14.7

Information flows

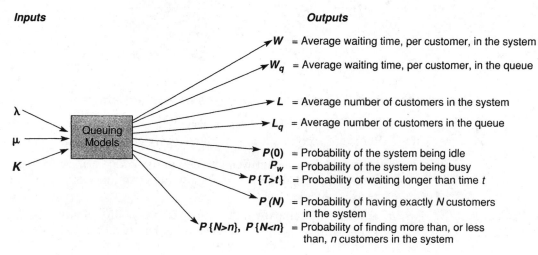

W	= Average waiting time, per customer, in the system
W_q	= Average waiting time, per customer, in the queue
L	= Average number of customers in the system
L_q	= Average number of customers in the queue
$P(0)$	= Probability of the system being idle
P_w	= Probability of the system being busy
$P\{T>t\}$	= Probability of waiting longer than time t
$P(N)$	= Probability of having exactly N customers in the system
$P\{N>n\}, P\{N<n\}$	= Probability of finding more than, or less than, n customers in the system

Solved Problem 14.1

The All American Aviation Company toolroom is staffed by one clerk who can serve 12 production employees, on the average, each hour. The production employees arrive at the toolroom every six minutes, on the average. Find the measures of performance expressed in Equations 14.1–14.12.

Solution

It is necessary first to change the time dimensions of λ and μ to a common denominator: λ is now given in minutes, μ in hours. We will use hours as the common denominator.

The problem states that $\mu = 12$ per hour. For λ, the arrival of one customer every six minutes means one customer every $\frac{1}{10}$ of an hour. Therefore, the arrival rate, λ, is 10 customers per hour.

Thus, in the following formulas we shall use: $\lambda = 10$, $\mu = 12$.

1. Toolroom utilization:

$$\rho - \lambda/\mu - 10/12 - .833$$

2. Average waiting time in the system (toolroom):

$$W = \frac{1}{\mu - \lambda} = \frac{1}{12 - 10} = .5 \text{ hours, per employee}$$

3. The average waiting time in the line:

$$W_q = \frac{\lambda}{\mu(\mu - \lambda)} = \frac{10}{12(12 - 10)} = .417 \text{ hours, per employee}$$

4. The average number of employees in the toolroom area:

$$L = \frac{\rho}{1 - \rho} = \frac{.833}{.167} = 5 \text{ employees}$$

5. The average number of employees in the line:

$$L_q = \frac{\rho^2}{1 - \rho} = \frac{(.833)^2}{.167} = 4.17 \text{ employees}$$

6. The probability that the toolroom clerk will be idle:

$$P(0) = 1 - \rho = 1 - .833 = .167$$

7. The probability of finding the system busy:

$$P_w = \rho = .833$$

8. The chance of waiting longer than 30 minutes in the system. That is, $t = \frac{1}{2}$:

$$P\{T > t\} = e^{-(12-10)1/2} = \frac{1}{e} = .368$$

9. The probability of finding four employees in the system, $N = 4$:

$$P(4) = \rho^4(1 - \rho) = (.833)^4(1 - .833) = .0804$$

10. The probability of finding more than three employees in the system:

$$P\{N > 3\} = \rho^{3+1} = (.833)^4 = .482$$

In the following example, it will be shown how to use such measures of performance in a comparative analysis.

14.9 Cost Analysis of Queuing Systems

In certain situations, it is possible to express the waiting costs in terms of dollars and cents. Queuing systems can then be compared on the basis of their total cost (TC), which is composed of two components: the facility cost (C_F) and the total cost of waiting customers (C_W).

$$TC = C_F + C_W \qquad (14.13)$$

Costs are computed on one of two bases: either as "cost per unit of time (hourly, daily)," or as "cost per customer served." In this text, the cost-per-unit-of-time basis is used.

Computing the Cost of Waiting

Two different cost components can be distinguished. First, the cost of the total wait (W), including the time of service, may be of relevance; for example, in industrial settings, where employees are being paid for the time they are away from their work while waiting for tools or other services. In the second case, typical of retail situations, only the time *while waiting in the queue* (W_q) is relevant, because consumers harbor virtually no ill will while being served in a normal fashion. Here we will assume that the waiting cost (regardless if it is linked to W or W_q) is *proportional* to the waiting time; that is, if the cost of waiting for an hour is $12, then the cost of waiting two hours is $2 \times 12 = \$24$.

Cost is proportional to time

Let C be the cost of one customer waiting one unit of time. Then the *waiting cost* per unit time for the queuing system as a whole is given by:

$$C_w = W\lambda C = LC \qquad (14.14)$$

where W is the average time in the system *per customer* (use W_q if the cost is directly proportional to the time in the queue) and λ is the average arrival rate per unit of time under consideration.

The Cost of Service

The cost incurred by providing the service, C_F, is typically composed of both fixed and variable costs. The annual fixed cost (amortization, insurance, taxes) and the variable (hourly) cost must both be converted into the same time units as used in Equation 14.14 so that the cost components can be added together.

The costs of service

The cost of service can be given in any of the following ways:

a. Per hour (or other time unit) of service (e.g., $20 per hour).

b. Per customer served (e.g., $5 per customer). If four customers are served during the hour, then the hourly cost is $4 \times \$5 = \$20$.

  c. Per unit capacity of service (e.g., $2 for each customer that can be served). If the facility can serve 10 customers per hour, the hourly cost is $2 × 10 = $20.

14.10 Managerial Applications of Poisson-Exponential Queuing Systems

Solved Problem 14.2

The Comtec Corporation is considering leasing one of two possible self-service duplicating machines. The Mark I is capable of duplicating, on the average, 20 jobs each hour, at a cost of $50 per day. Alternatively, the Mark II can duplicate, on the average, 24 jobs per hour, at a cost of $80 per day. We will assume that the service rate for the duplicating jobs is random. In essence this implies that the number of copies is random. However, if exactly one (or n) copies were needed per job, then the service time would be constant. The duplicating center is open 10 hours a day with an average arrival of 18 jobs per hour. The duplication is performed by employees arriving from various departments, whose average hourly wage is $5. Should the company lease Mark I or Mark II?

Solution Based on Daily Costs (Table 14.1)

TABLE 14.1   Comparing Measures of Performance

	Mark I	Mark II
λ, given per hour	18	18
μ, given per hour	20	24
ρ, utilization $= \dfrac{\lambda}{\mu}$	$\dfrac{18}{20} = .9$	$\dfrac{18}{24} = .75$
W(Equation 14.1) hours per customer	$\dfrac{1}{20 - 18} = \dfrac{1}{2}$	$\dfrac{1}{24 - 18} = \dfrac{1}{6}$
L(Equation 14.3) customers	$\dfrac{18}{20 - 18} = 9$	$\dfrac{18}{24 - 18} = 3$
$P(0)$(Equation 14.5)	$1 - .9 = .1$	$1 - .75 = .25$

Mark I

Because each employee will spend $W = \frac{1}{2}$ hour in the duplicating center, and because 180 persons arrive at the center each day (18 per hour times 10 hours), there will be a total waiting time of $\frac{1}{2}(180) = 90$ employee-hours each day. At $5 an hour, this waiting time will cost the company $5(90) = $450 a day. The total cost is thus $450 + $50 daily machine cost = $500 per day (see Table 14.2).

TABLE 14.2   **Cost Comparison for the Duplicating Machine**

System	Cost of Service	Cost of Waiting				TC ($ per hour)	TC ($ per day)
	Facility cost, C_F	λ	W	C	$C_W = \lambda WC$		
Mark I	$50 per day = $5 per hour	18	$\frac{1}{2}$	5	$18 \times \frac{1}{2} \times 5 = 45$	$5 + 45 = 50$	500
Mark II	$80 per day = $8 per hour	18	$\frac{1}{6}$	5	$18 \times \frac{1}{6} \times 5 = 15$	$8 + 15 = 23$	230

Mark II

With $W = \frac{1}{6}$ hour per employee, there will be a total wait of $\frac{1}{6}(180) = 30$ employee-hours each day. The cost is now only $5(30) = \$150$. Add to this the $80 daily cost of renting Mark II for a total cost of $150 + $80 = 230, or $270 per day lower than the Mark I. Note that even though Mark II is only utilized 75 percent of the time, it is still the "better" machine to lease (considering costs only).

Note: In comparing Mark I and Mark II, notice that Mark II is only 20 percent faster (i.e., its service capacity is 1.2 times that of Mark I). Yet the waiting time was cut down by almost 67 percent (from one-half to one-sixth of an hour). This is one indication that a "commonsense" approach (such as double the service rate so the waiting time will be cut in half) is incorrect in queuing situations, which exhibit *nonlinear* relationships.

Solved Problem 14.3

A plant distributes its products by trucks. The average loading time is 20 minutes per truck. Trucks arrive at an average rate of two each hour. Management feels that the existing loading facility is more than adequate. However, the drivers complain that they have to wait "more than half the time." Analyze the situation and find how much money the company can save by speeding up loading if the waiting time of a truck is figured at $30 per hour and the plant is in operation eight hours each day.

Solution (Table 14.3)

Given $\lambda = 2$ and $\mu = 3$ (20 minutes service means 3 per hour). Using Equation 14.6, the chance of having to wait in line is equal to $\frac{2}{3}$, or 66.7 percent, so the drivers' complaints are legitimate. Using Equation 14.2, the average waiting time for a driver in the system is:

$$W = \frac{1}{(3 - 2)} = 1 \text{ hour}$$

Because there are $2 \times 8 = 16$ loads a day, there is a waiting time of 16 hours each day, which costs the company, at $30 an hour, a total of $480. Therefore, the company should consider justifiable alternatives that could reduce this cost.

Solved Problem 14.3 (continued)

TABLE 14.3 **Cost Comparison for the Truck Loading Problem**

System	Facility Cost, C_F ($)	λ	W	TC ($ per hour)	TC ($ per day)
Existing system	Irrelevant	2	1	60	480
Proposed (automatic)	200 per day = 25 per hour	2	.125	.125(60) + 25 = 32.50	260

Automatic Device

The reader is encouraged to examine the following situation: An automatic device that can load 10 trucks an hour is available at a cost of $200 per day over the cost of the existing facility. Should management replace the existing facility? [Solution: Yes, because W is reduced to .125 hours and the daily cost of waiting to $60. Total daily savings: $480 − (200 + 60) = $220.]

The results are summarized in Table 14.3.

14.11 Concluding Remarks

Waiting line (queuing) theory is a tool used mainly for computing measures of performance of systems providing services. This information is used by management to design service systems and to improve their operations.

How Waiting Lines Are Formed

The main reason a queue forms, even when the average service rate is *faster* than the average arrival rate, is that both are fluctuating in an unpredictable manner. As a result, there are short-term variations in both the arrival and service rates. This leads to idle capacity at some points in time (which is usually lost since it cannot be accumulated) and to periods of waiting at other times. This sporadic variation in arrival and service rates results, for example, in a bank teller being idle for a while and then swamped with customers a little later.

Loss of capacity

Verifying the Statistical Distributions

The models discussed so far, as well as some of those to be discussed in Part B of this chapter, assume Poisson arrival rates and exponential service times. The question now is how to find out if a certain arrival rate or a certain service time indeed follows these distributions.

To begin with, one must collect data. This can be done through continuous observation, through a sample observation, or through an analysis of historical (logged) data

Data are required

(e.g., arrival times to emergency rooms are usually recorded). The first step is to determine how much data to collect. This question can be answered with the aid of statistical theory. Next, one should check if λ and μ remained unchanged throughout the period of data collection (again, statistical methods are available). It is necessary that these measures be stable, otherwise the formulas cannot be applied.

Stable conditions

Once λ and μ are found to be stable, frequency distributions can be constructed. The general shape and the amount of spread around the mean of the distributions should suggest certain standard probability distributions.

A quick way to check a distribution is to compute its mean and standard deviation. In the exponential distribution, the mean and the standard deviation must be equal, and in the Poisson, the mean must equal the variance. Such a test can rule out distributions that are not Poisson or exponential. However, in order to be sure, the chi-square goodness-of-fit test should be applied. This is a measure of the goodness-of-fit of a theoretical frequency distribution to an actual distribution. It is a simple yet powerful nonparametric test particularly useful for judging how close the observed frequency distribution is to the expected frequency distribution. (For the application of such a test, see the texts listed in Appendix B.) Graphical examination of the histograms and comparison with probabilities in statistical tables can be used as an approximation.

Check mean and standard deviation

Solution Approaches

"Commonsense" solutions are least desirable in waiting line situations. For example, most managers are likely to assume that to obtain the most efficient operations, they must make the average service rate approximate the average arrival rate; that is, have a utilization close to 1.0. Such a design will ordinarily be far from efficient when arrivals and service times are subject to chance variations. "Doubling the speed will cut waiting time in half" is another commonsense fallacy. Therefore, the use of models for queuing situations is very important.

In the event that the arrival rate and the service time follow certain theoretical distributions, formulas and/or charts can be used to compute the operating characteristics of queuing systems. However, if the theoretical distributions are not close to reality, or if the system is complex, then the technique of simulation must be used.

14.12 Problems for Part A*

1. The number of customers arriving at the loan department of the Swiss National Bank was logged over a period of 100 hours. The following table indicates the number of customers that arrived during each hour:

---

*For the problems in this chapter, unless otherwise stated, assume random arrivals (Poisson) and a negative exponential service time.

Customers per Hour	Number of Times Observed
0	10
1	20
2	30
3	15
4	15
5	10
Total	100

Compute:

a. The average arrival rate per hour.

b. The average interarrival time in minutes. Graph the distribution of arrivals.

2. Given below is the distribution of repair times, as recorded for 550 repairs:

Hours per Repair	Number of Times Recorded
1	110
2	165
3	165
4	85
5	25
Total	550

Determine:

a. The average repair time in hours.

b. The average number of repairs per day (24 hours). Graph the distribution of service times.

3. A physician schedules checkup patients at the rate of one every 15 minutes. Assume that the patients arrive exactly on schedule. Assume a constant checkup rate of four patients per hour.

a. Calculate the waiting line that is likely to be generated after four hours.

b. Assume that the physician can see five patients in an hour. What will be the waiting time after four hours, and what will be the physician's rate of utilization?

c. What will happen if the physician can see only three patients an hour? How long will the line be after four hours?

4. Identify the customers and the servers in the following systems:

a. Telephone booth.

b. Airport runways.

c. Parking lot.

d. Secretarial pool.

e. Maintenance center.

f. Hospital.

g. Automobile assembly line.

h. Elevators in a building.

i. Traffic lights.

5. Vic's Vending Corporation operates vending machines in one town. The machines break down at an average rate of two per hour. An hour of downtime of a machine is considered as a loss of $13. Currently, the machines are serviced by the company maintenance crew, which is capable of repairing each machine in 24 minutes. The hourly cost of the maintenance team is $20. A maintenance contractor offered to take over the maintenance work. The contractor can repair three machines each hour, with an hourly charge of $40. Should management accept the contractor's offer?

6. A service system has an average interarrival time of two minutes and an average service rate of 60 per hour. *Find:*

a. The probability that a customer will have to wait.

b. The probability that four persons are in the system.

c. The probability of finding more than three in the system.

d. The probability of waiting more than three minutes for service.

e. The probability that fewer than four are in the system.

f. The probability of being through the system within 10 minutes.

7. A toolroom clerk at British Light Industries, Ltd., is serving a maintenance department with a large number of employees who earn £8 per hour. The clerk earns £5 per hour. The workers arrive at the toolroom at an average rate of 6.2 per hour. The average service time is eight minutes.

a. What is the probability of finding no workers at the toolroom (either waiting or being served)?

b. What is the average waiting time (before being served) per worker?

c. What is the average number of workers waiting in line (excluding the one being served)?

d. Would you recommend installing an incentive plan that will reduce the average service time to 6.4 minutes and will cost the company £2 per hour?

e. Another clerk can be hired at £5 per hour. The two clerks will operate as a single team serving one line with an average service time of four minutes. Would you recommend hiring the additional clerk? (Assume no incentives.)

f. If you had the alternative of installing the incentive plan with the existing system or hiring a second clerk, which one would you recommend?

g. Two more clerks can be hired (at £5 each per hour) to help the single clerk, reducing the average service time to two minutes. Would you recommend this over hiring only one more clerk? Why (or why not)?

8. Given an arrival rate $\lambda = 3$, find values of L_q and W_q for the following values of μ: 3.1, 3.5, 4, and 6. When does speed of service become important?

9. Given a waiting line system with:

   1. Average interarrival times of six minutes.
   2. Space necessary for accommodating a waiting customer = 5 square feet.
   3. Cost per hour of waiting time per customer = $2.

   It was also observed that the facility is idle 20 percent of the time. *Find:*

   a. The area necessary to accommodate the average waiting line.

   b. Is it profitable to invest $5 an hour in the facility if the service rate can be doubled (twice as fast)?

10. Sunny Engineering Corporation is designing a special machine for processing chickens. The chickens arrive from the farms on trucks, in cages, at a rate of 10 trucks per hour. If the chickens are kept in the cage in the waiting area more than three hours, they will start to dehydrate, lowering their quality and causing damage to the processor. Determine the minimum average processing rate (in truckloads per hour) that must be designed for the machine in order to ensure that the cages will be processed, on the average, in three hours or less. That is, waiting and processing time is three hours or less.

11. Lima Airport currently operates with one runway for landings. The average landing time is three minutes. Airplanes arrive at the airport at the rate of 17 per hour. The estimated average fuel consumption for an airplane waiting for a landing is 10 liters per minute. A liter of fuel costs 2 thousand Peruvian sol. *Find:*

    a. The average number of airplanes circling the airport in a "holding pattern," that is, waiting for permission to land. Do not include the landing plane.

    b. The average cost of fuel "burned" by an airplane waiting to land.

    c. The chance of finding less than three airplanes in the airport vicinity (in the waiting line and landing).

    d. The utilization of the runway.

12. Five cars arrive at an emissions testing station each hour. The average service time is six minutes. The station can accommodate only three cars (waiting and being served). Any car that cannot be accommodated in the station is parked in a No-Parking area on the street, where there is a 40 percent chance of being fined $10. The owner of the station pays the fines. The station is in operation 48 hours per week. Cars completed are picked up immediately by the customers.

    Find the weekly fines paid (in $).

13. The Jamaican Pelican is a one-man yogurt shop where people arrive at the average rate of 20 per hour. Big Joe, the proprietor, serves a customer, on the average, in two minutes. During the noontime rush, the arrival rate increases to one arriving customer every two minutes. *Find:*

    a. How fast must Big Joe work to ensure that a noontime customer will not wait for service, on the average, more than 10 minutes?

    b. What is the probability that six or more people are in the shop during the nonrush period?

    c. What is the average waiting time during the nonrush hours?

14. Customers arrive at a service facility one every 12 minutes, on the average. The average service time is 10 minutes. The operation of the existing system costs $5 an hour. The facility is in operation eight hours a day.

Find:

a. If the waiting (prior to service) area, which can accommodate three customers, is sufficient 70 percent of the time.

b. It is proposed to speed up the service so 10 customers can be served in an hour, at an additional cost of $240 per day. If an hour waiting time (prior to service), per customer, is worth $10, is the investment justified?

15. Customers arrive at a one-person barbershop with an average interarrival time of 20 minutes. The average time for a haircut is 12 minutes.

a. The owner wishes to have enough seats in the waiting area so that no more than 5 percent of the arriving customers will have to stand. How many seats should be provided?

b. Suppose there is only sufficient space in the waiting area for five seats. What is the probability that an arriving customer will not find a seat?

16. The industrial engineering department of First National Bank conducted a study to determine the effectiveness of its two drive-in stations. These stations operate independently of each other and each has its own waiting line. The study involved random observations of the number of cars in a line (including the one being served). The results of the first day of the study are given below:

Time	Cars in Station 1	Cars in Station 2
9:12	3	2
9:37	5	3
10:04	2	2
11:30	0	4
11:58	4	2
12:20	3	3
12:39	2	2
1:23	5	1
1:37	4	5
2:06	2	3
2:19	1	0
2:46	3	4

In addition, it was noted that line 1 served 84 customers and was open six hours, whereas line 2 served 79 customers and was open six hours and 15 minutes. Find the utilization of each line and which is better utilized.

17. The following are observations taken at South London Bank Drive-In regarding the number of cars in the waiting line (prior to service):

Time	Cars in Line
10:30	6
10:37	7
10:53	2
11:06 (0 in service)	0
12:12	1
12:44	4
1:20	3
1:40	6
1:50 (1 car in service)	0
2:06	5
2:50	2
3:00	8

The Drive-In opened at 10:30 A.M. and at 3:00 P.M. no more cars were allowed to join the line. The last car left at 3:20 P.M. *Find:*

a. The average number of cars in the system.

b. The average number of cars in the waiting line.

18. "Commonsense" tells us that $L - L_q + 1$. Moreover, $W = W_q + 1/\mu$, as further evidence. Explain why this logic is wrong.

PART B: EXTENSIONS

14.13 Multifacility Queuing Systems (*M/M/K FCFS/∞/∞*)

The multifacility (multichannel) queuing systems considered here are composed of several identical and parallel service facilities. Such a situation is depicted in Figure 14.8. Note that only one waiting line exists that feeds the multiple service facilities. Whenever a server is free, the first customer in the queue goes to that service facility. An example of such a situation is an IRS (Internal Revenue Service) office, where arrivals get a number as they arrive and then the numbers are called sequentially as the examiners become free. Another example is airplanes circling a large airport with two runways; whenever a runway becomes free, an airplane is directed to that runway.

"Take a number
please"

There are several managerial problems in a multifacility system. For example, management is concerned with determining the proper number of servers, whether to use identical or nonidentical servers (e.g., whether or not to open an express lane in the supermarket), and the organization of the waiting line (one line for all servers, one line per server). Such decisions are based on the computation of the *measures of performance*.

An express lane?

In this section, the simplest multichannel system is analyzed. In such a system, the following assumptions are made:

1. Poisson-exponential systems, as described in Part A of this chapter.
2. Identical service facilities (channels).
3. One waiting line exists.
4. The arrival rate λ is smaller than the combined service rate $(K\mu)$ of all K service facilities.

FIGURE 14.8

*The multifacility
waiting line system*

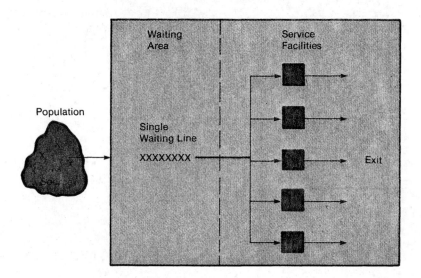

Formulas for Computing the Measures of Performance

Let:

λ = Mean arrival rate

μ = Mean service rate of *each* facility

K = Number of servers (service facilities)

ρ = Utilization factor $\dfrac{\lambda}{\mu}$ of each facility (as in the single facility system)

$\bar{\rho}$ = Utilization factor of the entire system:

$$\bar{\rho} = \frac{\rho}{K} = \frac{\lambda}{K\mu} \tag{14.15}$$

Assuming that $\lambda < K\mu$ (a necessary condition to avoid an explosive queue), then some of the most common measures of performance are:

1. The probability of finding no customers in the system (an "idle" system):

$$P(0) = \frac{1}{\dfrac{\rho^K}{K!\,(1 - \bar{\rho})} + \displaystyle\sum_{i=0}^{K-1} \frac{\rho^i}{i!}} \tag{14.16}$$

where i = index of summation.

2. The probability of finding exactly N customers in the system:

$$P(N) = \begin{cases} P(0)\dfrac{\rho^N}{N!} & \text{when } N \leq K \\[2ex] \dfrac{P(0)\bar{\rho}^N K^K}{K!} & \text{when } N > K \end{cases} \tag{14.17}$$

3. The average number of customers in the waiting line:

$$L_q = \frac{P(0)\rho^K \bar{\rho}}{K!\,(1 - \bar{\rho})^2} \tag{14.18}$$

Given L_q, this equation yields the following for $P(0)$:

$$P(0) = \frac{L_q K!\,(1 - \bar{\rho})^2}{\rho^K \bar{\rho}}$$

4. The average number of customers in the system:

$$L = L_q + \rho \tag{14.19}$$

TABLE 14.4 P(0) for the Multichannel Queue

Number of Channels, K

$\frac{\lambda}{K\mu}$	2	3	4	5	6	7	8	10	15
.02	.9608	.9418	.9231	.9048	.8869	.8694	.85214	.81873	.74082
.04	.9231	.8869	.8521	.8187	.7866	.7558	.72615	.67032	.54881
.06	.8868	.8353	.7866	.7408	.6977	.6570	.61878	.54881	.40657
.08	.8519	.7866	.7261	.6703	.6188	.5712	.52729	.44933	.30119
.10	.8182	.7407	.6703	.6065	.5488	.4966	.44933	.36788	.22313
.12	.7857	.6975	.6188	.5488	.4868	.4317	.38289	.30119	.16530
.14	.7544	.6568	.5712	.4966	.4317	.3753	.32628	.24660	.12246
.16	.7241	.6184	.5272	.4493	.3829	.3263	.27804	.20190	.09072
.18	.6949	.5821	.4866	.4065	.3396	.2837	.23693	.16530	.06721
.20	.6667	.5479	.4491	.3678	.3012	.2466	.20189	.13534	.04979
.22	.6393	.5157	.4145	.3328	.2671	.2144	.17204	.11080	.03688
.24	.6129	.4852	.3824	.3011	.2369	.1864	.14660	.09072	.02732
.26	.5873	.4564	.3528	.2723	.2101	.1620	.12492	.07247	.02024
.28	.5625	.4292	.3255	.2463	.1863	.1408	.10645	.06081	.01500
.30	.5385	.4035	.3002	.2228	.1652	.1224	.09070	.04978	.01111
.32	.5152	.3791	.2768	.2014	.1464	.1064	.07728	.04076	.00823
.34	.4925	.3561	.2551	.1812	.1298	.0925	.06584	.03337	.00610
.36	.4706	.3343	.2351	.1646	.1151	.0804	.05609	.02732	.00452
.38	.4493	.3137	.2165	.1487	.1020	.0698	.04778	.02236	.00335
.40	.4286	.2941	.1993	.1343	.0903	.0606	.04069	.01830	.00248
.42	.4085	.2756	.1834	.1213	.0800	.0527	.03465	.01498	.00184
.44	.3889	.2580	.1686	.1094	.0708	.0457	.02950	.01226	.00136
.46	.3699	.2414	.1549	.0987	.0626	.0397	.02511	.01003	.00101
.48	.3514	.2255	.1422	.0889	.0554	.0344	.02136	.00820	.00075
.50	.3333	.2105	.1304	.0801	.0496	.0298	.01816	.00671	.00055
.52	.3158	.1963	.1195	.0721	.0432	.0259	.01544	.00548	.00041
.54	.2987	.1827	.1094	.0648	.0382	.0224	.01311	.00448	.00030
.56	.2821	.1699	.0999	.0581	.0336	.0194	.01113	.00366	.00022
.58	.2658	.1576	.0912	.0521	.0296	.0167	.00943	.00298	.00017
.60	.2500	.1460	.0831	.0466	.0260	.0144	.00799	.00243	.00012
.62	.2346	.1349	.0755	.0417	.0228	.0124	.00675	.00198	.00009
.64	.2195	.1244	.0685	.0372	.0200	.0107	.00570	.00161	.00007
.66	.2048	.1143	.0619	.0330	.0175	.0092	.00480	.00131	.00005
.68	.1905	.1048	.0559	.0293	.0152	.0079	.00404	.00106	.00004
.70	.1765	.0957	.0502	.0259	.0132	.0067	.00338	.00085	.00003
.72	.1628	.0870	.0450	.0228	.0114	.0057	.00283	.00069	.00002
.74	.1494	.0788	.0401	.0200	.0099	.0048	.00235	.00055	.00001
.76	.1364	.0709	.0355	.0174	.0085	.0041	.00195	.00044	
.78	.1236	.0634	.0313	.0151	.0072	.0034	.00160	.00035	
.80	.1111	.0562	.0273	.0130	.0061	.0028	.00131	.00028	
.82	.0989	.0493	.0236	.0111	.0051	.0023	.00106	.00022	
.84	.0870	.0428	.0202	.0093	.0042	.0019	.00085	.00017	
.86	.0753	.0366	.0170	.0077	.0035	.0015	.00067	.00013	
.88	.0638	.0306	.0140	.0063	.0028	.0012	.00052	.00010	
.90	.0526	.0249	.0113	.0050	.0021	.0009	.00039	.00007	
.92	.0417	.0195	.0087	.0038	.0016	.0007	.00028	.00005	
.94	.0309	.0143	.0063	.0027	.0011	.0005	.00019	.00003	
.96	.0204	.0093	.0040	.0017	.0007	.0003	.00012	.00002	
.98	.0101	.0045	.0019	.0008	.0003	.0001	.00005	.00001	

5. The average waiting time per customer, before service:

$$W_q = \frac{L_q}{\lambda}$$

(14.20)

6. The average time a customer spends in the system (waiting and service):

$$W = \frac{L}{\lambda} = W_q + \frac{1}{\mu}$$

(14.21)

Use of a Table to Solve Multifacility Problems

In order to save computational time, a table to $P(0)$, Table 14.4, can be used. The process, illustrated in Figure 14.9, is simple: $P(0)$ is read from the table for various values of λ, μ, and K. Then L, L_q, W, or W_q can be computed.

Example

Given $\lambda = 36$ per hour, $\mu = 10$ per hour, and $K = 5$, find $P(0)$, L, L_q, W, and W_q.

Solution

Step 1. Find $\lambda/K\mu = 36/50 = 0.72$ (notice that $\lambda/K\mu = \bar{\rho}$).

Step 2. From the table, the value of $P(0)$ that corresponds to $K = 5$ is $P(0) = 0.0228$.

FIGURE 14.9

*The multifacility
solution process*

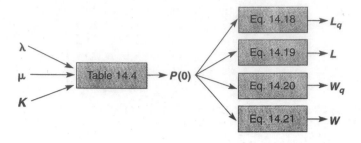

Step 3. From $P(0)$ compute the other variables, using Equations 14.18–14.21. For our example:

$$\rho = 36/10 = 3.6 \text{ (notice that } \rho/K = \bar{\rho} = 3.6/5 = .72)$$

$$L_q = \frac{P(0)\rho^K\bar{\rho}}{K!\,(1 - \bar{\rho})^2} = \frac{0.0228(3.6)^5.72}{5!\,(1 - .72)^2} = 1.055$$

$$L = 1.055 + 3.6 = 4.655$$

$$W_q = \quad 1.055/36 = 0.029$$

$$W = 4.655/36 = 0.129$$

Solved Problem 14.4

Parishioners arrive randomly to church for confession, at an average rate of 5.8 per hour. Father Bailey estimates that an average confession lasts 10 minutes. However, he is worried about the possibility of a long queue and wonders if he should ask more priests to hear confessions.

Solution

In this problem, it is given that:

$$\lambda = 5.8 \text{ per hour}$$

$$\frac{1}{\mu} = 10 \text{ minutes} = \frac{1}{6} \text{ hour}$$

$$\mu = 6 \text{ per hour}$$

If only one priest hears confession, then it is a system with a single server. Therefore:

$$L = \frac{\lambda}{\mu - \lambda} = \frac{5.8}{.2} = 29 \text{ parishioners in the church}$$

$$L_q = \frac{\lambda^2}{\mu(\mu - \lambda)} = \frac{5.8(5.8)}{6(.2)} = 28.03 \text{ parishioners in the waiting line}$$

$$W = \frac{1}{\mu - \lambda} = \frac{1}{.2} = 5 \text{ hours average time in the church (waiting and service) per parishioner}$$

$$W_q = \frac{\lambda}{\mu(\mu - \lambda)} = \frac{5.8}{6(.2)} = 4.83 \text{ hours average wait per parishioner}$$

Solved Problem 14.4 (continued)

The results above certainly corroborate Father Bailey's anxieties: an expected line length of 28 parishioners and a total time of five hours before they may leave for home.

Solution with Two Priests

For this situation, Table 14.4 will be used. Using the values $\rho = .967$ and $\bar{\rho} = .4835$ with $K = 2$ in Table 14.4 (round $\bar{\rho}$ to .48), we find $P(0) = .3514$:

$$L_q = \frac{.3514(.967)^2.484}{2! \ (.516)^2} = .299$$

$$L = .299 + .967 = 1.266$$

$$W_q = .299/5.8 = .052 \text{ hours (or 3.12 minutes)}$$

$$W = 1.266/5.8 = .218 \text{ hours (or 13.10 minutes)}$$

Notice that adding just one more priest to hear confessions did not cut the queue length and waiting time just in half (that would have resulted in a line of 14 parishioners and a total time of 2.5 hours); instead, the results indicate an average waiting line of only .2 persons and an average waiting time prior to the confession of only 2.16 minutes. This amazing result is due to the *randomness* of the arrivals.

Solved Problem 14.5

Star Oil service station (full service only) is considering how many of its eight identical gasoline pumps to staff during the night. Past experience indicates that there are an average of 16 random arrivals per hour during the 9 P.M.–7 A.M. period. Each customer brings the station a revenue of $15. The service time takes three minutes on the average, and follows a negative exponential distribution.

Long waiting lines create ill will. In addition, customers may not enter the station if they see long lines. Therefore, the management of Star Oil estimates that each total customer-hour of waiting time in the service station effectively costs $30. The operating cost of manning each pump is $15 per hour. Find how many pumps should be manned so that the total profit is maximized.

Solution

In this system, $\lambda = 16$, $\mu = 60/3 = 20$. The waiting time of interest is W_q, because this is a retail situation.

For One Pump:

$$W_q = \frac{\lambda}{\mu(\mu - \lambda)} = \frac{16}{20(20 - 16)} = \frac{16}{20(4)} = \frac{16}{80} = .2 \text{ hours per customer}$$

Because there are 16 customers each, the cost of ill will is $16(.2)(\$30) = \$96$ per hour.

The total profit per hour is:

Gross income: 16 customers $\times$ 15 = $240
Less operating expenses = $15
Less ill-will expense = $96
Profit = 240 − (15 + 96) = $129 per hour

(continued)

TABLE 14.5   Optimal Number of Service Facilities

Number of Pumps	Facility Cost	L_q	Cost of Waiting ($L_q \times \$30$)	Total Cost	Net Profit = $\$240$ − Total Cost	
1	15	3.2	$96.00	$111.00	$129.00	
2	30	0.152	4.60	34.60	205.40	←Maximum
3	45	0.028	.84	45.84	194.16	
4	60	negligible	negligible	60.00	180.00	

Two Pumps.   To compute W_q for two pumps, Table 14.4 is used, with $\rho = 0.8$, $K = 2$, and $\bar{\rho} = 0.4$. The result is $P(0) = 0.4286$. Thus:

$$L_q = \frac{0.4286(0.8)^2 0.4}{2(0.6)^2} = 0.152$$

and the cost of ill will is:

$$(W_q\lambda)\text{Cost} = L_q(\text{Cost}) = 0.152(\$30) = \$4.60$$

The profit is $240 - 15(2) - 4.60 = \$205.40$, which is considerably better than the case of one pump.

Three Pumps.   From Table 14.4, $P(0) = 0.2941$:

$$L_q = \frac{0.2941(0.8)^3 0.4}{3! \, (0.6)^2} = 0.028$$

and the cost of ill will is $0.028(\$30) = \$0.84$. The profit is thus $240 - 45 - 0.84 = 194.16$, which is less than two pumps.

Four Pumps or More.   There is no need to check: because the cost of ill will is minimal, adding more pumps will increase total costs.

Comparison

These computations are summarized in Table 14.5. The best number of pumps is two, with an hourly net profit of $205.40.

14.14 Other Queuing Situations

Finite Source Queuing Systems (M/M/1 FCFS/∞/n)

If the number of customers is limited

All waiting line situations discussed thus far assumed an infinite population source. However, in some real-life situations, the number of customers is small and cannot be considered infinite. For example, there may be only 9 production employees coming to the toolroom, or the number of airplanes arriving at a small airport each day may be limited to 12. Another very common situation is the so-called machine repair problem.

Companies often have maintenance teams whose primary function is to repair certain machines used for production when they break down. For instance, there may be one service person and five bottling machines. Another example is a production employee who supervises 15 textile machines. In such cases, the machines are viewed as the "customers" that require service.

Let M denote the finite number of customers in the source and λ denote each (identical) customer's individual average arrival rate (*not* the group of all M customers). The basic formulas, assuming a Poisson-exponential system and a *single* server, are:

$$P(0) = 1 \bigg/ \sum_{i=0}^{M} \left[\frac{M!}{(M-i)!} (\rho)i \right] \tag{14.22}$$

where i = summation index

$$P(N) = P(0)\rho^{N} \frac{M!}{(M-N)!} \tag{14.23}$$

$$L_q = M - \frac{\lambda + \mu}{\lambda}(1 - P(0)) \tag{14.24}$$

$$L = L_q + (1 - P(0)) \tag{14.25}$$

$$W_q = \frac{L_q}{\mu(1 - P(0))} \tag{14.26}$$

$$W = W_q + \frac{1}{\mu} \tag{14.27}$$

These equations could be applied to a situation such as the following:

Example

The ABC Bottling Corporation has five machines. Each breaks down once every $2\frac{1}{2}$ weeks, on the averge. Thus, $\lambda = 1/2.5 = .4$ per week. The repair capacity is one machine per week: $\mu = 1$. Find the operating characteristics of the system.

Rather than manually solving the equations, employing a computer program that already has been programmed with the above equations is faster and less susceptible to error. Equations for the multiple server case, which are even more complex, can be included as well. This will be demonstrated in Section 14.16, Use of Computers.

Queuing Systems with a Maximum Queue Length (M/M/1 FCFS/n/∞)

Limited space—customers may balk

In all the previous situations, no limits were set on the size of the waiting line. In the real world, however, there are many situations where the capacity of the waiting line is limited. For example, at some gas stations, there is only so much room for cars to wait. Any customers that arrive while the waiting area is full will leave the system (balk because they have no choice) without being served.

The maximum capacity of the system is designated by n. For a single server, the probability computation is given in Equation 14.10. For the multiserver situation, see Hillier and Yu [6]. The computer approach is discussed in Section 14.16.

Queuing Systems with a Constant Service Time and Poisson Arrivals (M/D/1 FCFS/∞/∞)

Human-machine systems

In some situations, the service time can be considered as constant. For example, automated servers such as vending machines perform service at essentially a constant rate. Also, humans servicing nonhuman customers (an oil change on a car) frequently perform at an approximately constant rate.

Due to lack of space, we will not discuss the equations for this case but instead rely again on computers (see Section 14.16).

14.15 Serial (Multiphase) Queues

Service in stages

In certain service situations, a customer receives service at a number of stations. The customer (product) moves from station to station and possibly from queue to queue. This is known as a *serial* or *multiphase* queue. Under certain assumptions, such a process may be analyzed rather easily. Multiple servers may even be included in the process.

Poisson in . . .

Poisson out

The first two necessary assumptions are that the source is infinite and the queues in each station are not limited in length. Second, in the case of multiple servers within each station, all servers must have the same exponential service time distribution. Third, the customers at the first station arrive randomly (Poisson). Finally, $\lambda < K\mu$ at every station, where K = number of servers, so that an explosive queue is not formed somewhere in the system. Under the above assumptions, the output from each station will also be Poisson, with the average rate λ. Because each station has Poisson arrivals, it may be treated independently of the others, and Table 14.4 can be used for computing the measures of performance throughout the entire process.

Example

Consider a three-station process, where the arrival rate $\lambda = 5$ per hour. The number of servers and the service rates are:

$$K_1 = 1; \mu_1 = 6 \quad \text{(for station 1)}$$

$$K_2 = 3; \mu_2 = 2 \quad \text{(for station 2)}$$

$$K_3 = 2; \mu_3 = 4 \quad \text{(for station 3)}$$

The problem is shown schematically in Figure 14.10. Find the waiting times within the process.

Solution (All Times Are Given in Hours)

Station 1 (Single Server, Use Formulas of Section 14.8).

$$\frac{\lambda}{\mu_1} = .833, \qquad L_{q1} = 4.5; \qquad W_{q1} = \frac{4.5}{5} = .90$$

Station 2 (Multiple Servers, Use Table 14.4). Given:

$$\lambda = 5, \qquad \mu_2 = 2, \qquad K_2 = 3$$

Compute:

$$\rho_2 = \lambda/\mu_2 = 5/2 = 2.5$$

$$\bar{\rho}_2 = 5/3 \times 2 = 0.833 \text{ (round to 0.84)}$$

From Table 14.4: $P(0) = 0.428$:

$$L_{q2} = \frac{0.428(2.5)^3 0.833}{(3 \times 2)(1 - 0.833)^2} = 3.33 \qquad W_{q2} = L_{q2}/\lambda = 3.33/5 = 0.66$$

FIGURE 14.10

A serial queue situation (combined with parallel servers)

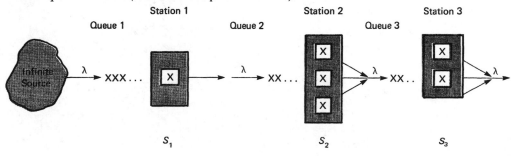

Station 3 (Multiple Servers, Use Table 14.4). For $\lambda = 5$, $\mu_3 = 4$, $K_3 = 2$ we get:

$$\rho_3 = 1.25 \qquad \bar{\rho}_3 = 5/8 = 0.625 \text{ (round to 0.62)}$$

From Table 14.4: $P(0) = 0.2346$:

$$L_{q3} = \frac{0.2346(1.25)^2 0.625}{2(0.375)^2} = 0.815 \qquad W_{q3} = 0.815/5 = 0.16$$

The total waiting time for service is:

$$W_q \text{ (system)} = 0.90 + 0.66 + 0.16 = 1.72 \text{ hours}$$

14.16 Use of Computers

As mentioned earlier, computers are ideal for queuing computations. The following examples of computer printouts use Nelson's program [7] for several models; some include a cost analysis. In all the computer analyses, the waiting cost is based on W, not W_q, and all data are on a per-hour basis.

Example 1

Single server ($M/M/1$).

Average Time Between Arrivals:	.05	Average Arrival Rate: $\lambda = 20.0$
Average Time for Service:	.04	Average Service Rate: $\mu = 25.0$

Number of Servers: 1
Queue Discipline: First Come, First Served
Maximum Queue Length: ∞
Source (Population) Size: ∞
Service Cost: 18
Waiting Cost: 5

QUEUING MODEL RESULTS

PROBLEM NAME: q1   SOLUTION METHOD: ANALYZE MODEL

ITEM	SYMBOL	ANALYSIS
Average Waiting Time in the System	W	0.200
Average Waiting Time in the Queue	Wq	0.160

Average No. of Units in the System	L	4.000
Average No. of Units in the Queue	Lq	3.200
Utilization Rate	P	0.800
Probability the System Is Idle	P(0)	0.200
Total System Cost	TC	38.00

The probability of finding exactly 3 units in the system:
  P(3) = 0.102400
The probability that more than 3 units are in the system:
  P(n > 3) = 0.409600
The probability of being in the system longer than .2:
  P(W > .2) = 0.367879
The probability of waiting for service longer than .15:
  P(Wq > .15) = 0.377893

Example 2

Single server (*M/M/*1) with queue limitation of six in the system (see Section 14.14). (*Note:* The balking rate refers to the percentage of customers that do *not* join the queue). The remaining input data are the same as for Example 1.

QUEUING MODEL RESULTS		
ITEM	SYMBOL	ANALYSIS
Average Waiting Time in the System	W	0.115
Average Waiting Time in the Queue	Wq	0.075
Average No. of Units in the System	L	2.140
Average No. of Units in the Queue	Lq	1.400
Utilization Rate	P	0.746927
Probability the System Is Idle	P(0)	0.253073
Total System Cost*	TC	28.70
Balking Rate Percentage	P(n > M)	6.634

*This figure does not include the cost of balking, if relevant. For examples where it is included, see the problems.

Example 3

Multiple server (*M/M/K*).

```
Average Time Between Arrivals:    .1           Average Arrival Rate: 10.0

Average Time for Service          .25          Average Service Rate:  4.0

Number of Servers: 3
Queue Discipline: First Come, First Served
Maximum Queue Length: ∞
Source (Population) Size: ∞
Service Cost: 8
Waiting Cost: 12
```

	QUEUING MODEL RESULTS	
PROBLEM NAME: q3	SOLUTION METHOD: ANALYZE MODEL	
ITEM	SYMBOL	ANALYSIS
Average Waiting Time in the System	W	0.601
Average Waiting Time in the Queue	Wq	0.351
Average No. of Units in the System	L	6.010
Average No. of Units in the Queue	Lq	3.510
Utilization Rate	P	0.955056
Probability the System Is Idle	P(0)	0.044944
Total System Cost	TC	96.12

Commercial Software

Several comprehensive MS/OR packages offer limited queuing modeling (e.g., SAS/OR from the SAS Institute, Cary, N.C.). A sophisticated package, $M^x/D/C$, is offered by A&A Pub., Kingston, Ontario, Canada.

14.17 Problems for Part B

Note: Assume a Poisson-exponential system unless otherwise specified.

19. Refer back to Problem 14. An alternative solution suggests three parallel, identical facilities serving one line. Each facility is capable of serving three customers per hour at a cost of $2 per hour facility. Analyze this alternative. Would you recommend it?

20. One branch of the post office in Calcutta would like to know how many windows to staff so the average number of customers waiting for service does not exceed eight. The average service time is three minutes and the post office uses a single queue system, as illustrated on the next page. How many windows should the post office staff on Monday

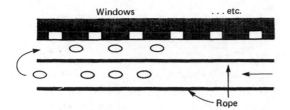

Windows ... etc.

Rope

mornings when the average arrival rate is 60 customers per hour?

21. Mrs. Grouch and Mr. Mean each have a private secretary who can type letters at the average rate of four per hour. The letters are generated by each manager at the average rate of three per hour. The managers have been wondering if they would benefit by pooling the two secretaries. What would you suggest? (Show calculations.)

22. The supervisor of the maintenance department of Everglade City is faced with a decision regarding maintenance of the city's heavy equipment. He is considering three alternatives:

a. Hire a first-class mechanic, which will cost the city $14.20 per hour (including fringe benefits). Such a mechanic can repair five units per eight-hour day.

b. Hire two second-class mechanics, each of whom will cost the city $11.50 per hour and would work separately. When the two serve one waiting line, they can each fix four units a day.

c. Subcontract the maintenance to ABC Engineering at a cost of $50 per unit repaired. The average repair time is one hour.

The quality of repairs in all three alternatives is considered the same. Currently, there is an average of four units of heavy equipment requiring daily repair (assume random arrivals). A unit of heavy equipment not in operation costs the city $25 per hour, because the city must lease alternative equipment. Find the total daily cost of the three alternatives.

23. Trucks are loaded by a forklift at a rate of four per hour. An hour of forklift operation costs $10. The trucks arrive at an average rate of one every 20 minutes. An idle hour (waiting for loading) for a truck is estimated to cost $16. Find how many forklifts should be used. Assumption: Only one forklift can be used per truck.

24. The keen competition in the successful fast-food industry has forced the management of Burger Corporation to study the operation of their various restaurants. At their Northwestern restaurant, where they receive the most complaints, an analysis revealed the following:

During rush hours, customers arrive at an average rate of one every minute. The attendants can serve, on the average, 66 customers per hour. Burger's president cannot understand why there are so many complaints about the Northwestern restaurant. As the president states: "Why do they complain? We can serve even 10 percent more without any problems."

a. Explain to the president why you think there are so many complaints.

b. What will happen if the average number of customers grows by 10 percent?

c. It was proposed that two teams, each with an hourly serving capacity of 33 customers, replace the existing team, which can serve 66 customers per hour. If there is no additional cost involved in such a change, would you recommend it? Show why or why not. (Assume that the two teams serve a single waiting line.)

Hint: Assume that the number of complaints is a function of waiting time per customer.

25. Hong Kong Machine Company has a toolroom with two clerks. Both clerks issue spare parts and tools to maintenance workers. Maintenance workers arrive at the rate of 20 per hour, each wanting either a part (40 percent) or a tool (60 percent), but not both. The average issuing time is five minutes per order (service by one clerk). Each clerk currently issues both parts and tools. A maintenance worker not at his or her bench costs the company $5 per hour. It was proposed that the two clerks be specialized, namely: One will issue spare parts only, and the other will issue tools only.

a. Would you advise specialization of the clerks if the service time does not change?

b. Would you advise specialization if the service time is reduced to four minutes per order?

Hint: Treat the current situation as a multiple station system with two servers. Treat the specialization as two single stations.

26. Toulouse Bakeries serves 480 customers during eight hours of operation. The average service time per customer is four minutes. Currently, there are five servers at the bakery serving one line.
    Find:
    a. The utilization of the bakery.
    b. The average number of customers at the bakery.
    c. The average waiting time (prior to service) in the bakery (per customer), in minutes.
    d. The average number of customers being served.
    e. The probability of finding no customers in the bakery.
    f. The probability of finding exactly three customers in the bakery.

27. A mechanic-operator services five machines. When a machine needs an adjustment, it is shut down. An adjustment takes 15 minutes, on average. Each machine needs an adjustment, on the average, once every two hours. *Compute* (use a computer):
    a. The average number of operating machines.
    b. The average number of inoperative machines.
    c. The utilization rate of the machines.
    d. The probability that all five machines are working.
    e. The weekly cost of inoperative machines if one hour of downtime costs $10 and the machines are in operation eight hours each day, five days a week.

28. Five factory servicepersons maintain 20 old machines that break down at an average rate of 15 per week. If the machines are repaired, one by each serviceperson, at an average rate of two per week, what is the expected line length of inoperative machines? Use a computer.

29. A gasoline station is served by one employee, who is capable of serving 30 customers per hour. There is a maximum space for five cars in the station (served and in line). Cars arrive at the station at an average rate of one every three minutes. Cars that do not have parking space leave and do not return. Use a computer.
    Find:
    a. The average number of cars *waiting* for service.
    b. The average waiting time in line per car.
    c. The probability of finding the station without any cars.
    d. The probability of finding three cars in the station.

e. It was proposed to increase the space so that 10 cars could be accommodated. The investment in such a case is $.50 per car space per hour. A car that leaves the station means a loss of $1 profit. Should the space be enlarged or not?

30. A restaurant with an 85-seat capacity has a bar that can accommodate 15 additional waiting customers. Customers who cannot be seated in the bar leave the restaurant. There are 10 waitresses at the restaurant, each capable of serving three customers per hour. Customers arrive at the restaurant at a rate of 29 per hour.

    Find the average number of customers waiting for service in the restaurant and bar. Assume that all customers go into the restaurant on arrival if room is available. Use a computer.

31. A five-stage manufacturing process receives raw materials (in units) randomly and must process an average of 12 units each day (eight hours). The data of the system are as follows:

Stage	Number of Parallel Servers in Stage (K)	Service Capabilities (per Eight-Hour Day, per Server)
1	2	7
2	1	15
3	5	3
4	3	4.5
5	1	30

a. Find the *expected time* that a unit will spend in the entire processing system (from arrival until finished in stage 5).
b. Find the average waiting time prior to entering the processing system.
c. The cost of a server in the system is $6 per hour. Unit waiting time costs $1 per hour. Would it be profitable to add more servers to the system? If yes, in what stage(s) should they be placed?
d. As an alternative to adding more servers, would a transfer of servers among stages be profitable?

Assume:

(1) The arrival rate cannot be changed.

(2) Servers are paid on an hourly basis; if they work a portion of an hour, they are paid proportionally.

32. Team Oil is a gas station with four pumps selling unleaded gasoline. The arrival rate during rush hours is 60 per hour. The service time is three minutes. What is the chance that an arriving customer will find no cars in the station? (Assume one waiting line.)

33. Refer to computer examples 1 and 2 in Section 14.16.

   a. Assume the system is in operation 300 days a year, 10 hours a day. Find the difference in the annual cost and comment on it.

   b. Use a computer to find out the cost impact of increasing the waiting space from six to seven units (on an annual basis).

34. Access to the freeway system in Los Angeles is controlled by a signaling system. The system permits one car to enter the freeway every few seconds. The time is constant (e.g., three seconds). However, it is changed during rush hours to a larger value.

   a. Explain in queuing terminology the reason for such an arrangement.

   b. Devise a freeway system with three lanes and use your own numbers to prove your point.

35. A system has the following input data: $\lambda = 10$, $\mu = 12$, service costs \$150 per hour, and waiting costs \$35 per hour.

   a. Find the total cost if the maximum number of customers in the system is four. Find the cost for five. For six. If the cost of balking is \$10 per person who balks, which alternative is the least expensive?

   b. Which alternative is the least expensive if the cost of balking is \$1 per customer?

   Note: In both cases, ignore any additional cost associated with adding more waiting space.

36. Given the computer printout of two service systems, A and B, below; data are for one hour of operation. The company operates 2 shifts, 5 days a week, 50 weeks per year, 8 hours per shift, to meet a demand of 360 customers per day. The company operates now with system A. It is estimated that each customer that leaves the line (balks) costs the company \$25. System

B is a proposed system that is faster. Replacing the system requires \$1 million. The company uses a three-year payback as a criterion for determining the acceptability of capital budgeting (investment) projects. Namely, the savings should return the investment in three years or less. Based on the computer printouts, show the calculations and the recommended action.

```
              System A

BALKING RATE (PERCENT) 5.7
EXPECTED NUMBER IN SYSTEM 1.53
EXPECTED NUMBER IN QUEUE .87
EXPECTED TIME IN SYSTEM .046
EXPECTED TIME IN QUEUE .026


ECONOMIC ANALYSIS RESULTS (PER HOUR)
COST OF SERVICE : 48
COST OF WAITING : 244.8
     TOTAL COST : 292.8
```

```
              System B

BALKING RATE (PERCENT) 2.9
EXPECTED NUMBER IN SYSTEM 1.15
EXPECTED NUMBER IN QUEUE .59
EXPECTED TIME IN SYSTEM .034
EXPECTED TIME IN QUEUE .017


ECONOMIC ANALYSIS RESULTS (PER HOUR)
COST OF SERVICE : 48
COST OF WAITING : 184
     TOTAL COST : 232
```

37. Patients arrive with minor injuries at City of Help's walk-in urgency clinic at random. The average arrival rate is 12 per hour. The urgency room is organized as follows:

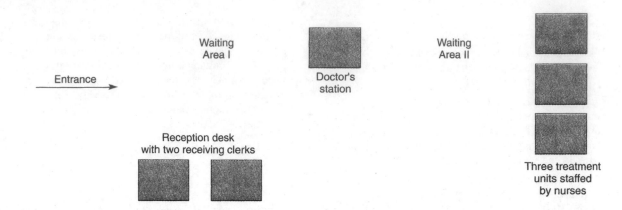

Patients enter the urgency room and go to the reception desk, where two clerks fill out the necessary paperwork (independently). The average time required to do the paperwork, per patient, is 7.5 minutes. The patient is then given a number and seated in the waiting area. When the number is called, the patient sees the doctor (the average examination time is 4 minutes). The patient then waits for the first available treatment unit; here a nurse treats the patient (following the doctor's orders). How long does the average patient spend in the clinic?

38. The City of Cincinnati is designing a new customer service building. The average number of customers expected to arrive at the center is 30 per hour. To serve a customer takes, on the average, six minutes. Management is interested in knowing how many service windows to plan for (assuming that there will be only one waiting line). The city would like to meet the following goals:
    a. There will be no more than five customers in the waiting area.
    b. The average time in the facility, including service, should be eight or fewer minutes.

39. Customers arrive at the First Western drive-in window at a rate of 10 per hour during *regular* periods. The average interarrival time during *peak hours* is 4 minutes. The average service time is 4.1 minutes.
    Determine:
    a. The probability a customer is in the system 12 or fewer minutes during a period of regular demand.
    b. The probability of finding fewer than six customers in the system during a period of regular demand.
    c. First Western wants to implement a policy that any customer who arrives during *peak time* will *not* have to wait (prior to service), on the average, more than 10 minutes. Is this goal achievable today? If not, determine what service rate is necessary to attain this goal.
    d. The operation of the drive-in window costs $20 an hour. The estimated loss due to decreased goodwill, because of the time spent in line, is figured at $1 per hour per customer. Management can expedite the service time to three minutes per customer at a cost of $15 per hour. Would you recommend it for the regular hours? For the peak hours? Why or why not?

CASES
I: NEWTOWN MAINTENANCE DIVISION

The city of Newtown, like many other cities today, is caught in a severe financial squeeze. Up to now, previous city managers have taken a short-term approach to Newtown's maintenance and repair services in the expectation that future tax receipts would improve. However, Newtown's voters have just rejected the fourth proposed tax increase on the ballot for city services in as many years, and the expected relief of future tax revenues now looks hopeless.

The new city manager has decided that a long-term policy must finally be established that recognizes the reality of continued low funding for city services. One portion of this problem is the manner of making daily repairs to the city's streets. Calls for repairs arrive randomly at the average rate of two per day. It is the mayor's declared policy that the city will respond to all calls for street repairs within one week (five eight-hour working days) of the call.

The city manager has two alternatives for servicing street repairs:

1. He can use any number of standard city crews, which cost $79 per hour and can each repair a street, on the average, in 10 hours.
2. He can lease special heavy-duty street repairing equipment and use smaller crews, resulting in an hourly cost of $90 per crew. These special crews can repair the average street in only seven hours.

Make a recommendation to the city manager concerning these two alternatives. How soon can the city respond to calls under the cheaper of the above two policies? What would happen if the mayor insisted that the response time be reduced to *two* working days?

II. A QUEUING CASE STUDY OF DRIVE-IN BANKING*

This case is a summary of the efforts of two students in the Applied Operations Research course taught in the University of Oklahoma School of Industrial Engineering in the fall of 1972. The case involved the effort of a local bank to expand its drive-in facilities. Two options were basically available: a "robo-window" system and a traditional expansion of the current system, which involved teller stations approximately 8 feet by 8 feet stationed on a traffic lane. The robo system involved a

─────────
*B. L. Foote, *Interfaces* August, 1976, pp. 31–36, copyright 1976, The Institute of Management Sciences.

small cube (approximately 3 feet in each dimension) that had a speaker system and a pneumatic tube to deliver cartridges back to a central location. Space was at a premium and expansion of the present system was limited to five teller stations (they now have three), whereas up to seven stations would be available if the robo system were used. The robo station was, of course, much cheaper (by about one-half) than an 8 foot by 8 foot room for a teller. The bank was less concerned about the costs than the quality of customer service. Our team was called in to assess the two systems.

The first concern was finding a measure of performance. Interviews with bank officials rapidly dismissed total costs as a consideration. The prime consideration was lost customers due to poor service. Bank officials then defined poor service as causing a customer to wait longer than five minutes. This choice was not as arbitrary as it sounds, as further questions showed that customers base their impatience on the movement of the minute hand between two marks, which on most watches represents five minutes. Bank officials then set four minutes as the maximum waiting time. The team then suggested a risk level of approximately .05 and this was agreed to.

The team also suggested that the cost criterion should be evaluated as a backup piece of information, and suggested that for any design the imputed cost of waiting should be determined and submitted to bank officials for their judgment. This was agreed to as well. The team cheerfully set to work with a set of formulas (from H. A. Taha, *Operations Research* [New York: Macmillan, 1987]). Time studies were immediately taken, using two observers to facilitate data collection. (Initial tests disclosed that observing the cars, operating the watch, and recording were too much for one student to do without substantial error.) Table 1 and similar tables were computed for various days and time intervals.

The expected frequency computations assumed that interarrival times were distributed exponentially. Be-

TABLE 1   Friday 2:15–6:30

Interval (Seconds)	Observed Frequency	Expected Frequency	Chi-Square ($\lambda = .03$ Arrivals per Second)
0–19	208	206	.019
20–39	109	113	.142
40–59	64	62	.016
60–79	33	34	.029
80–99	19	19	.000
100–119	13	10	.900
120+	10	12	.333
	456	456	1.439

cause $\chi^2_{.01}$ with five degrees of freedom is 15.086, this looked like a good fit.

Other tables had similar results. A plot of the arrival rates in Exhibit 1 gave rise to some second thoughts. The queue was obviously always in a state of flux and the theory of the transient behavior of queues was probably needed. A look at some basic references was discouraging. The formulas were so complex that elaborate programming or simulation seemed to be called for in

EXHIBIT 1

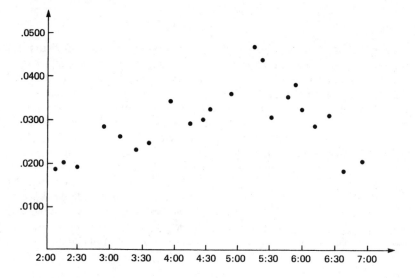

Exhibit 2

Time line diagram

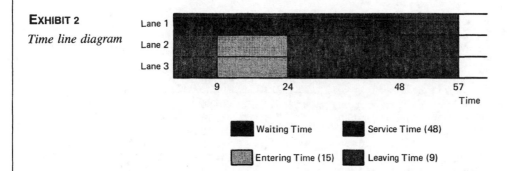

order to compute the probability of waiting in the system longer than four minutes. Further, the team could find no solid information on how long the "transient" state of a queue lasted. Someone remembered reading something about four hours. References were examined with no solid information found.

The bank operated by adding tellers as the waiting line grew. When about four were waiting, another window opened up. This rule of thumb would be used in the new system, so the team thought perhaps that this might "smooth out" the transient behavior and perhaps some simple formulas could still be used.

The team next studied the service time. Because waiting times can be lessened either by adding servers or decreasing service times, the layout of the workstation was studied and service times during busy periods were taken. No improvements in layout or work methods could be seen. Further, service times also were textbook fits of the χ^2 distribution. However, a fortunate observation was made. The service time of the system and the service time of the teller were two different times. The service time of the system consisted of the following events: realize the car in front had moved, move to the teller window, give the teller instructions or requests plus material items, teller actions, move out. On three of these actions the teller was forcibly idle. The total of the five actions the team called block time. The block time was 72 seconds and service time was 48 seconds. These were average figures, of course. A little machine interference speculation was conducted. Perhaps two tellers could serve three lanes. Two tellers could sit in a teller station and serve the station lane and two robo lanes.

Exhibit 2 shows a sample of the machine interference diagramming done. The conclusion was that this assignment was a possibility. Of course, the diagram was idealized based on averages, but it was felt that short service times would balance out in this case. When the time line was extended, the waiting times vanished. The time of vanishing of waiting time (115 seconds) was used as an estimate of transient state time. The relationship between 72 and 48 was too good to be true, but rechecks verified the figures.

The team then began calculations to see if the formulas could predict average waiting times. About two minutes after a window opened, observations were taken. One-, two-, and three-server cases were observed. Table 2 gives the results.

Table 2 and tables like it were intriguing. The predictions seemed good except for one "outlier." Further, the last calculation was *very* interesting. It seemed a variable teller window number policy could be approximated by formulas based on the maximum number of windows open at all times. Upon reflection, this seemed very reasonable.

If we assume the cost of a server is constant (probably not true), Taha gives an inequality that can be used to estimate imputed cost of waiting per hour.

These calculations showed the bank's current policy-imputed customer waiting time at somewhere between $3 and $24 per hour. These figures seemed acceptable to bank officials. The important calculation was still to come.

The formulas were good for expected times, but what about the waiting time distribution? For the transient case the waiting time distribution is not known ex-

TABLE 2   Predicted versus Observed System Average Waiting Times

Ws (Seconds) Observed	Ws (Seconds) Predicted	
89	85	(1 Teller, $\lambda = .0214$, $\mu = .0138$)
106	86	(3 Tellers, $\lambda = .0216$, $\mu = .0138$)
100	174	(2 Tellers, $\lambda = .0211$, $\mu = .0138$)
90	94	(3 Tellers, $\lambda = .025$, $\mu = .0138$)
208	202	(3 Tellers, $\lambda = .0356$, $\mu = .0138$)
125*	125*	(3 Tellers, $\lambda = .0305$, $\mu = .0138$)

λ = Arrival rate per second.
μ = Service rate per second.
Ws = Average waiting time in system.
*Observed and expected values for Ws for the entire period, assuming three open windows at *all* times.

TABLE 3   Observed System Waiting Times

Interval	Seconds	Observed Frequency
I	0–50	56
II	51–100	112
III	101–150	56
IV	151–200	24
V	201–250	13
VI	251–300	7
VII	300+	8

TABLE 4 $\alpha = 2$

Interval	Observed Frequency	Expected Frequency	χ^2
I	56	67	1.81
II	112	88	6.55
III	56	66	1.52
IV	24	30	1.20
V	13	13	0
VI	7	8	.13
VII	8	4	4.00
Totals	276	276	15.21

TABLE 5 $\alpha = 3$

Interval	Observed Frequency	Expected Frequency	χ^2
I	56	48	1.33
II	112	105	.47
III	56	69	2.45
IV	24	37	4.57
V	13	9	1.78
VI	7	6	.17
VII	8	2	18.00
Totals	276	276	28.77

plicitly. For the steady state case, the distribution has the form of a gamma distribution. It was hoped that using steady state as an approximation would work here also. Using Table 3, some empirical tests were made.

The gamma distribution depends on two parameters, α and β, where $\alpha\beta$ = mean value. For convenience, α was chosen as 1, 2, 3, . . . because, if α is noninteger, we no longer have $(\alpha - 1)!$ in the function definition, but a very complicated evaluation. β was determined by $\alpha\beta = W_s$; $\alpha = 2$ and $\alpha = 3$ are tested in Tables 4 and 5. $\chi^2_{.005} = 16.750$. $\alpha = 2$ was chosen, of course.

The team then set to work. They calculated W_s for various combinations of c; $1 \leq c \leq 7$. Using $\alpha\beta = W_s$, $\alpha = 2$, they computed $P(W_s \leq 4)$ by integration.

These evaluations "showed" the new system could handle the projected arrival rates in the future with some room to spare. An expansion to five lanes with two robos added to the current three lanes was recommended, with an assurance that adding a teller when the waiting line exceeded three or four would handle the projected volume and a customer would run less than a 5 percent chance of waiting more than four minutes.

The students happily handed in their report knowing they would be gone before the robo lanes would be built, and the instructor waited for the results of the bank decision.

Epilogue

The robo lanes were built and worked as predicted. There was an exception. The phenomenon of jockeying is well known in queuing systems. Here we had a single lane that emptied into one or two car queues in front of each of the tellers. This was a departure from the basic single queue multichannel service system that was used to model the system. The system worked fine as long as customers in the single queue drove to the empty lane. But, on occasion, customers would go into a nonempty queue in front of a teller station rather than a shorter queue on a robo lane (see Exhibit 3). Waiting times, of course, expanded. As the system continues to be used, the robo lanes have become more popular (the customers have become used to them). The system is now functioning normally.

Questions for Discussion

1. What measure of performance was used in the queuing model in this situation? Can you suggest additional measures of performance that would be appropriate in this case?
2. What is the purpose of applying the chi-square test to the distribution of interarrival times?
3. Discuss the concept of *imputed cost*. Is it possible to calculate the imputed cost of waiting in a queue?

EXHIBIT 3

Layout of final system

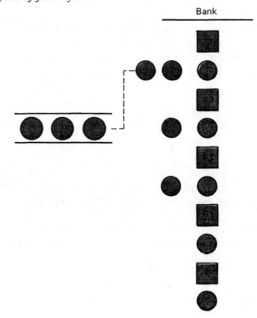

4. In the context of queuing models, what is meant by the *transient case* and by the *steady state case*?
5. Can you think of, or glean from the literature, situations where the application of standard queuing theory would be extremely limited?

Glossary

Arrival rate   The number of customers arriving for service in one unit of time.

Balking   Refusing to join a waiting line.

Calling population   See Source.

Cycling   Returning to the queue following service.

Explosive queue   A situation where the customers arrive faster than the service and the queue builds up continuously.

FCFS   The first-come, first-served service discipline.

Interarrival time   The average time between customer arrivals at the service facility.

Jockeying   Shifting back and forth between queues.

LCFS   Last-come, first-served; a priority system used in warehouses and stores.

Multifacility   A service facility with multiple service stations in parallel, each providing the same service.

Negative exponential   A type of continuous statistical distribution.

Parallel   Providing service at the same time; simultaneous.

Poisson   A type of discrete statistical distribution.

Poisson-exponential single-server system   The elementary queue with random arrivals and services.

Preemptive priority   When one can interrupt an ongoing service.

Queue   A waiting line.

Queue discipline   The policy of selecting customers for service.

Random   Based completely on chance.

Reneging   Leaving the system before service.

Serial   One following the other.

Service facility   The station where customers are served.

Service rate   The number of units that can be served in a unit of time

Source   The population of customers for a queue.

Utilization ratio   The fraction of time the facility is busy.

References and Bibliography

1. Boxma, O. J., and R. Syski, eds. *Queuing Theory and Its Applications*. Amsterdam: North-Holland, 1988.
2. Bunday, B. D. *Basic Queuing Theory*. London: Edward Arnold Pub. Co., 1986.
3. Cooper, R. B. *Introduction to Queueing Theory*. 2nd ed. New York: Elsevier North-Holland Publishing, 1981.
4. Gross, D. and C. Harris. *Fundamentals of Queueing Theory*. 2nd ed. New York: Wiley, 1985.
5. Hall, R. *Queueing Methods for Service and Manufacturing*. Englewood Cliffs, NJ: Prentice-Hall, 1991.
6. Hillier, F. S., and O. S. Yu. *Queuing Tables and Graphs*. New York: Elsevier North-Holland Publishing, 1981.
7. Nelson, T. *The Management Service System*. Homewood, Ill.: Richard D. Irwin, 1988.
8. Solomon, S. L. *Simulation of Waiting Line Systems*. Englewood Cliffs, N.J.: Prentice-Hall, 1983.
9. Walrand, J. *An Introduction to Queuing Networks*. Englewood Cliffs, N.J.: Prentice-Hall, 1988.

Part A: Basics

Part B: Extensions

The application of the management science tools described in the earlier chapters is frequently limited to relatively simple managerial problems. When managerial problems become complex, they often no longer fit the standard problem classifications that are solved by the standard tools. Development of special optimization models to handle such problems may be too costly in terms of dollars and time or the task may even be impossible. For such cases, simulation models are useful. A simulation model involves trial-and-error experimentation with a mathematical model in order to describe and evaluate the system's behavior. Five types of simulation models will be discussed in this chapter: Monte Carlo, visual simulation, business games, corporate planning, and system dynamics.

PART A: BASICS

Sunny Goldman was delighted with her new job as director of the Tourist Information Center for the city of Miami Beach. She had completed her graduate work in the Hotel and Entertainment Services program of a highly rated college in New York and accepted the offer for the new position from her former internship employer, the city of Miami Beach.

The city manager, Cy Bushnell, had been impressed with Sunny's analytical skills during her summers as an intern working at the Senior Citizens Center. There, she had been instrumental in instituting programs that raised the quality of the center's services while simultaneously cutting their costs. Cy had been straightforward in his expectations when offering Sunny the permanent position of director for this new center: the center was severely underfunded, yet the city council had high expectations for the center. If the first year was successful, the center would be much better funded the second year. If not, the city council might well cancel the entire concept.

Sunny saw her first task as determining the needs for service at the center. This required statistics concerning the tourists' arrival rates, their waiting times, and the service times they required to meet their needs. Following this, Sunny would look into more detail concerning the variety of services the tourists required. Special brochures and posters might handle a significant portion of their information requirements, for example. Or perhaps some form of "express line" for commonly asked questions or senior citizens was desirable.

We will return to Sunny's situation and describe some tools that Sunny might find helpful a bit later in the chapter.

15.1 The General Nature of Simulation

The example just presented is a simple case of one server (possibly more) in a waiting line situation. Unfortunately, as we will show, the case cannot be solved by the formulas in Chapter 14 because the arrival rate does not follow the Poisson distribution, nor is the service time exponential.

Formulas will not work

Sunny's first approach to the data collection problem was to log tourist arrivals and services in the facility. Her results for the first 10 tourists are shown in Table 15.1. Based on this quick preliminary sample, Sunny concluded that the average tourist waited 7/10 of a minute and the employee was busy during 41/50 minutes or 82 percent of the time. Several questions came to Sunny's mind:

How long should she clock the operation of the information clerk?
How do the employees feel about being clocked?
How do the tourists feel about being clocked?
What other kinds of measurements should she take?

What Sunny did not know then was that she could conduct all her experiments on a model of the Tourist Agency and get answers to each of her questions by using the technique of simulation. (The solution to Sunny's problem is given in Section 15.6.)

Simulation is not limited to waiting line problems. Other familiar simulations are the mock war games that national armies regularly schedule, primarily for their reservists, and Monopoly, the real estate game. Other, not so familiar, simulations are:

War games and Monopoly.

· Simulation models of urban systems.

TABLE 15.1 **Tourist Information Center Data**

Tourist Number	Arrival Time	Start of Service	End of Service	Tourist Waiting from–to	Employee Idle from–to
1	9:00	9:00	9:08	—	9:08–9:10
2	9:10	9:10	9:14	—	—
3	9:12	9:14	9:17	9:12–9:14	—
4	9:13	9:17	9:20	9:13–9:17	—
5	9:20	9:20	9:23	—	—
6	9:22	9:23	9:28	9:22–9:23	9:28–9:31
7	9:31	9:31	9:34	—	9:34–9:35
8	9:35	9:35	9:40	—	—
9	9:40	9:40	9:45	—	9:45–9:48
10	9:48	9:48	9:50	—	—
Total				7 minutes	9 minutes

- Corporate organizational (policy) models.
- Business games used for training.
- Flights to the planets and the moon.
- Plant and warehouse location models.
- Determination of the proper size of repair crews.
- Econometric models of national economies.
- Network models of traffic intersections to determine the best sequencing of traffic lights.
- Queuing models of airport runway takeoffs and landings.
- Air basin models to determine pollution sources, concentrations, and dynamics.
- Dam and river basin models to determine the effect of weather and operating policies on the hydroelectric output and water supply.
- Financial models (short and long run).

A flexible tool

From the above list, it can be seen that simulation is one of the most flexible techniques in the tool kit of management scientists. It can be applied to many different types of problems and yields a great deal of information concerning the effectiveness of different operating policies under various conditions and assumptions.

What Is Simulation?

Simulation has many meanings, depending on the area where it is being used. To *simulate,* according to the dictionary, means to assume the appearance or characteristics of reality. In management science, it generally refers to *a technique for conducting experiments with a digital computer on a model of a management system over an extended period of simulated time.*

Major Characteristics

Imitation—not just
representation

Conducting
experiments

To begin, simulation is not strictly a type of model; models in general *represent* reality, whereas simulation *imitates* it. In practical terms, this means that there are fewer simplifications of reality in simulation models than in other models.

Second, simulation is a technique for *conducting experiments*. Therefore, simulation involves the testing of specific values of the decision variables in the model and observing the impact on the output variables.

Simulation is a *descriptive* rather than a normative tool; there is usually no automatic search for an optimal solution. Instead, a simulation describes or predicts the characteristics of a given system under different circumstances. Once these characteristics are known, the best policy can be selected. However, the true optimal policy that could have been identified by an analytical model may not be considered at all in the simulation. The simulation process often consists of the repetition of an experiment many, many times to obtain an estimate of the overall effect of certain actions. It can be executed manually in some cases, but a computer is usually needed for the process.

Finally, simulation is usually called for only when the problem under investigation is too complex to be treated by analytical models or by numerical optimization techniques. Complexity here means that the problem either cannot be formulated mathematically (e.g., because the assumptions do not hold, as in Sunny's case) or the formulation is too involved for a practical or economic solution.

Advantages and Disadvantages of Simulation

The increased acceptance of simulation at higher managerial levels is probably due to a number of factors:

1. Simulation theory is relatively straightforward.

2. The simulation model is simply the aggregate of many elementary relationships and interdependencies, much of which is introduced slowly by request of the manager and in a patchwork manner.

3. Simulation is descriptive rather than normative. This allows the manager to ask what-if type questions (especially when used with an on-line computer). Thus, managers who employ a trial-and-error approach to problem solving can do it faster and cheaper with less risk, using the aid of simulation and computers.

4. An accurate simulation model requires an *intimate* knowledge of the problem, thus forcing the management scientist to constantly interface with the manager.

5. The model is built from the manager's perspective and in his or her decision structure rather than the management scientist's.

Primary advantages
of simulation

6. The simulation model is built for one particular problem and, typically, will not solve any other problem. Thus, no generalized understanding is

required of the manager; every component in the model corresponds one to one with a part of the real life system.

7. Simulation can handle an extremely wide variation in problem types such as inventory and staffing, as well as higher managerial level functions like long-range planning. Thus, it is "always there" when the manager needs it.

8. The manager can experiment with different factors to determine which are important and with different policies and alternatives to determine which are the best. The experimentation is done with a model rather than by interfering with the system.

9. Simulation, in general, allows for inclusion of the real-life complexities of problems; simplifications are not necessary. For example: simulation utilizes the real-life probability distributions rather than approximate theoretical distributions.

10. Due to the nature of simulation, a great amount of **time compression** can be attained, giving the manager some feel as to the long-term (1 to 10 years) effects of various policies, in a matter of minutes.

11. The great amount of time compression enables experimentation with a very large sample (especially when computers are used). Therefore, as much accuracy can be achieved as desired at a relatively low cost.

The primary disadvantages of simulation are:

Disadvantages

1. An optimal solution cannot be guaranteed.
2. Constructing a simulation model is frequently a slow and costly process.
3. Solutions and inferences from a simulation study are usually not transferable to other problems. This is due to the incorporation in the model of the unique factors of the problem.
4. Simulation is sometimes so tempting to apply that analytical solutions that can yield optimal results are often overlooked.
5. In contrast to real-world sampling, there may be model specification errors.

15.2 The Methodology of Simulation

Simulation involves setting up a model of a real system and conducting repetitive experiments on it. The methodology consists of a number of steps (Figure 15.1).

FIGURE 15.1

*The process of
simulation*

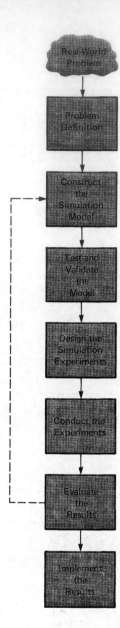

The Simulation Process

Problem Definition
The real-world problem is examined and classified. We should specify why simulation is necessary. The system's boundaries and other such aspects of problem clarification (see Chapter 2) are attended to here.

Construction of the Simulation Model
This step involves gathering the necessary data. For example, in Sunny's case, information is needed about arrivals, the Center's policies, and the nature of the service pro-

cess. In many cases, a flowchart (to be discussed in Section 15.5) is used to describe the process. Then, if the simulation is to be conducted by a computer, a program is written, often in a special computer language. Alternatively, a manual simulation may be conducted instead.

Testing and Validating the Model
The simulation model must properly imitate the system under study. This requires validation (Section 15.9).

Design of the Experiment
Once the model has been proven valid, the experiment is designed. Included in this step is determining how long to run the simulation (when to stop the experiment) and whether to consider all the data or to ignore the transient start-up data. This step thus deals with two important and contradictory objectives: *accuracy* and *cost*. These, as well as other issues of design, are also discussed in Section 15.9.

Conducting the Experiments
There are several types of simulation (see Section 15.3). Conducting the experiment may involve issues such as random number generation, stopping rules, and derivation of the results. Again, these issues are discussed in Section 15.9.

Evaluating the Results
The final step, prior to implementation, is the evaluation of the results. Here, we deal with issues such as: "What constitutes a significant difference?" "What do the results mean?" In addition to statistical tools, we may also use a sensitivity analysis (in the form of what-if questions). At this stage, we may even change the model and repeat the experiment.

Implementation
The implementation of simulation results involves the same issues as any other implementation. However, the chances of implementation are better because the manager is usually more involved in the simulation process than with analytical models and these simulation models are closer to reality.

15.3 Types of Simulation

There are several types of simulation. The major ones described in this book are:

Probabilistic Simulation
In this type of simulation, one or more of the independent variables (e.g., the arrival rate in a waiting line problem, or the demand in an inventory problem) is probabilistic. That is, it follows a certain probability distribution. Two subcategories are recognized: *discrete distributions* and *continuous distributions* (see Appendix B).

Discrete or
continuous?

1. *Discrete distributions* involve a situation with a limited number of events (or variables that can only take a finite number of values).

2. *Continuous distributions* refer to a situation involving variables with an unlimited number of possible values that follow density functions such as the normal distribution.

The two types of distributions are shown in Table 15.2.

Probabilistic simulation is conducted with the aid of a technique called Monte Carlo (Sections 15.4–15.7, 15.11, 15.12, and 15.15). Deterministic simulation is discussed in Section 15.17.

Time Dependent and Time Independent Simulation

Time independent refers to a situation where it is not important to know exactly when the event occurred. For example, we may know that the demand is three units per day, but we do not care *when* during the day the item was demanded. Or in some situations, such as organizational simulation, time may not be a factor (see Sections 15.5, 15.16, and 15.17). On the other hand, in waiting line problems, it is important to know the precise time of arrival (to know if the customer will have to wait or not). In this case, we are dealing with a **time dependent** situation (Sections 15.6 and 15.11).

Visual Simulation

This interactive computerized tool is one of the more successful new developments in computer-human problem solving. It is described in Section 15.13.

Business Games

The simulation of competitive decision making, which may also involve probabilistic simulation, is presented in Section 15.14.

Large System Simulation

Complex simulations of corporations or even national economies are possible. These methods are presented in Sections 15.15–15.17.

TABLE 15.2   Discrete and Continuous Distributions

Discrete		Continuous
Daily Demand	*Probability*	
5	.10	Daily demand is normally distributed with a mean of
6	.15	7 and a standard deviation of 1.2
7	.30	
8	.25	
9	.20	

15.4 The Monte Carlo Methodology

Sampling from the probability distributions

Managerial systems of decisions under risk exhibit chance elements in their behavior. As such, they can be simulated with the aid of a technique called **Monte Carlo** (named after the famous gambling kingdom). The technique involves random *sampling* from the probability distributions that represent the real-life processes.

Recall that in the Tourist Information Center case, we timed the arrivals and lengths of service. These two variables are usually probabilistic. What the Monte Carlo method does is to generate *simulated* arrival times and service times from a given distribution by the use of *random sampling*.

Monte Carlo is only a mechanism

Thus, the Monte Carlo mechanism is not a simulation model per se, although it has become almost synonymous with probabilistic simulation. It is a mechanism used in the process of a probabilistic simulation. Before we show how this is done, let us define some basic terms.

Uniform Distribution

A uniform distribution is one where each value of the variable has exactly the same chance of occurring (see Table 15.3). This distribution is shown graphically in Figure 15.2.

TABLE 15.3 An Example of the Uniform Distribution

Demand	Probability
5	.25
6	.25
7	.25
8	.25

FIGURE 15.2

A uniform distribution shown graphically

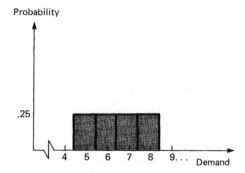

Random Number

A **random number (RN)** is a number picked, at random, from a population of uniformly distributed numbers. That is, each number in the population has an equal probability of being selected. Random numbers can be arranged in various ways, depending on the population:

Population	RN
0 to 1	Decimal — .62 or .876
0 to 9	Single digit — 6, 8, 0, 3
00 to 99	Two digits —16, 83, 42
000 to 999	Three digits—123, 306, 027, 815

Tables of Random Numbers.   Random numbers can be generated in several ways. The simplest way is to write each of the digits 0 to 9 on a card. Then shuffle the cards, randomly draw one, record the number, and return the card to the deck. Reshuffle the deck, draw a second card, and repeat the process. The numbers then can be arranged in tables where several digits (e.g., 6) are clustered together, forming rows and columns, such as in Table C2 in Appendix C. In 1955, the RAND Corporation used an electromechanical process that resulted in the generation of one million random digits. These numbers are used in many simulations. Also, many computer programs can generate random numbers on demand.

Assigning the Random Numbers.   The first decision concerns the number of digits to include in the simulation. For example, to sample the states of the United States requires two digits (for 50 states). Then, 01 might represent Alabama (if we use alphabetical order). To sample continents requires only one digit, because there are less than ten. Then, 0 might represent North America (or we could start with 1), 1 would represent Asia, and so on. To represent countries would require three digits because there are hundreds of different countries but less than a thousand.

The Process

The Monte Carlo process involves four steps (see Figure 15.3), illustrated for Sunny's problem.

Example: Sunny's Problem

Assume that more historical data collected through a time study or by estimation make it possible to express the service time in the Tourist Information Center by the probability distribution shown in the second column of Table 15.4.

Step 1. Construct the Cumulative Probability Distribution

This is constructed in the third column of Table 15.5 and shown in Figure 15.4. The cumulative distribution is obtained by adding the probabilities in Table 15.4 to the previous cumulative probabilities. At this point, the process can continue with either a graphical (steps 3 and 4; step 2 has been eliminated here because the graph provides the RN range assignments) or a tabular approach (steps 2, 3, and 4).

FIGURE 15.3

The Monte Carlo process

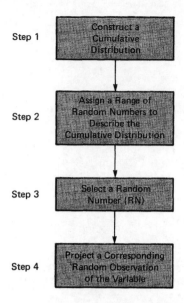

Step 1

Step 2

Step 3

Step 4

The Graphical Approach

Step 3. Generate a Random Number

A random number may be selected in several ways (see Section 15.9). A convenient way is to use a table of random numbers, such as Table C2 in Appendix C. The first number is 7823. Because we are working with three-decimal accuracy, we need only a three digit RN (782), and because we are in the 0 to 1 population, we will label it 0.782.

Step 4. Project a Service Time

This is done with the aid of the cumulative distribution, Figure 15.4.

   a. Locate the RN = .782 on the cumulative probability axis.

   b. Go horizontally to the cumulative probability, point *K*.

TABLE 15.4 Assigning a Range of RNs

Service Time	Probability	Cumulative Probability	Range of RNs
3	.156	.156	000–155
4	.287 (.156 + .287=) .443		156–442
5	.362	.805	443–804
6	.195	1.000	805–999

TABLE 15.5 Generating Random Service Times

RN (from Table C2):	782	430	922	871	477
Service time:	5	4	6	6	5

FIGURE 15.4

*Cumulative probabil-
ity distribution
shown graphically*

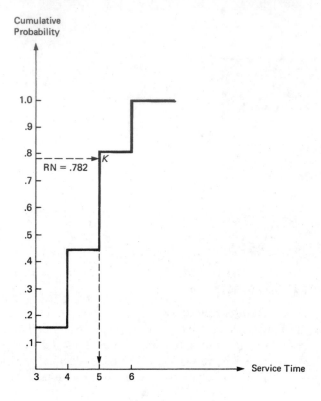

c. Turn downward and go vertically until the "Service Time" axis is reached.

d. Read the value of service time (5 in our case).

The Tabular Approach

This approach starts with Step 2.

Step 2. Assign a Range of RNs

Using the cumulative probability (Table 15.4) as guide, a representative range (or interval) is assigned to every value of the "service time" variable. This is done as follows
(refer to Table 15.4). Because this case involves three-digit data, the numbers 000 to
999 shall be used.

**Maintain
proportionality**

The assignment of representative numbers must be such that the *proportion* of the
various states of nature (the number of minutes of service in this case) is maintained.
For example, the assignment for three minutes service time requires 156 three-digit
numbers. This is because the proportion of three minutes is .156 and out of *all* existing
three-digit numbers (1,000), .156 translates into 156 (i.e., 1,000 × .156). The numbers to be used in each category are somewhat arbitrary. *Any* 156 three-digit numbers
can be used. For the sake of uniformity, one can start with 000. Starting with 000 and

counting 156 numbers, one will end with the number of 155. However, because it does not make any difference which numbers are used, one can also use the numbers 001 to 156.

In assigning the representative numbers, it is common to use, as an auxiliary instrument, the *cumulative* probability distribution. Notice, then, that the *lower limit* of the representative numbers (say, 156 in the case of four minutes) corresponds to the cumulative probability of three minutes (observe the arrows in Table 15.4).

Step 3. Generate an RN
This is done in exactly the same manner as in the graphical method (Use Table C2).

Step 4. Predict a Specific Value of the Variable of Interest
(Make a Random Observation)
Take the generated RN (782 in our case, dropping the unneeded digit 3) and find the range in which this number falls. In Table 15.4 the range is 443–804. Therefore, the RN 782 is said to correspond to five minutes service time. In a similar fashion, the Monte Carlo method will generate a sequence of random service times from a corresponding sequence of RNs (see Table 15.5). These predicted values are then used in the simulation process.

Simulation Experimentation: A Preview

The simulation experimentation in this book involves cases of risk, and therefore the Monte Carlo mechanism is used constantly. However, in deterministic simulation, the Monte Carlo mechanism is omitted. The following is a list of the nine steps involved in the simulation experimentation (including Monte Carlo):

Nine steps in
simulation

1. Describe the system and obtain the probability distributions of the relevant elements of the system. This is a crucial step requiring intimate familiarity with the system. Frequently, incorrect assumptions are made at this point that invalidate the rest of the simulation.
2. Define the appropriate measure(s) of system performance. If necessary, write it in the form of an equation(s).
3. Construct cumulative probability distributions for each of the stochastic elements.
4. Assign representative numbers in correspondence with the cumulative probability distributions.
5. Set up the initial conditions. Insert the values needed to start the simulation.
6. For each probabilistic element, take a random sample (generate a number at random or pick one from a table of random numbers).
7. Derive the measures of performance and their variances.
8. If steady-state results are desired, repeat Steps 6 and 7 until the measures of system performance "stabilize" (discussed in Step 8 of Section 15.5).

9. Repeat Steps 6–8 for various managerial policies. Given the values of the performance measures and their confidence intervals, decide on the appropriate managerial policy.

The above procedure will next be demonstrated with an inventory control example.

15.5 Time Independent, Discrete Simulation

Note: Some of the material presented in this section and the next, as well as the corresponding homework problems, are simple enough to be handled by analytical models. More complex examples would unnecessarily complicate and extend the presentation.

The Problem

Marvin's Service Station sells gasoline to boat owners. The demand for gasoline depends on weather conditions and fluctuates according to the following distribution:

Weekly Demand (Gallons)	Probability
2,000	.12
3,000	.23
4,000	.48
5,000	.17

Shipments arrive once a week. Because Marvin's Service Station is located in a remote place, it must order and accept gasoline once a week. Joe, the owner, faces the following problem: If he orders too small a quantity, he will lose, in terms of lost business and goodwill, 12 cents per gallon demanded and not provided. If he orders too large a quantity, he will have to pay 5 cents per gallon shipped back due to lack of storage. For each gallon sold, he makes 10 cents profit. At the present time, Joe receives 3,500 gallons at the beginning of each week before he opens for business. He feels that he should receive more, maybe 4,000 or even 4,500 gallons. The tank's storage capacity is 5,500 gallons. The problem is to find the best order quantity.

This problem can be solved by trial and error. That is, the service station can order different weekly quantities during, say, 10 weeks, and then compare the results. However, simulation can give an answer in a few minutes and a simulated loss is only a loss on paper.

Solution by Simulation

To find the appropriate ordering quantity, it is necessary to compute the profit (loss) for the existing order quantity (3,500 gallons) and for other possible order quantities. For example, 4,000 and 4,500 (as suggested by Joe), or any other desired figure. Each quantity is a proposed solution, and the first seven out of nine steps must be executed for each; the ninth step then concludes the analysis. Assume that today is the first day of the week and a shipment had just arrived, resulting in an inventory of 3,800 gallons. (*Note:* All quantities in this example are in gallons.)

Using a flowchart

Before constructing a simulation, particularly if computerized, it is wise to construct a **flowchart** or flow **diagram** of the tasks. A flowchart is a schematic presentation of all computational activities used in the simulation. Its major objective is to help the computer programmer in writing the computer program. Figure 15.5 shows a

FIGURE 15.5

Flow diagram for the inventory example

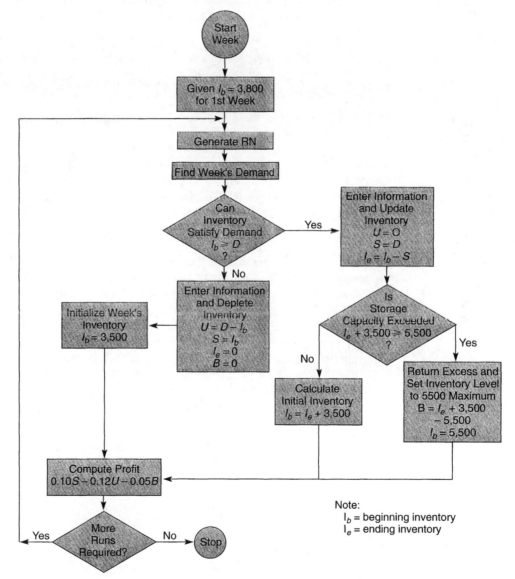

Note:
I_b = beginning inventory
I_e = ending inventory

flowchart for the inventory problem. We discuss equations and variables later, but the logic flow for the simulation process is clear. Therefore, let us begin the nine steps for the simulation and then follow the steps in the flowchart.

Step 1: Describe the System and Determine the Probability Distributions. There is only one probability distribution in this case; it describes the demand. In more complicated Monte Carlo simulations, there are several distributions involved.

Step 2: Decide on the Measure of Performance. The primary measure of performance is the average weekly profit, which is computed as:

$$\text{Average weekly profit} = 10\cancel{c} \times (\text{Sales}) - 12\cancel{c} \times (\text{Unsatisfied demand}) \tag{15.1}$$
$$- 5\cancel{c} \times (\text{Quantity shipped back})$$

Several less important measures such as the average shortage are discussed at the end of this example.

Step 3: Compute Cumulative Probabilities. The cumulative probabilities are computed in Table 15.6. (Columns (A) and (B) are given; column (C) is computed from column (B), and column (D) is assigned according to column (C).) The cumulative probability column indicates the chance for a certain demand or less to occur. For example, there is a .35 chance for a demand of 3,000 or less.

Representative ranges

Step 4: Assign Representative Ranges of Numbers. For each possible demand, a **representative range of numbers** is assigned in proportion to the probability distribution. For example, there is a chance of .12 for a demand of 2,000 to occur. Therefore, out of 100 numbers (all two-digit numbers), 12 will be assigned to represent a demand of 2,000. (*Note:* In this case, a two-digit random number is used. If the probability of demand were given by three-digit figures—for example, .115—then three-digit random numbers would have to be used.) An easy way of doing this is to assign the numbers 01, 02, 03, . . ., 12. (This information is entered in Table 15.6.) Next, the demand of 3,000 is represented by 23 numbers, because it has a .23 chance of occurring.

TABLE 15.6   Assignment of Representative Numbers

(A) Weekly Demand	(B) Probability	(C) Cumulative Probability	(D) Representative Numbers (Range)
2,000	.12	.12	01–12
3,000	.23	.35	13–35
4,000	.48	.83	36–83
5,000	.17	1.00	84–00

Because numbers 01–12 have already been used, it is logical to use the next 23 two-digit numbers, 13–35, and *any* number in this range will signify a demand of 3,000.

Note: Similarly, ranges for 4000 and 5000 are assigned. For the sake of consistency, we should have started the assignment of numbers from 00 and not from 01. However, we elected to start from 01 in order to stress the point that one can assign the range with *any* set of numbers. Starting with 0 or 00 (or 000) is most convenient. Therefore, our future examples start from 0.

Step 5: Initial Conditions. The simulation starts with a set of initial conditions. For example, $I_b = 3800$ in our example. In some cases, arbitrary numbers may be used. The stabilization (step 9) will take care of such situations.

Step 6: Generate Random Numbers and Compute the System's Performance. The first inventory system that will be considered is the current order policy of 3,500 gallons per week. For purposes of demonstration, Step 6 is repeated here only 10 times to simulate 10 weeks. In reality, it should continue until the measure of performance (average weekly profit) achieves *stability*, as will be explained later in Step 8. The detailed computations are shown in Table 15.7 and are executed as follows:

Column (1) designates the simulated week. In this example, only 10 weeks are simulated.

Column (2) is a list of random numbers (RNs) taken from the right-hand side of Table C2 in Appendix C. Here, we are interested in two-digit numbers, so the first and second of the four-digit numbers are used, starting with 32, then the next two, 08, and so on. (*Note:* The table of RNs is entered at some random location, not necessarily the top-left corner, and the digits read in *any* direction: horizontally, downwards, diago-

TABLE 15.7 **The Simulation for 10 Weeks**

(1) Week Number	*(2)* RN	*(3)* Inventory at Beginning of Week $I_b = I_e + 3,500$	*(4)* Simulated Demand D	*(5)* Sold S	*(6)* Inventory at End of Week $I_e = I_b - S$	*(7)* Unsatisfied Demand $U = D - I_b$	*(8)* Shipped Back B	*(9)* Weekly Profit	*(10)* Average Weekly Profit
1	32	3,800	3,000	3,000	800			300.00	300.00
2	08	4,300	2,000	2,000	2,300			200.00	250.00
3	46	5,500	4,000	4,000	1,500		300	385.00	295.00
4	92	5,000	5,000	5,000	0			500.00	346.25
5	69	3,500	4,000	3,500	0	500		290.00	335.00
6	71	3,500	4,000	3,500	0	500		290.00	327.50
7	29	3,500	3,000	3,000	500			300.00	323.57
8	46	4,000	4,000	4,000	0			400.00	333.12
9	80	3,500	4,000	3,500	0	500		290.00	328.33
10	14	3,500	3,000	3,000	500			300.00	325.50
Total	—	40,100	36,000	34,500	5,600	1,500	300	3,255.00	—
Weekly Average	—	4,010	3,600	3,450	560	150	30	325.50	325.50

nally, and so on. This procedure results in a set of random numbers because the table is generated in such a manner that every numeric location has the same chance (10 percent) of being occupied by a zero or any number from 1 to 9.)

Column (3) represents the inventory at the beginning of each week (I_b). The column is computed by adding the 3,500-gallon shipment to the inventory at the end of the previous week (I_e). The *maximum inventory* is 5,500 gallons, due to limited storage capacity. Thus, $I_b = I_e + 3,500$ (up to 5,500 as an upper limit).

Column (4) represents the forecasted demand, D, based on the RN in column 2 and the range of RNs in Table 15.6. For example, the first RN, 32, falls in the representative range of 13–35, which is equivalent to a weekly demand of 3,000. Once the second column (RN) is generated, the entire fourth column can be computed quickly.

Column (5) represents the amount sold. Two cases may occur.

Two sales possibilities

1. The demand, D, is equal to or smaller than the inventory on hand, I_b. In this case, sales equal demand (i.e., $S = D$ as in weeks 1, 2, 3, and 4).

2. Demand is *larger* than the inventory on hand. In this case, sales are limited to the inventory on hand, I_b (i.e., $S = I_b$). The difference between the demand and the inventory on hand, $D - I_b$, is thus the unsatisfied demand, U (column 7). For example, in week 5 there is a demand of 4,000, but an inventory of 3,500. Therefore, the sales are 3,500 and there is an unsatisfied demand of 500.

In Column (6) the inventory at the end of each week, I_e, is listed. It is computed by subtracting the amount sold (column 5) from the beginning inventory (column 3), $I_e = I_b - S$.

Column (7) designates the unsatisfied demand, U. This column shows the difference between the demand and the beginning inventory whenever demand is larger (e.g., in week 5). Thus, $U = D - I_b$.

Column (8) designates the amount shipped back, B. Such a situation occurs when the "end-of-the-week inventory" plus the shipment (3,500 gallons in the system under study) exceed the 5,500-gallon tank capacity. In this case, the excess supply is shipped back and the beginning inventory is 5,500. For example, in week 3, the shipment of 3,500, added to the weekend inventory of week 2 of 2,300, gives a total of 5,800 gallons. Therefore, $5,800 - 5,500 = 300$ gallons are shipped back.

Column (9) shows the measure of performance in this problem—profit. The profit is calculated, every week, according to the formula:

$$\$ \text{ profit} = .10S - .12U - .05B$$

For example:

In week 1: $S = 3,000$, $U = 0$, $B = 0$.   Profit $= .1(3,000) = \$300$

In week 3: $S = 4,000$, $U = 0$, $B = 300$. Profit $= .1(4,000) - .05(300) = \$385$

The resulting values are plotted in Figure 15.6a and compared to a "theoretical" continuous distribution that may, in reality, be the underlying distribution of weekly profit.

FIGURE 15.6

Profit results

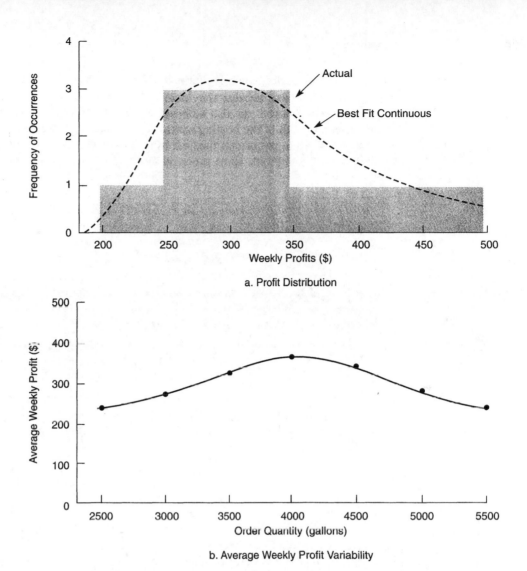

a. Profit Distribution

b. Average Weekly Profit Variability

Column (10) represents the *average* weekly profit at any week which is computed by totaling the weekly profits up to that week (cumulative profit) and dividing it by the number of weeks. The results are shown in Figure 15.6b. For example:

In week 3: Cumulative profit = $300 + $200 + $385 = $885

Weekly average: $885/3 = $295

Multiple trials

Step 7: Computing the Measures of Performance. Each simulation run is composed of multiple **trials.** The question of how many trials to have in one run (or finding the *length* of the run) involves statistical analysis. The longer the run, the more accurate the results, but the higher the simulation time and cost. This issue concerns what are called *stopping rules*. The stopping rules are usually built into the simulation program. For example, the number of trials could be terminated when a desired standard error in the measures of performance is attained. These measures are computed continuously during the simulation, because they determine stability and the stopping time (see Step 8). The length of a run can also be based on the length of an actual phenomenon. For example, the length of the boating season in Chicago is 10 weeks.

The simulation performed thus far indicated an average weekly profit of $325.50. In addition to total profit, some other measures of performance can be computed:

Multiple measures of performance

a. *The probability of running short and the average size of the shortage.* In 3 out of the 10 weeks, there was an unsatisfied demand. Therefore, there is a $3/10 = 30$ percent chance of running out of stock. The average shortage, per week, is $1,500/10 = 150$ gallons.

b. *The probability of shipping back and the average quantity shipped back.* In 1 out of the 10 weeks, some gasoline was shipped back. On the average there is a $1/10 = 10$ percent chance of shipping back; the average amount is $300/10 = 30$ gallons per week.

c. *The average demand.* The average weekly demand is computed as 3,600, which is close to the expected value of the demand (from Table 15.6) of 3,700. (In a stabilized process, these two numbers will be very close.)

d. *The average beginning inventory* is computed as 4,010 gallons.

e. *The average weekly sales* are computed as 3,450 gallons.

f. *The average ending inventory* is computed as 560 gallons.

Step 8: Stabilization of the Simulation Process. In all the examples in this text and the homework problems, we use only the initial data generated by the simulation to achieve brevity in presentation, even if the measures of performance have not stabilized. In reality, however, we recognize that the simulation begins to represent reality only after stabilization has been achieved. Stabilization is equivalent to what we called *steady state* in Markov analysis. Therefore, we distinguish a *start-up transient* period during which the data results are not yet valid. Usually, though not always, the decision maker is interested in finding the long-run, steady-state average values of the performance measures rather than the short-run, transient values.

Stabilization means steady state

Examination of column 10 in Table 15.7 indicates that the process, although close to stabilizing, has not yet stabilized (see Figure 15.7). That is, the *average* weekly profit is still fluctuating. Notice, however, that after six weeks, the differences are becoming very small. The end of this transient start-up period is determined from estimates of "serial correlation" in the measure of performance. Once this period is determined, *then* simulation runs are made to extend past this point into the stabilization period, and the measures of performance and their variances are recorded to determine their average value and confidence intervals.

Stabilization is essential

If there exist several measures of performance, then the stabilization analysis must be performed for *each* measure. Only after stabilization is achieved in *all* measures of performance (or at least in *all important* measures) should the simulation be stopped.

FIGURE 15.7

Stabilization of the simulation process

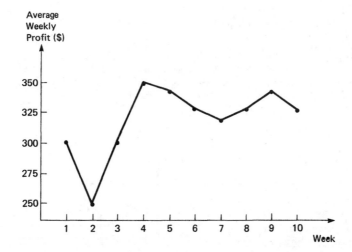

Step 9: Find the Best Ordering Policy. Steps 6, 7, and 8 are now repeated for other ordering policies in order to find the best. In the example just presented, the ordered quantity Q was 3,500; other values of Q (e.g., 3,300, 3,700, 4,000) should be considered next. Each Q constitutes an independent system for which the various measures of effectiveness such as average profit, average sales, and unsatisfied demand are computed. Normally, the same set of random numbers is used for all trials in order to increase their comparability (refer to variance reduction subsection in Section 15.9). Each such experiment is called a **simulation run.** The results for average weekly profit are shown in Figure 15.6b; the best results seem to occur at about 4,100 gallons.

In this case, the most important measure of performance has been assumed to be the average profit, and therefore the policy with the highest average profit will be selected (lack of space prevents us from showing the computations or calculating a 99 percent confidence interval). In other systems, two or more measures of performance may have to be compared, using a multiple objective method such as those presented in Chapter 8.

15.6 Time Dependent, Discrete Simulation

A Waiting Line Example

As you may recall, Sunny needed some tools to support her job as a director of the Tourist Information Center. To use simulation required extensive historical data concerning both the demand for services as well as the service capabilities. She has now collected the following information: The Tourist Information Center is staffed by one employee and is open from 9 A.M. to 5 P.M. The length of service required by tourists varies according to the probability distribution in Table 15.8a and they arrive at the center according to the distribution in Table 15.8b.

TABLE 15.8   **Arrival and Service Distributions**

a. Service		b. Arrivals	
Length of Service (Minutes)	Probability (Percent)	Time between Two Consecutive Arrivals (Interarrival Time, Minutes)	Probability (Percent)
3	15.6	3	20.2
4	28.7	4	23.6
5	36.2	5	31.2
6	19.5	6	18.4
		7	6.6

Sunny now wishes to find:

  a. The average waiting time per tourist, in minutes.

  b. The percentage of time that the employee is busy (utilization).

  c. The average number of tourists in the center.

  d. The probability of finding two tourists in the center.

Analysis

For illustrative purposes, we will simulate 10 arriving tourists (including the first arrival, we assume, at 9 A.M.) using the following random numbers for arrivals: 826, 058, 489, 643, 781, 321, 590, 187, 962; and the following random numbers for service: 242, 318, 876, 408, 630, 027, 716, 203, 130, 297.

The Simulation

Step 1.   Assign representative numbers for the two distributions (cumulative probabilities omitted) in Table 15.9.

Step 2.   Generate arrival and service times (in minutes). This is done in Table 15.10.

TABLE 15.9   **Assigning Representative Numbers**

a. Arrivals			b. Service		
Interarrival Time	Probability	Representative Numbers	Time in Minutes	Probability	Representative Numbers
3	20.2	000–201	3	15.6	000–155
4	23.6	202–437	4	28.7	156–442
5	31.2	438–749	5	36.2	443–804
6	18.4	750–933	6	19.5	805–999
7	6.6	934–999			

TABLE 15.10   **Simulation of Tourist Information Center**

| Tourist Number (1) | Arrivals | | | Service | | | | Measures of Performance | |
	RN (2)	Predicted Interarrival Time (3)	Time Arriving (4)	RN (5)	Predicted Length (Minutes) (6)	Start (7)	End (8)	Wait (Min.) (9)	Idle (Min.) (10)
1	—	—	9:00	242	4	9:00	9:04	—	—
2	826	6	9:06	318	4	9:06	9:10	—	2
3	058	3	9:09	876	6	9:10	9:16	1	—
4	489	5	9:14	408	4	9:16	9:20	2	—
5	643	5	9:19	630	5	9:20	9:25	1	—
6	781	6	9:25	027	3	9:25	9:28	—	—
7	321	4	9:29	716	5	9:29	9:34	—	1
8	590	5	9:34	203	4	9:34	9:38	—	—
9	187	3	9:37	130	3	9:38	9:41	1	—
10	962	7	9:44	297	4	9:44	9:48	—	3

Total (performance):   5   6
Average: 5/10   6/48

Explanation

Table 15.10 is divided into 10 columns: the first four deal with arrivals, the next four with service, and the last two with measures of performance. The time of the first arrival is given as 9:00. Next, a random number is selected to predict the length of service for this customer (242, column 5, is in the 156–422 range, meaning four minutes of service). The second tourist is predicted to arrive six minutes (column 2) after the first one because the first RN of 826 is in the range of 750 to 933, which corresponds to six minutes interarrival time.

In a similar manner, we generate all arrival and service times. Next, we compute the starting and ending times for service (columns 6 and 7). If the employee is busy with the previous customer, the tourist will have to wait, as happened to tourist 3, who waited from 9:09 until 9:10 (column 9). If no one is in the center, the employee is idle, as is the situation between 9:04 and 9:06 (column 10).

Analysis of the Measures of Performance

The Average Waiting Time (W).   For the 10 arriving tourists, only five minutes of waiting were recorded. Thus, the average waiting time per tourist was $5/10 = 0.5$ minutes.

The Utilization of the Service Facility.   The center was simulated during 48 minutes (from 9:00 to 9:48). During this period, there were six minutes of idle time; thus, $48 - 6 = 42$ minutes of utilization or $42/48 = 87.5$ percent utilization.

The Average Number of Tourists in the Center.   During six minutes, there were no tourists in the center, but during five minutes, there were two (during times of waiting). During the remaining 37 minutes ($48 - 6 - 5 = 37$), there was one tourist.

On the average, there were:

$$L = \frac{0(6) + 1(37) + 2(5)}{48} = .98 \text{ tourists}$$

This average corresponds to L in Chapter 14.

The Probability of Finding Two Tourists in the Center.   This situation happened in 5 out of the 48 minutes, or 10.4 percent of the time. In a similar manner, it is possible to find other measures of performance for this service system.

Time-Dependent, Continuous Distributions

Continuous distributions

In the case above, both the interarrival times and the service times followed discrete distributions. If one or both of these follow a continuous distribution, we must use the procedure outlined in Section 15.12 to generate the times of arrival and the lengths of service. Other than that, the procedure is identical (see Problem 27).

15.7 Risk Analysis

In Chapter 9 we presented simple examples of risk analysis in the form of a decision tree or a decision table. Simulation can deal with much more complicated risk analysis problems. Such problems involve many possible combinations and probabilities, and may also include some constraints. Thus, the standard decision analysis approach cannot do the necessary job. The example we use here is fairly simple, but it will illustrate the application of simulation in risk analysis.

Simulation for risk analysis

Let us assume that we want to predict the profit from product M-6. The profit is given by the following formula:

> Profit = [(Unit price − Unit cost) × Volume sold] − Advertising cost

Now let us assume that the unit selling price can take three levels: either $5, $5.50, or $6, depending on market conditions. We also assume that the probabilities of these market conditions are known. Similarly, the unit cost may assume several levels (depending on the commodity markets). The volume is a function of the economic conditions, and the advertising cost depends on competitors' actions. All this information is summarized in Table 15.11.

Using RNs, we can simulate the four random variables and compute the profit, or any other measures of performance. First, a RN range is assigned (Table 15.12). The simulation is conducted with RNs taken from Table C2 in Appendix C. The first 10 trials are shown in Table 15.13. For example, in trial 1, the profit $= (5.00 - 3.50)18,000 - 30,000 = -3,000$.

TABLE 15.11   Data for Simulation Risk Analysis, Product M-6

Selling Price	Prob- ability	Unit Cost	Prob- ability	Volume	Prob- ability	Advertising Cost	Prob- ability
$5.00	.20	$2.50	.35	15,000	.30	$20,000	.50
5.50	.50	3.00	.50	18,000	.45	25,000	.30
6.00	.30	3.50	.15	20,000	.25	30,000	.20

TABLE 15.12   Assigning Ranges

Selling Price	RN Range	Unit Cost	RN Range	Volume	RN Range	Advertising Cost	RN Range
5.00	00–19	2.50	00–34	15,000	00–29	20,000	00–49
5.50	20–69	3.00	35–84	18,000	30–74	25,000	50–79
6.00	70–99	3.50	85–99	20,000	75–99	30,000	80–99

TABLE 15.13   First 10 Trials

Trial	Price RN	Price Prediction	Cost RN	Cost Prediction	Volume RN	Volume Prediction	Advertising RN	Advertising Prediction	Profit	Cumulative Average Profit
1	17	5.00	91	3.50	42	18,000	82	30,000	−3,000	−3,000
2	05	5.00	89	3.50	31	18,000	17	20,000	7,000	2,000
3	21	5.50	17	2.50	60	18,000	51	25,000	29,000	11,000
4	66	5.50	94	3.50	71	18,000	44	20,000	16,000	12,250
5	43	5.50	85	3.50	76	20,000	75	25,000	15,000	12,800
6	54	5.50	44	3.00	55	18,000	58	25,000	20,000	14,000
7	11	5.00	62	3.00	52	18,000	41	20,000	16,000	14,280
8	61	5.50	09	2.50	38	18,000	38	20,000	20,000	16,750
9	35	5.50	66	3.00	59	18,000	29	20,000	25,000	17,667
10	39	5.50	37	3.00	97	20,000	61	25,000	25,000	18,400

Based on the simulation, we can find:

   a. The average profit.
   b. The probability of having a loss.
   c. The probability of having a profit.
   d. The probability of making $10,000 or more.
   e. The probability of losing $20,000 or more.

A risk profile

This information is then summarized in a *risk profile* probability distribution function and a cumulative probability distribution, such as in Figure 15.8. Such functions

FIGURE 15.8

Risk profile

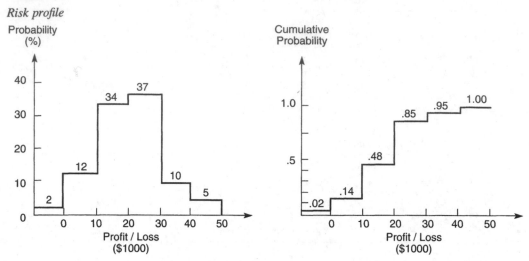

are extremely important in risk analysis. What these figures show is that the range of profit varies between a *loss* (−$3,000) and $50,000 profit. The mean is about $23,000 (based on 100 trials). If we compute the *most likely profit* (based on the most likely values of the variables) we would get:

$$(5.50 - 3.00)18,000 - 20,000 = \$25,000$$

a $2,000 difference compared to the long-run mean. The cumulative probability curve also shows us that there is a 2 percent chance of *losing* money on this product and a 14 percent chance of making less than $10,000. On the other hand, there is a 15 percent chance of making over $30,000 and a 5 percent chance of making more than $40,000. For further discussion, see Neelamkavil [11].

15.8 The Role of Computers in Simulation

Because simulation models involve only a few simplifications of the system, then the functions expressing the internal relationships are frequently many and/or quite complex, involving numerous variables and equations. In addition, each simulation run involves a large number of trials, as required for stabilization. On top of that, the entire simulation must be repeated each time a change is made in some of the input data. Finally, it is necessary to frequently check dozens of different system configurations. The end result of all the above is the necessity of a large computational effort. Therefore, computers are usually necessary for conducting simulation studies. Simulation problems can be programmed for computers with relative ease, because there is no need to develop algorithms or optimize functions. Also, special simulation languages can speed up the construction.

The need for a computer

Simulation Languages

Once a simulation problem is formulated, it is usually followed by a flowchart as a basis for computer programming. As with other models, the program may be written in a general-purpose language such as BASIC or Pascal, but this process can be very lengthy and expensive for large simulation problems. For this reason, there are many *special-purpose* simulation languages and packages. For a list and description of 56 packages see Swain [13]. Some representative packages are listed below:

Product	Vendor	Comments
Comnet	CACI, La Jolla, CA	Mainframe
DYNAMO	M.I.T.	For system dynamics
FACTOR	Pritsker Co., Indianapolis, IN	PCs and minis; shop scheduling
G2	Gensym Corp, Cambridge, MA	Minis and workstations
GPSS/H	Wolverine Software, Annandale, VA	Workstations; communication
GPSS/PC	Minuteman Software, Stow, MA	PCs
GPSS	IBM	Mainframe
Micro Saint	Micro Analysis & Design, Boulder, CO	PCs; discrete event
PC Model	SimSoft, Brookings, OR	PCs; manufacturing
SIGMA	Scientific Press, San Francisco, CA	PCs; discrete event
SIMAN	System Modeling Corp., Sewickley, PA	Flexible manufacturing
SIMFactory	CACI, La Jolla, CA	Factory simulation, flexible
SIMSCRIPT	CACI, La Jolla, CA	General purpose, powerful
SLAMSystem	Pritsker Corp., Indianapolis, IN	General purpose, flexible

Special languages (margin note)

15.9 Issues in Simulation

To fully understand simulation, it is helpful to elaborate some of the major issues involved.

Model Validation

Validation concerns (margin note)

The **validation** of simulation models involves practical as well as theoretical questions concerning the use of simulation techniques. How do we know that a model represents the process under study? How are we to understand what is going on in a model of a complex system? How do we use the results to yield predictions that are empirically accurate?

Analogies between wind tunnel models and simulation models are frequently drawn, but these analogies break down when one considers the complex underlying structure. The same fundamental laws of nature govern the behavior of an airplane model in a wind tunnel as govern the full-scale airplane. But a simulation model is usually a numerical representation of a system and is not governed by any physical laws that make it behave similar to the system that is being modeled.

A valid simulation model should behave similar to the underlying phenomena. This is a necessary validation condition, but by itself may not be sufficient to allow us to rely on its predictive abilities. Theoretical insights into the underlying phenomena that govern the behavior of the business, economic, and social system that is being simulated are critical to the construction of a valid model. There is, however, little consensus on the proper method to validate a simulation model.

Internal versus external validity

Validation may be viewed as a two-step process. The first step is to determine whether the model is internally correct in a logical and programming sense. The second is to determine whether it represents the phenomena it is supposed to represent (called "external" validity).

When a model is intended to simulate a new or proposed system for which no actual data are available, there is no good way to verify that the model, in fact, represents the system. Under these circumstances, there is little choice but to test the model thoroughly for logical or programming errors (especially at extreme values of the data) and be alert for any discrepancies or unusual characteristics in the results obtained from the model.

Experimental Designs

Some simulation models are very complex to design because the number of runs that are required to test all the feasible alternatives is very large.

Design issues

For example, consider investment problems (like our risk analysis example) with 10 possible investment alternatives (e.g., stocks, bonds), each of which may assume only five values. All together, there are 5^{10} different possibilities (close to 10 million). To simulate 10 million runs is very time-consuming and costly. The design of simulation experiments is similar to the usual design of experiments. Issues such as the *structure, sample size, cost, quality,* and the use of *statistical tools* to analyze the results are frequently involved. Other issues are: What constitutes a *significant difference* between alternatives? What is the *relative importance* of the different independent variables? For further discussion, refer to the bibliography.

Length of the Run

The longer the simulation run, the more accurate the results, but the costlier the experiment. "Stopping rules" have been developed (using statistical theory) to determine the most appropriate run size (see Jensen [9]). With the decreasing cost of computer time, it is usually worthwhile to make longer runs.

Variance Reduction

To save computer time, it is possible to design the simulation so that the greatest precision is achieved for a given sample size, or equivalently, the sample size needed to achieve a desired level of accuracy is reduced to the minimum. Several techniques are available for decreasing the variance of the distribution of the measures of performance (**variance reduction**). An example is *stratified sampling,* where the data are divided into portions (called *strata*) and each stratum is individually sampled. Again, see Jensen [9].

Generating Random Numbers

For teaching purposes, we use random number tables to conduct the simulation. These tables were originally generated by a physical device (such as a spinning disk or an electronic randomizer). In real-life simulation, instead of feeding a table of random numbers into the computer, the computer itself generates the random numbers. There are several methods of **random number generation.** The numbers generated by a computer are not called random numbers (strictly speaking) because they are *predictable* and *reproducible*. Rather, they are called **pseudorandom numbers** but for our simulation purpose, as well as most simulations, they are as good as the usual random numbers.

Start-up Conditions

It is usually necessary to wait until the model stabilizes before conducting the simulation, whereupon the start-up data are discarded.

Range of Acceptable Values for Decision Variable

Simulation is a trial-and-error approach, so an important issue is to determine the range of variables within which the simulation is conducted. For example, in determining an inventory level, should we test the range of 500–5,000 or 53,000–72,000? Especially important is the starting point. One approach is to start from any point and continue incrementally, following the development of a trend. For example, if the inventory level is being increased and so is the cost, try reducing the inventory level. It is advisable also to check *several* starting points so local optima may be located, improving the chance of finding the global optimal solution (or close to it).

Conducting Experiments with Simulation: Trade-offs

In the previous chapter, we illustrated several cases of conflicting costs (e.g., ordering costs versus storage costs in inventory and costs of service versus waiting in waiting lines). Such situations occur frequently when we simulate not only inventory and queuing problems but many other managerial problems. Because simulation may have several *independent variables,* it may be difficult to analyze the results of a simulation without establishing some trade-offs among the dependent variables. By doing so, one may also determine the appropriate values of the decision variables discussed earlier.

Sensitivity Analysis

Trial and error to check sensitivity

Sensitivity analysis is performed in simulation in two ways. First, using a trial-and-error approach, one can change the input values of the simulation (especially the uncontrollable parameters) to find how sensitive the proposed solutions are to changes in the input data. This is usually done by rerunning the simulation, either by using a what-if feature or simply using the computer's editing capabilities. Second, there is the issue of the value of additional information. One should explore the issue of if and where efforts should be directed to obtain better estimates or parameter values. The latter can be done either quantitatively (if possible) or qualitatively (nonmathematical approach).

Management Science in Practice

Simulation Improves Productivity at Burger King

From the time the first Burger King restaurant opened in Miami in 1954, coping with growth has been a constant challenge for the company. For example, when Burger King introduced the original "drive-thru" service concept, it had an overwhelming impact on sales—to the point where drive-thru now accounts for virtually 50 percent of food sales. But it also completely obsoleted their existing food service system, requiring an intensive analysis to redesign their restaurants to handle two intermingled food delivery systems. And in 1973, the "have it your way" concept required another massive restructuring of the food delivery system from one of mass production to that of a job-shop.

When meat prices began to fluctuate wildly in late 1977 and early 1978, the Operations Research Department of Burger King developed a computer model to determine what kinds of meat to buy from which suppliers so as to have the proper formulation of hamburger meat at minimum cost. The result was an average reduction in purchase cost of three-quarters of a cent per pound of hamburger. For a corporation that buys half a million pounds of hamburger meat a day, this resulted in a savings of over a million dollars a year. Further analysis by the OR Department of the shipping and distribution of this hamburger from a nationwide network of suppliers to a nationwide system of Burger King restaurants saved an additional two million dollars a year.

As operations grew more complex and more items were added to the menu, top management realized that a comprehensive computer restaurant model was needed to maintain peak operating efficiency with the ever-changing environment. This model would be used to test out new ideas and their impact on operations, service, sales, and profitability. Originally, a linear programming model was formulated, and it yielded valuable results, but it didn't permit the analysis of the increasingly dynamic aspects of restaurant operation. Thus, a simulation was subsequently developed that consists of three main models: a customer system, a production system, and a delivery system.

The simulation program handles some unusual characteristics typical of the fast food business: sales volumes can vary 1000 percent within 30 minutes (total daily sales are about four times the lunch-hour sales), the shelf life of most of the products is only 10 minutes, and all systems activities—production, inventory, distribution, and most consumption—occur under a single roof. The model was tested by comparing its simulated results to that of a live operation specially constructed in a warehouse to test all variations of extreme conditions. The videotaped results of the live test were compared to the model predictions and validated the accuracy of the simulation model. Today, virtually no decision concerning operations is made without having been subject to model analysis.

The model is used intensively, averaging 300 runs a month. Some of the applications have been:

1. Determining the optimal length of the drive-thru "stack size" (the distance from the order station to the pickup window), which increased hourly capacity by 12 cars.
2. Analyzing the effect of a second drive-thru window installed in series (rather than in parallel with two drive-thru lanes), which increased sales 14 percent.
3. Determining the operational impact of introducing a variety of new products.
4. Determining the optimal restaurant size for a given location (three basic sizes are now used).
5. Tailoring the amount and position of labor for a restaurant as a function of its configuration, product mix, drive-thru percentage, and sales volume (increased the typical restaurant's annual profit over $11,000).

The benefit of this computer simulation of Burger King, in conjunction with the capital investments recommended through the analysis of the program results, was estimated to be in excess of $170,000 in annual sales per restaurant.

Source: W. Swart and L. Donno "Simulation Modeling Improves Operations, Planning, and Productivity of Fast Food Restaurants." *Interface,* December, 1981, pp. 35–48.

Questions:

1. Why would the addition of a drive-thru necessitate changing the food service management and information system? (The menu did not change.)

2. How does a job-shop differ from a mass production system?

3. What are the advantages of simulation over linear programming for Burger King? What may be the disadvantages?

4. What is different about Burger King compared to most manufacturers who make all their products under one roof?

5. Identify the tradeoffs inherent in each of the five simulation applications described. For example, what are the benefits of having a short stack size as opposed to a long stack size?

15.10 Problems for Part A

Start all simulations with 0 or 00, unless otherwise instructed.

1. Given a distribution of daily demand:

Daily Demand	Probability
6	.15
7	.25
8	.38
9	.22

   a. Construct a cumulative probability distribution.
   b. Show the cumulative probability graphically.
   c. Graphically predict the demand for the following RNs: 91, 06, 85, 57, 31, 72.

2. Assign ranges of RNs to the daily demand in Problem 1. Predict the demand that corresponds to the following RNs: 43, 90, 12, 36, 51.

3. A community in South Florida is composed of 15 percent blacks, 40 percent Cubans, and 45 percent "others." Use random numbers to indicate the races of the first 10 people from the community to enter a room. Use the following RNs: 23, 74, 50, 96, 82, 79, 40, 06, 67, 31.

4. There is a 30 percent chance that a company will sell 100 units, a 50 percent chance that they will sell 110 units, and a 20 percent chance they will sell 120 units. The profit per unit is $14.

   a. Use simulation to find the average profit. (Use 15 trials. Random numbers are: 4, 7, 3, 6, 0, 9, 8, 2, 1, 1, 8, 6, 5, 7, 3, 0, 9, 4, 6, 8. Start the representative numbers from 1.)
   b. Compare it to the results of the expected value.

5. The U.S. Department of Agriculture estimates that the yearly yield of limes per acre is distributed as follows:

Yield in Bushels per Acre	Probability
350	.10
400	.18
450	.50
500	.22

   The estimated average price per bushel is $7.20.

   a. Find the expected annual per acre lime crop yield generated over the next 10 years. Use simulation; compare to the theoretical expected value results. Use RNs: 37, 23, 92, 01, 69, 50, 72, 12, 46, 81, 31, 89.
   b. Find the average yearly revenue.

6. The following information is known to you: A rainy day in Paris has a 40 percent chance of being

followed by a rainy day. A nonrainy day has an 80 percent chance of being followed by a nonrainy day.

a. Use simulation to predict what the weather is going to be over the next 20 days. (Today is a nonrainy day.) Use two-digit RNs from Table C2 in Appendix C. Start at the top left and go down the columns. Start the representative numbers from 01.

b. Based on the information collected in part (a), estimate the number of rainy days in Paris in one year (365 days).

7. A company has two cars. Car 1 is in use 40 percent of the time and car 2, 30 percent of the time. The president wishes to go somewhere; what is the chance that there will be a car available?

a. Draw a simulation flowchart.

b. Manually simulate for 20 periods. Use as many as you need of the following RNs: 7, 4, 9, 8, 4, 8, 8, 2, 0, 1, 5, 5, 0, 1, 4, 7, 0, 3, 2, 2, 7, 1, 0, 9, 8, 1, 4, 5, 4, 8, 6, 1, 2.

c. Find the theoretical answer (use probability theory) and compare with the simulation results.

d. Show graphically the stabilization process for 20 runs. What are your conclusions?

e. If a company car is unavailable, a cab is used, with an average cost of $15 per ride. Find the annual cost if the president makes 100 trips per year.

8. The B & T car dealership sells 13 cars, on the average, each week. The sales statistics show that of all cars sold, 20 percent are small, 45 percent are of medium size, and the remainder are large. The profit from the sale of the cars and the commission paid are shown in the following table:

Type of Car	Price per Car	Per Car Profit to Dealership	Per Car Commission Paid
Small	$5,200	$310	$62
Medium	6,050	425	70
Large	7,800	500	80

Find, with the aid of simulation (simulate for one week):

a. The size of the last car sold during the week.

b. The commissions paid in an average week.

c. The total dollar sales volume generated in one month (four weeks).

d. The chance of selling two large cars in a row.

e. The weekly profit to the car dealership. Use the following RNs: 08, 48, 16, 78, 37, 91, 82, 31, 54, 25, 69, 94, 41.

9. A newscarrier sells newspapers and tries to maximize profit. The exact number of papers purchased daily by customers can't be predicted. An elaborate time study was performed on the demand each day, and the following table was developed (for 125 days):

Demand per Day	Number of Times
15	10
16	20
17	42
18	31
19	12
20	10
Total	125

The following ordering policy was used by the news-carrier: The amount ordered each day is equal to the quantity demanded the preceding day. Assume that demand the previous day was 18.

A paper costs the carrier 15 cents; the carrier sells it for 30 cents. Unsold papers are returned, and the carrier is credited 8 cents per paper out of the 15 cents she paid. An unsatisfied customer is estimated to cost 7 cents in goodwill.

Determine the average daily profit if the news-carrier follows the ordering policy. Also determine the average loss of goodwill. Simulate for 15 days; use three-digit RNs: 782, 430, 922, 871, 477, 838, 872, 276, 198, 520, 076, 452, 702, 042, 297.

10. Kojo Corporation stocks small motors for their textile machines. The weekly demand for the motors follows the distribution below:

Demand	5	6	7	8
Probability	.2	.3	.4	.1

Motors arrive at the end of each week (after the plant is closed for the weekend) either 6 in a package (60 percent chance) or 10 in a package (40 percent chance).

Simulate 15 weeks of operation to find:

a. The average inventory on hand (at the beginning of the week).

b. The probability of stockout (in terms of number of times).

c. The inventory at the end of 15 weeks (before the last shipment arrives).

d. If the process has stabilized (check for the inventory level situation).

e. Comment on the existing inventory policy.

Assume:

1. The current inventory, at the beginning of week 1, is 5.

2. Unsatisfied demand is provided from stock whenever a supply arrives.

3. RNs for demand: 7, 8, 1, 6, 9, 0, 5, 9, 3, 2, 5, 4, 0, 4, 1, 7, 9, 3, 8, 2.

4. RNs for arrivals: 3, 1, 8, 0, 6, 7, 2, 4, 9, 0, 2, 8, 3, 5, 1, 9, 5, 7, 0, 4. Start the representative numbers from 1.

11. Customers arrive at a service facility according to the following distribution:

Number of Arrivals per Hour	Probability
4	.22
5	.68
6	.10

The service time is always exactly 11 minutes. The facility opens for service at 8 A.M. At the opening time, the first customer is there waiting.

Simulate for 15 customers. RNs: 73, 06, 62, 45, 93, 15, 69, 54, 37, 81, 26, 18, 81, 96, 31. *Find:*

a. Average waiting time, W_q.

b. Average time in the system, W.

c. Average number of customers in the system.

d. The utilization ratio.

12. Southern Airline has 15 daily flights from Miami to New York. The average profit per flight is $6,000.

Each flight requires one pilot. Flights that do not have a pilot are canceled (passengers are transferred to other airlines). Because pilots get sick from time to time, the airline has a policy of keeping three reserve pilots on standby to replace sick pilots. The probability distribution of sick pilots on any given day is given as:

Number Sick in One Day	Probability
0	.20
1	.25
2	.20
3	.15
4	.10
5	.10

Use Monte Carlo simulation to simulate 10 days. Use the following random numbers: 24, 57, 77, 68, 64, 88, 98, 50, 91, 55. Start assigning representative numbers from 01.

Note: The answers to the questions must be derived by *simulation* and not by statistics. The reserve pilots are assumed to always be available. *Find:*

a. The average daily utilization of the reserve pilots (in percent).

b. The average daily lost revenue due to canceled flights caused by lack of pilots (in dollars).

c. The chance that one or more flights will be canceled in a day.

d. The utilization of the aircraft (in percent).

e. A standby pilot is paid $2,000 per day. Find the optimal number of standby pilots.

f. Assume now that the standby pilots may get sick, too, with the same probability distribution. How should the simulation be conducted? Explain and execute.

13. A special medical diagnosis and treatment machine contains three identical radiation devices that cost $2,000 each. If any of the devices fail, the machine is shut down for one hour and the failed device is replaced. Management considers each hour of downtime as having an opportunity loss of $1,000.

The life expectancy of the radiation devices, in hours of operation, is listed below.

Life Expectancy (Hours)	Probability
500	.05
550	.08
600	.12
650	.15
700	.21
750	.14
800	.10
850	.07
900	.05
950	.03

Management is considering three replacement policies:

a. Replace each device when it fails.
b. Replace *all* the devices whenever *one* fails.
c. Replace a failed device and at that time check the life of the other two. If a device has been in use 850 hours or more, replace it, too.

The replacement costs are:

Replacing one device: $30 labor and 1 hour downtime.

Replacing two devices at a time: $40 labor, 1 hour and 20 minutes downtime.

Replacing all three devices at one time: $45 labor, and 1 hour and 30 minutes downtime.

Replaced devices with some remaining life are sold to a South American hospital for $15 each, regardless of age.

a. Write a flow chart for this problem.
b. Write a computer program.
c. Run each policy for approximately 10,000 hours of operation.
d. What are the results?

14. Conduct a risk analysis for Fiji Corporation's proposed portable word processor. The price can be set at $300 or $400; it is believed that the lower price will increase sales by 30 percent. The monthly fixed cost is $1 million and the variable costs are a function of the number of shifts used. If one shift is used, the variable cost is expected to be either $200 or $250 with a 50 percent chance of each. With two shifts, the variable cost will be either $250 or $270, again with a 50 percent chance of each. With one shift, the monthly maximum volume is 40,000 units; with two shifts, the maximum volume is 60,000 units. Assuming a $400 price, there is an equal chance of achieving either 20,000, 30,000, or 40,000 units of sales per month. What should Fiji's decision be concerning price and shifts?

PART B: Extensions

15.11 Complex Queuing Situations

Simulation for waiting lines

One of the most useful roles of Monte Carlo simulation is for solving waiting line problems. Analytical solutions, such as those demonstrated in Chapter 14, become extremely difficult, or even impossible, when the waiting line system increases slightly in complexity; for example, when the arrival or the service rate does not follow a standard distribution (such as the Poisson) or when priorities are considered. In Part A of this chapter we gave one example. The following example is more complicated. (Again, we skip the calculation of the confidence intervals for brevity.)

The Toolroom Problem

Manufacturing firms use a central toolroom to lend out tools to employees. Consider a typical situation with one clerk in the toolroom. Two different types of employees are

TABLE 15.14 **The Arrival Rates**

Production Employees			Maintenance Employees		
Time between Arrivals (Hours)	*Probability*	*Assigned Numbers*	*Time between Arrivals (Hours)*	*Probability*	*Assigned Numbers*
.2	.1	0	.4	.25	00–24
.3	.1	1	.6	.60	25–84
.5	.4	2–5	1.0	.15	85–99
.8	.3	6–8			
1.0	.1	9			

served by it: production employees and maintenance employees. Each has a different rate of arrival, as shown in Table 15.14. Note that the arrival rates do not follow standard distributions. The table also shows the assigned numbers that are required for the simulation. The number of employees in both groups is large enough so that the source of arrivals may be assumed infinite.

Currently, the production employees have priority over the maintenance employees; that is, a production employee will always be placed at the head of the waiting line. However, if a maintenance employee is being served, the service will continue uninterrupted (i.e., the production employee has a regular priority and not a "preemptive" priority over the maintenance employee).

Table 15.15 gives the distribution of service times, assuming that service can take only three time values: .1, .2, and .3 hours. The table also includes the assigned numbers required for the simulation.

Skip some numbers

Note that an *exact* duplication of the $\frac{1}{3}$ ratios is achieved by assigning only 999 out of all 1,000 three-digit numbers. (If we do not assign some numbers such as 999 in this case, then when such numbers appear as RNs, they are skipped over.) The assignment of three digits was arbitrary in this case (one digit is actually sufficient).

The toolroom clerk earns $8 per hour. A production employee earns $10 per hour, and a maintenance employee earns $12 per hour. The problem is to find the optimal number of clerks in the toolroom. Management also wishes to know if the existing priority system should be maintained.

TABLE 15.15 **Service Times**

Length of Service Time (Hours)	*Probability*	*Assigned Numbers*
.1	$\frac{1}{3}$	000–332
.2	$\frac{1}{3}$	333–665
.3	$\frac{1}{3}$	666–998

Solution

Simulating the Arrivals.   For the purpose of presentation, the time between arrivals of 15 employees of each type is simulated, using random numbers from Table C2 in Appendix C. The results are shown in Table 15.16. The table also indicates the clock time of arrivals.

For example, assume that employee 1 arrived at opening time, 7 A.M. Then, for arrival 2, the one-digit RN 5 is selected as the first RN from Table C2. According to Table 15.14 for production employees, an RN of 5 is in the assigned numbers zone of 2–5, which corresponds to .5 hours between arrivals. Because the process starts at 7:00, then the clock time is 7:30. The generation of arrivals then continues. For the third production employee, an RN of 2 is selected. The equivalent time between arrivals is again .5 hours, and the clock time is therefore 7:30 + 30 minutes = 8:00. The process continues for as many arrivals as desired (15 in the example) or for a specific period of time. Once the generation of the production employees is completed, the generation of the maintenance employee arrivals is conducted. The only difference in the process is the use of different RNs, this time with two digits.

Simulating the Length of Service.   The lengths of service are generated using three-digit RNs and Table 15.15. The process is similar to the generation of arrivals. The results are shown in Table 15.17, where 30 services are generated. A different set of random numbers is used this time.

TABLE 15.16   Generating Arrivals (Number 1 Arrives at Time Zero, 7:00 A.M.)

Production Employees				Maintenance Employees			
Arrival Number	*Random Number*	*Time between Arrivals (Hours)*	*Clock Time*		*Random Number*	*Time between Arrivals (Hours)*	*Clock Time*
2	5	.5	7:30		52	.6	7:36
3	2	.5	8:00		02	.4	8:00
4	0	.2	8:12		73	.6	8:36
5	2	.5	8:42		48	.6	9:12
6	7	.8	9:30		06	.4	9:36
7	3	.5	10:00		15	.4	10:00
8	4	.5	10:30		94	1.0	11:00
9	8	.8	11:18		12	.4	11:24
10	0	.2	11:30		95	1.0	12:24
11	6	.8	12:18		87	1.0	1:24
12	1	.3	12:36		04	.4	1:48
13	5	.5	1:06		99	1.0	2:48
14	9	1.0	2:06		40	.6	3:24
15	4	.5	2:36		98	1.0	4:24

TABLE 15.17   Generating 30 Services

Service Number	RN	Generated Length of Service (Hours)
1	782	.3
2	309	.1
3	194	.1
4	308	.1
5	421	.2
6	392	.2
7	283	.1
8	682	.3
9	871	.3
10	744	.3
11	244	.1
12	773	.3
13	264	.1
14	283	.1
15	879	.3
16	978	.3
17	477	.2
18	752	.3
19	016	.1
20	579	.2
21	260	.1
22	241	.1
23	643	.2
24	056	.1
25	861	.3
26	565	.2
27	029	.1
28	970	.3
29	958	.3
30	713	.3

Simulating the Process. Figure 15.9 presents what happened during the first six hours of operation. Assume that at 7 A.M., a production employee and a maintenance employee are waiting at the toolroom. The production employee is served first (has priority). Table 15.17 indicates (based on the first random number of 782) a service of .3 hours (18 minutes), from 7:00 to 7:18. During this time, the maintenance employee waits. The second production employee arrives after .5 hours at 7:30 (according to Table 15.16).

The first maintenance employee will start receiving service at 7:18. This service will be completed at 7:24 (random number of 309 for a service time of .1 hours = 6

FIGURE 15.9

The first six hours

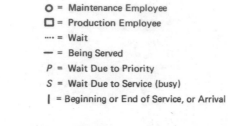

- ○ = Maintenance Employee
- □ = Production Employee
- ···· = Wait
- ─ = Being Served
- P = Wait Due to Priority
- S = Wait Due to Service (busy)
- I = Beginning or End of Service, or Arrival

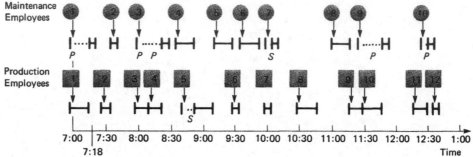

minutes, in Table 15.17). The second production employee arrives at 7:30 and is served from 7:30 to 7:36. The second maintenance employee arrives at 7:36 (random number 52 indicates that the second maintenance employee arrives .6 hours after the first one, Table 15.16). Because there is no line in the toolroom, this employee is served immediately (length of service is .1 hours as per Table 15.17). The third production employee and the third maintenance employee arrive at 8 A.M. (check Table 15.16 for computed times of arrival). Due to priority, the production employee is served first. Production employee 3 is served for .2 hours, from 8:00 to 8:12 (according to Table 15.17). Then, production employee 4 arrives (check Table 15.16) and, due to priority, is served before maintenance employee 3. Figure 15.9 shows the process for the first six hours. (This process could also be shown in an equivalent tabular form.)

Computing the Measures of System Effectiveness

The process that was simulated for six hours should be continued until stabilization is achieved. However, for the purpose of demonstration, let us examine the results of the six hours of simulation.

Arrivals

Ten maintenance employees arrived, or $10/6 = 1.67$ each hour, on the average. Twelve production employees arrived, or $12/6 = 2$ per hour.

Service

All 22 arrivals were served. The total service time was 4.2 hours. This means that the toolroom clerk was busy $4.2/6 = 0.70$ (or 70%) of the time. The average service time was $4.2/22 = 0.19$ hours.

Measures of policy effectiveness

Probability of Waiting

Of the 10 maintenance workers, 5 had to wait for service. Thus, the probability of a maintenance worker having to wait is $5/10 = 50$ percent. There was only one production employee out of 12 (8.34 percent probability) who had to wait.

Length of Wait

Total waiting time was 1.5 hours; thus, an employee waited $1.5/22 = .07$ hours (about four minutes) on the average. However, the average waiting time for a maintenance employee was $1.3/10 = .13$ hours, versus $.2/12 = .02$ hours for a production employee.

The Total Cost of Waiting

For production employees $= \quad .2$ hours $\times \$10 = \$2.0$ (for the 6-hour period)

For maintenance employees $= 1.3 \times \$12 \qquad = \underline{\$15.6}$

    Total $\qquad\qquad\qquad\qquad\qquad \$17.6$

$$\text{Waiting cost per hour} = \frac{17.6}{6} = \$2.94$$

Priorities

In five cases (50 percent of all maintenance employees), priorities were utilized by the production employees.

Conclusion

In this case, the system seems to be efficient. The cost of waiting is only $2.94 per hour. There is no sense in adding a second clerk to the toolroom at a cost of $8 per hour, because the maximum possible saving is only $2.94. The priority for the production employees is questionable. A second simulation run on a first-come, first-served basis should be run to compare the results. Also, a third simulation, giving priority to maintenance employees, could be run. (They earn more!) Results should then be compared.

Under a different system, it could have been possible for the waiting line to be longer and the cost of waiting very high. In such a system, a simulation run should be conducted to check if two or even three clerks were justified. Also, if one or more clerks are added, they could operate in various configurations. For example, each clerk could serve one group only, or both could serve one customer at one time (one doing the paperwork, one doing the material handling), and so on. Simulation can handle all such cases readily.

15.12 Simulation with Continuous Probability Distributions

The simulation procedure described so far involves random variables with discrete distributions. However, real-life situations may involve random variables whose probability density functions are continuous. The problem, then, is how to generate random values (demand, sales, and so on) from continuous distributions. Two approaches exist.

a. The Graphical Method

The graphical method involves plotting the *cumulative probability* function. This method can be used for any distribution, *including a discrete distribution,* as long as we can plot the cumulative distribution. Once the distribution is plotted, we use the following procedure:

Graphical or formula approach

A random number between 0 and 1.0 is first obtained from a uniform distribution such as the table of random numbers (C2), putting a decimal point in front of the number. For example, if the RN is 8, then we use .8. Next, we go to the cumulative probability axis (Figure 15.10) and find the value 0.8. Next we draw a *horizontal* line over to the cumulative function until the line hits the curve (point K), make a 90° turn, and go straight down to the random observation axis and read off the desired value. In our case, point L reads approximately 56.

b. The Use of a Formula

If it is possible to write the equation of the cumulative distribution function (or to use a table or chart) that describes it, then the following process can be followed. Construct a cumulative distribution function:

$$F(x) = P(X \leq x) \tag{15.2}$$

where x is the random variable of interest. Next, generate a random number (RN) between 0 and 1. Finally, set $P(X \leq x) = $ RN and solve for x.

The following examples will illustrate both approaches: Tables will be used for the normal distribution and a formula for the exponential distribution.

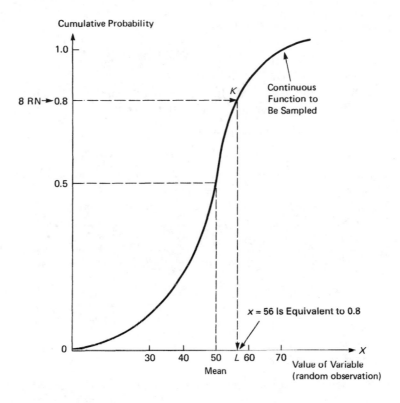

FIGURE 15.10

A cumulative distribution

Cumulative Probability

1.0

8 RN → 0.8

0.5

K

Continuous
Function to
Be Sampled

x = 56 Is Equivalent to 0.8

0

30   40   50   *L* 60   70

Mean

Value of Variable
(random observation)

X

Use of Tables: Normal Distribution

To illustrate, consider a variable that is normally distributed with mean $\mu = 100$ and standard deviation $\sigma = 10$.

Step 1
Generate a RN. Let us assume that the three-digit random number 695 is selected from a table.

Step 2
Put a decimal point in front of the RN; that is, the 695 is changed to .695.

Step 3

Using tables

Use Table C1 in Appendix C, the "area under the normal curve." Because it is known that:

$$Z = \frac{X - \mu}{\sigma} \tag{15.3}$$

then:

$$X = \mu + Z\sigma \tag{15.4}$$

The number .695, when spotted in the middle of Table C1, is equivalent to $Z = .51$. Using Equation 15.4 with $\mu = 100$ and $\sigma = 10$:

$$X = \mu + Z\sigma = 100 + .51 \times 10 = 105.1$$

Because Table C1 includes only numbers larger than .5, it is necessary to subtract any RN that is less than .5 (after the decimal point is added) from 1.0, or else use only numbers larger than 500. For example, the RN of 273 is changed to .273 and then $1.0 - .273$ results in .727. The corresponding value of Z is found in Table C1 ($Z = .605$ is equivalent to .727) and then Equation 15.5 is used to find X.

$$X = \mu - Z\sigma \tag{15.5}$$

That is:

$$X = 100 - .605 \times 10 = 93.95$$

Use of a Formula

Exponential formula

The exponential distribution is extensively used in waiting line problems (both for the interarrival times and the service rate). The distribution is described in Appendix B. Its density function is:

$$f(t) = \lambda e^{-\lambda t} \qquad 0 \le t \le \infty \tag{15.6}$$

where t is the time and λ is the mean arrival rate. The mean of this distribution is $1/\lambda$. Also, remember that the exponential distribution for *arrival time* describes the same thing as the Poisson distribution for arrivals per unit of time (*arrival rate*).

To generate random interarrival times, we can use Equation 15.7:

$$t = (-1/\lambda)\log_e(RD) \tag{15.7}$$

where RD = random decimal (between 0 and 1) generated from a uniform distribution, and $\log_e$ = natural logarithm.

Example

Generate arrival times for a waiting line system if $\lambda = 6$ per hour. Use the RNs 828, 135, 619, 430, and 015.

TABLE 15.18   Random Arrival Times

RD	$\log_e(RD)$	Interarrival Time, t	Time of Arrival
.828	− .1887	1.88 ≃ 2	2
.135	−2.0000	20.00	22
.619	− .4790	4.78 ≃ 5	27
.430	− .8440	8.44 ≃ 8	35
.015	−4.2000	42.00	77

Solution

Because $\lambda = 6$ per hour, then $1/\lambda = 1/6$ of an hour, or 10 minutes. This type of simulation is done in minutes (round results to the nearest minute). Thus, $t = -10 \log_e RD$. Table 15.18 presents the results.

15.13 Visual Interactive Simulation

VIS with computers

One of the most interesting developments in computer graphics is **visual interactive simulation (VIS).** The technique, also known as visual interactive modeling or visual interactive problem solving, has been used in the area of management science with an unusually high success rate.

VIS uses computer graphic displays to present the impact of various managerial decisions. These decisions can be implemented interactively while the simulation is running. It differs from regular computer graphics that use the screen simply as a communication device for presenting numeric data after decisions are made. Also, VIS can represent either a static or dynamic system. Static models display a visual image of the result of one decision alternative at a time. (With computer windows, several results can be compared on one screen.) Dynamic models display systems that *evolve* over time, the evolution being represented by *animation*.

Decision simulation

VIS is a decision simulation using visual interactive modeling. The end user watches the progress of the simulation in an animated form on a graphics terminal and can interact with and alter the simulation through various decision strategies.

Benefits

Conventional simulation does not usually allow a decision maker to see how a solution to a complex problem is developing over time, nor does it give him or her the ability to interact with it. The simulation only gives statistical answers at the end of a set of particular experiments. As a result, the decision maker is not an integral part of the simulation, and his or her experience and judgment cannot be used to directly assist in the analysis. Thus, any conclusions obtained by the model must be taken on faith. If the conclusions do not agree with the intuition or practical judgment of the decision maker, a confidence gap will exist about the model. The very nature of simulation studies means that a significant part of the analysis must appear to the manager as a "black box." For this reason, a solution derived by simulation may not be implemented.

A black box

The basic philosophy of VIS is that, because decision makers can watch the simulation of problem situations develop through time, they can also contribute to the validation of the model. Decision makers will have more confidence in its use because of their own participation. They are also in a position to be able to use their knowledge and experience to interact with the model in order to explore alternative strategies.

Testing the model

In order to gain insight into how systems operate under different conditions, it is important to be able to interact with the model while it is running so that alternative suggestions or directives can be tested. VIS has also been used in conjunction with artificial intelligence. The integration of the two techniques adds several capabilities that range from the ability of graphically building systems to learning about the dynamics of the systems.

A simple example of VIS is its application in the area of waiting lines (queuing). Complex waiting line problems typically require simulation, and the VIS can display the size of the waiting line or the value of the waiting time as it changes during the simulation runs. The VIS can also graphically present the answers to what-if questions regarding changes in the input variables.

Commercial software

General-purpose, dynamic VIS software is commercially available for both mainframe and microcomputers (e.g., see Bell, et al. [3] and Swain [13]). Most of the products listed in Section 15.8 have animation and VIS capabilities.

How VIS Helps a Manager*

The first exposure to VIS sets the manager on unfamiliar ground. A large color screen lights up with a graphic display that may include moving icons and blinking colors. The first response is usually a comparison to a videogame, and indeed, the program creating the display has much in common with game software. The comparison is, however, short-lived. The power of the technique emerges in stages.

Stage 1
The manager recognizes the screen display as a graphic representation of a familiar process or situation.

Stage 2
The manager observes the screen carefully, perhaps along with several other screen displays, and accepts the picture(s) as a sufficiently detailed image of the real process, with any motion showing realistic process evolution.

---

*This subsection is adapted from Bell, et al. [3].

Stage 3

The manager interacts with the model and observes that the screen image responds in accordance with his or her understanding of the real system.

Stage 4

Through experimentation and observation, the manager gains confidence in the visual model and becomes convinced that the model producing the displays is a valid representation of the real system.

Stage 5

Once convinced of the validity of the visual model, the manager can begin to ask what-if questions and the visual model becomes a powerful decision-making aid.

The power of VIS as a decision-making tool comes from the confidence in the model that grows as the manager sees the model confirm his or her understanding of the real system. Managerial validation of the model occurs because:

- A picture is recognizable as a model of the real world more readily than a table or set of numbers—a street map of a city is easier to recognize as a city than a list of the coordinates of street intersections.
- A visual model is not a "black box." The interior workings of the model are in full view and nothing has to be taken on trust.
- Dynamic visual models show the same transient behavior of the process that the manager sees every day, rather than average behavior over a long period of time.
- VIS enables the manager to interact directly with the model rather than working with a mathematical model through an analyst.

Once confidence in the visual model is achieved, VIS provides the manager with a decision-making environment very much like that of a scientist working in a laboratory. The manager chooses experiments to be conducted and evaluates them using results provided by the model. Explicit measures of the quality of alternative solutions can be incorporated into the model. For example, in a bus-routing problem, it may be desirable to keep the routes as short as possible and so, after changing stops around, the total length of the routes can be computed and displayed. Optimizing procedures can also be built into the model. When a stop is moved from one route to another, the routes can be redrawn so that the distance traveled is a minimum.

VIS is particularly powerful when the decision maker has multiple decision criteria, or where decision criteria are implicit or difficult to formalize. VIS allows the decision maker to choose a best solution, using whatever criteria are deemed appropriate. VIS is also a powerful training device, allowing the exposure to operations that appear to be very real.

Management Science in Practice

Log-Cutting Decisions at Weyerhaeuser Company

Weyerhaeuser Company (of Tacoma, Washington) is a large timber processor. The company developed several applications of visual interactive simulation (VIS) that have contributed approximately $7 million per year to the firm's profits. One of these involves the log-cutting decision.

Timber processing consists of harvesting trees, which are then delimbed and topped. The resulting "stems"

are crosscut into logs of various lengths. These logs are allocated among different mills, each of which makes a different end product such as plywood, lumber, or paper. For each tree, there may be hundreds of reasonable cutting and allocating combinations. The cutting and allocation decisions are the major determinant of revenues of the company and its profitability. The decisions are made on a stem-by-stem basis, because each

YOUR DECISION PROFIT $23.95

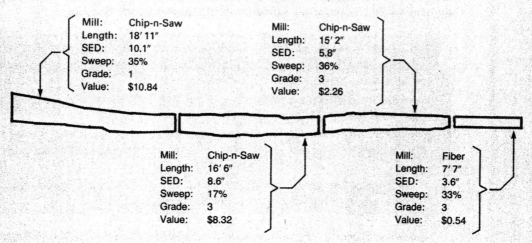

Mill:	Chip-n-Saw
Length:	18' 11"
SED:	10.1"
Sweep:	35%
Grade:	1
Value:	$10.84

Mill:	Chip-n-Saw
Length:	15' 2"
SED:	5.8"
Sweep:	36%
Grade:	3
Value:	$2.26

Mill:	Chip-n-Saw
Length:	16' 6"
SED:	8.6"
Sweep:	17%
Grade:	3
Value:	$8.32

Mill:	Fiber
Length:	7' 7"
SED:	3.6"
Sweep:	33%
Grade:	3
Value:	$0.54

MAXIMUM POTENTIAL PROFIT $27.92

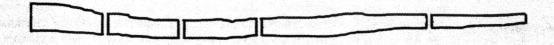

tree is physically different from every other tree. Many variables determine the manner in which a stem is to be cut, but these decisions usually do not affect cost significantly; thus, the larger the revenue generated, the larger the profit.

Management scientists developed a theoretical optimization model for the cutting and allocating decisions, using the technique of dynamic programming. However, the employees in the field were reluctant to use solutions that resulted from an unfamiliar, somewhat intimidating "black box" algorithm. Furthermore, like any other mathematical model, this one too is based on several assumptions that do not always fit reality. Therefore, the recommended solutions proved to be, on occasion, inferior to the solutions suggested by the operators. Thus, the operators had a legitimate reason for not following the computer's recommendations.

The VIS now allows the operators to deal with the proposed solutions on their own terms. This is done by letting them simulate on a video display a realistic representation of each stem (see exhibit). The simulator allows the operator to roll, rotate, cut, and allocate each stem the way he wants, on the computer screen, of course. He can *see* the end product and the resultant profit contribution of his suggested solution (upper part). He then can compare it with the profit resulting from the recommendation of the dynamic programming model (lower picture). If not satisfied, the operator can recut the same stem repeatedly (on the screen) to explore alternate decisions. The final decision, how to cut, is always made by the operator; therefore, the system is nonthreatening. Furthermore, the repeated cutting experimentation on the screen improves the operator's decision-making skill. The system is also used by management to evaluate alternative stem-processing strategies.

Source: M. R. Lembersky and U. H. Chi, "Decision Simulators Speed Implementation and Improve Operations," *Interfaces,* July–August 1984, pp. 1–15.

Questions:

1. In what ways did VIS help in implementation here?
2. How is the simulation conducted?
3. How does dynamic programming relate to the simulation?

15.14 Business Games

Business games are simulation models involving several participants who are engaged in playing a game that simulates a realistic competitive situation. Typically, a number of teams are organized as an **oligopoly** (a market where only a small number of sellers operate). Each team trys to maximize its own profit by making periodic decisions in areas such as production, inventory, marketing, investment, maintenance, research, and financing. Similar games exist for the services and nonprofit sectors. For example, hospital games allow the examination of decisions concerning staffing, room rates, expansion, and fund drives.

The two primary purposes of games are for *training* and *research*.

Training

Operational games

Operational gaming, or more generally, **management games,** have been very popular for training—both in industry and in academic settings. The advantages this method claims are: (1) a participant learns much faster and the knowledge is more permanent when he or she is active in the training process than when he or she is passive, and (2) the game introduces interfunctional dependencies (such as the relationship between production and marketing) in the organization in a congenial manner.

A great advantage of games, as in any other simulation, is the time compression factor—many years of operating experience can be obtained over the duration of a short period. This gives participants an opportunity to test unusual tactics that they would not be able to try in real organizations.

Research

Games are used for research purposes to provide insight into the behavior of organizations, the decision-making process, and the interactions within a team. When used to study managerial decision making, the manager's rate of learning as he or she continues to play the game is also analyzed. Observing the dynamics of team decision making sheds light on important research areas such as the roles assumed by individuals, the

Politics and conflict

effect of personality types and managerial styles, the emergence of "politics," and team conflict and cooperation.

Example: A Business Game

A business game uses a computer to simulate an industry in which there are a few companies (oligopoly) manufacturing and selling one product. Participants are organized into teams that manage their hypothetical companies in competition with each other. Decisions are made at regular intervals (e.g., "quarterly" decisions that may require 45 minutes in the game), and the outcome is determined by the interactions between the teams and the framework of the economic structure programmed into the computer. The models are basically deterministic, but the results may also be affected by probabilistic elements, because chance events and luck are sometimes programmed into the process as well.

A typical set of decisions made by each of the firms during each decision period (usually simulating a quarter of a year) is shown in Figure 15.11 for Firm #5. When decisions have been made, they are entered into the computer system. The computer, having been programmed to simulate the industry's operations, computes the financial and operational results and prints this information, as well as other useful reports, for each firm, each quarter, as in Figure 15.12. In addition, there is an "annual report" after every fourth quarter.

FIGURE 15.11

Typical decisions in a business game

Price of Product	Plant Investment
Marketing	Purchase of Raw Materials
Research and Development	Issue Stocks or Bonds
Maintenance	Dividend Declared
Production Scheduled	Financing

FIGURE 15.12

Typical game print-out

EXECUTIVE GAME

MODEL 2 PERIOD 3 JFM PRICE INDEX 101.2 FORECAST, ANNUAL CHANGE 5.5 0/0
SEAS. INDEX 90 NEXT QTR. 100 ECON. INDEX 110 FORECAST, NEXT QTR. 113

INFORMATION ON COMPETITORS

	PRICE	DIVIDEND	SALES VOLUME	NET PROFIT
FIRM 1	$ 6.19	$ 100000	794363	$ 150120
FIRM 2	$ 6.30	$ 200000	950000	$ 335424
FIRM 3	$ 6.20	$ 0	350091	$ -53503
FIRM 4	$ 6.15	$ 200000	1314660	$ 275325
FIRM 5	$ 6.10	$ 100000	741021	$ 39519
FIRM 6	$ 6.15	$ 100000	462704	$ 53713
FIRM 7	$ 6.15	$ 150000	522485	$ -34884
FIRM 8	$ 6.10	$ 30000	519784	$ 22190
FIRM 9	$ 6.15	$ 100000	830413	$ 179052

FIRM 5
OPERATING STATEMENTS

MARKET POTENTIAL	741021
SALES MARKET	741021
PERCENT SHARE OF INDUSTRY SALES	11
PRODUCTION, THIS QUARTER	820000
INVENTORY, FINISHED GOODS	147336
PLANT CAPACITY, NEXT QUARTER	431503

INCOME STATEMENT

RECEIPTS, SALES REVENUE		$ 4520230
EXPENSES, MARKETING	$ 900000	
RESEARCH AND DEVELOPMENT	200000	
ADMINISTRATION	419762	
MAINTENANCE	120000	
LABOR (COST/UNIT EX. OVERTIME $ 1.43)	1176310	
MATERIALS CONSUMED (COST/UNIT 1.55)	1269597	
REDUCTION, FINISHED GOODS INV.	-239218	
DEPRECIATION (2.500 0/0)	221630	
FINISHED GOODS CARRYING COSTS	74218	
RAW MATERIALS CARRYING COSTS	63590	
ORDERING COSTS	50373	
SHIFTS CHANGE COSTS	100747	
PLANT INVESTMENT EXPENSES	0	
FINANCING CHARGES AND PENALTIES	0	
SUNDRIES	90348	4447357
PROFIT BEFORE INCOME TAX		72873
INCOME TAX (IN. TX. CR. 7 0/0, SURTAX 0/0)		33354
NET PROFIT AFTER INCOME TAX		39519
DIVIDENDS PAID		100000
ADDITION TO OWNER'S EQUITY		-60481

CASH FLOW

RECEIPTS, SALES REVENUE		$ 4520230
DISBURSEMENTS, CASH EXPENSE	$ 3195348	
INCOME TAX	33354	
DIVIDENDS PAID	100000	
PLANT INVESTMENT	0	
MATERIALS PURCHASED	1350000	4678702
ADDITION TO CASH ASSETS		-158472

FINANCIAL STATEMENT

NET ASSETS, CASH		$ 204863
INV. VALUE, FINISHED GOODS		445307
INVENTORY VALUE, MATERIALS		1352205
PLANT BOOK VALUE (REPLACE. VAL. $	8912324)	8643557
OWNERS EQUITY (ECONOMIC EQUITY)	10914699)	10645932

SOURCE: Reprinted from R. C. Henshaw and J. R. Jackson, *The Executive Game*, 5th ed. (Homewood, Ill.: Richard D. Irwin, 1990). © 1990 by Richard D. Irwin, Inc.

After a certain number of periods have been simulated, the game is stopped and the instructor discusses the policies used by the firms, their results, the techniques of analysis employed or employable, and so on. A number of specialized games exist for financial management, banking, marketing management, production management, and maintenance, to name just a few. Several such games are available for microcomputers.

Specialized games

15.15 Corporate and Financial Planning Models

Long-range planning

One of the most important applications of simulation is in corporate planning, especially the financial aspects. Corporate planning involves both long- and short-range plans. These simulation models can be considered to be the first generation of early decision support systems. The development of corporate models differs from corporation to corporation. Some of them are *deterministic* (see Section 15.17) in nature, whereas others allow for risk analysis. Many large corporations (e.g., Sears, GM, J. C. Penney, New York Times, Eli Lilly, Monsanto, AVCO, United Airlines, and Kraft) have developed corporate simulation models. These models integrate production, finance, and marketing modules into one model (see Figure 15.13).

The development of a corporate model usually starts with determining the appropriate planning horizon (e.g., five years), then goals and objectives are determined, and only then is simulation used to project activities (such as sales, production levels,

FIGURE 15.13

An integrated corporate planning model

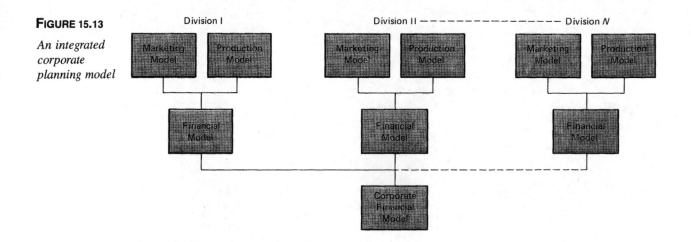

Short-run plans

or cash flow). Once the long-range plan is completed, the short-run (one year) plan can be generated. The model enables management to examine the impact of various policies, to conduct a sensitivity (what-if) analysis, and to perform a risk analysis.

Financial hub

The financial planning submodel is usually the center of the corporate planning model. A comprehensive conceptual corporate planning model was developed by Hamilton and Moses [7]. The schematic presentation of this model is shown in Figure 15.14.

A simple example of a corporate operational planning model is given next.

Simulation of a Paper Manufacturer

The simulation starts with the raw materials: the existing forest timber and the used paper available for recycling (see Figure 15.15). A set of equations effectively "translates" the timber into available pulp. Another set of equations does the same thing for the used paper. The plant itself is then simulated by equations that "translate" the conversion of pulp into paper and waste. Lag times between pulp input and paper output are included, as well as the lag time for shipping to distributors and wholesalers, from there to customers, and from customers to waste or back into the plant as used paper.

Under this system simulation, management can test the effect of varying environmental conditions on such dependent variables as annual costs, profits, revenues, reserve timberland, and total assets. The conditions tested include:

Test various
conditions

· Fire destruction of timberland,
· Decreased customer demand,
· Increased land values, and
· Transportation strikes.

In addition, the impact of various managerial (controllable) policies on the dependent variables can be tested. These include:

Test various policies

· Alternative uses of the timberland,
· Increased prices,
· Decreased production,
· Faster transportation, and
· Earlier knowledge of customer demand.

The result is a significantly improved basis for managerial decision making. Risk can be evaluated against potential profits. Frequently, the system simulation also gives the manager greater insight into the dynamic workings of the system itself, thus further improving his or her managerial decision-making ability. A detailed discussion of the dynamic aspects is presented in the next section.

FIGURE 15.14

*A corporate planning
model (from Hamil-
ton and Moses [7])*

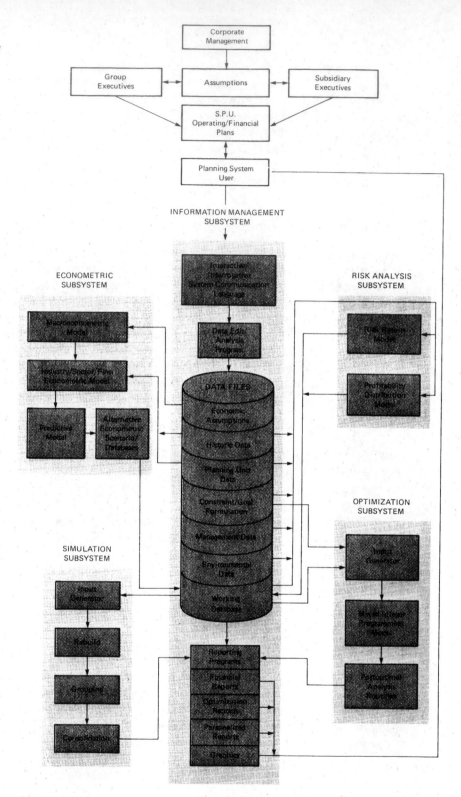

FIGURE 15.15

Paper manufacturer system dynamics

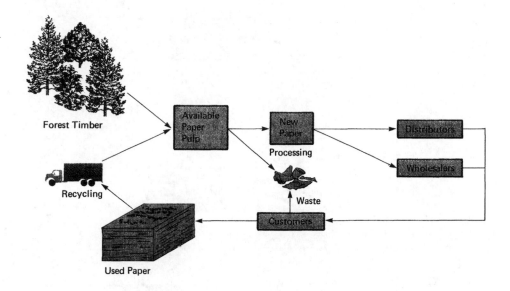

Forest Timber

Recycling

Used Paper

Available Paper Pulp

New Paper
Processing

Waste

Customers

Distributors

Wholesalers

15.16 System Dynamics

Nonequilibrium models

One of the most interesting types of simulation is **system dynamics.** Regular simulation models are most commonly meant to be evaluated in steady state (equilibrium) conditions. The same applies to Markov chains, queuing models, inventory, and almost all other management science models. But the real world is not static; it continuously changes. Therefore, a model is needed that will allow for dynamic behavior.

Industrial dynamics

Initiated in the 1960s by J. W. Forrester [6] under the name **industrial dynamics,** this engineering-oriented method is based on the concept that complex systems are usually composed of chains of causes and effects known as *feedback loops*. A decision or policy in one area (the cause) produces a result (effect) in another area, which in turn produces the need for another decision or creates another result. Two types of loops are

Positive versus negative loops

considered: *positive*, where an increase in the cause results in an *increase* in the effect; and negative, where an *increase-decrease* relationship is observed (see Figure 15.16).

Disaster!

Forrester used the system dynamics model to study the effects of population growth on the use of natural resources. The results of his model indicated a potential disaster for the human species. Population was predicted to reach a peak in the year 2020 and then decline rapidly. Additional computer runs were made involving other assumptions, such as doubling the estimate of natural resource reserves; unlimited resources; population controls; pollution controls and increased agricultural productivity; and perfect birth control. Although the timing varies, all runs eventually ended with disaster.

System dynamics has been used to encompass social, political, corporate, governmental, and even world systems. As with any other simulation, the method permits experimentation with a model of the system under study. However, in contrast to the other simulation models, which are more precise and deal with decision-making situa-

FIGURE 15.16

*System dynamics
feedback loops
(adapted from For-
rester [6])*

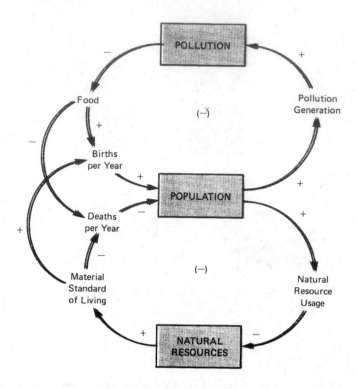

Policymaking

tions, system dynamics deals with policies. For example, a policy might state that our company will reduce the price whenever our major competitor reduces price. A *decision* would be the *specific amount* of price reduction (e.g., 5 percent). System dynamics models allow the manager to formulate several different policies and observe their effect through the feedback loops. However, a precise impact is not given, only the *general* directions (e.g., if price is increased, the sales volume will decline). The model, therefore, provides the manager with new insight about the system and its relationship with the environment.

System dynamics is composed of flowcharts coupled with equations that describe how the various elements of the system interact. An example of an industrial firm is shown in Figure 15.17. Note that in addition to the feedback loops (shown as information flows — — —), other flows are also shown. Note that inventory, inventory reorders, backlog, and manufacturing form a closed loop. The policy that we might test is whether to manufacture or to supply a backlog from existing inventory. Questions such as how to stabilize the employment level can also be analyzed through this diagram.

System dynamic models are generally associated with large computer simulations (via the special language DYNAMO). However, they now can be run on PCs.

FIGURE 15.17

System dynamics flowchart

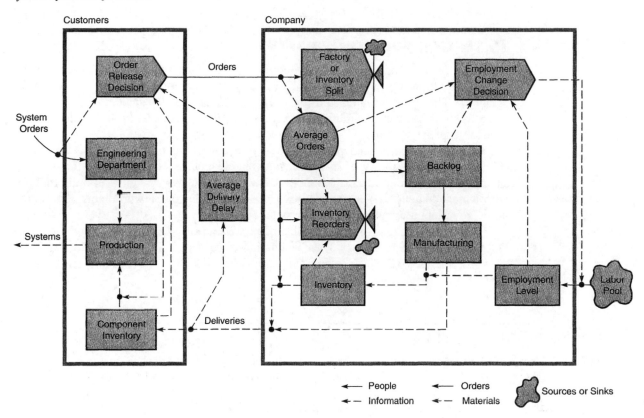

15.17 Other Simulation Models

Deterministic models

There are several other types of simulation models in use. Most of the examples presented in this chapter were of a probabilistic nature. In some cases, however, simulation is strictly deterministic, where all the variables are assumed to be certain. Several corporate planning models, especially financial models, are deterministic. In contrast to Monte Carlo simulation, the operating characteristics and relationships of the situation under study are *explicitly specified* rather than being random. Deterministic simulation models are normally less accurate than analytic representations of a system, but the additional simplification of ignoring the random elements is frequently justified and thereby results in a less complex, faster solution. These models are used to predict the impact of changes or to compare alternative courses of action or policy. Most of the

What-if capability   more advanced models involve a what-if capability so the sensitivity to changes can be tested.

15.18 Concluding Remarks

The advances in computer technology, combined with their reduced cost, make simulation one of the most popular techniques of management science, especially for top management. The more complex the problems and the more departments involved, the more likely is the use of simulation. Further, simulation is one of the foundations for decision support systems.

Complex organizational problems are often composed of many interacting variables, with the possibility of several uncontrollable chance variables also affecting the situation. Therefore, optimization models are usually not very helpful. Simulation thus allows management science to widen its scope and tackle complex problems in corporations, government organizations, and social agencies.

Simulation is a much more complicated task than using an analytical model such as EOQ or linear programming. The formulation is very complex and lengthy, and the programming may take weeks or even months to complete. Yet it is one of the most flexible management science tools.

15.19 Problems for Part B

15. Identify which types of simulation can be used in each of the following tasks:
    a. Writing poetry.
    b. Analyzing biblical passages to determine the author.
    c. Determining the effect of monetary policy on a national economy.
    d. Locating the most profitable sites for a chain of restaurants.
    e. Learning how to run a blast furnace.
    f. Imitating a controller's bond purchasing decision.

16. Describe visual interactive decision making and explain its contribution to improved problem solving.

17. How can a "hospital game" make a nurse aware of interdependencies in her hospital that she never knew existed?

18.* People arrive at an elevator in groups once every three minutes (there is a pedestrian crossway in front

of the building with a traffic light that switches every three minutes). The arrivals have the following frequencies:

Number of People in Group	Probability P(x)
3	.10
4	.15
5	.35
6	.25
7	.15

The elevator can accommodate at most five persons. It takes the elevator an average of two minutes to go up and return to the ground floor if it doesn't go beyond the eighth floor. If it goes beyond the eighth floor, it takes an average of four minutes to return. In 75 percent of the trips, the elevator does not go

_____

*Developed by Professor Dieter Klein, Worcester Polytechnic University, Worcester, Mass.

beyond the eighth floor. If a person waits for an elevator and the elevator returns, that person takes it *without* waiting for next group to arrive.

Simulate for 10 arriving groups until all people are accommodated. The elevator is at the ground floor at the beginning of the simulation and should return to the ground floor at the end of the simulation.

Find (by simulation):

a. The average number of people arriving each time.
b. The average number in an elevator ride.
c. The average time a person has to wait for the elevator.
d. The probability that a person will have to wait for the elevator.
e. The utilization of the elevator.
f. How many trips the elevator will make in *one hour*.

Use the following RNs:

I. For arrivals: 15, 81, 22, 55, 91, 48, 06, 58, 37, 74, 26, 87.

II. For the elevator: 09, 28, 93, 65, 31, 71, 42, 18, 68, 80, 52, 22, 60, 03.

Assign representative numbers from 01.

19. Of all the customers entering Swiss National Bank, 20 percent go to the receptionist, 15 percent to the loan department, 55 percent to the cashier windows, and 10 percent to the credit card department.

Of all who see the receptionist, one-half then go to the loan department, one-fourth go to the credit department, and one-fourth leave the bank.

Of all those who go to the cashier windows, 80 percent leave the bank and 20 percent go to the loan department.

Of all those who go to the credit card department, 50 percent will leave the bank. and 50 percent will go to the cashier windows.

Of all those who go to the loan department, 50 percent will go to the cashier windows, 15 percent will go to the credit department, and 35 percent will leave the bank.

Simulate the paths of five customers going through the bank. Assume that a customer may return to a service area more than once. Use the following random numbers: 78, 54, 16, 24, 58, 03, 90, 88, 48, 42, 59, 94, 80, 86, 14, 29, 36, 63, 12, 37, 89, 41. (Start the first customer with the first random number, and so on.)

Find:

a. In how many service areas each of the customers will stop.
b. How many times the first customer will show up at the cashier windows.
c. The average time at the receptionist's desk is 2 minutes, at the cashier windows 3 minutes, and at the loan and credit card departments 10 minutes. Estimate how the *workload,* in terms of minutes of service, is divided among the four service areas.
d. How many visits were paid, in total, to the cashier windows?
e. The floor area of the bank is 5,000 square feet. How would you allocate this area to the various service areas if the area needed is considered proportional to the number of visits?

20. Pump-It-Yourself, Inc., is an independently owned and operated service station. As such, it does not receive regular deliveries from the local wholesale gasoline distributorship, which is controlled by a major oil company. Instead, the station has the opportunity of purchasing any or all of the excess gasoline remaining on the distributor's truck after all regular deliveries have been made each day. There is no delivery charge if all the gasoline remaining in the truck is taken, but if not, there is a back-shipping charge. The delivery truck stops each day *after* the station has closed for business. The amount of gasoline remaining on the truck is a random variable with the following distribution:

Gallons Remaining	Probability
0	.20
500	.25
1,500	.30
2,500	.15
3,500	.10

The station has a 3,000-gallon storage capacity, and the demand for gasoline varies according to the following distribution:

Gallons Demanded	Probability
660	.10
1,200	.20
1,800	.30
2,400	.25
3,000	.15

Assume that unsatisfied demand is lost (customer goes to a competitor). Simulate the activities involving the supply and demand of gasoline for 12 days. Start with an inventory on hand of 2,100 gallons. Use the following random numbers:

RNs for demand: 79, 25, 03, 19, 28, 91, 58, 52, 68, 13, 46, 67.

RNs for supply: 69, 07, 95, 41, 49, 76, 08, 37, 83, 57, 12, 29.

Given:
Profit from a gallon sold = 20 cents
Cost of ill will = 5 cents per gallon
Cost of shipping back = 2 cents per gallon

Determine:
  a. The average daily demand for gasoline (compare to the "expected value").
  b. The percentage of time that storage capacity will not be sufficient for taking all gasoline from the truck.
  c. The percentage of time that demand cannot be met.
  d. The average daily beginning inventory.
  e. The average daily ending inventory.
  f. The average daily loss of unmet demand.
  g. The percentage of times that sales equaled demand.
  h. The daily net profit.

21. Given an inventory system with the following information:

  • Replenishment arrives at the beginning of the week (Monday).
  • Demand occurs during the week.
  • Inventory is taken at the end of the week (Friday) and orders are placed at that time.
  • Lead time: orders are placed at the *end* of a week and are delivered at the beginning of the week after next (nine days lead time).

Ordering policy:
If inventory on hand at the end of a week is I (can be negative for shortage) and replenishment due at the beginning of the following week is R, then: If $I + R \leq 5$, order so that $I + R + Q = 10$, where Q is the size of the order. If $I + R > 5$, do not order.

The probability of demand in each given week is shown below:

Number of Units	Probability
3	.05
4	.20
5	.35
6	.25
7	.15

Start with an inventory of six at the beginning of the first week (after replenishment arrived). Then:

1. Write a simulation flowchart.
2. Manually simulate for 20 weeks (use the RNs from Problem 20).

Find:
  a. The percent of times the system will be in a stockout.
  b. The average number of units stocked out per week.
  c. The percent of times the system will have a zero inventory at the end of the week.
  d. The frequency of placing replenishment orders.
  e. The average inventory on hand.

22. Assume that in Problem 21, the cost of a stockout is $50 per unit per occurrence, and the storage (holding) cost is $5 per unit per week. Explain how you would simulate to find if a different inventory policy is more profitable.

23. Dr. Z has an appointment schedule where patients are scheduled to come every 20 minutes. The office is open from 9 A.M. to noon, four days a week. The last patient is scheduled at 11:40 A.M. each day. Assume that patients arrive exactly on time. The time required for treatment or examination is distributed as

follows:

Minutes	Percent
10	14
15	25
20	41
25	20

The doctor will see all patients that are scheduled. Simulate for *two days* to find:

a. The average waiting time (prior to treatment) per patient (in minutes).

b. The average utilization of the physician (percentage that working time is of the total time in her office). *Note:* If the physician completes her examinations before noon, she will stay in the office until noon.

c. The average overtime (*in hours*) worked by the physician each week. Overtime is considered any time beyond noon.

d. The length of the last treatment on the second day (in minutes).

e. The average number of breaks the physician will have in a day between seeing patients.

f. The exact time the doctor will finish the treatment of the last patient on the second day.

RNs for the simulation: 52, 02, 73, 48, 06, 15, 94, 12, 95, 87, 04, 99, 40, 98, 58, 68, 08, 81.

Start assigning RN with 00.

24. Mexivalve, Inc., produces valves on a weekly schedule. Shipments are made to two customers, A and B. The customers enter orders by phone every Friday, after their weekly maintenance inspection is completed, and they want immediate delivery. Past experience indicated the following demand pattern: customer A orders either 15 valves (35 percent of the time) or 20 valves (65 percent of the time). Customer B orders 25 valves in 20 percent of the cases, 30 valves in 40 percent of the cases, and 35 valves in the remaining cases.

   The company would like to be able to meet all demand at least 95 percent of the time. The production manager thinks that he can do it with a weekly production schedule of 48 valves. Valves not demanded on Friday are used as safety stock, which currently stands at five units. Demand that cannot be met from production is met from the safety stock.

Demand that cannot be met at all is considered a lost opportunity.

   Simulate for 12 weeks.

   RNs for customer A: 63, 87, 06, 51, 33, 93, 15, 75, 26, 68, 41, 58.

   RNs for customer B: 34, 66, 12, 87, 43, 04, 53, 92, 27, 72, 49, 81.

   Start assigning RNs from 00.

Find:

a. Is the production level of 48 sufficient to meet the company's service policy? Why?

b. What is the average weekly profit if one valve brings 275,000 pesos?

c. What will be the safety stock at the end of the 12th week?

d. The average weekly number of valves demanded that are considered as a lost opportunity.

25. A certain service time is normally distributed, averaging 15 minutes with a standard deviation of 2. Three RNs were generated: 386, 628, 953. Find the length of service time of the first three services.

26. Demand for a perishable liquid product is known to be normally distributed, with an average daily demand of 23 gallons and a standard deviation of 4 gallons.

a. Generate demand for 10 days. Use RNs: 783, 430, 922, 871, 477, 838, 872, 276, 198, 520.

b. Round the average daily demand found in part (*a*) to one decimal point (e.g., 25.2). Assume that an inventory of 23.6 gallons is being kept daily. If demand in a given day is more than the inventory on hand, the company incurs a loss of $100 for each gallon short (proportion of $100 for fraction of a gallon). If there is some left over, the company's demurrage is $120 per gallon (proportion for a fraction). Find the average daily profit (loss) if each gallon sold contributes $50 to profit.

c. Based on the result of part (*b*), estimate the chance of not meeting the demand on any specific day.

27. Solve the waiting line problem of Section 15.6, using the following data:

a. The interarrival time is five minutes, on the average, with a standard deviation of 1.0 minute (normally distributed).

b. The service time is constant—five minutes. Use the same RNs as in the example.

28. *Given:*

   1. A waiting line situation with Poisson arrivals of $\lambda = 10$ per hour.
   2. The service time is four minutes (exponentially distributed).

   Simulate for 12 arrivals to find:
   a. The average waiting time.
   b. The utilization of the system (round to the nearest whole minute).

   Use RNs from Table C2; column 1 for arrivals, column 2 for service. Use three digit RNs.

29. A survey of 100 arriving customers at a drive-in window of North Eastern Bank resulted in the following information:

Time Between Arrivals (Minutes)	Frequency
.5	6
1.0	10
1.5	15
2.0	18
2.5	20
3.0	15
3.5	12
4.0	4
	100

The service time (from the time the car enters the service position until the car leaves) was distributed as follows:

Service Time (Minutes)	Frequency
1.0	12
1.5	18
2.0	30
2.5	25
3.0	15

a. Convert the distributions to cumulative probability distributions.

b. Use the graphical approach to generate 12 arrivals:

RNs for arrivals: 81, 13, 66, 58, 43, 76, 06, 33, 96, 50, 88, 39.
RNs for service: 26, 48, 04, 62, 98, 17, 51, 58, 73, 86, 21, 35.

c. Find the average waiting time per customer.
d. Find the utilization (in percent) of the drive-in window.

30. Moscow University has an information center staffed by one employee. Historical data indicate that people arrive at the center according to the following distribution:

Interarrival Time (Minutes)	Frequency
4	.223
5	.481
6	.275
7	.021

The time of service is normally distributed with an average of five minutes and a standard deviation of one minute. The center opens at 8:30 sharp. Simulate for 12 customers (including the first one). Use the following RNs:

For arrivals: .621, .326, .907, .698, .018, .434, .715, .246, .168, .540, .992.
For service: .319, .625, .428, .912, .037, .446, .721, .173, .268, .819, .396, .527.

Note:
1. Round the minutes to the nearest whole minute.
2. Round all other numbers to the nearest possible figure.
3. End the simulation after the last customer is served.

Find:
a. The utilization of the center.
b. The average number of customers in the center (waiting and/or being served).
c. The probability that a customer will have to wait.
d. The probability that a customer will be in the center more than five minutes in total.
e. The average waiting time, W_q, in the queue.

31. The demand for Orange Microcomputer II for the next 10 weeks is known (from existing orders) as: 520, 314, 618, 240, 590, 806, 430, 180, 300, 250. It takes two weeks to receive micros from the factory. The current inventory on hand is 600; an additional 400 will arrive next week. The costs are:

    Ordering costs are $300 plus $5 per unit.

    Carrying cost is $10 per unit per week.

    Shortage cost is $30 per unit short (special rush shipment).

    The existing ordering policy is to order 500 units whenever the inventory is 100 units or less.

    a. Simulate for a period of 10 weeks.
    b. Calculate the average inventory and shortage cost per week.
    c. Design a better ordering rule and find how much money you can save.

32. Simulation is often used to examine the tradeoffs of changing the values of the decision variables, similar to Figures 12.8 and 14.2. What costs trade off in the example of Section 15.11? Section 15.5?

In early October, Mr. Hans Huber, operations manager of Express A. G., received a request from Mr. Max Retter, the traffic manager at Stuttgart, Germany for an increase in the number of dispatchers assigned to the Stuttgart operation from two (the present number) to four. Mr. Retter claimed that with only two dispatchers the delivery van drivers were spending too much idle time waiting to report in and to receive new instructions. When Mr. Huber asked Retter how he had arrived at "four dispatchers" as the appropriate number, Retter replied, "Based on my observations, four dispatchers should clear up most of the waiting time." Mr. Huber then promised to look into the matter and to advise Retter of his decision.

The Delivery Van Operations of Express A. G.

Express A. G. is an integrated transportation company operating throughout Germany. Its headquarters is in Frankfurt, and other major operations centers are at München, Stuttgart, Hamburg, Bremen, and Aachen. An important segment of Express' business is the delivery van operation. In each major center, Express operates a fleet of delivery vans that serves the metropolitan area around the center. The delivery vans make home deliveries for many of the large department stores. In addition, the vans deliver goods locally that are brought into the metropolitan area warehouses by the large transcontinental trucking firms.

For each trip, the driver of the delivery van receives instructions from the dispatcher as to the particular requirements of the assignment. Upon return to the motor pool, the driver reports to the dispatcher either the successful completion of his assignment or any difficulties that he may have encountered. At the completion of the "trip report," the dispatcher assigns the driver to a new job.

The Operation at Stuttgart

Following the receipt of Mr. Retter's request, Mr. Huber became quite concerned. He felt that Retter's request should not be looked upon in isolation—if, as Retter claimed, the number of dispatchers at Stuttgart was inadequate, then it was probable that most of the other delivery van centers were also understaffed. Therefore, he decided to send Felix Stamm, a staff operations analyst, to Stuttgart to investigate the problem.

Mr. Stamm spent several days at Stuttgart and then returned to Frankfurt. He showed Mr. Huber the data he had gathered about the Stuttgart operation (see Exhibit 1) and promised to prepare a report within the next few days.

EXHIBIT 1 Information about Delivery Van Operation at Stuttgart

Number of dispatchers	2
Number of delivery vans	30
Average length of trip	2 hours
Arrival rate per hour at dispatcher's office	Random, approximately normally distributed, with mean = 15 and standard deviation = 4.*
Time with dispatcher	Random, approximately normally distributed, with mean = 8 minutes and standard deviation = 3 minutes. Minimum service time = 1 minute.
Wage rate per hour—dispatchers	12 DM†
Wage rate per hour—drivers	10 DM
Billing rate (revenue) per hour for van with driver	30 DM

* Within the hour, the arrivals appear to follow a completely random pattern.
† DM stands for the German currency deutsche mark.

---

*Adapted from a case prepared by Professor A. A. Robichek, Stanford University, Graduate School of Business. Copyright 1967, by l'Institut pour l'Etude des Méthodes de Direction de l'Entreprise (IMEDE), Lausanne, Switzerland. Reproduced by permission.

Questions for Discussion:

1. What is the optimal number of dispatchers for Stuttgart under each of the following assumptions:
   a. While the driver is waiting to see a dispatcher, the van is being serviced by the service department.
   b. The van and the driver are both idle during the waiting period.

   (In resolving this problem, make any additional assumptions you consider necessary.)

2. What additional information would have been of assistance in resolving this problem?

Notes:

a. Simulate for two hours. Use the waiting times for the second hour to arrive at a decision (waiting time for the first hour is too far from a stabilized condition).
b. Round the time to whole minutes.
c. Simulate the exact minute of arrival by using the formula: random number $\times$ (60/100). After computing the average number of arrivals within an hour, arrange by the "order of arrivals."
d. Use Table C2 for estimated service time and arrival rate values.

Glossary

Business games   Operational games that deal with decision making at the top executive level of a business corporation.

DYNAMO   A special-purpose simulation language for system dynamics.

Flowchart (or diagram)   A schematic presentation of all computational activities used in the simulation written in a symbolic language.

GASP   A simulation language written in FORTRAN.

GPSS   A flowchart-oriented simulation language.

Industrial dynamics   A computerized system simulation of a whole company or industry.

Monte Carlo simulation   Simulation that uses a random number mechanism to describe the behavior of systems with probabilistic elements.

Oligopoly   A market where only a small number of sellers operate.

Operational (management) games   Simulation of a competitive situation arranged in the form of a game. Participants make periodic decisions and the results are then analyzed. Such games are used mainly for training purposes.

Pseudorandom number   A random number generated by a mathematical process.

Random number (RN)   Numbers sampled from a uniform distribution. Each number has the same chance of being drawn.

Random number generation   A process of generating random numbers, usually by a computer. Can be done manually by drawing pieces of papers with numbers from a hat or from a specially constructed table.

Representative range of numbers   A range of numbers with the same number of digits that corresponds to the frequency distribution of the factor under consideration.

SIMSCRIPT   A special computer programming language.

Simulation   A procedure that involves the use of a mathematical model that imitates reality for the purpose of conducting experiments on the model. These trial-and-error-type experiments intend to *predict* the behavior of the system under different situations.

Simulation runs   A simulation run is one simulation experiment with one set of input data.

System dynamics   Simulation of large systems that allow for dynamic behavior. Used mainly for policy analysis.

Time compression   The ability to simulate years of operations in seconds or minutes of computer time.

Time dependent   Simulation where the exact time of each event is required and tracked.

Time independent   Simulation where the exact time of each event is *not* needed.

Trial   One period in a simulation run. A run is composed of many trials.

Validation   Determining how accurately the model predicts the behavior of the system.

Variance reduction   A technique for increasing the precision for a fixed sample size (or decreasing the sample size required to obtain a desired level of precision).

Visual interactive simulation   Visual interactive decision making in real time using simulation and computer graphics.

15.22 References and Bibliography

1. Aburdene, M. F. *Computer Simulation of Dynamic Systems,* Dubuque, Ia.: Wm. C. Brown, 1988.

2. Banks, J., and J. S. Carson. *Discrete Event System Simulation,* Englewood Cliffs, N.J.: Prentice-Hall, 1984.

3. Bell, P. C., et al. "Visual Interactive Problem Solving—A New Look at Management Problems." *Business Quarterly,* Spring 1984.

4. Condon, A. *Computational Models of Games.* Cambridge, Mass.: MIT Press, 1989.

5. Curry, G. L., et al. *Discrete Simulation: Fundamentals and Microcomputer Support.* Oakland, Calif.: Holden Day, 1989.

6. Forrester, J. W. *World Dynamics,* Cambridge, Mass.: Write-Allen Press, 1971.

7. Hamilton, W. F., and M. A. Moses, "A Computer-Based Corporate Planning System." *Management Science,* October 1974, pp. 148–159.

8. Hoover, S. V., and R. F. Perry. *Simulation: A Problem Approach.* Reading, Mass.: Addison Wesley Publishing, 1989.

9. Jensen, R. L. *A Management Experience.* Homewood, Ill.: Richard D. Irwin, 1990.

10. Law, A. M. and W. Kelton. *Simulation Modeling and Analysis.* 2nd ed. New York: McGraw-Hill, 1990.

11. Neelamkavil, F. *Computer Simulation and Modeling.* New York: John Wiley & Sons, 1987.

12. Pidd, M. *Computer Simulation in Management Science.* 2nd ed. New York: John Wiley & Sons, 1988.

13. Swain, J. *World of Choices—Simulation Software Survey. OR/MS Today,* Oct. 1991.

14. Watson, H. J., and J. H. Blackstone, Jr. *Computer Simulation.* 2nd ed. New York: John Wiley & Sons, 1989.

Dynamic Programming

The managerial problems presented in the previous chapters dealt with situations involving a single decision. Management, however, must frequently consider a *sequence* of decisions where each decision affects future decisions. The tool used for solving certain types of such sequential decision problems is called dynamic programming. Dynamic programming also facilitates dividing complex problems into simpler subproblems that can be solved and then recombined to solve the original problem.

No single model for solving dynamic programming problems exists. Therefore, these problems are classified into groups, each with its own formulation and method of solution. However, the basic approach and logic for solving all dynamic programming problems is the same. In Part A of this chapter, the basic structure and terminology of dynamic programming are discussed. Some examples are also given to illustrate the prototype problems and their solution approaches. In Part B of the chapter, the mathematics of the dynamic programming method are formulated and additional examples are given.

PART A: BASICS

Jeff knew that he was in trouble. It had been only three days since he received the job he had waited so long for, that of a dinner cook at the prestigious Queen's Hotel. The recipe for dinner that evening called for 7 ounces of wine; but Jeff, new on the job, could only find a 5-ounce cup and an 8-ounce cup.* The problem was that dinnertime was quickly approaching and no time remained to search for other measuring cups or to buy or borrow one. Jeff was tempted to use the 8-ounce cup, filling it not quite to capacity; but as a good cook he knew that accuracy in the use of wine was very important.

Jeff did some quick thinking. Clearly, if 7 ounces of wine were to be contained in one of the cups, it must be the 8-ounce cup. The problem then became one of getting 7 ounces into the 8-ounce cup. Proceeding in the same manner, he realized that if 2 ounces of wine were already in the 8-ounce cup, his problem would have been solved. He could the use a full 5-ounce cup of wine to add to the 2 ounces. How then could he pour 2 ounces of wine into the 8-ounce cup? Presumably by filling one of the cups and then pouring some out. using the 8-ounce cup meant filling it up and pouring out 6 ounces. Using the 5-ounce cup, it would be necessary to pour out 3 ounces. In either case, he needed a 6-ounce or a 3-ounce cup, but he had neither. Which alternative should he explore further? Jeff felt that he was getting nowhere, and dinnertime was almost at hand. The problem, however, intrigued him, and he considered it a bit longer.

After a moment of reflection he was sure that his problem could be solved. If 5 ounces of wine were in the 8-ounce cup (which could be accomplished by filling the 5-ounce cup and pouring it into the 8-ounce cup) and he then refilled the 5-ounce cup and poured it into the 8-ounce cup until the latter was full, then there would be *exactly 2 ounces* left in the 5-ounce cup! All that was left to do then was to empty the 8-ounce cup, pour the 2 ounces from the 5- to the 8-ounce cup refill the 5-ounce cup and add it to the 2 ounces in the 8-ounce cup to get exactly the required 7 ounces.

"Eureka!" cried Jeff. Only a minute or so was required to pour exactly 7 ounces of wine over the dinner beef. Jeff did not realize that his thinking followed the general thought process of perhaps the most fascinating tool of management science—*dynamic programming* (DP).

---

*This problem is adapted from G. L. Nemhauser *Introduction to Dynamic Programming* Wiley, 1966.

16.1 The Nature of Dynamic Programming (DP)

Jeff's approach to the solution of his problem is typical of DP (developed by Bellman [1]), because it has the characteristics of segmentation and a rollback approach.

Segmentation

Jeff approached the problem as follows: Because he could not solve the problem in one shot, he asked himself if there were any intermediate position which, if achieved, could take him to his target of 7 ounces. He soon realized that if 2 ounces were already in the 8-ounce cup, then he could solve his original problem. At this point, two things actually happened:

1. Jeff *created* and *solved* a second problem; namely, if there were 2 ounces of wine in the 8-ounce cup, then, in order to get 7 ounces, all that remained to do was to add 5 ounces from the second cup to the original 2 ounces.
2. Jeff *created* a third problem; namely, how to place 2 ounces of wine in the 8-ounce cup.

Two problems from one

Each problem is a stage

Overall, the original problem was **segmented** into two smaller ones. Once the two smaller problems were solved, the solution to the original problem was achieved. The segmentation of the complex problem into smaller problems resulted in a *sequence of decisions*. Jeff actually made two decisions. Each of the smaller problems created is labeled a **stage.**

In a multistage decision problem, a sequence of interrelated decisions either exists already or must be constructed. For example, the decision about how much preventive maintenance to give to an automobile this year is interrelated with the maintenance (or replacement) decision to be made next year. If the intent is to sell or replace the car next year, less maintenance will probably be prescribed this year. However, if the intent is to keep the car for several years, more extensive maintenance may be recommended.

Rollback Approach

Start from the end first

Jeff started the analysis by first solving the last of the newly created problems. Namely, how to achieve the goal of 7 ounces once 2 ounces were in the cup. Only then did he proceed to solve the next to last problem; namely, how to get 2 ounces in the cup. Such an approach is called the **rollback** (or backward) approach, because the problem closest to the target is solved first. Most DP problems are solved in this manner. There are, however, certain DP problems that are solved "forward"; that is, starting with the problem farthest from the goal first. The approach to be selected depends on the convenience and speed of computation.

Problems Solved by Dynamic Programming

DP for segmented problems

Dynamic programming solves problems that can either be segmented into a sequence of decisions (such as Jeff's problem) *or* are composed of a series of small problems to begin with.

Before considering the general structure and terminology of DP, the **sequential decision-making** process is illustrated in more detail with another example.

16.2 The Stagecoach Problem

In the good old days, stagecoaches were the only means of public transportation. A traveling salesman, living in San Francisco, decided to cross the country to New York. Figure 16.1 depicts the available stagecoach routes. Each circle on the map represents an exchange point. At an exchange point, the traveler moved to another stagecoach, because the horses needed to rest. The exchange points are numbered from **1** to **11** as a matter of convenience. The distance in "travel days" is marked above the routes. The problem is to find the route from San Francisco to New York that requires the fewest days of travel. (This single problem can also be formulated as a shortest route problem, but if complications are added, it cannot be solved by the shortest route algorithm.)

Solution by Complete Enumeration

There are only eight possible routes, as shown in Table 16.1. Thus, by complete enumeration, route $1 \to 2 \to 5 \to 8 \to 11$ (doubled in Figure 16.1 by a broken line) is found to be the fastest, requiring only 15 days.

FIGURE 16.1

The stagecoach problem

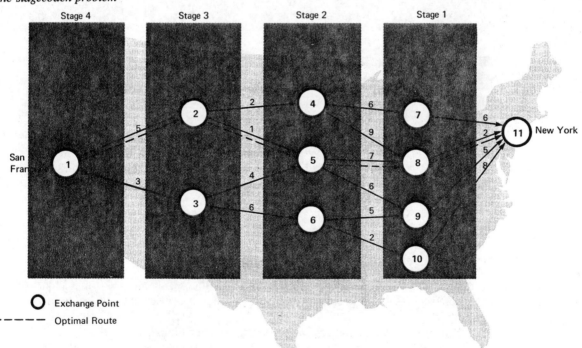

TABLE 16.1 **Possible Routes and Days of Travel—Complete Enumeration**

Route	Days of Travel	
①→②→④→⑦→⑪	19	
①→②→④→⑧→⑪	18	
①→②→⑤→⑧→⑪	15	←*Minimum*
①→②→⑤→⑨→⑪	17	
①→③→⑤→⑧→⑪	16	
①→③→⑤→⑨→⑪	18	
①→③→⑥→⑨→⑪	19	
①→③→⑥→⑩→⑪	19	

Enumeration may not be practical

In large travel networks, a complete listing and computation of all possible routes may be cumbersome, especially when constraints on travel (e.g., fares and delays) are taken into consideration. Also, the problem may be more complicated when additional objectives (such as safety and fun) are taken into consideration. For those cases, DP is prescribed.

Solution by Dynamic Programming

Four stagecoaches, 11 states

The first step of DP is the segmentation of the given problem into smaller problems or *stages*. A stage, in this example, is a decision point where the traveler must decide which stagecoach to take next. This segmentation is done as follows: In San Francisco, the traveler must decide on going to either **2** or to **3**. Once the traveler gets to either **2** or **3**, he or she must make another decision that will lead to either **4** or **5** (if the traveler went to **2**) or to **5** or **6** (if the traveler went to **3**). A decision at **4, 5,** or **6** will take the traveler to **7, 8, 9,** or **10,** from which the traveler may go directly to New York, **11.** Thus, no matter which route the traveler selects, the trip will require *four stagecoaches.* Therefore, the problem can be broken into four smaller problems, each made at a zone (stage) regarding what stagecoach to take next. The stages are marked backward, from 4 to 1, for convenience in employing the rollback concept.

In each stage, the decision maker can be at one and only one exchange point. The exchange points in these examples correspond to what are called **stages** in DP. A state is the condition that a system, or the problem, can occupy in a particular stage.

DP eliminates some routes

The use of DP eliminates the need to investigate *all* possible routes, as is done in complete enumeration. In this example, the computational work involved in DP is larger than that involved in complete enumeration. However, for large DP problems, the savings over complete enumeration can be substantial.

Details of the Solution

The solution procedure uses a rollback analysis; that is, the end of the problem is ana-lyzed first. The traveler thus starts from New York. The traveler then considers the question of how to proceed from any given exchange point (state) to New York so as to minimize the travel time. This computation begins with the *last* stage, which is labeled 1. Once this decision is made, the traveler considers another question; namely, how to get (in the best manner) to each of the possible exchange points of stage 1. The process then is repeated until San Francisco is reached.

Stage 1

Once the traveler is in New York, he or she has reached the goal. Immediately before that, he or she must be in one of the exchange points **7, 8, 9,** or **10.** These points are the states of stage 1. Note that there is *only one* possible way of getting from each of these points to New York. That is, if the traveler is, for example, in exchange point **7,** then the *best* and only choice is to travel by route **7 → 11.** In other words, it does not matter how the traveler reached exchange point **7;** once there, he or she should travel by route **7 → 11.** A similar analysis is made for all other exchange points at stage 1. The results are shown in Table 16.2, and should be treated on an "if-then" basis (e.g., *if* the traveler is at exchange point **7,** *then* the best way to continue traveling is **7 → 11** for six days of travel).

The evaluation of effectiveness in this case is based on "days of travel." The smaller the number of days, the better. The number of days of travel is the payoff or the **reward.**

Stage 2

In order to reach any of the stage 1 exchange points—**7, 8, 9,** or **10**—the traveler must be in one of the stagecoaches that started at exchange points **4, 5,** or **6.** Hence, these exchange points are the states of *stage 2.*

From each of these states, the best possibility of getting to New York is examined. However, instead of enumerating all routes to New York, only the routes to the states of stage 1 are examined. This is done because it is *already known* how to get from each state in stage 1 to New York in the best way.

TABLE 16.2   The First Stage

State	Alternative Route	Days of Travel to New York	Best Route (Days)
7	⑦ → ⑪	6	6
8	⑧ → ⑪	2	2
9	⑨ → ⑪	5	5
10	⑩ → ⑪	8	8

Considering state **4** first, there are two alternative ways of reaching stage 1: **4 → 7** or **4 → 8.** The former requires 6 days plus the optimal time to New York, computed in stage 1 as 6, for a total of 12. The latter requires 9 days + 2 days = 11 days. Of the two, the better is **4 → 8** with 11 days. Similar computations are executed for states **5** and **6.** The results are shown in Table 16.3. Notice that the best solution is computed for each state independently.

Stage 3

In order to get to one of exchange points **4, 5,** or **6** in the previous stage, it is necessary to exchange stagecoaches at points **2** or **3.** These points are the states of stage 3.

Table 16.3 summarizes the computations for the third stage as well. Note that the best results found in stage 2 above are used as an input for computing stage 3.

TABLE 16.3   The Second, Third, and Fourth Stages

	State	Alternative Route	Distance to Stage 1	Best Distance from Stage 1 to New York (From Table 16.2)	Total Distance	Best Route
Second stage	4	④→⑦	6	6	12	
		④→⑧	9	2	11	←
	5	⑤→⑧	7	2	9	←
		⑤→⑨	6	5	11	
	6	⑥→⑨	5	5	10	←
		⑥→ 10	2	8	10	←

	State	Alternative Route	Distance to Stage 2	Best Distance from Stage 2 to New York (From Second Stage)	Total Distance	Best Route
Third stage	2	②→④	2	11	13	
		②→⑤	1	9	10	←
	3	③→⑤	4	9	13	←
		③→⑥	6	10	16	

	State	Alternative Route	Distance to Stage 3 (Immediate Reward)	Best Distance from Stage 3 to New York (From Third Stage)	Total Distance (Reward)	Best Route
Fourth stage	1	①→②	5	10	15	←
		①→③	3	13	16	

Stage 4

Finally, the traveler is at the initial point. There are two alternatives here: either go to exchange point **2** or to exchange point **3**. There is only one state to be examined, state **1**. These computations are also shown in Table 16.3.

Now it is possible to reconstruct the optimal solution for the entire problem, this time going forward. In stage 4, the solution is route **1 → 2**. In stage 3, we know that *if* one is at state **2**, it is best to go to state **5**. In stage 2, we know that if one is at state **5**, it is best to go to state **8**. Finally, Table 16.2 tells us that from state **8** the best way to get to New York is **8 → 11**. The optimal travel route is thus:

$$1 \rightarrow 2 \rightarrow 5 \rightarrow 8 \rightarrow 11$$

for a total of 15 travel days (Table 16.3 gives this total).

Note that in each of the stages and for each state the following computations were executed (see Table 16.3):

> *a.* Total distance (reward) = Distance to previous stage (immediate reward) + Best distance from previous stage to New York (optimal reward in previous stage).
>
> *b.* Best route (optimal reward) = Smallest total distance (reward).

These two computational procedures are the backbone of DP.

16.3 Terminology and Structure

The stagecoach example will be used to help define the major terms and concepts of DP.

Major Terms in DP

Stages

The stagecoach problem was solved by breaking it into four subproblems, each of which is considered a *stage*. Thus, the first step in any DP solution is to divide the problem into stages if it is not originally so divided.

A stage as a decision point

> *Definition:* A stage refers to a particular decision point on the solution routes. For example, each time a decision about the next stagecoach has to be made, a stage is encountered.

States

A state as an exchange point

At each stage, the traveler could have been in one (and only one) of several possible exchange points, each of which is considered a *state*. As the traveler journeyed along the route, he or she moved from state to state. Sometimes the states in each stage are the same; sometimes they are completely different.

The Decision Process

A DP solution is viewed as a process of moving from stage to stage, making a decision at each. The direction of the move can be either forward (sometimes called a *forward pass*), from the *initial* to the *final* stage, or backwards (termed *rollback* or *backward pass*), from the *final* to the *initial* stage. At each stage, a decision about what state to move to is made. However, in some DP problems, the system may not change its state even though it goes through several stages. For example, a machine may remain in good condition for several weeks in a case where each stage is considered to be one week and the possible conditions of the machine are the states.

Reward

Three types of rewards

The dependent variable in the stagecoach example was the "days of travel." In DP, the dependent variable is called the *reward*. Three types of rewards are distinguished:

1. Immediate Reward. This is the reward associated with a move between two adjacent stages. For example, in Table 16.3, the column "Distance to Stage 3" designates the reward. This reward is an **immediate reward** for each alternative route (state to state) between two adjacent states.

2. The Total Reward. An examination of Table 16.3 indicates that at each stage, and *for each state in that stage,* the total reward (i.e., the total distance from each state to New York) was derived as the sum of the *immediate reward* (distance to previous stage) plus the *optimal reward* obtained in the previous stage.

3. Optimal Total Reward. In each stage, and for each state, there are usually several alternatives to reach the next stage and eventually the goal. For each alternative, the total reward is computed (according to 2). The best of all total rewards in each state, for each given stage, is the *optimal total reward.*

In terms of the stagecoach example, the optimal total reward for each exchange point (state) is the shortest route from the exchange point to New York.

Notice that the optimal total reward from the final decision state (San Francisco) gives the optimal solution for the original unsegmented problem.

The Recursive Relation

The recursive relation

The function that ties together the immediate reward, the total reward, and the optimal total reward is called the **recursive relation.** This function will be discussed in more detail in Part B. This relationship is derived from the **principle of optimality.**

Policy

A policy as a contingency plan

A **policy** in DP refers to a complete, predetermined plan for selecting a course of action under every possible circumstance. In addition to solving the original problem, DP solves several subproblems. The solution of these is in the form of a policy. For example, in the stagecoach problem, the solution in Table 16.3 says: *if* you are at state **2,** it is best to go to **5;** *if* you are at state **3,** go also to **5.** Overall, DP dictates an *optimal policy* to follow, which is the *best* of all possible policies for the entire problem derived from the collection of policies for the subproblems.

Optimal policy

The Basic Idea—the Principle of Optimality

In DP, the analysis is based on Bellman's *principle of optimality* [2], which states:

> An optimal policy has the property that whatever the initial state and initial decision are, the remaining decisions must constitute an optimal policy with regard to the state resulting from the decision.

In the stagecoach example, this principle implies that:

> If an exchange point is on the optimal route, then the shortest path from that exchange point to New York is also on the optimal route.

The basic principle of DP

The implication of the principle of optimality is that, starting at a current stage, the optimal policy (decision) for the remaining stages depends only on the state at the current stage and not on the means that the system used in arriving at that state. (That is, the optimal policy is independent of the policies [decisions] adopted at prior stages.)

The Structure of Dynamic Programming

To illustrate the general structure of a DP problem, let us visualize what happened in an *intermediate stage* (3) of the stagecoach problem (Table 16.3) by viewing it as an input-output system.

Assume that we arrived at any point (state) in stage 3 somehow; then a question may be asked: What is the best route to go from *each* of these points to stage 2? (Remember, this is exactly how Jeff approached his problem: "Assume that 2 ounces are in the large cup. What is the best way to get 7 ounces in that cup?")

The answer to such a question depends on what state we are in at stage 3. If we are in state **2,** then route $2 \rightarrow 5$ will be selected. If we are in state **3,** then route $3 \rightarrow 5$ will be selected.

Input-decision-reward-output

The actual location (state **2** or state **3**) can be determined only after stage 4 is analyzed (see Table 16.3). Therefore, the ultimate *input* to stage 3 is the *output* of stage 4. In a similar manner, the *output* of stage 3 is the *input* to stage 2. In graphical terms, this is shown as follows:

Let:

$s_3 =$ Input into stage 3 (state **2** or **3**)
$d_3 =$ Decision at stage 3
$r_3 =$ Reward at stage 3
$s_2 =$ Output to stage 2 (stage **4, 5,** or **6**)

FIGURE 16.2

FIGURE 16.2

Stage 3 input and output

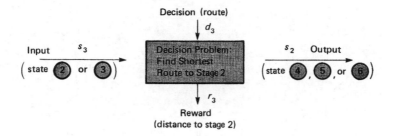

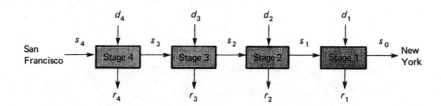

FIGURE 16.3

The stagecoach problem

Then the input-output relationship can be viewed as a diagram, as shown in Figure 16.2. Diagrams like that of Figure 16.2 can be drawn for every stage in the problem. Because the stages are connected, the entire DP process can be shown as a chain of input-output relationships. The stagecoach problem is displayed in this manner in Figure 16.3. Diagramming the DP problem in this manner helps its formulation in mathematical terms, as will be shown in Part B.

Prototype Dynamic Programming Problems

Unlike most other mathematical models, no *standard* recursive relation exists for DP. Therefore, it is impossible to use a general computational tool (such as the simplex method in LP). However, it is possible to classify DP problems into "families" (or prototypes) and build a special computational procedure for each. Although these prototypes differ in their structures and computational procedures, they share the general approach of DP. These prototypes are:

Families of DP problems

Typical DP problems

1. *Allocation process.* These processes (to be discussed in the next section) are segmented into smaller allocation problems.
2. *Multiperiod processes.* These processes are originally segmented, having two or more time periods. These are also known as smoothing or scheduling processes.
3. *Network processes.* PERT and other networks can often be viewed as DP problems and solved as such. The stagecoach problem is one example of a network process.

4. *Multistage production processes.* These problems arise in industrial production situations.
5. *Feedback control processes.* Feedback problems occur in electronics, aerospace, and automated production.
6. *Markov decision processes.* These problems were discussed in Chapter 13.

The remainder of this chapter is primarily devoted to illustrating some of these prototype problems; other examples can be found in Bellman and Dreyfus [2].

16.4 Allocation Processes

The allocation of resources among potential recipients is a major problem of organizations. In cases with a linear objective function and constraints, the problem may be presented as an LP problem. However, in many cases, the mathematical programming formulation leads to integer or nonlinear models that require difficult or costly solution procedures. DP offers a better way to handle some of these complicated cases.

An Investment Example

DP for investment decisions

The management of the Eastern Illinois Corporation is considering the allocation of $4 million among its three plants. It has already been decided that the allocation per plant is to be either $0, $1, $2, $3, or $4 million. (An investment is made in whole units of $1 million.)

Each plant has submitted its forecast of yearly returns corresponding to different levels of money invested. The forecast returns are given in Table 16.4. For example, an initial investment of $2 million in plant A will yield an annual return of $.5 million. The problem is to determine the optimal allocation of money to each plant in order to

TABLE 16.4   Eastern Illinois Corporation Investment Alternatives

Amount Allocated (in Million $)	Annual Return (Reward) ($ Million) to:		
	Plant A	Plant B	Plant C
0	0	0	0
1	.2	.3	.4
2	.5	.6	.9
3	1.5	1.2	1.1
4	1.4	1.5	1.6

FIGURE 16.4

An allocation problem

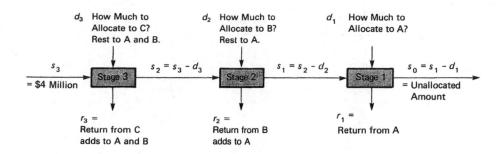

maximize the overall expected annual return. This problem cannot be solved as an LP, because it is an integer programming problem with nonlinear returns.

Formulation

The problem is segmented into three stages; each stage represents an allocation to one plant. That is, the process will be viewed as a sequence of decision-making subproblems. The relationship between the stages is shown in Figure 16.4. Again, a rollback approach will be followed. First, an allocation will be made to plant A (arbitrarily considered the "last" plant), then to B, and then to C.

States

In each stage, there are five possible states of money left to allocate: either 0, 1, 2, 3, or 4.

Solution

Stage 1

In this stage, either $0, $1, $2, $3, or $4 million (*labeled* s_1) will be available for allocation to plant A. The computed returns from the investment in plant A are given in Table 16.5. The optimal policy is: If 0, 1, 2, or 3 are available, the best solution is to allocate all the money. But if $4 million are available, then it is best to allocate only $3 million, because the optimal return from $3 million is larger than the return from $4 million (a situation that is unusual but possible). This information is shown in Table 16.5; the last column is composed of the highest reward (optimal) in each row. The numbers that are shaded are the highest and they point to the optimal policy (decision).

Stage 2

At this stage, it is necessary to determine how to split the available dollars between A and B. Let us designate the amount available for allocation to both A and B as s_2.

Thus, of the allocated amount s_2, plant B gets d_2, whereas the remaining $s_2 - d_2 = s_1$ is made available for allocation to plant A in the best possible way (as already computed in stage 1).

For each value of s_2 (0, 1, 2, 3, or 4), there are several alternatives for allocation; they must all be considered. This is done by examining all five possible states.

TABLE 16.5   Stage 1: Allocation to Plant A

Amount s_1, Available for Plant A	Decision d_1: How Much to Give to Plant A, by State					Optimal Reward
	0	1	2	3	4	
0	0					0
1	0	.2				.2
2	0	.2	.5			.5
3	0	.2	.5	1.5		1.5
4	0	.2	.5	1.5	1.4	1.5

For State $s_2 = 0$. No allocation, no return.

For State $s_2 = 1$. Either 1 to B and 0 to A (total return of .3 + 0 = .3) or 0 to B and 1 to A (total return of 0 + .2 = .2). It is clear that 1 to B is a better allocation. That is, *if* \$1 million is ever left to be allocated between A and B, B should get it. This information is then entered in Table 16.6. Table 16.6 includes the computations for all the remaining states. In each state, the optimal total reward is computed.

In general, the computations in the body of the table are those of the *total reward*, which is the sum of the immediate reward plus the optimal reward from stage 1.

Example for state $s_2 = 3$

Row 3 in Table 16.6 was computed as shown in Table 16.7. Once all total rewards are computed for each row, then the *highest* one is selected and designated as the "optimal total reward."

Stage 3

In this stage, an allocation decision is made to C, and the remaining amount is then *best allocated* between A and B according to the policy described in stage 2. At this final stage, only one state will be shown: $s_3 = 4$. (The other states are inferior and therefore are omitted.) The computations are shown in Table 16.8 in the standard manner used before, and in a somewhat more detailed manner in Table 16.9. Thus, the best allocation is: $d_3 = 1$, $d_2 = 0$, $d_1 = 3$; that is, 1 to C and 3 to A, with a return of \$1.9 million.

Some Observations

Several valuable observations can be made from the example shown here.

1. For every value of s, at every stage, the optimal return is computed in the analysis.
2. The marginal return for a given allocation policy, as s is increased (decreased) in units of \$1 million, can easily be observed from previously computed tables.

TABLE 16.6 Computation for s_2

Amount s_2, Available for Plants A and B	Decision d_2: How Much to Allocate to B; the Remainder Goes to A in an Optimal Manner					Optimal Total Reward
	0	1	2	3	4	
0	0					0
1	0 + .2 = .2	.3 + 0 = .3				.3
2	0 + .5 = .5	.3 + .2 = .5	.6 + 0 = .6			.6
3	0 + 1.5 = 1.5	.3 + .5 = .8	.6 + .2 = .8	1.2 + 0 = 1.2		1.5
4	0 + 1.5 = 1.5	.3 + 1.5 = 1.8	.6 + .5 = 1.1	1.2 + .2 = 1.4	1.5 + 0 = 1.5	1.8

TABLE 16.7 Detailed Computation of $s_2 = 3$

d_2 Allocation to B	Remainder to Allocate to A	Immediate Reward	Optimal from Stage 1	Total Reward	Optimal Total Reward
0	3	.0	1.5	1.5	←
1	2	.3	.5	.8	
2	1	.6	.2	.8	
3	0	1.2	.0	1.2	

TABLE 16.8 Stage 3: Allocation to Plant C, State $s_3 = 4$

s_3, Amount Available for Plants A, B, and C	Amount Allocated to C, d_3					Optimal Total Reward
	0	1	2	3	4	
4	0 + 1.8 = 1.8	.4 + 1.5 = 1.9	.9 + .6 = 1.5	1.1 + .3 = 1.4	1.6 + 0 = 1.6	1.9

TABLE 16.9 Stage 3, State $s_3 = 4$

Alternatives	Reward to C	Reward from Best Allocation among A and B (as Computed in Stage 2)	Optimal Total Reward	
d_3 = 4 to C, 0 to A & B	1.6	0	1.6	
d_3 = 3 to C, 1 to A & B*	1.1	.3 (1 to B)	1.4	
d_3 = 2 to C, 2 to A & B	.9	.6 (2 to B)	1.5	
d_3 = 1 to C, 3 to A & B	.4	1.5 (3 to A)	1.9	←Maximum (best)
d_3 = 0 to C, 4 to A & B	0	1.8 (1 to B, 3 to A)	1.8	

*Allocated between A and B in an optimal manner, as computed in stage 2.

Management Science in Practice

Optimal Overbooking for Scandinavian Airlines No-Shows

When passengers fail to show up for a flight, they have the right in some cases (e.g., first class) to refuse to pay for their reservations; thus, the airline loses money. "No-shows," as they are called, vary from 5 percent to as high as 30 percent. Because most major airlines are sold out for at least 100 flights every day, these no-shows cost each airline about $50 million dollars a year. To forestall this large loss, the airlines are forced to overbook flights; that is, accept reservations in excess of the plane's capacity. This policy has a cost also, however, in ill-will and compensating passengers who volunteer to take a later flight.

In the early 1970s, management at Scandinavian Airlines (SAS) decided to develop a fully automated system for overbooking. After 10 years of development and implementation, the system now seems to work extremely well.

The system operation is based on a stochastic dynamic programming process. Reservations and cancellations are stochastic variables with known probability distributions. SAS found that the probability of a reservation being canceled was independent of the time the reservation was made, which simplified the analysis. However, SAS, like most airlines, sells reservations by class (such as first class or coach fare), which complicates the analysis. The states of the process for a given flight are thus defined as the number of reservations existing for each class in the flight at each of the days preceding departure. The system changes state from time to time according to the probability distributions of passenger reservations and cancellations.

The objective in the process is to determine an optimal booking policy for the different classes so as to minimize the expected total losses. The computer program considers the cost of ill will in refusing boarding

to passengers, the cost of alternative flight arrangements (and what alternatives are available), the cost of empty seats, the cost of upgrading or downgrading the reservation class of the passenger, and so on.

For SAS's DC-9 fleet of aircraft with 110 seats, the computer program initially required 100 hours to run on a large computer, just to solve the problem for a single flight. Clearly, this was unacceptable. Thus, the solution process was modified to improve its speed. A number of efficiency routines were installed to avoid analyzing alternatives that either made no sense or had little probability of offering solutions. However, one major assumption was also added that helped in significantly reducing the computer time; that passengers tend to cancel in groups. For families traveling, or for groups of executives, this is probably not a bad assumption.

By installing the above modifications, SAS was able to reduce the computer time to under a minute. By conducting an extensive analysis that compared this optimal computer program to a heuristic process, such as those used by employees with a good "feel" for the right level of booking of a plane, it was found that the computer program would increase SAS's net revenue by about $2 million a year.

Source: J. Alstrup, et al, "Booking Control Increases Profit at Scandinavian Airlines," *Interfaces*, July–August 1989, pp. 10–19.

Questions:

1. What costs are incurred from underbooking? From overbooking?
2. How did the group assumption help?
3. Why is dynamic programming an appropriate tool for this situation?

3. A sensitivity analysis can easily be performed. For example, if management decides to consider only two plants, then the optimal solution can be found in the intermediate computations. (For example, if only A and B are considered, the best solution is read from Table 16.6 as: $d_2 = 1$ and $d_1 = 3$, for a total return of $1.8 million.)

DP advantages and characteristics

4. The DP procedure also identifies the *second* best alternative. In this case, it is (Table 16.8): $d_3 = 0$; that is, allocate nothing to C, 1 to B, and 3 to A, with an expected profit of $1.8 million. Similarly, the third best solution, and so on, can be found. These solutions are frequently important when qualitative factors have to be considered.

5. Adding a new plant to the problem merely adds an additional stage to the computations.

6. Adding more money to be allocated merely adds more states to the computations.

7. The DP process required 18 calculations for this problem. A solution by complete enumeration would have required only 15 calculations. Again, there is no saving of computational effort in such small problems. However, the savings would have been large had the problem been larger.

16.5 Concluding Remarks

Dynamic programming is an approach for finding an optimal solution to a problem by breaking it into smaller subproblems, each labeled a *stage*. In each stage (that is, for each subproblem) there exist several *states*, or positions, that the system under study can occupy.

The DP procedure considers one subproblem (stage) at a time, usually beginning from the *ending* stage. For each stage, a set of optimal solutions is derived for each state in that stage, with the aid of complete enumeration or an algorithm such as LP. This set is then used for the stage next in line. The process continues until all the subproblems are solved. The solution to the subproblems then leads to an optimal solution for the original problem.

Some limitations of DP

The application of DP is limited by two factors. First, the approach has to be tailored for each different type of problem. Every time a problem differs slightly, then a new formulation must be designed. Second, DP can be used to solve complex problems where other tools fail, such as when the rewards are not linear in an allocation problem.

The curse of dimensionality

However, it suffers from the "curse of dimensionality." The primary effect of this "curse" is an exponential growth in the amount of computation with problem size; that is, if the problems doubles in size, the amount of computation quadruples. Despite the meager number of applications of DP, it has tremendous potential due to its ability to attack difficult problems that other optimization tools fail to solve.

16.6 Problems for Part A

1. Given the following network:

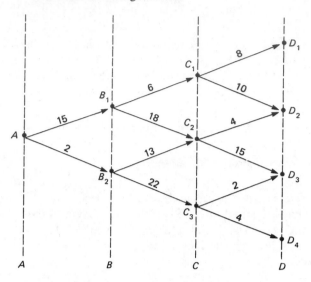

Determine by DP the shortest path going from point A to *any* point on the line D.

2. XYZ Publishing Company divides the country into two zones: eastern, with headquarters in Philadelphia; and western, with headquarters in Los Angeles. Regional sales centers in the eastern zone are in Atlanta, Boston, and Chicago. Regional sales centers in the western zone are in Seattle, Denver, Houston, and Reno.

The president wants to fly from Philadelphia to Los Angeles and stop in one eastern and one western sales center. The estimated travel expenses from Philadelphia to the eastern centers (assuming that the eastern center is visited first), are: Boston, $100, Atlanta, $130, Chicago, $110. The estimated travel expenses between the eastern centers and the western centers are:

	Denver	Reno	Houston	Seattle
Boston	160	150	180	180
Atlanta	80	130	110	200
Chicago	130	100	140	150

The travel expenses from each of the western centers to Los Angeles are: Seattle, $230, Denver, $190, Houston, $140, Reno, $180.

Find which cities the president should visit in order to minimize travel expenses.

3. Tijuana Auto Repair Shop, Inc., has three departments: metal, painting, and testing. Cars are repaired through all three departments. The metal department has three parallel workstations: M, N, and O. The painting department has two parallel workstations: P and Q. And the testing department has three parallel workstations: T, U, and V.

Whenever a car is towed in, its repair costs are estimated. This morning a car was brought in, and management would like to know through which stations the car should be processed to minimize the cost.

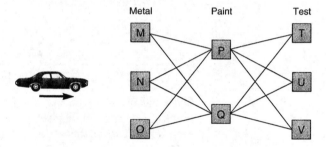

The costs at stations M, N, and O are 200, 220, and 230 thousand pesos, respectively. The cost at painting and testing depends on what happened in the previous stations. For example, if the metal work is not perfect, as is frequently the case in station M, the painting cost is slightly higher. The conditional cost relationships are:

Cost in the Painting Department (Thousand Pesos)

to

		P	Q
If car moved from	M	95	92
	N	80	85
	O	85	88

Cost in the Testing Department

to

If car moved from		T	U	V
	P	25	30	32
	Q	32	30	26

Find the sequence of stations that will minimize the repair cost (use dynamic programming).

4. Phillipine Electric Corporation produces and sells CB radios. A new model has just been developed with an estimated life of four years. The company must decide on an initial price that, in order to be competitive, must be either 90, 100, or 110 thousand pesos. The company's policy is to change prices, if necessary, only once a year. When a change is made (up *or* down), it is a 10,000-peso change.

The anticipated yearly profit from making and selling the CB radios, for each price/year combination, is given in the following table (in millions of pesos):

Year Price	1	2	3	4
90	20	18	30	24
100	24	18	35	28
110	25	15	32	31

For example, if the price in the third year is 90 thousand pesos, then the company will make 30 million pesos.

Find the optimal prices the company should set each year. Use dynamic programming. *Hint:* Stages are years; states are price levels. Assume the price levels are either 90, 100, or 110 thousand pesos all the time.

5. ABC Development Corporation plans to use one or more of three subcontractors to build six cooling units. The corporation would like to determine the best allocation of cooling units to subcontractors.

The table below shows the bids submitted by each subcontractor. The data are in thousands of dollars.

Units (Number)	Subcon- tractor A	Subcon- tractor B	Subcon- tractor C
1	5	4	5
2	10	8	9
3	14	11	12
4	17	18	18
5	20	25	24
6	27	30	30

For example, subcontractor A would build two units for $10,000 and three units for $14,000. Differences in the bids result from locational considerations and other such variations. Determine the best allocation of six cooling units among the subcontractors.

6. A sales manager must decide how to allocate her four available salespersons among three districts in her territory. The sales results (in thousands of dollars per month) are shown below as a function of the number of salespeople assigned to a district.

   a. Find the assignment of salespersons to districts that maximizes sales.

District	Salespeople Assigned	0	1	2	3	4
A		5	10	13	15	17
B		6	10	14	17	15
C		4	9	11	15	18

   b. Without resolving the problem, find the second best assignment.
   c. Without resolving the problem, find the best solution if only three salespeople are available.

7. A fancy Jamaican restaurant operates a fleet of vans for deliveries. A new van costs $10,000. It is estimated that in the future, the vans will continue to cost $10,000. The annual operating cost and the

resale value, as related to the age of the van, are given below:

Age of Van	Operating Cost ($)	Resale Value ($)
1	2,000	7,000
2	2,500	5,000
3	3,000	3,500
4	3,700	2,200
5	4,500	1,000
6	5,500	600

All the data, including the cost of new vans, are given in present values. Replacement decisions are made once a year. The restaurant buys only new vans. Find the replacement policy (i.e., at what age a van should be replaced) that minimizes the total cost. *Note:* A van cannot be kept beyond 6 years.

PART B: EXTENSIONS

16.7 Probabilistic Problems

DP can deal with risk

The previous two examples of DP dealt with deterministic situations. DP, however, can deal effectively with probabilistic problems as well.

Example: The Purchasing Agent's Problem

A purchasing agent must buy, for her company, a special beryllium alloy in a market that trades only once a week. Each week, there is a 20 percent chance that the alloy will cost $10,000; 50 percent that is will cost $11,000; and 30 percent that it will cost $12,000. At the present time, the agent knows that in order to meet the company's

Buy now or wait

production schedule, the alloy must be bought within the next month (four trading weeks). The agent worries that if she waits too long, price rises may force her to buy the alloy at a premium. On the other hand, if she buys early, future prices may be lower and she may miss an opportunity to economize. Thus, the timing of the purchase poses a delicate managerial problem.

Formulation

The agent's decision of "when to buy" can be viewed as a sequence of decisions. In each of the four trading weeks, a decision must be made between two alternatives: either to buy or to wait. The analysis starts from the final week and proceeds *backwards* in time.

Stages.   Each week is considered a stage; therefore, there will be four stages.

States.   There are two states in each week, to buy or to wait.

Reward. The expected (average) price is used as the criterion. It is labeled r_i, where i designates the stage.

Solution

Stage 1. Rolling back, the first stage occurs at week 4. At that time, there is no choice; if the alloy has not already been bought, it *must* be bought then. The expected price of the alloy is computed as the expected value, designated by $E(r_1)$.

$$E(r_1) = .2 \times \$10,000 + .5 \times \$11,000 + .3 \times \$12,000 = \$11,100$$

This situation is shown in a decision tree presentation in Figure 16.5.

Stage 2 (Third Week). The agent can either *buy* at the price prevailing that week (either \$10,000, \$11,000, or \$12,000) or she can *wait* until the fourth week. The decision is based on the following criterion:

If the prevailing price at the third week is *more* than the expected price in the last week (already calculated as \$11,100), the agent should *wait* until the final week. If the prevailing price is *less* than the expected price in the final week, the agent should buy. If the prices are the same, the agent is indifferent between the two alternatives. The agent may now extend the decision tree (Figure 16.6) for the analysis.

Because the price at any week can take only three possible values, it is possible to compute the expected reward in much the same way as was done for stage 1:

- There is a 30 percent chance of waiting, in which case the reward will be \$11,100, realized in week 4.
- There is a 20 percent chance of buying at \$10,000.
- There is a 50 percent chance of buying at \$11,000.

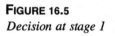

FIGURE 16.5

Decision at stage 1

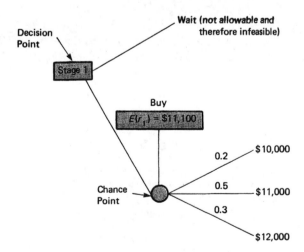

FIGURE 16.6

Decision at stage 2

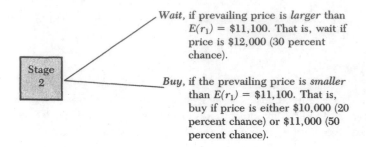

Wait, if prevailing price is *larger* than
$E(r_1) = \$11,100$. That is, wait if
price is $12,000 (30 percent
chance).

Buy, if the prevailing price is *smaller*
than $E(r_1) = \$11,100$. That is,
buy if price is either $10,000 (20
percent chance) or $11,000 (50
percent chance).

The expected reward at stage 2 is therefore:

$$E(r_2) = \overbrace{.2(\$10,000) + .5(\$11,000)}^{\text{Immediate reward}} + \overbrace{.3(\$11,100)}^{\substack{\text{Best reward from} \\ \text{previous stage}}} = \$10,830$$

Stage 3 (*Second Week*). The agent will buy if the price is less than $E(r_2)$ and wait if
it is more. The situation is shown in Figure 16.7. The expected reward is:

If *wait* (80 percent): the expected price will be $10,830.
If *buy* (20 percent): the price will be $10,000.

$$E(r_3) = .2(\$10,000) + .8(\$10,830) = \$10,664$$

Stage 4 (*Initial Week*). The agent will buy if the price at the first week is smaller
than $E(r_3)$, otherwise she will wait. Figure 16.8 shows this situation. The expected reward is:

$$E(r_4) = .2(\$10,000) + (.5 + .3)(\$10,664) = \$10,531$$

Summary

If the purchasing agent pursues the *optimal policy*, then the expected price she will pay is
$10,531. the decision rules for each week are summarized in Figure 16.9.

FIGURE 16.7

Decision at stage 3

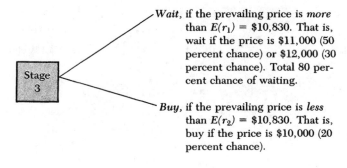

Wait, if the prevailing price is *more*
than $E(r_1) = \$10,830$. That is,
wait if the price is $11,000 (50
percent chance) or $12,000 (30
percent chance). Total 80 percent chance of waiting.

Buy, if the prevailing price is *less*
than $E(r_2) = \$10,830$. That is,
buy if the price is $10,000 (20
percent chance).

FIGURE 16.8

Decision at stage 4

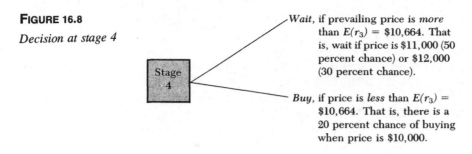

Wait, if prevailing price is *more* than $E(r_3) = \$10,664$. That is, wait if price is \$11,000 (50 percent chance) or \$12,000 (30 percent chance).

Buy, if price is *less* than $E(r_3) = \$10,664$. That is, there is a 20 percent chance of buying when price is \$10,000.

FIGURE 16.9

Decision rules for the purchasing agent

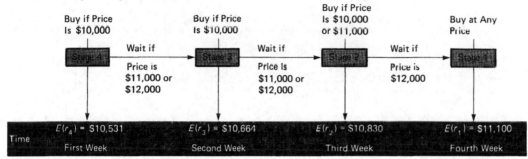

16.8 Mathematical Presentation and Optimization Techniques

The recursive relation

In all previous examples, we avoided mathematical symbols whenever possible. However, we stated over and over again that the relationship between the reward at each stage and the optimal reward is the key to the DP process. This reward relationship is called the *recursive relation*. In DP, it is necessary to write a recursive relation for each problem. Once such an equation has been written, it is much easier to execute the DP computations. The recursive relation says that an optimal reward, at any given stage, for any given state, is given as the value of the best alternative (when each alternative includes the total of the immediate reward and the optimal reward computed in the previous stage).

General Formulation

Let:

n = Index for the current stage. This index tells how many stages exist from the current stage to the end of the process (problem)

$n - 1$ = Previous stage

$$s_n = \text{State of the system in the current stage for which the recursive relations hold}$$

$$s_{n-1} = \text{State in the previous stage}$$

$$f_n(s_n, d_n) = \text{Total reward realized for each alternative, starting from state } s_n \text{ with decision } d_n \text{ in stage } n \text{ to the end of the process}$$

$$f_n^*(s_n) = \text{Optimal total reward; that is, the best } f_n(s_n) \text{ from state } s_n \text{ in stage } n$$

$$f_{n-1}^*(s_{n-1}) = \text{Optimal total reward obtained in the previous stage}$$

$$r_n(s_n, d_n) = \text{Immediate reward realized in stage } n, \text{ when decision } d_n \text{ is made for a specific value } s_s \text{ of the state variable}$$

$$d_n = \text{Decision among alternatives made at stage } n \text{ in the state under consideration.}$$

The recursive relation (minimization) for state s, at stage n, is then:

$$f_n^*(s_n) = \min_{d_n}[r_n(s_n, d_n) + f_{n-1}^*(s_{n-1})] \tag{16.1}$$

We will fit this formulation to a DP problem in Section 16.9.

Optimization Techniques

The basic approach of DP is to reduce a complex problem into a series of simpler subproblems. However, once such a reduction has been performed, it is still necessary to solve the subproblems. The following methods can be used in solving these subproblems; see the bibliography for details.

Enumeration

In many cases, complete enumeration is very efficient, because the number of possible solutions in the subproblems is usually finite and small. In some cases, it is possible to approximate an infinite number of possible solutions by using a finite number (e.g., replace a continuous function by a discrete one) and then employing enumeration.

Classical Calculus

The classical calculus methods can be used for certain unconstrained optimization problems, as well as for simple cases of constrained optimization.

Lagrange Multipliers and the Kuhn-Tucker Conditions

Equality constraints can be handled with the aid of the Lagrangian function. Inequality constraints are treated with the help of Kuhn-Tucker conditions.

Mathematical Programming

In certain cases, the subproblems are actually linear, integer, or nonlinear programming problems, and can be solved as such.

Sequential Search

In some cases, iterative procedures may be used where the solution is improved step by step.

Other Techniques

Several other **optimization techniques** can be used.

16.9 The Knapsack Problem

What should go in the knapsack?

A knapsack or a container has a limited weight and/or volume capacity. It is to be loaded with different items, each with a given weight (or volume). Each item has a certain value. The problem is to find what items to include in the knapsack to maximize the total value.

An example of a **knapsack problem** is a satellite whose weight is limited. The problem is: What instruments to include so that the scientific utility of the mission is maximized.

Another example involves production scheduling, where it is necessary to determine how many units to produce among several products on one machine. The value of the products is known, and so is their use of machine time, which is limited. The problem is: What products to produce and in what quantities (integer) so that the value is maximized. The knapsack problem appears in various forms and can often be formulated as an integer programming problem. Integer programming problems are, however, often difficult to solve, especially if they are nonlinear. Therefore, DP is used.

Example

Four types of items are considered for loading on an airplane, with an unlimited supply of each type. The weights and values of the types of items are given in Table 16.10. Find which items should be loaded on the plane, and in what quantities, if the maximum capacity of the plane is 11 tons and the objective is to maximize the value of the shipment.

TABLE 16.10   Knapsack Items

Item	Weight (Tons)	Value
A	2	18
B	4	25
C	5	30
D	3	20

Mathematical Presentation
Let:

n = The stage (item) under consideration
x_n = Number of items of type n to load
v_n = Value of one type n item
w_n = Weight of one type n item
K = Maximum available capacity

Integer Programming Formulation
The problem is:

$$\text{maximize } z = \sum_{n=1}^{4} v_n x_n$$

$$\text{subject to:}$$

$$\sum_{n=1}^{4} w_n x_n \leq K$$

and x_n is a nonnegative integer

(16.2)

For our example:

$$\text{maximize } z = 18x_1 + 25x_2 + 30x_3 + 20x_4$$

$$\text{subject to:}$$

$$2x_1 + 4x_2 + 5x_3 + 3x_4 \leq 11$$

and x_1, x_2, x_3, x_4 are nonnegative integers.

Dynamic Programming Formulation
This problem is an extension of the allocation problem discussed in Section 16.4.

Stages.　Each type of item is considered a stage.

States.　The remaining capacity (in integer tons) available for allocation; that is, the states are 0, 1, 2, . . . , 11.

The Decision at Each Stage.　How many units of each item to include in the optimal mix.

The Recursive Relation.　The recursive relation for this problem is:

$$f_n^*(s_n) = \max_{x_n}[v_n x_n + f_{n-1}^*(s_n - w_n x_n)]$$

(16.3)

where:

$$s_n = \text{The amount of the remaining weight available for allocation at stage } n$$
$$v_n x_n = \text{Immediate reward}$$
$$f_n^*(s_n) = \text{Optimal total reward starting at stage } n, \text{ for state } s_n$$
$$f_{n-1}^*(s_n - w_n x_n) = \text{Optimal reward at the previous stage}$$

Solution
Because there are four items, there will be four stages.

Stage 1 (Item D). Table 16.11 shows the states on the left side. On the top, the possible number of units of D that can be loaded are shown. Because the weight of D is 3 tons, then either 0, 1, 2, or 3 units can be loaded. The body of the table gives the reward computed by the formula given at the top of the table.

Mathematical Statement of Stage 1
The reward function is given by $v_1 x_1 = 20 x_1$, where x_1 designates the number of units of D.

The optimal solution column is designated by $f_1^*(s_1) = \text{maximum } [v_1 x_1]$, where $f_1^*(s_1)$ is the optimal reward starting from state s_1 and using an optimal policy from stage 1 to the end.

Stage 2 (Item C). At this stage, an allocation is made to item C, with the remaining weight utilized according to the best policy recommended in stage 1. Table 16.12

TABLE 16.11 Stage 1: Item D

State s_1 (Tons Available for Allocation to Item D)	$f_1(s_1) = v_1 x_1 = 20 x_1$ (Number of D Units to Load at 3 Tons Each)				$f_1^*(s_1)$
	$x_1 = 0$	$x_1 = 1$	$x_1 = 2$	$x_1 = 3$	
0	0				0
1	0				0
2	0				0
3	0	20			20
4	0	20			20
5	0	20			20
6	0	20	40		40
7	0	20	40		40
8	0	20	40		40
9	0	20	40	60	60
10	0	20	40	60	60
11	0	20	40	60	60

TABLE 16.12   Stage 2: Item C

State s_2 (Tons Available for C and D)	$f_2(s_2) = 30x_2 + f_1^*(s_2 - 5x_2)$ (Number of C Units at 5 Tons Each)			$f_2^*(s_2)$
	$x_2 = 0$	$x_2 = 1$	$x_2 = 2$	
0	0			0
1	0			0
2	0			0
3	20			20
4	20			20
5	20	30		30
6	40	30		40
7	40	30		40
8	40	50		50
9	60	50		60
10	60	50	60	60
11	60	70	60	70

shows the rewards for the various states. The total rewards are $f_2(s_1) = 30x_2 + f_1^*(s_2 - 5x_2)$; and the optimal reward is the maximum of $f_1(s_2)$. For example, in state 10, if 10 tons are available, then the following three alternatives are available:

a. Zero to C, then 10 goes to D. From Table 16.11 we know that the optimal allocation of 10 to D yields 60.

b. One to C, then there are 5 tons remaining. The best allocation of 5 (from stage 1) yields 20 plus the 30 achieved from the allocation of one to C, for a total yield of 50.

c. Two to C which takes 10 tons; that is, nothing remains. Therefore, the reward is $2 \times 30 = 60$.

The computations are similar to the allocation problem of Section 16.4.

Stage 3 (Item B).   The results are shown in Table 16.13. The total reward function is:

$$f_3(s_3) = 25x_3 + f_2^*(s_3 - 4x_3) \quad \text{and } f_3^*(s_3) = \max_{x_3} f_3(s_3)$$

Stage 4 (Item A).   The results for stage 4 are shown in Table 16.14. The optimal policy is given by $f_4^*(s_4) = \max_{x_4} [18x_4 + f_3^*(s_4 - 2x_4)]$.

TABLE 16.13   Stage 3: Item B

State s_3 (Tons Available for B, C and D)	$f_3(s_3) = 25x_3 + f_2^*(s_3 - 4x_3)$ (Number of B Units at 4 Tons Each)			$f_3^*(s_3)$
	$x_3 = 0$	$x_3 = 1$	$x_3 = 2$	
0	0			0
1	0			0
2	0			0
3	20			20
4	20	25		25
5	30	25		30
6	40	25		40
7	40	45		45
8	50	45	50	50
9	60	55	50	60
10	60	65	50	65
11	70	65	70	70

TABLE 16.14   Stage 4: Item A

State s_4 (Tons Available for A, B, C, and D)	$f_4(s_4) = 18x_4 + f_3^*(s_4 - 2x_4)$ (Number of A Units at 2 Tons Each)						$f_4^*(s_4)$
	$x_4 = 0$	$x_4 = 1$	$x_4 = 2$	$x_4 = 3$	$x_4 = 4$	$x_4 = 5$	
11	70	78	81	84	92	90	92

Optimal Solution

The starting state is $s_4 = 11$, and its solution is the solution to the entire problem. The optimal solution is read as: $x_4 = 4$; that is, four units of A (weighing 8 tons). The remaining $11 - 8 = 3$ tons are allocated in the optimal manner according to stage 3 (Table 16.13). Thus, $x_3 = 0$, and no units of B are included. The check then continues to stage 2 (Table 16.12). According to this table, $x_2 = 0$. Moving finally to stage 1 (Table 16.11), the optimal solution for 3 tons is $x_4 = 1$.

Therefore, the best solution is:

$$x_4 = 4 \text{ units of A}$$

$$x_1 = 1 \text{ unit of D}$$

The total reward is:

$$18 \times 4 + 20 \times 1 = 92$$

The knapsack problem has several variations. For example, it may be required that at least one unit (or no more than one unit) of each item be included. Cost minimization can be the objective. Additional constraints may also be added, such as volume limits.

16.10 Computerization

Due to the special structure of DP, it is difficult to design a standard program for computers. Either a special program must be built for each problem, or else an extremely large variety of options must be constructed.

16.11 Problems for Part B

8. You own 1,000 shares of a certain company that you *must* sell, for tax reasons, on or before the end of the fifth forthcoming trading day. The price of a share fluctuates between $20 and $22. At any given day, there is a chance of 25 percent of selling the shares at $20, 45 percent of selling them at $21, and 30 percent of selling them at $22. You pay 25 cents commission per share.

   a. Suggest an optimal policy. Assume that all shares are sold in one trade.

   b. How much money will you receive for your shares?

9. Reconsider problem 1. Suppose that the result of the choice made at each node is probabilistic. Namely, when one selects a route, there is only a 60 percent chance of pursuing that route. For example, if a decision made at node A was to go to B_1, the actual result would be 60 percent at B_1 and 40 percent at B_2. Use DP to find the path with the lowest expected value of the sum of the numbers along the arcs.

10. Suppose you own an option to buy 100 shares of the ABC Corporation at a certain price. Such options are traded on Mondays through Fridays on the American and Chicago exchanges. Today is Monday, and your option will expire on Friday; at that time, you will be able to sell it for $175. From your experience, you know that the price movement of this type of option during the last week of expiration will behave in the following manner:

Monday: 60 percent chance for $300, 40 percent chance for $200.

Tuesday: 40 percent chance for $350, 40 percent chance for $250, 20 percent chance for $150.

Wednesday: 20 percent chance for $400, 60 percent chance for $200, 20 percent chance for $150.

Thursday: 50 percent chance for $300, 50 percent chance for $200.

Friday: 100 percent chance for $175.

   The reason for such sharp movements is that in the last days before the expiration date, some traders who sold the option short must buy it back. Also, the stock itself moves up and down quickly.

   The commission for selling an option is $25, regardless of its price. Find the best trading policy.

11. A truck can carry a total of 10 tons. Three types of boxes are available for shipment. The boxes weigh 2, 1, and 3 tons, respectively, and their value is $50, $30, and $70, respectively. The truck delivers 10 times a day. It is required that at least one unit of each type of box be delivered in each shipment.

   a. Determine the loading policy that will maximize the value of the shipments.

b. Find the daily dollar value of the shipment.

c. Formulate as an integer programming problem.

12. Peru Trucking Company delivers four types of containers between two cities. The company wants to load *at least* 14 tons on each truck. The weight and the handling cost that is paid to porters for each type of container is given as:

Container	Weight (Tons)	Handling Cost (Thousands of Sols)
A	4	20
B	2	15
C	5	23
D	3	18

Find how many containers of each type should be loaded on each truck in order to minimize the total handling cost.

a. Formulate as an integer program.

b. Formulate and solve by DP.

13. Formulate the recursive relations for:

a. The allocation example of Section 16.4.

b. The stagecoach problem of Section 16.2.

c. The purchasing agent problem of Section 16.7.

16.12 CASE
THE PERSONNEL DIRECTOR

Bud Friendly, personnel director for Glades Corporation, was on the phone explaining his problem to the manager of marketing research:

"Mrs. Rich, with only three days to hire that customer rep, we won't be able to interview many applicants. It takes a full day to screen each one, including interviews, reference checks, and appraisals, so the most we can consider is three applicants. Obviously, if the first or second candidate is excellent, we will hire that candidate, but what if they're not?

"Look, Bud. In the past, we have found that of every 10 candidates you screen, 3 are 'excellent,' 5 are 'good,' and 2 are 'poor.' Surely, in three days you can come up with a superior candidate."

"But, Mrs. Rich, if I delay an early decision on a 'good' candidate, hoping to find an 'excellent' one, he or she might take another job instead and then we might have to settle on a 'poor' candidate on the last day."

"Well, I don't know what to advise you. I can say this though. A 'good' candidate is worth twice as much as a 'poor' one and an 'excellent' candidate is worth twice that again. Good luck, Bud."

Questions for Discussion:

1. Advise Bud on hiring policy.

2. What will be the candidate's expected worth if an optimal policy is followed?

Glossary

Immediate reward   The reward resulting from a move between two adjacent stages. It is the value added to the objective function when moving from stage to stage.

Knapsack problem   A classical allocation problem that determines the optimal mix of items to be put in a limited space (knapsack, bag, container) such that the total value of the items is maximized.

Policy   A complete, predetermined choice plan under every possible circumstance.

Principle of optimality   Bellman's principle, which is the basis for solving DP problems.

Optimization techniques   Mathematical routines that can be used to optimally solve DP subproblems.

Recursive relation   The function used in DP to compute the value of the objective function.

Reward   The payoff (value) of the objective function.

Rollback   A solution approach in which the subproblems that are closest to the end point are solved first.

Segmentation   Breaking up a complex problem into a sequence of smaller subproblems.

Sequential decision making   A sequential solution process involving several interrelated decisions.

Stage   A decision point in a sequence of decisions. A subproblem.

State   A condition or a possible alternative for each subdecision or stage.

References and Bibliography

1. Bellman, R. *Dynamic Programming*. Princeton, N.J.: Princeton University Press, 1957.

2. Bellman, R., and S. E. Dreyfus, *Applied Dynamic Programming*. Princeton, N.J.: Princeton University Press, 1962.

3. Bertsekas, D. P. *Dynamic Programming: Deterministic and Stochastic Models*. Englewood Cliffs, N.J.: Prentice-Hall, 1989.

4. Denardo, E. V. *Dynamic Programming Models and Applications*. Englewood Cliffs, N.J.: Prentice-Hall, 1982.

5. Esogbue, A. D. *Dynamic Programming for Optimal Resource Systems Analysis*. Englewood Cliffs, N.J.: Prentice-Hall, 1989.

6. Ross, S. *Introduction to Stochastic Dynamic Programming*. New York: Academic Press, 1983.

7. Sacco, W., et al. *Dynamic Programming: An Elegant Problem Solver*. Providence, R.I.: Janson Pub., 1987.

Special and Emerging Technologies

The technologies introduced in the previous chapters are the most common ones that can be found in the tool kit of the management scientist. However, the management scientist may use some special tools in complex or unusual situations. Part A of this chapter describes the special approaches of heuristic programming, a nonoptimizing technique, and game theory, the evaluation of situations involving conflict. Part B describes some of the newer technologies for semistructured or unstructured problems. To aid the decision maker, the new technologies of decision support and expert systems have recently been developed. Neural computing and genetic algorithms are still in the exploratory phase and new applications are continuously being developed for them.

PART A: HEURISTIC PROGRAMMING AND GAME THEORY

17.1 Heuristic Programming: An Overview

Heuristic

Heuristic: "serving to discover"

As an adjective, heuristic means (Michael [24], p. 75) serving to discover. As a noun, a heuristic is an *aid* to discovery. A heuristic contributes to the reduction of search in a problem-solving activity. An example of a heuristic is a rule of thumb that leads to a solution.

Intuitive exploitation

And yet another definition is provided by Silver, et al. [32, p. 153] "A heuristic method is a procedure for solving a well-defined mathematical problem by an intuitive approach in which the structure of the problem can be interpreted and exploited intelligently to obtain a reasonable solution."

Heuristic Problem Solving

Heuristic problem solving is the implementation of heuristics in problem-solving or decision-making situations.

Problem solving based on heuristics is a very old practice in comparison to science based on reason. Several terms are used in practice to describe the use of heuristics: hints, intuition, judgment, rules-of-thumb, and inspiration.

To help understand these various definitions and distinctions, consider the examples of simple heuristics given in Table 17.1.

The application of heuristics for solving well-structured problems is referred to as **heuristic programming.** (For a comprehensive review of several hundred applications,

---

TABLE 17.1   Some Examples of Heuristics

Sequencing jobs through a machine: Do the jobs that require the least time first.
Purchase of stocks: Do not buy stocks whose price-to-earnings ratio is larger than 10.
Commuting to work: Avoid the Golden Coast freeway (north bound) between 8 and 9 A.M.
Capital investment projects: Consider only projects whose estimated payback period is less than two years.
Buying a house: Buy in a good neighborhood but in the lower price range.
Marketing programs: Advertising expenditures for newspapers should be at least twice as much as those for television.
Inventory management: Follow a FIFO (first in, first out) policy.
Engineering: It costs $2 million to build one mile of a highway.
Personnel management: Increase salaries this year by adding 5 percent to last year's salaries.
Financial management: Keep the firm's current ratio greater than two-to-one.

TABLE 17.2 Typical Problems Solved by Heuristic Programming

Bus driver scheduling.	Assembly-line sequencing problems.
Cutting stock problems.	Traveling salesperson problems.
Vehicle dispatch (routing) problems.	Lot-sizing problems.
Knapsack problems.	Multiechelon inventory problems.
Pallet loading problems.	Aggregate planning problems.
Facility (warehouse) location problems.	Resource leveling in PERT/CPM
Facilities layout problems.	(also with multiprojects, multiresources).
	Resource scheduling problems.

see Zanakis, et al. [43].) Typical problems solved by heuristic programming are listed in Table 17.2.

Each of the problems in Table 17.2 appears in several variations: single and multiple stage, with or without capacity constraints, single versus multiple products, deterministic versus probabilistic, with or without bottlenecks, symmetric versus asymmetric, and static versus dynamic. However, heuristic thinking can also be used to solve ill-structured problems (mainly in artificial intelligence and expert systems). Also, it is worth noting that several heuristics may be used to solve a single problem. The use of heuristics has many potential benefits (Section 17.2), but it also has some drawbacks and limitations (Section 17.3), especially for well-structured, mathematically oriented situations.

17.2 The Benefits of Heuristics*

A technique to facilitate other techniques

Heuristics can be used to solve problems directly by forming a kind of formula or algorithm. But they can also be used to facilitate the use of almost all other MS techniques. This can be done in several different ways. For example, the application of many formulas requires some judgmental factors. These can be provided by heuristics in the form of a policy set (if–then type). For example, an initial solution can be found for mathematical programming, and a decision of what statistical test to use can facilitate the use of simulation.

Another use of heuristics is to speed up the search process of tools such as branch and bound. The problem is partitioned into subproblems whose solutions are then divided into feasible (integer) and infeasible sets. Throughout the setting of upper and lower bounds, against which solutions are compared, solutions are either discarded or maintained. When a branch is discarded, a large number of potential solutions is eliminated. Heuristics can be used to improve the efficiency of branch and bound by indicating which branches should be discarded and which should be kept.

*Based in part on Silver, et al. [32] and Zanakis and Evans [44].

The following are the major benefits of heuristics:

Flexible

1. They have an inherent flexibility, which allows them to be used on ill-structured and complex problems that do not fit the stringent conditions required for the application of most MS techniques.

2. Although an exact (either analytic or numeric) solution procedure may exist, it may be computationally prohibitive to use, or unrealistic in its data requirements. This is particularly true of enumerative methods that, *in theory*, are often applicable where analytic or numeric procedures cannot be found. For example, **combinatorial**-type **problems** can be solved by **enumeration**, but it may require years, even with high-speed computers.

Enumeration of combinatorial problems

Very fast

3. Generally, a solution using heuristics can be derived very fast.

A Combinatorial Problem

Explosion of alternatives

Certain managerial problems have a very large number of possible solutions. For example, there are n! = 3,628,800 different combinations of matching 10 candidates to 10 jobs. A major characteristic of combinatorial problems is that the number of alternative solutions increases much faster (usually exponentially) than the size of the problem. For example, by increasing the number of candidates and jobs from 10 to 11 (a 10 percent increase), the number of alternative matchings increases by 1,100 percent to 39,916,800. An increase from 10 to 12 (20 percent increase) will cause the number of alternatives to increase to about 480,000,000 or by about 13,200 percent.

Simpler

4. The heuristic method, *by design*, may be simpler for the decision maker to understand, especially when it is composed of (or supported by) qualitative analysis. Hence, the chances of implementing the proposed solution are much higher.

Educational

5. For a well-defined problem that can be solved optimally, a heuristic method can be used for teaching purposes; for example, to develop an intuitive feeling as to what variables are important. It can also help in training people to be creative and come up with heuristics for other problems.

Helper

6. A heuristic may be used as part of an iterative procedure that guarantees the finding of an optimal solution. Two distinct possibilities exist: (*a*) to easily and quickly obtain an initial feasible solution (e.g., the Northwest Corner Rule in the transportation problem), and (*b*) to make a decision at an intermediate step of an exact solution procedure (e.g., the rule for selecting the variable to enter the basis in the simplex method).

17.3 Disadvantages and Limitations of Heuristics

Some disadvantages

Despite the potential advantages, the use of heuristics should not be considered as an easy way out. Heuristics do have several disadvantages and limitations. They are (based in part on Geoffrion and von Roy [12]):

1. The inherent flexibility of heuristics can foster misleading manipulations and solutions.
2. Certain heuristics may contradict other heuristics that are applied to the same problem, generating confusion and lack of trust in heuristic methods.
3. Optimal solutions are not identified. **Local improvement** heuristics can short-circuit the best solution because they lack a global perspective. The gap between the optimal solution and the one generated by heuristics may be very large, with the potential losses exceeding the benefits. Because an optimal solution is not generated, it is frequently difficult to evaluate the recommendations generated by heuristic problem solving.
4. A major difficulty with heuristics is that they are not as general as algorithms. Therefore, they can normally be used only for the specific situations intended. For this reason, it is necessary to write special computer programs for each heuristic.
5. Enumeration heuristics that consider all possible combinations in practical problems can seldom be achieved.
6. Sequential decision choices can fail to anticipate future consequences of each choice.
7. Interdependencies in one part of a system can sometimes have a profound influence on the whole system.

Arbitrary approaches

Commonsense approaches and heuristics can fail because they are *arbitrary*. They are arbitrary in the choice of a starting point, in the sequence in which assignments or other decision choices are made, in the resolution of ties, in the choice of criteria for specifying the procedure, and in the level of effort expended to demonstrate that the final solution is in fact best or very nearly so. The result is erratic and unpredictable behavior—good performance in some specific applications and bad in others.

17.4 Measuring the Quality of Heuristics

A key to the successful application of heuristics is measuring their quality. A good heuristic should possess the following five properties:

Five qualities of a "good" heuristic

1. Realistic computational effort to obtain the solution.
2. The solution should be close to the optimum on the average; that is, we want good performance on the average.
3. The chance of a very poor solution (i.e., far from the optimum) should be low.
4. The heuristic should be as simple as possible for the user to understand (preferably explainable in intuitive terms), particularly if it is to be used manually. Carefully prepared documentation should help in this regard.
5. It should yield consistent results.

Silver, et al. [32] provide a detailed methodology for evaluating heuristics as they relate to these properties.

TABLE 17.3 **Factors Influencing the Quality of Heuristic Programming**

Nature of the problem
Frequency of the decision
Amount of computational effort needed
Analytical qualifications of the decision maker
Number of decision variables
Number of uncontrollable variables
Size of the problem
Number of discrete and continuous variables
Number of deterministic and probabilistic variables
Clarity of the heuristics
Implementability of the heuristics
Accuracy and consistency
Cost-benefit ratio

Wiest [40] has suggested that the user of heuristics ask the following questions in evaluating the quality of the output of heuristic programming:

- Does it produce better results than the present methods?
- Are there incremental savings in resources?
- Are computational effort and expenses reduced without sacrificing the quality of work?
- Is the information produced more timely, and are decisions reached earlier than by present methods?

The more positive answers we get, the better the quality of the heuristic (see Table 17.3 for additional factors).

17.5 Example: Heuristic Sequencing of Jobs*

An interesting sequencing problem occurs when several different jobs must be processed through a single production facility such as a printing press, boring mill, or a computer. The facility must be shut down after finishing each job in order to prepare it for the next job. The time periods that the facility is shut down are frequently referred to as *setup* or *changeover* times. Although the processing time of the jobs is usually independent of the sequence used, the setup times may depend on both the job being re-

The cost of
changing jobs

---

*Based on Gavett [11].

moved and the job being introduced. Management desires to sequence the jobs that are required to be processed in such a way that the total setup time will be minimized.

The difficulty in solving such a problem is that the sequencing can be done in many different ways; to be exact, *n* different jobs can be sequenced in *n*! different ways. For example, if there are only 10 jobs, there will be 10! = 3,628,800 different sequencing alternatives.

Unfortunately, there is no simple analytical model that can tell us which sequence is the best. One way to find the best sequence is to compare all alternatives (complete enumeration). The complete enumeration of as few as 20 jobs may take a long time, even with the aid of high-speed computers. Heuristic rules, although they do not guarantee an optimal solution, can usually identify a satisfactory solution very quickly.

Assume the following situation. A manager has three jobs assigned to a printing press in a certain day. The press is currently empty. The setup times for the jobs are indicated in Table 17.4. In this simplified case there are only six possible alternatives; therefore, it is possible to enumerate all of them rather easily. The results are given in Table 17.5. By complete enumeration it is seen that the sequence 1–3–2 is the best, with a minimum total setup time of 55 minutes.

The Next Best Rule

In many practical cases, workers do not enumerate the alternatives, even when only a small number of jobs is involved. Instead, they use an interesting rule of thumb called the *next best rule*. According to this rule, the worker sorts all jobs and selects, as the first job to be processed, the job that requires the least setup time from the "empty" condition (job 2 in the example, with only 20 minutes setup time). Then the employee searches for that job that will require the *least* setup time from job 2 (job 3 in this case) and so on, until all jobs are sequenced.

Next job with least time

TABLE 17.4 Setup Times in Minutes

From Job \ To Job	1	2	3
Empty	25	20	30
1	0	35	20
2	50	0	45
3	45	10	0

TABLE 17.5 **Enumeration Results**

Sequence Job Number	Setup Times	Total (Minutes)	
1–2–3	25 + 35 + 45	105	
1–3–2	25 + 20 + 10	55	←Minimum
2–3–1	20 + 45 + 45	110	
2–1–3	20 + 50 + 20	90	
3–1–2	30 + 45 + 35	110	
3–2–1	30 + 10 + 50	90	

In this case, the selected sequence 2–3–1 will result in 110 minutes of setup time, a solution that is far from the best. On the average, however, the next best rule results in a savings of 8 percent to 76 percent over a random selection. Although this procedure *is* better than a random arrangement, it can be improved further. The reason is that this procedure does the best it can in each *single step*. Such an approach is labeled **Greedy approach** a **greedy algorithm** (because it is shortsighted). This is in contrast to other heuristic methods that use a so-called "look-ahead" approach, viewing all the steps at once.

The Next Best with Adjustments Rule

Look-ahead approach This heuristic is also greedy but it yields much better results, on the average, than the previous one. According to this rule, the original setup time matrix is modified as follows: The minimum time in each column is subtracted from all other times in that column (ignore the zero values). This calculation is shown in Figure 17.1.

Once the reduced matrix is constructed, the next best rule is employed on it. Thus, from "empty," the least setup time is for job 1 with a value of 0. From 1, the least setup time is to number 3; from 3, one goes to 2. The solution is sequence 1–3–2 with 55 minutes of setup time (the optimal solution). *Note:* The advantage of these rules is that they can be executed manually by the employees themselves.

FIGURE 17.1

Decision matrix using "next best with adjustments" rule (Minimum column values circled.)

From	To 1	2	3		To 1	2	3		To 1	2	3
Empty	(25)	20	30		25 − 25 = 0	20 − 10 = 10	30 − 20 = 10		0	10	10
Job 1	0	35	(20)	→	X	35 − 10 = 25	20 − 20 = 0	→	X	25	0
Job 2	50	0	45		50 − 25 = 25	X	45 − 20 = 25		25	X	25
Job 3	45	(10)	0		45 − 25 = 20	10 − 10 = 0	X		20	0	X

| Original matrix | Reduction process | Resultant (reduced) matrix |

Management Science in Practice

Snow and Ice Removal in an Urban Environment

Snow storms can paralyze large cities, causing accidents, injuries, economic losses, and even deaths. Cities thus try to keep their streets and highways open, but the cost in the largest cities can exceed $10 million a year. The specifics of the problem are unique to each city and vary from year to year.

Snow and ice removal is done by plowing and/or spreading salt (or sand). Streets are divided into two categories: priority 1—snow routes, and priority 2—other streets. The objective is to minimize the time required to clear the snow routes. Studies show that the accident rate in the case of light snow or freezing rain can be reduced by more than 50 percent if the streets are cleaned quickly. The potential annual saving in large cities is several million dollars plus significant reductions in deaths and injuries.

Cities operate trucks for the plowing (spreading), with each truck assigned to a specific route. The problem is to minimize the clearing time of the entire city. The problem can be formulated as a complex combinatorial problem. A heuristic was developed for spreading salt (or sand) as follows: A spreader truck is assigned to a street (route) such that:

1. The route can be covered with one load of salt.
2. Assignments are made only to unsalted streets.
3. Make the next assignment to the nearest unassigned street first (the closest to the salt pile facility).

The authors give an example of a city with 2 trucks and 40 street segments, each 1 mile long. The authors used the above simple heuristic to schedule the trucks and compared the results against a typical scheduling policy where trucks are *preassigned* to certain routes. Using a hypothetical example, the city was cleared in 180 minutes with the heuristic, versus 252 minutes with the preassigned plan (a reduction of 29 percent in clearing time).

Other advantages of using this heuristic are: (1) balanced utilization of the trucks, (2) less interruptions because the trucks will travel to their routes over streets that have already been salted, and (3) automatic coverage in case of a truck breakdown. The cost of implementing the heuristic is minimal.

The authors tested the heuristic via a simulation for the city of Tulsa, Oklahoma. The heuristic yielded a time reduction of 36 percent over the preassigned routes method. Because a simulation model was constructed anyway, the city was able to test several proposals for the improvement of operations. For example, they tested increasing the number of salt pile locations from one to two or three and increasing the numbers of trucks and/or their tonnage (capacity). These proposals were found to be unattractive. The city of Tulsa adopted the recommendations derived by this study.

Source: Cook, T. M. and B. S. Alprin. "Snow and Ice Removal in an Urban Environment." *Management Science*, November 1976.

Questions:

1. Would this be considered a "greedy" heuristic?
2. Suggest some other possible heuristics for this problem.
3. How much improvement do you think an optimizing routine could gain over this heuristic?

17.6 The Traveling Salesperson Problem (TSP)

In the problems for Chapter 2, we introduced the TSP, a classical combinatorial problem. The problem is to minimize the travel time (or distance) in a tour in which the traveler starts from home, visits all cities once, and returns home. Several constraints can be added to make the problem more realistic; for example, the travel time from city A to city B may be different than that from B to A, a situation called asymmetric (e.g., going uphill versus returning downhill). Also, travel between certain cities may not be feasible, or it may be necessary to visit a certain city prior to another one. Let us first formulate the problem in its simplest form.

Formulation

The TSP is an optimization problem that can be viewed as a variation of the transportation problem. The problem, for n cities, can be stated as:

$$\text{minimize } z = \sum_{i=1}^{n} \sum_{j=1}^{n} c_{ij} \, x_{ij}$$

$$\text{subject to: } \sum_{j=1}^{n} x_{ij} = 1 \qquad i = 1, 2, \ldots, n \text{ (the traveler must embark from all cities)}$$

$$\sum_{i=1}^{n} x_{ij} = 1 \qquad j = 1, 2, \ldots, n \text{ (the traveler must visit all cities), and}$$

$$x_{ij} = 0 \text{ or } 1$$

The Possible Number of Solutions

In the asymmetric case, there are $(n - 1)!$ possible routes (in the symmetric case there are $.5(n - 1)!$ possibilities). For example, a 15-city asymmetrical problem will have 87,178,291,200 possible routes. Thus, the problem is combinatorial in nature, similar to the job scheduling problem. The problem can be formulated as a 0–1 integer program. For a problem with many cities, especially when constraints are added, the existing algorithms of integer programming prove to be either inefficient or even infeasible. The following are two simple heuristics that can be used for solving the TSP.

The Nearest-Neighbor Rule (Rosenkrantz et al. [14])

This heuristic employs the following procedure: Start at a particular city and go to the nearest city. From there, continue to the nearest city that has not yet been visited. Continue in this manner until all cities are visited.

Greedy but not efficient

    This procedure, another example of a greedy algorithm, is very simple and logical. But on the average, it is not very efficient for the reasons discussed earlier.

A Graphical Heuristic

According to this heuristic (which has been proven to be fairly efficient), draw a map (with distances shown to scale) and follow this rule:

Exterior approach

    Take a pencil and, starting from any city, draw a line to a nearby city such that you always stay in the exterior of the map as much as possible. In addition, do not cross over existing lines and do not backtrack. Finally, return to the original city. (See Figure 17.2.)

FIGURE 17.2

Heuristic solution to the traveling salesperson problem

Source: A. J. Rowe, "The Meta Logic of Cognitively Based Heuristics," *Special Report,* Los Angeles, Calif.: University of Southern California, April 1988.

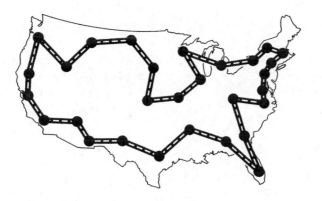

Management Science in Practice

Heuristics Improve the Production of Printed Circuit Boards

Metelco S. A. is a medium-sized manufacturer of printed circuit boards (PCBs) in Athens, Greece. To compete in the extremely competitive, high-technology European market requires constant attention to the production process in order to offer high-quality work with timely deliveries at low prices.

A major bottleneck in the production of PCBs for Metelco was the drilling of the holes for the electronic component pins that are to be soldered to the board. A typical PCB requires about 500 holes, although some may need as many as 1,000 holes. Moving the drill to the exact location of each hole is a time-consuming process. The normal procedure is to have the operator perform an initial setup run while the computer on the programmable drill monitors and records the motions the operator takes the drillhead through. By means of a joystick and digital X–Y readout, the operator can determine when he has reached the precise location of each hole. The routings and hole locations are then saved on a tape for later use in drilling the batch of PCBs for that order.

Usually, the operator simply follows the order of holes listed by the customer on the specification sheet. These are in random order so the drillhead frequently is moving from one end of the board to the other, or from one side to the other and then back again. However, on small boards with few holes, the operator can greatly speed up the drilling operation by resequencing the route so the drillhead moves smoothly and efficiently around the board in one continuous motion. Unfortunately, this requires so many hours of the operator's time that it is not usually possible for any but the smallest of boards.

This problem was clearly related to the traveling salesperson problem (TSP) and was thus attacked in that fashion. A limitation on the solution was that Metelco's management preferred that the solution be implementable on their new, limited-storage microcomputer. A number of approaches, some optimal and some heuristic, have been developed for the TSP, with various amounts of computer time and storage required and various accuracies in approximating the optimal solution.

Using known approximations for optimal TSP solutions, Metelco estimated that the absolutely minimal travel time to move to N holes on a PCB with an area of A square centimeters at a drillhead speed of V centimeters per second was about $0.69 \times V \times N \times A$ seconds. Also, knowing that it takes Metelco's drills about 1 second to drill one hole, it was determined that the minimal travel time constituted about half of the total throughput time (travel plus drilling). A deviation of X percent above this, therefore, resulted in about $0.5X$ reduction in throughput volume. Examining the current process for drillhead travel, Metelco found that they currently exceeded this minimal travel time by 50 percent, with a resulting reduction in throughput (relative to the maximum) of about 25 percent.

On the basis of this potential improvement, Metelco approved the project. The heuristic implemented, one that begins with the convex hull (external boundary of the points), was chosen for its small memory requirements yet good approximation ability. Tests on 20 cases showed it to be within about 10 percent of the optimum solutions, on average, and never worse than 15 percent.

On implementation of the process, a 35 percent reduction in travel time was achieved, a bit better than expected. Processing the tape on Metelco's computer for the drill takes about five minutes for a 500-hole board and 20 minutes for a 1,000-hole board, which is fully acceptable. Following implementation, it was estimated that PCB drilling section throughput increased about 10 percent and errors and defects decreased substantially.

The drilling section's workload has been reduced significantly and their operation is now more reliable and productive.

Source: V. F. Magirou, "The Efficient Drilling of Printed Circuit Boards," *Interfaces*, July–August 1986, pp. 13–23.

Questions:

1. Describe this problem in terms of the TSP.
2. What was the purpose of the first set of calculations to address this problem?
3. By using an optimal solution, how much would the throughput increase?
4. How much would they have had to speed up the drilling process to achieve the same benefits as obtained here?

17.7 Introduction to Game Theory

In 1943, General Kenney, commander of the Allied Air Forces in the Southwest Pacific, was faced with a problem. The Japanese were about to reinforce their army in New Guinea from their base in New Britain. Kenney's mission was to bomb and destroy the convoy of reinforcements. The Japanese had a choice of alternative sailing routes. They could either sail north of New Britain, where the weather was rainy and visibility poor for reconnaissance, or southward, where the weather was generally fair (see Figure 17.3). In either case, the journey would take three days. Kenney's problem was to decide where to concentrate the bulk of his reconnaissance aircraft to search for the convoy. The Japanese wanted their ships to have minimal exposure to enemy bombers and, of course, Kenney wanted as many days of bombing exposure as possible.

The following were the possible "days of bombing exposure":

1. If Kenney concentrated his aircraft on the northern route and the Japanese sailed north, the Japanese would not be found until the second day. There would thus be two days of exposure.
2. If Kenney concentrated on the northern route and the Japanese sailed south, they might easily be missed on the first day. There would again be two days of exposure.

FIGURE 17.3

The convoy's alternatives

Source: O. G. Haywood, Jr., "Military Decisions and Game Theory." *Journal of the Operations Research Society of America* (November 1954), p. 366.

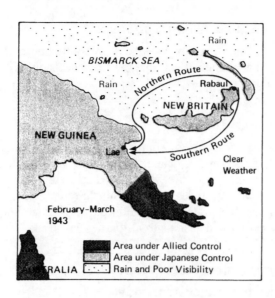

3. If Kenney concentrated on the southern route and the Japanese sailed north, they would not be discovered until the third day, resulting in only one day of exposure.

4. If Kenney concentrated on the southern route and the Japanese sailed south, they would be sighted immediately for three full days of exposure.

The problem faced by both sides was what course of action to take.

The Nature of Game Theory Problems

Decision under conflict

The military situation just presented illustrates decision making *under* **conflict** or *competition*. Its main characteristic is that two or more decision makers are involved and the consequences (payoff) to each depend on the courses of action taken by all. Further, objectives do not coincide and may, as illustrated in the military example, be completely opposed. As a matter of fact, each party is usually trying to maximize his or her overall welfare at the expense of the others.

"Game" presentation

Such situations are similar to parlor and other types of games. For this reason, the name *game theory* was adopted. Yet, situations analyzed with the aid of this tool are a far cry from "games." Marketing strategies, international military conflicts, labor-management negotiations, and potential takeovers are just a few examples of real-life game theory problems.

The Complexity of Game Theory Problems

The presence of two or more decision makers with conflicting objectives makes decision making complex for mathematical analysis. The decision tables discussed earlier cannot handle such situations.

Methodology of Game Theory

Optimal strategies

The managerial situation, problem, or conflict is presented in game format. The decision makers are viewed as players. Game theory aims at prescribing optimal playing strategies for the participants. A **strategy** is defined as a complete, predetermined plan for selecting a course of action, under every possible circumstance. An *optimal strategy* is the best among all possible strategies. In addition, the model computes the long-run payoffs or consequences of the decisions to all parties involved.

Format, Assumptions, and Classification of Games

The Format of Games and Major Assumptions
Games are arranged in a standard format. Certain rules and regulations that express the assumptions apply, and a specially developed terminology is used. The major aspects of the format concern:

The game situation

1. *The number of participants* (termed *players*). The military example involved two players. In other situations, three or more players may participate. A player can be a single individual or a group of individuals with the same objective.
2. *Timing*. It would have been easier for Kenney if he could have delayed his decision until the Japanese made their move (and vice versa). However, both had to decide simultaneously. *Simultaneous* decisions are assumed in all game situations.
3. *Conflicting goals*. Each party is interested in maximizing his or her welfare at the expense of the other.

Games composed of repetitive plays

4. *Repetition*. The military conflict is an example of a one-shot decision, which is termed a **play.** A series of repetitive decisions (plays) is called a **game.** It is generally assumed that most instances involve repetitive situations. However, using expected value allows us to justify the use of game theory in the case of a single play.

Zero value = Fair game

5. *Payoff*. The consequence of the decisions of the opponents in the military conflict was measured in terms of *days of bombing exposure*. Such results are called *payoffs*. The *average payoff per play* is termed the **value of the game.** A game whose value is zero is called a **fair game.**

6. *Information availability.* In general, it is assumed that each player knows *all* possible courses of action (finite number) open to the opponent as well as *all* anticipated payoffs. The cost of collecting this information is not considered relevant to the formal analysis.

7. *Rational players.* It is assumed that players play in a rational manner.

Presentation of Games

Tree or normal form

Games are presented either in tabular (termed *normal*) or tree (termed *extensive*) form.

Normal Form (a Tabular Presentation). A game is said to be in *normal form* when the entire sequence of decisions that must be made throughout the game is lumped together in a single strategy. This is the common form of games and the one used in this section. This form is limited to the case of two players.

An Example of Normal Form Presentation For the Military Conflict. In this situation, there were two decision makers: Kenney, with two possible courses of action: a_1 or a_2; and the Japanese, who had to decide either to sail north (b_1), or south (b_2). The above situation is presented in normal form as a payoff table in Table 17.6.

The payoff table

A game payoff table is similar to a decision payoff table. The difference between the two is that in a decision table, there is only one decision maker, who makes decisions in uncertain environments (expressed as "states of nature"). In the game table, on the other hand, there are two decision makers, one on the left and the other at the top. The information in the cells is the payoff (number of days exposure, in this case). A *positive* number means a *gain* to the player situated at the *left* side of the table (Allies in Table 17.6). This gain is the loss of the player situated at the top of the table (Japan). A *negative* number means a *loss* to the player situated at the left and a gain to the player at the top of the table.

TABLE 17.6 **The Military Conflict as a Game Payoff Table**

Allies \ Japan	North, b_1	South, b_2
Northern, a_1	2	2
Southern, a_2	1	3

Classification of Games

Games may be classified according to the number of players (e.g., **two-person games,** three-person games) and whether the game is *zero-sum* or *nonzero-sum*. These latter terms are defined next.

Your loss is my gain!

1. *Zero-sum games.* In **zero-sum games,** the winner(s) receives the entire amount of the payoff that is contributed by the loser(s). Such a game is always strictly competitive. The players' objective is to win as much as they can at the expense of the rival. Zero-sum games with two decision makers are labeled "two-person, zero-sum games" and are the major subject of this section. Two assumptions are necessary for the analysis of these games:
   a. All two-person, zero-sum games are solvable.
   b. The utility functions of the players, with respect to the outcome of the game, are identical. In other words, the payoffs are transferable to either player with the same value to each.
2. *Nonzero-sum games.* In a **nonzero-sum game** the gains of one player differ from the losses of the other. Therefore, nonzero-sum games are not strictly competitive and there is sometimes a possibility of cooperation.

17.8 Solving Game Theory Problems

The solution tells us the best strategy and resulting payoff

Solving Games

A solution to game problems provides us with answers to these two questions:

1. What strategy should each player follow to maximize his or her payoff?
2. What will the payoff to each player be if the recommended strategy is followed?

Unfortunately, clear answers can be given only in a few instances of conflicts; namely, for two-person, zero-sum games. The following subsections deal with such solutions. Two-person, zero-sum games are divided into two groups: those with a pure strategy solution and those with a mixed strategy solution.

Two-Person, Zero-Sum Games—Pure Strategy

A pure strategy versus a mixed strategy

The Allies-Japanese conflict presented earlier is an example of a pure-strategy game. The term **pure strategy** refers to a prescribed solution in which one alternative is repeatedly recommended to each player, regardless of what the other player does. This is in contrast to a *mixed strategy,* where players change from alternative to alternative when the game is repeated.

Analysis of the Allies-Japanese Conflict

Refer again to the Allies-Japanese conflict in Table 17.6. It was assumed that the Allies will try to *maximize* the days of exposure whereas the Japanese will try to *minimize* them.

The Allies can get the maximum "days of exposure" (three) if they select a_2 and the Japanese select b_2. However, the Allies realize that the Japanese, being rational competitors, will not select b_2. The reason for that is that *no matter what the Allies do, the Japanese will be at least as well off, or better off, selecting b_1 rather than b_2!* If the Allies select a_1, the Japanese will be subjected to two days of bombing exposure regardless of whether they had taken b_1 or b_2. But if the Allies follow a_2, the Japanese choice of b_1 would subject them to only one day of exposure, as compared to three if b_2 were selected. Therefore, knowing that the Japanese will select b_1, the Allies will select a_1. This minimax approach implies that:

1. Both players determine the *worst possible payoff* associated with each of their alternatives.

2. Then, they each select that alternative that yields *the best* of these worst payoffs.

Solving the game

The choices of both players are illustrated in Table 17.7. The steps involved in solving the game of Table 17.7 using this approach are:

For the Allies.

Step 1. Find the *minimum* value in each row. The minimum is 2 in row a_1 and 1 in row a_2.

Step 2. Select the row with the maximum of the minimums computed in Step 1. The highest value is 2. Hence, the Allies should select a_1 (the northern route).

TABLE 17.7   Pessimistic Selection

Allies \ Japan	b_1	b_2	Row Minimum (Worst Results to Allies)	
a_1	②	2	②	← *Maximum (best of worst)*
a_2	1	3	1	
Column Maximum (Worst Loss to Japan)	②	3		

Minimum (best of worst)

For the Japanese.

Step 1. Find the maximum in each column. In this case, the maximum is 2 in column b_1 and 3 in column b_2. Write them in a new, bottom row.

Step 2. Select the column with the *minimum* of the *maximums* of Step 1 (column b_1).

Notes: (1) In a pure strategy game, the value selected (2 in this case) must be the same for each player and it is called *the value of the game,* meaning a gain of 2 to the Allies and a loss of 2 to the Japanese. (2) This solution was actually adopted by both sides during the war, with a resultant two days of bombing exposure.

Dominance

An alternative course of action is said to *dominate* another when all the payoffs in the row (or the column of that alternative are as good as *and at least one is better than* the corresponding payoffs of the other. For example, in Table 17.8, alternative a_4 is better than alternative a_3 for player A, no matter what player B does. Thus, alternative a_4 is said to *dominate* a_3.

Row dominance does not seem to exist, at first sight, in Table 17.7; but column b_1 dominates column b_2 for the Japanese. Thus, the table can be reduced to that shown in Table 17.9. *Now,* however, row a_1 dominates row a_2, resulting in the final solution of (a_1, b_1). Thus, row (column) dominance should always be *rechecked* if a column (row) has just been deleted by dominance.

Two-Person, Zero-Sum Games—Mixed Strategy

Some two-person, zero-sum games are not pure strategy games. The way to judge if a game is one of pure strategy or not is to try to solve it by the pessimistic approach. If the "best of the worst" value is *the same* in value and sign for both players (as was

---

TABLE 17.8 **Multiple solution case**

	Player B			
	b_1	b_2	b_3	Minimum
a_1	7	−1	2	−1
a_2	4	4	6	④ ←Maximum
a_3	6	3	0	0
a_4	7	4	5	④ ←Maximum
Maximum	7	④	6	

Player A (label at left)

Minimum (↑ under the ④ in column b_2)

TABLE 17.9 Reduced table

	b_1
a_1	②
a_2	1

A mixed strategy

shown to be the case in Table 17.7), the game is a pure strategy game. Otherwise, it is necessary to treat the game as one requiring a **mixed strategy.**

A Marketing Example

Two competing companies are about to make a decision regarding an investment in a new promotional campaign. Company A considers two alternative courses of action:

$$a_1 = \text{Advertise in all media}$$

$$a_2 = \text{Advertise in newspapers only}$$

Company B considers two alternatives:

$$b_1 = \text{Run a sweepstakes}$$

$$b_2 = \text{Run a big sale}$$

If company A advertises in all media and company B runs a sweepstakes, then company A will increase its share of the market, at the expense of B, by 4 percent. If A advertises in all media and B runs a big sale, A will lose 1 percent of the market. If A advertises in newspapers only and B runs a sweepstakes, A will lose 2 percent; and if A advertises in newspapers only and B runs a big sale, then A will gain 1 percent. The information is summarized in Table 17.10. It is assumed that the objective of the companies is to maintain as large a share of the market as possible.

Analysis of the Marketing Example Game

Suppose that a pessimistic approach is attempted (see Table 17.11). The solution recommends that player A use a_1 and the player B use b_2. Note that the maximum value

TABLE 17.10   A Marketing Problem

A \ B	b_1 *Run a Sweepstakes*	b_2 *Run a Big Sale*
a_1 *Advertise, All Media*	4	−1
a_2 *Advertise, Newspaper Only*	−2	1

TABLE 17.11   **Minimax Approach to the Marketing Problem**

A \ B	b_1	b_2	Row Minimum	
a_1	4	−1	⓵−1	← *Maximum (of minimums)*
a_2	−2	1	−2	
Column Maximum	4	①		

↑
Minimum (of maximums)

Minimax ≠ Maximin

for player A of −1 (circled) is *not* equal to the minimum value for player B of 1. Assume that on the first play, player A selects alternative a_1 (his proposed maximin) and player B selects alternative b_2 (his proposed minimax). As soon as A finds out that B is consistently playing b_2, player A's next move will be a shift to a_2, because he will receive a larger payoff than by playing a_1. When B finds out that A has shifted to a_2, he will shift to b_1. Then, as A finds out about this shift, he will change back to a_1, and so on.

Both players will soon find out that:

1. It is better to shift from alternative to alternative (*mix* the alternatives) rather than play the same alternative all the time (as with a pure strategy approach).

Maintain secrecy

2. They should practice maximum secrecy with their plans so that the opponent will not be able to guess the next move.

3. The average payoff is determined by the fraction of time (proportion) that each of the alternatives is played, and there is a certain fraction that is best for each player, regardless of the other player's choices.

> Therefore, a solution to a mixed strategy problem includes:
>
> 1. *Computation of the best proportion mix of the alternatives.*
> 2. *Computation of the value of the game,* which is the expected (average) gain or loss, per play, to player A.

Analytical Solution to a Mixed Strategy Game with Two Choices Open to Each Player (2 × 2 Game)

Let us consider the data in Table 17.10 for illustrating a mixed strategy game. This information is reproduced in Table 17.12 with corresponding generalized symbols. *Note:*

TABLE 17.12 **Solving a Mixed Strategy Game**
(c_{ij} = **Payoff**)

			Player B	
Proportions			(q)	($1 - q$)
	Choices	b_1	b_2	
Player A (p)	a_1	$c_{11} = 4$	$c_{12} = -1$	
($1 - p$)	a_2	$c_{21} = -2$	$c_{22} = 1$	

With two choices, the proportions for A could be denoted as p_1 and p_2; however, because $p_1 + p_2 = 1$ or $p_2 = 1 - p_1$, there is only one unknown, which is designated as p in this case. A similar designation is made for B, using q instead of p.

Calculating the expected payoff

Solution. Let us assume that player B plays alternative b_1 consistently and player A plays a_1 in p of the cases and a_2 in $(1 - p)$ of the cases. The *expected payoff* (V_1) to player A is then (using an expected value formula and treating the proportion as a probability):

$$V_1 = p(4) + (1 - p)(-2)$$

Similarly, when B plays b_2 consistently, the expected payoff to A is:

$$V_2 = p(-1) + (1 - p)(1)$$

Player A desires to mix his strategies so that player B cannot reduce A's gain by shifting strategies. To do so, the expected payoff to A when B plays either strategy b_1 or strategy b_2 should be the same. By doing so, A becomes *independent* of B's decision. B can mix b_1 and b_2 in any proportion and A will receive the guaranteed minimum. That is, the two expected payoffs V_1 and V_2 must be equal:

$$\overbrace{p(4) + (1 - p)(-2)}^{V_1,\ \text{when B plays } b_1} = \overbrace{p(-1) + (1 - p)(1)}^{V_2,\ \text{when B plays } b_2}$$

or

$$4p - 2 + 2p = -p + 1 - p$$
$$8p = 3$$
$$p = 3/8$$

The proportion for a_1 is $\frac{3}{8}$ and for a_2 is $1 - \frac{3}{8} = \frac{5}{8}$.

The General Case. The requirement that $V_1 = V_2$ yields the following equation:

$$pc_{11} + (1 - p)c_{21} = pc_{12} + (1 - p)c_{22}$$

Rearrangement of this equation yields the following:

$$p = \frac{c_{22} - c_{21}}{c_{11} - c_{12} - c_{21} + c_{22}}$$

In our example, the proportion p, for playing a_1, is prescribed for player A as:

$$p = \frac{1 - (-2)}{4 - (-1) - (-2) + 1} = \frac{3}{8}$$

and the proportion for playing a_2 is:

$$1 - p = 1 - \frac{3}{8} = \frac{5}{8}$$

For player B, the proportion q of playing b_1 is derived by the equation $V_1 = V_2$ (for the columns), which, in this case, yields the following equation:

$$qc_{11} + (1 - q)c_{12} = qc_{21} + (1 - q)c_{22}$$

Computing B's proportions   or

$$q = \frac{c_{22} - c_{12}}{c_{11} - c_{12} - c_{21} + c_{22}}$$

In our example:

$$q = \frac{1 - (-1)}{4 - (-1) - (-2) + 1} = \frac{2}{8} = .25$$

and the proportion for playing b_2 is $1 - q = .75$.

Calculating the value of the game   ***The Value of the Game.***   Once p and q are established, the *value of the game, V,* can be determined. Assuming that player A plays with the prescribed probability p, his or her payoff can be found using *one* of the following four equations:

either	$V = pc_{11} + (1 - p)c_{21}$
or	$V = pc_{12} + (1 - p)c_{22}$
or	$V = qc_{11} + (1 - q)c_{12}$
or	$V = qc_{21} + (1 - q)c_{22}$

In our example:

$$V = \frac{3}{8} \times 4 + \frac{5}{8} \times (-2) = \frac{1}{4} \qquad \text{or,}$$

$$V = \frac{3}{8} \times (-1) + \frac{5}{8} \times 1 = \frac{1}{4} \qquad \text{or,}$$

$$V = \frac{1}{4} \times 4 + \frac{3}{4} \times (-1) = \frac{1}{4} \quad \text{or,}$$

$$V = \frac{1}{4} \times (-2) + \frac{3}{4} \times 1 = \frac{1}{4}$$

Thus, the value of the game is $\frac{1}{4}$. Because a game matrix is in terms of the payoff to A, there is an expected gain of $\frac{1}{4}$ to A and an expected loss (per play) of $\frac{1}{4}$ to B. To summarize the solution for our example: Player A: Play a_1 $\frac{3}{8}$ of the time and a_2 $\frac{5}{8}$ of the time. Player B: Play b_1 $\frac{1}{4}$ of the time and b_2 $\frac{3}{4}$ of the time. The value of the game is $\frac{1}{4}$.

A solution procedure for games larger than 2×2 is found through linear programming (see Schrage [31]). *Note:* The solutions to mixed strategy games are based on the assumption of repetition (or multiplicity of conflicts) so that an expected value approach is justified. However, most conflicts are nonrepetitive. Also, using utilities will change the game to nonzero sum, which is much more complex.

17.9 Problems for Part A

1. Give some examples of heuristics.

2. You are looking for syrup in a new grocery store. What heuristics do you employ?

3. You have the following weekend jobs facing you:

   Hanging a picture.

   Mowing a lawn.

   Walking a dog.

   Tuning up the car.

   Cleaning out the garage

   In what order would you choose to do these? What heuristic decision rules did you employ to choose this order?

4. There are 150 million cars in the United States. It has been suggested that a *national* plate to register all cars be used. The plate will include four letters followed by three digits. Whereas some people say that four letters and three digits will be sufficient for identifying all cars, others say, "No way!" Who do you think is right and why? (Be specific).

5. Heuristic problem: Little Billie is famous as the best junior burglar in Beverly Hills. He only robs from the filthy rich and is very selective in what he is willing to "lift" (because his goodies sack will only hold 27 cubic feet). Also, being small, he can only carry up to 92 pounds in his pack. On this particular night, he

has the items in the following table from which to choose.

Item	Value ($)	Volume (ft.^{3})	Weight (lb.)
A	300	2	25
B	100	1	10
C	500	3	20
D	900	5	30
E	600	5	15
F	400	1	35
G	200	2	10
H	300	3	15
I	500	4	15
J	700	8	10
K	200	4	20
L	800	7	20

Clearly, he wishes to maximize his "haul," but isn't sure which items to choose first. Test each of the following heuristic rules and advise Little Billie on their soundness:

a. If smaller items are chosen first, there might not be enough room left in the sack for the bigger, more valuable items, and the sack may have to be left partly empty. Therefore, because value is somewhat proportional to volume, fill the sack with the largest items first, tucking in the smaller items as space allows.

b. By the same reasoning, perhaps the heaviest items should be chosen first.

c. Choose the items in order of their value.

d. Choose the items in order of their value per unit volume

e. Choose the items in order of their value per unit weight.

f. Choose the items in order of their value per unit volume per unit weight.

6. Find the best sequence by using "next best" and "next best with adjustments" rules. The times are setup times.

From \ To	1	2	3	4	5	6	7	8
Initial Condition	9	29	9	14	29	34	18	16
1	0	23	30	15	18	17	11	24
2	24	0	22	8	22	10	24	16
3	7	7	0	8	33	26	20	25
4	7	18	11	0	27	18	6	34
5	4	15	22	10	0	22	30	35
6	26	33	26	9	22	0	35	15
7	23	19	29	33	7	24	0	30
8	31	24	19	28	10	21	19	0

7. A doctor has the following patients waiting to see him with the corresponding projected treatment times.

Patient	Treatment Time (Hours)
A	1.0
B	.2
C	2.0
D	1.5
E	.1
F	.7

The doctor wishes to schedule them to minimize average waiting time. Formulate two heuristic rules and compare them with taking the patients in the order given.

8. You are a designer of a computer system that may be attacked by n different hazards (e.g., a virus or an earthquake). Each hazard has a known chance of occurrence and known damage if it occurs. Each hazard can be prevented by a control, whose cost and probability of success is known. You have a limited amount of money to invest in the control.

The problem is to determine which control to include in the design.

a. Formulate the problem.

b. Why may it be difficult to solve?

c. Devise a heuristic to solve it.

9. Your company must decide in which magazines to advertise. The cost of the ad in each magazine is known and so is the percentage of the target audience that is reached by each magazine.

a. Develop a greedy algorithm for magazine selection, subject to a budget constraint.

b. Discuss some of the limitations of such a procedure.

c. You want to select 5 magazines from a list of 40 magazines. The number of combinations will be approximately 658,000. Show how this number has been derived.

10. Find the best strategy (strategies) for each player in the following two-person, zero-sum games. Also find the value of the game to both players. Circle the points of maximin and minimax.

a.

	b_1	b_2
a_1	1	3
a_2	7	4

b.

	b_1	b_2
a_1	−1	0
a_2	1	3

c.

	b_1	b_2	b_3
a_1	1	−2	3
a_2	−2	−5	−3
a_3	−1	−6	−5

d.

	b_1	b_2	b_3	b_4	b_5
a_1	3	3	1	6	0
a_2	−1	1	2	0	8
a_3	6	−3	2	1	4
a_4	5	3	3	6	4

11. Two companies are competing in a duopolistic market (a market with only two competitors). Both attempt to increase their share of the market, which is now equally divided. Company A plans to have a weekly advertising campaign that can increase its share of the market by 3 percent (of the total market) if company B does nothing. Company B, however, plans a weekly price cut that will result in a 4 percent gain to B if A does nothing and 1 percent gain to B if A uses the advertising campaign. No change in the market is foreseen if both companies do nothing.
    a. Arrange the problem in a payoff table.
    b. Suggest the best strategy for each company to follow.

12. Solve the following game:

	b_1	b_2
a_1	3	−2
a_2	1	5

13. Given below is a payoff table for two manufacturers, A and B, competing in one market. Each has to make a decision between two alternatives.

A \ B	b_1	b_2
a_1	−2	3
a_2	1	0

    a. Assuming that this is a repetitive decision, what is the best policy for the manufacturers?

    b. Let the figures in the payoff table be percentage of change in market share; what will the average gain (loss) to each manufacturer be?
    c. As a manager of Company B, would you follow the prescribed strategy? Why or why not?

14. A and B play a game in which each has three coins. A has a 2-cent coin, a nickel, and a dime. B has a penny, a nickel, and a dime. Each selects one of his coins without knowledge of the other's choice. If the sum of the two coins adds to an odd number, A wins B's coin. If the sum is an even number, B wins A's coin.
    a. Arrange the payoff table.
    b. Find the best strategy for both players.
    c. If you had to play the game, would you rather be A or B? Why?

15. Given three game tables:

a.

	b_1	b_2
a_1	3	−2
a_2	−3	0

b.

	b_1	b_2
a_1	5	0
a_2	−1	2

c.

	b_1	b_2
a_1	6	−4
a_2	−6	0

Solve the games. What can you conclude about the relationship among the three games in this case?

16. Two French companies plan a TV advertising campaign for a competitive product. TV ads run during four basic periods: morning (*M*), afternoon (*A*), evening (*E*), and night (*N*), as listed in the table below. Advertising time is available in units; company A can afford one unit only, but company B can afford two units. Thus, company A has four choices (advertise in *M*, *A*, *E*, or *N*), whereas company B has 10 alternatives as shown below.

    The payoff table shows the conditional share of the market captured by company A. For example, if A uses one unit in the morning and B uses two units in the morning, then A gets 30 percent of the market and B gets the remaining 70 percent. It is assumed that the objective of each company is to maximize its share of the market and that the cost of advertising is the same per unit. View this situation as a zero-sum game.
    a. What action should each company take?
    b. How will the market then be divided?

17. Two competing companies consider the advertising alternatives below. The table shows the alternatives and the percent increase in market share for company A. One percent of the share of the market is considered equal to $10,000.

B

A

	b_1	b_2	b_3	b_4	b_5
a_1	1	0	−1	−8	−9
a_2	5	3	5	−7	−3
a_3	7	−1	1	7	9

Find:

a. The optimal strategy of each company.

b. The average, per period, monetary gain (loss) of company B.

18. Recent suburban development in the city of Mid-America resulted in the construction of three new shopping centers: Eastland, Westland, and Northland. The location of these centers and the number of shoppers expected in each, per week, is shown on the following page.

Burgerqueen (BQ) and McBurger (MB) are each planning to open a restaurant in the new section of MidAmerica, and both must soon decide on the exact location. The location decision is a top secret at both

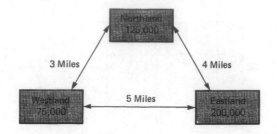

companies. However, a reputable independent market research company provided both of them with the following data:

a. If BQ is closer to a shopping center than MB, then 80 percent of the business in that center will be captured by BQ.

b. If MB is closer to a shopping center than BQ, then BQ will get 30 percent of the business there, leaving 70 percent for MB.

c. If both BQ and MB open a restaurant at the same distance from a shopping center, then MB will capture 55 percent and BQ will get 45 percent of the market.

1. Set up the problem as a game.

2. Find the best strategies for the two companies.

3. Assume that 10 percent of all shoppers eat at a fast-food restaurant. Find how many shoppers will eat in each establishment during the first week of operation if the optimal locations are selected.

B

A

	M(2)	A(2)	E(2)	N(2)	M(1) A(1)	M(1) E(1)	M(1) N(1)	A(1) E(1)	A(1) N(1)	E(1) N(1)
M	.30	.25	.20	.30	.25	.20	.30	.20	.25	.25
A	.35	.25	.20	.40	.30	.25	.30	.20	.25	.30
E	.40	.30	.25	.50	.30	.35	.35	.25	.30	.35
N	.25	.20	.10	.25	.20	.15	.20	.15	.20	.20

17.10 CASE
THE VIDEOTAPE STRATEGY

The Soonie Company is a manufacturer of videotapes. Being a leader in its field, the company runs national ads comparing its products to those of Pany, its major competitor. Soonie uses three advertising strategies: a_1—a direct attack on their competitor; a_2—an indirect attack; and a_3—no attack at all.

Pany is a more conservative company. It uses these advertising strategies: b_1—"our products are of the highest quality"; b_2—"our products give you more for your money"; and b_3—"sure, you can buy other products, but. . . ."

Soonie's advertising budget amounts to hundreds of thousands of dollars annually. Basic ad decisions are made monthly. Recent sales results indicate that the company's market share actually fluctuates too much and has periodic sharp declines. In its last meeting, the board of directors asked Soonie's president to study the situation.

Yuki White, the newly appointed director of marketing research, was authorized to investigate the problem. Using computerized time series and regression analyses, she attempted to find the relationship between advertising policies and sales levels. After analyzing historical data for the past few years, she decided there was no correlation between the two. Then she realized that Soonie's market share also depended on Pany's strategy. However, it was impossible to know exactly what the competition had in mind in the past.

"We should record what level of ads Pany uses," Yuki thought to herself. For a moment, she felt hopeless. Then she called a meeting of all key sales representatives, asking them to indicate the effectiveness of Soonie's ads in relation to various strategies used by Pany. Ad effectiveness was based on the following four-point scale: 4 = excellent; 3 = good; 2 = fair; and 1 = poor.

Although the sales reps disagreed on several of the possible results, she constructed an average response that looked like this:

If Soonie employs strategy a_1 and Pany employs b_1, the response to Soonie's strategy is *good*. Similarly, for the other possibilities the results were:

If Soonie Employs	If Pany Employs	The Results for Soonie
a_1	b_2	Excellent
a_1	b_3	Fair
a_2	b_1	Poor
a_2	b_2	Good
a_2	b_3	Fair
a_3	b_1	Fair
a_3	b_2	Good
a_3	b_3	Excellent

A quick review of these results indicated that there was no one superior strategy. Poor to fair results were possible for each of Soonie's alternatives. "I can see now why my computerized programs failed to show any conclusive results. I wish we had a better information system," Yuki sighed.

At this point, the company's president called Yuki and requested "specific recommendations for future ad strategies." For a moment, Yuki thought that she should tell him that she had found no relationship between strategy and sales level. Then she figured that this was probably not true.

What should Yuki do? Consider such factors as the lack of collusion between the competitors, possible cooperation between the competitors, and overall market size.

PART B: EMERGING TECHNOLOGIES*

17.11 Decision Support Systems

Houston Minerals Corporation was interested in a proposed joint venture with a local petrochemicals company to develop a chemical plant. Houston's executive vice president responsible for the decision wanted an analysis of the risks involved in the areas of supplies, demands, and price. Bob Sampson, manager of planning and administration, and his staff built a DSS model in a few days by means of a specialized planning language. The results strongly suggested the project should be accepted.

Then came the real test. Although the executive vice president accepted the validity and value of the results, he was worried about the potential downside risk of the project—the chance of a catastrophic outcome. As Sampson tells it, his words were something like this:

"I realize the amount of work you have already done, and I am 99 percent confident with it. However, I would like to see this in a different light. I know we are short on time and we have to get back to our partners with our yes or no decision." Sampson replied that the executive could have the risk analysis he needed in less than an hour's time. Sampson concluded, "Within 20 minutes, there in the executive boardroom, we were reviewing the results of his "what-if?" questions. Those results led to the eventual dismissal of the project, which we otherwise would probably have accepted."

DSS to apply management science

The mystique surrounding computers and quantitative models has resulted in a significant *gap* between existing technology and its use by the practicing manager. The Houston Minerals Corporation case just presented demonstrates some of the major features of **decision support systems (DSS).** A decision support system (DSS) is a flexible, easy-to-use, interactive, computerized system that may significantly reduce this gap. The case demonstrates that the analysis started with the application of simulation modeling, which was the first cut, based on the decision maker's initial definition of what was needed. Then, the executive vice president, using his experience, judgment, and intuition, felt that the model should be modified. The initial model, although mathematically correct, was incomplete. With regular modeling, a modification would have taken a long time, but the DSS provided a *very quick* analysis. Furthermore, the DSS was flexible and responsive enough to allow managerial intuition and judgment to be followed in the end. The major differences between MS and DSS are outlined in Table 17.13.

Decision support systems can be viewed as a philosophy and a new approach to managerial decision making. It is not at the present time a well-defined methodology with specific features and techniques. DSS use MS analytical models, other quantitative models, and possibly simulation in conducting an analysis. Traditional MS and other quantitative techniques operate quite well outside DSS in many organizations. However, DSS can greatly increase the extent of applications of these techniques.

---

* Note: Portions of this part were condensed from Turban [38].

TABLE 17.13 **Comparing Management Science and Decision Support Systems**

Operations research/management science

The impact has mostly been on structured problems (rather than tasks), where the objective, data, and constraints can be prespecified.

The payoff has been in generating better solutions for given types of problems.

The relevance for managers has been the provision of detailed recommendations and new methodologies for handling complex problems.

Decision support systems

The impact is on decisions in which there is sufficient structure for computer and analytic aids to be of value but where managers' judgment is essential.

The payoff is in extending the range and capability of managers' decision processes to help them improve their effectiveness.

The relevance for managers is the creation of a supportive tool (under their own control) that does not attempt to automate the decision process, predefine objectives, or impose solutions.

Source: P. G. W. Keen and M. S. Scott-Morton, *Decision Support Systems, An Organizational Perspective* (Reading, Mass.: Addison-Wesley Publishing, 1978.)

Definitions

Management decision systems

The concepts involved in DSS were first articulated in the early 1970s under the term *management decision systems*. A DSS was defined as an interactive computer-based system that helps decision makers utilize *data* and *models* to solve unstructured problems. Another classical definition of DSS, provided by Keen and Scott-Morton [6], states:

> Decision support systems couple the intellectual resources of individuals with the capabilities of the computer to improve the quality of decisions. It is a computer-based support system for management decision makers who deal with semistructured problems.

Four characteristics

The foregoing definitions indicate the four major characteristics of DSS:

- DSS incorporate both data and models.
- They are designed to *assist* managers in their decision processes in *semistructured* or *unstructured* tasks.
- They *support*, rather than *replace*, managerial judgment.
- The objective of DSS is to improve the *effectiveness* of the decisions, not the *efficiency* with which decisions are made.

It should be noted that DSS is a "content free" expression; that is, it means different things to different people.

> **Definition of a DSS**
>
> A DSS is an interactive, flexible, and adaptable computer-based information system that utilizes decision rules, models, and a model base joined with a comprehensive database and the decision maker's own insights. Using the DSS leads to specific, implementable decisions in solving problems that would *not* be amenable to management science optimization models per se.

Characteristics and Benefits

Ability to Support the Solution of Complex Problems
A DSS aids the solution of complex problems that ordinarily cannot be solved by other computerized approaches (or can be solved but at a much slower pace).

Fast Response to Unexpected Situations that Result in Changed Inputs
A DSS enables a thorough, quantitative analysis in a very short time. Even major changes in a scenario can be evaluated objectively in a timely manner.

Ability to Quickly and Objectively Try Several Different Strategies Under Different Configurations
As demonstrated in the preceding case, a complete what-if analysis was carried out in 20 minutes.

New Insights and Learning
The user can be exposed to new insights through the composition of the model and an extensive sensitivity/what-if analysis.

What if . . .

Facilitates Communication
Data collection and model construction/experimentation are executed with active users' participation, thus greatly facilitating communication among managers. The what-if analysis can be used to satisfy skeptics and, in turn, improve teamwork and implementation.

Improved Management Control and Performance
Decision support systems can increase management control over expenditures and improve the performance of the organization.

Cost Savings
Routine applications of DSS may result in considerable cost reduction or in reduction (elimination) of the cost of wrong decisions.

Objective Decisions
Consistent and objective decisions

The decisions derived from DSS are more consistent and objective than complex decisions that are made intuitively.

FIGURE 17.4

A conceptual model of a DSS

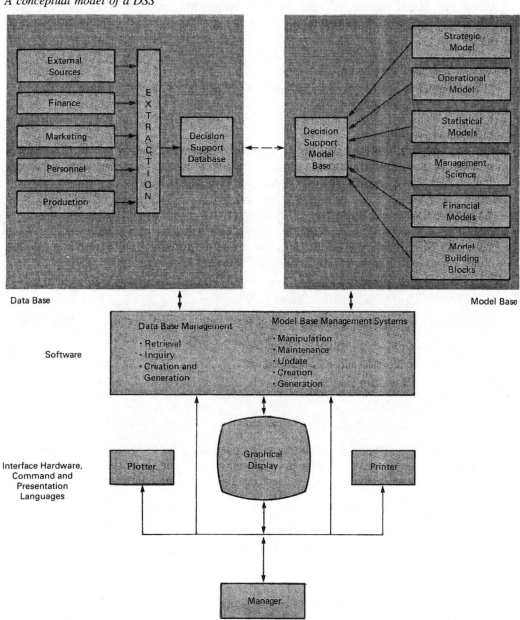

Improving Managerial Effectiveness

All of the above capabilities can improve managerial effectiveness (and personal efficiency) by allowing managers to perform a task in a way that uses less time and effort.

Support to Individuals and/or Groups

Decision support systems can be used to support individual managers and/or groups of managers at all managerial levels.

Graphical Display

Decision support systems provide an extensive graphical display of the information needed by managers. Computer graphics enable a user to view the data in several forms, such as bar graphs, scatter diagrams, or pie charts.

Extensive Range of Support

Decision support systems can support managers in *all steps* of decision making. Conventional MS models are limited to only one or two steps in the process. For a discussion of how DSS interface with the decision-making steps, see Turban [38].

The Structure of Decision Support Systems

A decision support system is composed of three major components (see Figure 17.4):

    a. The database and its management.

    b. The model base and its management.

    c. The user-system interface.

a. The Database and its Management

A **database** is a collection of data that is organized in such a way that it corresponds to the needs and structure of a company and can be used for more than one application. Most DSS have their own database, constructed by extracting data from internal and external sources.

Database Management System (DBMS)

The database is created, accessed, and updated by a **database management system (DBMS).** The DBMS is a series of *software programs*. DBMS provides six major features:

Six DBMS features

1. Capability of obtaining answers to queries.
2. Establishing data relationships.
3. Achieving data independence.
4. Quick retrieval (recovery) of data.
5. Quick updating of data.
6. Comprehensive data security.

An Application: Gotaas-Larsen Shipping Corp. (GLSC)*

One of the most promising uses of DSS is in the area of corporate planning and control, especially in strategic (long-range) planning. Strategic planning is one of the most difficult tasks of modern management. It involves all the functional areas in the organization and several outside factors which complicates the analysis, especially with the uncertainties of the long run. With the advances in computer technology and simulation, it is possible to find more and more corporations that use some kind of quantitative analysis in their strategic management process. However, regular MIS-type systems are less effective than DSS, because they lack the what-if and other on-line capabilities of DSS.

GLSC, a subsidiary of International Utilities, operates cargo ships all over the world. GLSC developed a comprehensive decision support system for executing both short- and long-term planning.

The *database* includes both external data (such as port or canal characteristics, competition, and prices) and internal data (such as existing plans, availability of resources, and individual ships' characteristics).

The *model base* includes standard accounting/financial analysis models (such as cash flow computations and pro forma income and expenses) organized on a per ship, voyage, division, and entire company basis. These models enable elaborate financial analyses. A simulation model is used to analyze alternative short- and long-term plans and projects. In addition, the system interfaces with commercially available time-sharing programs for analyzing individual voyages (time-charter analysis).

A highly decentralized, 15-month operational planning and control document is prepared within the framework of the long-term, strategic plan. This 15-month document is used as a basis for detailed goal formation for the various ships and the individual voyages. A detailed monitoring and control mechanism is also provided, including a regular variance report and diagnosis analysis. In addition, a detailed performance tracking report is executed (by voyage, ship, division, and for the entire corporation).

Once the assessment of the opportunity of individual projects (such as buying a ship or contracting a voyage) is examined by a charter analysis, an aggregation is performed. The objective is to determine whether a series of individually profitable projects add up to a feasible and desirable long-range plan. The DSS utilizes a simulation model that examines various configurations of projects in an attempt to conduct a "fine-tuning" of the aggregate plan. Specifically, when several projects are executed, the resources (such as financial arrangements) might be insufficient. Therefore, modifications in scheduling and financial arrangements, for example, might be necessary. This fine-tuning provides a trial-and-error approach to feasibility testing and sensitivity analysis. The what-if capabilities of DSS are especially important in this case. The strategic plan of GLSC is very detailed and accurate because of the contractual nature of both the sales and some of the expenses.

---

*Condensed from Alter [1], p. 47.

---

b. The Model Base and its Management

Two parts to model base

The **model base** is divided into two major parts:

1. Prewritten computer programs (or packages). These may include standard mathematical and statistical models as well as special models developed for an individual manager, an organization, or an industry. Notable are strategic, long-range planning models, financial planning models, and tactical and operational models. In addition, the model base includes simulation programs and sensitivity analysis routines. Of special interest are the "what-if" and "goal-seeking" routines.

2. Model building blocks. Some of the prewritten programs and subroutines can be used to *construct* ad hoc applications, such as a random number generator.

Management Science in Practice

AT&T's Site Selection System

Telemarketing is a marketing discipline that uses telecommunications and information systems to execute a marketing program. It is estimated that in 1993 there were over 200,000 telemarketing centers in the U.S. employing about 2.5 million people. This industry is growing fast and is expected to employ 8 million people by the year 2000. This rapid growth, together with corporate reorganizations, poses questions such as: (1) How many telemarketing centers should be opened by a specific company? (2) Where should the centers be located? (3) What geographic region will be served by each center? and (4) How many attendant positions are required at each location?

The answer to such questions is not simple, because there are thousands of potential scenarios to be considered. There is also a large number of impacting variables and considerable uncertainty due to strong competition and turbulent environments: business, technological, and economic. AT&T developed a site selection model to help their customers answer such questions. Here is how this model saved over a million dollars a year for one customer (a national manufacturer and distributor).

As a result of a corporate takeover, the customer went through a consolidation of its 42 existing telemarketing centers and expansion into new areas. Many factors determined the site locations, such as the cost of communication, the cost of labor, and the cost of real estate. Potential markets and existing facilities were also considered. And there were many environmental and legal constraints to take into account. The AT&T model is based on an optimization technique called mixed-integer programming, which minimizes the labor, communication, and real estate costs, while answering the four questions posed earlier. The customer simply provided AT&T with a list of criteria and requirements to guide the data collection for the model, and the first suggested solution was developed in a week. The customer then eliminated some potential lo-

cations and added a few more for consideration. The new list was tested again by the model for one-, three-, and five-year forecasts. A modified solution was presented to the customer within two weeks. The customer asked for an additional "what-if" analysis that included estimates of penalties of continuing to do business in existing locations. (Such penalties helped management to justify maintaining some existing locations.) Four weeks after the beginning of the study, the final recommendation was submitted.

AT&T also helped the customer to locate specific buildings in the selected cities by providing computerized maps using a geographical information system. Furthermore, while the customer was negotiating leases for the buildings, AT&T ran a simulation model to determine the implementation requirements for providing the necessary telephone lines and the number of attendants the customer would need in each location.

Source: T. Spencer, "AT&T Telemarketing Site Selection System Offers Customer Support," *Interfaces*, Jan.–Feb. 1990, pp. 83–96.

Questions:

1. Identify all the management science tools used in this situation.
2. The company admitted that using their own intuitive solution would have resulted in over a million dollars a year in extra costs. Why was AT&T's model superior?
3. The model was developed by AT&T for their customers and provided free of charge, enabling AT&T to generate more business. Why would a client use this service instead of developing its own model and having a choice in selecting a phone company?
4. In the final solution, the customer decided to use some existing centers at a penalty cost of $700,000 a year over the AT&T solution. Why?

What-if Analysis. A **what-if** sensitivity analysis attempts to check the impact of changes in the input variables on the proposed solution (the dependent variable). The what-if analysis is structured as: *"What* will happen to the solution *if* an input variable, an assumption, or a parameter value is changed?"

A what-if analysis may appear in several ways. For example:

- What is the impact on the total inventory cost if there is a 10 percent change in carrying cost?
- What is the impact on the economic order quantity if there is a 5 percent change in ordering cost?

The manager can ask these types of questions in English. Furthermore, he or she can change the percentage or any other data in the question as desired.

Goal Seeking. **Goal seeking** is a property that is similar to the what-if analysis. It has the capability of a "backward" solution of a model; that is, the manager is able to set a goal such as profit, and adjust another variable such as sales. For example, let us say that our initial analysis yielded a profit of $2 million. Management would then like to know what sales volume is necessary to generate a profit of $2.5 million, or what market share is required to achieve a 15 percent growth rate by 1995.

The opportunity to conduct a sensitivity analysis is very important because it can be used to improve confidence in the model and thus increase the rate of application and implementation of quantitative analysis. With many MS models, it is difficult to conduct such an analysis because the prewritten routines usually present only a limited opportunity for what-if and goal-seeking questions.

The Model Base Management System (MBMS)

The model base management system (MBMS) is a software system that generates new routines and reports, model updates and changes, and data manipulation. The MBMS is capable of interrelating models with the appropriate linkages through the database.

c. The User-System Interface

This component includes languages and devices with which information is entered into the computer and/or displayed.

17.12 Expert Systems

Introduction and Basic Concepts

An **expert system (ES)** employs human knowledge captured in a computer to solve problems that ordinarily require human expertise. Well-designed systems imitate the reasoning processes of experts in solving specific problems. They can be used by non-experts to improve their problem-solving abilities. They can also be used by experts as knowledgeable assistants. Expert systems are used to propagate scarce knowledge resources for improved, consistent results. Ultimately, such systems could function better than any single expert in making judgments in a specific, usually narrow, area of expertise (referred to as a *domain*).

The following are the major concepts involved in ES*:

---

*ES and DSS are read as either singular or plural.

Expertise

Expertise is the extensive, task-specific knowledge acquired from training, reading, and experience. The following types of knowledge are examples of what is included in expertise:

Examples of expertise

- Facts about the problem area.
- Theories about the problem area.
- Hard-and-fast rules and procedures regarding the general problem area.
- Rules (heuristics) of what to do in a given problem situation (i.e., rules regarding problem solving).
- Global strategies for solving these types of problems.
- Metaknowledge (knowledge about knowledge).

Experts

Expert knowledge

It is difficult to define what an expert is because we usually talk about a *degree* (or a level) of **expertise.** Nevertheless, it has been said that the nonexperts outnumber experts in any field by a ratio of 100 to 1. Also, the distribution of expertise appears to be of the same shape regardless of the type of knowledge being evaluated.

Experts can take a problem stated in some arbitrary manner and convert it to a form that lends itself to a fast and effective solution. Problem-*solving* ability is necessary, but not sufficient by itself. An expert should be able to *explain* the results, to *learn* new things about the domain, to *restructure knowledge* whenever needed, to *break rules* whenever necessary (i.e., know the exceptions to the rules), and to determine whether his or her expertise is *relevant*. Finally, experts *"degrade gracefully,"* meaning that as they get close to the boundaries of their knowledge, they gradually become less proficient at solving problems.

Graceful degradation

To mimic the human expert, it is necessary to build a computer that will be able to exhibit all these characteristics. To date, work in ES has primarily explored the second and third of these activities.

Transferring Expertise

The objective of an expert system is to transfer expertise from an expert to a computer and then transfer the knowledge and advice from the machine to other humans, usually nonexperts. This process involves three activities: *knowledge acquisition* (from the experts), *knowledge representation* (in the computer), and reasoning (or inferencing). The knowledge is stored in the computer in a component called a *knowledge base*.

Reasoning

A unique feature of an expert system is its ability to reason. Given that all expertise is stored in the knowledge base and that the program can access databases when needed, the computer is programmed so that it can make inferences. The reasoning is performed in a component called the *inference engine,* which includes procedures regarding problem solving.

The inference engine

Rules

Most commercial ES are rule-based; that is, the knowledge is stored mainly in the form of rules or heuristics, as are the problem-solving procedures. A simple rule is structured in an if–then format.

Explanation Capability

Another unique capability of an ES is its ability to explain its advice or recommendations and even to justify why a certain action was not recommended. The explanation and justification is done in a subsystem called the *justifier* or the explanation subsystem. It enables the system to examine its own reasoning and to explain its operation.

Justifier

The Structure of Expert Systems

Expert systems can be viewed as composed of two major parts: the **development environment** and the **consultation environment** (see Figure 17.5). The expert system development environment is used by the ES builder to build the components and *introduce* expert knowledge into the ES knowledge base. The consultation environment is used by a nonexpert to *obtain* the knowledge and advice.

The following components exist in a sophisticated expert system:

ES components

- Knowledge acquisition (an expert and a knowledge engineer).
- Knowledge base.
- Inference engine.
- Blackboard (workplace, database).
- User interface.
- Explanation (justifier).
- Reasoning capability improvement (knowledge refinement).

Note: Most existing expert systems do not contain the knowledge refinement component.

A brief description of these components follows.

Knowledge Acquisition Subsystem

Knowledge acquisition is the accumulation, transfer and transformation of problem-solving expertise from some knowledge source to a computer program for constructing or expanding the knowledge base. Potential sources of knowledge include human ex-

FIGURE 17.5

*The structure of an
expert system*

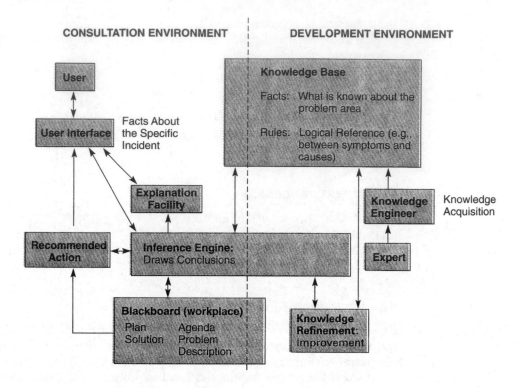

perts, textbooks, databases, special research reports, and the user's own experience
(see McGraw and Harbison-Briggs [23]).

The Knowledge Base
The information in the knowledge base is everything that is necessary for understanding and formulating the problem and then solving it. The knowledge base includes two
basic elements: (1) *facts*—for example, the problem situation and theory of the prob-

Heuristics   lem area; and (2) **heuristics** or rules that direct the use of knowledge to solve problems
in a particular domain.

The Inference Engine
The brain   The "brain" of the ES is the **inference engine,** also known as the *control structure* or
the *rule interpreter* (in rule-based ES). This component is essentially a computer program that provides a methodology for reasoning about information in the knowledge
base and the blackboard, as well as for formulating conclusions.

The Blackboard (Workplace)
The blackboard   The **blackboard** is an area of working *memory* set aside for description of a current
problem, as specified by the input data. It is also used for recording intermediate results. It is basically a database.

User Interface
Expert systems contain a language processor for friendly, problem-oriented communications between the manager-user and the computer

Explanation Subsystem (Justifier)
The ability to trace responsibility for conclusions to their sources is crucial both in the transfer of expertise and in problem solving. The **explanation subsystem** can trace such responsibility and explain the ES behavior by interactively answering questions such as:

- *Why* was a certain question asked by the expert system?
- *How* was a certain conclusion reached?

Knowledge Refinement
A human expert can analyze his or her own performance, learn, and improve it for future use. Similarly, such evaluation is necessary in computerized learning so that the program will be able to analyze the reasons for its success or failure.

How an Expert System Works
Three major activities take part in ES development and use: development, consultation, and improvement.

TABLE 17.14   Benefits and Limitations of Expert Systems

Benefits
- Cost reduction (human expertise is expensive)
- Increased productivity (ES can work faster than humans)
- Improved quality (ES provides consistent advice)
- Reduced downtime (quick diagnosis by ES means less downtime)
- Capturing scarce expertise (experts can leave or die)
- Training (training using ES is much faster)
- Reduced response time (response time of an ES is very fast)
- Operates in a hazardous environment (the system is there but not the human)
- Reliable service (ES do not become tired, bored, or sick; they are always available)
- Operate complex equipment (with an ES assistant it is possible)
- Can use incomplete information (as with a human expert)
- Solves complex problems (like a group of experts)
- Cost effective (pays for itself quickly)

Limitations
- Expertise is hard to extract from experts
- Knowledge is not always readily available
- ES works well only in narrow domains and certain problem categories
- It is difficult to identify the right solution approach
- Maintaining the ES may be costly
- Knowledge validation and verification can be difficult or expensive

---

Development

The development of an expert system involves the construction of a *knowledge base* by acquiring knowledge from experts and/or from documented sources. The knowledge is represented in the knowledge base such that the system can draw conclusions by emulating the reasoning process of human experts.

Consultation

Once the system is developed, it is transferred to the users. When the user wants advice, he or she comes to the ES, which conducts a conversation with the user. The system asks the user to provide *facts* about the specific incident. Based on the user's answers, the ES attempts to reach a conclusion. The effort is done by the inference engine.

Improvement

The improvements include the addition of new rules (to deal with unique cases), modification of rules (to deal with changing conditions or to correct rules), and deletion of rules that are no longer relevant.

The special structure of the ES results in many benefits. However, there are also some limitations to the use of the technology, as identified in Table 17.14.

Expert Systems and Management Science

One of the most interesting sessions at a national meeting of The Institute of Management Sciences in San Francisco was titled: "Will Artificial Intelligence (AI) Provide the Rebirth of Management Science?" The session was chaired by Karl M. Wiig, who presented the following beliefs:

MS rebirth

- MS needs to be reborn.
- Expert systems and natural language processors are the major branches of AI technology that will affect managerial decision making.
- MS needs ES and AI to automate decision support systems.
- MS will be combined with ES, mainly in such complex decision areas as long-range planning, socioeconomic models, and complex operational support (e.g., job shop scheduling).

In summary, Wiig concluded that ES (and other AI technologies) can and will provide the rebirth of MS. The following issues will be discussed here:

- Expert systems as a consultant and assistant to the management scientist.
- Expert systems as a modeling tool and intelligent DSS.
- ES as a management science consultant to the manager.
- ES as a tutor.

ES as a Consultant and Assistant to the Management Scientist

The scientist's consultant and assistant

Expert systems can serve the management scientist in several ways. First, the management scientist can use the ES as a source of information. Second, he or she can use the ES as a tutor, to learn the expertise of top specialists in MS or in related fields. Finally, the ES can be used as a personal assistant to execute routine activities (e.g., provide answers to routine questions and/or conduct standard training).

Expert Systems as a Modeling Tool and an Intelligent Support System

Expert systems can be used as a tool to help in modeling; for example, in constructing simulation models (see O'Keefe and Roach [27]), in conducting a complex PERT analysis by providing estimates, or by conducting a statistical analysis (see Gale [10]).

A DSS–ES

Expert systems can be used to model situations involving symbolic processing as well as analysis. The latest support is called an "intelligent DSS."

There are many ways that an expert system can be integrated with MS models and/or a DSS. For an overview, see Lee [21] and Turban [39]. Some examples of such integration are described below.

Logistics Management System (LMS)

Sullivan and Fordyce [35] report that IBM has constructed several integrated systems. One such system is called the *Logistics Management System* (LMS). LMS combines ES, simulation, traditional DSS, and computer-based information systems. In addition, the system includes computer-aided manufacturing and distributed data processing. The system provides IBM Burlington's manufacturing management a tool to assist in handling a "crisis" (e.g., non-functioning machines) and in planning.

DSS/Decision Simulation (DSIM)

DSIM is the outcome of combining traditional DSS, management science, statistics, database management, query capabilities, and AI. AI, especially the natural language interfaces and expert systems, provides three capabilities to DSIM:

DSIM capabilities

 a. Easing the communication of pertinent information to the computational algorithm or display unit.
 b. Assisting in finding the appropriate model, computational algorithm, or data set.
 c. Finding a solution to a problem where the computational algorithm(s) alone is not sufficient, appropriate, or applicable.

Expert Systems as an MS Consultant to the Manager

Automated consultant

Goul, et al. [15] have developed a DSS–ES system that replicates a manager-consultant-machine team and operates as follows: The computer attempts to diagnose the manager's problem by determining the general nature of the problem (e.g., allocation, inventory, investment—Step 1 in Figure 17.6). Once the general nature of the problem

Figure 17.6

Expert system as a consultant

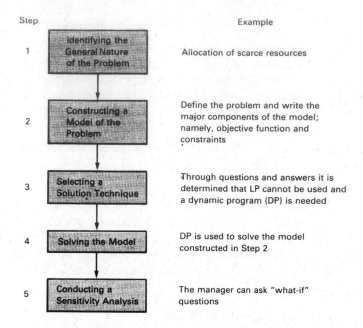

has been determined, the characteristics of the situation are analyzed and a model is jointly constructed (Step 2). For example, if Step 1 diagnosed an allocation problem, Step 2 will attempt to construct the objective function and the constraints. The third step is the suggestion of the specific MS tool (e.g., linear programming or dynamic programming). In Step 4, the computer uses the tool to solve the problem. Finally, a what-if analysis can be conducted (Step 5).

A tutor

It is assumed that the decision maker is not an MS expert; therefore, the ES acts also as a nonhuman tutor with the ability to explain terminology, concepts, and computational procedures. Further, the computer can provide a supportive bibliography, examples of typical applications, and other information as requested by the manager. In addition, the system can explain why a certain model was used and discuss the underlying assumptions.

During the man-machine interaction, the user may disagree with the logic of "why a certain action was undertaken." In such a case, the user can change the decision rules that generated the specific action.

Expert Systems as a Tutor

Computer-aided instruction

Expert systems are intended to transfer the expert's knowledge to the computer and then to the nonexpert. It makes sense that an instructor can be viewed as an expert, but the students are not. This idea is being implemented in the area of Intelligent Computer Aided Instruction (ICAI), which is based on AI. In the past 25 years, there has been considerable progress in the area of CAI (e.g., see Kearsley [19]). Lately, we have seen some evidence of tutoring MS via expert systems.

Management Science in Practice

An Expert System Helps GE Repair Locomotives

GE's top locomotive field service engineer, David I. Smith, had been with the company for more than 40 years. He was the top expert in troubleshooting diesel-electric locomotive engines. Approaching retirement, Mr. Smith was very busy traveling throughout the country to determine what was wrong with locomotives in need of repair and to advise young engineers about what to do. When Smith retired, GE would have to rely on a younger, less-trained generation of engineers, some of whom, being less loyal to the company, could move to another employer at any time.

GE's traditional approach to such a situation was to create teams that paired senior and junior engineers. The pairs worked together for several months or years, and by the time the older engineers finally did retire, the young engineers had absorbed enough of their senior's expertise to carry on troubleshooting or other tasks. This practice proved to be a good short-term solution, but GE still wanted a more effective and dependable way of disseminating expertise among its engineers and preventing valuable knowledge from retiring with the worker. Furthermore, having railroad service shops throughout the country required either extensive travel or moving the locomotives to an expert, because it was not economically feasible to have an expert in each shop.

In 1980, GE decided to build an expert system to model the way a human troubleshooter would work. The system builders spent several months interviewing Mr. Smith and transferring his knowledge to a computer. The computer programming was developed over a three-year period, slowly increasing the information and the number of decision rules stored in the computer. Finally, the system was able to "reason" much the way an experienced locomotive engineer reasons.

The new diagnostic technology enables a novice engineer or a technician to uncover a fault by spending only a few minutes at the computer terminal. The system also teaches the user the logic of its advice. Furthermore, the system can lead its users through the required repair procedures, presenting a detailed computer-aided drawing of parts and subsystems and providing specific "how to" instructions.

The system is based on a flexible, humanlike thought process rather than rigid procedures expressed in flowcharts or decision trees. The system, which was developed on a PDP 11/23 but operates on a microcomputer, is currently installed at every railroad repair shop served by GE, thus eliminating delays and boosting maintence productivity.

Source: P. P. Bonissone and H. E. Johnson, Jr., "Expert System for Diesel Electronic Locomotive Repair," *Human Systems Management* 4 (1985).

Questions:

1. Why doesn't GE provide expert systems for all their retiring experts?
2. Why does the ES only *emulate* the expert instead of attempting an optimal solution?
3. Why doesn't GE just keep Mr. Smith on the payroll, perhaps as a consultant?

The major advantage of an expert system as a tutor is that it can make learning an active, as opposed to a passive, process. It also can be designed to adapt to the requirements of the individual learner (e.g., speed of learning, terminology used).

Conclusions

Expert systems can be viewed as a powerful tool in the arsenal of the management scientist. But they are much more than that. The integration of an intelligent component into MS could provide the catalyst to revitalize the MS field. It seems that there is an evolution of MS toward inclusion of DSS and ES. This evolution, which is discussed by Wynne [21], could greatly expand the scope of MS operations. Using ES, the MS field could deal with complex problems of strategy that are of great interest to top executives. Further, as Wynne concluded, we should view the MS–DSS–ES relationship as sequential steps along the same path, with each step dominating some parts of the previous one. For example, DSS dominate MS by moving less structured situations from the MS world into the framework of DSS. Similarly, expert systems will dominate DSS in applications where human judgment needs to be extended rather than merely regularized.

17.13 Neural Computing and Genetic Algorithms

Automated problem solving has been a target for generations, long before computers were invented. Consider these examples: statistical models such as regression or forecasting, management science models such as inventory level determination and allocation of resources, and financial models such as make-versus-buy decisions and equipment replacement schedules. Unfortunately, such methods deal with what is called shallow knowledge. When problems are complex, they cannot be solved by these standard models. Instead, additional knowledge is needed. Such knowledge can be provided in some cases by expert systems, either by themselves or when integrated with other computer-based information systems. However, ES employ a *reasoning* approach, and therefore their use is limited to narrow domains. For more complex situations we

Machine learning

use a different approach called *machine learning*. Machine learning refers to a set of methods that attempt to teach machines to solve problems, or to support problem solving, by applying historical cases.

This task, however, is not simple. One problem is that there are many models of learning. Sometimes it is difficult to match the learning model with the type of problem (e.g., in job scheduling) that needs to be solved. Two methods of machine learning are briefly described here: *neural computing* and *genetic algorithms*.

An Introduction to Neural Computing

The tools of AI have been mostly restricted to sequential processing and only certain representations of knowledge and logic. A different approach to intelligent systems involves constructing computers with architectures and processing capabilities that mimic certain processing capabilities of the brain. The results are knowledge representations based on massive parallel processing, fast retrieval of large amounts of information, and the ability to recognize patterns based on experience. The technology that attempts to achieve these results is called *neural computing,* or *artificial neural networks* (ANNs).

Biological Neural Networks

Neurons— brain cells

Artificial neural networks are biologically inspired. Specifically, they borrow ideas from the manner in which the human brain works. Estimates of the number of neurons in a human brain cover a wide range—up to 100 billion—and there are more than a hundred different kinds of neurons. Neurons are separated into groups called networks. Each network contains several thousand neurons that are highly interconnected. Thus, the brain can be viewed as a collection of neural networks.

The ability to learn and react to changes in our environment requires intelligence. Thinking and intelligent behavior are controlled by the brain and the central nervous system. Those who suffer brain damage, for example, have difficulties learning and reacting to changing environments.

Artificial Neural Networks

An *artificial* neural network is a *model* that emulates a biological neural network. Today's neural computing uses a very limited set of concepts from biological neural systems. The concepts are used to implement software simulations of massive parallel processes that involve processing elements (also called artificial neurons or neurodes) interconnected in a network architecture. The artificial neuron receives inputs that are analogous to the electrochemical impulses that the biological neurons receive from other neurons. The output of the artificial neuron corresponds to signals sent out from a biological neuron. These artificial signals can be changed in a manner similar to the way the signals occurring in the human brain change. Neurons in an ANN receive information from other neurons or from external sources, perform transformations on the information, and pass on the information to other neurons or to external outputs. The manner in which information is processed by an ANN depends on its structure and on the algorithm used to process the information.

ANN emulates a biological neural network

Components and Structure of ANN

Processing Elements
An ANN is composed of artificial neurons, the processing elements (PEs). Each of the neurons receives input(s), processes the input(s), and delivers a single output. This process is shown in Figure 17.7. The input can be raw data or output of other processing elements. The output can be the final product or it can be an input to another neuron.

FIGURE 17.7

Processing information in an artificial neuron

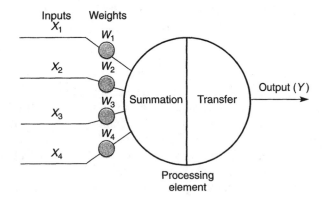

FIGURE 17.8

*Neural network with
one hidden layer*

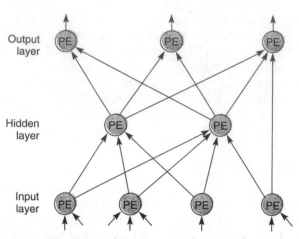

PE   = Processing element

A Network
Each ANN is composed of a collection of neurons that are grouped in layers. A typical structure is shown in Figure 17.8. Note the three layers: input, intermediate (called the hidden layer), and output. Several hidden layers can be placed between the input and output layers.

Structure of the Network
Similar to biological networks, an ANN can be organized in several different ways (topologies); that is, the neurons can be interconnected in different ways. Therefore, ANNs appear in many configurations. In processing information, many of the processing elements perform their computations at the same time. This *parallel processing* resembles the way the brain works, and it differs from the serial processing of conventional computing.

Parallel processing

Processing Information in the Network

Once the structure of a network is determined, information can be processed. Several major concepts related to the process are:

Inputs
Each input corresponds to a single attribute. For example, if the problem is to decide on the approval or disapproval of a loan, an attribute can be an income level, age, or ownership of a house. The numeric *value* of an attribute is the input to the network. Several types of data can be used as inputs. Neural computing can process only numbers. If a problem involves qualitative attributes or pictures, they must be *preprocessed* to numeric equivalencies before they can be treated by the artificial neural network.

Examples of inputs to neural networks are pixel values of characters and other graphics, digitized images and voice patterns, digitized signals from monitoring equipment, and coded data from loan applications. In all cases, an important initial step is the design of a suitable coding system so that the data can be presented to the neural network, commonly as sets of 1s and 0s.

Outputs

The output of the network is the solution to a problem. For example, in the case of a loan application it may be "yes" or "no." The ANN assigns numeric values—for example, +1 for "yes" and 0 for "no." The purpose of the network is to compute the values of the output.

Weights

Inputs are weighted

A key element in an ANN is the weight. Weights express the *relative strength* (or mathematical value) of the initial entering data or the various connections that transfer data from layer to layer. In other words, the weights express the *relative importance* of each input to a processing element. Weights are crucial; it is through repeated adjustments of weights that the network "learns."

Summation Function

The **summation function** finds the weighted average of all the input elements entering each processing element. A summation function multiplies each input value (X_i) by its weight (W_i) and totals them together for a weighted sum, Y. The formula for n inputs in one processing element (Figure 17.9) is:

$$Y = \sum_{i=1}^{n} X_i W_i$$

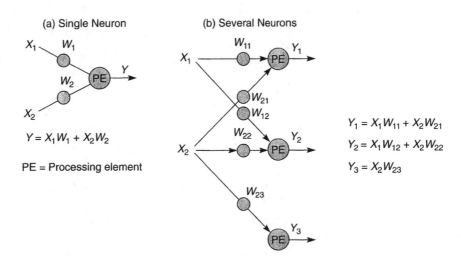

FIGURE 17.9

Summation function for single neuron (a) and several neurons (b)

(a) Single Neuron

$Y = X_1 W_1 + X_2 W_2$

PE = Processing element

(b) Several Neurons

$Y_1 = X_1 W_{11} + X_2 W_{21}$

$Y_2 = X_1 W_{12} + X_2 W_{22}$

$Y_3 = X_2 W_{23}$

For several (j) processing neurons (Figure 17.9b), the formula is:

$$Y_j = \sum_{i=1}^{n} X_i W_{ij}$$

Transformation (Transfer) Function

The summation function computes the internal stimulation, or activation level, of the neuron. Based on this level, the neuron may or may not produce an output. The relationship between the internal activation level and the output is expressed by a **transformation (transfer) function,** and there are several different types of these functions. The selection of a specific function determines the network's operation. One popular nonlinear transfer function is called a sigmoid function (or logical activation function):

Sigmoid function

$$Y_T = \frac{1}{1 + e^{-Y}}$$

where Y_T is the transformed (or normalized) value of Y.

The purpose of this transformation is to modify the output levels to a reasonable value (e.g., between zero and one). This transformation is done *before* the output reaches the next level. Without such transformation, the value of the output may be very large, especially when several layers are involved. Sometimes, instead of a transformation function, a *threshold value* is used. For example, any value of 0.5 or less is changed to zero; any value above 0.5 is changed to one.

A transformation can occur at the output of each processing element, or it can be performed at the final output of the network.

Learning

An ANN learns from its experiences. The usual process of learning involves three tasks:

1. Compute outputs.
2. Compare outputs with desired targets.
3. Adjust the weights and repeat the process.

The learning process starts by setting the weights, either by rules or randomly. The difference between the actual output (Y or Y_T) and the desired output (Z) is called the delta. The objective is to minimize the delta (or better, to reduce it to zero). The reduction of delta is done by changing the weights. The key is to change the weights in the *right* direction; that is, to make changes that further reduce delta. Different ANNs compute the delta in different ways, depending on the learning algorithm that is being used. More than a hundred learning algorithms are available for various situations and configurations.

Pattern recognition

Information processing with an ANN consists of an attempt to recognize patterns of activities (pattern recognition). During the learning stages, the interconnection weights change in response to training data presented to the system.

Benefits of Neural Networks

The value of neural network technology includes its usefulness for pattern recognition, learning, classification, generalization and abstraction, and the interpretation of incomplete and noisy inputs.

Neural networks have the potential to provide some of the human characteristics of problem solving that are difficult to simulate using the logical, analytical techniques of MS or even expert systems. For example, neural networks can analyze large quantities of data to establish patterns and characteristics in situations where rules are not known. Neural networks may be useful for financial applications such as measuring stock fluctuations or determining an appropriate portfolio mix. Likewise, neural networks can provide the human characteristic of making sense of incomplete or noisy data. These features have thus far proven too difficult for the symbolic/logical approach of traditional AI.

Neural networks have several other benefits:

- *Fault tolerance:* Because there are many processing nodes, each with primarily local connections, damage to a few nodes or links does not bring the system to a halt.
- *Generalization:* When a neural network is presented with noisy, incomplete or previously unseen input, it generates a reasonable response.
- *Adaptability:* The network learns in new environments.

Neural networks can be applied in areas where data are multivariate with a high degree of interdependence between attributes, data are noisy or incomplete, or many hypotheses are to be pursued in parallel and high computational rates are required.

Beyond its role as an alternative, neural computing can be combined with MS to produce powerful hybrid systems. Such integrated systems could include an MS model database, an expert system, and other technologies to produce computerized solutions to the most complex problems.

Areas of Application

In general, ANNs do not do well at tasks that are not done well by people. For example, arithmetic and data processing tasks are not suitable for ANNs and are best accomplished by conventional computers. Current applications of ANNs excel in the areas of classification and pattern recognition. Some areas of application are:

Interpretation of data where analytical tools are needed to make generalizations or draw conclusions from large amounts of data from different sources or from sensors:

Financial services—identification of patterns in stock market data and assistance in bond trading strategies (e.g., see Trippi and Turban [36]).

Loan application evaluation—judging worthiness of loan applications based on patterns in previous application information.

Jet and rocket engine diagnostics—training neural networks with sensor data.

Medical diagnosis—training neural networks with cases of previous patients.

Credit card information—fast detection of fraud from purchasing patterns.

DNA sequencing—analysis of patterns in DNA structures and rapid comparison of patterns in new sequences.

Airline forecasting—prediction of seat demand after training with historical data; rapid modification by retraining with new data as they become available.

Evaluation of personnel and job candidates—matching personnel data to job requirements and performance criteria; allows flexibility and tolerance of incomplete information.

Optimization. Several techniques (such as the Boltzmann machine and simulated annealing) can find acceptable solutions to problems involving many parameters.

Resource allocation based on historical, experiential data.

Genetic Algorithms

An algorithm is a set of instructions that is repeated to solve a problem. The word *genetic* refers to a behavior of algorithms that would be similar to biological processes of evolution. A basic goal of **genetic algorithms** is to develop systems that demonstrate

Adapting to change

self-organization and adaptation on the sole basis of exposure to the environment. Attaining such a goal would provide special capabilities in pattern recognition, categorization, and association; that is, the system would be able to learn to adapt to changes.

Grefenstette [16] defines a genetic algorithm as "an iterative procedure maintaining a population of structures that are candidate solutions to specific domain changes. During each temporal increment (called a *generation*), the structures in the current population are rated for their effectiveness as domain solutions, and on the basis of these evaluations, a new population of candidate solutions is formed using specific 'genetic operators' such as reproduction, crossover and mutation." This process is shown in Figure 17.10.

Most genetic algorithms use three primary operators:

1. **Reproduction:** Through reproduction, genetic algorithms produce new generations of improved solutions by selecting parents with higher fitness ratings or by giving such parents greater probability to be contributors.

2. **Crossover:** Many genetic algorithms use strings of binary symbols to represent solutions. Crossover means choosing a random position on the string (e.g., after two digits) and exchanging the segments either to the right or to the left of this point with another string partitioned similarly.

FIGURE 17.10

Flow diagram of the genetic algorithm process

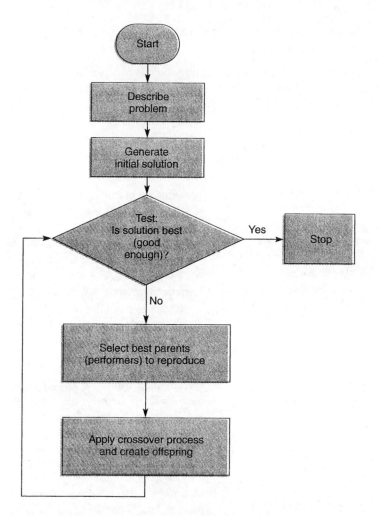

3. **Mutation:** Mutation is an arbitrary change in a situation. Sometimes it is needed to keep the algorithm from getting "stuck." The procedure changes a 1 to 0 or a 0 to 1 instead of duplicating them. However, such a change occurs at a very low probability (say, one in a thousand).

Genetic algorithms can be viewed as a type of machine learning for automatically solving complex problems. Austin [2] has indicated some general areas of applications:

- Dynamic process control.
- Induction for optimization of rules.
- Discovering new connectivity topologies (e.g., neural computing connections).
- Simulating biological models of behavior and evolution.

- Complex design of engineering structures.
- Pattern recognition.

A genetic algorithm is an exciting tool. It receives information that enables it to reject inferior solutions and to accumulate good ones. Also, genetic algorithms are suitable for parallel processing (see Austin [2]).

Glossary

Ad hoc reports   Reports for special purposes, nonroutine.

Artificial intelligence   The behavior of a computer programmed to react to situations in much the same manner as a human being would.

Artificial neural network (ANN)   Experimental computer technology that attempts to build computers that will operate like a human brain. The machines possess simultaneous memory storage and work with ambiguous information.

Combinatorial problem   A problem with a very large number of possible solutions. This number increases much faster than the size of the problem and can reach an astronomical value very quickly.

Consultation environment   The part of the expert system that is used by the nonexpert to obtain expert knowledge and advice.

Database   A collection of interrelated data stored together with minimum redundancy to serve multiple applications.

Database management system (DBMS)   The software to establish, update, or query a database.

Decision support system (DSS)   An advanced, interactive computer system that is easy to use and quick to respond.

Development environment   The part of the expert system that is used by the builder.

Enumeration   A process in which one compares alternative courses of action (e.g., two at a time). Once all alternatives are checked (complete or exhaustive enumeration), the optimal solution must be identified.

Expert systems (ES)   Computer systems that achieve high levels of performance in task areas that, for human beings, require years of special education and training.

Expertise   The set of capabilities that underlies the high performance of human experts, including extensive domain knowledge and heuristic rules.

Explanation subsystem   The component that can explain the system's reasoning and justify its conclusions.

A fair game   A game whose value is zero.

A game   A series of repetitive decisions (plays).

Genetic algorithm   Software program that learns from experience in a similar (simplified) manner to the way in which biological systems learn.

Goal seeking   The capability of asking the computer what values certain variables must have in order to attain desired goals.

Greedy algorithm   A procedure that does the best it can in a single step at a time. This shortsighted approach is in contrast to a procedure that reviews all the steps at once (look-ahead approach).

Heuristic programming   A step-by-step procedure using heuristics that, in a finite number of steps, arrives at a satisfactory solution.

Heuristics   Decision rules that are developed on the basis of logical problem analysis and, possibly, designed experimentation.

Inference engine   The component that controls ES operation by selecting (in a rule-based system) the rules to use, accessing and executing those rules, and determining when an acceptable solution has been found.

Interactive   The capability of both the user and computer to ask questions and to reply to questions while the user is on-line.

Knowledge acquisition   The extraction and formulation of knowledge derived from experts and documented sources.

Knowledge refining   The ability of the program to analyze its own performance, learn, and improve it.

Knowledge representation   A formalism for representing knowledge as facts and rules.

Machine learning   A set of methods used to teach computers to learn from experience (e.g., programs that can learn from historical cases).

Minimax theorem   Each player acts to maximize his or her minimum possible gain (or minimize his or her maximum loss).

Mixed strategy   A case where the decision maker should change the alternative courses of action at random, according to a predetermined proportion.

Model base   A collection of computer programs of various mathematical models.

Neural computing   (see artificial neural networks)

Neuron   Nerve cell in a biological nervous system.

Nonzero-sum game   A game where the winner(s) receives either less or more than what the loser(s) contributed.

On-line   Connected directly to the computer.

Pattern recognition   Technique of matching an external pattern to one stored within a computer's memory; used in inference engines, image processing, neural computing, and speech recognition (e.g., the process of classifying data into predetermined categories).

Value of the game   The average payoff per play.

What-if   The capability of "asking" the computer what the effect will be of changing some of the input data.

Zero-sum game   A game where the winner(s) receives, and the loser(s) contributes, the entire amount at stake.

References and Bibliography

1. Alter, S. L. *Decision Support System, Current Practice and Continuing Challenges*. Reading, Mass.: Addison-Wesley Publishing, 1980.
2. Austin, S. "Genetic Solution to XOR Problems." *AI Expert* (December 1990).
3. Brown, D. E. and C. C. White III (eds.). *Operations Research and Artificial Intelligence: The Integration of Problem Solving Strategies*. Hingham, MA: Kluwer Academic Pub., 1991.
4. Carter, C. M., et al. *Building Organizational Decision Support Systems*, Boston: Academic Press, 1992.
5. Caudill, M., and C. Butler. *Naturally Intelligent Systems*. Cambridge, MA: MIT Press, 1990.
6. Cave, J. *Introduction to Game Theory*. Santa Monica, Calif.: Rand Corporation, 1987.
7. Davis, L. *Handbook of Genetic Algorithms*. New York: Van Nostrand Reinhold, 1989.
8. Drissen, T. *Cooperative Games, Solutions, and Applications*. Norwell, Mass.: Kluwer Academic, 1988.
9. Feigenbaum, E. A., et al. *The Rise of the Expert Company*. New York: Times Books, 1988.
10. Gale, W. A. *Artificial Intelligence and Statistics*. Reading, Mass.: Addison-Wesley Publishing, 1985.
11. Gavett, J. W. "Three Heuristic Rules for Sequencing Jobs to a Single Production Facility." *Management Science* 11, no. 7, (1965).
12. Geoffrion, A. M., and T. J. von Roy. "Caution: Common Sense Planning Methods Can Be Hazardous to Your Corporate Health." *Sloan Management Review*, 1979.
13. Goldberg, D. E. *Genetic Algorithms in Search, Optimization and Machine Learning*. Reading, MA: Addison-Wesley, 1989.
14. Golden, B. L., and A. A. Assad. "A Decision-Theoretic Framework for Comparing Heuristics." *European Journal of Operational Research* 18 (1984).
15. Goul, M., et al. "Designing the Expert Component of a Decision Support System." Paper presented at the ORSA/TIMS meeting, San Francisco, May 1984.
16. Grefenstette, J. "Optimization of Control Parameters for Genetic Algorithms." *IEEE Transactions on Systems, Management and Cybernetics* 16 (no. 1, 1982).
17. Hecht-Nielsen, R. *Neurocomputing*. Reading, MA: Addison-Wesley, 1990.
18. Kahneman, D., et al. *Judgment under Uncertainty—Heuristics and Biases*. Cambridge: Cambridge University Press, 1982.
19. Kearsley, G., et al. *AI and Instruction: Applications and Methods*. Reading, Mass.: Addison-Wesley Publishing, 1987.
20. Keen, P. G. W., and M. S. Scott-Morton. *Decision Support Systems, An Organizational Perspective*. Reading, Mass.: Addison-Wesley Publishing, 1978.
21. Lee, J., ed. "Expert Systems and MS/OR—Special Issue." *Expert Systems with Applications*, Fall 1990.
22. Lundberg, B. G. "On the Evaluation of Heuristic In-

formation Systems," *Decision Support Systems,* Vol. 6, 1990.

23. McGraw, K. L., and B. K. Harbison-Briggs *Knowledge Acquisition: Principle and Guidelines.* Englewood Cliffs, N.J.: Prentice-Hall, 1989.

24. Michael, G. A. "A Review of Heuristic Programming." *Decision Sciences* 3 (1972).

25. Muller-Merbach, H. "Heuristics and Their Design: A Survey." *European Journal of Operational Research,* no. 8 (1981).

26. Nygard, K. E., et al., "Genetic Algorithms," *OR/MS Today,* Aug. 1992.

27. O'Keefe, R. M., and J. W. Roach, "Artificial Intelligent Approaches to Simulation," *Journal of the Operational Research Society* 38, no. 8 (1987).

28. Olson, D. L. and J. F. Courtney, Jr. *Decision Support Models and Expert Systems.* New York: Macmillan, 1992.

29. Rockart, J. F., and D. W. Delong, *Executive Support Systems.* Homewood, Ill.: Dow Jones-Irwin, 1988.

30. Rosenkrantz, D. J., et al. "Approximate Algorithms for the TSP." *Proceedings, 15th IEEE Symposium on Switching and Automata Theory,* 1974.

31. Schrage, L. *Linear, Integer, and Quadratic Programming with LINDO,* 3rd ed. Palo Alto, CA: Scientific Press, 1986.

32. Silver, E. A., et al. "A Tutorial on Heuristic Methods." *European Journal of Operational Research,* no. 5 (1980).

33. Sprague, R. H., Jr., and E. D. Carlson. *Building Effective Decision Support Systems.* Englewood Cliffs, N.J.: Prentice-Hall, 1982.

34. Sprague, R. H., Jr., and H. J. Watson, eds. *Decision Support Systems: Putting Theory into Practice.* 2nd ed. Englewood Cliffs, N.J.: Prentice-Hall, 1989.

35. Sullivan, G., and K. Fordyce. "The Role of Artificial Intelligence in Decision Support Systems." Paper presented at the International Meeting of TIMS, Copenhagen, Denmark, June 1984.

36. Trippi, R., and E. Turban (eds.). *Neural Network Applications in Investment and Financial Services.* Chicago: Probus Publishers, 1993.

37. Turban, E., and R. Trippi. "Integrating Expert Systems and Operations Research: A Conceptual Framework." *Expert Systems with Applications,* Fall 1990.

38. Turban, E. *Decision Support Systems and Expert Systems.* 3rd ed. New York: Macmillan, 1993.

39. Turban, E. *Expert Systems and Applied Artificial Intelligence.* New York: Macmillan, 1992.

40. Wiest, J. D. "Heuristic Programs for Decision Making." *Harvard Business Review,* September–October 1966.

41. Wilson, R. and R. Sharda. "Neural Networks," *OR/MS Today,* August 1992.

42. Wynne, B. "A Domination Sequence—MS/OR, DSS, and the Fifth Generation." *Interfaces,* May–June 1984.

43. Zanakis, S. H., et al. "Heuristic Methods and Applications: A Categorized Survey." *European Journal of Operational Research,* no. 43 (1989).

44. Zanakis, S. H., and J. R. Evans. "Heuristic Optimization: Why, When and How to Use It." *Interfaces,* October 1981.

Illustrative Integrated Cases

The application of the MS tools presented in this book was illustrated in previous chapters through the use of simplified cases and problems, usually on the basis of one tool to one problem. However, real management science problems are frequently more complex, requiring several MS tools. Also, sometimes it is possible to solve one problem by alternately using different tools. Both of these situations are illustrated in the cases of this chapter.

18.1 Execugraphics, Inc.*

The marketing group of EXECUGRAPHICS is considering advertising alternatives for a new product. After a great deal of work, the group has identified a number of options with the following characteristics:

	TV	Newspaper	Radio	Trade Magazine	Popular Magazine	Sales Promotion
Customers reached	1,000,000	300,000	400,000	200,000	450,000	450,000
Cost ($)	500,000	300,000	250,000	150,000	250,000	100,000
Designers needed (worker-hours)	700	200	200	250	300	400
Salespersons needed (worker-hours)	200	100	100	100	100	1,000

The objective of the advertising campaign is to reach as large an audience as possible. The total advertising budget for the project is $1.8 million. The total number of hours available for the designers is 1,500 and the total hours available for salespersons is 1,200. Only one ad per media type can be used. In addition, the following restrictions apply:

a. If the campaign is undertaken, advertising must appear on either radio or in a popular magazine (or both).

b. The company is not willing to advertise in both trade and popular magazines.

Questions

1. What is the managerial problem?
2. Show one possible solution. Specify all assumptions made.
3. How many alternative solutions exist?
4. Assume you added two more advertising options. Answer question 3 now.
5. What factors can make this situation complex? (List and discuss at least two of them.)
6. In which of the given data do you have the most and the least confidence? Why?
7. Are any of the data in the table unnecessary?
8. What type of model is this?
9. Solve the problem.

---

*Contributed by EXECUCOM Systems, Inc., a subsidiary of Comshare Corp., Austin, Texas.

Analysis

The answers to the specific questions are:

1. The problem is to find out how to allocate the advertising budget among six competing alternatives such that the audience is maximized.

2. Let: T = TV, N = newspaper, R = radio, TM = trade magazines, P = popular magazines, and S = sales promotion. One possible solution is: $N + R + TM + S$. Checking this solution via trial and error, we get:

   a. TC = 300,000 + 250,000 + 150,000 + 100,000 = \$800,000; OK (budget constraint).

   b. 200 + 200 + 250 + 400 = 1,050; OK (design hours).

   c. 100 + 100 + 100 + 1,000 = 1,300; no good (sales hours exceed the limit).

   This solution is not feasible (it violates the availability of sales hours). A feasible solution can be achieved if we drop any of the media or we can try another solution: $T + N + R + TM$.

   Checking: 500 + 300 + 250 + 150 = \$1,200; OK (Budget)

   700 + 200 + 200 + 250 = 1,350; OK (Design hours)

   200 + 100 + 100 + 100 = 500; OK (Sales hours)

   Audience = 1,900,000

   Assumptions: All data are correct, no competitive interferences, independence (no influence of one advertisement on another).

3. $2^6 = 64$.

4. $2^8 = 256$ (i.e., this is a combinatorial problem but it does not grow very fast).

5. Instead of a lump sum per media, allow buying inserts of spots at a fixed (or even variable, due to quantity) fee. This will increase the number of alternatives several times. Also, the number of customers reached (audience) per dollar invested may become nonlinear, complicating the problem further. Several additional constraints may be imposed.

6. Least confidence is in customers (audience) reached (uncontrollable variable), salesperson hours needed (can vary). Most: cost, budget, and available resources (controllable).

7. No, they all are relevant.

8. Allocation of resources, subject to constraints. An optimization problem ("reach as large an audience as possible"). Type of model: 0–1 integer, linear programming.

9. Several solution approaches can be attempted in this case. The following two were provided by Execucom Systems Corporation.

a. Trial and Error Using IFPS/Plus®—A DSS Approach

As we saw earlier, one can use a trial-and-error approach to determine the composition of media. Each solution is then computed and checked against the constraints. Those solutions that are feasible are compared and the best of them is selected. To expedite the computation, one can write a computer program from scratch—but this requires a programmer. The DSS approach allows *the user* (the marketing group in this case) to write a program very quickly (with minimum training).

As discussed, this is a 0–1 integer programming problem. If an advertising medium is selected, it will be marked with a value of 1; if not, it is zero. For example: the solution *N, R, TM, S* proposed earlier is expressed as: 0, 1, 1, 1, 0, 1.

The DSS program, written in the programming language IFPS, is shown in Figure 18.1. It automates the manual solution we showed earlier. The solution is shown in Figure 18.2 and it is infeasible. To move from one solution to another, one can use the what-if capability of the software or use the editor. All that is necessary is to change the values of the "Select" row. This approach is very practical if the number of possible alternatives is relatively small. Otherwise, more sophisticated tools are needed.

FIGURE 18.1

The IFPS basic model

```
MODEL ADVER VERSION OF 09/23/93  16.11
10 COLUMNS TV, NEWS, RADIO, TRADEMAG, POPMAG, PROMO,
20         RADIOPOP, TRADEPOP, TOTAL
30 *
40 SELECT = 0,1,1,1,0,1,
42 *
45 * RATES FOR EACH OPTION
46 *
50 AUDIENCE RATE      = 1000000,300000,400000,200000,450000,450000
60 COST RATE          = 500000,300000,250000,150000,250000,100000
70 DESIGN HOURS RATE  = 700,200,200,250,300,400
80 SALES HOURS RATE   = 200,100,100,100,100,1000
90 *
100 * CALCULATION OF ACTUALS
101 *
110 AUDIENCE       = SELECT * AUDIENCE RATE
120 COST           = SELECT * COST RATE
130 DESIGN HOURS   = SELECT * DESIGN HOURS RATE
140 SALES HOURS    = SELECT * SALES HOURS RATE
150 *
160 COLUMN RADIOPOP FOR SELECT = C RADIO + C POPMAG
170 COLUMN TRADEPOP FOR SELECT = C TRADEMAG + C POPMAG
180 COLUMN TOTAL FOR SELECT, AUDIENCE THRU SALES HOURS = SUM (C TV THRU C PROMO)
190 *
END OF MODEL
```

---

* IFPS/Plus is a registered trademark of Execucom Systems Corporation.

b. An Integer Programming Approach
The problem can also be formulated as an integer program:

Maximize $1{,}000{,}000x_1 + 300{,}000x_2 + 400{,}000x_3 + 200{,}000x_4$
$+ 450{,}000x_5 + 450{,}000x_6$

Subject to:
$500{,}000x_1 + 200{,}000x_2 + 250{,}000x_3 + 150{,}000x_4 + 250{,}000x_5$
$+ 100{,}000x_6 \leq 1{,}800{,}000$
$700x_1 + 200x_2 + 200x_3 + 250x_4 + 300x_5 + 400x_6 \leq 1{,}500$
$200x_1 + 100x_2 + 100x_3 + 100x_4 + 100x_5 + 1{,}000x_6 \leq 1{,}200$
$x_3 + x_4 \geq 1$
$x_4 + x_5 \leq 1$

and $x_1 \ldots x_6$ can take only values of either 0 or 1.

Solving a larger integer programming problem of this nature is a fairly lengthy process. IFPS/Optimum, an optimization routine available in IFPS/Plus, includes an efficient procedure for handling such cases. It includes three steps:

1. Formulate the problem as a linear program. This is done by simply adding the right-hand-side value as well as the requirements of the constraints to the DSS program of Figure 18.1. This addition is shown in Figure 18.3.

2. Next, solve the problem (with the integer requirements) by using a heuristic. The results are compared to the regular LP solution (which is not feasible). The difference between the two will be shown as a percentage (4.97, here). In this

---

FIGURE 18.2

The solution employing N, R, TM, and S

	TV	NEWS	RADIO	TRADEMAG	POPMAG	PROMO
SELECT	0	1	1	1	0	1
AUDIENCE RATE	1000000	300000	400000	200000	450000	450000
COST RATE	500000	300000	250000	150000	250000	100000
DESIGN HOURS RATE	700	200	200	250	300	400
SALES HOURS RATE	200	100	100	100	100	1000
AUDIENCE	0	300000	400000	200000	0	450000
COST	0	300000	250000	150000	0	100000
DESIGN HOURS	0	200	200	250	0	400
SALES HOURS	0	100	100	100	0	1000

	RADIOPOP	TRADEPOP	TOTAL
SELECT	1	1	4
AUDIENCE RATE			
COST RATE			
DESIGN HOURS RATE			
SALES HOURS RATE			
AUDIENCE			1350000
COST			800000
DESIGN HOURS			1050
SALES HOURS			1300

(Sales hours exceed 1200; infeasible)

FIGURE 18.3

*The commands for the
LP formulation*

```
DIRECT ADVER VERSION of 09/24/93 10:26
100 OBJECTIVE
110   MAXIMIZE AUDIENCE (TOTAL)
120 *
130 DECISIONS
140    DECISIONS-DISCRETE
150    ALL DECISIONS POSITIVE
160    SELECT (TV THRU PROMO) BETWEEN 0 AND 1
170 *
180 CONSTRAINTS
190    COST (TOTAL) .LE. 1800000
200    DESIGN HOURS (TOTAL) .LE. 1500
210    SALES HOURS (TOTAL) .LE. 1200
220 *CHOICE MUST INCLUDE EITHER RADIO OR POPMAG.
230    SELECT (RADIOPOP) .GE. 1
240 *CHOICE CAN INCLUDE EITHER TRADEMAG OR POPMAG, BUT NOT BOTH.
250    SELECT (TRADEPOP) .LE. 1
260 *
END OF DIRECT
READY FOR EDIT
```

solution, the audience increased from 1,900,000 (the best in the trial-and-error approach) to 2,150,000 (solution not shown).

3. If the user is satisfied with the results (i.e., the difference from the regular LP solution is small), the process is stopped. If not, or if the heuristic fails, the user can try to use a branch and bound optimization approach. Such an approach will find the optimal solution, but in problems with many 0–1 variables it may take a long time, even when large computers are used.

If a decision is made that the 4.97 percent difference between the LP and integer solutions is *not* satisfactory, a request for a branch and bound analysis is entered by adding the following two lines to the program shown in Figure 18.3.

```
270 CONTROL
280 BRANCH Yes
```

The results (not shown) indicate that the solution previously generated by the heuristic was indeed optimal.

Once a solution is derived, the user can use the standard features of IFPS to conduct sensitivity analysis (what-if, goal-seeking). In addition, the user may change the constraints. For example, instead of one insert per medium, one may allow two inserts in each medium. This change will be reflected in line 160. The new line will read:

```
160 SELECT (TV THRU PROMO) BETWEEN 0 AND 2.
```

This means that instead of 0–1 variables, the results can be 0, 1, or 2 (2 means two inserts). The solution of this option is not shown.

Discussion

This case illustrates a flexible approach for solving a complex problem. If you have the appropriate software, you can save a tremendous amount of time and effort solving problems of this nature.

18.2 Illinois Parts for Farming, Inc.

In a business world with frequent technological changes, continuous improvements in equipment, and frequent changes in products, it makes a lot of sense to lease rather than to buy equipment. Illinois Parts for Farming (IPF), a medium-sized company (100,000 square feet of manufacturing floor space) in eastern Illinois, has been using leasing as a prime business strategy. IPF makes parts for various agricultural machines as a subcontractor to Agra Corporation of Iowa. The company works eight hours a day, five days a week, 50 weeks a year. This arrangement cannot be changed due to contracts with the unions.

Last Monday morning, the executive committee discussed the possibility of leasing the necessary equipment for making a special gas monitoring instrument (GMI) that is being installed on several types of agricultural machines in order to reduce gasoline consumption. IPF has just signed a contract with Agra to provide up to 100,000 units of GMI per year for the next three years. Agra will pay $79 per unit. Agra also agreed to advance enough money to pay all necessary advances paid by IPF to its suppliers (working capital).

IPF's policy is to lease the equipment necessary for the production of the monitoring instruments. Three vendors (A, B, and C) offer this specialized equipment. The following table gives some information regarding the vendors and their products (all data are for *one* unit):

	Vendor A	*Vendor B*	*Vendor C*
Model number	A73	B13	C99
Annual fee (first year)	$50,000	$60,000	$70,000
Lease period	3 years	2 years	1 year
Renewal options	None	After 2 years (for 1 year)	After 1 year (for 1 year—twice)
Annual fees— during renewal	None	$40,000 per year	$60,000 first time $50,000 second time
Space required per unit	350 square feet	420 square feet	500 square feet
Annual production— capacity	10,000 units	9,000 units	7,000 units
Labor requirements per unit	2 employees	1.5 employees	1 employee
Delivery time	2 weeks	3 weeks	3 weeks
Annual maintenance— cost per machine	$2,000	$3,000	By vendor

IPF estimates its own costs as follows:

Materials for each monitoring instrument: $28.30.
Average direct labor cost per employee: $10 per hour.
Indirect labor cost: 15 percent of the direct cost.
Fringe benefits: 28 percent of the total labor cost.

There is a fixed cost of $206,800 per year for the entire manufacturing facility. This cost is prorated among the different products in direct proportion to the floor space used for each product. The production of GMI is estimated to occupy 4,500 square feet (regardless of the type of equipment leased). The company uses the following policies in assessing leases:

    a. Analyses are prepared for a three-year period.
    b. The discount rate is 12 percent per year.
    c. All costs are assumed to occur at the beginning of the year.
    d. It is possible to lease equipment from more than one vendor.
    e. The company is willing to allocate up to $600,000 each year for leasing the necessary equipment.
    f. The company is willing to add resources to the project. However, a clear-cut monetary justification must be prepared whenever such an addition is requested.

Questions

1. What is the managerial problem?
2. Show one possible solution (make any necessary assumptions and specify them).
3. Is your solution the best? Why or why not?
4. Are you looking for the best solution in this case?
5. What information provided in the case was not used in your analysis? Why not?
6. What factors that are not discussed here may influence the solution?
7. How would you justify increasing the annual leasing fee budget ceiling?
8. What kind of a model is this?
9. Solve the problem.

Analysis

These are the answers to the questions:

1. The problem is how many units to lease from each vendor to maximize profits subject to the constraints.
2. A feasible solution is to buy one unit of equipment from each of the three vendors. This solution does not violate any of the requirements.

3. We do not know how good the solution is unless some comparison is made.
4. We may search for an optimal solution. It depends on the objective; if it is to *maximize* profit, then the best solution can be searched for. Otherwise, a good enough solution may be sufficient.
5. The unnecessary information is the model number and the delivery times, which *are not* referred to in the case and are not required for the solution.
6. The solution may be affected by issues such as: Is leasing the best approach to use? Is subcontracting available? What are the fees of the above alternatives? Technological developments? Specific delivery dates and the cost and feasibility of overtime may be factors as well.
7. Justification is done by showing the potential benefits of extra leasing. However, you may not *need* more money; that is, the existing fee limit may be sufficient to produce the 100,000 units. Therefore, you need to perform a sensitivity analysis for the purpose of such justification.
8. The model is a deterministic LP allocation model. It is static in nature.
9. The solution to this problem depends on the simplifications that are made (using assumptions). For example, we will disregard the tax impact. Also, we assume that no major technological breakthroughs occur, the discount rate is 12 percent, and all costs occur at year end. The analysis compares leases for three years. Based on these assumptions, it is possible to formulate and solve this problem. We follow the steps below, using a DSS approach.

   a. Develop a model.
   b. Generate all necessary input data.
   c. Run the model and obtain results.
   d. Perform a sensitivity analysis.
   e. How would a risk analysis be conducted?

a and *b.* This is a linear programming problem. However, in order to solve it, one needs to first compute the profit contribution of each unit of equipment purchased from all vendors each year. A spreadsheet analysis can be used (with IFPS or Lotus 1-2-3 or the Lotus templates with this text). The results are shown below (for the first year).

	Vendor A	Vendor B	Vendor C
Annual sales	790,000	711,000	553,000
Material cost	283,000	254,700	198,100
Labor (direct)	40,000	30,000	20,000
Labor (indirect)	6,000	4,500	3,000
Fringe (28 percent)	12,880	9,660	6,440
Lease	50,000	60,000	70,000
Maintenance	21,000	3,000	0
Contribution Margin	396,120	349,140	255,460

Note: The fixed cost is not relevant in this case.

Using the present value function of the spreadsheet, with 12 percent discount, one can find the present value of the contribution margin (for the second and third years) for each piece of equipment for each vendor:

	A	B	C
Year 1	396,120	349,140	255,460
Year 2	353,696	311,747	237,029
Year 3	315,787	294,278	219,597
Total	1,065,603	955,165	712,086

These figures then are used in the objective function of the linear program.

Let x_1 = Number of units purchased from A in year 1
Let x_2 = Number of units purchased from A in year 2
Let x_3 = Number of units purchased from A in year 3
Let x_4 = Number of units purchased from B in year 1

$$\vdots \qquad\qquad \vdots$$

Let x_9 = Number of units purchased from C in year 3

The linear programming model is:

$$\text{Max } z = 396{,}120\, x_1 + 353{,}696\, x_2 + 315{,}787\, x_3 + 349{,}140\, x_4 + 311{,}747\, x_5$$
$$+ 294{,}278\, x_6 + 255{,}460\, x_7 + 237{,}029\, x_8 + 219{,}597\, x_9$$

subject to

2) $50{,}000\, x_1 + 60{,}000\, x_4 + 70{,}000\, x_7 \leq 600{,}000$
3) $50{,}000\, x_2 + 60{,}000\, x_5 + 60{,}000\, x_8 \leq 600{,}000$
4) $50{,}000\, x_3 + 40{,}000\, x_6 + 50{,}000\, x_9 \leq 600{,}000$
5) $350\, x_1 + 420\, x_4 + 500\, x_7 \leq 4{,}500$
6) $350\, x_2 + 420\, x_5 + 500\, x_8 \leq 4{,}500$
7) $350\, x_3 + 420\, x_6 + 500\, x_9 \leq 4{,}500$
8) $x_1 - x_2 = 0$
9) $x_1 - x_3 = 0$
10) $x_4 - x_5 = 0$
11) $x_4 - x_6 = 0$
12) $x_7 - x_8 = 0$
13) $x_7 - x_9 = 0$
14) $10{,}000\, x_1 + 9{,}000\, x_4 + 7{,}000\, x_7 = 100{,}000$
15) $10{,}000\, x_2 + 9{,}000\, x_5 + 7{,}000\, x_8 = 100{,}000$
16) $10{,}000\, x_3 + 9{,}000\, x_6 + 7{,}000\, x_9 = 100{,}000$

and $x_1, x_2, \ldots, x_9$ are integers

c. The optimal solution is:

$x_1 = x_2 = x_3 = 10$; that is, lease 10 units from vendor "A" for 3 years. The total profit is: $10,656,030.

d. Sensitivity analysis
Ranges in which the basis is unchanged:

OBJ Coefficient Ranges

Variable	Current Coefficient	Allowable Increase	Allowable Decrease
X1	396,120.000000	INFINITY	4,308.611000
X2	353,696.000000	INFINITY	4,308.610000
X3	315,787.000000	INFINITY	4,308.611000
X4	349,140.000000	3,877.750000	INFINITY
X5	311,747.000000	3,877.750000	INFINITY
X6	294,278.000000	3,877.750000	INFINITY
X7	255,460.000000	33,836.130000	INFINITY
X8	237,029.000000	33,836.130000	INFINITY
X9	219,597.000000	33,836.130000	INFINITY

Right-Hand-Side Ranges

Row	Current RHS	Allowable Increase	Allowable Decrease
2	600,000.000000	INFINITY	100,000.000000
3	600,000.000000	INFINITY	100,000.000000
4	600,000.000000	INFINITY	100,000.000000
5	4,500.000000	INFINITY	1,000.000000
6	4,500.000000	INFINITY	1,000.000000
7	4,500.000000	INFINITY	1,000.000000
8	.000000	.000000	.000000
9	.000000	.000000	.000000
10	.000000	.000000	.000000
11	.000000	.000000	.000000
12	.000000	.000000	.000000
13	.000000	.000000	.000000
14	100,000.000000	'.000000	.000000
15	100,000.000000	.000000	.000000
16	100,000.000000	.000000	.000000

The analysis is complicated because $x_1 = x_2 = x_3$ and $x_4 = x_5 = x_6$ and $x_7 = x_8 = x_9$.

e. The first issue is to identify the potential risks. One potential risk is that Agra will cancel their order. A probability for such an event needs to be assessed for each year, as well as the potential damages.

Costs may change too. Using a DSS approach one can try different "what-if" scenarios with the various input data (e.g., see what happens if the labor cost increases 5–15 percent).

Note: This problem can actually be run as a deterministic simulation first (on Lotus 1-2-3 or IFPS) because there are less than 100 feasible solutions (because of the integer requirements) that need to be considered. Then, using IFPS/Plus or any other package that allows for Monte Carlo, one can conduct a risk analysis.

18.3 Brunswick Corporation*

This well-known case possesses several elements that can be found today in many MS problems. The following points should be observed when reading the case:

a. Three different MS tools are used to address the situation, yielding essentially the same solution.

b. The data required for the use of these tools were not obvious. In certain cases, approximations and "guesstimates" were applied.

c. Constraints and resources may force management to use solutions that may not look optimal otherwise.

d. Behavioral considerations are important.

e. Managers' jargon and way of thinking differ from that of the management scientist.

f. Most real-life decisions are made under risk.

g. In approaching a problem, it is fairly easy to identify poor alternatives, but it is difficult to choose among good ones. A quantitative trade-off analysis is frequently required in order to evaluate a recommended solution.

The Problem

In mid-April 1967, Gerry O'Keefe, vice president for marketing of Brunswick Products, was trying to decide how many Snurfers he should request the manufacturing plant to produce for the 1967–68 winter season.

The Snurfer was a new item, first introduced to the consumer market by Brunswick during July and August 1966; but because of the difficulty of predicting the actual sales requirements, the factory had produced more Snurfers than were eventually sold. Mr. O'Keefe was anxious to avoid the same situation occurring in the 1967–68 selling season.

---

*This case was made possible by the cooperation of the Brunswick Corporation. It was prepared by Richard G. C. Hanna, Research assistant, under the supervision of Associate Professor Paul A. Vatter. Copyright © 1967 by the President and Fellows of Harvard College. Rev. 1/73. Reproduced by permission.

The Snurfer

The Snurfer was a surfboard-like device designed for use on snow. It consisted of a molded wooden plank 48 inches long by 7 inches wide upon which the rider stood and skied/surfed down snow-covered slopes. The company described the Snurfer in its specification brochure:

> Snurfing is the all-new and exciting winter fun sport. Children, teens, and young adults can now combine the many thrills and skills of surfing and skiing on the new Brunswick Snurfer. It's really maneuverable, fun-filled, and easy to learn. Goes on a minimum of snow—where saucers and sleds won't go. The Snurfer is just the thing for action-packed snow outings! Also fun for sand surfing.

The Snurfer was produced in two types, the regular and the super. Exhibit 1 shows the regular model. The regular model consisted of a molded laminated wood shell, painted yellow with black stripes, that used metal staples as foot grips. The Super Snurfer was the same basic shape as the regular but incoporated a metal keel for greater maneuverability. In place of the painted finish the super had a genuine natural wood surface, included deluxe metal traction button-type Snurf treads (foot grips), was decorated with an official red racing stripe and was sold complete with Snurf-Wax. The wax allowed the bottom surface to be polished for even greater speeds.

The Development of the Snurfer, January 1966–March 1967

The idea for the Snurfer had originated in Muskegon, Michigan, in early 1966. A plumbing supply salesman had converted a water ski for his children to use in the snow.

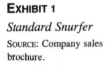

EXHIBIT 1

Standard Snurfer

SOURCE: Company sales brochure.

The idea interested him, and he experimented with different sizes and shapes and coined the name Snurfer.

During February, the product came to the notice of a Brunswick employee who felt that the item might be of interest to the corporation. On April 1, 1966, after some negotiation, Brunswick bought both the rights to the design and the registered name from the Muskegon salesman. The contract involved a lump-sum payment and a royalty that was based on Brunswick's gross sales of the product. The royalty was not to become effective, however, until a set number of Snurfers had been sold.

Following the signing of the contract, the Brunswick engineers commenced a careful study aimed at optimizing the shape of the Snurfer. Many samples were made, and field tests were conducted on the rapidly disappearing snow fields. By the end of April, the design had been finalized and the engineers were ready to turn the project over to the production personnel.

While the engineers had been working on the design, Noel Biery, a product manager, and Mr. O'Keefe, the marketing vice president, had been attempting to determine the size of the potential market and to settle upon channels of distribution. Because the product had been proved to be more readily usable by children than adults, Brunswick had decided to distribute the product through toy channels. After making rather slow progress with the local toy stores and jobbers, the decision was made to show the Snurfer at the New York Toy Show in late March. Only one prototype Snurfer was available at that time, yet the response at the show was encouraging. During the show, manufacturers' representatives covering 38 states were appointed. The product at this time, which consisted of only a single model (which later became the regular), was sold at a factory price of $3.60 with a suggested retail price of $5.95. During the second week in April, engineering prototypes together with specification sheets were sent to all representatives and Brunswick asked them to sound out the market and push for orders during the remainder of April.

By the end of April, Mr. O'Keefe had to make the decision whether or not to continue with the Snurfer and, if so, to decide how many units he would order from the factory. The Brunswick production people were insistent that if the units were to be produced in time for the winter selling season, they must have the firm annual production requirements for the Snurfer by the end of April. With only one firm order for 3,000 units, Mr. O'Keefe decided to go ahead with the project and ordered 60,000 units from the factory for delivery during the 1966–67 winter season. Fifty thousand units were to be the regular Snurfer and 10,000 units the super.

The tooling, capable of producing up to 150,000 units, was ordered at a cost of $50,000, and production scheduled to commence in early September.

By June, no further orders of note had been received and both Mr. Biery and Mr. O'Keefe became concerned as to what action should be taken. Brunswick's own full-time representative in New York was asked to investigate the reasons why the Snurfer was not being sold. With this assignment, and a Snurfer in hand, he visited several sporting good stores (as distinct from toy shops) and found the reaction to be very good. By July, Mr. Biery realized that the original decision to sell through toy jobbers and manufacturers' representatives had probably been a mistake; consequently the original distribution channels were closed down and Brunswick made an all-out effort to generate interest through their own dealer salespersons. However, by this time most sporting good stores had completed their winter buying; and although a good reaction was forthcoming, many stores were unwilling to order in quantity for the current season because of the late date. During August the decision was made to retrench, and the factory managed to cut back production from 60,000 to just over 50,000 units. In addition they agreed to change the product mix between regulars and supers.

The total number of Snurfers sold during the 1966–67 season only reached 35,000 units, with the ratio between supers and regulars being approximately 40:60. By mid-March 1967 there were nearly 17,000 Snurfers in inventory, consisting of 12,000 regulars and 5,000 supers.

Too high inventory

The Production Decision—April 1967

Because of the difficulties and setbacks that they had experienced during 1966, Mr. O'Keefe and Mr. Biery were anxious to ensure that the plans for 1967 were firmly based on what they had already learned.

In reviewing the situation, they had reason to believe that most of the early problems had arisen from the decision to class the Snurfer as a toy. Experience had shown that a considerable degree of skill could be developed by Snurfer enthusiasts and that speeds in excess of 30 miles per hour were attainable. This fact, coupled with the good, although somewhat late, response received from the sporting goods shops, suggested that by careful distribution and promotion, 1967 sales were potentially well in excess of the 1966 predictions. Although both Mr. Biery and Mr. O'Keefe were convinced that the immediate prospects for the Snurfer were excellent, they were uncertain as to the actual market demand for the coming year and as to the share of this market that would be taken by the Super Snurfer. They were certain, however, that in order to maximize the overall profitability of the product they would have to estimate the size of the production order in a careful and systematic manner. The factory order for the 1967–68 production run had to be in the hands of the production people by the end of April.

As a first step in determining this quantity Mr. Biery decided to review the new cost estimates for the two Snurfer models. The production department advised him that the existing tooling, which had been purchased at a cost of $50,000, was in good shape and would be capable of producing a total of 150,000 units per year in any mix of models. To produce anywhere between 150,000 and 200,000 units would require an additional $15,000 of tooling. To increase the production above 200,000 units per year would require yet another $55,000 in addition to the extra $15,000 already mentioned. This latter step-up in tooling would allow the factory to produce up to 500,000 Snurfers a year. In calculating costs, Mr. Biery planned to amortize tooling completely during the year in which it was ordered.

Cost analysis

After consultation with the salespersons, it had been decided to sell the Snurfers in 1967 at an average price from the factory (quantity discounts were involved) of $4.30 for the standard and $5.50 for the super. Brunswick's direct costs for these items were $2.50 and $3.20, respectively. In addition to direct costs, Mr. Biery estimated that 9 percent of the gross margin for both models would be required for selling expenses, royalties, and discounts, and a further 3 percent would be allocated to advertising and promotion. Also, there would be a penalty for overproduction in the form of an inventory-carrying cost that was charged at the rate of 2 percent per month based on Brunswick's direct costs. Mr. Biery estimated that any excess inventory could be considered as being carried for an average of six months.

Having outlined the costs involved, Mr. Biery turned his attention to the question of demand. Although he was uncertain as to what figure he should choose, he believed that it was unlikely that there would be any major intrusion into the 1967 market from competitive manufacturers. In addition, he realized that the Snurfer was something of a novelty item, and as such, might follow the trend of the skate board or Hula-Hoop™ with sales rising extremely rapidly for one or two years and then trailing off just as quickly. Because of the extreme uncertainty arising from these factors, he determined to concentrate solely on the demand for the 1967–68 season.

Range of demand

Point probabilities

To help in ascertaining the demand he called on Mr. O'Keefe, and together they considered the possible sales figures for Brunswick's Snurfers. They finally decided that the median demand was 150,000 units. They were certain that the demand would not be below 50,000 or above 300,000 units, and they believed that there was one chance in four that demand would be at least 190,000 units, and three chances in four that the demand would be at least 125,000 units.

In order to decide on what quantity of units to order from the factory, Mr. O'Keefe felt that they should estimate how this demand would be broken down between the super and standard model Snurfers. This was necessary because the factory had to order raw materials well in advance, and Mr. O'Keefe didn't want to be left carrying standard Snurfers in inventory while the market was demanding supers, or vice versa. Both Mr. Biery and Mr. O'Keefe believed that this breakdown of demand between models was independent of the overall level of demand. They reasoned that the consumer would purchase either the standard or the super entirely on each one's distinctive selling features, and this decision as to which to purchase would in no way be influenced by the total number of Snurfers being sold.

Mr. Biery and Mr. O'Keefe felt that the super Snurfer would most likely account for 40 percent of the total Brunswick demand, although it might rise to as high as 60 percent of the demand. In no circumstances, they believed, would it fall below 30 percent. In addition, they thought there was a 75 percent chance that the share would be 45 percent of demand and a 25 percent chance that the supers would account for 36 percent of the total demand for Snurfers.

Possible Production Quantities

The product mix problem

Mr. Biery now felt that he had all the information necessary to decide how many standard and super Snurfers he should order.

Proposed Solutions

To help in determining what production quantities he should consider, Mr. Biery decided to look at the suggestions he had received from the various people associated with the project. He prepared the following summary of recommendations from letters and memos that he had in his files:

> Field sales personnel argued that the gross margins on both standard and super Snurfers far outweighed the storage costs if some were left unsold. They requested that a total quantity of 225,000 be ordered. This was to be made up of 130,000 regulars and 95,000 supers.
>
> On the other hand, the production manager advised total production of 150,000 units, split 70,000 super and 80,000 regulars. He argued that until the Snurfer caught on, there was no point in incurring an additional investment cost. Realizing the super sales contributed a higher gross margin, he had suggested raising the proportion of supers to around 47 percent rather than at the level of 40 percent which was more in line with previous selling experience.

Mr. Biery himself felt that each of these arguments had its merits but suspected that a product quantity of 200,000 units, split 85,000 supers and 115,000 regulars, might decrease the cost of lost sales without incurring too high an investment cost in tooling. To ensure that he made the correct decision, however, he decided that he would analyze all three alternatives in order to determine which suggestion formed the best course of action.

Analysis

Overview Points of Note

1. Mr. O'Keefe desired to avoid overproducing as he had done in 1966−67; such a situation would have cast him in a bad light.
2. Factory price increased between 1966−67 and 1967−68 from $3.60 to $4.30, or about 20 percent.
3. We do not find out what the New York representative learned about toy store sales. Because response at the toy show was good, it seems there may exist an unexploited opportunity here.
4. Distribution through sporting goods stores allowed the firm to use their own full-time representatives instead of outsiders.
5. Based on the preceding, Biery and O'Keefe estimated that 1967−68 sales could be "well in excess of the 1966 predictions." Normally, this phrase would probably be interpreted to mean "anywhere between 20 to 100 percent over the 60,000 value," or 72,000−120,000 units.
6. Even if the equipment is amortized in the year it is ordered, it would still be useful in following years, or at least have a significant salvage value.
7. If inventory is carried an average of six months, then the assumption is that it *will* be sold in the next snow season.
8. The "no competition" assumption appears reasonable.
9. The boom−bust possibility is a serious assumption. If this is indeed that type of product, all demand projections could be extremely low for 1967−68. Following any final conclusion, this possibility should be checked.

Managers use
qualitative
statements

10. The demand distribution given is not symmetric and hence not normal. Based on the figures given and the interpretation of the case (boom–bust possibility), a Beta distribution appears more reasonable.

11. The same comments as in (10) hold for the production of supers. Here, however, we have a definite market result to go by (40 percent).

Cost Data

	Regular	Super
Inventory cost:		
.02 × 6 × DC		
(if *overproduced*)	$ .300	$ .384
Factory price	4.300	5.500
Direct cost (DC)	2.500	3.200
Gross margin	1.800	2.300
Selling expenditures		
royalty, discount (9%)	.162	.207
Promotion, ads (3%)	.054	.069
Net margin*	$1.584	$2.024

* Net margin is used throughout this case rather than the more common "profit." The difference is that the net margin can be applied toward fixed costs and is a more meaningful term to managers than profit, where some unknown allocation has already been made for fixed costs.

Probability Distributions

Regardless of what method is selected to analyze this case, the probability distributions of demand and fraction of supers (or regulars) in the total must be determined. The data in the case are as follows:

Demand, D:

> Median: 150,000
> Range: Lower limit: 50,000
> Upper limit: 300,000
> Point Probabilities: $P(D \geq 190{,}000) = .25$
> $P(D \geq 125{,}000) = .75$
> 1967 sales: 14,000 supers; 21,000 regulars
> Inventory: 5,000 supers; 12,000 regulars

Fraction of supers, F (independent of demand):

> Mode (most likely): 40 percent
> Range: Upper limit: 60 percent
> Lower limit: 30 percent
> Point Probabilities: $P(F \leq .45) = .75$
> $P(F \leq .36) = .25$

Beta, Gamma, or
lognormal
distribution?

Note: Notice Mr. Biery's poor phrasing of these probabilities in the case. Literally, the case states that the *point* probabilities are $P(F = .45) = .75$ and $P(F = .36) = .25$. If true, these would be the *only* values that F could attain and the "most likely" value of .40 could never occur.

From the above data the demand and fraction distributions can now be approximated. Because of the given form of the data (upper and lower limits) and the fact that the distributions are nonsymmetrical, a Beta distribution appears to be a reasonable form to try. Other possibilities are a Gamma or a lognormal distribution. Each of these could be checked with a statistical goodness-of-fit test to see how close it matched the given data at the upper and lower quartile points and, if acceptable, the best fit could be taken.

Such a procedure is beyond the scope of this textbook, however, and a simpler approximation will be used here instead. Exhibits 2 and 3 display the cumulative probability functions for the demand and fraction, with the given data marked by the dots. (The mode is used here as an estimate of the median for the fraction distribution.) The

Invoking a piecewise
linear approximation

approximation will be to simply join the dots with a straight line of the form $P = a + bR$, where R is either demand, D, or fraction, F, depending on which distribution is being approximated.

For a straight line, the values of a and b are given (for each line segment) by:

$$b = \frac{P_1 - P_2}{R_1 - R_2}; \qquad a = P_1 - bR_2$$

Let us now calculate each of the line segments $j \ldots z$ in Exhibit 4.

EXHIBIT 2

Demand

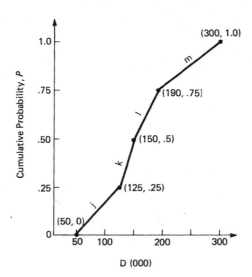

EXHIBIT 3

Fraction of supers

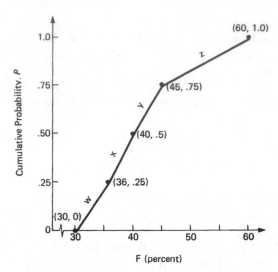

EXHIBIT 4

Line segment coefficients

Segment	$b = \dfrac{P_1 - P_2}{R_1 - R_2}$	$a = P_1 - bR_1$
j	.25/75 = .00333 per 1,000	.25 − .00333 (125) = −.16625
k	.25/25 = .010 per 1,000	.50 − .010 (150) = −1.0
l	.25/40 = .00625 per 1,000	.75 − .00625 (190) = −.4375
m	.25/110 = .00227 per 1,0000	1.0 − .00227 (300) = .319
w	.25/6 = .04167 per 1%	.25 − 4.167 (.36) = −1.25
x	.25/4 = .06250 per 1%	.50 − 6.25 (.40) = −2.0
y	.25/5 = .500 per 1%	.75 − 5.0 (.45) = −1.5
z	.25/15 = .01667 per 1 %	1.0 − 1.667 (.60) = 0

Now that the distributions have been approximated, analyses of the case may be conducted. Three different approaches are illustrated here: incremental analysis, decision tree analysis, and simulation.

Solution by Incremental Analysis

The net margin at median demand

The median expected demand was 150,000 units, with a most likely split of 40 percent supers/60 percent regulars. At this production level, no additional tooling would be necessary. The total net margin to the company (assuming all were sold and the 17,000 inventory maintained) would therefore be:

$$.4(150,000)(2.024) + .6(150,000)(1.584) = \$264,000$$

Sensitivity analysis

Before proceeding to the optimal production level analysis, we might look at the sensitivity of the margin to product-mix demand.

a. Assuming the products will *not* substitute for each other, a 1 percent demand *decrease* in proportion of supers *reduces* the year's margin calculated above by:

$$\left(\begin{array}{c}\text{Reduction in super net margin}\\(.01)(150,000)(2.024)\end{array}\right)+\left(\begin{array}{c}\text{Overproduction inventory cost}\\(.01)(150,000)(.384)\end{array}\right)=\$3,612$$

and a 1 percent *increase* in supers (or reduction in regulars) would reduce the margin by:

$$\left(\begin{array}{c}\text{Reduction in regular net margin}\\(.01)(150,000)(1.584)\end{array}\right)+\left(\begin{array}{c}\text{Overproduction inventory cost}\\(.01)(150,000)(.300)\end{array}\right)=\$2,826$$

b. If the products *will* substitute for each other, the corresponding reductions are:

$$(.01)(150,000)(2.04)-(.01)(150,000)(1.584)=3,036-2,376=\$660;$$

and, by symmetry, $\$-660$ respectively. This latter figure of $\$-660$ means that if customers buy supers when regulars are out of stock, our "reduction" is really an *increase* in net margin (per 1 percent change in product mix).

The anticipated impact of producing one more unit

Incremental analysis is also known by many other names, such as *critical fractile, newsboy problem,* and *marginal analysis.* The idea is to see if increasing the production by *one unit* (or 1 percent) will improve or hurt the present situation. At the median demand:

Expected increase in margin = (Probability of sale, $1-P$) [Average net margin]
$-P$ [Average "loss" from carrying inventory]
$= (.5)[.4(2.024)+.6(1.584)] - .5[.4(.384)+.6(.300)]$
$= .5[1.76] - .5[.333] = .713$

where P is the cumulative probability in Exhibit 2 of demand *not* reaching the level D; that is, not selling one more unit and then having to carry it in inventory until the following season.

Thus, the expected rewards of having one more Snurfer available for sale are considerably greater than the expected losses (when we are starting at the median demand figures). Note that the calculations assumed a hypothetical Snurfer that exhibited the margin and inventory cost characteristics of the super and regular models in the 40/60 proportion expected. Also note that the loss figures assumed no substitutability between the two models, and thus the loss was in holding the Snurfer in inventory for the next season (when it would be sold).

The critical probability

Clearly, at some point in the demand distribution, the probability of not selling the next unit is so large that the expected return (M) doesn't compensate for the probable loss (L). Calling this critical probability $P*$:

$$(1-P*)M = P*L$$

or:

$$P^* = \frac{M}{M + L}.$$

$$P^* = \frac{1.76}{1.76 + .333} = .84$$

Using the data on line segment m in Exhibit 4, with P given and solving for D, results in:

$$.84 = .319 + .00227D$$

or:

$$D = 229 \text{ (thousand units)}$$

Because there are 17,000 units in inventory already, this then implies a *production level* of $229 - 17$, or 212 (thousand units). But will the anticipated increase in returns at this production level justify the cost of the additional tooling? To reach 200,000 production units from 150,000 requires $15,000 in extra tooling. To go beyond 200,000 units requires another $55,000. It certainly seems doubtful that it would be worth the extra $55,000 to produce 12,000 more units, because the net margin is only about $2, but the $15,000 investment might be worthwhile.

Justifying the extra tooling

This can be checked by calculating how much extra return the $15,000 tooling can generate. *Without* the tooling, demand (sales) up to $150,000 + 17,000 = 167,000$ units could be satisfied. *With* the tooling, an extra 50,000 units could be produced, or a maximum of 217,000 *sold*. Both line segments l and m in Exhibit 2 will have to be used to calculate the expected increase in net margin. This would be the probability of a sale $(1 - P_D)$ times the margin (M_D), less the probability of not making the sale (P_D), times the loss (L_D) for every thousand units (D) from 167 to 217. Average margins and losses based on the 40/60 product mix are again assumed.

Expected increase in margin:

$$= \sum_{D=167}^{190} [(1 - P_D) - P_D l_D] \text{ (segment } l) + \sum_{D=191}^{217} [(1 - P_D)M_D - P_D L_D] \text{ (segment } m)$$

$$= \sum_{167}^{190} [(1 + .4375 - .00625 D)1.76 - (-.4375 + .00625 D).333]$$

$$+ \sum_{191}^{217} [(1 - .319 - .00227 D)1.76 - (.319 + .00227 D).333]$$

$$= \sum_{167}^{190} (2.6757 - .01308 D) + \sum_{191}^{217} (1.0923 - .00475 D)$$

$$= (2.6757)24 - .01308 \sum_{167}^{190} D + (1.0923)(27) - .00475 \sum_{191}^{217} D$$

$$= 64.217 - .01308 \left(\frac{167 + 190}{2}\right) 24 + 29.492 - .00475 \left(\frac{191 + 217}{2}\right) 27$$

$$= 11.51 \text{ thousand dollars}$$

Qualitative
considerations and
risk

It is therefore concluded that the extra tooling is *not* worth the cost. However, it is *almost* worth the cost, and faith in the probability distribution of demand is not strong—the Snurfer might become a fad item. Thus, for another $3,500, Brunswick can obtain "insurance," so to speak, so that they aren't left out in the cold if the Snurfer "catches on."

The optimal product
mix

Still to be resolved is the question of the best production mix, because it is clear that the demand will not be *exactly* 40 percent−60 percent. Because each product results in different net margins, an *optimal* mix between the two models will give the highest expected yield. Again, marginal analysis can be used to find this mix. Because Brunswick expects to lose more (at the median mix) by a 1 percent decrease in proportion of supers available for customers ($3,612 versus $2,826 for regulars), the proportion of supers should be *increased* until the expected loss from each model is the same:

$$(1 - P*)3,612 = (P*)2,826$$

Solving:

$$P* = \frac{3,612}{3,612 + 2,826} = .56$$

where $P*$ is the probability of not selling at least one more super model. Using the data on line segment y from Exhibit 4 results in the optimal product mix:

$$.56 = -1.5 + .05F$$

or:

$$F = 41.2 \text{ percent supers}$$

Therefore, Brunswick should have available for sale:

$$.412(167,000) = 68,804 \text{ supers}$$

$$.588(167,000) = 98,196 \text{ regulars}$$

Because Brunswick already has 5,000 supers and 12,000 regulars in stock, they should *produce:*

63,804	supers
86,196	regulars
150,000	total

Note: Previous calculations based on the median 40/60 mix should now be "corrected"; but because the correction is small (.2 percent for the margin), it is not considered significant.

Solution by Decision Tree

Here the approach is to handle the variability of demand by "discretizing" it into branches of a decision tree. If the number of branches is sufficiently large, the discrete approximation will be accurate enough for practical purposes. The method is illustrated with only a few branches.

A bivariate
distribution

The joint probabilities of the bivariate level/mix distribution are formed from the marginal probabilities. We work with only four branches, each with a probability of $(.5)(.5) = .25$:

1. Demand of 125,000; fraction of supers of .36.
2. Demand of 125,000; fraction of supers of .45.
3. Demand of 190,000; fraction of supers of .36.
4. Demand of 190,000; fraction of supers of .45.

This simplification assumes that the given values properly represent the range of values they replace, akin to an "expected value." For example, 190,000 units with a probability of .5 represents from 150,000 to 300,000. A better approximation would have been to use all four segments of Exhibit 2 with each of the four segments of Exhibit 3, resulting in 16 branches.

Four or 16
branches?

Three policies to
consider

The number of alternatives to consider is very large: a production level anywhere between 0 and 500,000 and a mix from 0 percent supers to 100 percent. Let us just consider the three proposed alternatives because they generally fall at natural break points in demand. The decision tree then appears as shown in Exhibit 5, assuming no costs for shortage (such as ill will). The tree assumes the use of the available existing inventory.

Calculating the first
outcome

The outcomes listed in the far-right column of Exhibit 5 are calculated in the following manner. Consider the first outcome, where 95,000 supers and 130,000 regulars are produced; 100,000 supers and 142,000 regulars are available for sale. Then, $125,000 \times .36 = 45,000$ supers and 80,000 regulars are demanded and, because they are available, are sold (in some cases the number demanded is not available, so sales are limited). On each super the margin is $2.024, and on each regular $1.584. There remains unsold $100,000 - 45,000 = 55,000$ supers and 62,000 regulars, each at a storage cost of $.384 and $.300, respectively. The outcome is $178,100.

Same answer as
before

The result of the decision tree is the same as that by incremental analysis—by keeping the current tooling and only producing 150,000 units, the expected outcome is $5,100 better than spending the $15,000 and producing 200,000 units. The incremental analysis showed $3,500 better; but the product mix was quite different also: 41 percent supers instead of the 46.6 percent here ($70,000/150,000 = .466$).

The pros and cons
of the three
proposals

The pros and cons of the three proposals are as follows. The extra tooling cost for the 225,000-unit proposal simply cannot be justified on the basis of the 25,000 extra units produced. On the other hand, if this is a hula-hoop–type product, then O'Keefe would certainly be glad they had the extra capacity. The advantage of the 150,000-unit proposal is the lack of a necessity to put more money into tooling without something definite to show for it. Up to now, they have only sold 35,000 units. In addition, O'Keefe didn't wish to repeat his previous overproduction mistake. However, with the high profit potential of the units and low costs of storage of any overproduction, it would appear a greater mistake on O'Keefe's part to underorder. In that case, he would look even more foolish than just being an optimist—he would have overordered when the demand *wasn't* there, and then underordered when the demand *was* there. The last proposal may be the best compromise. It requires a small additional investment but

EXHIBIT 5

Decision tree

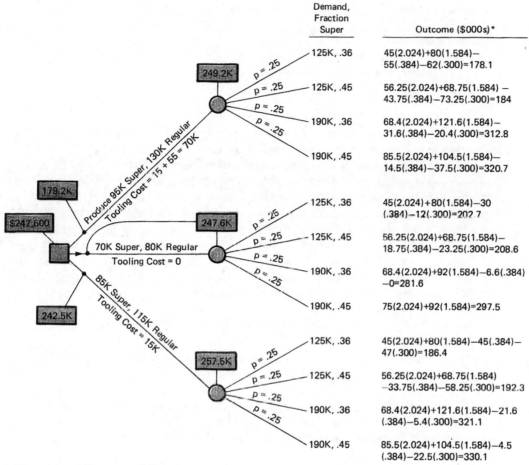

	Demand, Fraction Super	Outcome ($000s)*

Demand, Fraction Super / Outcome ($000s)*

125K, .36 — 45(2.024)+80(1.584)−55(.384)−62(.300)=178.1

125K, .45 — 56.25(2.024)+68.75(1.584)−43.75(.384)−73.25(.300)=184

190K, .36 — 68.4(2.024)+121.6(1.584)−31.6(.384)−20.4(.300)=312.8

190K, .45 — 85.5(2.024)+104.5(1.584)−14.5(.384)−37.5(.300)=320.7

125K, .36 — 45(2.024)+80(1.584)−30(.384)−12(.300)=202.7

125K, .45 — 56.25(2.024)+68.75(1.584)−18.75(.384)−23.25(.300)=208.6

190K, .36 — 68.4(2.024)+92(1.584)−6.6(.384)−0=281.6

190K, .45 — 75(2.024)+92(1.584)=297.5

125K, .36 — 45(2.024)+80(1.584)−45(.384)−47(.300)=186.4

125K, .45 — 56.25(2.024)+68.75(1.584)−33.75(.384)−58.25(.300)=192.3

190K, .36 — 68.4(2.024)+121.6(1.584)−21.6(.384)−5.4(.300)=321.1

190K, .45 — 85.5(2.024)+104.5(1.584)−4.5(.384)−22.5(.300)=330.1

* 12K regulars and 5K supers available in inventory already.

generates a sufficient amount of extra capacity to minimize risk if high demand should occur.

Solution by Simulation

Determining the actual distribution of net margin, stockouts, and so on

The procedure here would be to try several different policies (such as the three alternatives Mr. Biery is considering) with a computerized simulation. Each trial would constitute one possible reaction of the market. Repeating the process many many times would then give distributions for the variables of interest: net margin, shortages, sales mix, remaining inventory to carry over, and the like.

Such a simulation was programmed for a computer and run for 500 trials. The three proposals were then tested (where K is 000's):

Alternative	Production Strategy
I	70K super, 80K regular, no extra tooling
II	85K super, 115K regular, $15K tooling
III	95K super, 130K regular, $70K tooling

It was also assumed that there was no substitution by customers of regulars for supers and vice versa. This assumption is relaxed later.

Stabilization of the measures

The stabilization history of three measures of performance is illustrated in Exhibit 6. In the lower section of the figure, the average net margins of the three alternatives jump around quite a bit for the first 40 trials. The graphs only show every 20th trial, so the true variation can't be seen; but the average net margin for Alternative III goes

Stable by trial 140

from $144,000 in trial 1 (as shown) to $133,000, to $208,000, to $228,000 in trial 4 (trials 2, 3, and 4 are not shown in the Figure). Thus, between trials 2 and 4 the average ranged through $95,000 (that is, $228,000 − $133,000). Note in the figure (c) that between trials 100 and 120 the difference shown is only about $7,000. By trial 140 the variations are almost completely gone for all three alternatives (as indicated by the vertical line in (c) at trial 140).

Average storage cost in (b) has much less variation and is essentially stable for all three alternatives in Exhibit 6 by trial 40. At the top of the exhibit, the average lost margin (by not having specific Snurfer models available when demanded) stabilizes for Alternatives II and III by trial 40, but Alternative I doesn't stabilize until about trial 120.

Plotting the distribution

Considering all three measures of performance, the number of trials needed was probably only 140 or so. Using 500 trials, however, allowed the plotting of more accurate frequency distributions of the three measures of performance for each of the alternatives, as shown in Exhibits 7, 8, and 9.

Net margin: I is best, III is never best

The most important measure, net margin, is graphed first. On a trial-by-trial basis, 64 percent of the time Alternative I had the highest net margin, and 36 percent of the time II was best. Alternative III was never best—the $70,000 tooling investment for Alternative III was always a heavy penalty at the demand levels that were observed.

As can be seen in Exhibit 7, Alternative I has a distribution whose mode is at a significantly higher net margin than II, which is itself higher than III. Furthermore, fully 30 percent of I's margins are at this mode ($280,000—$320,000), whereas only 20 percent of II's and III's margins are at their modes. The result is that the mean and median margins are highest for I, then II, and lastly III.

The assumption of no substitution between Snurfer models was also relaxed. When this was done, Alternative I was even more superior, being favored in 71 percent, rather than 64 percent, of the trials. Again, Alternative III was never best.

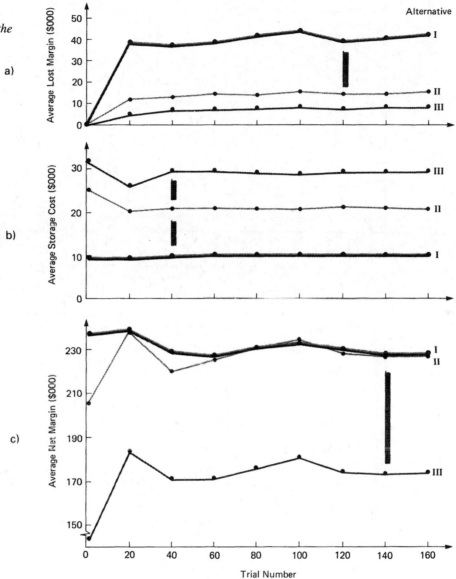

EXHIBIT 6

Stabilization of the simulation

a)

b)

c)

Storage cost: I is best again

Exhibit 8 illustrates the storage cost distributions of the three alternatives. As shown in the exhibit, Alternative I's highest frequency is near zero storage cost. Alternative II is the "more even" of the three distributions, with a lesser downward trend than I. And III's highest frequency cost is around $30,000. Therefore, in terms of storage cost, the preferred order of alternatives is, again, I, II, and III.

Exhibit 9 illustrates the distributions of margins lost due to insufficient production.

EXHIBIT 7

Distribution of net margins

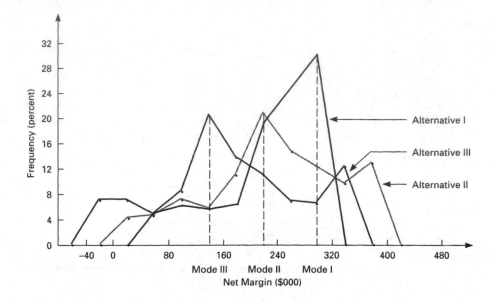

EXHIBIT 8

Storage cost distribution

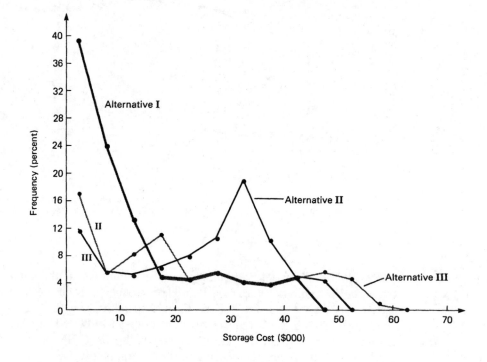

EXHIBIT 9

Distributions of lost margins

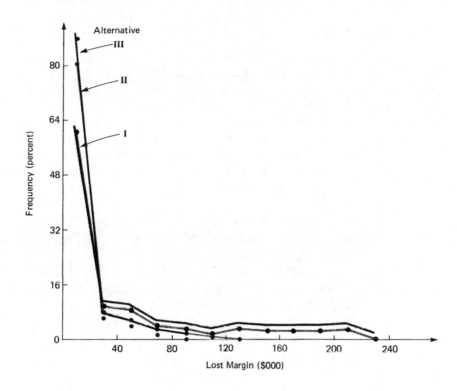

The majority of the time very little is ever lost, and all three alternatives look much the same up to about $35,000. Beyond this, Alternative I, which produces only 150,000 Snurfers, has a fairly constant (3 percent) probability of loss up to $220,000. Alternative II drops off quickly, with no loss beyond $130,000, and III drops off even faster.

Lost Margin: III is best

In summary, the simulation verifies the conclusion reached by the other two procedures: that Alternative I is the best of the three. The incremental analysis indicates Brunswick could increase their expected margin somewhat by reducing the number of supers in Alternative I from 70,000 to 64,000 and substituting the difference with regulars. It is seen from the net margin distributions in Exhibit 7 that Alternative I is superior for the majority of possible levels of demand, except for every high demands. At 175,000 total demand, Alternative II is about equivalent to Alternative I and, at 300,000 demand, II is $70,000 better than I. There is about a 37 percent chance of demand exceeding 175,000 (see Exhibit 2). The question then becomes: Is it worthwhile to spend $15,000 to try to gain this amount (computed earlier as an expected value of $11,510)? The answer: No, unless the money is important for some other reason (such as not looking like a fool again), or unless there is a good chance of this becoming a

Use II for "insurance"

boom product. Then the $15,000 tooling becomes "insurance."

18.4 Frazee Paint, Inc.*

The San Diego area is inundated with colorful vans belonging to Frazee Paint, Inc., a retailer of paint and wallpaper supplies. This developing company uses its vans to tell you, in vivid colors, about their products and services. In addition, the company is advertising in newspapers, TV, and on the radio. The company's sales have been increasing slowly. These increases are believed to be linked to the advertising budget and the population growth. Some relevant information is shown in Table 18.1.

A few days ago, the company was acquired by Worldwide Decorating, Inc. The first task of its new management is to prepare a six-year financial plan. The plan is based on the following assumptions:

a. The population growth rate will be the same as in the past.
b. The advertising budget will be $150,000 for the first year, increasing 10 percent per year thereafter.
c. The cost of goods sold is 75 percent of the sales plus a fixed cost of $500,000. The cost of goods sold in any particular department is $250,000 plus 75 percent of the sales in that department.
d. Sales will increase at the same rate as in the past and will be influenced by both the population and the advertising budget.
e. Taxes are about 35 percent of gross profit.

Part A

After a preliminary analysis that you conducted, the company realized that sales would reach only $64.14 million in six years with a net income of just above $9.9 million. These results were unacceptable to the new owners, who aspired to a sales level of $110.68 million in five years (double the sales realized in 1990).

Questions:

1. What is the managerial problem?
2. Build a model that will allow you to compute the projected sales and net income for the next six years.
3. Attempt to solve the model. (Hint: You will need to execute a statistical analysis in order to generate the input data for the model.) Show how the sales and income projections quoted earlier were derived.
4. Do you have any suggestions about how management can attain their sales goal? (Use only information provided in this case.)

---

*This case is based on a paper written by Ken Cambell and Fred Orton while they were students at United States International University in San Diego.

TABLE 18.1 **Historical Data**

Year	Sales ($ Thousands)	Population in Territory (Thousands)	Advertising Budget ($ Thousands)
1985	$40,898	806	$ 25
1986	47,472	840	85
1987	47,722	880	135
1988	52,043	925	120
1989	50,186	980	150
1990	55,340	1,048	180

Note: Dollars are constant for 1985.

Solution to Part A

1. The problem in 1990 was how to increase sales over the next six years.

2 and 3. In order to build such a model, one can use several methods. Our approach is to use a DSS model. The following are the steps:

    a. Employ a linear regression on the data in Table 18.1 (using population as the dependent variable and years as the independent variable). The result is:

    Population (thousands) = 745.667 + 47.86 × time (years)

    b. Use a multiple linear regression on the data in Table 18.1. Independent variables: population, advertising budget. Dependent variables: sales. The result:

    Sales (in $1000) = 22741 + 47.938 × advertising budget (in $1000) + 22,607 × population (thousands).

    c. Build a five-year income and profit model (use IFPS or Lotus 1-2-3). The model (written in IFPS) and its solution are given in Figure 18.4.

The results indicate that the projected sales in 1996 are $64.14 million and the net income is $9.94 million. These project sales were *not* acceptable to management.

4. The only thing that management can do to improve the situation is to increase advertising (other alternatives could be considered but they are outside the scope of this case). Because population is an uncontrollable variable, it cannot be controlled by management. To find the necessary increase in advertising, we conducted a goal-seeking analysis (using IFPS). The sales goal in 1996 was set as $110.68 million, doubling the sales of 1990. We "adjusted" the advertising as of 1991. In this manner, we get a gradual growth in sales. The results are impressive (see Table 18.2).

FIGURE 18.4

Six-year forecast with current advertising budget (all in thousands of dollars)

	1991	1992	1993	1994	1995	1996
TIME PERIOD	7	8	9	10	11	12
POPULATION	1080.687	1128.547	1176.407	1224.267	1272.127	1319.987
ADVERTISING	150	165	181.5	199.65	219.615	241.5765
SALES	54349.87	56150.01	58021.99	59973.01	62010.97	64144.56
COST OF GOODS SOLD	41262.4	42612.5	44016.49	45479.76	47008.23	48608.42
GROSS PROFIT	12937.47	13372.5	13824	14293.6	14783.13	15294.56
TAXES	4528.114	4680.376	4838.399	5002.761	5174.095	5353.098
NET INCOME	8409.354	8692.126	8985.599	9290.842	9609.033	9941.467

```
TIME = 7,8,9,10,11,12
POPULATION = 745.667 + 47.86*TIME
ADVERTISING = 150, 1.1 * PREVIOUS
SALES = 22.6 * POPULATION + 47.9 * ADVERTISING + 22741.344
COST OF GOODS SOLD = 500 + .75 * SALES
GROSS PROFIT = SALES - COST OF GOODS SOLD - ADVERTISING
TAXES = .35 * GROSS PROFIT
NET INCOME = GROSS PROFIT - TAXES
```

TABLE 18.2 Required Advertising to Double Sales by 1996 (in Thousands of Dollars)

	1991	1992	1993	1994	1995	1996
Time period	7.00	8.00	9.00	10.00	11.00	12.00
Population	1080.69	1128.55	1176.41	1224.27	1272.13	1319.99
Advertising	753.23	828.56	911.41	1002.55	1102.81	1213.09
Sales	83244.71	87934.33	92984.75	98432.05	104315.91	110680.00
Cost of goods sold	62933.54	66450.75	70238.57	74324.04	78736.94	83510.00
Gross profit	19557.95	20655.03	21834.78	23105.46	24476.17	25956.91
Taxes	6845.28	7229.26	7642.17	8086.91	8566.66	9084.92
Net income	12712.66	13425.77	14192.60	15018.55	15909.51	16871.99

Part B

In an attempt to conduct a fine-tuned analysis, management decided to separate both historical sales data and advertising expenditures along their major product lines: paint and wallcover supplies. Table 18.3 shows the available information.

Management was interested in finding the effect of splitting the advertising budget between the two departments. They wanted to find out what would happen over the next five years if the proposed advertising budget of Table 18.2 was split 50–50; if the budget was divided $\frac{1}{3}$ and $\frac{2}{3}$; if the budget was divided $\frac{2}{3}$ and $\frac{1}{3}$; and if 100 percent went

TABLE 18.3 Detailed Historical Data

	1	2	3	4	5	6	7
Year	Pop. (000)	Paint Advert. ($K)	Wallcov. Advert. ($K)	Total Advert. ($K)	Paint Sales ($K)	Wallcov. Sales ($K)	Total Sales ($K)
1985	806	10	15	25	20465	20433	40898
1986	840	50	100	150	21468	26004	47472
1987	880	50	85	135	24321	23401	47722
1988	925	50	70	120	24798	27245	52043
1989	980	65	85	150	25432	24754	50186
1990	1048	80	100	180	28102	27238	55340

to each department. The idea is to find, using trial and error, specifically, the best budget allocation between paint and wallcover supplies. Use the approach of part A to:

- a. Run a six-year projection under the five budget allocation policies. Comment on the results.
- b. Was it logical to split the analysis as described in Part B? Why?
- c. Frazee's customers are either individuals or contractors. If individuals are thought to be highly influenced by advertising, would they buy more paint or more wallpaper products than the average for the company? Would they buy the same? Explain.
- d. Can an optimal solution be found to this allocation problem?

Solution to Part B

- a. In this problem we are allocating the advertising money between wallpaper and paint in five different proportions. Each time we will run the IFPS model to see the results. In order to do this, it is necessary to separate the data in Table 18.3 into paint-related and wallpaper-related. Once this is done we conduct a multiple linear regression and obtain the following results:
  Paint sales = 13.3 ($ for paint ads) + 26.7 (population) − 963.94.
  Similarly, for wallpaper we obtain:
  Wallpaper sales = 49.4 ($ for wallpaper ads) + 9.17 (population) + 12,728.65. This is used in the IFPS model. We run the model five times, each time changing the allocation of paint vs. wallpaper. (The last two lines in the printout below indicate allocating 1/3 to paint and 2/3 to wallpaper.)

  Population = 1081, 1129, 1176, 1224, 1272, 1320
  Paint sales = 13.301*Paint advertising + 26.704*population − 963.938
  Paint cost of goods sold = 250 + .75*paint sales
  Paint gross profit = paint sales − paint cost of goods sold − paint advertising

Wall sales = 49.411*wall advertising + 9.166*population + 12728.648
Wall cost of goods sold = 250 + .75*wall sales
Wall gross profit = wall sales − wall cost of goods sold − wall advertising
Sales = paint sales + wall sales
Advertising = wall advertising + paint advertising
Gross profit = paint gross profit + wall gross profit
Taxes = .35*gross profit
Net income = gross profit − taxes
Advertising = 753,828,911,1002,1102,1213
Paint advertising = .333*advertising
Wall advertising = .667*advertising

	1991	1992	1993	1994	1995	1996
Population	1081	1129	1176	1224	1272	1320
Paint advertising	250.749	275.724	303.363	333.666	366.966	403.929
Wall advertising	502.251	552.276	607.637	668.334	735.034	809.071
Paint sales	31,238.3	32,852.28	34,475	36,159.85	37,884.56	39,658
Paint cost of goods sold	23,678.72	24,889.21	26,106.25	27,369.89	28,663.42	29,993.5
Paint gross profit	7,308.826	7,687.347	8,065.386	8,456.296	8,854.175	9,260.571
Wall sales	47,453.82	50,365.57	53,531.82	56,970.88	60,706.56	64,804.78
Wall cost of goods sold	35,840.36	38,024.18	40,398.86	42,978.16	45,779.92	48,853.58
Wall gross profit	11,111.2	11,789.12	12,525.32	13,324.39	14,191.61	15,142.12
Sales	78,692.12	83,217.85	88,006.81	93,130.73	98,591.13	104,462.8
Advertising	753	828	911	1,002	1,102	1,213
Gross profit	18,420.03	19,476.46	20,590.7	21,780.68	23,045.78	24,402.69
Taxes	6,447.01	6,816.762	7,206.746	7,623.239	8,066.024	8,540.943
Net income	11,973.02	12,659.7	13,383.96	14,157.44	14,979.76	15,861.75

b. Yes. By trial and error it was discovered that the more we shift to wallpaper advertising, the higher the total sales and profits. If we allocate all funds to wallpaper, total sales in 1996 would climb to $119.048 million with $18.23 million net income.

c. The regression analysis shows us that the money placed in paint advertising is less effective than the money invested in wallpaper advertising. Because contractors are less influenced by advertising, it is reasonable to assume that individuals will buy more wallpaper when advertising increases.

d. Yes. By trial and error we can get very close to the optimal solution. The problem can, however, be formulated and solved as an LP problem as well.

Part C

Once the total amount of advertising dollars is determined, as well as its distribution between paint and wallpaper, it is necessary to decide on the appropriate media. That is, determine how much to spend on advertising in TV, direct mail, newspapers, and so on. Historical data are available on the exposure of potential customers to the various media and on the success of such exposure. Because of the data availability, we can use the optimization approach of linear programming.

Frazee plans to allocate some or all of its advertising budget of $82,000 in the San Diego Metropolitan area. It can purchase local radio spots at $120 per spot, local TV spots at $600 per spot, and local newspaper advertising at $220 per insertion.

The company's policy requirements specify that the company must spend at least $40,000 on TV and allow newspaper expenditures up to either $60,000 or 50 percent of the TV expenditures, whichever is more profitable (overall) for the company.

The payoff from each advertising medium is a function of the size of its audience. The general experience of the firm is that the values of insertions and spots in terms of "audience points" (an arbitrary unit) are as follows:

Radio	40 audience points per spot
TV	180 audience points per spot
Newspapers	320 audience points per insertion

Find the optimal allocation of advertising expenditures among the three media.

Formulation

1. The decision variables

$$x_1 = \text{No. of spots allocated to radio}$$

$$x_2 = \text{No. of spots allocated to TV}$$

$$x_3 = \text{No. of insertions allocated to newspapers}$$

2. The objective function

$$\text{maximize } z = 40x_1 + 180x_2 + 320x_3$$

3. The constraints

$$120x_1 + 600x_2 + 220x_3 \leq 82,000$$

$$600x_2 \geq 40,000$$

and either

a.
$$220x_3 \leq 60,000$$

or

b.
$$220x_3 \leq 300x_2$$

where x_1, x_2, x_3 are integers.

Solution

Solve the problem twice using a software package:

With constraint 3a: $x_1 = 0$, $x_2 = 67$, $x_3 = 190$; $z = 72,860$ points (best)

With constraint 3b: $x_1 = 16$, $x_2 = 89$, $x_3 = 121$; $z = 55,380$ points

18.5 Problems

1. For the Brunswick Case:
   a. How would you respond to the arguments of field sales and the production manager, given the quantitative analyses just presented?
   b. Given the price of the Snurfer, how substitutable do you feel the two models are for each other?
   c. What are the important nonquantitative factors in this case?
   d. Which quantitative approach is most conceptually straightforward? Which is simplest? Which is the most difficult? Which is the most accurate? Which do *you* prefer?
   e. What are the key elements in this case that make the decision abnormally difficult?
   f. How does the "boom or bust" aspect of the product complicate Mr. Biery's decision?
   g. What decision is best for Brunswick? For Mr. O'Keefe? What would you decide in this situation?

2. Discuss a university's scheduling of classrooms for a known set of classes, known size of rooms, and size of classes subject to known variation. Specify:
   a. A statement of the problem.
   b. What model you would suggest using.
   c. What method(s) of solution you would recommend.
   d. What data are required.
   e. The likelihood of data availability.
   f. Possible implementation problems.

3. You have just been appointed president of a telephone company with two types of customers: residential and commercial. Your company serves the City of Hope, where 10,000 senior citizens are your customers. The company is a publicly held corporation whose shares are traded on the OTC market. The former president was fired because the shareholders decided that the company was not making enough money to suit them. The customers complain that the monthly fees are too high and that the repair service is too slow. As your first task, you must determine the most appropriate size of the repair crew at the City of Hope.
   a. What is the managerial problem?
   b. What information do you need in order to make a reasonable decision? Divide the information into quantifiable and nonquantifiable elements.
   c. Of the quantifiable information, which items do you think exist in a typical telephone company?

   d. What criteria would you use in order to evaluate any proposed solutions?
   e. How many possible solutions do you think might exist to your problem?
   f. Build a model of the situation.
   g. What type of a model is this?

4. Hess's Department Store is planning the replenishment of its supply of six popular items. The relevant data are given below:

| Item | Monthly Demand | Price per Unit | | Shelf Area for Monthly Demand (Cubic Feet) |
		Purchase (Dollars)	Selling (Dollars)	
A	3,000	2.40	3.95	3,000
B	2,000	6.60	11.95	5,000
C	1,200	3.20	5.95	2,500
D	4,000	2.00	.3.95	2,000
E	2,500	6.20	10.95	1,600
F	1,600	1.60	2.95	4,000

The store has a line of credit of $40,000 for these items and can spare up to 13,000 cubic feet of shelf area.
   a. Find the best ordering policy if the store's objective is to maximize profit. (Neglect inventory holding cost.) Assume immediate delivery.
   b. The line of credit can be increased to $80,000 a month at an extra cost of $600 (per month). Would you recommend taking this credit? Explain. If you take this extra cost, what will be the new best policy?
   c. The $600 can be used to increase shelf area rather than to increase available credit ($1 for each cubic foot per month). Would you suggest allocating the $600 to shelf area or to increasing credit?
   d. Hess's considers a policy of meeting *all demand* as a service to the community. If additional shelf area is available at $3 per cubic foot per month and additional credit is available for an extra $500 per month for each $10,000 of credit, will this policy cut Hess's net profits? Explain how to approach such a problem, but do not attempt to solve.

e. An additional product (G) is being considered. Its cost is $3 and it requires 1.2 square feet for each item. Hess's wants to sell 1,000 units on an experimental basis. What should be the selling price so that the store will make the same profit as in case (*a*)?

Note: It is advisable to use a computer.

5. You are asked to design a pipeline that is 8,000 feet long and has a total drop in elevation of 375 feet. When the slope of the land changes, a new span is defined. This pipeline consists of the following eight spans:

Span	Drop in Elevation (Feet)	Length (Feet)
1	75	1,500
2	100	500
3	50	1,000
4	−50	500
5	150	1,500
6	0	1,000
7	75	500
8	−25	1,500
	375	8,000

In each span, you may use any combination of three different sizes of pipe (for example, for $\frac{1}{4}$ of the length, size 1, and for $\frac{3}{4}$ of the length, size 3). The larger the diameter of the pipe, the lower the resistance to the flow of the liquid, but the more expensive the pipe. The resistance and cost of each size are given below:

Pipe Size	Resistance per Foot	Cost (Dollars per Foot)
1	0.08	1.00
2	0.04	1.20
3	0.02	1.40

The liquid enters the pipeline from a tank that has a constant level of 10 feet of liquid. The pipeline ends at a tank that must have at least a 20-foot liquid level maintained at all times. The resistance to the flow of the liquid at any point along the pipeline can never exceed the change in elevation (per foot) of the liquid from the beginning of the pipeline to this point. For example:

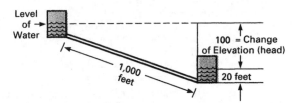

In the illustration, the change of elevation per foot is $100/1,000 = 0.1$; thus the maximum resistance to the flow allowed is 0.1 per foot. Design an optimal pipeline (meet all requirements at a minimum cost).

a. Formulate the problem.

b. Solve it.

Notes:

1. Within each span, if you use more than one size, put them in descending order (the largest one first).

2. The total drop is equal to the fluid pressure acting at that given point.

3. The length of the individual pipes times their resistance act against the fluid pressure (to reduce the fluid pressure).

4. Any difference, at any point, between the total pressure and the total resistance is equal to the flow.

6. Eddie Suarez, facilities manager, has just been charged with installing a new flexible manufacturing system in the machine shop. The job must be completed in twelve working days at minimum cost. To minimize the costs of installation, it is to Eddie's advantage to reduce the need to expedite, use overtime, or employ additional labor during the project. Eddie has broken the installation project into six definable phases: A—Inspect/Test Equipment, B—Prepare Floor Site, C—Prepare Utilities, D—Setup/Install Equipment, E—Install Computer Links, and F—Attach Utilities to Equipment. Phases A, B, and C can all start concurrently, but phases D and E cannot begin until phases A and B have been completed. Similarly, phase F cannot begin until phases C and D have been

completed. Eddie has made an estimate of the time and cost for each phase, as described below:

Phase	Time in Days, T_i Min.	Max.	Cost Function
A	3	7	$190 - 10(T_A - 3)$
B	4	8	$130 - 12(T_B - 4)$
C	3	7	$180 - 15(T_C - 3)$
D	1	6	$195 - 25(T_D - 1)$
E	5	9	$175 - 15(T_E - 5)$
F	2	10	$290 - 30(T_F - 2)$ if T_F is from 2 to 5
			$200 - 20(T_F - 5)$ if T_F is from 5 to 10

a. Draw the network.
b. Solve the problem by logical analysis for the duration of each project phase.
c. What is the "critical path?" Comment.
d. Formulate the problem as a linear program.

References and Bibliography

1. Assad, A. A., E. A. Wasil, and G. L. Lilien. *Excellence in Management Science Practice*. Englewood Cliffs, N.J.: Prentice-Hall, 1992.

2. Berry, W. L., et al. *Management Decision Sciences: Cases and Readings*. Homewood, Ill.: Richard D. Irwin, 1980.

3. Canadian Operational Research Society. *Successful Operational Research in Canada*. Ottawa, Canada: CORS-SCRO, 1988.

4. Dyer, J. S., and R. D. Shapiro. *Management Science/Operations Research: Cases and Readings*. New York: John Wiley & Sons, 1982.

5. Newson, P. *Management Science and the Manager: A Casebook*. Englewood Cliffs, N.J.: Prentice-Hall, 1980.

6. Render, B., and R. M. Stair, Jr. *Cases and Readings in Quantitative Analysis for Management*. Boston: Allyn & Bacon, 1982.

7. Turban, E. and P. Loomba. *Cases and Readings in Management Science*. Plano, Tex.: Business Publications, 1982.

Appendices

A—MATHEMATICS

The purpose of this appendix is to review the mathematical concepts that are used in this text.

A1 Definitions

Some notation is used throughout the text, independent of subject, and the student should be intimately familiar with these symbols:

!   "Factorial": $n! = n(n - 1)(n - 2) \ldots (1)$

Example:

$$5! = 5 \cdot 4 \cdot 3 \cdot 2 \cdot 1 = 120$$

Σ Summation

$\displaystyle\sum_i$ Sum over all values of the index i:

$\displaystyle\sum_i x_i = x_1 + x_2 + \cdots + x_n$,   where $i = 1, 2, \ldots, n$.

Alternatively, the symbol $\displaystyle\sum_{i=1}^{n} x_i$ can be used.

$\Sigma\Sigma$ Double summation

Example:

$$\sum_{i=1}^{3} \sum_{j=1}^{2} x_{ij} = x_{11} + x_{12} + x_{21} + x_{22} + x_{31} + x_{32}$$

Constant: A constant is a quantity that always maintains a fixed value.

Parameter: A parameter is usually constant throughout a problem but may change from problem to problem.

Variable: A variable is a quantity whose value may change throughout a problem.

Continuous variable: The variable may assume *any* value (e.g., 14.7638 . . .) within its acceptable range.

Discrete variable: The variable may only take on certain (countable) values (e.g., $\frac{1}{7}, \frac{2}{7}, \frac{3}{7}$, and so on), frequently *integers* (1, 2, 3, . . .).

Independent variable: In an equation, this variable is known. It is usually shown on the X-axis of graphs.

Dependent variable: In an equation, this variable, whose value is desired, is unknown. It is usually shown on the Y-axis of graphs.

Example:

In the equation for a circle's circumference, $C = \pi D$:

$C = $ A continuous dependent variable

$\pi = $ A constant (3.14159)

$D = $ A continuous independent variable (the diameter)

A2 Functions

A function is a mathematical expression that states a relationship between at least two variables. The expression $y = f(x)$ is read as follows: y is a function of x. This means that given a value for x, y can be determined, although $y = f(x)$ does not tell us how. It states that some relationship exists. This relationship may take the form of a table or an equation. For example, $C = \pi D$ means that C is a function of D. That is: given D, it is possible to determine C. This example demonstrates a *single-valued* function, because for each value of D there exists only one value of C. Similarly, the equation $y = 4 + x^2$ is a single-valued function. However, the equation $y^2 = 4 + x$ is an example of a *multiple-valued* function because y, *the dependent variable,* may take on more than one value for each value of the *independent variable* x (if $x = 0$, then $y = 2$ or -2). In the above examples, y was a function of the single variable x. However, in expressions like $y = f(x, z) = x^2 + 3z$, y is a function of *several variables*. Again, x and z would be the independent variables and y the dependent variable.

The *slope* of a function measures how much the dependent variable changes for a small amount of increase in each of the independent variables. If the function is a straight line, then the slope of the function is the same everywhere. However, for functions that are not straight lines, it is necessary to specify *where* the slope is to be measured and in what direction, because it may be different at different values of the independent variables. If the dependent variable *increases* (*decreases*) with small increases in the independent variables, then we say that the function is *positively* (*negatively*) *sloped.*

Continuous and Discrete Functions

In a manner similar to continuous and discrete variables, there exist continuous and discrete functions also. Examples of continuous functions are:

$$(1) \quad y = x^2 + 2x \quad \text{and} \quad (2) \quad y = 5$$

Some examples of discrete functions are:

$$(1) \quad y = 5x \quad \text{where } x = 0, 1, 2, \ldots$$

$$(2) \quad y = \begin{cases} 10 + 3x \\ 14 + x \end{cases} \quad \text{for} \quad \begin{cases} 0 \le x \le 2 \\ x \ge 2 \end{cases} \text{ and } x \text{ integer.}$$

Equalities

Functional relationships where the value of the dependent variable *equals* certain values of the independent variable are termed equations. For example, $y = 4x$.

Inequalities

If functional relationships cannot be written as equations but it is known that one exceeds the other, then they must be unequal and can be expressed as inequalities. Such relationships can be designated by the symbol $\neq$. For example $y \neq 5x$ means that y is *not* equal to $5x$.

When relationships are not equal, they can take *one* of four possible forms:

Form	Symbol	Example
Smaller than	$<$	$y < 6x + 2$
Smaller than or equal to	$\leq$	$y \leq 4x - 1$
Larger than	$>$	$y > 2x + 9$
Larger than or equal to	$\geq$	$y \geq 5x$

A3 Linear Equations

One of the most important functional relationships is the *linear equation,* due to its simplicity and wide range of applicability. A linear equation of two variables (one dependent, one independent) is a straight line. A linear equation of three variables is a plane, in three dimensions. The general form of a linear equation is:

$$y = a_1x_1 + a_2x_2 + \cdots + a_nx_n + b = \sum_i a_ix_i + b \tag{A1}$$

where the a_i and b are constants and the x_i are different variables. Let V_i designate each variable; that is, $x_1, x_2, \ldots, x_n$. Then a linear equation always satisfies the following rule:

If kV_i is substituted for each variable V_i in the original equation, $y = f(V_i)$, where k is a constant, then the result will be ky.

Mathematically:

$$\text{If } y = f(V_i) \text{ is linear, then } f(kV_i) = ky \tag{A2}$$

Example:

Is the function $y = 5x + 3(\omega - 4z)$ linear?

Solution

Substitute k times each variable in the equation and find:

$$5(kx) + 3[kw - 4(kz)] = 5kx + 3k(\omega - 4z) = ky$$

Thus, according to A2, the equation is linear.

The Slope of a Linear Equation

The slope of a linear equation is constant at all points of the function. In general, the equation of a straight line is given as:

$$y = ax + b \qquad (A3)$$

where a and b are constants. The slope of such a line is always a. The constant b also has a special name: the *intercept*. This is because when x is set to 0 (which is where the line "intercepts" the y-axis), the value of y equals b. The slope and intercept for the equation $y = 2x + 2$ are shown in Figure A1. Also shown in the figure are parts of the linear functions $y = 2$ and $y = 2x$, both of which differ from $y = 2x + 2$. The slope of $y = 2$ is 0, and its intercept is 2. The slope of $y = 2x$ is 2 and its intercept is 0.

Nonlinear Functions

Any function that does not meet the linearity requirement is considered nonlinear.

FIGURE A1

Slope of linear functions

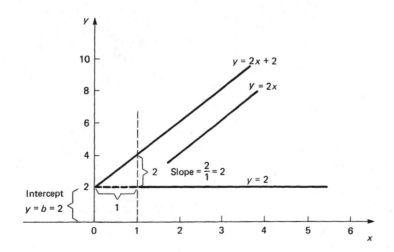

A4 Rules of Manipulation

Inequalities

The rules of manipulation of inequalities are the same as for equations with one exception: when multiplying or dividing the inequality by a negative number, the inequality sign is reversed. For example, given:

$$3 \geq -5$$

Multiplying by -1:

$$-3 \leq 5$$

As another example:

$$-4y + 10x \geq 2x - 8$$

Dividing by -2:

$$2y - 5x \leq -x + 4$$

Exponents

The definition of x^n (called x to the nth power) is x multiplied together n times, where n is called the *exponent*. The rules for manipulating exponents are:

1. *Rule of multiplication:*

$$x^a x^b = x^{a+b} \tag{A4}$$

For example, $x^2 x^3 = x^5$.

2. *Rule of division:*

$$x^a / x^b = x^{a-b} \tag{A5}$$

The second rule holds for cases where $b > a$ as well. This states, for example, that $x^3/x^4 = x^{3-4} = x^{-1}$. Invoking rule 1, it is possible to work backwards through cross-multiplication to obtain:

$$x^4 x^{-1} = x^{4-1} = x^3$$

Implications:

 a.

$$x^n / x^n = x^o = 1 \tag{A6}$$

for any nonzero value of x.

b. It can be seen that $1/x^2 = x^0/x^2 = x^{0-2} = x^{-2}$; that is, in general:

$$x^{-a} = 1/x^a \tag{A7}$$

c.

$$(x^a)^b = x^{a(b)} \tag{A8}$$

Example:

$$(x^2)^3 = (xx)(xx)(xx) = x^{2(3)} = x^6.$$

d.

$$\sqrt[b]{x^a} = x^{a/b} \tag{A9}$$

Example:

$$\sqrt[3]{x^6} = x^{6/3} = x^2$$

A5 Simultaneous Equations

Frequently in MS, sets of simultaneous equations are encountered that must be solved in order to determine the optimal answer to a problem. Sets of *linear* equations are particularly frequent, as in LP. A general set of *simultaneous linear equations* is indicated below, where there are m equations and n unknown variables x_i.

$$
\begin{aligned}
a_{11}x_1 + \ldots + a_{1n}x_n &= b_1 \\
&\ \ \vdots \\
\ldots + a_{ij}x_j + \ldots &= b_i \\
&\ \ \vdots \\
a_{m1}x_1 + \ldots + a_{mn}x_n &= b_m
\end{aligned}
\tag{A10}
$$

This system can be written as:

$$\sum_{j=1}^{n} a_{ij}x_j = b_i \qquad \text{for } i = 1, \ldots, m$$

The a_{ij} terms are the *coefficients* (constants) of the x variable in the ith row and jth column, x_j. Note that there are only n unknown x variables, one for each of j columns. There are also m right-hand constants, b_i. If all the b_i are zero, the linear system is called *homogeneous*. There are a number of techniques for solving a system of linear equations if, indeed, a solution exists. On the other hand, sometimes more than one solution exists.

Solution Methods

A common method is the *Gauss-Jordan* technique. Consider the following set of linear equations:

1. $$3x_1 + x_2 = 6$$

2. $$x_1 - 2x_2 = -1$$

The Gauss-Jordon solution procedure aims to eliminate x_j from all equations except the jth equation and to give x_j a coefficient of unity in that equation. Starting with x_1, Equation 1 is divided by 3:

1′. $$x_1 + \frac{1}{3}x_2 = 2$$

Next, the new Equation 1′ is subtracted from Equation 2 (a rule of algebra states that a multiple of one equation can be added to, or subtracted from, another equation without affecting the functional relationship):

2. $$x_1 - 2x_2 = -1$$

2′. $$-\left(x_1 + \frac{1}{3}x_2 = 2\right)$$

The result is that x_1 has been eliminated:

2′. $$0 - 2\frac{1}{3}x_2 = -3$$

The new set of equations is thus:

1′. $$x_1 + \frac{1}{3}x_2 = 2$$

2′. $$-2\frac{1}{3}x_2 = -3$$

Now consider the variable x_2. In order to have a coefficient of 1 for x_2, Equation 2′ is divided by $-2\frac{1}{3}$. The result is Equation 2″:

2″. $$x_2 = -3/-2\frac{1}{3} = \frac{9}{7}$$

Next, one third of Equation 2″ is subtracted from 1′ to eliminate x_2 in Equation 1′:

1′.
$$x_1 + \frac{1}{3}x_2 = 2$$

$$-\left(\frac{1}{3}x_2 = \frac{3}{7}\right)$$

The result is:

1″.
$$x_1 = 2 - \frac{3}{7} = \frac{11}{7}$$

Thus, the answer is:

$$x_1 = \frac{11}{7} \quad \text{and} \quad x_2 = \frac{9}{7}$$

Note: These solutions can be derived faster but our aim was a step-by-step explanation.

Other solution methods involve the use of matrices or determinants. For discussion, see any text in the bibliography of this appendix.

A6 Matrix Algebra

Matrices

A *matrix* is a rectangular (or square) array of numbers in m rows and n columns. Matrices are typically designated by capital letters. Alternately, small bracketed letters with two subscripts (the first refers to the row and the second to the column) to indicate elements of the matrix can be used. The general format of a matrix is:

$$A = [a_{ij}] = \begin{bmatrix} a_{11} & a_{12} & \cdots & a_{1n} \\ a_{21} & a_{22} & \cdots & a_{2n} \\ \cdot & \cdot & & \cdot \\ \cdot & \cdot & & \cdot \\ \cdot & \cdot & & \cdot \\ a_{m1} & \cdots & \cdots & a_{mn} \end{bmatrix} \tag{A11}$$

A is a matrix with m rows and n columns, or a matrix of $m \times n$ *dimension*. If $m = n$, the matrix is said to be a *square* matrix of *order n*. Each element in the matrix has an address designated by its row and its column. For example, a_{36} means a number in the third row and the sixth column. (For more than nine rows or columns, separate the subscripts with a comma.)

Row and Column Vectors

If a matrix has only one row and two or more, say n, columns, it is called an n-dimensional *row vector*; if there is one column and two or more rows, it is called a *column vector*. Vector elements are also designated by brackets [ ].

Examples:

Three-dimensional row vector:

$$S = [a_1 \quad a_2 \quad a_3] = [3 \quad 1 \quad -2]$$

Three-dimensional column vector:

$$T = \begin{bmatrix} a_1 \\ a_2 \\ a_3 \end{bmatrix} = \begin{bmatrix} 5 \\ 2 \\ 6 \end{bmatrix}$$

A matrix can be represented as a set of row or column vectors.

Example:

Given:

$$V = \begin{bmatrix} a_{11} \\ a_{21} \\ a_{31} \end{bmatrix} \quad W = \begin{bmatrix} a_{12} \\ a_{22} \\ a_{32} \end{bmatrix}$$

and:

$$X = [a_{11} \quad a_{12}] \qquad Y = [a_{21} \quad a_{22}] \qquad Z = [a_{31} \quad a_{32}]$$

then:

$$A = [VW] = \begin{bmatrix} X \\ Y \\ Z \end{bmatrix} = \begin{bmatrix} a_{11} & a_{12} \\ a_{21} & a_{22} \\ a_{31} & a_{32} \end{bmatrix}$$

The Null (Zero) Vector and Unit Vector

Two special vectors of importance are the *null vector,* with all elements zero; that is, [0 0 0 0], and the *unit vector*, with all elements zero except one element, whose value is unity (1); that is, [0 0 1 0].

The Null Matrix and Unit Matrix

Similar to the null vector and unit vector is the *null matrix,* with all elements zero; and the *unit (or identity) matrix,* denoted by I, with all elements zero except for ones along the main (top-left to bottom-right) diagonal:

$$I = \begin{bmatrix} 1 & 0 & 0 \\ 0 & 1 & 0 \\ 0 & 0 & 1 \end{bmatrix} \tag{A12}$$

The Transpose of a Matrix

The *transpose* of a matrix, A^T, is the matrix obtained by interchanging the rows and columns of the original matrix, A.

$$\text{If:} \quad A = \begin{bmatrix} a_{11} & a_{12} & a_{13} \\ a_{21} & a_{22} & a_{23} \\ a_{31} & a_{32} & a_{33} \\ a_{41} & a_{42} & a_{43} \end{bmatrix} \qquad \text{Then:} \quad A^T = \begin{bmatrix} a_{11} & a_{21} & a_{31} & a_{41} \\ a_{12} & a_{22} & a_{32} & a_{42} \\ a_{13} & a_{23} & a_{33} & a_{43} \end{bmatrix} \tag{A13}$$

Matrix Addition and Subtraction

In order to add or subtract matrices, they must be exactly of the same size. Then the corresponding elements in each matrix are added or subtracted. For example, in a 2×2 matrix:

$$\begin{bmatrix} a_{11} & a_{12} \\ a_{21} & a_{22} \end{bmatrix} + \begin{bmatrix} b_{11} & b_{12} \\ b_{21} & b_{22} \end{bmatrix} = \begin{bmatrix} a_{11} + b_{11}, & a_{12} + b_{12} \\ a_{21} + b_{21}, & a_{22} + b_{22} \end{bmatrix} \tag{A14}$$

Example:

$$\begin{bmatrix} 4 & 2 \\ 3 & 1 \end{bmatrix} + \begin{bmatrix} 5 & 3 \\ 0 & 4 \end{bmatrix} = \begin{bmatrix} 9 & 5 \\ 3 & 5 \end{bmatrix}$$

Matrix Multiplication

To multiply a matrix by a constant (called a *scalar*), it is necessary to multiply every element of the matrix by the constant. For example, given:

$$A = \begin{bmatrix} a_{11} & a_{12} \\ a_{21} & a_{22} \end{bmatrix}$$

then:

$$kA = \begin{bmatrix} ka_{11} & ka_{12} \\ ka_{21} & ka_{22} \end{bmatrix} \tag{A15}$$

Multiplying a matrix by a matrix is somewhat more complex. Let us use an example to demonstrate. Suppose that it is desired to multiply matrix A by matrix B where:

$$A = \begin{bmatrix} a_{11} & a_{12} \\ a_{21} & a_{22} \\ a_{31} & a_{32} \end{bmatrix} \qquad B = \begin{bmatrix} b_{11} & b_{12} \\ b_{21} & b_{22} \end{bmatrix}$$

Note that the number of columns of matrix A must equal the number of rows of matrix B. Otherwise they are not "comformable" for multiplication.

The product of $A \times B$ is:

$$C = \begin{bmatrix} a_{11} & a_{12} \\ a_{21} & a_{22} \\ a_{31} & a_{32} \end{bmatrix} \times \begin{bmatrix} b_{11} & b_{12} \\ b_{21} & b_{22} \end{bmatrix} = \begin{bmatrix} a_{11}b_{11} + a_{12}b_{21} & a_{11}b_{12} + a_{12}b_{22} \\ a_{21}b_{11} + a_{22}b_{21} & a_{21}b_{12} + a_{22}b_{22} \\ a_{31}b_{11} + a_{32}b_{21} & a_{31}b_{12} + a_{32}b_{22} \end{bmatrix} \tag{A16}$$

$$= \begin{bmatrix} c_{11} & c_{12} \\ c_{21} & c_{22} \\ c_{31} & c_{32} \end{bmatrix}$$

In General. An element in the resultant matrix C is the sum of the products of the elements of the ith row of A and the jth column of B. A simple way to derive the solution of matrix multiplication is as follows. First, represent the left matrix (A) by *row* vectors:

$$A = \begin{bmatrix} A_1 \\ A_2 \\ A_3 \end{bmatrix}$$

where A_1, A_2, and so on, are each a row vector: ($A_1 = [a_{11}\ a_{12}\ a_{13}\ \ldots]$). Then, represent the right matrix (B) by column vectors:

$$B = [B_1 \quad B_2]$$

where B_1, B_2, and so on, are each column vectors:

$$B_1 = \begin{bmatrix} b_{11} \\ b_{21} \\ . \\ . \\ . \end{bmatrix}$$

Then combine the matrices by forming the appropriate products:

$$A \times B = \begin{bmatrix} A_1 \times B_1 & A_1 \times B_2 \\ A_2 \times B_1 & A_2 \times B_2 \\ A_3 \times B_1 & A_3 \times B_2 \end{bmatrix} \tag{A17}$$

Note that this final matrix has as many rows as matrix A and as many columns as matrix B. The remaining step is to multiply each of the $A_i B_j$ vectors together, element by element, and sum.

Examples:

a.
$$\begin{bmatrix} 2 & 3 \\ 4 & 1 \\ 1 & 5 \end{bmatrix} \times \begin{bmatrix} 6 & 7 \\ 8 & 0 \end{bmatrix}$$

$$= \begin{bmatrix} 2 \times 6 + 3 \times 8 = 36 & 2 \times 7 + 3 \times 0 = 14 \\ 4 \times 6 + 1 \times 8 = 32 & 4 \times 7 + 1 \times 0 = 28 \\ 1 \times 6 + 5 \times 8 = 46 & 1 \times 7 + 5 \times 0 = 7 \end{bmatrix} = \begin{bmatrix} 36 & 14 \\ 32 & 28 \\ 46 & 7 \end{bmatrix}$$

b.
$$\begin{bmatrix} 2 \\ 4 \end{bmatrix} \times [6 \quad 7] = \begin{bmatrix} 2 \times 6 = 12 & 2 \times 7 = 14 \\ 4 \times 6 = 24 & 4 \times 7 = 28 \end{bmatrix} = \begin{bmatrix} 12 & 14 \\ 24 & 28 \end{bmatrix}$$

c.
$$[2 \quad 3] \times \begin{bmatrix} 6 \\ 8 \end{bmatrix} = [2 \times 6 + 3 \times 8 = 36] = 36$$

d.
$$\begin{bmatrix} 2 \\ 4 \end{bmatrix} \times \begin{bmatrix} 6 \\ 8 \end{bmatrix} = \text{not conformable for multiplication}$$

In general, $A \times B$ does not give the same results as $B \times A$. That is, the cumulative law of algebra *does not* hold with matrices. However, the *associative law* holds; that is:

$$(A \times B) \times C = A \times (B \times C) \tag{A18}$$

Also, the *distributive law* holds:

$$A \times (B + C) = (A \times B) + (A \times C) \tag{A19}$$

The Inverse of a Matrix

If square matrices A and D exist such that $AD = DA = I$ (the identity matrix), then D is said to be the inverse of A. *Note:* Only a square matrix can have an inverse. Also, a matrix whose determinant (to be presented soon) equals zero is called a *singular* matrix and does not have an inverse.

$$D = A^{-1} \qquad \text{(A20)}$$

Inverse matrices are important in solving systems of simultaneous linear equations. A simultaneous linear equation set, such as that of Equation A10, may be expressed in matrix form as follows:

1. All the coefficients a_{ij} are described in a matrix A:

$$A = \begin{bmatrix} a_{11} & \cdots & a_{1n} \\ \cdot & & \cdot \\ \cdot & & \cdot \\ \cdot & & \cdot \\ a_{m1} & \cdots & a_{mn} \end{bmatrix}$$

2. All the unknown variables x_j are expressed as a column vector X:

$$X = \begin{bmatrix} x_1 \\ \cdot \\ \cdot \\ \cdot \\ x_n \end{bmatrix}$$

3. The right-hand-side constants, b_i, are expressed as a column vector B:

$$B = \begin{bmatrix} b_1 \\ \cdot \\ \cdot \\ \cdot \\ b_n \end{bmatrix}$$

4. The entire system is expressed as:

$$AX = B \qquad \text{(A21)}$$

With matrix algebra, it is possible to solve for the vector X by multiplying the inverse of the vector A times B:

$$X = A^{-1}B$$

Finding the Inverse

Several methods are available for finding the inverse of a matrix, but one that works for *any* sized matrix utilizes the Gauss-Jordan system:

Example:

Find the inverse of the matrix:

$$A = \begin{bmatrix} a_{11} & a_{12} \\ a_{21} & a_{22} \end{bmatrix}$$

Step 1

Append an identity matrix to the right side of matrix A.

$$\begin{bmatrix} a_{11} & a_{12} & 1 & 0 \\ a_{21} & a_{22} & 0 & 1 \end{bmatrix}$$

Step 2

Manipulate the rows via the Gauss-Jordan method such that the identity matrix appears on the left side:

$$\begin{bmatrix} 1 & 0 & d_{11} & d_{12} \\ 0 & 1 & d_{21} & d_{22} \end{bmatrix}$$

The resulting right-hand matrix:

$$D = \begin{bmatrix} d_{11} & d_{12} \\ d_{21} & d_{22} \end{bmatrix}$$

will then be the inverse of A:

$$D = A^{-1}$$

As an example, let us use the Gauss-Jordan coefficients of Section A5:

$$A = \begin{bmatrix} 3 & 1 \\ 1 & -2 \end{bmatrix}$$

Step 1

$$\begin{bmatrix} 3 & 1 & 1 & 0 \\ 1 & -2 & 0 & 1 \end{bmatrix}$$

Step 2

Divide the first row by 3:

$$\begin{bmatrix} 1 & \frac{1}{3} & \frac{1}{3} & 0 \\ 1 & -2 & 0 & 1 \end{bmatrix}$$

Subtract row 1 from row 2:

$$
\begin{bmatrix}
1 & \frac{1}{3} & \frac{1}{3} & 0 \\
(1 - 1 = 0) & (-2 - \frac{1}{3} = -2\frac{1}{3}) & (0 - \frac{1}{3} = -\frac{1}{3}) & (1 - 0 = 1)
\end{bmatrix}
$$

Divide row 2 by $-2\frac{1}{3}$:

$$
\begin{bmatrix}
1 & \frac{1}{3} & \frac{1}{3} & 0 \\
0 & 1 & \frac{1}{7} & -\frac{3}{7}
\end{bmatrix}
$$

Subtract one-third of row 2 from row 1:

$$
\begin{bmatrix}
(1 - 0 = 1) & (\frac{1}{3} - \frac{1}{3} = 0) & (\frac{1}{3} - \frac{1}{21} = \frac{2}{7}) & (0 + \frac{1}{7} = \frac{1}{7}) \\
0 & 1 & \frac{1}{7} & -\frac{3}{7}
\end{bmatrix}
$$

The inverse is thus:

$$
\begin{bmatrix}
\frac{2}{7} & \frac{1}{7} \\
\frac{1}{7} & -\frac{3}{7}
\end{bmatrix}
$$

Check:

$$
\begin{bmatrix}
3 & 1 \\
1 & -2
\end{bmatrix}
\begin{bmatrix}
\frac{2}{7} & \frac{1}{7} \\
\frac{1}{7} & -\frac{3}{7}
\end{bmatrix}
=
\begin{bmatrix}
1 & 0 \\
0 & 1
\end{bmatrix}
$$

A7 Present Value

Many managerial decisions must reflect the value of time: "time is money." Thus, a dollar today is worth more than a dollar in the future (especially with inflation). This time value is accounted for by an interest rate (or, equivalently, a discount factor.) The following formulas present the basic mathematical notions of annuities, compound interest, and present value.

Formulas for Value of Compound Interest Factors.   Let:

P = Present value
A = Annuity, equal payments, of \$A each payment
n = Number of years
i = Interest rate

1. *To find P, given F, single payment.* The present worth of a single sum F, payable n years from now:

$$
P = \frac{F}{(1 + i)^n}
$$

(A22)

2. *To find P, given A:*

$$P = A\left[\frac{(1 + i)^n - 1}{i(1 + i)^n}\right]$$

(A23)

This is the present value of a series of uniform end-of-year payments, each of value *A*, for *n* years. This information is usually given in the form of tables in many finance, economics, and accounting texts.

Bibliography

1. Adams, B. *Fundamentals of Mathematics for Business, Social, and Life Sciences*. Englewood Cliffs, N.J.: Prentice-Hall, 1979.
2. Doe, M., and M. Warlum. *Business Mathematics: A Positive Approach*. 2nd ed. Homewood, Ill.: Richard D. Irwin, 1989.
3. Kemeny, J. G., A. Schleffer, Jr., J. L. Snell, and G. L. Thompson, *Finite Mathematics with Business Applications*. 2nd ed. Englewood Cliffs, N.J.: Prentice-Hall, 1972.
4. Vazsonyi, A. *Finite Mathematics, Quantitative Analysis for Business*. New York: John Wiley & Sons, 1977.

B—STATISTICS

This appendix includes a condensed presentation of the basic concepts of statistics and probability theory as related to this text. For more detailed explanations, the reader is referred to the bibliography for this appendix. The material here is divided into three main categories: probability, statistics, and distributions.

B1 Probability

The essence of probability is estimating the "odds," "risks," or "the long-run chances" of specific events occurring. An *event* is an *uncertain outcome*. The probability of a given event occurring is designated on a scale of 0 to 1. If the event *cannot* occur, then its probability is zero. If, on the other hand, the event is certain to occur, then its probability is one. Probability values other than 0 or 1 (expressed as a decimal fraction) represent an estimate of the random effect of chance. They measure the degree of belief that an event will occur. For example, a probability of .4 of showers today means that there is a .4 chance (or 40 percent chance) of rain.

Whenever probabilities are stated, a time frame must be specified. There is a certain chance of showers *today,* which may differ from the chances tomorrow, or over a week's duration. The classical definition of probability follows.

The probability of an occurrence is the relative frequency of an event when a situation is repeated many times under identical circumstances.

Formally, it is estimated as:

$$P(\text{event } A) = \frac{\text{Number of occurrences of event } A}{\text{Total number of occurrences}} \qquad (B1)$$

Basic Concepts

Range
Probabilities range between 0 and 1 and can never assume a negative value. Formally: $0 \leq P(A) \leq 1$, where $P(A)$ is the probability of event A.

Frequency and Probability
The terms *frequency* and *probability* express the same idea in slightly different ways. For example, it can be said that the frequency of a "head" in a coin toss is one out of two. The same information is given by saying that the *probability* of a "head" in a coin toss is .5, or 50 percent. The two terms are used interchangeably.

Example:

Suppose that you are in a hurry driving on a crowded street. You have driven down this street 80 times before. Out of these 80 times, you estimate, as best as you can, the relative frequency of occurrence of different speeds of traffic (events) on this street, as shown in Table B1.

TABLE B1   Estimated Probability Distribution of Traffic Speeds

Speed MPH (Event)	Number of Times Observed	Relative Frequency (Percent)	Cumulative Probability (Percent)
20	6	6/80 = 7.5	0 + 7.5 = 7.5
25	14	14/80 = 17.5	7.5 + 17.5 = 25.0
30	25	25/80 = 31.3	25 + 31.3 = 56.3
35	18	18/80 = 22.5	56.3 + 22.5 = 78.8
40	11	11/80 = 13.7	78.8 + 13.7 = 92.5
45	5	5/80 = 6.3	92.5 + 6.3 = 98.8
50	1	1/80 = 1.2	98.8 + 1.2 = 100.0
Total	80	80/80 = 100.0	100.0

Table B1 shows the frequency of the seven events. The table also shows the cumulative probability.

Cumulative Probability

The last column of Table B1 shows the probability of two or more events occurring on a cumulative basis. For example, the probability of traveling at 25 miles per hour or less is: 7.5 percent + 17.5 percent = 25.0. The *cumulative probability for all the events* is 100 percent, by definition. This property helps us to compute cumulative probabilities. For example, let us compute the cumulative probability of traveling faster than 40 MPH. Because the cumulative probability of traveling 40 MPH or less is 92.5 percent, then the probability of going faster than 40 MPH is 100 percent − 92.5 percent = 7.5 percent. The same result is achieved if the probability of 45 MPH is added to that of 50 MPH: 6.3 percent + 1.2 percent = 7.5 percent.

Assessment of Probabilities

Probabilities may be assessed in two ways: subjectively and objectively.

1. Subjective Probability.　If the chances of an event occurring are estimated by an individual, based on his or her beliefs and experience, but without hard data to back this belief, then the probability is termed *subjective*.

2. Objective Probability.　If the probability is based on hard facts, then it is termed *objective*. Three cases are distinguished:

   a. Probability that is *based on logic*. For example, the probability of a "head" in a coin toss is reasoned to be 50 percent.
   b. Probability that is *based on historical data*. For example, if 17 of the last 100 years had more than 3 inches of rain in April, then the probability of having more than 3 inches of rain in April is assessed as $17/100 = 17$ percent.
   c. Probability that is *based on experimentation*. For example, in order to find out the reliability of a new product, one may test 100 units of the new product to find out how many of these will work.

Random Variable

A variable whose value is determined by chance is referred to as a random variable. For example, the traffic speed in Table B1 is a random variable.

Event Relationships

Independent and Dependent Events

Events are classified as *independent* if the occurrence of one has no effect on the probability of others (and vice versa). Events are considered *dependent* if the occurrence of one of them *does* effect the probability of the others.

Mutually Exclusive Events

If the occurrence of an event *precludes* the occurrence of another event (that is, the two *cannot* occur together), then the events are said to be mutually exclusive.

Collectively Exhaustive Events

A set (collection) of events is called *collectively exhaustive* if one of them *must* occur.

Union of Events

An outcome that occurs whenever *any* event in a set of events happens is called the *union* of those events. It is expressed, for the case of two events, as:

$$(A \text{ or } B)$$

This situation occurs when the occurrence of either A, or B, or both together result in the same outcome.

Joint (Intersection of) Events

An outcome that occurs only whenever all events occur (together) is called the *intersection* of events. These are referred to as *joint* events. For the case of two events this situation is written as:

$$(A \text{ and } B)$$

Probability Relationships

Designations
Let:

$$P(A) = \text{Probability of } A \text{ occurring}$$

$$P(B) = \text{Probability of } B \text{ occurring}$$

Conditional Probabilities

The probability of two *mutually exclusive* events A and B occurring at the same time is zero, by definition. However, if A and B are *not mutually exclusive,* then it is possible to talk about the probability of A occurring *given* that B *has occurred* and vice versa. That is, if B happens first, what is the chance of A happening? The probability of A occurring, given that B has occurred, is called the *conditional* probability of A, given B, and is denoted $P(A|B)$. Similarly, $P(B|A)$ denotes the conditional probability of B, given that A has occurred.

Joint Probabilities

The probability of two or more events occurring jointly is labeled the *joint probability* of the events and is designated as $P(A \text{ and } B)$ for the case of two events. *Note:* This can also be written as $P(A, B)$.

Laws of Probability

These laws are given here for two events. They can be extended, as shown in some cases, to any number of events.

Multiplication

The multiplication rule is used to find the probability of the *joint occurrence* of two or more events. Two cases are distinguished:

1. Dependent Events. For the case of two events:

$$P(A \text{ and } B) = P(A) \times P(B|A) = P(B) \times P(A|B) \qquad \text{(B2)}$$

The Relationship Between Conditional and Joint Probabilities. It is possible to compute the conditional probability of two events if the probability of each event and their joint probability are given.

$$P(A|B) = \frac{P(A \text{ and } B)}{P(B)} \qquad \text{(B3)}$$

2. Independent Events. If the events are independent, then the outcome of one has no effect on the outcome of the other, and therefore the conditional probabilities are identical. For two events, this can be expressed as:

$$P(A|B) = P(A) \quad \text{and} \quad P(B|A) = P(B) \qquad \text{(B4)}$$

Inserting these values in Equation B2, we get a simplified multiplication law for independent events:

$$P(A \text{ and } B) = P(A) \times P(B) \qquad \text{(B5)}$$

This law can be extended to any number of independent events; that is:

$$P(A \text{ and } B \text{ and } C \text{ and } \ldots) = P(A) \times P(B) \times P(C) \times \ldots \qquad \text{(B6)}$$

Addition

This law predicts the chances of a *union* of events occurring. Three cases are distinguished:

1. Nonexclusive Joint Events. In such a case, the formula is (for two events):

$$P(A \text{ or } B) = P(A) + P(B) - P(A \text{ and } B) \qquad \text{(B7)}$$

2. Mutually Exclusive Events. The joint occurrence of mutually exclusive events is impossible (by definition). Thus, $P(A \text{ and } B) = 0$.

Therefore, Equation B7 becomes:

$$P(A \text{ or } B) = P(A) + P(B) \tag{B8}$$

3. *Mutually Exclusive and Collectively Exhaustive Events.* If a set of events is both mutually exclusive and collectively exhaustive, then the *union* of these events *must occur* (by definition); that is, the probability of (*A* or *B* or . . .) is certain (equal to one). This property can be expressed as:

$$P(A \text{ or } B \text{ or } \ldots) = P(A) + P(B) + \ldots = 1 \tag{B9}$$

Probabilities of events can also be designated as $p_i =$ probability of event *i*. Then Equation B9 is written as:

$$\sum_{i=1}^{n} p_i = 1$$

B2 Statistics

Definitions

Statistics

The word *statistic* generally is taken to mean an estimate of a population characteristic or a summarized presentation of a mass of data. There are two subtopics of statistics: *descriptive* and *inferential*.

Descriptive statistics is the methodology that reduces a large mass of data into a few summary statistics. The most common are: the *central tendency,* the *dispersion,* and the *frequency distribution.*

Inferential statistics is the methodology for inferring the characteristics of a large mass of data based on the examination of a sample.

Population and Samples

The description of data depends on what type of measurement is used. In general, two approaches exist: (1) measuring the entire population and (2) measuring a sample.

Population. A population is a complete set of individuals, objects, or measurements having some common observable characteristics. The observation of the entire population is normally more expensive and takes more time than the observation of a sample. On the other hand, observing the population generally yields more accurate results.

Samples. A sample is a small portion of data drawn from a larger group (the population). If properly drawn, it is possible to make reasonably accurate conclusions about the entire population from the study of the sample. This ability provides a powerful device for getting the information required for decision making cheaply and quickly.

Frequency Distribution

A frequency distribution is a function telling how many times each of a set of random events, x_i, occurred. In other words, given a set of mutually exclusive and collectively exhaustive events (such as shown in Table B1), then the set of relative frequencies of all events is called the *frequency distribution function*. Frequency distribution functions can be shown graphically as histograms (such as Figure B1) or curves (Figure B2). These figures and a detailed discussion of the most common frequency distribution functions used in this text are given in Section B3 of this appendix.

Measures of Central Tendency

The most common statistic is the central tendency, or the average. The purpose of the average is to represent a group of individual values in a concise manner. The most common measures of central tendency are: the *mean, the median,* and the *mode.*

The Population Mean

The population mean is given as:

$$\mu = \sum_i x_i P(x_i) \tag{B10}$$

where:

x_i = The value of the variable
$P(x_i)$ = The probability of obtaining the value x_i (or the relative frequency of x_i) in the population
μ = A Greek letter (pronounced mu) that designates the mean

FIGURE B1

The Poisson probability distribution

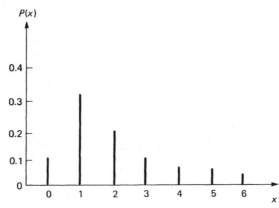

If the frequency of all values is the same, the formula is:

$$\mu = \frac{\sum x_i}{n} \tag{B11}$$

The Expected Value

The mean and expected value of a random variable are conceptually and numerically the same. The two are completely interchangeable. An expected value is designated by $E(x)$ (read as: the expected value of x).

The Median

The *median* is the middle value of the distribution. That is, if the number of observations is odd, then 50 percent of the observed data is smaller than the median and 50 percent is larger than the median. If the number of observations is even, then we average the middle two. For example, in Table B1, both the 40th and the 41st observations (which are 50 percent of the total of 80 observations) are 30 MPH. Thus, 30 MPH is the median speed.

The Mode

The *mode* is that data value with the highest frequency (there may be more than one). In Table B1, it is 30 MPH (25 observations). In this distribution, the median and mode fell in the same speed value, but that need not necessarily be true in other cases. Also, although the mode is always physically a realizable integer data point, the mean and the median may *not* be. For example, the mean family size in the United States is about 4.3 people. The mean, median, and mode apply to both populations and samples.

Measures of Dispersion

Measures of dispersion are measures of scatter around an average, or how data are scattered around the mean. The most important measure of dispersion in the context of this book is the standard deviation.

Standard Deviation and Variance of the Population

The standard deviation is designated by the Greek letter sigma (σ).

The formula for populations involving frequency distributions is:

$$\sigma = \sqrt{\sum_i (x_i - \mu)^2 P(x_i)} \tag{B12}$$

If the frequency of all values is the same, the formula simplifies to:

$$\sigma = \sqrt{\frac{\sum (x_i - \mu)^2}{n}}$$

(B13)

where n is the population size. The value σ^2 is known as the population *variance*.

Sample Distributions

The Mean

Data such as those presented in Table B1 (a sample of 80 observations) can be described by a sample mean (denoted by $\bar{x}$) according to the following formula:

$$\bar{x} = \sum_i x_i \frac{f_i}{n}$$

(B14)

The meaning of this notation can be explained by using the data of Table B1: x_i is the ith speed, f_i is the number of occurrences of that speed, and n is the sample size (80 in this case). The term f_i/n is the frequency of speed i.

The Standard Deviation and Variance

The sample standard deviation, s, is calculated from Equation B15.

$$s = \sqrt{\sum_i (x_i - \bar{x})^2 \frac{f_i}{n-1}}$$

(B15)

The value s^2 is known as the sample variance; that is, $V = s^2$.

Sample Error

Once $\bar{x}$ has been determined, it is possible to estimate the population mean. The difference between μ and $\bar{x}$ is termed the *sampling error*.

The Law of Large Numbers

Sampling is governed by the following law:

> As the size of a sample increases toward infinity, the difference between the true population mean and the sample mean tends toward zero.

Thus, it may be assumed that the sample mean is a good estimate of the population mean if the sample is "large enough" (30 is often considered the dividing point between a "small" and a "large" sample).

The Central Limit Theorem

It is possible to assess the *error* in estimating the population mean, indirectly, with the aid of the *central limit theorem*. The *central limit theorem* tells us that if one continues to take random samples of size *n*, from *any population distribution* with a standard deviation of σ, then the distribution of the *means of the samples* will tend to be normally distributed (the normal distribution is discussed in the next part of this appendix), with mean μ and standard deviation $\sigma/\sqrt{n}$, as *n* approaches infinity. Again, for practical purposes, if $n \geq 30$ ("large enough"), then a normal distribution of the samples' means can be assumed.

B3 Probability Distributions

Discrete and Continuous Probability Distributions

If a random variable may take only certain specific numerical values such as integer numbers, then the probability distribution that characterizes the process that generated that random variable is called a *discrete distribution*. However, if the random variable may take any value (within a specified interval), then the probability distribution is labeled *continuous*. In this appendix, the following distributions will be discussed: the Poisson (a discrete distribution) and the normal and exponential (continuous distributions).

The Poisson Distribution

The Poisson distribution describes situations where the number of occurrences per unit of time is constant; however, the timing of occurrence is random. In other words, occurrences have an equal chance of happening during any moment in the time interval under study. The distribution is shown in Figure B1.

The formula for the Poisson distribution is:

$$P(x) = \frac{\lambda^x e^{-\lambda}}{x!}$$

(B16)

where:

λ = The average number of occurrences per unit of time
e = 2.718 (the base of the natural logarithms), approximately
x = A variable that assumes integer values (such as $x = 0, 1, 2, \ldots$)
$P(x)$ = Relative frequency of each value of x

The mean and standard deviation of this distribution are:

$$\text{Mean} = \lambda \tag{B17}$$

$$\text{Standard deviation} = \sqrt{\lambda} \tag{B18}$$

Values of $e^{-\lambda}$ are tabulated in Table C3 of Appendix C.

The Normal Distribution

The normal distribution is a continuous distribution discovered over 200 years ago. It was then considered to be the law governing distributions of natural phenomena. This belief has been modified as other distributions were discovered; however, the distribution is still the most common one in statistics.

The normal distribution is shown in Figure B2 and its formula is:

$$f(x) = \frac{1}{\sigma\sqrt{2\pi}}\left[e^{-.5\left(\frac{x-\mu}{\sigma}\right)^2}\right] \tag{B19}$$

where:

$f(x) =$ The relative frequency of variable x
$\mu =$ The mean of the distribution
$\sigma =$ The standard deviation of the distribution
$\pi = 3.14$ (approximately)

FIGURE B2

The normal distribution

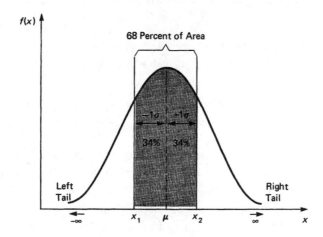

Note that in contrast to the Poisson distribution, we talk here about $f(x)$ being the relative frequency of point x, in the range of $-\infty$ to ∞. (In contrast, the $P(x)$ in the Poisson was the *probability* of x having a *particular value*.) Note also that the values of μ and σ are necessary and sufficient to describe the normal curve.

The Area Under the Normal Curve

Because the normal distribution is symmetrical, its midpoint is the mean. All x values (on the x-axis) are measured as deviations from the mean in standard deviation units. The area under the normal curve describes the proportion of the total distribution between two points on the x-axis. For example, in Figure B2, the shaded area between point x_1 (which is one standard deviation to the left of the mean) and point x_2 (which is one standard deviation to the right of the mean) is 68 percent of the total area. The area from point $-\infty$ (left side) to point x_2 is 84 percent (34 percent plus the mean, which is exactly at 50 percent). It is known that 95.4 percent of the curve lies between $\pm 2\sigma$ around the mean and 99.7 percent lies between $\pm 3\sigma$.

The Standard Normal Distribution

A normal distribution whose mean is zero and whose standard deviation is one is called a *standard* normal distribution. Such a distribution was used for the construction of Table C1, in Appendix C, which lists the area under the curve as a function of the number of standard deviations, Z. This table is extremely useful because it enables one to find the probabilities for *any* given normal distribution, using the relationship:

$$Z = \frac{x - \mu}{\sigma}$$

(B20)

where x is the value of the measured variable. Note that *if* (in Equation B20) $\mu = 0$ and $\sigma = 1$, then $z = x$.

The Use of the Area Under the Normal Curve (Table C1)

Tables that give the area under the normal curve appear in two alternative forms (Figure B3).

Alternative a   The entries in a table of this type represent the proportion of the total area under the normal curve (shaded) that falls between $-\infty$ and Z standard deviations to the right of the mean.

Alternative b   The entries in a table of this type represent the proportion of the total area under the normal curve (shaded) that falls between the mean and Z standard deviations to the right of the mean.

The difference between the same entry in the two tables is .5; that is, each entry in table type *a* is exactly .5 larger than that of type *b*. In this text, Table C1 is a type *a* table.

FIGURE B3

*Alternative presentation
of the area under the
normal curve*

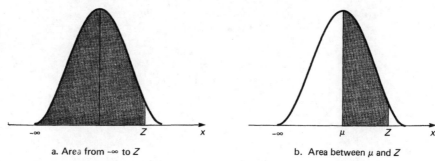

a. Area from −∞ to *Z*

b. Area between *μ* and *Z*

Using Table C1

Example 1

Find the area between −∞ and *Z* = 1.43 standard deviations to the right of the mean. First, find the entry in row *Z* = 1.4 that intersects with column .03; the reading is .9236 (that is, 92.36 percent of the area is covered).

Example 2

Find the area between the mean and .45 standard deviations to the *left of the mean*. Find the entry equivalent to *Z* = .45 (row *Z* = .4, column = .05), which is .6736. Then subtract .5 from this value. The result .6736 − .5 = .1736 means that the solution is 17.36 percent of the area.

See Figure B4 for a graphical presentation of these two examples.

FIGURE B4

*Graphical presentation
of the two examples*

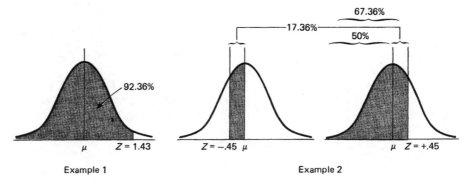

Example 1   Example 2

FIGURE B5

The negative exponential distribution

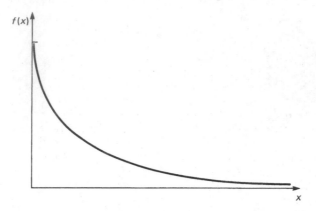

The Negative Exponential Distribution

The negative exponential distribution describes the probability "that it will take x time before the first occurrence of an outcome." The formula for the distribution is:

$$f(x) = \lambda e^{-\lambda x} \quad \text{for } \lambda \geq 0 \tag{B21}$$

where λ = the average number of occurrences per unit of time (e.g., service rate). The statistics of this distribution are:

$$\text{Mean} = \frac{1}{\lambda} \tag{B22}$$

$$\text{Standard Deviation} = \frac{1}{\lambda} \tag{B23}$$

The distribution is shown in Figure B5 and $e^{-\lambda}$ is tabulated in Table C3.

Bibliography

1. Iman, W. *Modern Business Statistics,* 2nd ed. New York: John Wiley & Sons, 1989.
2. Lapin, L. L. *Statistics for Modern Business Decisions,* 4th ed. New York: Harcourt Brace Jovanovich, 1987.
3. Madsen, R. W., and M. L. Mueschberger. *Statistical Methods for Business and Economics.* Englewood Cliffs, N.J.: Prentice-Hall, 1980.
4. Newbold, P. *Statistics for Business and Economics.* 2nd ed. Englewood Cliffs, N.J.: Prentice-Hall, 1988.
5. Sanders, D. H., A. F. Murph, and R. J. Eng. *Statistics—A Fresh Approach.* 2nd ed. New York: McGraw-Hill, 1980.
6. Wonnacott, T. H., and R. J. Wonnacott. *Introductory Statistics for Business and Economics.* 3rd ed. New York: John Wiley & Sons, 1984.

TABLE C1 Cumulative Probabilities of the Normal Probability Distribution (Areas under the Normal Curve from $-\infty$ to Z)

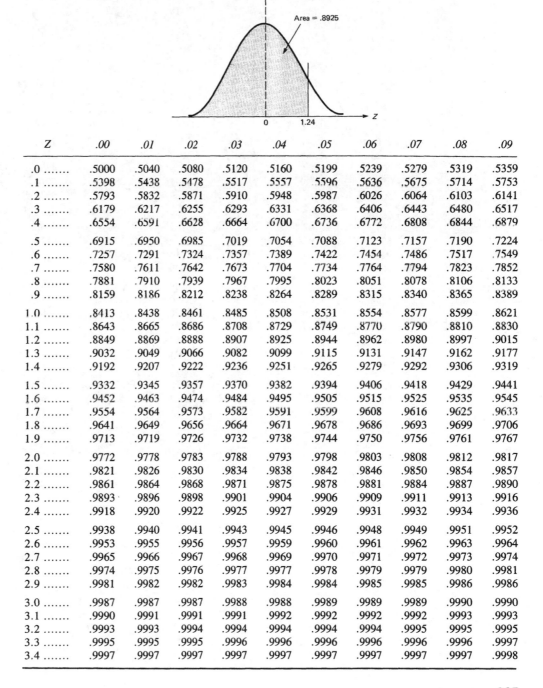

Area = .8925

0   1.24   Z

Z	.00	.01	.02	.03	.04	.05	.06	.07	.08	.09
.0	.5000	.5040	.5080	.5120	.5160	.5199	.5239	.5279	.5319	.5359
.1	.5398	.5438	.5478	.5517	.5557	.5596	.5636	.5675	.5714	.5753
.2	.5793	.5832	.5871	.5910	.5948	.5987	.6026	.6064	.6103	.6141
.3	.6179	.6217	.6255	.6293	.6331	.6368	.6406	.6443	.6480	.6517
.4	.6554	.6591	.6628	.6664	.6700	.6736	.6772	.6808	.6844	.6879
.5	.6915	.6950	.6985	.7019	.7054	.7088	.7123	.7157	.7190	.7224
.6	.7257	.7291	.7324	.7357	.7389	.7422	.7454	.7486	.7517	.7549
.7	.7580	.7611	.7642	.7673	.7704	.7734	.7764	.7794	.7823	.7852
.8	.7881	.7910	.7939	.7967	.7995	.8023	.8051	.8078	.8106	.8133
.9	.8159	.8186	.8212	.8238	.8264	.8289	.8315	.8340	.8365	.8389
1.0	.8413	.8438	.8461	.8485	.8508	.8531	.8554	.8577	.8599	.8621
1.1	.8643	.8665	.8686	.8708	.8729	.8749	.8770	.8790	.8810	.8830
1.2	.8849	.8869	.8888	.8907	.8925	.8944	.8962	.8980	.8997	.9015
1.3	.9032	.9049	.9066	.9082	.9099	.9115	.9131	.9147	.9162	.9177
1.4	.9192	.9207	.9222	.9236	.9251	.9265	.9279	.9292	.9306	.9319
1.5	.9332	.9345	.9357	.9370	.9382	.9394	.9406	.9418	.9429	.9441
1.6	.9452	.9463	.9474	.9484	.9495	.9505	.9515	.9525	.9535	.9545
1.7	.9554	.9564	.9573	.9582	.9591	.9599	.9608	.9616	.9625	.9633
1.8	.9641	.9649	.9656	.9664	.9671	.9678	.9686	.9693	.9699	.9706
1.9	.9713	.9719	.9726	.9732	.9738	.9744	.9750	.9756	.9761	.9767
2.0	.9772	.9778	.9783	.9788	.9793	.9798	.9803	.9808	.9812	.9817
2.1	.9821	.9826	.9830	.9834	.9838	.9842	.9846	.9850	.9854	.9857
2.2	.9861	.9864	.9868	.9871	.9875	.9878	.9881	.9884	.9887	.9890
2.3	.9893	.9896	.9898	.9901	.9904	.9906	.9909	.9911	.9913	.9916
2.4	.9918	.9920	.9922	.9925	.9927	.9929	.9931	.9932	.9934	.9936
2.5	.9938	.9940	.9941	.9943	.9945	.9946	.9948	.9949	.9951	.9952
2.6	.9953	.9955	.9956	.9957	.9959	.9960	.9961	.9962	.9963	.9964
2.7	.9965	.9966	.9967	.9968	.9969	.9970	.9971	.9972	.9973	.9974
2.8	.9974	.9975	.9976	.9977	.9977	.9978	.9979	.9979	.9980	.9981
2.9	.9981	.9982	.9982	.9983	.9984	.9984	.9985	.9985	.9986	.9986
3.0	.9987	.9987	.9987	.9988	.9988	.9989	.9989	.9989	.9990	.9990
3.1	.9990	.9991	.9991	.9991	.9992	.9992	.9992	.9992	.9993	.9993
3.2	.9993	.9993	.9994	.9994	.9994	.9994	.9994	.9995	.9995	.9995
3.3	.9995	.9995	.9995	.9996	.9996	.9996	.9996	.9996	.9996	.9997
3.4	.9997	.9997	.9997	.9997	.9997	.9997	.9997	.9997	.9997	.9998

TABLE C2 Random Numbers

7823	9505	7863	2976	4536	0062	2757	3281
4308	3826	1329	8318	5829	0986	2765	0874
9228	9903	9793	6938	9344	2120	1306	4629
8717	5407	0187	3141	7651	9415	2893	9213
4773	8866	4966	3964	8718	9311	5954	6955
8387	4641	6280	4467	4578	2349	7635	7109
8728	4950	9218	2101	8320	1526	8462	2968
2768	3615	2529	2812	3783	0934	3126	4600
1988	5102	1837	3864	1161	8517	7101	8024
5202	0158	0715	9539	4229	3874	6042	1437
9763	5760	9080	5720	1216	7843	5890	2789
7025	2332	6238	8043	1373	5162	6336	7402
6020	5070	7485	5620	3081	4854	8759	8005
0526	8974	8545	8541	6886	5014	2012	1843
5078	8581	1215	2189	8128	9536	5357	5700
5801	3622	6441	5059	8871	3844	7643	8809
8691	0747	7648	9165	7648	5068	5216	9526
6272	9181	7511	3217	8037	9114	8365	3502
9208	4589	5428	8676	3424	2980	7001	0478
0693	0665	0855	7396	5297	4919	1061	3722
0363	1856	9196	6949	6230	9456	9558	5963
5238	3367	2373	5890	6273	4141	4451	6709
1907	6029	5227	6050	2698	8500	1478	5049
3057	3784	1807	2634	8159	3015	9813	0030
2926	0519	2181	5244	1046	5367	5901	7474
0456	0663	0756	4094	4418	7953	4044	7590
4124	4389	1198	5571	6119	6540	7273	2009
9376	3496	0902	9923	2789	4477	6797	1870
1543	7954	9548	1232	4219	0236	6777	0342
2739	5811	1642	5979	2059	8088	3391	3480
0682	0604	2051	1375	8191	2566	3162	2572
0535	0605	6357	8278	3078	6929	5224	9124
7782	3184	4504	5879	3238	4159	5676	0418
0805	5265	6536	6506	9487	6087	9420	9063
6262	7289	3310	8731	3921	2095	5837	4218
8508	3313	2976	5658	3616	3361	9396	5188
6248	3796	5543	2582	2832	1983	4747	9837
5220	0327	3268	4413	3040	6358	8106	0776
5193	3007	3666	8084	1389	5026	2680	1549
2652	1375	4799	8832	3241	0752	5649	3029

TABLE C3 Poisson Values of $e^{-\lambda}$

λ	$e^{-\lambda}$	λ	$e^{-\lambda}$	λ	$e^{-\lambda}$	λ	$e^{-\lambda}$
0.1	0.90484	2.6	0.07427	5.1	0.00610	7.6	0.00050
0.2	0.81873	2.7	0.06721	5.2	0.00552	7.7	0.00045
0.3	0.74082	2.8	0.06081	5.3	0.00499	7.8	0.00041
0.4	0.67032	2.9	0.05502	5.4	0.00452	7.9	0.00037
0.5	0.60653	3.0	0.04979	5.5	0.00409	8.0	0.00034
0.6	0.54881	3.1	0.04505	5.6	0.00370	8.1	0.00030
0.7	0.49659	3.2	0.04076	5.7	0.00335	8.2	0.00027
0.8	0.44933	3.3	0.03688	5.8	0.00303	8.3	0.00025
0.9	0.40657	3.4	0.03337	5.9	0.00274	8.4	0.00022
1.0	0.36788	3.5	0.03020	6.0	0.00248	8.5	0.00020
1.1	0.33287	3.6	0.02732	6.1	0.00224	8.6	0.00018
1.2	0.30119	3.7	0.02472	6.2	0.00203	8.7	0.00017
1.3	0.27253	3.8	0.02237	6.3	0.00184	8.8	0.00015
1.4	0.24660	3.9	0.02024	6.4	0.00166	8.9	0.00014
1.5	0.22313	4.0	0.01832	6.5	0.00150	9.0	0.00012
1.6	0.20190	4.1	0.01657	6.6	0.00136	9.1	0.00011
1.7	0.18268	4.2	0.01500	6.7	0.00123	9.2	0.00010
1.8	0.16530	4.3	0.01357	6.8	0.00111	9.3	0.00009
1.9	0.14957	4.4	0.01228	6.9	0.00101	9.4	0.00008
2.0	0.13534	4.5	0.01111	7.0	0.00091	9.5	0.00007
2.1	0.12246	4.6	0.01005	7.1	0.00083	9.6	0.00007
2.2	0.11080	4.7	0.00910	7.2	0.00075	9.7	0.00006
2.3	0.10026	4.8	0.00823	7.3	0.00068	9.8	0.00006
2.4	0.09072	4.9	0.00745	7.4	0.00061	9.9	0.00005
2.5	0.08208	5.0	0.00674	7.5	0.00055	10.0	0.00005

D—ANSWERS TO EVEN-NUMBERED PROBLEMS

Chapter 2

2. *a.* A ≤ 400
   b. A + B ≥ 540
   c. A + B ≤ 720
   d. 800A + 1,150B ≤ 50,000

6. *f.* 362,880

Chapter 3

2. Two optimal basic solutions give $z = 95$;
   $x_1 = 12.6$, $x_2 = 6.4$; $x_1 = 8$, $x_2 = 11$

4. *c.* $x_1 = 9$, $x_2 = 7.5$
   d. 117

e.

Constraint	Slack	Surplus
1	0	0
2	0	0
3	0	12
4	25	0

f. #1,2 = 100 percent; #3 surplus of 80 percent;
#4 utiliz. = 37.5 percent.

g. $x_1 = 10.67$, $x_2 = 3.33$, $z = 105.34$

6. *a.* 600 pants, 1,200 shirts, $z = \$4,200$ per day
   b. The price of shirts must exceed $6 per unit

8. 37.5 hours (150 units) on line 1
   170 hours (850 units) on line 2
   Total cost = 1,150,000 won

10.   *Case* a   *Case* b
  a. #1   #6
  b. #4, #1   #4, #5
  c. None   #1
12. b. All points infeasible
14. $x_1 = 8.14$, $x_2 = 3.35$, $z = 95.74$
16. $x_1 = 8$, $x_2 = 3$ to $x_1 = 3.33$, $x_2 = 10$; $z = 30$
18. b. 5 (the number of constraints)
    c. If degenerate
    d. Bread 672.4 grams; carrots 134.2 g.; halibut
       118.0 g.; eggs 341.3 g. Cost: .89 pounds
       sterling per day
    e. 53.37 grams of protein
    f. Beef 100 grams; butter 44.8 g.; bread
       500 g.; carrots 476 g.; halibut 80.5 g.; eggs
       200 g. Cost: 1.024 pounds sterling, 41.2
       grams of protein
20. a. $x_1 = 10$, $x_2 = 8$, $z = 82$
    b. Solution is degenerate
    e. Additional basic solution: $x_1 = 11.45$,
       $x_2 = 6.18$, $z = 82$
22. $x_1 = 1$, $x_2 = 3$, $z = 14$
24. $x_1 = 1$, $x_2 = 3$, $z = 14$
26. Unbounded solution in x_2
28. Deluxe = 16, regular = 18, $z = 118$
30. Proportion of iron = 10/17, nickel = 2/17,
    $z = 1.71$ rupees/unit

Chapter 4

2. $x_1 = 6^2/_3$
    $x_2 = 1^2/_3$
    $x_3 = 1^2/_3$
    $z = 103^2/_3$
4. $x_1 = 1,000$
    $x_2 = 1,235.3$
    $x_3 = 352.9$
    $z = \$4,588.20$
8. a. Maximize $z = .25x_a + .32x_b + .15x_c + .28x_d$
       subject to: $x_a + x_b + x_c + x_d \leq 500$
                               $x_a \leq 250$
                               $x_b \leq 250$
                               $x_c \leq 250$
                               $x_d \leq 250$
                               $x_b \geq 50$
                     $x_a - x_c \leq 0$

10. $x_1 = \$3,400$
    $x_2 = 9,350$
    $x_3 = 4,250$
    $z = 223,550$ customers
12. a. 4,200,000 and 504,000
    b. 3,584,000 and 1,120,000
    c. \$4,564,000
    d. \$1,879,808
14. a. Maximize $z = .25x_C + .90x_D$
       subject to: $4x_C + 3x_D \leq 100,000$
                   $.1x_C + .2x_D \leq 9,000$
                   $.04x_C + .1x_D \leq 1,200$
                             $x_D \leq 3,500$
    c. $x_C = 21,250$
       $x_D = 3500$
       $z = 8,462.5$
       mtl. slack = 4,500
       power slack = 6,175
16. 7.5 ounces of liver at a cost of \$.703
18. $X_T = 112.50$, $X_S = 237.56$, $z = 91,875$

Chapter 5

2. $u_1 = 1^2/_3$, $u_2 = {}^2/_3$, $u_3 = u_4 = 0$, $w = 132$
4. a. Minimize $50u_1 - 20u_2 + 26u_3 - 26u_4$
       subject to:
       $5u_1 \quad + 2u_3 - 2u_4 \geq 5$
       $3u_1 - 2u_2 + 3u_3 - 3u_4 \geq 3$
           $- 1u_2 - 1u_3 + 1u_4 \geq 1$
    b. Minimize $-50u_1 + 20u_2 - 20u_3 + 45u_4$
       subject to:
       $-3u_1 + 1u_2 - 1u_3 + 2u_4 \geq -6$
       $-4u_1 + 2u_2 - 2u_3 + 3u_4 \geq 2$
6. a. $x_1 = .4$, $x_2 = .1$, $z = 200$
    b. The first, third, and fourth
    c. 1. None   5. Reduce cost by 50(.5)
       2. Infeasible   = \$25
       3. None   6. Infeasible
       4. None
8. a. $2,666.67 \leq x_1 \leq 8,000$
       $2,500 \leq x_2 \leq 7,500$
    b. No nonbasic variables
    c. $-\infty \leq b_1 \leq 11.50$
        $-16.50 \leq b_2 \leq \infty$
        $102.86 \leq b_3 \leq 240$
          $120 \leq b_4 \leq 233.33$
        $-\infty \leq b_5 \leq 205$

10. *a.* $x_1 = 0.5$, $x_2 = 0$, $z = 350$
   b. Coefficient of x_2 must exceed 35
   c. Can decrease by 3.5
   d. Coefficient can increase up to $2\frac{1}{3}$
   e. Infeasible solution

12. *a.* Yes, $916 > 120$ cost
   b. 16.10
   c. 66.3 percent
   d. 1, 3, and 4
   e. No, violates constraint 5
   f. No, violates constraint 4
   g. 36,956.3
   h. Decreasing the RHS will not help

14. *a.* 335.23
   b. 100
   c. x_1
   d. 45.703
   e. 234
   f. 0
   g. 4.297
   h. Slack exists
   i. Constraints not fully utilized
   j. #4 not fully utilized; #5 is
   k. 15.65
   l. 10% = nothing; 20% = no more x_4

16. Feasible, cost will decrease by 17.97

Chapter 6

6. *b.* $x_A = 8$, $x_B = 10$, $z = 18$
   d. $x_A = 12$, $x_B = 0$, $z = 12$

10. AM, BN, CO *or* AC, BN, CP; cost = 16

16. 2 type I, 10 type II, 1 type III, cost = $151,000

18. $x_1 = 12.86$, $x_2 = 12.20$, $z = 59.61$

20. A or B first on #1, C on #2 starting between 0–3 hours

22. 35,000 gallons on C at a cost of $2400

Chapter 7

2. *a.* Cost = $700
   b. Cost = $560
   c. Optimal solution cost = $560
   d. Yes, many

4. *a.* Optimal profit = $1,260
   b. Maximize $6x_{11} + 4x_{12} + 3x_{21} + 5x_{22} + 8x_{31} + 7x_{32} + 5x_{41} + 9x_{42}$
     subject to:
$$x_{11} + x_{12} \leq 50$$
$$x_{21} + x_{22} \leq 80$$
$$x_{31} + x_{32} \leq 60$$
$$x_{41} + x_{42} \leq 40$$
$$x_{11} + x_{21} + x_{31} + x_{41} = 80$$
$$x_{12} + x_{22} + x_{32} + x_{42} = 100$$

6. *b.* Several optimal solutions with a distance of 885 miles

8. *b.* Optimal minimum cost = $11,200; $x_{AC} = 1,000$; $x_{BD} = 1300$
   c. Minimize $6x_{AC} + 7x_{AD} + 9x_{AE} + 9x_{BC} + 4x_{BD} + 6x_{BE}$
     subject to $x_{AC} + x_{AD} + x_{AE} = 1,000$
           $x_{BC} + x_{BD} + x_{BE} = 1,300$

10. *a.* A–O, B–N, C–P, Minimum cost = $16

12. *a.* Several optimal solutions with minimum complaints of 21

14. *a.* $x_{AI} = 60$, $x_{AII} = 80$, $x_{BII} = 40$, $x_{BIII} = 80$, Cost = 8,500 rupees

16. $x_{AI} = 3,000$, $x_{B1} = 2,000$, $x_{C1} = 200$, $x_{C2} = 1,600$, $x_{D3} = 6,000$, Profit = $555,000

18. $x_1 = 0$, $x_2 = 1$, $x_3 = 1$, $x_4 = x_5 = 0$, $x_6 = x_7 = 1$, $x_8 = 0$; $z = 45$

20. 1–A, 2–B, 3–D, 4–C, loss = 42,000

22. Py-E, Rat-B, Asp-D, Cor-C, z = 156

24. B-III, C-II, D-I, $z = 281$

26. See previous solution

28. *a.* Degenerate, cost = 7900
   b. $x_{1A} = 200$, $x_{2A} = 400$, $x_{3C} = 500$, $x_{3D} = 100$, $x_{AB} = 400$, $x_{AE} = 300$, Cost = 6,000

30. $x_{AE} = 40$, $x_{CD} = 20$, minimum mileage = 3,800

32. See previous solution

Chapter 8

2. x_1 = hours on line 1
   x_2 = hours on line 2
   1) $5x_1 + 4x_2 + d_1^- - d_1^+ = 300$ (produce 300 units)
   2) $x_1 - 30 + d_2^- - d_2^+ = 4$ (overtime)

3) $15(x_1 - 30) + 12(x_2 - 30) + d_3^- - d_3^+ = 800$ (overtime cost)

4) $(30 - x_1) + (30 - x_2) + d_4^- - d_4^+ = 0$

5) $5x_1 + 4x_2 + d_5^- - d_5^+ = 0$

Minimize $z = P_1 d_1^- + P_2 d_2^+ + P_3 d_3^+ + 5P_4 d_4^- + P_5 d_5^-$

4. *a.* 106.67 and 61.67
   b. 21.67
   c. 40
   d. 333.44
   e. 100

6. 50,000 units of alpha; 33,333 units of beta; but violates budget and capacity constraints

8. $x_1 = 45$, $x_2 = 30$, profit = 75

12. 70, $2000

14. 70% of $20,000 and 30% of 0

16. *a.* 3.33   *b.* $1000   *c.* 0.6 for $20,000
    d. Buy new ($u = 6.1$ vs. 5.8)

18. A = 37, B = 38 (best)

20. John = 62.35, Mary = 63.95 (best)

22. *a.* Conservative
    b. P1 = 7.63 (best), P2 = 6.67

Chapter 9

2. Insure, 50,000 deductible: Expected cost = $825
   c. $500 total

4. *b.* 2.45 cars per day
   c. $174,195

6. Do not play; expected loss of playing is $0.167 per play

8. *a.* Select a_1: Expected profit 6.1, EOL = 1.1
   b. Select a_2: Expected profit 4.5, EOL = 1.6
   c. Select a_1: Expected profit 2.0, EOL = .3

10. Choose alternative *c* for a cost of $7,300

12. *a.* Order 11 crates
    b. Average daily profit $156.00

14. Convert now; expected cost 2,500 dollars

16. *a.* a_2
    b. $0.272 \le s_1 \le 0.615$

18. Do not insure: expected cost = $80

20. Do not repair: expected cost = $1,370

22. Attend at random: expected value is 1.74

24. Expand: expected present value = $695,000

26. Use no preparation: expected cost = $130.20

28. $.825 per day
    a. a_1
    b. a_3
    c. a_1
    d. a_3
    e. a_3
    Table 2:
    a. a_2 or a_3
    b. a_2
    c. a_3
    d. a_2
    e. a_2

32. *a.* a_2
    b. a_2
    c. a_3
    d. a_2
    e. a_2

34. 77.6 percent chance of purchase by the government

38. *c.* 0.62
    d. No, value is only 2,083

40. *a.* EVPI = 7; purchase
    b. No, value of 2,850

42. *a.* 3.50
    b. Vendor A (2.14 net profit vs. 1.99 for B)
    c. .09
    d. .32
    f. .17, .58, 0, .25, 0

44. *a, b.* 10,000 using new equipment
    c. $645
    d, e. EVII = $8.08; do not use!

Chapter 10

2. Final moving averages:

Order, *n*	Value
3	3.3
4	3.0
5	3.0

4. Alpha of: 0.05: 3.0
              0.30: 3.1
              0.90: 3.0

6.

	MAD	BIAS
Alpha = .05	0.51	−0.01
Order = 3	0.68	0.32

8. 12,350 for Q_3 of 1993

10. 2.87 Better than Chapter Table

12. 104,455
    R + 1%: − 4126
    C $1000: − 900
    I $1000: + 5100

14. $T = 4 + 0.167X$
    $S_1 = 1.22$
    $S_2 = 0.96$
    $S_3 = 0.72$
    $S_4 = 1.10$

16. 5.44
    MAD =   0.165
    Bias   = −0.0125

18. *a.* D = 3,361.3 − 56.33S
      2122 tires
      MAD = 174.3
      Bias = 0
    b. D = −810.1 + 112.6S
      1960 tires
      MAD = 44.5
      Bias = 0

20. Winter: 58,800
    Spring: 87,120
    Summer: 97,100
    Fall: 121,680
    Forecast (period 45) = 551.19
    Regression equation: $T_e = 484.79 + 1.67x$
    Seasonal indexes: 96.27, 109.91, 96.78, 97.04

22. *a.* 551.19
    b. 556.50
    c. 484.8 + 1.67x
    d. 1. 96.3
        2. 109.9
        3. 96.8
        4. 97.0

g. 584.21, 676.18
h. 2491.32

Chapter 11

2. *a.*

Event	T_E	T_L	Slack
1	0	0	0
2	3	3	0
3	5	8	3
4	10	10	0
5	16	16	0
6	19	19	0

  b. See *(a)* also.

Activity	Slack
a	0
b	3
c	0
d	3
e	0
f	7
g	6
h	5

  c. Critical path: *a–c–e–i*
  d. 3 on *b–d*
      7 on *b–f*
      6 on *b–g*

4. *a.* *a–d–e–g–i–j*
  b. 20 days
  c. 61 days
  d. 20 days

6. *b.* *b–f–h*
  c. *a–c*; 9 weeks
  e. 1 extra week: No effect
      2 extra weeks: Second critical path
      b–e–g
      3 extra weeks: One week delay and new
      critical path *b–e–g*

8. *b.* *b–e–g–h*
  c. new critical path *a–d–g–h*
  d. From *c* and *f* to *d*, then to *g*, lastly to *h*

10.

	ES	EF	LS	LF	TF	FF
a	0	3	0	3	0	0
b	0	5	3	8	3	0
c	3	10	3	7	0	0
d	5	7	8	10	3	3
e	10	16	10	16	0	0
f	5	9	12	16	7	7
g	5	13	11	19	6	6
h	10	14	15	19	5	5
i	16	19	16	19	0	0

Critical path is *a–c–e–i*

14. Critical path is **1–3–4–11–13–14–16**

16. *a.* 36.9 percent
    b. 84.1 percent
    c. 50 percent
    d. 17.32

18. *a.* 20.8 percent, 5.2 percent, 89 percent
    b. 0
    c. 23.057 weeks

20. *a.* 21.7 weeks
    b. **1–3–6–7**
    c. .3, 0
    d. 6, 0.7
    e. 17.88 percent
    f. 100 percent
    g. 24.728 weeks

22. Cost 160

24.

Date	Cost
17	0
16	25
15	55
14	105
13	165
12	245

26. Total distance = 271
28. Total distance = 156
30. Total distance = 64
32. 1–2–4–8 for 94

Chapter 12

2. 18,330 bags, .262 month's worth
4. *a.* 800 bags
   b. 0.8 month's worth
6. No, the cost would be $1,530, compared to $1,464 by ordering only 150 units (for which space is available)
8. *a.* Order $10,000 worth 20 times per year
   b. $2,000
   c. $3,200 more per year
   d. Order $10,488 worth
   e. $266.67 more per year
10. $.32 per unit per year
12. *a.* $11,100
    b. 1,200 units; $3,600
    c. 6
18. *b.* 40
    c. 10 days
    d. 40 days
       30 units maximum inventory
    e. Increases the cost from $750 to $812.50
20. *a.* 20 days
    b. 400
    c. 40 days
    d. $30,000 per year
22. *a.* 15
    b. No, total cost is $1,470 higher
    c. 7 percent
26. Release 140 on Oct. 29
28. *a.* $3,280
    b. 30
30. 7
32. 106 preferred but limit is 100, if rent; 108 if buy
34. Order 150 in week 10, 145 in week 13, and 155 in week 15
38. Order 50 for Jan. 3, 120 for Jan. 17, 120 for Jan. 24, 140 for Feb 7; TC = $480

Chapter 13

2. $Q(3) = [.456 \quad .544]$
4. *a.* 74 good; 74 fair; 32 poor
   b. 52.68 good; 83.42 fair; 43.90 poor

6. *a.* P(A operates) = .948; P(B operates) = .977; lease B
   b. If the lease for A is less than (948 ÷ .977) × lease for B, then A should be leased; otherwise, lease B

8. *a.* 21.74 in checking; 8.53 in loans, 9.72 in savings

10. 43.3 percent to A; 19.8 percent to B; 36.9 percent to C

12. *a.* $\begin{bmatrix} .765 & .210 & .025 \\ .033 & .914 & .053 \\ .040 & .020 & .940 \end{bmatrix}$

   c. 131, 199, 70
   d. 54, 170, 176

14.
Level	Days
1	7.01
2	10.50
3	24.05
4	40.15
5	50.50
6	51.47
7	77.35
8	59.80
9	44.17
Total	365.00

16. *b.* 39 at airport, 61 at beach
   c. $458.80
   d. 27 percent

18. *a.* 3.37 weeks
   b. ⁵⁄₃ weeks in good condition; 1 week in fair condition; ¹⁹⁄₂₇ weeks in poor condition.
   c. In the long run, 100 percent. Within a week, 10 percent if in good condition, 20 percent if fair, and 90 percent if poor

20. *a.*
	Paid	Bad	Current	Delinquent
			(in thousands)	
Nov. 1	950	150	500	200
Dec. 1	1,200	200	250	150

   b. 1.5 million
   c. 300,000
   d. 2 months in current + .4 months in delinq. = 2.4

22. *b.* $3,337,428
   c. .182 gas, .309 oil, .091 electricity, 0.418 solar
   d. 2. $1,273,872; 3. $65,760; $350,880
   e. 98 percent by 100 years

24. .0605, .615, $5.13

Chapter 14

2. *a.* 2.545 hours
   b. 9.44 repairs

6. *a.* 50 percent
   b. 3.12 percent
   c. 6.25 percent
   d. 11.16 percent
   e. 93.75 percent
   f. 99.32 percent

8.
μ	L_q	W_q
3.1	29.04	9.68
3.5	5.13	1.71
4	2.25	.75
6	0.5	.167

10. 10.33 truckloads per hour

12. $60

14. *a.* No, only 60 percent of the time
   b. Yes, since the investment will reduce the total hourly cost of the system from $46.67 to $40

16. Line 1 utilization is best: 73.9 percent

20. $P_0 = 0.038$, $L_q = 1.53$ so only 4

22. *a.* $913.60 *b.* $448 *c.* $300

26. *a.* 0.8
   b. $L = 6.22$
   c. 2.3 min.
   d. 4
   e. 0.013
   f. 0.139

28. $L_q = 2.77$

30. 30

32. $P(0) = 0.038$

36. 3 year savings only $918,600; do not invest

38. 4 windows for first goal, 5 for second goal

Chapter 15

2. 8, 9, 6, 7, 8

4. *a.* 108 units for $1,512 average profit
   b. 109 units

6. *b.* 54.75 days

8. *a.* Intermediate
   b. $944
   c. $342,800
   d. 15.4 percent
   e. $5,670

10. *a.* 13.27 units
    b. 20 percent
    c. 17 units
    d. No, inventory is increasing

12. *a.* 80 percent
    b. $3,000
    c. 30 percent
    d. 96.6 percent
    e. 3 (cost of 9,000)

14. One shift is better for either price; the $400 price is *much* more profitable

18. *a.* 5 people
    b. 3.846 people
    c. 0.94 minutes
    d. 54 percent
    f. 25.2 trips

20. *a.* 1,755 compared to $E(V) = 1,890$
    b. 8.33 percent
    c. 41.67 percent
    d. 1,816.67 gallons
    e. 441.67 gallons
    f. $22.75 due to ill will; $91.00 due to opportunity loss of 20¢ gallon
    g. $260.00 − 0.83 (shipped back) = $259.17. Opportunity loss of $22.75 might also be deducted

24. *a.* Unit demand was met (97.6%) but weekly demand was not (66.7%)
    b. 13,314,500 pesos
    c. Zero
    d. 1.16 valves per week

26. *b.* $830.50 per week
    c. 50 percent

28. *a.* 1.33 minutes per customer (prior to service)
    b. 762

30. *a.* .967   *d.* .545
    b. 1.02   *e.* .272
    c. 9.272

Chapter 16

2. P→A→H→LA, cost = $380

4.

Year	Price (thousands of pesos)
1	110
2	100
3	100
4	110

6. *a.* 1 to A, 2 to B, 1 to C; $33,000 per month
   b. 2 to A, 1 to B, 1 to C; $32,000 per month
   c. 1 to each; $29,000 per month

8. *a.* Sell on any day (except the fifth) if the price is ≥ 22; otherwise, wait. On the fifth day, sell at any price
   b. Net return = $21,526

10. Mon: Wait
    Tues: Sell if 350, otherwise wait
    Wed: Sell if 400, otherwise wait
    Thurs: Sell

12. *a.* Minimize $z = 20A + 15B + 23C + 18D$
    Subject to:
    $$4A + 2B + 5C + 32D \geq 14$$
    $$A, B, C, D \geq 0 \text{ and integer}$$
    b. 1A and 2C; Cost = 66 (thousands)

Chapter 17

6. *NB* rule: 3−2−4−7−5−1−6−8 for total of 73; *NBWA rule*: Same as above

10. *a.* $a_2, b_2, 4$
    b. $a_2, b_1, 1$
    c. $a_1, b_2, -2$
    d. $a_4, b_2, 3$

12. *a.* $a_1 = \frac{4}{9}$, $a_2 = \frac{5}{9}$
    b. $b_1 = \frac{7}{9}$, $b_2 = \frac{2}{9}$
    c. $V = \frac{17}{9}$

14. *a.* $a_1 = \frac{5}{6}$, $a_2 = \frac{1}{6}$
    b. $b_1 = \frac{2}{3}$, $b_3 = \frac{1}{3}$
    c. $V = 0$

16. *a.* A evening, B twice evening
    b. 50% to A and to B

18. Mix 50% each to E and N for both firms; value is $200,000 to BQ

Index